Francis Day

The Fishes of India - Being a natural history of the fishes known to inhabit the seas and fresh waters of India, Burma, and Ceylon.

Vol. 1

Francis Day

The Fishes of India - Being a natural history of the fishes known to inhabit the seas and fresh waters of India, Burma, and Ceylon.
Vol. 1

ISBN/EAN: 9783337241131

Printed in Europe, USA, Canada, Australia, Japan

Cover: Foto ©Andreas Hilbeck / pixelio.de

More available books at **www.hansebooks.com**

THE

FISHES OF INDIA;

BEING

A NATURAL HISTORY

OF

THE FISHES

KNOWN TO INHABIT THE SEAS AND FRESH WATERS

OF

INDIA, BURMA, AND CEYLON.

BY

FRANCIS DAY, F.L.S., & F.Z.S., &c.,

SURGEON-MAJOR MADRAS ARMY, AND INSPECTOR-GENERAL OF FISHERIES IN INDIA AND BURMA.

VOLUME I.

LONDON:

PUBLISHED BY BERNARD QUARITCH, 15 PICCADILLY.

1876.

THE FISHES OF INDIA.

CLASS PISCES.

Vertebrate animals which are, as a rule, exclusively adapted for an aquatic life, and have their extremities modified into fins. Respiring, almost invariably, solely by means of gills:* possessing a heart with only two cavities, and being cold-blooded. They are scaleless, partially or wholly scaled, the scales being sometimes in the form of osseous plates.

SYNOPSIS OF SUB-CLASSES.

I. Teleostei or Eleutherobranchii. Skeleton osseous. Brain distinct. Skull possessing cranial bones. Vertebræ completely separated, and the posterior extremity of the vertebral column bony, or having bony plates. Branchiæ free, and the water discharged through a single aperture on either side, protected by a bony gill-cover or opercle: branchiostegal rays present. A non-contractile bulbus arteriosus, having a pair of valves at its commencement.

II. Chondropterygii or Elasmobranchii. Skeleton cartilaginous. Brain distinct. Skull without cranial sutures. Gills pouch-like, and attached by their outer edge to the skin, whilst an intervening gill-opening exists between each. No gill-cover. Bulbus arteriosus contractile, and having three rows of valves at its commencement.

SYNOPSIS OF ORDERS AMONGST THE TELEOSTEI.

I. Acanthopterygii. A portion of the dorsal, anal, and ventral fins unarticulated, forming spines.† Air-vessel, when present, completely closed, not possessing a pneumatic duct.

II. Anacanthini. All the rays of the vertical and ventral fins articulated; the latter, when present, being jugular and thoracic.

III. Physostomi. All the fin rays articulated, with the exception of the first in the dorsal and pectoral which sometimes are more or less ossified. Ventral fins, when present, abdominal and spineless. Air-vessel, if existing, having a pneumatic duct (except in *Scombresocidæ*).

IV. Lophobranchii. Fishes possessing a dermal segmental skeleton, with the opercular pieces reduced to a single plate. Gill-openings small. Gills consisting of small rounded tufts, attached to the branchial arches. Muscular system very slightly developed. Snout produced: mouth terminal, but small. Teeth absent. Air-vessel stated to be destitute of a pneumatic duct.

V. Plectognathi. Fishes with the bones of the head completely ossified, whilst those in the remainder of the body are incompletely so: vertebræ few. Gill-openings small, situated in front of the pectoral fins. Gills pectinate. Head generally large. Mouth narrow: the bones of the upper jaw mostly united, sometimes produced into the form of a beak. Teeth in the jaws absent or present. There may be a single soft-rayed dorsal fin, belonging to the caudal portion of the vertebral column, and situated opposite the anal: in some a rudimental spinous dorsal is also present: ventrals when existing, have the form of spines. Skin either smooth, with rough scales, or ossified in the form of plates or spines. Air-vessel destitute of a pneumatic duct.

Geographical distribution. The Acanthopterygian Fishes do not exist in any numbers in the inland fresh-waters of India, being mostly confined to either within, or but a short distance removed from tidal

* Certain fish as the *Labyrinthici* and *Ophiocephalidæ* can live in water even with a bandage fastened round their gills, entirely preventing their use for respiratory purposes, provided they can obtain direct access to atmospheric air. Such a proceeding would however be fatal to the majority of fishes, thus showing that some forms possess means of depurating their blood which are not present to all.

† There are some genera in which the fins can hardly be said to possess any true spines as amongst the *Trachinidæ*, *Aulostomatidæ*, *Trachinidæ*, &c.

influence, or above the sea level. The larger the river, the greater is the probability of their extending their range up it. The hard rayed fishes captured in the fresh waters, mostly belong to one of the following genera. *Lates*, *Ambassis*, *Nandus*, *Badis*, *Pristolepis*, *Sciæna*, *Equula*, *Gobius* and allied genera, *Mugil*, members of the *Labyrinthiform* and *Ophiocephaloid* families, as well as the spined eels, and the *Etropli*.

SYNOPSIS OF FAMILIES AMONGST THE ACANTHOPTERYGII.*

First Group—Perciformes.

Body elevated or oblong, not elongate. No superbranchial organ. Spinous dorsal well developed, the soft dorsal similar to the soft anal: ventrals thoracic, 1/4 or 1/5.† Vent remote from the end of the tail, and posterior to the ventral fins. No prominent anal papilla.

1. *Percidæ*. Preopercle not articulated with the orbit. Neither molars nor cutting teeth. Vertical fins generally scaleless. Lateral line almost invariably present and uninterrupted.‡
2. *Squamipinnes*. Preopercle not articulated with the orbit. Body mostly elevated and compressed. Neither molars nor cutting teeth, setiform ones may exist in the jaws, or villiform ones on the palate. Vertical fins scaled. Lateral line uninterrupted.
3. *Mullidæ*. Preopercle not articulated with the orbit. Teeth feeble, jaws and palate variously armed or edentulous. Two long and stiff barbels below the chin.
4. *Nandidæ*. Preopercle not articulated with the orbit. Teeth feeble, but dentition more or less complete. Lateral line interrupted or absent.
5. *Sparidæ*. Preopercle not articulated with the orbit. Either rows of cutting or conical teeth in the front of the jaws, or a lateral row of molars, or both conjoined.
6. *Cirrhitidæ*. Preopercle not articulated with the orbit. Neither cutting nor molar teeth. Lower pectoral rays unbranched.
7. *Scorpænidæ*. Preopercle articulated with the orbit. Some of the bones of the head armed.
8. *Teuthididæ*. Each ventral fin having two spines and three intermediate soft rays.

Second group—Beryciformes.

Body oblong or elevated. Head with large, subcutaneous, muciferous cavities. Ventral fins thoracic, each with a spine, and less or more than five soft rays. Vent remote from the end of the tail, and posterior to the ventral fins.

9. *Berycidæ* as defined for the group.

Third group—Kurtiformes.

Body strongly compressed. A single dorsal fin, much less developed than the anal. Vent remote from the end of the tail, and posterior to the ventral fins.

10. *Kurtidæ* as defined for the group.

Fourth group—Polynemiformes.

Mouth on the lower side of a prominent snout: muciferous system on the head well developed. Two rather short dorsal fins: several free and articulated filaments below each pectoral. Scales more or less covering the vertical fins. Vent remote from the end of the tail, and posterior to the ventral fins.

11. *Polynemidæ* as defined for the group.

Fifth group—Sciæniformes.

Muciferous system on the head well developed. The second dorsal fin much more developed than the first, or the anal: no pectoral filaments. Vent remote from the end of the tail, and posterior to the ventral fins.

12. *Sciænidæ* as defined for the group.

Sixth group—Xiphiiformes.

The upper jaw produced into a long, sword-like process. Vent remote from the end of the tail, and posterior to the ventral fins.

13. *Xiphiidæ* as defined for the group.

* This synopsis of the Families of Acanthopterygian fishes existing in India, is taken, with as slight alterations as possible, from the elaborate one in the British Museum Catalogue of Fish, Vol. iii, **Appendix.** By adhering to this, it has been considered, that reference to the specimens in the national collection would be facilitated.

† There are exceptions; thus in some genera amongst the *Scorpænidæ*, the rays are rudimentary, and in Teuthididæ the ventral fin has 2/3.

‡ For exceptions, see Genus *Ambassis*, also Poey has recorded from Cuba a Genus nearly allied to *Lutianus*, but which, amongst other things, is distinguished by having an interrupted lateral line.

Seventh group—Trichiuriformes.

Body band-like and compressed. Cleft of mouth deep. Teeth in jaws and palate, several being strong and conical. Dorsal and anal fins many rayed: ventrals, when present, in the form of a pair of scales: caudal absent or forked. Vent remote from the end of the tail, and posterior to the ventral fins when such are present.

14. *Trichiuridæ*, as defined for the group.

Eighth group—Cotto-scombriformes.

Dorsal fins placed close together or continuous, having fewer spines than rays, or the spinous portion may be modified into tentacles, detached spines, or a suctorial disk: anal similar to the soft dorsal, sometimes both fins are modified posteriorly into finlets: ventrals, when present, jugular or thoracic, never forming a sucker. No prominent anal papilla. Vent remote from the end of the tail, and posterior to the ventral fins, when such are present.

15. *Acanthuridæ*. A single dorsal fin with less spines than rays. One or more bony spines on either side of the tail in the adult.

16. *Carangidæ*. Preopercle not articulated with the orbit. Body oblong, elevated, or subcylindrical and compressed. Teeth, when present, villiform or conical. Spinous portion of the dorsal fin sometimes rudimentary: the posterior rays of the dorsal and anal, may consist of detached finlets: ventrals, when present, thoracic. Vertebræ 10/14 (*Naucrates* 10/16).

17. *Stromateidæ*. Preopercle not articulated with the orbit. Body oblong, and compressed. Barbed teeth extend into the œsophagus. One long dorsal fin without any distinct spinous portion. Vertebræ exceed 10/14.

18. *Coryphænidæ*. Preopercle not articulated with the orbit. Body oblong or elevated, and compressed. No teeth in the œsophagus. One long dorsal fin without any distinct spinous portion. Vertebræ exceed 10/14.

19. *Nomeidæ*. Preopercle not articulated with the orbit. Body oblong, more or less compressed. Two dorsal fins, the spinous sometimes continuous with the soft portion, finlets occasionally present: anal spines mostly indistinct: caudal forked. Scales cycloid, of moderate or small size. Vertebræ exceed 10/14.

20. *Scombridæ*. Preopercle not articulated with the orbit. Body oblong, or slightly elongated and compressed. Two dorsal fins, the first being sometimes modified into free spines, or an adhesive disk, whilst the posterior dorsal and anal rays may be in the form of finlets. Scales, if present, small.

21. *Trachinidæ*. Preopercle not articulated with the orbit. Body low and more or less elongated. One or two dorsal fins. Vertebræ exceed 10/14.

22. *Batrachidæ*. Preopercle not articulated with the orbit. Body low, and more or less elongated. First dorsal fin consisting of a few free spines: ventrals jugular 1/2.

23. *Pediculati*. Preopercle not articulated with the orbit. The spinous dorsal, when present, composed of a few isolated spines which may be modified into tentacles: carpal bones forming a sort of arm for the pectoral fin: ventrals, when present, jugular, having four or five rays.

24. *Cottidæ*. Preopercle articulated with the orbit. Body more or less elongated. Some of the bones of the head usually armed. Pectoral fins with, or without filamentous appendages: ventrals thoracic. Body scaleless, scaled, or with a single row of plate-like scales.

25. *Cataphracti*. Preopercle articulated with the orbit. Head and body, more or less angular, cuirassed with plates, or keeled scales covering the body.

Ninth group—Gobiiformes.

Spinous dorsal short and composed of flexible spines, the soft dorsal and anal being of equal extent: ventrals when present, thoracic or jugular, having 1/5 or 1/4. A prominent anal papilla. Vent remote from the end of the tail, and posterior to the ventral fins when such are present.

26. *Gobiidæ*. Preopercle not articulated with the orbit. Ventrals either united so as to form a disk, or else placed close together: anal spines may be absent.

27. *Callionymidæ*. Preopercle not articulated with the orbit. Two dorsal fins, the first with from four to six flexible spines: ventrals wide apart.

Tenth group—Bleniiformes.

Body elongated and more or less cylindrical. Spinous portion of dorsal fin when distinct, may be as fully or even more developed than the soft part: anal more or less elongated: ventrals, if present, thoracic or jugular: caudal, when present, sometimes sub-truncated or rounded. Vent remote from the end of the tail, and posterior to the ventral fins when such are present.

28. *Blenniidæ*. Preopercle not articulated with the orbit. Ventral fins when present, jugular: anal spines few, or absent. Often a prominent anal papilla.

29. *Rhynchobdellidæ*. Body eel-like. Anterior portion of the dorsal fin consisting of numerous free spines: ventrals absent. No prominent anal papilla.

Eleventh group—Mugiliformes.

Two distinct dorsal fins, the anterior short, or similar to the posterior: ventrals well developed, abdominal, 1/5. Vent remote from the end of the tail and posterior to the ventral fins.

30. *Sphyrænidæ.* Body elongate, sub-cylindrical. Teeth large and cutting. Vertebræ 24.
31. *Atherinidæ.* Body more or less elongated, and somewhat sub-cylindrical. Dentition feeble, or moderate. Vertebræ usually exceeding 10/14.
32. *Mugilidæ.* Body more or less elongated, and somewhat sub-cylindrical. Dentition feeble. First dorsal fin consisting of four stiff spines. Vertebræ 24.

Twelfth group—Gasterosteiformes.

The spinous dorsal, when present, short or formed of isolated spines: ventrals abdominal* sometimes imperfectly developed. Vent remote from the end of the tail, and posterior to the ventral fins, when they are present.

33. *Aulostomatidæ.* Anterior bones of the head forming a tube having a small mouth at its extremity. Ventral fins with six rays.
34. *Centriscidæ.* Anterior bones of the head forming a tube having a small mouth at its extremity. Two dorsal fins, the first short, the soft and the anal of moderate extent: ventrals imperfectly developed.

Thirteenth group—Channiformes.

Body elongate. No labyrinthiform superbranchial organ, but a bony prominence on the epitympanic bone. Dorsal and anal fins long, all destitute of spines. Vent remote from the end of the tail, and posterior to the ventral fins, when such are present.

35. *Ophiocephalidæ.* Ventral fins present, or absent.

Fourteenth group—Labyrinthibranchii.

Body compressed, oblong or elevated. A labyrinthiform superbranchial organ arising from the branchial arches, and employed for respiratory purposes. Vent remote from the end of the tail, and posterior to the ventral fins.

36. *Labyrinthici.* Dorsal and anal spines present, and often numerous.

Fifteenth group—Trachypteriformes.

Body elongate and strongly compressed. Skeleton soft. Dentition feeble. Anal fin absent: caudal not in the longitudinal axis of the fish, or else rudimentary: ventrals thoracic.

37. *Trachypteridæ* as defined for the group.

Sixteenth group—Labriformes.

Body oblong, elongated, or elevated and compressed. The lower pharyngeal bones coalesced along the median line, and with or without a median longitudinal suture. A single dorsal fin, the number of spines and rays being nearly equal: soft anal similar to the soft dorsal: ventrals 1/5, thoracic.

38. *Pomacentridæ.* Bones of the head may be armed, or smooth. Scales ctenoid.
39. *Labridæ.* Scales cycloid.

* Dr. Günther observes that in the *Aulostomatidæ* "the ventrals have an abdominal position in consequence of the prolongation of the pubic bones, which are attached to the humeral arch." In the *Centriscidæ*, on the contrary, we find the "ventral fins truly abdominal, imperfectly developed."

FAMILY, I—PERCIDÆ.

Percoidei, pt., *Sciænoidei*, pt., et *Mænides*, pt., Cuv.: *Percidæ*, pt., *Theraponidæ*, pt., *Hæmulonidæ*, pt., Richardson: *Percidæ*, pt., et *Pristipomatidæ*, pt., Günther, Catal., and *Percidæ*, Fische d. Sudsee: *Ambassoidei*, pt. Bleeker.

Branchiostegals from five to seven: pseudobranchiæ present. Form of body generally oblong, and not elongated. Muciferous system of head rudimentary, or but slightly developed. Eyes lateral. No superbranchial organ. Preopercle entire or serrated: cheeks not cuirassed. Mouth in front of snout, having a lateral cleft, occasionally on the lower side: moderately or in some cases very protractile. Teeth in the jaws villiform, with or without canines, present or absent on the vomer, and palatines. Anterior portion of the dorsal fin spinous: ventrals thoracic, 1/5 or sometimes 1/4. Scales ctenoid or cycloid. Lateral line when present continuous, (except in some species of Ambassis.) Air-vessel usually present and more or less simple. Pyloric appendages in varying numbers.

SYNOPSIS OF INDIAN GENERA.

First group—Percina.

Form of body oblong. Opercles strongly denticulated or armed. Cleft of mouth rather oblique. Two dorsal fins: three anal spines. Scales of moderate size, usually ctenoid. Pyloric appendages few.

1. *Lates*. Branchiostegals seven. Preorbital and opercle serrated, the latter denticulated at its angle. Villiform teeth on jaws, vomer, and palate.

Second group—Serranina.

Form of body oblong, sometimes elevated. Opercles serrated or armed. Cleft of mouth rather oblique. One, or more rarely two dorsal fins.

2. *Cromileptes*. Branchiostegals seven. Opercles armed. Fine teeth in jaws, vomer, and palate, without canines. A single elevated dorsal fin: three anal spines. Scales small, cycloid.

3. *Serranus*. Branchiostegals seven. Opercles armed. Villiform teeth in jaws, vomer, and palate: canines present. A single dorsal fin: three anal spines. Scales small, cycloid or ctenoid.

4. *Variola*. Branchiostegals seven. Opercles armed. Villiform teeth in jaws, vomer, and palate: canines present: lateral conical teeth in lower jaw. A single dorsal fin: three anal spines: caudal deeply forked. Scales small, ctenoid.

5. *Anthias*. Branchiostegals seven. Opercles armed. Villiform teeth in jaws, vomer, and palate: canines present. A single dorsal fin: three anal spines: caudal deeply forked. Scales of moderate size.

6. *Grammistes*. Branchiostegals seven. Opercle spinate. Villiform teeth in jaws, vomer, and palate. Two dorsal fins: no anal spines. Scales minute.

7. *Diploprion*. Branchiostegals seven. Opercle spinate: preopercle with a double denticulated limb. Villiform teeth in jaws, vomer, and palate. Two dorsal fins: anal with two spines. Scales small, adherent.

8. *Lutianus*. Branchiostegals seven. Opercle scarcely spinate: preopercle serrated, and its vertical border may be notched to receive an interopercular spinate knob, which is sometimes present. Villiform teeth in jaws, vomer, and palate, generally canines in both jaws, and an outer row of conical lateral ones. A single dorsal fin: anal with three spines. Caudal more or less emarginate. Ctenoid scales of moderate or small size.

Third group—Priacanthina.

Lower jaw prominent. Cleft of mouth almost vertical. Scales ctenoid, small. Cæcal pylori few.

9. *Priacanthus* as defined in group.

Fourth group—Apogonina.

Form of body more or less elevated and compressed. Opercles mostly denticulated or armed. Cleft of mouth oblique or even nearly vertical. One or two dorsal fins.

10. *Ambassis*. Branchiostegals six. Horizontal limb of preopercle with a double serrated border: opercle without a prominent spine. Villiform teeth on the jaws and palate. A recumbent spine anterior to the first dorsal fin: three anal spines. Scales of moderate or small size, deciduous.

11. *Apogon*. Branchiostegals seven. Preopercle with a double border: serrated or entire. Opercle spinate. Villiform teeth in jaws, vomer, and palate. Two anal spines. Scales large, deciduous.

12. *Cheilodipterus*. Branchiostegals seven. Preopercle with an inner ridge, and sometimes with a double serrature: opercle not spinate. Canines, also villiform teeth in the jaws and palatines. Two anal spines. Scales large, deciduous.

Fifth group—Grystina.

Body oblong or elevated. Opercles entire, or variously serrated. Cleft of mouth more or less oblique. One or two dorsal fins.

13. *Dules.* Branchiostegals six. Preopercle serrated: opercle spinate. Villiform teeth in jaws, vomer, and palate. A single dorsal fin, deeply notched between the ninth and tenth spines: three anal spines. Scales ctenoid and of moderate size.

Sixth group—Theraponina.

Branchiostegals six. Opercle spinate: preopercle serrated. Cleft of mouth somewhat oblique. Dorsal fin single, but more or less notched: three anal spines. Air-vessel divided by a constriction into an anterior and posterior portion.

14. *Therapon.* Teeth villiform in jaws, deciduous on vomer and palate.
15. *Datnia.* Teeth villiform in jaws, palate edentulous. Snout rather produced.
16. *Helotes.* Palate edentulous, teeth in the outer row in the jaws having a small lobe on either side.

Seventh group—Pristipomatina.

Branchiostegals from five to seven. Preopercle serrated or entire. Mouth moderately protractile. Teeth in the jaws. Three anal spines. Air-vessel destitute of any constriction.

17. *Pristipoma.* Branchiostegals seven. Opercle with indistinct points: preopercle serrated. Cleft of mouth horizontal: a median groove along the under surface of the lower jaw. Dorsal fin single, but often with a deep cleft between the last two spines.

18. *Hapalogenys.* Branchiostegals six or seven. Preopercle serrated: opercle with short points: barbel-like papillæ on the mandible. Villiform teeth in jaws, vomer, and palate, with an outer enlarged row in the former. Spinous dorsal low, and deeply cleft: anal with three spines. Fins covered with fine scales.

19. *Diagramma.* Branchiostegals six or seven. Preopercle serrated. Mouth small: lips thick: pores on the under surface of the lower jaw, but no median groove. A single dorsal fin.

20. *Lobotes.* Branchiostegals six. Upper profile of the head concave. Preopercle serrated. Lower jaw the longer. A single dorsal fin.

21. *Scolopsides.* Branchiostegals five. Preopercle serrated. A backwardly-directed spine on the infraorbital ring of bones: opercle with a weak spine. A single dorsal fin.

22. *Dentex.* Branchiostegals six. Preorbital high. Preopercle entire. Generally strong canines. More than three rows of scales on the preopercle. A single dorsal fin. Air-vessel notched posteriorly.

23. *Synagris.* Branchiostegals six. Preorbital high. Preopercle serrated, or entire. Canines, not very strong, at least in the upper jaw. Three rows of scales on the preopercle. A single dorsal fin.

24. *Pentapus.* Branchiostegals six. Preorbital low. Preopercle entire. Generally strong canines. Three or more rows of scales on preopercle. A single dorsal fin.

25. *Smaris.* Branchiostegals six. Preopercle entire. Vomer edentulous. Mouth protractile. A single dorsal fin.

26. *Odontonectes.* Branchiostegals six. Preopercle serrated. Villiform teeth in jaws, vomer, and palatines. A single dorsal fin.

27. *Cæsio.* Branchiostegals six or seven. Preopercle entire or finely serrated. Palate edentulous. A single dorsal fin.

Eighth group—Gerrina.

Branchiostegals six. Body elevated or oblong. Preopercle serrated or entire. Mouth very protractile. Villiform teeth in the jaws. A single dorsal fin: three anal spines. Air-vessel simple.

28. *Datnioides.* Preopercle serrated: opercle with short spines. A deeply notched dorsal fin: caudal rounded.

29. *Gerres.* Preopercle mostly entire. Inferior pharyngeal bones united by a suture. Dorsal fin with a scaly sheath. Caudal forked.

Geographical distribution. The Indian PERCIDÆ are almost entirely marine fishes, if we are to judge from the localities where they breed, and the places in which they are most abundant. It is by no means uncommon to capture specimens of *Lates* long distances above tidal influence, but it is unusual to find any of the genera *Serranus, Lutianus, Therapon, Pristipoma, Lobotes, Datnioides,* or *Gerres,* many miles beyond the reach of the tides. The remainder of the genera (excluding *Ambassis*) are almost entirely marine. Amongst this last genus, which is considered by several excellent ichthyologists as forming a distinct family, some are confined to salt water, but the majority are spread through the larger rivers and tanks of the plains.

The colours and tints in fishes vary in different waters, if for instance the latter is opaque or muddy, its finny inhabitants will be found darker; whilst, on the other hand, in clear water they are brighter, and generally lighter.* Age and season likewise exercise an influence in this respect. Thus the *Lutianus marginatus* has a black lateral blotch in the young which generally, but not invariably, disappears in the adult; the same is seen in *Chætodon lunula, Etroplus Suratensis* and many other fishes. In some of the *Serrani,* and sometimes in

* Dr. Stark (Proc. Zool. Soc. 1833, p. 88) observed that the effect of keeping living fish in fresh water contained in vessels of different colours, created a tendency to their assuming the colour of the vessel in which they were kept. In marine forms it has been suggested that the depths of the ocean at which some reside may have an effect upon their colours.

Pristipoma, *Caranx*, *Osphromenus*, &c., vertical bands are found, as a sign that the fish is immature. Lateral longitudinal broad bands are frequently modified, two narrow ones taking the place of a single wider one, as seen in *Cheilodipterus*, *Diagramma*, &c. Likewise in stuffed examples, or in those which have been long macerated in spirit, marks which were distinct in the fresh specimen, become more or less obliterated. Irrespective of the foregoing, the period intervening between capture and examination, has a considerable bearing upon their fugitive colours, as well as whether they have been sodden in water, or kept dry by their captors: for instance, if a dark coloured fish is placed in a dry situation, and strips of moist cloth laid over it and kept wet, the portions of the body which have not been allowed to dry will be found to be of a lighter tint than those not so treated, and this banded appearance which can be so easily produced is indelible. It is by no means uncommon for the caudal fin to be white in the young, but black in the adult as in *Diagramma nigrum*.

The foregoing brief remarks on the colours of fishes will explain how it is that the descriptions in this work do not always agree with those of other observers. Such discrepancies indeed often merely mean, that the colours of the same species of fish may differ in different districts.

First group—Percina.

Form of body oblong. Opercles strongly denticulated or armed. **Cleft of mouth rather oblique. Two dorsal fins**: three anal spines. Scales of moderate size. Pyloric appendages **few.**

Genus, 1—Lates, *Cuv. and Val.*

Branchiostegals seven: pseudobranchiæ. Body oblong and somewhat compressed. Preorbital, and shoulder bone serrated: preopercle with strong spines at its angle, and denticulated along its horizontal limb: opercle spinate. Teeth villiform on jaws, vomer, and palatine bones, tongue smooth. Two dorsal fins united at their base, the first with seven or eight spines, the anal with three: caudal rounded. Scales finely ctenoid, and of moderate size. Cæcal pylori few.

Geographical distribution. Mouths of the Nile: from the coasts of Sind throughout the seas of India to the Malay Archipelago, China, and Australia.

Uses. Besides being in most places excellent as food, their air-vessels or sounds are dried, and appear in commerce as rough isinglass, much of which is exported from India to China, and some to Europe. Cantor observes that this fish "yields isinglass in the Straits, but little is collected, partly on account of the comparative scarcity of the fish, and partly owing to the thinness of the air-vessel. That of a large sized fish when dried weighs upwards of one ounce."

SYNOPSIS OF INDIVIDUAL SPECIES.*

1. *Lates calcarifer* D 7—8/$\frac{1}{11}$ $\frac{1}{12}$, A. $\frac{3}{8}$, L. l. 60. Colour greyish. Seas of India, China, and Australia.

1. Lates calcarifer, Plate I, fig. 1.

Holocentrus calcarifer, Bloch, t. 244.
Perca calcar, Bl. Schn. p. 89.
Perca pandoomacoo, Russell, Fish. Vizag., ii, p. 23, f. 131.
Holocentrus heptadactylus, Lacép. iv, pp. 344, 391.
Coius vacti, Ham. Buch. Fish. Ganges, pp. 86, 369, pl. 16, f. 28.
Lates nobilis, Cuv. and Val. ii, p. 96, f. 13; Richardson, Ich. China, p. 222; Bleeker, Perc. p. 27; Cantor, Catal. Mal. Fish. p. 1; Hageman, Nat. Tyds. Ned. Ind. 1851, p. 348.
Lates calcarifer, Günther, Catal. Fish. i, p. 68 & P.Z.S. 1870, p. 824; Day, Fishes of Malabar, p. 2.
Plectropoma calcarifer, Bleeker, Atl. Ich. Perc. t. xlv, fig. 3.
Dangara, Sind.; *Nuddee-meen* or *Nair-meen*, Mal.; *Painee-meen* or *Kodwa*, Tam.; *Pandu kopah* or *Pandu menu*, Tel.; *Durrnah* and *Bekkut*, Ooriah; *Begti*, Beng.; *Nga-tha-dyk*, Arme; *Koral*, or if large *Bhor*, Chittagong; *Tolok*, Andam.; *Cock-up* of Europeans.

B. vii, D. 7—8/$\frac{1}{11}$ $\frac{1}{12}$, P. 17, V. 1/5, A. $\frac{3}{8}$, C. 17, L. l. 52—60, L. tr. 6—7/13, Cæc. pyl. 3.

Length of head from 3/11 to 1/4, of caudal 1/5 to 1/6, height of body 3/10 to 3/11 of the total length. *Eyes*—diameter 1/5 to 1/6 of the length of the head, from 1 to 1½ diameters from end of snout, and 3/4 of a diameter apart. In the immature the eye is comparatively larger. The maxilla extends to below the posterior edge of the orbit. Preorbital and preopercle finely serrated, the latter with an obtuse angle, having a large tooth directed backwards, and three smaller but strong denticulations along its lower edge: opercular spine weak. Shoulder bone serrated. *Teeth*—villiform on jaws, vomer, and palatines. *Fins*—dorsal spines strong, the third the highest, equalling about the length of the post-orbital portion of the head, from it they decrease: third anal spine longest and strongest, their proportionate lengths varying according to age, thus at four inches long the

* Although only one species of this Genus has been described from India, it will be necessary here to indicate the mode which will be pursued in this work as to the position of each individual in Genera which possess more than one. An excellent method is to begin with that form which is most typical; a second plan is to commence with those having the greatest affinity to the preceding Genus and finish with those closely allied to the following one, in which case the most typical forms are in the middle: the third and least scientific is what I propose adopting in order to facilitate reference, it is to place first those possessing the largest number of spines, rays and scales, and continuing this plan throughout the Genus. Colour will not be adopted for reasons advanced under the next Genus. (See page 9.)

second spine is 3/4 as long as the third, but at 20 inches it is not above 1/4 so long: pectoral shorter than ventral, and rounded: caudal fan-shaped. *Air vessel*—thin, but furnishes a good isinglass. *Colours*—grey, with a dash of green along the back, and silvery on the abdomen: during the monsoon time it has a tinge of purple. The immature are usually darker than the adults.

Having examined Bloch's typical specimen still at Berlin, I find that it has as he states D. 7/$\frac{1}{10}$.

Deformities in this fish are by no means rare. In one case the last few dorsal rays were deflected to the left side of the free portion of the tail, and had there become continuous at their bases with the anal spines, which were likewise inserted along the same portion of the fish, whilst the anal rays were in their natural position.

It is very remarkable how in fishes which have died and stiffened with their mouths open, and the opercles and branchial rays distended, the appearance of the head becomes much changed, whilst it is difficult, or impossible to subsequently bring them back to their normal shape. Thus the profile of the head becomes more horizontal, whilst the posterior extremity of the maxilla does not reach so far back as when the mouth had been naturally closed.

Habitat.—Seas, backwaters, and mouths of tidal rivers in the East, up which last it often ascends long distances to prey upon its weaker neighbours. It is excellent eating when from the vicinity of large rivers. It salts well, and from it some of the best 'Tamarind-fish' is prepared.*

Second group—Serranina.†

Form of body oblong, sometimes elevated. Opercles serrated or armed. Cleft of mouth rather oblique. One, or more rarely two, dorsal fins.

Genus, 2—Cromileptes, *Swains.*

Serranichthys, Bleeker: *Liopercа*, Gill.

Branchiostegals seven: pseudobranchiæ. Body oblong, compressed. Eyes lateral, of moderate size. Preopercle with its vertical limb finely serrated, its horizontal one entire. Opercle with two or three spines. Teeth fine in the jaws, vomer, and palate, no canines; internal row in maxilla not fixed. Dorsal fin elevated, having ten or eleven spines, anal with three; caudal rounded. Scales small, cycloid.

SYNOPSIS OF INDIVIDUAL SPECIES.

1. *Cromileptes altivelis*, D. $\frac{10}{18-19}$, A. $\frac{3}{9-10}$, L. r. $\frac{120}{?}$. Upper profile of head concave. Covered with widely separated, black, white-edged spots. Seas of India to China and beyond.

* The above fish apparently belongs to the group *Percina* and may be a *Lates*. It is from a figure amongst the beautiful collection of coloured drawings made on the Coromandel coast of India by native artists, under the immediate supervision of Sir Walter Elliot, K.S.I. of the Madras Civil Service, who has most liberally placed the whole of them at my disposal for the purpose of this work. I have had it engraved in order to direct the attention of inquirers in India to it.

† Bleeker (Revis. des espèc. Ind-Arch. du groupe des Epinephelini, 1873) divides the Epinephelini (Serranini, pt.) as follows:—

I. Dorsal fin single or but slightly notched. Jaws and opercles scaled. Caudal fin with 15 divided rays.

A. Forehead, snout and suborbitals scaleless. Jaws with canines, which in the mandibles are both anterior and lateral.

1. *Paraserranus*, Blkr. Mandible scaleless. Inner row of teeth immoveable. Preopercle with a spine directed backwards. Dorsal with 10 spines; dorsal and anal scaleless. Scales of moderate size, ctenoid.

2. *Variola*, Swains.=*Pseudoserranus*, Klunz. Mandible scaleless. Inner row of teeth moveable. Preopercle feebly serrated, without any spine. Dorsal with 9 spines; dorsal and anal scaled. Scales very small, ctenoid.

3. *Paracanthistius*, Gill=*Plectropoma*, Gill (Cuv. and Val. ex. parte). Mandible scaled. Inner row of teeth moveable. Preopercle with its lower edge denticulated, the denticulations directed anteriorly. Dorsal with from 6 to 13 spines: dorsal and anal fins with scaly bases. Scales very small, ctenoid in the immature.

B. Forehead and lower jaw scaled. Inner row of teeth in the jaws moveable: mandibles without lateral canines. Dorsal and anal fins scaled. Scales small.

1. *Epinephelus*, Bloch=*Cephalopholis*, Bl. Schn.; *Labroperca, Mycteroperca, Bodianus, Enneacentrus, Petrometopon, Promicrops, Schistorus*, and *Menephorus*, Gill; *Prospinus*, Poey; *Prionanthichthys*, Day. Teeth on vomer, and palate: canines in the premaxillaries. Dorsal with 9 to 11 spines. Scales ctenoid or cycloid.

2. *Cromileptes*, Swains.=*Serranichthys*, Blkr.; *Liopercа*, Gill. Teeth on vomer, and palate: no canines in the jaws. Dorsal with 10 or 11 spines. Profile anteriorly concave. Scales cycloid.

3. *Anyperodon*, Günther=*Cerna*, Bp.? Palate edentulous: no canines in the mandibles. Dorsal with 11 spines. Scales ctenoid.

1. Cromileptes altivelis, Plate I, fig. 2.

Serranus altivelis, Cuv. and Val. ii, p. 324, pl. 35; Richards. Ich. China, p. 230; Bleeker, Perc. p. 33; Cantor, Catal. p. 10; Günther, Catal. i, p. 152; Kner, Denks. Ak. Wiss. Wien. xxiv. t. i, f. 1.

Cromileptes altivelis, Swains. Fish. ii, p. 201; Bleeker, Atl. Ich. Perc. t. 44, f. 3 & Epinephelini, p. 26.

B. vii, D. $\frac{10}{17}$ | $\frac{11}{19}$, P. 18, V. 1/5, A. $\frac{3}{9-10}$, C. 17, L. r. [illegible], L. tr. 36/—.

Length of head 2/7, of caudal about 1/5, height of body 2/7 of the total length. *Eyes*—diameter from 1/5 to 2/11 of the length of head, rather above 1 diameter from the end of snout, and 3/4 of a diameter apart. Upper profile of head concave. Mouth elongated and pointed, with the lower jaw much the longer. The maxilla reaches to below the last third of the orbit. Vertical limb of preopercle serrated; its lower limb, also sub- and inter-opercles entire. Opercular spines not well developed. *Teeth*—villiform in the jaws, the outer row in the maxilla, and inner in mandibles rather larger than the rest. *Fins*—dorsal spines moderately strong, the last being slightly longer than those preceding it, but only 2/3 or 3/4 as high as the highest dorsal ray; soft portions of dorsal and anal fins angularly rounded, and much elevated: pectoral as long as the head: ventrals reach the anus: second anal spine stronger than but not quite so long as the third: caudal fan-shaped. *Scales*—cycloid, about 22 rows between the base of the sixth dorsal spine, and the lateral-line. *Colours*—head and body greyish becoming lighter on the abdomen: fins grey: everywhere covered with round, black, white-edged spots, those on the body, dorsal, and caudal fins being the largest. Bleeker observes that the magnitude, and number of the spots varies with the size of the specimen.

Habitat.—Seas of India to the Malay Archipelago and China. The specimen figured was taken at the Nicobars by the late Dr. Stoliczka. It is about 9 inches in length. Cuv. and Val. type skin has only 10 spines as in this case exists in my specimen.

Genus 3—Serranus,* Cuv.

Epinephelus, sp. Bloch: *Cephalopholis*, sp. Bl. Schn.: *Paraserranus* and *Serraniclithys*, Blkr.: *Labroperca*, *Mycteroperca*, *Bodianus*, *Enneacentrus*, *Petrometopon*, *Promicrops*, *Schistorus*, and *Menephorus*, Gill: *Prospinus*, Poey: *Priacanthichthys*,† Day.

Branchiostegals seven: pseudobranchiæ. Eyes lateral, of moderate size. Preopercle with its vertical limb more or less serrated, its horizontal one generally entire, opercle with two or three flat spines. Teeth villiform in the jaws, vomer, and palate: canines present. Tongue smooth. Dorsal fin single, having from eight to twelve spines: anal with three: caudal cut square, obliquely, emarginate, or rounded. Scales small, ctenoid or cycloid. Pyloric appendages many, in moderate numbers, or few.

"Cavolini and Cuvier have, after repeated examinations, described the smooth Serranus (*S. cabrilla*), and some other species of this genus as true hermaphrodites, one portion of each lobe of roe consisting of true ova, the other part having all the appearance of a perfect milt, and both advancing to maturity simultaneously. A structure of a different kind which must be considered as accidental, has been observed by others in the perch, mackerel, carp, cod, whiting, and sole. This occasional malformation, to speak in a popular phrase, consists of a lobe of hard female roe on one side, and of soft male roe on the other side of the same fish."‡

The colour of these fishes, which varies so extensively in the same species, can hardly be accepted as a trustworthy guide for grouping. The form of the preopercle is not invariably identical in every specimen of the same species, or even on the opposite sides of a fish: whilst a spine is occasionally present at its angle in the immature, becoming more or less absorbed in the adult. The sub- and inter-opercles may be serrated or smooth in the same species as observed in *Serranus boenack*. The fins also alter with age, owing to the spines not increasing in length so rapidly as the rays, consequently they may be comparatively shorter in the adult than in the young. Even the rays in the mature fish are found less in their proportionate height to the entire length of the specimen, than they are in the immature. The same thing occurs in respect to the anal spines, the second is sometimes the longest in the immature but becomes shorter than the third in the mature, and this appears to be most frequent when the second spine is the strongest, augmenting in thickness whilst the third increases in length. Occasionally there is an excess of one spine and a deficiency of a ray in the dorsal fin, the first of the rays having apparently taken on a spinous character, as is seen more distinctly in some of the Sparidæ. The numbers of rows of scales is very important amongst these fishes, as so ably pointed out by Bleeker, and many a mistake in identification would have been saved, had his plan been adopted, which is to give the numbers of transverse rows going to the lateral-line from both above and below. As an example I would point to the *Serranus Sonnerati*, so easily distinguished when this plan is followed, but apparently so difficult where it is not attended to.

Geographical distribution.—The seas of temperate and tropical regions. The members of this genus in India may be considered as entirely marine, a few, it is true, ascend rivers not for breeding but predaceous purposes, restricting their range, however, to within tidal influence.

* Fishes of this genus are termed *Callawah*, Tam.

† In the Proc. Zool. Soc. 1868, p. 193, I described *Priacanthichthys Maderaspatensis* as the type of a new genus having a long serrated spine at the angle of the preopercle, and also a serrated ventral one, D. [illegible], A. [illegible], L. l. 70, L. r. above 100. Dark violet, with two light blue longitudinal bands. Dr. Günther suggests that it is the young of *Serranus latifasciatus*, Temm. & Schleg. which is by no means improbable, my largest specimen having been under two inches in length.

‡ Yarrell, British Fishes, i, p. 11.

Uses. Good as food, but coarse when very large. Isinglass is obtained from their air-vessels, but the amount is not very great.

SYNOPSIS OF SPECIES.

1. *Serranus Stoliczkæ*, D. [illegible], A. [illegible], L. r. [illegible], L. tr. 14/40. Preopercle emarginate, and its vertical border serrated. Caudal rounded. Reddish, with four vertical bands on the body: head and anterior half of body spotted with red, or reddish yellow. Coasts of Sind and Aden.

2. *Serranus areolatus*, D. [illegible], A. [illegible], L. r. 105, L. tr. 19/47. Preopercle slightly emarginate: vertical limb serrated, having coarser teeth at its angle. Caudal emarginate. Reddish-brown, with hexagonal markings over the head, body, and fins, which latter have dark margins edged with white. From Aden throughout the seas of India to the Malay Archipelago.

3. *Serranus Waandersi*, D. [illegible], A. [illegible], L. r. [illegible], L. tr. 25/56. Upper two thirds of body, dorsal fin, and upper third of caudal covered with hexagonal or rounded blotches. Seas of India to the Malay Archipelago.

4. *Serranus lineatus*, D. [illegible], A. [illegible], L. r. [illegible], L. tr. 28/48. Cæc. pyl. above 50. Preopercle with several denticulations at the angle, rather well developed. Caudal rounded. Brown, with four, five, or more blue longitudinal bands. India and China, attaining at least four feet in length.

5. *Serranus merra*, D. [illegible], A. [illegible], L. r. [illegible], L. tr. 16/32. Preopercle rounded, its vertical margin serrated, most coarsely at its angle. Pectoral fin as long as the head: caudal rounded. Reddish-brown everywhere covered with large brown spots.

6. *Serranus hexagonatus*, D. [illegible], A. [illegible], L. r. [illegible], L. tr. 13/16. Cæc. pyl. 32. Preopercle with strongest serrations at the angle. Caudal rounded. Brown, covered with large hexagonal, or rounded spots. Red Sea, East coast of Africa, seas of India, Malay Archipelago to the Pacific.

7. *Serranus maculatus*, D. [illegible], A. [illegible], L. r. [illegible], L. tr. 20/45. Preopercle rounded, vertical limb serrated, and most coarsely at its rather produced angle. Second, and third dorsal spines as long as the post-orbital portion of the head, and longer than the rays. Deep grey with round black spots on the head and some of the fins, becoming oval in the anterior half of the body, and rather sinuous on its posterior half. Coromandel coast of India, and the Andaman islands.

8. *Serranus flavo-cæruleus*, D. [illegible], A. [illegible], L. r. [illegible], L. tr. 22/. Serrations on preopercle weak, strongest at its angle. Caudal slightly emarginate. Purplish-blue, tail and fins gamboge-yellow, ventral and anal with black tips. From the East coast of Africa throughout the seas of India.

9. *Serranus fasciatus*, D. [illegible], A. [illegible], L. r. [illegible]. Preopercle rather strongly serrated, most so at its angle. Caudal rounded. Reddish or yellowish with indistinct vertical bands: dorsal, and caudal fins may be black edged. From the Red Sea, through those of India to the Malay Archipelago and beyond.

10. *Serranus [illegible]*, D. [illegible], A. [illegible], L. r. [illegible], L. tr. 21/. Preopercle serrated. Caudal rounded. Greyish-olive, darkest along the back. Body, and head covered with irregularly-sized pearly-white spots, whilst a black line exists on the maxilla. Fins dark grey, externally nearly black; the margins of the pectoral, ventral, soft dorsal, and caudal have a very narrow white border. The whole of the dorsal fin with white spots, as on the body. East coast of Africa, seas of India, and Burma, to the Malay Archipelago.

11. *Serranus diacanthus*, D. [illegible], A. [illegible], L. r. [illegible], L. tr. 20/45. Cæc. pyl. 11. Preopercle with strong teeth at its angle. Pinkish-brown on the back, rose coloured on the abdomen. Six vertical dark bands, the first on the head. Fins with dark margins. Found throughout the seas of India to Java. Is very common in Sind, and specimens reach 18 inches or more in length.

12. *Serranus sexfasciatus*, D. [illegible], A. [illegible]. Two spinate teeth at the angle of the preopercle. Brownish, with six vertical bands, and some irregular spots on the body. Dorsal, caudal, and anal yellow with black spots. Seas of India to the Malay Archipelago.

13. *Serranus lanceolatus*, D. [illegible], A. [illegible], L. r. [illegible], L. tr. 20/52. Cæcal pylori numerous, but very short. When young it is gamboge yellow, with five blackish-blue cross bands. Fins yellow with black bands, and spots. As it becomes adult the bands become broken up into irregular markings, and the yellow colour disappears, except from the fins, in which the black becomes also broken up into black spots. East coast of Africa, seas of India to the Malay Archipelago. Very numerous at Kurrachee: it attains a large size.

14. *Serranus erythrurus*, D. [illegible], A. [illegible]. Preopercular border rounded, and finely serrated in its vertical portion. Fins rounded. Head, and back greenish shot with red; under surface of the body silvery. Dorsal greenish; pectorals, ventrals, and anal yellowish; tail, and free portion of caudal reddish. Specimen 8 inches in length, but said to attain 4 feet. Malabar.

15. *Serranus Malabaricus*, D. [illegible], A. [illegible], L. r. [illegible], L. tr. 19/50. Cæc. pyl. 50-60. Vertical limb of preopercle serrated, strongest at the angle. Fins rounded. Brownish, with about eight cross bands, the first over the head, the second over the nape. Head, and body covered with large round yellow spots, that usually become brown in dead specimens: yellow spots also on the dorsal fin, which sometimes coalesce and form bands. East coast of Africa, seas of India to the Philippines. It attains a very large size.

16. *Serranus corallicola*, D. [illegible], A. [illegible], L. r. [illegible]. Greyish-brown with black spots. Madras to the Malay Archipelago.

17. *Serranus salmoides*, D. [illegible], A. [illegible], L. r. [illegible], L. tr. 24/50. Vertical limb of preopercle serrated, with three or four coarse teeth at the angle. Fins rounded. Brownish yellow: body, and fins entirely covered with black, or yellow spots. From the Red Sea, through the seas of India, to the Malay Archipelago.

18. *Serranus semipunctatus*, D. $\frac{11}{14}$, A. $\frac{3}{8}$. The serrations on the preopercle are fine. Caudal rounded. Body with six, or seven broad cross bands; head, and fins only are spotted. Pondicherry, to 1 foot in length.

19. *Serranus summana*, D. $\frac{11}{15-16}$, A. $\frac{3}{8}$. Canine teeth small. Preopercle serrated, with a shallow notch above its angle. Second anal spine longest and strongest: caudal rounded. Brown, body, and vertical fins covered with small, round, white dots. Scarcely any spots on the head: a black streak above the maxilla. Red Sea, East coast of Africa, and Andaman Islands, where it is very common.

20. *Serranus dermochirus*, D. $\frac{11}{15}$, A. $\frac{3}{8}$, appears to be a variety of the last species. Malabar.

21. *Serranus morrhua*, D. $\frac{11}{14}$, A. $\frac{3}{8}$, L. r. $\frac{112}{125}$, L. tr. 21/46. Preopercle with three strong teeth at its angle. Caudal rounded. Greenish-olive, becoming dull yellow on the abdomen; several irregular bluish-white bands radiate from the orbit, or exist on the head, whilst others are seen on the body. Red Sea, seas of India to Japan.

22. *Serranus angularis*, D. $\frac{11}{15-16}$, A. $\frac{3}{8}$, Cæc. pyl. 13-14. Three strong denticulations at the angle of preopercle. Caudal lunate. Greyish, head and body, covered with large closely-set yellow spots. Fins spotted, all, except the pectoral, with black white-edged margins. Andamans.

23. *Serranus fuscoguttatus*, D. $\frac{11}{14-15}$, A. $\frac{3}{8}$, L. r. $\frac{108}{98}$, L. tr. 22/56. Canine teeth feeble in the upper and not apparent in the lower jaw. Vertical limb of preopercle rather strongly serrated, but more coarsely at its angle: third anal spine longest, but not so strong as the second: caudal rounded. Greyish, with brown spots of a larger or smaller size irregularly disposed. East coast of Africa: Andaman Islands.

24. *Serranus grammicus*, D. $\frac{11}{15}$, A. $\frac{3}{8}$, L. r. $\frac{125}{122}$, L. tr. 17/44. Preopercle serrated, more coarsely at its angle. Caudal fin cut nearly square. Greyish, with three narrow black bands; the superior passes from the upper edge of the orbit to the last dorsal spine; the second from the upper third of the orbit over the superior opercular spine to the base of the sixth dorsal ray; and the third from the lower edge of the orbit to below the middle opercular spine, and on to the upper third of the caudal fin, where it takes the form of rounded blotches. Dorsal fin with a row of black spots along its centre, and edged with black; anal, and caudal edged with black, the latter with numerous black spots. Madras, to at least 15 inches in length.

25. *Serranus boenack*, D. $\frac{9}{15-16}$, A. $\frac{3}{9}$, L. r. 95, L. tr. 22/43. Preopercle most coarsely serrated at its angle. Caudal rounded. Yellowish-brown: snout pale blue: lips, and throat spotted with a darker blue: and about five fillets of the same colour diverge from the orbit and cross the opercles. Tortuous blue lines along the body. Seas of India to the Malay Archipelago, and China.

26. *Serranus miniatus*, D. $\frac{9}{14-15}$, A. $\frac{3}{9-10}$, L. r. $\frac{120}{98}$, L. tr. 14/40, Cæc. pyl. 12 (Madras) to 16 (Andamans). Sub- and inter-opercles serrated, as is also the vertical limb of the preopercle: opercle, with three spines, the upper the shortest. Caudal rounded. Scarlet: body, cheeks, dorsal, caudal, and anal fins covered with large blue spots. Two dark streaks from the orbit along the snout: fins darkest at their outer edges. Two rows of large blue spots along the hard dorsal, and six or eight over the soft, and the anal. Madras, Andamans, to the Malay Archipelago.

27. *Serranus guttatus*, D. $\frac{9}{14-16}$, A. $\frac{3}{9}$, L. r. $\frac{125}{125}$, L. tr. 21/43, Cæc. pyl. 8. Preopercle not emarginate: edge very slightly if at all serrated. Brownish-black, head, body, and all the fins with round blue black-edged spots, caudal, anal, and the posterior half of the dorsal with a white edge. Red Sea, seas of India to the Malay Archipelago, China, and Australia.

28. *Serranus leopardus*, D. $\frac{9}{14-15}$, A. $\frac{3}{9}$, L. r. $\frac{55}{}$, L. tr. 10/26. Reddish or yellowish: body spotted: a dark band from the eye to the opercle: one or two more over the free portion of the tail, and an oblique black band across either caudal lobe. Red Sea, through the seas of India to China.

29. *Serranus Sonnerati*, D. $\frac{9}{15}$, A. $\frac{3}{9}$, L. r. $\frac{110}{112}$, L. tr. 27/40, Cæc. pyl. 11 or 12. Vertical limb of preopercle finely serrated: caudal rounded. A dull lake colour, the head, and jaws covered with reticulated bright blue lines. Some very indistinct spots over the whole of the body. Fins lake colour, darkest at the edges. Soft dorsal, anal, and caudal sometimes with lightish badly-marked spots. East coast of Africa, seas of India to Sumatra, and the Louisiade Archipelago.

30. *Serranus Boelang*, D. $\frac{9}{15}$, A. $\frac{3}{9}$, L. r. $\frac{75}{}$, L. tr. 18/36. Preopercle rounded, and its vertical border finely serrated. Purplish, with eight or nine vertical bands on the body. East coast of Africa, Andamans to the Malay Archipelago.

1. Serranus Stoliczkæ, Plate I, fig. 3.

B. vii, D. $\frac{11}{17}$, P. 17, V. 1/5, A. $\frac{3}{8}$, C. 17. L. r. $\frac{132}{118}$, L. tr. 14/40.

Length of head, 3/11 to 2/7, of caudal 2/11 to 1/6, height of body 2/7 to 1/4 of the total length. *Eyes*—diameter 1/4 to 2/9 of length of head, 1 diameter from end of snout and also apart. The maxilla extends to below the posterior 1/3 or hind edge of the eye. Vertical border of the preopercle emarginate, rather coarsely serrated most so at its angle, its lower limb, sub- and inter-opercles entire. *Teeth*—canines in both jaws, the outer row in the maxilla and the inner in the mandible larger than the villiform bands. *Fins*—dorsal spines, excluding the two first, of about equal length, and from two-fifths to half the height of the body: pectoral as long as the head behind the middle of the orbit, and much longer than the ventral which reaches the vent: second anal spine strongest, the third somewhat the longest, equalling the third of the dorsal fin: caudal rounded. *Scales*—cycloid, extended over snout, suborbitals and hind half of maxilla. *Colours*—light brownish-red, becoming hyacinth-red on the sides and below, barred with four vertical darker bands, the anterior proceeding from the whole base of the spinous dorsal, these bands become indistinct in large specimens.

Head, and body, as far as the base of the soft dorsal, and anal, spotted with reddish-orange or gall-stone yellow, which on the head, and sometimes as far as the base of the pectoral fin, are in hexagonal blotches, divided by light lines. Base of pectoral white having a black crescentic band. Under surfaw of the throat and chest with large black marks sometimes enclosing lighter spaces. Dorsal fin with chestnut-brown spots: some white ones on the caudal, and anal.

I have dedicated this fish to the memory of my friend, and fellow worker in zoology, Dr. Ferdinand Stoliczka, whose untimely death, due to excess of zeal in the cause of Natural History, is referred to in the preface.

Habitat.—Coast of Sind, very common at Aden: it attains at least 12 inches in length, the specimen figured is 6 inches long.

2. Serranus areolatus, Plate I, fig. 4.

Perca areolata, Forsk. p. 42.

Perca tauvina, Geoff. Descr. de l'Eg. pl. 20, fig. 1.

Serranus tauvinus, Geoff. Poiss. d'Eg. p. 291.

Serranus areolatus (Japonicus), Temm. Schleg. Fauna Japon. p. 8; Cuv. and Val. ii, p. 350; Richards., Ich. China, p. 232; Peters, Wieg. Arch. 1855, p. 235; Günther, Catal. i, p. 149; Klunzinger, Verh. z. b. Ges. Wien, 1870, p. 675.

Serranus chlorostigma, Cuv. and Val. ii, p. 352; Günther, Catal. i, p. 151.

B. vii, D. $\frac{11}{15-17}$, P. 15, 1/5, A. $\frac{3}{8}$, C. 19, L. r. 105, L. tr. 19/47.

Length of head 3/10 to 2/7, of caudal 1/6, height of body 1/4 of the total length. *Eyes*—diameter 1/5 to 1/6 of length of head, $1\frac{1}{2}$ diameters from the end of snout and 1 apart. Lower jaw the longer: the maxilla reaches to below the posterior edge of the orbit. Vertical limb of preopercle oblique, serrated, and with much coarser teeth at its somewhat produced angle: sub- and inter-opercles entire. Central opercular spine the most developed. *Teeth*—small canines in both jaws, the outer row in the maxilla, and the inner in the mandible, rather larger than the villiform bands. *Fins*—the third to the fifth dorsal spines the longest, and equal to the highest rays: pectoral as long as the head behind the middle of the eyes: third anal spine $1\frac{1}{2}$ diameters of the orbit in length, not quite so strong, but longer than the second: caudal emarginate: in some specimens the outer rays are slightly produced, and the intermediate portion of the fin is cut square. *Scales*—slightly ctenoid. *Colours*—reddish-brown, with hexagonal markings, formed by fine bluish-white lines, which exist over the head, body, and fins, the last have dark margins edged with white. In Madras and Andaman specimens, the markings on the fins are not always so distinct, whilst there is generally a white upper half to the last third of the caudal fin. Sometimes the pectorals are of an uniform yellow and not marked.

The *S. chlorostigma* appears to be this species, with slightly stronger teeth at the angle of its preopercle than seen in typical *S. areolatus*, the markings are the same but lighter.

Habitat.—Coasts of India, from the Red Sea to the Malay Archipelago, attaining a considerable size. Largest specimen obtained 21 inches in length, the one figured is 9 inches.

3. Serranus Waandersi, Plate VIII, fig. 1.

Epinephelus Waandersi, Bleeker, Atl. Ich. Perc. t. xi, f. 3, and Epinephelini, p. 68.

B. vii, D. $\frac{11}{15}$, P. 18, V. 1/5, A. $\frac{3}{8}$, C. 17, L. r. [illegible], L. tr. 25/56.

Length of head 3/11, of caudal nearly 1/6, height of body 4/15 to 1/4 of the total length. *Eyes*—diameter 2/9 (in a specimen 10 inches long) to 2/11 (in a specimen 20 inches long) of length of head, $1\frac{1}{2}$ diameters from end of snout, and from 2/3 to nearly 1 apart. The posterior extremity of the maxilla reaches to below the middle of the orbit. Vertical limb of the preopercle rather strongly serrated, more especially at its angle, which is not produced, its lower limb, as well as sub- and inter-opercles entire: three distinct opercular spines, the central one being the most developed. *Teeth*—villiform, with an outer enlarged row in the upper and an inner in the lower jaw: small canines in both jaws: a narrow band along the centre of the tongue. *Fins*—dorsal spines of moderate length, increasing to the fourth which equals from 2/5 in the young to 1/3 in the height of the body below it, rays rather higher than the spines, soft portion of the fin and also of the anal rounded: pectoral longer than the ventral, and equalling the head behind the middle of the eye: anal spines rather strong, the third the longest, and equal to four-fifths that of the highest in the dorsal fin: caudal cut square in the young, but slightly emarginate in the adult, owing to the prolongation of the outer rays. *Scales*—rather strongly ctenoid, and thickly covering the snout, and suborbital ring of bones, as well as the posterior half of the maxilla. *Colours*—dark purplish, lightest on the abdomen, the whole of the head and body as low as the pectoral fin, the dorsal and upper third of the caudal, covered with large closely approximating rather dark edged blotches of yellow, which are rounded or hexagonal, those on the head being the smallest. Fins a little darker than the body, and stained with black at their edges: dorsal with a white margin: pectoral orange, upper half of caudal lighter than the lower (Male).

I first observed this species in the Madras Museum in 1867, where it was labelled *S. salmonoides*. I find it amongst Sir Walter Elliot's drawings. Jerdon (Madr. J. L. and Sc. 1851, p. 129) remarks under the head of *S. millus*, "In one specimen, of which I possess a drawing, only the upper half of the caudal is spotted."

Habitat.—Seas of India to the Malay Archipelago, attaining at least 2 feet in length, the specimen figured is 10 inches long.

4. Serranus undulosus, Plate II, fig. 1.

Bodianus undulosus, Quoy and Gaim. Voy. Freycinet, Poiss. p. 310 (not *Serranus undulosus*, Cuv. and Val.).

Serranus lineatus, Cuv. and Val. ii, p. 312; Jerdon, M. J. L. and Sc. 1851, p. 129; Günther, Catal. i, p. 156.

Serranus Amboinensis, Bleeker, Amb. and Ceram. p. 258; Günther, Catal. i, p. 156.

Epinephelus undulosus, Bleeker, Epinephelini, p. 65, and Atl. Ich. t. 228, Perc. t. 10, f. 3.

B. vii, D. $\frac{11}{17-18}$, P. 19, V. 1/5, A. $\frac{3}{8}$, C. 17, L. l. ca. 90, L. r. [illegible], L. tr. 20/48, Cæc. pyl. above 50.

Length of head from 2/7 to 3/11, of caudal 1/6, height of body 3/11 of the total length. *Eyes*—diameter 1/4 to 1/5 of length of head, from 1 to 1¼ diameters from the end of snout, and from 1/2 to 3/4 of a diameter apart. The maxilla reaches to below the last third or even the hind edge of the orbit. Preopercle serrated along its vertical edge, and with from two to four strong denticulations at its angle which is rather produced, especially in the adult; sub- and inter-opercles entire. Opercular spines distinct, the central one the most developed. In the fry a distinct spine exists at the angle of the preopercle. *Teeth*—one or two rather small canines on both sides of the symphysis in either jaw, those in the upper the larger: outer row of teeth in maxilla, and inner in the mandible larger than the villiform bands. *Fins*—dorsal spines of moderate strength, the third to the fifth the longest, equal to the distance between the hind edge of the orbit and the upper opercular spine, and nearly as high as the rays: pectoral and ventral of about the same size, and equal to the postorbital length of the head: second anal spine the strongest and nearly as long as the third, which equals one and a third diameters of the orbit in length. Soft portions of dorsal and anal fins somewhat rounded: caudal cut square in the adult, but rather rounded in the young. *Scales*—ctenoid. *Colours*—reddish-grey, becoming lighter on the abdomen: numerous oblique narrow brown (blue?) bands of varying length, and usually somewhat sinuous above the lateral-line not following the course of the scales, whilst they are more or less horizontal below it: dots and yellow lines on the head: fins rather dark, and stained at their edges.

I place this species as *S. undulosus*, in accordance with Bleeker's observations. There is no doubt but that it is identical with *S. lineatus* C.V., the type specimen of which (a skin) exists in Paris.

Amongst Sir Walter Elliot's drawings is one of this fish, termed *Seela punni*, October, 1848.

Habitat.—Seas of India to the Malay Archipelago and China. It is not uncommon at Madras where the young are numerous during the cold season. The longest specimen obtained was 12 inches.

5. Serranus merra, Plate II, fig. 2.

? *Perca tauvina*, Forsk. p. 39; Gmel. Linn. p. 1316.

Epinephelus merra, Bloch, t. 329; Bl. Schn. p. 300 (not Bleeker).

? *Holocentrus tauvina*, Bl. Schn. p. 321.

Serranus Gilberti, Richardson, Ann. Nat. Hist. 1842, p. 19, and Ich. China, p. 230; Günther, Catal. i, p. 148.

Serranus megachir, Richards. Ich. China, p. 230.

Serranus pardalis, Bleeker, Perc. p. 37.

Serranus Quoyanus, Günther, Catal. i, p. 153; (? Cuv. and Val. vi, p. 519).

Epinephelus pardalis, Bleeker, Ternate, p. 232.

Serranus tauvina, Klunz. Fisch. d. Roth. Meer. Verh. z. b. Ges. Wien, 1870, p. 683.

Epinephelus Gilberti, Bleeker, Epinephelini, p. 91.

B. vii, D. $\frac{11}{16-17}$, P. 18, V. 1/5, A. $\frac{3}{8}$, C. 17, L. r. [illegible], L. tr. 16/32.

Length of head 2/7 to 3/11, of caudal 2/9, height of body 3/11 to 1/4 of the total length. *Eyes*—diameter 1/4 to 2/9 of the total length, 3/4 of a diameter from the end of snout, and also apart. Snout obtuse. The maxilla reaches to below the hind edge of the orbit. Preopercle rounded, its vertical border coarsely but evenly serrated, its lower edge and also the sub- and inter-opercles entire. Central opercular spine well developed. *Teeth*—small canines in both jaws, the outer row of teeth in maxilla, and inner in mandible, slightly larger than the villiform bands. *Fins*—dorsal spines rather strong, the fourth somewhat the highest, equalling two-fifths of the length of the head, but not so long as the rays, from it they decrease to the last: soft portion of dorsal, and anal fins somewhat angularly rounded: pectoral large, as long as the head, and longer than the ventral: second anal spine strongest, and about as long as the third which slightly exceeds the second of the dorsal fin: caudal fan-shaped. *Scales*—ctenoid. *Colours*—reddish-brown, covered with large brown spots, except on the pectoral fin, on the head they appear to be usually somewhat hexagonal, with a light intervening reticulation: the marks on the body are larger, and also are usually hexagonal: pectoral with a dark semilunar mark over its base divided by a light band from the dark grey of the rest of the fin, which, as well as the ventral, and anal, has a black margin. A fine specimen in the Berlin Museum has a light edge to the pectoral fin.

Bloch's type specimen of *Epinephelus merra* (pl. 329) is 8½ inches in length, and still in Berlin amongst his fishes.

S. Quoyanus, apud Günther has its scales thus: L. r. [illegible], L. tr. 16/, and appears to me to be closely allied if not identical with *S. merra*, whilst it does not disagree with Valenciennes diagnosis, whose type specimen, however, I have not examined.

Habitat.—Red Sea, seas of India to the Malay Archipelago and China. The specimen figured is 8$\frac{7}{10}$ inches long, and was captured at the Andaman Islands.

6. **Serranus hexagonatus**, Plate II, fig. 3.

Perca hexagonata, Forster, Desc. An. p. 189.
Holocentrus hexagonatus, Bl. Schn. p. 323.
Holocentrus merra, Lacép. pp. 342, 384.
Serranus merra et *faveatus*, Cuv. & Val. ii, pp. 325, 329.
Serranus hexagonatus, Cuv. & Val. ii, p. 330; Guérin, Icon. Poiss. pl. 4, fig. 1; Richards. Voyage Sulphur, p. 82, pl. 38, fig. 1; Cantor. Catal. p. 7; Bleeker, Nat. T. Ned. Ind. vi, p. 191; Peters, Monat. Ak. Wiss. 1865; Günther, Catal. i, p. 141 & Fische d. Sudsee, p. 7, t. vii; Kner, Novara Fische, p. 25; Klunz. Fische d. Roth. Meer. Verh. z. b. Ges. Wien. 1870, p. 683.
Serranus confertus, Benn. Life Raffles, Fish. Sumatra, p. 686.
Serranus nigriceps, Cuv. & Val. vi, p. 517.
Epinephelus hexagonatus, Bleeker, Atl. Ich. Perc. t. 23, fig. 2.
Epinephelus merra, Bleeker, Epinephelini, p. 88 (not Bloch).
Naambu, Bel.: *Pulli-cullawah*, 'Spotted Perch' Tam.
B. vii, D. $\frac{11}{15-17}$, P. 16, V. 1/5, A. $\frac{3}{[illegible]}$, C. 17, L. r. [illegible], L. tr. 13/36, Cæc. pyl. 32, (24 Kner).

Length of head from 3/10 to 2/7, of caudal 1/6, height of body 2/7 to 1/4 of the total length. *Eyes*—diameter 1/4 to 2/9 of the length of head, 1 to $1\frac{1}{4}$ diameters from the end of snout, and from 1/3 to 1 apart. The maxilla reaches to below the hind edge of the orbit. Vertical limb of preopercle finely serrated in its upper two-thirds, more coarsely so in its lower third, especially at its angle, which, though usually rounded, is sometimes slightly produced and armed with one or two strong teeth, its lower limb and also the sub- and inter-opercles entire: the central opercular spine the most developed. *Teeth*—canines in the upper jaw stronger than those in the lower, the outer row of teeth in the maxilla and the inner in the mandibles stronger than the villiform bands. *Fins*—dorsal spines of moderate strength, the fourth the longest, from whence they slightly decrease to the last, which is not so high as the first ray: soft portion of the dorsal and anal fins angularly rounded: pectoral a little longer than the ventral and equal to the length of the head behind the middle of the eye: second anal spine strongest and slightly the longest: caudal obtusely rounded. *Scales*—ctenoid. *Colours*—reddish brown with a light reticulation causing the body, and also the pectoral, soft dorsal, and caudal fins to be covered with hexagonal, or sometimes rounded markings. In some specimens the dark blotches become more confluent, the light reticulations being indistinct.

Although Bloch's figure (t. 329) more resembles *S. hexagonatus* than the species under which I here place it, my reason for doing so is that Professor Peters has shown me the type specimen which unquestionably belongs to this species.

Serranus cylindricus, Günther, Catal. i, p. 151, in some respects very closely resembles this species, its scales are L. r. [illegible], L. tr. 13/, the diameter of its eye $4\frac{1}{2}$ in the length of the head, and 1 diameter from the end of the snout. Although the body is more elongated, it is wider than normal. I almost think that it will turn out to be a variety of this species.

In Cuv. & Val. it is suggested that *Trachinus Admensionis*, Osbeck, ii, p. 96 belongs to this species, he observes "the *body* is somewhat compressed and not quite round."

Habitat.—Red Sea, East coast of Africa, seas of India, Malay Archipelago to the Pacific. The specimen figured was taken at the Andaman Islands and is a little over 8 inches in length.

7. **Serranus maculatus**, Plate II, fig. 4.

Holocentrus maculatus, Bl. t. 242, fig. 3 (young); Bl. Schn. p. 315.
Holocentrus albofuscus, Lacép. iv, p. 384.
Serranus Gaimardi, Cuv. & Val. vi, p. 520; Quoy & Gaim. Voy. Astrol. Poiss. p. 656, pl. 3, fig. 3; Bleeker, Batav. p. 455; Günther, Catal. i, p. 150; Playfair, Proc. Zool. Soc. 1867, p. 847.
Serranus Sebr., Bleeker, Amb. p. 488; Günther, Catal. i, p. 137.
Serranus maculatus, Bleeker, Boeroe, p. 398.
Serranus albofuscus, Günther, Catal. i, p. 108.
Serranus longispinis, Kner, Voy. Novara, Poiss. p. 27, t. ii, f. 2: Playfair, Fish. Zanz. p. 10.
Epinephelus Gaimardi, Bleeker, Atl. Ich. Perc. vii, fig. 1.
Epinephelus albofuscus, Bleeker, l. c. Perc. xxvi, fig. 2.
Epinephelus maculatus, Bleeker, Epinephelini, p. 75, Atl. Ich. Perc. t. viii, fig. 3, & xi, fig. 2.
B. vii, D. $\frac{11}{16-17}$, P. 18, V. 1/5, A. $\frac{3}{[illegible]}$, C. 17, L. r. [illegible], L. tr. 20/45.

Length of head 3/10 to 2/7, of caudal 1/6, height of body nearly 1/4 of the total length. *Eyes*—diameter from 2/9 to 1/5 of the length of head, rather above 1 diameter from the end of snout, and 1 apart. The maxilla, which is rather wide posteriorly, reaches (in the young) to below the last third of the orbit, and in the adult to beneath its hind edge. Preopercle rounded, with its vertical border strongly but pretty evenly serrated, whilst its angle is a little produced and has about eight coarse denticulations. Opercle with the central spine well developed. *Teeth*—small canines in either jaw: the outer row in the maxilla, and the inner in the mandible larger than the villiform bands. *Fins*—dorsal spines of moderate strength: they increase to the third, which equals half the length of the head, and is one half longer than the rays: from thence they decrease, but the last is nearly as long as the rays; the soft portions of the dorsal and anal are somewhat angular: pectorals longer than the ventrals and equal to the length of the head from behind the middle of the orbit: second anal spine strongest but not so long as the third, which is nearly one third of the length of the head: caudal cut square but with rounded angles. *Scales*—ctenoid. *Colours*—deep grey, with round black spots somewhat distantly placed on the head, pectoral, and ventral fins: oval spots, having their longest diameter vertical, exist in the anterior half of the body, becoming more like short thick sinuous lines on the last half. A black edge along the top of the spinous dorsal, and some cloudy interspinous marks: the soft dorsal, anal, and caudal with a black edge and white margin.

Bleeker, in his excellent revision of the Epinephelini, observes that he possesses a beautiful series of specimens of this species showing the successive transitions in colour, which certainly varies very considerably. The young (*maculatus*), according to Bloch's figure, appears to have a light ground colour with a dark band over the head: a second, from the second to the fifth dorsal spine, passing downwards, encloses the pectoral, and ventral fins: a third from the soft dorsal passes down to the whole of the anal: one more exists over the free portion of the tail, and two on the caudal fin; a dark horizontal band appears to connect the others along the middle of the body.

The specimen figured (7 inches in length) from the Andaman Islands agrees with Kner's *S. longispinis*. The type specimens of *S. Guibardi* in the Paris Museum have a much higher body comparatively, whilst the longest dorsal spine scarcely exceeds the length of the rays.

Habitat.—East coast of Africa, seas of India, Andamans to the Malay Archipelago, and China.

8. Serranus flavo-cæruleus, Plate III, fig. 1.

Holocentrus flavo-cæruleus, Lacép. iv, pp. 331, 367.
Holocentrus gymnosus, Lacép. iii, pl. 27, fig. 2, and iv, pp. 335, 372.
Bodianus macrocephalus, Lacép. iii, pl. xx, f. 2, and iv, pp. 281, 293, 295.
Perca flavo-purpurea, Benn. Fish. Ceylon, p. 19, pl. 19.
Serranus Borbonicus, Quoy and Gaim. Voy. Uranie, Poiss. p. 313, pl. 57, f. 2.
Serranus flavo-cæruleus, Cuv. and Val. ii, p. 297; Peters, Wieg. Arch. 1855, p. 236; Günther, Catal. i, p. 145.
Cynichthys flavo-purpuratus, Swains. Fish. ii, p. 202, f. 42, c. (head).
Epinephelus flavo-cæruleus, Bleeker, Fish. Madagascar, p. 17.
Mungil callawah, Tam.: *Koha-lawyah*, Cingalese.

B. vii, D. $\frac{11}{16-17}$, P. 17, V. 1/5, A. $\frac{3}{8}$, C. 17, L. r. [illegible], L. tr. 22/—.

Length of head 3/10, of caudal about 1/5, height of body 3/10 of the total length. *Eyes*—diameter 2/9 to 2/11 of the length of head, $1\frac{1}{2}$ diameters from the end of snout and 1 apart. The maxilla reaches to below the hind edge of the orbit. Preopercle with its vertical limb finely serrated, more coarsely so at its angle, where occasionally they are almost spinate;* lower limb, sub- and inter-opercles entire. Central opercular spine rather strong. *Teeth*—small canines in either jaw, the outer row in the maxilla and the inner in the mandible, larger than the villiform bands. *Fins*—dorsal spines rather strong, increasing in length to the third which equals about 3/8 of the height of the body, and is rather longer than the soft portion of the fin which, as well as that of the anal, is rounded: pectoral as long as the head behind the middle of the eye: ventral reaches three-fourths of the distance to the vent: second anal spine not quite so long as the third: caudal emarginate. *Scales*—ctenoid on the body, thickly covering the snout, pre- and sub-orbitals, likewise the posterior half of the maxilla: about 18 rows between the lateral-line and the sixth dorsal spine: those on the chest and abdomen very small, about 65 rows between the lateral-line and the median line of the abdomen. *Colours*—head and body of a deep purplish blue: free portion of the tail and all the fins gamboge yellow: some yellow on the snout, maxilla, chest, and opercular spines: an indistinct darkish band along the base of the spinous and first third of the rayed portion of the dorsal fin: ventral, and caudal with fine black tips.

Jerdon says (M. J. L. and Sc. 1851), p. 129, "*Serranus flavo-purpureus*, Bennett. This very beautiful fish is very rare at Madras. I never saw but one specimen. I procured the very young at the Sacrifice rocks on the Malabar Coast, it looked like a living sapphire." Bennett observes that it is scarce on the southern coast of Ceylon, in the course of two years having met but with one specimen.

Habitat.—Seas of India to the West coast of Africa. The specimen figured was from the Andaman islands, and is nearly $10\frac{1}{2}$ inches in length.

9. Serranus fasciatus, Plate III, fig. 2.

Perca fasciata, Forsk. p. 40; Gmel. Linn. p. 1316.
Epinephelus marginalis, Bl. t. 328, fig. 1; Bl. Schn. p. 300.
Holocentrus erythræus, Bl. Schn. p. 320.
Holocentrus oceanicus, *marginatus*, *Forskalii* et *rosmarus*, Lacép. Poiss. iv, pp. 377, 384, 389, and 392, t. 7, fig. 2 and 3.
Serranus marginalis, Cuv. and Val. ii, p. 302; Richards. Ich. China, p. 233; Bleeker, Perc. p. 34; Peters, Fish. Mossamb. p. 235, and Monats. Ak. Wiss. Berlin, 1865, p. 109; Günther, Catal. i, p. 135; Kner, Novara Fische, p. 24; Playfair, Fish. Zanzibar, p. 7.
Serranus variolosus, Cuv. and Val. ii, p. 354; Günther, Catal. i, p. 139 (not syn.)

* On the right side of one specimen there are two almost spinate teeth at the angle, as described by Bleeker, they are not thus present on the left side, where however the serrations are somewhat coarse.

Serranus oceanicus, Cuv. and Val. ii, p. 292; Günther, Catal. i, p. 109.

Serranus fasciatus, Klunz. Fische d. Roth. Meer, Verh. z. b. Ges. Wien. 1870, p. 681; Günther, Fische d. Sudsee, p. 6, t. 6.

Epinephelus fasciatus, Bleeker, Epinephelini, p. 119.

B. vii, D. $\frac{11}{15-17}$, P. 18, V. 1/5, A. $\frac{3}{8-9}$, C. 17, L. r. [illegible].

Length of head from 3/10 to 2/7, of caudal 1/6, height of body 2/7 to 1/4 of the total length. *Eyes*—diameter 1/4 to 2/9 of the length of head, 1 diameter from end of snout, and 3/4 of a diameter apart. The maxilla extends to below the hind edge of the orbit. Preopercle rather strongly serrated along its vertical border, rather more coarsely so at its angle, above which it is somewhat emarginate, its lower limb entire. Sub- and inter-opercles either entire, or with a very few fine serrations. Central opercular spine the most developed. *Teeth*—canines in both jaws, the outer row of teeth in the maxilla, and the inner in the mandible larger than the villiform bands. *Fins*—dorsal spines from the third of about the same length, but not so high as the rays, the last are equal to two-fifths of the height of the body: pectoral slightly longer than the ventral, and equal to the length of the head behind the middle of the eye: ventral not reaching the vent: second anal spine the strongest, a little longer than the third which nearly equals the last in the dorsal fin: caudal rounded. *Scales*—on the body ctenoid: from 12 to 14 rows between the lateral-line and the base of the sixth dorsal spine. *Colours*—in *S. fasciatus* reddish or yellowish, with five dark vertical bands, a fine black edge along the whole of the dorsal fin. In *S. oceanicus* the cross bands may be absent. In *S. marginalis* brownish or yellowish, the dorsal, and caudal fins being black edged. In *S. variolosus* brownish, with spots over the head, body, and soft dorsal fins.

Sir J. Richardson directed attention to the *S. tsirimenara* of the 'Fauna Japonica' being distinguished from this fish, owing to its possessing a row of five or six irregular whitish and indistinct spots on the flanks. Bleeker observes that these spots are in two rows above, and below the lateral-line, irrespective of which on comparing specimens of the two species of the same length together, he found that in the *S. tsirimenara* the body is less rounded, the head more pointed, and the rows of scales above and below the lateral line are [illegible].

Habitat.—From the Red Sea through those of India to the Malay Archipelago and beyond. The specimen figured was taken at the Andaman islands, and is 7 inches in length.

10. Serranus tumilabris, Plate III, fig. 3.

Serranus summana, Cuv. and Val. ii, p. 344; Rupp. N. W. Fische, p. 102 and Atl. p. 104; Lefeb. Voy. Abyss. Zool. p. 229, pl. 5, f. 1; Klunzinger. Fische d. Roth. Meer, Verh. z. b. Ges. in Wien. 1870, p. 685 (not Forskal).

Serranus tumilabris, Cuv. and Val. ii, p. 346; Günther, Catal. i, p. 138; Playfair, Fish. Zanz. p. 8, pl. ii, f. 2.

Serranus Hoevenii, Bleeker, Verh. Bat. Gen. 1849, and Perc. p. 36; Günther, Catal. i, p. 138; Playfair, Fish. Zanz. p. 9, pl. ii, f. 3.

Serranus Kuhlartii, Bleeker, Sumatra, p. 169.

Epinephelus Hoevenii, Bleeker, Atl. Ich. Perc. t. iv, f. 1, t. viii, f. 4, & t. xii, f. 4, and Epinephelini, p. 110.

B. vii, D. $\frac{11}{16}$, P. 17, V. 1/5, A. $\frac{3}{8}$, C. 19, L. r. [illegible], L. tr. 21/—.

Length of head from 1/3 to 2/7, of caudal about 1/6, height of body from 2/7 to 1/4 of the total length. *Eyes*—diameter varies considerably, the following shows proportions in ten specimens in spirit. Four as *S. tumilabris* being as follows:—

1. Length of specimen $5\frac{3}{10}$ inches: diameter of eye 2/9 of length of head: third dorsal spine rather above 1/2 as long as head behind front edge of orbit.

2. Length of specimen $6\frac{1}{4}$ inches: diameter of eye 2/9 of length of head: third dorsal spine 1/2 as long as head behind the middle of the orbit.

3. Length of specimen 8 inches: diameter of eye 2/9 of length of head: third dorsal spine not quite 1/2 as long as head behind the front edge of orbit.

4. Length of specimen 9 inches: diameter of eye 1/5 of length of head: third dorsal spine 1/2 the length of the head behind the posterior nostril.

In No. 1, 2, and 3 the eye is 1 diameter from end of snout: in No. 4, $1\frac{1}{4}$ diameters.

Six marked as *S. Hoevenii* are as follows:—

1. Length of specimen $2\frac{7}{10}$ inches: diameter of eye 1/3 of length of head: third dorsal spine as long as the post-orbital portion of the head.

2. Length of specimen 6 inches: diameter of eye 2/9 of length of head: third dorsal spine 1/2 the length of the head behind the middle of the orbit.

3. Length of specimen $6\frac{3}{10}$ inches: diameter of eye $1/4\frac{1}{6}$ (6/25) of length of head: third dorsal spine 1/2 the length of the head behind the first 1/3 of the orbit.

4. Length of specimen $6\frac{7}{10}$ inches: diameter of eye $1/4\frac{1}{4}$ (4/17) of length of head: third dorsal spine 1/2 the length of the head behind the first 1/3 of the orbit.

5. Length of specimen $11\frac{1}{10}$ inches: diameter of eye $1/5\frac{1}{3}$ (3/16) of length of head: third dorsal spine half the length of the head behind the first 1/3 of the orbit.

6. Length of specimen 20 inches: diameter of eye 1/6 of length of head: third dorsal spine 1/3 the length of the head behind the front edge of the orbit.

In numbers 1, 2, 3, the eye is 1 diameter from the end of the snout: in number 4, 3/4 of a diameter: in number 5, $1\frac{3}{4}$ diameters: and in number 6, $1\frac{1}{2}$ diameters from the end of the snout.

The maxilla reaches to nearly or quite below the hind edge of the orbit. Vertical limb of preopercle slightly emarginate, with the angle rounded, the whole being finely serrated, most coarsely so at its angle: sub- and inter-opercles entire. In small specimens, e. g. $2\frac{1}{4}$ inches long, this species has a spine at its preopercular angle, which becomes absorbed as age advances: in some specimens some rather large denticulations are seen at this place, due to this absorption not having been so rapid as usual. *Teeth*—canines in both jaws, the outer row in the maxilla, and the inner in the mandible, rather larger than the villiform bands. *Fins*—dorsal spines from the third continue of about the same length, from 2/5 to 1/3 of the height of the body: the pectoral longer than the ventral, and equalling the length of the head behind the middle of the orbit: second anal spine the strongest, equal to or not quite so long as the third: caudal rounded. *Scales*—ctenoid, about 14 rows between the lateral-line and the base of the sixth dorsal spine. *Colours*—greyish olive, darkest along the back. Body and head covered with irregularly sized pearly-white spots, whilst a black line exists on the maxilla. Fins dark grey, externally nearly black, the pectoral, ventral, soft dorsal, and anal with a narrow white border: the whole of the dorsal fin white spotted. The colours vary much with age.

Habitat.—Red Sea, East coast of Africa, seas of India to the Malay Archipelago. The specimen figured is 6 inches long.

11. Serranus diacanthus, Plate III, fig. 4.

Cuv. & Val. ii, p. 319; Günther, Catal. i, p. 110; Kner, Novara Fische, p. 20.
Serranus sexfasciatus, Day, Fish. Malabar, (not Cuv. and Val.)
Dumbu, Sind: *Choundeka*, Belooch.

B. vii, D. [illegible], P. 18, V. 1/5, A. [illegible], C. 17, L. r. [illegible], L. tr. 19-21/45, Cæc. pyl. 11.

Length of head 1/3 to 3/10, of caudal 1/5 to 2/9, height of body 1/4 to 1/5 of the total length. *Eyes*—diameter 1/4 to 2/9 of the length of head, 1 diameter from the end of snout, and also apart. The maxilla reaches to below the hind edge of the orbit: lower jaw the longer. Vertical limb of preopercle strongly serrated, with two or three coarse teeth at its angle, its lower limb entire: sub- and inter-opercles entire. Three spines on the opercle, the centre of which is the largest. In a young specimen (3 inches long) the serratures at the angle of the preopercle are scarcely enlarged, but at $3\frac{1}{2}$ inches in length they commence to become coarser than those along the vertical border. *Teeth*—one or two canines on either side of each jaw, those in the mandible being the smaller: outer row in the upper jaw rather stronger than the villiform bands; inner row in the mandible a little the largest. *Fins*—dorsal spines rather weak, and being of nearly equal length from the third, which equals two-fifths of the length of the head: pectoral rather longer than the ventral: second anal spine rather longer than the third, and equal to the second of the dorsal fin: caudal rounded. *Scales*—ctenoid on body, and in about 20 rows between the first dorsal spine and the lateral-line. *Cœcal pylori*—eleven long ones. *Colours*—brownish, with a tinge of pink on the back, becoming rose-coloured on the abdomen. Six dark vertical bands, the first crossing the head: the second from the fourth to the sixth dorsal spines passing over the pectoral to the base of the anal: the remaining three take the same direction, the last crossing the free portion of the tail. A dark band passes from the orbit to the angle of the preopercle. Fins darkest at their margins. Occasionally the bands are continued on to the dorsal fin. A specimen in the British Museum has a white edge to the dorsal, caudal, and anal fins.

Dr. Jerdon, M. J. L. & Science, 1851, p. 129, observes of *S. nebulosus*, Cuv. & Val. "I procured one specimen of this at Madras and one at Tellicherry." The latter, a copy of the figure of which exists amongst Sir Walter Elliot's drawings, is the fish above described.

Habitat.—Seas of India to the Malay Archipelago: at Kurrachee I took them 18 inches in length.

12. Serranus sexfasciatus.

(Kuhl & v. Hass.) Cuv. & Val. ii, p. 360; Bleeker, Perc. p. 38; Günther, Catal. i, p. 108.
Epinephelus sexfasciatus, Bleeker, Atl. Ich. t. 281, Perc. t. iii, fig. 2 & Epinephelini, p. 103.

B. vii, D. [illegible], P. 17, V. 1/5, A. [illegible], C. 17, L. l. 85.

Length of head 3/11, of caudal 1/6, height of body 1/4 of the total length. *Eyes*—diameter 2/9 of length of head, 1 diameter from end of snout, and 3/4 of a diameter apart. The maxilla reaches to below the hind edge of the orbit. Vertical limb of preopercle rather coarsely serrated, with two large spinous teeth at its angle, the inferior of which is directed somewhat downwards. Opercular spines well developed. *Teeth*—small canines in both jaws, the inner row of teeth in the lower jaw, and outer one in the maxilla, longer than the villiform bands. *Fins*—dorsal spines moderately strong, increasing in length to the fourth and fifth, which equal nearly half the length of the head, but are not quite so high as the rays: soft portion of fin, also of the anal, and the caudal rounded: pectoral as long as the head excluding the snout: second anal spine stronger but not quite so long as the third. *Scales*—ctenoid. *Colours*—brownish, with about six vertical darker bands, about as wide as the ground colour: a few irregular dark spots about the body: dorsal, caudal, and anal yellow, with numerous round black spots, those at the hind edge of the caudal almost forming a black band with a white outer edge: pectoral and ventral greyish.

I examined two specimens of this species from Japan in the Berlin Museum, the largest being about 7 inches in length. This species I have not captured in India, the form I termed *S. sexfasciatus* being the

S. diacanthus as was pointed out to me by Professor Peters, who also showed me one of Val. typical specimens in the Berlin Museum.

13. Serranus lanceolatus, Plate IV, fig. 1.

Holocentrus lanceolatus, Bl. t. 242, f. 1; Bl. Schn. p. 315; Lacép. iv, pp. 380, 383.

Perca suggalathoo boutoo, Russell, Fish. Vizag. ii, p. 23, pl. 130.

Serranus lanceolatus, Cuv. & Val. ii, p. 316; Bleeker, Perc. p. 35; Cantor, Catal. p. 8; Günther, Catal. i, p. 107 & Zool. Record 1869, p. 128; Blyth, Proc. Asiatic Soc. of Beng. xxix, p. 111; Day, Fishes of Malabar, p. 4, pl. 1, fig. 1 & 2, & Proc. Zool. Soc. 1869, p. 512 & 1871, p. 635; Playfair, Fishes of Zanzibar, p. 4.

Serranus horridus, Cantor, Catal. p. 9 (not Cuv. & Val.)

Epinephelus lanceolatus, Bleeker, Epinephelini, p. 73.

Kurrupu, Mal.: *Commaree*, if young *Walla-collanak* or 'perch with a sore head,' Tam.: *Gussir*, Sind.: *Bole*, Chittagong: *Nga-towktoo-shewplow*, Arrak.

B. vii, D. $\frac{11}{14-15}$, P. 19, V. 1/5, A. $\frac{3}{8}$, C. 15, L. r. $\frac{95}{100}$, L. tr. 20/52, Cæc. pyl. many.

Length of head 4/13 to 2/7, of caudal 1/5 to 1/6, height of body 2/7 to 1/4 of the total length. *Eyes*—diameter 1/6 to 1/8 in the length of the head, 1 to $1\frac{1}{2}$ diameters from the end of snout, and from 1 in the young to $1\frac{1}{4}$ in the adult apart. The maxilla reaches to a little beyond the vertical from the hind edge of the orbit. Preopercle with its vertical edge having a shallow emargination above the angle, and finely serrated, becoming somewhat coarsely so at the angle: its lower edge, and also the sub- and inter-opercles entire. Opercle with the central spine most distinct. In the fry there is a well-developed spine at the angle of the preopercle. *Teeth*—a small canine on either side of upper jaw, and a still smaller one in the lower jaw: no enlarged row in the upper jaw, but the inner row in the mandible, especially posteriorly, much the largest. *Fins*—dorsal spines* not so high as the rays, its soft portion and also that of the anal rounded: pectoral longer than the ventral, and equal to the postorbital portion of the head: second anal spine stronger but shorter than the third: caudal rounded. *Scales*—cycloid, but usually with raised circular lines upon them, especially in the forepart of the body, about 15 rows between the 6th dorsal spine and the lateral-line. *Cæcal-pylori*—very short, consequently in the young appear almost like a gland. *Colours*—vary with age, the very young being of a fine citron or sulphur ground-colour, having irregular vertical bands and markings, which become more distinct as the age of the fish advances. About to a foot or even eighteen inches in length, the ground colour continues to be bright yellow, with five vertical, blackish-blue bands, the first passing from the orbit downwards over the preopercle; the second from the nape to the opercle joins the first band in its posterior margin, and coalesces with the third behind or above the pectoral fin: the third proceeding from the bases of seven dorsal spines (3-10), passes downwards to the abdomen: the fourth passes from the fifth to the last dorsal ray, and descends to the base of the anal fin: the last surrounds the free portion of the tail. *Fins*—yellow with black spots or blotches, forming confluent bars at their bases, which on the pectoral are disposed in three or four undulating arched bands. In the adult the black bands disappear, the ground colour becomes greyish-brown, the whole being reticulated with greyish-black lines. The fins retain most of their original yellow colour but the amount of the black decreases.

Amongst Sir Walter Elliot's drawings are two of the adult of this fish, termed *Pennl min* and *Pilli pusni*, having a remark attached "younger with transverse bars."

In "Fishes of Malabar," I considered, as Cantor had previously done, that *S. horridus* was the adult of this species. Dr. Bleeker, however, who appears to have inspected the specimen at Leyden, states it to be *Serranus fuscoguttatus*.

Habitat.—East coast of Africa and seas of India to the Malay Archipelago, attaining a large size. The specimen figured is about 15 inches long, and intermediate between the two figured in the "*Fishes of Malabar*," it is not included in the five referred to in the note. Respecting this fish, Cantor observes that "in one, the weight of which exceeded 130lbs., the stomach contained remains of *Stromateus*, *Sphyræna Blochii*, and of a *Limulus*."

14. Serranus erythrurus.

Cuv. & Val. ii, p. 320.

B. vii, D. 11/16, P. 17, V. 1/5, A. 3/9, C. 17.

Vertical border of preopercle finely serrated, its horizontal limb entire. *Fins*—rounded. *Colours*—on the back and upper surface of the head greenish, variegated with red, silvery-white below: dorsal greenish: ventral, anal, and pectoral yellowish: tail reddish.

* To show how the comparative length of the dorsal spines vary, not only with age, but with specimens, I subjoin the measurements of five in my collection:

1. Length of specimen $4\frac{5}{8}$ inches: of 4th dorsal spine equal to $\frac{1}{14}$ of the entire length of the fish.
2. " " $7\frac{1}{2}$ " " " " $\frac{1}{15}$ " "
3. " " 13 " " " " $\frac{1}{15}$ " "
4. " " 13 " " " " $\frac{1}{16}$ " "
5. " " 22 " " " " $\frac{1}{27}$ " "

The late Mr. Blyth having examined pl. 1, in the *Fishes of Malabar*, suggested my asserting on his authority, that they represented the identical species he referred to in the *Pro. of the Asi. Soc.* and were the young and old of one sort.

Habitat.—Malabar to 3 feet in length. I have not seen this species that I am aware of, unless it is a *Lutianus*. It may probably be Russell's *Rungoo*.

15. Serranus Malabaricus, Plate IV, fig. 2.

Holocentrus Malabaricus, Bl. Schn. p. 319, pl. 63.

Holocentrus pantherinus, Lacép. Poiss. iii, t. 27, f. 3 and iv, pp. 389 and 392.

Perca boutoo and *P. madinawa boutoo*, Russell, Fish. Vizag. ii, pp. 20, 21, pl. 127 and 128.

Bola? coioides, Ham. Buch. Fish. Ganges, pp. 82, 369.

Serranus boutoo, Cuv. and Val. ii, pp. 334, vi, p. 523; Cantor, Catal. p. 11; Günther, Catal. i, p. 138; Day, Fish. Malabar, p. 3.

Serranus suillus, Cuv. and Val. ii, p. 335; Bleeker, Verh. Bat. Gen. xxii, p. 9; Günther, Catal. i, p. 127; Playfair. Fish. Zanz. p. 5.

Serranus marulanus et *pantherinus*, Cuv. and Val. ii, pp. 332 and 333.

Serranus crapao, Cuv. and Val. iii, p. 494; Rich. An. and Mag. Nat. Hist. 1842, ix, p. 25; Bleeker, Verh. Bat. Gen. xxii, Perc. p. 37; Günther, Catal. i, p. 137.

Serranus diacopeformis, Benn. Life Raffles. Fish. Sumatra, p. 686.

Serranus nebulosus et *shihpan*, Richards. Ich. China, pp. 231, 232.

Serranus coioides, Cantor, Catal. p. 11.

Epinephelus crapao, Bleeker, Atl. Ich. Perc. t. viii, f. 1.

Epinephelus pantherinus, Bleeker, Epinephelini, p. 78.

Punni-cullawah, Tam.: *Boutoo*, Tel.: *Bool*, Chittagong: *Nga-towktoo*, Arrak.: *Kyouk-theyga-kakadit*, Burm.: *Rab-ua-dah* and *Ooroobun-dah*, Andamanese.

Variety, *S. boutoo*, *Madinawah boutoo*, Tel.: *Row-je-dah*, Andam.

B. vii, D. $\frac{11}{14-15}$, P. 19, V. 1/5, A. $\frac{3}{8}$, C. 15, L. l. 90, L. r. $\frac{100}{94}$, L. tr. 19/50, Cæc. pyl. 50-60.

Length of head $3\frac{1}{4}$ to $3\frac{1}{2}$, of caudal 1/5 to 1/6, height of body 2/7 to 1/4 of the total length. *Eyes*—diameter 1/5 to 1/6 of length of head, 1 to $1\frac{1}{2}$ diameters from the end of snout, and the same apart. Interorbital space flat: the premaxillary reaching to opposite the front edges of the orbit. The maxilla extends to below the posterior edges of the orbit, or even behind it in large specimens. Vertical limb of preopercle slightly emarginate, finely serrated, becoming more coarsely so at its rather square angle, where there exist from four to seven coarse teeth, its lower margin entire, as are also the sub- and inter-opercles, occasionally there are two or three serrations on the inter-opercle. Opercle with three spines, the central one being the longest. The fry has no spine at the angle of the preopercle. *Teeth*—one or two canines in either jaw, those in the upper usually the longer; the outer row of teeth in the upper jaw, and the inner in the lower, are the largest. *Fins*—the dorsal spines from the third are of about the same height, and equal to one-half the length of the post-orbital portion of the head, but not so high as the rays: the pectoral is longer than the ventral, and about equal the post-orbital portion of the head in length, soft portions of dorsal and anal fins rounded: the second anal spine in most estuary specimens equal the length of the third, but in marine ones it is often slightly shorter: caudal rounded. *Scales*—ctenoid, and in about 15 rows between the 6th dorsal spine and the lateral line. *Cæcal pylori*—from 50 to 60, but two or more open into a single basal tube. *Colours*—brownish, fading to grey or dirty white on the abdomen: the whole of the fish, even over to the branchiostegal rays covered with bright yellow or orange spots, which often become brown after death: three large blotches on the inter-opercle appear to be present in all varieties of this fish. In the *S. Malabaricus* Bloch, some brown spots are often during life intermingled with the orange ones, and it is vertically banded usually as follows; one passes from the first four dorsal spines to the pectoral fin: another from between the second and ninth to the abdomen: two more descend from the soft dorsal fin, and a fifth encircles the free portion of the tail: pectoral reddish spotted with yellow, sometimes the caudal, pectoral and ventral fins are unspotted but marked with darker shades, or the bands are continued on to them. This variety is the commonest, mostly marine, and the bands are unusually well marked in the young. In the variety *S. boutoo*, the bands when present bifurcate inferiorly, and the spots are all black; this is a marine and the rarest form, never appearing to attain to a large size. In the variety *S. coioides*, H. B. = *S. suillus*, C. V. the bands are absent, or else indistinctly visible; this is mostly taken in estuaries or large rivers, as the Hooghly at Calcutta.

Russell observed that the plate 128 (*S. boutoo*) may perhaps "be merely a variety" of plate 127 (*S. coioides*). Hamilton Buchanan, p. 82, remarked of his *coioides*, "this fish agrees so well with the description of the *madinawa boutoo* of Dr. Russell (Indian Fishes, vol. ii, no. 128) that I do not think them different species," p. 82. Cuvier considered Russell's species distinct: Playfair, "Fishes of Zanzibar," doubted if they might not be identical.

Russell records one taken at Vizagapatam in January 1786, which measured 7 feet in length, 5 in girth, and weighed upwards of three hundred pounds. Amongst Sir Walter Elliot's drawings is a figure of the banded variety *S. Malabaricus*, marked *Serranus suillus* and *Kullâwâoe*: a foot and a half in length is given as the size of the specimen.

The fish figured, pl. iv, fig. 2, is the variety *coioides*, the specimen being about 21 inches in length, and taken at Calcutta.

In one specimen of the variety *S. boutoo* $8\frac{7}{10}$ inches long, not only has it 12 dorsal spines, but the sixth has also two separate spinate terminations.

Habitat.—Seas of India to the Malay Archipelago, China, and beyond, attaining to a very large size.

16. Serranus corallicola.

(Kuhl. and v. Hass.) Cuv. and Val. ii, p. 336.
Serranus altivelioides, Bleeker, Perc. p. 38; Günther, Catal. i, p. 127; Kner, Novara Fische, p. 23.
Epinephelus altivelioides, Bleeker, Atl. Ich. Perc. t. xxx, f. 1.
Epinephelus corallicola, Bleeker, Epinephelini, p. 83.

B. vii, D. $\frac{11}{15|16}$, P. 18, V. 1/5, A. $\frac{3}{8}$, C. 17, L. r. [illegible] (Cæc. pyl. 9, Kner.)

Length of head from $3\frac{1}{2}$ to $3\frac{2}{3}$, height of body 2/7 to nearly 1/4 of total length. *Eyes*—diameter from $4\frac{1}{2}$ to 1/5 in the length of the head, and from 1/2 to 1 diameter apart. The maxilla reaches to below the hind edge of the orbit. Vertical edge of the preopercle serrated, its lower limb and also the sub- and inter-opercles entire: central opercular spine the most developed. *Teeth*—canines in both jaws. *Fins*—dorsal spines increase to the third or fourth which are about 2/5 of the height of the body, and 1/5 lower than the rays: pectoral as long as the head without the snout: second anal spine the strongest, a little longer than the third and equal in length to the last in the dorsal fin: caudal rounded. *Scales*—ctenoid on the body, about 14 rows between the lateral line and the base of the sixth dorsal spine. *Colours*—greyish-brown covered all over with black spots, soft dorsal, anal, pectoral, and caudal with a light edge.

Habitat—stated (Kner) to have been taken at Madras, found in the Malay Archipelago.

17. Serranus salmoides, Plate IV, fig. 3.

Holocentrus salmoides, Lacép. iii, pl. 34, fig. 3, iv, p. 346.
Serranus salmoides, Cuv. and Vol. ii, p. 343.
? *Serranus polypodophilus*, Bleeker, Perc. p. 37.
Serranus salmonoides, Günther, Catal. i, p. 128; Klunz. Verh. z. b. Ges. Wien. 1870, p. 682.
? *Epinephelus polyphekadophilus*, Bleeker, Atl. Ich. Perc. t. v. fig. 1, and Epinephelini, p. 101.

B. vii, D. $\frac{11}{15|16}$, P. 18, V. 1/5, A. $\frac{3}{8}$, C. 17, L. r. [illegible], L. tr. 24/50.

Length of head 3/10 to 2/7, of caudal 1/6, height of body 4/15 to 1/4 of the total length. *Eyes*—diameter 2/13 of length of head, $1\frac{1}{2}$ to 2 diameters from the end of snout, and $1\frac{1}{2}$ apart. The interorbital space rather convex: the posterior end of the premaxillary extends to behind the level of the front edge of the orbit. The maxilla reaches to rather beyond the posterior edge of the orbit. Preopercle slightly emarginate, serrated along its vertical margin, with five or six denticulations at its angle, lower limb entire, as are also the sub- and inter-opercles. Central opercular spine moderately distinct, the others indistinct. *Teeth*—small canines in both jaws: an outer enlarged row in the maxilla, and an inner in the mandible larger than the villiform bands. *Fins*—third dorsal spine one third of the length of the head, they gradually decrease to the last but none are so long as the rays: soft portions of the dorsal and anal fins rounded. Pectoral longer than the ventral, equalling the length of the postorbital portion of the head, it hardly reaches 2/3 of the distance to above the anal spines: second anal spine the strongest, but not so long as the third, which equals one-fourth to one-fifth of the length of the head: caudal rounded. *Scales*—cycloid on the head, ctenoid on the body. *Colours*—dark reddish-brown, having round black spots over the head, body, and fins, those on the head and jaws small. Large blotches or ill-defined bands on the body. In one of Val. specimens, these bands are well marked.

The specimen figured was captured at the Andaman islands, it is about 12 inches in length.

Habitat—Red Sea, seas of India to the Malay Archipelago. It is not common in India.

18. Serranus semipunctatus.

Cuv. and Val. ii, p. 341; Günther, Catal. i, p. 114.

B. vii, D. $\frac{11}{14}$, P. 17, V. 1/5, A. $\frac{3}{8}$, C. 17.

Length of head 3/10, of caudal 4/21, height of body 4/17 of the total length. *Eyes*—diameter 1/6 of length of head, $1\frac{1}{2}$ diameters from end of snout, and $1\frac{1}{4}$ apart. Upper surface of head broad and flat. The maxilla reaches to below the hind edge of the orbit. Serrations on preopercle strong, having three coarse teeth at its angle, but not spinate as in *S. sexfasciatus*. *Teeth*—moderately sized canines in both jaws, an outer enlarged row in the maxilla, and several irregularly pointed teeth mixed with the villiform ones in the mandible. *Fins*—dorsal spines moderately strong, increasing in length to the fifth, which equals half the postorbital length of the head, and is not quite so high as the rays: the soft portion of the fin, and also of the anal rather angular: pectoral as long as the postorbital portion of the head, and extending to nearly over the anal spines: ventral not quite so long: third anal spine a little the longest, and equalling the third of the dorsal, the second spine a little the strongest: caudal large, fan-shaped, and equal to the pectoral in size. *Colours*—body reddish-brown, with six or seven broad darker vertical cross bands: head and first portion of the body, as well as the free portion of the tail, with some small well-marked spots: dorsal and anal yellow, and likewise spotted: ventral grey.

It has been suggested that *Perca septemfasciata*, Thunb. (Nov. Ac. Stock. 1799, pl. i, f. 1) is this species; the specimen figured was obtained in Japan, and Professor Peters was good enough to show me one of Temm. and Schlegel's types of *Plectropoma susuki* from Japan, the two being compared appeared to entirely agree, whereas the *P. susuki* is evidently distinct from the *S. semipunctatus*.

Habitat—Pondicherry, attaining at least 12 inches in length.

19. **Serranus summana**, Plate IV, fig. 4.

Perca summana, Forsk. p. 42; Gmel. Linn. p. 1317.
Bodianus summana, Bl. Schn. p. 334.
Pomacentrus summana, Lacép. iii, p. 511.
Serranus polystigma, Bleeker, Sumatra, ii, p. 2; Günther, Catal. i, p. 129.
Serranus summana, Playfair, Fish. Zanz. p. 8, pl. ii, fig. 1 (not Cuv. and Val. &c.).
Epinephelus summana, Bleeker, Epinephelini, p. 105.

B. vii, D. $\frac{11}{15|16}$, P. 17, V. 1/5, A. $\frac{3}{8}$, C. 17, L. r. $\frac{120}{90}$, [illegible] tr. 21/48.

Length of head from 3/10 to 2/7, of caudal 2/11, height of body from 3/10 to 2/7 of the total length. *Eyes*—diameter from 1/4 to 1/5 of the length of head, $1\frac{1}{2}$ diameters from the end of snout, and also apart. The maxilla reaches to below the last third of the orbit. Preopercle with a very shallow emargination above its angle, its vertical border finely serrated, its lower as well as the sub- and inter-opercles entire. Central opercular spine the most developed. *Teeth*—moderate sized canines in both jaws, the outer row of teeth in the maxilla and the inner in the mandible rather larger than the villiform bands. *Fins*—dorsal spines of moderate strength, the third to the fifth being the longest, equalling $2\frac{1}{2}$ in the height of the body, and slightly decreasing to the last: the soft portion of the fin higher than the spinous, somewhat angular, as is also that of the anal: pectoral longer than the ventral, and equalling the length of the head, excluding the snout: second anal spine the strongest, rather longer than the third, and equalling the highest in the dorsal fin: caudal rounded. *Scales*—ctenoid on the body, about 13 rows between the lateral-line and the base of the sixth dorsal spine. *Colours*—brownish, the body and vertical fins covered with small round white dots, which are minute on the head or even absent, a black spot above the maxillary: soft portions of dorsal and anal fins with dark edges, having white margins.

Klunzinger observes that some specimens of *S. leucostigma*, C.V. are the young form of *S. summana*, C.V.=*S. tæniolabris*, C.V. Peters has shown that *Holocentrus cæruleopunctatus*, Bloch=*S. alboguttatus*, C.V.=*S. leucostigma*, C.V.

Habitat.—Red Sea, East coast of Africa, seas of India to the Malay Archipelago. It is very common at the Andamans, where the specimen figured, (10 inches long) was captured.

20. **Serranus dermochirus.**

Cuv. and Val. vi, p. 513.

B. vii, D. $\frac{11}{14}$, P. 17, V. 1/5, A. $\frac{3}{8}$, C. 17.

Length of head 4/13, of caudal 2/9, height of body 4/13 of the total length. *Eyes*—diameter 2/9 of length of head, 1 diameter from end of snout, and nearly 1 apart. The maxilla reaches to somewhat behind the hind edge of the orbit. Preopercle, with its vertical margin finely serrated, three well developed opercular spines, the central one being the longest. *Teeth*—a pair of canines on either side of both jaws, an outer enlarged row along the sides of the upper jaw, and an inner one in the lower. *Fins*—dorsal spines strong, increasing in length to the fourth, which equals two diameters of the orbit: pectoral longer than the ventral, and equal to the length of the head behind the front edge of the orbit. Although, doubtless, the skin covering the fins is thick, it does not appear to be remarkably so. *Colours*—the specimen appears to be covered with fine white spots along each row of scales. It much resembles and is probably identical with *S. summana*.

Habitat.—Malabar. The specimen is over 12 inches in length.

21. **Serranus morrhua**, Plate V, fig. 1.

Cuv. and Val. ix, p. 434; Günther, Catal. i, p. 154; Klunz. Verh. z. b. Ges. Wien. 1870, p. 678.
Serranus pœciliuotus, Temm. Schleg. Fauna Japon. Poiss. pl. iv, A. f. 1; Richards. Ich. China, p. [illegible]; Bleeker, Verh. Bat. Gen. xxvi, p. 61; Günther, Catal. i, p. 155.
Serranus radiatus, Day, Proc. Zool. Soc. 1867, p. 699.

B. vii, D. $\frac{11}{14|16}$, P. 19, V. 1/5, A. $\frac{3}{8}$, C. 17, L. r. $\frac{112}{112}$, L. tr. 21/46.

Length of head nearly 1/3, of caudal 1/6, height of body 2/7 of the total length. *Eyes*—diameter 1/4 of length of head, 1 diameter from end of snout, and 1/2 a diameter apart. The maxilla reaches to below the hind edge of the orbit. Vertical limb of preopercle slightly oblique, serrated, and with three or four strong denticulations at its angle, its horizontal edge as well as the sub- and inter-opercles entire: opercle with three spines, the central one the longest. *Teeth*—canines in both jaws, the outer row of teeth in the maxilla, and the inner in the mandible, larger than the villiform bands. *Fins*—dorsal spines moderately strong, increasing in length to the third which equals two-fifths of the height of the body, and is nearly as high as the rays: third anal spine the strongest, the second of nearly similar length and about equal to the third of the dorsal fin: pectoral as long as the head behind the middle of the eye: ventral nearly reaching the vent: caudal rounded. *Scales*—on body ctenoid, 14 rows between the lateral-line and the base of the sixth dorsal spine: none on the preorbital nor on the maxilla in the young. *Colours*—(in the young) greenish-olive, becoming dull yellow on the abdomen. A broad irregular-shaped bluish-white band passes from the posterior edge of the occiput to meet a similar one from the opposite side: two more descend from the lower and posterior edge of the orbit to the base of the pectoral fin: another proceeds from the upper margin of the preopercle, at first backwards, and opposite the posterior third of the pectoral it curves upwards to the middle of the spinous dorsal on to which it is continued.

A small patch of similar colour exists in front of the base of the dorsal. Another band goes from the hind edge of the pectoral to the front of the soft dorsal: two more similar bands cross the base of the tail, and several shorter marks exist over the body. Spinous dorsal nearly black, soft dorsal and other fins yellow. Eyes golden.

A young specimen exists in the Paris Museum, in which there are dark spots along the lines which bound the light spaces.

Adults are brownish, with about four curved longitudinal bands along the body, and four or five oblique bands on the head, radiating from the eye.

Amongst Sir Walter Elliot's drawings is a figure of this species, 3$\frac{4}{10}$ inches long, also of the young, 1$\frac{1}{10}$ inches, with the remark "taken at Waltair, March 9th, 1853."

Habitat.—From the Red Sea through those of India to Japan: the specimen figured (life size) was captured at Madras in 1867.

22. Serranus angularis, Plate V, fig. 2.

Serranus angularis, Cuv. and Val. vi, p. 353; Günther, Catal. i, p. 126.

Serranus Celebicus, Bleeker, Celebes, i, p. 117; Günther, Catal. i, p. 139; Klunz. Verh. z. b. Ges. Wien, 1870, p. 676.

Serranus areolatus, Playfair (not Cuv. and Val.) Proc. Zool. Soc. 1867, p. 848.

Serranus glaucus, Day, Proc. Zool. Soc. 1870, p. 678.

Epinephelus Celebicus, Bleeker, Atl. Ich. Perc. xi, fig. 3, and Epinephelini, p. 69.

B. vii, D. $\frac{11}{14|17}$, P. 17, V. 1/5, A. $\frac{3}{8}$, C. 17, L. l. 70, L. r. 105, L. tr. 23/40, Cæc. pyl. 13.14.

Length of head 2/7, of caudal 2/11, height of body 2/7 to 4/15 of the total length. *Eyes*—diameter 1/4 to 1/5 of the length of head, 1$\frac{1}{2}$ diameters from the end of snout, and 3/4 to 1 diameter apart. The maxilla reaches to below the last third of the orbit. Preopercle serrated, angle slightly produced, having two or three strong denticulations (more developed in some specimens than in others), the inferior of which sometimes is directed downwards: occasionally there are a few denticulations upon the sub- and inter-opercles. Opercular spines well developed, the central one the longest. *Teeth*—canines in both jaws, largest in the upper: outer row of teeth in maxilla and inner in mandible larger than the villiform bands. *Fins*—dorsal spines rather strong, increasing in length to the third which equals 3/7 of the height of the body, and is rather more than that of the rays: pectoral as long as the head, excluding the snout, and longer than the ventral: second anal spine strongest but not quite so long as the third, which equals one and a quarter diameters of the orbit: caudal emarginate. *Scales*—ctenoid. *Colours*—greyish, becoming dirty white along the abdomen: head and body studded rather closely with yellow spots, which become brown in preserved specimens: pectoral, dorsal, anal, and caudal also spotted, which spots sometimes form lines or bands, and all the fins with a black margin edged with white.

Habitat.—Seas of India and Ceylon to the Malay Archipelago, attaining two feet or more in length; the specimen figured is 7 inches long.

23. Serranus fuscoguttatus, Plate V, fig. 3.

Perca summana, var. fuscoguttata, Forsk. p. 42; Gmel. Linn. p. 1317.

Serranus fuscoguttatus, Rüpp. Atl. Fische, p. 108, t. 27, fig. 2; Peters, Wieg. Arch. 1855, p. 235; Günther, Catal. i, p. 127; Kner, Voy. Novara, Poiss. p. 22; Playfair, Fish. Zanzibar, p. 5; Klunz. Verh. zool.-bot. Ges. in Wien, 1870, p. 684.

Serranus horridus (Kuhl. and V. Hass.) Cuv. and Val. ii, p. 321; Bleeker, Perc. p. 36; Günther, Catal. p. 136.

Serranus geographicus, (Kuhl. and v. Hass.) Cuv. and Val. ii, p. 322; Günther, Catal. i, p. 150.

Serranus dispar, Playfair, Fish. Zanz. p. 6, pl. i, fig. 2 and 3; Günther, Fische d. Sudsee, Heft i, p. 9.

Epinephelus horridus, Bleeker, Atl. Ich. Perc. t. xxix, f. 3.

Epinephelus fuscoguttatus, Bleeker, Epinephelini, p. 83.

B. vii, D. $\frac{11}{14|15}$, P. 19, V. 1/5, A. $\frac{3}{8}$, C. 17, L. r. $\frac{120}{90}$, L. tr. 22/56 (Cæc. pyl. 24, Kner).

Length of head from 1/3 to 4/13, of caudal 1/6, height of body 4/13 to 2/7 of the total length. *Eyes*—diameter 2/9 to 1/6 of the length of head, 1$\frac{1}{2}$ diameters from the end of snout, and 1 apart. The maxilla reaches to beyond the vertical from the hind edge of the orbit. Preopercle usually convex, but in some specimens with a very shallow emargination above its rounded angle, serrated in its whole extent, most coarsely so at its angle, lower limb and also the sub- and inter-opercles entire. Opercle with rather badly developed spines, the central one the most conspicuous. *Teeth*—small canines in both jaws, the outer row in the maxilla and the inner in the mandible, larger than the villiform bands. *Fins*—dorsal spines rather strong, from the third of about equal length and not so long as the rays, the third equals about 2/7 of the length of the head: pectoral longer than the ventral, and as long as the postorbital portion of the head: third anal spine equal in length to the third dorsal one, and though longer, not so strong as the second: caudal rounded. *Scales*—cycloid. *Colours*—greyish, with brown spots of a larger or smaller size irregularly disposed, they are sometimes hexagonal on the head: pectoral and caudal may be banded: sometimes three or four narrow white lines cross the lower jaw. There are some larger blotches on the head and body, and one across the free portion of the tail. In some specimens only the large cloudy blotchings or markings are present on the body.

Habitat.—Red Sea, East coast of Africa, seas of India, Malay Archipelago and beyond. The specimen figured is $9\frac{1}{4}$ inches in length and from the coast of Sind.

24. **Serranus grammicus**, Plate V, fig. 4.

Day, Proc. Zool. Soc. 1867, p. 700.

B. vii, D. $\frac{11}{15}$, P. 19, V. 1/5, A. $\frac{3}{8}$, C. 17, L. l. 85, L. r. $\frac{120}{[illegible]}$, L. tr. 17/44.

Length of head about 2/7, of caudal 1/6, height of body 2/7 of the entire length. *Eyes*—diameter 1/5 of length of head, $1\frac{2}{3}$ diameters from the end of snout, and 1 apart. The maxilla reaches to below the posterior edge of the orbit. Vertical limb of preopercle oblique, finely serrated in its upper two-thirds, becoming coarser lower down, and having several large denticulations at its angle, which is slightly produced: its lower limb entire as are also the sub- and inter-opercles. Opercle with three spines, the central one the strongest. *Teeth*—a small canine on either side of the upper jaw: a slightly enlarged outer row in the maxilla, and an inner one in the mandible. *Fins*—dorsal spines of moderate strength, the fourth slightly the longest, and equal to one and a third diameters of the orbit in length, but not so long as the rays: pectoral as long as the postorbital portion of the head, and longer than the ventral, which latter only reaches half way to the vent: second anal spine the strongest, the third one-fourth longer, and equal to the second in the dorsal fin: soft portions of the dorsal and anal somewhat rounded: caudal very slightly rounded. *Scales*—cycloid, with raised roughened irregularly disposed lines upon them, those between the pectoral fin and the lateral-line being the largest. Snout and suborbital ring of bones scaled, very few on preorbital or maxilla. *Colours*—greyish with a golden gloss about the head. A narrow black line runs from the upper margin of the orbit to the last dorsal spine: a second passes from the upper third of the orbit to the superior opercular spine and on to the base of the sixth dorsal ray: a third from the lower edge of the orbit to below the central opercular spine and on to the upper third of the caudal fin, where it assumes the form of rounded blotches: an intermediate band exists on the head between the second and third. Dorsal fin with a row of black spots along its centre and tipped with black: caudal yellow, with numerous black spots, and the extremities of its rays black, anal with a black edge. Eyes golden.

Dr. Jerdon, in the Madras Journ. Lit. and Sc. 1851, p. 130, remarks: "I possess a drawing of another *Serranus* of a reddish-fawn-colour, brownish on the back, with three longitudinal brown lines," otherwise as described above. The figure he alludes to is amongst Sir Walter Elliot's illustrations.

Habitat.—Madras, where the above single male specimen, 15 inches in length, was taken in 1867.

25. **Serranus boenack**, Plate VI, fig. 1.

Bodianus boenack, Bloch, iv, p. 44, t. 226; Bl. Schn. p. 330.
Perca rohtee bontoo, Russell, Fish. Vizag. ii, p. 22, pl. 129.
Sciæna formosa, Shaw, Zool. Misc. p. 23, t. 1007.
Serranus formosus, Cuv. & Val. ii, p. 311; Richards. Ich. China, p. 233; Bleeker, Perc. p. 31; Günther, Catal. i, p. 154; Day, Fish. Malabar, p. 7; Kner, Novara Fische, p. 26.
Serranus boenack, Cuv. & Val. ii, p. 302.
Serranus boenack, Peters, Monats. d. Akad. Berlin, 1865, p. 105.
Epinephelus formosus, Bleeker, Epinephelini, p. 59.
Epinephelus boenack, Bleeker, Fish. Madagascar, p. 8.
Verri-cullaweah, Tam.

B. vii, D. $\frac{9}{15-16}$, P. 15, V. 1/5, A. $\frac{3}{8-9(10)}$, C. 17, L. l. 90-95, L. tr. 22/43.

Length of head 2/7 to 3/8, of caudal 1/5 to 1/6, height of body 1/3 to 3/10 of the total length. *Eyes*—diameter 1/5 to 2/11 of length of head, rather above 1 diameter from end of snout, and 3/5 of a diameter apart. The maxilla reaches to below the last third or hind margin of the orbit. Vertical limb of preopercle rather convex, and a little emarginate above its angle in the adult but not in the young, its upper two-thirds finely serrated, more coarsely so at its angle, where the serrations are rather irregularly disposed: lower limb entire, as are also the sub- and inter-opercles (in one specimen both sub- and inter-opercles are serrated). Three strong opercular spines, the central being the most developed. *Teeth*—one or two strong canines or either side of both jaws, the upper being generally somewhat the larger: the outer row in the upper jaw, and the inner in the lower, being larger than the others. *Fins*—dorsal spines from the third are of about the same length, the longest being 3/4 the length of the longest ray: soft portions of the dorsal and anal obtusely angular: second anal spine the strongest, equal in length to the third in the adult or even longer in the young: caudal rounded. *Scales*—ctenoid, covering the forehead and preorbital but none on maxilla. *Colours*—when alive very brilliant, but fading after death. Generally yellowish-brown, snout pale blue, lips and throat spotted with a deeper blue, whilst about five fillets of the same colour diverge from the orbit and cross the opercles and branchial membranes. Blue and rather tortuous horizontal lines pass from the head towards the tail below the lateral line, whilst above it are about eight more directed backwards, upwards, and continued on to the dorsal fin throughout its whole extent; these blue lines are likewise continued on to the other fins, except (occasionally on) the ventrals, which however become nearly black at their extremities. Some blue spots exist anterior to the base of the ventral fin (male), also occasionally on the jaws.

There are three figures of this fish amongst Sir W. Elliot's drawings, termed *Nama panni*, *Neela panni*, and *Panaina kullawaie*; one was captured at Waltair, March 24th, 1853.

The specimen termed *Serranus formosus*, "adult: stuffed Isle de France," in the British Museum Catalogue l. c. is, as Dr. Bleeker suggests (Fish. Madagascar, p. 20), identical with *Epinephelus Polleni*, Bleeker, l. c. p. 19: the caudal is cut nearly square instead of being rounded as in *S. boenack*. A beautiful specimen exists in the Paris Museum received from M. Liénard, of the Mauritius, but the description I am unable to recognise in his papers.

Habitat.—Seas of India and Malay Archipelago to China.

26. Serranus miniatus, Plate VI, fig. 2.

Perca miniata, Forsk. p. 41; Linn. Gmel. p. 1317.
Bodianus miniatus, Bl. Schn. p. 332.
Serranus miniatus, Rüpp. Atl. Fische, p. 106, t. xxvi, f. 3; Günther, Catal. i, p. 118, and in Garretts. Fische d. Sudsee, Heft. i, p. 5, pl. v; Klunz. Fische d. Roth. Meer. verh. z. b. Ges. Wien. 1870, p. 679.
Serranus guttatus, Cuv. and Val. ii, p. 357.
Diacope miniata, Cuv. and Val. ii, p. 433.
Cromileptes miniatus, Swains. Fish. ii, p. 201.
Serranus cyanostigmatoides, Bleeker, Verh. Bat. Gen. xxii, Perc. p. 31; Günther, Catal. i, p. 117.
Epinephelus cyanostigmatoides, Bleeker, Ternate, p. 232, and Atl. Ich. Perc. t. v, f. 3.
Epinephelus argus, Bleeker, Waigiou. p. 296.
Epinephelus miniatus, Bleeker Epinephelini, p. 53.

B. vii, D. $\frac{9}{14-15}$, P. 18, V. 1/5, A. [illegible], C. 17, L. l. 90, L. r. [illegible], L. tr. 14-16/40, Cæc. pyl. 12 (Madras)—16 (Andamans).

Length of head from 4/13 to 2/7, of caudal 1/7, height of body 2/7 of the total length. *Eyes*—diameter from 1/5 to 1/6 of length of head, 1 to 1½ diameters from the end of snout, and ⅘ of a diameter apart. The maxilla reaches to below the posterior third or hind edge of the orbit. Vertical limb of preopercle usually somewhat emarginate above its angle, the whole being finely and evenly serrated, as are also the sub- and inter-opercles. Opercular spines well developed, the central one being the largest. *Fins*—dorsal spines rather strong, the fourth or fifth somewhat the longest, and equal to one-third the height of the body, the last nearly as high as the first ray: pectoral as long as the head, exclusive of the snout, and longer than the ventral, which reaches three-fourths of the way to the vent: caudal rounded. *Scales*—ctenoid. *Colours*—uniform scarlet: body, cheeks, opercles, dorsal, caudal, and anal fins covered with large blue spots, the size of which equals the extent of from 2 to 5 scales: two blue spots opposite the base of the pectoral. Two dark streaks from the orbit along the snout. The fins darkest at their margins: two rows of large blue spots along the spinous portion of the dorsal, and six or eight over the soft dorsal and the anal: one or two spots near the base of the pectoral, which fin is sometimes spotted all over.

Peters (Wieg. Arch. 1855, p. 235) considered *S. cyanostigma* as identical with this species. Bleeker (Epinephelini), p. 56, observes that though closely allied they appear to be distinct, as the colour is constantly different: the scaling of the snout is not identical, and it has D. [illegible], P. 16-17, C. 19.

Habitat.—Red Sea, seas of India to the Malay Archipelago and beyond. The specimen figured is 9 inches in length.

27. Serranus guttatus, Plate VI, fig. 3.

Bodianus guttatus, Bl. t. 224; Bl. Schn. p. 330; Lacép. iv, p. 296.
Epinephelus argus, Bl. Schn. p. 301.
Cephalopholis argus, Bl. Schn. p. 311, pl. 61.
Serranus hemistictus, Rüpp. Atl. p. 109, t. xxvii, f. 3; Günther, Catal. i, p. 119; Klunzinger, Verh. z. b. Ges. Wien. 1870, p. 680.
Serranus myriaster, Cuv. and Val. ii, p. 365; Rüpp. Atl. p. 107, t. xxvii, f. 1; Richards. Ich. China, p. 233; Less. Voy. Coq. Poiss. pl. 37; Bleeker, Nat Tyds. Ned. Ind. vi, p. 192.
Serranus argus, Cuv. and Val. ii, p. 360; Günther, Catal. i, p. 115; Peters, Berlin. Monats. 1865, p. 103.
Serranus guttatus, Peters, Wieg Arch. 1855, p. 235; Günther, Catal. i, p. 119, and Fische d. Sudsee, p. 5, t. iv; Kner, Voy. Novara, p. 22; Klunz. Fische d. Roth. Meer. l. c. p. 686.
Epinephelus argus, Bleeker, Epinephelini, p. 57.

B. vii, D. [illegible], P. 16, V. 1/5, A. [illegible], C. 17, L. r. [illegible], L. tr. 21/43, Cæc. pyl. 8.

Length of head 1/3 to 2/7, of caudal 1/5, height of body 1/3 to 2/7 of the total length. *Eyes*—diameter from 1/5 to 2/13 of the length of head, 1½ diameters from the end of snout, and 1 apart. The maxilla reaches to beyond the vertical from the hind edge of the orbit. Preopercle, its vertical limb rounded and finely serrated, lower limb entire: a few serrations on the interopercle. Three well developed opercular spines, the central one being the longest. *Teeth*—rather small canines in both jaws, the outer row of teeth in the maxilla and the inner in the mandible are larger than the villiform bands. *Fins*—dorsal spines rather strong, increasing in length to the fourth and fifth, which equal about one-third the height of the body pectoral rather longer than the ventral: second anal spine strongest and slightly longer than the third: soft portions of the dorsal and anal fins angularly rounded: caudal rounded. *Scales*—ctenoid. *Colours*—usually reddish-brown and mostly with darker vertical bands; head, body, and all the fins (except occasionally the pectoral and ventral) covered with numerous small blue spots: dorsal, anal, and caudal with a fine white border.

In the variety figured, *S. hemistictus*, the cross bands are not seen: the spots on the upper half of the body are very few, and the pectoral has a broad yellow edge.

Habitat.—Red Sea, East coast of Africa, seas of India to the Malay Archipelago, China, Australia, and beyond. The specimen figured is 9 inches in length.

28. Serranus leopardus, Plate VI, fig. 4.

Labrus leopardus, Lacép. iii, p. 517, t. 30, f. 1.
Serranus leopardus, Cuv. and Val. ii, p. 336; Günther, Catal. i, p. 123 and Fische d. Sudsee, p. 4, t. 3, f. B. (excl. synonym. pt.)
Serranus spilurus, Cuv. and Val. vi, p. 433; Bleeker, Flores, p. 322.
Serranus Homfrayi, Day, Proc. Zool. Soc. 1870, p. 678.
Epinephelus suillus, Bleeker, Atl. Ich. Perc. t. x, fig. 2.
Epinephelus leopardus, Bleeker, Epinephelini, p. 61.

B. vii, D. $\frac{9}{15-16}$, P. 17, V. 1/5, A. $\frac{3}{8}$, C. 17, L. r. [illegible], L. tr. 10/26.

Length of head 2/7, of caudal 1/6, height of body 1/3 of the total length. *Eyes*—high up, diameter largest in the immature, from 1/5 to 1/6 of the length of the head in the adult, from 1 to $1\frac{1}{2}$ diameters from end of snout in the adult and nearly 1 apart. The maxilla reaches to below the hind edge of the orbit. Vertical limb of preopercle rounded and very finely serrated; the serrations extending along its angle but not to the lower limb: interopercle usually with a few fine serrations along its posterior half. *Teeth*—canines in both jaws, the outer row in the maxilla, and the inner in mandible larger than the villiform bands. *Fins*—dorsal spines strong, the fifth the longest but not equalling the length of the rays: soft dorsal and anal rounded: pectoral as long as the head exclusive of the snout: second anal spine the strongest and slightly the longest: caudal rounded. *Scales*—rather strongly ctenoid on the body, 8 rows between the lateral-line and the sixth dorsal spine, they cover the snout, preorbital and suborbital ring of bones and the posterior half of the maxilla. A badly marked line, very similar to the lateral-line, passes along the scales near the bases of the dorsal and anal fins. *Colours*—vary, red or yellow predominating. The body may be whitish covered with round or oval red spots which are extended over the dorsal, anal, and caudal fins. A dark band passes from the eye to above the upper opercular spine behind which it terminates in a black spot: one or two black bands with or without a white edging may be present over the free portion of the tail: caudal with a white or blue spot at either of its outer angles, and a triangular black band across its last third. This band may be broken up into an oblique mark across either side of the tail, or may even be seen quite white as in the lower one of the figure.

Habitat.—From the Red Sea through those of India to China; the one figured life size, was taken at the Andaman Islands.

29. Serranus Sonnerati, Plate VII, fig. 1.

Perca rubra, Sonnerat.
Serranus Sonnerati, Cuv. and Val. ii, p. 299; Günther, Catal. i, p. 122; Playfair, Fish. Zanz. p. 3, (exc. pl. iii, fig. 1.)
Serranus pachycentron, Cuv. and Val. ii, p. 295.
Serranus erythræus, Cuv. and Val. vi, p. 516; Günther, Catal. i, p. 116; Playfair, Fish. Zanz. p. 2, pl. i, f. 1.
Serranus pachycentrum, Günther, Catal. i, p. 116.
Epinephelus nigripinnis, Bleeker, Atl. Ich. Perc. t. vi, f. 2; and Epinephelini, p. 39; (*? Serranus nigripinnis,* Cuv. and Val. ii, p. 329).
Siggapu collaceah, Tam.

B. vii, D. $\frac{9}{15-16}$, P. 18-19, V. 1/5, A. $\frac{3}{8-9}$, C. 17, Cæc. pyl. 11-12, L. r. $\frac{122}{123}$, L. tr. 27/40.

Length of head 3/10 to 2/7, of caudal, 2/13 to 1/7, height of body, 4/13 to 2/7 of the total length. *Eyes*—diameter 2/11 to 2/13 of the total length, $1\frac{1}{4}$ to $1\frac{1}{2}$ diameters from the end of snout, and 3/4 of a diameter apart. Profile from the snout to above the eyes rather concave. The maxilla reaches to a slight distance beyond the hind edge of the orbit. Vertical limb of preopercle sometimes slightly oblique above its angle, it is very finely serrated in its whole extent: lower limb with irregular notches, and serrated, occasionally coarsely so: sub- and inter-opercles finely serrated: the two upper opercular spines more developed than the lower. *Teeth*—one or two well developed canines on either side of both jaws, largest in the lower: the outer row of teeth in the maxilla and the inner in the mandibles larger than the villiform bands. *Fins*—dorsal spines moderately strong, increasing in length to the third from whence they continue to very slightly augment in height to the last which equals 2/7 of that of the body, the inter-spinous membrane is slightly emarginate and not lobed, the rayed portion is about one-fourth higher than the spinous, it and the soft part of the anal rounded: pectoral as long as the head behind the front edge or middle of the eye, and rather longer than the ventral: second anal spine the strongest but not quite so long as the third, which nearly equals the third of the dorsal: caudal rounded. *Scales*—cycloid on the head, ctenoid on the body, fine ones are continued for some distance up the bases of the soft dorsal, anal, and caudal fins: fine ones over the snout, sub-orbital and the anterior and lower portion of the preorbital: the hind half of the maxilla sometimes has very fine ones, at other times it is destitute of any. There are 14 or 15 rows of scales between the sixth dorsal spine and the lateral line at its highest point which is below it. There exists a badly marked line, much similar to the lateral line, running along the scales near the bases of the dorsal and anal fins. *Colours*—of a dull lake, with the head and to below the first half of the spinous dorsal fin covered with a net-work of blue lines enclosing spots from one-sixth the diameter of the eye, to spaces larger than it. Some indistinct spots over the whole of the body. Fins of rather darker colour than the body, especially at their edges: caudal with some dull blue or white spots.

E

The specimen of *Serranus erythraeus*, figured in the "Fishes of Zanzibar" is identical with this species as suggested by Bleeker; also Kelaart's skin *a*, p. 116 of *S. pachycentron*,* which has L. r. [illegible], L. tr. 22/—, and is the same as the *large specimens* of *S. leopardus* in the British Museum. *S. Sonnerati*, Playfair, Fish. Zanzibar, p. 3, pl. iii, fig. 1, has L. r. [illegible] and 9 rows of scales between the lateral line and the base of the sixth dorsal spine, it appears to be identical, as already suggested by Bleeker with his *Epinephelus* (*Serranus*) *miltostigma*.

Amongst Sir Walter Elliot's drawings are three of this species showing variations of colour. Jerdon (M. J. L. and Sc. 1851, p. 129) observes that "the intensity of the red varies a good deal, and it is sometimes marked with white spots."

Habitat.—East coast of Africa, seas of India to the Malay Archipelago, and beyond. The specimen figured is that of a female 13 inches long captured in February, 1859, at Madras, where it is not uncommon and attains at least 3 feet in length.

30. Serranus boelang, Plate VII, fig. 2.

Serranus boelang, Cuv. and Val. ii, p. 308, vii, p. 504; Quoy and Gaim. Voy. Astrol. p. 657, pl. 3, fig. 1; Playfair, Fish. Zanz. p. 2.

Serranus nigrofasciatus, Hombr. and Jacq. Voy. Pol. Sud. Poissons, p. 36, t. 2, f. 1.

? *Merous unicolor*, Liénard, Nat. Hist. Soc. Maur. 1839, p. 31.

Serranus microprion, Bleeker, Amb. ii, p. 552; Günther, Catal. i, p. 116.

Serranus stigmapomus, Rich. Ich. China, p. 232.

Serranus boenack, Günther, Catal. i, p. 112 (not Bloch); Kner, Novara Fische, p. 21.

Epinephelus boelang, Bleeker, Epinephelini, p. 49.

Epinephelus microprion, Bleeker, Atl. Ich. Perc. t. ii, fig. 1, and Epinephelini, p. 47 (? variety).

B. vii, D. [illegible], P. 15, V. 1/5, A. [illegible], C. 17, L. r. [illegible], L. tr. 18/36 (Cæc. pyl. 6-7, Kner).

Length of head 4/13 to 2/7, of caudal 2/11, height of body nearly 2/7 of the total length. *Eyes*—diameter 1/5 of length of head, $1\frac{1}{2}$ diameters from end of snout, and 2/3 of a diameter apart. The maxilla reaches to some distance behind the posterior edge of the orbit. Preopercle with its vertical limb finely serrated, the serrations being continued along its angle and a short distance on to its horizontal border: fine serrations upon the sub- and inter-opercles. Opercular spines strong especially the central one. *Teeth*—small canines in both jaws, the outer row of teeth in the maxilla, and the inner in the mandible larger than the villiform bands which are comparatively of small size. *Fins*—dorsal spines rather strong and from the third are about equal in length but not so long as the rays: pectoral a little longer than the ventral and equalling the length of the head excluding the snout: second anal spine much the strongest and also the longest, being equal to two-fifths of the height of the body: soft portions of the dorsal and anal angularly rounded: caudal rounded. *Scales*—ctenoid on the body, ten rows between the lateral line and the base of the sixth dorsal spine. *Colours*—purplish, with from eight to nine vertical bands on the body not so wide as the ground colour: when freshly captured, the one over the free portion of the tail is very dark: a dark mark behind the two upper opercular spines, and a blackish edge to the dorsal, which in the soft portion of the anal and the caudal is margined with white.

S. microprion, Bleeker, which may be a variety of this species has blue spots over the head and shoulders.

Habitat.—Red Sea, East coast of Africa, through the seas of India to the Malay Archipelago. It does not appear to attain a large size. The one figured, life-size, came from the Andaman Islands.

Genus, 4—Variola, *Swains.*

Pseudoserranus, Klunz.

Branchiostegals seven: pseudobranchiæ. Body oblong, compressed. Eyes lateral, of moderate size. Preopercle with its vertical limb feebly serrated, its horizontal one entire. Opercle with three spines. Teeth villiform in the jaws, vomer and palate: canines present, and the inner row of teeth in both jaws moveable: some conical teeth along the rami of the mandibles. Dorsal fin single with nine spines: anal with three: caudal deeply emarginate. Scales small, ctenoid, none on the snout, suborbitals, or maxilla.

SYNOPSIS OF INDIVIDUAL SPECIES.

1. *Variola louti*, D. [illegible], A. [illegible], L. r. [illegible]. Vertical limb of preopercle slightly emarginate and finely serrated. Caudal deeply emarginate. Red, with small darker spots on the body and most of the fins, some of which last are edged with yellow. East coast of Africa, Ceylon.

1. Variola louti, Plate VII, fig. 3.

Perca louti, Forsk. p. 40.

Bodianus louti, Bl. Schn. p. 332; Lacép. iv, p. 286.

* Valenciennes observes that he had only seen one specimen and that was in the Leyden Museum, 7 French inches long. His especial reason for considering it a new species appears to be the character of the scales which were small and ctenoid. Those on the sides being slightly keeled, forming about 20 horizontal rows. This appearance is more seen in some specimens than in others, and is not peculiar to this species. In 1867, a *Serranus diacanthus* about $18\frac{1}{2}$ inches long, which was not quite fresh, was brought to me at Madras. I had it preserved as a skin and dried rather too rapidly, the result being that all the rows of scales on the body show a well developed keel. I have also seen this appearance caused in fish which have been immersed, from the first, in spirit of too great a strength.

Labrus punctatus, Lacép. iii, p. 431, pl. 17, f. 2.

Serranus louti, Rupp. Atl. p. 106, pl. 26, f. 2; Günther, Catal. i, p. 101, and Fische d. Sudsee, p. 2, t. i, (not Cuv. and Val.)

Serranus punctulatus, Cuv. and Val. ii, p. 367, ix, p. 435; Bleeker, Sumatra, i. p. 579; Quoy and Gaim. Voy. Astrol. Poissons. p. 654, pl. 3, f. 2.

Serranus phœnicosomus, Swains. Fish. ii, p. 201.

Variola longipinna, Swains. Fish. ii. p. 202.

Pseudoserranus louti, Klunz. Fische d. Roth. Meer. Verh. z. b. Ges. Wien. 1870, p. 687.

Variola louti, Bleeker, Epinephelini, p. 11.

B. vii, D. $\frac{9}{13-15}$, P. 18, V. 1/5, A. $\frac{3}{8}$, C. 17, L. r. [illegible], Vert. 10/14.

Length of head from 2/7 to 1/4, of caudal 2/9, height of body 2/9 of the total length. *Eyes*—diameter 2/9 to 1/5 in the length of head, upwards of $1\frac{1}{2}$ diameters from the end of snout, and 2/3 of a diameter apart. Lower jaw prominent, the maxilla reaches to below the hind edge of the eye. Vertical limb of preopercle with some feeble serrations at its angle, its lower limb, sub- and inter-opercles entire. *Teeth*—strong canines in the upper, and weaker ones in the lower jaw: outer row of teeth in the maxilla, shorter and thicker than the villiform band: some large teeth also present amongst the villiform ones in the mandible. *Fins*—dorsal spines rather weak, the soft portion of the fin, also of the anal, elongated and pointed: pectoral as long as the head without the snout: ventral one-third longer: second anal spine not quite so long as the third; caudal deeply emarginate and with pointed angles. *Scales*—ctenoid about 14 rows between the lateral-line and the base of the first dorsal spine. *Colours*—red with small darker spots everywhere: all the fins red, outer edge of pectoral and soft dorsal yellowish, as is also snout and abdomen. A yellow line along the inner edge of the two lobes of the caudal fin.

Habitat.—From the Red Sea through the seas of India to the Malay Archipelago. The specimen figured is from the collection in the British Museum.

Genus, 5—Anthias, (*Bl. Schn.*) *Cuv. & Val.*

Caprodon, Temm. and Schleg.: *Aylopon*, *Callanthias*, *Paranthias*, and *Elastoma*, Guichenot: *Holanthias*, Günther.

Branchiostegals seven: pseudobranchiæ. Body oblong, rather elongated, and compressed: preorbital of moderate height, entire. Preopercle serrated. Opercle with two spines. Villiform teeth in both jaws, with canines anteriorly, and an outer row of canine-like ones laterally: also villiform on the vomer and palate: if present on the tongue, minute. Dorsal fin single, with from nine to eleven spines: anal with three: pectorals pointed: caudal rather deeply forked: one, or more of the fins, as a rule, having elongated rays. Scales of moderate size, an enlarged row over the nape. Pyloric appendages few.

Geographical distribution, most of the seas of temperate and tropical regions.

SYNOPSIS OF INDIVIDUAL SPECIES.

1. *Anthias multidens*, D. $\frac{10}{17}$, A. $\frac{3}{7}$, L. l. 52. Rosy, with lateral golden bands on the body, and two on the head. Andamans.

1. Anthias multidens, Plate VII, fig. 4.

Mesoprion multidens, Day, Proc. Zool. Soc. 1870, p. 680.

B. vii, D. $\frac{10}{17}$, P. 16, V. 1/5, A. $\frac{3}{7}$, C. 16, L. l. 52, L. r. [illegible], L. tr. 7/17, Cæc. pyl. 5.

Length of head 4/15, of caudal 1/4, height of body 1/4 of the total length. *Eyes*—diameter 2/7 of length of head, $1\frac{1}{4}$ diameters from end of snout, and 1 apart. The distance between the eye and the angle of the mouth equals three-fourths of the diameter of the orbit. The maxilla reaches to below the first-third of the orbit. Vertical and horizontal limbs of preopercle finely serrated, most coarsely so at its rounded and somewhat produced angle. Opercle with two well developed spines. Seven rows of scales between the eye and the angle of the preopercle. *Teeth*—villiform in the jaws, with a large canine on either side of the premaxillary, and an outer lateral row of canine-like ones in the maxilla: likewise an outer row of canine-like teeth in the lower jaw: villiform ones on the vomer and palate. *Fins*—dorsal spines slender, the fifth the longest, and nearly equal to half the height of the body below it, the last spine upwards of two-thirds of the length of the fifth: pectoral as long as the head, and reaching to above the end of the base of the anal: last dorsal, and anal rays elongated to nearly twice as long as the one preceding each: second anal spine the strongest, the third the longest, and nearly equal to one-third of the length of the head: caudal deeply forked, the upper lobe slightly the longer. *Colours*—rosy, with about six longitudinal yellow bands along the body, and a golden one from the inferior angle of the eye to the snout, and another across the forehead.

Habitat.—Andamans, where it is common, attaining a large size: although the number of spines, rays, scales, and cæcal pylori are the same as in *Anthias oculatus*, Cuv. and Val. the form of the dorsal fin differs, as in this species the spines do not decrease to the last.

Genus, 6—Grammistes (*Artedi*) *Cuvier*.

Pogonoperca, Günther.

Branchiostegals seven: pseudobranchiæ. Body oblong and compressed. Snout short. Opercle and preopercle unserrated, but spinate. Eyes lateral. Teeth villiform in the jaws, vomer, and palatines, no canines: tongue smooth.

A barbel of a more, or less, rudimentary character on the chin. Two dorsal fins, the first with seven spines: anal spineless. Scales minute, adherent, and enveloped in the epidermis. Pyloric appendages few.

Geographical distribution—Red Sea, throughout those of India to the Malay Archipelago, and beyond.

SYNOPSIS OF INDIVIDUAL SPECIES.

1. *Grammistes Orientalis*, Bl. Schn. D. 7/$\frac{1}{12}$, A. 9-11. Three spinate denticulations on preopercle. Caudal rounded. Deep brown, with from three to seven narrow white longitudinal bands, which anteriorly are continued on to the head. Red Sea, seas of India, Malay Archipelago, and beyond.

1. Grammistes Orientalis. Plate IX, f. 1.

Grammistes Orientalis, Bl. Schn. p. 189: Cuv. and Val. ii, p. 203, pl. 27: Bleeker, Amboina, iv, p. 105; Günther, Catal. i. p. 171; Klunz. Fische. Roth. Meer. Verh. z. b. Ges. Wien. 1870, p. 707; Bleeker, Epinephelini, p. 129.

Perca lilineata, Thunb. Nov. Act. Hol. xiii, p. 142, t. 5.

Bodianus sex-lineatus, Lacép. iv, pp. 285, 302.

Sciaena vittata, Lacép. iv, p. 323.

Perca triacanthus et pentacanthus, Lacép. iv, pp. 398, 424.

Centropomus sex-lineatus, Lacép. v, pp. 688, 689.

B. vii, D. 7 | $\frac{1}{12}$-$\frac{1}{13}$, P. 16, V. 1/5, A. 9-11, C. 17.

Length of head 2/7 to 1/3, of pectoral 2/11, of caudal 1/5, height of body nearly 1/3 of the total length. *Eyes*—diameter 2/7 to 1/4 of the length of head, 3/4 of a diameter from end of snout, and 1 apart. Body oblong and elongated, sometimes with a slight concavity in the profile above the orbit: lower jaw the longer. The maxilla extends to below the hind edge of the orbit. Vertical limb of preopercle with three spinate denticulations on its border, the upper being the smallest; some indistinct ones along the lower limb. Three spines on opercle. A rudimentary barbel on the lower jaw, which in a fresh specimen, nearly 4 inches long, equalled half the length of the orbit. *Teeth*—villiform in jaws, vomer, and palate. *Fins*—third dorsal spine the longest equalling one-third of the height of the body below it: soft dorsal, anal, and caudal rounded. *Scales*—imbedded in epidermis and usually covered with mucus. *Colours*—of a deep chestnut brown, with three milk-white longitudinal bands, from the head along the body, the inferior ceasing opposite the posterior end of the base of the anal fin. A white median band from the snout to the base of the dorsal fin.

In some specimens there are six or more white longitudinal lines along either side of the body.

Seba figures this fish as *Grammistes*, pl. 27, f. 5.

Habitat—Seas of India, to the Malay Archipelago, and beyond, attaining only a few inches in length. The one figured is from the Andamans, and life size.

Genus, 7—Diploprion, *(Kuhl. and v. Hass.) Cuv. and Val.*

Branchiostegals seven: pseudobranchiae. Body oblong, compressed. Eyes lateral. Opercle spinate: preopercle with a double edge, the outer of which is denticulated. Teeth villiform in jaws, vomer, and palatines, no canines: tongue smooth. Two dorsal fins, the first with eight spines: anal with two. Scales small, adherent. Pyloric appendages few.

Geographical distribution.—From the seas of India to China and Japan. This fish I have not personally captured in India, nor found it in local Indian collections; those taken have been probably mere stragglers. Dr. Jerdon remarks, "this pretty fish is rare at Madras."—(Madr. Journ. Lit. and Science, 1851, No. 39, p. 129.)

SYNOPSIS OF INDIVIDUAL SPECIES.

1. *Diploprion bifasciatum*, D. 8 | 15, A. $\frac{3}{12}$. Yellow with two black vertical bands. Indian seas, Malay Archipelago to Japan.

1. Diploprion bifasciatum, Plate IX, f. 2.

(Kuhl. and v. Hass.) Cuv. and Val. ii, p. 137, pl. 21: Tem. and Schleg. Fauna Japon. p. 2, pl. 2, f. A.: Richards. Ich. China, p. 221; Bleeker, Verh. Bat. Gen. xxvi, p. 59 and Nat. Tyds. Ned. Ind. vi, 1854, p. 207 and Epinephelini, p. 124; Günther, Catal. i, p. 174; Kner, Novara Fische, p. 29.

Aswavah meen, Tam.

B. vii, D. 8 | 14-15, A. $\frac{3}{11-13}$, C. 17, L. r. $\frac{11}{100-110}$, L. tr. 12/—.

Length of head 2/7, of caudal 1/5, height of body 2/5 of the total length. *Eyes*—diameter 1/4 length of head, $1\frac{1}{4}$ diameters from end of snout, and 3/4 of a diameter apart. The maxilla reaches to below the middle of the orbit. Preopercle having a double edge the outer of which is serrated, the inner ridge is also stated to be sometimes serrated. Approximating portions of sub- and inter-opercles serrated. Opercle with its two upper spines large, followed inferiorly by several smaller ones. *Teeth*—generic. *Fins*—third and fourth dorsal spines the highest, and nearly equal to the length of the head behind the front edge of the orbit; they decrease in length to the last which is very short: anal spines also very short: caudal rounded. *Colours*—Gamboge yellow with two broad black cross bands.

Habitat—Seas of India, to China and Japan.

Sir John Richardson remarks, "specimens exist in every collection of Chinese fishes, and small ones are common in the insect boxes sold at Canton." The one figured is from a stuffed specimen in the Liverpool Free Museum, kindly lent me for this purpose by its curator, Mr. Moore.

Genus, 8—Lutianus, *Bloch.*

Diacope and *Mesoprion*, Cuv. and Val.: *Genyoroge*, Cantor: *Macolor*, Bleeker: *Proamblys*, *Hypoplites*, *Rhomboplites*, *Ocyurus*, *Evoplites*, *and Tropidinius*, Gill.

Branchiostegals seven: pseudobranchiæ. Body oblong, compressed: snout elongated, with the preorbital rather high and entire. Preopercle serrated, with or without a notch on its vertical border to receive a knob, which is sometimes developed on the interopercle. Opercle rarely with one, more generally with two or three indistinct points. Villiform teeth in both jaws: canines in the upper, with smaller ones in the anterior portion of the lower jaw, and laterally a row of canine-like teeth: villiform teeth likewise on the vomer, and palate: when present on the tongue minute. Dorsal fin single, with from nine to thirteen spines: anal with three: pectorals pointed: caudal rounded, truncated or emarginate. Scales ctenoid, of moderate or rather small size, one or two enlarged rows over the nape. Pyloric appendages few or absent. Air-vessel simple.

Geographical distribution.—From the Red Sea and East coast of Africa through the seas of India, the Malay Archipelago, and to the Pacific.

Uses.—As a rule all these fishes are good as food, though some are insipid: a few attain a large size. They are extensively salted and dried in many localities.

Amongst the *Lutiani* exist variations which require notice. Thus in some, when immature (as observed in a few *Serrani*), a spine exists at the angle of the preopercle: as age advances it is gradually absorbed, although occasionally in the adult coarse serrations may indicate its prior existence. Instead of one there may be several spinate denticulations at this spot in the fry, which also disappear, as in the case of the single spine. The interopercular knob, in those species which possess one (=Genus *Diacope*, Cuv. and Val., or *Genyoroge*, Cantor.) appears in two distinct modes—either as well formed from birth with a notch in the vertical border of the preopercle—or else the knob is gradually formed, and as it increases in size it presses against the vertical border of the preopercle causing absorption at the spot above it and thus creates a notch. Respecting the dorsal spines, it has been remarked of the *Serrani* that one ray may occasionally assume the form of a spine, thus changing the specific number (by the addition of one spine and the diminution of one ray) but this seems to be rather rare amongst the Indian *Lutiani* in which, although the spines may be increased, the rays are not usually diminished in number: an increase in the number of the rays is, however, of more frequent occurrence than in the spines.

In colouring there is one subject that requires further examination, and that is the lateral blotch: in those species in which it is present, it is sometimes most decided in the young, but whether it frequently exists in some specimens and is absent in others remains to be solved. That it disappears if the fresh specimen is left soaking in water is evident: that it sometimes is all but lost in those kept in spirit is also apparent, but the similarity of *Lutianus marginatus* without a lateral blotch to specimens in which it is present is so great, that I cannot separate them into distinct species; the same fact has been observed by Bleeker, in *L. Bengalensis* and *Amboinensis*. It is not a little remarkable that this mark is of a deep black colour on the Malabar coast, in *L. marginatus*; but much less apparent in specimens captured on the Coromandel coast, where also those of an identical size without any such blotch are numerous. Age then cannot be the sole cause, which may be sought for in locality and sex (provided they are the same species).

SYNOPSIS OF SPECIES.

1. *Lutianus Sebæ*, D. [illegible], A. [illegible], L. r. [illegible], L. tr. 9/22. Interopercular knob present, no lingual teeth. Scales in oblique rows. Reddish* with three curved black bands. Red Sea, seas of India, to the Malay Archipelago, and beyond.

2. *Lutianus Malabaricus*, D. [illegible], A. [illegible], L. r. [illegible], L. tr. 9/23. No interopercular knob. No lingual teeth. Scales in oblique rows above the lateral line. A violet-purple band on the back, along the base of the dorsal fin. Seas of India to the Malay Archipelago.

3. *Lutianus erythropterus*, D. [illegible], A. [illegible], L. r. [illegible], L. tr. 11-12/25. No interopercular knob. No lingual teeth. Scales in oblique rows. Red with marks varying with age. Red Sea, seas of India to the Malay Archipelago, and beyond.

4. *Lutianus dodecacanthus*, D. [illegible], A. [illegible], L. r. [illegible], L. tr. 8/23. No interopercular knob. No lingual teeth. Scales in oblique rows above the lateral-line. Scarlet. Seas of India to the Malay Archipelago.

5. *Lutianus Bengalensis*, D. [illegible], A. [illegible], L. r. [illegible], L. tr. 7-8/18. An interopercular knob. No lingual teeth. Scales in oblique rows above the lateral-line, superiorly reaching to above the front edge of the eye. Four blue bands from the eye along the sides. Red Sea, seas of India to the Malay Archipelago.

6. *Lutianus fulvus*, D. [illegible], A. [illegible], L. r. [illegible], L. tr. 9/21. An interopercular knob. No lingual teeth. Scales in oblique rows above the lateral-line. Yellowish-red. Andamans, Otaheite.

7. *Lutianus biguttatus*, D. [illegible], A. [illegible], L. r. [illegible], L. tr. 6/15. A small interopercular knob. Lingual teeth. Scales in oblique rows above the lateral-line. Olive with two milk-white spots on the back. Seas of India, to the Malay Archipelago.

* It is curious that from this as well as from some other species of red *Lutiani*, as *L. erythropterus*, *L. dodecacanthus*, and even *Odontonectes pinjalo*, the body colour has stained the cloth in which my specimens were enveloped whilst in spirit coming from India. In some white carps on the other hand, as *Barbus filamentosus*, and *B. arulius* the fish turns of a bright red after death, whether placed in spirit or skinned and stuffed, this colour being persistent except to incipient putrefaction, soaking in water or weak spirit and bleaching.

8. *Lutianus lineolatus*, D. $\frac{10}{12-13}$, A. $\frac{3}{8-9}$, L. r. [illegible], L. tr. 6-7/14. No interopercular knob. Lingual teeth. Scales in oblique sinuous rows above the lateral-line. Body horizontally banded. Red Sea, seas of India to the Malay Archipelago.

9. *Lutianus lemniscatus*, D. $\frac{10}{14}$, A. $\frac{3}{8}$, L. l. 56, L. tr. 8/21. A badly developed interopercular knob. Two wide dark horizontal bands from the eye to the caudal fin. Ceylon to the Malay Archipelago.

10. *Lutianus chrysotaenia*, D. $\frac{10}{13}$, A. $\frac{3}{8}$, L. r. [illegible], L. tr. 8/22. No interopercular knob. Lingual teeth. Scales in oblique rows above the lateral-line. Oblique bands from the eye, posteriorly. Nicobars to the Malay Archipelago.

11. *Lutianus rivulatus*, D. $\frac{10}{15}$, A. $\frac{3}{8-9}$, L. r. [illegible], L. tr. 8/19. An interopercular knob. No lingual teeth. Scales in oblique rows above the lateral-line. Brownish, spotted with blue: a black blotch, having a white front edge on the lateral-line. Red Sea, East coast of Africa, seas of India, to the Malay Archipelago, and beyond.

12. *Lutianus argentimaculatus*, D. $\frac{10}{13-14}$, A. $\frac{3}{8}$, L. r. [illegible], L. tr. 7-8/16. A very slight interopercular knob. Lingual teeth. Scales mostly in horizontal rows above lateral-line. Cherry-red, the young with narrow, white, vertical bands. Red Sea, East coast of Africa, seas of India, to the Malay Archipelago and beyond.

13. *Lutianus roseus*, D. $\frac{10}{14}$, A. $\frac{3}{8}$, L. r. [illegible], L. tr. 7/18. No interopercular knob. Lingual teeth. Scales in horizontal rows. Caudal fin rounded. Reddish-brown. Seas of India to the Malay Archipelago.

14. *Lutianus sillaoo*, D. $\frac{10}{14}$, A. $\frac{3}{8-9}$, L. r. [illegible], L. tr. 6/15. No interopercular knob. Lingual teeth. Scales in oblique rows above lateral-line. Reddish with varying colours. Seas of India.

15. *Lutianus lioglossus*, D. $\frac{10}{13-14}$, A. $\frac{3}{8-9}$, L. r. [illegible], L. tr. 6-7/15. A very slight interopercular knob. No lingual teeth. Scales in oblique rows above lateral-line. Roseate shot with gold: a black lateral blotch. Red Sea, seas of India to the Malay Archipelago and beyond.

16. *Lutianus jahngarah*, D. $\frac{10}{13-14}$, A. $\frac{3}{8}$, L. r. [illegible], L. tr. 6/13. No interopercular knob. No lingual teeth. Scales in horizontal rows. Reddish with varying colours. Seas of India.

17. *Lutianus quinquelineatus*, D. $\frac{10}{13-14}$, A. $\frac{3}{8-9}$, L. r. [illegible], L. tr. 8/21. No interopercular knob. Lingual teeth. Scales in oblique rows above the lateral-line. About six blue bands from the eye along the body: a black lateral blotch. Red Sea, East coast of Africa, seas of India to the Malay Archipelago and beyond.

18. *Lutianus lunulatus*, D. $\frac{10}{13-14}$, A. $\frac{3}{8-9}$, L. r. [illegible], L. tr. 7/21. No interopercular knob. Lingual teeth. Scales in oblique rows above the lateral-line. Reddish-crimson, a lunated black band on the caudal fin. Coast of India to the Malay Archipelago.

19. *Lutianus fulviflamma*, D. $\frac{10}{12-13}$, A. $\frac{3}{8}$, L. r. [illegible], L. tr. 7-8/16. No interopercular knob. Lingual teeth. Scales in oblique rows above the lateral-line. Golden with a black lateral blotch; and in the variety *Russellii* also oblique golden bands from the eye along the body. Red Sea, East coast of Africa, seas of India to the Malay Archipelago and beyond.

20. *Lutianus Johnii*, D. $\frac{10}{13-14}$, A. $\frac{3}{8-9}$, L. r. [illegible], L. tr. 7/13. A very indistinct interopercular tuberosity. Lingual teeth. Scales in horizontal rows. Golden with a black lateral blotch. Seas of India to the Malay Archipelago and beyond.

21. *Lutianus gibbus*, D. $\frac{10}{14}$, A. $\frac{3}{8-9}$, L. r. [illegible], L. tr. 8/23. A strong interopercular knob. No lingual teeth. Scales in oblique rows above the lateral-line. Crimson in the adult. In the young a black band covers the end of the dorsal fin, the last half of the free portion of the tail, and the whole of the caudal. Red Sea, Andamans to the Malay Archipelago.

22. *Lutianus bohar*, D. $\frac{10}{14}$, A. $\frac{3}{8}$, L. r. [illegible], L. tr. 7/18. A small interopercular knob. Lingual teeth. Scales in oblique rows above the lateral-line. Brownish with two milk-white spots, one below the spinous, the other below the soft portion, of the dorsal fin. Red Sea, seas of India to the Malay Archipelago and beyond.

23. *Lutianus marginatus*, D. $\frac{10}{13-14}$, A. $\frac{3}{8}$, L. r. [illegible], L. tr. 6-7/15. A strong interopercular knob. No lingual teeth. Scales in oblique rows above the lateral-line. Purplish-yellow, fins darker, edged with white. A black lateral blotch may be present, or absent. East coast of Africa, seas of India to the Malay Archipelago.

24. *Lutianus yapilli*, D. $\frac{10}{13}$, A. $\frac{3}{8}$, L. r. [illegible], L. tr. 6/14. No interopercular knob. Scales in horizontal rows. Caudal fin rounded. Silvery-grey, with yellow bands. Coromandel coast of India.

25. *Lutianus quinquelinearis*, D. $\frac{10}{13-14}$, A. $\frac{3}{8-9}$, L. r. [illegible], L. tr. 8/19. A strong interopercular knob. No lingual teeth. Scales in oblique rows above the lateral-line. Five blue bands from the eye along the body: a black lateral blotch. Seas of India to the Malay Archipelago.

26. *Lutianus vitta*, D. $\frac{10}{13}$, A. $\frac{3}{8}$, L. r. [illegible], L. tr. 8/12. No interopercular knob. Lingual teeth. Scales in oblique sinuous rows above the lateral-line. Yellowish-red with olive stripes. Seas of India to the Malay Archipelago.

27. *Lutianus Madras*, D. $\frac{10}{13-14}$, A. $\frac{3}{8-9}$, L. r. [illegible], L. tr. 6/16. No interopercular knob. Lingual teeth. Scales in oblique rows above the lateral-line. Roseate with olive or reddish lines following the rows of scales. East coast of Africa, seas of India to the Malay Archipelago.

28. *Lutianus decussatus*, D. $\frac{10}{13-14}$, A. $\frac{3}{8}$, L. r. [illegible], L. tr. 6-7/17. A slight interopercular swelling. No lingual teeth. Scales in oblique rows above the lateral-line. Six blackish longitudinal bands, and six more vertical ones cross them from the back. A black blotch at the base of the caudal fin. Seas of India to the Malay Archipelago and beyond.

1. Lutianus Sebæ, Plate IX, fig. 3.

Perca, Seba, iii, pl. 27, f. 2.
Sparus bottarco champah, Russell, Fish. Vizag. i, p. 77, pl. 99.

Diacope Sebæ, Cuv. and Val. ii. p. 411; Klunz. Fische Roth. Meer. Verh. z. b. Ges. Wien. 1870, p. 692.
Diacope Siamensis, Cuv. and Val. vi, p. 524.
Mesoprion Sebæ, Bleeker, Perc. p. 45; Kner. Novara Fische. p. 30.
Genyoroge sebæ, Günther, Catal. p. 176.
Lutjanus Sebæ, Bleeker, Siam. p. 173, and Lutjani, p. 53.
Veri-cutta-day, or *Nai-keruchi*, "smelling like a dog," Tam.

B. vii, D. $\frac{11}{15-16}$, P. 17, V. 1/5, A. $\frac{3}{10-11}$, C. 17, L. l. 50-55, L. r. [illegible], L. tr. 9/22: Cæc. pyl. 4-5. Vert. 10/14.

Length of head 4/13 to 2/7, of caudal 1/5, height of body 2/5 of the total length. *Eyes*—diameter 2/7 of length of head, $1\frac{1}{4}$ diameters from end of snout, and 2/3 of a diameter apart. The distance from the eye to the upper edge of the maxilla equals one-fourth of the diameter of the orbit. The maxilla reaches to below the middle of the eye. Both the vertical and horizontal limbs of the preopercle serrated, the former having a deep emargination in the adult to receive a well developed interopercular knob which in the young is not so distinct. *Teeth*—canines in the premaxillaries, an outer row of curved canine-like teeth in the jaws: villiform in a Λ-shape in the vomer, and in a band on the palate, none on the tongue. *Fins*—third dorsal spine the longest, rather above half the length of the head, from thence they decrease to the last but one: soft portion of the fin and also of the anal, elevated and pointed, much higher than long at its base. Pectoral nearly as long as the head. Third anal spine somewhat the longest and nearly equal to the post-orbital portion of the head. *Scales*—in oblique rows above the lateral-line and horizontal ones below it: superiorly they reach to above the hind edge of the orbit: caudal emarginate. *Colours*—reddish, a black band passes from before the dorsal fin, through the eye to the snout: a second from the second to the sixth dorsal spines to the ventral fin: a third from the soft dorsal, curving downwards to the lower half of the caudal: ventrals and lower half of anal black.

Bleeker observes that he possesses a very young specimen (35''' long) in which the soft dorsal and anal are more rounded, and in colour it appears as if it were brownish, traversed by two narrow white bands.

Habitat.—From the Red Sea, and East coast of Africa, through the seas of India to the Malay Archipelago. Longest specimen captured at Madras 8 inches.

2. Lutianus Malabaricus, Plate IX, fig. 4.

Sparus Malabaricus, Bl. Schn. p. 278.
Mesoprion Malabaricus, Cuv. and Val. ii, p. 480.
Mesoprion Malabaricus, Bleeker, Sumatra, iii, p. 3, and Günther, Catal. i, p. 204 (not synonym.)
Lutjanus Malabaricus, Bleeker, Atl. Ich. Perc. t. xv, fig. 1, and Lutjani, p. 50 (not synonym.)

B. vii, D. $\frac{11}{14}$, P. 17, V. 1/5, A. $\frac{3}{8}$, C. 17, L. l. 55, L. r. [illegible], L. tr. 9/23.

Length of head 2/7, of caudal nearly 1/6, height of body 4/11 of the total length. *Eyes*—diameter 1/4 of length of head, $1\frac{1}{2}$ diameters from the end of snout, and 3/4 of a diameter apart. Form of the body not so compressed as in *L. erythropterus*, its width being equal to two-fifths its height: a slight concavity over the orbits: lower jaw the longer: height of preorbital equals 4/5 of diameter of eye. The maxilla reaches to below the first third of the orbit. Preopercle with a very shallow emargination on its vertical border which is finely serrated; at its angle the serrations become larger, whilst four or five of diminished size exist along the posterior half of the lower limb. *Teeth*—two or three rather strong curved canines on either side of the premaxillaries; an outer row of curved conical canine-like teeth in either jaw: villiform ones in a Λ-shape on the vomer, a broad band on the palatines, none on the tongue. *Fins*—dorsal spines moderately strong, from the third they are of about equal length but shorter than the rays, the third spine equals about one-third of the length of the head; the last spine equals one diameter of the orbit: the seventh or eighth ray is the longest, and equals four-fifths of the extent of the base of the fin, soft dorsal and anal both somewhat angularly rounded and of the same height. Pectoral longer than the ventral, almost as long as the head and reaching to above the anal spines: second and third anal spines of about equal strength, the latter slightly the longer and nearly equalling the third of the dorsal fin: the fourth ray is the longest, slightly exceeding the highest in the dorsal fin: caudal slightly emarginate. *Scales*—rows not tortuous, those above the lateral-line oblique, as are also those below it above the level of the lower edge of the orbit, below which they are horizontal: two broad rows over the nape, and eight across the cheek: they extend along the back as far as to a level with the hind edge of the eye. *Colours*—having a roseate tinge in life with narrow oblique yellow streaks above the lateral-line, and longitudinal ones below it: a longitudinal violet-purple band passes from behind the eye along the base of the dorsal fin opposite the end of which it is interrupted by a light band over the commencement of the tail, subsequently it reappears in a lighter form across the middle of the free portion of the tail. Fins reddish, the dorsal and caudal with a fine black edge: anal spines dark grey, those of ventrals white.

Schneider's type specimen is still in good preservation at Berlin, and identical with the one figured which I took (a little over 8 inches in length) off the Meckran coast. It is closely allied to *L. erythropterus*; but the dorsal spines are much lower, the eye and the colours &c. differ.

Valenciennes remarks that as Bloch received his specimen from the Coromandel coast of India it is difficult to perceive why Schneider gave to it the term *Malabaricus*. The reason is that Tranquebar (from whence it came) and the southern portions of the Coromandel coast were then termed 'Malabar,' and to this day the natives of Madras call those residing to the south 'Malabars.'

Habitat.—Coasts of Sind and India.

3. Lutianus erythropterus, Plate X, figs. 1 (young), 2 (adult).

Lutianus erythropterus, Bl. t. 249; Bl. Schn. p. 325 (not Bleeker).
Sparus chirtah, Russell, Fish. Vizag. i, p. 74, pl. 93.
Diacope annularis, Rüpp. Atl. p. 91, and N. W. Fische, p. 74, pl. 93; Klunz. Fische Roth. Meer. Verh. z. b. Ges. in Wien. 1870, p. 697.
? *Diacope erythrina*, Rüpp. N. W. Fische, p. 92, t. 25, f. 3; Klunz. Fische Roth. Meer. Verh. z. b. Ges. in Wien. 1870, p. 702.
Diacope sanguinea, (Ehren.) Cuv. and Val. ii, p. 437 (adult).
Mesoprion rubellus, Cuv. and Val. ii, p. 475.
Mesoprion erythropterus, Cuv. and Val. ii, p. 478.
Mesoprion annularis, Cuv. and Val. ii, p. 488, and iii, p. 497: Quoy and Gaim. Voy. Astr. p. 666, pl. 5, fig. 4; Richards. Ich. China, p. 229; Bleeker, Perc. p. 67; Cantor, Catal. p. 14; Günther, Catal. i, p. 201; Kner. Novara Fische, p. 33.
Diacope metallicus, (Kuhl. and v. Hass.) Bleeker, Batav. p. 525.
Mesoprion sanguineus, Bleeker, Perc. p. 48.
Mesoprion erythrinus, Günther, Catal. i, p. 192; Playfair, Proc. Zool. Soc. 1867, p. 849.
Mesoprion chirtah, Day, Proc. Zool. Soc. 1868, p. 150, and 1869, p. 297.
Lutjanus annularis, Bleeker, Obi. p. 240.
Lutjanus chirtah, Bleeker, Atl. Ich. Perc. t. xxiii, fig. 1, and Lutjani, p. 42.
Soosta, Ooriah.

B. vii, D. $\frac{10}{13-14}$, P. 17, V. 1/5, A. $\frac{3}{8}$, C. 17, L. l. 52-55, L. r. [illegible], L. tr. 11-12/25, Cæc. pyl. 5-6, Vert. 10/14.

Length of head $3\frac{3}{4}$ to $3\frac{1}{2}$, of caudal 1/5 to 1/6, height of body from $2\frac{3}{4}$ to $3\frac{1}{4}$ in the total length. *Eyes*—diameter 1/5 to 1/6 of the length of the head in the adult, but much larger in the young,* $1\frac{1}{2}$ to 2 diameters from end of snout, and $1\frac{1}{4}$ to $1\frac{1}{2}$ apart. Body compressed, dorsal profile more convex than that of the abdomen, and slightly concave about the orbit. The maxilla, in the adult, scarcely reaches to below the front edge of the orbit. Preopercle with a very shallow emargination on its vertical limb which is finely and evenly serrated to above its angle where the serrations become coarser, they extend for a short distance along its horizontal border: sometimes a very small interopercular knob exists. *Teeth*—one or two canines on either side of the premaxillary, an outer row of curved canine-like teeth in either jaw, villiform ones in a triangular patch on the vomer, and in a rather narrow band on the palatines: none on the tongue. *Fins*—dorsal spines of moderate strength increasing in length to the fourth which equals two-fifths to one-third of the height of the body, from it to the last they are slightly lower and sub-equal in length, the soft portion of the fin more angular in the adult than in the young, the seventh to the tenth rays being the highest, half as long again as the fourth spine, and their height equalling the length of the base of the soft portion of the fin. Pectoral reaching as far as the ventral, and equalling the length of the head behind the posterior nostril: ventral spine as long as the fourth of the dorsal fin: second anal spine somewhat the strongest, but not quite so long as the third which equals the third of the dorsal fin: caudal slightly emarginate or cut square in the young. *Scales*—in somewhat tortuous rows going in a direction upwards and backwards, they extend over the base of the dorsal fin reaching highest on the rays, they are equally developed over the bases of the caudal and anal. *Colours*—crimson with orange reflections: a broad blackish band passes from the eye to the commencement of the dorsal spines, and is sometimes slightly apparent along the whole base of the fin: eight to twelve narrow and nearly horizontal black lines exist below the lateral-line, and several more above it, some being the continuations of those which commence below the lateral-line. A black band crosses the back over the free portion of the tail, having a white one before it, and a narrow pink one posterior to it. Pectoral flesh-coloured: ventral either black or stained black in its outer half or two-thirds: dorsal dark grey in some specimens with a nearly black base and a black edge: caudal pink with a narrow black border: anal darkest anteriorly. In *adults* (12 inches) the black lines disappear, and each row of scales has a golden line: a trace exists of the band from the eye to the dorsal fin: whilst that over the free portion of the tail is somewhat indistinct.

Amongst Bloch's typical collection in the Berlin Museum, Professor Peters showed me two of this species, one being young with the distinct colours of the *annularis*; the other more adult. Bleeker considers the *erythropterus* of Bloch to be identical with *L. lineolatus*, and certainly the body and fins in the figure appear more to resemble that species than the present: the head, (especially the eyes,) differs considerably from the *lineolatus*. The type specimens have their original names upon them.

Although Ruppell's figure of *Diacope erythrina* very closely resembles an adult of this species, he states it to have only 10 dorsal spines. Col. Playfair obtained a "fine specimen" now in the British Museum, termed *erythrinus*, which is the adult of this species, but it has 11 dorsal spines, it is nearly 18 inches long, and the eye is $5\frac{3}{4}$ in the length of the head.

In the Berlin Museum is a fine specimen (21 inches in length) of *Diacope sanguinea*, (Ehren.) Cuv. and

* The following are the measurements as to the *size of the eye* compared with the length of the head in specimens of various ages:

At 6 inches in length, $3\frac{1}{4}$ in the length of the head.
" $8\frac{1}{2}$ " " " $4\frac{1}{2}$ " " " "
" 12 " " " $5\frac{1}{4}$ " " " "
" 18 " " " $5\frac{3}{4}$ " " " "
" 21 " " " 1/6 " " " "

Val. type of the species. It appears identical with this fish. Length of head $\frac{1}{4}$, of caudal [illegible], height of body nearly $\frac{1}{3}$ of the total length. *Eyes*—diameter $5\frac{1}{2}$ in the length of the head, 2 diameters from end of snout, and $1\frac{1}{2}$ apart. *Fins*—fourth and fifth dorsal spines of equal height, and $2\frac{3}{4}$ in the length of the head.

The type specimen of *Mesoprion rubellus*, C. V., in the Paris Museum is a skin from Pondicherry of this species, its scales are L. r. 67, L. tr. 12/25.

Habitat.—Red Sea, East coast of Africa, seas of India to the Malay Archipelago and beyond. It is captured all the year round at Madras, but is most abundant during the cold months when its fry are also about. Fig. 1 is from a specimen 6 inches in length, and represents the immature fish: Fig. 2, or the mature fish is from a specimen a little over 12 inches long. Both are from Madras.

4. Lutianus dodecacanthus, Plate X, Fig. 3.

Mesoprion Malabaricus, Bleeker, Sumatra, v, p. 497; Günther, Catal. i, p. 204 (not Bloch, Schn.)
Lutjanus dodecacanthus, Bleeker, Amb. ii, p. 278 and Atl. Ich. Perc. t. xxiv, f. 2.
Mesoprion dodecacanthus, Günther, Catal. i, p. 206.
Lutjanus Malabaricus, Bleeker, Atl. Ich. Perc. t. lxxv, fig. 1 and Lutjani, p. 50 (in part).

B. vii, D. [illegible], P. 17, V. 1/5, A. $\frac{3}{8}$, C. 17, L. l. 52, L. r. [illegible], L. tr. 8/23.

Length of head $3\frac{1}{4}$, of caudal 1/5, height of body $3\frac{1}{3}$ of the total length. *Eyes*—diameter 1/4 of length of head, $1\frac{1}{2}$ diameters from end of snout, and nearly 1 apart. Body compressed, profile above the orbit somewhat concave: the distance between the eye and the upper edge of the maxilla equals a little more than one diameter of the orbit. The maxilla extends to beneath the front edge of the orbit. Vertical limb of preopercle having a shallow emargination, the whole being finely serrated superiorly, but more coarsely so at its angle: lower limb finely serrated in its anterior half. A small interopercular knob. *Teeth*—a pair of moderately sized, curved canines in the premaxillaries, and having two smaller intermediate ones: an outer row of curved, canine-like teeth in both jaws, largest in the mandible, especially about its centre: none on the tongue. Villiform ones in a A-form on the vomer, and in a band on the palatines. *Fins*—dorsal spines of moderate strength, the fourth and fifth the longest, and equal to $3\frac{1}{2}$ in the height of the body, they gradually decrease to the last, which is only two-thirds as long as the fourth: the soft portion of the dorsal angular, and one-fifth higher than its base is long. Pectoral reaches to above the anal spines, and is as long as the head: ventral just reaches the vent. Second anal spine not quite so long as the third, which equals the longest in the dorsal fin: its soft portion angular, one-fourth higher than the length of its entire base: caudal slightly emarginate. *Scales*—in oblique, straight (not sinuous) rows above the lateral line, and also as low as a level with the eye, below which all are horizontal: twelve rows between the occiput and base of the dorsal fin, and six across the cheeks. *Colours*—uniform scarlet, with a golden line along each row of scales and a nacreous spot across the free portion of the tail just behind the base of the dorsal fin. A narrow black edge to the dorsal, caudal, and anal fins.

This species seems to be identical with Bleeker's: he observes that three of his specimens have twelve dorsal spines, but which appears to be due to the transformation of the first ray into a weak spine.

There are two fine specimens in the British Museum, one about 16 inches in length, wherein the eye is 2 diameters from the end of the snout: the other is 15 inches long, the diameter of the eye 1/4 of the length of the head, and $1\frac{1}{2}$ diameters from the end of the snout.

Habitat.—Seas of India to the Malay Archipelago. The specimen figured is $14\frac{1}{2}$ inches in length and from Madras.

5. Lutianus Bengalensis, Plate X, Fig. 4.

? *Sciæna kasmira*, Forsk. p. 46.
Holocentrus Bengalensis, Bloch, t. 246, fig. 2; Bl. Schn. p. 316; Lacép. iv, p. 330.
Perca polyzonias, Forst. Mss. p. 225.
Diacope octolineata, Cuv. and Val. ii. p. 418, vi, p. 526 (in part); Rüppell, Atl. p. 75; Tem. & Schleg. Fauna Japon. p. 12, t. vi, f. 2; Richards. Ich. China, p. 229.
Diacope octovittata, Cuv. and Val. vi, p. 528.
Mesoprion pomacanthus, Bleeker, Amb. p. 407 (in part); Günther, Catal. i, p. 210.
Genyoroge Bengalensis, Günther, Catal. i, p. 178 (in part.)
Genyoroge octovittata, Günther, Catal. i, p. 180.
Evoplites pomacanthus, Gill, Cuban Fish, Proc. Ac. Nat. Sc. Phil. 1862, p. 234.
Genyoroge Amboinensis, Day, Proc. Zool. Soc. 1870, p. 679.
Diacope kasmira, Klunz. Fische d. R. M. Verh. z. b. Ges. Wien, 1870, p. 695.
Lutjanus Bengalensis, Bleeker, Atl. Ich. Perc. t. xxiv, f. 3 and Lutjani, p. 34.
Veri-keechan, Tam.

B. vii, D. [illegible].* P. 16, V. 1/5, A. $\frac{3}{8}$, C. 17, L. l. 48, L. r. [illegible], L. tr. 7-8/18, Cæc. pyl. 0.

Length of head from 2/7 to 4/15, of caudal 1/5, height of body 2/7 of the total length. *Eyes*—diameter from 1/4 to 2/9 of the length of head, $1\frac{1}{4}$ diameters from the end of snout, and 3/4 apart. The distance from the eye to the upper border of the maxilla equals half the diameter of the orbit. The maxilla reaches to below the middle of the orbit. Vertical limb of preopercle with a moderately deep notch above its rounded angle,

* Bleeker has found the following amongst specimens of this species: D. [illegible] or 10 | [illegible] or [illegible] or 11 | [illegible].

superiorly it is finely serrated, but very coarsely so at its angle, some serrations are also continued along its lower limb. Interopercular knob distinct. *Teeth*—moderate-sized canines in the premaxillaries, an outer row of curved conical teeth in either jaw: villiform ones in a ʌ-form on the vomer, in a band on the palatines, but none on the tongue. *Fins*—dorsal spines rather strong, the fourth the longest and one-fourth higher than the rays: soft portion of the fin rounded, half as high as its base is long. Pectoral as long as the head and reaching to above the anal spines: ventral does not reach the vent. Second anal spine stronger and usually rather longer than the third (it is sometimes slightly shorter), which equals the length of the postorbital portion of the head, anterior rays the highest and as long as the entire base of the fin, its lower edge slightly convex; caudal emarginate. *Scales*—in oblique rows above the lateral-line and in horizontal ones below it: six or eight rows across the cheeks, whilst superiorly they extend as far forwards as to above the front edge of the eye: none on the preorbital, except in large specimens, but I possess one nine inches long that has several rows there. *Colours*—yellowish-brown superiorly becoming yellowish-white inferiorly. Four bright blue black-edged and slightly sinuous bands pass from the orbit across the opercles, the superior to about the ninth dorsal spine, the second to the fourth dorsal ray, the third to behind the last dorsal ray, and the fourth to rather below the centre of the base of the caudal. Fins yellowish, the dorsal with a dark edge and a light outer margin.

Bleeker observes that three species have the upper surface of the head scaled, the vomerine teeth in a ʌ-form, a deep preopercular emargination and an edentulous tongue. They are as follows, and may be thus divided for convenience sake:—

Lutianus Bengalensis, D. [illegible], L. r. [illegible], L. tr. 8-9/20-21, Cæc. pyl. 0.
Lutianus quinquelinearis, D. [illegible], L. r. [illegible], L. tr. 6-7/18-19, Cæc. pyl. 5.
Lutianus Amboinensis, D. [illegible], L. r. [illegible], L. tr. 7-8/17-18, Cæc. pyl. ?.

Bennett, Proc. Zool. Soc. 1832, p. 182, briefly describes a fish as *Diacope spilura*, from Ceylon: D. [illegible], A. [illegible]. Five parallel red lines on either side; the second and third go from the eye, the fourth from the axilla, the fifth from the angle of the mouth: a large black spot before the base of the caudal fin: spinous portion of the dorsal with a black base and outer edge. It is stated to be allied to *D. octolineata*.

Specimens under the name of *Genyoroge notata*, in the British Museum, have D. [illegible], A. [illegible], L. r. [illegible], L. tr. 9/. *Eyes*—diameter $3\frac{1}{2}$ in the length of the head, 1 diameter from the end of snout, and 3/4 of a diameter apart. Scales over suborbital, and a few on preorbital. The second anal spine equals half the length of the head. They are coloured as in this species.

Habitat.—Red Sea, seas of India, to the Malay Archipelago, and beyond; it attains at least 10 inches in length.

6. Lutianus fulvus, Plate X, fig. 5.

Perca fulva, Forst. Mss. p. 193.
Holocentrus fulvus, Bl. Schn. p. 318.
Diacope fulva, Cuv. and Val. ii, p. 435.
Genyoroge fulva, Günther, Catal. i, p. 184.

B. vii, D. [illegible], P. 17, V. 1/5, A. [illegible], C. 17, L. l. 51, L. r. [illegible], L. tr. 9/21.

Length of head 2/7, of caudal 2/11, height of body 3/10 of the total length. *Eyes*—diameter $3\frac{1}{2}$ of the length of head, $1\frac{1}{2}$ diameters from the end of snout, and 3/4 of a diameter apart. A considerable rise from the snout to the commencement of the dorsal fin: abdominal profile not so convex as that of the back: thickness of body equal to 4/7 of its height. The maxilla reaches to below the front fourth of the orbit. Vertical limb of preopercle with a very deep emargination and a produced rounded angle, above the notch the limb is serrated, on the angle it becomes almost spinate, whilst a few fine serrations exist on the lower limb. Interopercular knob very well developed in a pyramidal form. *Teeth*—small curved canines in the upper jaw, an outer rather numerous row of canine-like curved teeth in either jaw, villiform ones in a triangular spot on the vomer, in a band on the palatines, none on the tongue. *Fins*—dorsal spines strong, increasing in length to the fourth, which equals that of the postorbital portion of the head, or $2\frac{1}{4}$ in the height of body, from it they decrease to the last, which is scarcely above two-thirds as high: the soft portion of the fin rounded, the height of the rays being equal to about two-thirds of the highest spine. Pectoral as long as the head, reaching to above the anal spines. Second anal spine much the strongest, third slightly the longest, equalling the second of the dorsal fin, height of the longest rays a little more than that of its entire base; caudal emarginate. *Scales*—in oblique rows above the lateral-line and in horizontal ones below it. *Colours*—uniform yellowish-red with a dark spot in the axil: fins yellow: the upper third of the dorsal black with a white margin: caudal also with a black edge and white margin: a dark black mark across the middle of the first third of the anal.

Habitat.—Andamans, Otaheiti. The specimen figured is upwards of 10 inches in length.

7. Lutianus biguttatus, Plate X, fig. 6.

Serranus biguttatus, Cuv. and Val. vi, p. 507; Günther, Catal. i, p. 155.
Mesoprion lineolatus, Bleeker, Perc. p. 46 (not Rüppell.)
Mesoprion Bleekeri, Günther, Catal. i, p. 208.
Lutjanus Bleekeri, Bleeker, Halmah. i, p. 155.
Lutjanus biguttatus, Bleeker, Lutjani, p. 32.

B. vii, D. [illegible], P. 16, V. 1/5, A. [illegible], C. 17, L. l. 50, L. r. [illegible], L. tr. 6/15.

Length of head 2/7, of caudal 1/7, height of body 1/4 to 2/9 of the total length. *Eyes*—diameter 3/10 to 2/7 of length of head, 1 diameter from the end of snout, and 3/4 of a diameter apart. Body elongated, its dorsal and abdominal profiles nearly horizontal. The maxilla reaches to below the first third of the orbit: interorbital space flat. Vertical limb of preopercle with a moderately deep emargination to receive a very badly developed interopercular knob, its angle rounded, the whole limb finely serrated, and the lower limb almost entire. Two small sharp points on the opercle. *Teeth*—villiform in the jaws, with a large canine on either side of the premaxillary, between which are two smaller curved canine-like teeth in the outer row, and several more similar ones along the upper jaw: in the lower jaw exists an outer row of curved, canine-like teeth, becoming larger posteriorly: in a triangular spot of villiform ones on the vomer, the base being behind, and from the centre of which a narrow band passes a short way backwards: those on the palatines in a narrow line: an oblong patch on the tongue. *Fins*—spines weak, those of the dorsal increase in length to the third and fourth, which are half as long as the head, from these they decrease to the last: soft portion of the fin, (as is also that of the anal,) rounded and not half so high as the spines, the longest ray equalling two-thirds the length of the base of the fin. Pectoral extends rather beyond the ventral, but hardly to above the anal, it is two-thirds as long as the head: third anal spine rather the longest, equal to the diameter of the orbit but not so long as the rays, anterior anal rays one-third higher than those of the dorsal, last anal ray as short as the spine, lower edge of fin straight: caudal slightly emarginate. *Scales*—in parallel rows below and oblique ones above the lateral line. *Colours*—yellowish-grey superiorly, becoming yellowish-white on the sides and abdomen, a broad black band passes from the eye to the middle of the caudal fin, dividing the dark back from the light sides, and a second band is continued from below the jaws to above the posterior end of the base of the anal, where it becomes indistinct. A white pearly spot exists on the back under the middle of the spinous dorsal, and a second under the commencement of the rayed portion of the fin.

Professor Peters showed me one of this species, nearly 4 inches in length, received from Paris as *Serranus biguttatus*, and I subsequently saw several more of the types in the Paris Museum.

Habitat.—Seas of India to the Malay Archipelago. The type specimen of Cuv. and Val. came from Ceylon, the one figured ($7\frac{1}{2}$ inches in length) I procured at the Andaman islands.

8. **Lutianus lineolatus**, Plate XI, fig. 1 and 2.

Perca karoo, Russell, Fish. Vizag. ii, p. 19, pl. 125.
Diacope lineolata, Rüpp. Atl. Fische, p. 76, t. 19, f. 3; Klunz. Verh. z. b. Ges. in Wien. 1870, p. 698.
Serranus woolcay, Cuv. and Val. ii, p. 247; Günther, Catal. i, p. 126.
Mesoprion caroui, Cuv. and Val. ii, p. 489; Cantor, Catal. p. 16.
Mesoprion xanthopterygius, Bleeker, Perc. p. 46.
Mesoprion lineolata, Bleeker, Perc. p. 46 (not syn.); Günther, Catal. i, p. 205; Kner. Novara Fische, p. 36; Playfair, Zanz. p. 17.
Mesoprion erythropterus, Bleeker, Perc. 47; Günther, Catal. i, p. 205 (not Bloch.)
Mesoprion dodecacanthoides, Günther, Catal. i, p. 206 (not Bleeker.)
Lutjanus erythropterus, Bleeker, Atl. Ich. Perc. t. xx, fig. 2, and Lutjani, p. 29 (not Bloch.)
Nooleai, Tam.

B. vii, D. $\frac{10}{12}|\frac{1}{13}$, P. 16, V. 1/5, A. $\frac{3}{8-9}$, C. 17, L. l. 50, L. r. $\frac{45}{55}$, L. tr. 6-7/14, Cæc. pyl. 4.

Length of head 2/7 to 3/11, of caudal 1/6, height of body 2/7 to 4/15 of the total length. *Eyes*—diameter 1/3 to 2/7 of length of head 3/4 of a diameter from end of snout and also apart. The depth of the cheek from the eye to the maxillary bone equals two-thirds of that of the maxillary bone. The maxilla reaches to below the middle of the orbit. Vertical limb of the preopercle with a slightly produced angle and almost horizontal lower limb, its vertical limb finely serrated, more coarsely so at its angle, the serrations being continued along the posterior half of its lower limb: opercle with two points, the lower being the most distinct. No interopercular knob. *Teeth*—canines in the premaxillaries and an outer row of curved canine-like teeth in both jaws: villiform ones in a triangular patch, having a posterior median elongation in the vomer, and in a narrow band on the palatines; an oblong patch widest anteriorly of very fine teeth on the tongue. *Fins*—dorsal spines moderately strong, the third to the fifth being the longest and nearly equal to half the length of the head, from thence they decrease to the last which is about two-thirds of their height and equal to that of the rays. Pectoral pointed, nearly as long as the head, and reaching to above the anal spines: second anal spine the strongest and nearly equal to the length of the third or to the postorbital portion of the head, anal rays one-fourth higher than those of the dorsal fin. *Scales*—in oblique sinuous rows above the lateral-line to opposite the end of the soft dorsal fin where they become horizontal, as are also those below the lateral-line: on the summit of the head the scales extend forwards to above the anterior third of the eye. *Colours*—purplish-red along the back, becoming more yellow below the lateral-line. In the upper third of the body there are oblique and in places sinuous golden lines along each row of scales, whilst below the lateral-line there are bands of dark pink, one passes along the first-third of the lateral-line and for the depth of half a scale below it: next is a golden band, one scale deep, ending on the lateral-line beneath the middle of the soft dorsal: below this is a rather wider reddish band passing from the eye to the lateral-line below the end of the soft dorsal: next follows a yellow band one scale deep going to the middle of the tail. Below this the fish is longitudinally banded with pink and yellow alternately. Fins yellow, with a light band, along the centre of the dorsal.

Jerdon observed, (M. J. L. and Sc. 1851, p. 129) "I am inclined to think that Russell's figure (125 *woodeni*) is intended for this fish and not for a species of *Mesoprion (? Serranus)* to which Cuvier refers it without however having seen a specimen. His account of the colour corresponds exactly with that of the *woodeni* of Madras. It is a very beautiful fish but one of very soft and flabby texture." The figure of *woodeni* is amongst Sir W. Elliot's drawings (No. 15), and to it Jerdon has attached the name of *Serranus woodeni*. Irrespective of this he sent a specimen to the British Museum where it still exists, and is placed in the catalogue (i, p. 206) as *Mesoprion dodecacanthoides*, *a*. Half-grown; not good state. Madras. Presented by J. C. Jerdon, Esq.

In the unrivalled Paris collection, Cuv. and Val.'s two specimens of *Serranus woodeni*, C. V. still exist and are, as suggested by Jerdon, identical with the species described above.

Bleeker first pointed out that the *lineolata* Rüppell and Russell's *karwi* are identical. I have figured both varieties owing to the great difference I observed in their colouration, the size of the eye, &c. Fig. 1 is from the coast of Sind ($7\frac{1}{2}$ inches in length) and its tints resemble those shown by Rüppell: fig. 2 is from Madras (7 inches long) and its colours are as described by Russell.

In the 'Fishes of Zanzibar,' three varieties are recorded, (1) yellow with pale blue streaks above the lateral-line, and about seven below it: (2) olive-brown with the lines darker blue: (3) violet above, muzzle rosy, the oblique and longitudinal lines yellow. The form, however, with blue streaks has a well-developed interopercular knob, and can hardly be considered as a mere variety of this species.

Habitat.—Red Sea, East coast of Africa, seas of India to the Malay Archipelago. It is very common off Madras.

9. Lutianus lemniscatus.

Serranus lemniscatus, Cuv. and Val. ii, p. 240; Günther, Catal. i, p. 155.
Lutjanus melanotaenia, Bleeker, Obi, p. 245, and Atl. Ich. Perc. t. vii, fig. 2, and Lutjani, p. 66.

B. vii, D. $\frac{10}{14}$, P. 17, V. 1/5, A. $\frac{3}{8}$, C. 17, L. l. 56, L. tr. 8/21.

Length of head 3/10, of caudal 4/21, height of body 4/13 of the total length. *Eyes*—diameter 1/4 of length of head, $1\frac{1}{2}$ diameters from end of snout, and 3/4 of a diameter apart. Dorsal profile more convex than that of the abdomen, and slightly concave between the snout and the eye. The maxilla reaches to below the front edge of the eye. Vertical limb of preopercle serrated and with a shallow emargination: interopercle with a badly developed knob. *Teeth*—canines large in the upper jaw. *Fins*—dorsal spines rather strong, increasing in length to the fourth which equals the postorbital length of the head, and a little higher than the rays: pectoral not quite so long as the head: the second and third anal spines of about the same length and equal to the third of the dorsal fin: caudal emarginate. *Scales*—in oblique rows above the lateral-line, and horizontal ones below it. *Colours*—appear to have been dark red or yellow, with a wide brown or black band going from the eye to the centre of the caudal fin, and another less defined and narrow one below it but parallel to it. The above description is from Valenciennes specimen in the Paris Museum, which is in a good state of preservation. It was obtained from Ceylon.

Habitat.—Ceylon to the Malay Archipelago.

10. Lutianus chrysotænia, Plate XI, fig. 3.

Mesoprion chrysotænia, Bleeker, Nat. Tyds. Ned. Ind. ii, 1851, p. 170, and Act. Soc. Ned. Ind. Manado, i, p. 49; Günther, Catal. i, p. 192; Kner. Novara Fische, p. 34.
Lutjanus chrysotænia, Bleeker, Ternate, p. 233, and Atl. Ich. Perc. t. xxiv, fig. 4, and Lutjani, p. 22.

B. vii, D. $\frac{10}{13}$, P. 16, V. 1/5, A. $\frac{3}{8}$, C. 17, L. l. 52, L. r. $\frac{7}{13}$, L. tr. 8/22.

Length of head 2/7, of caudal 1/5, height of body 4/13 to 2/7 of the total length. *Eyes*—diameter 4/15 of length of head, $1\frac{1}{3}$ diameters from end of snout, and 1 apart. Abdominal profile nearly horizontal, that of the dorsal more convex, but from the orbit to the nape it is straight, or slightly concave: snout pointed: jaws of nearly equal length anteriorly: preorbital under the front third of the eye equals three-fourths of the diameter of the orbit in height. The maxilla reaches to below the anterior third of the orbit. Vertical limb of preopercle having a very shallow emargination, its angle rounded but not produced, both limbs finely serrated. No interopercular knob. Opercular points indistinct. *Teeth*—a pair of large curved canines in the premaxillaries, an outer row of curved canine-like teeth in the upper jaw more closely set but smaller than one which is present in the lower jaw: villiform teeth on vomer in a T-form (or a lanceolate patch, Bleeker): in a band on the palate: and in an oblong patch, rather largest anteriorly, on the tongue. *Fins*—dorsal spines weak, increasing in length to the third which equals that of the postorbital portion of the head, from thence they decrease to the last, which is two-thirds in the same distance: soft portion of the fin rounded, the highest ray equals two-fifths of the length of its base and is much lower than the spinous portion. Pectoral pointed, as long as the head, posterior to the hind nostril and reaching to nearly above the anal spines: ventral reaches two-thirds of the distance at the anal: second anal spine strongest but scarcely so long as the third which equals $1\frac{1}{4}$ diameters of the orbit in length, its first rays highest and are as long as the base of the entire fin, its lower edge rounded, caudal emarginate. *Scales*—in oblique rows above the lateral-line, and in horizontal ones below it: nine to ten rows across the cheek. *Colours*—olive-green with a dark band passing from the upper edge of the eye to the end of the spinous dorsal: a second through the upper fourth of the eye to the last few dorsal rays, and a third from the centre of the eye to the upper half of the base of the caudal fin and having a golden band below it, inferior to which is another dark horizontal band, and the abdomen beneath it golden: a deep black spot in the axil of the pectoral. Fins golden, a light edge along the upper margin of the spinous dorsal and first five or six rays: caudal with a darkish edge. Bleeker gives the colour of the body as greenish, with eight or more yellow shining bands somewhat oblique above the lateral-line and horizontal below it, also some yellow spots on the head.

The specimen I have figured is very different in colouration from Dr. Bleeker's type, but the proportions of the fish are the same, as well as the direction of the bands, which however are darker in colour, and wider. The description I have given is that of my specimen.

In the British Museum there is a very interesting specimen, 4 inches long, taken at Amboina, and received from Mr. Franks, as *Mesoprion chrysotænia*, young. It is of the same colour as the one I have figured, except that it has a black blotch on the lateral-line from the 22nd to the 32nd scale. The proportions are much the same, allowing for size, but lingual teeth are not well discernible, and its scales are as follows, L. r. $\frac{55}{?}$, L. tr. 9/20.

Habitat.—Nicobars, from whence the late Dr. Stoliczka brought the specimen figured ($7\frac{3}{4}$ inches long) to the Malay Archipelago.

11. **Lutianus rivulatus**, Plate XI, fig. 4.

Sparus kallee mace, Russell, Fish. Vizag. i, p. 75, pl. 96.
Diacope rivulata, cœruleopunctata, et *alboguttata*, Cuv. and Val. ii, pp. 414, 424, 445, pl. 38.
Mesoprion myriaster, Liénard, Nat. Hist. Soc. Mauritius, 1839, p. 32.
Mesoprion cœruleopunctatus, Bleeker, Perc. p. 169.
Lutjanus cœruleopunctatus, Bleeker, Amb. p. 278.
Genyoroge rivulata et *cœruleopunctata*, Günther, Catal. i, p. 182; Day, Fishes of Malabar, pp. 7, 9.
Diacope rivulata, Klunz. Verh. z. b. Ges. in Wien. 1870, p. 694.
Lutjanus rivulatus, Bleeker, Lutjani, p. 81.
Cuttu pirima, Tam.

B. vii, D. $\frac{10}{14}$, P. 17, V. 1/5, A. $\frac{3}{8}$, C. 17, L. l. 45-50, L. r. $\frac{50}{60}$, L. tr. 8/19, Cæc. pyl. 5.

Length of head 3/10 to 2/7, of caudal 1/5, height of body 1/3 of the total length. *Eyes*—diameter 2/9 of length of head, $1\frac{1}{2}$ diameter from the end of snout, and rather above 1 apart. The maxilla reaches to below the anterior edge of the orbit. Vertical limb of preopercle finely serrated even in the well-developed notch that is above its angle to receive the interopercular knob; horizontal limb of preopercle more coarsely serrated in its posterior portion than it is on its vertical border. Sub- and inter-opercles entire, the latter have a large triangular tuberosity directed a little upwards and backwards and received into the preopercular notch. Opercle with two flattened points, the lower the larger. In the very young the preopercular notch is badly formed, but as the interopercular knob increases in size, it by pressure causes absorption above it and thus forms a notch in the preopercular border. *Teeth*—one or two curved canines on either side of the premaxillaries, and an external row of curved canine-like teeth in either jaw, villiform ones in a triangular spot on the vomer, a narrow band on the palate, but none on the tongue. *Fins*—dorsal spines strong increasing in length to the third, fourth, and fifth, which are equal to about one-third of the height of the body, but not quite so long as the highest of the dorsal rays, they decrease in length to the last which equals two-thirds the height of the longest one: soft portion of the fin angularly rounded, the ninth to the eleventh rays being the longest. Pectoral as long as the head: ventral reaches the anus. Anal spines strong, especially the second which is slightly longer than the third and equals the highest of the dorsal fin: soft portion of the fin angular and one-third more than that of the dorsal: caudal slightly emarginate. *Scales*—in oblique rows above the lateral-line, and in horizontal ones below it, a strongly serrated shoulder scale, and two rows of broad scales over the nape. *Colours*—(in the immature) back olive, with a slate coloured spot in the centre of each scale, thus forming lines passing upwards and backwards; abdomen greyish with horizontal golden lines crossing the centre of each scale, and vertical dark ones along their bases. Several bright blue lines pass downwards and backwards over the preopercle and opercle, and two larger ones along the snout. A large white blotch on the lateral-line opposite the third to the fifth soft ray, having a wide black edge anteriorly and posteriorly in its upper third. This white mark covers four scales transversely, is one below and three above the lateral-line. Dorsal, slate coloured, superiorly reddish with a narrow white edge: pectoral reddish: ventrals slaty with a dark edge: caudal bluish, tipped with red. Generally vertical bands are more or less distinct. (In the *adult*) as about 15 inches in length, the mark on the lateral-line becomes indistinct, the golden shade is wanting, but the blue spots remain. The white edge to the fins is also usually absent.

Habitat.—Red Sea, East coast of Africa, seas of India to the Malay Archipelago, and beyond.

12. **Lutianus argentimaculatus**, Plate XI, fig. 5.

Sciæna argentimaculata, Forsk. p. 47.
Sciæna argentata, Gmel. Linn. p. 1300.
Perca argentata, Bl. Schn. p. 86.
Alphestes gembra et *sambra*, Bl. Schn. p. 236, t. 51.
Lobotes argentatus, Lacép. iii, pp. 426, 467.
Sparus rangoo, Russell, Fish. Vizag. i, p. 74, pl. 94.

Diacope argentimaculata, Cuv. and Val. ii, p. 432; Rüpp. Atl. Fische, p. 71, t. 19, f. 1; Klunz. Verh. z. b. Ges. in Wien. 1870, p. 688.
Mesoprion rangus, Cuv. and Val. ii, p. 482; Day, Fishes of Malabar, p. 10; Kner. Novara Fische, p. 34.
Mesoprion gembra, Cuv. and Val. ii, p. 485; Cantor, Catal. p. 15; Günther, Catal. i, p. 193; Bleeker, Sumatra, iv, p. 246.
Mesoprion taeniops, Cuv. and Val. vi, p. 543.
Mesoprion immaculatus, Bleeker, Perc. p. 45 (not C.V.)
Mesoprion argentimaculatus, Günther, Catal. i, p. 192.
Lutjanus gembra, Bleeker, Ceram. ii, p. 187.
Lutjanus argentimaculatus, Bleeker, Lutjani, p. 84.
Mesoprion sindera, Peters, Monats. Ak. Wiss. Berlin, 1865, p. 111.
Rangoo, Tel.: *To-go-re-dah*, Andam.

B. vii, D. $\frac{10}{13-14}$, P. 16, V. 1/5, A. $\frac{3}{8}$, C. 17, L. l. 45-50, L. r. [illegible], L. tr. 7-8/16, Cæc. pyl. 4.

Length of head $3\frac{1}{2}$ to 2/7, of caudal 1/6 to 2/11, height of body 1/3 to 2/7 of the total length. *Eyes*—diameter 1/3 to 1/5 of the length of head, 1 to $1\frac{1}{2}$ diameter from end of snout, and 2/3 to 1 diameter apart. The distance from the eye to the upper edge of the maxilla, equals from a little more to a little less than one diameter of the orbit in height. The maxilla reaches to below the first third or middle of the eye. Vertical limb of preopercle with a very shallow emargination, a rounded angle, and an oblique lower limb, the vertical border very finely serrated, most coarsely so at its angle and especially along its lower limb. A slight swelling on the interopercle. Opercle with two blunt points. *Teeth*—large canines in the premaxillaries; an outer row of canine-like ones in either jaw, those in the mandible being much the largest. Villiform teeth in a lanceolate or Λ-form, which sometimes has a central posterior projection, also in a band on the palate, and in the adult, a large sabulous patch along the centre of the tongue with small ones anterior to it: in the very young the tongue may be found destitute of teeth. *Fins*—dorsal spines not very strong, increasing in length to the third, fourth, and fifth, which are from one-third to two-fifths of the height of the body, from thence they decrease to the last which is two-thirds their height: soft portion of the fin rather angular, its longest ray equalling three-fourths of the length of its base. Pectoral nearly as long as the head, and reaching to above the anal spines: ventral nearly reaches the vent. Second anal spine the strongest and about equal in length to the third or nearly to the sixth of the dorsal: its soft portion angular, one fourth longer than its entire base: caudal emarginate, in some specimens rather deeply lunated. *Scales*—in horizontal rows above the lateral-line, in some specimens (especially young) they are a little sinuous but do not become regularly oblique until under the soft portion of the fin: below the lateral-line they are horizontal. *Colours*—cherry-red, darkest at the bases of the scales. The front edge of the anal fin pinkish-white as is also the first ventral ray. Upper margin of spinous dorsal orange. In some specimens there are dark spots on the dorsal, caudal, and anal fins. The very young have from six to nine narrow, vertical, silvery-white bands, which become more or less lost as age increases.

This species more especially differs from *L. roseus* by the latter having a rounded caudal fin, and from *L. sillaoo* in the latter having a higher spinous dorsal, and the rows of scales above the lateral-line being oblique in their direction. It appears questionable however whether the last is not merely a variety.

Habitat.—From the Red Sea and East coast of Africa, through the seas of India to the Malay Archipelago and beyond. It attains upwards of two feet in length and is good eating.

13. Lutianus roseus, Plate XI, fig. 6.

Mesoprion rangus, Cantor, Catal. p. 14 (not C. V.)

B. vii, D. $\frac{10}{14}$, P. 16, V. 1/5, A. $\frac{3}{8}$, C. 17, L. l. 48, L. r. [illegible], L. tr. 7/18.

Length of head 2/7, of caudal 1/7, height of body 4/13 of the total length. *Eyes*—diameter 2/9 to 1/4 of length of head, $1\frac{1}{2}$ diameter from end of snout, and 1 apart. Height of preorbital equals three-fourths of the length of the eye. The maxilla reaches to below the first third of the orbit. Vertical limb of preopercle emarginate, and having an oblique lower limb, the whole being finely serrated, but most coarsely at its angle and along the lower limb. No tuberosity on the interopercle: sub- and inter-opercles entire: opercle with two obtuse points. *Teeth*—one or two rather large and curved canines on either side of the premaxillaries: an outer row of slightly curved canine-like teeth in both jaws, largest in the lower: a triangular patch of villiform ones on the vomer, without any posterior prolongation, a very narrow band on the palate, and an elongated band of minute ones on the tongue. *Fins*—dorsal spines moderately strong, the fourth the highest, and equal to the length of the postorbital portion of the head; from it they decrease to the last, which is three-fourths as high as the second, the soft portion of the fin rather rounded, as high as four-fifths of the length of its base and equal to the fourth spine. Pectoral as long as the head behind the posterior nostril: ventral reaching nearly two-thirds of the distance to the anal: second anal spine stronger and rather longer than the third and equal to the length of the sixth of the dorsal fin, soft portion of the fin one-fifth higher than that of the dorsal: caudal rounded. *Scales*—in horizontal rows below the lateral-line, and also above it so far as to below the middle of the dorsal spines, where they commence going obliquely to the base of the soft dorsal, but becoming horizontal beyond the base of that fin: 15 rows between the occiput and base of the first dorsal spine. *Colours*—dark reddish-brown, becoming dull cherry-red below the lateral-line: fins with dark edges.

This fish is so like the *L. argentimaculatus*, that had I not seen many specimens, I should have hesitated separating them further than varieties. It differs in its rounded instead of emarginate tail: in its vomerine teeth: its second anal spine and slightly in its scaling, &c. Cantor's specimen appears to be identical with it. He observes: "according to Russell this fish is not much esteemed. At Pinang and Singapore, where single individuals occur at all seasons, it is of excellent flavour and considered a great acquisition for the table. At Malacca it is plentiful, and in our settlements and in the Straits it is known under the denomination of 'red rock cod.'" He gives D. $\frac{10}{14}$, and as growing to 20 inches in length.

Habitat.—Seas of India to the Malay Archipelago. The specimen figured (8 inches long) is from Madras.

14. Lutianus sillaco, Plate XII, fig. 2.

? *Sparus silaoo*. Russell, Fish Vizag. i, p. 78, pl. 100.
Mesoprion rubellus, Day, Fish. Malabar, p. 2, pl. 2, fig. 2 (not C. V.)

B. vii, D. $\frac{10}{14}\left(\frac{11}{13}\right)$, P. 16, V. 1/5, A. $\frac{3}{8}$, C. 17, L. l. 44, L. r. [illegible], L. tr. 6/15.

Length of head $3\frac{1}{4}$, of caudal 2/11, height of body $3\frac{1}{4}$ of the total length. *Eyes*—diameter $4\frac{1}{4}$ in length of head, $1\frac{1}{2}$ diameter from end of snout, and 1 apart. Upper profile of head slightly concave: the distance from the eye to the maxilla equals rather more than one diameter of the orbit. The maxilla reaches to below the first third of the eye. Vertical limb of preopercle with scarcely any trace of an emargination, angle rounded, and lower limb very oblique: the whole of the vertical limb is very finely serrated with a few coarser serrations at its angle. No trace of an interopercular knob. Opercular points blunt. *Teeth*—a pair of large curved canines in the premaxillaries, an outer row of curved canine-like teeth in both jaws: villiform ones in a Λ-shape on the vomer and in a band on the palate. A long oval patch of teeth along the centre of the tongue, with two more small ones side by side near its tip. *Fins*—dorsal spines weak, the third and fourth of about the same length, nearly as long as the postorbital portion of the head, and two-fifths the height of the body, from thence they decrease to the last, which is only a little above half the height of the fourth: soft portion of the fin angular, and nearly as high as the spines, its longest ray equalling two-thirds of the length of its base. Pectoral as long as the head behind the first nostril, and reaching to above the last anal spine: ventral extending to the vent: second anal spine stronger but not so long as the third, which equals that of the seventh of the dorsal: its soft portion angular, its longest ray equalling the length of the entire base of the fin. Caudal slightly emarginate. *Scales*—the rows above the lateral-line first go rather obliquely towards the dorsal fin, more so under its soft portion: below the lateral-line they are horizontal. There are twelve rows anterior to the dorsal fin, and seven across the checks. *Colours*—back greyish-brown, chest orange, abdomen and sides of a light violet, each scale having a white edge. Spinous portion of dorsal greyish, but the soft with a more yellow tinge: pectoral reddish: caudal red with a black edge.

Russell gives 11 dorsal spines, otherwise the fish resembles either this species or the *L. johngarah*. My reason for considering that I wrongly identified them in the "Fishes of Malabar" is that I find that it is this species which has lingual teeth, and the *L. johngarah* in which they are deficient, as observed by Russell.

This fish is evidently very closely allied if not a mere variety of, *L. rangus*, but its dorsal spines appear higher, the rows of scales on its back more oblique, its colours differ, and before referring it to that species, further investigations are required. A figure is given for the purpose of drawing attention to it.

Habitat.—Seas of India, attaining at least four feet in length.

15. Lutianus lioglossus, Plate XII, fig. 1.

Lutjanus monostigma, Bleeker, Halmaheira, Ned. T. Dierk. I, p. 155 (not Cuv. and Val.)*
Diacope monostigma, Klunz. Fische d. Roth. Meer, Verh. z. b. Ges. Wien. 1870, p. 702.
Mesoprion monostigma, Günther, Fishe d. Sudsee, p. 14, t. xvi.
Lutjanus lioglossus, Bleeker, Lutjani, p. 74.

B. vii, D. $\frac{10}{14}$, P. 16, V. 1/5, A. $\frac{3}{8}$, C. 17, L. r. [illegible], L. tr. 6.7/15.

Length of head 2/7, of caudal 2/13, height of body $3\frac{3}{4}$ to 1/4 in the total length. *Eyes*—diameter 2.7 to 2.9 of length of head, $1\frac{1}{2}$ to 2 diameters from end of snout, and 3/4 of a diameter apart. The distance from the eye to the maxilla equals one diameter of the orbit. The maxilla reaches to below the middle of the eye. Vertical limb of preopercle with a very shallow emargination, and serrated in its whole extent: a very obscure interopercular knob. *Teeth*—strong curved canines in the premaxillaries, an outer row of curved canine-like teeth in both jaws, largest in the lower: villiform teeth in a Λ-form in the vomer and a band on the palatines: no lingual teeth. *Fins*—dorsal spines of moderate strength, increasing in length to the fourth, which equals from two-fifths to one-third in the height of the body, the last spine is one-third shorter: soft portion of the fin somewhat rounded and its height rather less than half its length. Pectoral about as long as the head: ventral reaching rather above half the distance to the anal. Anal spines rather short, the third slightly the longest, and equal to three-fourths of the diameter of the orbit in length, soft portion of the fin highest in front, equalling about the length of its base, lower edge straight: caudal emarginate. *Scales*—in oblique rows above the lateral-line and in horizontal ones below it: 12 rows of scales between occiput and first dorsal spine: six or seven rows across the cheeks. *Colours*—roseate, lightest below, with a black blotch on the lateral-line below the first portion of the soft dorsal fin.

* *Mesoprion monostigma*, C. and V.=*Lutianus fulviflamma*, see p. 41. Kelaart's specimen of *Mesoprion rangus*, from Ceylon, has the rows above the L. l. oblique, and L. r. [illegible], L. tr. [illegible].

The small eye, short anal spines, and edentulous tongue divide this species from *fulviflamma*, which it much resembles, whilst its scales L. r. [illegible] likewise show that it cannot be *L. jahngarah* having L. r. [illegible].

Habitat.—Red Sea, seas of India to the Malay Archipelago; attaining at least 18 inches in length.

16. Lutianus jahngarah.

Sparus erythrinus, ? Russell, Fish. Vizag. i, p. 72, *Jahngarah*, pl. 90.
Mesoprion sillaoo, Day, Fish. Malabar, p. 12, pl. 11, fig. 1 (not C. V.)
Parrameen, Ooriah.

B. vii, D. [illegible], P. 16, V. 1/5, A. $\frac{3}{8}$, C. 17, L. l. 46, L. r. [illegible], L. tr. 6/17.

Length of head 2/7, of caudal 1/6, height of body 2/7 of the total length. *Eyes*—diameter 1/5 of length of head, $1\frac{2}{3}$ diameter from end of snout, and 1 apart. Dorsal profile more convex than that of the abdomen. The distance between the eye and the upper edge of the maxilla equals one diameter of the orbit. The maxilla reaches to below the middle of the orbit. Vertical limb of preopercle with a shallow emargination above its rounded angle, which appears continuous with its oblique lower limb; the whole of its vertical limb is finely serrated, but about the angle they increase in size, and along the lower limb are more widely apart. A distinct though small interopercular knob. Opercular points blunt. *Teeth*—a pair of large slightly curved canines in the premaxillaries, an outer row of curved, conical, canine-like teeth in both jaws, those in the lower being the largest: villiform ones in a ʌ-shape in the vomer, in a band on the palate but none on the tongue. *Fins*—dorsal spines moderately strong, the third the longest and nearly equal to one-third the height of the body, from it they decrease to the last, which is only half its height; soft portion of the fin rather rounded, not so high as the spinous, and its highest ray equal to two-thirds the length of its base. Pectoral as long as the head behind the front nostril, and not reaching to above the anal spines, the ventral reaches a little above half way to the anal fin. Second anal spine stronger but shorter than the third, which equals the length of the seventh dorsal spine or one diameter of the orbit, soft portion of the fin angularly rounded, central rays the highest and equal the length of its entire base: caudal emarginate, being lobed in its last fourth, the upper being slightly the longer. *Scales*—in almost parallel rows to the dorsal profile both above and below the lateral-line, but becoming a little irregular below the soft dorsal, where they ascend obliquely upwards and backwards, but become horizontal again beyond the end of the fin: seven rows across the cheeks: 11 rows between the occiput and base of dorsal fin. *Colours*—back brownish-red, the base of each scale being darkest, whilst below the lateral-line it becomes of a lake-colour, having a tinge of orange along the lower surface of the body. A blue zig-zag line crosses the preorbital. Spinous portion of dorsal and anal greyish, the soft scarlet tinged with orange: pectorals scarlet: front edge of anal whitish.

This species is evidently closely allied to *L. rangus*, it differs greatly in colours, in wanting lingual teeth, in the number of its scales, the length of its spines, and the size of its eye. *L. lioglossus*, Bleeker, has no lingual teeth, but its scales are oblique above the lateral-line, and much more numerous, being L. r. [illegible]. This species differs from *L. sillaoo* in having a small interopercular knob, its lower spinous dorsal, the direction of its scales above the lateral-line, &c.

Habitat.—Seas of India, attaining two feet or more in length. It is esteemed good eating.

17. Lutianus quinquelineatus, Plate XII, fig. 3.

Holocentrus quinquelineatus, Bloch, iv, p. 84: Lacép. iv, p. 329.
Sparus sawagi wapadi, Russell, Fish. Vizag. ii, p. 8, pl. 110.
Mesoprion quinquelineatus, Cuv. and Val. ii, p. 445: Günther, Catal. i, p. 209.
Diacope coeruleolineata, Rüpp. N. W. Fische, p. 93, t. 24, f. 3: Klunz. Verh. z. b. Ges. in Wien, 1870, p. 701.

B. vii, D. [illegible], P. 16, V. 1/5, A. [illegible], C. 17, L. l. 51, L. r. [illegible], L. tr. 8/21.

Length of head 2/7, of caudal 2/11, height of body 2/7 of the total length. *Eyes*—diameter 2/9 of length of head, $1\frac{1}{2}$ diameter from end of snout, and 3/4 of a diameter apart. Body rather strongly compressed, dorsal profile having a considerable rise from the snout and being somewhat concave above the orbit. The maxilla reaches to below the middle of the orbit. Height of preorbital below the first third of the eye equals three-fourths of the diameter of the orbit. Preopercle with a shallow emargination above its angle, the whole of its vertical limb finely serrated, most coarsely so at its angle, lower limb entire: no interopercular knob: opercle with two very blunt points. *Teeth*—an exceedingly strong curved canine on either side of the premaxillary, and two intermediate small ones, an outer row of curved canine-like teeth in both jaws, largest in the lower: villiform ones in a ʌ-shape on the vomer, in a narrow band on the palatines and in an oblong patch along the centre of the tongue. *Fins*—dorsal spines moderately strong, increasing in height to the fourth, which equals the length of the postorbital portion of the head; they subsequently gradually decrease to the last, which is two-thirds the height of the longest; soft portion of the fin rounded, as high as the spinous, and its longest ray equal to two-thirds of the length of its base. Pectoral equals the length of the head behind the posterior nostril: the ventral does not quite reach the anal spines. Second anal spine stronger but not so long as the third, which equals the length of the last dorsal spine, soft portion of the fin one-third higher in front than the last ray, its lower edge rounded: caudal lunated. *Scales*—in oblique rows above the lateral-line and horizontal ones below it: they extend forwards on the back to above the hind edge of the eye: seven rows on the cheeks. *Colours*—a blue band goes from the eye to the base of the last dorsal spine: two from the posterior-superior angle of the eye coalesce under the sixth dorsal spine and proceed to the middle of the base of the soft dorsal: the fourth, also arising from the eye, goes along the lateral-line and opposite the sixth dorsal spine curves upwards, going to the end of the base of the soft dorsal: the fifth band, which is the broadest, commences just above the middle of the hind edge of the eye and goes to the upper half of the base of the caudal fin: the sixth from the lower edge of the eye to the middle of the base of the caudal. A dark mark exists at the base of the pectoral, a black blotch on the lateral-line below the commencement of the soft dorsal fin.

In the 'Fishes of Zanzibar' it is observed: "*Diacope cæruleo-lineata*, Rüpp. N. W. Fische, p. 93, t. 24, f. 3 [not *M. quinquelineatus*,* Cuv. and Val.]." *Bleeker*, Lutjani, p. 40, observes: *M. quinquelineatus*, C. V. is described from the *Mangi nugidi*, Russell, and has blue lines which superiorly are parallel to the profile of the back and are continued to the base of the caudal. He doubts if Rüppell's fish with the lines going obliquely to the back is the same species.

The specimen of Bloch's, *Lutianus quinquelineatus*, 9 inches long, No. 229, is undoubtedly this species, and differs widely from the figured *quinquelineatus*, the type of which is likewise in existence, both being in a good state of preservation at Berlin.

Habitat.—Red Sea, East coast of Africa, seas of India: the specimen figured is 6 inches in length and from the Andaman Islands.

18. Lutianus lunulatus, Plate XII, fig. 4.

Perca lunulata, Mungo Park, Trans. Linn. Soc. iii, p. 35, pl. 6.
Lutjanus lunulatus, Lacép. iv, p. 213; Bl. Schn. p. 329; Bleeker, Atl. Ich. Perc. t. xvii. f. 1, and Lutjani, p. 64.
Mesoprion lunulatus, Cuv. and Val. ii. p. 477; Bleeker, Sumatra, p. 75.

B. vii, D. $\frac{10}{13-14}$, P. 17, V. 1/5, A. $\frac{3}{8-9}$, C. 19, L. l. 55, L. r. $\frac{11}{..}$, L. tr. 7/21.

Length of head 2/7, of caudal 1/6, height of body 1/3 to 2/7 of the total length. *Eyes*—diameter 1/4 of length of head, $1\frac{1}{2}$ diameters from end of snout, and nearly one apart. The distance from the eye to the upper edge of the maxilla equals three-fourths of the diameter of the orbit. The maxilla reaches to below the first third of the orbit. Vertical limb of preopercle with a shallow emargination and an oblique lower limb, its vertical limb is finely, its angle more coarsely serrated, lower limb entire. No interopercular knob. *Teeth*—large curved canines in the intermaxillaries, an outer row of curved canine-like teeth in both jaws, largest in the lower: villiform ones in a Λ-shaped band on the vomer, a narrow one on the palatines, and a small patch near the anterior end of the tongue. *Fins*—dorsal spines weak, the fourth the longest and nearly equalling the length of the postorbital portion of the head, from it they decrease to the last which is about two-thirds its height: soft portion of the fin rounded, its highest ray equalling one-half the length of its base but not so high as the fourth spine. Pectoral much longer than the ventral, being nearly as long as the head: ventral reaching two-thirds of the distance to the anal. Second anal spine longer and stronger than the third: the anterior rays the highest, equalling the length of the base of the entire fin, its lower edge straight, caudal emarginate. *Scales*—in oblique rows above the lateral-line and in horizontal ones below it: superiorly they extend forwards to nearly above the hind edge of the orbit. *Colours*—reddish-crimson superiorly becoming silvery-white on the abdomen: golden lines along each row of scales: dorsal, caudal, and anal with a black outer edge and an external white margin: a lunated black band at the base of the caudal fin extending along its outer edges to the end of the fin: pectoral and ventrals yellow.

Bleeker places *Diacope bitæniata*, C. V. as a synonym of this species, but the type specimen in the Paris Museum has a distinct and rather well-developed interopercular knob, although the emargination of the preopercle is not very deep. The specimen however is not an adult.

Habitat.—Coast of Sind (where the specimen figured, 10 inches long, was captured) to the Malay Archipelago.

19. Lutianus fulviflamma, Plate XII, fig. 5 and 6.

Sciæna fulviflamma, Forsk. p. 45; Gmel. Lin. p. 1299.
Perca fulviflamma, Bl. Schn. p. 90.
? *Lutjanus notatus*, Bl. Schn. p. 325 (not Bloch).
Centropomus hober, Lacép. iv, p. 255.
Sparus vatika doondiawah, Russell, Fish. Vizag. i, p. 76, pl. 98.
Diacope fulviflamma, Rüpp. Atl. Fische, p. 72, t. 19, f. 2, and N. W. Fische, p. 94; Cuv. and Val. ii, p. 423; Klunz. Verh. z. b. Ges. Wien, 1870, p. 700.
Mesoprion unimaculatus, Quoy and Gaim. Zool. Freyc. p. 304; Cuv. and Val. ii, p. 441; Bleeker, Perc. p. 42; Quoy and Gaim. Voy. Astrol. p. 665, pl. 5, f. 3.
Mesoprion aurolineatus, Cuv. and Val. iii, p. 496; Day, Fish. Malabar, p. 14, pl. iii.
Mesoprion Russellii, Bleeker, Verh. Bat. Gen. xxii, Perc. p. 41; Day, Proc. Zool. Soc. 1867, p. 701.
Lutjanus notatus, Bleeker, Ternate, p. 233.
Genyoroge notata, Cantor, Catal. p. 12; Day, Fishes of Malabar, p. 8 (not C. V.)
Mesoprion fulviflamma, Bleeker, Amb. ii, p. 532; Günther, Catal. i, p. 201; Day, Fish. Mal. p. 13; Kner, Novara Fische, p. 35.

* The specimen probably referred to is thus marked in the Catalogue, "a. Adult. sine patria. D. $\frac{10}{13}$, A. $\frac{3}{8}$, L. l. 80," and which (omitting the black blotch, which is now imperceptible) I would suggest is *L. chrysotænia*: is such a modification of this species?

Lutjanus Russellii, Bleeker, Atl. Ich. Perc. t. xxii. f. 2, and Lutjani, p. 76.
Lutjanus unimaculatus, Vaillant, Soc. Phil. Paris, May 23rd, 1874.
Lutjanus fulviflamma, Bleeker, Halmah. p. 155, Lutjani, p. 61.
Villa-chembolay, Mal.; *Shemkara* and *Carrumay*, Tam.

B. vii, D. $\frac{10}{13-14}$, P. 16, V. 1/5, A. $\frac{3}{8}$, C. 17, L. l. 50-54, L. r. $\frac{80}{100}$, L. tr. 7-8/16, Cæc. pyl. 4-6.

Length of head 2/7, of caudal 1/5, height of body 1/3 to 2/7 of the total length. *Eyes*—diameter 2/7 to 1/4 of length of head, 3/4 to 1¼ diameters from end of snout, and 3/4 of a diameter apart. Snout rather pointed, the maxilla reaches to below the first third of the orbit: height from the eye to the upper edge of the maxilla equal to two-thirds of the diameter of the orbit. Vertical limb of preopercle with a shallow emargination, its angle rather produced, and its lower limb oblique, the whole being finely serrated, most coarsely so at its angle, whilst the serrations are continued half way along the vertical limb. No interopercular knob: two opercular points. *Teeth*—strong curved canines in the premaxillaries, an outer row of curved, conical, canine-like teeth in both jaws, largest in the lower villiform teeth in a Λ-shape or T-shape on the vomer, in a band on the palatines, and an oblong patch on the tongue (in the adult) which is widest anteriorly. *Fins*—dorsal spines not very strong, the third of nearly the same height as the fourth and fifth, from whence they gradually decrease, the third is one-third higher than the rays and from two-fifths to half as long as the head: rayed portion rounded, two-thirds as high as its base is long. Pectoral as long as the head behind the front nostril: ventral not reaching the vent. Third anal spine about equal in strength but slightly shorter than the second, which equals one diameter and a quarter of the eye in length, and is of equal length with the first ray, which is twice as long as the last, lower edge of the fin concave: caudal slightly emarginate. *Scales*—in oblique rows above the lateral-line and horizontal ones below it: from six to eight rows on the cheeks: superiorly they extend forwards to above the hind edge of the eye. *Colours*—yellow or rosy along the back, with three or four, in the variety *L. Russellii*,* narrow and brilliant golden bands passing obliquely upwards and backwards from the lateral-line, and three or four similar golden bands below it, the first of which goes from the posterior edge of the orbit to the finger mark: the second from the middle of the opercle to opposite the end of the soft dorsal, where it becomes lost on the lateral-line: the third from below the orbit to the base of the caudal fin: and the fourth from below the base of the pectoral to the base of the anal. A large black blotch exists on the lateral-line opposite the commencement of the soft dorsal fin from the 22nd to the 28th or 31st scales, most of it being below the line and only reaching to one or two scales above it: in the variety *L. Russellii*, however, this mark is mostly above the lateral-line.

The type specimen of *Mesoprion monostigma* at Paris is 3$\frac{1}{10}$ inches in length. The eye is a little less than 1/3 of the length of the head, and 1 diameter from the end of the snout. The second anal spine is of nearly the same length as the third and equal to 2½ in the length of the head.†

The *Lutianus fulviflamma* is found in two very distinct varieties: in one there are the yellow lines such as I have described and also figured (in pl. xii, fig. 6), and in this form, *L. Russellii*, the distance from the eye to the snout and the size of the lateral blotch is a little more than we perceive it to be in the typical *L. fulviflamma*, of which I have also given a figure (pl. xii, fig. 5.) The two specimens were 7½ and 10 inches respectively in length, and, examined together, certainly appear to be distinct species: but in comparing a large number of specimens, every intermediate variety in form and colour (except the yellow fillets of the *L. Russellii*) are to be seen.

Habitat.—Red Sea, East coast of Africa, seas of India to the Malay Archipelago, and beyond.

20. Lutianus Johnii, Plate XIII, fig. 1.

Anthias Johnii, Bloch, t. 318; Bloch. Schneid. p. 303.
Lutjanus Johnii, Lacép. iv, p. 235; Bleeker, Lutjani, p. 20; Vaillant, Soc. Phil. de Paris, May, 1874.
Sparus doondiawah, Russell, i, p. 76, pl. 97.
Coius catus, Ham. Buch. pp. 90, 369, pl. 38, f. 30.
Sparus Malabaricus, Shaw, Zool. iv, p. 471.
Serranus pavoninus, (young) Cuv. and Val. vii, p. 443; Günther, Catal. i, p. 126.

* In a specimen of this fish (var. *Russellii*) at 1$\frac{3}{10}$ inches long, not only are the vertical and horizontal limbs of the preopercle serrated, but the bone has the appearance of a double edge as seen in *Ambassis* and *Apogon*, having a few serrations upon it. The interopercle is likewise serrated in its last half.

† The following lengths of the 3rd anal spine have been carefully made from 10 specimens:

		Inches.		
L. fulviflamma (*Russellii*).	Length of specimen	5½ :	Length of anal spine	2½ in the length of head.
" "	" "	5¾	" "	2¼ " "
" "	" "	8	" "	3¼ " "
" "	" "	10	" "	2¾ " "
" "	" "	16	" "	4½ " "
" "	" "	7½	" "	3¾ " "
" "	" "	8	" "	4⅓ " "
" "	" "	12	" "	4¼ " "
" "	" "	13	" "	4$\frac{1}{12}$ " "
" "	" "	15	" "	4$\frac{1}{12}$ " "

Mesoprion Johnii, Cuv. and Val. ii, p. 443; Cantor, Catal. p. 13; Günther, Catal. i, p. 200; Day, Fish. Malabar, p. 11; Kner, Novara Fische, p. 35.

Mesoprion flavipinnis, Cuv. and Val. ii, p. 475.

Mesoprion unimaculatus, Richardson, Ich. China, p. 222 (not Quoy and Gaim.)

Chembolay, Mal.: *Nga-pi-nee*, Burm.

B. vii, D. [illegible], P. 16, V. 1/5, A. $\frac{3}{8}$, C. 17, L. l. 48, L. r. [illegible], L. tr. 7/13, Cæc. pyl. (4 Kner.)

Length of head 4/13 to 2/7, of caudal 1/5 to 2/11, height of body 2/7 of the total length. *Eyes*—diameter 1/4 to 1/5 or even 1/6 in large specimens of the length of head, $1\frac{1}{3}$ to $1\frac{1}{2}$ diameters from the end of snout, and from 3/4 to 1 apart. Dorsal profile more convex than that of the abdomen. Preorbital equals three-fourths of the diameter of the orbit in height. The maxilla reaches to below the first third or middle of the orbit. Vertical limb of preopercle finely serrated, becoming more coarsely so at its angle, which is somewhat produced and rounded, its lower limb with a few serrations and crenulations. A very indistinct tuberosity on the interopercle is sometimes present: opercle with two flat points the lower being the longer. The fry up to about $1\frac{1}{2}$ inches in length have a spine at the angle of the preopercle, which becomes absorbed as age advances, the lower limb of the preopercle is also strongly serrated: in a specimen $2\frac{1}{4}$ inches long the spine remains only in the form of a strong denticulation, whilst there are seven more strong serrations along the lower limb. *Teeth*—curved canines of moderate strength in the premaxillaries, an outer curved row of canine-like teeth in both jaws: villiform ones in a triangular patch or elongated Λ-form on the vomer, in a band on the palatines, and in an elongated patch on the tongue in the adult. *Fins*—dorsal spines strong, increasing in length to the fourth, which is two-fifths of the height of the body, from this spine they decrease to the last, which is about one-fourth shorter, the soft portion of the fin somewhat rounded, its longest rays equal to five-sixths of the length of its base and exceed that of the highest spine. Pectoral nearly as long as the head: ventral reaches the vent: second anal spine usually slightly the longest and strongest, it equals the height of the third spine of the dorsal, the rayed portion rounded and rather higher than that of the dorsal: caudal slightly emarginate. *Scales*—the rows above the lateral-line are parallel with the profile of the back, whilst those below it are horizontal. Scales on the dorsal profile only extend forwards to a level with the hind edge of the orbit. *Colours*—yellowish, lightest on the abdomen, with a large black finger mark, of varying depths of colour, on the lateral-line between the 22nd and 31st scales; age, season, and locality all exercise an influence on this blotch: a dark line is almost invariably present along each row of scales. Fins yellow dashed with red: anal with a light front edge.

In the young the ocellus on the side is larger, in a specimen $2\frac{1}{4}$ inches long it commences on the 19th scale, and is surrounded by a light ring, thus constituting *Serranus pavonius*, Val., whose single specimen was a little over an inch in length: the observation of its having a strong spine at the angle of the "opercle" is evidently a misprint for "preopercle."

Hamilton Buchanan points out the affinity of *Coius catus* with the *Doondiawah* of Russell as well as with his *Mungi sanpadee* (No. 110), also that *Anthias Johnii*, Bloch, is nearly allied. It is readily distinguished from all allied species of *Lutianus*, with lateral blotches, recorded from the seas of India, by its having no oblique rows of scales on the body, all those above the lateral-line being parallel to the back and those below it being horizontal.

The type specimen of *Mesoprion flavipinnis*, C. V. (a skin) belongs to this species, the lateral blotch has been omitted from the short description.

Habitat.—Seas of India, Malay Archipelago and beyond, attaining a foot or more in length. The specimen figured is $6\frac{1}{2}$ inches long and from Madras.

21. Lutianus gibbus, Plate XIII, fig. 2 (adult): 3 (young).

Sciæna gibba, Forsk. p. 46.

Holocentrus bottonensis, Lacép. iv, pp. 331, 367.

Lutjanus gibbus, Bl. Schn. p. 326.

Diacope coccinea, (Ehren.) Cuv. and Val. ii, p. 437; Rüpp. N. W. Fische, p. 91, t. 23, f. 3.

Diacope gibba, Cuv. and Val. ii, p. 438; Klunz. Fische d. Roth. Meer. Verh. z. b. Ges. Wien, 1870, p. 693.

Diacope bottonensis, Cuv. and Val. ii, p. 434, and vi, p. 535.

Diacope borensis, Cuv. and Val. vi, p. 532.

Diacope tiea, Less. Voy. Duperr. Poiss. p. 231, pl. 23.

Mesoprion bottonensis, Bleeker, Nat. Tyds. Ned. Ind. ii, p. 170; Kner, Nov. Fische, p. 32, f. 6.

Mesoprion janthinus, Bleeker, l. c. vi, p. 52.

Genyoroge gibba, Günther, Catal. i, p. 180.

Genyoroge bottonensis, Günther, l. c. p. 181.

Genyoroge melanura, Günther, l. c. p. 183.

Mesoprion borensis, Günther, l. c. p. 199.

Mesoprion gibbus, Günther, Fische d. Sudsee, p. 12, t. xii, and xiii, f. A.

B. vii, D. [illegible], P. 18, V. 1/5, A. [illegible], C. 17, L. l. 50, L. r. [illegible], L. tr. 8/23, Cæc. pyl. 4-5.

Length of head 3/11, of caudal 1/5, height of body 3/10 of the total length. *Eyes*—diameter

$4\frac{1}{2}$ (in the adult) to $3\frac{1}{4}$ (in the young) in length of head, $1\frac{1}{2}$ diameters from end of snout, and 1 apart. Body compressed, profile above the eyes concave: the distance from the eye to the upper edge of the maxilla equals $1\frac{1}{4}$ diameters of the orbit in height. The maxilla reaches to below the front edge of the orbit. Vertical limb of preoperele with a very deep emargination succeeded by a broad and deep angle, its height forming half of that of the vertical limb, above the notch the serrations are very fine, on the rounded, produced angle they are coarse, and a few are continued along its oblique lower limb. Interopercular knob well developed. *Teeth*—large canines in the premaxillaries, an outer row of curved canine-like teeth in both jaws, the most posterior of those in the upper jaw being directed slightly forwards; villiform teeth in a Λ-form in the vomer, and in a band on the palatines, none on the tongue. *Fins*—the third to the fifth dorsal spines the longest and equal to two-sevenths of the height of the body, posteriorly they gradually decrease, the last being three-fourths of their height: soft portion of the fin rounded in the young, more pointed in the adult, the length of the highest ray being three-fifths of that of its base. Pectoral reaches to nearly above the anal, and is as long as the head behind the posterior nostril: ventral reaches the vent. Second anal spine strongest and slightly the longest, it equals the highest in the dorsal fin: soft portion of the fin angular, the middle rays rather longer than its entire base. Caudal slightly notched in the young, more emarginate in the adult, the upper portion being the longer. *Scales*—go in oblique rows, directly upwards and backwards, above the lateral-line, and in sinuously oblique ones, taking the same course, below the lateral-line: six rows on cheeks: superiorly they extend forwards to above the hind edge of the eye. Free portion of the tail rather higher than long. *Colours*—uniform crimson, dorsal and anal fins having a black edge with a white external margin, and a white tip to the caudal lobes: a dark band along the base of the dorsal and anal fins; pectorals and ventrals yellow, the latter with a dark tip: caudal dark purple. In the *young*—body crimson, with a black band commencing at the end of the dorsal fin, and covering a part of the hind end of the free portion of the tail and the caudal fin, except that it has a white outer edge.

Bleeker suggests whether *Diacope axillaris*, C.V. vi, p. 532, may not be this species, but Cuv. and Val. observe that perhaps it is merely a variety of the *marginata*.

Habitat—Red Sea, Andaman islands to the South Sea, the largest specimen obtained ($11\frac{1}{2}$ inches) is figured as the adult, one of the smaller ones is given (fig. 3) life-size. This fish attains at least 16 inches in length.

22. Lutianus bohar, Plate XIII, fig. 4.

Sciæna bohar, Forsk. p. 46, No. 47.
Sparus lepisurus, Lacép. iii, t. 15, f. 2.
Lutjanus bohar, Bl. Schn. p. 325; Bleeker, Lutjani, p. 57.
Diacope bohar, Cuv. and Val. ii, p. 433; Rüpp. Atl. Fische, p. 73, and N. W. Fische. p. 103; Klunz. Verb. z. b. Ges Wien, 1870, p. 699.
Diacope quadriguttata, Cuv. and Val. ii, p. 427, vi, p. 533.
Mesoprion quadriguttatus, Bleeker, Banda, p. 233.
Mesoprion bohar, Günther. Catal. i, p. 190, and Fische d. Sudsee, p. 13, t. xv.

B. vii, D. $\frac{10}{14}$, P. 17, V. 1/5, A. $\frac{3}{8}$, C. 17, L. l. 50, L. r. [illegible], L. tr. 7/18.

Length of head 2/7, of caudal 2/9, height of body 1/3 of the total length. *Eyes*—diameter 2/7 of length of head, $1\frac{1}{4}$ diameter from end of snout, and also apart. The distance from the eye to the upper edge of the maxilla equals two-thirds of the diameter of the orbit. The maxilla reaches to below the middle of the eye. Vertical margin of the preopercle with a shallow notch, the whole of it serrated, most strongly so at its rounded and slightly produced angle, its lower limb oblique and likewise serrated: interopercle with a very small knob. *Teeth*—a pair of large canines in the premaxillaries, an outer row of conical canine-like teeth in either jaw: villiform ones in a Λ-shape on the vomer, in a band on the palatines, and in one or two long patches on the tongue. *Fins*—dorsal spines of moderate strength, the fourth the longest and equalling the length of the post-orbital portion of the head, last dorsal spine slightly exceeding one diameter of the orbit in length: soft portion of the fin rounded, the highest ray equalling two-thirds of the length of its base. Pectoral reaching to nearly above the anal spines, the ventrals scarcely so far: second anal spine strongest and somewhat the longest, equalling the third of the dorsal: soft portion of the fin rounded and the height of the rays equalling the length of the entire base of the fin, its lower edge straight: caudal somewhat deeply emarginate. *Scales*—in oblique rows above the lateral-line and in horizontal ones below it: on the upper surface of the body they reach to above the hind edge of the orbit. *Colours*—brownish along the back becoming whiter on the sides and below: two milk-white spots along the base of the dorsal fin, the first below the sixth to the eighth spines, the second below the last third of the soft dorsal: first dorsal deep blackish-brown, which is continued along the upper edge of the first half of the soft dorsal: outer edges of caudal and front edge of anal blackish, the latter fin having a narrow white anterior margin: ventral black, with a white outer edge.

Habitat.—From the Red Sea through those of India to the Malay Archipelago and beyond. The specimen figured is 6 inches in length.

23. Lutianus marginatus, Plate XIII, fig. 5.

Diacope marginata, Cuv. and Val. ii, p. 425; Peters, Wieg. Arch. 1855, p. 238.
Diacope xanthopus, Cuv. and Val. iii, p. 495.

Diacope axillaris, Cuv. and Val. vi, p. 532.

Mesoprion marginatus, Bleeker, Amboina, 1852, ii, p. 554; Kner, Novara Fische, p. 31; Günther. Fische d. Sudsee, p. 13, t. xiv.

Mesoprion Gaimardi, Bleeker, Act. Soc. Sc. Ind. Neerl. vi, Enum. Pisc. p. 23.

Genyoroge marginata, Günther, Catal. i, p. 181.

Lutjanus marginatus, Bleeker, Halmah, p. 155, and Lutjani, p. 72.

Sangarah, Tam.

B. vii, D. $\frac{10}{13-14}$, P. 16, V. 1/5, A. $\frac{3}{8}$, C. 17, L. l. 50, L. r. [illegible], L. tr. 6-7/15, Cæc. pyl. (7 Kner.)

Length of head 2/7 to 1/4, of caudal 1/5, height of body 1/3 to 2/7 of the total length. *Eyes*—diameter 2/7 of length of head, 1¼ diameters from end of snout, and 2/3 of a diameter apart. The height of the preorbital equals two-thirds of the length of the orbit. The maxilla reaches to below the first third of the orbit. Vertical limb of preopercle finely serrated above its emargination, which is deep and situated in its lower third, angle rounded where the serratures are coarsest, whilst some are continued along its horizontal edge: sub- and inter-opercles entire, the latter having a large tuberosity directed upwards and slightly outwards and which is received into the preopercular notch: opercle with two small points. *Teeth*—moderately strong canines in the premaxillaries, an outer row of curved canine-like teeth in both jaws, a narrow villiform Λ-shaped series in the vomer, and a narrow palatine band: none on the tongue. *Fins*—dorsal spines strong, the fourth the longest and equal to two-fifths the height of the body, from it they gradually decrease in length to the last which equals the length of the orbit, the soft portion of the fin rounded, three-fourths as high as the fourth spine, and its height equal to half the length of its base. Pectoral nearly as long as the head and reaching to above the first anal spine: ventral reaches the vent. Second anal spine the strongest and equal to or rather longer than the third, and as long as the highest in the dorsal fin: soft portion of the fin one-third higher than that of the dorsal: caudal emarginate. *Scales*—in oblique rows above the lateral-line to opposite the end of the dorsal fin where they become horizontal, as they likewise are below the lateral-line; they extend forwards on the back to above the hind edge of the eye. *Colours*—purplish-yellow above the lateral-line and golden below it. Generally no lateral blotch. The colours of the back are continued on to the lower third of the dorsal fin and cease at a dark grey longitudinal band which has a lighter one above it, edged superiorly with black and margined with white: caudal dark purplish-red having a white edge: pectoral, ventral and anal flesh-coloured having a yellowish tint.

On the Malabar coast of India specimens are frequently taken that have a black lateral-blotch: also on the Coromandel coast some few have the lateral-mark faintly developed, but it is more commonly absent. This does not depend upon size or season, but may upon sex or locality: in specimens preserved in spirit the mark is liable to disappear. The one figured is 7 inches long, and from Madras.

Habitat.—East coast of Africa, seas of India to the Malay Archipelago, attaining at least 16 inches in length.

24. Lutianus yapilli, Plate XIII, fig. 6.

Sparus yapilli, Russell, Fish. Vizag. i, p. 75, pl. 95.

Mesoprion yapilli, Cuv. and Val. ii, p. 483.

B. vii, D. $\frac{10}{14}$, P. 17, V. 1/5, A. $\frac{3}{8}$, C. 17, L. l. 47, L. r. [illegible], L. tr. 6/14.

Length of head nearly 1/4, of caudal 1/8, height of body 3/11 of the total length. *Eyes*—diameter 1/6 of length of head, 2 diameters from end of snout, and 1¼ apart. The distance from the eye to the upper edge of the maxilla equals one diameter and a quarter the length of the orbit: lower jaw the longer. The maxilla reaches to below the front edge of the orbit. Vertical limb of preopercle with a very shallow emargination above its rounded angle, the whole of the limb being finely serrated, the serrations becoming a little more coarse and widely separated at its angle and along its horizontal border. Sub- and inter-opercles entire. No interopercular knob. *Teeth*—large canines in the premaxillaries, an outer row of curved canine-like teeth in either jaw: villiform ones in a Λ-form on the vomer, and in a band on the palate. The specimen having had the tongue removed the existence or not of lingual teeth cannot be ascertained. Russell also omits to mention whether it is rough or smooth, a subject which he generally notices. *Fins*—dorsal spines strong, the third being three-quarters the height of the fourth which is nearly half the height of the body, they decrease to the ninth which is only 4/11 of that of the fourth spine: soft portion of the dorsal rounded, its height being rather more than half the length of its base. Pectoral nearly as long as the head: the ventral does not reach half the way to the anal fin. Second anal spine the strongest but not quite so long as the third, which equals the length of the head anterior to the orbits: its soft portion a little higher than long at its base, lower edge rounded. *Scales*—in rows parallel to the back above the lateral-line, and horizontal below it: 7 rows on the cheeks, none on the preorbital: superiorly they extend to above the hind edge of the eye, ten rows between the occiput and the first dorsal spine. *Colours*—silvery-grey on the back becoming yellowish white on the abdomen: longitudinal yellowish bands along each row of scales, which in the dry specimen appear sometimes in the form of occasional black spots: cheeks dashed with purple. Fins yellowish, dorsal, anal, and caudal edged with orange.

The foregoing description is from a single specimen 26½ inches long, stuffed, and in the British Museum, it came from Madras where I was not so fortunate as to meet with the species. Jerdon remarks, in Ichthyological Gleanings in Madras (M. J. L. and Sc. 1851, p. 139) "*Vella kadirup*, Tam. Russell, pl. 95. Not very common, of soft texture." A figure of it exists amongst Sir W. Elliot's drawings.

Habitat.—Coromandel coast of India.

25. Lutianus quinquelinearis, Plate XIV, fig. 1.

Holocentrus quinquelinearis, Bl. iv, p. 84, t. 239.
Grammistes quinquevittatus, Bl. Schn. p. 187.
Diacope octolineata, Cuv. and Val. ii, p. 418 and vi, p. 526, (in part); Richardson, Ich. China, p. 228.
Mesoprion etaape, Less. Voy. Coq. ii, p. 229.
Diacope decemlineata, Cuv. and Val. vi, p. 528.
Mesoprion octolineatus, Bleeker, Perc. p. 40.
Mesoprion pomacanthus, Bleeker, Amb. p. 407 (in part).
Genyoroge Bengalensis, Günther, Catal. i, p. 178 (in part).
Genyoroge grammica, Day, Proc. Zool. Soc. 1870, p. 679 (not Bleeker).
Mesoprion Bengalensis, Kner, Novara Fische, p. 31.
Lutjanus quinquelineatus, Bleeker, Lutjani, p. 37.

B. vii, D. $\frac{10}{13-14}$, P. 16, V. 1/5, A. $\frac{3}{8}$, C. 17, L. l. 56, L. r. [illegible], L. tr. 8/19, Cæc. pyl. 5.

Length of head 2/7, of caudal 1/6, height of body 3/10 to 2/7 of the total length. *Eyes*—diameter 3/10 to 1/3 of the length of head, about 1 diameter from end of snout, and 3/4 of a diameter apart. Dorsal profile more convex than that of the abdomen, which is nearly horizontal: lower jaw slightly the longer: distance from the eye to the upper edge of the maxilla equals a little more than half the diameter of the orbit. The maxilla reaches to below the first third of the orbit. Vertical limb of preopercle with a very deep emargination and a rounded angle, the whole being serrated, the serrations at the lower angle being coarse, lower limb also serrated. A strong interopercular knob: opercular points indistinct. *Teeth*—a pair of moderate sized curved canines in the premaxillaries, an outer row of curved canine-like teeth in either jaw, those in the upper being the largest: villiform ones in a Λ-form in the vomer, a band on the palatines, but none on the tongue. *Fins*—dorsal spines of moderate strength, increasing in length to the fourth which equals $2\frac{1}{2}$ in the height of the body, from it they slightly decrease to the last which equals one diameter of the orbit in length, the soft portion of the fin rounded, the highest ray equal to half the length of its base. Pectoral not quite so long as the head, second anal spine rather longest and strongest, it equals half the height of the body, the rayed portion highest anteriorly where its rays equal the length of its base, its lower edge rounded: caudal emarginate. *Scales*—in oblique rows above the lateral-line, and in horizontal ones below it, superiorly they extend forward to above the anterior third of the eye: the suborbital ring of bones is more or less scaled, and in adults some are even present on the preorbital. *Colours*—olive-yellow, with a deep black finger-mark on the lateral-line below the last few dorsal spines and the first few rays: some lines above the nape formed by a dark spot on each scale. Five blue bands pass from the eye, the first three from above it to the dorsal fin or its termination, the two next from the middle and lower edge of the eye join on the end of the opercle and pass direct to the middle of the base of the tail: the lowest from the snout is continued past the pectoral fin to the end of the base of the soft anal: fins yellow: caudal with a light tip.

Neither Bloch's specimen* or figure shows any lateral blotch, which according to Bleeker is sometimes absent, all my specimens possess it, and in all that I examined I found 5 cæcal appendages, whereas the *Bengalensis* has none.

Genyoroge notata Günther, has D $\frac{10}{13}$, and 9 rows of scales between the lateral-line and the first dorsal spine, otherwise it resembles the fish described above, and of which I consider it is a variety.

Habitat.—Seas of India to the Malay Archipelago. The specimen figured (6 inches long) is from the Andaman islands, but the species is common at Madras.

26. Lutianus vitta, Plate XIV, fig. 2.

Serranus vitta, Quoy and Gaim. Voy. Frey. p. 315, pl. 58, f. 3; Cuv. and Val. ii, p. 239, vi, p. 505; Richards. Ich. China, p. 234.
Diacope vitta, Temm. and Schleg. Fauna Japon. p. 13, t. 6, fig. 1.
Mesoprion enneacanthus, Bleeker, Perc. p. 40 (D. $\frac{9}{14}$): Günther, Catal. i, p. 209.
Mesoprion phaiotæniatus, Bleeker, Perc. p. 43.
Mesoprion vitta, Bleeker, Perc. p. 44; Günther, Catal. i, p. 207; Kner, Novara Fische, p. 37.
Mesoprion ophuysenii, Bleeker, Sumatra, p. 74.
Lutjanus vitta, Bleeker, Ternate, p. 233 and Lutjani, p. 25.

B. vii, D. $\frac{10}{12}$, P. 16, V. 1/5, A. $\frac{3}{8}$, C. 17, L. l. 50, L. r. $\frac{11-12}{13-15}$, L. tr. 8/12.

Length of head from 2/7 to 3/11, of caudal 1/6, height of body 2/7 of the total length. *Eyes*—diameter 2/7 to 1/4 of length of head, $1\frac{1}{4}$ to $1\frac{1}{2}$ diameter from end of snout, and 2/3 of a diameter apart. Body somewhat compressed, dorsal profile more convex than that of the abdomen, but above the eyes it is somewhat concave. Lower jaw slightly the longer: the maxilla reaches to below the first third of the orbit. Suborbital ring of bones below the front third of the orbit equalling three-fourths of the diameter of the eye in depth. Vertical limb of preopercle with a shallow emargination, its angle slightly rounded but not produced, its lower edge rather oblique, it is finely serrated along both limbs, most coarsely so at its angle: opercle with two small and flat

* Bloch's specimen is $5\frac{7}{10}$ inches long, and in good preservation at Berlin, it is marked thus by Valenciennes, *Holocentrus quinquevittatus*, Bl. t. 239; *Diacope decemlineata*, C.V.

points. Sometimes there is a very indistinct interopercular swelling. *Teeth*—large canines in the premaxillaries, an outer row of curved canine-like teeth in either jaw, villiform ones in a triangular spot on the vomer, which patch may be produced posteriorly in the median line, a similar narrow band on the palatines, and in a band pointed behind rounded anteriorly on the tongue (in a specimen 11 inches long). *Fins*—dorsal spines of moderate strength, the fourth being the longest, and equal to two-thirds of the length of the head, from it they gradually decrease to the last which is two-thirds as high as the first ray, whilst the soft portion is slightly lower than the third spine : pectoral nearly as long as the head : second anal spine a little the strongest, but not quite so long as the third which equals the length of the eye : caudal lunated. *Scales*—in oblique and sinuous rows above the lateral-line as far as the end of the dorsal fin, beyond which as well as below the lateral-line they are horizontal. *Colours*—yellowish-red along the back, becoming rosy below the lateral-line : olive stripes follow each row of scales above the lateral-line and brilliant yellow ones those below it. Fins orange, dorsal, anal, and tips of caudal marginal with white. Sometimes, but not invariably (especially at Madras), a broad black band passes from the eye to above the centre of the caudal fin, and in such specimens the olive stripes in the upper third of the body are nearly black.

Habitat.—Seas of India to the Malay Archipelago, and beyond. The specimen figured is 7 inches in length.

27. Lutianus Madras, Plate XIV, fig. 3.

Lutianus lutianus, Bl. t. 245; Bl. Schn. p. 324; Bleeker, Lutjani, p. 27, and Atl. Ich. Perc. t. xxxvi, f. 3.

Lutjanus Blochii, Lacép. iv, pp. 178, 210.*

Mesoprion lutjanus, Cuv. and Val. ii, p. 479; Kner, Novara Fische, p. 37.

Mesoprion Madras, Cuv. and Val. vii, p. 446; Bleeker, Perc. p. 44; Günther, Catal. i, p. 200; Day, Fish. Malabar, p. 14.

? *Lutjanus rangus*, Bleeker, Bali, p. 154, Atl. Ich. Perc. t. xxi, fig. 3, Lutjani, p. 59.

B. vii, D. $\frac{10}{12}|\frac{0}{11}$, P. 16, V. 1/5, A. $\frac{3}{8}$, C. 17, L. l. 50, L. r. [illegible], L. tr. 6/16.

Length of head 2/7, of caudal 1/6, height of body 1/3 to 2/7 of the total length. *Eyes*—diameter 1/3 to 2/7 of length of head, 1 diameter from end of snout, and 2/3 of a diameter apart. The depth of the preorbital equals about half the length of the eye : dorsal profile more convex than that of the abdomen. The maxilla reaches to below the front third of the orbit. Vertical limb of preopercle not emarginate, its angle slightly produced and rounded having an oblique lower limb, the whole being serrated, most coarsely so at its angle : no interopercular knob : opercle with two points, the lower most distinct. *Teeth*—rather large curved canines in the upper jaw, and an outer row of curved canine-like teeth in either jaw : villiform ones on the palate either in a lanceolate patch or else in a triangular spot prolonged posteriorly in the median line : in a band on the palatines, also a patch on the tongue. *Fins*—dorsal spines moderately strong, increasing in length to the fourth, which equals that of the postorbital portion of the head, they subsequently decrease to the last which is rather above half the same length : soft portion of the fin rounded, its height being equal to one-third of the length of its base, and being much lower than the spinous. Pectoral pointed, nearly as long as the head but not reaching to above the anal spines : ventral reaches two-thirds of the distance to the anal spines, the second of which is as strong as the third but slightly shorter, its length not being quite equal to the diameter of the eye : soft portion of the fin as high in front as it is long at its base, its last ray half the height of its first, lower edge of the fin straight : caudal emarginate. *Scales*—in oblique rows above and horizontal ones below the lateral-line, they extend forwards to between the centre of the orbits. *Colours*—roseate, with oblique line above the lateral-line, but which to below the first four dorsal spines are sinuous, below the lateral-line the sides and abdomen are yellow, with narrow red horizontal bands. One specimen captured December 1869, had a lateral band as seen in *L. vitta*.

Bleeker's figure of *L. rangus* appears to resemble this fish, but the upper surface of the head is said to be scaleless.

Habitat.—From the Seychelles through the Indian seas to the Malay Archipelago, attaining about a foot in length.

28. Lutianus decussatus, Plate XIV, fig. 4.

Mesoprion decussatus, Cuv. and Val. ii, p. 487; Bleeker, Perc. p. 43; Günther, Catal. i, p. 210; Kner, Novara Fische, p. 34.

Mesoprion therapon, Day, Proc. Zool. Soc. 1869, p. 514.

Lutjanus decussatus, Bleeker, Ternate, p. 233, and Lutjani, p. 79.

B. vii, D. $\frac{10}{12}|\frac{0}{14}$, P. 15, V. 1/5, A. $\frac{3}{8}$, C. 17, L. l. 50-54, L. r. [illegible], L. tr. 6-7/17, Cæc. pyl. 3.

Length of head 4/15 to 2/7, of caudal 1/6, height of body 1/3 to 2/7 of the total length. *Eyes*—diameter 1/4 to 2/9 of length of head, $1\frac{1}{2}$ diameter from end of snout, and nearly 1 apart. Snout pointed, lips rather thick : depth below the orbit to edge of the upper jaw equal to 1 diameter of the eye. The maxilla reaches

* Lacépède describes his fish, p. 178, as having D. $\frac{3}{17}$, and the general colour white : the back yellowish, and above the lateral-line blue transverse bands, &c., he subsequently, p. 210, considers his fish identical with Bloch's.

to below the front edge of the orbit; jaws of equal length in front. Vertical limb of preopercle with a shallow emargination, having fine serrations which are lost at the angle: a slight interopercular knob. *Teeth*—one or two large curved canines in the premaxillaries, and an external row of curved canine-like teeth in the upper jaw, rather larger ones, less curved and wider apart in the lower jaw: villiform ones in a Λ-shaped band in the vomer, an elongated one on the palatines, but none on the tongue. *Fins*—third to fifth dorsal spines the longest, nearly equal to the length of the postorbital portion of the head and two-fifths the height of the body, posteriorly they decrease to the last: soft portion of the fin rounded and lower than the spinous, its longest ray equal to one half the length of its base. Pectoral as long as the head behind the anterior nostril, or even longer in some specimens: ventral reaches two-thirds of the distance to the anal. Second anal spine the strongest, usually not quite so long as the third which equals one diameter and a quarter of the eye in length, its first rays highest, its lower margin rounded: caudal forked, upper lobe the longer. *Scales*—in oblique rows above the lateral-line, and in horizontal ones below it: they extend forwards to above the hind edge of the orbit: seven or eight rows across the cheeks. *Colours*—whitish, with six longitudinal black bands along the body, and six badly marked short vertical ones in its upper third, descending from the base of the dorsal fin, the crossing of these two sets of bands leaves large uncovered whitish spots of ground colour; a deep black spot at the root of the caudal fin. A white band across the occiput, which is continued on to the preopercle. Fins greyish, anal with a white front edge.

Habitat.—Seas of India to the Malay Archipelago, and beyond. The one figured ($9\frac{1}{2}$ inches long) is from the Andamans, where it is a very common species and readily captured with a bait.

Third group—Priacanthina.

Lower jaw prominent. Cleft of mouth almost vertical. Scales ctenoid, small. Cœcal appendages few.

Genus, 9—PRIACANTHUS, Cuv. and Val.

Branchiostegals six: pseudobranchiæ. Body oblong and somewhat elevated. Eyes large. Lower jaw prominent. Preopercle serrated on both limbs as well as on the angle which is produced into a flattened spine-like point: opercle with a point. Teeth villiform in the jaws, vomer, and palate, none on the tongue. A single dorsal fin, with nine to ten spines; anal with three. Scales small and ctenoid, extended on to the snout.

Geographical distribution.—Tropical seas. They do not appear to be very common in India, none have been seen by me in the fresh state: Russell does not figure any. Amongst Sir Walter Elliot's drawings named by Jerdon are two of this Genus: the first appears to be *P. Blochii:* the second termed *Priacanthus kë-süie* has D. $\frac{10}{11}$, A. $\frac{3}{11}$, and is of the same shape but of a much lighter colour: the ventral fin is spotted with brown, whilst there are two or more large blackish-brown blotches between the inner rays and the body: the length of the longest figure is $4\frac{1}{2}$ inches.

SYNOPSIS OF INDIVIDUAL SPECIES.

1. *Priacanthus Blochii.* D. $\frac{10}{12}$, A. $\frac{3}{13}$. Light lake red, the vertical and ventral fins with a narrow black edge. Seas of India to the Malay Archipelago.

1. Priacanthus Blochii, Plate VIII, fig. 2.

Anthias macrophthalmus, Bl. vi, p. 115, t. 319; Bl. Schn. p. 304.
Priacanthus Blochii, Bleeker, Nat. Tyds. Ned. Ind. iv, p. 456; Günther, Catal. i, p. 218.

B. vi, D. $\frac{10}{12|13}$, P. 18, V. 1/5, A. $\frac{3}{13|14}$, C. 17, L. r. 110-120.

Length of head 3/11, of caudal 2/13, height of body 3/11 of the total length. *Eyes*—large, in the middle of the length of the head, 1/2 a diameter from the end of snout and the same distance from the posterior end of the opercle. Lower jaw strongly prominent. The angle of the preopercle provided with a strong spinate point, it and the vertical as well as the horizontal edges of the preopercle serrated: preorbital also serrated along both its upper and lower borders. The maxilla reaches to almost below the first third of the orbit. *Teeth*—villiform in the jaws, vomer, and palate. *Fins*—dorsal spines of moderate strength, increasing in length to the last, which however is not quite so long as the rays; the first few are roughened anteriorly. Pectoral short, equalling two-fifths of the height of the body: ventral spine serrated on both edges: anal spines serrated anteriorly, the third being the longest: caudal cut square. *Colours*—of a light lake-red, all the vertical as well as the ventral fins having a narrow black border.

Amongst Sir W. Elliot's drawings is one named *Priacanthus? Pasoowa* which appears to be this species from Madras: it wants however the black edge to the fins, which also is very slightly apparent in Bloch's specimen. Jerdon remarks, (M. J. L. and Sc. 1851, p. 131.) "*Priacanthus.* I possess drawings of apparently two species of this genus. The one is entirely of a fine red colour, and was named *Paruwa*, Tam. The other is reddish above, white on the sides, and the ventral fins spotted with dusky: D. $\frac{10}{11}$, A. $\frac{3}{11}$, it was named *Kowai.*"

Habitat.—Red Sea, East coast of Africa, seas of India, to the Malay Archipelago. The figure is from a specimen in the British Museum collection, $8\frac{1}{2}$ inches in length.

Fourth Group—Apogonina.*

Form of body more or less elevated and compressed. Opercles mostly denticulated or armed. Cleft of mouth oblique or even nearly vertical. One or two dorsal fins.

Genus, 10—AMBASSIS,† (Comm.) *Cuv. and Val.*

Chanda, pt. Ham. Buch.: *Hamiltonia* et *Ambassus*, Swains.: *Bogoda*, *Parambassis*, et *Pseudambassis*, Bleeker.‡

Branchiostegals six: pseudobranchiæ well developed. Body compressed, more or less diaphanous. Lower limb of preopercle with a double serrated edge: opercle without prominent spine. Villiform teeth on jaws, vomer, and palate, sometimes on the tongue: canines rarely present. Two dorsal fins, the first with seven spines, the anal with three: a forwardly directed recumbent spine in front of the base of the dorsal fin. Scales cycloid, of moderate or small size, frequently deciduous. Lateral-line complete, interrupted, incomplete or absent.

Geographical distribution.—From the Red Sea, and East coast of Africa, through the seas of India and Malay Archipelago to North Australia and even beyond. Some are exclusively found in fresh water.

Uses.—Although this genus consists of little bony fishes, which rarely exceed six inches in length, and are generally far less, still they have their economic uses. The poorer classes eat them, they are extensively consumed by the larger fishes, forming much of their sustenance during the dry months of the year, whilst owing to their formation they are easily dried without the employment of salt. Buchanan observes of his genus *Chanda*, which is mostly composed of species of *Ambassis*, that they "are very small, and of little value, although in many places abundant and used in considerable quantities: but as food they are insipid, and filled with small bones, for which defect their size does not compensate." Cantor remarks that the "species of *Apogon* and *Chanda* are of little value as articles of food. At Pinang, they, as well as numerous other small fishes, the daily residue of the market, are used as manure."

Some difficulty exists in ascertaining the species of this genus to which a specimen belongs, and for the following reasons. The comparative length of the second or third dorsal spine to that of the body often differs in accordance with the size of the specimen: and local variations on this point seem to exist. The number of the soft rays is not constant. Scales are distinctly apparent in the adult of species in which they are hardly visible in the very young. The lateral-line is subject to variation. Colours likewise are not constant, but the character least subject to change appears to be the serrations on the sub- and inter-opercles, the preorbital, and around the orbit, but those on the vertical border of the preopercle are inconstant in some species.

SYNOPSIS OF SPECIES.

1. *Ambassis nama.* D. 7/$\frac{1}{13-17}$, A. $\frac{3}{[illegible]}$. Blunt serrations along horizontal limb of preopercle and on preorbital. Large curved canines in lower jaw. Yellowish-olive with a dark shoulder mark. Fresh waters of India, Assam, and Burma.

2. *Ambassis ranga.* D. 7/$\frac{1}{13-14}$, A. $\frac{3}{13-15}$, L. r. 60-70. Vertical limb of preopercle serrated or entire, both edges of its lower limb and preorbital serrated. Golden with vertical bands and black margins to the fins in the young. Fresh waters of India and Burma.

3. *Ambassis baculis.* D. 7/$\frac{1}{[illegible]}$, A. $\frac{3}{[illegible]}$, L. r. 60. Double lower edge of the preopercle serrated, also the preorbital and upper edge of the orbit. No canines. Yellowish-olive with a golden occipital spot. Fresh waters of Bengal to the Punjab and Orissa.

4. *Ambassis Thomassi.* D. 7/$\frac{1}{11-12}$, A. $\frac{3}{9-10}$, L. l. 35-41. Vertical limb and double lower edge of preopercle and posterior half of interopercle serrated: preorbital also serrated. Silvery, spotted. Malabar coast in fresh water.

5. *Ambassis Commersonii.* D. 7/$\frac{1}{[illegible]}$, A. $\frac{3}{[illegible]}$, L. l. 30-33. Double lower edge of preopercle serrated, interopercle entire: preorbital also serrated. Silvery. Seas of India.

6. *Ambassis nalua.* D. 7/$\frac{1}{10-11}$, A. $\frac{3}{9-10}$, L. l. 26-27. Double lower edge of preopercle and posterior half of interopercle serrated: preorbital also serrated. Silvery. Fresh waters of India near the coast.

7. *Ambassis interrupta.* D. 7/$\frac{1}{10-11}$, A. $\frac{3}{9-10}$, L. l. 28. Double lower edge of preopercle serrated: interopercle with a few denticulations at its angle: preorbital serrated. Second dorsal spine high. Lateral line interrupted. A dark band along either caudal lobe. Andamans to the Malay Archipelago.

8. *Ambassis Dayi.* D. 7/$\frac{1}{10-11}$, A. $\frac{3}{10}$, L. l. 30. Snout pointed. Vertical limb of preopercle minutely serrated: its double lower border more coarsely so, also the posterior half of the interopercle and the preorbital. Malabar.

* Bleeker places the *Ambassini* or *Bogodini* distinct from this group of *Apogonini*: Klunzinger has a Family *Ambassoidei* with a group of *Apogonini*, which together equal the above "fourth group."

† Gu-nas-si, Mugh.

‡ Bleeker's genera of his Bogodini are as follows:—

1. *Ambassis.* Preorbital serrated: teeth small: scales 30-46: dorsal and anal rays, 8-11.

2. *Parambassis.* Preorbital serrated: outer row of teeth in premaxillary enlarged, rather widely separated, and almost developing canines: scales of medium or small size: dorsal and anal rays 9-11.

3. *Pseudambassis.* Strong teeth in premaxillary, dorsal fin 12-14 rays, anal 14-17.

4. *Bogoda.* Preorbital entire. Strong teeth in jaws, but more obtuse and conical, with a slight outward direction: dorsal and anal fins many rayed: scales small.

9. *Ambassis gymnocephalus.* D. $7/\frac{1}{9-10}$, A. $\frac{3}{9-10}$, L. l. 27-29. Double lower edge of preopercle serrated: interopercle entire: preorbital serrated: two rows of scales on suborbitals. Lateral-line interrupted. Silvery, with a burnished lateral band. Seas of India, ascending estuaries and rivers.

10. *Ambassis urotænia.* D. $7/\frac{1}{9-10}$, A. $\frac{3}{9-10}$, L. l. 27-28. Double lower edge of preopercle serrated: interopercle entire: preorbital serrated; one row of scales on the suborbitals. Lateral-line entire. Silvery, with a burnished lateral band. Seychelles, Andamans, to the Malay Archipelago.

Amongst the preceding 10 Indian species, *the interopercle is serrated* in *A. Thomassi*, L. l. 35-41; *A. nalua*, L. l. 27-28; *A. interrupta*, L. l. 28 and an interrupted lateral-line, and *A. Dayi*, L. l. 30. The six which have the *interopercle entire* are, *A. nama* with curved canines: *A. ranga*, L. l. 60-70; *A. baculis*, L. l. 80; *A. Commersonii*, L. l. 30-33: *A. gymnocephalus*, L. l. 27-29, and an interrupted lateral-line, and *A. urotænia*, L. l. 28.

1. Ambassis nama, Plate XIV, fig. 5.

Chanda nama, Ham. Buch. Fish. Ganges, pp. 109, 371, pl. 39, f. 37.
Chanda phula et bogoda, Ham. Buch. l. c. pp. 111, 371.
Ambassis nama, phula et bogoda, Cuv. and Val. ii, pp. 185, 186, 187; Day, Proc. Zool. Soc. 1869, p. 298.
Ambassis oblonga, Cuv. and Val. ii, p. 185; Günther, Catal. i, p. 228.
? *Ambassis Indica*, McClell. Cal. Journ. Nat. Hist. ii, p. 585.
Bogoda nama, Bleeker, Beng. en Hind. p. 89.
Ambassis bogoda, Günther, Catal. i, p. 228.
Muckee and *Chal-du-ah*, Punj.: *Soondah*, Assam.: *Pud-da* and *Pat-to-bah*, Sind.: *Ak-ku-rati*, Tel.: *Buck-ra* and *Pon-pi-ah*, N. W. Prov.: *Cart-kona* and *Gon-chappi*, Ooriah.

B. vi, D. 7 | $\frac{1}{13-17}$, P. 13, V. 1/5, A. $\frac{3}{14-17}$, C. 17.

Length of head 1/4 to 2/9, of caudal 1/4 to 2/9, height of body from 4/11 to 1/3 of the total length. *Eyes*—diameter about 1/3 of length of head, 2/3 to 3/4 of a diameter from end of snout, and also apart. Body compressed, the dorsal and abdominal profiles equally convex, a considerable rise from the occiput to the base of the first dorsal fin. Lower jaw much longer than the upper. The maxilla reaches to below the anterior third of the orbit. Preorbital with three denticulations along its posterior-superior margin: also a denticulation behind them at the middle of the front edge of the orbit, and another at its posterior-superior angle. Vertical limb of preopercle entire, except near its angle, where there are two or three denticulations which become blunted with age: the double border, very slightly denticulated at its lower edge in the young, often entire. Sub- and inter-opercles entire. *Teeth*—two or three large and crooked canines directed forwards on either side of the symphysis of the lower jaw: an outer and an inner enlarged row in both jaws: fine ones on the vomer and palatines. *Fins*—dorsal spines of moderate strength, a recumbent one anterior to the fin, the second spine the longest (in a few specimens the third) and equal in length to the head behind the anterior edge or middle of the eye, or to about half the height of the body below it, the seventh dorsal spine somewhat longer than the sixth: the spine of the second dorsal as long as the first ray, the rays gradually decrease in height: ventral reaches a little beyond the anus but not so far as the anal fin: the third anal spine the longest and strongest equalling the height of the longest in the dorsal fin: caudal deeply forked, the lobes of equal length. *Scales*—minute, scarcely visible on the head; in young specimens captured from stagnant pieces of water, the mucous often causes the scales to be overlooked. *Lateral-line*—is always indistinct, in some specimens it is entire, in others it ceases after proceeding a short way, or it may even be absent. *Pseudobranchiæ*—well developed. *Colours*—yellowish-olive covered all over with minute black dots which on the shoulder are collected into an oblong patch, having its longest diameter vertical: summit of the head and top of the eyes black. Fins orange, the upper half of the first dorsal deep black: a dark upper edge to the second dorsal: caudal dark with a light outer margin: anal with a black mark over the bases of the spines. In some specimens taken at Hurdah, in Bombay, the caudal was black tipped.

This fish shows considerable local variations, which have caused its being described under more than one name. Buchanan observed of the *phula*, that it is "devoid of scales," "strongly resembles the *nama*, but seldom exceeds two inches," "nor indeed, except in the number of the rays which support the fins, is there any considerable difference between the two species." In *nama*, D. $7/\frac{1}{17}$, A. $\frac{3}{17}$: in *phula*, D. $7/\frac{1}{13}$, A. $\frac{3}{13}$, are the numbers he records.

As regards the *bogoda*, he observes it has 16 soft rays in the dorsal and 17 in the anal fin, and "a long transparent body devoid of scales," "but that it differs in nothing remarkable from the two former (*nama* and *phula*) except in the number of soft rays contained in the back and vent fins, and in that contained in the pectorals, each of which has twelve."

Amongst Buchanan's MSS. drawings in Calcutta, is one $1\frac{7}{10}$ inches long, termed *Centropomus phulchanda*, which his notes show to be the *phula*, and a second $2\frac{1}{10}$ inches long of the *bogoda*.

Having brought together upwards of thirty specimens from different localities of India and Burma, I find that this species is subject to variation, but some points remain the same in all. Although the comparative length of the longest dorsal spine varies, it retains its proportion to the third of the anal, which appears to be invariably the longest in that fin: the last dorsal and anal rays are divided to their bases, (counting each as 1) and the following numbers exist in my specimens, D. 7/[illegible], A. [illegible], certainly the most common is D. $7/\frac{1}{14}$, A. $\frac{3}{14}$: but of course if we count the last dorsal and anal rays divided to their bases as two, which

Buchanan frequently did, it would cause my figures to stand thus D. [illegible], A. [illegible]. In Cuv. and Val. it is observed that the *A. oblonga* has D. 7/$\frac{1}{12}$, A. $\frac{3}{11}$, and the black dots and the shoulder mark appear to have been absent, but these dots often disappear in specimens which have been long kept, that on the base of the anal is generally first lost, and subsequently the others. The variation in the number of rays has been already referred to. McClelland observes *A. Indica* has D. $\frac{1}{5}$ an evident misprint; he also mentions the depth of the body equal to its length.

Habitat.—Throughout the fresh waters of India, Assam, and Burma, attaining three or four inches in length.

2. Ambassis ranga, Plate XIV, fig. 6.

Chanda ranga, Ham. Buch. Fish. Ganges, pp. 113, 371, pl. 16, f. 38.

Chanda lala, Ham. Buch. l. c. pp. 114, 371, pl. 20, f. 39; Bleeker, Beng. en Hind. p. 88, and Verh. Bat. Gen. xxv, t. i, f. 1.

Ambassis ranga et *lala*, Cuv. and Val. ii, pp. 183, 184.

Ambassis Barlovi,* Sykes, Fishes of Dukhun. Trans. Zool. Soc. i, p. 350, pl. 60, f. 1.

Ambassis alta, Cuv. and Val. ii, p. 183; Günther, Catal. i, p. 227.

Ambassis lala, McClelland, Cal. Journ. Nat. Hist. v, p. 150, t. 4, fig. 1.

Ambassis lala, Blyth. Proc. Asi. Soc. Beng. 1860, p. 138.

Chandee, Beng. and N.W. Prov.: *Pee-dah*, Sind.: *Laal-chandee*, Ooriah.

B. vi, D. 7/$\frac{1}{13-14}$, P. 11, V. 1/5, A. $\frac{3}{13-16}$, C. 17, L. r. 60-70, L. tr. 13/—.

In the adult, length of head 4/13 to 1/4, of caudal 1/4 to 2/9, height of body 2/5 to 3/7 of the total length. *Eyes*—diameter 2/5 of length of head, 1/2 a diameter from end of snout, and 3/4 of a diameter apart. Dorsal and abdominal profiles both very convex, but the profile over the eyes is slightly concave. The maxilla reaches to below the middle of the orbit. Vertical limb of preopercle sometimes entire, more commonly finely serrated, but in some specimens, especially on the Bombay side of India, and in Burma, rather coarsely so: the double margin of horizontal limb of the preopercle serrated; sub- and inter-opercles entire. Preorbital with about six denticulations on its inferior edge, and a strong one on its anterior superior angle directed towards the eye and about five more along the upper edge of that bone. Another spine at the middle of the posterior edge of the orbit, with five more, but decreasing in size along its upper half. *Teeth*—villiform in the jaws, vomer, and palate, none on the tongue. *Fins*—second spine of the dorsal equals the distance from the middle of the orbit to the posterior end of the head, and is generally as long although sometimes shorter than the third: the ventral almost reaches to the commencement of the anal; second anal spine of equal strength but slightly shorter than the third which equals two-fifths of the height of the body above it: caudal deeply forked. In Burma the second anal spine is comparatively shorter than in Indian specimens. *Colours*—olive, having a dark mark composed of spots on the shoulder, being the remains of a band present in the young. The margins of the vertical fins are usually somewhat dark.

In the *young*, termed by Buchanan *lala*, the fish is of a bright yellow or orange colour, with four or five dark vertical bands which are formed of fine black dots. The first dorsal is nearly black, the second and the anal as well as occasionally the ventral have deep black edges. Buchanan mentions yellow spots as sometimes present.

This species appears to be subject to greater variations in accordance with age than is seen in any other species of *Ambassis*. In examining the highest dorsal spine in comparison with the length of the fish, in 8 specimens, I found it to be as follows:

		inches.		inch.		inches.			
No. 1,	total length	$1\frac{3}{10}$	: of body	1	: height of dorsal spine	3/10	or	$3\frac{1}{4}$	in the length of the body excluding the caudal fin.
No. 2	„ „	$1\frac{4}{10}$	: „	$1\frac{1}{10}$	: „ „ „	3/10	„	$3\frac{2}{3}$	„ „ „
No. 3	„ „	$1\frac{6}{10}$	: „	$1\frac{2}{10}$	: „ „ „	3/10	„	1/4	„ „ „
No. 4	„ „	$1\frac{7}{10}$	: „	$1\frac{3}{10}$	: „ „ „	3/10	„	1/4	„ „ „
No. 5	„ „	$2\frac{1}{10}$	: „	$1\frac{7}{10}$	: „ „ „	4/10	„	$4\frac{1}{4}$	„ „ „
No. 6	„ „	$2\frac{4}{10}$	: „	2	: „ „ „	4/10	„	1/5	„ „ „
No. 7	„ „	$2\frac{6}{10}$	: „	2	: „ „ „	4/10	„	1/5	„ „ „
No. 8	„ „	3	: „	$2\frac{4}{10}$	: „ „ „	9/20	„	1/5	„ „ „

Irrespective of the above, demonstrating how the average proportional length of the dorsal spines to that of the body decreases with age, it is remarkable that in all under $1\frac{1}{2}$ inches in length the second anal spine is the longest: as their size increases the second and third become of equal length: but in the adult the third is almost invariably the longer.

Habitat.—Throughout India and Burma, to a few inches in length.

3. Ambassis baculis, Plate XV, fig. 1.

Chanda baculis, Ham. Buch. Fish. Ganges, pp. 112, 371.

Ambassis baculis, Cuv. and Val. ii, p. 187.

* I find on Sykes' original drawing, *Gandreechee*, given as the native name of this species, and *Chanda ranga*, Buch. for which *Ambassis Barlowii* was subsequently substituted.

Ambassis notatus, Blyth. Proc. As. Soc. of Beng. 1860, p. 138.
Kung-gi, Punj.: *Nga-kona-wa*, or *Nga-zin-zat*, Burm.

B. vi, D. $7 \mid \frac{1}{13}$, P. 12, V. 1/5, A. $\frac{3}{13}$, C. 17, L. r. 80.

Length of head 1/4, of caudal 1/4, height of body 1/3 of the total length. *Eyes*—diameter 1/3 of length of head, 1/2 to 2/3 of a diameter from end of snout, and also apart. Body compressed: lower jaw rather shorter than the upper. The maxilla reaches to below the first third of the orbit. Preorbital strongly serrated along its lower edge and having a sharp spine directed towards the orbit at its anterior-superior angle followed by several more along its upper edge. The whole of the upper edge of the orbit serrated. Vertical limb of preopercle entire, the whole of the lower edge of the horizontal limb strongly serrated, and a few serrations near the angle of its upper edge: sub- and inter-opercles entire. *Teeth*—villiform in jaws, vomer, and palate. *Fins*—second spine of the first dorsal fin the highest and equal to the length of the head behind the hind edge of the orbit, and rather more than half the height of the body below it; the seventh spine rather longer than the sixth. Ventral reaches three-quarters of the distance to the anal. Third anal spine slightly the longest: caudal forked, lower lobe slightly the longer. *Lateral-line*—complete, it becomes straight opposite the first-third of the second dorsal fin. *Colours*—yellowish-olive: a golden spot on the occiput: black along the top of the first dorsal fin: second dorsal and anal darkest externally: front of each anal ray blackish: caudal dark along its base and also with blackish tips to each lobe.

Buchanan observes that it has "the body short and transparent, and devoid of scales and with a yellow mark on the nape." It is said to resemble the *bogala* in colour, and the *chanda* in shape. A figure of it exists amongst his MSS. drawings $1\frac{3}{10}$ inches in length and marked *Centropomus ? bakral*.

The *Ambassis baculis* principally differs from the *A. nama* in its form being higher, its lower jaw the shorter and not crooked to one side, its vertical limb of the preopercle being strongly serrated, and its possessing no canine or enlarged teeth in its jaws.

Habitat.—Fresh waters of Orissa, Bengal, and as far north as the Punjab: also in Burma. The figure is taken from a specimen $1\frac{7}{10}$ inches in length, captured at Lahore.

4. Ambassis Thomassi, Plate XV, fig. 2.

Day, Proc. Zool. Soc. 1870, p. 369.
Mulla-cherá, Mal.: *Mulla-tharu*, Tel.: *Mulla-jubbu*, Canarese.

B. vi, D. $7/_{1} \mid \frac{1}{9-10}$, P. 15, V. 1/5, A. $\frac{3}{9-10}$, C. 15, L. l. 35-41, L. tr. 7/17.

Length of head $3\frac{1}{2}$ to 2/7, of caudal 4/17 to 1/4, height of body 1/4 to 1/3 of the total length. *Eyes*—diameter from 1/3 to $3\frac{1}{2}$ of length of head, 3/4 of a diameter from end of snout, and 1/2 a diameter apart. The younger specimens are rather more oval than the adults: lower jaw the longer: a slight concavity over the orbits, owing to a rise from the nape to the base of the dorsal fin. The maxilla reaches to below the middle of the orbit. Vertical limb of preopercle finely serrated, its lower double edge more coarsely so especially at the angle: posterior half of lower edge of interopercle strongly serrated. Lower edge of preorbital with about nine denticulations, sometimes becoming more numerous (up to 15) and smaller with age, and a raised usually serrated edge along its upper third, which sometimes becomes blunted with age. One spine at the posterior-superior angle of the orbit (becoming bifurcated with age,) and the lower two-thirds of its margin serrated (these becoming blunted with age). *Teeth*—in villiform bands in jaws, vomer, and palate, an outer rather enlarged row in both jaws, none on tongue. *Fins*—second dorsal spine strong and nearly as long as the head without the snout: the ventral reaches as far as the anal spines: second anal spine equals that of the third and half the length of the head: caudal deeply forked. *Lateral-line*—continuous. *Pseudobranchiæ*—well developed. *Colours*—greyish, spotted with silvery, there are also brownish basal spots on many of the scales, more especially along the back.

Habitat.—The coasts of Canara as low as Cochin: it is found some distance inland even in elevated localities: it attains to at least $6\frac{1}{2}$ inches in length.

5. Ambassis Commersonii, Plate XV, fig. 3.

? *Sciæna safgha*, Forsk. Desc. Anim. p. 53.
? *Perca safgha*, Bl. Schn. p. 86.
Centropomus ambassis, Lacép. iv, p. 273.
Ambassis Commersonii, Cuv. and Val. ii, p. 176, pl. 25; Rüpp. N. W. Fische, p. 89; Bleeker, Perc. p. 30, and Ambassis, p. 95; Günther, Catal. i, p. 223; Day, Fishes of Malabar, p. 15.
Ambassis macracanthus, Bleeker, Perc. p. 30; Günther, Catal. i, p. 227; Day, Fishes of Andamans, P. Z. S. 1870, p. 681 (not synonym.)

B. vi, D. $7/_{1} \mid \frac{1}{9-11}$, P. 13, V. 1/5, A. $\frac{3}{9-10}$, C. 15, L. l. 30-33, L. tr. 4/9, Vert. 9/15.

Length of head about 1/4, of caudal 2/9, height of body $3\frac{1}{4}$ to 2/7 of the total length. *Eyes*—diameter 1/3 to 2/7 of length of head, 1/2 a diameter from end of snout, and also apart. Dorsal and anal profiles about equally convex: lower jaw the longer, its cleft very oblique, so that when closed it forms a portion of the anterior profile. The maxilla reaches to below the first third of the orbit. Preorbital rather strongly serrated, the serratures being directed downwards and slightly backwards. Vertical limb of preopercle entire, its inferior having its double edge serrated, two or three coarser teeth being at the angle: lower margin of interopercle entire. Two or three small and very blunt denticulations at the posterior superior angle of the orbit and in a line between it and the posterior-superior angle of the opercle. *Teeth*—villiform in the jaws, in a single Λ-shaped row in the vomer, and also present on the palatines: tongue usually with a narrow band along its centre. *Fins*—dorsal spines strong, transversely lineated, giving a serrated appearance to the second, which is the longest, and equal to the length of the head behind the front margin of the orbit, or even slightly longer: the ventral does not extend to the anal: second anal spine the strongest and nearly as long as the third, which almost equals the third of the dorsal: caudal deeply forked, upper lobe usually the longer. *Lateral-line*—continuous. *Pseudobranchiæ*—well developed. *Colours*—silvery, with purplish reflections: a bright silvery line from the eye to the caudal fin: interspinous membrane between the second and third dorsal spines dark.

In examining six specimens of this fish, the following were the proportions of the highest dorsal spine as compared with the length of the body.

No.	total length (inches)	without caudal fin (inches)	dorsal spine (inches)	of length of body
No 1	3 [illegible]	2 4/10	[illegible]	3 [illegible]
2	3 [illegible]	2 [illegible]	[illegible]	3 [illegible]
3	3 [illegible]	2 [illegible]	[illegible]	3 [illegible]
4	4	3 [illegible]	[illegible]	3 [illegible]
5	4 [illegible]	3 [illegible]	[illegible]	3 [illegible]
6	[illegible]	3 [illegible]	[illegible]	4 [illegible]

The specimens in the British Museum, marked *A. Batjanensis*, Bleeker, have the preorbital serrated and not entire as stated in the Catalogue (Vol. i, p. 225), and otherwise closely resemble this species.

Habitat.—This common species extends from the Red Sea through those of India to North Australia: it ascends rivers and estuaries, attaining to six inches in length.

6. Ambassis nalua, Plate XV, fig. 4.

Chanda nalua, Ham. Buch. Fish. Ganges, pp. 107, 371, pl. 6. f. 36; Cantor, Catal. p. 6.?

Ambassis nalua, Cuv. and Val. ii, p. 182; Bleeker, Perc. p. 29, and Ambassis, p. 94; Günther, Catal. i. p. 225.

Ambassis Commersonii, Kner, Novara Fische, p. 41.

Kyoung-nga-seh, Burm.

B. vi, D. 7/[illegible], P. 15, V. 1/5, A. [illegible], C. 15, L. l. 26-28, L. tr. 3/12.

Length of head 1/4, of caudal 1/4, height of body 2/5 of the total length. *Eyes*—diameter 2/5 of length of head, nearly 1/2 a diameter from end of snout, and 1 apart. A great rise in the dorsal profile from the snout to the commencement of the dorsal fin, but with a concavity over the eyes: lower jaw the longer: cleft of mouth very oblique. The maxilla reaches to below the middle of the orbit. Preorbital rather strongly serrated on both its inferior and superior borders: two short spines directed backwards at the posterior superior angle of the orbit. Vertical limb of preopercle entire, except a few serrations just above the angle, its double edge on its horizontal border strongly serrated, also the posterior half of the lower border of the interopercle. *Teeth*—villiform in jaws, vomer, and palate, a narrow band of teeth along the middle of the tongue. *Fins*—dorsal spines strong, the second the longest and equal to the length of the head behind the front edge of the orbit: the ventral does not quite reach to the anal: the pectoral extends to above the anal spines, the second and third of the latter of the same length, and almost equal to the third of the dorsal fin: caudal deeply forked. *Lateral-line*—continuous. *Pseudobranchiæ*—present. *Colours*—silvery, with a burnished lateral band: interspinous membrane dark between the second and third dorsal spines: a dark longitudinal band along either caudal lobe.

Cantor remarks, as observed by M. M. Cuvier and Valenciennes, that this species differs from *Lutjanus gymnocephalus*, Lacép. (syn. *Sciæna safgha*, Forsk.? *Centropomus ambassis*, Lacép. *Ambassis Commersonii*, Cuv. and Val.) by its comparatively shorter head, blunter muzzle and greater depth of the body (p. 6). Also in this species the interopercle is serrated, whilst it is entire in the *Ambassis Commersonii*.*

Habitat.—Calcutta in fresh and brackish water: Malabar coast and Andamans to the Malay Archipelago.

7. Ambassis interrupta, Plate XV, fig. 5.

Bleeker, Ceram, ii, p. 696, Atl. Ich. Perc. t. lxx, f. 5, and Ambassis, p. 97: Günther, Catal. i, p. 226.

Ambassis macracanthus, Day, Proc. Zool. Soc. 1870, p. 681.

B. vi, D. 7/[illegible], P. 13, V. 1/5, A. [illegible], C. 18, L. l. 28, L. tr. 6/8.

Length of head 2/7, of caudal 2/7, height of body 2/5 of the total length. *Eyes*—diameter 2/5 of length of head, 1/2 a diameter from end of snout, and 3/4 of a diameter apart. Lower jaw the longer: cleft of mouth oblique. The maxilla reaches to below the front edge of the orbit. Preorbital with both its upper and lower edges serrated. Anterior edge of orbit serrated and two spines at its posterior-superior angle. Vertical limb of preopercle entire, the double edge of its horizontal limb serrated: interopercle with four denticulations at its angle. *Teeth*—villiform in jaws, vomer and palate. *Fins*—second dorsal spine nearly half the length of the body in the adult; the ventral does not extend to the anal fin: third anal spine slightly the longest:

* In some rare cases the posterior inferior angle of the interopercle has 2 or 3 very badly marked serrations in *A. Commersonii*.

caudal forked. *Scales*—a row along the bases of the dorsal and anal fins: two rows on the suborbitals. *Lateral-line*—interrupted. *Colours*—silvery with a narrow lateral band: second spine of the dorsal bright orange, the membrane between it and the third black: a dark longitudinal band along either caudal lobe.

As in other species of this genus, the comparative length of the highest dorsal spine varies with age, and in examining the 5 specimens in the British Museum, I find the following proportions exist.

Total length	$2\frac{3}{10}$ inches :	of body	2 inches :	highest dorsal spine	7/10 of an inch	or nearly	1/3 of length of body.
"	$2\frac{7}{10}$ " :	"	2 " :	" "	8/10	" " "	$2\frac{1}{2}$ " "
"	3 " :	"	$2\frac{3}{10}$ " :	" "	8/10	" " "	$2\frac{3}{4}$ " "
"	$3\frac{3}{10}$ " :	"	$2\frac{5}{10}$ " :	" "	9/10	" " "	$2\frac{3}{4}$ " "
"	$3\frac{3}{10}$ " :	"	$2\frac{5}{10}$ " :	" "	8/10	" " "	$2\frac{3}{4}$ " "

But the comparative length of the same spine in my specimen from the Andamans is still greater:

Total length $1\frac{8}{10}$ inches: of body $1\frac{5}{10}$ inches: highest dorsal spine $\frac{7}{10}$ or nearly 1/2 of body.

Habitat.—Sea at the Andamans and Batavia: the specimen which is figured was taken at the Andamans, and is nearly 2 inches in length.

8. Ambassis Dayi, Plate XV, fig. 7.

? *Ambassis Malabaricus*, (C. & V.) Jerdon, Madr. Journ. Lit. & Science, 1849, No. xv, p. 140.
Ambassis nalua, Day, Fish. Malabar, p. 15, (not H. Buch.)
Ambassis Dayi, Bleeker, Nat. Verh. d. Holland. Maats. d. Weten. 3de Verz. Deel II, No. 2, 1874, p. 95.
B. vi, D. $7\,|\,\frac{1}{11}$, P. 16, V. 1/5, A. $\frac{3}{10}$, C. 16, L. l. 30, L. tr. 4/—.

Length of head 2/7, of caudal about 4/17, height of body 1/3 of the total length. *Eyes*—diameter 1/4 to 2/9 of length of head, 3/4 to 1 diameter from end of snout, and also apart. Snout pointed, lower jaw the longer, cleft not very oblique. The maxilla reaches to below the middle of the orbit. Preorbital serrated along its lower border, and one spine at its anterior-superior angle. Vertical limb of preopercle with some very minute serrations in the largest specimen, its lower limb serrated along both edges: interopercle serrated in its posterior half: subopercle entire. One spine at the posterior-superior angle of the orbit. *Teeth*—villiform, with a rather stronger outer row in the upper jaw. *Fins*—the following is the comparative height of the second dorsal spine to that of the body in two specimens:—

No. 1, total length, $1\frac{8}{10}$ inches: without caudal fin $1\frac{4}{10}$ inches: dorsal spine $\frac{4}{10}$ inches or $3\frac{1}{2}$ in length of body.
" 2, " " 7 " " " " $5\frac{4}{10}$ " " " $1\frac{1}{10}$ " " $4\frac{3}{4}$ " " "

The ventral reaches two-thirds of the distance to the base of the anal: the second and third anal spines of about equal length even in the young, but the second is the stronger: caudal deeply forked. *Lateral-line*—continuous. *Colours*—silvery glossed with purple, a broad lateral burnished band: interspinous membrane between the second and third dorsal spines dark: second dorsal, anal, and caudal stained dark at their edges.

The serrated interopercle and pointed snout at once show its distinction from *A. Commersonii* and *A. nalua*.

This may be Jerdon's *A. Malabaricus* (C. V.) of which he observes—"Height not a third of its length. Fin rays D. $7\,|\,\frac{1}{11}$, A. $\frac{3}{9}$ &c. 5 inches long;" but as this short definition is equally applicable to three or four other species found in Malabar, and the type appears to have been lost, it becomes impossible to be certain. Bleeker *l.c.* observed on this species differing from *A. nalua*.

Habitat.—Malabar coast of India, attaining at least 7 inches in length.

9. Ambassis gymnocephalus, Plate XV, fig. 6.

Lutjanus gymnocephalus, Lacép. iii, t. 23, f. 3, and iv, p. 216.
Priopis argyrozona, (K. & v. H.) Cuv. & Val. vi, p. 503.
Ambassis Dussumieri, Cuv. and Val. ii, p. 181, vi, p. 503, and ix, p. 431; Quoy and Gaim. Voy. Astrol. Poiss. p. 651, pl. i, f. 3; Bleeker, Perc. p. 30; Günther, Catal. i, p. 225; Day, Fish. Malabar, p. 16; Kner, Novara Fische, p. 41.
Chanda Dussumieri, Cantor, Catal. p. 6.
Ambassis Vachelli, Peters. Mon. ber. Preuss. Akad. Wiss. 1868, p. 255, (not Richards.)
Ambassis gymnocephalus, Bleeker, Ambassis, p. 99.
Chandee, Ooriah.
B. vi, D. $7/\,|\,\frac{1}{9-10}$, P. 15, V. 1/5, A. $\frac{3}{9-10}$, C. 17, L. l. 27-29, L. tr. 3/8.

Length of head 2/9 to 1/4, of caudal 2/7 to 1/4, height of body 2/7 of the total length. *Eyes*—diameter dependant on age, in the young 2/5, in the adult nearly 1/3 of the length of the head, 1/2 a diameter from the end of snout, and also apart. Lower jaw the longer. The maxilla reaches to below the front edge of the orbit. Preorbital with six or seven denticulations directed downwards and backwards on anterior-inferior edge, and a few serrations on its posterior: the double edge on the inferior limb of the preopercle finely serrated, its vertical limb entire. Sub- and inter-opercles entire. Two or three strong spines directed backwards at the posterior-superior angle of the orbit, and another rather larger posterior to them, occasionally a small spine on the shoulder just before the commencement of the lateral line. *Teeth*—a single row of fine ones in jaws, vomer, and palate: a band along the centre of the tongue. *Fins*—dorsal spines strong, the second being nearly or quite as high as the third, or in a few cases a little longer, the longest is generally two-thirds the height of the body below it, and the second is very minutely striated on its posterior edge, as is also the spine of the second dorsal, the other spines are striated all across: the ventral reaches about two-thirds of the distance to the anal: the third anal spine is longer but not quite so strong as the second, its length equals that of the fourth of the dorsal fin: caudal deeply forked, its upper lobe slightly the longer. *Scales*—two rows on the suborbital ring of bones, the lower of which is much the deeper. *Lateral-line*—interrupted after about from the eighth to the twelfth scale, in some specimens it ceases entirely. *Pseudobranchiæ*—well developed. *Colours*—silvery with a bright longitudinal lateral band, some brown spots on the upper third of the body in its front half: blackish between its second and third dorsal spines, also a black edge to the caudal.

In examining a large number of these fish the first thing that strikes one's attention is the variation in the length of the second and third dorsal spines, sometimes one, sometimes the other being the longer. Not only do they vary between themselves, but likewise as regards their comparative length to that of the remainder of the body. The undermentioned specimens are taken at random from upwards of fifty in my collection.

		inches.		inch.			inch.		
No. 1.	total length	1[illegible],	exclusive of tail	1:	height of dorsal spine		3/10:	or $3\frac{1}{4}$	in length of body, excluding the caudal fin.
" 2.	"	2	"	1[illegible]:	"	"	4/10:	" $3\frac{3}{4}$	" " "
" 3.	"	2[illegible]	"	1[illegible]:	"	"	4/10:	" 1/4	" " "
" 4.	"	2[illegible]	"	1[illegible]:	"	"	4/10:	" $4\frac{1}{2}$	" " "
" 5.	"	2[illegible]	"	1[illegible]:	"	"	4/10:	" $4\frac{1}{4}$	" " " "
" 6.	"	2[illegible]	"	1[illegible]:	"	"	4/10:	" $4\frac{1}{2}$	" " " "
" 7.	"	2[illegible]	"	2[illegible]:	"	"	5/10:	" $4\frac{1}{2}$	" " " "
" 8.	"	2[illegible]	"	2[illegible]:	"	"	5/10:	" $4\frac{3}{4}$	" " " "
" 9.	"	2[illegible]	"	2[illegible]:	"	"	5/10:	" $4\frac{1}{2}$	" " " "
" 10.	"	3	"	2[illegible]:	"	"	4/10:	" $5\frac{1}{4}$	" " " "

The foregoing distinctly shows how the comparative length of the dorsal spines to that of the remainder of the body decreases with age, and renders it probable that *Ambassis Buruensis*, Bleeker (Boeroe, p. 396), is very closely allied to this species.

Habitat—East coast of Africa, seas of India to the Malay Archipelago and China: it attains at least 4 inches in length. Although generally captured in the sea or saline backwaters, I obtained a specimen from the fresh water in the Cochin State several miles inland.

10 **Ambassis urotænia**, Plate XV, fig. 8.

Bleeker, Amb. and Comm. p. 257; Günther, Catal. i, p. 224.
? *Ambassis denticulata*, Klunz. Verh. z. b. Ges. in Wien, 1870, p. 719.

B. vi, D. $7|\frac{1}{9}$-$\frac{1}{10}$, P. 13, V. 1/5, A. $\frac{3}{9}$-$\frac{3}{10}$, C. 18, L. l. 27-28, L. tr. 3-4/10.

Length of head 1/5, of caudal 1/4, height of body 4/13 of the total length. *Eyes*—diameter 2/5 of length of head, 1/2 a diameter from end of snout, and 3/4 apart. Lower jaw the longer: cleft of mouth very oblique. The maxilla reaches to below the front edge of the orbit. Preorbital with seven sharp teeth along its inferior edge: a spine at the posterior-superior angle of the orbit. Vertical limb of preopercle entire except two serrations just above its angle; its horizontal double edge serrated, the lower the most coarsely so: sub- and inter-opercles entire. *Teeth*—villiform in jaws, vomer, and palate: a small central band at the root of the tongue. *Fins*—second spine of the dorsal longest and equal to one quarter or two-ninths of the total length, and rather above half the height of the body below it: ventral reaches two-thirds of the way to the anal fin: third anal spine usually slightly the longest but not equalling the longest of the dorsal. *Scales*—a single row along the suborbital ring of bones. *Lateral-line*—curves downwards under the middle of the soft dorsal, but in an interrupted or semi-interrupted manner. *Colours*—Silvery with a burnished lateral band: the interspinous membrane between the second and third dorsal spines black: a dark longitudinal band along either lobe of the caudal.

Dr. Günther observes, P.Z.S. 1871, p. 655, that *Ambassis miops*, Günther, differs from *A. urotænia*, Bleeker, by the smaller size of the eye, and by the lateral-line being continuous. The diameter of the eye in *A. urotænia* is equal to the length of the postorbital portion of the head. In *A. miops* the lateral-line forms a distinct and continuous curve from opposite the end of the dorsal fins, whilst there are two rows of scales along the suborbitals.

Habitat,—Seychelles, Andamans, and the Malay Archipelago. It closely resembles the *A. gymnocephalus*, but its lateral-line is entire: it has only one row of scales along the suborbitals and the comparative height of its body differs. It appears to be common at the Andamans.*

* **Bogota infuscata.**

Blyth. J.A.S. of Bengal. 1860, p. 139; Day, Proc. Zool. Soc. 1869, p. 515.
D. $10|\frac{1}{13}$, V. 1/5, A. 3/8, C. 17.

Preopercle strongly serrated with large teeth at its angle. A spine directed backwards, apparently on the subopercle. A long spine on the opercle. Preorbital entire. Lower jaw the longer. *Teeth*—in jaws villiform. *Fins*—second anal spine the longest. *Scales*—none now visible. *Colours*—brownish-black, except the fins, which are of a dirty yellowish white.

The specimen is half an inch long and in a very bad condition. The occiput is broken across: in fact it is now too damaged to admit of a complete description. One thing is evident, that it does not belong to the genus *Ambassis*, it may be the fry of a species of *Priacanthus*. For these reasons I refer to it in a note.

Blyth described it thus: "a minute species (if adult) $\frac{7}{10}$ in. long by $1\frac{1}{2}$ in. depth, minus the fins: with the tail much less forked

Genus, 11—Apogon, *Lacép.*

Amia, Gronovius: *Apogonichthys*, Bleeker: *Monoprion*, Poey: *Mionorus*, Krefft: *Archamia*, *Lepidamia*, and *Glossamia*, Gill.

Branchiostegals seven: pseudobranchiæ present, usually well developed. Opercle not spinate. Preopercle with a double edge, either or both of which may be serrated, crenulated, or entire. Teeth villiform in the jaws, vomer, and palatines, without canines: tongue smooth. Two separate dorsal fins, the first with six or seven spines; the anal with two. Lateral-line distinct and entire. Scales ctenoid, as a rule large and deciduous, but occasionally they are rather small. Cæcal appendages when present few.

Geographical distribution.—From the Red Sea and East coast of Africa, through the seas of India and Malay Archipelago to Australia, and even beyond. These small fishes are marine, and are numerous in sheltered spots as inside harbours, and some have been captured at the mouth or even a short distance up tidal rivers and backwaters. In the Indian region they are most numerous off the Sind and Bombay coasts, and Andaman islands.

Uses.—Although small, they are eaten fresh, dried, or salted, by the natives of India.

The fishes of this Genus, after having been primarily divided in accordance with the number of spines in the first dorsal fin, have undergone various subdivisions, the most popular of which seems to be as regards their colours. The longitudinally or transversely banded ones, those which possess or are deficient in the caudal blotch, have been separated on several plans, and although such may possess advantages they appear to be counterbalanced by marks sometimes disappearing or perhaps never having existed in the specimen. Consequently colour will still be omitted from indicating the position of any species, and the number of spines, rays, and scales employed for this purpose. It seems also questionable whether any considerable value can be placed upon the serrations about the bones of the head, especially of the orbits, as such appear to be more distinct in some specimens than in others, and may vary with age.

SYNOPSIS OF SPECIES.

1. *Apogon multitæniatus*, D. 7/$\frac{1}{9}$, A. $\frac{2}{8}$, L. l. 38. Outer edge only of preopercle serrated. Pinkish, with violet lines, along the body: fins scarlet, the vertical ones having black borders. Red Sea, coasts of India.

2. *Apogon kalosoma*, D. 7/$\frac{1}{9}$, A. $\frac{2}{8}$, L. l. 35-36. Outer edge only of preopercle serrated. Reddish, with a dark band from the snout to the end of the centre of the caudal fin: another above it: a black spot at the base of the tail: a dark mark on first dorsal fin, a band along the base of the second dorsal. Seas of India to the Malay Archipelago.

3. *Apogon nigricans*, D. 7/$\frac{1}{9}$, A. $\frac{2}{8-9}$, L. l. 25-26. Outer edge of preopercle and shoulder serrated. Greyish, with dark vertical bands and spots on the head. Madras.

4. *Apogon frenatus*, D. 7/$\frac{1}{9}$, A. $\frac{2}{8}$, L. l. 27-28. Both edges of preopercle serrated, also the lower edge of the orbit. Three or four longitudinal bands along the body: a black spot sometimes present at the base of the caudal fin: a basal band along both soft dorsal and anal. Seas of India to the Malay Archipelago and beyond.

5. *Apogon tæniatus*, D. 7/$\frac{1}{9}$, A. $\frac{2}{8}$, L. l. 27. Outer edge of preopercle and shoulder bone serrated. Reddish brown: two vertical dark bands and a dark mark at the base of caudal fin. Red Sea to Madras.

6. *Apogon endekatænia*, D. 7/$\frac{1}{9}$, A. $\frac{2}{8}$, L. l. 26. Outer edge of preopercle, lower edge of orbit and shoulder serrated. A dark median and four or five lateral bands, a dark spot at the base of the caudal fin. Seas of India to the Malay Archipelago.

7. *Apogon quadrifasciatus*, D. 7/$\frac{1}{9}$, A. $\frac{2}{8}$, L. l. 26. Outer edge of preopercle and lower edge of orbit serrated. No median band: two along either side of the body. Seas of India to the Malay Archipelago.

8. *Apogon fasciatus*, D. 7/$\frac{1}{9}$, A. $\frac{2}{8}$, L. l. 25. Outer edge of preopercle and shoulder serrated. Four longitudinal bands along the body, one along soft dorsal and anal fins. Seas of India to the Malay Archipelago and beyond.

9. *Apogon Savayensis*, D. 7/$\frac{1}{9}$, A. $\frac{2}{8}$, L. l. 26. Outer edge of preopercle serrated. Olive, with 4 or 5 narrow vertical bands on the anterior half of the body: a dark band over the upper half of the free portion of the tail: a streak from the eye to the angle of the preopercle: numerous brown spots on the head. Coasts of Africa, India, and beyond.

10. *Apogon nigripinnis*, D. 7/$\frac{1}{9}$, A. $\frac{2}{8}$, L. l. 26. Outer edge of preopercle and shoulder bone serrated. Greyish, with vertical bands over the body and free portion of the tail. Neither spots nor streaks on the head. Vertical fins black, except the caudal which is yellow, with a dark edge. Seas of India.

11. *Apogon Wassinki*, D. 7/$\frac{1}{9}$, A. $\frac{2}{8}$, L. l. 25-26. Outer edge of preopercle serrated. Golden, with a black head, four white longitudinal bands: fins orange. Andamans to the Malay Archipelago.

12. *Apogon aureus*, D. 7/$\frac{1}{9}$, A. $\frac{2}{8}$, L. l. 25-26. Outer edge of preopercle serrated. Pinkish, with a broad black band over the free portion of the tail: vertical fins reddish, with a narrow black border. Red Sea, seas of India to the Malay Archipelago.

than in B. nama (B.H.) Bleeker; and of a dusky or infuscated hue, having silvery gill-covers and a greenish silvery stripe on each side: fins paler than the body, with a blackish tinge on the anterior half of the first dorsal.

D. 10—1-10?—A. 3-8?

One specimen only from the Matla. Presented by Major W. S. Sherwill."

13. *Apogon bifasciatus*, D. 7/$\frac{1}{9}$, A. $\frac{2}{8}$, L. l. 25. Outer edge of preopercle serrated. Grey, with two dark vertical bands: a black spot at the root of the caudal: fins dark. Red Sea, through those of India to the Malay Archipelago, and beyond.

14. *Apogon glaga*, D. 7/$\frac{1}{9}$, A. $\frac{2}{8}$, L. l. 24. Lower limb of preopercle crenulated. Yellowish-green above, becoming redder on the abdomen: scales dotted at their edges, with a pearly spot in their centres forming three light stripes: a dark interorbital band: upper half of first dorsal and edges of second dorsal and caudal black. Seas of India to the Malay Archipelago.

15. *Apogon auritus*, D. 7/$\frac{1}{9}$, A. $\frac{2}{8}$, L. l. 23. Preopercle entire. Spotted and marbled with brown: a circular black spot on the opercle surrounded by a narrow white ring. Red Sea, through seas of India.

16. *Apogon Ellioti*, D. 7/$\frac{1}{9}$, A. $\frac{2}{8}$, L. l. 26. Outer edge of preopercle and lower edge of orbit serrated. Golden: upper half of first dorsal black, a similar coloured band along the centre of the second dorsal and anal: soft dorsal and anal with black edges. East coast of Africa, seas of India to Japan.

17. *Apogon maculosus*, D. 7/$\frac{1}{9}$, A. $\frac{2}{8}$. Brown, with four rows of darker spots along either side: fins brown, dotted with black. Seas of India.

18. *Apogon macropterus*, D. 6/$\frac{1}{9}$, A. $\frac{2}{8-9}$, L. l. 22-26. Outer edge of preopercle serrated. White, with pinkish reflections: a black spot at the root of the tail. Seas of India to the Malay Archipelago.

19. *Apogon Sangiensis*, D. 6/$\frac{1}{9}$, A. $\frac{2}{8}$, L. l. 25. Outer edge of preopercle serrated. Golden tinged with red: a wide band from the snout through the eye to a little below the shoulder: a spot on the side of the free portion of the tail. Upper half of first dorsal black. Andamans to the Malay Archipelago.

20. *Apogon hyalosoma*, D. 6/$\frac{1}{9}$, A. $\frac{2}{8}$, L. l. 24-25. Outer edge of preopercle serrated. Olive, with a spot on either side of the tail: fins grey, blackish between the second and third dorsal spines. Seas of India to the Malay Archipelago.

21. *Apogon orbicularis*, D. 6/$\frac{1}{9}$, A. $\frac{2}{8}$, L. l. 22. Outer edge of preopercle and shoulder bone serrated. Olive-brown, a dark zone round the body from in front of the dorsal fin to behind the ventrals: head with black spots: ventrals nearly black. Andamans, to the Malay Archipelago and beyond.

22. *Apogon Ceramensis*, D. 6/$\frac{1}{9}$, A. $\frac{2}{8}$, L. l. 21. Outer edge of preopercle serrated. Greenish-brown, with some dark spots on the head: a dark band from the eye to the root of the caudal fin, where it ends in a black spot. Black between the second and third dorsal spines. Nicobars to the Malay Archipelago.

1. Apogon multitæniatus, Plate XVI, fig. 1.

Apogon multitæniatus, (Ehren.) Cuv. and Val. ii, p. 159; Klunz. Fische d. Roth. Meeres, Verh. z. b. Ges. Wien, 1870, p. 45, (not Bleeker).

B. vii, D. 7/$\frac{1}{9}$, P. 15, V. 1/5, A. $\frac{2}{8}$, C. 17, L. l. 37-38, L. tr. $3\frac{1}{2}$/12.

Length of head 3/10, of caudal 2/11, height of body 2/7 of the total length. *Eyes*—diameter 2/7 of length of head, 3/4 of a diameter from end of snout, and 4/5 of a diameter apart. Jaws of about equal length, the maxilla reaches to rather behind the middle of the orbit. The outer edge of both the vertical and horizontal limbs of the preopercle finely and nearly evenly serrated: shoulder bone and edges of orbit entire: a small flat opercular spine. *Teeth*—villiform in jaws, vomer, and palate. *Fins*—dorsal spines stout, the third and fourth are the highest, and equal in length to the postorbital portion of the head, or $2\frac{1}{4}$ in the height of the body; second dorsal nearly two-thirds as high as the body, its upper edge nearly straight: pectoral rounded, reaching to above the anal spines: ventral not reaching the anal, the rayed portion of which latter fin equals in height that of the second dorsal: caudal slightly emarginate. *Lateral-line*—tubes very arborescent. *Pseudobranchiæ*—well developed. Free portion of tail about as high at its base as it is long. *Colours*—of a slaty tinge along the back, becoming reddish on the head, sides, and abdomen: violet lines along the body, narrower than the ground colour, between the rows of scales, but which are most apparent after death. Fins, dorsal scarlet, black along its base, between the last two spines, and in its upper three-fourths: second dorsal scarlet, with a light edge and black tip: caudal scarlet, also with a light edge and black tip: pectoral and ventral scarlet: anal as second dorsal. Eyes scarlet in their anterior halves, with some black markings.

Dr. Bleeker having been good enough to compare my figure of this species with *A. Noordzieki*, observes that it appears to be distinct. The latter has the head more pointed, the profile from the snout to the dorsal a little concave, the rostro-ventral one less concave, and the cleft of the mouth less oblique.

Habitat.—One specimen $5\frac{3}{4}$ inches in length was obtained in Madras, April 3rd, 1867: and two more in Bombay, April, 1874, one of which latter is figured. This is the species of which Jerdon remarks (M. J. L. and S. 1851, p. 129): "*Cheilodipterus*, a species apparently belonging to this genus was once brought me without a name—its colours were reddish, with longitudinal brown lines, fins bright pink, edged with blackish. D. 6, 1-9, A. 2-8." A figure exists amongst Sir W. Elliot's drawings.

2. Apogon kalosoma, Plate XVI, fig. 2.

Bleeker, Banka, p. 418; Günther, Catal. i, p. 240.
Lepidamia kalosoma, Gill, Catal. Fish. Nat. Hist. Soc. Phil. 1863, p. 81.
Amia kalosoma, Bleeker, Apogonini, p. 16.

B. vii, D. 7/$\frac{1}{9}$, P. 15, V. 1/5, A. $\frac{2}{8}$, C. 17, L. l. 35-36, L. tr. 3/13.

Length of head 2/7, of caudal 1/5, height of body 2/7 of the total length. *Eyes*—diameter $2\frac{1}{2}$ to $2\frac{3}{4}$ in the length of head, 1/2 a diameter from end of snout, and also apart. Jaws of about equal length, or the lower slightly the longer: the maxilla reaches to below the middle of the orbit. Preopercle having both its vertical and horizontal limbs finely and evenly serrated along their outer edges: no serrations on the shoulder bones. *Teeth*—villiform in the jaws, vomer, and palate. *Fins*—dorsal spines of moderate strength, the two first short, the third and fourth of nearly the same height and equal to half the length of the head, first spine of second dorsal two-thirds as high as the rays, and equalling the longest in the first dorsal fin: the pectoral reaches to over the anal spines: the caudal slightly emarginate. *Lateral-line*—tubes well developed, with small lateral branches. *Colours*—reddish, more especially over the head: a dark band proceeds from above the eye and passes to the upper edge of the free portion of the tail: a second from the snout goes through the eye to the base of the caudal fin where there exists a large black spot, it is subsequently continued along the middle of the caudal fin: a third band passes from the lower edge of the eye to the end of the base of the anal fin. Fins reddish, the front half of the first dorsal and the upper portion of its last half black, the remainder scarlet. A black band along the base of the second dorsal and anal: second dorsal, anal, and caudal, scarlet with black tips.

Habitat.—Madras to the Malay Archipelago. The specimen figured was captured at Madras, April 3rd, 1867.

3. **Apogon nigricans**, Plate XVI, fig. 3.

B. vii, D. 7/$\frac{1}{9}$, P. 13, V. 1/5, A. $\frac{2}{8-9}$, C. 17, L. l. 25-26, L. tr. 2/7.

Length of head $3\frac{1}{4}$, of caudal 1/4 to 2/9, height of body $3\frac{1}{4}$ in the total length. *Eyes*—diameter 1/3 of length of head, 1 diameter from end of snout, and 3/4 of a diameter apart. Dorsal profile more convex than that of the abdomen. Lower jaw slightly the longer: the maxilla reaches to below the middle of the orbit. Both the vertical and horizontal limbs of the preopercle finely serrated on their outer edges, shoulder also serrated, orbit entire. *Teeth*—villiform in jaws, vomer, and palate. *Fins*—dorsal spines rather weak, the first two short, the third nearly as long as the fourth, which is rather more than half as long as the head. The spine of the second dorsal much higher than the third of the first dorsal and the rays much more elevated than the spine, being equal to 4/5 of the height of the body: pectoral and ventral both reach as far as the anal, the spine of which is half as high as the body, and the rays as long as those of the dorsal: caudal notched. Free portion of tail longer than it is high at its base. *Lateral-line*—nearly straight, tubes laterally expanded at their bases. *Colours*—greyish shot with yellow, several badly marked vertical dark bands narrower than the ground colour exist on the body and over the free portion of the tail. Head covered with dark brown spots, some of which have a light centre: opercles with purplish reflections: no streaks on the jaws or head. The whole of the body finely spotted with brown. Vertical fins black: pectoral with a dark base.

Habitat.—Madras.

4. **Apogon frenatus**, Plate XVI, fig. 4.

Val. Nouv. Ann. Mus. Hist. Nat. 1832, p. 57, pl. iv, f. 4: Bleeker, Amboina, p. 25, Günther, Catal. i, p. 241, and Fische d. Sudsee, p. 19, pl. xix, f. A.

Apogon vittiger, Bennett, Proc. Zool. Soc. 1833, p. 32.

Apogon melanorhynchos, Bleeker, Amb. and Ceram. p. 255, and l. c. p. 26 (ex parte.)

Amia frenata, Bleeker, Atl. Ich. Perc. t. lxiv, fig. 2, and Apogonini, p. 42.

B. vii, D. 7/$\frac{1}{9}$, P. 16, V. 1/5, A. $\frac{2}{8}$, C. 17, L. l. 27-28, L. tr. 2/7.

Length of head 3/10, of caudal 1/5, height of body 2/7 of the total length. *Eyes*—diameter 1/3 of length of head, 1/2 a diameter from end of snout, and 3/4 of a diameter apart. Jaws of about equal length. The maxilla reaches to below the last third of the orbit. The outer edge of the vertical and horizontal limbs of the preopercle serrated, its intramarginal crest likewise more or less serrated, also some serrations along the lower edge of the orbit: none on the shoulder: a small opercular spine. *Teeth*—villiform in jaws, vomer, and palate. *Fins*—first and second dorsal spines short, the third nearly as long as the fourth which is the highest in the fin, and equals the length of the postorbital portion of the head. Pectoral nearly as long as the head excluding the snout: the ventral reaches two-thirds of the distance to the anal: caudal notched, upper lobe slightly the longer. *Lateral-line*—with well developed tubes having a small enlargement on either side near the base of each tube, which becomes arborescent in the adult. Free portion of the tail longer than it is high at its commencement. *Colours*—reddish, a dark band passes from the eye to the middle of the caudal fin: a narrower one from the upper edge of the orbit to the upper part of the caudal on which it is lost near its base: a third from below the eye to the lower portion of the caudal. A black band along the bases of the second dorsal and anal: dorsal, caudal, ventral, and anal black tipped. A black spot may be present at the base of the caudal fin.

Some specimens of this last variety were shown to me at the British Museum, as *A. quadrifasciatus*, but they are not identical with Cuv. and Val. species; the type specimen of this latter fish ($3\frac{1}{10}$ inches long), from Pondicherry, has only the free border of the preopercle serrated, its intramarginal crest being smooth. Two other specimens are marked by Valenciennes as *A. quadrifasciatus* from Bourbon, and are similar to the Pondicherry one.

Pristipogon frenatus, (C.V.) Klunz. Fische R. M. Verh. z. b. Ges. Wien, 1870, p. 715, is considered by Günther to be this species; by Bleeker to be *Amia* or *Apogon melanorhynchus*, Blkr. (ex parte), being distinguished from *A. frenatus* by its higher body ($3\frac{3}{4}$ to 1/4 in the total length) a serrated shoulder bone, a smooth intramarginal edge to the preopercle, and a black spot at the base of the caudal fin, &c.

Habitat.—Mauritius, seas of India to the Malay Archipelago and beyond.

5. Apogon tæniatus, Plate VIII, fig. 4.

? *Apogon tæniatus*, (Ehrenb.) Cuv. and Val. ii, p. 159; Rüpp. Atl. p. 48, and N. W. Fische, p. 87; Günther, Catal. i, p. 234.

Apogon tæniatus, Klunz. Fische R. M. Verh. z. b. Ges. Wien, 1870, p. 44.

B. vii, D. $7/\frac{1}{9}$, P. 15, V. 1/5, A. $\frac{2}{8}$, C. 17, L. l. 27, L. tr. 2/8.

Length of head $3\frac{1}{4}$, of caudal 2/9, height of body $3\frac{1}{4}$ in the total length. *Eyes*—diameter 2/7 of length of head, nearly one diameter from end of snout, and 3/4 of a diameter apart. Jaws of equal length: the maxilla reaches to below the last third of the eye. The outer edge of both the vertical and horizontal limbs of the preopercle, and the shoulder bone serrated; orbit entire. A flat opercular spine. *Teeth*—villiform in jaws, vomer, and palate. *Fins*—first dorsal spines rather strong, the fourth being the longest and equal to $2\frac{1}{4}$ in the height of the body: soft dorsal much higher than the spinous, being equal to 3/5 of the height of the body, its upper edge as well as the outer one of the anal slightly rounded: last dorsal and anal rays divided to their bases. Pectoral as long as the head behind the middle of the eye: ventral slightly longer and reaching the anal: caudal forked. *Lateral-line*—tubes arborescent, most distinctly so anteriorly. Free portion of tail rather longer than it is high at its base. *Colours*—reddish-brown shot with gold, having a black band from the bases of the first three dorsal spines to the axil of the pectoral fin: a second from the middle of the second dorsal to the commencement of the anal fin: a small black spot near the end of the lateral-line: inner third of ventral nearly black: a narrow dark band across the soft dorsal fin.

This species is evidently closely allied to *A. nigripinnis*.

The British Museum has received a specimen of this fish determined as above by Dr. Klunzinger. In Cuv. and Val. it is stated to be brownish, with five longitudinal bands. Dr. Klunzinger considers it a variety of *bifasciatus*, but the difference between the first dorsal fins in the two has led me to rather leave them as distinct species.

Habitat.—Red Sea and Madras, from whence the specimen figured (life size) was obtained.

6. Apogon endekatænia, Plate XVI, fig. 7.

Apogon endekatænia, Bleeker, Banka, p. 449.

Apogon novemfasciatus, Temm. and Schleg. Fauna Japon. Poiss. p. 2, t. ii, f. 2.

Apogon Schlegeli, Bleeker, Japan, p. 55.

Apogon fasciatus, Günther, Catal. i, p. 241; Kner, Novara Fische, p. 43; Klunz. Fische R. M. Verh. z. b. Ges. Wien, 1870, p. 713.

Amia endekatænia, Bleeker, Atl. Ich. Perc. t. xxxii, f. 2, and Apogonini, p. 31.

B. vii, D. $7/\frac{1}{9}$, P. 13, V. 1/5, A. $\frac{2}{8}$, C. 17, L. l. 26, L. tr. 2/7.

Length of head 2/7, of caudal 1/5, height of body 2/7 of the total length. *Eyes*—diameter 2/5 of length of head, 1/2 a diameter from end of snout, and also apart. The jaws equal in front: the maxilla reaches to below the last third of the orbit. Outer edges only of the vertical and horizontal limbs of the preopercle serrated: edges of orbit smooth: shoulder bone serrated. *Teeth*—villiform in jaws, vomer, and palate. *Fins*—first and second dorsal spines short, the third equal to two-thirds the height of the body below it. Pectoral equals the length of the head behind the middle of the eye: the ventral scarcely reaches so far as the anal: caudal slightly notched. *Lateral-line*—tubes distinct, those in the first half of the body with lateral arborescent branches. *Colour*—of a reddish-brown tinge, with a dark band from the upper edge of the orbit to the end of the second dorsal and continued along the upper margin of the free portion of the tail and caudal fin: the second passes below it to the base of the upper half of the tail, and then curves downwards: the third from the head along the body below the lateral-line to the tail: the fourth along the upper part of the lower jaw through the eye to the base of the pectoral fin. Sometimes intermediate, narrower and short dark bands are present between those described. A black spot at the base of the tail. First dorsal fin black in its front half, a black band along the centre of the second dorsal, a similar one along the base of the anal and continued to its last ray: dorsal, caudal, and anal fins with darkish edges.

Habitat.—From the Red Sea through those of India to the Malay Archipelago and beyond.

7. Apogon quadrifasciatus.

Cuv. and Val. ii, p. 153; Bleeker, Perc. p. 28; Cantor, Catal. p. 3; Peters, Wieg. Arch. 1855, p. 234; Günther, Catal. i, p. 239; Kner, Novara Fische, p. 43.

Amia quadrifasciata, Bleeker, Atl. Ich. Perc. t. lvii, f. 1, and Apogonini, p. 30.

B. vii, D. $7/\frac{1}{9}$, P. 14, V. 1/5, A. $\frac{2}{8}$, C. 17, L. l. 26, L. tr. 2/6.

Length of head $3\frac{1}{3}$, of caudal 1/5, height of body $3\frac{1}{4}$ to $3\frac{1}{2}$ in the total length. *Eyes*—diameter $3\frac{1}{2}$ in the length of the head, 3/4 of a diameter from end of snout, and also apart. Lower jaw slightly the longer: the width of the head equals half its length. The maxilla reaches to below the last third of the orbit. Some serrations along the lower edge of the orbit: the shoulder entire. The outer edge of the vertical and horizontal limbs of the preopercle rather strongly serrated, its intramarginal crest entire. *Teeth*—villiform in jaws, vomer, and palate. *Fins*—dorsal spines of moderate strength, the first very short, the second scarcely above one-third of the length of the third, which is about the same height as the fourth and fifth, being equal to half the height of the body and two-thirds of the rays: soft portion of the fin with its upper edge cut square or slightly emarginate. Pectoral as long as the head behind the middle of the eye: the ventral reaches the anal. Second anal spine 2/5 of the height of the body: caudal emarginate. *Lateral-line*—tubes well developed with a basal enlargement which in some appears to be slightly arborescent. *Colours*—a broad brown band passes from the snout through the eye and is continued to the end of the caudal fin: another from the upper edge of the eye to above the free portion of the tail and continued to the base of the caudal fin. No median band from the eye to the base of the dorsal fin. A badly developed basal band along the soft dorsal and another on the anal fin: no black spot at the base of the caudal.

Habitat.—Seas of India, to the Malay Archipelago and beyond.

8. Apogon fasciatus.

Mullus fasciatus, White, N. S. Wales, p. 268, fig. 1.

Apogon novemfasciatus, Cuv. and Val. ii, p. 154; Bleeker, Timor, i, p. 163; Peters, Wieg. Arch. 1855, p. 234; Kner, Novara Fische, p. 43.

Apogon Baliensis, Bleeker, Perc. p. 28, and Verh. Bat. Gen. xxii. Bali, p. 5.

Apogon Aroubiensis, Hombr. and Jacq. Voy. Pôle Sud. Poiss. p. 31, pl. i, fig. 1.

Apogon fasciatus, Quoy and Gaim. Voy. Freyc. p. 344; Günther, Fische d. Sudsee, p. 19, t. xx. fig. A and B.

Amia fasciata, Gill, Proc. Nat. Soc. Phil. 1863; Bleeker, Atl. Ich. t. xlviii, fig. 4, and Apogonini, p. 36.

B. vii, D. 7/ $\frac{1}{9}$, P. 13, V. 1/5, A. $\frac{2}{8}$, C. 17, L. l. 25, L. tr. 2/6.

Length of head $3\frac{1}{2}$, of caudal 1/5, height of body $3\frac{1}{3}$ to $3\frac{1}{2}$ in the total length. *Eyes*—diameter 1/3 of length of head, 3/4 of a diameter from end of snout, and the same apart. The width of the head equals two-thirds of its length: jaws of about equal length. The maxilla reaches to below the hind edge of the orbit. Outer edge of preopercle serrated along both limbs, its intramarginal crest entire. Edges of orbit smooth or sometimes a little roughened: shoulder serrated. *Teeth*—villiform in jaws, vomer, and palate. *Fins*—dorsal spines rather stout, the first short, the second about half as high as the third which is the longest and equal to two-thirds of the height of the body, and nearly as high as the rays: soft portion of the fin with its upper edge oblique. Pectoral as long as the head behind the middle of the eye: the ventral does not reach the anal: caudal emarginate. *Lateral-line*—tubes distinct, with arborescent lateral projections. *Colours*—reddish-brown with four lateral longitudinal bands, the third of which commencing at the snout passes through the eye to the centre of the base of the caudal fin, along which it is sometimes continued to its termination, this band is usually edged below by a narrow white one commencing at the pupil of the eye. The second and fourth bands may either end at the upper and lower edges of the base of the caudal fin, or be continued along it in a converging direction forming an arch near the end of the fin. A dark band runs along the first dorsal fin, and is continued as a black band along the middle or base of the second dorsal: the anal has also a basal band.

Habitat.—Seas of India to the Malay Archipelago and beyond.

9. Apogon Savayensis, Plate XVI, fig. 5.

Apogon savayensis, Günther, Proc. Zool. Soc. 1871, p. 656, and Fische Sudsee, p. 21, t. xix, fig. B.

B. vii, D. 7/$\frac{1}{9}$, P. 12, V. 1/5, A. $\frac{2}{8}$, C. 17, L. l. 26, L. tr. 2/6.

Length of head $3\frac{1}{3}$, of caudal 1/5, height of body $3\frac{1}{4}$ to $3\frac{1}{3}$ in the total length. *Eyes*—diameter 2/5 of length of head, 1/3 of a diameter from end of snout, and 1/2 a diameter apart. The head is very slightly longer than high: lower jaw rather the longer. The rise from the snout to the dorsal fin is not considerable. The maxilla reaches to below the last fourth of the orbit. Vertical and horizontal limbs of preopercle serrated in their outer edges. Shoulder bone crenulated or entire: edges of orbit smooth. *Teeth*—in villiform bands in jaws, vomer, and palate. *Fins*—dorsal spines weak, the first very short, the second short, and the third not so high as the fourth, which equals the length of the post-orbital portion of the head and nearly half the height of the body below it. The pectoral reaches the anal, as does also the ventral: caudal slightly notched. *Lateral-line*—tubes well developed but rather short and having a slight lateral enlargement, it forms a moderate curve becoming straight below the end of the second dorsal. *Colours*—olive, with four or five narrow dark vertical bands from the first dorsal and first half of the second dorsal descending to the abdomen: a dark band, three scales wide, over the free portion of the tail and only reaching to half a scale below the lateral-line. A black streak from the lower edge of the eye to the angle of the preopercle; numerous small brown spots on the head and also on the body, more especially above the lateral-line. Fins grey, the anterior half of the first dorsal black: caudal with a dark edge externally margined with white.

Habitat.—Coast of Africa, seas of India and beyond, attaining to at least 3 inches in length.

10. Apogon nigripinnis, Plate XVI, fig. 6.

Cuv. and Val. ii, p. 152: Temm. and Schleg. Fauna Japon. Poissons, p. 3; Richardson, Ich. China, p. 221 (not Günther).

Amia nigripinnis, Bleeker, Apogonini, p. 64.

B. vii, D. 7/$\frac{1}{9}$, P. 15, V. 1/5, A. $\frac{2}{8}$, C. 17, L. l. 26, L. tr. $2\frac{1}{2}$/$6\frac{1}{2}$.

Length of head 1/3 to $3\frac{1}{2}$, of caudal 2/11 to 1/5, height of body 1/3 to $3\frac{1}{4}$ in the total length. *Eyes*—diameter 1/3 to $3\frac{1}{2}$ in length of head, 1/2 to 2/3 of a diameter from end of snout, and 3/4 of a diameter apart. No very considerable rise from the snout to the base of the dorsal fin: snout rather elevated. Lower jaw slightly the longer: the maxilla reaches to below the last third or even hind edge of the orbit. Vertical and horizontal limbs of preopercle strongly and evenly serrated along their outer edges: shoulder-bone serrated. *Teeth*—villiform in jaws, vomer, and palate, an outer slightly enlarged row in each jaw. *Fins*—dorsal spines strong, the two first short, and the third not so high as the fourth which equals the length of the postorbital portion of the head and half the height of the body below it. The pectoral does not reach the anal, but the ventral does: second anal spine $1\frac{1}{2}$ diameters of the eye in length: caudal rounded. *Lateral-line*—very slightly curved: tubes distinct, having a low lateral enlargement. *Colours*—greyish, with a dark vertical band from in front of the base of the first dorsal which passes backwards and downwards, increasing in width, and is lost below the whole length of the pectoral fin: a second goes from the base of the second dorsal to the lateral-line, and a third over the free portion of the tail. No black spots or streaks on the head, vertical fins black except the caudal, which is yellow and has a dark edge.

Cuv. and Val. type specimen is in excellent preservation in Paris, and identical with the above.

Habitat.—Madras, where it is common; it grows to at least $3\frac{3}{10}$ inches in length. The figure is life-size.

11. Apogon Wassinki.

Bleeker, Timor, p. 258.
Apogon chrysotænia ?, Day, Proc. Zool. Soc. 1870, p. 682.
Amia Wassinki, Bleeker, Apogonini, p. 38.

B. vii, D. 7/$\frac{1}{9}$, P. 14, V. 1/5, A. $\frac{2}{8}$, C. 17, L. l. 25-26, L. tr. 2/7.

Length of head $3\frac{1}{3}$ to $3\frac{1}{2}$, of caudal $4\frac{1}{2}$ to $4\frac{3}{4}$, height of body $3\frac{1}{4}$ in the total length. *Eyes*—diameter $2\frac{1}{4}$ to $2\frac{1}{2}$ in the length of head, 1/2 a diameter from the end of snout, and also apart. The width of the head at the opercles equals $1\frac{2}{3}$ in the height of the body, the greatest height of the head equals its length excluding the snout. Lower jaw slightly the longer, the maxilla reaches to below the middle of the eye. Vertical and horizontal limbs of preopercle serrated in their outer edges, other bones of the head and shoulder entire. *Teeth*—villiform bands in jaws, vomer, and palate. *Fins*—first dorsal spine short, the second half the length of the third and fourth, which are the longest, and equal to $1\frac{1}{2}$ in the height of the body, and 1/5 less than the longest ray, the spine of the second dorsal is a little shorter than the highest in the first dorsal fin: upper edge of first dorsal slightly emarginate. Pectoral 4/5 as long as the body is high. Ventral nearly reaching the anal. Second anal spine equal to half the height of the body, the rays similar to those of the soft dorsal. Caudal lobed. *Lateral-line*—makes a gradual curve, tubes well developed and having rather distinct lateral expansions, especially in the anterior portion of the body. *Colours*—brilliant golden with a black head. A silvery-white median band exists along the top of the head, it divides, one branch proceeding along the back on either side to the upper half of the tail: a second goes from above the orbit to the middle of the tail; a third through the orbit to the lower half of the tail: and a fourth from the angle of the mouth to below the base of the pectoral. Fins orange.

As my largest specimen is only $1\frac{2}{3}$ inches in length it is not improbable that it is the young of some species which in the more adult stage has another name. It appears to agree with Bleeker's *A. Wassinki*, of which he procured one specimen 60mm in length.

This fish is very common amongst the coral-reefs on the Andaman islands. As soon as the water is splashed they all crowd into the coral, concealing themselves amongst its sticks, apparently afraid that the splash has been occasioned by some large carnivorous fish.

Habitat.—Andamans and Nicobars.

12. Apogon aureus, Plate XVI, fig. 8.

Ostorhinchus Fleurieu, Lacép. iv, p. 24, iii, t. 32, f. 2.
Dipterodon hexacanthus, Lacép. iv, pp. 166, 168, iii. t. 30, f. 2.
Centropomus aureus, Lacép. iv, pp. 253, 273.
Apogon annularis, Rüppell, Atl. p. 48, and N. W. Fische, p. 85; Günther, Catal. i, p. 239; Klunz. Fisch. Roth. M. p. 713.
Apogon roseipinnis, Cuv. and Val. iii, p. 490, vi, p. 553; Bleeker, Amb. and Ceram. p. 253; Quoy and Gaim. Voy. Astrol. Poissons, p. 649, pl. i, f. 5; Peters, Wieg. Arch. 1855, p. 234.
Apogon aureus, Bleeker, Enum. pisc. p. 6.
Amia aurea, Bleeker, Atl. Ich. Perc. t. lix, f. 1, and Apogonini, p. 48.
Calallumbia, Tam.

B. vii, D. 7/$\frac{1}{9}$, P. 14, V. 1/5, A. $\frac{2}{8}$, C. 17, L. l. 25-26, L. tr. $2\frac{1}{2}$/6. Cæc. pyl. 4.

Length of head 2/7, of caudal 2/9, height of body 1/3 to 2/7 of the total length. *Eyes*—diameter 2/5 to $2\frac{1}{4}$ in length of head, 1/2 a diameter from end of snout, and 3/4 apart. The lower jaw slightly the longer: the maxilla reaches to below the middle of the orbit. Vertical limb of preopercle with its outer edge minutely serrated in its upper half, becoming more coarsely so at the angle and along the outer edge of its horizontal limb: edges of orbit and shoulder-bone entire. *Teeth*—villiform, in a single row on vomer and palate. *Fins*—dorsal spines rather slender, the first two short, the third not quite so long as the fourth, which equals half the length of the head and nearly half the height of the body below it; soft portion of the fin highest, and cut square or even slightly emarginate, especially in large specimens: pectoral reaches to above the anal: ventral reaches the anus: caudal emarginate. *Lateral-line*—tubes distinct, with numerous short lateral branches. *Pseudobranchiæ*—well developed. *Colours*—body pinkish shot with gold, a rather broad, black band at the root of the caudal fin over the free portion of the tail: some minute black spots around the jaws, on the upper portions of the opercles, and on the crown of the head. Fins reddish, first dorsal black tipped; ventral spine and outer ray black, and a narrow black edge to second dorsal, anal, and caudal. Variety *A. roseipinnis* has a violet band along the base of the anal fin.

In a female specimen 4 inches long, captured at Madras, January 9th, 1868, a black band passes through the eye to the opercle, which also has a vertical band of dots upon it: the ring round the free portion of the tail ends one row of scales below the lateral-line.

Habitat.—Red Sea, East coast of Africa, through the seas of India to the Malay Archipelago. Very common at Madras up to 5 or 6 inches in length, in June and July they are usually abundant. Specimen figured life-size.

13. **Apogon bifasciatus**, Plate XVI, fig. 9.

Rüppell, N. W. Fische, p. 86, t. 22, f. 2; Günther, Catal. i, p. 238;* Kner, Novara Fische, p. 42; Klunz. Fische d. Rothen Meeres, p. 711.

Apogon trimaculatus, Richardson, Ich. China, p. 221 (not C. V.)

? *Amia taeniata*, Bleeker, Nat. Verh. d. Holl. Maats. d. Weten. 3de Verz. Deel. ii, No. i, 1874, p. 24, and Apogonini, p. 24.

B. vii, D. 7/$\frac{1}{9}$, P. 15, V. 1/5, A. $\frac{2}{8}$, C. 17, L. l. 25, L. tr. 2/7½, Cæc. pyl. 3 (4 Kner.)

Length of head 3½ to 2/7, of caudal 2/11, height of body 4/11 in the total length. *Eyes*—diameter 4/11 of length of head, 1/3 of a diameter from end of snout, and 2/3 apart. A considerable rise from the snout to the dorsal fin. The maxilla reaches to below the posterior third of the orbit. Vertical limb of preopercle finely serrated in its outer edge, rather more coarsely so at its angle, becoming very indistinct along the lower limb, the inner edge entire. Shoulder-bone serrated in the young, becoming nearly entire in the adult. *Teeth*—villiform in jaws, and in a band on the vomer and palatines. *Fins*—dorsal spines strong, the two first short, the third and fourth of about the same height and equal to two-thirds of the length of the head in the adult (proportionately higher in the young), or half the height of the body beneath: the spine of the second dorsal strong, and equal to half the length of the head. The pectoral reaches to above the anal spines: caudal emarginate in the adult, more rounded in the young. *Lateral-line*—forms a curve in the first part of its extent, which becomes straight opposite the end of the base of the anal fin: the tubes anteriorly are very arborescent laterally, but less so in the posterior half of the body. *Colours*—slaty-grey with bronze reflections: a dark vertical band from the first half of the dorsal fin passing down the side to below the pectoral fin, and a shorter but similar band from the first half of the second dorsal: a black spot at the root of the caudal. Fins, except the pectoral, blackish, or with black edges, due to fine black points, which are also spread over the jaws, head, and very finely over the body.

Habitat.—Red Sea, through the seas of India, to the Malay Archipelago and China. Very common at Madras up to 6 inches in length. It is very closely allied to *A. taeniatus*, which latter, however, has a much lower first dorsal fin.

14. **Apogon glaga**, Plate XVI, fig. 10.

Apogon glaga, Bleeker, Perc. p. 29.

Apogonichthys glaga, Bleeker, Japan, p. 57, and Atl. Ich. Perc. t. xxxiii, fig. 1; Günther, Catal. i, p. 247.

Amia glaga, Bleeker, Apogonini, p. 66.

B. vii, D. 7/$\frac{1}{9}$, P. 16, V. 1/5, A. $\frac{2}{8}$, C. 17, L. l. 24-25, L. tr. 2/7.

Length of head 2/7, of caudal 1/5, height of body 2/7 of the total length. *Eyes*—diameter 2/7 of length of head, 1/2 a diameter from end of snout, and 1 apart. Lower jaw the longer: the maxilla reaches to below the last third of the orbit. Both limbs of preopercle entire, but the outer edge of the horizontal limb somewhat crenulated, its outline being sinuous: the other bones of the head entire, except the lower border of the orbit which is roughened. *Teeth*—villiform in the jaws, the outer row in the maxilla rather enlarged, and a few canine-like ones in the mandible: those in the vomer and palate in a single row of rather larger-sized ones than exist in the jaws. *Fins*—dorsal spines weak, the first short, the fourth the highest, equal to the length of the postorbital portion of the head, and nearly one-fourth higher than the spine of the second dorsal; soft dorsal fin considerably higher than the spinous. Pectoral reaches to above the anal spines. Caudal rounded. *Lateral-line*—tubes distinct, having a lateral basal enlargement. *Colours*—yellowish-green superiorly, becoming more roseate along the abdomen: a dark band between the hind fourth of the orbits. The approximating edges of

* Dr. Günther observes that *A. bifasciatus* has both the margins of the preopercle strongly serrated, the denticulations on the inner ridge being coarse, and gradually becoming more so at the angle: vomerine teeth in a single row.

the scales having minute black dots, forming horizontal lines, which are most distinct along the back: the scales in the second and third rows having a pearly white spot at the base of each. Upper half of the first dorsal black; second dorsal and caudal with black edges. A moderately wide band along the middle of the second dorsal, which appears to be sometimes spotted with blue.

Habitat.—Madras to $3\frac{3}{4}$ inches in length, as far as the Malay Archipelago.

15. Apogon auritus, Plate XVII, fig. 2.

Apogon auritus, Cuv. and Val. vii, p. 443; Günther, Fische d. Sudsee, p. 23.
Apogon punctulatus, Rüppell, N.W. Fische, p. 88, t. xxii, f. 4; Bleeker, Ceram. p. 696.
Apogonichthys polystigma, Bleeker, Amboina, p. 484, and Ternate, p. 372; Günther, Catal. i, p. 246.
Apogonichthys punctulatus, Bleeker, Aroe, p. 36.
Apogonichthys auritus, Günther, Catal. i, p. 246; Day, Proc. Zool. Soc. 1870, p. 682.
Amia polystigma, Bleeker, Apogonini, p. 67.

B. vii, D. $7/\frac{1}{9}$, P. 12, V. 1/5, A. $\frac{2}{7-8}$, C. 17, L. l. 23-24, L. tr. 2/6.

Length of head 1/3, of caudal 2/9, height of body 2/7 to 1/4 of the total length. *Eyes*—diameter 1/3 to 2/7 of the length of head, 1/2 to 1/3 of a diameter from end of snout, and also apart. Jaws of about equal length: the maxilla reaches to slightly behind the posterior edge of the orbit. Edges of preopercle, also of the other bones of the head and shoulder entire. *Teeth*—villiform in the jaws, vomer, and palate. *Fins*—first dorsal spine very short, the third and fourth the highest, equal to the length of the postorbital portion of the head, and three-fourths as high as the rayed fin. Pectoral as long as the postorbital portion of the head. Ventral reaches two-thirds of the way to the anal, the second spine of which last fin is equal to two-fifths of the height of the body. Caudal rounded or cut rather square. *Lateral-line*—either ceases under the middle of the soft dorsal fin, or reappears lower down going direct to the centre of the base of the caudal fin: tubes distinct, generally with a basal swelling. *Colours*—body and head spotted and marbled all over with brown. A circular black spot on the opercle enclosed by a narrow white ring, which is present even in the fry.

Bleeker observes that he formerly considered this species as identical with *A. punctulatus*, Rüppell= *A. auritus*, C. V. the interrupted lateral line and the distribution of colours being much the same. He now divides them, as Ruppell's fish appears to have a higher body, 4 longitudinal yellow bands over the preopercle, and only 20 rows of scales.

Having examined specimens taken in the Red Sea and elsewhere, I have not found less than 23 scales along the lateral-line, and in two specimens from Zanzibar the lateral-line is continuous.

Specimen	from Suez,	$1\frac{1}{2}$	inches	long:	height of	body	$3\frac{1}{2}$	in the	total length.
"	"	$1\frac{7}{10}$	"	" :	"	"	$3\frac{1}{4}$	"	"
"	Andamans,	$1\frac{1}{2}$	"	" :	"	"	$2\frac{3}{4}$	"	"
"	Massowah,	$1\frac{9}{10}$	"	" :	"	"	1/3	"	"
"	"	$1\frac{1}{2}$	"	" :	"	"	$3\frac{1}{3}$	"	"
"	Andamans,	2	"	" :	"	"	$2\frac{3}{4}$	"	"
"	Zanzibar,	$2\frac{7}{10}$	"	" :	"	"	$3\frac{1}{2}$	"	"
"	Andamans,	3	"	" :	"	"	$3\frac{1}{4}$	"	"
"	Zanzibar,	$3\frac{1}{2}$	"	" :	"	"	$3\frac{1}{3}$	"	"

The foregoing measurements lead me to doubt the specific difference between *A. auritus* from the Red Sea, and my species from the Andamans which=*A. polystigma*, Bleeker.

Habitat.—Red Sea, East coast of Africa, seas of India to the Malay Archipelago and beyond.

16. Apogon Ellioti, Plate XVII, fig. 1.

Apogon nigripinnis, Jerdon, M. J. L. and Sc. 1851, p. 128, and Günther, Catal. i, p. 235, and Fische d. Sudsee, p. 21, (not Cuv. and Val.)

B. vii, D. $7/\frac{1}{9}$, P. 15, V. 1/5, A. $\frac{2}{8}$, C. 16, L. l. 26, L. tr. $2/6\frac{1}{2}$.

Length of head $3\frac{1}{4}$, of caudal 2/11, height of body 2/7 in the total length. *Eyes*—diameter 2/7 of length of head, 1/2 a diameter from end of snout, and 1 apart. Lower jaw very slightly the longer: the maxilla reaches to below the posterior edge of the orbit.* Vertical limb of preopercle entire, or very finely serrated on its lower half and outer edge, more distinctly round its angle and on the outer edge of its horizontal limb, there may also be a few serrations likewise along its inner angle: lower edge of orbit roughened: shoulder entire. *Teeth*—fine in jaws, vomer, and palate. *Fins*—spinous much lower than the soft dorsal, its third, fourth and fifth spines the highest, and equal to two-fifths of that of the body: the second dorsal three-fourths as high as the body, its upper edge and also that of the anal being rounded. Pectoral as long as the ventral, which does not reach the anal: caudal rounded. *Pseudobranchiæ*—present. Free portion of tail rather longer than high at its base. *Lateral-line*—at first arborescent, but posteriorly with a lateral plate-like prolongation on either side of the base of each tube. *Colours*—golden, upper surface of head and jaws, also upper portion of opercle with black spots:

* In examining some immature specimens of this fish in the British Museum, I found that at $1\frac{1}{10}$ inches in length, the diameter of the eye was 2/5 of the length of the head, and the maxilla reached to nearly below its centre. At 2 inches in length, the diameter of the eye was 1/3 of the length of the head, and the maxilla reached to below the last third of the orbit.

a greyish band along the side, terminating in the young in an indistinct lateral blotch by the side of the free portion of the tail. First dorsal white, with its upper half deep black: second dorsal yellow, having a black band along its centre, and a black outer edge: anal likewise with a black median band: caudal grey, with a white band margined with black, and an external white edge.

Habitat.—East coast of Africa, seas of India to China and Japan. Madras two specimens to 4 inches in length. Amongst Sir W. Elliot's drawings is one of this fish named *A. nigripinnis* by Jerdon.

17. Apogon maculosus.

Cuv. and Val. iv, p. 493; Günther, Catal. i, p. 236.

B. vii, D. $7/\frac{1}{9}$, V. 1/5, A. $\frac{2}{8}$.

Colours—brown, darkest anteriorly, having four rows of brown spots along either side, but none on the head. Fins brown, spotted with black.

Habitat.—This fish is said to have come from the seas of India, from whence M. de Ketlitz, a Russian naturalist, brought figures (? specimens), and from whom Cuv. and Val. obtained their information.

It is stated to attain three inches in length.

18. Apogon macropterus, Plate XVII, fig. 3.

(K. and v. H.) Cuv. and Val. ii, pp. 160; Bleeker, Perc. p. 168; Günther, Catal. i, p. 244.
? Apogon Zeylonicus, Cuv. and Val. iii, p. 492; Günther, Catal. i, p. 232.
Apogon argenteus, Val. Nouv. Ann. Mus. Hist. Nat. 1832, p. 60.
Apogon fucatus, Cantor, Catal. p. 4; Günther, Catal. i, p. 241.
Apogon macropteroides, Bleeker, Banka, p. 724; Günther, Catal. i, p. 245; Playfair, Fish. Zanz. p. 20.
Apogon Bleekeri, Günther, Catal. i, p. 245.
Archamia Bleekeri, Gill, Nat. Hist. Soc. Phil. 1863, p. 81.
Amia macropteroides, Bleeker, Amb. p. 280.
Apogon subata, Day, Proc. Zool. Soc. 1870, p. 686.
Amia macroptera, Bleeker, Ternate, p. 233, Atl. Ich. Perc. t. lxviii, f. 2, and Apogonini, p. 72.

B. vii, D. $6/\frac{1}{9}$, P. 13, V. 1/5, A. $\frac{2}{17}$ ($\frac{2}{15}$-$\frac{2}{17}$), C. 17, L. r. 22-26 (Cæc. pyl. 0, Cantor.).

Length of head 2/7, of caudal 1/6, height of body $3\frac{1}{4}$ to $3\frac{3}{4}$ in the total length. *Eyes*—diameter 2/5 to 1/3 of length of head, 1/2 of a diameter from end of snout, and also apart. Body rather elongated in shape and compressed. Lower jaw slightly the longer. The maxilla reaches to below the middle of the orbit. Angle of the preopercle rounded, the outer edge of vertical and horizontal limbs finely serrated, the other bones of the head entire. *Teeth*—villiform in jaws, vomer, and palate. *Fins*—dorsal spines weak, the third the highest and equal in length to the postorbital portion of the head, or behind the middle of the eye. The pectoral reaches to above the third or fourth anal ray: caudal forked. *Colours*—whitish, having a pink tinge, fins pinkish: a round black spot on the side close to the base of the caudal fin.

Habitat.—East coast of Africa, seas of India to the Malay Archipelago. It does not appear to attain more than 3 or 4 inches in length in India, and is very common at Madras.

19. Apogon Sangiensis, Plate XVII, fig. 4.

Bleeker, Sangi, p. 375; Günther, Catal. i, p. 235, and Fische d. Sudsee, p. 20.
Amia sangiensis, Bleeker, Atl. Ich. Perc. t. xli, f. 4, and Apogonini, p. 56.

B. vii, D. $6/\frac{1}{9}$, P. 13, V. 1/5, A. $\frac{2}{8-9}$, C. 17, L. l. 24-25, L. tr. $1\frac{1}{2}/7$.

Length of head 1/3 to $3\frac{1}{3}$, of caudal $4\frac{3}{4}$ to $4\frac{1}{2}$, height of body 1/3 to $3\frac{1}{4}$ in the total length. *Eyes*—diameter 1/3 of length of head, 2/3 of a diameter from end of snout, and also apart. Jaws of about equal length. The maxilla reaches to below the middle of the orbit. Outer edge of both vertical and horizontal limbs of preopercle very finely serrated, orbital edge rough, the other bones of the head and shoulder entire. *Teeth*—villiform. *Fins*—dorsal spines very weak, the third generally the longest and $1\frac{2}{3}$ in the height of the body. Ventral almost reaches the anal: caudal notched. *Lateral-line*—tubes distinct, having a lateral basal enlargement. *Colours*—golden tinged with red: a wide brown band passes from the snout, through the eye, ending on the posterior edge of the opercle, or else in a black spot a little below the shoulder: a round black spot on the side of the free portion of the tail close to the base of the caudal fin: a minute black spot on the back, close behind the base of the last dorsal ray. Upper half of first dorsal black. The anal fin is said to be sparingly spotted with blue in specimens from the Malay Archipelago.

Habitat.—Andamans to the Malay Archipelago.

20. Apogon hyalosoma, Plate XVII, fig. 5.

Apogon thermalis, Bleeker, Perc. p. 27, (not Cuv. and Val.)

Apogon hyalosoma, Bleeker, Singapore, p. 63, and Amboina, iv, p. 329; Günther, Catal. i, p. 321; Kner, Novara Fische, p. 42.

Amia hyalosoma, Bleeker, Atl. Ich. Perc. xxxi, f. 1, and Apogonini, p. 57.

B. vii, D. $6/\frac{1}{9}$, P. 12-14, V. 1/5, A. $\frac{2}{8}$, C. 17, L. l. 24-25, L. tr. $2\frac{1}{2}/8\frac{1}{2}$.

Length of head 1/3 to $3\frac{1}{4}$, of caudal 1/5, height of body 1/3 of the total length. *Eyes*—diameter 2/7 to $3\frac{1}{4}$ in length of head, 3/4 of a diameter from end of snout, and 1 apart. Snout rather elevated. Lower jaw slightly the longer: the maxilla reaches to below the hind edge of the orbit. Both limbs of preopercle serrated along their outer edges, most slightly so on the vertical one: the other bones of the head and shoulder entire. *Teeth*—fine in jaws, vomer, and palate. *Fins*—dorsal spines of moderate strength, the second and third of about the same length, and equal to $2\frac{1}{4}$ in the height of the body, but not so high as the soft dorsal. Pectoral rather longer than the ventral, which latter reaches two-thirds of the distance to the base of the anal fin: soft anal as high as the soft dorsal: caudal lobed. *Lateral-line*—tubes distinct, some having a slightly arborescent base. *Colours*—olive, with a darkish blotch on the side at the base of the caudal fin: blackish between the second and third dorsal spine; fins grey.

Habitat.—Seas of India and Malay Archipelago, attaining at least six inches in length.

21. Apogon orbicularis, Plate XVII, fig. 7.

Apogon orbicularis, (Kuhl. and v. Hass.) Cuv. and Val. ii, p. 155, and vi, p. 495; Quoy and Gaim. Voy. Astrol. Poiss. p. 648, pl. i, fig. 4; Bleeker, Amb. & Ceram. p. 254, and Act. Soc. Ned. i, Amboina, p. 28; Günther, Catal. i, p. 233, and Fische d. Sudsee, p. 22, pl. xx, fig. D.

Amia orbicularis, Bleeker, Ceram. p. 188, and Nat. Verh. Holl. Maats. Weten. 3de Verz. Deel. II, No. i, 1874, p. 19.

B. vii, D. 6/$\frac{1}{9}$, P. 12, V. 1/5, A. $\frac{2}{8}$, C. 17, L. l. 24-26, L. tr. $2\frac{1}{2}$/7.

Length of head 2/7, of caudal 1/4, height of body 2/5 of the total length. *Eyes*—diameter $2\frac{1}{2}$ to $2\frac{3}{4}$ in the length of head, 1/2 to 2/3 of a diameter from the end of snout, and 3/4 of a diameter apart. Lower jaw the longer: the maxilla reaches to below the middle of the orbit. The outer edges of both limbs of the preopercle serrated, as is also the shoulder-bone, the other bones of the head entire. *Teeth*—villiform in the jaws, vomer, and palate. *Fins*—second and third dorsal spines slightly higher than the fourth, two-thirds the height of the body and in length about equal to the rays in the second dorsal fin. Pectoral as long as the head excluding the snout. Ventrals reach the anal fin, the second spine of which last is two-fifths the height of the body, whilst the rays are similar to those of the soft dorsal. Caudal forked, its three outer rays on either side rather spinate and projecting. *Lateral-line*—tubes well-developed. Free portion of the tail slightly longer than high at its commencement. *Colours*—olive-brown, a dark zone round the body from in front of the first dorsal fin, and passing to behind the ventral. Head spotted with black. A cloudy band below the second dorsal fin: free portion of the tail with some black spots and blotches. First dorsal with some dark spots: ventral nearly black.

Habitat.—Andamans, Malay Archipelago and beyond. The specimen figured (life-size) is from the Andamans.

22. Apogon Ceramensis, Plate XVII, fig. 6.

Bleeker, Amb. and Ceram. p. 256; Günther, Catal. i, p. 235.

Amia Ceramensis, Bleeker, Atl. Ich. Perc. t. lviii, f. 1, and Apogonini, p. 45.

B. vii, D. 6/$\frac{1}{9}$, P. 14, V. 1/5, A $\frac{2}{8}$, C. 17, L. l. 23-25, L. tr. 2/7.

Length of head $3\frac{1}{4}$, of caudal 1/5, height of body $3\frac{1}{4}$ in the total length. *Eyes*—$3\frac{1}{2}$ diameters in length of head, 3/4 of a diameter from end of snout, and 2/3 of a diameter apart. Dorsal profile rather concave over the eyes. Upper jaw slightly the longer: the maxilla reaches to below the last third of the orbit. Both limbs of the preopercle serrated along their outer edges, the other bones of the head and shoulder entire. *Teeth*—villiform. *Fins*—third dorsal spine is slightly the highest, and as long as the head behind the middle of the eye. The ventral does not reach the anal. Caudal notched. *Lateral-line*—tubes well developed, having lateral basal enlargements. *Colours*—greenish-brown with some dark spots on the head: a narrow blackish-brown band passes from the head to the root of the caudal fin, where it ends in a round black blotch: in its anterior half it is margined on either side by a bluish-white streak, which gradually decreases in width: there is a brownish blotch on the shoulder. The interspinous membrane between the second and third dorsal spines is black.

Habitat.—Nicobars, from whence Dr. Stoliczka brought the specimen which is figured: it is found in the Malay Archipelago.*

Genus, 12—CHEILODIPTERUS, (*Lacép.*) *Cuv. & Val.*

Paramia, Bleeker.

Branchiostegals seven: pseudobranchiæ well developed. Opercles spineless: preopercle with a double edge, both

---

* **Apogon quinquevittatus.**

Blyth. P. A. S. of Bengal, 1858, p. 272.

D. 13/10, P. 15, A. $\frac{3}{9}$, V. 5, L. l. 24, L. tr. 3/10.

Eyes—diameter 2/5 of the vertical height of the head. Form compressed: mouth small. *Fins*—pectoral reaching beyond the second lateral band: the posterior dorsal and anal fins projecting similarly as far as the base of the tail fin. *Colours*—four vertical black bands, a fifth at the base of tail, and the occipital region also of this colour.

Habitat.—Andamans, about 1 inch in length. Unless some typographical error has occurred, this fish having three anal spines, &c., cannot be referred to *Apogon*.

of which, or the outer only, may be serrated. Villiform teeth in the jaws, vomer, and palate: canines present generally in both jaws and lateral canine-like ones. Two dorsal fins separated by an interspace, the first with six spines; the anal with two. Scales ctenoid, large and deciduous. Lateral-line distinct.*

Geographical distribution.—From the Red Sea and East coast of Africa, through the seas of India and the Malay Archipelago to the Pacific. Along the coasts of India they appear to be most abundant off Sind, and in the Andamans and Nicobars. The specimen of this genus recorded from the Coromandel coast of India, by Dr. Jerdon, in the 'Madras Journal Literature and Science' (1851, No. 39, p. 129) was, as I have already observed (p. 57), *Apogon multitæniatus*.

SYNOPSIS OF SPECIES.

1. *Cheilodipterus lineatus*, D. 6/$\frac{1}{9}$, A. $\frac{2}{8}$, L. l. 26. Silvery-red with from seven to sixteen narrow black longitudinal bands, and a dark spot at the base of the caudal fin: first dorsal black between the second and third spines. Red Sea, East coast of Africa, and Sind.

2. *Cheilodipterus quinquelineatus*, D. 6/$\frac{1}{9}$, A. $\frac{2}{8}$, L. l. 25. Similar to the last with five bands. Red Sea, Nicobars to the Malay Archipelago.

1. Cheilodipterus lineatus, Plate XVIII, fig. 8 and 9 (var. *Arabicus*).

Perca lineata, Forsk. Desc. Anim. p. 42, No. 43; Rüpp. N. W. Fische, p. 89.
Perca Arabica, Linn. Syst. Nat. p. 1312.
Cheilodipterus lineatus, Lacép. iii, p. 543, pl. xxxiv, fig. 1; Günther, Catal. i, p. 248; Klunz. Verh. z. b. Ges. Wien, 1870, p. 717.
Centropomus macrodon, Lacép. iv, p. 273.
Cheilodipterus octovittatus, Cuv. and Val. ii, p. 163; Klunz. Verh. z. b. Ges. Wien, 1870, p. 717.
Cheilodipterus Arabicus, Cuv. and Val. ii, p. 165, pl. 23.
Cheilodipterus heptazona, Bleeker, Perc. p. 29.
Paramia octolineata, Bleeker, Atl. Ich. Perc. t. xxvii, fig. 2, and Apogonini, p. 75.

B. vii, D. 6/$\frac{1}{9}$, P. 13, V. 1/5, A. $\frac{2}{8}$, C. 17, L. l. 26-27, L. tr. $3\frac{1}{2}$/$7\frac{1}{2}$.

Length of head nearly 1/3, of caudal $4\frac{1}{2}$ to 1/5, height of body 1/4 in the total length. *Eyes*—diameter from $4\frac{1}{4}$ to 1/4 in length of head, 1 to $1\frac{1}{2}$ diameters from end of snout, and 3/4 to 1 diameter apart. The maxilla reaches to below the last third of the orbit. Vertical limb of preopercle very finely serrated in its outer edge, as is also that of the horizontal limb, where however the serrations are coarser and blunter; the other bones of the head entire. *Teeth*—canines in both jaws, and lateral canine-like ones. *Fins*—dorsal spines weak, the second and third of the same height and equal to two-thirds of that of the body. Pectoral reaches to above the anal spines: ventral two-thirds of the distance to the anal. Caudal forked. *Colours*—silvery-red, with horizontal bands along the head and body, the number of which appears to increase with age. In Sind some specimens had only seven, others as many as sixteen. One black band commencing above the snout proceeds to the base of the first dorsal fin: a second arising on the snout in common with that of the opposite side just anterior to the upper one and passes along the back above the lateral-line to the upper side of the caudal fin: the third commences on the side of the snout and passes through the eye, from the hind edge of which about four bands arise and are continued along the body: there are also generally two more from below the eye. A black spot exists at the base of the caudal fin, which is surrounded by a light edge. Fins red, the first dorsal black between the second and third spines. In adults intermediate bands appear between those described as existing in the young.

In the variety (fig. 9) which= *C. Arabicus*, C.V. it is bright yellow around the caudal blotch. The specimen came from Gwadar.

Habitat.—Red Sea, East coast of Africa, seas of India, Andamans to the Malay Archipelago and beyond.

2. Cheilodipterus quinquelineatus.

Cuv. and Val. ii, p. 167; Rüpp. N. W. Fische, p. 89; Lesson. Zool. Voy. Duperr. ii, p. 237; Bleeker, Mol. p. 252; Klunz. Verh. z. b. Ges. Wien. 1870, p. 716.
Apogon novemstriatus, Rüppell, N. W. Fische, p. 85, t. 22, f. 1.
Chilodipterus quinquelineatus, Günther, Catal. i, p. 248.
Paramia quinquelineata, Bleeker, Bouro, p. 147, Atl. Ich. Perc. t. xlviii, fig. 2, and Apogonini, p. 76.

B. vii, D. 6/$\frac{1}{9}$, P. 15, V. 1/5, A. $\frac{2}{8}$, C. 17, L. l. 25, L. tr. 2/7.

Length of head about 2/7, of caudal 1/5, height of body 2/9 of the total length. *Eyes*—diameter 1/3 of length of head, 3/4 of a diameter from end of snout, and also apart. Vertical limb of preopercle serrated along its outer edge. *Teeth*—generic. *Fins*—dorsal spines weak, second and third of the same height, and about equal to half of that of the body. Caudal forked. *Colours*—with a reddish tinge having five black bands

* Bleeker has separated those species in which (although their dentition is similar) the scales are smaller and cycloid, and the caudal fin convex instead of emarginate, into a distinct genus, *Pseudamia*.

along the side: and a black spot surrounded by a yellow ocellus at the root of the caudal fin. It otherwise resembles the last species, of which it might be considered a variety.

Fifth group—Grystina.

Body oblong or elevated. Opercles entire or variously serrated. Cleft of mouth more or less oblique. One or two dorsal fins.

Genus, 13—Dules, *Cuv. and Val.*

Moronopsis & Plectroplites, Gill: *Paradules*, pt. Bleeker.

Branchiostegals six; pseudobranchiæ. Eyes of moderate size. Chin moderately prominent. Preopercle serrated. Opercle with spines, but destitute of any membranous lobe. Villiform teeth in the jaws, vomer, and palatines, no canines. A single dorsal fin with ten spines, having a deep notch between the two last: anal with three spines. Scales ctenoid and of moderate size.

Geographical distribution.—From the Red Sea and East coast of Africa through the seas of India to the Malay Archipelago and beyond, being found in most intertropical seas, some being said to enter fresh waters.*

Uses.—Owing to their small size, these fishes are of but little economic value.

SYNOPSIS OF SPECIES.

1. *Dules marginatus*, D. $\frac{10}{11}$, A. $\frac{3}{10-11}$, L. l. 42. An oblique wide greyish band with an outer white margin across either caudal lobe: another along the top of the soft dorsal. Seas of India to the Malay Archipelago and beyond.

2. *Dules argenteus*, D. $\frac{9}{1}|\frac{1}{10}$, A. $\frac{3}{10-11}$, L. l. 52. A central black band on caudal fin and two oblique yellowish-black ones across either lobe: soft dorsal with a grey band along its upper edge, having a white outer margin. East coast of Africa, seas of India, to the Malay Archipelago and beyond.

1. Dules marginatus, Plate XVIII, fig. 1.

Cuv. and Val. iii, p. 116, pl. 52, and vii, p. 474; D'Urville, Voy. Pôle Sud. Poissons, p. 41, pl. iii, f. 3; Bleeker, Sumatra, i, p. 573; Günther, Catal. i, p. 268, and Fische d. Sudsee, p. 24.

Dules malo, Cuv. and Val. vii, p. 479; D'Urville, l. c. pl. iii, f. 4; Günther, Catal. i, p. 270.

Dules malo, Less. Voy. Coq. Zool. ii, p. 223.

Dules leuciscus, Jenyns, Voy. Beagle, Fishes, p. 17.

Kuhlia ciliata, Gill, Nat. Hist. Soc. Phil. 1861, p. 48.

Moronopsis ciliatus, Bleek. Arch. Néerl. 1872, p. 376, and Atl. Ich. Perc. t. xxxviii, f. 1, and l. c. t. xlvi, f. 2.

Paradules marginatus, Bleeker, Ceram. p. 257.

B. vi, D. $\frac{10}{11}$, P. 15, V. 1/5, A. $\frac{3}{10}$, C. 17, L. l. 42, L. tr. 5/8.

Length of head 2/7, of caudal 1/5, height of body 4/13 of the total length. *Eyes*—diameter 2/7 of length of head, 1 diameter from end of snout and also apart. The maxilla reaches to below the middle of the orbit. Preorbital very finely serrated along its lower margin, most distinctly so in the young. Horizontal limb of preopercle serrated. Opercle with two spines of which the lower is the longer. *Teeth*—villiform in jaws, vomer, and palatines. *Fins*—dorsal spines moderately strong, the fifth the highest and equal in length to the postorbital portion of the head, the tenth is longer than the ninth: third anal spine the longest: caudal moderately forked. *Colours*—greyish along the back, becoming silvery-white on the sides and abdomen; a greyish band, having a white tip, across the posterior third of the caudal fin: a similar but darker band, having a white upper edge, along the top of the soft dorsal: the other fins tinged externally with grey and edged with white.

Perca ciliata, (K. v. H.) Cuv. & Val.=*Percichthys ciliata*, (C.V.) Günther=this species according to Bleeker.

Habitat.—Seas of India, to the Malay Archipelago and beyond, attaining at least eight inches in length.

2. Dules argenteus, Plate XVIII, fig. 2.

Perca argentea, Bennett, Fish. Ceylon, p. 22, pl. 22.

Dules tæniurus, Cuv. and Val. iii, p. 114; Bleeker, Perc. p. 49: Günther, Catal. i, p. 267; Kner, Novara Fische, p. 47.

? *Dules Guamensis*, Cuv. and Val. vii, p. 474; D'Urville, l. c. p. 42, pl. 3, f. 1; Günther, Catal. i, p. 269.

Dules Bennetti, Bleeker, Bengal, p. 36; Peters, Wiegm. Arch. 1855, p. 238; Günther, Catal. i, p. 270.

Dules argenteus, Klunzinger, Verh. z. b. Ges. Wien, 1870, p. 730; Günther, Fische d. Südsee, p. 25, t. xix, f. C.

Moronopsis tæniurus, (Gill) Bleeker, Arch. Néer. Sc. 1872, p. 374.

Paradules tæniurus, Bleeker, China, p. 139.

B. vi, D. $\frac{9}{1}|\frac{1}{10}$, P. 15, V. 1/5, A. $\frac{3}{10-11}$, C. 17, L. l. 52, L. tr. 6/12.

Length of head nearly 1/4, of caudal nearly 1/5; height of body 4/15 of the total length. *Eyes*—diameter 2/5 of length of head, 1/2 a diameter from end of snout, and 3/4 of a diameter apart. The maxilla reaches to below the first third of the orbit. Preorbital very finely serrated along its lower edge. Horizontal

* According to Mr. Garrett's observations in the *Fische d. Sudsee*, p. 24, these fishes appear sometimes to prefer fresh water to saline.

limb of preopercle regularly and evenly serrated. Opercle with two spines, the lower somewhat the longer. *Teeth*—villiform in jaws, vomer, and palate. *Fins*—dorsal spines not very strong, the fifth and sixth the highest, and equal to half the length of the head: second anal spine slightly shorter but stronger than the third: caudal forked. *Colours*—bluish, becoming silvery-white on the sides and abdomen, soft dorsal greyish-black along its upper third and having a white outer margin: caudal milk-white, with two oblique yellowish-black bands and a narrow central black longitudinal one.

Young—in a specimen $1\frac{1}{2}$ inches in length, taken at the Andamans, the colour differs from that of the adult;—body blue, with a narrow black longitudinal band passing from the upper edge of the orbit along the back, nearer to the base of the dorsal fin than the lateral-line, and ending in the lower of the two bands crossing the upper lobe of the caudal fin: a narrow black band runs along the bases of both dorsal fins, whilst each have black tips: the anal has a black mark on the front of its highest portion: caudal with one central band, and two oblique ones across either lobe.

Habitat.—East coast of Africa, seas of India to the Malay Archipelago and beyond: it attains six inches or more in length.

Sixth group—Theraponina.

Branchiostegals six. Opercle spinate: preopercle serrated. Cleft of mouth somewhat oblique. Dorsal fin single, but more or less notched: three anal spines. Air-vessel divided by a constriction into an anterior and posterior portion.

Genus, 14—Therapon,* Cuv.

Pelates, sp. Cuv.†

Branchiostegals six: pseudobranchiæ. Eyes of moderate size. Opercle with spines. Preopercle and sometimes preorbital serrated. Teeth villiform in both jaws, the outer row being sometimes the larger: deciduous ones on the vomer and palatines. Dorsal fin single, but more or less notched, having from eleven to thirteen spines: anal with three. Scales of moderate or small size. Air-vessel divided by a constriction. Pyloric appendages few or in moderate numbers.

Geographical distribution.—From the Red Sea and East coast of Africa through the seas of India to the Malay Archipelago and Australia. These fishes in India are almost strictly marine, but some are occasionally found in brackish water within tidal influence; and having entered during very high tides, or in the monsoon season, their return to salt water may be cut off, when they live in the brackish or even fresh water ponds until the return of the next spring tide or the succeeding year's monsoon. The *T. jarbua* is frequently captured in the Hooghly as high as Calcutta.

Uses.—Not esteemed as food, as they are reputed to feed on carrion, but they are eaten by the poorest class of natives.

The colour of these fish is usually silvery, with longitudinal bands, but in some species cross bands are present in the immature. This may especially be noticed in the *T. quadrilineatus*, whilst in the adult the only remnant existing of such is the black blotch on the shoulder, which originally formed a portion of the first body-band. As might be expected, the serrations and spines about the head vary with age; but it is worthy of special notice, that the sub- and inter-opercles may be serrated in some specimens and yet be entire in others, and this is most apparent in the *T. jarbua*. The existence of teeth on the vomer and palate appears to be often confined to the immature.

SYNOPSIS OF SPECIES.

1. *Therapon puta*, D. $\frac{11}{10}|\frac{1}{9}$, A. $\frac{3}{8}$, L. l. 90-100. Large teeth at preopercular angle. Four straight longitudinal blackish-brown bands along the body: a dark blotch on the spinous dorsal, and two oblique bands across either caudal lobe. Seas of India to the Malay Archipelago.

2. *Therapon jarbua*, D. [illegible], A. [illegible], L. l. 80-90. Serrations at preopercular angle strong, but pretty even. Three longitudinal, convex, reddish-brown bands along the body: a dark blotch on the spinous dorsal: two oblique bands across either caudal lobe. Red Sea, East coast of Africa, seas of India, to the Malay Archipelago and beyond.

3. *Therapon quadrilineatus*, D. $\frac{11}{10}|\frac{1}{9}$, A. $\frac{3}{10}$, L. l. 70. Serrations at preopercular angle strong, but pretty even. Four or five horizontal blackish bands along the body: a black blotch on the spinous dorsal, another on the shoulder: no bands on the caudal. Seas of India to the Malay Archipelago and China.

4. *Therapon theraps*, D. [illegible], A. $\frac{3}{8}$, L. l. 50-55. Evenly serrated on its preopercular angle. Three or four horizontal blackish-brown bands along the body: two across either caudal lobe. East coast of Africa, seas of India to the Malay Archipelago and beyond.

1. Therapon puta, Plate XVIII, fig. 3.

Perca keelputa, Russell, Fish. Vizag. ii, p. 19, pl. 126.
Therapon puta, Cuv. and Val. iii, p. 131, Règ. Anim. Ill. Poissons, pl. xii, fig. 2; Bleeker, Perc. p. 50.

* *Sabah-ra*, Mugh.

† Bleeker divides this genus by adopting the following, with reference to their dentition, as sub-genera:
1. *Datnia*; teeth in jaws conical, entire, and in many rows.
2. *Pelates*; teeth in jaws conical, entire, in 3 rows in the upper and 2 in the lower jaw.
3. *Helotes*; teeth in the jaws in many rows, and tricuspidate.

Therapon ghebul, (Ehren.) Cuv. and Val. iii, p. 133; Bleeker, Perc. p. 51; Günther, Catal. i, p. 281; Klunz. Verh. z. b. Ges. Wien, 1870, p. 728.

Therapon trivittatus, Günther, Catal. i, p. 280; Day, Fish. Malabar, p. 17; Kner, Novara Fische, p. 45; Bleeker, Therapons, 1872, p. 375.

Kore keetchan, Tam. (Madras): *Keelputa*, Tel.: *Keetchan*, Tam. and Mal.

B. vi, D. $\frac{11}{1|9}$, P. 15, V. 1/5, A. $\frac{3}{8}$, C. 17, L. l. 90-100, L. tr. 13-14/24, Cæc. pyl. 7, Vert. 10/13.

Length of head 1/4 to $4\frac{1}{2}$, of caudal 1/5, height of body 1/4 in the total length. *Eyes*—diameter $3\frac{1}{2}$ to $3\frac{2}{3}$ in length of head, 1 diameter from end of snout, and 2/3 of a diameter apart. The maxilla reaches to below the anterior edge of the orbit. Preopercle with five or six strong denticulations on its vertical limb, the second above the lowest being generally the largest, whilst the two inferior are larger than the superior ones, the serrations are also continued along its horizontal limb. Sub- and inter-opercles entire. Opercle with two spines, the inferior the longest and strongest, and about equal to the largest of those on the preopercle. Shoulder-bone serrated (or crenulated), as is also the one in the axilla but more strongly so. *Teeth*—villiform in the jaws with an outer enlarged row, rudimentary ones present on the vomer and palate in the young, but lost as age advances. *Fins*—dorsal spines rather slender, the fourth to the sixth about equal and the longest, higher than the rays and equal to about 3/5 of the height of the body, from whence they decrease to the last but one, the last being a little higher. Pectoral as long as the head behind the middle of the eye. Second anal spine a little shorter than the third, which equals from 1/2 to 4/9 the height of the body: caudal emarginate. *Colours*—greyish, with three or four longitudinal straight blackish-brown bands: spinous portion of dorsal in its upper three quarters blackish between the third or fourth and seventh or eighth spines. Two oblique bands pass across the upper caudal lobe, and one, sometimes two, across its lower one. The *young* are similar to the adult, except that they look as if light spots were present along the interspace between the first three horizontal bands, giving the appearance of sinuous oblique dark bands.

Habitat.—Seas of India to the Malay Archipelago.

2. Therapon jarbua, Plate XVIII, fig. 4.

Sciæna jarbua, Forsk. Desc. Anim. p. 50; Gm. Linn. p. 1303; Shaw, Zool. iv, p. 541.

Holocentrus servus, Bloch, t. 238, f. 1.

Holocentrus jarbua, Lacép. iv, pp. 348, 355.

Grammistes servus, Bl. Schn. p. 185.

Coius trivittatus, Ham. Buch. Fish. Ganges, pp. 92, 370.

Therapon Timoriensis, Quoy and Gaim. Voy. Uran. Poiss. p. 341.

Therapon servus, Cuv. and Val. iii, p. 125, and vii, p. 479; Rüppell, N. W. Fische, p. 95; Bleeker, Perc. p. 50, and Atl. Ich. Perc. t. xxxiv, f. 2; Richards. Ann. and Mag. Nat. Hist. ix, p. 125; Günther, Catal. i, p. 278, and Fische d. Sudsee, p. 26; Day, Fish. Malabar, p. 18; Kner, Novara Fische, p. 45.

Pterapon trivittatus, Gray and Hardw. Ind. Zool. (from H. B. Mss.)

Therapon trivittatus, Cantor. Catal. p. 19.

Therapon jarbua, Klunzinger, Verh. z. b. Ges. Wien, 1870, p. 729.

Therapon (Datnia) jarbua, Bleeker, Therapons, 1872, p. 377.

Palia keetchan, Tam.: *Gahun*, Ooriah: *Nga-saban-sa*, 'Paddy eating fish,' Arrac.: *Boorgooni* and *Jerry-?*, Beng.-Chitt.

B. vi, D. $\frac{12}{1|10}$, P. 13, V. 1/5, A. $\frac{3}{8}$, C. 17, L. l. 80-90, L. tr. 15/30, Vert. 10/15.

Length of head from 3/11 to 1/4, of caudal 1/5, height of body $3\frac{1}{2}$ to $3\frac{2}{3}$ in the total length. *Eyes*—diameter $3\frac{1}{2}$ to 1/4 in length of head, 1 diameter from end of snout, and also apart. The maxilla reaches to below the first third of the orbit. Preorbital moderately serrated in the last two-thirds of its lower edge. Vertical limb of preopercle with from 12 to 14 serrations, the two at its rounded angle being much the strongest, along the lower limb are about eight weaker ones. Sub- and inter-opercles with fine serrations at their approximating edges, which may or may not be blunted with age, those from the Malabar coast appear to be the most strongly serrated. Upper opercular spine small, the lower large and strong, and its length equal to about two-thirds of the diameter of the orbit. Shoulder-bone, also the one in the axilla, serrated, very strongly so in the young. *Teeth*—an outer somewhat enlarged row in the jaws, fine ones likewise generally present on the vomer and palatines, more especially in the young. *Fins*—dorsal spines moderately strong, the third and fourth the longest, of about the same height and equal to half that of the body below them: second anal spine usually the strongest, and slightly shorter than the third: caudal forked. *Colours*—back bluish-grey, becoming white on the abdomen, with a tinge of gold along the cheeks and snout. Three longitudinal reddish-brown bands, having a slight convexity downwards, pass along the body: the upper from in front of the dorsal spines to the eighth or ninth: the second from the occiput to the end of the soft dorsal having reached the lateral-line in its concave course: the third from the back of the head to the lower opercular spine, and continued in a curved direction to the centre of the caudal fin. Sometimes a fourth band is present along the abdomen. Ventral and anal with a yellow tinge along their centres. Dorsal interspinous membrane milk-white, with a black mark in its upper two-thirds between the third and sixth spines: a second commences at the eighth spine, and is continued along the whole base of the soft dorsal: upper edge of first three dorsal rays tipped with black: caudal with two oblique bands across each lobe: eye yellowish-red.

In the *young* there are two strong spines at the preopercular angle.

Dr. Klunzinger, *l.c.* observes upon having only found 10 spines in the first dorsal fin. Dr. Günther, 'Fische d. Sudsee,' p. 26, in answer to this, remarks that during a London fog he has found 11. I may complete the discussion by stating that in my collection I have specimens representing both numbers.

Col. Tickell, MS. remarks that this fish is termed the Paddy or rice eater in Arracan, in consequence of the young being so frequently found in the inundated rice or paddy-fields.

Habitat—From the Red Sea and East coast of Africa through the seas and estuaries of India to the Malay Archipelago and north coast of Australia. It is a common fish, attaining 12 or 13 inches in length. Hamilton Buchanan left an excellent figure of this fish illustrative of his *Coius trivittatus*: it is labelled *Holocentrus kathoya*, and was reproduced by General Hardwicke. The species is not uncommon at Calcutta in the tidal Hooghly, whilst the *T. puta*, to which Buchanan's description has been referred, does not appear to ascend so high, although I have taken it, along with other marine fishes, in the Sunderbunds.

3. Therapon quadrilineatus, Plate XVIII, fig. 5.

Holocentrus quadrilineatus, Bloch, t. 238, fig. 2.

Pristipoma sexlineatum, Quoy and Gaim. Voy. Freyc. Poiss. p. 320.

Therapon quadrilineatus, Cuv. and Val. iii, p. 134; Richards. Ich. China, p. 239; Bleeker, Perc. p. 51; Günther, Catal. i, p. 282; Kner, Novara Fische, p. 46.

Therapon xanthurus, Cuv. and Val. iii, p. 135.

Pelates sexlineatus, quadrilineatus, et quinquelineatus, Cuv. and Val. iii, p. 146, pl. 55; Less. Voy. Coq. ii, p. 223; Cuv. Reg. An. Illus. Poiss. pl. xii, fig. 1; Griff. An. King. Fish. t. xii, fig. 1.

Helotes polytænia, Bleeker, Halmah, p. 53 and Atl. Ich. Perc. t. xxvi, f. 1.

Therapon Cuvieri, Bleeker, Timor, p. 211; Günther, Catal. i, p. 282.

Therapon sexlineatus, Steindach. Fischf. Port Jackson, Sitz. Ak. Wiss. liii, p. 429.

Therapon (Pelates) quadrilineatus, Bleeker, Therapons, 1872, p. 389.

B. vi, D. $\frac{12}{10}$, P. 15, V. 1/5, A. $\frac{3}{9-10}$, C. 17, L. l. 70, L. tr. 13/26, Cæc. pyl. 18.

Length of head 1/4, of caudal 1/6, height of body 1/4 of the total length. *Eyes*—diameter 1/3 of length of head, 2/3 of a diameter from end of snout, and also apart. The maxilla reaches to below the front edge of the orbit. Preorbital slightly serrated on its lower border. Preopercle serrated along both limbs, coarsest at its rounded angle, becoming indistinct along its horizontal limb. Sub- and inter-opercles entire. Opercle with two rather weak spines. Shoulder-bone entire, that in the axilla serrated. *Teeth*—villiform in 3 rows in the upper and two in the lower jaw, and having the external row in the maxilla enlarged. *Fins*—dorsal spines moderately strong, becoming highest about the fifth, which equals half the height of the body below it: second anal spine strongest, the third the longest; caudal emarginate. *Pyloric appendages*—very short. *Colours*—silvery, with five horizontal black bands, the first to the anterior portion of the soft dorsal: the second to the end of its base: the third to the upper third of the base of the caudal: the fourth to its lower third: the fifth (sometimes absent) to the end of the base of the anal. A large black blotch on the shoulder. Dorsal fin with a black blotch between its third and seventh spines, a black mark along the middle of the soft dorsal, and a black tip. Pectoral canary colour, as is also the ventral and anal, the last of which is darkest externally, and has a dark basal band: caudal yellowish with a dark edge but no bands.

The *young* have six light vertical cross bands, four times as wide as the ground colour, passing from the back to the fourth horizontal band; they are distinct in the specimens up to $3\frac{1}{2}$ inches in length. The black shoulder blotch in the adult is the upper portion of the first body band.

Habitat.—Seas of India to the Malay Archipelago and China; attaining at least 6 inches in length.

4. Therapon theraps, Plate XVIII, fig. 6.

Therapon theraps, Cuv. and Val. iii, p. 129, pl. 53; Bleeker, Perc. p. 50, and Atl. Ich. Perc. t. xliii, fig. 1; Richards. Ann. Nat. Hist. 1842, p. 126; Rüpp. N. W. Fische, p. 95; Günther, Catal. i, p. 274, and Fische d. Sudsee, p. 26; Day, Fish. Malabar, p. 19; Kner, Novara Fische, p. 44; Klunz. Verh. z. b. Ges. Wien, 1870, p. 728.

Therapon obscurus, Cuv. and Val. iii, p. 135; Cantor, Catal. p. 20; Günther, Catal. i, p. 275.

Therapon squalidus, Cuv. and Val. iii, p. 136 (Cæc. pyl. 13?); Günther, Catal. i, p. 275.

Therapon transversus, Cuv. and Val. iii, p. 136 (Cæc. pyl. 11?)

Therapon cinereus, Cuv. and Val. iii, p. 138 (Cæc. pyl. 10?); Günther, Catal. i, p. 276.

? *Datnia virgata*, Cuv. and Val. vii, p. 480.

? *Therapon rubricatus*, Richards. Ann. Nat. Hist. 1842, p. 127.

? *Therapon virgatus*, Günther, Catal. i, p. 276.

Therapon (Datnia) theraps, Bleeker, Therapons, 1872, p. 379.

Kutta keetchan, Tam.

B. vi, D. $\frac{(12)}{(9)}\frac{12}{10}$, P. 15, V. 1/5, A. $\frac{3}{8}$, C. 17, L. l. 50-55, L. r. [illegible], L. tr. 11/16, Vert. 10/15, Cæc. pyl. (7 Kner.)

Length of head 1/4, of caudal 2/11 to 1/5, height of body 2/7 of the total length. *Eyes*—diameter $3\frac{1}{4}$ to $3\frac{1}{2}$ in length of head, 1 diameter from end of snout, and also apart. The maxilla reaches to below the first third of the orbit. Preorbital very finely serrated on its lower edge in the adult but more distinctly in the young. Preopercle nearly evenly serrated, most coarsely at its angle: sub- and inter-opercles entire, in some of the young they are rough or even serrated at their approximating edges. Lower opercular spine the longer, about 2/3 as long as the orbit, but not equalling the length of *T. jarbua*. *Teeth*—villiform in the jaws, with an outer somewhat enlarged row: deciduous ones present in the young on the vomer and said also to exist on the palate. Shoulder-bone serrated, and two or three strong spines on the bone at the axilla. *Fins*—dorsal spines moderately strong, the fourth slightly the longest and equal to half the height of the body below it, their length decreases to the last but one, which is only two-thirds or three-fourths as high as the last: second anal spine the strongest, but rather shorter than the third: caudal emarginate. *Scales*—above the lateral-line a little smaller than those below it. *Colours*—silvery, with four horizontal blackish-brown lines, the first from the second to the last dorsal spine leaving a narrow yellow intervening space between them: the second from the nape to the last few dorsal rays, and ending by being continued on to the fin as well as joining the line below it: the third (which is often the last) from the snout to upper part of the tail: the lowest (often absent) from the base of the pectoral to the lower caudal lobe. Dorsal fin with a black blotch between its third and its seventh spines, and a dark band along the upper portion of the rays. An horizontal black band along the first half of the anal fin. Caudal with two oblique bands across its lower lobe, and two also across its upper, the superior of which is interrupted in the adult, the lobe has likewise a black tip.

In the *young* the colours are much darker, and due to innumerable fine brown spots they appear as if they were dark with two light bands only half the width of the darker ones. The anal fin has two large black spots, one on the interspinous membrane and continued on to the first three rays: the second is confined to the last three rays. A large black shoulder spot is sometimes visible. There are teeth on the vomer.

Variety.—In a small specimen from Madras, 2¼ inches long, there are D. $\frac{10}{10}$, the two first spines apparently being absent, it is otherwise identical with the young of this species.

Therapon cinereus (Cuv. and Val.) Günther in the British Museum is this species, in which the bands, though very faint, may still be traced: as the condition of the specimen is good, either it must have been somewhat of an albino variety, or else it has been kept in such a light that etiolation has resulted.

Habitat.—East coast of Africa, seas of India, through the Malay Archipelago to China, attaining at least six inches in length.

Genus, 15—Datnia, *Cuv. and Val.*

Mesopristis, sp. Bleeker.

Branchiostegals six; pseudobranchiæ. Body elevated, with a somewhat rectangular or concave profile; snout pointed and somewhat produced. Eyes of moderate size. Opercle with spines; preopercle serrated. Teeth villiform in both jaws; palate edentulous. Dorsal fin single, but slightly notched, spines strong (12-13) *and occupying a considerable amount of the length of the fin; anal with three spines. Scales of moderate size.*

SYNOPSIS OF INDIVIDUAL SPECIES.

1. *Datnia argentea*, D. $\frac{12}{10}$, A. $\frac{3}{8}$, L. l. 56. Second anal spine strong. Seas of India to the Malay Archipelago.

Datnia argentea, Plate XVIII, fig. 7.

Datnia argentea, Cuv. and Val. iii, p. 139, pl. 54; Bleeker, Perc. p. 52.
Mesopristis macracanthus, Bleeker, Batavia, p. 523.
Datnia cancelloides, Bleeker, Sumatra, p. 247 (*young*).
Therapon argenteus, Günther, Catal. i, p. 283.
Therapon (Datnia) argenteus, Bleeker, Therapons, 1872, p. 382 (not Kner.)

B. vi, D. $\frac{12}{10}$, P. 14, V. 1/5, A. $\frac{3}{8}$, C. 17, L. l. 56, L. tr. 30-35, Cæc. pyl. 11.

Length of head 1/4, of caudal 1/5, height of body 1/3 to 3½ in the total length. *Eyes*—diameter 1/4 of length of head, 1¼ diameters from end of snout, and 4/5 of a diameter apart. The maxilla does not quite extend to beneath the anterior edge of the orbit. Snout pointed. Preorbital serrated along the last half of its lower edge. Preopercle serrated along its vertical margin. *Teeth*—villiform in jaws, none on the palate. *Fins*—fourth and fifth dorsal spines the longest and rather more than half the height of the body: second anal spine very strong, longer than the third, and exceeding the length of the longest in the dorsal fin: caudal notched. *Colours*—silvery, darkest along the back: a narrow black outer edge to the dorsal fin: a band along the middle of the anal, which also has a dark margin.

The *young* appear to have longitudinal bands.

As Cuvier observes, this fish has a more elevated body than in the typical *Therapons*, a somewhat concave profile, and pointed snout, the dorsal spines being stronger and their bases occupying a comparatively greater extent of the back than the rays, and there being a very slight notch between the last two. In fact it is his first species of *Datnia*, a genus which some Ichthyologists consider ought not to be retained.

Habitat.—Cape seas, seas of India to the Malay Archipelago and beyond. I never obtained it in India, saw it in a local collection there, or observed any figure of it amongst drawings of Indian fishes, but as it is found in the Malay Archipelago, stray ones may very possibly be occasionally captured on the coast of India.

Genus, 16—Helotes, Cuv.

Branchiostegals six. Eyes of moderate size. Cleft of mouth rather small, jaws nearly equal in front. Preopercle serrated; opercle with weak spines. The outer row of teeth in the jaws having a small lobe on each side; palate edentulous. Dorsal fin single, not deeply notched, having twelve spines; anal with three. Scales small, ctenoid. Air-vessel divided by a constriction into an anterior and posterior portion. Pyloric appendages in moderate numbers.

Geographical distribution.—Ceylon* ? to the Malay Archipelago and beyond.

Sixth group—Pristipomatidæ.

Branchiostegals from five to seven. Preopercle serrated or entire. Mouth moderately protractile. Teeth in the jaws. Three anal spines. Air-vessel destitute of any constriction.

Genus, 17—Pristipoma, Cuv.

Genytremus, Genyatremus, Anisotremus and *Pristocantharus*, Gill: *Hemulopsis*, Steind.

Branchiostegals seven; pseudobranchiæ. Body oblong, compressed. Eyes of moderate size. Cleft of mouth horizontal; gape not very wide; premaxillaries moderately protractile; jaws of nearly equal length; a central longitudinal and deep groove below the symphysis of the lower jaw, and two small open pores under the chin; no barbels. Preopercle serrated; opercle with indistinct points. Teeth in the jaws villiform without canines; palate edentulous. Dorsal with from eleven to fourteen spines, and sometimes having a deep notch between the last two; anal with three spines. Vertical fins scaleless or only so along their bases. Scales ctenoid and of moderate or small size, present on the head, including the preorbital and lower jaw. Air-vessel simple, destitute of any constriction. Pyloric appendages few.

Geographical distribution.—All tropical seas and likewise found in the Mediterranean; the young of the Indian species are often taken in backwaters.

Uses.—Fair as food but not much esteemed: the air-vessel in some places collected as isinglass. Many breed about April or May.

SYNOPSIS OF SPECIES.

1. *Pristipoma stridens*, D. [illegible], A. [illegible], L. r. [illegible]. Purplish on the back, becoming white on the abdomen. Three golden bands along the body and a dark mark on the upper third of the opercle. Red Sea, along the Meckran coast to Sind.

2. *Pristipoma olivaceum*, D. [illegible], A. [illegible], L. r. [illegible]. Olive-grey, the head glossed with purple: a black mark on the opercle. Beloochistan and Sind.

3. *Pristipoma furcatum*, D. [illegible], A. [illegible], L. l. 55-60. Silvery, with six sinuous blackish-brown bands, three of which are above the lateral-line: a dark mark on the opercle: spinous dorsal with three rows of brown spots and a dark edge: upper half of dorsal dark, and a band along the anal. Seas of India to the Malay Archipelago.

4. *Pristipoma hasta*, D. [illegible], A. [illegible], L. l. 45-50. Four or five lines of dark grey along the sides, sometimes coalescing and forming bands: two or three rows of spots along the dorsal fin. Red Sea, East coast of Africa, seas of India to the Malay Archipelago and beyond.

5. *Pristipoma Commersonii*, D. [illegible], A. [illegible], L. l. 50. Sinuous rows of black dots over upper two-thirds of body, and several rows along the dorsal fin. Madras.

6. *Pristipoma maculatum*, D. [illegible], A. [illegible], L. l. 52-56. Greyish, becoming white beneath: a black band over the nape, and six black blotches along the side, three above and three below the lateral-line, not forming bands but placed like squares on a chess board. Red Sea, East coast of Africa, through the seas of India to the Malay Archipelago and beyond.

7. *Pristipoma Dussumieri*, D. [illegible], A. [illegible], L. l. 50-54. Greyish, becoming lighter below: two golden lateral bands: fins with dark edges. Seas of India.

8. *Pristipoma guoraka*, D. [illegible], A. [illegible], L. l. 45-47. Silvery, an olive spot on the opercle. Seas of India to the Malay Archipelago.

9. *Pristipoma operculare*, D. [illegible], A. [illegible], L. l. 57. Silvery, with a black blotch at the posterior-superior angle of the opercle: upper half of the body with numerous black spots, sometimes forming undulating bands: a dark spot at the base of each dorsal spine and ray. East coast of Africa to Sind.

1. Pristipoma stridens, Plate XVIII, fig. 8.

Sciæna stridens, Forsk. p. 50.
Perca stridens, Bl. Schn. p. 87.
Pristipoma simmena, Cuv. and Val. v, p. 260.
Pristipoma stridens, Rüppell, N. W. Fische, p. 122, t. 31, f. 1; Günther, Catal. i, p. 300; Klunzinger, Fische Roth. Meeres, Verh. z. b. Ges. Wien, p. 732.

* In the list of the Acanthopterygian fishes of Ceylon, prepared by Dr. Günther (Sir E. Tennent's Nat. Hist. of Ceylon, 1861, p. 360), is *Helotes polytænia* Bleeker, as that species = *Therapon quadrilineatus*, I conclude that Dr. Günther's species, which I have not seen, may be identical.

B. vii, D. [illegible], P. 17, V. 1/5, A. [illegible], C. 17, L. r. [illegible], L. tr. 8-9/18, Cæc. pyl. 5-6.

Length of head 1/4, of caudal 1/6, height of body 1/4 of the total length. *Eyes*—diameter 2/7 to 1/4 of length of head, 1 to $1\frac{1}{2}$ diameters from end of snout, and 1 apart. Upper profile of head somewhat rounded: jaws of about equal length. The maxilla reaches to below the front edge or first third of the orbit. Vertical margin of preopercle oblique, angle rounded, serrated in its whole extent, its two or three lowest serrations the strongest: horizontal limb entire, as are also the sub- and inter-opercles. Shoulder-bone serrated. *Teeth*—villiform in jaws, the outer row being slightly the largest. *Fins*—dorsal interspinous membrane moderately notched, the spines slender, the fifth the highest and half as long as the head. Pectoral as long as the head without the snout. Second anal spine stronger than, but not quite so long as the third, which equals 4/11 of the height of the body: caudal forked in its last third. *Colours*—they much resemble those of a *Therapon*, purplish on the back becoming dirty white on the abdomen, a golden band from the occiput to the end of the base of the soft dorsal: a second from the shoulder passes along the lateral-line to be lost on the summit of the free portion of the tail: a third from the eye to the middle of the caudal fin: a dark mark at the upper third of the opercle: dorsal interspinous membrane covered with fine black spots, outer edge and also that of the caudal and anal stained grey: many fine dots over the head and body.

Variety.—At Aden I procured a variety of this species, which was nearly black, from the numerous dark spots all over it.

Habitat.—Red Sea, along the Meckran coast, and very common at Kurrachee in Sind: attaining at least 6 inches in length.

2. Pristipoma olivaceum, Plate XIX, fig. 1.

B. vii, D. [illegible], P. 17, V. 1/5, A. 3/7, C. 17, L. l. 55, L. r. [illegible], L. tr. 9/15, Cæc. pyl. 6.

Length of head 4/15 to 1/4, of caudal 2/11 to 1/6, height of body 3/10 to 1/3 of the total length. *Eyes*—diameter 2/7 to 1/4 of length of head, 1 diameter from end of snout, and $1\frac{1}{2}$ apart. Dorsal profile more convex than that of the abdomen: body compressed. The maxilla reaches to below the posterior nostril or even front edge of the eye. Vertical limb of preopercle emarginate, its angle rounded, and the whole strongly serrated: a deep groove below and behind the symphysis of the lower jaw and two open pores. *Teeth*—villiform in both jaws: the outer row rather the largest. *Fins*—dorsal spines, the fourth the highest and equal to half the length of the head, the interspinous membrane notched. Pectoral pointed and nearly as long as the head: second anal spine the strongest, and nearly as long as the third which equals the eighth of the dorsal fin. Caudal emarginate. *Scales*—in oblique rows above and horizontal ones below the lateral-line. *Cœcal appendages*—six which are rather long and enlarged at their extremities. *Colours*—olive-grey, the head glossed with purple, a large black blotch bordered in front with yellow at the upper angle of the opercle: pectoral yellow, as is also the ventral in its front half, whilst its posterior portion is black with a white edge: the other fins stained with blackish and having fine deep brown dots. Eyes golden.

Habitat.—Coasts of Beloochistan and Sind, attaining at least a foot in length (the specimen figured is a little over 8 inches long). It appears to be common during the cold months.

3. Pristipoma furcatum, Plate XIX, fig. 2.

Grammistes furcatus, Bl. Schn. p. 187, t. 43.

Perca paikeeli, Russell, Fish. Vizag. ii, p. 16, pl. 121.

Pristipoma paikeeli, Cuv. and Val. v, p. 259; Cantor, Catal. p. 74; Bleeker, Verh. Bat. Gen. xxiii, Sciæn. p. 20; Günther, Catal. i, p. 292.

Pristipoma furcatum, Bleeker, Revis. Pristipoma, 1873, p. 304, (not Agass).

Paikeeli, Tel.: *Kullu-koorake*, Tam.

B. vii, D. [illegible], P. 17, V. 1/5, A. 3/7, C. 17, L. l. 55-60, L. tr. 7/18.

Length of head from 1/4 to 4/17, of caudal 1/6, height of body 1/3 of the total length. *Eyes*—diameter from $3\frac{1}{2}$ to $4\frac{1}{2}$ in length of head, from 1 to $1\frac{1}{2}$ diameters from end of snout and also apart. A deep groove under the symphysis of the lower jaw and two open pores. The maxilla reaches to below the anterior nostril. Preopercle serrated, most strongly so at its somewhat produced angle. *Teeth*—in villiform rows, with an outer enlarged one in the upper jaw, and a slightly enlarged one in the lower jaw. *Fins*—third or fourth dorsal spine the highest and equal in length to the head behind the middle of the eye, or $2\frac{1}{2}$ in the height of the body, every alternate one being broader. Pectoral a little longer than the head: ventral does not reach the anal. Second anal spine much the strongest and also the longest, being higher than the fourth of the dorsal fin and about 1/2 as high as the body: caudal notched. *Colours*—silvery with six horizontal brownish-black bands, darkest externally, three of which are above the lateral-line: spinous portion of the dorsal fin with three rows of brown spots and a dark edge: upper half of soft dorsal dark: a dark band along the anal.

Bloch Schneider's specimen, a little over 7 inches in length, is still preserved in the Berlin Museum, leaving no doubt as to its identity with the *paikeeli* of Russell.

Habitat.—Seas of India to the Malay Archipelago. The specimen figured is 6 inches long and from Madras, there is a stuffed one from the same locality in the India Museum, 11 inches in length.

4. Pristipoma hasta, Plate XIX, fig. 3, and 4 (young ?).

Lutjanus hasta, Bl. t. 246, f. 1.

Coius gutystia, Ham. Buch. p. 94, 370.
Pristipoma kaakan, Cuv. and Val. v, p. 244; Rüppell, N. W. Fische, p. 123.
Pristipoma Commersonii, Cantor, Catal. p. 72.
Pristipoma hasta, Cuv. and Val. v, p. 247; Günther, Catal. i, p. 289; Day, Fishes of Malabar, p. 20; Klunzin. Verh. z. b. Ges. Wien. 1870, p. 733; Bleeker, Revis. Pristip. 1873, p. 308.
Pristipoma chrysobalion, (K. and v. H.) Cuv. and Val. v, p. 248.
Mesoprion gutystia, (Cuv. and Val.) Blyth, Proc. A. S. of Bengal, 1860, p. 111.
Pobotes nitidus, Blyth, Proc. A. S. of Beng. 1858, p. 283, & 1860, p. 111.
Corona and *Corake*, Tam.: *Coompoo*, Bel.

B. vii, D. $\frac{12}{13-14}$, P. 17, V. 1/5, A. $\frac{3}{7-8}$, C. 17, L. l. 45-50, L. tr. 7/10, Cæc. pyl. 6-7.

Length of head 1/3 to 2/7, of caudal 1/5 to 1/6, height of body 1/3 to 3/10 of the total length. *Eyes*—diameter from 1/3 to 1/5 of length of head, from 2/3 to $1\frac{1}{2}$ diameters from end of snout and also apart. The maxilla reaches to beneath the anterior edge or even first third of the orbit. Preopercle emarginate posteriorly, its angle rounded and produced, serrated in its whole extent, very coarsely so at its angle, and most distinctly so in the immature. Opercle with two rounded points. Shoulder bone serrated. *Teeth*—villiform, outer row somewhat the largest. *Fins*—dorsal spines strong, the third or fourth the longest and equal to 1/2 the height of the body, from it they decrease to the 11th which equals 2/3 the height of the second, whilst the 12th is almost 1/3 longer. Pectoral nearly as long as the head: ventral reaches 2/3 of the way to the anal. Second anal spine longest and strongest, equalling 1/2 of the height of the body and longitudinally fluted, the 3rd thinner and 1/4 shorter. Caudal emarginate. *Colours*—four or five interrupted lines of grey along the sides, three or four being above the lateral-line: sometimes they coalesce and form bands. Two or three rows of spots along the dorsal fin, and in the adult a single row of dull blotches at the base of the fin.

Habitat.—Red Sea, East coast of Africa, seas of India, Malay Archipelago to North Australia, attaining $1\frac{1}{2}$ feet or more in length.

The specimen from which fig. 3 is taken is 7 inches long, whilst fig. 4 of one of the young is twice the natural size, it shows how with age the length of the last dorsal spines comparatively decrease to the size of the fish.

5. Pristipoma argenteum, Plate VIII, fig. 3.*

Sciæna argentea, Forsk. p. 51.
? *Anthias Lineatus*, Bl. t. 326, f. 1.
? *Labrus Commersonii*, Lacép. iii, pp. 431, 477, t. xxiii, fig. 1: Shaw, Zool. iv, p. 493.
? *Lutjanus microstomus*, Lacép. iv, pp. 181, 216, and iii, t. xxxiv, f. 2.
? *Pristipoma Commersonii*, Cuv. and Val. v, p. 252.
Pomadasis argenteus, Lacép. iv, p. 516.
Pristipoma argenteum, Cuv. and Val. v, p. 249; Günther, Catal. i, p. 291.

B. vii, D. $\frac{12}{14}$, P. 15, V. 1/5, A. $\frac{3}{7}$, C. 17, L. l. 50, L. tr. 5/13.

Length of head 2/7, of caudal 2/13, height of body 3/10 of the total length. *Eyes*—diameter $3\frac{1}{2}$ in the length of head, 1 diameter from end of snout, and 2/3 of a diameter apart. The maxilla reaches to below the front edge of the eye. Preopercle serrated along its vertical limb and angle. Shoulder bone serrated, the one in the axilla entire. A deep groove under the symphysis of the lower jaw, and two small open pores anterior to it. *Teeth*—villiform, with the external row enlarged, most distinctly so in the upper jaw. *Fins*—dorsal spines of moderate strength, each alternate one thicker on one side, first short, second nearly twice its height but only half of the third which equals 3/7 of the height of the body, the fourth is nearly as high and the rest gradually decrease to the eleventh which equals the height of the second, the twelfth is a very little longer but more than 1/2 the height of the rays. Pectoral as long as the head: ventral almost reaches the anal. First anal spine short, the second moderately strong, having a raised keel along its anterior surface, and being nearly 1/2 as high as the body: third spine much weaker, and a little more than 1/3 shorter. *Lateral-line*—tubes expand posteriorly into a wedge-shape. Free portion of tail about as long as high. *Colours*—silvery, covered with black spots in the upper two-thirds of the body forming sinuous lines: a dark spot on the opercle. A row of basal spots along the dorsal fin, two more above it in the spinous portion, and a dark line along the soft fin.

This species has a less deeply cleft dorsal fin than is seen in *P. hasta* (except in the very young); irrespective of which it also differs from it or *P. nageb*, in its more obtuse snout, &c.

Habitat.—Red Sea and seas of India.

6. Pristipoma maculatum, Plate XIX, fig. 5.

Anthias maculatus, Bloch, t. 326, f. 2; Bl. Schn. p. 306.
Lutjanus maculatus, Lacép. iv, p. 233.
Perca caripa, Russell, Fishes Vizag, ii, p. 18, pl. 124.
Pristipoma caripa, Cuv. and Val. v, p. 261; Rüpp. N. W. Fische, p. 124; Cantor, Catal. p. 75; Bleeker, Sciæn. p. 21.
Pristipoma maculatum, Günther, Catal. i, p. 293; Day, Fishes of Malabar, p. 21; Kner, Novara Fische, p. 52; Klunzinger, Verh. z. b. Ges. Wien, 1870, p. 735; Bleeker, Rev. Pristip. 1873, p. 306.

* Marked *Pristipoma Commersonii*, on the plate.

Corps, Tel.: *Eeratten coroh*, Mal.: *Curruteke*, Tam.

B. vii, D. [illegible], P. 17, V. 1/5, A. [illegible], C. 17, L. l. 52-56, L. tr. 8/12, Cæc. pyl. 6.

Length of head 2/7, of caudal 1/6, height of body 1/3 to nearly 4/13 of the total length. *Eyes*—diameter 2 7 to 1/4 of length of head, $1\frac{1}{4}$ diameters from end of snout, and also apart. Maxilla extends to nearly or quite below the anterior edge of the orbit. Vertical limb of preopercle slightly emarginate and finely serrated, angle rounded and having two or three very small serrations; inferior limb crenulated or entire. Shoulder-bone entire. *Teeth*—villiform in the jaws, the outer row slightly the largest. *Fins*—fourth dorsal spine the highest, equalling the length of the postorbital portion of the head. Pectoral as long as the head: ventral does not reach the anal. Second anal spine a little longer and much stronger than the third, it equals 1/3 the height of the body: caudal emarginate. *Scales*—in oblique rows above the lateral-line and horizontal ones below it. *Colours*—greyish, becoming white beneath, and having a purplish tinge about the head: a blackish band over the snout: a second from the occiput touches the posterior edge of the orbit, and descends over the opercles. A vertical black band, about eight scales wide, passes over the nape and terminates about three scales below the lateral-line: posterior to this are six black blotches, three or four above, and two or three below the lateral-line, not forming bands, but placed like squares on a chess board. Spinous dorsal with a large black mark between its fourth and seventh or even eighth spines: soft dorsal with a dark band along its centre, and both dorsals with their edges stained black, as is also the caudal.

In *young specimens*, as $2\frac{3}{10}$ inches in length, the preopercle is strongly serrated along its vertical border: at $3\frac{1}{2}$ the serrations are still strong: at $4\frac{1}{2}$ there is but slight difference, whilst at $6\frac{1}{2}$ they are even less apparent.

Abnormal development.—In one specimen an extra spine is developed on one side of the second spine of the dorsal fin.

Habitat.—From the Red Sea and East coast of Africa, through the seas of India to the Malay Archipelago and New Guinea: it attains at least 16 inches in length: the specimen figured is 9 inches long.

7. Pristipoma Dussumieri, Plate XIX, fig. 6.

Cuv. and Val. v, p. 259; Günther, Catal. i, p. 291.
Pristipoma Neilli,* Day, Proc. Zool. Soc. 1867, p. 936.
Cutdah-kee, Tam.

B. vii, D. [illegible], P. 15, V. 1/5, A. [illegible], C. 19, L. l. 50, L. r. [illegible], L. tr. $6\frac{1}{2}$/15.

Length of head 1/4, of caudal 1/5, height of body rather more than 1/3 of the total length. *Eyes*—diameter 1/3 of length of head, nearly 1 diameter from end of snout, and 3/4 of a diameter apart. Jaws of about equal length anteriorly. The maxilla extends to nearly beneath the front edge of the orbit. Preopercle having its vertical limb slightly emarginate, its rounded angle being a little produced, and the whole serrated but most coarsely so at the angle, its horizontal limb with a few serrations along its posterior portion. *Teeth*—villiform in the jaws. *Fins*—dorsal spines strong, every alternate one being broader, interspinous membrane slightly notched, the fourth spine the longest and equal to two-fifths of the height of the body: pectoral as long as the head: ventral does not reach the anal, its first ray with a filamentous prolongation: second anal spine strong, one-fourth longer than the third, and equal to two-thirds the length of the head: caudal emarginate, being deeply lunated. *Colours*—greyish, becoming white on the abdomen: a brilliant golden band passes from the eye to the base of the caudal fin, a second above it runs along a few rows of scales. Fins silvery dashed with gold, a dark band along the base of the dorsal and its spinous portion with a black margin: upper portions of soft dorsal and the last half of spinous dorsal dark grey. Stuffed specimens lose their golden bands and appear uniform.

Habitat.—Seas of India, more common on the East than on the West coast, but nowhere numerous. Jerdon only obtained it on the Malabar coast (Madr. Journ. Lit. and Science, 1851, p. 132.)

8. Pristipoma guoraka, Plate XX, fig. 1.

? *Perca grunniens*, Forst. p. 294.
? *Anthias grunniens*, Bl. Schn. p. 308.
Perca guoraka, Russell, Fish. Vizag. ii, p. 24, pl. 132.
Pristipoma guoraka, Cuv. and Val. v, p. 256; Cantor, Catal. p. 73; Bleeker, Sciæn. p. 23, and Revis. Prist. 1873, p. 315, and Atl. Ich. Perc. t. xlv, fig. 1; Day, Fishes Malabar, p. 22; Kner, Novara Fische, p. 53.
Pristipoma argyreum, Cuv. and Val. ix, p. 485; Bleeker, Sciæn. p. 22, and Atl. Ich. Perc. t. xiii, fig. 4, and Revis. Prist. 1873, p. 313; Günther, Catal. i, p. 292; Day, Proc. Zool. Soc. 1870, p. 683.

B. vii, D. [illegible], P. 16, V. 1/5, A. [illegible], L. l. 45-47, L. tr. 6/12, Cæc. pyl. 5 (Kner).

Length of head 2/7, of caudal 1/6, height of body a little above 1/3 of the total length. *Eyes*—diameter $3\frac{1}{3}$ to $3\frac{3}{4}$ in length of head, 1 to $1\frac{1}{3}$ diameters from end of snout and also apart. A considerable rise from the snout to the base of the first dorsal. The maxilla hardly reaches to below the front edge of the orbit. Vertical limb of preopercle coarsely serrated, as is also its produced and rounded angle, where the serrations are wide apart, along the horizontal limb they are much blunter. Shoulder-bone serrated. *Teeth*—villiform, with the

* In the Zoological Record for 1867, p. 159, Dr. Günther observes: "*Pristipoma guoraka* (Cuv. and Val.) is described as *Pristipoma Neilli* (sp. n.) by Day." The type specimen is therefore figured, it is $6\frac{7}{10}$ inches in length.

outer row in the upper jaw somewhat enlarged. *Fins*—dorsal spines rather strong, the third and fourth the longest, and equal to half the height of the body below, but rather less in the young, interspinous membrane rather deeply notched, the last dorsal spine rather longer than the one preceding it. Pectoral equals the length of the head: second anal spine the longest,* and in the adult a fourth longer than the fifth of the dorsal, it is striated in grooves along its front edge: caudal cut square or slightly emarginate. *Colours*—silvery, darkest along the back, and in the young with an indistinct darkish band along the middle of the body: a dark spot, having steel blue reflections, exists on the opercle: snout dark: a dark streak along the dorsal fin most distinct in the immature. In a specimen 3¾ inches long the snout is dark, and there is a large black blotch covering 2/3 of the opercle.

Bleeker considers that *P. argyreum* is distinct from *P. guoraka*, the former being distinguished by a more obtuse and more convex profile, by the eyes being considerably larger, and by the second anal spine being weaker and shorter.

In examining a series of specimens of these fishes, it appears to me that one can hardly separate one species from the other, the difference being probably due to age and perhaps sex. In the young the eye is 1/3 the length of the head and only 1/2 a diameter from the end of the snout, and the second anal spine generally only equals the length of the postorbital portion of the head.

Habitat.—Seas of India to the Malay Archipelago, said to have been captured in fresh water. Russell observed that his fish was 2 feet in length, if it was this species, his specimen must have been a most extraordinarily large one.

9. Pristipoma operculare, Plate XX, fig. 2.

Playfair, Fish. Zanz. p. 24, pl. iv, f. 1.

B. vii. D. $\frac{12}{14}$, P. 19, V. 1/5, A. $\frac{3}{7}$, C. 17, L. l. 57, L. r. [illegible], L. tr. 9/19, Cæc. pyl. 5.

Length of head 2/7, of caudal 2/11 to 1/6, height of body 2/7 of the total length. *Eyes*—diameter 1/5 to 2/11 of length of head, 1¾ diameters from end of snout, and 1½ apart. Snout pointed and somewhat compressed: jaws of equal length. The maxilla reaches to below the posterior nostril. Preopercle emarginate, finely serrated, most coarsely so at its rounded angle. *Teeth*—in jaws villiform, the outer row being scarcely enlarged. *Fins*—dorsal spines strong, the fourth the highest, equal to the length of the postorbital portion of the head and higher than the rays. Pectoral as long as the head reaching to above the anal fin: the ventral does not reach to the anal: second anal spine the strongest and longest equal to the third of the dorsal: caudal emarginate. *Cæcal appendages*—very long. *Colours*—silvery, with a black blotch at the posterior-superior corner of the opercle: upper half of body with numerous black spots, which in some do, in others do not, form undulating bands: a black spot at the base of each dorsal spine and ray: dorsal and caudal dark edged: anal blackish in its front half.

The *young* are silvery, with the opercular spot distinct, a black mark in the axilla, and a few dark spots over the base of the pectoral fin: dark spots on the dorsal almost form bands along its upper and lower thirds: a dark band is likewise present along the centre of the soft portion: last half of caudal dark grey.

The form of this species is very similar to *P. sueb*, Rüppell, which, however, has D. $\frac{12}{13-14}$, L. l. 42-43, and the eye 1/6 of length of head. The second anal spine comparatively longer. In the specimen in Berlin, 16 inches long, the spots are sprinkled over one side of the body, but in bands as shown in Rüppell's figure on the other. A specimen of *P. sulliaa*, C.V. at Berlin from the Cape of Good Hope makes it doubtful whether *P. operculare* may not prove to be a variety of that species.

Habitat.—East coast of Africa to Sind, where it is common: attaining at least 15 inches in length.

Genus, 18—Hapalogenys, *Richards.*

Pogonias, sp. Tem. and Schleg.

Branchiostegals six or seven: pseudobranchiæ. Body rather elevated and compressed. Eyes of moderate size. Cleft of mouth horizontal: the anterior and under surfaces of the lower jaw and the lips covered with fine barbel-form papillæ. Preopercle serrated: opercle with short spines. Villiform teeth in the jaws, vomer, and palatines: an outer row of conical but somewhat obtuse teeth in either jaw, but no canines: tongue smooth. A deeply notched dorsal fin having eleven spines: anal with three: caudal convex or slightly notched. Scales ctenoid, of moderate or small size, and extended over the fins. Air-vessel simple. Pyloric appendages few.

Geographical distribution.—Seas of Sind to China and Japan.

The specimen captured off Sind differs from the usual definition of the Genus,† and I am indebted to the kind services of Professor Peters for suggesting its present position.

* In six specimens in my collection the following are the comparative lengths as regards the second anal spine:

	Total length	of body without caudal fin	anal spine	in length of body
1.	3[illegible] inches	2[illegible] inches	[illegible] inches	or 5[illegible]
2.	3[illegible] "	3[illegible] "	[illegible] "	" 5½ "
3.	4[illegible] "	3[illegible] "	[illegible] "	" 5[illegible] "
4.	4[illegible] "	3[illegible] "	[illegible] "	" 5[illegible] "
5.	4[illegible] "	3[illegible] "	[illegible] "	" 5[illegible] "
6.	5[illegible] "	4[illegible] "	[illegible] "	" 5[illegible] "

† The single species recorded here has seven (not six) branchiostegal rays: its spinous dorsal is very low, and divided by a notch from the soft portion of the fin, making one almost doubt the propriety of including it in this Genus. On the other hand the general form of the body, the dentition, &c. being the same, it is placed as an aberrant form of *Hapalogenys*.

SYNOPSIS OF INDIVIDUAL SPECIES.

1. *Hapalogenys Petersi*, D. $\frac{11}{15}$, A. $\frac{3}{8}$, L. l. 100. Colours dark slatey, with the fins nearly black. Sind.

1. Hapalogenys Petersi, Plate XX, fig. 3.

B. vii, D. $\frac{11}{15}$, P. 19, V. 1/5, A. $\frac{3}{8}$, C. 17, L. l. ca. 100.

Length of head 2/7, of caudal nearly 1/6, height of body 4/13 of the total length. *Eyes*—diameter 2/7 of length of head, rather above 1 diameter from end of snout, and 3/4 of a diameter apart. Dorsal profile much more convex than that of the abdomen, a considerable rise from snout to the base of the dorsal fin, with a shallow concavity over the forehead. Lower jaw somewhat the longer, the maxilla reaches to below the hind third of the orbit. Vertical limb of preopercle somewhat emarginate and finely serrated in its whole extent, but the serrations are concealed by the scales: preorbital, sub- and inter-opercles entire. Two very obtuse spines on opercle. Lips thick, they, the chin, and under surface of lower jaw with innumerable closely-set fine papillæ, having barbel-like prolongations, but without any groove or deep pores. *Teeth*—villiform ones in jaws, vomer, and palate, the upper jaw with an outer row of from twenty to thirty conical ones, of no great size, and a similar row but of lesser number in the lower jaw. *Fins*—dorsal spines of moderate strength, very low in proportion to the rays, they increase in height to the third which equals three-fourths of the diameter of the eye in length, those posterior to it gradually decrease in length to the last but one, the last being higher and its length equal to three-fourths of that of the third spine: interspinous membrane deeply notched: soft portion of the fin highest anteriorly where the rays equal the length of the postorbital portion of the head, whereas the last only equals the height of the third dorsal spine: the pectoral equals the length of the head excluding the snout: the ventral reaches a little more than half way to the base of the anal: third anal spine much longer and stronger than the second, its length equal to the highest in the dorsal fin, soft portion of the fin similar to that of the soft dorsal: caudal emarginate. *Scales*—small, finely ctenoid, and covering all the fins. *Colours*—blackish-grey with the fins darker.

Habitat.—Sind and Meckran coast, being termed *Dah-ri*, at Gwadur. Although the species was not uncommon the specimens were so large, I was unable to bring away more than the skin of the smallest one, 18 inches in length, which was preserved in spirit, and from which the figure was taken.

Genus, 19—Diagramma, *Cuv.*

Plectorhynchus, pt. Lacép.

Branchiostegals six or seven: pseudobranchiæ. Body oblong, compressed, with the upper profile of the head parabolic. Eyes of moderate size. Mouth small, slightly protractile: lips thick and folded back. Preopercle serrated: suborbitals entire. Four or six open pores on the under surface of the lower jaw but no median groove. Teeth in jaws villiform, without canines: palate edentulous. One dorsal fin more or less receivable into a groove along its base, having from nine to fourteen spines: anal with three. Caudal not forked. Scales ctenoid, usually small, but of a moderate size in some species, present on the head excluding the lower jaw, and usually continued on to the soft dorsal and anal fins. Air-vessel simple, destitute of any constriction. Pyloric appendages few.

Geographical distribution.—From the Red Sea and East coast of Africa, through the seas of India to the Malay Archipelago and beyond. These fishes are much more abundant off Sind and as far as Bombay, than they are down the Malabar or Coromandel coasts of India. In fact Russell does not figure one of the genus.

Uses—generally not in much esteem as food, but some are good eating.

The species forming this genus are subject to considerable variations in the number of the dorsal rays, whilst a spine* more or less may exist. Irrespective of the differences observable in the dorsal fin, the colour varies almost as widely as amongst the *Serrani* (see page 9, ante). The ground colour is usually white or yellow in those which are striped longitudinally: there are, as a rule, component parts of two very distinct bands, the upper commencing above the eye by a wide base including the second dorsal spine and ending in a wedge-shaped form along the soft dorsal, both the roots of this band and its terminal extremities may be composed of several narrow ones which coalesce: next there is a central broad one going from the eye to the middle of the caudal fin, also terminating in a wedge-shaped form, this broad band may be made up of two parallel narrow ones, separated by an interspace: below this central band may be a lower or third one, either single or constituted of one or more narrow ones. If this is the correct solution of the composition of the ornamental colouring of these fishes, it seems by no means unlikely that some of those now recognised as species, will have to be considered as varieties. The form of the caudal fin often varies considerably in the same species, and this does not appear to be simply due to age.

SYNOPSIS OF SPECIES.

1. *Diagramma crassispinum*, D. [illegible], A. $\frac{3}{7}$. Black, tail and edges of dorsal and anal fins white in the immature. Seas of India to the Malay Archipelago and beyond.

2. *Diagramma lineatum*, D. [illegible], A. [illegible]. Yellowish-white with about six longitudinal chestnut bands, which may be reduced by amalgamation into three broad ones: anterior dorsal spines not much higher than the others. Red Sea, seas of India to the Malay Archipelago and beyond.

* Regarding the dorsal spines "in fact the height of these spines appear to vary very much, and I fully believe that *D. balteatum* is a variety of *D. pictum*."—Günther, Catal. i, p. 328. If therefore the number of spines and rays likewise vary, and the colours are subject to considerable modifications, great caution becomes necessary to prevent falling into the error of considering a variety as a distinct species.

3. *Diagramma Orientale*, D. [illegible], A. [illegible]. Yellowish-white, with four or five complete or interrupted chestnut bands. Red Sea, seas of India to the Malay Archipelago and beyond.

4. *Diagramma cinctum*, D. [illegible], A. [illegible]. Slatey-grey, covered with large black blotches which also exist on the fins. Sind, China, and Japan.

5. *Diagramma griseum*, D. [illegible], A. [illegible]. Grey: fins blackish. East coast of Africa, seas of India.

6. *Diagramma pictum*, D. [illegible], A. [illegible]. Front portion of spinous dorsal elevated. Caudal rounded. Longitudinally banded. Red Sea, East coast of Africa, seas of India to the Malay Archipelago and beyond.

7. *Diagramma punctatum*, D. [illegible], A. [illegible]. Front portion of spinous dorsal not elevated: caudal notched, spotted and blotched with yellow. Red Sea, seas of India to the Malay Archipelago.

8. *Diagramma picoides*, D. [illegible], A. [illegible]. Four large light blotches. Indian seas.

1. **Diagramma crassispinum**, Plate XX, fig. 4.

Diagramma crassispinum, Rüppell, N. W. Fische, p. 125, t. 30, f. 4; Bleeker, Sciæn. p. 26; Günther, Catal. i, p. 319; Klunz. Verh. z. b. Ges. Wien, 1870, p. 738.

Pristipoma nigrum, Cantor, Catal. p. 74; ? Cuv. and Val. v, p. 258; Günther, Catal. i, p. 289.

Diagramma affine, Günther, Catal. i, p. 319;* Playfair, Fishes of Zanzibar, p. 26.

Diagramma nigrum, Day, Malabar Fishes, p. 23.

Diagramma altum, Day, Proc. Zool. Soc. 1869, p. 514 *(young)*.

Plectorhynchus crassispina, Bleeker, Ternate, p. 232 and Rev. Plec. 1873, p. 277.

B. vii, D. [illegible], P. 17, V. 1/5, A. [illegible], C. 17, L. l. 50-60, L. r. [illegible], L. tr. 10/17, Cæc. pyl. 6.

Length of head 2/7, of caudal 1/6, height of body in the adult 1/3 of the total length. *Eyes*—diameter in the adult 2/9 of length of head, $1\frac{1}{2}$ diameters from end of snout, and more than one apart. The maxilla does not reach so far in the adult as to below the front edge of the orbit. Open pores but no groove below the mandible. Vertical limb of preopercle finely serrated in the adult, more coarsely so in the young, and its angle rounded, posterior half of its horizontal limb serrated. *Teeth*—villiform in the jaws. *Fins*—dorsal spines strong, the alternate ones thicker on one side, the fourth the highest, nearly equalling the length of the head without the snout: pectoral rather longer than the highest dorsal spine, it reaches to rather beyond the ventral, which latter extends three-fourths of the way to the anus. Second anal spine much stronger than the third, it equals the highest of the dorsal fin. Free portion of tail rather longer than high at its commencement. *Colours*—greyish, or slatey-grey, with a violet tinge over the head, and a brassy one on the body: fins nearly black. A few irregular coppery spots on the body, and a tinge of the same colour over the spinous dorsal: the other fins of a violet slate-colour, lightest along their centres. In the *young* the caudal is yellowish-white, and in one specimen having a dark caudal, which I kept a few years in spirit I now find the fin nearly white, the colouring matter having disappeared.

This fish appears to alter considerably with age. The height of the body is at first equal to nearly half of the total length. In some the maxilla extends to below the first third of the orbit, in others to beneath the posterior nostril; whilst the size of the eye varies in individual specimens.

The specimen marked *Diagramma crassispinum* in the British Museum, received from Zanzibar, is a skin under 10 inches in length, and not in a good state; the spines are a little shorter than in a Malabar specimen of the same size, irrespective of which it has several narrow black bands passing backwards and downwards from the base of the dorsal fin over the body.

Jerdon, M. J. L. and S. 1851, observes of *Scolopsides*: "a fourth species is also found, of which, however, I only saw one specimen. Its colours were inky black, with the edges of the soft dorsal white, and the caudal pale yellowish-white. It was called *Tawoolee pinnel*." The figure is amongst Sir W. Elliot's collection named as above by Jerdon, and is this species.

Habitat.—Red Sea, seas of India to the Malay Archipelago and beyond. It attains two feet or more in length and is good eating.

2. **Diagramma lineatum**, Plate XX, fig. 5.

Sciæna lineata, Linn. Mus. Ad. Frid. t. xxxi, f. 4.

Perca diagramma et lineata, Gmel. Linn. p. 1319.

Grammistes lineatus, Bl. Schn. p. 186.

Diagramma lineatum, Cuv and Val. v, p. 309: Bleeker, Amboina, iv, p. 112; Günther, Catal. i, p. 330; Klunz. Verh. z. b. Ges. Wien, 1870, p. 735.

Diagramma Lessonii, Cuv. and Val. v, p. 313; Less. Voy. Coq. Zool. ii, p. 119, pl. 24; Bleeker, Bat. p. 463; Gunther, Catal. i, p. 329, and Fische d. Sudsee, p. 28, t. xxiii.

Diagramma albovittatum, Rüpp. N. W. Fische, p. 125, t. xxxi, fig. 2; Bleeker, Makass. p. 46; Günther, Catal. i, p. 330; Klunz. l. c. p. 736.

Plectorhynchus lineatus, Bleeker, Atl. Ich. Perc. t. xxviii, f. 4, Ternate, p. 232 and Revis. Plector. p. 286.

Plectorhynchus Lessoni, Bleeker, Atl. Ich. Perc. t. xxxix, fig. 3 and Revis. Plector. p. 288.

Plectorhynchus albovittatus, Bleeker, Revis. Plector. p. 280.

* References to the plates and figures cited in the British Museum Catalogue are omitted as misleading, for such have not been published, and the figures do not now exist.

B. vi, D. [illegible], P. 19, V. 1/5, A. 3/7, C. 17, L. l. 59, L. r. [illegible], L. tr. 13/24.

Length of head about 1/4, of caudal 1/6, height of body from 4/13 to 2/7 of the total length. *Eyes*—diameter from 1/3 to 2/7 of length of head, 1 diameter from end of snout, and nearly 1 apart. Dorsal profile much more convex than that of the abdomen, profile of head parabolic. The maxilla reaches to below the front third of the orbit. The depth of the preorbital nearly equals the diameter of the eye. Vertical limb of preopercle very slightly emarginate, its angle rounded, and the whole finely and evenly serrated. *Teeth*—fine. *Fins*—dorsal spines strong, every alternate one broadest on one side, they increase in height to the fourth, which equals two-fifths or one-third of that of the body, the last being about one-fifth shorter, soft portion of the fin gradually increasing in height, its middle third being higher than the spinous. Pectoral as long as the head without the snout: ventral reaching three-fourths of the distance to the anal, the second spine of which latter fin is stronger and slightly longer than the third, equalling the length of the head behind the middle of the orbit: caudal rounded, or cut rather square. *Colours*—*D. lineatum*, yellowish-white superiorly, becoming white along the sides and on the abdomen: about six chestnut-coloured bands, the upper being wider than the ground colour, extend from the head along the body, the two first below the soft dorsal fin, coalescing and being continued along its centre as far as its termination in a wedge-shaped form: the third passes through the upper third of the eye along the side to a little above the centre of the caudal fin, and in its course touches the lower edge of the soft dorsal: the fourth arises by one or two roots below the eye, and goes to the lower third of the caudal, and joining with the last band, is continued in a pointed manner to its termination: the fifth proceeds from the angle of the mouth to the lower edge of the base of the caudal, and the sixth from below it to the lower edge of the soft portion of the anal: fins yellow, with sometimes one or more dark blotches: dorsal with a dark edge, which may be confined to its soft portion: three oblique bands across either caudal lobe, which are occasionally broken up into blotches: a band along the middle of the anal fin.

Variety.—*Diagramma albovittatum*, silvery-white above, becoming yellowish-white below, a dark chestnut median band commences on the occiput opposite the middle of the eye, and goes to the anterior dorsal spine, being continued first along the bases of the spines, but attaining their middle posteriorly, it joins the second band: the second chestnut band commences on the snout and passes above the eye, and gradually increasing in width posteriorly, arrives at the base of the soft dorsal, and is continued along its middle as far as its termination in a wedge-shaped form: the third band, which may be considered the coalescence of the two in *D. lineatum*, extends from the snout through the eye, becomes the widest, and arriving at the centre of the base of the tail, diminishes in width, and is continued in a wedge-shape to the termination of the fin. Fins yellow, a narrow dark edge to the spinous dorsal, which increases in width over the soft portion: two oblique dark bands across the upper caudal lobe and one along the lower: a darkish edge to ventrals, and the outer half of anal with a dark band.

In some specimens a wide chestnut coloured band appears to extend from below the eye, covering the abdomen, and leaving only a very narrow interspace of whitish ground colour between it and the band immediately above it; in such specimens the colour of the body appears to be chestnut, with three narrow white or light longitudinal bands. It must, however, be evident that other points being identical, this form is merely the *D. lineatum** with three instead of six longitudinal body bands, which, due to their decrease in number, show an increase in width.

Bleeker (Revis. Plector. p. 282) observes that *albovittatum* has no dark border to the spinous dorsal, nor spots on the paired fins, whilst the dorsal spines are of about equal length. A frontal profile little or not at all convex. L. r. [illegible]. The specimen I have figured has L. r. [illegible], and appears to so connect the two species that it is difficult to say to which it belongs, the colours and form of the spinous dorsal being such as refers it more to *lineatum* than *albovittatum*, but the number of scales, absence of spots on the paired fins, and a black edge to the spinous dorsal, being such as have been pointed out as characteristic of *albovittatum*.

In the Catalogue of Fishes of the British Museum, i, p. 330, *Bodian Cuvier*, Bennett Fish. Ceylon, p. 13, fig. 13 is referred to *Diagramma lineatum*.† In the "Fishes of Zanzibar," p. 28, under the head of *Diagramma Cuvieri*, is Seba, iii, 27, 19, *Bodian Cuvier*, Bennett, and *Diagramma Sebæ*, Bleeker, whilst *D. Lessonii* (*l. c.*) is recorded as a distinct species. In the "Fische d. Sudsee," p. 28, the synonyms for *D. Lessonii* are *D. sebæ*, Bleeker, but Bennett's fish is not referred to. Bleeker in his revision of these fishes (pp. 288-9) observes that *Lessonii* is very near *lineatus*, and may represent its adult age, the formula of the scales and rays being identical.

Turning to Bleeker's figure of *D. Sebæ*, = *D. Lessonii*, Günther, the anterior dorsal spines in the former appear to be more elevated. If the two longitudinal bands from the eye in the figure referred to were amalgamated, and the fin marks reduced to blotches or spots so frequently the case in large specimens,

* Klunzinger (Verh. z. b. Ges. Wien, 1870, p. 736) observes that *D. Bleekii* differs from *D. albovittatum* in having 10 dorsal spines, &c., and places *D. lineatum* (l. c. p. 735) as a variety of *D. punctatum*.

† It is also a subject worthy of consideration whether *Plectorhynchus polytænia* = *P. polytænioides*, Bleeker, L. r. [illegible], is not identical with *P. Goldmanni*, = *P. hæmatochir*, L. l. [illegible], the former having a bluish instead of a yellowish-white ground colour, and the bands being light brown instead of dark chestnut, whilst the deficiency of colouring matter accounts for the absence of spots on the fins of the former but present in the latter. The colouring of *P. Goldmanni* again approaches very nearly that of *P.* or *Diagramma Sebæ*, Bleeker, L. l. [illegible], which, as observed, is considered by Dr. Günther as identical with *D. Lessonii*, which is a variety of *D. lineatum*.

the colours would considerably resemble those of *lineatum*; the three upper bands would only have to be conjoined and continued on to the dorsal fin, when *albovittatum* would be reproduced. But Bleeker observes that the scales are L. r. $\frac{100}{88}$, and more than are found in *lineatum* or *Lessonii*: were it not for that fact, one would almost feel inclined to agree with Dr. Günther, and place it as another synonym of *lineatum*.

It is very desirable that some one residing where these fishes are to be obtained in quantities, as Sind or the Andamans, would bring together a large number, of all sizes, at different seasons of the year, carefully examine the sexes, and the number of their cæcal appendages whilst they are in a fresh state, making a comparison between all the differently coloured ones, the result I anticipate would be, as in the *Serrani*, that a conclusion must be arrived at, that there are many varieties but comparatively few species.

Habitat.—Red Sea, seas of India to the Malay Archipelago and beyond. The specimen figured was given me by Dr. Shortt, Inspector General of Vaccination for the Madras Presidency, who received it whilst fresh at Cuddalore in 1867. Personally I never obtained a specimen of this genus along the Coromandel coast.

3. **Diagramma Orientale**, Plate XX, fig. 6.

Anthias Orientalis, Bloch. t. 326, fig. 3; Bl. Schn. p. 306.
Lutjanus aurantius, Lacép. iv, p. 239.
Serranus Orientalis, Cuv. and Val. ii, p. 318.
Diagramma pica, Cuv. and Val. v, p. 297; Günther, Catal. i, p. 326, and Fische d. Sudsee, p. 27, t. xxii, fig. A.
Diagramma Orientale, Cuv. and Val. v, p. 299, pl. 124; Bleeker, Verh. Bat. Gen. xxiii, Sciaen. p. 23; Günther, Catal. i, p. 326 and Fische d. Sudsee, p. 28, taf. xxii, fig. B and C.
Diagramma Sibbaldii, Bennett, Proc. Zool. Soc. 1832, p. 182.
Plectorhynchus Orientalis, Swains. Fish. ii, p. 218; Bleeker, Atl. Ich. Perc. t. xxviii, fig. 3, and Revis. Plectorh. p. 295.

B. vi, D. $\frac{13}{11}|\frac{1}{15}$, P. 17, V. 1/5, A. $\frac{3}{7}$, C. 17, L. r. $\frac{100}{85}$, L. tr. 13/25.

Length of head from 3/13 to 2/9, of caudal 1/6 to 1/7, height of body 2/7 of the total length. *Eyes*—diameter from 1/3 to 2/7 of length of head, 1 diameter from the end of snout. Dorsal profile much more convex than the abdominal: profile of head parabolic. The maxilla reaches to below the front third of the orbit: the depth of the preorbital nearly equals the diameter of the eye. Vertical limb of preopercle serrated, its angle not produced. *Teeth*—generic. *Fins*—dorsal spines of moderate strength, every alternate one strongest on one side, the second nearly as high as the third which is the longest in the fin and equals from half to two-fifths of the height of the body, the last being from one-third to one-half shorter: soft portion of the fin gradually increasing in height, its middle third being higher than the spinous. Pectoral as long as the head without the snout: ventral reaching three-fourths of the distance to the anal, the second spine of which latter fin is stronger and longer than the third, equalling the length of the head posterior to the middle of the eye: caudal rounded or cut rather square. *Colours*—yellowish superiorly, becoming white on the sides and beneath, the body with several chestnut bands nearly or quite as wide as the ground-colour. There may be four or five complete or interrupted horizontal bands along the snout and head, which form three or four on the body: the highest going to the base of the spinous dorsal: the second, usually interrupted, to the first two-thirds of the base of the soft dorsal: the third bifurcating beyond the end of the pectoral fin divides into two, the superior, often interrupted, going to the upper portion of the caudal fin, and the inferior to its lower portion, on the caudal these two bands gradually approximate or even coalesce, and are so continued to the centre of the fins termination: the lowest body band goes from below the pectoral fin to the end of the base of the anal. Spinous dorsal with a narrow dark upper edge: a dark angular band along its base, which is anteriorly two-thirds as high as the spines, but ending in a point at the base of the last spine: a similar wedge-shaped band exists on the soft dorsal, its base being along the origin of the first ten or twelve rays and its apex at the upper termination of the same rays. Pectoral yellowish, with a dark blotch covering all but its margin: a black band along the middle of the anal and an oblique one across either lobe of the caudal, the lower being sometimes divided into two, or having a light spot in its centre.

The *Orientale* figured in Bloch, Cuv. and Val., and in Garrett's Fische d. Sudsee shows much of the colouring of *D. pica*:—a band passes vertically from the upper surface of the head behind the eye to the angle of the mouth, and from it proceeds a wide single horizontal one along the body which is more or less interrupted but eventually constitutes a central caudal band: from this lateral band one may proceed directly upwards and form the basal blotch on the spinous dorsal, or it may be interrupted in this course; a second band proceeds upwards and forms the blotch on the soft dorsal: a lower band likewise proceeds from the base of the pectoral to the end of the anal joining the band on that fin: the marks on the fins are as in the first variety.

That this species is very closely related to *D. lineatum* is apparent: its colouring is evidently a modification of identical bands somewhat differently disposed. The dorsal spines however differ, and to judge by this question solely would cause Bennett's figure of *Bodian Cuvier*, p. 13, fig. 13, to be a *Diagramma* with much the form of *Orientale* and the colouring of *D. lineatum*. Cantor indeed observes of it, "in the absence of a detailed description * * the species cannot be determined."

Habitat.—Red Sea, seas of India, to the Malay Archipelago, and beyond.

4. Diagramma cinctum, Plate XXI, fig. 1.

Diagramma cinctum, Temm. and Schleg. Fauna Japonica, Pois. p. 61, pl. 26, f. 1; Richardson, Ich. China, p. 226; Günther, Catal. i, p. 325.

B. vii, D. [illegible], P. 17, V. 1/5, A. $\frac{3}{7}$, C. 17, L. l. 56, L. r. [illegible], L. tr. 11/20.

Length of head 3/11, of caudal 1/6, height of body 1/3 of the total length. *Eyes*—diameter $4\frac{1}{2}$ in length of head, $1\frac{1}{2}$ diameters from end of snout, and 1 apart. A considerable rise from the snout to the base of the dorsal fin: upper jaw slightly the longer. The maxilla reaches to below the front edge of the orbit. Vertical margin of preopercle also shoulder-bone serrated. *Teeth*—villiform in the jaws. *Fins*—dorsal spines strong, increasing in length to the fourth and fifth, which are equal in height to nearly half that of the body, from the fifth they decrease in length: soft portions of dorsal and anal rounded. Pectoral half as long as the body is high, it does not reach so far as the ventral, which last extends three-fourths of the way to the anal: second anal spine much stronger and longer than the third, it equals nearly 1/3 the height of the body and the length of the postorbital portion of the head: caudal cut square. *Colours*—slaty-grey, the upper half of the anterior and the whole of the posterior portion of the body covered with large black blotches. Two rows of black blotches and an outer black margin to the dorsal fin, usually an additional row on the soft portion: caudal and soft portion of the anal likewise with black blotches and a black margin: ventral nearly black: pectoral yellow. The bands on the body alluded to in the 'Fauna Japonica' and shown in the plate do not exist in my Indian specimens.

Habitat.—Sind, where it is not uncommon, attaining to two feet in length; also in China and Japan. In the British Museum is a specimen marked "*g*. adult: skin. Nepal? Presented by B. H. Hodgson, Esq." (Catal. vol. i, p. 326); this marine fish, it is almost unnecessary to observe, could not have been captured in such a locality, but was probably obtained from the mouth of the Hooghly along with several other sea fish, which are likewise recorded as from Nepal and sent by Mr. Hodgson.

5. Diagramma griseum, Plate XXI, fig. 2.

Cuv. and Val. v, p. 306; Günther, Catal. i, p. 321; Playfair, Fishes of Zanzibar, p. 26, pl. iv, fig. 3, var. *b*. and Proc. Zool. Soc. 1867, p. 851.*

B. vii, D. [illegible], P. 17, V. 1/5, A. $\frac{3}{8}$, C. 17, L. l. 63, L. r. [illegible], L. tr. 13/26, Cæc. pyl. 9.

Length of head 3/11 to 1/4, of caudal 1/6, height of body 1/3 of the total length. *Eyes*—diameter from 2/7 in the young to 1/4 of length of head, $1\frac{1}{2}$ diameters from end of snout, and 1 apart. The profile from the snout to occiput more obtuse in adults than in the young. The maxilla reaches to below the posterior nostril. Vertical limb of preopercle rather strongly and evenly serrated, angle rounded and also serrated. Shoulder-bone serrated. *Teeth*—villiform in the jaws. *Fins*—dorsal spines of moderate strength, the third or fourth the highest and equal to the length of the postorbital portion of the head, from thence they gradually decrease to the last; height of soft dorsal scarcely exceeds that of one-third of the body. Pectoral as long as head without the snout and of about equal length to the ventral: second anal spine strongest and longest, equalling the distance between the middle of the orbit and the end of the head in the young or merely the postorbital portion in the adult: caudal slightly emarginate. Free portion of tail as deep at its commencement as it is long. *Scales*—in oblique rows above the lateral-line, some are present on the preorbital. *Colours*—uniform grey or olive-grey with the fins nearly or quite black. In the *young* the general colour is olive, with some sinuous and narrow light blue lines over the snout and cheeks, but which usually fade shortly after death. There are also several sinuous blue lines taking an oblique direction from the head upwards, and which extend to nearly the length of the body. Also a black mark over the posterior end of the free portion of the tail.

Variety.—"Colour grey above, white below, with four whitish curved cross bands; the first crosses the forehead and terminates at the angles of the operculum and preoperculum: the second proceeds from the second dorsal spine, in the direction of the root of the ventrals: the third runs parallel to the last from the seventh and eighth dorsal spines; and the last, also parallel, runs from the first anal ray to the posterior of anal. Fins blackish, immaculate. Length $4\frac{1}{2}$ to 17 inches." ("Fishes of Zanzibar," p. 26.)

Diagramma sordidum, Klunz. (Verh. z. b. Ges. Wien, 1870, p. 67) = ? *Sciæna schotaf*, Forsk. (p. 51) has the sixth dorsal spine the highest and slightly longer than in *D. griseum*, D. [illegible], A. $\frac{3}{8}$. The above is from one of the type specimens which closely resembles *D. griseum*.

Habitat.—East coast of Africa, Beloochistan and seas of India, attaining at least 18 inches in length. It is very common in Sind and Bombay. Specimen figured 6 inches long.

6. Diagramma pictum, Plate XXI, fig. 3.

Perca picta, Thunb. Nya Handl. xiii, 1792, p. 142, pl. v, fig. 1.
Sciæna albo-sagittata, Forsk. p. 51.

* Col. Playfair observes that "several specimens of this fish were caught in a mountain-torrent in Seychelles, which loses itself in a sand-bank without reaching the sea. The only direct communication between the two is after unusually heavy floods, so that it would appear that this salt water species not only visits, but habitually lives in fresh water." This conclusion requires modification, the species perhaps, as is common with many other marine forms in the East, entered the river with the rain floods, and owing to a sudden cut-off, its return to the ocean became cut off, and those which did not die were waiting for the next rains to allow them to escape to the sea (see page 68 ante).

Anthias diagramma, Bloch, t. 320 (var. *Blochii*).
Grammistes pictus, Bl. Schn. pp. 184, 190.
Holocentrus radjabau, Lacép. iv, pp. 335, 374.
Lutjanus pictus, Lacép. v, pp. 687, 688.
Diagramma Blochii, Cuv. and Val. v, p. 312; Günther, Catal. i, p. 329.
? *Diagramma pœcilopterum*, Cuv. and Val. v, p. 314; Temm. and Schleg. Fauna Japon. Poiss. p. 61; Günther, Catal. i, p. 329.
Diagramma pictum, Cuv. and Val. v, p. 315; Tem. and Schleg. Fauna Japon. p. 62; Richardson, Ich. China, p. 227; Günther, Catal. i, p. 327.
Diagramma balteatum, (Kuhl. and v. Hass.) Cuv. and Val. v, p. 316.
Plectorhynchus Blochii, Cantor, Catal. p. 77.
Plectorhynchus balteatus, Cantor, Catal. p. 78.
Plectorhynchus punctatus, Bleeker, Atl. Ich. Perc. xxii, fig. 1, Ceram, p. 187, and Revis. Plector. p. 298.

B. vi, D. $\frac{9}{19}$ [illegible], P. 17, V. 1/5, A. $\frac{3}{7}$, L. r. [illegible], L. tr. 15/26.

Length of head 2/9, of caudal 2/13, height of body 4/15 of the total length. *Eyes*—diameter 2/7 (in the young) to 2/9 of the length of head, $1\frac{1}{2}$ to 2 diameters from the end of snout, and nearly 1 apart. The maxilla reaches to below the front edge of the orbit. *Teeth*—generic. *Fins*—dorsal spines of moderate strength, the first short, the third usually the highest and equalling about one half the depth of the body, the second and fourth spines are of nearly the same height but variations are constantly found, the last dorsal spine is about one fourth of the height of the body, and the rays a little higher than the anterior or most elevated portion of the spines. Pectoral as long as the head excluding the snout: the second and third anal spines of about the same length and equal to about half the length of the head or the height of the sixth dorsal spine: caudal cut nearly square, or with rounded angles. *Colours*—This fish having been divided into several species due to variations in colour, I propose describing such in accordance with what appears to me to be that most readily explained. *Diagramma Blochii* (variety) orange yellow or white, with chestnut brown or black longitudinal bands, the upper three of which commence between the eye and the base of the first dorsal spine, the superior narrow runs along the base of the spinous dorsal and joins the one on the dorsal fin: the second and third are broader and coalesce above the middle of the pectoral fin, becoming lost below the base of the soft dorsal and on the upper edge of the free portion of the tail: the fourth and fifth proceed from the snout, through the eye, and go direct to the centre of the base of the caudal, where they join and are continued to the end of the fin in a wedge-shaped form: below these bands are one or two more, the upper of which goes to the lower edge of the free portion of the tail. Dorsal fin with a narrow black margin, a broad dark band runs from the upper two-thirds of its second spine backwards and downwards to the base of the fin, leaving the lower third of the second and third spines uncovered, this band is sometimes interrupted (as shown by Bloch), causing a black spot to exist between its third and fourth spines; if continuous (as in Pl. xxi, fig. 3), it coalesces with the upper body band, and is continued in a wedge-shaped form to the posterior-superior angle of the soft dorsal fin. Caudal with a central wedge-shaped dark band, and a cross-band over its upper and lower angles, these are frequently broken up into spots: the lower half of the anal and the end of the ventral black.*

A very interesting form of colouring exists in a specimen with D. [illegible] from Madras, presented by Dr. Jerdon to the British Museum, it is the intermediate form of ornamental colouring between *D. Blochii* and *D. pictum*, the two bands which pass backwards from the eye to the caudal fin become merged into one below the middle of the soft dorsal.

Diagramma pictum has the same ground colour as *D. Blochii* with fewer but wider longitudinal bands: the first, second, and third bands coalesce much sooner, the upper two below the middle or end of the spinous dorsal, and the second and third on the nape: whilst the two bands which pass backwards from the eye to the caudal fin, and which coalesce in Dr. Jerdon's specimen below the middle of the soft dorsal, in the typical *pictum* form a single broad one by the amalgamation of them in their whole length from the eye to the tail. The fins are coloured as described for *D. Blochii*, in short the immature appear to be generally coloured as in the typical *D. pictum*.

Bleeker's figure of *Plectorhynchus punctatus* is this species, the ornamental colouring being increased by the addition of some extra intermediate bands which are broken up into spots: the ventral and anal are likewise darker, due to the existence of additional colour.

In a bad skin in the British Museum, marked *D. Blochii* with D. $\frac{13}{17}$, all the longitudinal bands are broken up into a series of elongated spots or blotches.

Having remarked how the wide bands in the typical *D. pictum* are liable to be varied by the existence of more numerous but narrower ones in *D. Blochii* it remains to be observed that they may be further modified by being broken up into rows of oblong blotches or spots; or when narrow bands exist they may be alternately complete or interrupted as in *D. pœcilopterum*.

* Col. Playfair, Fish. Zanz. p. 28, apparently on the authority of a single skin, asserts "the colour of the adult is dark grey, with darker longitudinal lines and series of spots; fins blackish, except pectorals, which are grey." But as specimens with the colouring of the typical *Blochii* exist as large as the grey lineated one, I think it would be preferable to consider such as having a peculiar form of colouring. However, a doubt is raised as to whether *Diagramma Blochii*, Cuv. and Val., is *Anthias diagramma*, Bloch, as he remarks "the younger specimen agrees perfectly with the *Anthias diagramma* of Bloch, although it is doubtful whether it is the same as the *D. Blochii* of Cuvier and Valenciennes, which is only known from a figure taken at Trincomalee."

Habitat.—Red Sea, East coast of Africa, seas of India to the Malay Archipelago and beyond. The specimen is figured life-size.

7. Diagramma punctatum, Plate XXI, fig. 4.

(Ehren.) Cuv. and Val. v, p. 302; Temm. and Schleg. Fauna Japon. p. 60, pl. xxvi, A; Rüpp. Atl. Fische, p. 126, t. 32, f. 2, and N. W. Fische, p. 125; Quoy and Gaim. Voy. Astrol. Poiss. p. 689, pl. xii, fig. 2; Günther, Catal. i, p. 323; Kner, Novara, Fische, p. 54; Klunzinger, Verh. z. b. Ges. Wien, 1870, p. 734 (part).

Diagramma cinerascens, Cuv. and Val. v, p. 307; Rupp. Atl. p. 127.

? *Diagramma centurio*, Cuv. and Val. v, p. 308; Playfair, Fish. Zanz. p. 27.

Plectorhynchus punctatus, Bleeker, Ceram. p. 187 and Atl. Ich. Perc. t. xxii, f. 1.

B. vii, D. [illegible], P. 17, V. 1/5, A. $\frac{3}{7}$, C. 17, L. r. [illegible], L. tr. 15/20.

Length of head from 4/17 to 2/9, of caudal from 1/8 to 1/9, height of body 2/7 of the total length. *Eyes*—diameter from 2/9 to 1/4 of length of head, $1\frac{1}{2}$ to 2 diameters from end of snout, and about 1 apart. Dorsal profile much more convex than that of the abdomen. The maxilla reaches to below the hind nostril. Vertical border of preopercle serrated, as is also its rounded angle. Shoulder-bone serrated. *Teeth*—villiform. *Fins*—dorsal spines moderately strong, the second and third being the longest and equal to two-fifths of the length of the head: second anal spine slightly the strongest but the third a little the longest: caudal lunated: the distance the ventral fins extend varies considerably with the age of the fish, becoming comparatively very much shorter in the larger specimens. *Colours*—greyish, several rows of large brilliant golden spots along the upper half of the body: three short bluish bands pass from the eye across the opercle, and two more in the same direction between the eye and the angle of the mouth, these bands are continued on to the body between the rows of spots. Two rows of brownish spots dashed with yellow exist on the hard dorsal as well as a light longitudinal band: soft dorsal with similar spots much wider than the ground colour: caudal the same: anal and ventral likewise spotted, the latter being greyish externally: pectoral golden.

In a specimen $27\frac{1}{2}$ inches in length the colouring varied, it being of an uniform greyish-brown, some small ill-defined spots on the soft dorsal: the caudal covered with small circular brown marks as well as the outer half of the anal: ventral externally greyish.

Bleeker (Revis. Plector. p. 301) considers *D. pictum* and *D. punctatum* as the young and adult of one species, the colours and the form of the dorsal changing with age. My specimens however show *D. pictum* (figured life-size) with L. r. [illegible], and *D. punctatum* (at 10 inches in length, Pl. xxi, fig. 4), with L. r. [illegible], and a specimen $27\frac{1}{2}$ inches with L. r. [illegible]. But Dr. Bleeker having, as he observes, 43 specimens which show the gradations, make one very doubtful whether this species may not be the adult of *pictum*.

Habitat.—Red Sea, seas of India to the Malay Archipelago.

8. Diagramma picoides.

Peters, Monatsb. Akad. Wiss. Berl. 1866, p. 94.

B. vii, D. [illegible], P. 17, V. 1/5, A. $\frac{3}{7}$, C. 17, L. l. 100, L. r. [illegible], L. tr. 16-17/31-32.

Length of head 2/9, of caudal nearly 1/7, height of body 4/17 of the total length. *Eyes*—diameter 2/9 of length of head, $1\frac{1}{2}$ diameters from end of snout, and $1\frac{1}{3}$ apart. *Fins*—the spines of the dorsal are of moderate height, the third being a little more than 1/3 of the height of the body: ventral spine longer than the third of the dorsal fin: the second anal spine is slightly longer and much stronger than the third, and one-third longer than the highest in the dorsal fin. *Colours*—upper 1/2 of body black with four large light blotches, one being over the snout: a second across the nape: a third under the commencement of the dorsal rays, and the last over the free portion of the tail. The white colour of the abdomen is divided in a zig-zag or wavy line from the black of the back. On the tail where there is a row of black spots, the white colour merges into the upper spot. Dorsal fin with a black base and upper edge, and having a white median longitudinal band. The anal and caudal with irregular black spots.

Habitat.—A dried example nearly 12 inches long was obtained by Lamare Pigout, most probably in the East Indies, but it might have come from the Mauritius, or even the Cape of Good Hope.

Genus, 20—Lobotes, *Cuv.*

Branchiostegals six: pseudobranchiæ. Body and fins somewhat elevated: upper profile of head concave. Eyes rather small. Mouth moderately protractile, its cleft oblique, lower jaw the longer. Opercle with obtuse points: preopercle serrated. Villiform teeth in the jaws having an external enlarged and somewhat conical row, but without canines: palate edentulous. One dorsal fin with twelve stout spines: anal with three: caudal rounded. Scales ctenoid, of moderate size, extended over the head. Air-vessel simple, without any constriction.

Geographical distribution.—Seas of India, China, and Atlantic coasts of America.

SYNOPSIS OF INDIVIDUAL SPECIES.

1. *Lobotes Surinamensis*, Bloch, D. $\frac{12}{15-16}$, A. $\frac{3}{11-12}$, L. l. 48. Brassy-brown blotched with darker. East coast of Africa, seas of India to the Malay Archipelago and beyond.

Lobotes Surinamensis, Plate XXI, fig. 5.

Holocentrus Surinamensis, Bloch, t. 243; Bl. Schn. p. 316.

Lobotes Surinamensis, Cuv. and Val. v, 319; Day, Fishes of Malabar, p. 24.

Lobotes erate, Cuv. and Val. v, p. 322; Bleeker, Sciæn. p. 26, and Atl. Ich. Perc. t. xviii, fig. 1; Cantor, Catal. p. 80.

Lobotes Farkharii et *somnolentus*, Cuv. and Val. v, p. 324.

Lobotes auctorum, Günther, Catal. i, p. 338.

Paramadee, Mal.: *Musselli*, Tam.: *Chota bekkut*, Ooriah.

B. vi, D. $\frac{12}{15-16}$, P. 15-17, V. 1/5, A. $\frac{3}{11-12}$, C. 17, L. r. [illegible], L. tr. 9-11/22, Cæc. pyl. 4 (3), Vert. 13/11.

Length of head from $3\frac{1}{2}$ to $3\frac{2}{3}$, of caudal 1/6, height of body $2\frac{1}{2}$ to 1/3 in the total length. *Eyes*—diameter 1/6 to 1/7 of the length of head, 1 diameter from the end of snout, and $1\frac{1}{2}$ to 2 apart. A concavity in the dorsal profile over the eyes. The maxilla reaches to below the anterior third of the orbit. Vertical limb of preopercle denticulated, with spinate teeth at its rounded and slightly produced angle: horizontal limb entire. Shoulder-bone and one in axilla denticulated. *Teeth*—fine. *Fins*—dorsal spines strong, the fourth to the seventh of about the same height and the longest equal to half the length of the head; soft portion of the fin higher than the spinous. Pectoral rounded, half as long as the head: third anal spine longer than the second, and equal to 1/4 or 2/9 of height of body: soft portions of dorsal and anal rather angular: caudal rounded. *Air-vessel*—large, thin, and lanceolate in shape. *Colours*—brassy-brown blotched with darker, and having the extremity of the caudal and the pectoral of a dirty yellowish-white: the other fins are of a slate colour.

This fish varies considerably with age; and Dr. Günther, under the designation of *Lobotes auctorum*, gives as its range, "Atlantic coasts of America from New York to the coast of Surinam; Caribbean sea; Ceylon, Bay of Bengal, Sunda, Molucca, and Chinese seas."—Catal. i, p. 338.

Habitat.—East coast of Africa, seas of India to the Malay Archipelago and beyond, attaining at least $2\frac{1}{2}$ feet in length. It is excellent as food.

Genus, 21—Scolopsis, *Cuv. and Val.*

Scolopsides, Cuv.

Branchiostegals five: pseudobranchiæ. Body oblong. Eyes of moderate or large size. Mouth moderately protractile: jaws of nearly equal length anteriorly: cleft of mouth horizontal. Infraorbital arch with a spine directed backwards: preopercle as a rule serrated, and often the suborbital ring: opercle with a weak spine. A single dorsal fin with ten spines: anal with three: caudal emarginate or forked. Scales ctenoid. Air-vessel without any constriction, simple. Pyloric appendages few.

Geographical distribution.—From the Red Sea, and East coast of Africa, through the seas of India to the Malay Archipelago and beyond. The largest numbers and greatest varieties of species in this Genus are taken off the coasts of Sind and Bombay, also at the Andamans and Nicobars.

SYNOPSIS OF SPECIES.

1. *Scolopsis bimaculatus*, D. $\frac{10}{9}$, A. $\frac{3}{7}$, L. l. 48, L. tr. $4\frac{1}{2}$/14. Greyish, a broad white opercular band: two black blotches on the lateral-line, the first from the eleventh to the twenty-second scale: the second behind the end of the dorsal fin. Red Sea, seas of India to China.

2. *Scolopsis phæops*, D. $\frac{10}{9}$, A. $\frac{3}{7}$, L. l. 46-48, L. tr. 5/16. A light band along the base of the dorsal fin: a blue band from the eye to the upper jaw; a second to the axilla where it ends in a blue spot. East coast of Africa, and seas of India.

3. *Scolopsis bilineatus*, D. $\frac{10}{9}$, A. $\frac{3}{7}$, L. l. 46, L. tr. 4/14. A white band from snout to base of dorsal spines: a second from above the orbit to a little way below the last dorsal spine: a third from the upper edge of the eye to the lateral-line. A wide yellow, black-edged band from the mouth to the soft dorsal. A large yellow blotch below the last half of the soft dorsal, which latter is anteriorly edged with black: anal with its front half black. Andamans and Malay Archipelago.

4. *Scolopsis ghanam*, D. $\frac{10}{9}$, A. $\frac{3}{7}$, L. l. 46, L. tr. 4/14. A light band from the snout to the base of the dorsal spines: a second from above the eye to the end of the dorsal fin: a third from the eye to the shoulder where it divides into two and is continued backwards: a black spot in the axilla. Red Sea and Andamans.

5. *Scolopsis monogramma*, D. $\frac{10}{9}$, A. $\frac{3}{7}$, L. l. 44, L. tr. 5/14. A deep black band from the eye to above the base of the caudal fin. Andamans to the Malay Archipelago.

6. *Scolopsis cancellatus*, D. $\frac{10}{9}$, A. $\frac{3}{7}$, L. l. 44, L. tr. $3\frac{1}{2}$/14. A white streak from snout to first dorsal spine: a second from over orbit to the end of the base of the dorsal: a third from the upper third of the eye to opposite the end of the pectoral: a fourth from the middle of the eye to the upper third of the caudal. Several irregular and wide vertical body bands. A black spot between first and third dorsal spines. Andamans to the Malay Archipelago and beyond.

7. *Scolopsis Vosmeri*, D. $\frac{10}{9}$, A. $\frac{3}{7}$, L. l. 42-44, L. tr. $3\frac{1}{2}$-4/14. Serrations on preopercle directed backwards in the immature, outwards in the adult. A light band over the opercles, and a longitudinal light line along the body. Red Sea, seas of India to the Malay Archipelago and beyond.

8. *Scolopsis leucotænia* [illegible], D. $\frac{10}{9}$, A. $\frac{3}{7}$, L. l. 3[illegible], L. tr. $3\frac{1}{2}$/13. A light band edged with dark above and below, going from the eye to the upper half of the caudal fin: usually a dark spot on the dorsal fin. Bombay to the Malay Archipelago.

9. *Scolopsis ciliatus*, D. $\frac{10}{9}$, A. $\frac{3}{7}$, L. l. 40, L. tr. 4/15. A silvery line from between the lateral-line and the back, from near the head to the commencement of the soft dorsal: most of the scales below the lateral-line with a golden spot. Andamans to the Malay Archipelago and beyond.

1. Scolopsis bimaculatus, Plate XXII, fig. 1.

Rüppell, Atl. Fische, p. 8, t. ii, f. 2, and N. W. Fische, p. 126; Günther, Catal. i, p. 357; Klunz. Verh. z. b. Ges. Wien, 1870, p. 740; Bleeker, Revis. Scolop. p. 367.
Scolopsides bimaculatus, Cuv. and Val. v, p. 340.
Scolopsides inermis, Cuv. and Val. v, p. 340; Richards. Ich. China, p. 236, (not Tem. and Schleg.)
Scolopsides monogramma, Bleeker, Sciæn. p. 29, (ex parte.)

B. v, D. $\frac{10}{9}$, P. 18, V. 1/5, A. $\frac{3}{7}$, C. 17, L. l. 48, L. tr. $4\frac{1}{2}$/14.

Length of head about 1/4, of caudal 1/6, height of body 4/13 to 2/7 of the total length. *Eyes*—diameter 1/3 of length of head, 1 diameter from end of snout, and 3/4 apart. The maxilla reaches to nearly beneath the front edge of the orbit. Preorbital 1/2 as high as the diameter of the orbit, having a strong spine, with four or five denticulations along the posterior margin of its plate. Vertical limb of preopercle serrated, most strongly so at the angle. *Teeth*—fine. *Fins*—dorsal spines strong, the fourth the highest being rather longer than the post-orbital portion of the head. Pectoral nearly as long as the head. Second anal spine stronger but shorter than the third, which equals one-third the length of the head: caudal lunated. *Colours*—greyish, becoming dull white on the abdomen: a broad light opercular band. Branchiostegal membranes blood-red. A brownish band over the snout, and one or two blotches on the lateral-line, the first large, being from the eleventh to the twenty-second scales, the second smaller and behind the posterior extremity of the dorsal fin, or the two may be conjoined. Fins orange, becoming reddish externally. Eyes silvery.

Habitat.—Red Sea, seas of India and China. The specimen which is figured was captured at Madras in June, 1867, and is nearly $8\frac{1}{2}$ inches in length. Instead of having a long single blotch on the side, it has taken the form of two distinct ones.

2. Scolopsis phæops, Plate XXII, fig. 2.

Scolopsides phæops, Bennett, Proc. Zool. Soc. 1831, i, p. 165.
Scolopsis phæops, Günter, Catal. i, p. 358.
Scolopsis notolænia, Playfair, Fish. Zanz. p. 29, pl. v, fig. 2.

B. v, D. $\frac{10}{9}$, P. 16, V. 1/5, A. $\frac{3}{7}$, C. 17, L. l. 46-48, L. tr. 5/16.

Length of head 1/4 to $4\frac{1}{2}$, of caudal nearly 1/5, height of body $3\frac{2}{3}$ to $3\frac{1}{2}$ in the total length. *Eyes*—diameter 2/9 of length of head, $1\frac{1}{2}$ diameters from end of snout, and $1\frac{1}{3}$ apart. Interorbital space rather convex transversely. Cleft of mouth somewhat oblique, the maxilla reaching to below the front edge of the orbit. Preorbital spine of moderate size, with a strong denticulation on the posterior-inferior edge of the plate. Vertical limb of preopercle slightly emarginate, the angle being rounded and somewhat produced: on the vertical limb the serrations are strongest, superiorly decreasing in strength to above the angle where they become almost spinate. *Teeth*—in the jaws fine. *Fins*—dorsal spines of moderate strength, increasing in length to the fourth which equals 1/3 of the height of the body. Pectoral equals the length of the head excluding the snout: third anal spine longer but not quite so strong as the second, and equalling 2/7 of the height of the body: caudal forked, upper lobe somewhat the longer. *Colours*—greenish-olive above the lateral-line, becoming yellowish-white below it: a narrow light band runs along the back close to the base of the dorsal fin. A wide bright blue band passes from the eye over the preorbital and upper maxillary bone ceasing a short distance between the centre of the upper jaw and the angle of the mouth: a second goes from the posterior edge of the eye to the axilla where it ends in a blue spot: fins reddish.

In the dried skin shown me in the British Museum of *S. notolænia*, Playfair, and as I understood the type, the anal spines are correctly described as "the two last spines are nearly equal in length, but the second is the stronger, they are about one-third of the length of the head:" (Fish. Zanz. p. 30,) but they have evidently been injured and grown again in an irregular manner.

Habitat.—East coast of Africa, seas of India. Not uncommon off Sind. The specimen figured is [illegible] inches in length.

3. Scolopsis bilineatus, Plate XXII, fig. 3.

Anthias bilineatus, Bloch, t. 325, fig. 1; Bl. Schn. p. 306.
Lutjanus ellipticus, Lacép. iv, p. 213.
Scolopsides bilineatus, Cuv. and Val. v, p. 336; Bleeker, Verh. Bat. Gen. xxiii, Sciæn. p. 28.
Scolopsides lineatus, Bleeker, Solor. p. 73, (not Rüpp.)
Scolopsis bilineatus, Günther, Catal. i, p. 357; Bleeker, Revis. Scolop. p. 359.
Scolopsis bleekeri, Günther, Catal. i, p. 361.

B. v, D. $\frac{10}{9}$, P. 16, V. 1/5, A. $\frac{3}{7}$, C. 17, L. l. 46, L. tr. 4/14, Cæc. pyl. 5.

Length of head 1/4 or a little less, of caudal 1/5, height of body 2/7 of the total length. *Eyes*—diameter 4/11 to 2/5 of length of head, 2/3 of a diameter from end of snout, and 1 apart. The maxilla reaches to below the front edge of the orbit or even to its first third in the adult. Vertical limb of preopercle serrated, and its angle rather produced and rounded. A strong preorbital spine, with three teeth below it along the edge of the plate. Opercular spine distinct. *Teeth*—villiform. *Fins*—dorsal spines not strong, increasing in height to the fourth which equals 3/7 of the height of the body. Pectoral extends nearly to above the anal spines, the second of which is very strong, longer than the third, and equal to rather more than half of the height of the body: soft dorsal and anal angularly rounded; caudal forked. *Colours*—a white band from the snout to the base of the dorsal spines: a second from above the orbit to a little way below the last dorsal spine: a third from the upper edge of the eye to the lateral-line. A wide yellow, black-margined band passes from the mouth to the commencement of the soft dorsal fin. A large yellow blotch exists below the last half of the soft dorsal, which latter fin is anteriorly edged with black: anal black in its front half and white posteriorly.

In the young, *S. Bleekeri*, Günther, the light band bordered with black is nearly straight, and terminates where the white spot exists in the adult, near the end of the base of the soft dorsal: another light band proceeds from the upper edge of the eye to the base of the spinous portion of the dorsal fin; whilst a third median one goes from the snout to the base of the first dorsal spine.

Habitat.—Andamans and Malay Archipelago. The specimen is figured life-size.

4. Scolopsis ghanam, Plate XXII, fig. 4.

Sciæna ghanam, Forsk. p. 50, No. 56.
Holocentrus ghanam, Lacép. iv, p. 347.
Scolopsis lineatus, Rüpp. Atl. Fische, p. 7, pl. 2, fig. 1, and N. W. Fische, p. 126.
Scolopsides ghanam, Cuv. and Val. v, p. 348.
Scolopsis ghanam, Günther, Catal. i, p. 362; Klunzinger, Verh. z. b. Ges. Wien, 1870, p. 739.

B. v, D. $\frac{10}{9}$, P. 17, V. 1/5, A. $\frac{3}{7}$, L. l. 46, L. tr. 4/14, Cæc. pyl. 6 (4).

Length of head 1/4 to $4\frac{1}{2}$, of caudal 1/5, height of body $3\frac{1}{3}$ to $3\frac{2}{3}$ in the total length. *Eyes*—diameter 1/3 of length of head, 3/4 of a diameter from end of snout, and 1 apart. Scaleless portion of the head covered with numerous small pores. The maxilla reaches to below the first fourth of the orbit. Preorbital spine strong, the plate denticulated on the edge beneath it: lower edge of suborbital ring of bones serrated. Vertical limb of preopercle strongly serrated, most coarsely so upon its produced angle. Opercular spine well developed. Shoulder-bone serrated. *Teeth*—fine. *Fins*—the dorsal spines which are rather weak increase in length to the fifth, the height of which nearly equals half the length of the head. Pectoral not quite so long as the head: anal spines of equal strength, the longest equalling the extent of the postorbital portion of the head: caudal deeply forked. *Lateral-line*—curves to opposite the end of the dorsal fin, from whence it proceeds direct to the centre of the caudal. *Colours*—back olive, a yellowish-white band goes from the snout to the base of the dorsal spines: a second from above the orbit to the end of the base of the dorsal fin: a third from the snout, where it arises in common with the one for the opposite side, passes through the upper portion of the eye and at the shoulder divides into two, one being above the lateral-line and becoming lost on the back of the tail, the other going below the lateral-line being lost on the last fourth of the body: a fourth goes along the preorbital and suborbital ring of bones being lost above the base of the pectoral fin which has a black spot in its axil. Most of the scales below the lateral-line in the anterior two-thirds of the body have a black spot at their bases. A violet mark is present at the base of either lobe of the caudal fin.

Habitat.—Red Sea and Andaman islands, where it is very common. Specimen figured is $6\frac{1}{10}$ inches in length.

5. Scolopsis monogramma, Plate XXII, fig. 5.

Scolopsides monogramma, (Kuhl and v. Hass.) Cuv. and Val. v, p. 338.
Scolopsis monogramma, Günther, Catal. i, p. 358; Bleeker, Revis. Scolop. p. 369.

B. v, D. $\frac{10}{9}$, P. 17, V. 1/5, A. $\frac{3}{7}$, C. 17, L. l. 44, L. tr. 5/14.

Length of head 1/4, of caudal 1/5, height of body 4/15 of the total length. *Eyes*—diameter 1/3 of length of head, nearly 1 diameter from end of snout and also apart. Upper surface of the head flat, and the scales extend forwards nearly to the nostrils. Preorbital bone with one flat spine having three small teeth at the anterior-inferior edge of the plate, the depth of which equals half the diameter of the orbit: infraorbital ring of bones finely serrated. The maxilla reaches to below the front edge of the orbit. Vertical limb of preopercle almost evenly serrated as well as its rounded and somewhat produced angle. Shoulder-bone serrated. *Teeth*—villiform. *Fins*—dorsal spines slender, increasing in length to the fourth which equals 3/7 of the height of the body. Second anal spine stronger but not so long as the third which equals 3/10 of the height of the body: caudal forked. *Lateral-line*—makes a very gradual curve to below the end of the soft dorsal fin. *Colours*—olive with a deep black band, one scale wide, passing from the snout through the eye to above the base of the caudal fin, until it arrives below the end of the dorsal fin it is inferior to the lateral-line: fins immaculate.

Habitat.—Andamans to the Malay Archipelago. Specimen figured is 5 inches long.

6. Scolopsis cancellatus, Plate XXII, fig. 6.

Scolopsides cancellatus, Cuv. and Val. v, p. 351;* Bleeker, Sciæn. p. 28.

* It is suggested by Cuv. and Val. that *Scolopsis lineatus* Quoy and Gaim. Voy. de M. Freycinet. Zool. pl. 60. f. 3, may be this species badly delineated.

Scolopsis cancellatus, Günther, Catal. i, p. 361, and Fische d. Sudsee, p. 30; Bleeker, Atl. Ich. Perc. t. xxxi, fig. 2, and Revis. Scolop. p. 355.

Scolopsis Bleekeri, Bleeker, Atl. Ich. Perc. t. xvi, fig. 1, (not Günther.)

B. v, D. $\frac{10}{9}$, P. 15, V. 1/5, A. $\frac{3}{7}$, C. 17, L. l. 44, L. tr. $3\frac{1}{2}$/14.

Length of head 1/4, of caudal 2/9, height of body 1/4 of the total length. *Eyes*—diameter 2/5 of length of head, 1/2 a diameter from end of snout, and 3/4 apart. Dorsal profile more convex than that of the abdomen. Interorbital space flat. Scaleless portion of the head studded with fine open pores. The maxilla reaches to below the front edge of the orbit. Preorbital spine of moderate length and strength, fluted and with one or two denticulations along the inferior edge of the plate. Some serrations on the suborbital ring of bones. Vertical limb of preopercle serrated, most coarsely so superiorly and at its slightly produced and rounded angle. *Teeth*—fine. *Fins*—dorsal spines weak, increasing in length to the fifth which is more than half as long as the head: pectoral as long as the head behind the front edge of the orbit: second anal spine stronger but a little shorter than the third which equals half the length of the head. *Lateral-line*—curves to opposite the end of the dorsal fin, from whence it proceeds direct to the centre of the caudal. *Colours*—greyish above and whitish below the lateral-line: a white streak goes from the snout to the base of the first dorsal spine: a second from over the orbit to the end of the base of the dorsal fin: a third from the upper third of the eye to opposite the end of the pectoral: a fourth from the middle of the eye to the upper third of the caudal. Several wide but irregular vertical bands pass from the back to the middle of the body. A black spot between the first and third dorsal spines in their lower half. Bleeker observes that the longitudinal bands are more distinct and regular in the young than in the adult, whilst the black spot on the spinous dorsal usually disappears with age.

Habitat.—Andamans, to the Malay Archipelago, and beyond. The specimen is figured life-size.

7. Scolopsis Vosmeri, Plate XXIII, fig 1 (young): 2 (semi-adult): 3 (adult).

Anthias Vosmeri, Bloch, t. 321.

Anthias Vosmeri, Bl. Schn. p. 304.

Anthias Japonicus, Bloch, t. 325, f. 2; Bl. Schn. p. 307.

Perca aurata, Mungo Park, Trans. Linn. Soc. iii, p. 35.

Lutjanus Japonicus, Lacép. iv, p. 31.

Lutjanus Vosmeri, Lacép. iv, p. 213.

Lutjanus aurovittatus, Lacép. iv, p. 216.

Pomacentrus cuneodactylus, Lacép. iv, pp. 505, 508.

Lutjanus auratus, Bl. Schn. p. 328.

Sparus kurite, Russell, Fish. Vizag. ii, p. 5, pl. 106.

Scolopsides kurite, Cuv. and Val. v, p. 331.*

Scolopsis kurite, Rüpp. Atl. Fische, p. 9, t. 2, f. 3.

Scolopsis kate, Cuv. and Val. v, p. 329.

Scolopsides Rüppellii, Cuv. and Val. v, p. 332†; Richards. Ich. China, p. 236.

Scolopsides vosmeri, Cuv. and Val. v, p. 333‡; Bleek. Verh. Bat. Gen. xxiii, Sciæn. p. 27.

Scolopsides torquatus, Cuv. and Val. v, p. 345; Bleeker, l. c. p. 28.

Scolopsis torquatus, Günther, Catal. i, p. 356; Kner, Novara, Fische, p. 59; Bleeker, Revis. Scolopsis, p. 355.

Scolopsides aurata, Cantor, Catal. i, p. 81.

Scolopsis Japonicus, Günther, Catal. i, p. 354; Day, Fish. Malabar, p. 25; Klunz. Verh. z. b. Ges. in Wien 1870, p. 749.

Scolopsis auratus, Günther, Catal. i. p. 355.

Scolopsis Vosmeri, Bleeker, Revis. Scolop. p. 361.

Kaalal, Tam.

B. v, D. $\frac{10}{9}$, P. 17, V. 1/5, A. $\frac{3}{7}$, C. 17, L. l. 42-44, L. tr. $3\frac{1}{2}$-4/13-14, Cæc. pyl. (3 Kner.)

Length of head 1/4 to 3/14, of caudal 4/21 to 2/9, height of body 1/3 to 2/5 of the total length. *Eyes*—diameter 2/5 to 1/3 (in the adult) of length of head, 2/3 of a diameter from end of snout, and 3/4 to 1 apart. The maxilla reaches to below the anterior fourth or in the adult to beneath the front edge of the orbit. Preorbital with rather a deep plate, armed superiorly with one strong fluted spine projecting backwards and from about three to seven or eight denticulations below it: above this spine the suborbital plate is armed with another directed both forwards and backwards, in some specimens these are very small, especially the anterior one. In one specimen this anterior projection of the suborbital spine is imperceptible, so it is probable that Sir John Richardson's statement of "two suborbital teeth pointing backwards, one under the other and more slender, none pointing forwards," may have been quite correct: it is scarcely necessary to observe that he considered the preorbital spine as a suborbital one. Preopercle with its vertical limb slightly emarginate, due to its projecting

* Cuv. and Val. remark upon Russell's figure showing 10 soft rays in the dorsal fin, and his description giving 11, consequently a new name was bestowed on the species, which however only possesses 9 rays.

† Cuv. and Val. bestowed this designation on Rüppell's fish because the vertical limb of the preopercle is not shown so emarginate as figured by Russell and as existing in nature.

‡ *Scolopsis argyrosomus*, Kuhl and v. Hass. MSS, apud Cuv. and Val.

and rounded angle: it is serrated in its whole extent, but the character of these serrations alters considerably with age. In the young, *S. torquatus*, the serrations are moderately coarse and directed backwards, sometimes a small cusp exists at the base of some, at other times it does not, the vertical limb and rounded angle may be said to be serrated, the serrations being directed backwards. As the size of the specimen augments, *S. Japonicus*, we find that these basal cusps begin to be more distinctly developed, and a blunt one as a rule is present at the base of every serration, in some specimens the posteriorly directed teeth now begin to disappear. As the adult, *S. aureatus*, is reached the appearance becomes remarkable, the posteriorly directed serrations on the vertical limb (not on the angle) have become absorbed, and the cusps at their bases have augmented in size and consequently the serrations project outwards instead of backwards. Opercle with a moderately developed spine. *Teeth*—generic. *Fins*—dorsal spines strong, each alternate one being broader, they increase in length to the fourth or fifth, from whence they continue of about the same height, or equal to about half the length of the head, whilst the rays are of about the same height. Pectoral equal to the length of the head posterior to the nostrils: ventral almost reaching the anus. Anal spines strong, the third nearly equal to the highest in the dorsal fin but one-fourth shorter than the second in a specimen 8½ inches in length; in younger specimens the difference in length is sometimes not so great, in such cases the second spine is generally the longer, as will be alluded to: caudal forked. *Colours*—adult of a pale dull-red, usually having a whitish band round the opercles, from the upper edge of which bone a longitudinal wide line of the same colour passes backwards below the lateral-line, being lost beneath the end of the base of the dorsal fin. Every scale on the body has generally a dark basal mark. In the medium size fish, *S. Japonicus*, the ground colour is often the same as given for the adult, but in others it is of an ashy grey: the opercular band is generally distinct and of a cream-yellow colour. A deep arterial blood-red spot exists behind the opercular spine, and the fins are of a pale yellow. In the young, *S. torquatus*, the band of the opercles is very distinct and of a light lemon-yellow colour, whilst the blood-red spot behind the opercular spine is very well marked: the inside of the mouth is likewise red.

If we divide this fish into three distinct species merely in accordance with the colours observed, the difficulty arises amongst specimens from India, of ability to discover any very young *S. aureatus* or *S. Japonicus*, unless the *S. torquatus* is admitted to be such. Of course, however, it is by no means improbable that some immature might from the first adopt the livery seen in the adult, but such a mere anomaly would be insufficient to constitute a valid species. In Cuvier and Valenciennes, it is observed that Ruppell's figure of *S. kurite*, does not show such an emargination of the preopercle as is exhibited in Russell's, this however appears to have been merely an accident. The question of the direction of the preopercular serrations deserves however more consideration, and it was not until I had collected a large number of specimens of all ages and examined those in the British and Madras Museums, that I arrived at the conviction that such were merely due to maturity or the reverse of the specimen. In the young, although the serrations project backwards, they have a small cusp at their base, which, did it grow, would project outwards: in middle age this outer projection increases in development whilst the posterior one shows signs of atrophy: in the adult stage the change is completed, the earliest serrations have become almost or entirely absorbed, the original basal cusp has developed into an outwardly directed serration, having sometimes the original ones in the form of a backwardly projecting cusp at the base of each.

Bleeker, *l. c.* places *S. torquatus* as nearly allied but distinct from *S. Vosmeri*, being distinguished from it by a more convex profile, a larger head, larger eyes and a lower anal fin. In colours by an absence of the light lateral band and a purple triangular spot at the base of the pectoral fin. He gives in *S. torquatus* length of head 4 to 4½, height of body 2¾ to 3 in the total length; eyes, diameter 2 to 2¼ in the length of head: in the *S. Vosmeri*, length of head 4⅓ to 4⅔, height of body 2¼ to 3 in the total length; eyes, diameter 2⅓ to 3 in the length of head.

Pl. xxiii, fig. 1, represents a specimen of *S. torquatus*, life-size, no longitudinal band exists and the pectoral blotch is distinct, but the comparative length of the second anal spine is as great as in any specimen of the typical *S. Vosmeri*, which I have seen. In four other specimens 6, 6$\frac{1}{10}$, 6½, and 7 inches respectively in length, the second anal spine is only 1/2 the length of the head. Therefore variations do exist, and to prove such I have figured (Pl. xxiii, fig. 2) an intermediate form, 6¾ inches in length, which agrees with Bleeker's *torquatus*.

Habitat.—Red Sea, East coast of Africa, seas of India to the Malay Archipelago and beyond, attaining at least 12 inches in length.

8. Scolopsis leucotænia, Plate XXIII, fig. 4.

Scolopsides leucotænia, Bleeker, Banka, p. 451, Atl. Ich. Perc. t. xvi, fig. 4, and Revis. Scolop. p. 351; Günther, Catal. i, p. 363.

Scolopsides leucotænioides, Bleeker, Celebes, p. 439; Günther, Catal. i, p. 363.

B. v, D. $\frac{10}{9}$, P. 17, V. 1/5, A. $\frac{3}{7}$, L. l. 39, L. tr. 3½/13.

Length of head equals one fourth less than the height of the body. *Eyes*—diameter 2/5 of length of head, 1/2 a diameter from end of snout, and 1 apart. Interorbital space flat: dorsal profile more convex than that of the abdomen. Cleft of mouth somewhat oblique: the maxilla reaches to below the first third of the orbit. Preorbital one-third as high as the diameter of the eye, its spine weak, and the hind edge of the plate with a few indistinct serrations: suborbital ring of bones serrated. Vertical limb of preopercle slightly emarginate, serrated along its whole extent but most coarsely so at its rounded angle. Shoulder-bone serrated. *Teeth*—fine

Fins—dorsal spines strong, increasing in length to the fourth which equals half the length of the head: pectoral equals the length of the head without the snout: the ventral nearly reaches the anal: second anal spine much the strongest and considerably the longest, equalling the length of the head behind the middle of the eye. *Colours*—a broad yellowish-white streak from above the eye to the upper edge of the free portion of the tail, it is margined both above and below with a dark purple stripe; above it the body is reddish-brown, below it yellowish: a dark purplish vertical band extends down the opercle. Fins reddish, the dorsal with a fine black upper edge and a dark band along the centre of its spinous portion.

In the typical *S. leucotænia*, no black mark exists on the dorsal fin, and the second anal spine is longer and stronger than the third.

In *S. leucotænioides* a black blotch exists between the first and fourth dorsal spines, and the second and third anal spines are of about equal length and strength.

In the specimen figured, a dark band passes along the spinous dorsal and the anal spines are as in *S. leucotænia*.

Habitat.—Bombay to the Malay Archipelago.

My single specimen having its tail injured must be the excuse for the way in which I have given the proportions, but Bleeker observes, length of head 1/4, height of body 2/7 to 1/4 of the total length.

9. Scolopsis ciliatus, Plate XXIII, fig. 5.

Holocentrus ciliatus, Lacép. iv, pp. 333, 371.
Scolopsides lycogenis, Cuv. and Val. v,* p. 346, pl. 127; Bleeker, Sciæn. p. 27.
Scolopsis ciliatus, Günther, Catal. i, p. 355.

B. v, D. $\frac{10}{9}$, P. 17, V. 1/5, A. $\frac{3}{7}$, C. 17, L. l. 44, L. tr. $3\frac{1}{2}$-4/15, Cæc. pyl. 5, Vert. 10/14.

Length of head 1/4 to $4\frac{1}{2}$, of caudal nearly 1/5, height of body $3\frac{1}{4}$ to $3\frac{1}{2}$ in the total length. *Eyes*—diameter 2/5 to 3/8 of length of head, 2/3 of a diameter from end of snout, and 1 apart. A prominent ridge having a serrated edge exists on the maxilla, and that bone extends to below the front margin of the orbit. Preorbital with a strong spine directed backwards, two smaller ones on the plate below it and a few serrations beneath. Vertical edge of preopercle serrated, most strongly so at its angle which is not produced. A conspicuous spine on the opercle: shoulder-bone serrated. *Teeth*—villiform. *Fins*—dorsal spines slender, increasing in length to the fifth, the height of which nearly equals half the length of the head: anal spines not strong, the third weaker but longer than the second, and nearly equalling the longest in the dorsal fin: caudal forked. *Colours*—greenish-olive above, becoming lighter on the abdomen: a silvery white band extends between the lateral-line and the back, from near the head to opposite the commencement of the soft dorsal: the position of this white line Bleeker observes is liable to change with age: the scales below the lateral-line have a golden spot. Fins reddish.

Habitat.—Andamans, Malay Archipelago, &c. The specimen figured is 7 inches in length and from the Andaman islands.

Genus, 22—Dentex, *Cuv.*

Gymnocranius, pt. Klunz.: *Paradentex*, pt. Blkr.: *Synagris*, (Klein) Bleeker.

Branchiostegals six or seven: pseudobranchiæ. Body oblong, rather elongate, and a little elevated. Eyes of medium or rather large size. Mouth moderately protractile, its cleft more or less horizontal: jaws of about equal length. Preopercle entire or feebly serrated: opercle without any or with a not very prominent spine: the distance between the eye and the angle of the mouth considerable. Generally strong canines from 4 to 6 in number in both jaws, almost invariably present in the upper: a conical outer lateral row in either jaw: vomer, palate, and tongue edentulous. One scaleless dorsal fin having from 10 to 13 spines, anal with three and nine to eleven rays: the spines generally weak, and being more or less provided with a scaly groove: caudal forked. Scales ctenoid, of moderate size, more than three rows between the eye and the angle of the preopercle, none on the front of the snout, jaws, or preorbital. Air-vessel not constricted but notched posteriorly. Pyloric appendages few.

This Genus has been subdivided from *Synagris*, mostly owing to the existence of upwards of three rows of scales across the preopercle. Even thus restricted it has been farther subdivided and *Gymnocranius*, Klunz.=*Paradentex*, Bleeker, consists of those species in which the scales do not extend forward on the upper surface of the head so far as the eye: none on the outer limb of the preopercle: the upper jaw is rather more protractile, and the canines are weaker.

Geographical distribution.—The fishes of this Genus have a wide range, being found in the Mediterranean, Atlantic, Red Sea, and through those of India to the Malay Archipelago, and beyond.

SYNOPSIS OF INDIVIDUAL SPECIES.

1. *Dentex rivulata*, D. $\frac{12}{10}$, A. $\frac{3}{10}$. Canines in both jaws. Sinuous blue lines on the sides of the head. Red Sea, Ceylon.

* *Lycogenis argyrosoma*, Kuhl. and v. Hass. Mss. apud Cuv. and Val.

1. Dentex rivulatus.

Rüpp. N. W. Fische, p. 116, t. 29, fig. 2; Günther, Catal. i, p. 372.
Gymnocranius rivulatus, Klunz. Verh. z. b. Ges. Wien, 1870, p. 765.

D. $\frac{11}{10}$, P. 15, V. 1/5, A. $\frac{3}{10}$, C. 17, L. l. 48, L. tr. 7/20.

Length of head 4/17, of caudal 2/11, height of body 3/10 of the total length. *Eyes*—diameter 3/11 of the length of head, 1¾ diameters from the end of snout, and 1¼ apart. The depth of the preorbital rather exceeds the length of the diameter of the orbit. The maxilla reaches to below the front nostril. Hind limb of preopercle almost vertical and entire, a few serrations exist along its rounded angle. *Teeth*—an outer row of strong canines in the upper jaw, and a strong lateral row of conical ones: lower jaw with six canines in front and a lateral conical row which posteriorly become rather obtuse. *Fins*—dorsal spines rather strong, increasing in length to the fourth from whence they decrease to the last, the height of the fourth equals the distance from the eye to the end of the preorbital bone, the last dorsal spine equals the length of the third and is slightly longer than the ninth: second anal spine two-thirds as long as the third which equals the length of the post-orbital portion of the head: caudal deeply forked. *Scales*—five rows on the cheeks: superiorly they do not extend so far as to opposite the posterior edge of the orbit. *Colours*—greenish, glossed with golden on the sides: wavy blue lines along the snout and over the preorbital.

Habitat.—Red Sea and Ceylon.

Genus, 23—Synagris (*Klein*) *Günther.*

Dentex, pt. Cuv. and Val: *Nemipterus*, Swains.: *Spondyliosoma*, sp. Cantor: *Heterognathos*, pt. Steind.: *Dentex* (C. V.) Bleeker.*

Branchiostegals five or six; pseudobranchiæ. Body oblong, rather elongate and a little elevated. Eyes of medium or rather large size. Mouth moderately protractile, its cleft more or less horizontal: jaws of about equal length. Preopercle entire or feebly serrated: opercle without any or with a not very prominent spine: the distance between the eye and the angle of the mouth considerable.† Moderately sized curved canines in the upper and generally feeble ones in the front of the lower jaw: an inner villiform band in either jaw and usually an outer conical row: vomer, palate, and tongue edentulous. One scaleless dorsal fin having ten spines and nine rays: anal also scaleless having three spines and seven rays: all the spines weak: caudal forked. Scales ctenoid, of moderate size, three rows on the preopercle none along its outer border, on the snout, preorbital, or jaws. Air-vessel not constricted but notched posteriorly. Pyloric appendages few.

Swainson's genus *Nemipterus* is founded on *Dentex filamentosus*, C. and V. = *D. striatus* = *Synagris*, Günther, and consequently might perhaps (to prevent further confusion) be employed instead of *Synagris*.

Geographical distribution.—Red Sea, East coast of Africa, seas of India to the Malay Archipelago and beyond.

SYNOPSIS OF SPECIES.

1. *Synagris striatus*, D. $\frac{10}{9}$, A. $\frac{3}{7}$, L. l. 48. Preopercle serrated: only 2 rows of teeth in the lower jaw, no conical ones. Two first dorsal rays and upper lobe of caudal prolonged. Silvery, with purplish bands. Seas of India to Surinam.

2. *Synagris tolu*, D. $\frac{10}{9}$, A. $\frac{3}{7}$, L. l. 48. Preopercle entire. Lateral conical teeth in either jaw. Dorsal spines elongated and interspinous membrane deeply notched. Roseate, with yellow longitudinal bands. Seas of India to the Malay Archipelago.

3. *Synagris Bleekeri*, D. $\frac{10}{9}$, A. $\frac{3}{7}$, L. l. 48. Preopercle entire. No outer conical row in the upper jaw, a single conical lateral row in the mandible. No elongated spines or rays: interspinous membrane slightly notched. A spot on the opercle. Seas of India.

4. *Synagris filamentosus*, D. $\frac{10}{9}$, A. $\frac{3}{7}$, L. l. 48. Preopercle serrated. A lateral outer row of small conical teeth in the upper jaw only. Upper caudal lobe prolonged: interspinous membrane slightly notched. Yellowish-red, with roseate longitudinal bands. Seas of India.

5. *Synagris notatus*, D. $\frac{10}{9}$, A. $\frac{3}{7}$, L. l. 47. Preopercle entire. An outer row of small conical teeth in the upper jaw, also a similar row in the mandible, but becoming very small in the last fourth of the jaw. No elongated spines or rays; interspinous membrane slightly notched. A brilliant spot on the first 5 scales below the lateral-line. Andamans.

1. Synagris striatus, Plate VIII, fig. 5.‡

? *Coryphæna striata*, Bl. Mss.
? *Coryphæna lutea*, Bl. Schn. p. 297, t. lviii.
Dentex striatus, (? Cuv. and Val. vi, p. 252); Jerdon, M. J. L. and Sc. 1851, p. 131.

* Genus *Synagris* (Klein) Bleeker = *Dentex* (C. V.) Günther in part, and is not similar to *Synagris*, Günther.

† The preorbital in the following species of this genus is high and consists of two pieces, the posterior of which ends in a point at its posterior-superior angle, but this point, which is of varying extent, does not form a spine as in the genus *Scolopsis*. The posterior border of this preorbital plate is free, the skin covering it not passing directly on to the cheeks, but being first reflected on to the posterior surface of the plate.

‡ Marked *Synagris luteus* on the plate.

Dentex filamentosus, Cuv. and Val. vi, p. 244, pl. 155 (not Val. Isles Canar. nor *Cantharus filamentosus*, Rüpp.)

Nemipterus filamentosus, Swains. Fish. ii, p. 223.

? *Synagris luteus*, Günther, Catal. i, p. 380.

Synagris macronemus, Günther, Catal. i, p. 380.

B. vi, D. $\frac{10}{9}$, P. 17, V. 1/5, A. $\frac{3}{7}$, C. 17, L. l. 48, L. tr. $3\frac{1}{2}/10$.

Length of head $4\frac{1}{2}$, of caudal (without its prolongation) $4\frac{3}{4}$, height of body one-fourth of the total length (excluding the prolonged caudal ray). *Eyes*—diameter $3\frac{1}{4}$ in length of head, 1 diameter from end of snout, and 2/3 of a diameter apart. The height of the head equals its length exclusive of the opercle: lower jaw slightly the longer: the maxilla reaches to below the front edge of the orbit. Height of preorbital equals 2/3 of the diameter of the eye, it terminates posteriorly in a point below the last third of the eye. Vertical limb of preopercle finely and evenly serrated in its middle third, its angle rounded and entire. Opercle without any distinct spine. *Teeth*—villiform along the whole of the upper jaw, with 4 canine-like ones anteriorly in either premaxillary, laterally the outer row is composed of about 30 closely set conical ones: the inner ones in the mandible are villiform just above the symphysis, whilst laterally they are in two rows of which the inner is slightly the larger. *Fins*—dorsal spines rather weak, the two first elongated, the second reaching to the base of the caudal fin: interspinous membrane very slightly notched, the height of the last eight spines gradually increases, the last equalling rather more than the length of the postorbital portion of the head but is not so high as the rays. Pectoral as long as the head. Ventral reaches the anal. Third anal spine the longest, and equalling 1/3 of the length of the head. Caudal forked, upper lobe with a filamentous prolongation. *Scales*—extend forwards superiorly to between the eyes. *Lateral-line*—the tubes divide posteriorly into two branches. *Colours*—silvery, with pinkish longitudinal bands: fins pinkish stained with yellow.

The specimen described and figured is from Sir W. Elliot's Madras collection, the coloured figure is named *Dentex striatus* C. V. by Jerdon, and is alluded to in M. J. L. and Sc. 1851, p. 131.

This species, a specimen of which, from Vizagapatam, has been given me by Sir Walter Elliot, cannot be *Spondyliosoma gulimiuda* (C. V.) Cantor,* Catal. p. 50, which is not Russell's *Sparus lunua gulimiuda*=*Synagris tolu*, of which I have both male and female specimens. It is very similar to *S. Japonicus*, but (irrespective of the spines being weaker and longer, it has only 9 instead of 10 rows of scales between the lateral-line and the base of the anal fin). I have a male of that species which has no prolongation of the dorsal fin. There are two of Bloch's specimens marked *Dentex luteus* at Berlin, one evidently the skin from which Bl. Schn.'s figure has been taken, the artist not having reversed it, whilst he has delineated the eye too small, and the (?) elongated dorsal spines are broken. On the second specimen, which has no elongated dorsal spine, is Val.'s label, "C'est le vrai *C. luteus*, Bl. Schn." Bloch's may be this species, but it has several rows of villiform teeth in the mandibles of about the same size and very similar to *S. Japonicus*, which it appears to resemble. This (*Synagris striatus*) is certainly Jerdon's *Dentex striatus*.

Bl. Schn.'s figure is probably coloured from a description in which it was said to have been striated or banded, and instead of placing such longitudinally he has given them as vertical.

Habitat.—Coromandel coast of India: the specimen figured was captured November 25th, 1852. *Dentex filamentosus*, C.V., came from Surinam.

2. Synagris tolu, Plate XXIII, fig. 6.

Sparus lunua gulimiuda, Russell, Fish. Vizag. ii, p. 6, pl. cvii.

Dentex tolu, Cuv. and Val. vi, p. 249; Bleeker, Spar. p. 13, Atl. Ich. Perc. t. xxvii, fig. i, and Revis. Dentex. p. 20 (not Klunz.)

Cantharus gulimiuda, Cuv. and Val. vi, p. 344 (not *Spondyliosoma gulimiuda*, Cantor.)

Cowlil, Tam.

B. vi, D. $\frac{10}{9}$, P. 17, V. 1/5, A. $\frac{3}{7}$, C. 17, L. l. 48, L. tr. 3/10, Cæc. pyl. 10-11.

Length of head 2/9, of pectoral 1/6, of caudal 2/9 to 1/4, height of body 2/9 to 1/4 of the total length. *Eyes*—transversely oval, diameter 1/3 of length of head, 1 diameter from end of snout, and 2/3 apart. Jaws of equal length, the maxilla reaches to below the front edge of the orbit. The lower edge of the preorbital obliquely convex in its posterior half, its height equals half the diameter of the orbit. Preopercle entire. Opercle with a small flattened spine. *Teeth*—villiform along the whole of the upper jaw, with from 4 to 6 canine-like ones anteriorly in either premaxillary, laterally the outer row is composed of about 16 closely set pointed ones: the inner ones in the mandible also villiform, opposite the symphysis in several rows, laterally in a single one, the outer row in front of the lower jaw is rather larger than the villiform ones, but not so large as the outer lateral row which equals those in the side of the upper jaw. *Fins*—dorsal spines very slender and flexible, the interspinous membrane deeply notched. The spines increase in length to the sixth, seventh, and eighth, which equal two-thirds the height of the body, the last spine equals two-fifths of the height of the body and is of the same length as the last ray: pectoral fin as long as the head excluding the snout: ventral with its outer ray elongated, scarcely reaches so far as the anus: second anal spine of equal strength to but not so long

* In Cantor's fish the dentition is slightly different. It has villiform teeth in both jaws, with 5 or 6 small curved canines in the front of the upper jaw, whilst laterally its outer row is slightly enlarged: the canines in front of the lower jaw are very small, whilst laterally the outer row is scarcely larger than the villiform teeth.

as the third which equals one third of the height of the body; caudal deeply forked the upper lobe the longer. As regards sexes the dorsal spines are equally prolonged in males and females: the pectoral is a little longer in the males, extending to the anus, but the caudal lobes are the same. *Colours*—rosy, with four or five yellowish longitudinal bands between the rows of scales from immediately above the base of the pectoral fin. Fins pinkish: tips of dorsal spines orange.

Russell's figure, although defective, is sufficient to distinguish the species by: it is the most common kind in Madras from October to March, and may be at once recognised from the other recorded forms by its long and flexible dorsal spines and deeply emarginate interspinous membrane. The caudal fins of some males examined in October had no filamentous prolongations.

Cuv. and Val. specimens are in good preservation at Paris and coincide with the above described, but not with *Spondyliosoma gulinuda*, Cantor, whose type is in the British Museum.

Habitat.—Seas of India to the Malay Archipelago.

3. Synagris Bleekeri, Plate XXIV, fig. 1.

B. vi, D. $\frac{10}{9}$, P. 17, V. 1/5, A. $\frac{3}{7}$, C. 17, L. l. 48, L. tr. $3\frac{1}{2}$/11.

Length of head one-fourth to 2/9, of caudal $4\frac{2}{3}$, height of body $4\frac{1}{2}$ in the total length. *Eyes*—transversely oval, diameter $3\frac{3}{4}$ in the length of head, $1\frac{1}{3}$ diameters from end of snout, and 1 apart. Interorbital space flat. The maxilla reaches to below the first third of the orbit. Preorbital three-fourths as high as the length of the transverse diameter of the orbit, its posterior margin oblique gradually passing into the inferior one. Preopercle entire. A small flat spine on the opercle. *Teeth*—in villiform bands in the upper jaw, four small canines in the front of each premaxillary, no enlarged lateral row: villiform teeth above the symphysis in the lower jaw, but continued a very short distance laterally, and canine-like teeth in front of the lower jaw, and a single row of conical ones in the last two-thirds of the mandible. *Fins*—dorsal spines of moderate strength with the interspinous membrane scarcely notched, the spines increase in length to the last, the height of which equals the length of the post-orbital portion of the head or two-fifths of the height of the body, the last rays somewhat elongated and equal to half the height of the body. Pectoral nearly as long as the head: ventral with its outer ray elongated and nearly reaching the anal spines: anal spines of equal strength, the second not so long as the third which is rather longer than the diameter of the orbit: caudal deeply forked, the upper lobe the longer, but no filamentous prolongation was observed in Madras specimens. *Colours*—reddish superiorly, becoming silvery along the sides and beneath, where yellow bands exist: a bluish spot on the opercle: fins reddish, dorsal edged with orange and having a golden band along its base.

This species is closely allied to *S. notatus*, from which it differs both in its dentition and colouring.

Habitat.—Seas of India. The specimen figured is from Madras, and 8 inches in length.

4. Synagris Japonicus, Plate XXIV, fig. 2.

Sparus Japonicus, Bl. t. 277, f. 1 (not *Synagris Japonicus*, Günther).
Cantharus filamentosus, Rüpp. Atl. p. 50, t. xii. f. 3 (not *Dentex filamentosus*, C. V.).
Dentex tambulus, Cuv. and Val. vi, pp. 249, 558 (? Rüppell, not Bleeker).
? *Dentex bipunctatus*, (Ehren.) Cuv. and Val. vi, p. 247.
Synagris filamentosus, Günther, Catal. i, p. 378.
Synagris grammicus, Day, Fish. Malabar, p. 26, pl. iv.
Chavajarah, Tam.

B. vi, D. $\frac{10}{9}$, P. 17, V. 1/5, A. $\frac{3}{7}$, C. 17, L. l. 48, L. tr. $3\frac{1}{2}$/10.

Length of head 1/4, of caudal 2/9, height of body 1/4 of the total length excluding the filamentous prolongation of the upper caudal lobe. *Eyes*—diameter $3\frac{1}{4}$ to $3\frac{1}{2}$ in length of head, $1\frac{1}{4}$ to $1\frac{1}{2}$ diameters from end of snout, and nearly 1 apart. The maxilla reaches to below the first third of the orbit. Vertical limb of preopercle finely and evenly serrated in its lower half: its angle rounded and entire. Opercle without any distinct spine. *Teeth*—in villiform bands in both jaws, from four to six small curved canines in the front of either premaxillary, whilst the outer row is a very little the largest: in the mandible the last six or eight teeth only are conical and a little enlarged. *Fins*—dorsal spines rather weak with the interspinous membrane scarcely notched, the height of the spines increase to the last which equals the length of the postorbital portion of the head; the last ray equals half the length of the head. Pectoral reaches to above the anal spines. Ventral, having its first ray prolonged, reaches as far as the anal fin. Third anal spine slightly weaker than the second but longer, equalling one-third the length of the head. Caudal deeply forked, having a filamentous prolongation. (This may be peculiar to the males, but I have reason to believe it is present in the females. In a specimen captured at Madras, $9\frac{1}{2}$ inches in length to the end of the caudal lobes, the upper one is produced beyond this $2\frac{3}{10}$ inches in addition.) *Colours*—yellowish-red, having longitudinal reddish lines along each row of scales. Dorsal and anal fins with a yellow streak along their centres, a grey base and pinkish edge.

Dentex Blochii, Bleeker (Sciæn. p. 176, and Revis. Dentex, p. 27)=*Synagris Japonicus*, Günther (Catal. i, p. 378) is not synonymous with the above, its preopercular limb being entire. The statement in Cuv. and Val. of the preopercular edge being entire is erroneous, as I have convinced myself by examining the type specimen at Berlin, and Val.'s identification of it with *Sparus Japonicus* was perfectly correct.

S. grammicus appears to be a variety of this fish, its preorbital being considerably higher than is seen in specimens from the Red Sea and East coast of Africa, in the former the height equalling almost 1 diameter of the orbit; in the latter 1/2 or 2/3 of a diameter.

Habitat.—Red Sea, East coast of Africa, and seas of India.

5. Synagris notatus, Plate XXIV, fig. 3.

? *Dentex furcosus*, Cuv. and Val. vi, p. 244.
Synagris furcosus, Günther, Catal. i, p. 373.
Synagris notatus, Day, Pro. Zool. Soc. 1870, p. 684.

B. vi, D. $\frac{10}{9}$, P. 15, V. 1/5, A. $\frac{3}{7}$, C. 17, L. l. 47, L. tr. $3\frac{1}{2}$/10.

Length of head $3\frac{3}{4}$ to one-fourth, of caudal 2/9 to one-fifth, height of body one-fourth of the total length. *Eyes*—diameter $3\frac{1}{2}$ to 1/4 in the length of head, $1\frac{1}{3}$ diameters from the end of snout, and nearly 1 apart. Height of the head nearly equals its length. The maxilla reaches to below the front edge of the orbit. Preorbital under the commencement of the eye is nearly as high as the transverse diameter of the orbit, whilst its hind edge is more angular than in *S. Bleekeri*. Preopercle entire. Opercle with a small flat spine. *Teeth*—villiform in the upper jaw with four large curved canines in either premaxillary, and laterally an outer conical row which are not very large: villiform ones in the front third of the lower jaw with six well-developed anterior canine-like ones, laterally a row of conical teeth which become small in the last fourth of the jaw. *Fins*—dorsal spines weak, interspinous membrane very slightly emarginate, the spines increase in length to the fifth from whence they continue of about the same height or 1/3 of the length of the head to the last which is a little longer being $2\frac{3}{4}$ in the same distance: the length of the last rays equal that of the postorbital portion of the head. Pectoral equals 3/4 of the height of the body. Caudal forked, upper lobe the longer. *Colours*—rosy with a brilliant spot on the first five scales below the lateral-line, the upper half red, the lower yellow. Five or six longitudinal yellow bands are present below the lateral-line, and three silvery-white ones: fins pinkish, with a yellow band along the bases of the dorsal and anal.

This appears to be a slight variety of *S. furcosus*, Günther, in which latter the dorsal spines increase in length to the third from whence they slightly decrease to the last which equals the length of the head behind the eye.

Dentex furcosus, C. V. has an elongated body and the caudal lobes very prolonged.

Habitat.—Seas of India.

Genus, 24—Pentapus, *Cuv.*

Leiopsis, Bennett: *Gnathodentex*, pt. Bleeker.

Branchiostegals six: pseudobranchiæ. Body oblong. Eyes of medium size. Cleft of mouth more or less horizontal and not deep: jaws of about equal length: a serrated ridge may extend along the upper jaw. Preopercle entire: opercle without any or with a very feeble spine: preorbital narrow, entire, the distance between the eye and the mouth small. Villiform teeth in the jaws with canines, palate edentulous. One scaleless dorsal fin receivable into a groove at its base, having ten spines and from eight to ten rays: anal with three spines and from eight to ten rays: caudal forked. Scales ctenoid, of moderate or small size, with three or more rows on the preopercle. Air-vessel simple. Pyloric appendages few.

Dr. Bleeker separates *Gnathodentex* from *Pentapus* due to its possessing a serrated longitudinal ridge on the upper jaw, &c.

Geographical distribution.—Seas of India to Australia.

SYNOPSIS OF INDIVIDUAL SPECIES.

1. *Pentapus aurolineatus*, D. $\frac{10}{10}$, A. $\frac{3}{7\text{-}8}$, L. l. 74-78. Golden bands along the body, a white spot on the back behind the last dorsal ray. Ceylon to the Malay Archipelago and beyond.

1. Pentapus aurolineatus.

Sparus aurolineatus, Lacép. iv, p. 132.
Dentex lycogenis, Benn. Proc. Zool. Soc. i, p. 127.
Pentapus aurolineatus, Cuv. and Val. vi, pp. 269, 550, pl. 157; Bleeker, Halma. p. 55; Günther, Catal. i, pp. 381, 507, and Fische d. Sudsee, p. 33, t. xxv, f. B.
Gnathodentex aurolineatus, Bleeker, Atl. Ich. Perc. t. xl, fig. 3, and Revis. Dentex, p. 49.

B. vi, D. $\frac{10}{10}$, P. 16, V. 1/5, A. $\frac{3}{7\text{-}8}$, C. 17, L. l. 74-78, L. tr. 6/20.

Length of head $4\frac{1}{2}$ to one-fourth, of caudal nearly one-fifth, height of body two-sevenths of the total length. *Eyes*—diameter 2/5 of length of head, 3/4 of a diameter from end of snout, and 1 apart. The maxilla reaches to below the front nostril, a serrated ridge extends along the centre of the upper two-thirds of its outer surface. *Teeth*—about six canines in the front of the upper jaw, and an equal number in front of the lower, the outer of which is enlarged. *Fins*—dorsal spines rather weak, increasing in length to the fourth which is two-fifths of the height of the body below it, the hind ones are a little shorter, the rays are rather higher than the spines, interspinous membrane slightly notched: pectoral nearly as long as the head: ventral nearly reaches the anal, the spines of the latter are not strong, the third the longest but not quite equal to the fourth of the dorsal:

caudal deeply forked. *Colours*—silvery, with four or five horizontal golden bands along the sides, and a silvery mark on the back behind the last dorsal ray: fins rosy, the dorsal, caudal, and anal being margined with red.

Habitat.—Mauritius, Ceylon to the Malay Archipelago, and beyond. This species exists in the Netley Hospital Museum, it was received from Ceylon.

Genus, 25—Smaris, *Cuv.*

Branchiostegals six; pseudobranchiæ. Body oblong or cylindrical. Eyes of medium or large size, mouth very protractile. Preopercle entire. Teeth in the jaws, none on the vomer. A single, sometimes deeply notched scaleless dorsal fin, with from nine to fifteen feeble spines; anal with three. Scales ctenoid, rather small. Air-vessel not constricted, but generally forked posteriorly. Pyloric appendages few.

Geographical distribution.—Mediterranean and Atlantic ocean, one species from Ceylon.

SYNOPSIS OF INDIVIDUAL SPECIES.

1. *Smaris balteatus*, D. $\frac{11}{13}$, A. $\frac{3}{10}$. A silvery band from the eye to the tail.

1. Smaris balteatus.

Cuv. and Val. vi, p. 424; Günther, Catal. i, p. 389.

B. vi, D. $\frac{11}{13}$, P. 17, V. 1/5, A. $\frac{3}{10}$.

Length of head $4\frac{1}{2}$, of caudal $5\frac{1}{2}$, height of body one-fourth in the total length. *Eyes*—diameter $2\frac{3}{4}$ in the length of the head, 2/3 of a diameter from the end of snout. Body cylindrical and somewhat elongated: mouth protractile: the maxilla reaches to below the front edge of the orbit. *Teeth*—fine. *Fins*—division between the spinous and soft portions of the dorsal well marked. *Colours*—reddish-brown along the back, dotted with small brilliant silvery spots: the coloured part of the back streaked with the brilliant silver of the sides, whilst below this coloured portion is a wide silvery longitudinal band, which passes from the superciliary region across the opercle, and proceeds to the tail. Fins pale coloured.

Habitat.—Ceylon, to 4 inches in length.

Genus, 26—Cæsio, (*Comm.*) *Cuv.*

Cæsio, sp. Cuv. and Val.: *Paracæsio*, Bleeker; *Odontonectes*, Günther.

Branchiostegals six or seven: pseudobranchiæ. Body oblong, sometimes somewhat elevated. Mouth moderately protractile, its cleft oblique, lower jaw sometimes the longer. Preopercle entire or minutely serrated. Fine teeth in the jaws, sometimes deciduous ones on the vomer or palate. A single dorsal fin, more or less scaled (rarely scaleless) with the anterior portion the higher and having from nine to thirteen feeble spines: anal with three. Scales very finely ctenoid, of moderate or small size, and as a rule extended over the bases of the vertical fins. Air-vessel not constricted.*

Bleeker (Fish. Madag. p. 38) has instituted a Genus *Paracæsio* for the reception of those species in which the dorsal fin is scaleless.

Geographical distribution.—From the Red Sea, through those of India to the Malay Archipelago.

SYNOPSIS OF SPECIES.

1. *Cæsio pinjalo*, D. $\frac{11}{14}$, A. $\frac{3}{10}$, L. l. 50-55, L. tr. 9/18. Roseate and yellow: dorsal and caudal edged with black. Seas of India to the Malay Archipelago.
2. *Cæsio caning*, D. $\frac{10}{15}$, A. $\frac{3}{11}$, L. l. 53. Bluish-green above, rosy below. Seas of India to the Malay Archipelago.
3. *Cæsio chrysozona*, D. $\frac{10}{15}$, A. $\frac{3}{11-12}$. A golden longitudinal band: a black spot in the axil and a black band along the middle of either caudal lobe. Red Sea, seas of India to the Malay Archipelago.

1. Cæsio pinjalo, Plate XXIV, fig. 4.

Pinjalo typus, Bleeker, Bydr. Topog. Batav. p. 521 and Revis. Cæsio, p. 25.

Cæsio pinjalo, Bleeker, Mænid. p. 10, Java, i, p. 102, and Atl. Ich. Perc. t. xiv, fig. 3; Günther, Catal. i, p. 391.

Mesoprion Mitchelli, Günther, Ann. and Mag. Nat. Hist. xix, 1867, p. 257, pl. ix.

B. vii, D. $\frac{11}{14}$, P. 21, V. 1/5, A. $\frac{3}{10}$, C. 17, L. l. 50-55, L. r. [illegible], L. tr. 9/18.

Length of head 2/9, of caudal 1/5, height of body 2/7 of the total length. *Eyes*—diameter 2/7 to 1/4 of length of head, 3/4 to 1 diameter from end of snout, and also apart. Body oval and compressed. Lower jaw the longer. The maxilla reaches to below the front edge of the orbit. Height of preorbital equal to half the diameter of the orbit. Vertical limb of preopercle serrated, most coarsely so at its angle which is considerably produced. Opercle with a weak, flat spine. *Teeth*—villiform, with one or two, sometimes three, small conical ones on either

* Referring to *C. cærulaureus*, Dr. Günther remarks that "from the extremely delicate structure of the fin-rays, it is very difficult to count them and to give the correct numbers, but which is the more necessary, as we do not yet know to what extent they vary in the species of this genus."—Catal. i, p. 372.

side of the middle of the upper jaw, in a narrow band in a Λ-form on the vomer, and also on the palatines, occasionally absent from the latter bone, and in some specimens from the former. *Fins*—dorsal spines weak, the fourth and fifth the highest and equal to rather more than the length of the postorbital portion of the head, from thence they slightly decrease to the last which nearly equals the height of the first ray, these latter being shorter than the longest spine: pectoral slightly longer than the head, pointed, and reaching to below the first dorsal ray. Second anal spine* of equal length to, or slightly shorter than the third: caudal lunated. *Colours*—yellowish-red along the back, becoming rosy below the lateral-line: dark olivaceous stripes along the rows of scales above the lateral-line, but having a more yellow-tinge below it: pectoral, ventral, and anal orange, dorsal and caudal yellowish edged with black.

A coloured figure, eight inches long, exists in Sir Walter Elliot's collection, labelled *Mette mirrei, Cœsio?*

Habitat.—Coromandel coast of India, Malay Archipelago, attaining at least 16 inches in length. The specimen figured is 9 inches long.

2. Cæsio cuning.

Sparus cuning, Bloch, t. 263, f. 1; Lacép. iv, p. 115.
Cichla cuning, Bl. Schn. p. 336.
Cæsio erythrogaster, (Kuhl. and v. Hass.) Cuv. and Val. vi, p. 442, pl. 166; Bleeker, Verb. Bat. Gen. xxiii, Mænid. p. 9, and Atl. Ich. Perc. t. xxxiv, f. 3, and Revis. Cæsio, p. 8; Kner, Novara Fische, p. 64.
Cæsio cuning, Cuv. and Val. vi, p. 444; Günther, Catal. i, p. 390.
Odontonectes erythrogaster, Günther, Catal. i, p. 265.

B. vi, D. $\frac{10}{15}$, P. 20, A. $\frac{3}{11}$, C. 17, L. l. 53, L. tr. 7/13, Vert. 10/14, Cæc. pyl. 5.

Length of head 4/19 to 1/5, of caudal 1/4, height of body 4/15 to 2/7 of the total length. *Eyes*—diameter 1/4 of length of head, and 3/4 to 1 diameter from end of snout, and $1\frac{1}{2}$ apart. The upper maxilla reaches to slightly behind the vertical from the front edge of the orbit. Preopercular angle rounded and finely serrated. *Teeth*—villiform in jaws, small ones on vomer, and mostly some deciduous ones on the palatine bones. *Fins*—dorsal spines slender and flexible, the fourth the longest. Second and third anal spines of nearly the same height, and equal to 1/3 of the length of the head: caudal deeply forked. *Colours*—bluish-green superiorly becoming rosy along the abdomen.

Dr. Jerdon observes, "I once procured a specimen 18 inches long of this handsome fish, which the fishermen called *Cul kilchi*, Tam., but which did not appear well known to them, D. $\frac{10}{14}$, A. $\frac{3}{12}$." Madr. J. L. and Science, 1851, p. 133. The late Col. Tickell also considered he obtained it in Burma. It is very probable that it is found in the seas of India, although I have not obtained specimens from thence.

Habitat.—Seas of India to the Malay Archipelago and beyond.

3. Cæsio chrysozona, Plate XXIV, fig. 5, (var. *aurolineatus*.)

(Kuhl. and v. Hass) Cuv. and Val. vi, p. 440; Bleeker, Mænid. p. 9, and Atl. Ich. Perc. t. xxix, f. 2, and Revis. Cæsio, p. 19; Günther, Catal. i, p. 392; Kner. Novara Fische, p. 65.
Cæsio striatus, Bleeker, Batav. p. 521.
Pristipomatoides aurolineatus, Day, Proc. Zool. Soc. 1867, p. 937 (variety).

B. vi, D. $\frac{10}{14}\frac{|}{-15}$, P. 19, V. 1/5, A. $\frac{3}{11-12}$, C. 15, L. l. 72, L. tr. 8/16.

Length of head $4\frac{1}{4}$, of caudal 2/9, height of body $4\frac{1}{4}$ in the total length. *Eyes*—upper margin close to the profile, diameter $2\frac{1}{2}$ in the young to $3\frac{1}{4}$ in the adult in length of head, 3/4 of a diameter apart, 1/2 to 1 diameter from end of snout. Body rather elongated and compressed. Lower jaw the longer; the maxilla extends to below the anterior third of the orbit. Preorbital long, narrow, and at least three times as long as wide, and with elevated striæ upon it. Preopercle wide, its horizontal wider than its vertical limb; both striated at their edges, and irregularly serrated, in the adult the angle is rather produced. Opercle with a moderately developed spine. *Fins*—dorsal spines weak, third and fourth the longest, and equal to half the height of the body: interspinous membrane very slightly emarginate: rays of about equal length. Pectoral reaching to opposite the anus. First anal spine one-quarter the length of the second, which is of equal strength but slightly shorter than the third, which equals the height of the second in the dorsal fin. Caudal deeply lobed, the lower being the largest and longest. *Scales*—ctenoid, a few rows of scales along the bases of the dorsal and anal fins. *Colours*—bluish with a golden band along the lateral-line and a black one on either lobe of the caudal: a black spot in the axilla. In *C. aurolineatus*, above the lateral-line it is of a light lake colour: from the eye to the base of the caudal below the lateral-line exists a shining golden band, three scales deep anteriorly, decreasing to one posteriorly: below this band pinkish-white: caudal lobes tipped with black.

A figure nearly five inches in length exists amongst Sir W. Elliot's drawings, labelled, Nat. size, *Perooa kilchi* and *Woongoomi?*

The colours of *C. chrysozona*, K. v. H. given in Bleeker's Atl. Ich. Perc. xxix, fig. 2, are blue instead of a lake colour, and it has a narrow yellow band along the back close to the base of the dorsal fin, D. $\frac{10}{14}$, A. $\frac{3}{12}$, L. l. 65. In a fine specimen in the British Museum the height of the body is 2/9 of the total length.

* The proportionate strength of the second anal spine to that of the third varies:—out of six specimens in my collection from 6 to 10 inches in length, in two the former is the stronger.

the first anal spine is very short, the general colour is steel blue with a golden lateral band two scales wide: the caudal lobes are of equal length.

Bleeker observes that *Caesio chrysozona* is closely allied to *C. caerulaureus*, but the body is more elongated in the former than in the latter. The temporal band of scales is largest in the *C. caerulaureus*, which has its golden lateral band above instead of below the lateral line.

Habitat.—Red Sea, seas of India.

Eighth group—Gerrina.

Branchiostegals six. Body elevated or oblong. Preopercle serrated or entire. Mouth very protractile. Villiform teeth in the jaws. A single dorsal fin: three anal spines. Air-vessel simple.

Genus, 28—Datnioides, *Bleeker*.

Branchiostegals six: pseudobranchiæ. Body elevated. Eyes of moderate size. Premaxillaries very protractile. Preopercle serrated. Villiform teeth in the jaws without canines; vomer, palate, and tongue edentulous. A single dorsal fin having twelve stout spines: anal with three: caudal rounded. Scales ctenoid. Air-vessel simple. Pyloric appendages few.

Geographical distribution.—Mouths of large rivers from the Hooghly throughout Burma to the Malay Archipelago. Rarely found beyond tidal reach although it frequently ascends into fresh water.

SYNOPSIS OF INDIVIDUAL SPECIES.

1. *Datnioides polota*, D. $\frac{12}{13-14}$, A. $\frac{3}{8-9}$, L. l. 48. Brown with several cross bands. Estuaries of the Ganges to the Malay Archipelago.

1. Datnioides polota, Plate XXIV, fig. 6.

Coius polota, Ham. Buch. pp. 95, 370, pl. 38, f. 31; Temm. and Schleg. Fauna Japon. Poiss. p. 17; Richards. Ich. Sulphur, p. 83.
Coius binotatus, Gray and Hard. Ind. Zool.; Temm. and Schel. l. c. p. 17; Richards. l. c. p. 83.
Datnia polota, Cantor, Catal. p. 16.
Lobotes hexagona, Bleeker, Nat. Tyds. Ned. Ind. i, p. 9, and ii, p. 165.
Datnioides polota, Bleeker, l. c. v, p. 441, and Atl. Ich. Perc. t. xxvii, f. 1; Günther, Catal. i, p. 339.
Nga-kyn and *Nga-wet-mu*, Burm.; *Nga-pree-gryn* and *Nga-thak-kon*, Arrac.

B. vi, D. $\frac{12}{13-14}$, P. 19, V. 1/5, A. $\frac{3}{8-9}$, C. 17, L. l. 48, L. r. [illegible], L. tr. 12/25, Cæc. pyl. 5.

Length of head 2/7 to 1/3, of caudal 2/11 to 1/6, height of body 2/5 to 1/3 of the total length. *Eyes*—diameter 1/5 of length of head, $1\frac{1}{2}$ diameters from end of snout, and 1 apart. The posterior processes of the premaxillaries reach to behind the orbit. The maxilla extends to below the middle of the orbit. Preopercle serrated along both limbs: both shoulder-bone and the one in the axilla serrated. *Teeth*—fine in the jaws, with the outer row slightly enlarged. *Fins*—dorsal spines strong, every alternate one being thickened on one side, the fifth and sixth the longest and equal to two-fifths of the height of the body or half of the length of the head: second anal spine the strongest and longest, equalling the highest in the dorsal fin: caudal rounded. *Colours*—brownish, glossed with copper, having six or seven narrow brown vertical bands on the body and similar ones radiating from the orbit.

Habitat.—Estuaries and within tidal influence of the Ganges and rivers of Burma to the Malay Archipelago, attaining at least 1 foot in length: though not esteemed as food it is eaten by the poorer classes. The specimen figured ($6\frac{3}{4}$ inches in length) is from Calcutta.

Genus, 29—Gerres, *Cuv.*

Diapterus, Ranz.: *Chanda*, sp. Ham. Buch.: *Catochaenum*, Cantor: *Synistius*, Gill: *Eucinostomus*, Baird, Gir.

Branchiostegals six: pseudobranchiæ. Body elevated or oblong, and compressed. Mouth very protractile and descending when produced. Preopercle as a rule entire, rarely serrated. Eyes comparatively large. Villiform teeth in the jaws. Inferior pharyngeal bones firmly united by a suture. Length of the bases of the spinous and soft portions of the dorsal fin of nearly equal extent, and having a scaly sheath into which it can be wholly or partially received: the spines numbering nine or ten, the rays ten or eleven: anal with three spines: caudal forked. Scales of moderate size, when ctenoid very slightly so. Air-vessel simple. Pyloric appendages few.

Gill places the Gerrini as a distinct family.

Geographical distribution.—All the tropical seas, entering estuaries. Some apparently being mostly confined to the latter situations, and ascending into brackish or fresh waters as high as tidal influence extends.

Uses.—As food these fishes are mostly eaten by the indigent classes, being little esteemed whilst fresh on account of their numerous bones and deficiency in flavour. As they salt and dry well, large numbers are extensively prepared in this manner for future use or as a matter of export trade.

The species comprising this genus are somewhat difficult of determination unless a good collection is brought together, but even then some important considerations have to be borne in mind prior to deciding whether the specimen belongs to a known or an unknown species. The eye, certainly in some, increases in comparative size with the head as age advances, as occurs in *Megalops cyprinoides*, &c. The first few dorsal spines may be compressed or rounded: and the second and third slightly or very elongate, but this elongation often varies considerably, as seen in *G. filamentosus*, in which it may be only two-thirds the height of the body or even extending so far as the base of the caudal fin, and though this difference is generally, it is not always due to age, but in the young it is mostly shorter than in the adult. Even in the anal spines the second may be equal in length to the third or a little longer or shorter in the same species. As regards colour the young are generally vertically banded, and these bands may be indistinct or even entirely absent in the adult. In those with longitudinal bands they sometimes become interrupted in large specimens, showing rows of long oval blotches or marks placed one over the other, the reason usually being that these marks are apparent in the adult where the vertical bands existed in the immature.

SYNOPSIS OF SPECIES.

1. *Gerres setifer*, D. $\frac{9}{10}$, A. $\frac{3}{7}$, L. l. 38, L. tr. 5/10. Preopercle serrated along its lower limb. Highest dorsal spine 2/5 of that of body. Silvery, a narrow dark edge to spinous dorsal, and a brown spot on the middle of each ray. Hooghly.

2. *Gerres oblongus*, D. $\frac{9}{10}$, A. $\frac{3}{7}$, L. l. 48-50. Highest dorsal spine 3/4 of that of the body. Silvery. Seas of India to the Malay Archipelago and beyond.

3. *Gerres filamentosus*, D. $\frac{9}{10}$, A. $\frac{3}{7}$, L. l. 45-48. Highest dorsal spine elongated sometimes reaching the caudal fin. Silvery, with rows of short, oblong, horizontal, bluish spots along the upper half of the body: a spot at the base or centre of each dorsal spine and ray. Seas of India to the Malay Archipelago and beyond.

4. *Gerres oyena*, D. $\frac{9}{10}$, A. $\frac{3}{7}$, L. l. 38-40, L. tr. 5/10. Highest dorsal spine as long as head excluding the snout. Red Sea, through those of India, to the Malay Archipelago and beyond.

5. *Gerres lucidus*, D. $\frac{9}{10}$, A. $\frac{3}{7}$, L. l. 41, L. tr. 5/10. Highest dorsal spine two-fifths as high as the body. Dorsal fin with a black blotch, a dark spot on each spine and ray just above the sheath. Seas of India.

6. *Gerres abbreviatus*, D. $\frac{9}{10}$, A. $\frac{3}{7}$, L. l. 37-40, L. tr. 6/11. Highest dorsal spine almost as long as the head: pectoral long. Seas of India to the Malay Archipelago.

7. *Gerres poeti*, D. $\frac{9}{10}$, A. $\frac{3}{7}$, L. l. 40, L. tr. 6/11. Highest dorsal spine as long as the head excluding the snout. Red Sea, seas of India to the Malay Archipelago and beyond.

8. *Gerres limbatus*, D. $\frac{9}{10}$, A. $\frac{3}{7}$, L. l. 35, L. tr. 4/10. Highest dorsal spine as long as the head behind the middle of the orbit. Seas of India.

1. Gerres setifer, Plate XXV, fig. 1.

Chanda (?) setifer,* Ham. Buch. Fish. Ganges, pp. 105, 370.
Gerres altispinis, Günther, Catal. iv, p. 258.

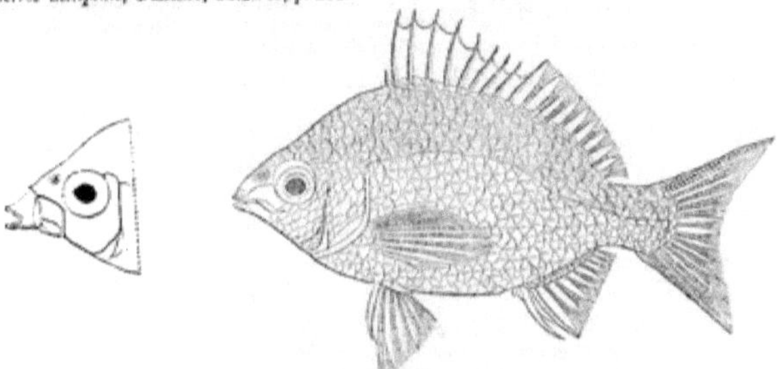

Chanda (?) setifer, (H. Buchanan's MSS. figure).

B. vi. D. $\frac{9}{10}$, P. 17, V. 1/5, A. $\frac{3}{7}$, C. 19, L. l. 38, L. tr. 5/10.

Length of head 4/17 to 1/4, of caudal 1/5, height of body 1/3 of the total length. *Eyes*—diameter 1/3 of length of head, nearly 1 diameter from end of snout, and 1 apart. The groove for the posterior process of the premaxillary reaches to opposite the first third of the orbit, it is posteriorly rounded and scaleless. The maxilla

* Buchanan observes of his *Genus*, *Chanda*, or "Silvery fishes," that "the first (*Chanda setifer*) has the strongest affinity to the *Zeus insidiator*, so that all of them no doubt belong to the same genus with that fish, although I cannot help thinking that, to include them in the same genus with *Zeus ciliaris* and *Zeus faber* is an unnatural arrangement" (Buchanan l. c. p. 103), "as in the genera already described there are, as it were, certain intermediate species, so in this the two first (*Chanda setifer* and *C. ruconius*) * * * have but little of the transparency, which forms part of the generic character" (l. c. p. 104).

reaches to below the front edge of the orbit. Lower margin of preopercle serrated in its last half, in the British Museum specimen these serrations are less apparent than in mine. *Teeth*—fine. *Fins*—dorsal spines of moderate strength, the second not quite so high as the third and fourth which are equal to two-fifths the height of the body: last dorsal spine rather longer than the one preceding it, and one third shorter than the third or fourth. Pectoral reaches to nearly above the anal: ventral three-fourths of the distance to the anal: anal spines of about equal length or the second slightly the longer: caudal deeply forked. *Scales*—the sheath to the dorsal and anal fins high. Free portion of the tail as wide at its commencement as it is long. *Colours*—silvery, with a narrow dark edge to the dorsal interspinous membrane and a brown spot at the middle of each dorsal ray just above the sheath.

Hamilton Buchanan states that *Chanda setifer* has ten prickles in its dorsal fin, the first of which is very short; but irrespective of his description he has left a drawing of it, labelled *katchanda*, whilst amongst the collection of fishes received by the British Museum from Mr. Waterhouse exists one, the type of *Gerres altispinis*, Günther, having ten dorsal spines, not nine as stated in the Catalogue. It is closely allied to *G. lucidus*, but possesses one more dorsal spine, a more or less serrated border along the horizontal edge of the preopercle, and one more row of scales between the lateral-line and the base of the dorsal fin. Bleeker in his "Pisces Hindostan, &c." gives "p. 38, Scolopsides (?) setifer, Blkr. Chanda (?) setifer, Buchan."

Habitat.—River Hooghly at Calcutta, where it is common, attaining to 4 inches in length.

2. Gerres oblongus, Plate XXV, fig. 2.

Cuv. and Val. vi, p. 479; Günther, Catal. i, p. 354, and iv, p. 264.

Gerres gigas, Günther, Catal. iv, p. 262, and Fische d. Sudsee, p. 30, pl. xxiv, fig. A.

B. vi, D. $\frac{9}{10}$, P. 17, V. 1/5, A. $\frac{3}{8}$, C. 17, L. l. 48-50, L. tr. 5½/.

Length of head 3/13, of caudal 2/9, height of body nearly 1/4 of the total length. *Eyes*—diameter 1/3 of length of head, 3/4 (in the young 1) of a diameter from end of snout, and 1 apart. Snout rather elevated. The maxilla reaches to below the front edge of the orbit. Preopercle entire. The groove for the posterior process of the premaxillary reaches to opposite the middle of the eye, it is rounded behind and scaleless. *Teeth*—fine. *Fins*—dorsal spines not very strong, compressed, the second curved and much the highest, being almost as long as the head, and three-fourths of that of the body below it: pectoral long, reaching to above the anal spines: anal spines weak, the third rather the longest and equalling the length of the post-orbital portion of the head: caudal deeply forked, with some fine scales upon it. *Scales*—5½ rows between the lateral-line and the base of the dorsal fin. The scaly sheath of both dorsal and anal fins moderately developed. Free portion of the tail as high at its commencement as it is long. *Colours*—silvery, eye golden. The *young* are considerably darker above the lateral-line, and show indistinct bands.

Habitat.—It would seem to extend throughout the seas of India to the Malay Archipelago and beyond. The young are sometimes captured at Madras, and I have also taken this fish at the Andaman islands, where I procured the specimen figured, which is a little over nine inches in length.

3. Gerres filamentosus, Plate XXV, fig. 3.

Zeus wodawakah, Russell, i, p. 52, pl. 67.

Gerres filamentosus, Cuv. and Val. vi, p. 482; Günther, Catal. i, p. 345, and iv, p. 261; Day, Fishes of Malabar, p. 159; Kner, Novara Fische, p. 56 (not C.V.); Klunz. Verh. z. b. Ges. Wien, 1870, p. 773.

Gerres punctatus, C. V. vi, p. 480; Bleeker, Batav. p. 521; Günther, Catal. i, p. 346, and iv, p. 260; Day, Fish. Malab. p. 159.

Catochaenum filamentosum Cantor, Catal. p. 56.

Diapterus filamentosus, Bleeker, Ternate, p. 231, and Révis. Gerrini, p. 5.

Diapterus punctatus, Bleeker, Révis. Gerr. p. 9.

Jaggari, Tel. (Ganjam): *Oodan*. Tam.: *Nga-wet-sat*, Arrak.

B. vi, D. $\frac{9}{10}$, P. 15, V. 1/5, A. $\frac{3}{7}$, C. 17, L. l. 45-48, L. tr. 6/14, Cæc. pyl. 3.

Length of head 1/4 to 4/17, of caudal 2/9, height of body rather above 1/3 of the total length. *Eyes*—diameter 1/3 of length of head, 4/5 to 1 diameter from the end of snout and also apart. The maxilla extends to below the front edge or first fourth of the orbit. Preopercle entire, its angle rounded. Opercle with two blunt points. *Teeth*—fine in the jaws. *Fins*—dorsal spines of moderate strength, the second prolonged, sometimes, especially in the adult, extending to the caudal fin, in others as in the immature, it is not so high as the body: last four or five dorsal spines shorter than the rays: pectoral rather longer than the head: ventral reaching three-fourths of the way to the anal: second anal spine stronger but not quite so long as the third which equals half the length of the head: caudal deeply forked. Free portion of the tail as high at its commencement as it is long. *Scales*—the sheath along the bases of the dorsal and anal fins well developed, five or six fine rows of scales between the lateral-line and the base of the dorsal sheath. *Colours*—silvery in the adult, with rows of short oblong horizontal bluish spots along the upper half of the body, on the scales being rubbed off they are found to be continuous, forming lines: snout black: a blackish spot anteriorly on the base of each dorsal spine and ray just above the scaly sheath, and usually a dark edge to the soft dorsal: caudal greyish externally: the other fins yellow with numerous fine dots on the fin membrane.

The *young* have vertical bands, the alternate ones being the shortest.

Habitat.—Seas of India to the Malay Archipelago and beyond, attaining 8 inches or more in length.

4. Gerres oyena, Plate XXV, fig. 4.

Labrus oyena, Forsk. p. 35; Bl. Schn. p. 245; Lacép. iii, p. 463.

Labrus longirostris, Lacép. iii, p. 467, pl. 19, fig. 1.

Sparus britannus, Lacép. iv, pp. 132, 134.

Smaris oyena, Rüpp. Atl. p. 11, t. 3, f. 2.

Gerres oyena, Cuv. and Val. vi, p. 472; Bleeker, Verh. Bat. Gen. xxiii, Mænid. p. 12; Günther, Catal. i, p. 353, and iv, p. 261; Klunz. Verh. z. b. Ges. Wien, 1870, p. 772.

Gerres equula, Temm. and Schleg. Fauna Japon. p. 76, pl. 40, fig. 1.*

Diapterus filamentosus, Bleeker, Ternate, p. 232, and Revis. Gerr. p. 29.

B. vi, D. $\frac{9}{10}$, P. 15, V. 1/5, A. $\frac{3}{7}$, C. 19, L. l. 38-40, L. tr. 5/10, Cæc. pyl. 3.

Length of head 1/4, of caudal 2/9, height of body 4/11 of the total length. *Eyes*—diameter 2/7 of length of head, 1 diameter from end of snout and also apart. The groove for the posterior processes of the premaxillaries reaches to opposite the middle of the orbit. The maxilla extends to below the first third of the orbit. Preopercle roughened along its vertical limb but not serrated. *Teeth*—fine. *Fins*—dorsal spines pretty strong, the anterior ones somewhat compressed and a little arched, the second longest and equal to nearly the length of the head without the snout; the last spine nearly as high as the rays and rather longer than the postorbital length of the head: pectoral longer than the head and reaching to beyond the anal spines: ventral almost touching the anal. Second anal spine strongest but shorter than the third, which equals half the length of the head; caudal forked. *Scales*—fine ones covering the caudal fin: sheath to the dorsal and anal fins high: four rows of scales between the lateral-line and the base of the sheath opposite the fourth dorsal spine. Free portion of the tail as high at its commencement as it is long. *Colours*—silvery, dorsal fin black edged, and a dark spot on each spine and ray at about half their height: a darkish mark may exist over the free portion of the tail: a narrow black posterior edge to the middle of the caudal: the fins yellow.

Habitat.—Red Sea, East coast of Africa, seas of India to the Malay Archipelago and beyond. The specimen figured was taken at Mangalore and is 7½ inches in length, its second anal spine is rather abnormally strong, and the lower caudal lobe is a little shortened, as is so frequently the case with littoral and estuary fishes.

5. Gerres lucidus, Plate XXV, fig. 5.

Gerres lucidus, Cuv. and Val. vi, p. 477.

B. vi, D. $\frac{9}{10}$, P. 15, V. 1/5, A. $\frac{3}{7}$, C. 17, L. l. 40, L. tr. 5/10, Cæc. pyl. 3.

Length of head 2/9, of caudal 2/9, height of body 1/3 of the total length. *Eyes*—diameter 2/5 of length of head, 2/3 of a diameter from end of snout, and 1 apart. The groove for the posterior process of the premaxillary is ovate, scaleless, and reaches to nearly opposite the first third of the orbit. The maxilla reaches to below the first third of the orbit. Preopercle entire, in a few specimens it is a little roughened along its horizontal edge, but not serrated. *Teeth*—fine. *Fins*—dorsal spines of moderate strength and not curved, the first very short, the third slightly longer than the second and equal to two-fifths of the height of the body, or the length of the head posterior to the middle of the orbit: pectoral longer than the head and reaching to above the anal spines: ventrals reach two-thirds of the way to the anal: second anal spine stronger† but generally not quite so long as the third which is a little longer than the third of the dorsal: caudal forked. Free portion of the tail as high at its commencement as it is long. *Scales*—the sheath for the dorsal fin is rather more developed than that for the anal: a few scales over the caudal: four rows between the lateral-line and the base of the fourth dorsal spine. *Colours*—silvery, with an indistinct vertical dark band over the nape, a second from below the dorsal spines, and two more below the soft portion of the dorsal fin: snout black: fins canary-yellow, the upper half of the membrane between the second and fifth dorsal spines deep black,‡ the rest of the fin dark edged with a black margin: a row of dark spots along the dorsal spines and rays at half their height: caudal grey-edged, the inferior caudal lobe with a very narrow white lower edge and a white tip.

As this fish increases in length the height of the body becomes proportionately a little less, thus at 5 inches in length it is 4/13 of the total: and the eye 3/4 of a diameter from the end of the snout.

This species is closely allied to *G. setifer*, but the latter appears to be confined to the tidal Hooghly, whereas this is a marine form having one dorsal spine less, &c., as already pointed out (see p. 98).

Habitat.—Seas of India to the Malay Archipelago and China: it is the most common Indian species, visiting the coasts in enormous numbers.

6. Gerres abbreviatus, Plate XXV, fig. 6.

? *Sparus erythrourus*, Bloch, t. 261.

* The type specimen is still in good preservation in the Leyden Museum, the artist has given his figure too elongated a shape, in fact resembling *G. oblongus*.

† The second anal spine is much stronger in this species than in specimens of *G. Japonicus*, which however it very strongly resembles.

‡ This deep black colour of the dorsal interspinous membrane, is liable to be diminished in specimens which have been kept long in spirit, especially if their condition at first had not been very good or the liquor tainted.

? Cichla erythrura, Bl. Schn. p. 336.

Gerres abbreviatus, Bleeker, Java, i, p. 103, and Mænid. p. 11; Günther, Catal. i, p. 345, and iv, p. 257; Kner, Novara Fische, p. 56, t. iii, f. 3a (Pharyngeal teeth).

Diapterus abbreviatus, Bleeker, Révis. Gerr. p. 16.

B. vi, D. $\frac{9}{10}$, P. 15, V. 1/5, A. $\frac{3}{7}$, C. 17, L. l. 37-40, L. tr. 6/11.

Length of head 1/4, of caudal 2/9, height of body 2/5 to 3/8 of the total length. *Eyes*—diameter 2/5 to 1/3 of length of head, 2/3 to 3/4 of a diameter from end of snout, and 1 apart. Snout somewhat spatulate: the posterior process of the premaxillary reaches to opposite the first third of the orbit. Preoperele entire or finely serrated along its vertical limb.* *Teeth*—fine. *Fins*—dorsal spines strong, the second rather longer than the third, and almost equal to the length of the head, both rather curved. Pectoral reaching to opposite the middle of the base of the anal and longer than the head: second anal spine the strongest, the third slightly the longest, equalling the distance from the posterior edge of the orbit to the end of the snout: caudal deeply forked, upper lobe slightly the longer. Free portion of the tail higher at its commencement than long. *Scales*—five rows between the lateral-line and the base of the fifth dorsal spine: scaly sheaths to dorsal and anal fins well developed. *Colours*—silvery-white, darkest along the back, each scale with a rather indistinct spot, but forming longitudinal bands: fins yellowish, dorsal with a blackish edge and a spot on each spine and ray just above the sheath.

Longest specimen obtained $7\frac{1}{10}$ inches in length.

Bloch's specimen of a *Gerres* is still in a good state of preservation in the Berlin Museum, it is about 9 inches long, and as the height of the body is $3\frac{3}{4}$ inches, it is difficult to understand how Val. could have considered it identical with *G. oyena*, having the height of the body equal to about 1/4 of the total length. It is so unlike the figure of *Sparus erythrurus* that I consider it better to leave the fish under Bleeker's name.

Habitat.—Seas of India to the Malay Archipelago.

7. Gerres poeti, Plate XXVI, fig. 1.

Cuv. and Val. vi, p. 468; Bleeker, Mænid. p. 11; Günther, Catal. i, p. 341, and iv, p. 256; Kner, Novara Fische, p. 55.

Diapterus poeti, Bleeker, Saparona, p. 360, and Révis. Gerr. p. 18.

B. vi, D. $\frac{9}{10}$, P. 15, V. 1/5, A. $\frac{3}{7}$, C. 17, L. l. 40, L. tr. 6/11.

Length of head 2/9, of caudal 2/11, height of body 1/3 of the total length. *Eyes*—diameter 2/5 of length of head, 2/3 of a diameter from end of snout, and 1 apart. The groove for the premaxillary reaches to opposite the middle of the eye: the maxilla to below the first third of the orbit. *Teeth*—fine. *Fins*—dorsal spines not very strong, the second and third compressed and somewhat arched, the second being slightly the longer, and equal to the length of the head excluding the snout, the last spine nearly as high as the rays and equal to the postorbital portion of the head. Pectoral as long as the head and reaching to above the anal spines: the ventral extends three-fourths of the distance to the anal: second anal spine the strongest, stouter than any in the dorsal fin, and slightly longer or of the same length as the third which equals three-fourths of the height of the second of the dorsal fin: caudal forked. *Scales*—the sheath to the dorsal fin moderately developed: no scales on the caudal: five rows between the highest point of the lateral-line and the base of the dorsal fin. Free portion of the tail higher at its commencement than it is long. *Colours*—silvery, with a dark edge to the dorsal fin, and the outer edge of the caudal greyish: spots along the base of each dorsal spine and ray, and more or less distinct lines along the rows of scales on the body.

Habitat.—Red Sea, East coast of Africa, seas of India, Malay Archipelago, and beyond. My longest specimen is 7 inches.

8. Gerres limbatus.

Cuv. and Val. vi, p. 476; Günther, Catal. iv, p. 259; Day, Fishes Malabar, p. 109.

Catochænum limbatum, Cantor, Catal. p. 55.

Diapterus limbatus, Bleeker, Révis. Gerr. p. 17.

B. vi, D. $\frac{9}{10}$, P. 15, V. 1/5, A. $\frac{3}{7}$, C. 17, L. l. 35, L. tr. 4/10.

Length of head 1/4, of caudal 3/13, height of body 4/13 of the total length. *Eyes*—diameter 1/3 of length of head, 2/3 of a diameter from end of snout, and 1 apart. The maxilla reaches to below the first third of the eye. *Fins*—dorsal spines not very strong, the second and third of about equal length, compressed and somewhat arched, the third being slightly the longer and equal to the length of the head behind the middle of the orbit, the last spine nearly equal to half the height of the rays and almost as long as the postorbital portion of the head; pectoral as long as the head and reaching to nearly above the anal spines: ventral extends three-fourths of the distance to the anal: second anal spine much the strongest, also stronger than those in the dorsal fin but slightly shorter than the third which nearly equals the second of the dorsal fin: caudal deeply forked. *Scales*—the sheath of the dorsal fin moderately developed: numerous fine scales over the caudal: three rows between the summit of the lateral-line and the base of the dorsal fin. Free portion of the tail as high at its

* In a specimen from the Malabar coast, which has 40 scales along its lateral-line, the second dorsal spine is only equal to three-fourths of the length of the head, and the second of the anal is slightly shorter in proportion than in my Andamanese specimens which latter however have the spines not quite so strong. The Andamanese specimens have the angle and lower limb of the preopercle crenulated but not serrated: others from the Malay Archipelago have neither serrations nor crenulations.

commencement as it is long. *Colours*—silvery, with a dark margin to the dorsal and anal fins, and a spot on each spine and ray of the dorsal fin about its middle.

Habitat.—Seas of India. The type specimen at Paris is $4\frac{1}{2}$ inches in length, and from it the above description has been taken. I obtained a specimen 5 inches in length at Madras. It much resembles *G. lucidus* but is destitute of the dark blotch on the dorsal fin.

Genus, 30—PENTAPRION, *Bleeker.*

Clara, Gill.

This Genus differs from Gerres in having the inferior pharyngeal bones separate: 14 to 15 rays in the dorsal fin: 5 anal spines, and 13 or 14 rays.

SYNOPSIS OF INDIVIDUAL SPECIES.

1. *Pentaprion longimanus*, D. $\frac{5}{14-15}$, A. $\frac{5}{13}$.

1. Pentaprion longimanus, Plate LII, fig. 6.

Equula longimanus, Cantor, Catal. p. 152; Günther, Catal. iii, p. 505.

Pentaprion gerroides, Bleeker, Mænid. p. 13, Java, p. 104, and Révis. Pentaprion, p. 22; Günther, Catal. i, p. 396.

B. vi, D. $\frac{5}{6}\,|\,\frac{10(11)}{14-15}$, P. 15, V. 1/5, A $\frac{5}{13}$, C. 17, L. l. 40.

Length of head $4\frac{1}{3}$, of caudal $4\frac{1}{3}$, height of body $3\frac{1}{4}$ in the total length. *Eyes*—diameter $2\frac{2}{3}$ in the length of head, 2/3 of a diameter from end of snout, and 1 apart. Body of a long oval shape: dorsal and anal profiles equally convex. Snout slightly swollen. The posterior process of the premaxillary reaches to opposite the first third of the eye. No spines or serrations around the orbit. The maxilla reaches to below the front edge of the eye. Mandible not concave inferiorly. Lower preopercular edge serrated. *Teeth*—villiform in the jaws, vomer and palate edentulous. *Fins*—dorsal spines weak, the first very short, the second one-third the height of the third which equals 4/7 of the length of the head. Pectoral equals the height of the body. Ventral reaches two-thirds of the distance to the anal. Second anal spine the longest and equal to 1/3 of the height of the body: caudal forked, upper lobe the longer. Free portion of tail rather higher than it is long. Scales very deciduous, they extend forwards over the back to opposite the middle of the eyes. *Colours*—silvery, with a silvery stripe from the eye to the base of the caudal fin.

Cantor erroneously gave 4 spines instead of 5 to the anal fin, in this he appears to have been copied by Dr. Günther. The specimen is much mutilated but 5 spines are still visible.

On mentioning this fish to Dr. Bleeker he at once showed me his types of *Pentaprion gerroides*, which are identical.

Habitat.—Madras, where I procured several specimens, to the Malay Archipelago. Cantor observes that "in the Straits of Malacca this species is very abundant at all seasons, and quantities, both fresh and dried, are consumed by the natives."

ADDENDA AND CORRIGENDA.

Page 18. Serranus lanceolatus.

After this portion of my work had been printed I went over to Leyden to examine the types of *S. horridus* and *S. geographicus*. *S. horridus* (K. and v. H.) Cuv. and Val. ii, p. 321 is $9\frac{1}{2}$ inches in length; *S. geographicus* (K. and v. H.) Cuv. and Val. ii, p. 322 is much larger; both are stuffed, painted and varnished, and I consider are forms of *S. lanceolatus*, Bloch, and not of *S. fuscoguttatus*, under which they are placed at p. 22.

Page 57. Apogon tæniatus.

"(Not Bleeker)" has to be omitted, and the following reference to be added:—

Apogon Noordzieki, Bleeker, Java, p. 330.

Amia Noordzieki, Bleeker, Révis. Apogonini, p. 15.

Page 59. Apogon tæniatus.

Having seen Valenciennes types I have no doubt but that they represent this species as stated by Klunzinger. One specimen still shows traces of longitudinal bands.

Page 60. Apogon Savayensis.

This fish is identical with *A. Bandanensis*, Bleeker, whose name has the priority. Dr. Bleeker showed me specimens of his fish with the markings as well seen as in Dr. Günther's specimen and figure. The following references have to be added:—

Apogon Bandanensis, Bleeker, Banda, p. 95; Günther, Catal. i, p. 238.

Amia Bandanensis, Bleeker, Boeroe, p. 147, and Révis. Apogonini, p. 27.

FAMILY, II—SQUAMIPINNES, *Cuv.*

Chætodontidæ, pt. Richardson.

Branchiostegals six or seven (Zanclus four): pseudobranchiæ well developed. Body elevated and compressed. Eyes lateral and of moderate size. Mouth generally small, with a lateral cleft, and situated in front of snout. Teeth villiform or setiform, neither incisors nor canines: in most of the genera the palate is edentulous, soft portion of the dorsal fin of greater extent than the spinous, sometimes considerably more, rarely slightly so: anal with three or four spines, its soft portion similar to that of the dorsal: lower pectoral rays branched: ventrals thoracic, with one spine and five rays. Scales cycloid, or very finely ctenoid, extending to a greater or less extent over the vertical fins, but occasionally absent from the spinous portion. Air-vessel present, generally simple. Intestines usually much convoluted; stomach cæcal. Pyloric appendages in moderate numbers.

Geographical distribution.—These fishes are, as a rule, marine, and although some have been recorded as taken in rivers and estuaries, they are rarely captured above tidal reach.

The *Squamipinnes* have been divided by Dr. Günther into three groups:—*First*, those which have the palate edentulous (*Chætodontina*): *secondly*, those which have teeth on the palate, but the dorsal fin is situated in the posterior half of the length of the back (*Toxotina*): and *thirdly*, some Australian forms wherein there are palatine teeth, and the dorsal fin occupies the middle of the length of the back, (*Scorpidina*).

In some species a prolongation of the dorsal fin, owing to sex, may be present as in *Holacanthus imperator*, *H. annularis*, &c.

SYNOPSIS OF GENERA.

First group—Chætodontina.

No palatine or vomerine teeth: no concealed spine in front of the base of the dorsal fin in the adult.

1. *Chætodon.* Snout of moderate length or short: no preopercular spine: a single un-notched dorsal fin without an elongated spine: anal with 3 or 4 spines.

2. *Chelmo.* Snout much produced: no preopercular spine: 9 to 13 dorsal spines none of which are elongated.

3. *Heniochus.* Snout of moderate length: no preopercular spine: 11 to 13 dorsal spines, the fourth being much elongated.

4. *Zanclus.* Snout of moderate length: no preopercular spine: 7 dorsal spines, the third being much elongated.

5. *Holacanthus.* Snout of moderate length: a strong preopercular spine: 11 to 15 dorsal spines, none of which are elongate.

6. *Scatophagus.* Snout of moderate length: no preopercular spine: dorsal fin notched and no scales on the spinous portion: anal with 4 spines.

7. *Ephippus.* Snout short: no preopercular spine; dorsal fin deeply notched, with 8 or 9 spines several of which are elongated and flexible.

8. *Drepane.* Snout short: no preopercular spine: dorsal fin deeply notched, with 8 or 9 spines, none of which are elongated.

Second group—Toxotina.

Vomerine and palatine teeth: no concealed spine in front of the base of the dorsal fin which is situated in the last half of the back.

9. *Toxotes.* Snout somewhat produced. Dorsal fin with 4 or 5 spines.

The young fishes in some of the above genera of the first group show considerable enlargement of the bones of the head which more or less disappear in the adult,* in a few a concealed spine pointing forwards may be present in the immature in front of the base of the dorsal fin.

---

* Genus—THOLICHTHYS, *Günther.*

Dr. Günther (Annals and Mag. of Nat. History, 1868, p. 457) described and figured a very small fish, 11 millims. long, as a new Cyttoid Genus, which he termed *Tholichthys*. I obtained several (I think thirteen) larger ones at Madras 1 1/10 inches long, which I described (Proc. Zool. Soc. 1870, p. 687,) as *T. osseus*, but drew attention to their belonging to the Family *Squamipinnes*, giving it a strong resemblance to *Heniochus* or *Chætodon*. I personally deposited my largest specimen in the British Museum, but as it has been mislaid I have figured my next largest at twice the natural size; it is unfortunately dried, all my specimens in spirit, irrespective of the one previously mentioned, having become spoiled during their transit from India.

First group—Chætodontina.

No palatine or vomerine teeth: no concealed spine in front of the base of the dorsal fin in the adult.

Genus, 1—CHÆTODON, *Cuv.*

Rabdophorus and *Microcanthus*, Swains.; *Megaprotodon*, Guich.; *Sarothodus*, Gill.

Branchiostegals six. Body elevated and strongly compressed. Snout of moderate length or short. Preopercle entire, or slightly serrated, but destitute of any spine at the angle. Palate edentulous. Spinous and soft portions of the dorsal fin not separated by a notch, the rays of slightly or considerably larger number than the spines, none of the latter elongated: anal with three or four spines. Scales of large, moderate, or small size. Lateral line continuous, sometimes incomplete. Air-vessel may be constricted or with horns. Intestines much convoluted.

SYNOPSIS OF SPECIES.

A. *With four anal spines.*

1\. *Chætodon plebeius.* D. [illegible], A. [illegible], L. l. 50. A black ocular band with white edges: a black white-edged ocellus at the base of the caudal fin. Andamans to the South Seas.

B. *With three anal spines.*

2\. *Chætodon xanthocephalus.* D. [illegible], A. [illegible], L. l. 38. A small dark blotch above the orbit: body with five indistinct vertical streaks. Ceylon and Zanzibar.

3\. *Chætodon falcula.* D. [illegible], A. [illegible], L. r. 28. A narrow ocular band, two wide triangular bands pass downwards from the dorsal fin, another exists over the free portion of the tail. Twelve or more narrow black bands on the body. Seas of India to the Malay Archipelago and beyond.

4\. *Chætodon pictus.* D. [illegible], A. [illegible], L. r. [illegible]. An ocular band descending to the chest. Several dark lines descend downwards and forwards from the first half of the dorsal fin to the head, whilst in the last half of the body others go backwards and downwards. Dorsal and anal fins dark: caudal with a dark base and two dark vertical bands. Red Sea, seas of India, to the Malay Archipelago.

5\. *Chætodon vagabundus.* D. [illegible], A. [illegible], L. r. [illegible]. An ocular band descending to the interopercle. Many dark bands pass downwards to the middle of the body when they go backwards. Dorsal and anal fins margined with black: two vertical black bands on caudal. From the Red Sea throughout those of India to Polynesia.

6\. *Chætodon Mertensii*, D. [illegible], A. [illegible], L. l. 34. A narrow interrupted ocular band: anterior two-thirds of body violet, with narrow vertical, angular, bands: last third of body, soft dorsal, and anal fins yellow: a vertical band on caudal: a narrow dark intramarginal line to soft dorsal and anal fins. Red Sea, Seas of India, and beyond.

7\. *Chætodon auriga.* D. [illegible], A. [illegible], L. l. 42. Fifth dorsal ray prolonged. An ocular band descends to the interopercle. A dark ocellus on the middle dorsal rays. Red Sea, through those of India to Polynesia.

8\. *Chætodon Kleinii.* D. [illegible], A. [illegible], L. l. 34. Brownish, with a broad ocular band extending to a black ventral fin: edges of soft dorsal, caudal, and anal black. Seas of India to the Malay Archipelago.

9\. *Chætodon guttatissimus*, D. [illegible], A. [illegible], L. l. 38. An ocular band descends to the interopercle: brown spots on the body scales, and small ones on the soft dorsal and anal fins: caudal with a black vertical band.

10\. *Chætodon vittatus*, D. [illegible], A. [illegible], L. r. [illegible]. Body with numerous fine dark lines passing backwards: a dark band along the base of the dorsal fin, another along the centre of the soft dorsal: a dark band on the last third of the caudal: ventrals white. From the Red Sea to Polynesia.

11\. *Chætodon unimaculatus*, D. [illegible], A. [illegible], L. l. 46. A narrow ocular band: a black blotch on the side above the lateral-line beneath the last four dorsal spines. Ceylon to the Malay Archipelago.

12\. *Chætodon collaris*, D. [illegible], A. [illegible], L. l. 34. Each scale with a light centre: a whitish band from in front of the dorsal fin to the chest, another to the eye, and a third over the snout. Seas of India to the Malay Archipelago.

13\. *Chætodon lunula*, D. [illegible], A. [illegible], L. l. 40. A wide ocular band descends to the preopercle: a second from the first dorsal spine joins it: a third goes to the base of the pectoral, and another over the free

---

Tholichthys osseus, Pl. XXVI. fig. 2 (twice life size.)

Day, Proc. Zool. Soc. 1870, p. 687.

D. 11/23, P. 15, V. 1/5, A. [illegible], C. 17, L. l. 41.

Length of head nearly 1/3, of caudal 1/5, height of body 1/2 of the total length. *Eyes*—diameter from 1/2 to 2/5 of the length of head, 1/2 in diameter from the end of snout, and 1 apart. In the specimen figured the angle of the preopercle is much enlarged, reaching to almost below the origin of the pectoral fin: the shoulder scale and those over the shoulder girdle considerably dilated. *Fins*—third dorsal spine the longest and strongest, the fin notched: ventrals rounded: caudal cut almost square. *Scales*—ctenoid. *Lateral line*—ceases opposite the end of the soft dorsal fin.

This is evidently the same species as the one I formerly described, l. c. but the development of the cranial bones differs. Probably in *Holacanthi* the preopercular spine is the remains of the elongated and dilated preopercular angle seen in this species.

In the very young, as figured by Dr. Günther, the developments mentioned above are greatly magnified, showing that atrophy occurs as age advances.

portion of the tail. Young with a large ocellus on the soft dorsal fin. Seas of India to the Malay Archipelago.

14. *Chætodon melanotus*, D. [illegible], A. [illegible], L. l. 37-40. A narrow ocular band; body yellow, with its upper fourth stained with black and black lines along each row of scales: a yellow vertical band on caudal: a short black one at the base of the first four anal rays. Red Sea, seas of India, to the Malay Archipelago.

15. *Chætodon octofasciatus*, D. [illegible], A. [illegible], L. l. 50. Light vertical bands on the body and head. Seas of India to the Malay Archipelago and beyond.

16. *Chætodon oligacanthus*, D. [illegible], A. [illegible], L. l. 46-48. Five vertical brown bands: a dark ocellus at the base of the eighth to twelfth dorsal rays. Seas of India to the Malay Archipelago and beyond.

A. *With four anal spines.*

1. Chætodon plebeius, Plate XXVI, fig. 3.

Brouss. MS. Brit. Mus.; Gmel. Linn. p. 1269 (?); Cuv. and Val. vii, p. 68.
Chætodon plebejus, Günther, Catal. ii, p. 5, and Fische d. Sudsee, p. 35, t. xxxii, f. D.

B. vi, D. [illegible], P. 15, V. 1/5, A. [illegible], C. 17, L. l. 50, L. tr. 7/15.

Length of head 1/4, of caudal 1/7, height of body nearly 1/2 of the total length. *Eyes*—diameter 2/7 of length of head, and 1 diameter from end of snout. Preopercle finely serrated: the maxilla reaches half way to below the front edge of the orbit. *Fins*—dorsal spines strong, the fourth slightly the longest, the soft portions of the dorsal and anal rounded: second anal spine longest and strongest: caudal slightly rounded. *Colours*—yellow, with a black ocular band which has a white edge: a black white-edged ocellus at the base of the caudal fin.

Habitat.—Andaman islands to the South seas; the specimen figured is from the British Museum collection, and is $4\frac{1}{2}$ inches in length.

B. *With three anal spines.*

2. Chætodon xanthocephalus, Plate XXVI, fig. 4.

Bennett, Proc. Zool. Soc. ii, p. 182; Günther, Catal. ii, p. 33.

B. vi, D. [illegible], P. 15, V. 1/5, A. [illegible], C. 17, L. r. [illegible], L. tr. 11/18.

Length of head $4\frac{1}{3}$, of caudal one sixth, height of body $1\frac{3}{4}$ in the total length. *Eyes*—diameter 1/4 of length of head, $1\frac{1}{2}$ diameter from end of snout, and also apart. Preopercle indistinctly serrated. *Fins*—soft portions of the dorsal and anal rounded. *Colours*—a small dark blotch above the orbit: body brownish-yellow, with six indistinct dark vertical streaks: dorsal and anal fins dark violet, having white edges: caudal and ventrals yellowish.

Habitat.—Ceylon and Zanzibar, the figure and description are from the type specimen in the British Museum.

3. Chætodon falcula, Plate XXVI, fig. 5.

Bloch, ix, p. 102, t. 425, f. 2; Bl. Schn. p. 225; Cuv. and Val. vii, p. 41; Bleeker, Batoe. p. 311; Günther, Catal. ii, p. 17, and Fische d. Sudsee, p. 39, t. xxvii, f. C.
Chætodon ulietensis, Cuv. and Val. vii, p. 39; Bleeker, Amboina, p. 38; Günther, Catal. ii, p. 18.

B. vi, D. [illegible], P. 15, V. 1/5, A. [illegible], C. 17, L. r. 28, L. tr. 6/12.

Length of head $3\frac{1}{4}$ to one fourth, of caudal $6\frac{1}{2}$, height of body $1\frac{3}{4}$ in the total length. *Eyes*—diameter 1/4 of length of head, nearly 2 diameters from the end of snout, and 1 apart. The maxilla reaches half way to below the front edge of the orbit. Preopercle serrated along its vertical limb, but almost entire along its angle and vertical edge. *Teeth*—brush-like. *Fins*—dorsal spines of moderate strength, the last being the longest, the soft portion of the fin rounded: caudal cut almost square: ventral reaching as far as the anal spines: pectoral equal to the length of the head behind the angle of the mouth: second anal spine strongest and rather the longest, being equal to the last of the dorsal fin. *Colours*—body and head of a rather red-lilac-purple, becoming of a primrose colour posteriorly, and also on the fins. A dark ocular band, narrower than the orbit, commences a short distance anterior to the dorsal fin, and is continued through the eye on to the interopercle, it has a white edge. A black band, widest above, arises from the first four or five dorsal spines, and is continued to a short distance below the lateral-line:* a second angularly pointed in front, begins from the last three spines and descends to the lateral-line: a third passes over a free portion of the tail. Twelve to fourteen vertical narrow black bands pass down either side. Soft dorsal fin with a narrow black upper margin: caudal with a black and white posterior edge: anal with a black intramarginal band having a white outer margin, and two more superiorly parallel to it.

Habitat.—Seas of India to the Malay Archipelago and beyond. The specimen figured was taken at the Nicobars, the species attains to at least 8 inches in length.

* A different distribution of colours is shown in Garrett's "Fische d. Sudsee," in which the body is lighter than described above. The two dark vertical bands from the dorsal fin are conjoined superiorly and only extend forwards so far as the fourth dorsal spine, but they descend lower than in my specimen. Likewise the band over the free portion of the tail is reduced to a blotch. The body bands are stated to have sometimes white edges.

4. Chætodon pictus, Plate XXVI, fig. 6.

Forsk. p. 65; Bl. Schn. p. 226; Cuv. and Val. vii, p. 55; Bleeker, Nat. Tyds. Ned. Ind. ii, p. 177; Günther, Catal. ii, p. 24; Klunz. Fische d. Roth. Meer, Verh. z. b. Ges. Wien. 1870, p. 751.

Chætodon vagabundus? Russell, Fish. Vizag. i, p. 65, pl. 83; Bennett, Fish. Ceylon, p. 7, pl. 7.

Chætodon decussatus, Cuv. and Val. vii, p. 54; Bleeker, l. c. xiii, p. 328; Kner, Nov. Fische, p. 101.

Painah, Tel.: *Khyoay-khayock*, Arrak.

B. vi, D. [illegible], P. 15, V. 1/5, A. [illegible], C. 17, L. l. [illegible], L. tr. 6/14.

Length of head above 2/7, of caudal 2/11, height of body 4/7 of the total length. *Eyes*—diameter 1/3 of the length of head, 1 diameter from the end of snout, and also apart. Preopercle finely serrated. *Teeth*—brush-like. *Fins*—dorsal spines of moderate strength, soft portions of both dorsal and anal fins angular. Pectoral as long as the head behind the anterior nostril: ventral reaches to the anal: second anal spine stronger but of equal length to the third. *Colours*—snout with a black band: a dark ocular one descends through the eye over the interopercle to the chest: numerous fine dark lines descend downwards and forwards from the first half of the dorsal fin to the middle of the body, whilst in the posterior half of the body there are others having a direction downwards and backwards. Dorsal and anal fins dark, having a black margin and a light external edge, the dark line is continued over the posterior third of the body: there is another dark line over the free portion of the tail, and a dark semilunar mark on the caudal fin. Ventral darkest in its centre.

Amongst Sir Walter Elliot's drawings exists a figure of this species marked *Kunnadee* or *Kalloodi*: a second labelled September, 1848, shows the red bands across the snout, this is the variety, No. 83, figured by Russell and identical with *C. decussatus*, C. and V.

Habitat.—Red Sea, those of India to the Malay Archipelago, attaining at least 10 inches in length. The specimen figured is life-size from one captured at the Andamans.

5. Chætodon vagabundus, Plate XXVII, fig. 1.

Chætodon vagabundus, Linn. Mus. Ad. Fried. ii, p. 71 and Sys. i, p. 465; Gmel. Linn. p. 1251; Bl. p. 1192, t. 204, f. 2; Bl. Schn. p. 222; Cuv. and Val. vii, p. 50; Bleeker, Verh. Bat. Gen. xxiii, Chætod. p. 18; Günther, Catal. ii, p. 25 and Fische d. Sudsee, p. 43.

Pak-noo-dah, Andam.

B. vi, D. [illegible], P. 15, V. 1/5, A. [illegible], C. 17, L. r. [illegible], L. tr. 4/15.

Length of head about one fourth, of caudal from $6\frac{1}{2}$ to one sixth, height of body $1\frac{3}{4}$ of the total length. *Eyes*—diameter 3/10 of the length of head, $1\frac{1}{4}$ diameters from the end of snout, and also apart. Snout rather produced and pointed. The maxilla reaches to below the front nostril. Preopercle finely serrated, most strongly so at its angle. *Teeth*—brush-like. *Fins*—dorsal spines of moderate strength, the interspinous membrane deeply notched: soft portions of the dorsal and anal obtusely angular: pectoral as long as the head behind the angle of the mouth: ventral nearly reaching the anal: second anal spine equals the length of the third: caudal rounded. *Colours*—a black ocular band having white edges descends to the angle of the interopercle. Numerous dark bands pass downwards and forwards to the centre of the depth of the body, where others pass backwards. Dorsal and anal fins margined with black. Two black vertical bands on the caudal, the anterior of which is concave.

Habitat.—From the Red Sea, through those of India to Polynesia.

6. Chætodon Mertensii, Plate XXVII, fig. 2.

? *Chætodon chrysurus*, Brouss.

? *Pomacentrus chrysurus*, Cuv. and Val. v, p. 423; Günther, Catal. iv, p. 29 (not synom.)

Chætodon Mertensii, Cuv. and Val. vii, p. 47; Günther, Fische d. Sudsee, p. 45, t. 36, fig. B. (from a drawing).

B. vi, D. [illegible], P. 15, V. 1/5, A. $\frac{3}{16}$, C. 17, L. r. [illegible], L. tr. 5/14.

Length of head $4\frac{1}{2}$, of caudal $6\frac{1}{2}$, height of body $2\frac{1}{4}$ of the total length. *Eyes*—diameter $3\frac{1}{4}$ of the length of the head, $1\frac{1}{2}$ diameters from end of snout and also apart. The maxilla reaches to about half way below the front edge of the orbit. Preopercle entire, its angle very oblique. *Teeth*—brush-like. *Fins*—dorsal spines of moderate strength, increasing in length to the fifth, the soft portion of the fin as high as the spinous and rounded posteriorly: ventral spine strong, as long as the head excluding the snout: caudal cut nearly square: anal spines of moderate strength but long, the third rather the longest exceeding the highest of the dorsal by nearly one fourth, soft portion of the fin similar to that of the dorsal. *Colours*—head and anterior two-thirds of the body lavender, its posterior third yellow: interorbital space yellow: a narrow dark white-edged band commences a little in front of the dorsal fin, then ceases, but reappears a little above the eye, through which it descends and passes down the preopercle to a little in front of its angle. Anterior two-thirds of the body with narrow black vertical bands, which form an angle at the middle of the body directed forwards. A narrow dark intramarginal line having a white outer edge exists on both the dorsal and anal fins: a narrow dark vertical band in the last third of the caudal, followed by a rather wider yellow one, whilst externally the fin is grey.

In Garrett's "Fische d. Sudsee," the formula given is D. [illegible], A. $\frac{3}{16}$, and if it is the same species the figure is not exact.

P

Habitat.—A specimen in the Berlin Museum is from the Red Sea. I have the species from Ceylon, and Valenciennes' fish in Paris is from the Mauritius, labelled "*Chætodon chrysurus*, v. p. 423," by Valenciennes, but does not correspond with the description of *C. chrysurus*. Some other specimens are likewise thus labelled by Valenciennes, but the locality from which they were procured is unknown.

7. **Chætodon auriga**, Plate XXVII, fig. 3 (var. *setifer*).

Forsk. p. 60; Bl. Schn. p. 226; Cuv. and Val. vii, p. 79; Rüpp. N. W. Fische, p. 28; Günther, Catal. ii, p. 7; Klunzing. Fische d. Roth. Meer. Verh. z. b. Ges. Wien, 1870, p. 775.

Chætodon setifer, Bloch, t. 425, f. 1; Bl. Schn. p. 225; Cuv. and Val. vii, p. 76; Guérin, Icon. Poiss. pl. 22. f. 1; Less. Voy. Coq. Zool. ii, p. 175, Poiss. pl. 29, f. 2; Richards. Ich. China, p. 246; Cuv. Règ. Anim. Ill. Poiss. pl. 38, f. 1; Jenyns, Zool. Beagle, Fish. p. 61; Günther, Catal. ii, p. 6 and Fische d. Sudsee, p. 36, t. xxvi, f. B; Kner, Novara Fische, p. 97.

Pomacentrus filamentosus, Lacép. iv, pp. 506, 511.

Chætodon sebanus, Cuv. and Val. vii, p. 74.

Chætodon auriga, var. Rüpp. N. W. Fische, p. 28.

Chætodon lunaris, Gronov. ed. Gray, p. 70.

Linophora auriga, Kaup, Arch. d. Naturg. 1860, pt. 2, pp. 137 and 156.

B. vi, D. [illegible], P. 15, V. 1/5, A. [illegible], C. 17, L. r. [illegible], L. tr. $3\frac{1}{2}$-$4\frac{1}{2}$/13.

Length of head 3/11 to 2/7, of caudal 1/7, height of body 4/7 to 1/2 of the total length. *Eyes*—diameter 2/7 of length of head, nearly $1\frac{1}{2}$ diameters from end of snout, and 1 apart. Snout pointed. The maxilla reaches half way to below the front edge of the orbit. Preopercle very finely serrated. *Teeth*—brush-like. *Fins*,—in the specimen figured there are only eleven dorsal spines of moderate strength, the fifth ray is produced into a short filament, soft portions of dorsal and anal angularly shaped: pectoral equals the length of the head posterior to the nostrils: third anal spine the longest: caudal slightly emarginate. *Colours*—in *C. auriga* a brown ocular band, having a white anterior edge, passes through the orbit to over the interopercle. Body with darkish lines, passing upwards and backwards in the anterior third of the body, and downwards and backwards posteriorly. A darkish band passes from the base of the soft dorsal across the free portion of the tail and to the lower half of the anal. A dark band goes through the middle of the anal fin. Dorsal, anal, and caudal edged with white. In the variety *C. setifer* the ocular band, which has white edges, widens after it has passed the orbit and extends to the interopercle. Body with narrow darkish bands passing upwards and backwards in the anterior third of the body, and downwards and backwards in the last two thirds. A dark ocellus on the centre of the middle dorsal rays. Anal with a fine black intramarginal band having a white outer edge, upper and hind margins of the anal edged with black: two fine vertical lines on the caudal fin which enclose a semilunar space.

Habitat.—From the Red Sea, through the seas of India to Polynesia. The specimen figured was captured at the Nicobars, and is $4\frac{4}{10}$ inches in length.

8. **Chætodon Kleinii.**

Bloch,* t. 218, f. 2; Bl. Schn. p. 225; Günther, Catal. ii, p. 22.

Chætodon virescens, Cuv. and Val. vii, p. 30; Bleeker, Verh. Bat. Gen. xxiii. Chæt. p. 18.

Chætodon flavescens, Bennett, Proc. Zool. Soc. 1831, p. 61.

B. vi, D. [illegible], P. 15, V. 1/5, A. [illegible], C. 17, L. l. 33, L. tr. 5/11.

Length of head $4\frac{1}{2}$, of caudal 1/6, height of body nearly 1/2 of the total length. *Eyes*—diameter 1/3 of length of head, 1 diameter from end of snout, and $1\frac{1}{4}$ apart. The maxilla reaches to below the front nostril. Preopercle entire. *Fins*—dorsal spines of moderate strength increasing in length to the fifth, the soft portion of the fin rounded and rather higher than the spinous: caudal rounded: second and third anal spines of about equal strength, their length about equal to the fifth of the dorsal. *Colours*—uniform brownish, becoming darkest posteriorly: a rather broad ocular band extends from in front of the dorsal fin, through the eye over the pre- and inter-opercles to the chest and goes to the base of the ventral fin: a black band over the snout. Ventrals black: edges of the soft dorsal, anal, and caudal black.

Habitat.—Seas of India to the Malay Archipelago.

9. **Chætodon guttatissimus**, Plate XXVII, fig. 4.

Bennett, Proc. Zool. Soc. ii, p. 183; Günther, Catal. ii, p. 26; ? Klunz. Verh. z. b. Ges. Wien, 1870, p. 780.

Chætodon tachetè, Liénard, Nat. Hist. Soc. Mauritius, 1839, p. 36.

B. vi, D. [illegible], P. 15, V. 1/5, A. [illegible], C. 19, L. l. 38, L. r. [illegible].

Length of head 4/17, of caudal 2/11, height of body 1/2 of the total length. *Eyes*—diameter 1/3 of length of head, 1 diameter from end of snout and also apart. Preopercle serrated: the posterior extremity of the maxilla reaches nearly half way to below the orbit. *Fins*—soft portions of dorsal and anal rounded posteriorly. *Colours*—a brown white-edged ocular band one third the width of the eye passes from the nape to the lower edge of the interopercle. Body yellow, each scale having a brown spot: dorsal and anal fins with an

* Klein, MSS. iv, t. 10, f. 2, p. 255.

outer narrow black edge and a broader white outer band, followed externally by a yellow margin, the rest of the fins covered with fine dark brown spots: caudal yellow with a black vertical band.

Habitat.—Ceylon, Zanzibar, and Red Sea. The figure is taken from Bennett's type specimen.

10. Chætodon vittatus, Plate XXVII, fig. 5.

Chætodon trifasciatus, Lacép. iv, p. 498; Mungo Park, Trans. Linn. Soc. iii, p. 34.

Chætodon vittatus, Bl. Schn. p. 227; Cuv. and Val. vii, p. 34; Bleeker, Verh. Bat. Gen. xxiii, Chætod. p. 18; Beechey, Voy. Zool. p. 61, pl. 17, f. 3; Günther, Catal. ii, p. 23, and Fische d. Sudsee, p. 41; Kner, Novara Fische, p. 100; Klunz. Fische d. Roth. Meer, 1870, p. 782.

Chætodon austriacus, Rüpp. N. W. Fische, p. 30, t. 9, f. 2 (var.).

B. vi, D. [illegible], P. 15, V. 1/5, A. [illegible], C. 18, L. r. [illegible], L. tr. 5/13.

Length of head 4/17 to 1/4, of caudal 1/6 to 1/7, height of body 2/3 to 1/2 of the total length. *Eyes*—diameter 1/3 of length of head, 1 diameter from end of snout, and $1\frac{1}{2}$ apart. Snout obtuse: the maxilla reaches nearly half way to below the front edge of the orbit: preopercle finely serrated. *Fins*—the soft portion of the dorsal, anal and also of the caudal rounded. *Colours*—a dark line passes over the snout, separated by a thin white band from the ocular one, which is half as wide as the orbit, and passes to the chest. Another dark line exists parallel to it, with an intermediate fine light one. Body with about fifteen fine dark lines passing backwards. A dark band along the base of the soft dorsal fin, becoming wider over the free portion of the tail: another band along the centre of the soft dorsal. A light yellow band along the base of the anal with a dark one above it, whilst it has a white outer edge. Fins margined with dark and edged with orange. A dark vertical band on the posterior third of the caudal. Ventrals white.

Habitat.—From the Red Sea to Polynesia.

11. Chætodon unimaculatus.

Bl. p. 1181, t. 201, f. 1; Bl. Schn. p. 221; Cuv. and Val. vii, p. 72; Bleeker, Banda, i, p. 241; Günther, Catal. ii, p. 11.

B. vi, D. [illegible], P. 15, V. 1/5, A. [illegible], C. 17, L. l. 46, L. tr. 8/19, Vert. 10/14.

Length of head 1/4, of caudal 1/6, height of body about 1/2 of the total length. *Eyes*—diameter $3\frac{1}{2}$ of the length of head, rather above 1 diameter from the end of snout, and $1\frac{1}{4}$ apart. Lower jaw slightly the longer: the maxilla does not quite reach to below the front edge of the orbit. Preopercle entire. *Fins*—the dorsal spines strong, increasing in length to about the seventh from whence they slightly decrease, the soft portion of the fin, also of the anal, and the caudal rounded. *Colours*—yellowish, with a narrow brownish black ocular band descending from just in front of the dorsal fin through the middle of the eye to the angle of the preopercle and on to the chest: a black blotch on the side above the lateral-line* below the last four spines and two first rays: posterior edge of soft dorsal with a narrow black band which is continued over the free portion of the tail on to the hind edge of the anal rays.

Habitat.—Ceylon, (from whence the above specimen came,) to the Malay Archipelago, attaining at least 5 inches in length.

12. Chætodon collaris, Plate XXVII, fig. 6.

Bloch, t. 216, f. 1; Gmel. Linn. p. 1263; Bl. Schn. p. 223; Cuv. and Val. vii, p. 53; Bleeker, Chætod. p. 19; Günther, Catal. ii, p. 21.

Chætodon unifasciatus, Gronov. ed. Gray, p. 69.

Chætodon prætextatus, Cantor, Catal. p. 156, pl. iii; Günther, Catal. ii, p. 22; Day, Fishes of Malabar, p. 31.

B. vi, D. [illegible], P. 15, V. 1/5, A. [illegible], C. 17, L. r. [illegible], L. tr. 7/15.

Length of head 2/7, of caudal 2/11, height of body 3/5 in the young to 2/3 in the adult of the total length. *Eyes*—diameter 1/3 of length of head, 1 diameter from end of snout, and 5/7 apart. The maxilla reaches two-thirds of the distance to below the orbit. A few fine serrations at the angle of the preopercle. *Teeth*—brush-like. *Fins*—fifth and sixth dorsal spine the longest; second anal spine the strongest and longer than the third: caudal cut nearly square. *Colours*—brownish olive, each scale light citron colour in its centre. A bluish-white band passes from in front of the dorsal fin over the opercles and on to the throat, where it expands: a second across the preorbital and over the cheek to the throat: opposite the orbit it gives off another branch which passes to the angle of the mouth and the throat. Another similar line exists on the forehead and is lost opposite the anterior edge of the orbit. Dorsal and anal fins tinged with reddish violet, the upper fourth of the soft portion being margined with six coloured bands in the following order from without: white, black, scarlet, black, pearl white, and black: anal tipped with three rows, white, black, and scarlet. Posterior half of caudal pearly white, divided by a black band from a scarlet base. Ventrals, black.

Jerdon (M. J. L. and Science, 1853, p. 134), under the head of *Chætodon prætextatus*, Cantor, observed, "I possess a dried specimen which appears to be this species." I also obtained mine at Cochin where I found

* In Bloch's type specimen, a little more than 4 inches in length (No. 1957) the blotch is partly (about 1/3) below the lateral-line.

P 2

they were common for about a fortnight in June, after the commencement of the monsoon (Proc. Zool. Soc. 1865, p. 16).

Bloch's type is of about equal length to Cantor's ($5\frac{3}{4}$ inches), which it closely resembles. The specimen I have figured appears to be the young and proportionately much higher. The specimens of *C. collaris* in the British Museum resemble those of *C. reticulatus* at Paris.

Habitat.—Seas of India to the Malay Archipelago.

13. Chætodon lunula.

Pomacentrus lunula, Lacép. iv, pp. 507, 510, 513.

Chætodon lunula, Cuv. and Val. vii, p. 59, pl. 173; Bleeker, Gilolo, p. 57; Günther, Catal. ii, p. 25 and Fische d. Sudsee, p. 42, t. xxxiii, A, B, C, D.

Chætodon biocellatus, Cuv. and Val. vii, p. 62; Less. Voy. Duperr. Zool. Poiss. p. 176; Bleeker, Borneo, p. 403; Günther, Catal. ii, p. 9.

B. vi, D. $\frac{12}{24-26}$, P. 19, V. 1/5, A. $\frac{3}{18-19}$, C. 17, L. r. $\frac{42}{45}$, L. tr. 7/14.

Length of head 2/7 to 4/11, of caudal 1/6 to 2/13, height of body 4/7 of the total length. *Eyes*—diameter 2/7 of length of head, $1\frac{1}{4}$ diameters from end of snout, and 1 apart. Preopercle serrated. *Fins*—the soft dorsal and anal rounded, caudal slightly rounded. *Lateral-line*—ceases below the last third of the soft dorsal fin. *Colours*—ocular band of a deep chestnut colour with white edges, and rather wider than the orbit, ending on the edge of the preopercle: a second brown band passes from the five first dorsal spines and unites with the occipital one: a third band from the fifth and sixth dorsal spines gradually widens and goes as low as the base of the pectoral fin: a band along the base of the soft dorsal passes over the free portion of the tail: caudal with a dark band in its posterior third; dorsal and anal with a dark edge and white margin.

In the *young* the ocular band is edged with white, the vertical bands are badly developed, and a large black white-edged ocellus exists in the centre of the soft dorsal.

Habitat.—Seas of India, Andaman islands to the Malay Archipelago.

14. Chætodon melanotus, Plate XXVIII, fig. 1.

Bl. Schn. p. 224 (not Reinw.); Klunz. Verh. z. b. Ges. Wien, 1870, p. 777.

Chætodon dorsalis, (Reinw.) Cuv. and Val. vii, p. 70; Rüpp. Atl. p. 41, t. 9, f. 2 and N. W. Fische, p. 28; Bleeker, Banda, i, p. 240; Günther, Catal. ii, p. 28.

Chætodon marginatus, (Ehren.) Cuv. and Val. vii, p. 57.

Chætodon abhortani, Cuv. and Val. vii, p. 58.

B. vi, D. $\frac{12}{19}$, P. 15, V. 1/5, A. $\frac{3}{17}$, C. 17, L. l. 37-40, L. tr. 6/16.

Length of head 1/4, of caudal nearly 1/7, height of body 4/7 of the total length. *Eyes*—diameter 1/3 of length of head, 1 diameter from end of snout, rather more apart. The maxilla does not quite reach to below the front edge of the orbit. Preopercle very finely serrated. *Fins*—dorsal spines rather strong, increasing in length to the fifth from whence they again diminish in height: soft portion of the fin also of the anal and the caudal rounded. *Colours*—yellowish, having a narrow black ocular band descending from in front of the dorsal fin through the middle of the eye, over the preopercle, interopercle, and on to the chest. The upper fourth of the body stained with black and black lines along each row of scales, a black band over the free portion of the tail but interrupted in the middle. Fins yellow, a narrow black intramarginal band along the soft portions of the dorsal and anal fins with a white outer edge: a yellow band with a narrow black external edge down the centre of the caudal, the last third of which fin is grey. A short black band at the base of the first four anal rays.

Habitat.—Red Sea, seas of India to the Malay Archipelago and beyond, attaining at least 5 inches in length. Schneider's type still exists in Berlin, it is about $4\frac{3}{10}$ inches long.

15. Chætodon octofasciatus.

Chætodon octofasciatus, Gmel. Linn. i, p. 1262; Bloch, t. 215, f. 1; Bl. Schn. p. 223; Cuv. and Val. vii, p. 17; Bleeker, Verh. Bat. Gen. xxiii, Chætod. p. 16; Günther, Catal. ii, p. 17; Kner, Novara Fische, p. 98.

Chætodon octolineatus, Gronov. ed. Gray, p. 69.

B. vi, D. $\frac{11}{20-22}$, P. 19, V. 1/5, A. $\frac{3}{17}$, C. 18, L. l. 50, L. tr. 12/24.

Length of head 1/4, of caudal nearly 1/6, height of body 2/3 of the total length. *Eyes*—diameter 1/3 of length of head, nearly 1 diameter from end of snout and also apart. Preopercle a little rough along its edge, especially at the angle, but not serrated. *Fins*—dorsal spines strong, increasing in length to the fourth, the interspinous membrane deeply emarginate, soft portions of it and of the anal rounded: second anal spine the strongest but not quite so long as the third: caudal cut almost square. *Colours*—buff, vertically banded, with a central band along the snout to between the eyes: ocular band commences a short distance in front of the dorsal fin, and passing through the eye (which is about twice its width), it crosses the cheeks and is lost on the chest: the second goes from the third and fourth dorsal spines to behind the base of the ventral: the third from the seventh dorsal spine to before the commencement of the anal: the fourth from the two last spines to the first anal rays: the fifth from the first few dorsal rays to the anterior third of the soft anal: the sixth down the last third of the soft dorsal across the free portion of the tail (where it increases in width) to near the posterior extremity of the soft anal: the last over the base of the caudal: soft dorsal and anal with a dark outer edge and light margin.

Amongst Sir W. Elliot's drawings is a very good representation of this species marked *C. octofasciatus*, but with no note as to where it was obtained, Jerdon however remarks (M. J. L. and Sc. 1851, p. 134) that it is rarely met with in Madras, where its Tamil designation is *Munja cooli min*.

Habitat.—Seas of India to the Malay Archipelago and beyond.

16. Chætodon oligacanthus.

Platax ocellatus, Cuv. and Val. vii, p. 209; Cantor, Catal. p. 170.

Chætodon oligacanthus, Bleeker, Verh. Bat. Gen. xxiii, Chæton. p. 16; Günther, Catal. ii, pp. 34, 516; Kner, Novara Fische, p. 102.

Parachætodon oligacanthus, Bleeker, Nov. Typi Gen. Pisc. neg. 1875, p. 5.

B. vi, D. $\frac{13-14}{19-20}$, P. 15, V. 1/5, A. $\frac{3}{17-18}$, C. 17, L. l. 46-48.

Length of head 4/15 to 1/4, of caudal 1/6, height of body 2/3 of the total length. *Eyes*—diameter 4/13 of the length of head, 1 diameter from the end of snout and also apart. Both limbs of preopercle serrated, the inferior being most coarsely so. *Fins*—anterior portions of soft dorsal and anal the highest. *Lateral-line*—ceases opposite the posterior fourth of the dorsal fin. *Colours*—yellowish white, with five vertical brown bands, the anterior four of which have black edges, the ocular one is brown and narrower than the orbit: three more similar bands pass from the back to the abdomen: at the upper part of the last is a dark ocellus at the base of the 8th to 12th dorsal rays inclusive: the fifth band is over the free portion of the tail. The posterior half of the ventrals is sometimes black.

Habitat.—Seas of India, the Malay Archipelago to the Philippine Islands.*

Genus, 2—CHELMO, *Cuv.*

Branchiostegals six or seven: pseudobranchiæ. Body elevated and compressed. Snout produced as a long round tube by the horizontal elongation of the premaxillaries and mandibles† which are laterally connected by membrane, the gape of the mouth anteriorly being small. Preopercle without any spine, it and the preorbital may be serrated. Teeth on the jaws: none on the palate. One dorsal with from nine to thirteen spines, none being elongated: anal with three. Scales of moderate or small size.

Geographical distribution.—East coast of Africa, seas of India to the Malay Archipelago and beyond.

SYNOPSIS OF SPECIES.

1. *Chelmo longirostris*, D. $\frac{11-12}{24-25}$, A. $\frac{3}{18-19}$, L. l. 70-75. Yellow, with a black triangular patch from the first dorsal spine to the snout, and extending to the opercle: a round black spot at the posterior angle of the anal fin. East coast of Africa, seas of India to the Malay Archipelago.

2. *Chelmo rostratus*, D. $\frac{9}{29-31}$, A. $\frac{3}{22-24}$, L. l. 47-50. Five orange white-edged cross bands. East coast of Africa, seas of India to the Malay Archipelago and China.

1. Chelmo longirostris.

Chætodon longirostris, Brouss. Ich. t. 7.

Chelmon longirostris, Cuv. and Val. vii, p. 89, pl. 175; Bleeker, Verh. Bat. Gen. xxiii, Chætod. p. 20.

Chelmo longirostris, Günther, Catal. ii, p. 38, and Garrett's Fische d. Sudsee, p. 48.

D. $\frac{11-12}{24-25}$, P. 15, V. 1/5, A. $\frac{3}{18-19}$, C. 18, L. l. 70-75, L. tr. 11/30.

Length of head 3/7, of caudal 1/7, height of body 2/5 of the total length. *Eyes*—diameter 2/15 of the length of head, 1¼ diameters in the postorbital portion of the head. Angle and lower edge of the preopercle serrated, some fine serratures along the upper edge of the orbit and a few along the lower edge of the preorbital. *Fins*—dorsal spines strong, the interspinous membrane very deeply emarginate, the fourth spine somewhat the longest, equalling that of the head behind the front nostril, and exceeding the length of the rays, which latter portion of the fin is rounded: pectoral equals two-thirds the height of the body: third anal spine the longest. *Colours*—yellow, with a black triangular patch extending from the base of the first dorsal spine to the snout, and its lower edge going through the eye to the opercle. Posterior edge of the dorsal with a black margin: a small round black spot at the posterior angle of the anal fin: caudal grey with a rather wide dark band over its base at and anterior to the commencement of the rays.

Habitat.—East coast of Africa, seas of India, to the Malay Archipelago and beyond.

* ADDENDA.

Chætodon ?

D. $\frac{14}{26}$, A. $\frac{3}{23}$.

"I also have a drawing and the dried skin of another species of Chætodon which I procured at Tellicherry. It has the ground colour of the body, a sort of lavender colour, line from the first dorsal down to the muzzle yellow; chin, throat and lower part of face, and a line from top of opercle to base of pectoral bright orange, membrane between the dorsal spines yellow, with a blue spot which continues in a line on to the upper portion of the soft dorsal, and also on the anal; soft dorsal green with a yellowish margin. Anal and ventral yellow. Caudal lavender, the rays purple and margined on the sides with yellow and exteriorly with orange. Lips red. D. 14-26, A. 3-23. Length 6 inches."—Jerdon. M. J. L. and S. 1851, p. 134.

† Due to this tubular elongation of the snout, these fishes are able to employ it as a blow pipe, from which they discharge globules of water at insects flying above them.

2. Chelmo rostratus, Plate XXVIII, fig. 2.

Chætodon rostratus, Linn. Mus. Ad. Fried. i, p. 61, t. 34, f. 2; Gmel. Linn. p. 1244; Bl. p. 1184, t. 202, f. i; Bl. Schn. p. 221; Shaw, Zool. iv, p. 337, pl. 47; Gronov. Sys. ed. Gray, p. 73.

Chætodon enceladus, Shaw, Nat. Misc. p. 2, pl. 67.

Chelmon rostratus, Cuv. Règ. Anim. ii, p. 190, and Illus. Poiss. pl. 40, f. i; Bennett, Life of Sir S. Raffles, p. 689; Cuv. and Val. vii, p. 87; Cantor, Catal. p. 158; Bleeker, Verh. Bat. Gen. xxiii, Chætod. p. 20.

Chelmo rostratus, Günther, Catal. ii, p. 36; Kner, Novara Fische, p. 103.

D. $\frac{9}{29-30}$, P. 16, V. 1/5, A. $\frac{3}{20-21}$, C. 17, L. l. 47-50, L. r. [illegible], L. tr. 8/20 (Vert. 10/14).

Length of head nearly or quite 1/3, of caudal 2/13 to 1/7, height of body about 1/2 of the total length. *Eyes*—diameter 1/5 of length of head, $2\frac{1}{2}$ diameters from the end of snout, and nearly 1 apart. Preopercle finely serrated along both limbs: lower edge of preorbital and supra-orbital margin likewise serrated in the young. *Teeth*—brush-like. *Fins*—dorsal spines moderately strong, the soft portions of the dorsal and anal obtusely angular: caudal rounded. In the young the ventral reaches the anal rays, but not so far in larger specimens: pectoral equal in length to the head behind the front nostril. *Scales*—seven rows between lateral-line and base of sixth dorsal spine. *Colours*—head and body with five orange cross-bands edged with brown and with white outer margins: a round black white-edged spot in the middle of the soft dorsal and within the fourth cross band: a dark band round the free portion of the tail: soft dorsal, caudal and anal with blue and white edges.

Habitat.—East coast of Africa through the seas of India, the Malay Archipelago and China. The specimen figured is $4\frac{6}{10}$ inches in length.

Genus, 3—Heniochus, *Cuv. and Val.*

Taurichthys, Cuv. and Val.: *Diphreutes*, Cantor.

Branchiostegals five: pseudobranchiæ. Body elevated and strongly compressed: mouth short, or of moderate length. Preopercle finely serrated or entire. Teeth villiform, none on the palate. A single dorsal fin, with from eleven to thirteen spines, the fourth of which is elongated and filiform, anal with three. Scales ctenoid or cycloid, of moderate size, and more or less covering the vertical fins. Lateral-line continuous. Air-vessel present. Pyloric appendages few.

Geographical distribution.—Seas of India to Polynesia, &c.

SYNOPSIS OF INDIVIDUAL SPECIES.

1. *Heniochus macrolepidotus*, D. $\frac{11-12}{24-25}$, A. $\frac{3}{17-18}$, L. l. 52-60. Three purplish vertical bands.

1. Heniochus macrolepidotus, Plate XXVIII, fig. 3.

Chætodon macrolepidotus, Artedi, species, p. 94; Linn. Syst. i, p. 464; Gmel. Linn. p. 1247; Bl. p. 1177, t. 200, f. 1; Lacép. iv, p. 455, pl. 11, f. 3 and pl. 12, f. 1; Bl. Schn. p. 231; Klunz. Fische d. Roth. Meer. Verh. Zool. Bot. Ges. in Wien, 1870, p. 784.

Chætodon acuminatus, Linn. Mus. Ad. Fried. t. 33, f. 3; Gmel. Linn. 1241; Bl. Schn. p. 229.

Chætodon bifasciatus, Shaw, Zool. iv, p. 342; Gronov. ed. Gray, p. 75.

Heniochus acuminatus, Cuv. and Val. vii, p. 98.

Heniochus macrolepidotus, Cuv. Règ. Anim. ii, p. 191; Cuv. and Val. vii, p. 93, pl. 176; Temm. and Schleg. Fauna Japon. p. 82, pl. 44, f. 1; Richards. Ich. China, p. 246; Bleeker, Verh. Bat. Gen. xxiii, Chætod. p. 21; Günther, Catal. ii, p. 39 and Fische d. Südsee, p. 48, t. xxxvii; Day, Fish. Malabar, p. 23; Klunzing. Verh. z. b. Ges. Wien, 1870, p. 784.

Diphreutes macrolepidotus, Cantor, Catal. p. 159.

Parrowmee, Mal.: *Chuddukun*, Tam.: *Pak-noodah*, Andam.

B. v, D. $\frac{11-12}{24-25}$, P. 17, V. 1/5, A. $\frac{3}{17-18}$, C. 17, L. l. 52, L. r. [illegible], L. tr. 9/22, Cæc. pyl. 6, Vert. 10/14.

Length of head 1/4, of caudal 1/5, height of body 2/3 of the total length. *Eyes*—diameter from 4/13 to 1/3 of length of head, $1\frac{1}{2}$ diameters from end of snout, and nearly 1 apart. A slight protuberance above each orbit but none on the neck. The maxilla reaches to half way between the snout and the front edge of the orbit. Vertical limb of preopercle finely serrated, more coarsely so at its angle: sub- and inter-opercles entire: opercle with two points. *Teeth*—villiform in the jaws. *Fins*—dorsal spines rather strong, the fourth having a filamentous prolongation reaching to the caudal fin or even beyond, the fifth is also somewhat elongated: ventral reaches the anal: the second and third anal spines of about equal length and strength: caudal cut nearly square. *Scales*—about 5 rows between the lateral-line and the base of the eighth or ninth dorsal spines. *Colours*—pearly white, with a dark purplish band over the summit of the snout, another over the eyes: a third broad one extending from the three first dorsal spines and posterior two-thirds of the opercle, passing downwards includes the whole of the ventral fin and extends backwards to the anal: the last commences at the summit of the fifth dorsal spine, passes downwards to the base of the seventh, is as wide as to the first ray, and ends in the posterior third of the anal fin. Pectoral, soft portions of dorsal, anal, and caudal fins bright yellow.

In Cuv. and Val. a *variety* figured by Bennett, Ms. wherein the colours have become transposed, the dark bands being where the light ones ordinarily are, is named *H. permutatus*, (Ed. Benn.) l. c. p. 99.

Habitat.—East coast of Africa, through the Indian Ocean and Malay Archipelago: it is said to attain 18 inches in length.

Genus, 4—ZANCLUS,* *Cuv. and Val.*

Gnathocentrum, Guich.; *Gonopterus*, (Gronov.) Gray.

Branchiostegals four: pseudobranchiæ. Body elevated and compressed. Snout of moderate length. Preopercle without any spine, it and the preorbital may be serrated. Teeth in the jaws, none on the palate. One dorsal fin with seven spines, the third of which is very elongate: anal with three. Scales small. Air-vessel present. Pyloric appendages in moderate numbers.

Geographical distribution.—Seas of India to the Malay Archipelago and beyond.

SYNOPSIS OF INDIVIDUAL SPECIES.

1. *Zanclus cornutus*, D. [illegible], A. [illegible]. Yellowish-white, with three vertical dark bands. Seas of India to the Malay Archipelago and beyond.

1. Zanclus cornutus, Plate XXVIII, fig. 4.

Chætodon cornutus, Linn. Syst. p. 461; Bl. p. 1179, t. 200, f. 2; Bl. Schn. p. 221; Lacép. iv, p. 473, pl. 2, f. 1.

Zanclus cornutus, Cuv. and Val. vii, p. 102, pl. 177; Swainson, Fish. ii, p. 212; Bleeker, Verh. Bat. Gen. xxiii, Chætod. p. 22; Günther, Catal. ii, p. 493.

Gonopterus mærens, Gronov, ed. Gray, p. 77.

B. iv, D. [illegible], P. 19, V. 1/5, A. [illegible], C. 16, Cæc. pyl. 14, Vert. 9/13.

Length of head nearly 1/3, of caudal 4/17, height of body 5/7 of the total length. *Eyes*—diameter 2/7 of length of head, 1 diameter apart, and twice the length of the postorbital portion of the head. Upper edge of orbit serrated in its front half and a parallel serrated ridge just above it. *Fins*—dorsal spines very elongated and filiform, the last rays are very short: anal much the highest anteriorly: caudal emarginate. *Scales*—minute. *Colours*—yellowish-white, with three broad, dark, vertical brown bands, the anterior from the two first dorsal spines and upper profile as far forwards as the orbit, descends over the opercles and cheeks to the ventral fin: the second band commencing from the base of the fourth spine to the first ray passes downwards to the highest portion of the anal, it has a white hind edge: the last goes over the caudal fin, having a concave posterior margin and a white front edge. There is also a band over the snout: pectoral yellow.

Habitat.—Seas of India to the Malay Archipelago and beyond.

Genus, 5—HOLACANTHUS, *Lacép.*

Genicanthus, Swains.

Branchiostegals six: pseudobranchiæ. Body compressed, and as a rule much elevated. Preopercle serrated, with one or more strong spines at its angle directed backwards. No palatine teeth. A single dorsal fin with from twelve to fifteen spines: anal with three or sometimes four. Scales of moderate or small size, more or less covering the vertical fins. Air-vessel with two horns posteriorly. Pyloric appendages many.

Geographical distribution.—Throughout the seas of India and generally in those of the tropics.

SYNOPSIS OF SPECIES.

A. *Scales small.*

1. *Holacanthus imperator*, D. [illegible], A. [illegible]. Bluish, with three narrow blue bands on the head and about nineteen narrow oblique canary coloured bands on the body; chest brownish, caudal yellow. From seas of East Africa through those of India to the Malay Archipelago.

2. *Holacanthus Nicobariensis*, D. [illegible], A. [illegible]. Blue, with light vertical more or less semicircular bands on the body. Red Sea, East coast of Africa, India to the Malay Archipelago and beyond.

3. *Holacanthus annularis*, D. [illegible], A. [illegible]. Brown, with a blue ring on the shoulder, and six or seven blue body bands radiate from the eye: caudal yellow. Seas of India to the Malay Archipelago and beyond.

B. *Scales of moderate size.*

4. *Holacanthus diacanthus*, D. [illegible], A. [illegible], L. r. 52. Yellowish, with eight to twelve vertical blue brown-edged bands. Seas of India to the Malay Archipelago.

5. *Holacanthus xanthurus*, D. [illegible], A. [illegible], L. l. 50. Greyish, with a light opercular band and a yellow shoulder spot. Seas of India.

6. *Holacanthus xanthometopon*, D. [illegible], A. [illegible], L. l. 47. Blue, with yellow black-edged spots on the cheeks a yellow interorbital band, a blue spot on each scale on the body. Andamans to the Malay Archipelago.

* This genus is included by Dr. Günther amongst the *Carangidæ*. Respecting the skeleton he observes of *Z. cornutus*, which has vertebræ 9/13, that "the anterior and posterior portions of its vertebral column are so shortened in their longitudinal diameter, that, at both extremities, one vertebra has not been developed." Catal. ii, p. 493. One of his definitions of the Family *Carangidæ* being "Vertebræ 10/14" l. c. p. 417.

A. *Scales small.*

1. Holacanthus imperator, Plate XXVIII, fig. 5.

Chætodon imperator, Bloch, p. 1164, t. 194; Gmel. Linn. p. 1255; Bl. Schn. p. 217.

Holacanthus imperator, Lacep. iv, pp. 527, 534, pl. 12, f. 3; Cuv. and Val. vii, p. 180; Bleeker, Celebes, iii, p. 758, and Act. Soc. Neder. i, Man. en Makass. p. 49; Günther, Catal. ii, p. 52, and Fische d. Sudsee, p. 53, t. xli, fig. A; Klunz. Verh. z. b. Ges. Wien, 1870, p. 787.

B. vi, D. $\frac{14}{19-20}$, P. 21, V. 1/5, A. $\frac{3}{19-21}$, C. 17.

Length of head 1/4 to 3/13, of caudal 1/7, height of body 1/2 to 4/7 of the total length. *Eyes*—diameter 1/3 to 1/4 of the length of head, $1\frac{1}{4}$ to $1\frac{1}{2}$ diameters from the end of snout, and 1 apart. Body oval, strongly compressed: snout elevated. The maxilla reaches half-way to below the front edge of the orbit. Vertical limb of preopercle rather oblique and serrated, as is also its horizontal limb; angle with a strong, smooth, curved spine, one and a quarter diameters of the orbit in length, and reaching to below the base of the pectoral fin. *Teeth*—in closely set rows, some of them with a small lobe on either side of their base. *Fins*—dorsal spines strong, gradually increasing in length, with the interspinous membrane deeply notched, its soft portion as well as that of the anal rounded. Pectoral as long as the head behind the angle of the mouth: ventral reaching to the anal: anal spines strong, the third the longest and equal to the last of the dorsal or the head excluding the snout: caudal rounded. *Scales*—small, covering the vertical fins. *Colours*—Body blue, having a greenish tinge along the back: about nineteen canary-coloured lines pass upwards to the dorsal, horizontally to the caudal, or downwards towards the anal fin. A large black descending band with a blue anterior edge, on the shoulder; chest chestnut. A light blue stripe across the snout, round the cheeks, and to the preopercular spine, which is nearly black. A brown band superiorly edged with blue crosses the eye and passes on to the preopercle. Opercle yellow, edged with blue, and the branchiostegals black. A narrow black edge to the caudal: ventral dark with orange coloured rays: pectoral blackish.

A coloured drawing nearly 8 inches in length, labelled *Kulloo koli meen* and *Holacanthus imperator*, exists amongst Sir Walter Elliot's figures of fish.

Habitat.—From the East coast of Africa through the seas of India to the Malay Archipelago.

2. Holacanthus Nicobariensis, Plate XXVIII, fig. 6 (variety *semicirculatus*).

Chætodon Nicobarensis, Bl. Schn. p. 219, t. 50.

Holacanthus geometricus, Lacép. iv, pp. 528, 537, pl. xiii, fig. 1; Cuv. and Val. vii, p. 189.

Holacanthus striatus, Rüppell, N. W. Fische, p. 32, t. x, f. 2; Bleeker, Amb. iv, p. 414; Günther, Catal. ii, p. 53.

Holacanthus semicirculatus, Cuv. and Val. vii, p. 191, pl. 183; Bleeker, Amb. vi, p. 414 and Banka, p. 452; Voy. Coq. Zool. Poiss. p. 173, pl. xxx, fig. 3; Günther, Catal. ii, p. 53.

Holacanthus Nicobariensis, Bleeker, Amb, vi, p. 413; Günther, Catal. ii, p. 52 and Fische d. Sudsee, p. 54, t. xli, f. B.

B. vi, D. $\frac{13}{21-22}$, P. 19, V. 1/5, A. $\frac{3}{20-21}$, C. 18, L. r. [illegible].

Length of head 1/4, of pectoral 1/4, height of body 1/2 to 4/9 of the total length. *Eyes*—diameter 1/3 to 2/7 of length of head, 1 diameter from end of snout, and 3/4 to 1 diameter apart. Preopercle serrated, its spine smooth reaching to opposite the posterior edge of the opercle and equal in length to 3/4 or 1 diameter of the orbit. *Teeth*—brush-like. *Fins*—dorsal spines shorter than the rays, the soft dorsal angularly-rounded in the adult: caudal rounded. *Scales*—minute, about thirteen rows between lateral-line and base of sixth dorsal spine. *Colours*—this fish shows different distributions of the same colours, some dependant on age, others not so. In the young (*H. striatus*) it is deep blue with slightly curved vertical bands, alternately white and bluish-white, the white ones being the broader. Caudal white, with or without a narrow black outer margin. In a specimen in my collection there are reticulated blue lines between the broad white band behind the eye and on one descending from the centre of the spinous dorsal. In the adult (*H. semicirculatus*) the vertical bands have a more curved direction, the convexity being forwards. In the *Nicobariensis* this is still more apparent, a white spot or short transverse band being the centre around which the body bands are curved. In both these last varieties the tail fin is coloured.

In my *H. striatus* $2\frac{4}{10}$ inches in length, the preopercular spines are bifurcated at their extremities, in a specimen in the British Museum ($1\frac{7}{10}$ inches) they are not so.

Klunzinger, Verh. z. b. Ges. Wien, 1870, p. 789, enumerates *Holacanthus striatus*, Rüpp. Blkr. &c., *H. lineatus*, Rüpp. *H. cœrulescens*, Rüpp. *Chætodon asfur*, var. b. Forsk. *Holacanthus haddaja*, C.V., *Chætodon maculosus*, Forsk.=*Holacanthus maculosus*, *Holacanthus arusel*, Lacép., *Pomacanthus asfur*, Lacép. as varieties of *Chætodon asfur*, Forsk.=*Holacanthus asfur*.

Habitat.—Red Sea, East coast of Africa, seas of India to the Malay Archipelago and beyond.

3. Holacanthus annularis, Plate XXIX, fig. 1.

Chætodon annularis, Bl. t. 215, f. 2; Gmel. Linn. p. 1262; Bl. Schn. p. 219; Shaw, Zool. iv, p. 330, pl. 47.

Holacanthus annularis, Lacép. iv. pp. 526, 533; Cuv. Rég. Anim. ii, p. 192; Cuv. and Val. vii, p. 178; Cantor, Catal. p. 164; Bleeker, Verh. Bat. Gen. xxiii, Chætod. p. 26; Günther, Catal. ii, p. 42.

Chætodon sakritschapi, Russell, Fish. Vizag. i, p. 69, pl. 88.
Chætodon cristatus, Gronov. Syst. ed. Gray, p. 71.
Nga-dyk-pye, Arrak.: *Daakhrasal*, Chittagong.

B. vi, D. [illegible], P. 20, V. 1/5, A. [illegible], C. 17.

Length of head 2/9, of caudal 1/6, height of body 4/7 of the total length. *Eyes*—diameter 2/7 of length of head, $1\frac{1}{4}$ diameters from end of snout, and also apart. Preoperele finely serrated along its vertical limb, the spine at its angle smooth and as long as the diameter of the orbit. *Teeth*—brush-like. *Fins*—dorsal spines increase in length to the last, none of the rays prolonged: the soft portion of the fin angular, in adults it is often produced, that of the anal rounded: third anal spine the longest. *Scales*—small. *Colours*—sienna, with a blue ring on the shoulder. One narrow blue interorbital band is continued behind the eye over the opercle on the hind edge of which it curves upwards towards the ring: a second across the snout passes under the eye across the opercle and joins the third on the body: six or seven arched blue bands radiate from the head and are continued along the body converging towards the soft dorsal fin: pectoral yellow, with a blue band at its base. Dorsal and anal fins dark, the six body bands are continued on to the former, where there are also some intermediate narrow blue lines, the fin with a blue upper edge: anal with three blue lines on it and a light blue margin: caudal yellow, with a narrow orange tip.

Russell observed, "the present subject bears a strong resemblance to *Chætodon annularis*, Linn., but differs principally in two circumstances; the one the setaceous elongation of the dorsal fin, resembling that of *Chætodon setifer*, Bloch; the other (less material) in the remarkable ring on the shoulder being rather square than of a circular figure."

Amongst Sir Walter Elliot's drawings is one of this fish, which was coloured from an individual captured at Waltair, March, 1853, its native names are recorded as *Jutipyan*, Tel.: *Ledha terate*, Mal. Jerdon remarks, M. J. L. and Sc. 1851, p. 134, "I only once procured this beautiful fish." The specimen figured was taken at Singapore by the late Dr. Stoliczka.

Habitat.—Seas of India to the Malay Archipelago, China, and beyond. It attains at least a foot in length. The specimen figured is 6 inches long.

B. *Scales of moderate size.*

4. Holacanthus diacanthus.

Chætodon diacanthus, (Boddaert), Bl. Schn. p. 220.
Chætodon dux et Boddaertii, Gmel. Linn. pp. 1243, 1255.
Chætodon fasciatus, Bloch, t. 195; Gmel. Linn. 1266; Bl. Schn. p. 217.
Holacanthus dux, Lacép. iv, p. 534; Cuv. and Val. vii, p. 184; Rüpp. N. W. Fische, p. 37; Bleeker, Celebes, iii, p. 757.
Acanthopus Boddaertii, Lacép. iv, pp. 559, 560.
Holacanthus diacanthus, Günther, Catal. ii, p. 48; Klunz. Verh. z. b. Ges. Wien, 1870, p. 786.

B. vi, D. [illegible], P. 19, V. 1/5, A. [illegible], C. 17, L. r. 52, L. tr. 7/25.

Length of head 1/5, of caudal 1/6, height of body 3/7 of the total length. *Eyes*—diameter 2/9 of length of head, $1\frac{1}{2}$ diameters from end of snout, and also apart. Preopercle strongly serrated, its spine strong, equal in length to about 2 diameters of the orbit, and extending to below the base of the pectoral fin. *Fins*—soft dorsal and anal rounded: third anal spine longest and strongest: caudal rounded. *Colours*—yellowish, with from eight to twelve vertical blue brown-edged bands, those on the body being continued on to the vertical fins. A short one exists along the snout, two descend from the summit of the head to the eye and to a little below it: one traverses the opercle, and about eight exist on the body: caudal yellow. Anal has bluish streaks parallel to its base.

Habitat.—Seas of India to the Malay Archipelago.

5. Holacanthus xanthurus, Plate XXIX, fig. 2.

Bennett, Proc. Zool. Soc. 1832, p. 183; Günther, Catal. ii, p. 51.

B. vi, D. [illegible], P. 17, V. 1/5, A. [illegible], C. 17, L. l. 50, L. r. [illegible], L. tr. 7/22.

Length of head 1/4 to 4/17, of caudal excluding its prolongation 1/6, including it 1/4, height of body 1/2 of the total length excluding caudal filament. *Eyes*—diameter 1/3 to 2/7 of the length of head, 1 diameter from the end of snout, and also apart. Body compressed: dorsal and abdominal profiles about equally convex. The maxilla reaches half way to below the orbit. Vertical limb of the preopercle serrated, and having a strong smooth spine which is equal to or rather above one diameter of the orbit in length at its angle, and reaching nearly to the base of the pectoral fin. *Teeth*—in jaws fine, pointed, with the outer row the largest. *Fins*—dorsal spines and rays almost parallel to the dorsal profile, the fourth dorsal spine slightly the longest, the last being equal to the third: soft portion of the fin slightly rounded: pectoral a little longer than the head excluding the snout: the ventrals reach the vent: third anal spine longest, strongest, and one-third longer than the longest in the dorsal fin, the soft portions of the two similar: caudal rather rounded, with its upper ray produced

Q

into a filament.* *Scales*—strongly ctenoid, and longitudinally fluted, much smaller above than below the lateral line. *Colours*—body greyish-brown, darker along the back, and becoming black over the tail as well as on the vertical fins, head, and chest: a lightish opercular band and a small but brilliant yellow shoulder spot: dorsal and anal fins edged with yellowish-white: caudal canary colour. After death each scale seems to have a light semilunar band.

A coloured figure, nearly 6 inches in length, exists in Sir Walter Elliot's collection, termed *Kal kasi*, and *Holacanthus nicobariensis*.

Habitat.—Ceylon and Madras to 6 inches in length.

6. Holacanthus xanthometopon.

Bleeker, Sumatra, ii, p. 258; Günther, Catal. ii, p. 51.

B. vi, D. $\frac{13}{17}$, P. 17, V. 1/5, A. $\frac{3}{18}$, C. 17, L. r. 47, L. tr. 7/25.

Length of head 2/9, of caudal 2/11, height of body 4/9 of the total length. *Eyes*—diameter 1/4 of length of head, $1\frac{1}{2}$ diameters from end of snout, and also apart. Vertical limb of preopercle with widely set serrations, a strong spine at the angle of the preopercle not quite half so long as the head. *Fins*—soft dorsal and anal fins angular: caudal rounded. *Colours*—blue, cheeks and opercles with numerous golden spots externally edged with black: some fine black lines on the lips and chin: a broad yellow interorbital band: body violet, each scale with a brilliant blue spot: a yellow shoulder spot. Dorsal, caudal, and pectoral yellow, with a black spot at the base of the last seven dorsal rays, caudal with a black edge: ventral and anal white with a blue edge.

Habitat—Andamans and Malay Archipelago. A specimen, $7\frac{1}{2}$ inches in length, exists in the Calcutta Museum. A native artist attempted for a whole week to figure it but unsuccessfully.

Genus, 6—Scatophagus, *Cuv. and Val.*

Cacodoxus,† Cantor.

Branchiostegals six: pseudobranchiæ. Body much compressed and elevated, snout of moderate length. Preopercle spineless. Palate edentulous. Two dorsals, united at their bases, the first having ten or eleven spines, and anteriorly a recumbent one directed forwards; the soft dorsal covered with scales: anal with four spines. Scales very small. Air-vessel simple. Pyloric appendages rather numerous.

Geographical distribution.—East coast of Africa; Seas of India, to the Malay Archipelago and beyond.

SYNOPSIS OF INDIVIDUAL SPECIES.

1. *Scatophagus argus*, D. 10 | $\frac{1}{16-17}$, A. $\frac{4}{14-15}$. Purplish, blotched all over with dark spots. Seas of India, to China and Australia.

1. Scatophagus argus, Plate XXIX, fig. 3.

Chætodon argus, Gmel. Linn. p. 1248; Bloch, p. 1191, t. 204, f. 1; Bl. Schn. p. 232; Shaw, Zool. iv, p. 332; Russell, Fish. Vizag. i, p. 61, pl. 78.

Chætodon pairatalis, Ham. Buch. Fish. Ganges, pp. 122, 372, pl. 16, f. 41.

Chætodon atromaculatus, Bennett, Fish. Ceylon, p. 18, pl. 18.

Scatophagus argus, Cuv. and Val. vii, p. 136; Richards. Ich. China, p. 245; Günther, Catal. ii, p. 58 and Ann. and Mag. Nat. Hist. 1867, p. 58; Day, Fishes of Malabar, p. 34; Kner, Novara Fische, p. 106.

Cacodoxus argus, Cantor, Catal. p. 163.

Scatophagus ornatus, Günther, Catal. ii, p. 58.

Sargus maculatus, Gronov. ed. Gray, p. 65.

Qu-ee, Sind.; *Chitallee* and *Eepatti*, Tel.; *Sipili*, Tam.; *Natchar char*, Mal.; *Nga-pa-thoung*, Arrak.; *Beeshotara*, Chittag.; *Po-ra-deh*, Andam.

B. vi, D. 10 | $\frac{1}{16-17}$, P. 20, V. 1/5, A. $\frac{4}{13-14}$, C. 16, Cæc. pyl. 18 (20).

Length of head 1/5, of caudal 2/11, height of body 1/2 of the total length. *Eyes*—diameter 2/7 of length of head, 1 diameter from end of snout, and $1\frac{1}{4}$ apart. Body somewhat quadrangular, strongly compressed, and the dorsal profile more curved than the abdominal. The maxilla reaches to about half way between the end of the snout and the front edge of the orbit. Preorbital with the last half of its lower edge finely serrated. Sometimes a few very fine teeth at the angle of the preopercle and also along its lower limb; sub- and inter-opercles entire. Opercle with a weak spine. *Teeth*—villiform in the jaws. *Fins*—dorsal spines strong, each alternate one thicker on one side, interspinous membrane deeply notched, fourth spine the highest equalling the length of the head behind the posterior nostril, anterior rays much the longest, but not quite equalling the length of the fourth spine: anal spines all about the same length, each alternate one being the stronger: caudal fan-shaped, its central rays rather the longest. *Scales*—minute, in about 110 irregular rows, and continued over the soft portions of the dorsal, anal, and caudal fins, likewise on the head and opercles; about 30 rows between the 6th dorsal spine and the lateral-line. *Colours*—purplish, becoming white on the abdomen: large round blackish or

* Having seen many specimens and all with this prolongation, I think it unlikely that such is a sexual distinction.

† Substituted for *Scatophagus*, C. V. pre-occupied by *Scatophaga*, Meigen, 1803 *(Diptera.)*

greenish spots on the body, most numerous along the back, and varying in size and tints. First dorsal brownish-blue, having a few minute spots: second dorsal yellowish, with slight brown markings between the rays.

In the *very young*, a bony ridge, ending in a spine, passes from the eye to above the opercle on to the shoulder, it is serrated along the upper edge of the orbit and the lower edge of the preorbital.

Dr. Günther. Ann. and Mag. *l. c.* considers *Scatophagus argus*, C.V., the young of *S. argus*, C.V.

Habitat.—Indian Ocean, to China and Australia, attaining a foot in length: it enters backwaters and rivers, but is a foul feeder,* and, so far as I have observed, is not in request as food. Hamilton Buchanan remarks of it that "when newly caught it is a fish of great beauty, easy digestion, and excellent flavour: but after death it soon becomes soft and strong tasted." Cantor states that at Pinang "it is eaten by the natives, though many reject it on account of its reputed disgusting habits." In Ceylon, where it is termed *Dewi barakeyah*, "it is generally esteemed, its flesh partaking the flavour of trout."—*Bennett, l. c.*

Genus, 7—EPHIPPUS, *Cuv.*

Selene, Lacép.; *Harches*, Cantor.

Branchiostegals six: pseudobranchiæ. Body much compressed and elevated. Snout short, the upper profile parabolic. Preopercle without a spine. No teeth on the palate. Dorsal with eight or nine spines, several of which are flexible and elongated, all are receivable into a groove at their base, interspinous membrane deeply cleft, and a deep notch between the spinous and soft portions of the fin: three anal spines; pectoral short. Scales of moderate or small size, some over the soft dorsal, anal, and caudal fins. Air-vessel bifurcated anteriorly, and with two long horns posteriorly. Pyloric appendages few.

Geographical distribution.—Seas of India, to the Malay Archipelago, and beyond.

SYNOPSIS OF INDIVIDUAL SPECIES.

Ephippus orbis, D. [illegible], A. [illegible], L. l. 42, L. tr. 7/15. Silvery. Seas of India, to the Malay Archipelago and beyond.

1. **Ephippus orbis**, Plate XXIX, fig. 4.

Chætodon orbis, Bloch, p. 1187, t. 202, f. 2; Gmel. Linn. 1244; Lacép. iv, pp. 458, 491; Bl. Schn. p. 232; Shaw, Zool. iv, p. 339.

Ephippus orbis, Cuv. Règ. Anim. ii, p. 191; Cuv. and Val. vii, p. 127; Swainson, Fishes, ii, p. 213; Richards. Ich. China, p. 245; Günther, Catal. ii, p. 62; Day, Fish. Mal. p. 35.

Harches orbis, Cantor, Catal. p. 160.

Nulla torriti, Tam.: *Kol-lid-dak*, Andam.

B. vi, D. [illegible], P. 19, V. 1/5, A. [illegible], C. 19, L. l. 42, L. r. [illegible], L. tr. 7/15, Cæc. pyl. 2-4.

Length of head 1/4 to 2/9, of caudal 1/5, height of body nearly 2/3 of the total length. *Eyes*—diameter $2\frac{1}{3}$ of the length of head, nearly 1 diameter from end of snout, and also apart. The upper profile is much elevated, rising abruptly from the snout to the first dorsal fin: the abdominal contour is much less convex. The maxilla extends to opposite the anterior margin of orbit. Preopercle narrow, finely denticulated on its vertical limb and at its angle. Sub- and inter-opercles entire, opercle ending in two obtuse points connected by a shallow emargination. *Fins*—dorsal spines moderately strong at their bases, interspinous membrane at first deeply emarginated, but not that between the last spine and the soft rays: the third, fourth and fifth spines are elongated and filiform at their extremities, especially the third. The anterior rays of the dorsal from the 3rd are somewhat the longest: the fin rounded.† Ventral having its first ray elongated. Second anal spine the strongest, equal to the seventh in the dorsal in length: anterior rays the longest. Ventral pointed. Caudal slightly produced in the centre, and somewhat emarginate above and below. *Scales*—some over the bases of the vertical fins. *Air-vessel*—thick, with one tendinous attachment on either side, having horns anteriorly and two long bifurcations posteriorly. The intestines in this species are much convoluted, and possess two, sometimes four, long pyloric appendages. May 11th, 1868, a female was taken in which the ova was well developed. *Colours*—back and head greyish-green, sides and abdomen silvery shot with pink: fin membranes diaphanous finely dotted with black, more especially in their marginal halves: rays bluish white. The young have a dark grey orbital band, another over the nape, and two over the body: the fins are edged with grey.

Habitat.—Seas of India and the Malay Archipelago, attaining at least 6 inches in length; the one figured is $5\frac{3}{4}$ inches long.

Genus, 8—DREPANE, *Cuv. and Val.*

Harpochirus, Cantor; *Cryptosmilia*, Cope.

Branchiostegals, six: pseudobranchiæ. Body elevated and much compressed. Snout short. Preopercle spineless. Palate edentulous. Dorsal having anteriorly a concealed spine directed forwards, and eight or nine spinous

* Col. Tickell, MS. disputes this and asserts that he has eaten this fish taken some distance off the coast, of the most delicate flavour. My reason for believing the natives to be correct as to its love for foul feeding is that I have opened many specimens, and those taken from near inhabited localities had, as a rule, their stomachs full of ordure.

† In two specimens [illegible], and $2\frac{1}{4}$ inches in length respectively, a recumbent, anteriorly directed spine exists in front of the base of the dorsal fin.

rays, which, as well as those of the anal, are receivable into a groove at their bases; interspinous membrane deeply notched; pectoral long and falciform. Scales of moderate size. Air-vessel posteriorly prolonged into two horns. Pyloric appendages few.

Geographical distribution.—Red Sea, throughout those of India, and beyond.

SYNOPSIS OF INDIVIDUAL SPECIES.

1. *Drepane punctata*, D. $\frac{8-9}{19-22}$, A. $\frac{3}{17-19}$. Silvery, with or without vertical bands and black spots.

1. Drepane punctata, Plate XXIX, fig. 5.

Chætodon punctatus, Gmel. Linn. p. 1243; Bl. Schn. p. 231; Shaw. Zool. iv, p. 365.

Chætodon longimanus, Bl. Schn. p. 229.

Chætodon falcatus, Lacép. iv, pp. 452, 470.

Chætodon totte, Russell, Fish. Vizag. i, p. 62, pl. 79.

Chætodon terla, A and B, Russell, l. c. i, pp. 63, 64, fig. 80, 81.

Ephippus punctatus et longimanus, Cuv. Reg. Anim. ii, 191.

Drepane punctata, Cuv. and Val. vii, p. 132, pl. 179; Swainson, ii, 213; Dampier, Voy. New Holland, ii, pl. 4; Richards. Ich. China, p. 244, and Ann. and Mag. Nat. Hist. x, 1842, p. 28; Bleeker, Verh. Bat. Gen. xxii, p. 5; Günther, Catal. ii, p. 62, and Fische d. Sudsee, p. 55; Day, Fish. Malabar, p. 36; Kner, Novara Fische, p. 107.

Drepane longimana, Cuv. and Val. vii, p. 133; Richards. l. c. p. 245; Bleeker, Verh. Bat. Gen. xxiii, Chætod. p. 23.

Harpochirus punctatus et longimanus, Cantor, Catal. pp. 162, 163.

Cryptosmilia luna, Cope, Trans. Am. Phil. Soc. xiii, p. 401.

Púnnar, Sind.; *Shak*, Belooch.; *Páwlhee*, Mal.; *Pelli* or *Torrili*, Tam.; *Thetti*, Tel.; *Roopi-chanda*, Chittag.; *Sheengwa-neet*, Arrak.; *Nga-shingna*, Burm.

B. vi, D. $\frac{8-9}{19-22}$, P. 17, V. 1/5, A. $\frac{3}{17-19}$, C. 15, L. l. 50-55, L. r. [illegible], L. tr. 14/33, Cæc. pyl. 2-3.

Length of head from 4/13 to 1/4, of pectoral 1/2, of caudal 1/4 to 1/5, height of body 2/3 to 3/4 of the total length. *Eyes*—diameter from 3/7 to 1/3 of the length of head, 1 to $1\frac{1}{2}$ diameters from end of snout, and 2/3 to 3/4 of a diameter apart. Dorsal profile considerably elevated, the abdominal much less curved. Mouth small, the maxilla extends to below the first third of the orbit. Preorbital high, its depth generally exceeding the diameter of the eye. Preopercle with a few serrations on its lower limb; sub- and inter-opercles entire.

In *young* specimens the upper edge of the orbit and the upper edge of the occipital process are serrated, whilst there exist about eight strong teeth along the horizontal limb of the preopercle. In a very young specimen ($1\frac{1}{2}$ inches long), in addition to the foregoing, an elevated roughened ridge passes from the upper hind edge of the orbit to the lateral-line.

Fins—dorsal spines strong, and considerable differences are perceptible, in a young individual (at $1\frac{3}{10}$ inches long), the last *six* are of equal height. Should there be nine dorsal spines, the fourth is the longest in the adult; if only eight then the third; this spine equals the length of head behind the middle or front edge of the eye; interspinous membrane deeply notched, and the rays longer than the spines; pectoral sometimes reaching to the base of the caudal; second anal spine the strongest and generally the longest; caudal with its central rays slightly produced. *Colours*—silvery, having a gloss of gold and tinge of purple, with or without vertical bands and black spots; edges of the fins stained with grey, and a similar band along the middle of the dorsal.

The *D. punctata* has been considered a distinct species, and it may be that such an opinion is correct.* At $1\frac{1}{2}$ inches in length is the earliest age at which I have seen distinct spots existing on the vertical body bands. Out of twelve specimens of this variety, and in which every individual is distinctly spotted, nine dorsal spines invariably exist, as given by Russell, and in Cuv. and Val. vii, pl. 179.

In *D. longimana*, the black spots are absent, and out of eleven specimens examined, eight had only eight dorsal spines, the number given by Russell, whilst the horizontal one before the dorsal fin was as a rule more apparent than in the other variety: in some of the remaining three the spots may have disappeared.

In the very young the fish are covered all over with minute dark spots giving them a grey appearance.

Jerdon observes that *D. punctata* is termed *Pooli tarate*, and *D. longimana*, *Sipu tarate*. M. J. L. and S. 1851, p. 134.

Habitat.—Red Sea, East coast of Africa, seas of India to Australia, attaining at least 15 inches in length, and in most places esteemed as food.

Genus, 9—Toxotes, *Cuv.*

Branchiostegals seven; pseudobranchiæ. Body oblong, compressed, back depressed. Eyes of moderate size. Snout rather produced; lower jaw the longer. Villiform teeth on jaws, vomer, and palatine bones. A single dorsal

* "Except the colours, no external character can be assigned to distinguish the two species, but anatomical differences have been pointed out by M. M. Cuv. and Val."—Cantor, l. c.

fin having four or five strong spines situated in the posterior half of the back: anal with three spines. Scales cycloid, of moderate or rather small size, some are extended to over the soft portions of the vertical fins. Air-vessel simple. Pyloric appendages in moderate numbers.

Geographical distribution.—Seas and estuaries of India, to the Malay Archipelago and Polynesia.

SYNOPSIS OF SPECIES.

1. *Toxotes microlepis*, D. $\frac{5}{13}$, A. $\frac{3}{17}$, L. l. 42. Two to four rows of large black patches or stripes along the sides, most being above the lateral-line. Estuaries and large rivers of Burma and Siam near their mouths.

2. *Toxotes chatareus*, D. $\frac{5(4)}{12}$, A. $\frac{3}{16-17}$, L. l. 31. Five or six oblong black patches along the upper half of the head and back. Estuaries and rivers of India, Bengal and Burma to the Malay Archipelago.

3. *Toxotes jaculator*, D. $\frac{4}{11-12}$, A. $\frac{3}{15-17}$, L. l. 27. Four triangular blotches descend from the back to the lateral-line. Red Sea, seas of India to the Malay Archipelago.

1. Toxotes microlepis, Plate XXX, fig. 1.

Blyth, Jour. As. Soc. of Bengal, 1860, p. 142; Günther, Catal. ii, p. 68.
Nga-kyet-oo, Burmese.

B. vii, D. $\frac{5}{13}$, P. 12, V. 1/5, A. $\frac{3}{17}$, C. 19, L. l. 42, L. r. [illegible], L. tr. 6/14, Cæc. pyl. 8.

Length of head 3/10 to 2/7, of caudal 2/11 to 1/6, height of body 2/5 of the total length. *Eyes*—diameter 1/3 to 2/7 of length of head, 1 diameter from end of snout, and $1\frac{1}{4}$ apart. Body compressed, dorsal profile horizontal and flat. The maxilla reaches to below the centre of the orbit. Preopercle and preorbital with their lower edges finely serrated. *Teeth*—villiform in the jaws, vomer, and palate. *Fins*—the dorsal commences slightly in advance of the anal, but is in the last third of the length of the body, its posterior three spines the longest, as is also the third of the anal. *Colours*—golden, with two to four large black oblong blotches or stripes along the sides, most being above the lateral-line: dorsal blotched with black and having dark edges: anal dark: caudal yellow.

Habitat.—Burma and Siam. The specimen figured is from the Irrawaddi, and $4\frac{1}{2}$ inches in length.

2. Toxotes chatareus, Plate XXIX, fig. 6.

Coius chatareus,* Ham. Buch. Fish. Ganges, pp. 101, 370, pl. xiv, fig. 34.
Toxotes jaculator, Cuv. and Val. vii, p. 314 (part); Cantor, Catal. p. 176; Günther, Catal. ii, p. 67 (part).
Nga-prong-gyee, *Kalrya* and *Pauloung-gyee*, Arrac.

B. vii, D. $\frac{5(4)}{12}$, P. 13, V. 1/5, A. $\frac{3}{16-17}$, C. 17, L. l. 31, L. tr. 4-5/11-10.

Length of head $3\frac{3}{4}$ to $3\frac{1}{3}$, of caudal $5\frac{1}{2}$ to 1/6, height of body 2/5 of the total length. *Eyes*—diameter $3\frac{1}{2}$ to 1/4 of length of head, 1 to $1\frac{1}{3}$ diameters from end of snout, and $1\frac{1}{4}$ apart. The maxilla reaches to below the middle of the orbit. Preorbital and preopercle serrated along their lower edges. *Teeth*—villiform in the jaws, vomer, and palate. *Fins*—dorsal spines strong, the fourth somewhat the longest and equal to the length of the head behind the middle or front margin of the eyes. In the specimen with only four dorsal spines, the third equals the fourth as described. Anal commences slightly behind the dorsal, the third spine a little the longest and equal to 2/5 the length of the head. Pectoral as long as the head without the snout. Caudal cut nearly square. *Scales*—from 26 to 28 rows between the snout and the base of the dorsal fin: 6 rows between the lateral-line and the base of the last dorsal spine. *Colours*—silvery shot with gold, dorsal profile greenish-brown, six or seven oblong spots between the eye and the end of the base of the dorsal fin. Some black blotches on the soft dorsal: anal with its lower edge black. In the *young* the blotches are larger and darker, the ventral is black, and there is a black band along the base of the caudal.

Habitat.—Rivers and estuaries of India, Burma, and the Malay Archipelago. My largest specimen is 8 inches in length, but it attains upwards of a foot. The specimen figured is 6 inches long and from the Irrawaddi.

3. Toxotes jaculator.

Sciæna jaculatrix, Pallas, spic. viii, p. 41.
Scarus Schlosseri, Gm. Linn. p. 1282; Lacép. iv, pp. 5, 17; Shaw, Zool. iv, p. 398.
Labrus jaculatrix, Lacép. iii, pp. 425, 464; Shaw, l. c. p. 485, pl. 68.
Toxotes jaculator, Cuv. Règ. Anim. ii, p. 196; Cuv. and Val. vii, p. 314, pl. 192 (pt.); Swainson, ii, p. 214; Bleeker, Verh. Bat. Gen. xxiii, Chætod. p. 31; Günther, Catal. ii, p. 67 (part).

B. vii, D. $\frac{4}{11-12}$, P. 15, V. 1/5, A. $\frac{3}{15-17}$, C. 17, L. l. 27, L. tr. 4-5/10-9.

Length of head 1/3, of caudal 1/6, height of body 1/3 of the total length. *Eyes*—diameter $3\frac{1}{2}$ to 1/4 of

* I have to thank Dr. Bleeker for directing my attention to the difference between *T. chatareus* and *T. jaculator*. All my fresh water and estuary specimens have five dorsal spines, except one individual having four, and they = *chatareus*; my marine forms have only four and = *jaculator*. Valenciennes remarks on the difference seen in the spines and rays, but considers the fish varieties of one species.

length of head, 1 to $1\frac{1}{4}$ diameters from end of snout, and from $1\frac{1}{3}$ to $1\frac{1}{2}$ apart. The maxilla reaches to below the middle or last third of the orbit. Preorbital and preopercle very finely serrated along their lower edges. *Teeth*—villiform in the jaws, vomer, and palate. *Fins*—dorsal spines strong, the third the longest and equal to from $1\frac{1}{2}$ to 2/5 in the length of the head. Anal commences below the first dorsal spine, the third spine the longest and equal to from $2\frac{1}{3}$ to $3\frac{1}{4}$ in the length of the head. Pectoral as long as the head without the snout. Caudal rather emarginate. *Scales*—24 rows between the snout and base of the dorsal fin: five rows between the lateral line and base of the last dorsal spine. *Colours*—brownish shot with golden: four triangular black blotches pass downwards from the back to the lateral-line, most developed in the young. Fins dark.

Habitat.—Red Sea, seas of India, to the Malay Archipelago and beyond. The two specimens described are $3\frac{3}{4}$ and $9\frac{1}{2}$ inches in length from the Andaman islands.

RUIN OF PORTUGUESE CATHEDRAL AT COCHIN (1864.)

FAMILY, III—MULLIDÆ,* *Swainson.*

Branchiostegals four: pseudobranchiæ. Body rather elongate. Profile of head more or less parabolic. Eyes of moderate size, lateral. Mouth in front of snout, rather small, and with a lateral cleft. Two stiff barbels below the chin belonging to the hyal apparatus. Teeth feeble and variously inserted. Two dorsal fins situated at some distance asunder: the anal similar to the second dorsal: ventral with one spine and five rays. Scales large, feebly ctenoid, and rather deciduous. Air-vessel, when present, simple. Pyloric appendages few or in moderate numbers.

Geographical distribution.—Seas of temporate parts of Europe and those of most of the tropics, many young and some adults have been captured in rivers.

Uses.—Usually excellent as food. We are informed that they were originally termed *Mullus* by the Romans, with reference to the scarlet colour of the sandals that their Consuls wore, and which were subsequently adopted by their Emperors under the designation of *Mulleus*. These fish kept in vivaria did not increase in size. The liver was considered the most delicate portion of the Red Mullets, which are now frequently termed the "Woodcock of the seas," due, it is asserted, to the fact that they are dressed similarly to those birds.

SYNOPSIS OF GENERA.

1. *Upeneoides.*—Teeth in both jaws, on the vomer, and palatine bones. Red Sea, East coast of Africa, seas of India, to the Malay Archipelago and beyond.
2. *Mulloides.*—Teeth in several rows in both jaws, palate edentulous. From the Red Sea and East coast of Africa, through the seas of India, to the Malay Archipelago and beyond.
3. *Upeneus.*—Teeth in a single row in both jaws, palate edentulous. From the Red Sea and East coast of Africa, through the seas of India, to the Malay Archipelago and beyond.
4. *Upeneichthys.*—Teeth in both jaws and on the vomer, none on the palatines. Australian seas.
5. *Mullus.*—Teeth in the lower jaw, none in the upper: present on the vomer and palatines. Mediterranean and temperate parts of Europe.

Amongst these fishes a minute first spine to the dorsal fin appears to be sometimes wanting; in other instances, where it is of a larger size, it seems rarely to be absent. There are likewise several other points that should not be overlooked. The comparative length of the barbels appears liable to increase with age; sometimes a sharp spine exists at the shoulder in the young, mostly disappearing as the adult stage is arrived at, although in such it may remain or even be present on one side and absent on the other, as a rule it atrophies into a blunt point. The preorbital may be scaled or scaleless.

In the "Fishes of Zanzibar," 1866, Messrs. Günther and Playfair reunited all the genera into that of *Mullus* (p. 40). Dr. Günther observed in the "Zoological Record" for 1865, p. 183: "The Recorder regrets to have formerly adopted the genera proposed in this family by Bleeker * * the Recorder regards the *Mullidæ* as one natural genus." However, in Garrett's "Fische d. Sudsee," 1874, Dr. Günther still retains Bleeker's genera, and they appear to have been generally adopted by other Ichthyologists as based on distinct anatomical characters. Still it does not seem superfluous to suggest that specimens of the genus *Upeneoides* may be taken in the Indian seas with a more or less edentulous vomer and palate.

Dr. Bleeker however changes his nomenclature in revising this family in 1874, considering the genus he formerly termed as *Upeneoides* = *Upeneus*, Cuv. and Val. thus cancelling *Upeneoides*; *Mulloides* he retains, but includes all his other fish of this family under the generic term *Parupeneus*, chiefly characterised by a single row of conical teeth in both jaws; vomer, and palate edentulous. Scales along the median line of the abdomen, having an obtuse keel. Dorsal and anal fins scaleless.

Genus, 1—UPENEOIDES, *Bleeker.*

Megalepis, Bianc.; *Upeneus*, sp. Cuv.; *Upeneus*, (C. V.) Bleeker, 1874.

Definition as in the family, except:—teeth fine in the jaws, vomer, and palatine bones.

Geographical distribution.—From the Red Sea and East coast of Africa through the seas of India, to the Malay Archipelago and beyond.

SYNOPSIS OF SPECIES.

1. *Upeneoides vittatus*, D. 8 | $\frac{1}{8}$, A. 7, L. l. 38-39. Air-vessel present. Body, dorsal and caudal fins striped. Red Sea, through those of India to the Malay Archipelago and beyond.
2. *Upeneoides sulphureus*, D. 8 | $\frac{1}{9}$, A. 7, L. l. 36-38. No air-vessel. A golden stripe from the orbit to the upper third of the tail: dorsal banded. Seas of India to the Malay Archipelago.

* In Cuv. and Val. iii, p. 419, it is remarked "Ce genre est tellement isolé, que l'on peut le considérer comme formant à lui seul une famille particulière."

3. *Upeneoides cœruleus*, D. 7-8 | 9, A. 7, L. l. 32-34. Air-vessel present. Leaden colour, bands on dorsals and caudal. Madras.

4. *Upeneoides tragula*, D. 7-8 | $\frac{1}{8}$, A. 7, L. l. 30-32. Head and body with brown spots; a brown stripe from eye to the base of the caudal: dorsal and caudal barred. East coast of Africa, seas of India to the Malay Archipelago.

5. *Upeneoides bensasi*, D. 7 | $\frac{1}{8}$, A. $\frac{1}{6}$, L. l. 30-32. Air-vessel absent. A silvery stripe from the eye to the caudal fin, body with red spots: dorsal and upper lobe of caudal barred. Madras to the Malay Archipelago.

6. *Upeneoides tæniopterus*, D. 7 | $\frac{1}{9}$, A. 7. Air-vessel present. A large triangular reddish blotch on the free portion of the tail: dorsal and caudal banded. Ceylon.

1. Upeneoides vittatus, Plate XXX, fig. 2.

Mullus vittatus, Forsk. Fauna Arab. p. 31; Gmel. Linn. p. 1341; Lacép. iii, pp. 382, 401, pl. 14, fig. 1; Bl. Schn. p. 79; Shaw, Zool. iv, p. 616, t. 89.

Mullus seraunletus, Russell, ii, p. 43, fig. 158 (*Bandi goolivinda*).

Mullus subvittatus, Schleg. Fauna Japon. Poiss. p. 30.

Upeneus vittatus, Cuv. and Val. iii, p. 448; Rüppell, N. W. Fische, p. 101; Bleeker, Révis. Mull. p. 6.

Upeneus bitæniatus, Bennett. Proc. Zool. Soc. 1830-31, p. 59.

Upeneoides vittatus, Bleeker, Amb. p. 42; Günther, Catal. i, p. 397; Day, Fish. Malabar, p. 27; Kner, Novara Fische, p. 67; Klunz. Verh. z. b. Ges. Wien, 1870, p. 742.

Cheerul, Mal.: *Chak-ti-ing-ul-dah*, Andam.

B. iv, D. 8 | $\frac{1}{8}$, P. 15-17, V. 1/5, A. $\frac{1}{6}$, C. 15, L. l. 38-39, L. tr. $2\frac{1}{2}$-3/7, Cæc. pyl. 11, Vert. 7/17.

Length of head 4/17, of caudal 1/5, height of body 4/17 to 2/9 of the total length. *Eyes*—diameter $3\frac{1}{2}$ to $3\frac{3}{4}$ of length of head, $1\frac{1}{2}$ diameters from end of snout, and 1 apart. Interorbital space nearly flat. The maxilla reaches to below the first third of the orbit. Barbels to below the angle of the preopercle or even beyond. *Teeth*—in several villiform rows in both jaws and palatines, and in a single one on the vomer. *Fins*—spines of first dorsal weak, its first one minute, the second and third of nearly the same length, and equal to two-thirds of the height of the body, and 1/3 higher than the second dorsal: six rows of scales between the two dorsal fins; origin of anal below the third or fourth dorsal ray, its spine minute; ventrals reach rather above half-way to the anus: caudal somewhat deeply forked. *Scales*—ctenoid, extending over the head to the snout, none on the preorbital bone: two rows between lateral-line and first dorsal fin, and three between it and the second: those along the median line of the abdomen with a dull keel along their centres. *Lateral-line*—in an arborescent form on each scale, especially anteriorly. *Air-vessel*—present. *Colours*—chestnut on the back; golden below. Two or three bright yellow longitudinal bands along the sides: first dorsal fins black-edged and with two blackish bands; pectoral pinkish edged with white: upper caudal lobe crossed by six yellowish-brown bars having dark edges and a black tip, whilst on the lower lobe there are three oblique dark bars and a white tip.

Habitat.—Red Sea, East coast of Africa, seas of India, to the Malay Archipelago and beyond.

2. Upeneoides sulphureus, Plate XXX, fig. 3.

Upeneus sulphureus, Cuv. and Val. iii, p. 450; Bleeker, Révis. Mull. p. 4.

Upeneus bivittatus, Cuv. and Val. vii, p. 520.

Hypeneus vittatus, var. Cantor, Catal. p. 35.

Upeneoides bivittatus, Bleeker, Perr. p. 64 (in part); Day, Proc. Zool. Soc. 1867, p. 702 (variety).

Upeneoides sulphureus, Bleeker, Act. Soc. Ned. ii, Amboina, p. 45; Günther, Catal. i, p. 398; Kner, Novara Fische, p. 67.

Upeneoides fasciolatus, Day, Proc. Zool. Soc. 1868, p. 151.

B. iv, D. 8 | $\frac{1}{8}$, P. 15, V. 1/5, A. 7, C. 15, L. l. 35-38, L. tr. $2\frac{1}{2}$/7.

Length of head 1/4 to 5/21, of caudal 1/6, height of body $4\frac{1}{2}$ to 2/9 of the total length. *Eyes*—diameter 2/7 to 4/15 of length of head, $1\frac{1}{4}$ diameter from end of snout, and 1 apart. The maxilla reaches to below the first third of the orbit. Interorbital space nearly flat. Barbels reach to opposite the posterior edge of the orbit in the young, but to nearly below the angle of the preopercle in the adult. *Teeth*—in several villiform rows in both jaws, in an uninterrupted semilunar band on the vomer, and also present on the palate. *Fins*—first dorsal spine very small, the third a little longer than the second or the fourth, and 3/4 the height of the body below it: six rows of scales between the two dorsal fins: second dorsal 2/3 as high as the spinous: origin of anal below the second or third dorsal ray: ventrals reach rather above half-way to the anus: caudal rather deeply forked. *Scales*—ctenoid, on the head extending as far forwards as the snout, none on the preorbital bone. *Lateral-line*—tubes in an arborescent form on each scale. *Air-vessel*—absent. *Colours*—of a reddish-chestnut on the back, becoming silvery on the abdomen which in the adult is shaded with yellow. A purplish blotch on the opercle descending on to the subopercle. A brilliant golden stripe, two-thirds as wide as a scale, passes from the orbit to the upper third of the tail, there are generally two or three more below and parallel with it, and in the larger specimens a light band passes along the row of scales above the lateral-line. First dorsal milk-white edged with black, having two horizontal yellow lines finely dotted with black: second dorsal with only one band: caudal reddish, with a black white-edged margin. In some specimens I have found the caudal with bands much as in *U. vittatus*, but fewer in number and lighter in shade. They possessed no air-vessel.

A species much similar exists in Madras, differing in that the eye is a little smaller, the maxilla reaches to below the front edge of the orbit: preorbital scaled. A few villiform teeth on the vomer, some also on the palate. *Fins*—second and third dorsal spines as high as the body. No band or marks on the fins. A female specimen full of roe a little above $6\frac{1}{10}$ inches long was captured in December, 1867.

Habitat.—Seas of India to the Malay Archipelago, attaining at least 5 inches in length.

3. Upeneoides cæruleus.

Day, Proc. Zool. Soc. 1868, p. 194.

B. iv, D. 7-8/9, P. 15, V. 1/5, A. 7, C. 15, L. l. 32-34, L. tr. $2\frac{1}{2}$/7.

Length of head 2/9 to 1/5, of caudal 1/6, height of body 2/9 to 1/4 of the total length. *Eyes*—diameter 2/7 of length of head, 1 diameter from end of snout, and also apart. The maxilla reaches to below the first third of the eye. Interorbital space flat. Opercle with two spines. Barbels do not reach so far as to below the angle of the preopercle. *Teeth*—in fine villiform rows in both jaws, in a single row on the vomer and palate. *Fins*—the first spine of the dorsal fin is minute or wanting, the longest equals the length of the head behind the middle of the eye, or two-thirds of that of the body below it: seven or eight rows of scales between the two dorsal fins: ventral reaches about half way to the anus, but is not quite so long as the pectoral: caudal forked. *Scales*—finely ctenoid, none on the preorbital bone. *Lateral-line*—the tubes are rather long and bifurcate in the first portion of the lateral-line, the branches subsequently are short and mostly spring from its upper side. *Air-vessel*—present. *Colours*—leaden colour superiorly, becoming dirty white below. First dorsal with a black tip, a whitish band along its centre and a badly marked one at its base: second dorsal dark with a light band along its centre: extremities of caudal stained with black and a band across the upper lobe: pectoral, ventral and anal yellowish.

Considering the time of year at which all the specimens have been captured and their small size, it is not improbable that they are the young of a larger species, as *U. vittatus*.

Habitat.—Madras, to 4 inches in length, most common during the months of June and July.

4. Upeneoides tragula, Plate XXX, fig. 4.

Upeneus tragula, Richardson, Ich. China, p. 220; Bleeker, Révis. Mull. p. 11.
Upeneoides variegatus, Bleeker, Perc. p. 64, and Act. Soc. Ned. ii, Amboina, p. 48.
Upeneoides tragula, Günther, Catal. i, p. 398; Kner, Novara Fische, p. 66.
Mullus tragula, Playfair, Fish. Zanz. p. 40.

B. iv, D. 7-8/$\frac{1}{8}$, P. 13, V. 1/5, A. $\frac{1}{6}$, C. 15, L. l. 30-32, L. tr. 2/7, Cæc. pyl. 6.

Length of head 2/9 to $4\frac{1}{3}$, of caudal 1/5, height of body 1/5 to 4/17 of the total length. *Eyes*—diameter 4/15 to 1/4 of the length of head, $1\frac{1}{2}$ diameters from end of snout, and 1 apart. The maxilla reaches to beneath the first third of the eye. Snout rather obtuse anteriorly. A strong preopercular spine, a smaller one at the shoulder just below the commencement of the lateral-line. Barbels reach to opposite the hind edge of the preopercle. *Teeth*—villiform in jaws, vomer, and palate. *Fins*—first spine of the dorsal fin minute or even absent. first dorsal very little higher than the second: anal commences slightly behind the origin of the second dorsal. *Scales*—ctenoid, covering snout and preorbital bone: two entire rows between the lateral-line and bases of the dorsal fin: some over forepart of dorsal and anal fins: four rows between the two dorsal fins. *Colours*—silvery, head and body spotted with brown, a brown longitudinal band passes from the eye through the snout to the base of the caudal fin: dorsal fin with dark, almost black, bands: each caudal lobe with five or six oblique black bars.

Habitat.—East coast of Africa, Andamans to the Malay Archipelago, attaining at least $4\frac{1}{2}$ inches in length. The specimen figured is from the Andaman islands.

5. Upeneoides bensasi, Plate XXX, fig. 5.

Mullus bensasi, Tem. and Schleg. Faun. Japon. Poissons, p. 30, pl. xi, f. 3.
Upeneoides bensasi, Bleeker, Verh. Bat. Gen. xxvi, Japan, p. 71; Günther, Catal. i, p. 399.
Upeneoides guttatus, Day, Proc. Zool. Soc. 1867, p. 938.
Upeneoides tragula, Günther, Zool. Record, 1867, p. 160 (not Richardson).

B. iv, D. 7/$\frac{1}{8}$, P. 15, V. 1/5, A. $\frac{1}{6}$, C. 15, L. l. 32-34, L. tr. 2/7.

Length of head from 4/17 to 2/9, of pectoral 2/13, of caudal 1/5, height of body 1/5 to 2/11 of the total length. *Eyes*—diameter from $4\frac{1}{4}$ to $4\frac{1}{2}$ in length of head, nearly or quite 2 diameters from end of snout, and $1\frac{1}{2}$ apart. The maxilla extends to beneath the front edge of the orbit. The barbels reach to below or rather behind the posterior margin of the preopercle. Preopercular spine small. Interorbital space nearly flat. *Teeth*—villiform in either jaw, in vomer, and palate. *Fins*—four rows of scales between the two dorsals, the first of which fins is higher than the second, the longest dorsal spine is two-thirds the height of the body below it and 1/3 more than the second dorsal: caudal forked. *Scales*—ctenoid. Two entire rows between the lateral-line and the bases of either dorsal fin. The central row along the median line of the abdomen with a blunt keel: scales on preorbital. *Lateral-line*—the tubules are very arborescent posteriorly, especially on their upper side. *Air-vessel*—absent. Free portion of tail one half longer than high at its base. *Colours*—chestnut along the back, becoming golden on the abdomen: head reddish: a silvery stripe from the eye to the centre of the caudal fin, with a row of red spots above and another below it. Dorsals tipped with black and having two reddish bands across them: caudal reddish, the upper lobe having four oblique chestnut bars. Pectorals, ventrals, and anal yellow.

Jerdon observes (M. J. L. and S. 1851, p. 141) of the sea fishes of Madras, "I have common drawings of two other species of this genus, one of them spotted all over with small red spots, and dorsals and caudal barred with the same, called *Te urere*, Tam. 4 inches long."

Habitat.—Madras to the Malay Archipelago. It appears to be abundant all the year round on the Coromandel coast attaining to five inches in length.

6. Upeneoides tæniopterus.

Upeneus tæniopterus, Cuv. and Val. iii, p. 451.

B. iv, D. 7/$\frac{1}{8}$, P. 15, V. 1/5, A. 7, L. l. 38, L. tr. 3/7, Cæc. pyl. 2.

Length of head, of caudal and height of body each 4/19 of the total length. *Eyes*—diameter 2/9 of length of head, $1\frac{2}{3}$ diameters from end of snout, and $1\frac{1}{3}$ apart. Interorbital space flat, a very slight rise from snout to the base of the first dorsal fin, a slight swelling over the snout in front of the eye. Opercular spine weak. Barbels reach to below the first third of orbit. *Teeth*—villiform in jaws, vomer and palate. *Fins*—first spine of the dorsal fin the highest and equal to two-thirds of the height of the body, the second very nearly as long: six rows of scales between the bases of the two dorsal fins: pectoral equal in length to the first dorsal spine: caudal deeply forked. *Lateral-line*—the tubes very arborescent posteriorly. *Air-vessel*—large. *Colours*—back reddish, becoming white on the abdomen. A large triangular reddish spot said to have existed on the free portion of the tail but not now apparent. First dorsal fin with three brownish longitudinal bands, second dorsal likewise banded: caudal with six oblique streaks across either lobe.

Habitat.—Ceylon to Australia, attaining at least 12 inches in length. The description is taken from Val.'s type specimen in the Jardin des Plantes at Paris.

Genus, 2—Mulloides, *Bleeker.*

Upeneus, sp. Cuv. and Val.

Definition as in the family, except that the teeth in the jaws are in several rows: palate edentulous.

Geographical distribution.—From the Red Sea and East coast of Africa, through the seas of India to the Malay Archipelago and beyond.

SYNOPSIS OF INDIVIDUAL SPECIES.

1. *Mulloides flavolineatus*, D. 7/$\frac{1}{8}$, A. 7, L. l. 36-37. Barbels thick and reach the hind edge of preopercle. A yellow band from eye to middle of base of caudal. From Red Sea, through those of India to the Malay Archipelago and beyond.

1. Mulloides flavolineatus, Plate XXX, fig. 6.

? *Mullus auriflamma*, Forsk. p. 30; Gmel. Linn. p. 1340; Bl. Schn. p. 79.

Mullus flavolineatus, Lacép. iii. p. 406.

Mullus aureovittatus, Shaw, Zool. iv, p. 618.

Upeneus flavolineatus, Cuv. and Val. iii, p. 456; Rüpp. N. W. Fische, p. 101, t. 26, f. 1; Jenyns, Voy. Beagle, Fishes, p. 24.

Upeneus Zeylonicus, Cuv. and Val. iii, p. 459, and vii, p. 520.

Upeneus auriflamma, Cuv. and Val. iii, p. 461.

? *Hypeneus flavolineatus*, var. Cantor, Catal. p. 36.

Mulloides flavolineatus, Bleeker, Cerum. ii, p. 697, and Révis. Mull. p. 15; Günther, Catal. i, p. 403, and Fische d. Sudsee, p. 56; Kner, Novara Fische, p. 69 (not syn.).

Mulloides Zeylanicus, Bleeker, Nieuw-Guinea, p. 8, and Révis. Mull. p. 16; Günther, Catal. i, p. 404.

Mulloides auriflamma, Klunz.* Fische d. roth. Meer. Verh. z. b. Ges. Wien, 1870, p. 742.

B. iv, D. 7/$\frac{1}{8}$, P. 17-19, V. 1/5, A. $\frac{1}{6}$, C. 15, L. l. 35-36, L. tr. 2/6, Cæc. pyl. 18.

Length of head 3/13, of caudal from 2/9 to 1/5, height of body from 4/21 to 1/5 of the total length. *Eyes*—diameter $3\frac{1}{2}$ to 1/4 in length of head, $1\frac{1}{2}$ of a diameter from end of snout, and 1 apart. The maxilla reaches two-thirds of the distance to below the front edge of the orbit. Interorbital space flat. The barbels, which are thick, extend to opposite or rather posterior to the hind margin of the preopercle. Opercular spine rather weak. Snout somewhat compressed and pointed. *Teeth*—in villiform bands in jaws. *Fins*—first three dorsal spines of about the same length and equal to three-fourths of the height of the body. Five rows of scales between the two dorsal fins. Second dorsal anteriorly half to two-thirds as high as the first, its last rays only half as long as its front ones. The length of the pectoral equals that of the head in front of the hind edge

* Bleeker considers *Mulloides ruber*, Klunz. l. c. p. 75 this species: in Garrett's Fische d. Sudsee, t. 43, f. A, is a figure of Klunzinger's species life-size, showing about 40 rows of scales along the lateral-line. Gunther gives it at 42-43.

of the orbit. Anal of the same shape as the second dorsal, its first spine minute: it commences slightly behind the origin of the second dorsal. Caudal deeply forked, its lobes pointed. Free portion of the tail $1\frac{1}{2}$ times as long as it is high at its commencement. *Scales*—ctenoid, extending as far forwards as the snout, none on the preorbital bone: three rows on the cheeks, also between the lateral-line and the base of the second dorsal fin. *Lateral-line*—tubes very arborescent, especially anteriorly. *Air-vessel*—large. *Colours*—upper surface of the head and back reddish-chestnut, becoming whitish along the sides, and tinged with yellow on the abdomen. A narrow yellow band from the upper edge of the eye to the snout, and a second from below the eye joins it. A brilliant golden band, rather above one scale in width, passes from the hind edge of the eye to the middle of the base of the caudal fin. Fins flesh-coloured, a yellow band along the base of the second dorsal: lower lobe of caudal grey.

Having examined Val.'s type of *Upeneus Zeylonicus* I consider it to be this species.

Habitat.—Red Sea, through those of India to the Malay Archipelago and beyond. The specimen figured is 10 inches long and from the Andamans.

Genus, 3—Upeneus, (*Cuv. and Val. pt.*) *Bleeker*.

Mullupeneus, Poey; *Parupeneus*, Bleeker (1874).

Definition as in the family, except that only a single row of teeth exists in either jaw, whilst the palate is edentulous.

Geographical distribution.—From the Red Sea and East coast of Africa, through the seas of India to the Malay Archipelago and beyond.

1. *Upeneus macronemus*, D. 8/9, A. 7, L. l. 29-30. Last dorsal and anal rays produced. A black band from the eye to below the end of the soft dorsal, a black blotch at the base of the caudal: a deep black band along the base of the second dorsal: ventral blackish externally. Red Sea, through those of India to the Malay Archipelago and beyond.

2. *Upeneus barberinus*, D. 8/9, A. 7, L. l. 29-31. Last dorsal and anal rays not produced. A black lateral band from the eye to below the end of the soft dorsal: a black spot at the base of the caudal: in some specimens a dark band along the base of the second dorsal. Red Sea, those of India to the Malay Archipelago and beyond.

3. *Upeneus multifasciatus*, D. 8/9, A. 7, L. l. 30-32. A dark vertical band from below the second dorsal to the lateral-line: a second over the free portion of the tail. A black band along the base of the second dorsal: dark lines on the anal. Seas of India to Polynesia.

4. *Upeneus luteus*, D. 8/9, A. 7, L. l. 30. Eyes, diameter $6\frac{1}{2}$ in length of head. Light lines about the head: golden spots on many of the scales: second dorsal and anal with three to five longitudinal lines. East coast of Africa through the seas of India.

5. *Upeneus dispilurus*, D. 8/9, A. $\frac{1}{7}$, L. l. 29. Eyes, diameter $4\frac{2}{3}$ in length of head. Some light lines upon the head and golden spots on most of the scales of the body. Second dorsal and anal with narrow bands: caudal reticulated. Coasts of Sind.

6. *Upeneus Indicus*, D. 8/9, A. $\frac{1}{7}$, L. l. 30. Purplish-red, with a large oval shining golden blotch on the lateral-line opposite the interspace between the two dorsal fins; a purplish-black mark on the side of the free portion of the tail. Seas of India to China.

7. *Upeneus cinnabarinus.* Red vermilion: upper caudal lobe orange, lower red. A large purplish blotch over the opercle and subopercle. Ceylon.

1. Upeneus macronemus, Plate XXXI, fig. 1.

Mullus macronemus, Lacép. iii, pp. 383, 404, pl. 13, f. 2.
Mullus auriflamma, Lacép. iii, p. 406, pl. 13, f. 1 (not Forsk.).
Upeneus lateristriga, Cuv. and Val. iii, p. 463; Rüppell, N. W. Fische, p. 101; Bleeker, Celebes, p. 242.
Upeneus macronemus, Bleeker, En. Pisces, Arch. Ind. p. 37; Günther, Catal. i, p. 405; Klunz. Fische d. roth. Meer, p. 744.
Mullus macronemus, Playfair, Fish. Zanz. p. 40.
Parupeneus macronemus, Bleeker, Amboina, p. 281, and Révis. Mull. p. 24.

B. iv, D. 8/9, P. 16, V. 1/5, A. 7, C. 15, L. l. 29-30, L. tr. $2\frac{1}{2}$/7.

Length of head 3/11 to 1/4, of caudal 1/5, height of body 1/4 to $4\frac{2}{3}$ in the total length. *Eyes*—diameter 1/5 of length of head, $2\frac{1}{2}$ diameters from end of snout, and $1\frac{1}{2}$ apart. Greatest height of head equals its length excluding the opercle. The maxilla reaches two-thirds of the distance to below the front edge of the eye. Lips thick. Interorbital space rather convex. Opercular spine rather strong. Barbels reach to nearly opposite the hind edge of the opercle. *Teeth*—in a single row in both jaws. *Fins*—first spine of dorsal short, the third and fourth equal the length of the head in front of the hind edge of the orbit, and nearly or quite twice as high as the anterior dorsal rays: last dorsal and anal rays very elongated: ventral a little longer than the pectoral: caudal forked. *Scales*—finely ctenoid, present on the snout, maxilla and cheeks, not on the preorbital: three rows between the two dorsal fins, and two entire ones between the lateral-line and the bases of the dorsal fins. No enlarged pores on the snout. *Lateral-line*—with several short bifurcations posteriorly. Free portion of tail longer than high at its commencement. *Colours*—a black band passes from the snout through the eye, at first just below the lateral-line, subsequently upon it, and ending below the end of the soft dorsal, it is 1½ scales in depth at its widest part: a black blotch at the base of the caudal fin, these two marks are divided by a light oblique vertical band which passes over the free portion of the tail just behind the second dorsal fin: some golden spots exist on the scales along the sides of the body. A purplish stripe goes from the eye to the snout. First dorsal violet, second dorsal with a deep black band along its base, it has several irregular transverse lines along its upper half: pectoral with a dark base: ventral blackish externally, reticulated internally: anal with narrow transverse lines as in the upper half of the soft dorsal, but of a violet colour: caudal with a black edging.

A specimen in the Calcutta Museum has on it an old label with *Apogon Amherstianus*. It was probably brought from Amherst by Blyth, but I am unable to find any record of the name having been published.

Habitat.—Red Sea, those of India to the Malay Archipelago and beyond, attaining at least 8½ inches in length.

2. Upeneus barberinus.

Mullus barberinus, Lacép. iii, p. 406, pl. 13, f. 3.

Upeneus barberinus, Cuv. and Val. iii, p. 642; Rüpp. N. W. Fische, p. 101; Bleeker, Perc. p. 172; Günther, Catal. i, p. 405; Kner, Novara Fische, p. 70; Klunz. Fische d. roth. Meer. Verh. zool. bot. Ges. Wien, 1870, p. 745; Garrett, Fische d. Sudsee, t. 42.

Parupeneus barberinus, Bleeker, Ternate, p. 234, and Révis. Mull. p. 25.

B. iv, D. 8/9, P. 18, V. 1/5, A. 7, C. 15, L. l. 29-31, L. tr. 2½/7.

Length of head 2/7 to 1/4, of caudal 1/5, height of body 2/9 to 1/5 of the total length. *Eyes*—diameter 2/11 of length of head, 3 diameters from end of snout, and 1½ apart. The maxilla reaches to nearly midway between the end of the snout and the front edge of the eye. Opercular spine rather strong. Barbels reach to rather beyond the vertical from the angle of the preopercle. *Teeth*—in a single row of moderately sized ones in the jaws. *Fins*—first spine of dorsal fin very short, the third, sometimes also the fourth, the highest and equalling the length of the head in front of the hind edge of the orbit, in a large specimen rather more, and about twice the height of anterior dorsal rays: second dorsal fin not having its last rays prolonged: pectoral nearly as long as the longest dorsal spine and equal to the ventral: caudal forked. *Scales*—finely ctenoid, present on snout and cheeks but none on the preorbital bone. Three rows between the two dorsal fins, and two entire ones between the lateral-line and bases of the dorsal fins. *Lateral-line*—tubules with several rather long bifurcations posteriorly. Free portion of tail longer than high at its base. *Colours*—a black band passes from the eye along the lateral-line and from below the middle of the second dorsal it becomes above that line ending 2/3 of a scale above it below the end of the second dorsal: a round black spot at the root of the caudal. In some specimens there is a darkish band along the dorsal fins.

The similarity between this species and *U. macronemus* is so great that I have not considered it necessary to figure both. In *U. barberinus* the bands, especially on the fins, are much lighter, and the last dorsal and anal rays not elongated as in *U. macronemus*. Both are abundant at the Andamans, and I would suggest an examination of their sexes and the number of cæcal appendages in either sex.

Habitat.—Red Sea, through those of India, to the Malay Archipelago and beyond, attaining at least 12 inches in length.

3. Upeneus multifasciatus.

Mullus multifasciatus, Quoy and Gaim. Voy. Uranie, p. 330, Atl. t. lix, f. 1.

Upeneus trifasciatus, Cuv. and Val. iii, p. 468; Jenyns, Voy. Beagle, Fish. p. 25; Bleeker, Banda, p. 237; Günther, Catal. i, p. 407 (Synonym. in part); Kner, Novara Fische, 71; Garrett's Fische d. Sudsee, pl. 44, B.C.

Parupeneus multifasciatus, Bleeker, Madagascar, p. 42, t. xix, f. 3.

B. iv, D. 8/9, P. 17, V. 1/5, A. 7, C. 15, L. l. 30-32, L. tr. 2½/7, Vert. 10/14.

Length of head 1/4 to 4/15, of caudal 4¾ to 1/5, height of body 1/4 to 4½ in the total length. *Eyes*—diameter 1/5 to 1/6 of length of head, 3½ diameters from end of snout, and 1½ apart. Interorbital space very convex, no open pores on preorbital bone. The maxilla, which is very broad posteriorly, reaches a little above half way to below the orbit. Barbels extend 1 diameter of the orbit behind the posterior edge of the preopercle. *Teeth*—in a single conical row in the jaws. *Fins*—first spine of dorsal minute, third the longest and equal to the length of the head in front of the middle of the eye, and twice as high as the anterior dorsal rays: three rows of scales between the bases of the two dorsal fins. Pectoral as long as the head anterior to the hind edge of the eye: anal commences on the vertical below the third or fourth dorsal ray, it is usually longer at its base than it is high, but in a beautiful figure of this species in Bleeker's Madagascar, l. c. the last dorsal ray is elongated: ventral reaches the anus: caudal forked. *Scales*—ctenoid, present on the snout, cheeks and upper jaw, but not on the preorbital bone: 2½ rows between the lateral-line and the bases of the dorsal fins. *Lateral-line*—tubes arborescent posteriorly. Free portion of tail somewhat longer than it is high at its base. *Colours*—purplish, a black horizontal band usually exists on the snout, and is continued through the eye sometimes to a good distance behind it. Two or three wide black bands descend from the two dorsal fins or the interspace between them to the middle of the body, their number may be decreased by their amalgamating into one, or increased by their being split up into several. There is usually a third band over the free portion of the tail or a spot on the side of its base. Second dorsal, anal, and sometimes the outer half of the ventral finely banded, occasionally a dark basal band exists on the second dorsal.

Habitat.—Seas of India, to the Malay Archipelago and beyond.

4. **Upeneus luteus**, Plate XXXI, fig. 2.

Upeneus luteus (? Cuv. and Val. vii, p. 521); Bleeker, Perc. p. 63.

Upeneus cyclostoma, Günther, Catal. i, p. 409 (not Cuv. and Val.); (? Klunz. Fische R. M. Verh. z. b. Ges. Wien, 1870, p. 745.)

Mullus luteus, Playfair, Fish. Zanz. p. 41.

Parupeneus luteus, Bleeker, Amb. p. 281, and Révis. Mull. p. 32.

B. iv, D. 8/9, P. 15, V. 1/5, A. 7, C. 15, L. l. 30, L. tr. 2/7.

Length of head 1/4, of caudal 1/5, height of body 1/4 of the total length. *Eyes*—diameter $6\frac{1}{2}$ in the length of the head, $3\frac{1}{2}$ diameters from the end of snout, and $1\frac{1}{2}$ apart. Height of head nearly equals its length. Interorbital space a little convex: the profile from the snout to the base of the first dorsal fin is in a moderate and even curve. No open pores on the preorbital. The maxilla reaches to about midway between the snout and the hind margin of the orbit. Barbels with roughened elevations along their whole length and extending to a little behind the posterior edge of the preopercle. Opercular spine of moderate size. *Teeth*—a single row of conical ones in either jaw. *Fins*—first spine of dorsal minute, the third and fourth the longest and equal to $1\frac{1}{2}$ in the height of the body and nearly twice as high as the anterior dorsal rays: three rows of scales between the bases of the two dorsal fins: pectoral three-fourths as long as the head: caudal deeply forked, the lobes pointed. *Scales*—ctenoid, present on snout, maxilla and cheeks, none on the preorbital bone. Two entire rows between the lateral-line and the bases of the dorsal fins. *Lateral-line*—the branches of the tubes very short but numerous. Free portion of tail rather longer than high at its base. *Colours*—reddish, the edges of the scales somewhat the darkest. A broad purplish band, having a light yellow edge on either side, goes from below and in front of the eye to the snout: the lower band is continued backwards across the upper edge of the opercle where it joins another from the lower edge of the eye: a third narrow yellow band goes from the upper edge of the eye backwards. Outer edge of preopercle purplish. The centre of each scale on the body, except the first thirteen of the lateral-line, has a golden spot: abdomen yellowish. Second dorsal and anal with from three to five bluish longitudinal lines.

This species very nearly resembles the figure of *U. Vlamingii*, C. V. iii, pl. 71, but has its second dorsal much lower.

Habitat.—East coast of Africa and seas of India, attaining at least a foot in length. Specimen 12 inches long.

5. **Upeneus displurus**, Plate XXXI, fig. 3.

Mullus displurus, Playfair, Fish. Zanzibar, p. 41, pl. v, fig. 4 (not 3) adult.

Mullus pleurotænia, Playfair, l. c. fig. 3 (not 4) young.

B. iv, D. 8/9, P. 15, V. 1/5, A. 1/7, C. 16, L. l. 31, L. tr. 2-$2\frac{1}{2}$/7.

Length of head $3\frac{3}{4}$ to almost 1/4, of caudal 1/5, height of body 2/9 to $4\frac{2}{3}$ in the total length. *Eyes*—diameter 3/14 to 1/5 of length of head, $1\frac{1}{3}$ to $1\frac{1}{2}$ in the postorbital portion of the head, $2\frac{1}{3}$ to $2\frac{1}{2}$ from end of snout, and $1\frac{1}{4}$ apart. Snout pointed, compressed. The maxilla reaches to rather more than half way below the front edge of the orbit. Barbels extend to below the hind margin of the preopercle. Interorbital space slightly convex: opercular spine of moderate strength. *Fins*—fourth dorsal spine rather the longest and equal to three-fourths of the height of the body below it: three rows of scales between the two dorsal fins: front portion of the second dorsal equals two-thirds the height of the first dorsal: pectoral as long as the head anterior to the hind edge of the orbit: anal commences slightly behind the origin of the second dorsal: caudal deeply forked and the lobes pointed. *Scales*—on snout and head including most of the preorbital bone: the uncovered portion has some rather large pores. *Colours*—reddish, the edges of the scales being slightly darkest. A broad purplish band, having a light silvery edge, passes from in front of the eye to the snout: two more narrow silvery lines, formed of short oblong spots, proceed from hind edge of orbit for a short distance: the two rows above the lateral-line, and generally the three below, have a golden-yellow spot in the centre of each scale: a light golden band over the free portion of the tail. First dorsal marbled with brown, the second with four and the anal with three reddish bands: caudal reticulated with light grey markings. Specimens from the East coast of Africa are said to have two shining light longitudinal bands, the first from the orbit to the middle of the soft dorsal, and the second, which is broader, from the upper lip to the middle of the back.

Some confusion appears to have occurred respecting Colonel Playfair's two species, the markings stated to exist on the fins of *pleurotænia* are shown on those of *displurus* by the artist. In the type specimens I am unable to trace any spots on the fins, whilst the two shining longitudinal bands are very distinct, but they are also slightly apparent in the large specimen. Also the dark band over the tail is present in the smaller specimens as well as in the large one. The situation of the eyes as shown by the artist appear to me to be correct although at variance with the text.

If the foregoing species are merely to be recognised by their markings, then the one I procured in Sind, where it is abundant, can hardly be more than another form of colouring, consequently those who hold the *displurus* and *pleurotænia* to be distinct, would probably consider this as a separate species.

Habitat.—Sind, where it attains at least 9¼ inches in length, probably also found in East Africa. The specimen figured is 8¾ inches long.

6. Upeneus Indicus, Plate XXXI, fig. 4.

Mullus Indicus, Shaw, Zool. iv, pt. ii, p. 614.
Mullus barbatus, Russell, ii, p. 42, pl. 157 (not Linn.).
Upeneus Russellii, Cuv. and Val. iii, p. 465; Richards. Ich. China, p. 220; Bleeker, Perc. p. 62.
Upeneus Waigiensis, Cuv. and Val. iii, p. 466.
Upeneus Malabaricus, Cuv. and Val. iii, p. 467; Günther, Catal. i, p. 407, and Fische d. Sudsee, p. 58, pl. xlv, f. B.
Upeneus Indicus, Günther, Catal. i, p. 406; Day, Fishes of Malabar, p. 28.
Parupeneus Russellii, Bleeker, Ternate, p. 234.
Mullus Malabaricus, Playfair, Fish. Zanz. p. 41.
Parupeneus Indicus, Bleeker, Bouro, p. 148, and Révis. Mull. p. 27.
Rahtee goolivinda, Tel.: *Mussara*, Tam.

B. iv, D. 8/9, P. 16, V. 1/5, A. 1/7, C. 15, L. l. 30, L. tr. 2½/7.

Length of head from 4/15 to 1/4, of caudal 1/5 to 3/16, height of body 4/15 to 1/4 of the total length. *Eyes*—situated in the anterior portion of the posterior half of the head, or even a little behind it, and from 2/11 to 2/13 (larger in the young) of its length, 1¼ diameters apart. Snout somewhat pointed. The maxilla reaches rather more than half way to below the front edge of the orbit. Interorbital space more or less convex. Barbels reach to beyond the angle of the preopercle. Opercular spines small. *Teeth*—generic. *Fins*—first spine of anterior dorsal minute, the third and fourth the longest, 1/2 higher than the rays, and equalling three-fourths of the height of the body. Pectoral as long as the head in front of the hind edge of orbit: anal commences slightly behind the level of the second dorsal and is as high as it: caudal deeply forked, the lobes pointed. *Scales*—finely ctenoid, extending on the head as far forwards as the snout, but none on the preorbital bone: two entire rows between the lateral-line and the bases of either dorsal fins. Free portion of the tail longer than high at its commencement. *Lateral-line*—tubes becoming very arborescent posteriorly. *Air-vessel*—present. *Colours*—purplish-red, with a large oval shining golden blotch on the lateral-line opposite the interspace between the two dorsal fins, which usually disappears after death; a purplish-black mark, lightest in its centre, on either side of the free portion of the tail between the end of the dorsal and the base of the caudal fins: yellow lines or spots on the abdomen. Some light violet lines on the upper surface of the head. A broad purple band from the eye to the snout, having a narrow violet one on either side: cheeks pink, variegated with yellow and tortuous blue lines: a dark spot at the corner of the mouth. Dorsal purplish streaked with blue: a few yellow bands on anal, fins pinkish except the caudal, which has the rays purplish, but the membrane has a greenish tinge.

Amongst Sir W. Elliot's drawings is one of this species labelled *Upeneus Russellii* and *Kul nuceri*, Tam. Jerdon observes, M. J. L. and Sc. 1851, p. 140: "this very beautiful fish is rarely met with at Madras": Russell also made much the same remark—however, I have frequently obtained it there.

The species I considered *U. spilurus* from the Andamans I find to be *U. Indicus*: the *U. Malabaricus* has been considered to differ in wanting the spine to the anal fin and thus having only seven rays.

Habitat.—Red Sea, East coast of Africa, seas of India to the Malay Archipelago and beyond, attaining at least 16 inches in length.

7. Upeneus cinnabarinus.

Cuv. and Val. iii, p. 475.

B. iv, D. 8/9, P. 15, V. 1/5, A. 7, C. 15, L. l. 29, L. tr. 3/7.

Length of head 1/4, of caudal 1/5, height of body 4/17 of the total length. *Eyes*—diameter 1/4 of length of head, nearly 2 diameters from end of snout, and 1 apart. The dorsal profile makes a considerable rise from the snout to above the centre of the eyes. The maxilla reaches to below the front edge of the orbit. A rather strong opercular spine. Barbels rather thick and reach to below the front edge of the orbit. *Teeth*—conical and in a single row in either jaw. *Fins*—first spine of dorsal fin short, the second not quite so long as the third which equals rather above one-third of the height of the body below it: the pectoral as long as the head posterior to the front nostril: caudal deeply forked. *Scales*—three rows between the two dorsal fins. *Lateral-line*—the tubes very arborescent posteriorly. *Air-vessel*—small. *Colours*—of a vermilion, darkest on the back, now there appears to be a central silvery spot in the middle of each scale forming the two rows above and the two below the lateral-line. Dorsal and anal rays yellow, the membrane reddish: upper caudal lobe orange, the lower one red. A large purple spot covers the opercle and descends on to the subopercle. Barbels rosy.

Habitat.—Ceylon, where it is said to be abundant. The above description is taken from Valenciennes' type specimen in the Jardin des Plantes at Paris.

FAMILY, IV—NANDIDÆ, *Günther.*

Pseudochromoides, pt., et *Mænoidei*, pt. Müll. & Trosch.

Branchiostegals from five to six: pseudobranchiæ present in marine genera, but sometimes concealed or absent in those of the fresh-water. Body oblong and compressed. Teeth feeble, but dentition more or less complete. Dorsal fin single: the length of the base of the spinous portion of greater or equal extent to that of the soft: anal with three spines, its rays similar to those of the dorsal: ventrals thoracic, with one spine and four or five rays. Scales ctenoid, covering the body. Lateral line interrupted or absent. No super-branchial organ. Air-vessel present. Pyloric appendages few or absent.

Dr. Günther's family *Nandidæ* is composed of three groups, his *Nandina* being similar to *Nandoïdes*, Bleeker, containing the Genera *Nandus*, C.V., *Badis*, Bleeker, and *Pristolepis*, Jerdon = *Catopra*, Bleeker, which Bleeker observes belong to the great Family *Percidæ*.* Thus restricted, this small group would find a natural place between the *Centrarchini (Grystina*, pt.) and the *Osphromenoides (Labyrinthibranchii)* and the *Polycentroïdes*. It also approaches the *Pseudochromidoïdes* and the *Cichloïdes*. The dentition inside its mouth distinguishes it from the groups enumerated.

Geographical distribution.—Of the Asiatic Genera of Family *Nandidæ*, Günther, some are marine, others fresh-water fishes, extending their range from the Red Sea and East coast of Africa, through those of India, the Malay Archipelago and beyond.

The colours in some are liable to considerable variations, due to age, probably season, and the locality they inhabit. The number of spines, rays, and even scales, as in the indigenous fresh-water Acanthopterygian genera, *Ambassis*, *Anabas*, *Polyacanthus* and *Trichogaster* are by no means fixed, a few more or less being of no infrequent occurrence. The same remark applies to the serrations of the bones of the head as they often vary in specimens from different parts, which however can merely allow their being classed as local varieties and not distinct species.

SYNOPSIS OF GENERA.

First group—Plesiopina.

Pseudobranchiæ present: ventral with four rays.

1. *Plesiops.* Pseudobranchiæ. None of the bones of head serrated. Villiform teeth in jaws and palate, none on tongue. The first one or two of the ventral rays elongated and bifid. Red Sea, through those of India to the Malay Archipelago.

Second group—Nandina.

Pseudobranchiæ absent: ventral with five rays.

2. *Badis.* None of the bones of head serrated. Villiform teeth in jaws, palate, root of tongue and roof of cavity of mouth. Fresh waters of India and Burma.
3. *Nandus.* Opercles may be serrated or armed. Villiform teeth in jaws, palate, root of tongue and cavity of mouth. Fresh waters of India and Burma.
4. *Pristolepis.* Opercles serrated or armed. Villiform teeth in jaws and palate, with globular crowns at the root of tongue and roof of cavity of mouth. Fresh waters of India, Burma, Siam to the Malay Archipelago.

First group—Plesiopina.

Pseudobranchiæ present: ventral with four rays.

Genus, 1—PLESIOPS, *Cuv.*

Pharopteryx, Rüpp.

Branchiostegals six; pseudobranchiæ. Body oblong and compressed. Mouth moderately protractile. None of the bones of the head serrated. Villiform teeth on the jaws, vomer, and palatines, none on the tongue. Eleven to twelve spines in the dorsal fin, three in the anal; ventral with one spine and four rays, the outer ones being elongated and bifid. Scales cycloid, of moderate size. Lateral-line interrupted. Air-vessel present. Pyloric appendages absent.

Geographical distribution.—Red Sea, through those of India to the Malay Archipelago.

SYNOPSIS OF INDIVIDUAL SPECIES.

1. *Plesiops nigricans*, D. $\frac{11}{7}$, A. $\frac{3}{8}$, L. l. 23-28. Each scale on the body with a blue central spot: a large

* Dr. Günther's classification is adhered to for reasons stated in note at p. 2.

black blue-edged ocellus on the opercles, a blue line along the dorsal and anal fins which, as well as the caudal, have a light edge; blue spots on soft dorsal, anal and caudal fins. Red Sea, through those of India to the Malay Archipelago.

1. Plesiops nigricans, Plate XXXI, fig. 5.

Pharopteryx nigricans, Rüpp. Atl. p. 15, t. iv, f. 2, and N. W. Fische, p. 5.

Plesiops cœruleo-lineatus, Rüpp. N. W. Fische, p. 5, t. ii, f. 5; Bleeker, Amboina, iii, p. 116; Günther, Catal. iii, p. 363.

Plesiops melas, Bleeker, Verh. Bat. Gen. xxii, Bali, p. 9.

Plesiops corallicola, (K. and v. H.) Bleeker, Sumatra, ii, p. 280; Günther, Catal. iii, p. 364; Day, Proc. Zool. Soc. 1870, p. 685; Kner, Novara Fische, p. 214.

Plesiops nigricans, Günther, Catal. iii, p. 363; Klunz. Verh. z. b. Ges. Wien, 1871, p. 517.

B. vi, D. $\frac{11}{7}$, P. 21, V. 1/4, A. $\frac{3}{8}$, C. 16, L. l. 23-28, L. tr. $2\frac{1}{2}$/10.

Length of head from 4/15 to 1/4, of pectoral 2/11, of caudal 2/9, height of body 2/9 of the total length. *Eyes*—diameter 1/4 to 1/5 of length of head, 3/4 to 1 diameter from end of snout, and 1 apart. Snout obtuse. The maxilla reaches to behind the posterior edge of the orbit. *Teeth*—villiform in the jaws, vomer and palatines, none on the tongue, the outer row of teeth in the upper jaw are usually slightly enlarged. *Fins*—dorsal spines much shorter than the rays, the interspinous membrane (which extends beyond the tips of each spine) deeply emarginate, soft portion of the fin and also of the anal pointed: two outer ventral rays elongated: third anal spine the longest: caudal pointed. *Scales*—finely ctenoid in the last half of the body. *Colours*—brownish, each scale on the body with a blue centre, some of those on the shoulder and head with several blue spots. Opercle with a large black blue-edged ocellus. A blue band along the dorsal and anal fins: dorsal, caudal and anal with a white margin: soft dorsal and anal with blue streaks in the direction of the rays, they are also present on the caudal but in the form of transverse blotches.

Habitat.—From the Red Sea, through those of India to the Malay Archipelago and beyond. It is very common at the Andaman islands, attaining at least 6 inches in length.

Second group—Nandina.

Pseudobranchiæ concealed or absent: palatine and vomerine teeth: ventral with five rays.

Genus, 2—Badis, *Bleeker*.

Branchiostegals six: pseudobranchiæ apparently absent. Eyes lateral. Mouth protractile. Opercle with one sharp spine, none of the other bones of the head armed. Villiform teeth on the jaws, vomer and palatines, absent from the tongue. A single dorsal fin, the spinous portion being of much greater extent than that of the soft: anal with three spines, its rayed portion similar to that of the dorsal. Scales ctenoid, of moderate size. Lateral-line interrupted or absent. Air-vessel large and simple. Pyloric appendages absent.

Geographical distribution.—Fresh waters of the hills and plains of India and Burma.

Hamilton Buchanan observed of his two species of *Badis*, that "the two following species I refer to the genus *Labrus*, although their almost total want of teeth would perhaps require their forming a distinct genus. Notwithstanding the form of their tail fins, they approach nearer the *Labrus malapterus* of Bloch, (*Ichth.* t. ix, p. 26, pl. 296, f. 2) than to any other fish described by that author," p. 70.

SYNOPSIS OF SPECIES.

1. *Badis Buchanani*, D. $\frac{15-17}{7-10}$, A. $\frac{3}{6-7}$, L. l. 26-32 interrupted. Purplish and banded, or irregularly spotted or blotched. Fresh waters of India and Burma.

2. *Badis dario*, D. $\frac{14}{9}$, A. $\frac{3}{7}$, L. l. 26-30 absent. Stone colour, with several dark vertical belts, most being in the posterior half of the body. Bengal, Behar and Western ghauts.

1. Badis Buchanani, Plate XXXI, fig. 6.

Labrus badis, Ham. Buch. Fish. Ganges, pp. 70, 368, pl. 25, fig. 23.

Badis Buchanani, Bleeker, Verh. Bat. Gen. xxv, t. 2, f. 3; Günther, Catal. iii, p. 367.

Kala-poo-ti-ah and *Chiri*, Punj.: *Kundala* and *Ka-sundara*, Tel.: *Kahlee-poee* and *Bundei*, Ooriah: *Nalot* and *Ran-doh-nee*, Assam.: *Pin-lay-nga-ba-mah* and *Nga-mee-loung*, Burm.

B. vi, D. $\frac{16-17}{7-10}$, P. 12, V. 1/5, A. $\frac{3}{6-8}$, C. 16, L. l. 26-32, L. tr. $2\frac{1}{2}$/8.

Length of head 2/9 to 1/5, of pectoral 1/5, of caudal 2/9, height of body $2\frac{1}{4}$ to 2/9, in the variety figured, in the total length. Form of body an elongated oval, sides compressed. *Eyes*—diameter $3\frac{2}{3}$ (3/11) of the length of head, 2/3 of a diameter from end of snout, and 1 apart. The maxilla reaches to below the front edge of the orbit: lower jaw slightly the longer. *Teeth*—villiform in jaws, vomer and palatines, also on pre-sphenoid and epi-hyal. *Fins*—spines somewhat slender, the soft portion of the fin rather elevated and pointed: anal spines short, its soft portion similar to that of the dorsal: caudal pointed. Variations, as in other Acanthopterygian fresh-water fishes, exist in the number of spines and rays; in Bengal and Madras the formula is generally D. $\frac{15-17}{8-7}$, A. $\frac{3}{6-7}$, L. l. 26-28, but in Assam and Burma it is mostly as follows: D. $\frac{16-17}{7-10}$, A. $\frac{3}{6}$, L. l. 28-33.

Scales—ctenoid, extending over the body and head, there are two or three small rows along the bases of the dorsal and anal fins, and some minute ones are often present on the rays of the vertical fins, one entire row exists between the highest portion of the lateral-line and the small scales along the base of the dorsal fin. *Lateral-line*—interrupted below the posterior extremity of the dorsal fin. *Air-vessel*—large, with thin walls. *Colours*—subject to great variation. In India proper, including the Punjab and Sind, the body is variegated with alternate belts of black and green; but in old fishes, especially if captured in dirty water, these bands are black and dirty red. On each shoulder there is usually a bluish-black spot, another is often present on the opercle, and a third at the base of the caudal fin. In specimens from Assam and Burma a different mode of colouring obtains. In Assam, in the variety figured, they are of a dull red, blotched or spotted with black; but in Burma these spots take the form of six vertical bands, each being formed by four transverse blotches one above the other; a large one is situated on the shoulder, and another on the side of the free portion of the tail: all the vertical fins have a narrow white edge.

Habitat.—Fresh waters of India and Burma, attaining at least 3½ inches in length. I obtained several at Mandalay in Upper Burma from a canal which was being baled out.

2. Badis dario.

Labrus dario, Ham. Buch. Fish. Ganges, pp. 72, 368.
Badis dario, Günther, Catal. iii, p. 367.
Kundukie, Ooriah: *Ka-sondam*, Tel.

B. vi, D. $\frac{16}{8}$, P. 9, V. 1/5, A. $\frac{3}{6}$, C. 15, L. l. 26-30, L. tr. 11.

Length of head 1/4, of caudal nearly 1/4, height of body 1/4 of the total length. Under jaw slightly the longer. *Eyes*—diameter 1/3 of length of head, 1/2 a diameter from end of snout, and also apart. *Teeth*—minute as in the last species. *Fins*—dorsal spines slender, the soft portion as well as of the anal pointed: caudal wedge-shaped. *Scales*—rather large. *Lateral-line*—absent. *Colours*—stone-colour, with several black vertical bands, mostly in the last half of the body; but in dirty water the black colour extends all over.

Habitat.—Ponds, rivers and ditches in the northern parts of Bengal, Behar, and along the Western ghauts, attaining three inches in length: it is eaten by the natives.

Genus, 3—Nandus, *Cuv. and Val.*

Bedula, Gray.

Branchiostegals six: pseudobranchiæ absent. Body oblong, compressed. Eyes lateral. Mouth very protractile, its cleft deep. Opercle with one spine: preopercle serrated, or more or less entire, as are also the preorbital, sub- and inter-opercles. Teeth villiform on the jaws, vomer, palatines and tongue: the length of the base of the spinous portion of the dorsal fin longer than that of the rays: anal with three spines. Scales of moderate size, ctenoid. Lateral-line interrupted. Air-vessel large and simple. Pyloric appendages absent.

Geographical distribution.—Fresh waters of India, Burma and Siam.

SYNOPSIS OF INDIVIDUAL SPECIES.

1. *Nandus marmoratus*, D. $\frac{12-13}{11-13}$, A. $\frac{3}{5-8}$, L. l. 46-57. Brown, vertically marbled with wide darker bands.

This species shows great variation in accordance with the localities where it is taken, the serrations on the bones of the head being usually exceedingly indistinct or even absent in specimens obtained in Sind and India as far as Calcutta. But in Assam a considerable difference is perceptible, as most of the specimens have both limbs of the preopercle and also the lower edges of the sub- and inter-opercles serrated, sometimes rather coarsely so.

1. Nandus marmoratus, Plate XXXII, fig. 1.

Coius nandus, Ham. Buch. pp. 96, 370, pl. 30, fig. 32; McClell. Cal. J. N. Hist. ii, p. 574.
Nandus marmoratus, Cuv. and Val. vii, p. 482, pl. 207; Cantor, Catal. p. 17; Jerdon, Madras J. L. and Sc. 1848, p. 141; Günther, Catal. iii, p. 367; Day, Fish. Malab. p. 128; Bleeker, Nandioides, p. 3.
Bedula Hamiltonii, Gray and Hardw. Ill. In. Zool. ii, pl. 88, f. 3 (from H. B. Ms.)
Mootahree, Mal.: *Bodosi* and *Gossiporoh*, Ooriah: *Vaudhul*, Hind.: *Septi*, Tel.: *Latha* and *Gultha*, Beng.: *Mussossah*, Punj.: *Gad-gud-di* and *Bad-vaad-hi*, Assam.

B. vi, D. $\frac{12-13}{11-13}$, P. 16, V. 1/5, A. $\frac{3}{5-8}$, C. 15, L. l. 46-57, L. r. $\frac{42-48}{42-48}$, L. tr. 5½-6/17-20, Vert. 24.

Length of head 1/3, of pectoral 2/15, of caudal 1/6 to 2/11, height of body 1/3 to 3/10 of the total length. *Eyes*—diameter 1/5 to 1/6 of length of head, rather above 1 diameter from end of snout, and 1 apart. The profile over the orbit is rather concave, whilst the abdominal is not so convex as that of the dorsal. Premaxillaries very protrusible, reaching to one diameter behind the posterior border of the orbit. The posterior extremity of the maxilla reaches to some distance behind the eye. Preopercle may be entire, only finely serrated at its angle, or serrated along both limbs: the sub- and inter-opercles likewise may be entire, serrated along their approximating portions or in their whole extent. Preorbital with some minute serrations or entire. *Teeth*—in villiform bands in the jaws, in an elongated band, widest at either extremity, on the tongue; in a narrow row on the palatines and in a Λ-shaped band on the vomer, in some cases "intermixed with these in each jaw are several sharp teeth of a larger size." (Ham. Buch. l. c.) *Fins*—dorsal spines rather strong, their base occupying rather above three-fourths of the length of the fin and are receivable into a groove, interspinous membrane deeply emarginate, soft portion of the fin similar to that of the anal and almost square: anal spines of moderate strength the central one the longest and equal to two-thirds the length of the rays: caudal cut nearly square. *Scales*—rather smaller on the nape than on the body, some extend over the bases of the dorsal and anal rays, an enlarged one at the angle of the ventral fin and another between the two ventrals. *Lateral-line*—interrupted at about the 36th scale. *Colours*—greenish-brown with brassy reflections, vertically marbled with three broad patchy bands, and a fourth crosses the free portion of the tail, or occasionally there exists a black blotch there, some narrow dark bands radiate from the eye. Narrow bands of spots across the soft portions of the dorsal, anal, and the caudal fins.

In Assam and to the east of Bengal, as already observed (p. 129), the bones of the head are more strongly serrated than is usually seen in the other parts of India.

Bleeker has discriminated between the *Nandus marmoratus* C. V. of India, and the *N. nebulosus*, Gray and Hardw. which inhabits the islands of the Sound. Of this latter he observes amongst other peculiarities that its scales are [illegible], being much fewer in number than in *N. marmoratus*. In examining 10 specimens of this latter I find as follows:

Five from Madras and Malabar L. r. [illegible], L. tr. $5\frac{1}{2}$-6/17-20.
Five „ Assam . . . . . L. r. [illegible], L. tr. $5\frac{1}{2}$-6/18-19.

Habitat.—Fresh and brackish waters of India and Burma, attaining at least 7 inches in length. It is common in ditches and inundated fields where it preys on small *Cyprinidæ*. It is exceedingly tenacious of life.

Genus, 4—Pristolepis, *Jerdon* (1848).

Catopra, Bleeker (1851): *Paranandus*, Day.

Branchiostegals six: pseudobranchiæ absent. Eyes lateral. Mouth moderately protractile. Opercle with two flat (generally bifid) spines: preopercle and preorbital mostly serrated. Teeth villiform on the jaws and palate, villiform or globular on the vomer, obtusely globular on the base of the tongue, on the roof of the cavity of the mouth (pre-sphenoid), and sometimes on the vomer. Anal fin with three or four spines. Scales ctenoid, large, extended on to the interbranchial membrane. Lateral-line interrupted. Pyloric appendages two.

Geographical distribution.—Fresh waters of the plains and hills of India, Burma, Siam and the Malay Archipelago: those with villiform teeth in the adult on the vomer would appear to belong to India proper: those with globular teeth on that bone to Burma and the Eastwards.

SYNOPSIS OF SPECIES.

A. *With villiform teeth on vomer (Paranandus).*

1. *Pristolepis marginatus*, D. [illegible], A. [illegible], preorbital, preopercle, sub- and inter-opercles serrated. Wynaad.
2. *Pristolepis Malabaricus*, D. [illegible], A. [illegible]. Malabar ghauts descending to the plains.

B. *With globular teeth on vomer (Catopra).*

3. *Pristolepis fasciatus*, D. [illegible], A. [illegible]. Burma and to the East as far as the Malay Archipelago.

A. *With villiform teeth on the vomer (Paranandus).*

1. Pristolepis marginatus.

Jerdon, Madras Journal, Lit. and Sc. 1848, p. 141, and Ann. and Mag. Nat. Hist. 1865, xvi, p. 298; Day, Fishes of Malabar, p. 131.

Catopra tetracanthus, Günther, Proc. Zool. Soc. 1862, p. 192, pl. xxvi, fig. B.

B. vi, D. [illegible], P. 14, V. 1/5, A. [illegible], L. r. [illegible], L. tr. $3\frac{1}{2}$/11.

Length of head $3\frac{1}{3}$ to $3\frac{1}{2}$, of caudal 1/5, height of body, $3\frac{1}{2}$ in the total length. *Eyes*—diameter $3\frac{1}{4}$ to $3\frac{1}{2}$ of length of head, 1 diameter from end of snout, and 2/3 of a diameter apart. Length of head rather exceeds its height. Lower jaw very slightly the longer: premaxillaries reach to opposite the anterior margin of the orbit: the maxilla to below the front edge of the eye. Preopercle serrated at its angle and also for a short distance along its vertical border: sub- and inter-opercles likewise with some serrations at their approximating angles: opercle with two flat spines, the lower of which may be bifid: preorbital sometimes rather strongly serrated. *Teeth*—villiform in the jaws, with an outer rather widely placed row of curved ones: villiform teeth on the vomer and palatines, and granular at the root of the tongue and on the roof of the cavity of the mouth (pre-sphenoid). *Fins*—dorsal spines rather strong, increasing in length to the fifth: three last anal spines of about the same length: caudal rounded. *Scales*—two entire and two half rows between the lateral-line and the base of the dorsal fin: 13 rows between the base of the ventral and that of the dorsal fin. *Lateral-line*—interrupted opposite the last third of the soft dorsal on the twenty-first scale. *Colours*—as in the next species.

Habitat.—This form, originally described by Jerdon, was obtained from the "river of Manontoddy, flowing into the Cauvery: in the Cotiaddy river in North Malabar, and in the stream that runs near Canote in the same district." I have obtained one in Malabar $3\frac{3}{4}$ inches in length, with the *P. Malabaricus*. I believe it to be rather an elongated variety of the next, but for the present leave them distinct. Dr. Jerdon felt so satisfied that the fish he described was the *Catopra Malabarica*, Günther, and I obtained so many specimens from Malabar, all but one however with merely three anal spines, that I accepted his opinion that a misprint had occurred. The two original specimens of *tetracanthus* are in the British Museum, having been received without any indication of their habitat from the E. I. Museum, it is therefore open to enquiry whether they might not be Jerdon's types. This fish is said to attain a considerably larger size than 4 inches in length.

2. Pristolepis Malabaricus, Plate XXXII, fig. 2.

Catopra Malabarica, Günther, Ann. and Mag. Nat. Hist. 1864, p. 375; Day, Proc. Zool. Soc. 1865, p. 39.
Nandus Malabaricus, Day, Fish. Mal. p. 130, pl. viii.
Chetichi, Mal.

B. vi, D. [illegible], P. 14-15, V. 1/5, A. [illegible], C. 16, L. l. 25-27, L. r. [illegible], L. tr. $3\frac{1}{2}$/11, Vert. 13/11.

Length of head 4/13 to 1/4, of pectoral 1/4 to 2/9, of caudal 2/9, height of body 2/5 to 4/9 of the total length. *Eyes*—diameter 2/7 of length of head, 1 diameter from end of snout and also apart. Body compressed, a considerable rise to the dorsal fin: head as high as long: jaws equal in front; the premaxillaries reach posteriorly to opposite the first third of the orbit; the maxilla reaches to a little behind the front edge of the eye. Preopercle with its vertical limb roughened, in some cases serrated, most strongly so at its angle: sub- and inter-opercles with some fine serrations at their approximating portions. Opercle with two sharp flat spines which are generally bifid: preorbital entire. *Teeth*—villiform in the jaws, with the outer row somewhat enlarged, some specimens have merely two or four teeth enlarged in the lower jaw, and standing rather in front of the remainder: vomer and palatines with small villiform teeth; the presphenoid has small teeth, all but the outer row of which have rounded crowns, and there are some of the same description at the root of the tongue on the epi- and cérato-hyals, those on the cerato-hyal having rounded crowns, the outer row being somewhat smallest and pointed, they do not extend so far forwards as in the *P. nandioides*, neither are the middle ones so large: villiform teeth on both superior and inferior pharyngeals. *Fins*—dorsal spines rather stout, shorter than the rays, increasing in length to the third and having a groove for their reception along their base, interspinous membrane somewhat deeply emarginate: second anal spine thickest but not quite so long as the third, a groove along their base: caudal rounded. *Lateral-line*—interrupted, ceasing opposite the fourth ray on the twenty-first scale, commencing again in the centre of the side below the last ray, there are two entire and two half rows between the lateral-line and base of the dorsal fin, and 13 between the ventral and base of the dorsal. *Colours*—rifle-green with purplish reflections, fins with lighter edges: caudal with a white outer margin. In some specimens the fish is vertically banded.

Habitat.—Ghauts of Western India, where it seems to prefer clear and rapid streams, attaining at least 6 inches in length.

B. *With globular teeth on the vomer (Catopra).*

3. Pristolepis fasciatus, Plate XXXII, fig. 3.

Catopra fasciata, Bleeker, Borneo, p. 65, and Nandioides, p. 7, fig. 2; Günther, Catal. iii, p. 368.
Catopra nandioides, Bleeker, Selerop. &c. 1851, p. 172; Günther, Catal. iii, p. 368; Day, Proc. Zool. Soc. 1869, p. 615.
Catopra Siamensis, Günther, Proc. Zool. Soc. 1862, p. 191, pl. xxvi, fig. A.

B. vi, D. [illegible], P. 15, V. 1/5, A. [illegible], C. 14, L. l. 26-28, L. r. [illegible], L. tr. $4\frac{1}{2}$/12, Cæc. pyl. 2.

Length of head from 4/15 to 4/15, of pectoral 1/5, height of body $2\frac{1}{4}$ to $2\frac{1}{3}$ in the total length. *Eyes*—diameter nearly 1/4 of length of head, 1 diameter from end of snout, and $1\frac{1}{2}$ apart. Head as high as long. Snout in the adult convex; body oblong, compressed, the dorsal profile rising considerably to the base of the dorsal fin. The maxilla reaches to below the first third of the orbit. Preorbital and preopercle rather strongly serrated; fine serrations, which may be absent, on the contiguous portions of the sub- and inter-opercles: two sharp flat spines on the opercle, mostly bifid, and the lower the larger. *Teeth*—villiform in jaws and palatines, globular on vomer, base of tongue and roof of the cavity of the mouth, at the base of the tongue they extend forward nearly to its anterior extremity. In the young, *C. Siamensis*, the vomerine teeth are not quite so blunted as they become in the adult. *Fins*—dorsal spines strong, interspinous membrane deeply emarginate, central rays the longest: second anal spine the strongest but not so long as the third caudal rounded. *Lateral-line*—interrupted opposite the posterior end of the dorsal fin, being continued on the third row of scales below it. *Air-vessel*—large. *Scales*—four entire rows between the lateral-line and base of the dorsal fin, and 16 or 17 between the bases of the ventral and dorsal. *Cæcal appendages*—two. *Colours*—dull greenish, having a deep black spot in the axilla and over the upper part of the base of the pectoral fin, which otherwise is yellow: the other fins slate coloured.

Four specimens were procured in Burma varying from 4[illegible] to 8 inches in length. A small one from Prome had only 12 dorsal spines, but otherwise no difference was perceptible. Two from Sittang had each 13 spines: the immature is banded. I have likewise a specimen $3\frac{1}{2}$ inches long from Siam, collected by Dr. v. Martens, its opercular spines are not bifurcated.

Habitat.—Fresh-waters of Burma, Siam, and the Malay Archipelago.

Family, V—SPARIDÆ, *Cuv.*

Squamipinnes, pt. Cuv.: *Chætodontidæ*, pt. Richards.

Branchiostegals from five to seven: pseudobranchiæ well developed. Body oblong and compressed. Eyes of moderate size, lateral. Mouth in front of snout, having a lateral cleft. Bones of the head with a rudimentary muciferous system. No teeth on the palate (except in Genus *Pimelepterus*): more or less broad and cutting or conical teeth in front of the jaws, or a lateral series of molars, or both conjoined. A single dorsal fin formed by a spinous and soft portion, their bases being of nearly equal extent; anal with three spines: lower pectoral rays generally branched, but not so in some genera: ventrals thoracic, with one spine and five rays. Lateral-line continuous, not extending on to the caudal fin. Scales cycloid or minutely ctenoid.

Geographical distribution.—Seas of temperate and tropical regions, some entering fresh waters.

SYNOPSIS OF GENERA.

First group—Cantharina.

Broad cutting teeth in front of the jaws: no molars: palate edentulous. Lower pectoral rays branched.

1. *Crenidens.* One or more rows of broad cutting teeth and with a posterior band of granular ones: no pointed lateral teeth. Scales on cheeks and opercles, none on the vertical fins.

Second group—Sargina.

Cutting teeth in front of jaws: no molars. Lower pectoral rays simple.

2. *Sargus.* Molar teeth in several rows along the sides of the jaws.

Third group—Pagrina.

Cutting teeth in front of the jaws and molars along the sides.

3. *Lethrinus.* No scales on the cheeks.
4. *Sphærodon.* Scales on cheeks. Canine teeth and a single row of molars.
5. *Pagrus.* Scales on cheeks. Canine teeth, two rows of molars in the upper jaw.
6. *Chrysophrys.* Scales on cheeks. Canine teeth, three or more rows of molars in the upper jaw.

Fourth group—Pimelepterina.*

Cutting teeth in front of the jaws, and teeth on the palate.

Pimelepterus, as defined above.

First group—Canthamina.

Broad cutting teeth in front of the jaws: no molars: palate edentulous. Lower pectoral rays branched.

Genus, 1—Crenidens, *Cuv. and Val.*

Branchiostegals five: pseudobranchiæ. One or two rows of broad teeth in both jaws, with their cutting edges crenulated: a band of granular teeth posteriorly but no pointed lateral ones: neither molars nor vomerine teeth. A single dorsal with eleven spines which can be received into a groove: three anal spines: lower pectoral rays branched. Scales ctenoid, of moderate size, covering cheeks and opercles, but not the vertical fins. Air-vessel simple. Pyloric appendages in small numbers.

Geographical distribution.—Red Sea, coasts of Africa, seas of India to the Malay Archipelago and beyond.

SYNOPSIS OF SPECIES.

1. *Crenidens Indicus*, D. $\frac{11}{11-12}$, A. $\frac{3}{11-12}$, L. l. 53-57, L. tr. 7/13, Cæc. pyl. 5. Dorsal spines very strong. Greyish, fins black. Red Sea and seas of India.
2. *Crenidens Forskålii*, D. $\frac{11}{11}$, A. $\frac{3}{11}$, L. l. 52-54, L. tr. 5/15, Cæc. pyl. 3. Dorsal spines comparatively weak. Silvery, fins grey. Red Sea and seas of India.

1. Crenidens Indicus, Plate XXXII, fig. 4.

Day, Report on the Sea Fish and Fisheries of India, Nov. 15th, 1873, p. clxxxvi, No. 184.
? *Crenidens Forskålii*, Kner, Novara Fische, p. 74.

* Klunzinger, in his elaborate paper on the Fishes of the Red Sea, considers this group as distinct from the Sparidæ.

Crenidens macracanthus, Günther, Ann. and Mag. Nat. Hist. Nov. 1874, p. 368.
Keea-see, Belooch.: *Oodea*, Tam.

B. v, D. $\frac{10}{11}|\frac{11}{10}$, P. 15, V. 1/5, A. $\frac{3}{10-11}$, C. 17, L. l. 53-55, L. tr. 7/13, Cæc. pyl. 5.

Length of head 1/4 to 2/9, of caudal about 1/5, height of body 4/11 to 1/4 of the total length. *Eyes*—diameter 2/7 to 1/3 of length of head, 1 to $1\frac{1}{4}$ diameters from end of snout, and 1 apart. Form of body oval and compressed: a slight swelling above the eyes. The maxilla reaches to below the front edge of the orbit. Preorbital broad, scaleless, occasionally notched on its lower margin to receive the extremity of the maxilla. Opercle with a soft point. *Teeth*—a compressed row in the front of either jaw, eight in the upper, each being lobed at the sides, behind this row are three more of the same character but smaller in size and more in number: in large specimens there may be some with rounded crowns in the inner row: in the mandible there are ten in the front row smaller in size than those in the upper jaw each having about five notches, behind these are two or three rows as in the upper jaw. *Fins*—dorsal spines strong, the fourth which is the longest, equalling 2/5 to 1/3 in the height of the body, they are alternately wider on one side. Pectoral extending to above the base of the anal: second anal spine strong and nearly or quite as long as the fourth of the dorsal, the third which is weaker, is of about equal length: caudal emarginate. *Scales*—two or three rows on the cheeks, $6\frac{1}{2}$ or 5 entire and 2 half rows between the lateral-line and sixth dorsal spine, 17 rows between snout and base of dorsal fin, and 9 or 10 between base of ventral and lateral-line. *Colours*—greyish-silvery, the scales on the head and anterior portion of the body with black edges, dark lines along the rows on the body: dorsal and anal fins black except the last anal ray which is white: pectoral yellow, with its base orange, and a black spot in axilla: outer two-thirds of ventral black, the rest bluish-white: caudal dark grey with a black edge.

Habitat.—Very common along the Sind coast and not rare at Madras: attaining at least 12 inches in length. Also found at Suez. The specimen figured is from Sind and 10 inches long.

2. Crenidens Forskālii.

Sparus crenidens, Forsk. Desc. Anim. p. xv, No. 19.
Crenidens Forskālii, Cuv. and Val. vi, p. 377, pl. 162 quater; Rüppell, N. W. Fische, p. 120; Peters. Wieg. Arch. 1855, p. 243; Günther, Catal. i, p. 424.

B. v, D. $\frac{11}{11}$, P. 15, V. 1/5, A. $\frac{3}{9-11}$, C. 17, L. l. 52, L. tr. 5/15, Cæc. pyl. 3.

Length of head $4\frac{1}{2}$ to $4\frac{3}{4}$, of caudal 4/21 to 1/5, height of body $2\frac{3}{4}$ of the total length. *Eyes*—diameter 2/7 of length of head, 1 diameter from end of snout, and also apart. A swelling over the anterior-superior angle of the eye. The maxilla reaches to below the anterior nostril. Preorbital two-thirds as high as the orbit is wide. *Teeth*—in a compressed row in front of either jaw as in the last species *(C. Indicus)*, but with ten in the anterior row in the upper and twelve in the lower jaw. *Fins*—dorsal spines rather weak, with the fourth slightly the longest, and rather less than half the length of the head: pectoral much longer than the head, but not reaching to above the anal spines, which latter are weak, the third being equal to two-thirds of the length of the fourth dorsal spine, and not quite so strong as the second: caudal forked. *Scales*—11 or 12 rows between the base of the ventral fin and the lateral-line, and $5\frac{1}{2}$ or four entire and two half rows between the lateral-line and base of the sixth dorsal spine. *Colours*—silvery, the vertical fin being rather darker than the body.

Habitat.—Red Sea, seas of India, Sind, and the coast of Mozambique.

Second group—Sargina.

Cutting teeth in front of jaws: no molars. Lower pectoral rays branched.

Genus, 2—SARGUS, *(Klein)*, *Cuv.*

Branchiostegals five or six: pseudobranchiæ. Opercle either unarmed or with a blunt point. A single row of cutting teeth in the front part of the jaws, and several lateral rows of rounded molars. A single dorsal with from ten to thirteen spines receivable into a groove along its base: anal with three. Scales finely ctenoid, of moderate size, covering the cheeks. Air-vessel sometimes notched anteriorly and posteriorly. Pyloric appendages few.

Geographical distribution.—This genus has a wide range, being found in the Mediterranean, Atlantic, and the Western shores of India.

SYNOPSIS OF INDIVIDUAL SPECIES.

Sargus noct. D. $\frac{11}{12}|\frac{2}{14}$, A. $\frac{3}{9}$, L. l. 62-68, L. tr. 6/16. Eight flattened and compressed incisors in either jaw. A black spot on the lateral-line on either side of the tail. Red Sea, Beloochistan and Sind.

1. Sargus noct. Plate XXXII, fig. 5.

(Ehren.) Cuv. and Val. vi, p. 51: Rüppell, N. W. Fische, p. 110; Günther, Catal. i, p. 444; Klunz. Verh. z. b. Ges. Wien, 1870, p. 81.
Keen-ree, Belooch.

B. vi, D. $\frac{11}{12}|\frac{2}{14}$, P. 15, V. 1/5, A. $\frac{3}{9}$, C. 17, L. l. 62-68, L. tr. 7-8/16, Cæc. pyl. 8 (5), Vert. 10/13.

Length of head 1/4 to 2/9, of caudal 1/5, height of body 3/10 of the total length. *Eyes*—diameter 1/3 to 1/4 of the length of head, $1\frac{1}{4}$ to $1\frac{1}{2}$ diameters from end of snout, and also apart. Dorsal and abdominal profiles about equally convex. The maxilla reaches to below the front edge of the orbit: snout compressed, lips rather thick. The height of the preorbital equals two-thirds of the diameter of the orbit, preopercle and preorbital entire: opercle with a blunt point. *Teeth*—eight broad, compressed, rather forwardly directed incisors in either jaw, also three rows of rounded molars. *Fins*—dorsal spines of moderate strength, increasing in length to the fourth, which equals about half of that of the head, the rays much lower than the spines. Pectoral as long as the head; ventral does not reach the anus: second anal spine strongest and longest, equalling the length of the snout: caudal forked, the upper lobe usually the longer. *Scales*—five rows between the eye and the angle of the preopercle. *Colours*—greyish-silvery, fine dots on the scales, forming lines along the centre of each row, and a darkish spot at the base of the pectoral: a black blotch with a silvery lower border (lost in the adult) on the lateral-line between the end of the dorsal fin and the base of the caudal. *Fins*—blackish, except the pectoral, which is flesh-coloured, and the caudal which has an orange tinge. Eyes golden. *Young* with narrow vertical brown lines on the body.

Habitat.—Red Sea, very common at Suez, to the coast of Sind, attaining at least 12 inches in length.

Third group—Pagrina.

Cutting teeth in front of the jaws and molars along the sides.

Genus, 3—LETHRINUS, *Cuv.*

Branchiostegals six: pseudobranchiæ. Villiform teeth in the anterior portion of the jaws, having canines in front of them: lateral teeth in a single row and either conical or with rounded crowns: none on the palate or tongue. Dorsal fin single, receivable into a sheath at its base, and having ten spines and nine rays: anal with three spines. Scales of moderate size, none on the cheeks. Air-vessel generally notched posteriorly and having short lateral processes. Pyloric appendages few.

Bleeker in his revision of the fishes of this genus offers some excellent remarks. The *Lethrini* have the same number of spines and rays, whilst the number of pierced scales along the lateral-line only varies between about 45 and 50, and the scaling of the head is the same in all. One would imagine that specific characters might be found in the length of the snout, in the comparative height of the preorbital, and in the form of the posterior teeth in the jaws, but these characters have merely a relative value, because the snout becomes more elongated as age advances, the height of the preorbital increases, and the rounded molars in the adult are occasionally the remains of what were conical and pointed teeth in the young. The same variations are seen as to colours, the black lateral blotch present in the young disappears in some species as age advances, in fact the vivid colours of immature become more sober and uniform as age increases. The best characteristics are found in the number of rows of scales between the lateral-line and the dorsal fin, in the form of the profile: in the relative heights of the body and head, and in the strength and length of the dorsal and anal spines.

Geographical distribution.—Red Sea, East coast of Africa, seas of India, to the Malay Archipelago and beyond.

SYNOPSIS OF SPECIES.

A. *With the lateral teeth conical.*

1. *Lethrinus rostratus*, D. $\frac{10}{9}$, A. $\frac{3}{8}$, L. tr. 6/16. Height of body 1/4 of the total length: eyes 2 to $2\frac{1}{2}$ diameters from end of snout. Fourth dorsal spine longest. Olive-brown, with dark bands on the head, and generally a dark blotch between the pectoral fin and lateral-line. Red Sea, seas of India to the Malay Archipelago and beyond.

B. *With some or all of the lateral teeth molarform.*

2. *Lethrinus cinereus*, D. $\frac{10}{9}$, A. $\frac{3}{8}$, L. tr. 6/17. Head slightly longer than high. A quadrangular blotch between the pectoral fin and the lateral-line. Seas of India.
3. *Lethrinus karwa*, D. $\frac{10}{9}$, A. $\frac{3}{8}$, L. tr. 6/17. Head rather higher than long. A blue spot on each scale, a blood red edge to opercle. Seas of India.
4. *Lethrinus nebulosus*, D. $\frac{10}{9}$, A. $\frac{3}{8}$, L. tr. 6/16. Head rather longer than high: eyes $2\frac{1}{2}$ diameters from end of snout. Bands of blue and yellow spots. Red Sea and Indian Ocean.
5. *Lethrinus opercularis*, D. $\frac{10}{9}$, A. $\frac{3}{8}$, L. tr. 6/16. Colours as in *karwa*. Seas of India.
6. *Lethrinus ornatus*, D. $\frac{10}{9}$, A. $\frac{3}{8}$, L. tr. 6/15. Head as high as long. Eyes $1\frac{1}{2}$ diameters from end of snout. Several longitudinal bands and a violet one across the base of the pectoral fin. Andamans to the Malay Archipelago.
7. *Lethrinus ramak*, D. $\frac{10}{9}$, A. $\frac{3}{8}$, L. tr. 6/14. Head longer than high. Eyes 2 diameters from end of snout. Olive, with yellowish bands and a violet spot in the axilla. Red Sea and Ceylon.
8. *Lethrinus harak*, D. $\frac{10}{9}$, A. $\frac{3}{8}$, L. tr. $5\frac{1}{2}$/15. Eyes 2 diameters from end of snout. Head as high as long. An oblong black blotch below the lateral-line opposite the middle of the pectoral fin. Red Sea and seas of India.

A. *With the lateral teeth conical.*

1. Lethrinus rostratus, Plate XXXIII, fig. 1.

(Kuhl. and v. Hass.) Cuv. and Val. vi, p. 296; Bleeker, Verh. Bat. Gen. xxiii, Spar. p. 13 and Révis. Leth. p. 26; Günther, Catal. i, p. 454.

Lethrinus longirostris, Playfair, Fish. Zanz. p. 44, pl. vii, fig. 2.

B. vi, D. $\frac{10}{9}$, P. 13, V. 1/5, A. $\frac{3}{8}$, C. 19, L. l. 48-50, L. tr. 6/16, Cæc. pyl. 3.

Length of head 3/11, of caudal 1/5, height of body 1/4 of the total length. *Eyes*—diameter 1/5 of length of head, $2\frac{1}{2}$ diameters from end of snout, and $1\frac{1}{4}$ apart. Interorbital space nearly flat: snout pointed and compressed. Length of head 1/4 more than its height. The maxilla reaches to nearly below the front nostril. *Teeth*—three rather small curved canines in front of the upper jaw, and a small one on either side of the symphysis of the lower jaw; from 18 to 20 compressed, conical, and pointed teeth along either ramus of the lower jaw, and about 15 similar ones in the upper, the most posterior of these last being occasionally a little rounded. *Fins*—dorsal spines rather weak, increasing in length to the fourth which equals one third of the height of the body or the postorbital length of the head, but is not quite so long as the rays: pectoral as long as the head, exclusive of its postorbital portion: ventral almost reaches the anal spines, the third of which is considerably longer than the second: caudal emarginate. *Scales*—four entire and 2 half rows between the lateral-line and base of sixth dorsal spine. *Colours*—olive-brown lightest on the abdomen. Head, more especially superiorly, having a tinge of purple: a dark brown blotch behind the posterior superior angle of the eye: three narrow dark bands pass from the anterior edge of the eye to the upper jaw: a fourth along the inferior and hind edge of the eye: an oblique one commences on the opercle and crosses to the angle of the mouth becoming very faint in its last portion: a large blotch on the opercle. Inside of mouth orange. The centre of each scale having a blue spot, darkest externally: about eight faint vertical bands descend from the back towards the middle of the body, and usually a dark blotch is apparent between the pectoral fin and the lateral-line. A black spot at the base of each dorsal ray and the fin lightly banded: ventrals slate-coloured: some indistinct vertical bands on the caudal.

L. borely, C. V. vi, p. 292, is said to be closely allied and very similar to *L. frenatus*, C. V., the first has the teeth larger and more rounded, and only two streaks between the end of the mouth and the eye. Its back is vinous brown, abdomen white and the dorsal spotted with red. The eye in the latter is only 1/3 the length of the head, rather above 1 diameter from the end of snout, and nearly 1 apart: the height of the body is about 1/3 of the total length, but the specimen is only about $4\frac{1}{2}$ inches in length.

The specimen figured was captured at Bombay and is 12 inches long.

Habitat.—Red Sea, through those of India to the Malay Archipelago and beyond.

B. *With some or all the lateral teeth molarform.*

2. Lethrinus cinereus.

Cuv. and Val. vi, p. 293.

? *Lethrinus maculatus*, Cuv. and Val. vi, p. 292.

B. vi, D. $\frac{10}{9}$, P. 13, V. 1/5, A. $\frac{3}{8}$, C. 17, L. l. 47-48, L. tr. 6/17.

Length of head 3/11, of caudal 3/17, height of body 1/3 to 4/13 of the total length. *Eyes*—diameter 2/7 to 1/4 of length of head, $1\frac{1}{2}$ diameters from end of snout, and nearly 1 apart. Interorbital space nearly flat. The height of the head nearly equals its length. The maxilla, 1/3 the length of the head, reaches to beneath the front nostril. Opercle with two points separated by a shallow emargination, the lower being the larger. *Teeth*—four small curved canines in the upper and six in the lower jaw, the lateral teeth conical and somewhat irregular in size, especially in the lower jaw, the posterior ones of which have rounded crowns. *Fins*—dorsal spines of moderate strength, increasing in length to the fourth and fifth which equal about 1/3 of the height of the body. Pectoral nearly as long as the head: ventral reaches the vent; second and third anal spines of moderate strength, of about equal length and as high as the third of the dorsal fin, highest anal ray not equal to the length of the base of the rays: caudal forked, lobes pointed. Free portion of the tail as high or higher at its commencement as it is long. *Scales*—5 entire and 2 half rows between the lateral-line and the base of the dorsal fin. *Colours*—of an olive brown, having a quadrangular black blotch between the pectoral fin and the lateral-line: faint vertical bands on the body which are more or less broken up: numerous white or blue spots on the scales in the upper half of the first two-thirds of the body: dorsal fin with brown spots and a red outer margin: pectoral pinkish: ventral slate-coloured: anal similar to the second dorsal: caudal with 3 faint brown vertical bands most distinct in the young.

Habitat.—Seas of India, to the Malay Archipelago and beyond: my longest specimen is 9 inches and from Madras.

3. Lethrinus karwa, Plate XXXIII, fig. 2.

Sparus karwa, Russell, i, p. 71, pl. 89.

Lethrinus karwa, Cuv. and Val. vi, p. 311; Day, Proc. Zool. Soc. 1867, p. 558.

? *Sparus borely*, Cuv. and Val. vi, p. 292.

Karwa, Tel.

B. vi, D. $\frac{10}{9}$, P. 13, V. 1/5, A. $\frac{3}{8}$, C. 17, L. l. 48, L. tr. 6/17.

Length of head 2/7 to $3\frac{3}{4}$, of caudal 1/6, height of body 2/7 of the total length. *Eyes*—diameter in the adult at 15 inches 1/4 to $4\frac{1}{2}$ of length of head, $2\frac{1}{2}$ diameters from end of snout, and 1 apart. Head rather higher than long. Interorbital space nearly flat: the maxilla ($2\frac{1}{4}$ in the length of the head) reaches to below the front nostril. Preopercle very oblique in adults: opercle with two blunt points separated by a somewhat deep emargination. *Teeth*—four large and strong canines in either upper jaw, and the same number in the lower, the outer of which are the largest, in the adult all the lateral row of teeth in the upper jaw with rounded crowns, increasing in size to the last but two; in the lower jaw the first five of the teeth are more or less conical and rounded, whilst those behind have rounded crowns widest transversely except the last two. In younger specimens the posterior teeth are not so rounded. *Fins*—dorsal spines of moderate strength increasing in length to the third, which equals rather more than $1\frac{1}{2}$ diameters of the orbit in height and scarcely so long as the longest ray, it is longer than the fourth. Pectoral nearly as long as the head: ventral reaches the vent: second anal spine rather strongest but not so long as the third, which equals the length of the second of the dorsal fin, and is nearly as high as the rays, the longest of which does not equal that of the base of the soft portion of the fin: caudal emarginate. *Scales*—$5\frac{1}{2}$ or 4 entire and 2 half rows between the lateral-line and the base of the spinous dorsal fin. *Colours*—olivaceous-brown becoming lighter on the abdomen, the centre of each scale having a cobalt-blue spot forming longitudinal lines in the direction of the rows of scales, in some specimens there are intermediate yellow bands: inside of mouth orange: pectoral flesh-coloured, base of its second ray bright blue: dorsal, caudal and anal slate-coloured, margined with orange, and having a line of spots along the centre of the rays; ventral externally slate-coloured. In most adult specimens a faint quadrangular spot is seen between the lateral-line and the middle of the pectoral fin and indistinct vertical bands. In some the edge of the opercle, sub-opercle and branchiostegous rays is of a blood-red colour, but this colour is likewise seen in some specimens of *L. nebulosus.*

Habitat.—Red Sea, seas of India: the specimen figured was captured at Madras in June, 1867, and is 16 inches in length.

4. Lethrinus nebulosus, Plate XXXIII, fig. 4.

Sciæna nebulosa, Forsk. p. 52.

Lethrinus nebulosus, Cuv. and Val. vi, p. 284; Rüpp. N. W. Fische, p. 118; Günther, Catal. i, p. 460; Klunz. Fische d. Roth. Meer. Verh. z. b. Ges. Wien, 1870, p. 86.

B. vi, D. $\frac{10}{9}$, P. 13, V. 1/5, A. $\frac{3}{8}$, C. 17, L. l. 46-48, L. tr. 6/16.

Length of head 3/11 to 2/7, of caudal 1/6 to 2/11, height of body 3/11 to 2/7 of the total length. *Eyes*—diameter 1/4 to 2/9 of length of head, 2 to $2\frac{1}{2}$ diameters from end of snout, and 1 apart. Height of the head rather less than its length. Interorbital space nearly flat, dorsal profile not much elevated. The maxilla, $2\frac{1}{4}$ in the length of the head, reaches to beneath the front nostril. Numerous fine open pores on the lower surface of the mandibles, and even on to the cheeks in the adult. Preopercle moderately oblique: opercle with two blunt points, separated by a shallow emargination. *Teeth*—four rather small canines in the front of either jaw, the first three of the lateral teeth in the upper jaw rather conical, the remainder with globular crowns, not wider transversely than in their antero-posterior diameter: the first six or seven lateral teeth in the lower jaw rather conical, the remainder with globular crowns and rather larger than in the upper jaw. *Fins*—dorsal spines of moderate strength, increasing in length to the fourth which equals rather more than $1\frac{1}{2}$ diameters of orbit in height, and is about equal to the longest ray. Pectoral nearly as long as the head: ventral reaches the anus: second anal spine nearly one-fourth shorter than the third which is nearly as long as the third of the dorsal fin, and as high as the anal rays, the highest of which last equals the length of the bases of the rays: caudal forked, lobes pointed. *Scales*—the row containing the lateral-line rather smaller than the one above or below it: five entire and two half rows between the lateral-line and base of the dorsal fin. Free portion of the tail about as long as high at its base. *Colours*—a blue, black-edged band passes from the eye to the posterior nostril, a second to the angle of the mouth: another blue line exists below the eye: preopercle spotted with blue. Inside of the mouth orange: opercular membrane yellow, sometimes blood-red. Body olivaceous, becoming lighter on the abdomen: scales orange along their centres, and every other row spotted with blue at it's base: in some specimens faint vertical bands are perceptible, and a darkish blotch between the pectoral fin and the lateral-line, whilst the rows of scales below the pectoral have a narrow dark line along their centres. A large specimen had a cobalt blue band over the last half of the eye, whilst the last row of occipital scales was of the same colour: upper surface of the head tinged with blue. Dorsal, caudal and anal slate-coloured, the dorsal edged with reddish, and having two rows of blue spots: faint lines along the soft dorsal and anal, the caudal with narrow blue transverse bars: upper pectoral ray blue in its basal half.

The specimen figured was captured at Aden: my longest specimen is from Sind, and $16\frac{1}{2}$ inches in length.

Lethrinus centurio,* C.V. has the height of the body about 1/3 of the total length. *Eyes*—in the commencement of the last half of the head, $2\frac{1}{4}$ diameters from end of snout, and $1\frac{1}{2}$ apart. Height of head 1/4 more than its length.

Habitat.—Red Sea and the seas of India: very common at Madras.

5. Lethrinus opercularis.

Cuv. and Val. vi, p. 289: Bleeker, Verh. Bat. Gen. xxiii, Spar. p. 14, Révis. Leth. p. 20; Günther, Catal. i, p. 463.

? *Lethrinus geniguttatus*, Cuv. and Val. vi, p. 304.

* *Lethrinus centurio*, C.V. vi, p. 301; Peters, Wieg. Arch. 1855, p. 243.
Lethrinus esculentus, C.V. vi, pl. 159.

B. vi, D. $\frac{10}{9}$, P. 13, V. 1/5, A. $\frac{3}{8}$, C. 17, L. l. 48, L. tr. 6/16.

Length of head 2/7, of caudal 2/11, height of body 2/7 of the total length. *Eyes*—diameter 1/4 of length of head, $1\frac{1}{4}$ diameters from the end of snout, and 1 apart. *Teeth*—as in *L. nebulosus*. *Fins*—as in *L. nebulosus*, except that the second anal spine is nearly as long as the third, equals one diameter of the eye in length, and is not quite so long as the second in the dorsal fin. *Colours*—as in *karwa*.

Habitat.—Seas of India and ? Malay Archipelago.

6. Lethrinus ornatus.

Cuv. and Val. vi, p. 231; Bleeker, Révis. Lethr. p. 18.

Lethrinus erythropterus, Cuv. and Val. vi, p. 293 (young).

Lethrinus xanthotænia, Bleeker, Sclerop. 1851, ii, p. 176; Günther, Catal. i, p. 461.

B. vi, D. $\frac{10}{9}$, P. 13, V. 1/5, A. $\frac{3}{8}$, C. 17, L. l. 48, L. tr. 6/15.

Length of head 4/15, of caudal nearly 1/5, height of body nearly 1/3 (4/13) of the total length in a specimen 7 inches long. *Eyes*—diameter 2/7 of length of head, $1\frac{1}{2}$ diameters from end of snout, and nearly 1 apart. Interorbital space nearly flat: dorsal profile somewhat elevated. Height of head equals its length. The maxilla is nearly 1/3 the length of the head, and reaches to almost below the front edge of the orbit. Preopercle scarcely oblique: opercle with two blunt points, separated by a very shallow emargination. *Teeth*—four conical canines in either jaw, the first five lateral teeth in the upper jaw conical and pointed, the remainder with globular crowns: the first five in the lower jaw similar to those in the upper but smaller, the posterior ones of moderate or rather small size and with rounded crowns. *Fins*—dorsal spines of moderate strength, increasing in length to the fourth which is the highest, as long as the longest ray, and equal to about 1/3 of the height of the body below it. Pectoral almost as long as the head: ventral reaches the anus: second anal spine rather stronger but shorter than the third which equals the length of the third of the dorsal fin, and is nearly as high as the rays, the height of which equals the length of the base of the soft portion of the fin: caudal forked. *Scales*—the row containing the lateral-line is much smaller than that above or below it. *Colours*—greenish-olive, with from six to seven yellow horizontal bands the opercular membrane red, caudal edged with red. A violet band across the base of the pectoral fin.

Young specimens have the dorsal and anal edged with reddish, and irregular blackish blotches about the body, the largest, which is somewhat quadrangular, being above the middle of the base of the pectoral fin.

Habitat.—Andamans to the Malay Archipelago.

7. Lethrinus ramak.

Sciæna ramak, Forsk. p. 52.

Lethrinus ramak, Rüpp. N. W. Fische, p. 117, t. 28, f. 3; Günther, Catal. i, p. 459; Klunz. Fische d. Roth. Meer. Verh. z. b. Ges. in Wien, 1870, p. 752.

Lethrinus fasciatus, Cuv. and Val. vi, p. 290.

? *Lethrinus Ehrenbergii*, Cuv. and Val. vi, p. 312.

B. vi, D. $\frac{10}{9}$, P. 13, V. 1/5, A. $\frac{3}{8}$, C. 17, L. l. 50, L. tr. 6/14.

Length of head $3\frac{1}{2}$, of caudal 1/5 to $5\frac{1}{2}$, height of body $3\frac{1}{3}$ in the total length. *Eyes*—diameter 1/4 to $4\frac{1}{2}$ in the length of head, 2 diameters from end of snout, and $1\frac{1}{4}$ apart. Interorbital space slightly convex from side to side. Height of head a little less than its length. The length of the maxilla is $2\frac{3}{4}$ in that of the head, it reaches to beneath the posterior nostril. Fine pores visible over most of the scaleless portion of the head. *Teeth*—canines rather small, the lateral row in the jaws are first compressed and pointed, the posterior 6 or 8 being rounded, the first few of which are largest and most obtuse. *Fins*—dorsal spines of moderate strength, increasing in length to the third and fourth, which equal one-third of the height of the body, but are not quite so long as the last rays. Pectoral nearly as long as the head: ventral reaches the anus. Second anal spine strongest but not so long as the third which equals the second in the dorsal fin: the longest ray not quite equal to the extent of the base of the soft portion: caudal forked. *Scales*—$5\frac{1}{2}$ or 4 entire and 2 half rows between the lateral-line and the base of the spinous dorsal. Free portion of the tail as high at its base as it is long. *Colours*—olive, with yellow longitudinal bands, a small violet spot in the axilla.

The canines in front of the jaws in Cuv. and Val.'s specimens are rather larger than described above, whilst a brown spot exists below the lateral-line above the first third of the pectoral fin.

Habitat.—Red Sea and Ceylon.

8. Lethrinus harak, Plate XXXIII, fig. 3.

Sciæna harak, Forsk. p. 52.

Lethrinus harak, Rüpp. N. W. Fische, p. 116, t. 29, f. 3; Bleeker, Spar. p. 15 and Révis. Lethr. p. 21; Günther, Catal. i, p. 458; ? Kner, Novara Fische, p. 81; ? Klunz. Fisch. R. M. Verh. z. b. Ges. Wien, 1870, p. 755.

Lethrinus rhodopterus, Bleeker, Singapore, p. 65.

? *Lethrinus Amboinensis*, Kner, Novara Fische, p. 80 (not Bleeker).

? *Lethrinus Bonhamensis*, Garrett's Fische d. Sudsee, t. xlvii.*

* Dr. Günther's description has not yet been published, it appears, from the figure, as if the species had only $4\frac{1}{2}$ rows of scales between the lateral-line and the base of the 6th dorsal spine, thus agreeing with Klunzinger's description.

Pootaung-alah, Andam.

B. vi, D. $\frac{10}{9}$, P. 12, V. 1/5, A. $\frac{3}{8}$, C. 17, L. l. 46-47, L. tr. $5\frac{1}{2}$/15, Cæc. pyl. 3.

Length of head 3/11, of caudal 2/11, height of body 2/7 of the total length. *Eyes*—diameter $3\frac{1}{4}$ to 1/4 in length of head, rather above 2 diameters from end of snout, and 1 apart. Height of head nearly equals its length. Snout rather elongated and pointed, having a slight swelling above the anterior superior edge of the eye. The maxilla reaches to below the front nostril. *Teeth*—canines in front of the villiform bands in both jaws, and of moderate size; the first four in the lateral row conically obtuse, whilst the hind ones are large and rounded. *Fins*—dorsal spines weak, increasing in length to the fourth which equals one-third of that of the body below it, or $2\frac{3}{4}$ in the length of the head, and is about equal to the length of the rays. Pectoral about equal in length to the head: ventral just reaches the anal spines, which are of moderate strength, the third being slightly the longest: caudal forked. The height of the free portion of the tail at its commencement equals its length. *Scales*—from $5\frac{1}{2}$ to 4 entire and 2 half rows between the lateral-line and the sixth dorsal spine. *Colours*—greenish-olive, with an oblong blackish blotch below the lateral-line opposite the middle of the dorsal fin.

Klunzinger gives only $4\frac{1}{2}$ rows of scales above the lateral-line; if such is not a typographical error his fish cannot be this species.

Habitat.—Red Sea, through those of India to the Malay Archipelago.

Genus, 4—Sphærodon, *Rupp.*

Chrysophrys, sp. Cuv. and Val.: *Pagrus*, sp. Bleeker.

Branchiostegals six: pseudobranchiæ. Jaws with conical canines anteriorly and a single row of molars laterally. A single dorsal fin with ten spines, receivable into a groove at their base: three anal spines. Scales of moderate size extending on to the cheeks. Pyloric appendages few.

Geographical distribution.—Red Sea, throughout those of India to the Malay Archipelago.

SYNOPSIS OF INDIVIDUAL SPECIES.

1. *Sphærodon heterodon*, D. $\frac{10}{10}$, A. $\frac{3}{8}$, L. l. 44-48. Rose-coloured, base of pectoral violet. Ceylon and Malay Archipelago.

1. Sphærodon heterodon.

Pagrus heterodon, Bleeker, Gilolo, p. 54.
Sphærodon heterodon, Günther, Catal. i, p. 465.

B. vi, D. $\frac{10}{10}$, P. 15, V. 1/5, A. $\frac{3}{8}$, C. 17, L. l. 44-48, L. tr. 5/14.

Length of head 1/4, of caudal 1/4 in the young to 2/9 in the adult, height of body 2/7 of the total length. *Eyes*—diameter 3/7 to 1/3 of length of head, 2/3 to 1 diameter from end of snout, and 1 diameter apart. A swelling over the anterior superior edge of the orbit. The maxilla reaches to below the first third of the orbit. *Teeth*—generic, the molars very broad. *Fins*—dorsal spines increasing in length to the third and fourth, from whence they continue about the same length: pectoral extends to above the anal: caudal deeply forked and elongated in the young. *Colours*—rosy, scales with darker edges: base of pectoral violet.

Habitat.—Ceylon and Malay Archipelago.

Genus, 5—Pagrus, *Cuv.*

Argyrops, Swains.

Branchiostegals six: pseudobranchiæ. Jaws with an anterior row of conical canines, and laterally two or even a rudimentary third row of rounded molars. A single dorsal fin with from eleven to twelve, sometimes elongated, spines, receivable into a groove at their base: anal with three. Scales of moderate size, extending on to the cheeks. Air-vessel simple. Pyloric appendages, when present, in small numbers.

Geographical distribution.—Mediterranean, Atlantic shores of America, Red Sea, and throughout those of Africa and India to Australia.

SYNOPSIS OF INDIVIDUAL SPECIES.

1. *Pagrus spinifer*, D. $\frac{11-12}{10-9}$, A. $\frac{3}{8-9}$, L. l. 53, L. tr. 6-7/18. Whitish, with pink vertical bands. Red Sea and seas of India to the Malay Archipelago.

1. Pagrus spinifer, Plate XXXIII, fig. 5.

Sparus spinifer, Forsk. p. 32; Gmel. Linn. i, p. 1273; Bl. Schn. p. 281; Russell, Fish. Vizag. ii, p. 1, pl. 101.

Pagrus spinifer, Cuv. and Val. vi, p. 156; Rüppell, N. W. Fische, p. 114; Günther, Catal. i, p. 472; Klunz. Fische d. Roth. Meer. p. 761.
Pagrus longifilis, Cuv. and Val. vi, p. 159; Bleeker, Celebes, iii, p. 756.
Soh-ru, Belooch.: *Kooroota*, Tel.: *Soh-ru*, Belooch.: *Pannatlai*, Tam.

B. vi, D. $\frac{11-12}{10-9}$, P. 15, V. 1/5, A. $\frac{3}{8-9}$, C. 17, L. l. 53, L. tr. 6-7/18, Cæc. pyl. 5.

Length of head 3/11 to 4/15, of caudal 1/5 to 2/11, height of body 3/7 to 2/5 of the total length. *Eyes*—

diameter $3\frac{1}{2}$ to 4/4 in length of head, $1\frac{1}{2}$ to 2 diameters from end of snout, and nearly one apart. Dorsal profile rather more convex than that of the abdomen, a more or less developed protuberance before the anterior superior angle of the eyes. The maxilla reaches to below the front edge of the orbit. Preorbital very deep, being equal to from 1 to $1\frac{1}{4}$ diameters of the orbit. Preopercle crenulated at its angle and along its lower limb: opercle high and narrow having two very blunt points. *Teeth*—four conical incisors in front of both jaws, with about three rows of rounded teeth immediately behind them: two rows of teeth with rounded crowns along the sides of either jaw, the most interior being small and in above two rows, the first few in the outer row of the maxilla may be more or less conical. *Fins*—dorsal spines of moderate strength and compressed, the young having filamentous prolongations, two first very short, just appearing above the scales, the third the longest in the fin, often longer than the head, and its interspinous membrane cleft to the base of the fourth spine, the membrane between the rest of the spines deeply emarginate. Pectoral one-third longer than the head; ventral reaches as far as the anus: the second anal spine a little stronger than the third and of about equal length, being $2\frac{1}{2}$ to $2\frac{2}{3}$ or even 1/3 in the length of the head: caudal emarginate. *Scales*—cycloid, about six rows between the orbit and the angle of the preopercle. *Colours*—whitish, with pinkish bands passing along the centre of every scale becoming rather indistinct below the middle of the height of the body. In specimens up to 4 inches in length there are five vertical bands on the body.

Dr. Günther, l. c. observes that a young specimen from China in the British Museum has A. $\frac{3}{9}$, a number I have not observed in Indian examples. In two young specimens (to 3 inches) from Sind the filamentous prolongation of the dorsal fin reaches to the base of the caudal.

A specimen from Sind, 11 inches long, has a very prominent protuberance above and in front of the orbits.

Habitat.—Red Sea, East coast of Africa, seas of India to the Malay Archipelago.

Genus, 6—Chrysophrys, *Cuv.*

Chrysoblephus, Swainson.

Branchiostegals six: pseudobranchiæ. Body oblong, compressed. Four to eight conical or compressed teeth anteriorly, and three or four rows of rounded molars laterally in either jaw. A single dorsal fin, with from eleven to thirteen spines, receivable into a groove at their base: anal with three spines. Scales of moderate size, extending over the cheeks. Air-vessel sometimes notched or with very short appendages. Pyloric appendages few.*

Geographical distribution.—Red Sea, coasts of Africa, seas of India to the Malay Archipelago and beyond.

Some stress has been laid in the discrimination of species in this genus as to whether the lower edge of the preorbital is straight or notched, in order to receive the posterior extremity of the maxillary bone. This sign however is of little if any value, for it may be straight, emarginate or deeply notched in the same species, as seen in *C. berda*, &c. The proportionate height of the preorbital to the diameter of the orbit varies with age, and its depth appears, as a rule, to increase, while that of the eye decreases, in comparison to the length of the head. Likewise, as is also the case in some other Genera, as *Pristipoma*, having the alternate dorsal spines broad on one side and not on the other,—it is not an invariable rule that the broad side shall be the first, third, fifth, and so on, for in specimens of the same species they may be the second, fourth, sixth, &c. The length of the second anal spine is subject to considerable differences, see *C. Cuvieri*, whilst the number of dorsal spines likewise varies.

SYNOPSIS OF SPECIES.

1. *Chrysophrys datnia*, D. $\frac{11}{11-12}$, A. $\frac{3}{8}$, L. l. 46-48, L. tr. 4-5/11, Cæc. pyl. 4. Six incisors in front of either jaw, an outer compressed row along a portion of the rami, and four or five rows of rounded molars in the upper and three or four in the lower jaw: $3\frac{1}{2}$ rows of scales between the lateral-line and the base of the dorsal spines. Greyish. Seas and estuaries of India.

2. *Chrysophrys berda*, D. $\frac{11}{11-12}$, A. $\frac{3}{8-9}$, L. l. 44-46, L. tr. 6/13, Cæc. pyl. 3. Six incisors in front of either jaw: an outer rather conical row along a portion of the upper jaw: four rows of rounded teeth in the upper and three in the lower jaw: four entire and two half rows between the lateral-line and the base of the spinous dorsal. Greyish, a dark opercular spot. Seas of India to the Malay Archipelago and beyond.

3. *Chrysophrys Cuvieri*, D. $\frac{11}{11-12}$, A. $\frac{3}{8}$, L. l. 48, L. tr. 4-5/12. Six conical incisors in front of either jaw, with villiform teeth behind them: the outer row at the sides rather conical and compressed: molars small, three rows in the upper and two in the lower jaw. Greyish, fins nearly black. Seas of India ? to the Malay Archipelago and beyond.

4. *Chrysophrys bifasciata*, D. $\frac{11-12}{13-15}$, A. $\frac{3}{10-11}$, L. l. 48-50, L. tr. 7/15. Dorsal, caudal and pectoral yellow, ventral and anal black. Two vertical black bands on the head. Red Sea and seas of India.

5. *Chrysophrys sarba*, D. $\frac{11-12}{12-13}$, A. $\frac{3}{11}$, L. l. 55-60, L. tr. 6-7/14. From four to six broad compressed incisors in front of the upper and six to eight in the lower jaw, three rows of large molars in the lower and four in the upper jaw. Silvery, with golden bands along each row of scales. Red Sea and seas of India.

6. *Chrysophrys haffara*, D. $\frac{11}{12}$, A. $\frac{3}{11}$, L. l. 60, L. tr. 7/14. Six compressed incisors in front of either jaw,

* "It must be considered, as a rule, *in those fishes with a truly single dorsal fin, composed of a spinous and soft portion, that often one or two soft rays, nearest to the spines are transformed into true spines*, the number of the latter thus appearing to be increased." Günther, Catal. i, p. 493. For instances advanced to the contrary, see l. c. p. 183, respecting *Genyoroge* and *Mesoprion*.

three rows of rounded teeth in the lower, four in the upper jaw. Second anal spine 1/3 of length of head. Silvery, with golden bands along the rows of scales on the body. Red Sea, seas of India to China.

1. Chrysophrys datnia, Plate XXXIV, fig. 1.

Coius datnia, Ham. Buch. Fish. Ganges, pp. 88, 369, pl. 9, f. 29.
Chrysophrys longispinis, Cuv. and Val. vi, p. 116; Bleeker, Beng. p. 93.
Chrysophrys Schlegelii, Bleeker, Japan, p. 400, and Verh. Bat. Gen. xxvi, p. 86.
Chrysophrys hasta, Günther, Catal. i, p. 490 (not *Sparus hasta*, Bl. Schn.); Day, Fish. Mal. p. 29; Kner. Nov. Fische, p. 88.

B. vi, D. $\frac{11}{11}$-$\frac{11}{13}$, P. 15, V. 1/5, A. $\frac{3}{8}$, C. 17, L. l. 46-48, L. tr. 4-5/11, Cæc. pyl. 4.

Length of head from 1/4 to 4/17, of caudal 1/6, height of body 4/11 of the total length. *Eyes*—diameter 1/4 to 1/5 of length of head, 1 to 1½ diameter from end of snout, and also apart. A slight protuberance above the anterior-superior angle of the orbit. Dorsal profile considerably elevated. Preorbital twice as long as deep, its lower edge usually almost straight, but occasionally notched. In a large specimen in the British Museum it is emarginate in the last three-fourths of its lower edge. The maxilla reaches to below the middle of the orbit. Vertical limb of preopercle very finely serrated: opercle with a well developed spine. *Teeth*—six incisors in front of either jaw, more closely set and less pointed than in *C. Cuvieri*, and with rounded teeth behind them; an outer compressed row, (neither so large or pointed as in the last species, and blunted in the adult,) extending for only four or five teeth, exists in either jaw, internal to which are three or four rows of rounded molars in the lower and four or five in the upper jaw: the inner teeth of the hind rows are the largest: there are no villiform teeth in either jaw. *Fins*—alternate dorsal spines strongest on one side, the fourth being the longest, and as long as the postorbital portion of the head: first anal spine short, the second as long as the head excluding the snout. *Lateral-line*—3½ rows of scales between it and the sixth dorsal spine, 10 rows between the base of the ventral fin and the lateral-line. *Colours*—silvery-grey, the bases of the scales darkest and their edges silvery, this is most distinct above the lateral-line: a dark interorbital band: dorsal and caudal with black edges, a dark band along the soft dorsal and the first few anal rays.

Dr. Günther (Catal. i, p. 490) considers *C. xanthopoda* and *C. aureipes*, Richardson, synonyms of this species. It differs from *C. berda* in its teeth, likewise in the strength of the dorsal spines, the number of pyloric appendages, and also of the rows of scales.

Habitat.—The specimen figured (6 inches long) is from the Hooghly at Calcutta, where it attains at least 18 inches in length. It is found from the Red Sea throughout those of India to the Malay Archipelago and beyond.

2. Chrysophrys berda, Plate XXXIV, fig. 2, and XXXV, fig. 2 (var. [illegible].)

Sparus berda, Forsk. p. 32; Lacép. iv, pp. 31, 105; Bl. Schn. p. 278 (not Risso.)
Sparus hasta, Bl. Schn. p. 275.
Sparus calamara, Russell, i, p. 63, pl. xcii.
Chrysophrys berda, Rüpp. N. W. Fische, p. 120, t. 27, f. 4; Cuv. and Val. vi, p. 113; Richards. Ich. China, p. 240; Günther, Catal. i, p. 494; Klunz. Fische d. Roth. Meer. 1870, p. 758.
Chrysophrys calamara, Cuv. and Val. vi, p. 117; Bleeker, Spar. p. 10; Cantor, Catal. p. 48; Günther, Catal. i, p. [illegible]; Day, Fish. Malabar, p. 30.
Dandee-a, Sind.: *Calamara*, Tel.: *Aree*, Mal.: *Coorrie* and *Cerrapu-mathara*, Tam.: *Kala-mulmas*, Hind.: *Nya-wah*, Mugh.: *Moorrock-oduk*, Andam.: *Jarree*, Sind.

B. vi, D. $\frac{11}{11}$-$\frac{11}{12}$, P. 15, V. 1/5, A. $\frac{3}{8\text{-}10}$, C. 17, L. l. 44-46, L. r. [illegible], L. tr. 6/13, Cæc. pyl. 3.

Length of head 1/4, of caudal 1/5 to 1/6, height of body 3/8 to 2/5 of the total length. *Eyes*—diameter 2/7 to 1/4 of length of head (in a young specimen 4$\frac{4}{10}$ inches long 1/3), 1¼ to 1½ diameters from end of snout, and also apart. Dorsal profile more convex than that of the abdomen, snout compressed and somewhat pointed. The maxilla reaches to below or slightly behind the front edge of the orbit. Preorbital narrow with its lower edge straight, emarginate or even notched above the end of the maxilla. Vertical limb of preopercle a little roughened or even minutely serrated: opercle with a distinct spine. *Teeth*—six incisors in front of either jaw, the remainder of the teeth with rounded crowns except a few in the outer row of the upper jaw, which are occasionally not so obtuse as the others: three or four rows in the lower jaw, four or five in the upper, the largest being the last of the inner series. *Fins*—each alternate dorsal spine strongest on one side, the fourth or fifth being slightly the longest and equalling from about 1/2 to 2/3 the length of the head. Pectoral slightly longer than the head. Ventral not reaching the anus. Second anal spine much the strongest equalling from 1/2 or a little more (in typical *berda*) to 3/4 of the length of the head (in the variety *calamara*), in which last it is much the strongest: caudal emarginate. *Scales*—four entire and two half rows between the lateral-line and the base of the spinous dorsal: nine rows between the base of the ventral and the lateral-line. *Air-vessel*—notched posteriorly. *Colours*—in *berda* silvery-grey. Scales darkest at their bases and usually a black spot behind the opercle on the shoulder. A black edge to the dorsal interspinous membrane, soft dorsal, caudal, and anal with black edges: a dark band along the anal fin. In specimens from Sind brownish bands usually radiate from the eye. In the variety *calamara* the fish is dark-greyish, the scales with dark edges, the fins black or edged with black. Some specimens are much darker than others.

Valenciennes vi, p. 115, observes that he has compared *Sparus hasta*, Bl. Schn. with *S. berda* (Forsk.) C. V. and that they are identical. "Valenciennes confounds under the name of *Chr. berda*, Bengal specimens of

Sparus hasta with eleven dorsal spines and *Sp. berda*, Forsk." (Günther, Catal. i, p. 491). Professor Peters having shown me a specimen $14\frac{1}{2}$ inches long with Bl. Schn.'s name *Sparus hasta* on it, marked as his type, and which was sent to Valenciennes, by whom it is also labelled, I certainly think that Valenciennes was correct and the specimen belongs to the variety *calamara*.

Habitat.—Red Sea, and seas of India to the Malay Archipelago and beyond. I have taken specimens of *berda* in Sind 30 inches in length. The *calamara* is known as "black rock cod" in the Madras Presidency, and is excellent eating: it is common in Malabar until July.

3. Chrysophrys Cuvieri, Plate XXXIV, fig. 3.

Dentex hasta, Cuv. and Val. vi, p. 255; Günther, Catal. i, p. 373 (not *Sparus hasta*, Bl. Schn.)

B. vi, D. $\frac{11}{11-12}$, P. 15, V. 1/5, A. $\frac{3}{8-9}$, C. 17, L. l. 48, L. tr. 4-5/13.

Length of head 2/7 to 1/4, of caudal 1/6, height of body from 2/7 to 1/3 in the young of the total length. *Eyes*—diameter 1/6 (to 1/4 in the young) of length of head, $1\frac{1}{4}$ to 2 diameters from end of snout, and $1\frac{1}{2}$ apart. Dorsal profile scarcely elevated in the adult, that of the abdomen almost horizontal. Preorbital low in the young with an almost straight inferior edge, in an adult (as $14\frac{1}{2}$ inches) the depth of the preorbital equals the diameter of the eye. The maxilla reaches to below the front third of the orbit or to under its centre in the adult. Vertical limb of preopercle very minutely serrated in the immature; opercle with a distinct spine. *Teeth*—four to six sharp, pointed and rather conical incisors in front of either jaw, with villiform teeth behind them: a pointed and compressed row along the outer side of either jaw, the last few of which are small and with rounded crowns; internal to these are two rounded rows of small molars in the lower and three in the upper jaw. In a fine specimen $14\frac{1}{2}$ inches in length this distribution of the teeth is still seen, and the size of the molars is far less than is apparent in any other of the genus taken in India; they approach very close to the dentition of *Dentex rufus*, pl. 34, f. 4, which was mislaid until too late to insert in its proper place. *Fins*—alternate dorsal spines strongest on one side, the fourth or fifth being the highest, and nearly equalling the length of the postorbital portion of the head in the young or 1/3 the height of the body in the adult: pectoral not quite so long as the head: first anal spine short, the second strong and equal to half the length of the head or even more in the young, but it greatly decreases in comparative length with age, being only $2\frac{1}{2}$ in the length of the head in the adult: caudal slightly lobed. *Scales*—seven rows between the eye and angle of the preopercle: a few over the base of the soft portion of the dorsal: a band at the base of the anal: the caudal with fine ones almost to its end: four entire and two half rows between the lateral-line and the base of the spinous dorsal: 10 rows between the base of the ventral fin and the lateral-line. *Lateral-line*—very slightly curved. *Colours*—silvery-grey, about eight lines radiate from the eye and posterior edge of the preorbital: each row of scales has a darkish band along its centre: dorsal and caudal fins black tipped, a grey band along the centre of the dorsal fin and a grey spot at the base of each spine and ray: anal spines grey, the membrane and rays black except the two last rays which are white.

This species differs from the *C. datnia* in its teeth and more pointed snout, whilst the head at its widest part only equals its postorbital length. It is identical with the two specimens of *Dentex hasta*, C. V. in the Paris Museum.

Habitat.—Seas of India to at least $14\frac{1}{2}$ inches in length: the figure is from a specimen captured at Mangalore measuring $14\frac{1}{2}$ inches.

4. Chrysophrys bifasciata, Plate XXXIV, fig. 5.

Chætodon bifasciatus, Forsk. p. 64.
Holocentrus rabaji, Lacép. iv, p. 725.
Sparus aries, Lacép. iii, pl. 26, f. 2, and iv, p. 131.
? *Labrus catenula*, Lacép. iii, p. 467, pl. 26, f. 3.
Chrysophrys bifasciata, Cuv. and Val. vi, p. 118; Rüpp. N. W. Fische, p. 112; Günther, Catal. i, p. [illegible]; Klunz. Fische d. Roth. Meer. Verh. z. b. Ges. Wien, 1870, p. 758.
Bak-areer, Bel.

B. vi, D. $\frac{11}{13-14}$, P. 15, V. 1/5, A. $\frac{3}{11-12}$, C. 19, L. l. 48-50, L. tr. 7/15, Cæc. pyl. 2.

Length of head 2/7, of caudal 2/11, height of body 2/5 of the total length. *Eyes*—diameter 2/9 of length of head, $1\frac{1}{2}$ to 2 diameters from end of snout, and $1\frac{1}{2}$ apart. Dorsal profile more convex than the abdominal: a slight elevation above the anterior angle of the eye. The maxilla reaches to below the middle of the orbit: preopercular margin a little roughened above its angle, its height equal to at least the diameter of the eye. *Teeth*—six large compressed incisors in the front of the upper and four in the lower jaw: five rows of rounded molars along the sides of the upper and four in the lower jaw. *Fins*—dorsal spines strong increasing in length to the fifth, which is two-fifths of the length of the head, whilst the rays are scarcely higher than the spines: pectoral a little longer than the head: ventral does not reach the anus: second anal spine much the strongest and equal in length to the third: caudal forked. *Colours*—silvery, with dark lines along each row of scales on the body, and having two black cross bands, the first through the eye, the second over the hind edge of the opercle: a yellow band before the eyes, snout black, dorsal, caudal and pectoral yellow, dorsal spine black, and a narrow black edge along soft dorsal: ventral and anal black except the last anal ray which is yellow.

Habitat.—Red Sea, East coast of Africa and seas of India, attaining at least 15 inches in length. The specimen figured is from Sind and 14 inches long.

5. Chrysophrys sarba, Plate XXXIV, fig. 6.

Sparus sarba, Forsk. p. 31; Gmel. Linn. p. 1275; Bl. Schn. p. 280; Lacép. iv, pp. 97, 106.
Sparus bufonites, Lacép. iv, pp. 141, 143, pl. 26, fig. 3.
Sparus psittacus, Lacép. iv, p. 141.
Sparus chitchilee, Russell, i, p. 73, pl. xci.
Chrysophrys sarba, Cuv. and Val. vi, p. 102; Rüpp. N. W. Fische, p. 110, pl. 28, f. 1; Günther, Catal. i, p. 488; Kner, Novara Fische, p. 88; Klunz. Fische d. Roth. Meer. 1870, p. 759.
Chrysophrys chrysargyra, Cuv. and Val. vi, p. 107.
Tin-til, Belooch.: *Chitchillee*, Tel.: *Vella-mattawa*, Tam.: *Suffeda-mucklawa*, Hind.

B. vi, D. $\frac{11}{12}$ $\frac{1}{13}$, P. 15, V. 1/5, A. $\frac{3}{11}$, C. 17, L. l. 55-60, L. tr. 6-7/14.

Length of head 1/4 to 4½, of caudal 2/11 to 1/5, height of body 2/5 to 4/11 of the total length. *Eyes*—diameter 1/3 to 3½ in the length of head, 1½ diameters from end of snout, and 1¼ apart. Dorsal profile slightly more convex than that of the abdomen. The maxilla reaches to below the front edge of the eye. Preorbital rather above one diameter of the eye in height. Vertical limb of preopercle entire, its angle and lower edge crenulated: opercle with a badly marked spine. *Teeth*—from four to six broad and compressed incisors in the front of the upper jaw and six to eight in the lower, the remainder of the teeth with rounded crowns the largest being in the inner row, about three rows in the lower and four in the upper jaw. *Fins*—dorsal spines of moderate strength alternately broader on one side, the fourth being the highest and equal to a little more than half the length of the head. Pectoral longer than the head: ventral not quite reaching the anal and its spine rather longer than the highest in the dorsal fin: second anal spine strongest, of equal length or a little shorter than the third and equal to the length of the sixth of the dorsal or 1/2 the length of the head: caudal emarginate or slightly lobed. *Scales*—five rows between the eye and the angle of the preopercle; some small ones over the caudal fin, about 5½ rows between its almost straight lateral-line and the base of the dorsal fin. *Colours*—silvery, with golden bands along each row of scales, parallel to the back above the lateral-line and horizontal below it: no dark blotch on the shoulder above the opercle: fins yellowish with a tinge of grey along the upper portion of the dorsal and the end of the caudal: a dark band along the middle of the former fin. Eyes golden.

Habitat.—From the Red Sea through those of India, attaining at least 16 inches in length. They abound in Madras about April, when the young ascend the rivers and backwaters. As food it is inferior to the *berda*.

6. Chrysophrys haffara, Plate XXXV, fig. 1.

Sparus haffara, Forsk. p. 33; Gmel. Linn. p. 1276; Bl. Schn. p. 279.
Chrysophrys haffara, Cuv. and Val. vi, p. 108; Rüpp. N. W. Fische, p. 111, t. 29, f. 1; Günther, Catal. i, p. 488; Klunz. Fische d. Roth. Meer. Verh. z. b. Ges. Wien, 1870, p. 760.
? *Chrysophrys aries*, Temm. and Schleg. Fauna Japon. Poiss. p. 68, pl. 31; Bleeker, Verh. Bat. Gen. xxvi, p. 87; Günther, Catal. i, p. 489.

B. vi, D. $\frac{11}{11}$, P. 15, V. 1/5, A. $\frac{3}{10}$, C. 17, L. l. 60, L. tr. 6-7/14, Cæc. pyl. 3.

Length of head 4½ to 4⅓, of caudal 4½ to 1/5, height of body 2¼ in the total length. *Eyes*—diameter 3½ to 4¼ in the length of the head, 1½ to 2 diameters from end of snout, and 1 apart. Dorsal profile more convex than that of the abdomen, a prominence over the forepart of the orbit causing the snout to appear somewhat vertical: posterior nostril very elongated. The maxilla reaches to below the first edge of the orbit. Preorbital deep, being 1 diameter of the orbit in height. Preopercle entire: opercle with a spine. *Teeth*—six conical and compressed ones in front of either jaw, sometimes only four in the lower, the remainder of the teeth with rounded crowns the largest being in the inner row, three rows in lower four in upper jaw. *Fins*—dorsal spines rather weak, their breadth on both sides being nearly equal, the fourth the highest and equal to two-fifths of the length of the head. Pectoral longer than the head: ventral reaches the anus, its spine a little longer than the fourth of the dorsal: anal spines comparatively weak, the second a little the strongest and slightly the longest, equal to 2¼ to 2¾ in the length of the head: caudal lobed. *Scales*—five rows between the eye and the angle of the preopercle, about 5½ rows between its slightly curved lateral-line and the base of the dorsal fin, a very long one at base of ventral fin. *Colours*—silvery, with golden bands along each row of scales as in *C. sarba*; usually no black mark on the shoulder, fins grey, ventral and anal almost black.

This species is evidently closely allied to the *C. sarba*, and I have only obtained it in Sind; it is however at once recognised by its comparatively short and weak anal spines.

Habitat.—Red Sea and Sind to (?) China: the largest specimen I obtained in Sind measured 12 inches in length.

Fourth group—Pimelepterina.

Cutting teeth in front of the jaws and teeth on the palate.

Genus, 7—PIMELEPTERUS *(Lacép.)* Cuv.

Kyphosus, (Lacép.) Cuv.

*Branchiostegals seven: pseudobranchiæ. Preopercle as a rule serrated. Villiform teeth in the jaws, with an outer row of cutting ones: fine teeth on the vomer, palatines, and tongue. A single dorsal with eleven spines, anal *with three. Scales of moderate size, fine ones over the soft portions of the vertical fins. Air-vessel divided posteriorly into two long processes, sometimes notched anteriorly. Pyloric appendages few or very numerous.*

Geographical distribution.—Red Sea, those of Africa, India, Malay Archipelago and beyond.

SYNOPSIS OF SPECIES.

1. *Pimelepterus fuscus*, D. [illegible], A. [illegible], L. r. [illegible]. Fifth to seventh dorsal spines one-third to one-half higher than the rays. Red Sea, seas of India to the Malay Archipelago.

2. *Pimelepterus cinerascens*, D. [illegible], A. [illegible], L. r. [illegible]. Fourth and fifth dorsal spines nearly as high as the rays. Red Sea, East coast of Africa, seas of India to the Malay Archipelago.

1. Pimelepterus fuscus.

Xyster fuscus, (Comm.) Lacép. pp. 484, 485.

Pimelepterus fuscus, Cuv. and Val. vii, p. 264; Rüpp. N. W. Fische, p. 34, t. 10, f. 3; Günther, Catal. i, p. 498; Klunz. Verh. z. b. Ges. Wien, 1870, p. 796.

? *Pimelepterus Waigiensis*, Quoy and Gaim. Voy. Frey. Zool. p. 386, pl. 62, f. 4; Günther, Catal. i, p. 498.

? *Pimelepterus marciac*, Cuv. and Val. vii, p. 267; Rüpp. l. c. p. 35; Bleeker, Waigiou, p. 3.

Pimelepterus fuscus, Klunz. Verh. z. b. Ges. Wien, 1870, p. 796.

B. vii, D. [illegible], P. 18, V. 1/5, A. [illegible], C. 17, L. l. 60, L. r. [illegible], L. tr. 10/23, Cæc. pyl. numerous.

Length of head 1/5, of caudal 1/5, height of body 1/3 of the total length. *Eyes*—diameter 1/4 of length of head, rather above 1 diameter from the end of snout, and $1\frac{1}{2}$ apart. Body oblong, compressed, and with a swelling opposite the front of the orbit. The maxilla reaches to nearly below the front edge of the orbit. Preopercle with its angle serrated. Sub- and inter-opercles entire: preorbital very finely serrated. *Teeth*—in a single compressed row, their horizontal portions being rather longer than their vertical: minute teeth on the vomer and palate. *Fins*—dorsal spines of moderate strength, increasing in length to the fifth, sixth, and seventh, which are 1/3 to one-half higher than the longest ray: pectoral slightly longer than the ventral, which equals the length of the head behind the middle of the eye: anal spines of moderate strength, the third much the longest and equal to half the length of the first ray: caudal emarginate. *Scales*—over vertical fins, 21 rows between the ventral fin and the lateral-line, and 11 or 12 between it and the base of the sixth dorsal spine. *Colours*—grey, darkest along the back and at the edges of the scales. A silvery band under the eyes.

The difference between the *cinerascens* and *fuscus* is chiefly to be found in the larger number of scales, the greater comparative height of the soft dorsal and anal fins in the latter to what exists in the former, and the size of the pectoral and ventral fins, as well as that of the eye. This *may* however be only a sexual difference, and the various species merely varieties. Klünzinger places *P. marciac*=*Waigiensis*, C.V. as synonyms to *P. tahmel*=*cinerascens*, Forsk.

Habitat.—Red Sea, throughout those of India to the Malay Archipelago and beyond; attaining upwards of 2 feet in length.

2. Pimelepterus cinerascens, Plate XXXV, fig. 3.

Sciæna cinerascens, Forsk. No. 64, p. 53.

Pimelepterus altipinnis, Cuv. and Val. vii, p. 270; Bleeker, Banka, ii, p. 727.

Pimelepterus tahmel,* Rüpp. N. W. Fische, p. 35, t. 10, fig. 4; Günther, Catal. i, p. 499; Bleeker, Solor, p. 5.

? *Pimelepterus Dussumieri*, Cuv. and Val. vii, p. 274.

Pimelepterus tahmel, Klunz. Verh. z. b. Ges. Wien, 1870, p. 795.

Thendala, Tam.

B. vii, D. [illegible], P. 18, V. 1/5, A. [illegible], C. 17, L. l. 60, L. r. [illegible], L. tr. 10/21, Cæc. pyl. numerous, short.

Length of head 2/9, of caudal 2/11, height of body nearly or quite 1/3 of the total length. *Eyes*—diameter 2/7 of length of head, 1 diameter from end of snout, and $1\frac{1}{3}$ apart. Body oblong, compressed, with a slight swelling opposite the front of the orbit. The maxilla reaches to below the front edge of the orbit. Preopercle with its angle serrated, sub- and inter-opercles entire: preorbital finely serrated. *Teeth*—in a single compressed row, their horizontal portions being about one-third longer than their vertical, minute ones on vomer and palate. *Fins*—dorsal spines of moderate strength, increasing in length to the fourth and fifth which are nearly as high as the middle rays, which are the highest in the fin, the whole being enveloped in scales: pectoral of the same length as the ventral and equal to the head excluding the snout: anal spines of moderate strength, the third slightly the longest but only half or two-fifths of the height of the anterior portion of the soft anal, which is scaled as is also the soft dorsal: caudal emarginate. *Air-vessel*—divided posteriorly, one portion passing along either side of the caudal vertebræ to above the hind end of the caudal fin: anteriorly it is not divided. *Scales*—19 rows between the ventral fin and lateral-line, and 9 between the latter and the base of the sixth dorsal spine. *Colours*—silvery-grey, with a dark band between each row of scales: a silvery band under the eye: fins nearly black.

Habitat.—Red Sea, East coast of Africa, seas of India to the Malay Archipelago.

* *Tahmel* is the Arabic name of this fish according to Forskål, whilst *cinerascens* is the specific term he applied to the [illegible]

Family, VI—CIRRHITIDÆ, *Gray*.

Percoidei, pt., et *Sciænoidei*, pt., Cuv.: *Theraponidæ*, pt., et *Polynemidæ*, pt. Richardson.

Branchiostegals three, five or six: pseudobranchiæ. Body oblong and compressed. Mouth in front of snout having a lateral cleft. Eyes of moderate size: cheeks not cuirassed. Teeth in the jaws villiform or pointed, sometimes canines as well; vomerine and palatine teeth present or absent. A single dorsal fin composed of spines and rays of nearly equal extent: anal with three spines. Lower pectoral rays simple, and generally thickened: ventrals thoracic, at some distance from the insertion of the pectorals, and having one spine and five rays. Scales cycloid: lateral-line continuous. Air-vessel absent, or with many appendages. Pyloric appendages few.

Geographical distribution.—Tropical seas, likewise in the temperate parts of the South Pacific.

SYNOPSIS OF GENERA.

1. *Cirrhites*. Branchiostegals six. Operclc unarmed. No teeth on the palatines. Seas of India to the Malay Archipelago and beyond.
2. *Cirrhitichthys*. Branchiostegals six. Opercle with spines. Teeth on the palatines. Seas of India to the Malay Archipelago and beyond.

Genus, 1—Cirrhites, (*Comm.*) *Cuv.*

Amblycirrhitus, Gill; *Paracirrhites*, Bleeker.*

Branchiostegals six. Preopercle denticulated: opercle unarmed. Villiform teeth in both jaws: canines generally present: teeth on the vomer, none on the palatines. A single dorsal fin with ten spines: the lower five to seven pectoral rays are unbranched. Scales of moderate size. Air-vessel absent. Pyloric appendages few.

SYNOPSIS OF SPECIES.†

1. *Cirrhites Forsteri*, D. $\frac{10}{11}$, P. 7+VII, A. $\frac{3}{6}$, L. l. 50. Head and chest with black spots: a broad brown or black band from the head to the upper half of the tail, and a yellow one below it. East coast of Africa, seas of India.
2. *Cirrhites fasciatus*, D. $\frac{10}{12}$, P. 9+V, A. $\frac{3}{6}$. Greyish, vertically banded with darker: white spots on head and nape. Pondicherry.

1. Cirrhites Forsteri, Plate XXXV, fig. 4.

Perca taeniata, Forster, Descrip. Anim. p. 224.
Grammistes Forsteri, Bl. Schn. p. 191.
Sparus pantherinus, Lacép. iv, p. 160, t. vi, fig. 1.
Cirrhites pantherinus, Cuv. and Val. iii, p. 70; Less. Voy. Coq. Poiss. p. 225, pl. 22, fig. 1; Bleeker, Banda, p. 232.
Gerreus Tankervillæ, Bennett, Ceylon, p. 27, p. 27.
Cirrhites Forsteri, Günther, Catal. ii, p. 71, and Garrett's Fische d. Sudsee, t. xliv, A; Gill, Proc. Am. Ac. Nat. Sci. Phil. 1862, p. 112; Klunz. Verh. z. b. Ges. Wien, 1870, p. 797.
Amblycirrhites Forsteri, Bleeker, Ned. T. Dierk. iii, p. 175.
Paracirrhites Forsteri, Bleeker, Cirrh. 1874, p. 6.

B. vi, D. $\frac{10}{11}$, P. 7+VII, V. 1/5, A. $\frac{3}{6}$, C. 15, L. l. 50, L. tr. 5/13, Cæc. pyl. 4, Vert. 10/16.

Length of head $3\frac{1}{3}$ to 1/4, of caudal 1/7, height of body $3\frac{1}{4}$ to $3\frac{1}{2}$ in the total length. *Eyes*—diameter

* Genus *Oxycirrhites*, Bleeker, has the premaxillary produced a considerable distance in front of the mouth. Genus *Paracirrhites* has the scales on the checks large and regularly imbricated, and those on the body smaller; whereas in *Cirrhites* the scales on the body are large, and those on the cheeks small.

† I have not included *C. punctatus*, C. and V. iii, p. 70, which Dr. Günther (in Catal. ii, p. 72) states comes from the "Indian Ocean?" as in the 'Histoire Naturelle des Poissons,' its locality is not given. In the British Museum Catalogue the existence of one specimen is thus recorded, "a, Adult: stuffed. Sine patria." On the stand this is now marked "W. Indies." The specimen is as follows.

D. $\frac{10}{11}$, P. 7+VII, V. 1/5, A. $\frac{3}{6}$, C. 16, L. r. 42, L. tr. 5/10.

Length of head $3\frac{1}{3}$, of caudal 2/11, height of body $3\frac{1}{3}$ of the total length. *Eyes*—diameter 2/9 of length of head, $1\frac{1}{2}$ diameters from end of snout, and 2/3 of a diameter apart. Vertical limb of preopercle finely serrated. Interorbital space deeply convex. A short tentacle at the anterior nostril. *Fins*—fifth dorsal spine the longest, equalling the length of the rays, or $2\frac{2}{3}$ the height of the body: second anal spine much the longest, equalling the highest in the dorsal fin.

2/9 to 2/11 of length of head, $1\frac{1}{2}$ diameters from end of snout, and 1 apart. The maxilla reaches to below the middle of the orbit. Vertical limb of preopercle finely serrated, angle oblique, its lower limb also the sub- and inter-opercles and the preorbital entire; a blunt opercular point. Anterior nostril rather valvular and fringed. *Teeth*—strong canines on either side of symphysis of the upper jaw, two large and some small lateral conical canine-like ones in the mandible: the villiform teeth on the vomer in a triangular patch, with its base behind. *Fins*—dorsal spines rather strong, increasing in length to the third and fourth which equal $2\frac{1}{4}$ in the height of the body, they slightly decrease in length to the last but one, the twelfth being rather longer than the eleventh; interspinous membrane with a fine prolongation from behind each spine, the highest rays of the dorsal fin as long as those of the anal: lower free rays of pectoral fin longer than the branched ones and equal to two-thirds of the length of the head: ventral reaches the vent: second anal spine the strongest, and as long as the third which is nearly one-third the height of the body: caudal cut square or slightly emarginate. *Scales*—cycloid, some between the rays of the vertical fins: the sub- and inter-opercles, and outer edge of the preopercle are covered with fine scales, as is also the preorbital and suborbital ring of bones, whilst on the cheeks and opercles there are many small ones amongst the rows of large ones, which about equal in size those on the body. *Colours*—reddish, head, chest and base of pectoral fin with black spots: a broad dark band along the middle of the body to the upper half of the caudal fin, becoming brown with black blotches in its last third. A wide yellow band from above the pectoral to the lower half of the caudal fin. Upper edge of the last half of the spinous dorsal black, continued as a black band along the base of the soft dorsal: front edge of anal and outer edge of soft caudal with narrow black margins.

Habitat.—Red Sea, East coast of Africa, seas of India to the Malay Archipelago and beyond. The specimen figured is $5\frac{1}{2}$ inches long, and was captured at the Andaman islands. Bennett observes, "the *Tik*[illegible] of the Cingalese inhabits rocky situations, seldom exceeds eighteen inches in length, and is a firm-fleshed and wholesome fish."

2. Cirrhites fasciatus.

Cuv. and Val. iii, p. 76, pl. 47; Günther, Catal. ii, p. 73 (not Bennett).

B. vi, D. $\frac{10}{12}$, P. 9+V, V. 1/5, A. $\frac{3}{6}$, C. 15.

Length of head 3/11, of caudal 1/7, height of body 2/5 of the total length. *Eyes*—diameter 2/7 of length of head, 1 diameter from end of snout. The maxilla reaches to below the first third of the orbit. *Teeth*—no canines. *Fins*—dorsal interspinous membrane very deeply emarginate, fourth dorsal spine the highest and equal to about 1/3 the height of the body, from it they decrease to the last but one, which is not so high as the last; soft portion of the fin as high as the spinous: second anal spine the longest, equalling rather more than the highest of the dorsal fin. *Colours*—greyish, becoming white below, it is vertically banded with darker: some white spots on the snout and nape.

Habitat.—Pondicherry.

Genus, 2—Cirrhitichthys, *Bleeker*.

Cirrhitopsis, Gill.

Branchiostegals six. Preopercle denticulated: opercle spinate. Villiform teeth and canines in the jaws: teeth also in the vomer and palatines. A single dorsal fin with ten spines; anal with three: five to seven of the lower pectoral rays unbranched. Scales of moderate size. Air-vessel absent. Pyloric appendages few.

SYNOPSIS OF SPECIES.

1. *Cirrhitichthys aureus*, D. $\frac{10}{12-13}$, P. 7+VI-VII, A. $\frac{3}{6-7}$, L. l. 43, L. tr. 4/12. First dorsal ray prolonged. Rosy, with badly defined blotches: some red spots on the caudal. Seas of India to the Malay Archipelago and beyond.

2. *Cirrhitichthys marmoratus*, D. $\frac{10}{12}$, P. 7+VII, A. $\frac{3}{6}$, L. l. 40, L. tr. 4/10. No elongated dorsal ray. Body and vertical fins with brown spots. Red Sea to the Malay Archipelago and beyond.

1. Cirrhitichthys aureus, Plate XXXV, fig. 5.

Cirrhites aureus, Temm. and Schleg. Faun. Japon. Poiss. p. 15, t. vii, f. 2.
Cirrhitichthys aureus, Günther, Catal. ii, p. 75.
Cirrhitichthys Bleekeri, Day, Sea Fishery Report, No. 207, p. cxci.
Shna-gon, Tam.

B. vi, D. $\frac{10}{12-13}$, P. 7+VI-VII, V. 1/5, A. $\frac{3}{6-7}$, C. 15, L. l. 43, L. tr. 4/12.

Length of head 1/4, of caudal 2/11, height of body 3/10 of the total length. *Eyes*—diameter 2/7 of length of head, $1\frac{1}{4}$ diameters from end of snout, and 2/3 of a diameter apart. Interorbital space concave. The maxilla reaches to below the first third of the orbit. Preopercle denticulated along its vertical border, as is also the shoulder scale: sub- and inter-opercles entire: preorbital nearly as deep as long, entire. A weak opercular spine. *Teeth*—villiform, with an outer rather enlarged row in the upper jaw, and two or more rather curved and conical lateral ones in the mandible: villiform bands on the vomer and palate. *Fins*—dorsal spines rather strong, increasing in length to the fifth and sixth, which equal two-fifths of the height of the body: first ray elongated, otherwise the soft portion only as high as the spinous: pectoral a little longer than the head, the two upper free rays the longest and reaching to above the anal spines, the free rays may be six or seven in number: ventral not reaching the vent; second anal spine strongest and much the longest, 1/4 higher than the longest in the dorsal fin: caudal slightly emarginate. *Scales*—large on the opercles, cheeks with a few small ones interspersed: none on the preorbital or suborbital ring. *Colours*—rosy, with lightish longitudinal lines and a large ill-defined blotch below the soft dorsal extending half way down the side, in some specimens two more descend from the spinous dorsal; a small dark blotch behind the upper edge of the preopercle. Dorsal and caudal fins more or less banded, soft dorsal darker than the spinous portion, and having a light outer edge: caudal with red spots.

Habitat.—Seas of India to the Malay Archipelago and Japan. It is rather common at Madras, attaining to about 4 inches in length.

This is the species once obtained by Jerdon (M. J. L. and Sc. 1851, p. 132) at Madras, and which he termed *Cirrhites fasciatus*, C.V.

2. Cirrhitichthys marmoratus.

Labrus marmoratus, Lacép. iii, p. 492, pl. v, fig. 3.
Cirrhites maculatus, Lacép. v, p. 3; Cuv. and Val. iii, p. 69.
Cirrhites maculosus, Bennett. Zool. Journ. 1829, p. 38.
Cirrhitichthys maculatus, Günther, Catal. ii, p. 74.

B. vi, D. $\frac{10}{11}$, P. 7+VII, V. 1/5, A. $\frac{3}{6}$, C. 15, L. l. 40, L. tr. 4/10, Vert. 10/16.

Length of head 2/7, of caudal 1/6, height of body 2/7 of the total length. *Eyes*—diameter 1/4 of length of head, $1\frac{1}{4}$ diameters from end of snout, and 3/4 of a diameter apart. The maxilla reaches to below the middle of the orbit. Vertical limb of preopercle serrated: sub- and interopercles entire. A broad fringed valve to the posterior nostril. *Teeth*—villiform in the jaws, vomer, and anterior portion of the palatines. *Fins*—dorsal spines increase in length to the fifth and sixth, which equal two-fifths the height of the body and are as long as the rays, the last spine is a little higher than the one preceding it, no prolonged dorsal ray: pectoral reaches as far as the ventral and equals the length of the head excluding the snout: the ventral extends to the anus: second anal spine strongest, longest, and equalling the highest in the dorsal fin. *Colours*—body and vertical fins with brown spots, and a row of dark spots along the base of the dorsal.

Habitat.—Red Sea, seas of India to the Malay Archipelago and beyond.

NATIVE OFFICIAL OF CUDDALORE AND FISHERMEN (1868)

FAMILY, VII—SCORPÆNIDÆ, *Swainson.*

Sclerogenidæ, pt. Owen.

Branchiostegals five to seven: pseudobranchiæ. Body oblong, compressed or subcylindrical. Eyes lateral. Cleft of mouth lateral. Some of the bones of the head armed: suborbital ring articulated with the preopercle. Teeth in villiform bands. A single dorsal fin in two distinct portions: the anal usually similar to the soft dorsal: ventrals thoracic. Body scaled or scaleless. Air-vessel generally present. Pyloric appendages when present, few or in moderate numbers.

Geographical distribution.—Some of these fishes are usually found in most seas.

SYNOPSIS OF GENERA.

1. *Sebastes.* Interorbital space convex, scaled. No occipital groove but usually a few spines on top of head: no skinny appendages. Teeth in jaws, vomer and palatines. A single dorsal fin: no free rays at base of pectoral: articulated fin-rays as a rule branched. Scales present.

2. *Sebastichthys.* Differs from *Sebastes* in having no teeth on the palatines.

3. *Scorpæna.* Interorbital space concave, generally scaleless, with a groove on occiput laterally bounded by spines. Teeth on jaws, vomer and palatines. A single dorsal fin deeply notched (D. 11 | [illegible]): no free rays at base of pectoral: articulated fin-rays as a rule branched. Scales present. Fleshy appendages of varying size on head and body.

4. *Scorpænopsis.* Differs from *Scorpæna* in having no teeth on the palatines.

5. *Pterois.* Interorbital space more or less concave: bones of the head armed: no occipital groove. Villiform teeth in jaws and vomer, none on the palatines. A single, deeply-notched dorsal fin (D. 11-12 | [illegible]): no free rays at base of pectoral: articulated fin-rays as a rule branched. Scales present. Fleshy appendages on head.

6. *Apistus.* Sharp preorbital and preopercular spines: bones of the head armed. Barbels present. Teeth in jaws, vomer and palate. A single dorsal fin (D. [illegible]): three anal spines: a free ray at base of pectoral which is elongated: articulated fin-rays as a rule branched. Scales present.

7. *Centropogon.* Sharp preorbital and preopercular spines: bones of the head armed. Teeth in jaws, vomer and palate. A single dorsal fin (D. [illegible]): three anal spines: no free ray at base of pectoral: articulated fin-rays as a rule branched. Scales present.

8. *Gymnapistus.* Sharp preorbital and preopercular spines: bones of the head armed. Teeth in jaws, vomer and palate. Two dorsal fins, the first with three spines: anal with three spines: no free ray at the base of pectoral: articulated fin-rays as a rule branched. Scales rudimentary or absent.

9. *Amblyapistus.* Head and body strongly compressed: no groove across occiput. Sharp preorbital and preopercular spines: bones of the head armed. Teeth in jaws, vomer and palate. A single dorsal fin (D. [illegible]): three anal spines: no free rays at base of pectoral: articulated fin-rays branched. Scales rudimentary or absent.

10. *Micropus.* Preorbital and preopercle with spines, also the sub- and inter-opercles: other bones of the head armed. No groove across occiput. Villiform teeth in the jaws only. A single or two dorsal fins with less spines than rays: two weak anal spines: no free rays at base of pectoral: ventral almost rudimentary. Articulated fin-rays branched. Scaleless.

11. *Minous.* Head large, a groove across occiput. Sharp preorbital and preopercular spines: bones of the head armed. Teeth in jaws and vomer, none on the palatines. A single dorsal fin (D. [illegible]): anal spines, if present, badly developed: pectoral with a free ray at its base. Articulated fin-rays unbranched. Scaleless.

12. *Cocotropus.* Head and body strongly compressed: no groove on occiput. Blunt preorbital and preopercular spines: bones of head armed. Teeth in jaws and vomer, none on palatines. A single dorsal fin (D. [illegible]): two weak anal spines: pectoral without free rays at its base. Articulated fin-rays unbranched. Scaleless.

13. *Pelor.* Head irregularly shaped, it and body with many skinny appendages: a groove across occiput. Bones of the head armed. Villiform teeth on jaws, vomer, and palatines. Articulated fin-rays generally branched. Scaleless.

14. *Choridactylus.* Head and body compressed: a groove on occiput. Sharp preorbital and preopercular spines: bones of the head armed. Teeth in the jaws, none on vomer or palate. A single dorsal fin (D. [illegible]): two anal spines: three free rays at base of pectoral. Articulated fin-rays branched. Scaleless.

15. *Synanceidium.* Head monstrous and irregularly shaped. Bones of the head with blunt spines. Teeth in jaws and vomer but not on the palate. A single dorsal fin (D. [illegible]): three anal spines: no free rays at base of pectoral. Articulated fin-rays branched. Scaleless.

16. *Synanceia.* Head monstrous, irregularly shaped. Bones of the head spineless. Teeth in jaws, none on vomer or palate. A single dorsal fin (D. [illegible]): three anal spines: no free rays at base of pectoral. Articulated fin-rays branched. Scaleless.

17. *Pseudosynanceia*. Eyes directed upwards. Villiform teeth in jaws and vomer. Dorsal spines strong (D. $\frac{12}{6}$); three anal spines: no free ray at base of pectoral. Articulated fin-rays unbranched. Scaleless.

18. *Polycaulis*. Body anteriorly sub-cylindrical, posteriorly compressed. Eyes directed somewhat upwards. Preopercle armed. Teeth villiform in the jaws, none on vomer or palate. A single dorsal fin (D. $\frac{12-14}{4-6}$): no anal spines (A. 11-15): no free rays at base of the pectoral fin. Articulated fin-rays unbranched. Scaleless.

M. Sauvage in his paper on *Triglidæ*, Cuv. and Val. (Sep. 1873) divides them as follows: 1, SCORPÆNIDÆ; 2, PLATYCEPHALIDÆ; 3, TRIGLIDÆ; and subdivides the first family thus:

SCORPÆNIDÆ.
- a. Body covered with ordinary scales as *Sebastes*, *Scorpæna*, *Pterois*, and group of *Apistus*—SCORPÆNI.
- b. Body scaleless or with spinate scales, as *Synanceidium*, *Synanceia*, *Minous*, *Pelor*, and group of *Cottus*, &c.—COTTINI.

Dr. Günther, "Fishes of Zanzibar," (p. xiv, errata) observes, "*before* SYNANCEIA insert Family COTTIDÆ," &c. I must refer to M. Sauvage's paper for my reasons for placing all the foregoing Genera in the present Family.

Genus, 1—SEBASTES, *Cuv. and Val.*

Branchiostegals seven: pseudobranchiæ. Head and body somewhat compressed. No groove on the occiput, usually a few small spines; preopercle armed. Villiform teeth on the jaws, vomer and palatines. Fins not elongated: a single dorsal, having the spinous portion more or less separated from the soft by a notch, spines twelve to fourteen: anal not elongated, with three spines: no free rays to the pectoral fin. Articulated fin-rays branched. Scales present and of moderate or small size, extending as far forwards as the orbit or even beyond: no skinny appendages. Air-vessel, as a rule, present. Pyloric appendages few or in moderate numbers.

SYNOPSIS OF INDIVIDUAL SPECIES.

1. *Sebastes Stoliczkæ*, D. $\frac{12}{10}$, A. $\frac{3}{5}$, L. l. 35. No spines on top of head. Reddish, marbled with brown: fins spotted or blotched. Nicobars.

1. Sebastes Stoliczkæ, Plate XXXVI, fig. 1.

B. vii, D. $\frac{12}{10}$, P. 14, V. 1/5, A. $\frac{3}{5}$, C. 16, L. l. 35, L. r. $\frac{42}{32}$, L. tr. 5/14.

Length of head 3/10, of caudal 2/13, height of body 3/11 of the total length. *Eyes*—diameter $3\frac{1}{4}$ in length of head, 3/4 of a diameter from end of snout, and also apart. Height of head equals its length without the snout. Interorbital space convex. The maxilla reaches to below the last third of the orbit. Vertical limb of preopercle serrated, and having three strong anteriorly-directed spines along its horizontal border: sub- and inter-opercles entire. No spines on the head: no groove below the eyes: a moderately strong opercular spine. A nasal tentacle nearly half the diameter of the orbit in length. *Teeth*—villiform in jaws, vomer, and palate. *Fins*—dorsal spines strong, increasing in length to the fourth which is more than half ($1\frac{3}{4}$) the height of the body, they gradually decrease to the last which equals three-fourths of the diameter of the orbit in length, the rays are almost of the same height as the spines. Pectoral as long as the head behind the front third of the eye and longer than the ventral which just reaches the vent: second anal spine much the strongest and longest, equalling the length of the pectoral fin: caudal rounded. *Scales*—finely ctenoid, those on the head and to below the third dorsal spine much smaller than those on the body: upper surface of head scaled as far as the snout, also along the suborbital ring of bones and on the cheeks and opercles: $4\frac{1}{2}$ rows between lateral-line and base of sixth dorsal spine: 10 between the ventral and the lateral-line. *Colours*—reddish, marbled with brown: some dark bands radiate from the eye: all the fins spotted, blotched and banded with brown or black.

Habitat.—Nicobars, from whence the specimen figured (life-size) was brought by the late Dr. Stoliczka.

Genus, 2—SEBASTICHTHYS, *Gill.*

Sebastodes, Ayres.

Differs from Sebastes in having no palatine teeth.

SYNOPSIS OF INDIVIDUAL SPECIES.

1. *Sebastichthys strongia*, D. 11-12 | $\frac{1}{9}$, A. $\frac{3}{5}$, L. l. 45. Seas of India to the Malay Archipelago.

1. Sebastichthys strongia.

Scorpæna strongia, Cuv. and Val. iv, p. 323; Quoy and Gaim. Voy. Astrol. Poissons, p. 683, pl. xi, f. 2; Less. Voy. Duperr. Zool. Poiss. p. 213; Klunz. Verh. z. b. Ges. Wien, 1870, p. 803.

Scorpæna cyanostigma, Bleeker, Buru, p. 400.

Sebastes strongensis, Günther, Catal. ii, p. 105.

B. vi, D. 11-12 | $\frac{1}{9}$, P. 19, V. 1/5, A. $\frac{3}{5}$, C. 15, L. l. 45, L. tr. 5/16.

Length of head 1/3, of pectoral 1/4, of caudal 2/11, height of body nearly 1/3 of the total length. *Eyes*—diameter a little more than 1/3 of length of head, 3/4 of a diameter from end of snout, 1/2 a diameter apart. Supraorbital ridge spined: two spinate lines given off posteriorly from the orbit, one towards the occiput, the other towards the lateral-line. A sharp spine on nostril: anterior edge of preorbital with obtuse spines. Ridge below the orbit to the angle of the preopercle also spiny, and two more strong spines on the lower margin of the preopercle. Three strong spines on preorbital and a very strong one at shoulder. Two tentacles above the orbit and several more about the head. The maxilla reaches to under the posterior third of the orbit. *Teeth*—villiform in both jaws, and also on the vomer. *Fins*—the lower eight rays of the pectoral with free extremities. Dorsal spines strong, increasing in length to the ninth. Second dorsal rather lower than the first. Second anal spine longest and strongest: caudal rounded. *Scales*—cover the body, the occiput, cheeks and opercles, also the bases of the soft rays of the fins. *Lateral-line*—in single tubes, with here and there tentacles. *Colours*—brownish, banded with darker, the first passing downwards through the eye: a large brown spot on opercle: fins irregularly banded in dotted lines.

Habitat.—Ceylon, Andamans, Malay Archipelago.

Genus, 3—Scorpæna, *Artedi.*

Scorpænopsis, Heck.; *Neosebastes*, Guichenot; *Pseudomonopterus*, Bleeker.

Branchiostegals seven: pseudobranchiæ. Head large, with a scaleless groove on the occiput, armed with spines and usually with skinny flaps. Villiform teeth on the jaws, vomer, and palatines. A single dorsal fin deeply notched, dividing the two portions, having twelve spines, and three in the anal, which latter fin is not elongated: pectoral large, without free rays. Air-vessel absent. Pyloric appendages few.

Geographical distribution.—Tropical seas, also in the Mediterranean and Atlantic coasts of America.

SYNOPSIS OF SPECIES.

1. *Scorpæna haplodactylus*, D. 11 | $\frac{1}{9}$, A. $\frac{3}{5}$, L. r. 43, L. tr. 6/22. An orbital tentacle. Brownish-black, banded and marbled. Andamans and Malay Archipelago.

2. *Scorpæna armata*, D. 11 | $\frac{1}{9}$, A. $\frac{3}{5}$, L. l. 35, L. tr. 9/19. No orbital tentacle. Roseate brown, with darker blotches. East Indies.

1. Scorpæna haplodactylus, Plate XXXVI, fig. 2.

Scorpæna aplodactylus, Bleeker, Ceram. ii, p. 698.
Scorpæna haplodactylus, Günther, Catal. ii, p. 117; Kner, Novara Fische, p. 116.

B. vii, D. 11 | $\frac{1}{9}$, P. 5+XII, V. 1/5, A. $\frac{3}{5}$, C. 15, L. l. 26, L. r. $\frac{42}{43}$, L. tr. 6/22.

Length of head 1/3, of pectoral 1/4, of caudal 1/7, height of body 3/10 of the total length. *Eyes*—diameter 1/4 of length of head, $1\frac{1}{2}$ diameters from the end of snout, and 1/2 a diameter apart. Width of head equals three-fourths of its length. The maxilla reaches to below the centre of the orbit. Interorbital space deeply concave, no groove below the eyes. Two spines on the posterior-superior edge of the orbit, the hind one of which is furnished with a tentacle. Three strong spines on the occipital and the same number on the temporal ridge, and one intermediate small spine. A strong turbinal spine: a suborbital spinate ridge: three strong spines on the vertical limb of the preopercle and two blunt ones along its horizontal border: two strong opercular spines. Several fleshy tentacles about the head. A strong spine above the base of the pectoral fin on the shoulder girdle. *Teeth*—villiform in the jaws, in a narrow V-shaped band on the vomer, and a few on the anterior end of the palatines. *Fins*—dorsal spines increase in length to the fourth, which equals half the height of the body, from it they decrease in length to the eleventh, between which and the next exists a deep notch, the twelfth spine twice as high as the eleventh: soft dorsal slightly higher than the spinous. Pectoral equals the length of the head behind the middle of the eyes, its twelve lower rays unbranched: second anal spine the strongest and longest, equalling half the height of the body: caudal rounded. *Scales*—on the cheeks, upper and hind edge of the opercles, and a few fleshy tentacles along the lateral-line. *Colours*—brownish-black, banded and marbled with darker: anal having a broad band along its basal half: one vertical band at the base of the caudal, another along its centre, and a dark margin edged with white: dorsal with brown marks.

Habitat.—Andamans (where the specimen figured life-size was procured) to the Malay Archipelago and beyond.

2. Scorpæna armata.

Sauvage, Nouv. Arch. du Museum, p. 49, t. ix, pl. 6, fig. 1.

B. vii, D. 11 | $\frac{1}{9}$, P. 6+XII, V. 1/5, A. $\frac{3}{5}$, C. 13, L. l. 35, L. tr. 9/19.

Length of head 4/11, of caudal 2/11, height of body 1/3 of the total length. *Eyes*—diameter 1/4 of length of head, $1\frac{1}{2}$ diameters from end of snout, and 3/4 of a diameter apart. The maxilla reaches to nearly below the hind edge of the orbit. Interorbital space very concave, with a quadrangular fossa, along which are two low ridges that terminate posteriorly in two spines: a deep groove below the eyes. Two or three spines along the upper margin of the orbit: a turbinal spine: two strong ones on the preorbital from which a ridge proceeds to a spine in the middle of the vertical border of the preopercle, below which are three smaller ones. Opercle with two spines. Occipital and temporal ridges spinate. *Teeth*—villiform in jaws, in a V-shaped band on the vomer, and a large band on the palatines. *Fins*—fifth dorsal spine rather above half the height of the body: pectorals and ventrals of the same length passing to slightly beyond the anus: third anal spine the longest, exceeding the highest in the dorsal fin: caudal slightly rounded. *Scales*—over body and head, none between the eyes. *Colours*—roseate brown, with darker blotches and a few yellowish-white spots: head spotted with black. Fins yellowish-brown, spotted with darker, sometimes forming lines.

Habitat.—Two specimens, obtained in the East Indies, were presented to the Paris Museum by M. Bosaré.

Genus, 4—Scorpænopsis, *Heckel*.

Scorpænichthys and *Parascorpæna*, Bleeker.

Differs from Scorpæna in having no palatine teeth.

Geographical distribution.—Tropical seas, also with those of the last genus.

SYNOPSIS OF SPECIES.

1. *Scorpænopsis Guamensis*, D. 12 | $\frac{1}{9}$, P. 9+X, A. $\frac{3}{5}$, L. r. 43. No orbital tentacle. Scales over cheeks and opercles. Brown, marbled with darker. East Indies to the Malay Archipelago.

2. *Scorpænopsis cirrhosa*, D. 11 | $\frac{1}{10}$, P. 6+XII, A. $\frac{3}{5}$, L. r. 56. Orbital tentacle, if present, small. Head scaleless. Pinkish brown marbled with darker.

3. *Scorpænopsis oxycephala*, D. 11 | $\frac{1}{10}$, P. 6+XII, A. $\frac{3}{5}$, L. r. 46. Orbital tentacle well developed. Scales on the upper portions of opercle and preopercle. Reddish brown, spotted and blotched with darker. Nicobars to the Malay Archipelago and beyond.

4. *Scorpænopsis rosea*, D. 11 | $\frac{1}{10}$, P. 6+XII, A. $\frac{3}{5}$, L. r. 43. An orbital tentacle. Scales on upper portion of opercles. Reddish brown, marbled. Seas of India.

5. *Scorpænopsis venosa*, D. 11 | $\frac{1}{9}$, P. 6+XII, A. $\frac{3}{5}$, L. l. 38. Apparently no orbital tentacle. Head scaleless. Reddish brown blotched with darker. Seas of India.

1. Scorpænopsis Guamensis.

Scorpæna Guamensis, Quoy and Gaim. Voy. Frey. Zool. p. 326.
? *Scorpæna polylepis*, Bleeker, Nat. Tyds. Ned. Ind. 1851, ii, p. 173.
Sebastes polylepis, Günther, Catal. ii, p. 106.*

B. vii, D. 12 | $\frac{1}{9}$, P. 9+X, V. 1/5, A. $\frac{3}{5}$, C. 13, L. r. 43.

Length of head 1/3, of caudal 1/5, height of body 2/7 of the total length. *Eyes*—diameter 2/7 of length of head, 1 diameter from end of snout, and 3/4 of a diameter apart. Interorbital space concave. No groove beneath the eyes. Supraorbital edge spinate. No orbital tentacle. The maxilla reaches to below the middle of the eye. Spines on head acute. *Teeth*—villiform in jaws and on the vomer. *Fins*—highest dorsal spines equal half of the height of the body. *Scales*—present on cheeks and opercles. *Colours*—brown marbled with darker.

Habitat.—Malay Archipelago, and said to have been brought from the East Indies.

2. Scorpænopsis cirrhosa.†

Perca cirrhosa, Thunb. Nya Handl. Stockh. xiv, 1793, p. 199, pl. 7, fig. 2.
Scorpæna cirrhosa, Cuv. and Val. iv, p. 318; Günther, Catal. ii, p. 120; Klunz. Verh. z. b. Ges. Wien, 1870, p. 801.
Scorpæna neglecta, Temm. and Schleg. p. 42, pl. 17, fig. 2, 3; Bleeker, Verh. Bat. Gen. xxvi, p. 79.
Scorpæna barbata, Rüpp. N. W. Fische, p. 105, t. 27, fig. 1.

B. vii, D. 11 | $\frac{1}{10}$, P. 6+XII, V. 1/5, A. $\frac{3}{5}$, C. 13, L. r. 56.

Length of head 1/3, of caudal 1/6, height of body 3/10 of the total length. *Eyes*—diameter 1/5 of length of head, $1\frac{1}{2}$ diameters from end of snout, and 2/3 of a diameter apart. Interorbital space deeply concave, with two low ridges along its whole extent which do not end in spines: a deep groove below the anterior edge of the orbit: a shallow groove over occiput: occipital and temporal ridges strongly spinate. Two strong spines along the upper edge of the orbit. Sometimes an orbital tentacle of small size, which is however mostly absent. A spinate ridge from the preorbital across the cheeks, preopercle spinate: opercle with two spines. *Tentacles*—besides the orbital one, there are many more about the head and a very large one above the angle of the mouth: there are also some on the body. *Teeth*—in jaws and vomer, none on the palate. *Fins*—dorsal spines increase in length to the fourth, which is half as high as the body, and usually shorter than the second of the anal, which equals half the length of the head: ventral reaches the anus: caudal cut nearly square. *Scales*—none on the head. *Colours*—Pinkish brown marbled with darker: fins spotted and blotched.

Habitat.—West coast of Africa, seas of India to Malay Archipelago and beyond.

3. Scorpænopsis oxycephala, Plate XXXVI, fig. 3.

Scorpæna oxycephalus, Bleeker, Sclerop. p. 20, and Verh. Bat. Gen. xxii, Sclerop. p. 7; Kner, Novara Fische, p. 116.
Scorpæna cirrhosa, Günther, Catal. ii, p. 120 (in part).
Scorpænopsis oxycephala, Sauvage, Nov. Arch. Mus. t. ix, p. 52, pl. 6, fig. 3 and 3a.

B. vii, D. 11 | $\frac{1}{10}$, P. 6+XII, V. 1/5, A. $\frac{3}{5}$, C. 13, L. r. [illegible], L. tr. 7/22.

* Specimens marked *Sebastes polylepis*, B. M. Catal. ii, p. 107, belong to this species, under which designation they are now placed.

† The specimen of *Scorpæna polyprion*, B. M. Catal. ii, p. 115, recorded as "d. Half grown, Ceylon, presented by Captain Gascoigne," appears to belong to this species.

Length of head 4/13, of caudal 2/11, height of body 4/17 of the total length. *Eyes*—diameter 1/5 of length of head, $1\frac{1}{2}$ diameters from end of snout, and 1 apart. Interorbital space deeply concave, with two low ridges along its whole extent, and which do not end in spines, between them anteriorly is a third: a deep groove below the front third of the orbit continued as a shallow one below the eye: a groove across the occiput having one spine anterior to it and two more belonging to the occipital ridge posterior to it. Three strong spines along the upper edge of the orbit with a tentacle between the last two. A strong turbinal spine. A tentacle to the front nostril. Preorbital with ridges in a star-shape, about seven in number, and ending in spines: a spinate ridge across the cheeks to a strong spine in the centre of the vertical border of the preopercle, which has two more below it and one blunt one along its lower limb: opercle with two spines. Temporal ridge spined and one spine between it and the occipital ridge. A spine on the shoulder girdle just above the base of the pectoral fin. *Tentacles*—besides those enumerated, there exists a large one above the angle of the mouth, some small ones along the margin of the preopercle, a few also on the lateral-line and on some of the body scales. *Teeth*—villiform in jaws and vomer. *Fins*—dorsal spines rather strong, the third very slightly longer than the fourth, and equal to two-fifths of the height of the body and about as long as the rays: pectoral as long as the head without the snout and reaching as far as the ventral: second anal spine much the strongest and equal to the length of the head behind the last third of the eye: caudal cut square. *Scales*—present on the upper portions of the opercle and preopercle, eight rows between sixth dorsal spine and lateral-line. *Colours*—reddish, clouded with brown, and having a few blackish spots: a dark band commences in the upper half of the interspinous membrane between the second and third dorsal spines, and passing along the upper third of the fin, descends between the sixth and seventh on to the back: many blotches on the fins: a dark band descends over the last half of the caudal: three narrow dark horizontal bands go across the lower half of the anal: undivided pectoral rays spotted; ventral with brown spots.

In a young specimen ($2\frac{3}{4}$ inches long) captured along with the one described above, the eye is comparatively much larger, the cheeks and opercles are scaled, there are two supraorbital tentacles and a short one on the upper angle of the eye, whilst the body is comparatively higher.

Habitat.—Nicobars to the Malay Archipelago and beyond: the specimen figured (over 6 inches in length) was obtained at the Nicobars.

4. Scorpænopsis rosea, Plate XXXVI, fig. 4.

Scorpæna rosea, Day, Proc. Zool. Soc. 1867, p. 703.

B. vii, D. 11 | $\frac{1}{\text{v-viii}}$, P. 6+XII, V. 1/5, A. $\frac{3}{5}$, C. 15, L. l. 43, L. tr. 7/18.

Length of head 1/5, of pectoral 1/4, of caudal 1/5, height of body 1/3 of the total length. *Eyes*—somewhat elevated, with a deep groove below, and anterior and posterior depressions: interorbital space deeply concave, with an elevated smooth ridge on either side: diameter of eyes 1/4 of length of head, $1\frac{1}{2}$ from end of snout, and 3/4 of a diameter apart. Snout rather elevated, a transverse depression between it and the orbit. The maxilla reaches to below the centre of the orbit: lower jaw the longer. A sharp turbinal spine; a broad fleshy fringed tentacle to the anterior nostril. Above the angle of the preopercle is a ridge with five more backwardly directed spines. Along the angle and lower edge of the preopercle are three denticulations, the superior strong and sharp, the others blunted, also three fleshy tentacles along its border and one on its surface. Interopercle with a blunt spine and tentacle. Opercle with a central bony ridge ending in two spines. Temporal ridge containing three spines, and occipital one likewise spiny; whilst there is one spine between it and the ridge below it. Orbit with a strong spine at its posterior-superior—and another at its superior—edge, the last with a long wide tentacle at its base. Several fleshy tentacles exist on the snout, a large one at the angle of the mouth, and two on the end of the upper jaw: also three rather large ones on the lower jaw. *Teeth*—villiform, a V-shaped patch on the vomer, none on the palatines. *Fins*—dorsal spines moderately strong, the third the longest, interspinous membrane rather deeply cleft and extended beyond each spine. Pectoral with its lowest twelve rays unbranched and minute fleshy appendages attached to them. Second and third anal spines of equal length, the former much the stronger. Caudal cut nearly square. *Scales*—present, some on the upper port of the opercle, head otherwise scaleless. Lateral-line in 23 or 24 tubes. *Colours*—rosy, marbled with greyish: one or two irregular vertical grey bands on the caudal fin: dorsal, anal, and ventral also banded: pectoral with numerous dark spots.

S. *Mauritiana*, C. V. appears very similar, it has 43 rows of scales above the lateral-line and 40 below it. Six branched pectoral rays but only 10 simple ones.

Habitat.—Madras.

5. Scorpænopsis venosa.

Scorpæna mooroo-lootoo, Russell, Fish. Vizag. i, p. 44, pl. 56.
Scorpæna venosa, Cuv. and Val. iv, p. 317; Swainson, Fish. ii, p. 266.

B. vii, D. 11 | $\frac{1}{9}$, P. 18, V. 1/5, A. $\frac{3}{5}$, C. 16, L. l. 38.

Length of head 1/3 of the total length. *Eyes*—rather above one diameter from the end of snout and also one apart. The maxilla reaches to below the last third of the eye. Interorbital space very concave with two longitudinal ridges that end posteriorly in spines: a groove before the eyes: a quadrangular space on the vertex bordered by spines: turbinal and preorbital spines, a spiny ridge across the cheeks: vertical limb of preopercle spinate: occipital and temporal ridges spinate. *Tentacles*—none apparent over the orbit (?): very distinct on lower jaw and different parts of the head. Valenciennes observes that its most remarkable character is that all the skin of the head between the spines is as if it were veined with small scooped out lines which join on all sides, and thus form a network which has the appearance of scales. *Teeth*—none on the palate. *Fins*—fourth dorsal spine the longest and equal in length to the second of the anal which is 2/5 of the length of the head. *Scales*—none on head, those on body oblong, ctenoid with a single row of minute spines along its marginal border. *Colours*—"head and body dark, with a mixture of dull red: the throat and belly are of a pink colour. The fins irregularly streaked black and red: the ventral at its root is pink like the belly."—(Russell.)

M. Sauvage, who has kindly compared Valenciennes' type specimen for me with a drawing I made of *S. rosea*, has furnished me with the additional information detailed above. He likewise observes "*S. rosea* differs from *S. rosea* (according to your figure) by the head being more elongated: the body also more elongated and the dorsal spines not being so high."

Habitat—Coromandel coast of India.

Genus, 5—Pterois, *Cuv.*

Macrochyrus, Pterolepius, Pteropterus and *Brachyrus*, Swainson.

Branchiostegals seven: pseudobranchiæ. Head rather large, armed with spines and having skinny flaps: no occipital groove. Villiform teeth in jaws and on vomer, none on the palate. A single deeply notched dorsal fin, having from twelve to thirteen spines: anal with two or three spines and five rays: rays, and sometimes spines, elongated: no pectoral appendages. Air-vessel large. Pyloric appendages few.

Geographical distribution.—Red Sea, coasts of Africa, through the seas of India to the Malay Archipelago and Polynesia.

It does not appear that any very great value can be placed on the comparative length of the dorsal spines, or pectoral rays in this Genus of Fishes, as they are subject to considerable modifications, some being dependant upon age, and others seem to be subject to variation in specimens of the same species. It has yet to be ascertained whether the orbital tentacle is equally developed in both sexes.

SYNOPSIS OF SPECIES.

1. *Pterois Russellii*, D. 12 | $\frac{1}{11-11}$, L. r. [illegible]. A short supraorbital tentacle. Interorbital space and nape scaled. Caudal unspotted. No white spot in axilla. Pectoral grey, with its two upper rays spotted. Seas of India to the Malay Archipelago.

2. *Pterois miles*, D. 12 | $\frac{1}{10-11}$, L. r. 92. A short supraorbital tentacle. Interorbital space and nape scaled. Dorsal, caudal, and anal spotted. A white spot in the axilla. Seas of India.

3. *Pterois zebra*, D. 12 | $\frac{1}{10}$, L. r. [illegible]. A long supraorbital tentacle. Interorbital space scaleless. Dorsal, caudal, pectoral and anal spotted. A white spot in the axilla.

4. *Pterois volitans*, D. 12 | $\frac{1}{10-11}$, L. r. 90. A long supraorbital tentacle. Interorbital space and nape scaleless, or with rudimentary scales. Dorsal, caudal and anal spotted. A white spot in the axilla. Red Sea, East coast of Africa, seas of India to Australia.

5. *Pterois cincta*, D. 11 | $\frac{1}{9}$, L. r. 45. A long supraorbital tentacle. Nape scaled. Soft dorsal, caudal and anal spotted. No white spot in axilla. Red Sea, seas of India and beyond.

1. Pterois Russellii, Plate XXXVI, fig. 5.

Gasterosteus volitans, Russell, Fish. Vizag. ii, p. 25, pl. 133 (*kodipungi*), (not *G. volitans*, Linn.)
Pterois Russellii, (Van Hass.) Bennett, Proc. Zool. Soc. 1831, p. 128.
Pterolepius longicauda, Swains. Fish. ii, p. 264.
Pterois miles, Cantor, Catal. p. 42 (not Bennett).
Pterois kodipungi, (Russell) Bleeker, Banka, p. 450; Günther, Catal. ii, p. 124.
Pseudomonopterus kodipungi, Bleeker, Fish. Madagascar, p. 87.

B. vii, D. 12 | $\frac{1}{11-11}$, P. 13, V. 1/5, A. $\frac{3}{5}$, C. 14, L. r. [illegible], L. tr. 11/33.

Length of head 1/4, of caudal 2/7, height of body 1/4 of the total length. *Eyes*—diameter 2/9 to 1/5 of the length of head, $1\frac{1}{2}$ diameters from the end of snout, and 3/4 of a diameter apart. The maxilla reaches to below the middle of the orbit. Preorbital with a spinate ridge traversing its centre, and continued over the cheek to the upper preopercular spine, below which latter there exist two or three more on its vertical, and two along its horizontal edge. A spine at the posterior-superior angle of the orbit and a short supraorbital tentacle. Interorbital space deeply concave, it and the occiput scaled. Occipital and temporal ridges spiny; a small turbinal spine. A rather long fleshy tentacle at the angle of the preorbital, one at the anterior nostril, and several more about the head. *Teeth*—villiform in jaws and vomer. *Fins*—dorsal spines increase in length to the fifth which equals the height of the body and is longer than the rays: the pectoral, with its membrane, especially between its four upper rays, deeply cleft, it reaches a little beyond the base of the caudal, or even further: ventral extends to the anal rays: third anal spine the longest, equalling the length of the snout: caudal pointed. *Scales*—eleven rows between lateral-line and 6th dorsal spine. *Colours*—reddish, with from eleven to twelve broad dark vertical bands, with intermediate narrow ones. A black spot on the shoulder behind the opercle, no white spot in the axilla. Pectoral grey, its upper two rays with black spots, its lowest five pinkish, in the adult all are spotted: ventrals grey, with obscurely marked white spots: dorsal spines grey, or white annulated with grey, soft dorsal, caudal, and anal flesh-coloured without spots, but having in adults a narrow black edge.

Bennett observes that Russell's fish, *Gasterosteus volitans*, is identical with *P. volitans* in Sir S. Raffles' life, but not with *P. volitans*, Linn.

Habitat.—Seas of India, Mauritius to the Malay Archipelago. Very common in Madras, the specimen figured is 7 inches long, the largest obtained 11½ inches. Jerdon (M. J. L. and Sc. 1851, p. 141) observes this fish is termed *Sia tumbi*, Tam. at Madras.

2. Pterois miles, Plate XXXVII, fig. 2.

Scorpæna miles, Bennett, Fish. Ceylon, p. 9, pl. 9.
Pterois miles, Günther, Catal. ii, pp. 125, 520; Day, Fish. Malabar, p. 40.
Pterois muricata, Cuv. and Val. iv, p. 363; Rüppell, N. W. Fische, p. 107; Kner, Novara Fische, p. 118; Klunz, Verh. z. b. Ges. Wien. 1870, p. 807.
? *Pterois geniserra*, Cuv. and Val. iv, p. 066.
Macrochyrus miles, Swainson, Fishes, ii, p. 264.
K[illegible] tumbi, Tam. "Flying dragon."

B. vii, D. 12 | $\frac{1}{10-11}$, P. 14, V. 1/5, A. $\frac{3}{6-7}$, C. 14, L. r. 92, L. tr. 12/[illegible], Vert. 10/14.

Length of head 2/9, of pectoral 4/11, of caudal 2/9, height of body 2/7 of the total length. *Eyes*—diameter 2/7 to 1/4 of the length of head, 1½ diameters from the end of snout, and 1 apart. The maxilla reaches to below the front edge of the orbit. Preorbital covered in its lower third with spinate elevations which are continued across the cheeks to the angle of the preopercle where they end in three spines in the young or clusters of them in the adult: two strong turbinal spines: upper edge of orbit spinate as is also the temporal ridge as far as the commencement of the lateral-line: interorbital space convex but not very deeply so: occipital ridge spinate, most strongly so posteriorly where it ends in a flattened blade-like spine which has several more near its base. A short orbital tentacle, one at the anterior nostril, a long preorbital one over angle of the mouth, and other short ones about the head. *Teeth*—villiform in jaws and vomer. *Fins*—dorsal spines moderately strong, highest from the 6th to the 12th, which equal the height of the body and are longer than the rays: pectoral with the inter-radial membrane most deeply cleft between the first three rays, and reaching to below the end of the base of the dorsal fin: ventral reaches the anal, the third spine of which last fin is the longest and equal to the length of the snout: caudal wedge-shaped. *Scales*—present in the interorbital space and on the nape. *Colours*—red, with many dark vertical bands much wider than the ground colour, in fact, in the first two-thirds of the body the ground colour appears like narrow light bands: in the last third of the body the dark bands are wider apart with from one to three intermediate narrow ones. Head banded, bands mostly radiating from the eye, two of an S-shape over the chest. A white spot surrounded by black in the axilla. Dorsal spines with from five to six dark rings: soft dorsal, caudal, and anal covered with small black spots: pectoral with large black blotches on a lighter ground: ventral nearly black, with white and light brown spots.

Habitat.—From the Red Sea through those of India, to the Malay Archipelago and beyond. The largest specimen captured at Madras measured 14 inches in length. Klunzinger considers this another form of *P. volitans*, from which it may be distinguished by its scaled nape, comparatively short pectoral, and the numerous spines on its head. In a specimen 9 inches long the pectoral reaches the root of the caudal.

3. Pterois zebra.

Cuv. and Val. iv, p. 367; Bleeker, Amb. and Ceram. p. 265; Quoy and Gaim. Voy. Uranie, p. 329, and Voy. Astrol. Poiss. p. 692, pl. xi, f. 6; Günther, Catal. ii, p. 125.

Brachyrus zebra, Swainson, Fishes, ii, p. 264.
Pseudomonopterus zebra, Bleeker, Fish. Madag. p. 87.

B. vii, D. 12 | $\frac{1}{10}$, P. 17, V. 1/5, A. $\frac{3}{5-6}$, C. 14, L. r. $\frac{45}{50}$, L. tr. 9/.

Length of head 2/7, of caudal 2/9, height of body 2/7 of the total length. *Eyes*—diameter 2/7 of length of head, (in a specimen 3½ inches long,) 1 diameter from end of snout, and 2/3 of a diameter apart. Interorbital space deeply concave, traversed by two low ridges which posteriorly end in a strong spine: interorbital space scaleless. The maxilla reaches to below the first third of the orbit. Preopercle with three spines on its vertical border at and above its angle: turbinal spines present. Two or three spines along the upper edge of the orbit, its hind margin likewise serrated. Ridges in a stellate form on the preorbital, one of which is continued backwards in a spinate form across the suborbitals and cheeks to the superior preopercular spine: three strong spines on the occipital and four along the temporal ridge. A long orbital tentacle equalling more than half the length of the head: fleshy tentacles along the lower edge of the preorbital, the hind one over the angle of the mouth being very large. *Teeth*—villiform in jaws and vomer. *Fins*—dorsal spines increase in length to the seventh, remaining about of equal height to the tenth, or as long as the height of the body and higher than the rays: pectoral with 17 rays, the upper four having filamentous prolongations, and reaching as far as the base of the caudal: ventrals reach the anal spines, the third of which is slightly the longest, and equal to 1½ diameters of the orbit in length: caudal wedge-shaped. *Colours*—body vertically banded with narrow intermediate ones: a black blotch with a white central spot in the axilla: dorsal spines annulated with black: soft dorsal and anal with black spots in irregular lines: four or five sinuous vertical bands on the caudal: pectoral and ventral with black transverse bands and lines as wide or wider than the ground-colour.

Habitat.—Seas of India to the Malay Archipelago and beyond. I have this species from the Andamans.

4. **Pterois volitans,** Plate XXXVII, fig. 1.

Gasterosteus volitans, Linn. Syst. Nat. XII, i, p. 491.

Scorpæna volitans, Bloch, t. 184; Gmel. Linn. p. 1217; Bl. Schn. p. 193; Lacép. iii, p. 282; Gronov. ed. Gray, p. 119; Bennett, Fish. Ceylon, p. 1, pl. 1.

Scorpæna miles, Lacép. iii, p. 278.

Pterois volitans, Cuv. and Val. iv, p. 352, pl. 88; Swainson, Fishes, ii, p. 264; Bleeker, Sclerop. p. 8; Rüppell, N. W. Fische, p. 107; Günther, Catal. ii, p. 122; Day, Fishes of Malabar, p. 38; Klunz. Verh. z. b. Ges. Wien, 1870, p. 806.

Pseudomonopterus volitans, Bleeker, Fish. Madagas. p. 87.

Pterois à nageoires lie de vin, Liénard, Nat. Hist. Soc. Mauritius, 1839, p. 33.

Purroo-ah, Mal.: *Cheeb-ta-ta-deh*, Andam.

B. vii, D. 12 | $\frac{1}{10-11}$, P. 14, V. 1/5, A. $\frac{3}{7-8}$, C. 14, L. r. 90, L. tr. 13/, Cæc. pyl. 3, Vert. 10/14.

Length of head 3/11 to 3/13, of caudal 3/11 to 4/13, height of body 4/13 to 1/3 of the total length. *Eyes*—diameter 1/4 to 2/9 of length of head, $1\frac{1}{2}$ to $1\frac{1}{4}$ diameters from end of snout, and 1 apart. Interorbital space deeply concave, it and the nape scaleless, or with some very rudimentary scales: it is traversed by two low ridges which do not terminate posteriorly in spines. The maxilla reaches to below the front edge or first third of the orbit. Preopercle with two or three spines along its vertical border, and three more along its lower limb: turbinal spines present: some blunt ones along the upper edge of the orbit: occipital ridge with two blade-like spines: two more, but less developed, on the temporal ridge: lower margin of preorbital with three blunt spines and a raised line, sometimes almost spinate, running across the cheeks from that bone to the upper preopercular spine. Opercular spine but slightly developed. A long tentacle from the upper edge of the orbit and about half the length of the head: also fleshy tentacles along the lower edge of the preorbital, the hind one of which is most developed. *Teeth*—villiform in jaws and vomer. *Fins*—the first ten dorsal spines are high, and equal to the height, or one half more, of the body, the interspinous membrane deeply emarginate: soft portion of fin not so high as the spinous: pectoral reaching to or beyond the root of the caudal, the membrane between the upper four rays deeply cleft: ventrals reach the anal rays: third anal spine the longest, being three-fourths as high as the first dorsal spine: caudal rather rounded or wedge-shaped. *Colours*—reddish, with vertical brown bands having narrower and lighter intermediate ones: three or four broad ones radiate from the eye: one passes over the nape, and seven or eight more are present on the body, the third and fourth usually coalescing under the middle of the pectoral fin. A black mark in the axilla, having a pure white spot in its centre. Dorsal spines annulated with black: soft dorsal, caudal, and anal spotted: pectoral greyish with light-coloured spots: ventral slate-coloured with white spots.

Habitat.—Red Sea, East coast of Africa, through the seas of India to Australia.

5. **Pterois cincta,** Plate XXXVII, fig. 3.

? *Pterois radiata*, (Park.) Cuv. and Val. iv, p. 369; Garrett, Fische d. Sudsee, t. lvi, fig. A.

Pterois cincta, Rüpp. N. W. Fische, p. 108, t. 26, f. 3; Günther, Catal. ii, p. 125; Klunz. Verh. z. b. Ges. Wien, 1870, p. 806.

B. vii, D. 11 | $\frac{1}{11-12}$, P. 16, V. 1/5, A. $\frac{3}{5}$, C. 15, L. l. 25, L. r. 45, L. tr. 7/25.

Length of head 3/11, of caudal 1/4 to 3/14, of pectoral 2/3, height of body 3/11 of the total length. *Eyes*—diameter 2/7 of length of head, 1 diameter from end of snout, and 2/3 of a diameter apart. Interorbital space very concave. The maxilla reaches to below the hind edge of the orbit. Tentacle above the orbit long, and reaching as far as the end of the snout. Margin of orbit serrated: occipital and temporal ridges spinate: other bones about the head comparatively feebly armed. Several fleshy tentacles on the head: long ones on the snout. *Teeth*—villiform in jaws and vomer. *Fins*—eighth to ninth dorsal spines the highest, equalling half the height of the body: pectoral reaches as far as the end of the caudal. *Scales*—on nape. *Colours*—snout uncoloured: a deep brown band edged with white extends from the eye to the angle of the interopercle: the second encircles the neck, and there are six more on the body, which looks as if it were traversed vertically by narrow milk-white bands. A dark band at the base of the pectoral, which is also stained in its outer half; a blackish mark in the axilla without any white spot. Ventral greyish, its spine white: caudal spotted.

The name *P. radiata* attached to a figure of this species in Garrett's Fische d. Sudsee, l. c. would appear* to show that Dr. Günther considers the figure of a *Pterois*, made at Otaheiti by Parkinson, to be identical with the above. See Cuv. and Val. iv, p. 369.

Habitat.—Red Sea, Andamans to the Malay Archipelago and beyond.

Genus, 6—Apistus, *Cuv.*

Pterichthys, Swainson; *Polemius*, Kaup.

Branchiostegals six. Head and body rather compressed. No groove across occiput. Strong and sharp

* Parts i-iii have been published in this country, including lx plates, but only 96 pages of letterpress.

preorbital and preopercular spines: opercles armed. A mandibular barbel. Villiform teeth in jaws, vomer and palate. A single dorsal fin with more spines than rays (D. [illegible]) *: three anal spines: pectoral elongated and having a free ray at its base. Articulated fin-rays branched. Scales present. Air-vessel with a constriction. A cleft behind the fourth gill.*

Geographical distribution.—From the Red Sea through those of India.

SYNOPSIS OF INDIVIDUAL SPECIES.

1. *Apistus carinatus*, D. [illegible], P. 12+1, A. $\frac{3}{7}$, L. r. 70. Body greyish above, rosy below: pectoral black and a black blotch on the spinous dorsal: soft dorsal and anal banded in spots. Seas of India to the Malay Archipelago and beyond.

1. Apistus carinatus, Plate XXXVII, fig. 4.

Scorpæna carinata, Bl. Schn. p. 193.
Trigla mooruk-wiroo, Russell, Fish. Vizag. ii, p. 45, pl. 160, B.
Apistus alatus, Cuv. and Val. iv, p. 392; Tem. Schleg. Fauna Japon, p. 49; Günther, Catal. ii, p. 131.
Apistus carinatus, Cuv. and Val. iv, p. 395.
Apistus Israëlitarum, (Ehrenb.) Cuv. and Val. iv, p. 396; Günther, Catal. ii, p. 131; Klunz. Verh. z. b. Ges. Wien, 1870, p. 809.
Pterichthys alatus et *carinatus*, Swainson, Fish. ii, p. 265.
Polemius alatus, Kaup. Wiegm. Arch. 1858, p. 333.

B. vi, D. [illegible], P. 12+1, V. 1/5, A. $\frac{3}{7}$, C. 12, L. r. 70.

Length of head from 2/7 to 3/11, of caudal 1/4 to 2/9, height of body 3/13 to 1/4 of the total length. *Eyes*—directed slightly upwards and outwards, diameter 2/7 to 1/4 of length of head, rather above 1 diameter from end of snout, and 1/3 of a diameter apart. Upper surface of the head rugose with two divergent lines passing from the snout between the eyes to the occiput where they terminate in small spines a little in front of either side of the base of the dorsal fin. The maxilla reaches to below the centre of the orbit. Preorbital spine as long as the orbit, having two small ones anteriorly on the lower edge of the bone. Preopercle with one strong spine and two or three small ones along its lower edge: opercle rugose, with two spines and a spinate temporal ridge. Barbels—a long slender one, equalling the diameter of the eye, is situated below the mandibular symphysis, and another a short distance behind it. *Teeth*—villiform in jaws, vomer and palate. *Fins*—first dorsal spines increase to the sixth, then decrease to the fourteenth; in some specimens the first few dorsal spines are shorter than in others: membrane deeply notched, fifteenth spine nearly twice as long as the preceding one: pectoral reaching to the base of the last dorsal ray, its single appendage to the first of the anal: ventral slightly longer: third anal spine the longest: caudal cut square. *Scales*—small, somewhat trefoil in shape. *Air-vessel*—thick, constricted in the centre. *Colours*—body greyish along the back, becoming rosy on the abdomen: pectorals deep black: appendage milk-white: dorsal diaphanous, tinged with grey and edged with black, a deep black blotch from the eighth to the fourteenth spine: three oblique brownish streaks on the soft dorsal, which also has a brown edging: upper pectoral ray white: caudal with four vertical black bands: anal greyish, with a yellow horizontal band.

Russell mentions a variety of a grey colour. Ehrenberg's specimen at Berlin has D. $\frac{14}{9}$, not $\frac{15}{9}$ as given by C.V. and Klunzinger.

Habitat.—Seas of India to the Malay Archipelago and beyond, attaining 5 inches in length.

Genus, 7—Centropogon, *Günther.*

Gymnapistes, sp. Swainson.

Branchiostegals six or seven. Head and body rather strongly compressed: no groove on occiput. Preorbital with a strong spine, preopercle likewise spinate, opercle armed. Villiform teeth in the jaws, vomer and palatine bones. A single dorsal fin with more spines than rays (D. [illegible]) *: anal with three spines: pectoral without any free rays at its base: articulated fin-rays branched. Scales present. (A narrow cleft behind the fourth gill.)*

Geographical distribution.—Seas of India to the Malay Archipelago and beyond.

SYNOPSIS OF INDIVIDUAL SPECIES.

1. *Centropogon Indicus*, D. $\frac{15}{8}$, A. $\frac{3}{5}$, L. r. 80. Pinkish, with irregular bands on the head: bars on body, anal and caudal fins. Madras.

1. Centropogon Indicus, Plate XXXVIII, fig. 2.

B. vii, D. $\frac{15}{8}$, P. 10, V. 1/4, A. $\frac{3}{5}$, C. 14, L. r. 80.

Length of head 3/10, of caudal 1/5, height of body 1/4 of the total length. *Eyes*—diameter 2/7 of length of head, 3/4 of a diameter from end of snout, and 2/3 of a diameter apart. The maxilla reaches to below the first third of the eye: lower jaw slightly the longer. Interorbital space slightly concave, traversed by two ridges which posteriorly have rather spinate terminations. Preorbital with a strong spine extending to below the last third or hind edge of the eye, and having a small one at its base. A strong preopercular spine equal to two-thirds of the diameter of the orbit in length, five more blunt ones along its angle and lower edge: opercle with two spines: occipital and temporal ridges sharp but not spinate. *Teeth*—villiform in jaws, vomer and palate. *Fins*—second and third dorsal spines the longest and about equal to two-thirds the height of the body, longer also than the rays: soft portion of the dorsal fin not joined to the caudal: pectoral as long as the head excluding the snout, all the rays branched: ventral reaches the anus: third anal spine considerably the longest and equal in length to the highest in the dorsal fin: caudal slightly rounded. *Scales*—distinct, none on the head. *Colours*—pinkish, with irregular markings over the head, the cheeks being barred with pinkish and brown vertical bands: three or four badly defined vertical bars on the body, the last being over the base of the caudal fin: a vertical brown band over the last third of caudal fin, and the posterior third of the anal banded: ventral nearly black in its last half.

Habitat.—Madras, the specimen figured is $2\frac{1}{4}$ inches long.

Genus, 8—GYMNAPISTUS, *Swains.*

Apistus, sp. Cuv. and Val.: *Trichosomus*,* sp. Swainson: *Prosopodasys*, Günther.

Branchiostegals six. Head and body somewhat compressed: no groove across the occiput. Preorbital and preopercle with strong, sharp spines: opercle armed. Villiform teeth in jaws, vomer and palate. Dorsal fin formed of two portions, the first of three spines which are connected by membrane with the second part, the spines in greater number than the rays: three anal spines, pectoral without any free rays at its base: articulated fin-rays branched. Scales rudimentary or absent.

Geographical distribution.—Seas of India to the Malay Archipelago and beyond.

SYNOPSIS OF SPECIES.

1. *Gymnapistus niger*, D. 3 | $\frac{9-10}{8}$, A. $\frac{3}{5}$. Scales absent. Nearly black. Seas of India to the Malay Archipelago.

2. *Gymnapistus dracæna*, D. 3 | [illegible], A. $\frac{3}{4-5}$. Scales rudimentary. Greyish-brown, with a black blotch on the dorsal fin between the third and seventh spines: other fins marked with black. Seas of India.

1. Gymnapistus niger, Plate XXXVII, fig. 5.

Apistus niger, Cuv. and Val. iv, p. 415.
Gymnapistes niger, Swainson, Fishes, ii, p. 266.
Prosopodasys niger, Günther, Catal. ii, p. 141.
Pon-the-cho-royno-dah, Andam.

B. vi, D. 3 | $\frac{9-10}{8}$, P. 10, V. 1/5, A. $\frac{3}{5}$, C. 9.

Length of head 3/10, of caudal 2/9, height of body 1/3 of the total length. *Eyes*—diameter 1/4 of length of head, 1 diameter from end of snout, and 3/4 of a diameter apart. Mouth oblique, lower jaw very slightly the longer; the maxilla reaches to below the last third of the orbit. Preorbital with a very strong sharp spine reaching to beyond the hind edge of the orbit. Preopercle with a sharp spine, as long as one diameter of the orbit, about the middle of its vertical border, with three obtuse ones below it and two along its horizontal limb, Interorbital space slightly concave. *Teeth*—villiform in jaws, vomer and palate. *Fins*—the first dorsal commences over the hind third of the orbit, the interspinous membrane of the two fins continuous, the second spine is two-thirds as high as the body and there is a short interspace between the two fins: the rayed portion is of equal height with the second part of the spinous, a membraneous prolongation goes from the end of the fin nearly to the base of the caudal. Pectoral, which is 1/5 of the total length, reaches to above the anus, but the ventral does not extend quite so far: third anal spine longer but weaker than the second: caudal cut square. All the articulated fin-rays branched at their extremities. *Scales*—absent except in the form of roughnesses here and there in the skin. *Colours*—brownish-black, caudal yellowish-white, striated with brown and having a dark band in its last fourth and a white external edge.

Habitat.—Seas of India to the Malay Archipelago: very numerous at the Andamans where the specimen (figured life-size) was captured. The natives assert that wounds from its spines are exceedingly venomous.

2. Gymnapistus dracæna, Plate XXXVIII, fig. 1.

Apistus dracæna, Cuv. and Val. iv, p. 403.
Apistus Belengeri, Cuv. and Val. iv, p. 412; Belenger, Voy. Ind. Orient. p. 349.
Trichosomus dracæna, Swainson, Fishes, ii, p. 265.
Prosopodasys dracæna, Günther, Catal. ii, p. 140; Day, Fishes of Malabar, p. 42.
Tetraroge Belengeri, Day, Fish. Malabar, p. 41.

B. vi, D. 3 | [illegible], P. 13, V. 1/5, A $\frac{3}{4-5}$, C. 13.

Length of head 2/7, of caudal 1/4, height of body 1/3 of the total length. *Eyes*—diameter 1/4 of length of head, 3/4 of a diameter from end of snout, and 2/3 of a diameter apart. Width of head equals its length behind the orbit. The maxilla reaches to below the first third of the orbit: lower jaw the longer and having a tubercle at the symphysis. Preorbital with a strong sharp spine directed backwards, three-fourths of the orbit

* Preoccupied by Trichosoma, Rud. Vermes, 1819, also (Ramb.) Boisdav. Lepidop. 1834.

in length and having a small one at its base. Preopercle with a sharp spine as long as the orbit, and three or four blunt points along its angle and lower limb. Opercle with two spines. *Teeth*—villiform in jaws, vomer and palate. *Fins*—dorsal spines sharp but slender; the first arises over the middle of the eye, the interspinous membrane is deeply notched, the second or third spine the longest equalling half the height of the body, all three are longer than the spines of the second dorsal, the membrane of which latter is deeply notched. All the articulated rays are branched. Pectoral a little longer than the head and reaching to above the middle rays of the anal: ventral reaches the anal spines, the third of which is the longest: caudal cut almost square. *Scales*—rudimentary. *Colours*—greyish-brown, a black blotch on the dorsal fin between the third or fourth and seventh or ninth spines: soft dorsal nearly black in its last three-fourths: pectoral blackish, as is also the outer half of the ventral and the anal: caudal yellowish-white with some small brown spots.

Habitat.—Common in the seas in Western India and Ceylon, especially off Canara, where it attains 3 inches in length.

Genus, 9—Amblyapistus, *Bleeker.*

Apistus, sp. Cuv. and Val.: *Platypterus*,* Swainson.

Branchiostegals five or six. Head and body strongly compressed: no groove across occiput. Strong and sharp preorbital and preopercular spines: opercle armed. Villiform teeth in jaws, vomer and palate. A single dorsal fin with more spines than rays (D. [illegible]) generally elevated anteriorly: three anal spines: pectoral without any free ray at its base. Articulated fin-rays branched. Scales, if present, rudimentary. Air-vessel present. Pyloric appendages few.

SYNOPSIS OF SPECIES.

1. *Amblyapistus tænianotus*, D. [illegible], A. [illegible]. Second dorsal spine as high as the body. Reddish, with irregular dark spots and blotches: a brown mark between the fifth and seventh dorsal spines. Andamans to the Malay Archipelago.

2. *Amblyapistus longispinis*, D. [illegible], A. [illegible]. Second dorsal spine two-thirds as high as the body. Scales minute. Pinkish, with blotches and a white spot on the side. Seas of India to China.

3. *Amblyapistus macracanthus*, D. [illegible], A. [illegible]. Brownish-black: pectoral with a white border. Andamans and Malay Archipelago.

1. Amblyapistus tænianotus, Plate XXXVIII, fig. 5.

Tænianotus litorilitulus, Lacep. iv, pl. 3, f. 2 (no description.)

Apistus tænianotus, Cuv. and Val. iv, p. 404; Richardson, Voy. Samarang, Fish. pl. 4, fig. 1 and 2; Bleeker. Amb. ii, p. 557.

Tetraroge tænianotus, Günther, Catal. ii, p. 136.

Platypterus tænianotus, Swains. Fish. ii, p. 265.

Amblyapistus tænianotus, Bleeker, Fish. Maur. p. 87.

B. v. D. [illegible], P. 12, V. 1/5, A. [illegible], C. 12.

Length of head 3/13, of pectoral 2/7, of caudal 4/17, height of body 2/7 of the total length. *Eyes*—diameter 3/10 of length of head, nearly 1 diameter from end of snout and 3/4 of a diameter apart. Body strongly compressed, the profile from the snout to the commencement of the dorsal fin almost vertical. The maxilla reaches to below the front edge of the orbit, lower jaw slightly the longer. Preorbital spine curved and very sharp, of moderate length and having a small basal one: preopercle with a sharp spine a little above its angle, and three or four blunt ones along its lower margin: two opercular spines, the upper the longer. *Teeth*—villiform in jaws, on vomer, and in a small patch on the palate. *Fins*—dorsal high anteriorly, its first spine a little above one diameter of the orbit in length, its second as high as the body, and its third a little shorter: from about the fourth spine to the end of the rays all are of about the same height: a slight membraneous continuation between the end of the dorsal and base of the caudal fins. All the articulated fin-rays branched.† The ventrals do not reach the anal and are shorter than the pectoral: third anal spine the longest: caudal slightly rounded. *Scales*—rudimentary. *Lateral-line*—first sixteen tubules distinct, subsequently they coalesce into one tube. *Colours*—reddish, with irregular brownish spots, a brown mark between the fifth and sixth or seventh dorsal spines.

Habitat.—Andaman islands, Malay Archipelago and beyond, attaining a few inches in length. The specimen figured is in the British Museum collection.

2. Amblyapistus longispinis, Plate XXXVIII, fig. 4.

Apistus longispinis, Cuv. and Val. iv, p. 408; Quoy and Gaim. Voy. Astrol. Poiss. p. 694, pl. xi, fig 4.

Apistes multicolor, Richardson, Voy. Samarang. Fishes, p. 3, pl. iv, fig. 3, 4.

Tetraroge longispinis, Günther, Catal. ii, p. 134.

B. vi, D. [illegible], V. 1/4 A. [illegible], C. 12.

* Preoccupied (K. and V. Hass.) Cuv. and Val. Fishes, 1837, &c.

† The specimen marked "5. Young. Madras. Presented by T. C. Jerdon. Esq.," has none of its articulated rays branched, it is *A. rosea*.

Length of head 4/15, of caudal 2/11, height of body 3/11 of the total length. *Eyes*—diameter 2/7 of length of head, one diameter from end of snout, and nearly one apart. Body strongly compressed, a rise from the snout to the base of the dorsal fin at about 45°. The maxilla reaches to below the middle of the orbit, lower jaw slightly the longer. Preorbital with one sharp spine reaching to below the hind edge of the orbit and having a small one at its base. A strong sharp spine at the angle of the preopercle, and some blunt ones along its lower edge: opercular spines moderately developed. *Teeth*—villiform in jaws, vomer, and palate. *Fins*—dorsal spines moderately strong, commencing over the middle of the eye, interspinous membrane deeply emarginate, the first dorsal spine equals the length of the head in front of the middle of the eye, the second and third are of equal length and as long as the head excluding the snout, last eight spines of about the same height as the rays: pectoral as long as the head, its articulated rays branched, and it extends as far as the ventral: second anal spine rather strong and nearly as long as the head anterior to the hind edge of the eye, third spine equals the length of the head behind the middle of the eye: caudal cut square. *Scales*—rudimentary, but distinct. *Lateral-line*—with 20 tubes. *Colours*—pinkish, a brown spot on the lateral line below the seventh dorsal spine, and a white one above and behind it: fins with brown spots, end of caudal blackish.

The specimen is figured life-size from one from China in the British Museum, presented by Mr. Reeves. I never obtained this species in India, but one stated to have come from thence was given the British Museum by General Hardwicke.

Habitat.—Seas of India to China, attaining a few inches in length.

3. **Amblyapistus macracanthus,** Plate XXXVIII, fig 3.

Apistus macracanthus, Bleeker, Ceram. p. 267.
Tetraroge macracanthus, Günther, Catal. ii, p. 133.

B. vi, D. $\frac{15}{9}\,\frac{7}{8}$, P. 12, V. 1/5, A. $\frac{3}{5}$, C. 12.

Length of head 2/9, of caudal 1/4, height of body 2/7 of the total length. *Eyes*—diameter 3/11 of length of head, 1 diameter from end of snout, and 3/4 of a diameter apart. Body strongly compressed. The maxilla reaches to below the first third of the orbit. Preorbital with two strong sharp spines: five along the angle and vertical limb of the preopercle, the upper being sharp and the strongest: opercle with two spines. Barbels absent. *Teeth*—villiform in jaws, vomer, and palate. *Fins*—dorsal fin commences before the eyes, is high anteriorly, the first three spines being at some distance from the others, the second dorsal spine the highest, being nearly as high as the body, the last spine as high as the rays. All the articulated fin-rays branched near their extremities. Pectoral rather longer than the height of the body: ventral reaches the anal: third anal spine the longest and equal to half the length of the head: caudal pointed, its lower border truncated, it is slightly joined to the base of the caudal by a membranous prolongation. *Scales*—a few small ones imbedded in the skin on the body. *Colours*—brownish-black, the pectoral with a white border.

Habitat.—Andamans and Malay Archipelago, the specimen figured (a female 3½ inches long) was captured at the Andaman islands.

Genus, 10—Micropus, *Gray.*

Caracanthus, Kröyer: *Amphiprionichthys*, Bleeker: *Centropus*, Kner: *Crossoderma*, Guichenot.

Branchiostegals four to six. Body strongly compressed. Preorbital, pre- sub- and inter-opercles armed. Villiform teeth in the jaws only. A single or two dorsal fins, the first with seven or eight spines, the anal with two: no free pectoral rays: ventrals rudimentary: some of the articulated fin-rays branched. Body scaleless, but covered with small tubercles, (no cleft behind the fourth gill.)

Geographical distribution.—These small fishes appear to be distributed through the seas of India to the Malay Archipelago and beyond.

SYNOPSIS OF INDIVIDUAL SPECIES.

1. *Micropus Zeylonicus*—D. 7/14, A. $\frac{3}{7}$, yellowish-brown, with darker reticulations. Malabar and Ceylon.

1. **Micropus Zeylonicus,** Plate XXXVIII, fig. 6.

Amphiprionichthys Zeylonicus, Day, Proc. Zool. Soc. 1869, p. 515.

B. iv, D. 7/14, P. 13, V. 1/3?, A. $\frac{3}{7}$, C. 15.

Length of head nearly 1/3, of caudal 1/5, height of body 4/9 to 1/2 of the total length. *Eyes*—high up, 1½ diameters from end of snout and 1 apart. Body elevated and compressed, the profile from the dorsal fin to the snout very steep. Mouth anterior, lower jaw rather the longer: the maxilla reaches to below the middle of the eye. Preorbital with a strong spine directed backwards and somewhat downwards: preopercle with five blunt spines, the two lowest being the longest: an equally long one but not so blunt exists on the interopercle: subopercle with one blunt spine: opercle with two badly developed spines. A serrated ridge passes from the back of the orbit towards the occiput. *Teeth*—villiform in the jaws, none on the vomer or palate. *Fins*—dorsal fin has a notch between its two portions, the third and fourth spines the highest, and equal to a little more than 1 diameter of the orbit: rays not so high as the spines: ventrals rudimentary: anal spines with a deep notch in the membrane separating them from the rays. *Scales*—absent, but slight elevations on the skin. *Colours*—bluish along the upper half of the body, becoming dirty brown on the abdomen: several irregular rows of yellowish blotches along the back and sides, separated by a darker reticulation: fins light-coloured, caudal marked as the sides of the body.

Habitat.—The specimen figured ($1\frac{1}{2}$ inches long) is from Malabar; some from Ceylon, dredged by Dr. Anderson in the Galle harbour, exist in the Calcutta Museum, the largest is $2\frac{1}{2}$ inches in length.

Genus, 11—Minous, *Cuv. and Val.*

Corythobatus, sp. Cantor.

Branchiostegals seven. Head large, body rather compressed: a groove across occiput. Preorbital with a strong spine, preopercle likewise spinate: opercle armed. Villiform teeth on jaws and vomer, palatines edentulous. A single dorsal fin with about the same number of spines as rays (D. [illegible])*: anal spines if present badly developed: pectoral with a free ray at its base. Articulated fin-rays single, unbranched. Scales absent. Cœcal appendages few. (A cleft behind the fourth gill.)*

SYNOPSIS OF INDIVIDUAL SPECIES.

1. *Minous monodactylus*, D. [illegible], P. 10+I, A. 9-11. Greyish, becoming flesh-coloured along the abdomen, fins marked with black. Seas of India to the Malay Archipelago and beyond.

1. Minous monodactylus, Plate XXXVIII, fig. 7.

Scorpæna monodactyla, Bl. Schn. p. 195.
Trigla morrah-minoo, Russell, ii, p. 44; fig. 149.
Apistus minous, Cuv. Règ. Anim.
Minous woora, Cuv. and Val. iv, p. 421; Richards. Ich. China, p. 213; Bleeker, Sumatra, ii, p. 251.
Minous monodactylus, Cuv. and Val. iv, p. 424, pl. 89, f. 2; Bleeker, Sclerop. p. 9, and Fish. Mauritius, p. 87; Günther, Catal. ii, p. 148; Day, Fish. Malab. p. 43.
Apistes Russellii et *monodactylus*, Swains. Fish. ii, p. 265.
Corythobatus woora, Cantor, Catal. p. 45.
Minous Adamsii, Richards. Voy. Samar. Fish. p. 7, pl. 2, f. 4, 5.
Cul-ploochee, Tam.

B. vii, D. [illegible], P. 10+I, V. 1/5, A. 9-11, C. 10, Cæc. pyl. 4.

Length of head 3/10, of caudal 1/4, height of body 4/17 to 1/4 of the total length. *Eyes*—diameter 2/7 to 1/4 of the length of head, $1\frac{1}{2}$ diameters from the end of snout, and also apart. The maxilla reaches to below the front edge of the orbit. Preorbital spine strong, sharp, and equal in length to 2/3 of the diameter of the orbit, and having another small one at its base. In one specimen there are two long preorbital spines on one side as well as the basal one, but the normal number on the other. Preopercle with a strong sharp spine at its angle and three other shorter and blunter ones, one or two short ones also at its lower limb. Temporal and occipital ridges spinate, and all or most of those on the head rugose, as are also the edge of the orbit and the superciliary ridge. *Teeth*—fine in jaws, on vomer, but none on the palate. *Fins*—dorsal spines moderately strong, the first distinct from the remainder, the membrane deeply cleft: pectoral large and as long as the head, reaching to below the commencement of the soft dorsal or even to its third ray, a single free ray below the pectoral fin which is nearly as long as the fin, in dried specimens it sometimes splits into two: caudal rays, and all the articulated ones, unbranched. *Scales*—absent. *Colours*—head greyish-brown above, sides and abdomen lighter or flesh-coloured, with dark blotches and marks: dorsal fin light brown margined with black: pectoral black, its appendage white: caudal buff, with three vertical brown bars.

Habitat.—Seas of India to China, attaining 4 or 5 inches in length.

Genus, 12—Cocotropus, *Kaup.*

Corythobatus, sp. Cantor; *Tetraroge*, pt. Günther.

Branchiostegals six. Head and body strongly compressed: no groove across the occiput. Preorbital with a strong blunt spine: preopercle with a similar one: opercle armed. Villiform teeth in jaws and vomer, palatines edentulous. A single dorsal fin with more spines than rays (D. [illegible])*: two weak anal spines: pectoral without any free ray at its base. Articulated fin-rays single, unbranched. Scales absent.*

SYNOPSIS OF SPECIES.

1. *Cocotropus echinatus*, D. [illegible], P. 11, A. [illegible]. Pinkish. Seas of India to the Malay Archipelago.
2. *Cocotropus roseus*, D. [illegible], P. 14, A. [illegible]. Pinkish, a white outer angle to each side of the caudal fin. Coromandel coast of India.

1. Cocotropus echinatus.

Corythobatus echinatus, Cantor, Catal. p. 45, pl. 13.
Cocotropus echinatus, Kaup. Wiegm. Arch. Naturg. 1858, p. 333.
Tetraroge echinata, Günther, Catal. ii, p. 136.

B. vi, D. [illegible], P. 11, V. 1/3, A. [illegible], C. 12.

Length of head 3/11, of pectoral 1/4, of caudal 1/6, height of body 2/7 of the total length. *Eyes*—

near the dorsal profile and below the base of the two first dorsal spines, diameter 2/9 of length of head, $1\frac{1}{2}$ diameters from end of snout, and 3/4 of a diameter apart. Body and head strongly compressed, the anterior profile ascends almost vertically from the snout to the base of the first dorsal spine. Maxilla reaches to below the centre of the orbit. Preorbital with a strong curved blunt spine, having a smaller but similar one at its base: four blunt spines along the margin of the preopercle and three on the opercle. *Teeth*—villiform in the jaws, and in a crescentic band on the vomer. *Fins*—the single dorsal commences over the front half of the orbit, the first spine being rather curved, and the longest equalling the head excluding the snout, the last spines as high as the rays which are unbranched: from the end of the dorsal fin a membraneous continuation extends to the base of the caudal. Anal spines very weak: caudal rounded. Body and head studded with small obtuse prickles. *Lateral-line*—indistinct. *Colours*—buff, with five brown lines radiating from the eye; upper edge of dorsal parple: some large brownish blotches in the upper half of the body, all the fins more or less dotted with brown, and a whitish spot at the upper and lower angle of the end of the caudal.

This species exists in the Calcutta Museum, where it was labelled *Apistes spinosa*, from the Andamans, it attains a few inches in length.

Habitat.—Andamans and Pinang.

2. **Cocotropus roseus**, Plate XXXVIII, fig. 8.

B. vi, D. $\frac{13}{9}|\frac{3}{10}$, P. 14, V. 1/3, A. $\frac{2}{7}$, C. 12.

Length of head 2/7, of caudal 1/7, height of body 2/7 of the total length. *Eyes*—placed high up, diameter 1/4 of length of head, $1\frac{1}{2}$ diameters from end of snout, and 3/4 of a diameter apart. Body strongly compressed: profile from dorsal fin to snout oblique: mouth slightly oblique, lower jaw a little the longer. Preorbital with two blunt spines, the longest going backwards to beneath the first third of the eye, the lower and shorter one a little downwards and backwards. A rough ridge passes across the suborbitals to a little above the angle of the preopercle on the vertical limb of which are two blunt spines, the upper the longer, and equal to the diameter of the orbit in length: two more smaller spines along its horizontal limb: three opercular spines: an elevated occipital ridge, and also a temporal one having three blunt spines. No barbels. *Teeth*—villiform in jaws and vomer, none on the palate. *Fins*—dorsal fin continuous, it commences over the middle of the eye; spines strong, the second being slightly the longest and equal to half the height of the body, they subsequently slightly decrease to the last which is as high as the first ray: a membraneous extension exists from the end of the dorsal fin, and nearly reaches the base of the caudal. All the articulated fin-rays are unbranched. Pectoral equals the length of the head and reaches to the commencement of the anal: ventral short, reaching half way to the anus, it has one spine and three rays: two weak anal spines only: caudal rounded. *Scales*—absent, skin with many widely spread rough elevations, becoming somewhat spinate in large specimens: tubes of lateral-line 10 or 11 distinct ones in number, which occupy its whole length. *Colours*—fleshy, the fins having more of a pinkish tinge. Dorsal fin edged with white, having a dull grey band along its centre, and most distinct in its last half: caudal edged with white, and having a dull base due to numerous grey spots: pectoral and anal reddish, the former having many black spots upon it: ventrals white.

These fish are very common in Madras in October, and through the cold months, but they rarely exceed $2\frac{1}{2}$ or 3 inches in length.

Jerdon observes (Madr. Journ. Lit. and Sc. 1851, p. 141), "*Agriopus* ——, I possess a drawing of a small species of this genus of a mottled red colour throughout. I only procured it once, it was named *Crusi tenashi*, Tam." The specimen is in the British Museum, as *Tetraroge taeniaunotus* (ii, p. 136), from which it may be readily distinguished, as the spines on its head are blunt, and its articulated fin-rays are unbranched, which is not the case in *A. taeniaunotus* (see p. 157).

My reasons for considering this distinct from *C. echinatus* are the more oblique profile from the snout to the dorsal fin: the second dorsal spine (instead of the first) being the highest: the pectoral having 14 (instead of 10) rays, &c.

Habitat.—Coromandel coast of India. The specimen is figured life-size.

Genus, 13—Pelor, *Cuv. and Val.*

Branchiostegals seven. Head irregularly shaped. Villiform teeth in the jaws and vomer. The three first dorsal spines connected by a membrane and are at a little distance from the others (12-14) *which are somewhat isolated one from another, due to the interspinous membrane being deeply cleft: two free rays at the base of the pectoral fin, having a connecting membrane: ventrals thoracic. Articulated fin-rays branched. Scales absent. Head, body and fins with skinny appendages. Air-vessel small. Pyloric appendages few.*

SYNOPSIS OF INDIVIDUAL SPECIES.

1. *Pelor didactylum*, D. 3 | $\frac{12}{8}\frac{1}{?}$, A. 11-12. Brownish-grey, irregularly banded. Andaman islands to the Malay Archipelago and beyond.

1. **Pelor didactylum**, Plate XXXIX, fig. 1.

Scorpaena didactyla, Pallas, Spic. Zool. Fas. vii, p. 26, t. 4.
Trigla rubicunda, Hornst. Ngn. Handl. ix, p. 45, t. 3.

Synanceia didactyla et *rubiginosa*, Bl. Schn. pp. 195, 196.

Pelor sinculatum, Cuv. and Val. iv, p. 437; Less. Voy. Coq. Poiss. p. 210, t. xx; Günther, Catal. ii, p. 150.

Pelor obscurum, Cuv. and Val. iv, p. 436; Less. Voy. Coq. Zool. ii, p. 211, Poiss. pl. 21, f. 2; Bleeker, Ceram. iii, p. 241; Kner, Novara Fische, p. 119.

Scorpæna digitata, Gronov. ed. Gray, p. 117.

Pelor didactylum, Günther, Catal. ii, p. 150; Bleeker, Révis. Synan. 1874, p. 7, t. iv, f. 1.

B. vii, D. 3 | $\frac{9}{2-3}$ | $\frac{1}{5}$, P. 10 + II, V. 1/5, A. 11-12, C. 12.

Length of head 2/7 to 1/4, of caudal 2/11, height of body 2/7 of the total length. *Eyes*—diameter 2/11 in the adult to 1/3 in the young of length of head, $2\frac{1}{2}$ diameters from end of snout, and from 1 to $1\frac{1}{2}$ apart. The maxilla reaches to nearly below the front edge of the eye: lower jaw considerably the longer: the width of the head at the opercles equals its length. Interorbital space deeply concave with a transverse ridge between the two eyes: a deep saddle-shaped depression across the occiput: a groove below the eyes. Upper edge of orbit with blunt spines: spinate occipital and temporal ridges: preopercle with spines on its vertical border: a suborbital spinate ridge: a turbinal spine: opercle mostly with two spines. Rather long fleshy tentacles on the lower jaw. *Teeth*—villiform in jaws and on vomer, none on the palate. *Fins*—second dorsal spine somewhat the longest of the three first, as high as the longest in the rest of the fin, and 3/5 of the length of the head: interspinous membrane deeply cleft and covered with skinny appendages. Pectoral equals the length of the head, and has two free rays at its base: caudal cut almost square. *Scales*—absent, but skinny appendages over the head, back, and fins. *Colours*—brownish-grey becoming dirty white beneath, with fine spots over the body and head. Dorsal coloured as the body, a dark band passes down the last few spines on to the body, and another over the last few rays takes the same course: caudal yellow with a dark vertical band across its base, and another in its last third: outer edge of anal dark coloured.

Habitat.—Andaman islands, from whence the one figured (a female $5\frac{1}{2}$ inches in length) was procured, to the Malay Archipelago, and beyond.

Genus, 14—Choridactylus, *Richardson*.

Branchiostegals six. Head and body compressed. Bones of the head with osseous ridges; the preorbital, preopercle and opercle with spines: a groove on the occiput. Villiform teeth on the jaws, palate edentulous. A single dorsal fin with more spines (13) than rays (9): anal with two spines: pectoral fin with three free rays: ventrals with one spine and five rays. Articulated fin-rays branched. Scales absent: some skinny appendages on the body. Air-vessel absent. Pyloric appendages few.

Geographical distribution.—Coromandel coast of India, and seas of China.

SYNOPSIS OF INDIVIDUAL SPECIES.

1. *Choridactylus multibarbis*, D. $\frac{13}{9}$, P. 9 + III, A. $\frac{2}{8}$. Brownish with darker markings: dorsal fin yellow with black marks: caudal yellow, with black basal and terminal bands: other fins dark, the ventral with white spots. Madras and China.

1. Choridactylus multibarbis, Plate XXXIX, fig. 2.

Choridactylus multibarbis, Richardson, Voy. Samarang, Fishes, p. 8, pl. 2, f. 1-3.

Chorismodactylus multibarbis, Günther, Catal. ii, p. 151.

B. vi, D. $\frac{13}{9}$, P. 9+III, V. 1/5, A. $\frac{2}{8}$, C. 15.

Length of head 1/4, of pectoral 1/4, of caudal 1/5, height of body 2/7 of the total length. *Eyes*—high up, with prominent orbits, diameter 2/7 of length of head, 1 diameter from end of snout, and rather more apart. Mouth anterior: lower jaw slightly the longer, the maxilla reaches to beneath the front edge of the orbit. Interorbital space concave, with two longitudinal ridges which posteriorly end in a transverse one connecting them together. Upper edge of orbit with points scarcely spinate. Preorbital with a sharp spine posteriorly, two-thirds the length of the orbit having a small one at its base pointing downwards, as well as two or three more spinate elevations. A spinate or rough ridge runs along the suborbitals and over the cheeks to the middle of the vertical limb of the preopercle, which is armed with a sharp spine that crosses the whole width of the opercle: it has a small one directed outwards at its base: there is likewise a spine at the angle of the preopercle, and three blunt points along its horizontal edge. Two spines on the opercle. Occipital and temporal ridges with blunt spines, one on the shoulder girdle above the base of the pectoral fin. A deep depression across the occiput, extending down behind the eyes. A fleshy tentacle over the centre of the eye, and some on the mandible. *Teeth*—villiform in the jaws. *Fins*—dorsal fin commencing just behind the eyes, the first three spines somewhat removed from the rest, the fourth likewise stands at some distance from those in front of or behind it, the third and fourth spines the longest, nearly equalling two-thirds the height of the body, interspinous membrane deeply emarginate: rays a little higher than the longest spine and branched near their extremities: pectoral rounded and having three free rays below its base: ventral large and attached by nearly the whole length of its inner edge by a skinny flap to the abdomen: anal spines small, the second one-third the longest: caudal rounded. *Scales*—absent. *Colours*—brownish, with a yellow shoulder mark, and two or three vertical orange bands: base of ventral and anal with fine white spots. Fins blackish brown, with a light band between the fourth and sixth dorsal spines: margins of pectorals orange: caudal with a black band at its base, and another in its last third having a light edge: outer two-thirds of anal blackish: free rays black, with white in their middle.

This is the species observed upon by Jerdon (Madr. J. L. and Sc. 1851, p. 141,) as follows:—"I have drawings and specimens of a very curious fish, which I have marked as *Apistes niger*, C. V. I however hardly think it can belong to this genus; it appears to me rather an aberrant form of *Pterois*, allied to Swainson's genus *Bembras*."

This fish is very common at Madras, attaining about 4 inches in length: the specimen figured (life-size) is from that locality.

Habitat.—Coromandel coast of India, and China.

Genus, 15—SYNANCIDIUM, *Müll.*

Bufichthys, Swains.

Branchiostegals seven. Head monstrous and irregularly shaped, but without sharp spines. Villiform teeth on the jaws and vomer, but not on the palatines. The soft dorsal continuous with the spinous, less rays (6-9) than spines (13); anal with 3 spines and few (5) rays: no pectoral appendages. Scales absent: body and sometimes the head with skinny flaps. Air-vessel small. Pyloric appendages few.

SYNOPSIS OF INDIVIDUAL SPECIES.

1. *Synancidium horridum*, D. $\frac{13}{6-7}$, A. $\frac{3}{5}$. Eyes elevated: a deep saddle-shaped depression across the occiput.

1. Synancidium horridum, Plate XXXIX, fig. 3.

Scorpæna horrida, Linn. i, p. 453; Bl. t. 183; Lacép. iii, p. 261, ii, t. 17, f. 2.

Synanceia horrida, Bl. Schn. p. 194; Cuv. and Val. iv, p. 449; Bleeker, Verh. Bat. Gen. xxii, Scler. p. 9, and Révis. Synan. 1874, p. 12.

Scorpæna monstrosa, Gronov. ed. Gray, p. 117.

Synanceia grossa, Gray and Hard. Ind. Zool. i, pl. 97.

Bufichthys horrida et *grossa*, Swainson, Fish. ii, p. 268.

Synanceia trachynis, Richards. Ann. and Mag. Nat. Hist. 1842. ix, p. 385.

Synancidium horridum, Müll. Akad. Wiss. 1844, p. 163; Günther, Catal. ii, p. 144; Kner. Novara Fische, p. 119.

B. vii, D. $\frac{13}{6-7}$, P. 16, V. 1/5, A. $\frac{3}{5}$, C. 12, Cæc. pyl. 3, Vert. 10/14.

Length of head 1/3, of caudal 2/11 to 1/6, height of body 1/3 of the total length. *Eyes*—diameter 1/8 of length of head, 3 diameters from end of snout. Crown of head irregularly saddle-shaped: a deep groove on the cheeks, orbit raised. *Teeth*—villiform in the jaws and on the vomer, which last, Bleeker observes, are not invariably present.* *Fins*—dorsal spines stiff, the three first the highest and somewhat separated from the others: the vertical fin more or less enclosed in skin. Articulated fin-rays branched. Skin with numerous large and small tubercles even when on the fins: some large fringed tubercles along the lower edge of preopercle and preorbital. *Colours*—brownish-fawn colour superiorly, becoming lighter below: irregular blotches on the body, and smaller ones on the fins.

Habitat.—Seas of India to the Malay Archipelago and beyond.

Genus, 16—SYNANCEIA, *Bl. Schn.*

Synanceichthys, Bleeker.

Branchiostegals seven. Head monstrous, irregularly shaped but spineless, no saddle-shaped fossa across the occiput: no transverse elevation between the orbits, nor deep groove below the eyes. Villiform teeth on the jaws, vomer and palatine bones edentulous. The soft dorsal continuous with the spinous, less rays (5-6) than spines (13-16): anal with 3 spines and few (5) rays, no pectoral appendages. Air-vessel present. Scales absent. Pyloric appendages few.

SYNOPSIS OF INDIVIDUAL SPECIES.

1. *Synanceia verrucosa*. D. $\frac{13}{6-7}$, A. $\frac{3}{5}$. From the Red Sea, through those of India to the Malay Archipelago and beyond.

1. Synanceia verrucosa, Plate XXXIX, fig. 4.

Bl. Schn. p. 195, t. 45; Rüpp. N. W. Fische, p. 109; Günther, Catal. ii, p. 146; Klunz. Verh. z. b. Ges. Wien, 1870, p. 811; Bleeker, Révis. Syn. 1874, p. 15.

Scorpæna brachio, Lacép. iii, pp. 259, 272, pl. 12, f. 1.

Scorpæna brachiata, Shaw, Zool. iv, pt. 2, p. 274.

Synanceia sanguinolenta, Ehren. Pisc. t. 3.

Synanceia brachio, Cuv. and Val. iv, p. 447; Bleeker, Sclerop. p. 9.

* Of course if the presence of vomerine teeth is inconstant, the genus *Synancidium* (which is chiefly separated from Synanceia owing to their presence) has no generic value.

B. vii, D. $\frac{13}{6-7}$, P. 1/8, V. 6, A. $\frac{3}{5-6}$, C. 10-12, Cæc. pyl. 0(4). Vert. 10/14.

Length of head 2/5, of caudal 1/7, height of body $2\frac{3}{4}$ in the total length. *Eyes*—diameter 1/6 to 1/7 of length of head and 2 diameters from end of snout. Head monstrous: interorbital space very concave: orbits but little elevated. A slight groove on the cheek: no saddle-shaped depression across the occiput. The anterior extremity of the lower jaw is on the dorsal profile. Body with cutaneous excrescences, and many filaments about the head. *Colours*—brownish, caudal with a vertical dark band down its centre and white margins: pectoral and ventral with dark edges and light borders: anal banded.

Lienard's *Synancée à trois bandes*, D. 13/7, P. 18, V. 1/5, A. $\frac{3}{5}$, C. 14 (Nat. Hist. Soc. Mauritius, 1839, p. 34) is apparently this species. Three vertical white bands, the first between the fifth and seventh dorsal spines: the second at the commencement of the rays: the third over the base of the caudal. Caudal with two brown bands between the white, and a third of yellow.

Le Juge, in the Transactions of the same Society (1871, v, p. 19), has observed that this fish termed 'Laffe' is very poisonous at the Mauritius; the poisonous instrument being its dorsal spines, each of which has a poison bag at its base.

Habitat—Red Sea, East coast of Africa, seas of India to the Malay Archipelago and beyond: attaining at least 13 inches in length.

Genus, 17—Pseudosynanceia.

Branchiostegals seven. Body elongated, anteriorly sub-cylindrical, posteriorly compressed: head broad depressed. Eyes on the upper surface of the head directed upwards. Preopercle and preorbital armed. Gill-opening with a superior as well as posterior orifice, the two being continuous. Villiform teeth in the jaws and on the vomer, none on the palate or tongue. A single dorsal fin with strong spines (16) *and* (5) *unbranched rays: anal with three spines and few rays* (7). *No pectoral appendage. Ventral thoracic with one spine and less than five* (3) *rays, and not united to the abdomen along its inner edge. Articulated fin-rays unbranched. Scales absent, skin smooth.*

This genus differs from *Leptosynanceia*, Bleeker, in having vomerine teeth. Should these teeth be inconstant, the fish described would belong to genus *Leptosynanceia*.

SYNOPSIS OF INDIVIDUAL SPECIES.

1. *Pseudosynanceia melanostigma*. D. $\frac{16}{5}$, A. $\frac{3}{7}$. Grey mottled with black. Some of the fins yellow with black edges or bands. Coast of Sind.

1. Pseudosynanceia melanostigma, Plate LV, fig. 6.

B. vii, D. $\frac{16}{5}$, P. 14, V. 1/3, A. $\frac{3}{7}$, C. 11.

Length of head $4\frac{1}{2}$, of caudal $4\frac{1}{2}$, height of body one-sixth in the total length. *Eyes*—diameter 1/7 of length of head, $1\frac{1}{2}$ diameters from end of snout, and 3 apart. The eyes are upon the upper surface of the head and directed upwards and slightly outwards. The maxilla, which expands posteriorly, reaches to below the middle of the eye. Upper surface of head depressed and its width rather exceeding its length. Preorbital with ridges placed in a star form and ending in two spines on its lower border. Upper surface of the head with sinuous, but not spinate, ridges. Preopercle with a moderately strong spine at its angle, and three short blunt ones along its lower limb. Opercle with a spine. Gill opening with a small rounded superior orifice, exclusive of, but continuous with the posterior one. Lower jaw the longer, its symphysis forming a portion of the dorsal profile. *Teeth*—villiform in the jaws, in a well-developed transverse band across the vomer, none on the palate or tongue. *Fins*—dorsal spines strong, commencing over the centre of the opercle, the posterior ones being somewhat the longest but not so high as the rays, which are unbranched; interspinous membrane deeply cleft, the soft dorsal not continuous with the caudal. Pectoral with its upper rays much the longest, it extends to over the anal. Ventral short. Anal spines short but pungent, its rays and those of the caudal unbranched. No skinny tentacles on head, body or fins. *Colours*—of a grey mottled with black on the top of the head and along the back, becoming yellow on the abdomen. Spinous dorsal also mottled, a vertical yellow band across the front half of the soft dorsal, and black in its last half. Pectoral yellow, with some grey spots at its base and a wide black edge. Ventral and anal yellow edged with black. Caudal yellow, with a black band down its last half, externally edged with yellow.

Habitat.—Kurrachee, in Sind, where I procured the specimen figured (7 inches long). It lives in the mud and is difficult to obtain, for although I saw several we only captured one.

Genus, 18—Polycaulis, Günther.

Synanceia, sp. Bloch: *Trachicephalus*,* Swainson.

Branchiostegals seven. Body anteriorly sub-cylindrical, posteriorly compressed: head broad, rather depressed. Eyes directed upwards. Preopercle armed. Gill-opening with a superior as well as posterior orifice, the two being continuous. Villiform teeth in the jaws, absent on the vomer. A single dorsal fin with flexible spines and rays: anal somewhat elongated: no pectoral appendages: ventral thoracic, united to the abdomen along its inner edge. Articulated fin-rays unbranched. Scales absent. Vertical fins more or less enveloped in skin.

Geographical distribution.—Seas of India to the Malay Archipelago and beyond.

* Preoccupied, Trachycephalus, Tsch. Rept. 1838.

SYNOPSIS OF INDIVIDUAL SPECIES.

1. *Polycaulis elongatus*, D. [illegible], A. 11-15. Brown, with the fins black-edged or else spotted with white. Seas of India to the Malay Archipelago and beyond.

1. Polycaulis uranoscopus, Plate XXXIX, fig. 6.

Synanceia uranoscopa, Bl. Schn. p. 195; Cuv. and Val. iv, p. 458.
Synanceia elongata, Cuv. and Val. iv, p. 456; Bleeker, Verh. Bat. Gen. xxii, Sclerop. p. 10; Griffith, Cuv. An. King. xi, pl. 8, fig. 3.
Trachicephalus elongatus, Swainson, Fishes, ii, p. 268.
Synanceia brevipes, Richardson, Voy. Sulph. Fishes, p. 71.
Uranoscopus adhesipinnis, Blyth, J. A. S. of B. 1860, p. 142.
Polycaulus elongatus, Günther, Catal. ii, p. 175; Kner, Novara Fische, p. 120.

B. vii, D. [illegible], P. 13, V. 1/5, A. 11-15, C. 11.

Length of head from 1/5 to 2/9, of caudal 1/5 to 2/11, height of body 1/5 to 2/9 of the total length. *Eyes*—diameter 2/9 to 1/5 of length of head, 1½ diameters from end of snout, and 2 apart. The maxilla reaches to below the middle of the eyes. Head as wide as long, and covered with bony ridges having numerous blunt points: a blunt preorbital spine having a short one at its base, five along the edge of the preopercle, two on opercle. Lower jaw the longer. Gill-openings having a small rounded superior orifice continuous with the posterior one. *Teeth*—villiform in the jaws, becoming very obsolete in old specimens. *Fins*—spines and rays enclosed in the skin, the dorsal commences between or rather in advance of the superior openings of the gills, its spines are low and more or less flexible. Pectoral pointed and a little longer than the head, ventral attached along its entire inner edge to the abdomen: caudal cut square. *Scales*—absent. *Colours*—brownish, with or without white dots: fins stained dark at their edges, sometimes spotted, the caudal with a white edge.

One of Bloch Schneider's specimens of *Synanceia uranoscopa*, in spirit, was shown me at Berlin as his type, it was identical with that described above. In the description he states it possesses D. 31 (probably a misprint for D. 21), and A. 20 (perhaps for 10, the first short ray having been overlooked). His specimen came from Tranquebar.

Jerdon (M. J. L. & Sc. 1851, p. 141) observes that this fish is termed *Cel tumbi*, Tam. at Madras, and is not very uncommon.

Habitat.—Seas and estuaries of India, to the Malay Archipelago and beyond, attaining at least 5 inches in length.

FAMILY, VIII—TEUTHIDIDÆ, *Cuv.*

Teuthyes, pt. Cuv.

Branchiostegals five: pseudobranchiæ well developed. Body oval and strongly compressed. Eyes of moderate size, lateral. Mouth slightly cleft, and but little protractile. A single row of cutting incisors in either jaw: palate edentulous. One dorsal fin with the spinous portion more developed than the soft: anal with seven spines. Ventrals thoracic, with two spines and three intermediate soft rays. Scales minute. A complete lateral line, but no armature, on the side of the free portion of the tail. Air-vessel present. Pyloric appendages few.

Several different opinions have been advanced respecting the position this family of Acanthopterygian fishes should hold. Cuv. and Val. placed them after their *Mænidæ* and next to their *Acanthuridæ*. Swainson observed (Fishes, ii, p. 247): "the procumbent advanced spine before the dorsal induces me to place this genus between *Seriola* and *Caranx* rather than with the *Acanthuri*."

SYNOPSIS OF INDIVIDUAL GENUS.

1. *Teuthis.*—Definition as in the family.

Genus, 1—TEUTHIS,* *Linn.*

Siganus, Forsk.: *Centrogaster*, Houtt.: *Amphacanthus*, Bl. Schn.: *Buro*, (Comm.) Lacép.

Branchiostegals five: pseudobranchiæ. Body oval, strongly compressed. Teeth small, denticulated. A single dorsal fin with thirteen spines as well as a horizontal one anteriorly; anal with seven; each ventral with two, an outer and an inner one, having three intermediate rays. Scales minute, cycloid. Air-vessel large, forked both anteriorly and posteriorly. Pyloric appendages when present† few (4-6).

Geographical distribution.—Red Sea, East coast of Africa, Seas of India to the Malay Archipelago and beyond.

SYNOPSIS OF SPECIES.

1. *Teuthis Java.* Neutral tint, with grey rounded spots on head, and along the back, becoming more elongated on the sides and lineated on the abdomen. Seas of India, to the Malay Archipelago and beyond.
2. *Teuthis vermiculata.* Light brown, with undulating bluish lines, about one-fourth as wide as the ground colour. Seas of India, to the Malay Archipelago and beyond.
3. *Teuthis marmorata.* More elongated than the last, colours much the same, but the blue lines are narrower and become sinuously-longitudinal on the sides. Seas of India, to the Malay Archipelago and beyond.
4. *Teuthis virgata.* Oblique lines and spots on the snout, blue spots on the upper third of the body: a wide brown blue-edged ocular band, and another from the spinous dorsal to the base of the pectoral fin. Andamans to the Malay Archipelago and beyond.
5. *Teuthis concatenata.* Blue bands on the head: orange spots over the body. Andamans to the Malay Archipelago.
6. *Teuthis margaritifera.* Brownish-olive, with scattered small blue spots, and a dark shoulder-mark: some marks and lines on the vertical fins. Andamans to the Malay Archipelago and beyond.
7. *Teuthis sutor.* Body higher, otherwise very similar to the last. Spots larger, those on the sides with a dark centre: a dark shoulder-mark. Seychelles and Malabar.
8. *Teuthis oramin.* White spots over the body: a dark shoulder-mark and barred caudal fin. Seas of India to the Malay Archipelago and beyond.
9. *Teuthis stellata.* Greyish, with purplish angular spots: a dark shoulder-mark sometimes present. Red Sea through those of India.

1. Teuthis Java, Plate XXXIX, fig. 5.

Teuthis Java, Linn. Syst. i, p. 507; Gmel. Linn. p. 1362; Cantor, Catal. p. 207; Günther, Catal. iii, p. 315; Day, Fish. Malabar, p. 125.

Sparus spinus? Russell, Fish. Vizag. ii, p. 2, and *Worahwah*, pl. 102.

Amphacanthus Javus, Cuv. and Val. x, p. 118; Bleeker, Verh. Bat. Gen. xxiii, Teuth. p. 9; Schleg. and Müll. Verh. Nat. Ges. Overz. Bezitt, p. 10; Kner, Novara Fische, p. 205.

Ottah, Tam.: *Thar-oar-dah*, Andam.; *Worahwah*, Tel.

B. v, D. $\frac{13}{10}$, P. 18, V. 2/3, A. $\frac{7}{9}$, C. 19.

Length of head 4/21, of pectoral 1/6, of caudal 1/5, height of body 3/8 to 4/11 of the total length. *Eyes*—

* *Worah*, Tam.; *Nya-gran-da*, Mugh. † Rüppell states that in *T. sigana* they are absent.

diameter 1/3 to 2/7 in the length of head, $1\frac{1}{2}$ diameters from end of snout and also apart. Interorbital space rather elevated, with a central shallow groove which narrows anteriorly: anterior superior edge of orbit serrated. The maxilla extends to below the posterior nostril: horizontal edge of preopercle roughened. The height of the soft portion of the cheek equals that of the orbit, whilst it is one-half wider than deep. *Teeth*—generic. *Fins*—dorsal spines strong, their base occupying five-sevenths of that of the entire fin, the spines increase in length to the fourth, which is as long as the head excluding the snout, and slightly higher than the rays, from it they decrease to the last which equals the length of the snout: soft portion of fin (as well as of the anal) obliquely rounded: anal spines strong, increasing in length to the third which equals the longest in the dorsal fin, from thence they decrease to the sixth, but the seventh is longer and equal to the third: caudal emarginate, its central rays being equal to two-thirds of the length of the longest of the outer ones. *Scales*—minute. *Colours*—head, back, and sides of a dark brownish neutral tint, becoming lighter on the abdomen. On the head and back many pale grey rounded spots, becoming more elongated on the sides and abdomen. The upper spots are not so wide as the ground colour. No streaks on the head as a rule, but to this there are exceptions, and in some instances the cheeks are reticulated: fins immaculate.

This doubtless is *Hepatus*, Gronov. Zooph. t. 8, fig. 4, and probably *Amphacanthus Russellii*, Bleeker.

Habitat.—Seas of India to the Malay Archipelago and beyond. Jerdon (M. J. L. and S. 1851, p. 138) mentions having procured both of Russell's species at Madras.

2. Teuthis vermiculata, Plate XL, fig. 1.

Amphacanthus vermiculatus, (Kuhl, and v. Hass.) Cuv. and Val. x, p. 126: Müll. and Schleg. Verh. Overz. Bez. Visseh. p. 11, pl. 3, fig. 3; Bleeker, Verh. Bat. Gen. xxiii, Teuth. p. 11.
Teuthis vermiculata, Günther, Catal. iii, p. 317; Day, Fishes of Malabar, p. 123.
Kat-e-rah, Mal.: *Chow-bul-dah*, Andam.

B. v, D. $\frac{13}{10}$, P. 16, V. 2/3, A. $\frac{7}{9}$, C. 17.

Length of head about 1/5, of caudal 2/13, height of body 3/7 to 2/5 of the total length. *Eyes*—diameter $3\frac{1}{2}$ in the length of head, upwards of $1\frac{1}{2}$ diameters from end of snout, and $1\frac{1}{2}$ apart. The maxilla reaches about half way to below the front edge of the orbit. Angle of preopercle slightly produced. *Teeth*—generic. *Fins*—Dorsal spines strong and occupying five-sevenths of the length of the base of the entire fin, from the fourth they are of about the same height, equalling half the length of the head, but are not so high as the first few rays: rayed portion of the fin angular: anal of the same form as the dorsal, but the spines are stronger and occupy three-fifths of the entire base of the fin, they are of about the same height from the third, equalling half the length of the head: pectoral two-fifths of the height of the body and longer than the ventral which does not quite reach the anal fin: caudal slightly emarginate. *Scales*—minute, but distinct over the body and cheeks. *Colours*—light brown, running into bluish green on the back, and nearly white on the abdomen. The whole of the body, head, and lips are lineated with undulating bluish lines of about one-fourth the width of the ground colour, being broadest near the abdomen: caudal fin with brown lines.

Habitat.—Seas of India, Malay Archipelago and beyond, attaining at least 11 inches in length.

3. Teuthis marmorata, Plate XL, fig. 2.

Amphacanthus marmoratus, Quoy and Gaim. Voy. Uranie, Zool. p. 367, pl. 62, fig. 1; Cuv. and Val. x, p. 124; Kner, Novara Fische, p. 208.
Teuthis marmorata, Günther, Catal. iii, p. 322.
Teuthis striolata, Günther, Catal. iii, p. 319, and Garrett, Fische d. Sudsee, t. 59, fig. A.

B. v, D. $\frac{13}{10}$, P. 18, V. 2/3, A. $\frac{7}{9}$, C. 17.

Length of head 3/16 to 1/5, of caudal 1/7, height of body 3/10 to 2/7 of the total length. *Eyes*—diameter 1/3 of length of head, 1 to $1\frac{1}{2}$ diameters from end of snout, and 1 apart. Interorbital space nearly flat, edge of orbit entire. The maxilla reaches to nearly below the hind nostril. The soft portion of the cheek (between the orbit, preopercular limb, and hind edge of preorbital and maxilla) is as high as the orbit, and but slightly longer than high. *Teeth*—generic. *Fins*—dorsal spines of moderate strength, increasing to the fourth and subsequently decreasing from the seventh, the highest spines equalling the length of the head behind the first third of the eyes, and being half as long again as the soft portion of the fin which is rounded: pectorals as long as the head excluding its post-orbital portion: ventral reaches more than half way to the anal: anal spines increase in length to the third, (which equals half the length of the head,) from whence they decrease to the last, which equals two-fifths of the same extent: caudal lobed, upper lobe the longer. *Colours*—brownish, covered all over the back with blue vermiculated lines, which become sinuously-longitudinal along the sides: head covered with similar lines. Dorsal, anal, and caudal with sinuous brown lines: pectorals yellow.

Habitat.—Seas of India to the Malay Archipelago.

4. Teuthis virgata, Plate XL, fig. 3.

Amphacanthus virgatus, Cuv. and Val. x, p. 133; Müll. and Schleg. Verh. Overz. Bez. Visseh. p. 14, pl. 3, fig. 1; Bleeker, Verh. Bat. Gen. xxiii, Teuth. p. 11; Kner, Novara Fische, p. 209.
Teuthis virgata, Günther, Catal. iii, p. 323.
Tuh-meer-dah, Andam.

B. v, D. $\frac{13}{10}$, P. 17, V. 2/3, A. $\frac{7}{9}$, C. 17, Cæc. pyl. 4.

Length of head 2/9, of caudal 2/9, height of body 2/5 to 3/7 of the total length. *Eyes*—diameter 1/3 of length of head, $1\frac{1}{2}$ diameters from end of snout, and $1\frac{1}{4}$ apart. A slight protuberance over the eyes: no serrations to orbit. The maxilla reaches to below the posterior nostril. Angle of preopercle slightly produced. *Teeth*—generic. *Fins*—dorsal spines rather strong, increasing in length to the fifth, from whence they remain of about the same height to the seventh, after which they decrease; the longest spines equal that of the head excluding the snout, and are of the same height as the longest of the rays, the soft portion rather angular: pectoral as long as the head excluding its post-orbital portion: ventral does not reach the anal; anal spines increase in length to the fourth, from which they continue of about the same length, or equal to the longest in the dorsal fin: caudal emarginate. *Scales*—minute. *Colours*—some oblique blue lines and spots on the snout. Upper two-thirds of body coppery yellow, covered with round blue spots, and having blue lines on the head. A brown band, as wide as orbit, extends from before the dorsal fin through the eye to below the jaws; a second from the sixth and seventh dorsal spines to the base of the pectoral, both these bands are edged with blue. Fins yellowish.

Habitat.—Andamans (where the specimen figured was taken) to the Malay Archipelago, and beyond.

5. **Teuthis concatenata**, Plate XL, fig. 4.

Amphacanthus concatenatus, Cuv. and Val. x, p. 127; Bleeker, Amboina, p. 46.
Teuthis concatenata, Cantor, Catal. p. 208; Günther, Catal. iii, p. 316.
Tha-war-dah, Andam.

B. v, D. $\frac{13}{10}$, P. 18, V. 2/3, A. $\frac{7}{9}$, C. 18, Cæc. pyl. 5-6, Vert. 10/13.

Length of head 4/19, of caudal 4/21, height of body 3/8 to 2/5 of the total length. *Eyes*—diameter 1/3 of length of head, $1\frac{1}{2}$ diameters from end of snout, and $1\frac{1}{4}$ apart. Dorsal profile more convex than that of the abdomen. Interorbital space with a broad shallow groove along its whole extent, bounded on either side by a low ridge: anterior-superior angle of the orbit feebly serrated: preopercular angle slightly produced. Soft portion of the cheek as deep as wide, and equal to 1 diameter of the orbit. *Teeth*—generic. *Fins*—dorsal spines increase in length to the fifth, which equals the length of the head excluding the snout; they subsequently slightly decrease to the twelfth, but the last is a little longer: soft portion of dorsal and anal fins angular and rather higher than the longest spine: pectoral almost as long as the head: ventral reaches the anal spines: anal spines increase in length to the third, which equals the highest in the dorsal fin, the last spine is a little longer: caudal emarginate. *Scales*—larger than in most of the known species. *Colours*—dark, greyish-brown, covered all over with light orange spots, which along the back are larger than the interspaces, but decrease in size towards the abdomen. A broad blue band extends from below the orbit to the angle of the mouth, and another passes along the preopercle: brown spots on the caudal fin.

Habitat.—Andaman islands and Malay Archipelago.

6. **Teuthis margaritifera**, Plate XL, fig. 5.

Amphacanthus margaritiferus, Cuv. and Val. x, p. 145; Bleeker, Java, iv, p. 331; Kner, Novara Fische, p. 206.

Teuthis margaritifera, Günther, Catal. iii, p. 317.

B. v, D. $\frac{13}{10}$, P. 17, V. 2/3, A. $\frac{7}{9}$, C. 17, Vert. 10/13.

Length of head 4/21, of caudal 2/11, height of body 4/13 to 2/7 of the total length. *Eyes*—diameter 1/3 of length of head, $1\frac{1}{2}$ diameters from end of snout, and also apart. Dorsal and abdominal profiles equally convex. The maxilla reaches to below the posterior nostril. Interorbital space nearly flat: no serrations along the edge of orbit. Soft portions of the cheek two-thirds as high as the orbit is long, and half longer than high. Angle of preopercle slightly produced. *Teeth*—generic. *Fins*—dorsal spines rather weak, increasing in length to the fifth which is a little above half the length of the head and one-third longer than the rays, subsequently they decrease to the last which equals the diameter of the orbit in length: pectoral rather pointed and as long as the head excluding its post-orbital portion: ventral does not reach the anal spines: third and fourth anal spines slightly longer than the second and equal to the third of the dorsal fin, from thence they decrease to the last which equals $1\frac{1}{4}$ diameter of the orbit in length: caudal lobed, the upper the longer, central caudal rays two-thirds as long as the longest of the outer ones. *Scales*—minute. *Colours*—brownish-olive, with small scattered blue spots on the back and sides, much smaller than the interspaces: a dark oval shoulder-mark: some dark lines on the spinous dorsal: soft dorsal and anal with brown spots.

Habitat.—Andamans to the Malay Archipelago and beyond.

7. Teuthis sutor.

? *Buro brunneus*, Comm. V.
Amphacanthus sutor, Cuv. and Val. x, p. 148.
Teuthis sutor, Günther, Catal. iii, p. 317; Day, Fish. Malabar, p. 126.
Teuthis margaritifera, Playfair, Proc. Zool. Soc. 1867, p. 855 (not Cuv. and Val.).

B. v, D. [illegible], P. 16, V. 2/3, A. $\frac{7}{10}$, C. 17.

Length of head 2/11, of caudal 2/11, height of body 4/11 of the total length. *Eyes*—diameter 2/7 of length of head, 1¼ diameters from end of snout, and 1½ apart. The maxilla reaches to below the front nostril. Anterior-superior edge of orbit indistinctly serrated. *Fins*—fifth dorsal spine the longest and equal to half the length of the head, from it they decrease to the last which equals 1¼ diameters of the orbit in length: third anal spine the longest equalling half the length of the head, from it they decrease to the last which is only two-fifths of the same distance: caudal emarginate, the central rays two and a quarter in the length of the outer ones. *Colours*—light brown, with pale blue spots, those in the middle of the side being the largest and having brown centres: a dark blotch on the shoulder.

In Cuv. and Val. it is observed as closely resembling *A. margaritiferus*, but having its pectorals a little more short and rounded.

Habitat.—Seychelles and coast of Malabar: the foregoing description is from Colonel Playfair's specimen, 11 inches in length, captured at the Seychelles.

8. Teuthis oramin, Plate XL, fig. 6.

Amphacanthus guttatus, var. oramin, Bl. Schn. p. 207, t. 48.
Amphacanthus albopunctatus, Temm. and Schleg. Fauna Japon. Poiss. p. 128.
Teuthis brevirostris, Gronov. ed. Gray, p. 142.
Teuthis oramin, Günther, Catal. iii, p. 318.
Teuthis albopunctata, Günther, Catal. iii, p. 318.

B. v, D. $\frac{13}{10}$, P. 16, V. 2/3, A. $\frac{7}{9}$, C. 17.

Length of head from 4¾ to 5½, of caudal 1/5, height of body 1/3 to 3½ in the total length. *Eyes*—diameter 2¾ in the length of head, 1 to 1¼ diameters from end of snout, and 1 apart. Interorbital space flat, anterior-superior edge of the orbit very finely serrated. The maxilla reaches to below the posterior nostril. The preopercular angle slightly produced: the soft portion of the cheek as high as the orbit and half longer than high. *Teeth*—generic. *Fins*—dorsal spines rather weak, increasing in length to the fourth which equals the length of the head excluding the snout, and is nearly twice as long as the rays, subsequently they decrease to the last which is only two-fifths of the length of the head: pectoral as long as the head excluding its postorbital portion: ventrals do not reach the anal: anal spines increase to the third and fourth which equal the highest in the dorsal fin, they subsequently decrease to the last which equals 1¼ diameters of the orbit in length: caudal with pointed lobes, the central rays being equal to two-thirds of the length of the outer ones. *Scales*—very minute. *Colours*—olivaceous, with indistinct longitudinal stripes in the upper half of the body, below silvery-white. A round black shoulder spot, and a black spot at the top of the eye: numerous pearl white spots on the upper half of the body. Dorsal fin spotted with brown: caudal with four or five vertical bars and a black outer edge. Spinous portion of anal with large black spots, the soft irregularly lineated: pectorals orange. In specimens over 7 or 8 inches in length, the markings on the fins generally become obsolete, the white spots on the body decrease in number, and have a blue tinge. The shoulder spot becomes dark, but the spot on the upper edge of the eye remains.

The black shoulder spot has been omitted in Bl. Schneider's figure, which otherwise is not incorrect: when freshly captured the bars across the caudal fin are very distinct.

Dr. Günther observes, "Professor Peters has informed us that the dried typical specimen mentioned by Schneider appears to have been lost." (l. c. p. 318). It must however be added that Schneider's specimen in spirit is still in good preservation at Berlin.

Habitat.—Common along the coasts of India, attaining at least nine inches in length. If it is the same as *Amphacanthus dorsalis*, C.V.=*Teuthis dorsalis*, Cantor, it would appear to be found at Pinang and Java.

9. Teuthis stellata.

Scarus stellatus, Forsk. p. 26, No. 10.
Amphacanthus stellatus, Bl. Schn. p. 209; Rüpp. N. W. Fische, p. 129.
Amphacanthus punctatus, Rüpp. Atl. Fische, p. 46, pl. 11, f. 2 (not Bl. Schn.)
Amphacanthus nuchalis, Cuv. and Val. x, p. 140.
Teuthis stellata, Günther, Catal. iii, p. 320.

B. v, D. $\frac{13}{10}$, P. 16, V. 2/3, A. $\frac{7}{9}$, C. 19.

Length of head nearly 1/4, of caudal 1/4, height of body about 1/3 of the total length. *Eyes*—diameter 1/3 of length of head, 1½ diameters from end of snout, and 1½ apart. The maxilla reaches to below the hind nostril. *Fins*—fourth dorsal spine the highest, soft dorsal and anal rather pointed: last anal spine the longest: caudal deeply lobed, the upper the longer. *Colours*—greyish, covered all over with small angular spots of a purplish-brown colour: a greenish-yellow spot in front of the dorsal fin: a dark shoulder spot sometimes present: dorsal and anal fins spotted with brown, the border of the soft rays and of the caudal yellowish.

A specimen in the Calcutta Museum from the Red Sea has fine white upper edges and dark lower ones to the spots on the body.

Habitat.—Red Sea, through those of India.

FAMILY, IX—BERYCIDÆ, *Lowe.*

Holocentrini, pt. Swainson.

Branchiostegals from four to eight: pseudobranchiæ present. Form of body oblong, or rather elevated and compressed. Opercles more or less armed. Head with large muciferous cavities. Eyes large, lateral. Cleft of mouth more or less oblique, extending to the sides of the muzzle. Teeth more or less villiform in both jaws, and usually so on the palate. Dorsal fin, when single, having the spinous portion of less extent than the soft, or with isolated spines in front of the fin: or there may be two dorsals, the first being spinous. Ventrals thoracic, each with either less or more than five soft rays. Scales ctenoid, seldom bony or absent: none on the head. Pyloric appendages numerous or in moderate numbers.

SYNOPSIS OF GENERA.

1. *Myripristis.* Branchiostegals seven to eight. Bones of the head serrated, no large spine at the angle of the preopercle. Tropical seas.

2. *Holocentrum.* Branchiostegals eight. Bones of the head serrated: a long, strong, spine at the angle of the preopercle. Tropical seas.

Genus, 1—MYRIPRISTIS, *Cuv.*

Branchiostegals usually eight, more rarely seven: pseudobranchiæ well developed. Eyes large, mostly lateral. Muzzle short, lower jaw prominent. Cleft of mouth oblique, in one species horizontal. Opercular pieces serrated: opercle generally with one spine, none on the preopercle. Teeth villiform on jaws, vomer, and palatines, there may be an outer widely separated row of small obtusely conical ones in the jaws. Two dorsal fins, scarcely united: ventral with one spine and seven rays: anal with four spines: caudal forked. Scales large, ctenoid. Air-vessel transversely contracted near its centre. Pyloric appendages in moderate numbers.

Although considerable prominence has been given to the presence or absence of black marks on the fins in species of this genus, I am convinced that it is subject to great variation, and present or absent in the same species.

Geographical distribution.—Tropical seas.

SYNOPSIS OF SPECIES.

1. *Myripristis botche*, D. 10 | $\frac{1}{13-14}$, A. $\frac{4}{11-13}$, L. l. 28-30, L. tr. 3/7½. Soft dorsal, anal, and caudal black edged, first dorsal also often more or less black. A dark opercular and axillary mark. East coast of Africa, seas of India to the Malay Archipelago and beyond.

2. *Myripristis murdjan*, D. 10 | $\frac{1}{13-15}$, A. $\frac{4}{11-13}$, L. l. 28-30, L. tr. 3½/7½. Red, with a dark mark at the gills and axilla. East coast of Africa, seas of India to the Malay Archipelago and beyond.

1. Myripristis botche, Plate XLI, fig. 1.

Sparus botche, Russell, Fish. Vizag. ii, p. 4, pl. cv.

Myripristis botche, Cuv. and Val. iii, p. 181; (Bleeker, Perc. p. 52, Kner, Novara Fische, p. 5, t. i, f. 1, not synon.)*

Myripristis adustus, Bleeker, Amboina, p. 108, Revis. Myrip. 1871, p. 16; Günther, Catal. i, p. 22; Playfair, Fish. Zanzibar, p. 51.

B. viii, D. 10 | $\frac{1}{13-14}$, P. 15, V. 1/7, A. $\frac{4}{11-13}$, C. 19, L. l. 28-30, L. tr. 3/7½.

Length of head 4/15, of caudal nearly 1/5, height of body nearly 1/3 of the total length. *Eyes*—diameter 2½ to 2¾ in the length of the head, 1/2 a diameter from end of snout, and 3/4 apart or nearly 1/4 in the length of the head. Head slightly longer than high. Chin prominent: the maxilla, which is not denticulated, reaches to below the last third of the orbit. Under surface of lower jaw roughly and irregularly furrowed: pre- and sub-orbitals serrated, also both limbs of the preopercle: a moderately strong opercular spine with two or three above and below it; the lower half of the opercle, the sub- and the inter-opercles serrated. *Teeth*—villiform. *Fins*—dorsal spines weak, the longest being half the length of the head: second dorsal higher than the first: pectoral equals the length of the head behind the front third of the orbit: the ventral reaches two-thirds of the way to the anal: fourth anal spine the longest and equalling the diameter of the orbit but not so strong as the third: caudal forked. *Scales*—seven to eight rows anterior to the dorsal fin: seven along the preopercle: two entire and two half rows between the lateral-line and the base of the dorsal fin. Free portion of the tail rather higher than long. *Colours*—scarlet, the edges of the scales violet, more especially above the lateral-line: longitudinal bands, alternately lighter and darker along each row of scales. First dorsal black, or black with a light longitudinal band, or simply rose-coloured: the other fins pinkish, with the outer third of the soft dorsal, anal, and caudal lobes black, which amount is sometimes reduced to a mere

* This species has been named *M. macrolepis* by Bleeker, Revis. Myr. p. 18.

spot. A deep black spot behind the gill-opening, a dark mark in the axilla. In some rare instances a dark spot may exist on the upper edge of the eye.

I have only collected two species of this genus on the Coromandel coast of India (see pl. xli.), and am of opinion that they are the two that Russell (plates civ. and cv.) obtained from the same place. Russell distinctly shows one has a band on its eye, pl. civ. (see also pl. xli. f. 2.) The one with the banded eye is by far the commonest, and I consider it as *M. murdjan.*

The second species is easily recognised by its more or less black fins, and appears to be *M. adustus.* Admitting that Russell's description does not coincide, neither does it with his own figure. He gives B. viii, D. $\frac{11}{13}$ ($\frac{12}{13}$), P. 15, V. 1/7 ($\frac{1}{6}$), A. $\frac{4}{7}$ ($\frac{4}{12}$), C. 21; his figure gives D. $\frac{11}{14}$, A. $\frac{4}{11}$, demonstrating that his numbers are not trustworthy.

Jerdon (M. J. L. and Sc. 1851, p. 131) observes: "*Myripristis botche,* C. V. *Moonda kan kalosi,* Tam. Russell, 105."

Dr. Günther, Catal. i, p. 21, considers Russell's fish (pl. cv.) is identical with *M. murdjan,* but Bleeker points out that the colours in the two are very differently disposed on the fins.

Habitat.—East coast of Africa, seas of India to the Malay Archipelago and beyond. The specimen figured is $8\frac{1}{2}$ inches in length and from the Coromandel coast of India. It is not nearly so common as the *M. murdjan.*

2. Myripristis murdjan, Plate XLI, fig. 2.

Sciæna murdjan, Forsk. p. 48; Gmel. Linn. p. 1301.
Perca murdjan, Bl. Schn. p. 86; Lacép. pp. 326, 418.
Sparus sallauerwakustee, Russell, Fish. Vizag. ii, p. 3, pl. civ.
Myripristis murdjan, Rüpp. Fische Roth. Meer. p. 86, t. xxiii, f. 2, and N. W. F. p. 95; Cuv. and Val. iii, p. 177 and vii, p. 495; Bleeker, Amb. p. 109, and Révis. Myrip. 1871, p. 11; Günther, Catal. i, p. 21; Kner, Novara Fische, p. 4; Playfair, Fish. Zanz. p. 51 (part); Klunz. Fische Roth. Meer, Verh. z. b. Ges. Wien, 1870, p. 726.
Myripristis melanophrys, Swains. Fish. ii, p. 207.

B. viii, D. 10 | $\frac{1}{13-15}$, P. 15, V. 1/7, A. $\frac{4}{12-13}$, C. 19, L. l. 28-30, L. tr. $3\frac{1}{2}/7\frac{1}{2}$.

Length of head $3\frac{3}{4}$ to $3\frac{1}{2}$, of caudal from 1/5 to 2/9, height of body from 1/3 to $3\frac{3}{4}$ in the total length. *Eyes*—diameter $2\frac{3}{4}$ to $2\frac{1}{2}$ in length of head, 1/3 of a diameter from end of snout, and about 1/2 a diameter apart, the width of the interorbital space equalling from 1/4 to $4\frac{1}{2}$ in the length of the head. Posterior edge of hind nostril usually serrated in the young. Lower jaw slightly the longer, having a rough, nipple-like projection on either side of the symphysis. The maxilla reaches to beneath the last third of the orbit, it has some blunt denticulations on its front near its lower end. Under surface of lower jaw furrowed by ten or twelve grooves: the maxilla, pre- sub- and inter-opercles also grooved. Preopercle serrated in its whole extent. Interopercle finely denticulated: opercle with a moderately strong spine, having a few denticulations above it, and the whole of its outer margin below it serrated. Sub-opercle with an emargination opposite the base of the pectoral fin. Shoulder-scale serrated. Upper surface of the head roughened by three or four raised lines, which, passing backwards, divide and subdivide, each terminating in a small spine. *Teeth*—villiform in the jaws, with an external row of widely separated ones which are larger and conically rounded, none on the tongue. *Fins*—dorsal spines increasing in length to the third which is about the same height as the three next or equal to one diameter of the orbit, the interspinous membrane rather deeply emarginate, front portion of the second dorsal higher than the first. Pectoral as long as the head behind the middle of the eye in the adult, longer in the young: ventral reaches two-thirds of the distance to the anal. Third anal spine the strongest but the fourth the longest and equal to 2/5 to one-third in the length of the head: caudal forked. Free portion of the tail about as high at its base as it is long. *Scales*—about seven rows along the preopercle. *Colours*—roseate, gill openings deep brownish-black, or else like coagulated blood, a dark mark in the axilla. A dark vertical band through the eye, sometimes confined to above the pupil. Dorsal, caudal, and anal fins with milk-white outer edges; a dark mark, often deep black, may be present or absent at the highest points of the soft dorsal and anal fins, also at the tips of the caudal. Rarely there is a dark mark along the first dorsal. Outer edge of ventral white.

Myripristis kuntee, Cuv. and Val. vii, p. 487, was considered in the Hist. Nat. des Poissons to be identical with Russell's fish, a conclusion doubted by Bleeker, whilst Dr. Günther considers it closely allied to *M. praslinius,* C. V.

Habitat.—From the Red Sea and East coast of Africa, through the seas of India to the Malay Archipelago and beyond. The specimen figured is a little over 6 inches in length, and from Madras: my longest is $11\frac{1}{4}$ inches long. It is very common at Madras especially about February.

Genus, 2—Holocentrum, *Artedi.*

Rhynchichthys, Cuv. and Val. (*young**); *Corniger,* Agassiz.

* The genus *Rhynchichthys,* Cuv. and Val., is probably formed of the young of *some* of these species, and is distinguished by an elongated, pointed, and more or less transparent snout, the same as is perceived in some immature fresh water Indian siluroids. A small

Branchiostegals eight. Eyes large, lateral. Jaws of equal length, or the lower slightly the longer; snout of moderate length. Opercles and suborbitals serrated; opercle with two spines: generally a large spine at the angle of the preopercle. Villiform teeth on the jaws, vomer, and palatines. Two dorsal fins scarcely united; ventral with one spine and seven rays; anal with four spines, the third being long and strong; caudal forked. Scales ctenoid, of moderate size. Air-vessel oval and simple. Pyloric appendages numerous.

Bleeker observes that amongst the characters by which these fishes may be distinguished one from another, especial notice should be taken of the number of rows of scales on the preopercle, the relative height of the two last dorsal spines, and the presence or absence of spines at the margin of the nostrils or the end of the snout. To show that these intra-nasal spines are not invariable I would refer to *H. Andamanense*, p. 172. It appears that in some at least of the species of *Holocentrum*, the comparative length of the preopercular spine to that of the body increases with age, whereas, as already observed (p. 9) in *Serrani* or *Lutiani* (p. 29), when one exists at this spot in the immature it becomes more or less absorbed in the adult.

SYNOPSIS OF SPECIES.

1. *Holocentrum diadema*, D. 11 | $\frac{1}{12}$, A. $\frac{4}{9}$, L. l. 47-48, L. tr. 3/7. Width of interorbital space 1/4 of length of head. No intra-nasal or rostral spine. Red, with silvery bands. Red Sea, East coast of Africa, seas of India to China.

2. *Holocentrum Andamanense*, D. 11 | 15, A. $\frac{4}{9}$, L. l. 42, L. tr. $3\frac{1}{2}/7\frac{1}{2}$. Width of interorbital space about 1/5 of length of head. Intra-nasal spine present or absent: a rostral one bifid at its extremity. Uniform rosy-scarlet. Andamans.

3. *Holocentrum caudimaculatum*, D. 11 | 13-14, A. $\frac{4}{9}$, L. l. 40-43, L. tr. $3\frac{1}{2}/7\frac{1}{2}$. Width of interorbital space about 1/5 of length of head. Intra-nasal and rostral spines present. Red, with longitudinal violet bands, a white spot on the free portion of the tail behind the end of the dorsal fin. Red Sea, seas of India to the Malay Archipelago.

4. *Holocentrum rubrum*, D. 11 | 12-13, A. $\frac{4}{9}$, L. l. 35-39, L. tr. $3/6\frac{1}{2}$. Width of interorbital space from 2/7 to 1/4 of length of head. No intra-nasal spines, but rostral ones present. Red, with more or less longitudinal bands: fins sometimes with dark marks.

5. *Holocentrum sammara*, D. 10 | $\frac{1}{11}$-$\frac{1}{12}$, A. $\frac{4}{7-8}$, L. l. 39-40, L. tr. 3/7. Width of interorbital space from $3\frac{1}{2}$ to 1/4 of length of head. No intra-nasal spines, but rostral ones present. Red, with or without violet longitudinal bands: usually a dark mark between the first four dorsal spines, and a dark spot at the base of each spine: vertical fins usually with some dark markings.

1. Holocentrum diadema.

Holocentrus diadema, Lacép. iv, pp. 372, 374, pl. 32, fig. 3; Rüppell, Atl. Fische, p. 84, t. xxii. f. 2.

Holocentrum diadema, Cuv. and Val. iii, p. 213; Less. Voy. Duperr. Zool. ii, p. 220, t. xxv. fig. 2; Bleeker, Moluc. p. 259 and Révis. Holoc. p. 13; Günther, Catal. i, p. 42; Klunz. Fische Roth. Meer. Verh. z. b. Ges. Wien, 1870, p. 723.

B. viii, D. 11 | $\frac{1}{12}$, P. 13, V. 1/7, A. $\frac{4}{9}$, C. 19, L. l. 47-48, L. tr. 3/7, Vert. 11/16.

Length of head 2/7, of pectoral 2/9, of caudal 1/6, height of body $3\frac{1}{4}$ to $3\frac{1}{2}$ in the total length. *Eyes*—diameter 2 to $2\frac{1}{4}$ in the length of the head, 1/2 a diameter from the end of snout, and from 1/2 to 2/3 of a diameter apart, the width of the interorbital space being about 1/4 of the length of the head. The height of the head equals its length without the snout; its width equals half its length. The maxilla reaches to below the anterior third of the orbit. Opercles, preorbital, and suborbitals denticulated, as is also the posterior half of the upper edge of the orbit. Lower edge of preorbital serrated and having a strong blunt spinate projection, directed downwards and forwards. Upper opercular spine the longest and strongest, but not equalling that on the preopercle. The posterior edge of the preopercle and the lower ones of the sub- inter- pre- and opercle spinate. No spines at

---

specimen of *Holocentrum* (*H. platyrhinum*, Klunz. $1\frac{7}{8}$ inches long) exists in the Berlin Museum, and does not possess this elongation of the snout, the latter being nearly 1/2 a diameter of the eye in length. The following may be the fry of a *Holocentrum* (? *rubrum*).

Rhynchichthys ornatus.

Day, Proc. Zool. Society, 1868, p. 149.

B. viii, D. 11/12, P. 15, V. 1/7, A. $\frac{4}{9}$, C. 17, L. l. 38, L. tr. 3/7.

Length of head $3\frac{1}{2}$, of pectoral 1/6, height of body $3\frac{1}{2}$ in the total length. *Eyes*—diameter 2/5 of length of head, 1/2 a diameter from end of snout, the width of the interorbital space equalling nearly 1/3 of the length of the head. Height of head nearly equal to its length. Upper jaw the longer, overhung by a projecting and transparent snout. The maxilla reaches to below the middle of the orbit. Preopercular spine equals about 1/2 the width of the orbit: the opercular pieces and shoulder-bone serrated, upper opercular spine the longer nearly equalling the length of that at the angle of the preopercle. *Teeth*—villiform. *Fins*—dorsal spines moderately strong, the second and third the longest equalling half the height of the body and much higher than the rays, its last two spines of about equal height, interspinous membrane deeply cleft. Third anal spine longest and strongest, equalling the one at the angle of the preopercle, caudal slightly forked. *Scales*—seven rows between the occiput and dorsal fin, and also along the preopercle. *Colours*—bluish-silvery along the back and sides, rosy on the abdomen: dorsal orange, with black spines; interspinous membrane between the first three spines and also between the sixth and last of a deep black colour, the other fins yellowish.

Habitat.—Madras, to $1\frac{7}{8}$ inches in length.

nostrils nor end of snout. *Fins*—the fourth to the sixth dorsal spines the longest and equal to about half the height of the body, interspinous membrane deeply cleft: the two dorsal fins of about the same height. Ventral reaches the vent. Third anal spine the longest and equal from about 1/5 of the total length in young specimens to 1/6 in adults. Caudal forked. *Scales*—not fluted, eight rows between the occiput and the base of the dorsal fin: seven or eight rows along the preopercle. *Colours*—red, with from eight to eleven longitudinal silvery bands: spinous dorsal brownish black, having a white longitudinal band, the other fins rosy.

Habitat.—Red Sea, East coast of Africa, seas of India, to the Malay Archipelago, China and beyond.

2. **Holocentrum Andamanense**, Plate XLI, fig. 3.

Day, Proc. Zool. Soc. 1870, p. 686.

B. viii, D. 11 | 15, P. 17, V. 1/7, A. 4/9, C. 22, L. l. 42, L. tr. 3½/7½.

Length of head 4/13 to 2/7, of caudal 1/6, height of body 3½ to 3¾ in the total length. *Eyes*—diameter 2/7 to 3¾ in length of head; 1 diameter from end of snout, and 3/4 apart, the width of the interorbital space being not quite 1/5 of that of the head. Height of head equals its length behind the posterior nostril: dorsal profile over the eyes slightly concave. Lower jaw a little the longer. The maxilla reaches to below the first third or middle of the orbit. The posterior process of the premaxillary extends to opposite the first third of the eye. Vertical and horizontal limbs of preopercle rather finely denticulated, and with an entire but fluted spine at its angle as long or 1/2 longer than the orbit. Opercle with two or three flat spines, the upper or central one being the longest, the margin of the opercle below it spinate. Sub- and inter-opercles wholly or partially serrated: preorbital with two or three triangular tooth-like processes directed downwards along its lower border, and the interspace serrated. Shoulder-bone rather strongly serrated. A spine directed inwards and rather upwards at the left nostril of one specimen, not on the right side nor in the other specimen, a bifid spine on either side at end of snout. *Teeth*—villiform, none on the tongue. *Fins*—third to fifth dorsal spines the highest and equal to the length of the postorbital portion of the head, the last spine much the shortest being less than half the diameter of the orbit in height, interspinous membrane very slightly notched. Pectoral reaching to the thirteenth scale. Third anal spine the strongest and equal to 1/6 of the total length. Caudal deeply forked. Free portion of the tail as high at its commencement as it is long. *Scales*—3½ rows between the lateral line and the dorsal spines, six before the dorsal fin, and seven or eight rows along the preopercle. *Colours*—uniform rosy-scarlet.

Habitat.—Andamans, from whence two specimens were procured, the longest (figured) being nine inches in length.

3. **Holocentrum caudimaculatum.**

Holocentrum spinifer, Rüpp. Atl. p. 86, t. xxiii, fig. 1 (not N. W. Fische, p. 97).
Holocentrum caudimaculatum, Rüpp. N. W. Fische, p. 97.
Holocentrum spiniferum, Cuv. and Val. iii, p. 206, vii, p. 498.
Holocentrum ruber, Bennett, Fish. Ceylon, p. 4, t. iv.
Holocentrum caudimaculatum, Günther, Catal. i, p. 41, and Garrett, Fische d. Sudsee, p. 95; Playfair, P. Z. S. 1867, p. 855; Klunz. Fische Roth. Meer, 1870, p. 724; Bleeker, Révis. Holoc. p. 22.
Holocentrum leonoides, Bleeker, Celebes, p. 71, and Perc. p. 54.

B. viii, D. 11 | 13-14, P. 14, V. 1/7, A. 4/9, C. 19, L. l. 40-43, L. tr. 3½/7½.

Length of head 3¾, of pectoral 1/5, of caudal 4½, height of body 1/3 to 3½ in the total length. *Eyes*—diameter 2/5 to 1/3 of the length of head, from 1/2 to 2/3 of a diameter apart and also from the end of snout, the width of the interorbital space about 1/5 of the length of the head. Height of the head equals its length excluding the snout, and its width equals half its length. Jaws of about equal length anteriorly, the maxilla reaches to below the middle of the orbit. Preorbital serrated and anteriorly with a rather large blunt spine pointing downwards. Opercular bones serrated, the upper opercular spine the longer: the preopercular spine as long as or longer than the orbit. Shoulder-bone serrated. Two intra-nasal spines. *Teeth*—villiform. *Fins*—the fourth dorsal spine the longest and equal to about 2/5 of the height of the body, but not so high as the soft dorsal: dorsal interspinous membrane rather deeply emarginate. Third anal spine longest and strongest equalling about 2/9 of the total length. Caudal forked. *Scales*—seven or eight rows between the occiput and the base of the dorsal fin: seven or eight rows along the preopercle. *Colours*—red, more or less longitudinally banded with violet, and having a white spot over the free portion of the tail behind the end of the dorsal fin.

Habitat.—Red Sea, seas of India to the Malay Archipelago.

4. **Holocentrum rubrum**, Plate XLI, fig. 4.

Sciæna rubra, Forsk. p. 48 (not Bl. Schn.)
Perca rubra, Bl. Schn. p. 90.
Perca praslin, Lacép. iv, p. 418.
Holocentre tilmeanthe, Lacép. iv, p. 334.
Holocentrum alborubrum, Lacép. iv, p. 372: Richards. Ich. China, p. 223; Bleeker, Fish. Ind. Arch. p. 2.
Holocentrum ruber, Rüppell, Atl. p. 83, t. xxii. f. 1, and N. W. Fische, p. 96.
Holocentrum Orientale, Cuv. and Val. iii, p. 197, vii, p. 497; Bleeker, Perc. p. 53; Jerdon, M. J. L. and Sc. 1851, p. 131.
Holocentrum marginatum et laticeps, Cuv. and Val. iii, pp. 216, 211, and vii, p. 500 (not Günther).

Holocentrum spinosissimum, Rich. Ich. China, p. 223 (not Tem. and Schleg.).

Holocentrum rubrum, Günther, Catal. i, p. 35, and Garrett, Fische d. Sudsee, p. 96; Day, Fish. Malabar, p. 1; Kner, Novara Fische, p. 7; Playfair, Fish. Zanz. p. 52; Klunz. Verh. z. b. Ges. Wien, 1870, p. 722; Bleeker, Révis. Hol. 1871, p. 27.

Cul-kuh-catchee, Tam.

B. viii, D. 11 | 12-13, P. 15, V. 1/7, A. $\frac{4}{9}$, C. 19, L. l. 35-39, L. tr. 3/6½, Cæc. pyl. 20, Vert. 11/16.

Length of head 2/7 to 3¾, of caudal 2/13, height of body 3¼ to 3½ in the total length. *Eyes*—diameter 2/7 to 2¾ in the length of head, 2/3 of a diameter from the end of snout, 3/4 of a diameter apart, the width of the interorbital space equalling from 2/7 to 1/4 of the length of the head. The maxilla reaches to below the centre of the orbit. The posterior process of the premaxillary shorter than the diameter of the eye. Upper surface of the head roughened with sinuous lines which posteriorly end in spinate points. Suborbital ring of bones narrow, fluted and serrated in their whole extent. Preoperele likewise fluted along its vertical limb, having a strong spine as long as the orbit at its angle and serrated along both limbs. Operele evenly fluted, armed with two spines (the lower being the shorter) and its outer edge strongly serrated: sub- and interopercles fluted and denticulated: shoulder-bones denticulated. Snout with two sharp nipple-shaped spines on the preorbital and intermediate serrations: no spines at nostrils. *Teeth*—villiform. *Fins*—dorsal spines strong, the third to the fifth the longest, the third equalling half the height of the body, but not so high as the soft portion of the fin. Pectoral reaches to the twelfth scale of the lateral-line, and the ventral three-fourths of the way to the anus. Third anal spine very strong, its height equalling about 2/3 of the height of the body, whilst it is 2/9 to 1/5 longer than the fourth spine. Caudal forked. *Scales*—six or seven rows between the occiput and the base of the first dorsal fin: seven rows along the preoperele. *Colours*—in the *young* silvery white with longitudinal dull rosy bands from the opercles, the second and third coalescing. In the *adult* it is red with seven or eight silvery bands. Head more or less rosy as are also the fins. Occasionally there is a little dark about the latter.

In the Fishes of Zanzibar, "Var. b, has a large black blotch at the base of the soft dorsal and anal, a third at the root of the caudal, and a fourth at the axil of the pectoral. This is clearly identical with that described by Bleeker as *H. melanospilos*. These varieties are structurally identical, and the difference in coloration is probably a sexual one; one specimen of Var. b proved to be a male fish, at or near spawning time." (p. 52).

Respecting colour, the one I have figured, destitute of any black, was a male. Jerdon's specimen (*sea-poorau*, Tam.) has a black spot at the base of both soft dorsal and anal fins, and a third above the superior opercular spine, whilst the margin of the preopercle is dark-edged; it has no vestige of a spine inside the nostril, as exists in *Holocentrum melanospilus*, Bleeker.

Habitat.—Red Sea, East coast of Africa, through the seas of India to the Malay Archipelago and beyond.

5. Holocentrum sammara.

Sciæna sammara, Forsk. p. 48; Lacép. iv, p. 314.

Perca sammara, Bl. Schn. p. 89.

Labrus angulosus, Lacép. iii, p. 430, t. xxii, f. 1.

Holocentrum sammara, Rüpp. Atl. Fische, p. 85, t. xxii, f. 3.

Holocentrum sammara, Cuv. and Val. iii, p. 216; Bleeker, Perc. p. 33, Amb. p. 555, and Révis. Holoc. p. 16; Günther, Catal. i, p. 46; Kner, Novara Fische, p. 9; Klunz. Verh. z. b. Ges. Wien, 1870, p. 720.

Holocentrum Christianum, (Ehren.) Cuv. and Val. iii, p. 219.

? *Holocentrum leo*, Günther, Catal. i, p. 47.

Holocentrum Tahiticum, Kner, Novara Fische, p. 9, t. i, f. 2.

B. viii, D. 10 | $\frac{1}{11-12}$, P. 14, V. 1/7, A. $\frac{4}{8}$, C. 19, L. l. 39-40, L. tr. 3/7, Vert. 11/16.

Length of head 3½ to 3¾, of caudal 1/5, height of body 3¾ to 1/4 of the total length. *Eyes*—diameter 2¼ to 1/3 in the length of head, 2/3 of a diameter from end of snout, and also apart, the interorbital space being equal to 3¼ to 1/4 of the length of the head. The height of the head equals its length excluding the snout: its width equals half its length. The lower jaw the longer: the maxilla reaches to below the middle of the eye. Both limbs of the preopercle serrated in their entire extent, the length of the preopercular spine equals about 1/3 of the diameter of the orbit. The external edges of all the opercles more or less serrated: two spines on the opercle, the upper of which is as large as the preopercular one, the lower rather smaller. Preorbital denticulations strong: suborbital likewise serrated. No spine at nostrils nor at the end of the snout. Shoulder-bone striated and serrated. *Teeth*—villiform. *Fins*—the dorsal spines from the second to the fourth are of about the same height and equal to 1½ in that of the body, subsequently they decrease to the tenth which is one-fourth of their height: interspinous membrane deeply emarginate: second dorsal highest anteriorly and rather higher than the highest dorsal spine. Pectoral nearly equals the head excluding the snout. Ventral reaches half way to the anal. Third anal spine strongest and longest, equalling from 5¼ to 4½ in the total length. Caudal forked. *Scales*—six to seven rows between the occiput and the base of the dorsal fin: seven along the preopercle. *Colours*—body with or without longitudinal violet bands, which may be composed of spots. A black spot may be present on either cheek. Usually a black spot between the first four dorsal spines, and sometimes a light mark between the bases of each spine. Anterior edge of soft dorsal and anal, also usually upper and lower edge of caudal, violet.

Habitat.—Red Sea, East coast of Africa, seas of India to the Malay Archipelago and beyond.

FAMILY, X—KURTIDÆ.

Branchiostegals seven: pseudobranchiæ absent. Body oblong and compressed. Eyes large. The infraorbital bones do not articulate with the preopercle. Cleft of mouth oblique: lower jaw prominent. Villiform teeth on jaws, vomer, and palatines. A single dorsal fin, the spinous portion being of less extent than the soft, some spines may even be rudimentary: anal elongated, with two or three spines: ventrals thoracic with one spine and five rays. Scales of moderate or small size. Air-vessel present. Pyloric appendages few.

SYNOPSIS OF GENERA.

1. *Kurtus.* Dorsal spines rudimentary, three anal ones. A horizontally directed spine between the ventral fins. Seas of India to the Malay Archipelago.

2. *Pempheris.* Six dorsal and three anal spines. Scales over the anal fin. Red Sea, seas of India to the Malay Archipelago.

Genus, 1—KURTUS, *Bloch.*

Branchiostegals seven: pseudobranchiæ absent. Body oblong and strongly compressed: back elevated. Cleft of mouth oblique and deep, the lower jaw prominent. Preopercle denticulated. Villiform teeth in the jaws, vomer, and palatines. A single dorsal fin of much shorter extent than the anal, its spines being rudimentary: between the ventrals is a horizontal backwardly directed spine. Scales very small. Air-vessel present, enclosed in a conical cavity made by the ribs, which are dilated, convex, and forming rings in contact with each other.

SYNOPSIS OF INDIVIDUAL SPECIES.

1. *Kurtus Indicus.* D. $\frac{1|5-6}{12-14}$, A. $\frac{2-3}{31-32}$. Silvery. Seas of India to the Malay Archipelago and beyond.

1. Kurtus Indicus, Plate XLII, fig. 1.

Kurtus Indicus, Bl. t. 169; Gmel. Linn. p. 1184; Shaw, Zool. iv, p. 185, pl. 25; Bl. Schn. p. 163; Bleeker, Verh. Bat. Gen. xxiv, Makr. p. 78; Günther, Catal. ii, p. 510.

Kurtus Blochii, Lacép. ii, pp. 516, 517; Cuv. and Val. ix, p. 421, pl. 277; Cuv. Règne Anim. Poiss. pl. 64, f. 2; Swainson, Fishes, ii, p. 253.

Blennius,? Russell, Fish. Vizag. i, p. 37, and *Sandrum-karo-woodike,* pl. 48.

Kurtus cornutus, Cuv. Règ. Anim. Poiss. pl. 64, f. 1; Cuv. and Val. ix, p. 426.

Cyrtus Indicus, Cantor, Catal. p. 145; Kner, Novara Fische, p. 172.

Kokosi, Tel.; *Oordah* and *Valloond-cutchal,* Tam.

B. vii, D. $\frac{1|5-6}{12-14}$, P. 21, V. 1/5, A. $\frac{2-3}{31-32}$, C. 17, Vert. 8/15.

Length of head 1/4 to 2/9, of caudal 1/4 to 2/9, height of body 1/3 to 2/7 of the total length. *Eyes*—in the anterior half of the head, 1 diameter from end of snout, and 1½ apart. Body strongly compressed, the males having a cartilaginous arched process directed forwards and situated a short distance in front of the dorsal fin. Lower jaw the longer, and having a tuberosity at the symphysis, when the mouth is closed its extremity forms a portion of the dorsal profile: the maxilla reaches to below the last third or hind edge of the orbit. A strong, short spine directed downwards at the angle of the preopercle, and two or three more along its lower edge: the occipital ridge rough. *Teeth*—in minute rows, in the jaws, vomer, and palatines. *Fins*—dorsal fin having five spines in front of its soft portion, preceded by a recumbent spine directed anteriorly: in front of this spine are some points appearing above the skin, most distinct in the fry, and similar to the rudimentary fins of *Stromateidæ,* &c.: soft portion of the dorsal fin highest anteriorly: ventral reaches as far as the anal, it has a short backwardly-directed spine in front of the base of the outer ray of either fin, and also a horizontally similar but larger one between the two fins. Second anal spine two-thirds as high as the rays: the length of the first few anal rays equals four-ninths that of the fins base: caudal deeply lobed. *Scales*—fine and irregular on the body.

Lateral-line—ceases opposite the end of the soft dorsal. *Colours*—silvery shot with steel-blue, or lilac: back with fine black dots which behind the occiput form a rounded black spot.

The young are not uncommon in the Sunderbunds about January and February.

Habitat.—Seas of India to the Malay Archipelago and beyond. It attains at least $4\frac{1}{2}$ inches in length, and is most numerous on the Coromandel coast during the cold months. The specimen figured is a male from Coconada.

Genus, 2—Pempheris, *Cuv. and Val.*

Branchiostegals seven. Body oblong, compressed: head obtuse. Eyes large. Cleft of mouth oblique, with the lower jaw prominent. Opercle with a small spine. Villiform teeth on the jaws, vomer, and palatine bones. A single short dorsal fin with six spines and nine rays: anal with three spines and many rays. Scales small, extended over the anal fin. Air-vessel divided into an anterior and posterior portion. Pyloric appendages few.

Geographical distribution.—Red Sea, seas of India, to the Malay Archipelago and beyond.

SYNOPSIS OF SPECIES.

1. *Pempheris mangula*, D. $\frac{6}{9}$, A. [illegible], L. l. 60-64. Eyes, diameter $2\frac{1}{4}$ to $2\frac{1}{2}$ in length of head: height of body $3\frac{1}{3}$ in the total. Silvery, dorsal black tipped. Seas of India to the Malay Archipelago and beyond.

2. *Pempheris Molucca*, D. $\frac{6}{9}$, A. [illegible], L. l. 56. Eyes, diameter half the length of head: height of body 2/5 of the total. Silvery, fins stained with darker. Red Sea, seas of India to the Malay Archipelago.

1. Pempheris mangula, Plate XLII, fig. 3.

Sparus mangula-kutti, Russell, Fish. Vizag. ii, p. 10, pl. 114.

Pempheris mangula, Cuv. and Val. vii, p. 304; Bleek. Chætod. p. 30; Günther, Catal. ii, p. 509; Kner, Novara Fische, p. 171; Klunz. Verh. z. b. Ges. Wien, 1871, p. 469; Garrett, F. d. Sudsee, t. lix, f. B.

Pempheris Otaitensis, Cuv. and Val. vii, p. 304, pl. 191; Less. Voy. Coq. p. 197; Günther, Catal. ii, p. 508; Kner, Novara Fische, p. 171.

? *Pempheris Vanicolensis* et *nesogallica*, Cuv. and Val. vii, pp. 305, 306.

B. vii, D. $\frac{6}{9}$, P. 17, V. 1/5, A. [illegible], C. 17, L. l. 60-64.

Length of head 1/5, of caudal 1/5, height of body 3/10 of the total length. *Eyes*—diameter from $2\frac{1}{4}$ to $2\frac{1}{2}$ in the length of head. Interorbital space slightly concave. The maxilla reaches to below the middle of the eye. Preopercle having rather a strong denticulation on its intramarginal edge near the angle. *Teeth*—villiform in jaws, vomer, and palate. *Fins*—soft dorsal highest anteriorly, rapidly decreasing in height to the last ray. Pectoral a little longer than the head. Ventral reaches the anal fin. Anterior portion of the anal the highest and equal to two-fifths of that of the body: caudal emarginate. *Colours*—violet-brown superiorly, becoming silvery below. Fins roseate with fine dots: axilla and base of pectoral light coloured.

Habitat.—Seas of India and beyond. The specimen figured (6 inches long) is from Madras, where at times it is abundant.. Jerdon, M. J. L. and Sc. 1851, p. 134, observes this fish is termed *Moonda-kua-kooree*, Tamil.

2. Pempheris Molucca, Plate XLII, fig. 2.

Pempheris Molucca, Cuv. and Val. vii, p. 306; Cuv. Règ. Anim. Ill. Poiss. pl. 44, f. 2; Temm. and Schleg. Fauna Japon, p. 85, pl. 44, fig. 3; Richards. Ich. China, p. 244; Cantor, Catal. p. 175; Günther, Catal. ii, p. 509; Day, Fishes of Malabar, p. 108.

Pempheris Malabarica, Cuv. and Val. vii, p. 308.

B. vii, D. $\frac{6}{9}$, P. 18, V. 1/5, A. [illegible], C. 17, L. l. 56, Cæc. Pyl. 6-7, Vert. 10/14.

Length of head $3\frac{3}{4}$, of caudal 1/5, height of body 2/5 of the total length. *Eyes*—diameter about 1/2 the length of the head, 3/4 of a diameter apart. The maxilla reaches to below the middle of the orbit. Preopercle entire, but having three somewhat spinate denticulations along its intra-marginal border. *Teeth*—in jaws, vomer, and palate. *Fins*—dorsal spines weak, increasing in length to the last which is scarcely so high as the first rays, the soft portion decreases posteriorly in height. Pectoral as long as the head. Ventral short: anal highest in front: caudal forked. *Scales*—the rows along the lateral-line larger than the others. *Colours*—silvery-grey, upper third of the dorsal rays black: pectorals orange, and usually having a dark base; anal rather dark anteriorly and inferiorly: caudal with its posterior margin stained grey.

It is suggested by Cuv. and Val. that *Cyrtus macrolepidotus*, Bl. Schn. p. 164, which is said to have large scales with their edges dotted with red, subvertical eyes and B. 2, D. [illegible], P. 12, V. 1/5, A. [illegible], C. 22, from Tranquebar, may be this species: the [illegible] being a misprint for [illegible]. More information is however necessary before this point can be decided.

This species is very abundant off the Sind coast, and found through the seas of India to Japan.

Habitat.—Red Sea, seas of India to the Malay Archipelago and beyond. The specimen figured (6 inches long) is from Kurrachee.

FAMILY, XI—POLYNEMIDÆ.

Branchiostegals seven: pseudobranchiæ. Body oblong, somewhat compressed. Eyes large, lateral, more or less covered by an adipose membrane: mouth on the lower side of a prominent snout, and having a lateral cleft. Muciferous system on the head well developed. Villiform teeth on the jaws, and palatines: present or absent on the vomer. Two dorsal fins: several free and articulated appendages below the pectoral fin: ventrals thoracic, with one spine and five rays. Scales finely ctenoid or cycloid, and more or less covering the vertical fins. Lateral-line continuous, continued on to the caudal fin. Air-vessel, when present, varying in form and structure. Pyloric appendages of varying numbers.

Geographical distribution.—Seas of India to the Pacific, also tropical portions of the Atlantic, not found in the Red Sea.

SYNOPSIS OF INDIVIDUAL GENUS.

Genus, 1—*Polynemus.* Definition as in the Family.

Uses.—These fish are all excellent as food, and from some, rough isinglass or fish-sounds are obtained and exported in large quantities.

Genus, 1—POLYNEMUS,* *Linn.*

Trichidion, Klein; *Polistonemus*, Gill; *Eleutheronema*, Bleeker.

Preopercle serrated. Teeth villiform on the jaws, palatines, vomer, and pterygoid bones. First dorsal fin with seven or eight weak spines; soft dorsal and anal of nearly equal extent: pectoral rays simple or branched and having a varying number of free ones (3-7) at the base of the fin. Scales ctenoid, rather small, extended on to the vertical fins. Air-vessel, when present, varying in form, size, and structure. Pyloric appendages few, in moderate numbers, or many.

SYNOPSIS OF SPECIES.

1. *Polynemus paradiseus*, D. 7 | $\frac{1}{15-16}$, A. $\frac{3}{12}$, L. l. 70. Seven free pectoral rays, the three upper being twice as long as the fish. No air-vessel. Golden colour. Upper part of Bay of Bengal to the Malay Archipelago, entering rivers.

2. *Polynemus heptadactylus*, D. 8 | $\frac{1}{12-13}$, A. $\frac{3}{11-12}$, L. l. 50-52. Seven free pectoral rays reaching the base of the anal. No air-vessel. Golden, pectoral black, vertical fins with dark edges.

3. *Polynemus xanthonemus*, D. 8 | $\frac{1}{16}$, A. $\frac{3}{11-12}$. Six free pectoral rays reaching beyond the tip of the ventral. No air-vessel. Fins edged with black. Seas of India to China.

4. *Polynemus sextarius*, D. 8 | $\frac{1}{13-14}$, A. $\frac{3}{12-13}$, L. l. 48-50. Six free pectoral rays reaching to the middle or end of the ventral fin. Air-vessel small and simple. Upper half of dorsal, pectoral, and outer part of ventral black. A large black shoulder-spot. Seas of India to the Malay Archipelago.

5. *Polynemus sexfilis*, D. 8 | $\frac{1}{12-13}$, A. $\frac{3}{11-12}$, L. l. 46. Six free pectoral rays reaching rather beyond the ventrals. Air-vessel large. Golden, pectoral black: dorsal and anal black-edged. Seas of India to the Malay Archipelago.

6. *Polynemus Indicus*, D. 8 | $\frac{1}{12-13}$, A. $\frac{2-3}{11-12}$, L. l. 70-75. Five free pectoral rays reaching nearly to the anal fin. Air-vessel long and narrow. Vertical fins dark edged. Seas of India to Australia.

7. *Polynemus plebeius*, D. 8 | $\frac{1}{13}$, A. $\frac{2-3}{11}$, L. l. 60-65. Five free pectoral rays reaching to the end of the ventral fin. Air-vessel present. Golden, with grey longitudinal bands. Seas of India to China.

8. *Polynemus tetradactylus*, D. 8 | $\frac{1}{13-15}$, A. $\frac{2-3}{14-17}$, L. l. 75-85. Four free pectoral rays reaching to the end of the ventral. Air-vessel absent. Seas of India to the Malay Archipelago and China.

1. Polynemus paradiseus, Plate XLII, fig. 4.

Polynemus paradiseus, Linn. Syst. Nat. p. 1401; Russell, ii, p. 69, pl. 185; Günther, Catal. ii, p. 320.
Polynemus risua, aureus, topsui, Ham. Buch. Fish. Ganges, pp. 228, 232, 381.
Polynemus longifilis, Cuv. and Val. iii, p. 395, and vii, p. 512; Bleeker, Bengal, p. 91, and Enum. Spec. Ind. Arch. p. 245, (not Borneo, ii, p. 268, and vi, p. 418.)
Trichidion paradiseus, Bleeker, Fish. Madagascar, p. 78.
Tupsee muchee, Beng.; *Nga-poonyan*, Burm. *Mango fish.*

B. vii, D. 7 | $\frac{1}{15-16}$, P. 15+vii, V. 1/5, A. $\frac{3}{12}$, C. 19, L. l. 70, L. tr. 5/14, Vert. 10/15, Cæc. pyl. 5(10).

Length of head 2/13 to 1/6, of pectoral 2/5 to 1/4, of caudal $3\frac{1}{4}$ to $3\frac{1}{2}$, height of body 2/13 to 1/6 of the total length. *Eyes*—minute in the young, in the adult diameter 1/8 of length of head, 2 diameters from end of

* *Kala*, Tam.: *Nut-tiah*, Mugh.

snout, and 3 apart. Height of head equals its length excluding the snout, its width equals its postorbital length. Snout overhanging the mouth. The maxilla extends to upwards of two diameters behind the posterior edge of the orbit. Preopercle serrated and having a soft, produced, and rounded, angle: the other opercles entire. A small spine on the shoulder. *Teeth*—villiform in jaws, vomer, and palate. *Fins*—spines of first dorsal weak, the second one slightly the longest: the height of the first ray of the second dorsal equals the length of the base of the fin which is highest anteriorly, its upper edge concave. Pectoral rays undivided, the fin has seven free rays below its base, the three superior being the longest, strongest, and about twice the length of the fish. Ventral does not quite reach the anal, the latter fin commencing under the second dorsal and being of the same height, its lower edge emarginate. Caudal deeply forked, upper lobe the longer. *Scales*—ctenoid, in regular horizontal rows, covering the body and head, with fine ones over the vertical fins. *Lateral-line*—forms a gradual curve, and becomes lost at the centre of the base of the caudal fin. Least depth of the free portion of the tail equals 2/5 of the length of the head. *Air-vessel*—absent. *Colours*—generally golden, with a shade of gray along the back, and the dorsal fins also stained grayish with a slight tinge of the same shade, so are also the caudal, the pectoral, and upper pectoral appendages.

Buchanan observes: "Those who officiate in the temple of *Sib* are called *Topasi* in the vulgar dialect, and *Topaswi* in Sangskritta, that is to say penitents. They ought not to shave, on which account a fish called *Mangoe* fish by the English of Calcutta, which has long fibres proceeding from near its head, is called by the same name."

Habitat.—Indian seas, Bay of Bengal at least as low as Coconada, also along the coasts of Burma to the Malay Archipelago, entering rivers for spawning purposes, and generally during the S. W. monsoon and the cold months. It is considered a great luxury for the table and commences to be taken in numbers about June. It attains 9 inches in length. Ham. Buch. observes: "I have, I think, observed three species included under this name (Mangoe fish), and Dr. Russell describes a fourth: but all have exactly the same qualities and manners, nor am I sure that the slight differences in the number of rays which I observed may not be accidental varieties, rather marking individual than specific differences" (p. 229).

2. Polynemus heptadactylus, Plate XLII, fig. 5.

Cuv. and Val. iii, p. 390; Bleeker, Perc. p. 60; Cantor, Catal. p. 34; Günther, Catal. ii, p. 321; Day, Fishes of Malabar, p. 59.

B. vii, D. 8 | $\frac{1}{12-13}$, P. 15+vii, V. 1/5, A. $\frac{3}{11-12}$, C. 19, L. l. 50-52, L. tr. 5/11, Cæc. pyl. 4.

Length of head 1/5, of caudal 1/4, height of body 1/4 of the total length. *Eyes*—diameter $3\frac{1}{4}$ in the length of head, 1/2 a diameter from end of snout, and 1 apart. Height of the head equals its length excluding the snout, the width of the head nearly equals half its length. The maxilla reaches to 1/2 a diameter behind the posterior edge of the eye: interorbital space nearly flat. Preopercle strongly serrated, having a well developed spine just above its angle, which is rounded and produced. A spine on shoulder at the commencement of the lateral-line. *Teeth*—villiform in jaws, vomer, and palate. *Fins*—first dorsal spine short, the third the longest and equal to 2/3 the height of the body, the last scarcely one-third of its height; second dorsal highest anteriorly where it equals 3/4 of that of the body, upper edge of the fin concave. Pectoral rays unbranched, the length of the fin equals 3/4 of the height of the body, its appendages reach to the base of the anal, the upper being the longest. Ventral reaches the vent. Anal highest anteriorly where it equals the first dorsal, its lower edge straight. Caudal deeply lobed. *Air-vessel*—absent. Free portion of the tail in its least depth equals $1\frac{1}{3}$ in the length of the head. *Colours*—golden, pectoral nearly black: edge of first dorsal, upper edge of second dorsal, margins of caudal, lower half of the anal and tip of ventral also black.

Habitat.—Seas of India to the Malay Archipelago, attaining at least 6 inches in length.

3. Polynemus xanthonemus.

Cuv. and Val. vii, p. 517; Richardson, Ich. China, p. 219; Günther, Catal. ii, p. 325.

B. vii, D. 8 | $\frac{1}{14}$, P. 15+vi, A. $\frac{3}{14-15}$, Cæc. pyl. 12.

It is observed that this fish more resembles *P. sextarius* than *P. sexfilis*. *Fins*—its six free pectoral rays extend beyond the end of the ventral but are shorter than in *P. hexanemus*, in which they reach to the end of the body. Although the caudal lobes are not more elongated than in *P. sextarius* (1/5 of the total length), the fin is more deeply cleft. *Air-vessel*—absent. *Colours*—back greenish, sides and abdomen silvery: the fins yellow with a black border, the free rays are the same colour as the fins.

Sir John Richardson observes of Reeves' figure, that it "has a zigzag blackish line above the base of the pectoral, which is not noticed in the 'Histoire des Poissons,' but in other respects it agrees with the description in that work."

Habitat.—Seas of India to China, attaining at least 6 inches in length. I have not recognised this species in India.

4. Polynemus sextarius, Plate XLII, fig. 6.

Bloch. Schn. p. 18, t. iv; Cuv. and Val. iii, p. 388, and vii, p. 514; Bleeker, Perc. p. 59; Cantor, Catal. p. 32; Günther, Catal. ii, p. 326; Day, Fish. Malabar, p. 60.

B. vii, D. 8 | $\frac{1}{12}|\frac{1}{13}$, P. 14 + vi, V. 1/5, A. $\frac{3}{11}|\frac{3}{12}$, C. 17, L. l. 48-50, L. tr. 5/10.

Length of head 1/4 to $4\frac{1}{2}$, of caudal 1/5 to 2/9, height of body 1/4 to 2/9 of the total length. *Eyes*—diameter 1/3 to $3\frac{1}{4}$ in the length of head, 2/5 to 3/4 of a diameter from end of snout, and about 1 apart. Height of head equals its length behind the middle of the eye, its width from $2\frac{1}{4}$ to $2\frac{1}{2}$ in its length. The maxilla reaches to behind the posterior edge of the orbit. Vertical margin of preopercle denticulated, with a rather strong tooth just above its angle, which latter is rounded, produced, and entire. *Teeth*—villiform, those on the vomer in a transverse band, whilst the palatine band is semi-interrupted. *Fins*—dorsal spines with rather filamentous terminations, the third being equal to $1\frac{1}{3}$ in the height of the body and as long as the highest ray in the second dorsal: the height of the second dorsal and of the anal are nearly the same, but the length of the base of the former is longer than that of the latter: upper edge of the second dorsal fin scarcely, if at all, emarginate. Pectoral rays branched; the free rays at the base of the fin reach to the middle of the ventral fin, occasionally to its end: caudal rather deeply forked. A spine on the shoulder at the commencement of the lateral-line. *Air-vessel*—small and simple. *Cæcal appendages*—long and rather numerous. Free portion of the tail in its lowest part equal to 1/2 the length of the head. *Colours*—golden, the upper half of the first dorsal black spotted: pectoral and ventral with numerous black spots sometimes occasioning the former to be almost black: other fins more or less numerously dotted with black and often black-edged. A large black spot on the shoulder on the lateral-line from the second to the eighth scales.

This fish is very numerous throughout the coasts of India up to $7\frac{1}{2}$ inches in length.

Habitat.—East coast of Africa, seas of India to the Malay Archipelago.

Jerdon in his Ichthy. paper on Madras (M. J. L. and Sc. 1851, p. 140) observes of the species of this genus he had obtained "*Polynemus tetradactylus*, C.V. *Yerra kala*, Tam.; *P. plebeius*, C.V. *Pole kala*, Tam.; *P. Indicus*, Shaw, *Wahan kala*; *P. sextarius*, C.V. *Kalli kala*, Tam.; *P. heptadactylus*, C.V. *Ma-kala*, Tam. The first three species are called Roeball at Madras and are considered good eating."

5. Polynemus sexfilis, Plate XLIII, fig. 1.

? Cuv. and Val. vii, p. 515; Günther, Catal. ii, p. 325 (not Playfair, Fish. Zanz.* p. 53).
Polynemus hexanemus, Cantor, Catal. p. 23 (not Cuv. and Val.).
Trichidion sexfilis, Bleeker, Fish. Madagascar, p. 79.

B. vii, D. 8 | $\frac{1}{12}|\frac{1}{13}$, P. 15 + vi, V. 1/5, A. $\frac{3}{11}|\frac{3}{12}$, C. 17, L. l. 46, L. tr. 5/10, Cæc. pyl. many.

Length of head $4\frac{1}{2}$, of caudal 2/7, height of body 2/9 of the total length. *Eyes*—diameter 2/9 of length of head, 1/2 a diameter from end of snout, and 1 apart. Height of head equals its length excluding the snout, its width equals 4/7 of its length. The maxilla reaches half a diameter behind the orbit. Vertical margin of preopercle strongly denticulated with a rather strong tooth above its rounded, produced, but entire angle. *Teeth*—villiform in jaws, in a semilunar band on the vomer, and in an interrupted one on the palatines. *Fins*—third dorsal spine 2/3 of the height of the body; second dorsal 1/4 higher anteriorly than the anal, its upper edge rather concave. The pectoral rays unbranched, the free ones reach to rather beyond the end of the ventral: base of the anal slightly longer than that of the second dorsal: caudal deeply forked. A spine on the shoulder at the commencement of the lateral-line. Free portion of the tail as high as it is long, its least height equal to nearly 1/2 the length of the head. *Cæcal appendages*—long and rather numerous. *Air-vessel*—large. *Colours*—golden, pectoral deep black, a black lower edge to the anal; ventral dark in the middle.

In Cuv. and Val. *P. sexfilis* is said to have no air-vessel. This species appears to closely resemble *P. Pfeifferi*, Bleeker, which also has a large air-vessel, and D. 8 | $\frac{1}{13}$, A. $\frac{3}{13}$, L. l. 48. Length of head 1/5, and of caudal lobes $3\frac{1}{4}$ in the total length.

This species differs from *P. sextarius* in its eye being smaller, its caudal lobes larger, the base of its anal longer than that of its second dorsal, its third dorsal spine 2/3 of the height of the body, some of its pectoral free-rays reaching beyond the end of the ventral, and its rays being simple, and likewise in having a black pectoral fin but no black shoulder-spot. From the *P. xanthonemus*, wherein only 12 pyloric appendages exist.

Cantor, whilst observing that "the second, third, and fourth filaments from the pectoral fin are the

* The fish alluded to by Colonel Playfair in the "Fishes of Zanzibar," is not identical with the above, and might be termed *Polynemus Playfairi*, if it is not *P. Kuru*: two other specimens exist in the British Museum: the species is as follows:—

B. vii, D. 8 | $\frac{1}{14}$, P. 18 + vi, V. 1/5, A. $\frac{3}{13}$, C. 17, L. l. 67, L. tr. 7/13.

Length of head $5\frac{1}{2}$, of caudal $3\frac{3}{4}$, height of body $4\frac{3}{4}$ of the total length. *Eyes*—diameter nearly 1/3 of length of head, 1/4 of a diameter from end of snout, and 1 apart. The maxilla reaches to a little behind the vertical from the posterior edge of the orbit. Height of head equals its length excluding the snout, its width two-thirds of its length. A spine at the shoulder. *Fins*—first dorsal two-thirds as high as the body below it: second dorsal nearly equal in height to the length of the head and having its upper edge deeply concave, its front rays being one-fifth higher than the first dorsal fin. Pectoral as long as the head behind the middle of the eye, its upper free-rays reach to a little beyond the end of the fin. The distance between the bases of the ventral and anal fins equals the length of the head excluding the snout. Anal not quite so high as the second dorsal, it commences below the fifth dorsal ray and has a very emarginate lower edge. Caudal deeply forked. Free portion of tail slightly higher at its base than it is long. *Colours*—body with lines along each row of scales and a black pectoral fin.

This species appears to be closely allied to *P. Kuru*, Bleeker, which however has the upper caudal lobe $3\frac{1}{4}$ in the total length. The specimen (Col. Playfair's) from which this description has been taken is about 14 inches in length.

Habitat.—East coast of Africa to the Malay Archipelago, and probably found in the seas of India, although I have not obtained it there. It would be interesting to see if it has or has not an air-vessel.

longest, greatly exceeding the length of the head almost extending to the anal fin," (p. 33), considers his fish identical with *P. hexanemus*, wherein some of them reach the *caudal fin*.

Habitat.—Seas of India and Mauritius. The specimen, which is figured life-size, is from Madras.

6. Polynemus Indicus.

Polynemus maga-booshee, Russell, ii, p. 68, pl. 184.

Polynemus Indicus, Shaw, Zool. v, p. 155; Swainson, Fishes, ii, p. 234; McClell. Cal. J. N. H. iii, p. 179,* pl. vi; Cantor, Catal. p. 29; Günther, Catal. ii, p. 326; Day, Fishes of Malabar, p. 60; Kner,† Novara Fische, p. 137.

Polynemus sele, Ham. Buch. Fish. Ganges, pp. 226, 381; McClelland, Cal. Journ. Nat. Hist. iii, p. 181.

Polynemus uronemus, Cuv. and Val. iii, p. 385.

Polynemus plebeius and *gelatinosus*, McClelland, C. J. N. H. iii, pp. 179, 181.

Tahlun-bola, Tam.: *Yeta*, Mal.: *Dara*, Bombay: *Bhât*, Mahr.: *Lukwah*, Arrac.: *Katha* or *Ka-ka-yan*, Burm.: *Kwey-yeng*, Tavoy.

B. vii, D. 8 | $\frac{1}{12-13}$, P. 15 + v, V. 1/5, A. $\frac{2-3}{11-12}$, C. 17, L. l. 70-75, L. tr. 7/13, Vert. 5/19, Cæc. pyl. many.

Length of head $4\frac{1}{4}$ to $4\frac{1}{2}$, of pectoral 1/6 to 2/13, of caudal 1/4, height of body 1/6 of the total length excluding the filamentous prolongation of the tail. *Eyes*—diameter 1/7 of length of head, 1 to $1\frac{1}{2}$ diameters from end of snout, and 2 apart. Height of head equals 2/3, and its width 2/5 of its length. The maxilla reaches to far behind the orbit. Preopercle with a rounded and produced angle, its posterior margin moderately serrated, and having a strong tooth above its angle. Interorbital space rather flat. *Teeth*—villiform in the jaws, in a somewhat semilunar band on the vomer, and in a wide cuneiform band broadest anteriorly on the palatines, the last being emarginate internally about its centre. *Fins*—spines of first dorsal weak, the third having rather a filamentous prolongation, the fin one-third higher than long, second dorsal highest in front where it equals the anal and is one-third higher than its base is long: upper edge of the fin concave. Pectoral with its rays branched, having five articulated free rays, the upper of which is the longest reaching nearly to the anal, which latter fin extends posteriorly some distance behind the vertical from the end of the second dorsal, its lower edge is concave. The distance between the bases of the ventral and anal fins is longer than the head. Caudal deeply lunated having pointed lobes which usually have filamentous terminations, the lower being mostly the longer. Free portion of the tail in its least depth equal to 2/5 of the length of the head. *Air-vessel*—oval and thick, occupying the entire length of the abdomen and posteriorly prolonged amongst the caudal muscles. It adheres to the vertebræ from the third to the seventh, whilst from either side towards the ventral surface it has from 28 to 35 appendages. *Lateral-line*—continued along the lower caudal lobe almost to its end. Vertical fins rather densely scaled. *Colours*—back purplish-black, abdomen silvery-white, dashed with gold. First and second dorsals also anal stained with black, as is likewise the lower half of the opercle. Caudal with many black points.

Habitat.—Seas of India to the Malay Archipelago and Australia. It attains 4 feet in length, but is rarely above 20lbs weight. A large fish yields about two ounces of rough isinglass. The largest specimens appear to be captured in the embouchures of large rivers: they take a bait freely.

7. Polynemus plebeius

Brouss. Ich. fasc. i, t. viii; Gmel. Linn. p. 1401; Bloch. t. cccc; Bl. Schn. p. 17; Shaw, Zool. v, pl. cxxv; Cuv. and Val. iii, p. 380; Temm. and Schleg. Fauna Japon. p. 29, t. xi, fig. 1; Bleeker, Perc. p. 58; Richards. An. and Mag. Nat. Hist. 1842, p. 210; McClell. Cal. Journ. Nat. Hist. iii, p. 185; Cantor, Catal. p. 27; Günther, Catal. ii, p. 329.

Polynemus lineatus, Lacép. v. pl. 13, f. 2, p. 410; Günther, Catal. ii, p. 327; Kner, Novara Fische, p. 137.

Polynemus tæniatus, Günther, Catal. ii, p. 526.

Trichidion plebejus, Bleeker, Fish. Madagascar, p. 79.

B. vii, D. 8 | $\frac{1}{13}$, P. 17 + v, V. 1/5, A. $\frac{3}{11-12}$, C. 17, L. l. 60-65, L. tr. 7-8/13, Cæc. pyl. many.

Length of head 2/9, of caudal 3/11, height of body 1/5 of the total length. *Eyes*—diameter $3\frac{1}{4}$ to $4\frac{1}{2}$ in the length of head, 1/2 to 3/4 of a diameter from end of snout, and 1 to $1\frac{1}{4}$ apart. Interorbital space rather convex. Height of the head equals its length excluding the snout, its width is not 1/2 its length. The maxilla reaches to about 1 diameter behind the posterior edge of the eye. Angle of preopercle rounded and produced; its vertical limb rather coarsely serrated and most so above the angle. *Teeth*—villiform. *Fins*—third dorsal spine with rather a filamentous prolongation and equal to 3/4 of the height of the body, the length of the base of the fin equals rather above 2/3 of its height. Second dorsal rather higher anteriorly than the first or than the anal, its upper edge deeply concave. Pectoral rays unbranched, its length equals 3/4 the height of the body, of its five free-rays the superior reaches rather beyond the ventral. Ventral reaches the vent, the distance between its

* McClelland observes (C. J. N. H. iii, p. 173) that "at Scinde (where it proves, as originally suggested by us, to be the source of the cod-sounds alluded to as an article of export from Kurrachee) it is called *seer*." However the Kurrachee fish is a *Sciænoid* (see p. 187) and not one of this family. See also paper by Mr. O. Reilly, l. c. ii, p. 450, and by Captain Hogle, ii, p. 615.

† Kner observes of Russell's figure "nicht gut." Cantor however more justly remarks that it was in his time "the only correct figure."

base and that of the anal equals the length of the head excluding the snout. First spine of anal minute or wanting: the lower edge of the fin deeply concave. Caudal with pointed lobes. Least depth of the free portion of the tail equals half the length of the head. *Air-vessel*—elongated, narrow, and simple. *Cœcal appendages*—numerous. Vertical fins rather densely scaled. *Lateral-line*—continued along the lower lobe of the caudal fin to the end of its second or third rays below its centre. *Colours*—golden, having a grayish tinge along the back and darkish lines along each row of scales: anal fin dashed with gray, ventral white and externally grayish: both dorsals, the caudal and pectoral gray-edged.

Habitat.—This species is exceedingly common in the seas and estuaries of India. I have captured females full of roe as early as March. It is found from Sind through the seas of India to the Malay Archipelago and beyond.

8. Polynemus tetradactylus.

Polynemus maga-jellee, Russell, Fish. Vizag. ii, p. 68, pl. 183.

Polynemus tetradactylus, Shaw, Zool. v, p. 155; Cuv. Règ. Anim. Ill. Poiss. pl. xix, f. 1; Cuv. and Val. iii, p. 375, vii, p. 514; Swainson, Fishes, ii. p. 234; McClell. Journ. As. Soc. Beng. 1839, p. 206; Royle on Isinglass, pp. 25, 26: Richards. Ich. China, p. 218; Bleeker, Perc. p. 57; Cantor, Catal. p. 25; Günther, Catal. ii, p. 328; Day, Fish. Malabar, p. 62; Kner, Novara Fische, p. 138.

Polynemus teria, Ham. Buch. Fish. Ganges, pp. 224, 381; Gray and Hard. Ill. Ind. Zool. pl. 92, f. 2.

Polynemus sælliah et quadrifilis, Cantor, Journ. Roy. As. Soc. v, p. 166.

Eleutheronema tetradactylus, Bleeker, Bintang, 1868, p. 5.

Polun-kala, Tam.: *To-bro-dah*, Andam.

B. vii, D. 8 | $\frac{1}{12-13}$, P. 17+iv, V. 1/5, A. $\frac{1-3}{15-17}$, C. 17, L. l. 75-85, L. tr. 8/14, Cæc. pyl. many.

Length of head 1/5, of caudal 1/5, height of body 1/5 to 1/6 of the total length. *Eyes*—diameter 2/9 to 1/5 of the length of head, 1/2 a diameter from end of snout, and 1 apart. Height of head equals its length excluding the snout or behind the middle of the eye, its width equals 2/5 of its length. The maxilla extends to 1 diameter behind the posterior edge of the orbit. Angle of preopercle produced and rounded, its vertical limb serrated and having its strongest denticulation just above the angle. *Teeth*—villiform. *Fins*—third dorsal spine equals 3/4 of the height of the body and is as long as the anterior rays of the second dorsal, the upper edge of which last fin is concave. Pectoral rays undivided, the free rays reach nearly to the end of the ventral, which latter extends to the vent. The distance between the bases of the ventral and anal fins equals the length of the head excluding the snout. Anal similar to second dorsal, its first spine minute or absent:* caudal deeply forked. *Air-vessel*—absent. *Cœcal appendages*—numerous. The least depth of the free portion of the tail equals nearly 1/2 the length of the head. *Colours*—silvery-green, becoming yellowish-white on the sides and abdomen: dorsal and caudal grayish with minute black points and nearly black at the edges: ventral and anal pale orange in their outer halves, pectoral filaments white. A dark mark on the upper portion of the opercle.

Habitat.—Seas of India to the Malay Archipelago and China, attaining 6 feet and upwards in length: it is excellent eating. This species appears to ascend higher up the rivers than any of the others, and the young are numerous in the Hooghly at Calcutta. Ham. Buchanan observes: "I have been assured by a credible native that he saw one which was a load for six men, and which certainly therefore exceeded in weight 320 lb. avoirdupois." (Fish. Ganges, p. 225.)

* Cantor gives three or four anal spines: Buchanan two: Russell and Cuvier one. I have specimens in which I can only discover two, others wherein three are distinct.

FAMILY, XII—SCIÆNIDÆ, *Cuv.*

Branchiostegals seven: pseudobranchiæ sometimes concealed, or even absent. Body somewhat compressed and rather elongate. Eyes lateral, of moderate or small size. Mouth in front of or below the snout. Cheeks unarmed; opercles sometimes with weak spines. Barbels present in a few genera. Muciferous system on the head well developed. Teeth in villiform bands, with the outer or inner row often enlarged: canines present in some genera but neither cutting nor molar-form ones in the jaws: palate edentulous. Two dorsal fins, the spines of the first usually feeble (8-12), the second much more developed (22-43 rays) than the first: anal with one or two spines and much fewer (5-16) rays than the second dorsal: pectoral rays branched: ventrals thoracic with one spine and five rays. Scales ctenoid or cycloid, covering the head and snout, placed in oblique and often sinuous rows on the body. Lateral line complete, often continued on to the caudal fin. Stomach cæcal. Air-vessel, when present, as a rule with branching or elongated appendages. Pyloric appendages generally few.

The number of rays in the soft dorsal fin are liable to considerable variation in species belonging to this family, whilst the caudal becomes more obtuse as the adult stage is arrived at. The scales, which are placed in oblique rows, often vary considerably in the number of pierced ones along the lateral-line, and in those descending or ascending to it, consequently it becomes necessary to enumerate what are present in each separate place. The eye is comparatively very much smaller in adults of this family than it is in the immature.

Bleeker, Mémoire sur les Sciénoides (1874), has shown that the dentition of these fishes forms a far better guide to classification than the size and length of the second anal spine, &c. He also questions the utility of separating *Sciæna* (Artedi) Bleeker = *Umbrina*, Cuv. and Val. from *Johnius* (Bloch) Bleeker, simply because the former has a central barbel under the symphysis of the lower jaw. In my investigations I have found another species, *Sciæna albida*, C. V. (or a *Pseudosciæna*, Bleeker), in which a rudimentary barbel exists at each of the first lateral open pores below the symphysis of the lower jaw, but obviously insufficient for the purpose of constituting a new genus.

Uses.—The air-vessels of many of these fishes are extensively collected along the coasts of India as they afford isinglass which is exported to China and elsewhere. As food however their flesh is rather tasteless whilst young, and coarse when large, consequently in many localities, as Kurrachee or in Beloochistan, the sounds or air-vessels are as valuable as the whole of the remainder of the fish.

Habitat.—Klünzinger observes that from the Red Sea no representatives of the true SCIÆNIDÆ have been recorded; a few appear to be present along the East coast of Africa, whilst from Beloochistan and Sind throughout the seas of India they are numerous, many entering estuaries and rivers, and although one species (*S. coitor*) is often found far above tidal reach it still is only a visitor from the ocean.

SYNOPSIS OF GENERA.

1. *Umbrina.* Upper jaw overlapping the lower. A central barbel under the symphysis of the lower jaw. Fins as in *Sciæna*.

2. *Sciæna.* Upper jaw overlapping the lower or both equal. Teeth villiform, with an outer enlarged row in the premaxillaries and sometimes an inner enlarged series in the mandibles. No central barbel beneath the chin; second dorsal fin rather long (23-32 rays).

3. *Sciænoides.* Eyes small: head broad and convex. Upper jaw overlapping the lower or both equal. Teeth villiform, with an outer much enlarged row in the premaxillaries, and an inner conical series in the mandibles. No barbels. Second dorsal fin elongated (27-43 rays).

4. *Otolithus.* Lower jaw prominent. Elongated and pointed canines in both jaws: a single row of widely separated conical teeth in the lower jaw. No barbels. Second dorsal fin rather long (28-31 rays).

Genus, 1—UMBRINA, *Cuv.*

Menticirrhus and *Cirrimens*, Gill: *Sciæna* (Artedi) Bleeker, 1874.

Branchiostegals seven: pseudobranchiæ. Body oblong and rather elongated. Eyes of moderate size. Interorbital space rather broad and somewhat concave. Snout rounded and overhanging the upper jaw, which latter is longer than the lower. A central barbel present below the symphysis of the lower jaw. Teeth villiform, with the outer row in the premaxillaries enlarged: no canines. Two dorsal fins, the first with 9-10 spines and connected at its base to the second which is of moderate length (24-30 rays): anal with two spines. Scales ctenoid or cycloid, extending over the head and snout, and more or less present on the vertical fins, and on that of the tail. Air-vessel present. Pyloric appendages in moderate numbers or few.

The open pores or orifices of some of the muciferous channels of the head are very distinct. There are 3 or 5 in a transverse row across the snout, whilst along the free edge of the skin as it crosses from one preorbital to

* Absent in some American species.

the other over the groove for the posterior limb of the premaxillaries, there are five more. The central one is mostly triangular, the largest, and at the upper surface: whilst along its free edge, sometimes below it, are two more on either side. The existence of a lateral-lobe is entirely due to these orifices, and its size is in accordance with their position.

On the lower surface of the mandible beneath the symphysis is a single central barbel having a pore at its base, occasionally it has one in front and another behind it. On either side of its base laterally and rather posteriorly are two more open orifices.

Habitat.—From the East coast of Africa, through the seas of India to the Malay Archipelago and beyond. They are found in the Mediterranean and Atlantic, and some in the rivers of North and South America.

SYNOPSIS OF SPECIES.

1. *Umbrina macroptera*, D. 10 | [illegible], A. [illegible], L. l. 48, Cæc. pyl. 11. Barbel half as long as the eye. First dorsal fin 2/5 the height of body. Scales cycloid on head and chest, elsewhere ctenoid. Grayish. Seas of India to the Malay Archipelago.

2. *Umbrina sinuata*, D. 10 | [illegible], A. [illegible], L. l. 44. Barbel one-quarter as long as the eye. First dorsal fin 1/2 height of body. Scales ctenoid except on snout, and below eyes. Dorsal, ventral, and anal fins nearly black; nine wide and sinuous brown bands from the back pass downwards and forwards. Sind.

3. *Umbrina Dussumieri*, D. 10 | [illegible], A. [illegible], L. l. 52. Barbel half as long as eye. First dorsal fin from 4/5 to as high as body. Scales cycloid. Usually dark coloured. Seas of India to China.

4. *Umbrina Russellii*, D. 10 | [illegible], A. [illegible], L. l. 44. Barbel sometimes nearly as long as the eye. First dorsal fin 4/9 of height of body. Scales ctenoid. Grayish, first dorsal tinged with black. Seas of India to the Malay Archipelago.

1. Umbrina macroptera.

Bleeker, Sumatra, p. 254; Günther, Catal. ii., p. 279.

Sciæna macropterus, Bleeker, Mém. Scién. 1874, p. 60.

B. vii, D. 10 | [illegible], P. 17, V. 1/5, A. [illegible], C. 17, L. l. [illegible], L. tr. 5-6/15, Cæc. pyl. 11.

Length of head 1/4 to 2/9, of caudal 1/6, height of body $3\frac{1}{2}$ to $4\frac{1}{2}$ in the total length. *Eyes*—diameter $3\frac{1}{2}$ to $4\frac{1}{2}$ in the length of head, $1\frac{1}{2}$ to $1\frac{1}{2}$ diameters from the end of snout, and 1 apart. Greatest width of the head equals half its length, and its height equals its length excluding the snout. The snout rather inflated and prominent. Cleft of mouth slightly oblique, the maxilla reaching to below the middle of the eye. The distance between the eye and the maxilla equals 1 diameter of the orbit. Preopercle serrated, most coarsely so at its angle: two opercular points. Three pores across the base of snout; outer fold of skin of snout laterally lobed, having five pores along its free border. Barbel below the symphysis of the lower jaw nearly half the diameter of the eye in length, having a deep pore on either side of its base and another rather more externally. *Teeth*—in villiform rows in both jaws, the outer row in the front half of the premaxillaries being somewhat enlarged. *Fins*—dorsal spines weak, the first very short, the second to the fourth about the same length and equal to 2/5 the height of the body and more than twice as high as the rays. Pectoral as long as the head excluding the snout. Ventral reaches nearly half way to the anal fin. Second anal spine of moderate strength, one-third shorter than the first ray, and equal to $2\frac{1}{2}$ in the height of the body. Caudal rather wedge-shaped. *Scales*—cycloid on the head, chest, and as high as the base of the pectoral fin, the remainder ctenoid. *Lateral-line*—becomes straight opposite the posterior end of the anal fin: the tubes give off a branch on either side which rarely subdivides. *Colours*—grayish, becoming silvery on the abdomen, and everywhere covered with minute black dots, but so small as not to interfere with the general light colour. Fins yellowish, dotted as the body. A dark mark on the opercle.

Habitat.—Seas of India to the Malay Archipelago. I took a female, 8 inches long, with fully developed ova in April, 1868, and found eleven cæcal appendages. It is not uncommon at Madras.

2. Umbrina sinuata, Plate XLVI, fig. 1.

B. vii, D. 10 | [illegible], P. 17, V. 1/5, A. [illegible], C. 17, L. l. [illegible], L. tr. 7/12.

Length of head $4\frac{1}{4}$, of caudal 1/5, height of body $3\frac{3}{4}$ in the total length. *Eyes*—diameter $3\frac{1}{2}$ in length of head, 3/4 of a diameter from end of snout, and 1 apart. Greatest width of head equals 1/2 its length, and its height equals its length excluding the snout. The distance between the eye and the upper jaw equals 3/4 of the diameter of the orbit. Snout obtuse, swollen, and overhanging the jaws. Upper jaw overlapping the lower: the maxilla reaching to below the middle of the eye. Preopercle serrated, most coarsely at its angle: two opercular spines. Shoulder-flap serrated. Three pores in a transverse line across the base of the snout, and five more orifices along the free edge of the skin, a lateral lobe present on either side. Central barbel below the symphysis of the lower jaw 1/4 the length of the orbit: two open pores on either side. *Teeth*—villiform in both jaws, an outer enlarged row in the anterior half of the premaxillaries, whilst a few of those in the front row of the lower jaw near the symphysis are larger than those posterior to them. *Fins*—dorsal spines weak, the third to the fifth the longest, 1/4 higher than the rays and equal to the length of the head behind the middle of the eyes. Pectoral as long as the head behind the anterior third of the eyes. Ventral reaches two-thirds of the distance to the base of the anal. Second anal spine strong, equal to half the length of the head and 1/3 shorter than the first ray; the length of the base of the fin equals 1/4 of that of the soft dorsal. Caudal wedge-shaped. *Scales*—ctenoid except on the snout and below the eyes, those on the summit of the head as far as the occiput very much smaller than those on the body. A dense band at basal third of soft dorsal and anal fins. *Lateral-line*—becomes straight above the end of the anal fin, its tubes with two, sometimes more, branches. *Colours*—brownish silvery, everywhere covered with minute dark points. A diffused bluish spot on the opercle. Nine sinuous brown bands on the body, wider than the ground-colour, passing from the back downwards and forwards: a dark spot in the axilla. First dorsal black, a black band along the whole length of the soft dorsal. Anal similar to soft dorsal. Ventral black. Caudal yellow, with a black tip and white outer edge.

Two specimens captured at Kurrachee up to 4 inches in length.

The dorsal fins show considerable similarity to *U. Dussumieri*, but the scales are ctenoid instead of cycloid.

3. **Umbrina Dussumieri**, Plate XLIII, fig. 2 and 3.

Umbrina Dussumieri, Cuv. and Val. ix, p. 481; Bleeker, Sciæn. p. 19; Günther, Catal. ii, p. 279; Day, Fishes of Malabar, p. 48.

Umbrina amblycephalus, Bleeker, Amb. p. 412; Günther, Catal. ii, p. 278.

Sciæna Dussumieri, Bleeker, Mémoire Sciénoid. p. 56.

Tara kattelee, Tam.

B. vii, D. 10 | [illegible], P. 17, V. 1/5, A. [illegible], C. 17, L. l. [illegible], L. tr. 6/17, Cæc. pyl. 7-9.

Length of head 1/4 to 4½, of caudal 1/7, height of body 4¼ to 2/9 of the total length. *Eyes*—diameter 2 7 to 3¼ in the length of head, 1¼ diameters apart and also from the end of snout. Height of head equals its length excluding the snout, and its thickness equals 2/3 of its length. Dorsal profile more convex than that of the abdomen. Snout obtuse, it and the cheeks inflated: cleft of mouth nearly horizontal: the maxilla reaches to below the middle of the eye. Distance between the eye and the upper maxillary bone equals one diameter of the orbit. Preopercle crenulated (scarcely denticulated) in its whole extent, its angle rounded: two opercular spines. Shoulder-lobe with smooth edges. Central barbel below the chin about half a diameter of the eye in length, a deep pore exists on either side of its base: pores on snout generic. *Teeth*—villiform in both jaws, a few of the outer row and in the anterior portion of the premaxillaries being enlarged, somewhat conical but scarcely curved. *Fins*—dorsal spines weak, the first short, the two next from 4/5 to as long as the height of the body and three times as long as the rays. Pectoral as long as the head excluding the snout. Ventral reaches half way to the anal. Second anal spine rather above half the height of the first ray. Caudal wedge-shaped in the young, more obtuse in the adult. *Scales*—cycloid on the body and head: a few over the bases of the soft dorsal and anal fins. *Lateral-line*—curves to above the end of the soft dorsal, it is in single tubes, which bifurcate posteriorly. *Colours*—usually of a dark brown or coppery tinge, often nearly black and shot with golden, lightest along the abdomen. Fins reddish-brown, the first dorsal stained with black: other fins with gray edges; ventrals yellow.

Fig. 2 is from Madras, and of the most common colour there: fig. 3 is from Bombay, has a dark shoulder-spot and generally gray colour, which is the most common appearance in the latter locality: the specimen figured is 7 inches long.

Habitat.—Seas of India to China, attaining at least 8 or 9 inches in length.

4. **Umbrina Russellii**, Plate XLIII, fig. 4.

Labrus qualar-katchelee, Russell, Fish. Vizag. ii, p. 13, plate 118.

Umbrina Russellii, Cuv. and Val. v, p. 178; Richards. Ich. China, p. 226; Cantor, Catal. p. 71; Jerdon, M. J. L. & Sc. 1851, p. 132; Günther, Catal. ii, p. 278; Kner, Novara Fische, p. 131.

Umbrina Kuhlii, Cuv. and Val. v, p. 179; Bleeker, Sciæn. p. 19.

Sciæna Indica, (K. and v. Hass.) Cuv. and Val. v, p. 179.

Sciæna Kuhli, Bleeker, Bintang, p. 293.

Sciæna Russellii, Bleeker, Mémoire Sciénoid. 1874, p. 58.

B. vii, D. 10 | [illegible], P. 17, V. 1/5, A. [illegible], C. 17, L. l. [illegible], L. tr. 6/15, Cæc. pyl. 7 (8 Kner).

Length of head 1/4 to 4½, of caudal 1/6, height of body 3¾ to 1/4 of the total length. *Eyes*—diameter 3½ to 1/4 of length of head, 3/4 to 1 diameter from end of snout, and 1 apart. Greatest width of head equals half its length, its height equals its length excluding the snout. Snout overhanging the jaws, the upper slightly the longer; the maxilla reaches to below the last third of the orbit. Nostrils opposite the lower third of the eye. Distance between the eye and the upper jaw equals 3/4 of a diameter of the orbit. Preopercle distinctly serrated: two opercular spines. Barbel equals from 2/5 of the diameter of the eye to nearly as long as it. Pores on snout and lower jaw generic: shoulder-flap serrated. *Teeth*—villiform in both jaws, with an outer enlarged row in the anterior half of the premaxillaries. *Fins*—dorsal spines moderately strong, the fourth equal to 2¼ in the height of the body and 1/3 longer than the rays. Pectoral equal to the head excluding the snout. Ventral reaches half way to the anal. Second anal spine strong, 4/5 as long as the first ray, and nearly equal to half the length of the head. Caudal wedge-shaped. *Scales*—ctenoid. *Lateral-line*—curves to above the middle of the anal fin where it becomes straight, tubes with one or two branches from either side. *Colours*—gray, becoming silvery-white on the abdomen: a steel-blue opercular spot: upper two-thirds of first dorsal nearly black: other fins yellow.

Habitat.—Seas of India to the Malay Archipelago, attaining at least 10 inches in length.

Genus, 2—Sciæna, (Artedi) Cuv.

Johnius, Bloch: *Corvina* and *Stellifer*, Cuv.: *Bola*, sp. Ham. Buch.: *Leiostomus*, Cuv. and Val.: *Corvinus*, Pall.: *Homoprion*, Holb.: *Amblyodon*, (Raf.) Gir.: *Cheilotrema*, v. Tsch.: *Gnypocerus*, *Plagioscion*. *Sciænops*, *Bairdiella*, *Haploidonotus*, *Rhinoscion* and *Ophioscion*, Gill: *Diplolepis*, Steind.: *Pseudosciæna*, Bleeker.

Branchiostegals seven: pseudobranchiæ. Body oblong, rather elongated, and compressed. Eyes of moderate size. Interorbital space rather broad and slightly convex. Snout rounded, sometimes overhanging the upper jaw, which last is longer than the lower, or both are of equal length. No central barbel below the symphysis of the lower jaw. Teeth villiform, with an outer enlarged row in the premaxillaries, and sometimes the inner row in the mandibles enlarged. No distinct canines. Two dorsal fins, the first with 9-10 spines, and connected at its base to the second which is of moderate length (23-32 rays). Anal with one or two spines. Scales ctenoid or cycloid, extending over the head and snout, and generally more or less present on the vertical fins and on that of the tail. Air-vessel present.† Pyloric appendages in moderate numbers or few.*

Pores or the orifices of muciferous canals are found in most of the species of this genus, identically as described in *Umbrina*. But a few, evidently approaching towards *Otolithus*, have some or all absent from both jaws.

In one species, *Sciæna albida*, a small, though distinct barbel, is present at the anterior of the lateral open pores on the lower jaw. Whether very great stress ought to be laid upon whether the scales are ctenoid or cycloid appears open to doubt. (See *S. coruttu*, *S. glaucus*.)

This genus has been subdivided by Bleeker into the following: 1. *Pseudosciæna*, in which the inner row of teeth in the lower jaw is distinctly larger than those external to it: 2. *Johnius*, destitute of any enlarged row of teeth in the lower jaw.

SYNOPSIS OF SPECIES.

A. An enlarged inner row of teeth in the lower jaw. (*Pseudosciæna*.)

1. *Sciæna Bleekeri*, D. 10 | $\frac{1}{27}$, A. $\frac{2}{7}$, L. l. 60, L. tr. 11/18. Eyes, diameter 1/5 of length of head. Second anal spine weak, $1\frac{1}{2}$ diameters of the orbit in length. Gray, with a dark axillary spot. First dorsal gray, fins edged with gray. Bombay.

2. *Sciæna miles*, D. 9-10 | $\frac{1}{22-24}$, A. $\frac{2}{7}$, L. l. 50, L. tr. 8/16. Eyes, diameter 2/9 to 1/5 of length of head. Second anal spine very strong and half the length of the head. Silvery, outer edges of vertical fins sometimes gray. Seas of India.

3. *Sciæna Vogleri*, D. 10 | $\frac{1}{28-30}$, A. $\frac{2}{7}$, L. l. 50, L. tr. 6/14. Eyes diameter 2/9 to 3/14 of length of head. Second anal spine weak, as long as the eye. Silvery, first dorsal dark. Seas of India to the Malay Archipelago.

4. *Sciæna sina*, D. 10 | $\frac{1}{27-29}$, A. $\frac{2}{7}$, L. l. 52. Eyes, diameter 1/4 of length of head. Second anal spine weak, 2/7 of length of head. Seas of India.

5. *Sciæna cuja*, D. 10 | $\frac{1}{27-29}$, A. $\frac{2}{7}$, L. l. 50. Eyes, diameter 1/5 of length of head. Second anal spine very strong, as long as the head behind the middle of the eyes. Oblique dark streaks above the lateral-line and horizontal ones below it. Estuaries of Ganges and Siam.

6. *Sciæna coitor*, D. 10 | $\frac{1}{27-29}$, A. $\frac{2}{7}$, L. l. 55. Eyes, diameter from 1/4 to 2/11 of length of head. Second anal spine strong, and as long as the postorbital portion of the head. Silvery. Large rivers of India and Burmah.

7. *Sciæna axillaris*, D. 10 | $\frac{1}{27-29}$, A. $\frac{2}{7}$, L. l. 50, L. tr. 6-7/14. Eyes, diameter 1/4 of length of head. Second anal spine strong, $2\frac{1}{4}$ in the length of the head. Silvery, upper two-thirds of first dorsal black, a dark axillary spot. Seas of India.

8. *Sciæna albida*, D. 9-10 | $\frac{1}{24-26}$, A. $\frac{2}{7}$, L. l. 52, L. tr. 7/18. Eyes, diameter 1/4 to 1/7 of length of head. Second anal spine strong, half as long as the head. Silvery, a diffused opercular blotch. Seas of India.

9. *Sciæna diacanthus*, D. 10 | $\frac{1}{23-27}$, A. $\frac{2}{7}$, L. l. 52, L. tr. 7/18. Eyes, diameter 2/9 to 1/6 of length of head. Second anal spine $2\frac{3}{4}$ in the length of the head. Brownish-gray superiorly, silvery below. Upper half of body, dorsal, and caudal fins spotted in the immature. Seas of India to the Malay Archipelago.

10. *Sciæna aneus*, D. 10 | $\frac{1}{23-27}$, A. $\frac{2}{7}$, L. l. 50, L. tr. 8-9/18. Eyes, diameter 1/4 to $4\frac{1}{2}$ in the length of head. Lower jaw the longer. Second anal spine weak, from 3/4 to 1 diameter of the orbit in length. Silvery, first dorsal gray. Seas of India to the Malay Archipelago.

11. *Sciæna maculata*, D. 10 | $\frac{1}{23-27}$, A. $\frac{2}{7}$, L. l. 45-48, L. tr. 8/16. Eyes, diameter $4\frac{1}{4}$ to 1/5 of length of head. Second anal spine 1/3 the length of head. Silvery, with five broad black bands, sometimes interrupted. Seas of India.

B. No enlarged inner row of teeth in the lower jaw. (*Johnius*.)

12. *Sciæna Belengeri*, D. 9 | $\frac{1}{27-30}$, A. $\frac{2}{7}$, L. l. 52, L. tr. 6/14. Eyes, diameter $3\frac{1}{4}$ to $3\frac{3}{4}$ of length of head. Second anal spine $2\frac{1}{2}$ in length of head. Slate-coloured, with the vertical fins nearly black. Seas of India to the Malay Archipelago.

* *Sciæna aneus*, Bloch, is an exception, forming a transitional state to genus *Otolithus* not only in this respect, but in the pores on the snout, and below the symphysis of the mandibles.

† Stated to be absent in some American species.

13. *Sciæna semiluctuosa*, D. 10 | [illegible], A. [illegible], L. l. 55-60, L. tr. 8-9/25. Eyes, diameter 2/9 to 1/6 of length of head. Second anal spine about 1/2 the length of head. Gray, with blackish bands going along each row of scales: fins black. Seas of India to China.

14. *Sciæna glauca*, D. 10 | [illegible], A. [illegible], L. l. 50, L. tr. 6/18. Eyes, diameter $3\frac{1}{4}$ to $4\frac{1}{2}$ in length of head. Second anal spine 2/5 of length of head. Gray, a diffused bluish opercular blotch: an axillary spot: first dorsal nearly black: vertical fins with gray edges. Seas of India.

15. *Sciæna carutta*, D. 10 | [illegible], A. [illegible], L. l. 50, L. tr. 5-6/18. Eyes, diameter 1/4 of length of head. Second anal spine 2/7 to 2/5 of length of head. Purplish-brown, with a light band along the lateral-line. Fins dark. Seas of India to the Malay Archipelago.

16. *Sciæna osseus*, D. 10 | [illegible], A. [illegible], L. l. 50, L. tr. 6/15. Eyes, diameter 1/5 of length of head. Second anal spine 1/4 as long as the head. Gray, with the fins stained at their edges. Malabar.

A. An enlarged inner row of teeth in the lower jaw (*Pseudosciæna*).

1. Sciæna Bleekeri, Plate XLV, fig. 4.

Soh-lee, Bel.

B. vii, D. 10 | [illegible], P. 17, V. 1/5, A. [illegible], C. 17, L. l. [illegible], L. tr. 9-10/18.

Length of head $4\frac{1}{2}$, of caudal $5\frac{1}{2}$, height of body $4\frac{3}{4}$ in the total length. *Eyes*—diameter 1/5 to 1/7 of length of head, $1\frac{3}{4}$ to 2 diameters from end of snout, and 1 apart. Greatest width of head equals 2/5 of its length, and the height equals its length excluding the snout. Dorsal profile more convex than that of the abdomen, a slight concavity over the eyes: head rather strongly compressed. Snout not overhanging the jaws, cleft of mouth somewhat oblique, the jaws of about the same length anteriorly, the maxilla reaches to below the last third of the eye, whilst superiorly its anterior extremity is on a level with the lower edge of the eye. The distance between the eye and the upper edge of the maxilla equals 2/3 of the diameter of the orbit. Preopercle with some rather strong denticulations and three well-marked ones at the angle: two opercular spines. Shoulder-scale strongly serrated. A pore above the centre of the free edge of the skin of the snout, and a smaller one on either side, but no lateral lobe. Five pores on under surface of lower jaw below the symphysis. *Teeth*—villiform in both jaws, with an outer row of curved conical ones in the premaxillaries: whilst the inner row in the lower is much larger than the rest of the teeth. *Fins*—fourth to sixth dorsal spines of about the same height, one-third higher than the rays and equal to about $2\frac{1}{2}$ in that of the body. Pectoral equals two-thirds of the height of the body. Ventral reaches half way to the anal fin. Second anal spine weak, half the length of the first ray and about equal to $1\frac{1}{4}$ diameters of the orbit, the length of its base equals $4\frac{1}{2}$ of that of the soft dorsal. Caudal wedge-shaped. *Scales*—cycloid on snout and under the eyes, ctenoid elsewhere. *Lateral-line*—curves to above the middle of the anal fin, the tubes have simple bifurcations. *Colours*—Silvery-gray along the back, becoming dull white below: a black spot in the axilla. First dorsal gray with a light line along its centre: caudal dark in its outer third, fins otherwise yellowish.

This species appears to be closely allied to *Johnius microlepis*, Bleeker, Sumatra, p. 11, or *Pseudosciæna microlepis*, Bleeker, Mem. Scién. 1874, p. 23, but its anal spine is not nearly so long and its eye is much smaller.

Habitat.—Bombay, from whence two specimens were procured, the largest, which is figured, being nearly 8 inches in length. Large specimens from 27 inches in length were not uncommon at Gwadur where the fish is extensively salted.

2. Sciæna miles, Plate XLIII, fig. 5.

Holocentrus miles, Lacép. iv, p. 244.
Labrus tella katchelee, Russell, Fish. Vizag. ii, p. 13, f. 117.
Corvina miles, Cuv. and Val. v, p. 94, ix, p. 479; Jerdon, M. J. L. and Sc. 1851, p. 131; Bleeker, Sciæn. p. 17; Günther, Catal. ii, p. 300.
Corvina soldado, Cantor, Catal. p. 70.
Corvina Waitii, Bleeker, Borneo, p. 65.
Corvina sampitensis, Bleeker, Borneo, p. 421.
Corvina Celebica, Bleeker, Celebes, p. 244.
Corvina dorsalis, Peters, Fische Mozam. p. 242.
Johnius Celebicus, Bleeker, Enum. Pisc. p. 35.
Johnius miles, Bleeker, Pinang, p. 75.
Pseudosciæna miles, Bleeker, Mémo. Scién. 1874, p. 25.
Vella katteloe, Tam.

B. vii, D. 9-10 | [illegible], P. 17, V. 1/5, A. [illegible], C. 17, L. l. [illegible], L. tr. 8/16.

Length of head $4\frac{3}{4}$ to $4\frac{1}{2}$, of caudal 1/6, height of body $3\frac{3}{4}$ to 1/4 of the total length. *Eyes*—diameter $4\frac{1}{2}$ to 1/5 of length of head, $1\frac{1}{2}$ diameters from end of snout, and 1 apart. Greatest width of head equals half its length, and its height equals its length excluding the snout. Cleft of mouth moderately oblique. Snout not overhanging the jaws which are of about equal length anteriorly, or the upper slightly the longer, the maxilla reaches to below the last third of the eye. Preopercle with some rather widely separated denticulations especially at its rounded angle: two opercular points. Free border of the skin of the snout with five orifices of canals and a small lateral lobe: five pores on the inferior surface of the lower jaw. *Teeth*—villiform in the upper jaw, with an outer row of large curved conical ones in the premaxillaries: villiform in the lower jaw with the inner row consisting of distantly placed enlarged ones. *Fins*—dorsal spines weak, nearly twice as long as the rays, and from $1\frac{2}{3}$ to 1/2 as high as the body. Pectoral as long as the head excluding the snout. Ventral reaches rather above half way to the anal. Second anal spine very strong, nearly as long as the first ray and equal from 1/2 the length of the head to its length behind the middle of the eyes: the extent of the base of the fin from 1/4 to 1/5 of that of the soft dorsal. Caudal wedge-shaped. *Scales*—cycloid on head and chest, ctenoid on the remainder of the body. *Lateral-line*—becomes straight above the hind edge of the anal, its tubes arborescent posteriorly. *Colours*—grayish darkened with green along the back, becoming white on the sides and abdomen, sometimes a small brown spot in front of each dorsal ray. Outer edges of the fins in some specimens dark, except the ventral which is white.

Habitat.—Seas of India to the Malay Archipelago, attaining at least 2 feet in length. The specimen figured, from Bombay is 10 inches long.

3. Sciæna Vogleri, Plate XLV, fig. 1.

Otolithus Vogleri, Bleeker, Sumatra, p. 253.
Sciæna Vogleri, Günther, Catal. ii, p. 294.
Pseudosciæna Vogleri, Bleeker, Mémoir. Scién. 1874, p. 35.

B. vii, D. 10 | [illegible], P. 19, V. 1/5, A. 2/7, C. 17, L. r. [illegible], L. tr. 6/14, Cæc. pyl. 9.

Length of head $3\frac{2}{3}$, of caudal $6\frac{1}{2}$, height of body 1/4 to $4\frac{1}{3}$ in the total length. *Eyes*—diameter $4\frac{1}{2}$ to $4\frac{2}{3}$ in the length of head, 1 to $1\frac{1}{4}$ diameters from the end of snout, and also apart. Body rather compressed, the dorsal profile more convex than the abdominal. Width of head equals $1\frac{3}{4}$ in its length, its height equals its length excluding the snout. The snout does not overhang the upper jaw which is very slightly longer than the lower, cleft of the mouth oblique, the maxilla reaching to below the middle of the orbit. Preopercle distinctly but finely serrated: two opercular spines: the distance between the eye and the maxilla equals 1 diameter of the orbit. Five large open pores under the symphysis of the lower jaw, also five orifices along the free edge of the skin of the snout. The shoulder-scale serrated. *Teeth*—villiform in both jaws, with an outer row of large, curved, and rather distantly placed ones in the premaxillaries: and an internal row of large conical and rather widely separated ones in the lower jaw. *Fins*—dorsal spines of moderate strength, the second to the fifth subequal in length, from 2 to $2\frac{1}{4}$ in the height of the body, and 1/3 higher than the rays. Pectoral as long as the head behind the first fourth of the eye. Ventral scarcely reaches half way to the anal. Second anal spine weak, half the height of the first ray, and $4\frac{1}{2}$ in that of the body. Caudal wedge-shaped. *Scales*—cycloid on the head, ctenoid over the chest and body: the base of the soft dorsal fin rather thickly scaled. *Lateral-line*—becoming straight opposite the posterior portion of the anal fin, its tubes with one or two branches. *Colours*—silvery, glossed with golden, first dorsal dotted with black, most distinctly so in its upper half: superior edge of soft dorsal and last half of caudal gray: a small dark spot sometimes present in the axilla: fins yellow.

Habitat.—Seas of India to the Malay Archipelago. The largest specimen I have taken is $10\frac{1}{2}$ inches in length.

4. Sciæna sina, Plate XLIV, fig. 2.

Johnius sina, Cuv. and Val. v, p. 122; Blyth, J. A. S. of Beng. 1860, p. 141.
Corvina sina, Bélang. Voy. Ind. Orient. Zool. p. 359; Bleeker, Verh. Bat. Gen. xxvi, p. 62; Jerdon, M. J. L. and Sc. 1851, p. 132.
Sciæna sina, Günther, Catal. ii, p. 292; Day, Fish. Malabar, p. 52.
Boorte and *Sowarch* or *Sowr*, Sind.: *Goal*, Bel.

B. vii, D. 10 | [illegible], P. 17, V. 1/5, A. [illegible], C. 17, L. r. [illegible], L. tr. 8/14, Cæc. pyl. 9.

Length of head 1/4 to 2/9, of caudal 1/5 to 2/11, height of body 2/7 to 1/4 of the total length. *Eyes*—diameter 1/4 of length of head, 1 diameter from end of snout, and $1\frac{1}{4}$ apart. Height of head equals its length excluding the snout, and its width $1\frac{1}{3}$ of its length. Snout rather inflated, scarcely overhanging the jaws: jaws of nearly equal length anteriorly cleft of mouth nearly horizontal, the maxilla reaching to below the last third or hind edge of the orbit. The distance from the eye to the upper jaw equals 1/2 to 3/4 of a diameter of the orbit. Preopercle rounded, generally some distinct spinate teeth at its angle. Snout with three pores across its base: the free edge of the skin with a large central opening, and another externally on either side, no large lateral lobe: shoulder-flap serrated. Five open pores under the symphysis of the mandible. *Teeth*—villiform, with an outer curved row of rather distantly placed ones in the upper jaw, and an inner enlarged row in the mandible. *Fins*—dorsal spines rather weak, third and fourth the longest and equal to $2\frac{1}{2}$ in the height of the body. Pectoral as long as the head without the snout. Ventral reaches nearly 1/2 way to the anal. Second anal spine more than half the height of the first ray, and equal to $3\frac{1}{4}$ in that of the body: the base of the fin equal to 2/7 of that of the soft dorsal. Caudal wedge-shaped. *Air-vessel*—large anteriorly, bulging on either side like a hammer, whilst from it descends an appendage on each side: posteriorly it ends in a sharp point. *Scales*—ctenoid, except on the head where they are cycloid, a few exist on the bases of the soft dorsal and anal fins. *Lateral-line*—becomes straight over the middle of the anal fin: each tube gives off a branch on either side. *Colours*—silvery, tinged with brownish along the back, and shot with gold on the abdomen: first dorsal blackish, especially in its outer half, the other fins gray.

This fish attains a very large size on the Western coast of India and Sind, even so far as Gwadur. They are not much valued as food but their air-vessels are extensively collected for isinglass. In Bombay and Sind there are daily to be seen in the markets examples of this fish and *S. glaucus* of 5 or 6 or even more feet in length. Females in full spawn are common in April.

Habitat.—Seas of India, attaining several feet in length, the one figured is 6 inches long. McClelland in his paper on isinglass in the Calcutta Journal of Natural History, refers the *Soor* (spelt *Seer*) fish from which the sounds are collected at Kurrachee, to a *Polynemus*, but it is a *Sciæna*, and as described above or *S. glaucus*.

5. Sciæna cuja.*

Bola cuja, Ham. Buch. Fish. Ganges, pp. 81, 369, pl. xii, f. 27.

Corvina cuja, Cuv. and Val. v, p. 96; Temm. and Schleg. Fauna Japon. Poiss. p. 58; Blyth, Journ. As. Soc. of Bengal, 1860, p. 141; Günther, Catal. ii, p. 300.

Sciænoides asper, Blyth, l. c. p. 140 (*young*).

B. vii, D. 10 | [illegible], P. 17, V. 1/5, A. 2/7, C. 17, L. l. [illegible], L. tr. 7/16.

Length of head 1/4 to 2/9, of caudal 1/8, height of body $3\frac{3}{4}$ to 1/4 of the total length. *Eyes*—diameter 1/5 of length of head, 1 diameter from end of snout, and also apart. Profile along the upper surface of the head somewhat concave: snout not swollen: jaws of nearly the same length anteriorly, or the lower slightly the longer. Greatest width of the head equals $2\frac{1}{4}$ in its length, and its height equals its length behind the front nostril. Cleft of mouth somewhat oblique, the maxilla reaches to below the hind edge of the orbit. The distance between the eye and the upper jaw equals 3/5 of the diameter of the orbit. In the fry the upper edge of the orbit is serrated and two rough ridges pass backwards from it. Preopercle scarcely denticulated: two opercular spines. Three open pores across the base of the snout, and five large ones along the edge of the free portion of the skin, but no lateral lobe. One central pore below the symphysis of the lower jaw, and two large ones on either side posterior to it. *Teeth*—villiform in either jaw, with an outer row of enlarged, curved, rather distantly placed and comparatively small ones in the anterior half of the premaxillaries: the inner row in the lower jaw is slightly larger than the villiform bands. *Fins*—dorsal spines strong, the second to the fourth the longest, one third higher than the rays, and equal to the length of the postorbital portion of the head. Pectoral as long as the head behind the middle of the eyes. Second anal spine very strong, nearly or quite as long as the first ray and equalling the length of the head behind the middle of the eyes. Caudal rounded. *Scales*—cycloid on the head, ctenoid on the body, the basal third of the soft dorsal and anal densely scaled: those on the summit of the head to the end of the occiput very much smaller than those on the body. *Lateral-line*—the tubes divide posteriorly into many branches. *Colours*—oblique dark streaks, following the rows of scales, exist above the lateral-line, horizontal ones below it. Both dorsals with two or three rows of black spots.

Habitat.—Estuaries of the Ganges, and Japan. It attains to several feet in length.

6. Sciæna coitor, Plate XLIV, fig. 3.

Bola coitor, Ham. Buch. Fish. Ganges, pp. 75 and 368, pl. 27, f. 24.

Corvina coitor, Cuv. and Val. v, p. 116; Günther, Catal. ii, p. 301.

Johnius coitor, Blyth, J. A. S. of Beng. 1860, p. 141.

Corvina wolla-kotchelee, Richards. Ich. China, p. 226.

Botold and *Patteriki*, Ooriah: *Nga-ta-dun* and *Nga-pok-thin*, Burm.

B. vii, D. 10 | [illegible], P. 17, V. 1/5, A. 2/7, C. 17, L. l. [illegible], L. tr. 5-6/15, Cæc. pyl. 6-7 (9 Madras).

Length of head $4\frac{1}{4}$ to $4\frac{2}{3}$, of caudal $5\frac{1}{2}$ to 1/6, height of body $4\frac{1}{3}$ to $4\frac{3}{4}$ in the total length. *Eyes*—diameter from 1/4 to $5\frac{1}{2}$ in the length of head, $1\frac{1}{2}$ to 2 diameters from the end of snout, and from 3/4 to $1\frac{1}{2}$ apart. Greatest width of head equals one and two-thirds in its length, its height equals its length excluding the snout. Snout scarcely overhanging the jaws but prominent and swollen superiorly, upper jaw somewhat the longer. Interorbital space nearly flat, and the profile over the eyes rather concave. The distance between the eye and the upper edge of the maxilla equals from 3/4 to 1 diameter of the eye. Preopercle serrated, most distinctly so at its angle: two weak opercular spines. Shoulder-flap finely serrated. Three small open pores across the snout, and five much larger ones along the free edge of the skin of the snout, whilst there is a well developed lateral lobe. One central and two lateral orifices below the symphysis of the lower jaw. *Teeth*—villiform in both jaws, with an external slightly enlarged row in the premaxillaries, and an inner similar one in the lower jaw. *Fins*—dorsal spines weak, the second to the fourth the longest and equal to 2/3 the height of the body and 1/4 more than the rays. Pectoral equal to the length of the head behind the front nostril. Second anal spine rather strong, 4/5 as high as the first ray and equal to the length of the postorbital portion of the head, the length of the base of the fin equals from $3\frac{1}{2}$ to 1/4 of that of the soft dorsal. Caudal wedge-shaped. *Scales*—cycloid on the snout and below the eyes, elsewhere ctenoid. *Lateral-line*—makes a gradual curve, and above the commencement of the anal becomes straight, its tubes give off a single branch on either side. *Colours*—silvery shot with gold and purple, upper half of first dorsal blackish: soft dorsal, caudal, and anal dark externally, whilst the last fin has a darkish basal band.

This fish appears to vary considerably. Burmese and Bengal adult specimens have six or seven cæcal appendages, and an eye from 1/5 to $5\frac{1}{2}$ in the length of the head. In southern Madras, adults have nine cæcal appendages and an eye about 1/4 the length of the head. *Sciæna (Corvina) sina*, Steind. Verh. z. b. Ges. Wien, 1866, p. 771, t. xv, f. 1, is probably this species.

* *Johnius serratus*, Bl. Schn. p. 76, has been referred to this fish, it came however from Tranquebar where *S. cuja* is not found.

A specimen of this fish, 6¼ inches in length, exists in the Berlin Museum, it was received from Paris with the label *Corvina furcrea*, and stated to have come from the Ganges. The true *Perca furcrea*, Lacép. or *Corvina furcrea*, Cuv. and Val. is described and figured by Steindachner as the *Pachypops furcreus* from the Brazils. (Verh. z. b. Ges. Wien, 1866, p. 4, t. i.)

Cantor's specimen of *Johnius Dussumieri* (Catal. p. 64), which is a skin, appears to me to be identical with the foregoing, but its anal spine is a little short, being 2¼ in the length of the head, whilst the length of the base of its anal equals 4½ in that of the length of the base of the soft dorsal. Another of the specimens in the British Museum seems to be *S. Vogleri*. The species I formerly (Fishes of Malabar, p. 51) described as *Sciæna Dussumieri* I now find is not identical with that species (see p. 192). It appears so doubtful as to what *Corvina Dussumieri* (C.V. v, p. 119) is, that I have omitted it. The description approaches most closely to that of *Sciæna sina* amongst the species of this Genus which I have collected in Malabar.

Habitat.—Throughout the larger rivers of India and Burmah, descending to the sea at certain seasons: it attains a foot in length. The one figured (an adult) is from the Irrawaddi.

7. Sciæna axillaris, Plate XLIII, fig. 6.

Corvina axillaris, Cuv. and Val. v, p. 113; Belanger, Voy. Ind. Orient. Zool. p. 356; Günther, Catal. ii, p. 302; Day, Fish. Malabar, p. 53.

B. vii, D. 10 | $\frac{1}{27-29}$, P. 17, V. 1/5, A. $\frac{2}{7}$, C. 17, L. l. $\frac{54}{52}$, L. tr. 6-7/14, Cæc. pyl. 9.

Length of head 4¼ to 4½, of caudal 1/6, height of body 3¾ to 3⅞ in the total length. *Eyes*—diameter 1/4 of length of head, 3/4 to 1 diameter from end of snout, and 1½ apart. Dorsal profile more convex than that of the abdomen. Greatest width of head equals half its length, and its height its length excluding the snout. Snout not overlapping the jaws, the jaws of about equal length anteriorly: the maxilla reaches to below the hind edge of the eye. Vertical limb of preopercle serrated, most strongly so at its angle. Two opercular spines. Distance from the eye to the maxilla equals two-thirds of the diameter of the orbit: shoulder-flap with smooth edges. No open glands visible across the snout nor lateral lobes. A knob below the symphysis of the lower jaw and two open pores behind it on either side. *Teeth*—villiform, with an outer curved row of rather strong ones in the premaxillaries, whilst the inner row in the lower jaw is twice as strong as the remainder. *Fins*—dorsal spines of moderate strength, the fourth and fifth the longest, equal to 2¼ in the height of the body, and 1/3 longer than the rays. Pectoral equals the head excluding the snout. Ventral reaches two-thirds of the way to the anal, its first ray elongated. Second anal spine strong, 3/4 as long as the first ray and equal to 2⅔ in the height of the body, the length of the fins base equals 3½ in that of the soft dorsal. Caudal wedge-shaped. *Scales*—cycloid on the head and as far as the bases of pectoral and ventral fins, superiorly they extend to below the middle of the first dorsal, posterior to these places they become ctenoid. *Lateral-line*—curves to opposite the commencement of the anal, its tubes are arborescent posteriorly. *Colours*—silvery dashed with purple, a black spot in the axilla: upper two-thirds of the first dorsal black, and a dark tinge along the top of the first portion of the second: fins greyish.

Habitat.—Seas of India. The specimen (figured life-size) from Orissa, was taken along with two others, the largest, captured at Madras in April, 1868, was a female 6¾ inches in length, and full of well developed ova.

8. Sciæna albida, Plate XLIV, fig. 4 and 6.

Bola coitor, Ham. Buch. Fish. Ganges, pp. 78, 368.

Corvina albida, Cuv. and Val. v, p. 93; Belanger, Voy. Ind. Zool. p. 355; Günther, Catal. ii, p. 304; Day, Fish. Malabar, p. 54.

Johnius anei, Blyth, Proc. Asi. Soc. Beng. 1860, p. 141 (not Bloch).

Corvina Neillii, Day, Fish. Malabar, p. 55.

Vella kattelee and *Korana kattelee*, Tam.

B. vii, D. 9-10 | $\frac{1}{27-30}$, P. 18, V. 1/5, A. $\frac{2}{7}$, C. 17, L. l. $\frac{48-50}{[illegible]}$, L. tr. 7/18, Cæc. pyl. 5.

Length of head 3¾ to 1/5, of caudal 1/6 to 1/7, height of body 1/4 of the total length. *Eyes*—diameter 1/4 in the young to 1/7 in the adult* in the length of head, and from 1 to 1½ diameters from the end of the snout. Dorsal and abdominal profiles about equally convex in the adult. Greatest width of head equals half its length, and its height equals its length excluding the snout. Interorbital space very slightly convex; snout not overhanging the mouth. Jaws equal in front, or the upper slightly the longer, cleft of mouth slightly oblique, the maxilla reaching to below the last third or hind edge of the eye. Preopercle with some serrations in the young most developed at its angle, but which become indistinct in the adult. Opercular spines indistinct. Three pores across the front of the snout: the free edge of the skin of the snout with five orifices and a slight lateral lobe. A bluntish knob below the symphysis of the lower jaw behind the base of which is a large open pore, and two more on the side of either ramus: a short barbel exists between the central pore and anterior lateral one, and a very minute one at the posterior pore. *Teeth*—villiform with an outer row of large curved ones in the premaxillaries: whilst the inner row in the lower jaw also consists of enlarged pointed teeth. *Fins*—dorsal spines increase in length to the third which is one-fourth higher than the rays, and equals from 1⅔ to 1/2 the height of the body. Pectoral as long as the head excluding the snout and a little longer than the ventral, which latter reaches half way to the anal. Second anal spine strong, nearly as long as the first ray and equal to 1/2 or 2/3 the height of the body. Caudal

* Specimens 8 inches long have the diameter of the eye 1/4 in the length of the head, 4½ at 11 inches: 5½ at 15 inches, and 1/7 in very large ones. This atrophy is not peculiar to this species.

wedge-shaped in the young, rounded in the adult. *Scales*—cycloid on head, elsewhere ctenoid, fine ones covering the bases of the soft dorsal and anal, and in the adult the whole of the caudal fin; those anterior to the base of the first dorsal fin are much smaller than those posteriorly. *Lateral-line*—becomes straight opposite the anal fin: the tubes are arborescent posteriorly. *Colours*—silvery, with a light streak along each row of scales, the first dorsal in the young with a black interspinous membrane, but only having a black outer edge in the adult: second dorsal stained gray at the upper third. A dark bluish mark on the opercles, most distinct in the young. Ventral, anal, and caudal yellowish.

In Indian specimens there are as a rule only nine spines in the first dorsal fin, and the first of these is very short.

The two figures show the marine form (fig. 4) at 8½ inches in length, the tail is longer and the colours much lighter. Fig. 6 is the estuary species as found off Calcutta, the back is dark and the lower surface brilliant golden: a dark spot on the axilla.

Habitat.—Seas of India (China?): termed *Sapé katelé* at Pondicherry. It is a common species, but not in much esteem for the table, it attains at least 3 feet in length.

9. Sciæna diacanthus.

Lutjanus diacanthus, Lacép. iv, pp. 195, 244.
Labrus ardla katchelee, Russell, ii, p. 11, pl. 115.
Labrus katchelee, Russell, ii, p. 12, pl. 116 (*young*).
Bola chaptis, Ham. Buch. Fish. Ganges, pp. 77, 368, pl. 10, f. 25.
Johnius cataleus, Cuv. and Val. v, p. 128; Blyth, J. A. S. of Beng. 1860, p. 141.
Johnius chaptis, Cuv. and Val. v, p. 130; Blyth, J. A. S. of Beng. 1860, p. 141.
Corvina catalea, Cuv. and Val. v, p. 128; Belanger, Voy. Ind. Orient. p. 360; Richards. Ich. China p. 226; Jerdon, M. J. L. and Sc. 1851, p. 131; Bleeker, Sciæn. p. 18.
Corvina platycephala, Cuv. and Val. v, p. 132.
Sciæna maculata, Gray and Hardw. Ill. Ind. Zool. ii, p. 89, f. 1 (*young*).
Johnius diacanthus, Cantor, Catal. p. 67; Bleeker, Java, p. 326; Kner, Novara Fische. p. 133.
Johnius Valenciennesi, Eyd. Soul. Voy. Bonite, i, p. 159, t. 4, f. 2.
Johnius maculatus, Blyth, J. A. S. of Beng. 1860, p. 141.
Sciæna diacanthus, Günther, Catal. ii, p. 290.
Pseudosciæna diacanthus, Bleeker, Mém. Scién. 1874, p. 27.

B. vii, D. 10 | $\frac{1}{22-25}$, P. 18-19, V. 1/5, A. 2/7, C. 17, L. l. [illegible], L. tr. 7/18, Cæc. pyl. 8.

Length of head 1/4 to 4½, of caudal 1/6, height of body 4½ to 1/5 of the total length. *Eyes*—diameter 4½ to 1/6 of length of head, 1½ to 1¾ diameters from end of snout, and also apart. Greatest width of the head equals 1¾ in its length, and the height equals its length excluding the snout. Snout slightly inflated, upper jaw a little the longer, cleft of mouth oblique, the maxilla reaches to below the last third of the orbit. The distance from the eye to the upper jaw equals 2/3 of the diameter of the orbit. Margin of preopercle crenulated in the adult, in the immature the angle is denticulated: two opercular points. Snout with three open pores across its base, and three openings along the free edge of the skin, but no lateral lobe. Five open pores under the symphysis of the lower jaw. Shoulder-flap finely serrated. *Teeth*—villiform in either jaw, with an outer row of curved, conical, and distantly placed ones in the premaxillaries, and an inner enlarged row in the mandibles. *Fins*—dorsal spines weak, increasing in length to the third and fourth which are 1/4 higher than the rays, and 2 to 2½ in the height of the body. Pectoral equals the length of the head behind the middle of the eyes. Ventral reaches nearly half way to the base of the anal. Second anal spine moderately strong, at least half as long as the rays and equal to 2¼ in the length of the head: the length of the base of the fin equals 1/3 to 2/7 of the base of the soft dorsal. Caudal wedge-shaped. *Scales*—ctenoid except on the snout and below the eyes. *Lateral-line*—becomes straight above the end of the anal fin, the tubes are arborescent posteriorly. *Colours*—brownish-gray shot with silver along the back, which below the lateral-line gradually fades to dull silvery-gray, head of the same colour glossed with purple. Fins yellowish, with black dots. Eyes golden. In the immature as up to a foot and a half in length or even more, the fins are grayish with dark edges, and the dorsal has two rows of dark spots: the caudal also has black spots and a black edge. In still younger specimens the back and upper half of the body has many black spots, and the young are as a rule vertically banded.

Russell observes that his plate 116, or the *maculata*, Gray and Hard. was believed by the fishermen to be the female: I have dissected many males however having this form of colour.

Habitat.—Seas of India to the Malay Archipelago and China, attaining at least 5 feet in length: it ascends tidal rivers and estuaries, and is found in the Hooghly as high as Calcutta.

10. Sciæna aneus, Plate XLV, fig. 5.

Johnius aneus, Bloch, t. 357.
Corvina anei, Cuv. and Val. v, p. 131.
? *Corvina sina*, Schleg. Fauna Japon, p. 58, pl. 24, f. 2 (not Cuv. and Val.)
Otolithus macrophthalmus, Bleeker, Sciæna, p. 16, and Java, Gen. et Spec. nov. p. 93.
Sciæna macrophthalmus, Günther, Catal. ii, p. 291.
Otolithus aneus, Day, Proc. Zool. Soc. 1867, p. 940.
Corvina macrophthalmus, Bleeker, Bintang, p. 292.

Pseudosciæna microphthalmus, Bleeker, Mém. Scién. 1874, p. 21.
Pravoh, Tam.: *Chalduvadah*, Andam.

B. vii. D. 10 | $\frac{1}{22-25}$, P. 18, V. 1/5, A. $\frac{2}{7}$, C. 17, L. l. $\frac{48}{50}$, L. tr. 8-9/18, Cæc. pyl. 10.

Length of head $3\frac{3}{4}$ to 1/4, of caudal 1/7 to 1/8, height of body 1/4 to $4\frac{1}{2}$ in the total length. *Eyes*—diameter 1/4 to $4\frac{1}{2}$ in the length of head, 1 to $1\frac{1}{4}$ diameters from end of snout and also apart. Greatest width of head equals 4/7 of its length, and the height equals its length behind the posterior nostril. Interorbital space nearly flat, snout not overhanging the mouth, the lower jaw the longer. Cleft of mouth oblique, the maxilla reaches to below the middle of the eye: the distance between the eye and the upper edge of the maxilla equals from 1/2 to 3/4 of the diameter of the orbit. Nostrils large and opposite the upper third of the orbit. Preopercle finely but widely serrated along both limbs, its lower edge very strongly serrated in the young: two opercular spines. Shoulder-flap entire. A small pore on either side of the snout just above the free edge of the skin. A small open pore on either side of the symphysis of the lower jaw on its under surface. *Teeth*—villiform in the upper jaw, with an outer conical row of distantly placed ones becoming canine-like near the symphysis. In the lower jaw an internal row of distantly placed conical teeth having a few villiform ones between or external to them. *Fins*—dorsal spines of moderate strength, the second to the fifth the longest, one-third higher than the rays, and equal to from 1/2 to $2\frac{1}{3}$ in the height of the body. Pectoral equals the length of the head excluding the snout. Ventral scarcely reaches half-way to the vent. Second anal spine weak, and from 3/4 to 1 diameter of the orbit in length, the length of the base of the fin equals from 1/4 to $4\frac{1}{2}$ in that of the soft dorsal. Caudal slightly rounded, cut square, or even a little emarginate. *Scales*—cycloid except in the posterior portion of the body where they are feebly ctenoid. *Lateral-line*—tubes become arborescent posteriorly. *Air-vessel*—oval with about 30 lateral processes on either side and extending the whole length of the abdomen. Dr. Ogg, chemical examiner at Madras (1867), found the isinglass very inferior. *Colours*—silvery-gray, becoming dull white along the abdomen: first dorsal black tipped or stained with dark gray: second dorsal grayish, lightest along its centre. Pectoral, ventral, and anal yellowish. Caudal tipped with gray.

In the Museum at Paris there is a specimen labelled as above and brought from Batavia by M. Raynaud.

Habitat.—Seas of India to the Malay Archipelago, it is very common at Madras up to 8 or 9 inches in length. It is not rare at Bombay or the Andamans: the specimen figured is $5\frac{1}{2}$ inches long and from Madras.

11. Sciæna maculata.

Johnius maculatus, Bl. Schn. p. 75; Cantor,* Catal. p. 68 (not synon.); Blyth, J. A. S. of Beng. 1860, p. 141 (not syn.).
Perca sari-kulleh, Russell, Fish. Vizag. ii, p. 17, pl. 123.
Corvina maculata, Cuv. and Val. v, p. 126; Jerdon, M. J. L. and Sc. 1851, p. 132.
Sciæna maculata, Günther, Catal. ii, p. 291; Day, Fish. Malabar, p. 50.
Cooroova and *Vari katcheler*, Tam.: *Cutlah*, Mal.: *Tomtah*, Bel.

B. vii, D. 10 | $\frac{1}{24-26}$, P. 18, V. 1/5, A. $\frac{2}{7}$, C. 17, L. l. $\frac{48-50}{75}$, L. tr. 8/16, Cæc. pyl. 8.

Length of head $3\frac{1}{2}$ to $3\frac{2}{3}$, of caudal from 1/5 to 1/6, height of body $3\frac{1}{2}$ to 1/4 of the total length. *Eyes*—diameter $4\frac{1}{2}$ to 1/5 of length of head, $1\frac{1}{4}$ diameters from end of snout, and 1 apart. Width of head equals 1/2 its length, and its height 4/5 of the same extent. Upper jaw overlapping the lower, and being itself overhung by the snout: the maxilla reaches to below the middle or last third of the eye. Preopercle with about six widely separated but rather strong denticulations at its angle, and its lower border crenulated in the young: opercle with two rather obtuse spines. Shoulder-flap serrated. A transverse row of four pores across the snout, the free edge of the skin with five orifices and a lateral lobe. A central pore below the mandibular symphysis, having two more on either side of it. *Teeth*—villiform in the upper jaw with an outer row of conical curved ones most developed near the median line: in the lower jaw villiform in several rows above the symphysis, whilst laterally the inner row consists of curved, enlarged teeth, and the outer villiform ones soon disappear. *Fins*—dorsal spines of moderate strength, the third to the seventh being the longest and equal to half the height of the body and one-third higher than the second dorsal fin. The pectoral equals the length of the head excluding the snout. Ventral reaches half way to the vent, its outer ray prolonged. Second anal spine 2/3 as long as first ray, and equals about 1/3 of the height of the body, length of the base of the fin 1/4 of that of the soft dorsal. Caudal wedge-shaped in the young, becoming more obtuse in the adult. *Scales*—ctenoid, except on the cheeks. *Lateral-line*—curves to below the middle of the soft dorsal when it proceeds straight, the tubes have usually a single branch on either side. *Air-vessel*—with 14 or 15 lateral processes on either side, each having two or three insertions. *Colours*—silvery-gray, abdomen whitish, cheeks tinged with golden. Five broad black bands, sometimes interrupted, extend over the back, the first from the nape passes backwards and downwards, and shortly after crossing the lateral-line abruptly terminates. The second commencing opposite from the fifth to the seventh dorsal spines passes backwards and downwards,

* The species termed *Johnius maculatus*, var. by Cantor, (Catal. p. 68), is still present in the British Museum, it has been termed by Bleeker (Mém. Scién. 1874, p. 51) *J. Cantori*. I would here add to Cantor's description the following remarks from his type. Height of head equals its length excluding the snout: the distance from the eye to the upper jaw equals three-fourths of a diameter of the orbit. *Teeth*—an enlarged outer row in the upper jaw: solely villiform ones in the lower. *Fins*—longest spines of first dorsal fin one-third higher than the rays and equal to 2/5 of the height of the body. Second anal spine nearly as long as the first ray and equals the length of the postorbital portion of the head, length of the base of the anal fin equals $3\frac{1}{2}$ in that of the soft dorsal. *Scales*—ctenoid, except on the snout and below the eyes; 48 rows along the lateral line, 50 above it, and 45 below it.

terminating opposite the middle of the ventral fin. The third arising opposite the second and third dorsal rays or between the two dorsal fins passes downwards parallel to the second band. The fourth commences below the centre of the second dorsal and descends to the lateral line: the fifth taking the same course is below the last few dorsal rays: occasionally there is a sixth over the free portion of the tail. Upper two-thirds of first dorsal stained black, becoming more indistinct with age: caudal slightly tinged with black, the other fins yellowish.

Habitat.—Seas of India, attaining at least a foot in length, it is not considered good eating.

B. No enlarged inner row of teeth in the lower jaw (*Johnius*).

12. **Sciæna Belengeri**, Plate XLIV, fig. 5.

Sparus, Russell, Fish. Vizag. ii, p. 8, pl. cxi.
Corvina Belengeri, Cuv. and Val. v, p. 120; Günther, Catal. ii, p. 303; Day, Fish. Malabar, p. 54.
? Corvina lobata, Cuv. and Val. v, p. 122, pl. cvii; Günther, Catal. ii, p. 304; Day, Fish. Malabar, p. 55.
Corvina Kuhlii, Cuv. and Val. v, p. 121; Bleeker, Sciæn. p. 18, and Enum. Pisc. p. 35.
Johnius Belengeri, Cantor, Catal. p. 65; Kner, Novara Fische, p. 133; Bleeker, Mémoire Sciénoid. 1874, p. 46.
Tonna kotteler, Tam.

B. vii, D. 9 | $\frac{1}{27-29}$, P. 17, V. 1/5, A. $\frac{2}{7}$, C. 17, L. l. $\frac{55}{[illegible]}$, L. tr. 6/14, Cæc. pyl. 5.

Length of head $4\frac{1}{3}$ to $4\frac{1}{2}$, of caudal $5\frac{1}{2}$, height of body 1/4 to $4\frac{1}{4}$ in the total length. *Eyes*—diameter $3\frac{1}{2}$ to $3\frac{3}{4}$ in the length of head, nearly 1 diameter from end of snout, and 1 apart. Height of head equals its length without the snout or behind front nostril, and its thickness equals from $1\frac{1}{4}$ to $1\frac{1}{3}$ in its length. Snout rounded, overhanging the upper jaw which last is in advance of the lower. The maxilla reaches to below the middle of the eye: cleft of mouth almost horizontal. Preopercle serrated, most coarsely so at its angle and along its horizontal limb: two opercular spines. The distance between the eye and the upper edge of the maxilla equals 1 diameter of the orbit. Snout with three open pores across its base: the free edge of the skin has one central and a second opening on either side dividing it into four lobes: five rather small open pores on the lower jaw. *Teeth*—villiform in both jaws with an outer row of enlarged and curved ones in the upper. *Fins*—dorsal fin having as a rule only 9 spines, the first of which is very short: the second and third equal from 2/3 to 1/2 the height of the body, and are 1/3 higher than the rays. Pectoral as long as the head excluding the snout. Ventral reaches half way to the anal, its outer ray prolonged. Second anal spine from a little above 1/2 to 2/3 the height of the first ray, and from $2\frac{1}{2}$ to 2/5 of that of the body: length of base of the fin equal to 1/4 of that of the soft dorsal. Caudal wedge-shaped. *Scales*—ctenoid except on snout and below the eyes where they are cycloid: they form a thick covering for the base of the soft dorsal fin. *Lateral-line*—curves to opposite the end of anal where it becomes straight, at first it is indistinct: the tubes with one or two branches. *Air-vessel*—"each side has ten branching processes, shorter, however, and apparently placed at a greater distance from each other than in *J. Dussumieri*. The three posterior pairs are much longer than the preceding, the eighth and ninth bipartite, the tenth pair is undivided, pointed."—(Cantor.) *Colours*—dark-gray, dorsals, anal, and caudal almost black: a dark blotch on the opercle: some specimens are much lighter. I have also a specimen $5\frac{1}{2}$ inches long marked as in *S. lobata*.

Out of 16 specimens from the coasts of India I find none with more than 9 dorsal spines. Kner gives 8 cæcal appendages, which are also said to exist in *S. lobata*, C. V., but I have never found above five in this species.

Habitat.—Seas of India to the Malay Archipelago and beyond: is much more common on the Western coast of India than in the Bay of Bengal. The specimen figured, life-size, is from Bombay.

13. **Sciæna semiluctuosa.**

Corvina semiluctuosa, Cuv. and Val. v, p. 97, p. 106; Jerdon, M. J. L. and Sc. 1851, p. 132; Günther, Catal. ii, p. 304; Day, Fish. Malabar, p. 53.
Johnius semiluctuosa, Kner, Novara Fische, p. 134.
Sakkua, Belooch.

B. vii, D. 10 | $\frac{1}{22-27}$, P. 19, V. 1/5, A. $\frac{2}{7}$, C. 17, L. l. $\frac{50}{[illegible]}$, L. tr. 8-9/25, Cæc. pyl. 7-8.

Length of head 2/7 to 1/4, of caudal 1/6 to 1/7, height of body 2/7 to 1/4 of the total length. *Eyes*—diameter $4\frac{1}{2}$ to 1/6 of length of head, 1 to 2 diameters from the end of snout, and 1 to $1\frac{1}{2}$ apart. Greatest width of head equals 4/7 of its length, the height its length without the snout. Upper profile of head rather convex: snout a little inflated. Upper jaw rather longer than the lower, the maxilla extends to below the middle of the orbit. Edge of preopercle crenulated: two blunt opercular points. Three open pores across the base of the snout, five more along the free margin of the skin, and a small lateral lobe. Five pores under the symphysis of the lower jaw. *Teeth*—villiform in either jaw, with an enlarged, curved, external row in the premaxillaries, and a few outer enlarged ones above the symphysis of the mandibles. *Fins*—dorsal spines weak, the third the longest, being 1/3 higher than the rays and equal to 3/7 of the height of the body. Pectoral as long as the head behind the middle of the eyes. Ventral reaches half way to the anal, its first ray prolonged. Second anal spine strong, nearly 3/4 as high as the first ray and equal to 3/7 of the height of the body, the length of the base of the fin equal to $4\frac{1}{2}$ in that of the soft dorsal. Caudal wedge-shaped or rounded.

Air-vessel—simple. *Cæcal appendages*—seven or eight, the longest equals about 3 diameters of the orbit. *Scales*—ctenoid except on the snout and below the eyes: the base of the soft dorsal fin thickly scaled. *Lateral-line*—tubes have short branches. *Colours*—deep gray with a blackish band running along the centre of each row of scales; head glossed with purple: fins deep black. In young specimens the lines along the rows of scales are very faint.

Habitat.—Seas of India to China, very common at Bombay along the coasts of Sind and Beloochistan. Jerdon observes, "I have only seen this species on the Malabar coast." I have never obtained it either along the Bay of Bengal: the largest specimen I found was 18 inches in length.

14. Sciæna glaucus, Plate XLVI, fig. 2.

Sciæna Dussumieri, Day, Fish. Malabar, p. 51, (not Cuv. and Val.)

B. vii, D. 10 | $\frac{1}{24-25}$, P. 16, V. 1/5, A. $\frac{2}{7}$, C. 17, L. l. [illegible], L. tr. 6/18.

Length of head $4\frac{1}{2}$ to $4\frac{1}{2}$, of caudal $7\frac{1}{2}$, height of body $4\frac{1}{2}$ in the total length. *Eyes*—diameter $3\frac{3}{4}$ to $4\frac{1}{4}$ in length of head, $1\frac{1}{2}$ diameters from end of snout and also apart. Greatest width of head equals half its length, the height equals its length without the snout. Snout rounded and slightly overhanging the jaws, the upper of which overlaps the lower: the upper jaw at its highest point is not on a level with the lower edge of the orbit. Distance between eye and upper jaw equals 3/4 of a diameter of the orbit. Preopercle with distinct and widely separated denticulations most developed at the angle: opercle with two spines. Shoulder-flap entire. Snout with three pores across its base, and five along its free border which has a distinct lateral lobe. Five open pores below the symphysis of the lower jaw. *Teeth*—villiform in both jaws, with an outer enlarged row of somewhat conical ones in the premaxillaries. *Fins*—dorsal spines moderately strong, the highest equal to $1\frac{2}{3}$ in the height of the body and nearly twice as high as the rays. Pectoral falciform, as long as the head excluding the snout. Ventral reaches 1/2 way to the anal, its outer ray prolonged. Second anal spine rather strong, from 1/2 to 2/3 as high as the first ray and equal from $2\frac{1}{4}$ to $2\frac{1}{2}$ in the height of the body, the extent of its base equals 2/9 that of the soft dorsal. Caudal rounded or wedge-shaped. *Scales*—cycloid on snout, cheeks, and anterior portion of the chest, ctenoid from behind the preopercle on the upper surface of the head from above the middle of the eye; 27 rows between snout and base of first dorsal fin. *Lateral-line*—becomes straight above the middle of the anal fin: tubes with one or two branches on either side. *Colours*—grayish-green along the back, becoming silvery below, a diffused bluish blotch on the opercles: a dark spot at base of pectoral, most distinct posteriorly, everywhere fine brown spots. First dorsal nearly black: upper two-thirds of second dorsal dark, due to fine spots, caudal and last half of pectoral grayish from the same cause.

This species in its proportions closely resembles *S. carutta*, but may be distinguished by wanting the light tint along the lateral line, by having a much stronger and longer second anal spine, and by most of the scales being ctenoid instead of cycloid.

Amongst my collection from the Andamans exists a species (?) having a close relationship to *S. glaucus*, and which may be a variety. It differs in that it has D. 11 | [illegible], L. r. [illegible]. Eyes, diameter [illegible] in the length of the head, 1 diameter from the end of snout. *Scales*—cycloid on snout and below the eyes, everywhere else ctenoid. The extra dorsal spine may be an anomaly, but the character of the scales suggests a doubt if the species are the same. Curiously, I have a specimen from Orissa exactly resembling the typical *glaucus*, except that it has ctenoid scales as in the Andamanese variety.

Habitat.—Seas of India, very common at Bombay, where it attains a large size. Its air-vessel, which is similar to that of *S. sina*, is collected at the same places, and the two species have the same native names.

15. Sciæna carutta, Plate XLIV, fig. 1.

Johnius carutta, Bloch, t. 356; Cantor, Catal. p. 66; Bleeker, Sciænoides, p. 48.
Corvina carutta, Cuv. and Val. v, p. 124; Günther, Catal. ii, p. 302; Day, Fish. Malabar, p. 53.
Corvina carouna, Cuv. and Val. l. c. p. 125.

B. vii, D. 10 | $\frac{1}{22-23}$, P. 17, V. 1/5, A. $\frac{2}{7}$, C. 17, L. l. [illegible], L. tr. 5-6/18.

Length of head 1/4 to $4\frac{1}{2}$, of caudal 1/7, height of body 1/4 of the total length. *Eyes*—diameter 1/4 of length of head, $1\frac{1}{4}$ diameters from end of snout and also apart. Greatest width of head equals 2/3 of its length, its height equals its length excluding the snout. Snout inflated overhanging the upper jaw, which slightly overlaps the lower, the maxilla reaches to below the middle of the eye: the distance between the eye and the upper edge of the maxilla equals that of the diameter of the orbit: cleft of mouth nearly horizontal. Preopercle crenulated, more especially along its lower border: opercle with two weak spines. A row of pores across the snout; 5 along the edge of its free border, and a lateral lobe. A central pore beneath the symphysis of the mandible having two more on either side of it. *Teeth*—villiform in both jaws, a few of the outer row and in the anterior portion of the premaxillaries being enlarged, somewhat conical but scarcely curved. *Fins*—dorsal spines weak, the second and third the longest, 1/3 higher than the rays and equal to 1/2 the height of the body. Pectoral as long as the head excluding the snout. Ventral reaches half way to the vent, its outer ray elongated. Second anal spine weak, nearly 2/3 as high as the first ray, and 2/7 to 2/5 of the length of the head. Caudal rhomboidal. *Scales*—mostly cycloid, a few ctenoid at the centre of their free edge between the pectoral fin and lateral-line: the ctenoid portion of the scale is only in a little patch about the middle of its free edge. Those on the head as large as those on the body. *Lateral-line*—curves gradually until above the end of the anal fin when it becomes straight, its tubes have short branches. *Air-vessel*—with several lateral branching attachments. *Colours*—purplish-brown due to numerous fine dots, but becoming golden in the lower fourth of the body, its lateral-line is generally lighter than the contiguous parts. Head glossed with purple. First dorsal fin dark, the others with gray edges.

Jerdon observes, M. J. L. and Sc. 1851, p. 132, that this fish is more abundant on the Malabar coast than at Madras, but I find on referring to Sir W. Elliot's drawings that he has marked one as *Corvina carutta*, and which he observes equals Russell's cxi. or *S. Belengeri*.

I have two specimens from the Malabar coast that appear to be *Corvina caroua*, Cuv. and Val. (v. p. 125). They are gray and have merely an indistinct trace of the light line along the lateral-line, so well marked in *S. carutta*. Irrespective of this however, all the scales (except those on the snout and below the eyes) are strongly ctenoid, offering a marked contrast to *carutta*, and the second anal spine is from 1/4 to 4½ in the length of the head. Otherwise I am unable to discover any difference.

Habitat.—Seas of India to the Malay Archipelago, it attains nearly a foot in length. The specimen figured is 8 inches in length, and from Madras.

16. Sciæna osseus, Plate XLVI, fig. 3.

B. vii, D. 10 | 1/25, P. 18, V. 1/5. A. 2/7, C. 17, L. l. [illegible] L. tr. 6/15.

Length of head 4¾, of caudal 1/6, height of body 4¾ in the total length. *Eyes*—diameter 1/5 of length of head, 1¾ diameters from end of snout, and 1½ apart. The greatest width of the head equals its post-orbital length; its height equals its length behind the front nostril. Snout obtuse, not inflated, the dorsal profile above the eyes is a little concave: cleft of mouth oblique, the anterior extremity of the lower jaw being on a level with the lower edge of the eye. The maxilla reaches to below the hind edge of the orbit; the upper jaw scarcely overlaps the lower. The distance from the eye to the upper jaw nearly equals one diameter of the orbit. Preopercle rather strongly denticulated in its whole extent. Two opercular spines. Shoulder-flap serrated. Three small pores across the snout, and five along the free edge of the skin but no lateral lobe. Two small central pores below the symphysis of the lower jaw and two more large ones laterally and posteriorly. *Teeth*—villiform in both jaws with an outer enlarged row in the premaxillaries. *Fins*—first dorsal spine very short, the second and third of equal length, the fourth the longest but only slightly higher than the posterior rays, and 2½ in that of the body. Pectoral as long as the head behind the middle of the eyes. Ventral reaches half way to the vent. Second anal spine weak, about 1/2 as long as the first ray and equal to 1/4 of the length of the head. Caudal wedge-shaped. *Scales*—cycloid on head and chest, ctenoid on the body. *Lateral-line*—forms a well marked curve to above the front edge of the anal fin: tubes very distinct, and giving off one short branch on either side. *Colours*—brownish-gray or stone-coloured along the back, becoming dull white on the sides and below. Opercle bluish-black. First dorsal black in its upper half, outer edges of pectoral, ventral, anal, and caudal gray.

Habitat.—Malabar coast of India, from whence the specimen figured (7 inches long) was procured.

Genus, 3—Sciænoides,* *Blyth* (January, 1860).

Bola, pt. Ham. Buch.; *Sciæna*, sp. Cuv. and Val.; *Collichthys*, Günther (June, 1860); *Hemisciæna*, Bleeker; *Plagioscion*, Gill.

Branchiostegals seven: pseudobranchiæ. Eyes small. Head broad, with its upper surface very convex. Cleft of mouth oblique and deep. Teeth villiform in the upper jaw, with an outer distantly placed row of curved conical ones in the premaxillaries, becoming canine-like anteriorly: an inner row enlarged and conical in the lower jaw, with an outer series of villiform ones. No barbels. Two dorsal fins, united at their bases, the second with many rays: two weak anal spines: caudal wedge-shaped. Scales small, cycloid or ctenoid. Air-vessel generally having a horn-like process on either side, and with many lateral appendages. Pyloric appendages few or in moderate numbers.

Uses.—Good as food, its air-vessel used for isinglass.

Habitat.—Seas of India to the Malay Archipelago and beyond.

SYNOPSIS OF SPECIES.

1. *Sciænoides pama*, D. 10 | [illegible], A. 2/7, L. l. [illegible], Cæc. pyl. 9. Brownish superiorly, light below: fins edged with gray. Bay of Bengal, entering estuaries and rivers.
2. *Sciænoides microdon*, D. 8-9 | [illegible], A. 2/7, L. l. [illegible], Cæc. pyl. 6. Brownish superiorly, becoming light beneath. Seas of India to the Malay Archipelago.
3. *Sciænoides biauritus*, D. 9 | [illegible], A. 2/7, L. l. [illegible], Cæc. pyl. 13. Brownish superiorly, golden below. Estuaries of India to the Malay Archipelago and China.
4. *Sciænoides brunneus*, D. 9 | [illegible], A. 2/7, L. l. [illegible]. Gray, with blackish fins. Bombay.

1. Sciænoides pama.

Bola pama, Ham. Buch. Fish. Ganges, pp. 79, 368, pl. 32, fig. 26.

* Blyth gives as the species forming his Genus, 1. *Sciænoides biauritus*; 2. *Sc. pama*; 3. *Sc. Hardwickii*=*S. pama*, young; 4. *Sc.* (?) *axyer*.

Sciæna pama, Cuv. and Val. v, p. 55, pl. 101; Bleeker, Verh. Bat. Gen. xxv, p. 92.
Sciænoides pama, Blyth, Proc. Asia. Soc. Beng. 1860, p. 139.
Collichthys pama, Günther, Catal. ii, p. 316.
Sciænoides Hardwickii, Blyth, J. A. S. of Beng. 1860, p. 139 (*young*).
Ven beyti, Ooriah and Hind.: *Coii bola*, Bengali: *Botal*, Ooriah: *Nga-pouss-wus*, Mugh.

B. vii, D. 10 | [illegible], P. 17, V. 1/5, A. [illegible], C. 17, L. l. [illegible], L. tr. 9/25, Vert. 24, Cæc. pyl. 9.

Length of head $4\frac{1}{3}$ to $4\frac{2}{3}$, of caudal $5\frac{1}{2}$, height of body 1/5 to 1/6 of the total length.* *Eyes*—diameter 1/7 to 1/8 of the length of head, 2 diameters from end of snout, and from $2\frac{1}{2}$ to 3 apart. Greatest width of the head equals $1\frac{3}{4}$ of its length: its height equals its length excluding the snout. Snout not much swollen. Cleft of mouth oblique, the maxilla reaching to below or even behind the hind edge of the orbit: lower jaw slightly the shorter. The distance between the eye and the maxilla equals about $1\frac{1}{2}$ diameters of the orbit. Preopercle crenulated, with denticulations at its angle most distinct in the young: opercle with two points. Snout with two open pores on its anterior surface, and two more opening on the free edge of the skin: lower jaw with a small open pore a little below and to one side of the symphysis. Shoulder-flap having its edge with numerous long ciliæ. *Teeth*—villiform in the upper jaw, with an outer row of large, distantly placed, curved, and conical ones, largest near the symphysis. An inner row of widely placed, conical teeth in the lower jaw, with an outer villiform series. *Fins*—dorsal spines weak, with filamentous terminations, the third and fourth the longest and equal to $2\frac{1}{2}$ in the height of the body, and nearly twice as long as the rays. Pectoral pointed and as long as the head. Ventral reaches half way to the vent. Second anal spine weak, 1/3 to 2/7 of the length of the rays and equal to 1 diameter of the orbit: length of the base of the fin equal to 1/8 of that of the soft dorsal. Caudal wedge-shaped, its central rays much the longest. *Scales*—cycloid on the head, ctenoid on the body. *Lateral-line*—on a raised row of scales, becomes straight above the middle of the anal fin, its tubes being very arborescent posteriorly. *Air-vessel*—dividing anteriorly into two short processes, whilst springing from near its posterior extremity are two more long processes which extend anteriorly as far as the auditory apparatus. *Colours*—light brownish along the back, becoming white beneath: head shot with gold and purple. Fins yellowish, the upper half of the dorsal gray, as is also the last half of the caudal.

It is termed '*whiting*' in Calcutta, and is light and wholesome if cooked whilst fresh, but it rapidly becomes soft and tasteless after death.

Habitat.—Bay of Bengal, entering estuaries and rivers as far as the tide extends, it attains at least 5 feet in length.

2. Sciænoides microdon, Plate XLV, fig. 2.

Otolithus microdon, Bleeker, Madura, p. 10, Sciæn. p. 16, Java, p. 99.
Sciæna microdon, Günther, Catal. ii, p. 294.
Collichthys microdon, Bleeker, Mém. Scién. 1874, p. 16.

B. vii, D. 8-9 | [illegible], P. 19, V. 1/5, A. [illegible], C. 18, L. l. [illegible], L. tr. 11/20, Cæc. pyl. 6.

Length of head 1/4, of caudal 2/9, height of body 2/11 of the total length. *Eyes*—diameter 1/6 of length of head, $1\frac{1}{2}$ diameters from end of snout, and $2\frac{1}{2}$ apart. The greatest width of head equals half to 2/3 its length, its height equals its length excluding the snout. Snout not overhanging the jaws, the lower slightly prominent opposite the symphysis. Cleft of mouth oblique, the maxilla at its anterior extremity on a level with the middle of the eye, posteriorly it reaches to below the hind edge of the orbit. Edges of the preopercle finely serrated: an opercular spine. Three open pores along the free edge of the skin at the snout, but no lateral lobe. Four large open pores along the under side of the lower jaw near the symphysis. *Teeth*—villiform in both jaws, an outer row of distantly placed, curved, conical ones in the premaxillaries: an inner row of widely separated conical ones in the lower jaw, and an outer villiform series. *Fins*—dorsal spines increase in length from the third to the fifth which are 1/4 higher than the rays and equal to 1/2 the height of the body. Pectoral equals the length of the head excluding the snout. Ventral reaches half way to the anal. Second anal spine equals half the height of the rays. Caudal wedge-shaped. *Scales*—cycloid in the young, ctenoid on the body, in larger specimens especially below the lateral-line. *Lateral-line*—curves to opposite the commencement of the anal fin. *Colours*—brown, becoming lighter on the sides and beneath. Fins yellow, dorsal and anal tipped with blackish.

Habitat.—The specimen which is figured life-size came from Bombay. If it is identical with Bleeker's species it is also found in the Malay Archipelago. A larger specimen (9 inches) from Orissa was a female, with the air-vessel as in *S. biauritus*.

3. Sciænoides biauritus, Plate XLVII, fig. 1.

Otolithus biauritus, Cantor, Catal. p. 57; Bleeker, Borneo, p. 3.
Sciænoides biauritus, Blyth, J. A. S. of Beng. 1860, p. 139.
Collichthys biauritus, Günther, Catal. ii, p. 315, and Zool. Record, iii, p. 143; Bleeker, Mém. Scién. 1874, p. 15.

B. vii, D. 9 | [illegible], P. 19, V. 1/5, A. [illegible], C. 17, L. l. [illegible], L. tr. 12/25, Cæc. pyl. 13.

* The fry do not appear at all like the adult. I took a number in the Sunderbunds, and at $2\frac{1}{2}$ inches in length the height of the body is only 1/4 to 2/9 of that of the total, the preopercle is strongly denticulated, with 2 or 3 spines at its angle.

Length of head 1/4 to 4½, of caudal 1/6, height of body 1/5 to 1/6 of the total length. *Eyes*—diameter 1/7 to 1/8 of length of head, 2 diameters from end of snout, and also apart. The greatest width of the head equals half its length, height of head equals its length excluding the snout. Cleft of mouth oblique, the anterior extremity of the upper jaw being on a level with the lower edge of the orbit: the maxilla reaches to below the last third or hind edge of the eye: upper jaw overlaps the lower. The distance from the eye to the upper jaw equals the diameter of the orbit. Posterior limb of preopercle oblique, and indistinctly crenulated along its vertical border: two opercular points. Five open pores along the free edge of the skin of the snout, no lateral lobe: four small open pores on the under surface of the lower jaw. Shoulder-flap fimbriated. *Teeth*—villiform in the upper jaw, with an outer row of distantly placed, curved, conical ones in the premaxillaries: an inner row of conical teeth in the lower jaw, with a few villiform ones externally. *Fins*—dorsal spines weak, and as high as the posterior rays of the soft dorsal fin, the highest equalling about 2/5 in that of the body. Pectoral equals the head behind the middle of the eyes. Ventral reaches half way to the anal. Second anal spine weak, half as long as the rays and equal to 1/4 of the length of the head: the length of the base of the fin is from 5½ to 1/6 of that of the soft dorsal. Caudal wedge-shaped. *Scales*—cycloid, except on the body below the lateral-line where they are feebly ctenoid. *Lateral-line*—on a row of thin scales, becoming straight above the front edge of the anal fin: tubes well developed. *Air-vessel*—with 25 lateral processes, and a single long projection on either side from the anterior extremity reaching to the posterior end of the air-vessel. *Colours*—of a light brownish superiorly, tinged with gold on the abdomen, head shot with purple.

Habitat.—Seas and estuaries of India to the Malay Archipelago and China. The longest specimen in the Calcutta Museum is 42 inches.

4. Sciænoides brunneus, Plate XLV, fig. 6.

Otolithus brunneus, Day, Journal Linn. Soc. 1873, p. 524.

B. vii, D. 9 | $\frac{1}{27-28}$, P. 18, V. 1/5, A. 2/7, C. 17, L. l. [illegible], L. tr. 21/34.

Length of head 1/4 to 2/9, of caudal 2/11 to 1/6, height of body 2/11 to 1/6 of the total length. *Eyes*—diameter 1/7 to 1/8 of length of head, 1½ diameters from end of snout, and 2 apart. Width of the head equals half its length, its height equals 3/5 of its length. The jaws of about equal length, or the lower slightly the shorter. Cleft of mouth somewhat oblique, the maxilla reaches to below the hind edge of the eye. Preopercle with a few widely separated serrations, most apparent at its rounded angle. Opercle with two obtuse points. No open glands on snout: two badly marked pores on the front of the lower jaw below the symphysis. Shoulder-lobe finely fimbriated along its free edge. *Teeth*—an outer row of curved conical teeth in the upper jaw, having about two villiform rows internally, a small curved canine on either side of the centre of the upper jaw: an outer villiform row and an inner single row of irregularly sized and rather distantly placed conical teeth laterally in the lower jaw, with a small canine-like one on either side of the symphysis, having a few villiform ones posteriorly, a few small teeth are present external to the enlarged row. *Fins*—dorsal spines weak and having filamentous terminations, the third to the sixth of somewhat the same length, and equal to about 2½ in the height of the body. Second dorsal highest in its last third, where it equals or exceeds that of the spinous dorsal. Pectoral as long as the head posterior to the middle of the eye: ventral only reaches one-third of the distance to the vent. Anal spines weak and short, 1/3 of length of rays, the length of the base of the fin equal to 5½ or 1/6 of that of the soft dorsal. Caudal pointed. *Scales*—rather oval, cycloid, and transversely elongated on the head, ctenoid and vertically elongated on the body: a few very fine ones over the bases of the soft dorsal and anal fins. *Lateral-line*—gently curves to below the first fourth of the second dorsal, where it becomes straight. *Colours*—brownish, becoming golden below: fins darkest externally.

A specimen of this fish in the Berlin Museum is marked as having been received from Valenciennes, marked *Sciæna pama*, Bombay, with it was also sent the *Sciænoides pama* from the Ganges, having the same designation.

Habitat.—Bombay, where it is common in October, it attains at least 18 inches in length, the specimen figured is 11 inches long.

Genus, 4—Otolithus, *Cuv.*

Cynoscion, *Anomiolepis*, *Apseudobranchus*, *Archoscion* and *Atractoscion*, Gill.

Branchiostegals seven: pseudobranchiæ. Body oblong. Eyes of moderate size. Snout a little pointed, the lower jaw being the longer. Preopercle crenulated, serrated, or denticulated. No barbels. Villiform teeth in both jaws with the outer row in premaxillaries enlarged: well developed conical canines in both jaws or merely in the upper,† they are usually received, when the mouth is closed, into fossæ in the opposite jaw. A single row of widely separated conical teeth in the lower jaw with occasionally a single outer row of villiform ones. Two dorsal fins united at their bases, the first with nine or ten weak spines: anal with one or two small ones, and few rays (6-11). Scales ctenoid or cycloid, and of moderate or small size. Air-vessel present, mostly with lateral appendages. Pyloric appendages few.*

Uses.—Employed as food: its air-vessels collected for isinglass.

* As a rule in the fry of Indian species the preopercle is denticulated or spinate.

† *Cynoscion*, Gill.

Habitat.—Seas of India, the Malay Archipelago and beyond; residents in most tropical seas, some are said to be found in fresh water. In India they are rarely if ever taken above tidal reach.

SYNOPSIS OF SPECIES.

1. *Otolithus maculatus*, D. 9-10 | [illegible], A. [illegible], L. l. [illegible]. Large canines in both jaws. Grayish, five or six rows of black spots along the body and caudal fin. Seas of India to the Malay Archipelago.

2. *Otolithus ruber*, D. 10 | [illegible], A. [illegible], L. l. [illegible]. Width of head 2¼ in its length. Large canines in both jaws. Brownish-red shot with silver. Seas of India to the Malay Archipelago.

3. *Otolithus argenteus*, D. 10 | [illegible], A. [illegible], L. l. [illegible]. Width of head equals 1¾ to 1/2 its length. Large canines in both jaws. Silvery, four narrow gray longitudinal bands along the sides. Seas of India to the Malay Archipelago.

1. Otolithus maculatus. Plate XLVI, fig. 4.

Cuv. Règn. Anim. Poiss. t. xxvii, f. 2; Cuv. and Val. v, p. 64; Cantor, Catal. p. 62; Blyth, J. A. S. of Beng. 1860, p. 140; Bleeker, Sciæn. p. 15, and Mémoire Scién. 1874, p. 12; Günther, Catal. ii, p. 310; Day, P. Z. S. 1865, p. 300.

? *Otolithus bispinosus*, Cuv. and Val. v, p. 65; Blyth, J. A. S. of Beng. 1860, p. 141; Günther, Catal. ii, p. 310 (? *young*).

Birralli, Ooriah.

B. vii, D. 9-10 | [illegible], P. 18, V. 1/5, A. [illegible], C. 17, L. l. [illegible], L. tr. 14/26.

Length of head 3½ to 4¼, of caudal 1/8, height of body 5¾ to one-sixth in the total length. *Eyes*—diameter 1/6 to 1/7 of length of head, 1½ diameters from end of snout, and 1½ apart. Greatest width of head equals from 1¾ to 2 in its length, its height equals its length behind the middle of the eye. Cleft of mouth oblique, lower jaw the longer, the maxilla reaches to below the last third or hind edge of the eye. Edge of preopercle more crenulated than denticulated (spinate in the young): opercle with two weak points. Skin of snout with three small open orifices along its free border but no lateral lobe. No open pores visible below lower jaw. Shoulder-flap crenulated. *Teeth*—a long strong canine on either side of the symphysis of the lower jaw, and on either side of the upper just external to those in the mandibles: a row of widely separated conical and pointed teeth along the sides of the lower jaw; and villiform teeth in the upper with an external row of conical and curved ones. *Fins*—dorsal spines weak with filamentous terminations, they increase in length to about the fifth which equals 2/3 of the height of the body and is a third higher than the rays. Pectoral equals the height of the head. Ventral reaches about one-third of the distance to the anal. Second anal spines weak, 1/2 the height of the first ray, and 1/4 of that of the body: length of the base of the anal fin equals 1/3 of that of the soft dorsal. Caudal wedge-shaped or rounded. *Scales*—cycloid, and in very irregular rows. *Lateral-line*—becomes straight above the middle of the anal fin. *Air-vessel*—with about 54 lateral appendages on either side. *Colours*—grayish in the upper part of the body, golden below: five or six rows of black spots along the body and caudal fin: the other fins stained with gray at their edges.

Some fry, apparently of this species, which I captured in the Sunderbunds, March 1874, had the body gray, fins black except the tail which was white.

Habitat.—Seas of India to the Malay Archipelago, attaining at least 16 inches in length. It is very common in the sea and estuaries of Orissa and lower Bengal.

2. Otolithus ruber.

Johnius ruber, Bl. Schn. p. 75, t. xvii.

Otolithus ruber, Cuv. and Val. v, p. 60, pl. 102; Swainson, Fishes, ii, p. 219; Cantor, Catal. p. 59; Jerdon, M. J. L. and Sc. 1851, p. 131; Günther, Catal. ii, p. 309; Day, Fish. Malabar, p. 57; Bleeker, Mémoire Scién. 1874, p. 11.

Otolithus submaculatus, Blyth, J. A. S. of Beng. 1860, p. 141.

B. vii, D. 10 | [illegible], P. 17, V. 1/5, A. [illegible], C. 17, L. l. [illegible], L. tr. 7/17, Cæc. pyl. 4-5.

Length of head 1/4 to 2/7, of caudal 1/6 to 2/13, height of body 1/4 to 5½ in the total length. *Eyes*—diameter 1/4 to 1/5 or even 1/6 of length of head, nearly 1 diameter from end of snout, and 1¼ apart. Greatest width of head equals 2¼ in its length, and its height its length excluding the snout. Cleft of mouth rather oblique, the maxilla reaches to below the last third of the eye: nostrils opposite the upper third of the orbit. Preopercle scarcely denticulated: two opercular spines. Shoulder-flap entire. The distance between the eye and the upper jaw equals two-thirds of the diameter of the eye in extent. *Teeth*—on either side of the symphysis of the upper jaw a pair of large canines, and an inner villiform band, also an outer row of conically curved ones, occasionally even between the canines: in the lower jaw a central (sometimes a second) curved canine having a few villiform teeth behind it, and a lateral row of distantly placed conical teeth. *Fins*—dorsal spines slender, the second and third equalling from 2 to 2½ times in the height of the body, and from 1/2 to 2/3 higher than the rays. Pectoral as long as the head excluding the snout. The ventral does not reach quite half way to the vent. First anal spine minute or wanting, the length of the second equals about 2/5 of that of the first ray, the length of the base of the anal fin about 1/6 in that of the soft dorsal. Caudal wedge-shaped. *Scales*—cycloid. *Lateral-line*—gradually curves to above the middle or end of the anal the tubes arborescent posteriorly. *Air-vessel*—somewhat contracted at its first fourth and having about 34 branching processes on either side. *Colours*—brownish-red, shot with silvery and white, sometimes glossed with gold in the lower third of the body. First dorsal stained black at its edge, soft dorsal and anal with grayish outer margins: pectoral, ventral, and anal yellow.

Having sent an air-vessel of this species to Mr. Broughton, the Government chemist, he observed that "it contains about 80 per cent of gelatine, isinglass containing about 90 per cent. It will set a jelly with about 26 times its weight of water."

Habitat.—Seas of India to the Malay Archipelago, attaining 2½ feet or more in length: it is the commonest form in the Indian seas, especially along the Coromandel coast. It is pretty good for the table. The ova appears to be deposited from about March to July.

3. Otolithus argenteus, Plate XLV, fig. 3.

(Kuhl. and v. Hass.) Cuv. and Val. v, p. 62; Richards. Ich. China, p. 225; Bleeker, Sciæn. p. 15, and Mémoire Sciénoides, 1874, p. 9; Cantor, Catal. p. 61; Günther, Catal. ii, p. 310; Day, Fish. Malabar, p. 58; Kner, Novara Fisch. p. 135, t. vi, f. 4 (air-vessel.)

Bu-ru, Sind.: *Golaree*, Tel. (at Gopalpore.)

B. vii, D. 10 | $\frac{1}{24-26}$, P. 16, V. 1/5, A. $\frac{2}{7}$, C. 17, L. l. $\frac{50-55}{70-75}$, L. tr. 7-8/21, Cæc. pyl. 6.

Length of head $3\frac{3}{4}$ to $4\frac{1}{4}$, of caudal $6\frac{1}{2}$ to 1/7, height of body $4\frac{1}{2}$ to 1/5 of the total length. *Eyes*—diameter 2/9 to 1/4 of length of head, 1 to $1\frac{1}{4}$ diameters from end of snout, and $1\frac{1}{2}$ apart. Greatest width of head equals from $1\frac{2}{3}$ to 1/2 its length: its height its length excluding the snout. Interorbital space almost flat. Cleft of mouth oblique: lower jaw the longer: the maxilla reaches to below the middle of the eye: the distance between the eye and the maxilla equals half a diameter of the orbit. Vertical limb of preopercle slightly serrated (in the young it is spinate): its angle and lower edge crenulated: two opercular spines. Free edge of skin across snout entire having an open pore above the vertical from the canine teeth: no open glands on the lower jaw. Edge of shoulder-flap serrated. *Teeth*—a villiform internal series in the upper jaw, two large pointed canines to the side of the symphysis. A single large central canine in the lower jaw and a lateral row of conical teeth: in some specimens there exists a few villiform teeth external to this row. *Fins*—dorsal spines increase in length to the third and fourth which equal half the height of the body, and are 1/3 higher than the rays. Pectoral as long as the head excluding the snout. Ventral reaches half way to the anal. Second anal spine weak, rather more $(2\frac{1}{2})$ than one-third the height of the first ray, and 3/4 of the diameter of the orbit: the base of the fin equals 1/5 of that of the soft dorsal. Caudal wedge-shaped. *Scales*—cycloid, except in the last half of the body in its lower half where they are more or less ctenoid, some over bases of caudal and anal fins. *Lateral-line*—tubes strongly arborescent posteriorly. *Air-vessel*—with 25 lateral processes on either side. *Colours*—silvery, darkest along the back: four dark longitudinal bands along the sides, one being along the lower edge of the dorsal fin, a second at 1/3 the distance between it and the lateral-line, the two others on either side of the lateral-line. A darkish spot on the opercle. Pectoral, ventral, and anal orange, outer edge of dorsal grayish.

Russell (Fish. Vizag. ii. p. 7, pl. 109) published the figure of what he termed a *Sparus?* Called by the natives *Pottee koraneh*, having D. 10/$\frac{1}{27}$, it he observed attained one foot two inches in length and its breadth was 1/4 of its length. Cuv. and Val. (v, p. 64) named the species *Otolithus versicolor*, and Cantor (Catal. p. 63) considered that he recognised it in a species from Pinang which has D. 10 | $\frac{1}{27}$, and has been called by Bleeker, *Otolithus lateoides* (Java, p. 98, Sciæn. p. 16, and Mém. Scién. 1874, p. 7.)

Having searched very many times for this fish on the Coromandel coast and always without any result, it has appeared to me that it may represent *O. argenteus*, which is very common at Vizagapatam: but on the other hand there is Cantor's specimen, and Bleeker's species from the Malay Archipelago, and which may still be found in the Bay of Bengal. It has D. 10 | $\frac{1}{27}$-$\frac{1}{28}$, P. 17, V. 1/5, A. $\frac{2}{7}$, C. 17, L. l. $\frac{1}{28}$, L. tr. 11/. Length of head 1/5, height of body 5 to $5\frac{1}{2}$ in the total length. *Eyes*—diameter $4\frac{1}{2}$ to 1/6 in the length of head, and 1 to $1\frac{1}{4}$ apart, &c.

Habitat.—The *O. argenteus* inhabits the seas of India to the Malay Archipelago and China, attaining upwards of $2\frac{1}{2}$ feet in length. The specimen figured is 8 inches long, and from Orissa.

FAMILY, XIII—XIPHIIDÆ, *Agass.*

Sword-fish.

Branchiostegals seven: pseudobranchiæ. Eyes lateral. Body compressed, the upper jaws (comprising ethmoid, vomer, and premaxillaries) produced into a long, sword-shaped process: cleft of mouth deep. Teeth absent or rudimentary. One or two dorsal fins, without any distinct spinous portion: ventrals when present, thoracic and rudimentary. Scales absent or in the form of rudimentary dermal productions. Air-vessel present. Pyloric appendages, when present, numerous.

The sword-fishes are well known to occasionally attack vessels in the Indian Ocean. "The ship, Royal George of about 500 tons, experienced the dreadful hurricane in the Bay of Bengal. So furious was the tempest that in addition to the loss of the main and mizzen masts the bowsprit was found broken off just outside the head of the stern, its diameter was 23 inches: and on looking at the bottom, the snout or horn of an unicorn fish was discovered projecting beyond the surface about 6 inches. A similar fact was remarked and the perforated piece of wood presented to the A. S. of Bengal, as noticed in the Proceedings of December 26th, 1833."* In the *Indian Daily News* (November, 1874), it is observed: "We have been shewn by the commander of the ship *Cashmere* a piece of the sword of a sword-fish which must have attacked the ship on her course from Bombay to Calcutta. Without any apparent cause the vessel began to make water, and all attempts to discover the cause were futile, until, after the removal of a large part of the cargo, the lightened ship rose in the water and the cause was discovered. The ship had been struck by a sword-fish, and the sword had pierced the copper and the timber of the ship, and penetrated some nine or ten inches beyond, breaking off by the copper, probably from the impossibility of withdrawing it. The sword not merely pierced the ship, but split the plank for a considerable distance on each side of the point of contact. The *Cashmere* is a new ship, and the timber perfectly sound." See also a paper by Dr. J. E. Gray, (An. and Mag. 1871, viii, pp. 338, 339), "On the injury inflicted on ships by the Broad-finned sword-fish of the Indian Ocean."

"The young of *Xiphias*, has a very long *Belone*-like beak; the supraorbital edge with conical prominences, no occipital spine, and with two short pointed teeth at the angle of the preopercle. The young of *Histiophorus* has the jaws comparatively shorter, the supraorbital edge very finely or not denticulated, a bony spine on each side of the occiput and at the angle of the preopercle."—Günther, Zool. Record, 1873, p. 110.

Habitat.—From the Mediterranean throughout the tropical seas.

SYNOPSIS OF GENERA.

1. *Histiophorus.* Ventral fins present. Seas between the tropics, also in the Mediterranean.
2. *Xiphias.* Destitute of ventral fins. Not as yet been found in the seas of India.

Genus, 1—HISTIOPHORUS, *Lacép.*

Notistium, Herm.: *Tetrapturus*, (Rafin.) Cuv. and Val.: *Zanclurus*, Swains.

Branchiostegals, seven: pseudobranchiæ. Body elongated. Upper jaw conical, much prolonged, and considerably longer than the lower. Minute teeth on the jaws and palatines: vomer edentulous. Two dorsal and two anal fins, the anterior of each of which is the longer: ventrals in the form of one, two, or even three rays. Scales absent, rudimentary dermal productions may be present. Air-vessel present. Pyloric appendages, when present, numerous.

The height of the dorsal fin, in comparison with that of the body, appears to be much more considerable in the young than in the adult.

SYNOPSIS OF SPECIES.

1. *Histiophorus gladius.* D. 40-50/7, A. 10/7. Dorsal fin much higher than the body. Dorsal fin covered with brilliant blue spots. Tropical seas or their vicinity.
2. *Histiophorus immaculatus.* D. 47/7, A. 10-11/7. Dorsal fin much higher than the body. Gray, dorsal blackish. Red Sea, and seas of India.
3. *Histiophorus brevirostris.* D. 35/7, A. 11/7. Dorsal fin not so high as the body. Gray, dorsal and pectoral tipped with black. Seas of India.

1. Histiophorus gladius.

Scomber gladius, Brouss. Mém. Acad. Sc. 1786, p. 454, pl. x; Bloch, t. 345.
Xiphias velifer, Bl. Schn. p. 93.
Istiophorus gladius, Lacép. iii, pp. 374, 375.
Xiphias ensis, Lacép. ii, p. 296.

* Proc. As. Soc. of Bengal, iv, p. 411.

Xiphias platypterus, Shaw, Zool. iv, p. 101.
Histiophorus Indicus, Cuv. Règ. Anim. Ill. Poiss. pl. 53, f. 1; Cuv. and Val. viii, p. 293, pl. 229; Jerdon, M. J. L. and Sc. 1851, p. 139.
Histiophorus Americanus, Cuv. and Val. viii, p. 303; Guichen, Cuba, p. 105.
Histiophorus gladius, Günther, Catal. ii, p. 513; Playfair, P. Z. S. 1867, p. 856.
Myl-meen, Tam. 'Peacock Fish.'

B. vii, D. 40-50/7, P. 15, V. 1-2, A. 10/7, C. 17, Vert. 14/10.

Length of entire head 1/4, height of body 1/7 to 1/8 of the total length. *Eyes*—a very abrupt ascent in the upper profile of the head. Snout produced and longer than the remainder of the head. *Teeth*—generic. *Fins*—dorsal fin commences on the nape and is much higher to twice as high as the body in its first portion, but becomes lower posteriorly, and considerably raised above its centre in young specimens. Pectoral equal to 1/6 or 1/7 of the total length. First anal commences under the last fourth of the first dorsal fin: the second, smaller, is below the second dorsal and similar to it. *Scales*—dermal productions lanceolate. Stomach elongated, intestines very short not exceeding the length of the fish. *Air-vessel*—in the last third of the abdominal cavity, consisting of two distinct lateral portions, each of which are subdivided internally into numerous cavities. *Cæcal-appendages*—absent (Ehrenberg found them innumerable). *Colours*—body bluish-gray, becoming dull white underneath. Dorsal fin of a bright Prussian-blue with darker spots: other fins dusky.

Habitat.—Tropical seas or their vicinity. I procured one 9 feet long at Madras, February 15, 1867, its stomach contained a full-sized *Scomber kanagurta*, two large *Hemiramphi* and numerous small fish. Common in the cold season off Madras, arriving about October and continuing until March.

2. Histiophorus immaculatus.

Rüpp. Proc. Zool. Soc. iii, p. 116, Trans. Zool. Soc. ii, p. 71, pl. xv, and N. W. Fische, p. 42, t. xi, f. 3; Günther, Catal. ii, p. 514.
Yeenaugolah, Tamil.

B. vii, D. 47/7, P. 16, V. 3, A. 10-11/7, C. 17.

Length of head (including the snout) 1/3, height of body 1/10 of the total length. *Eyes*—diameter about 1/3 in the postorbital portion of the head. A very slight ascent from the snout to the base of the first dorsal fin. The maxilla reaches to below the hind edge of the orbit. *Teeth*—generic. *Fins*—length of base of dorsal fin about 1/3 of the total length, eleventh to the fifteenth dorsal ray the longest, and at least three times higher than the body: the last few rays are low and reach to the base of the second dorsal fin. Ventral elongated. *Scales*—dermal productions lanceolate. *Lateral-line*—at first makes a very strong curve, but becomes straight above the hind extremity of the pectoral fin. *Colours*—gray, dorsal and ventral blackish.

Habitat.—Red Sea, and seas of India. A specimen in the Madras Museum is 5 feet 9 inches in length.

3. Histiophorus brevirostris, Plate XLVII, fig. 3.

? *Tetrapturus Indicus*, Cuv. and Val. viii, p. 286.
? *Histiophorus brevirostris*, Playfair, Fish. Zanz. pp. 53, 145. c. fig.
? *Histiophorus*, Knox, Trans. New Zealand Inst. ii, 1870, pp. 13-16, pl. 1.

B. vii, D. 35/7, P. 19, V. 2, A. 11/7, C. 17.

Length of head (including the snout) 3/10, of caudal lobes 1/5, entire length of upper jaw (including the snout) 2/9, height of body 1/8 of the total length. Greatest width of head equals 1/2 its depth. *Eyes*—diameter 1/3 in the postorbital portion of the head; a very slight ascent from the snout to the base of the first dorsal fin. Snout produced, its length, beyond the anterior extremity of the lower jaw, rather above 1/3 of that of the head. The maxilla reaches to rather behind the hind edge of the orbit. *Teeth*—generic. *Fins*—first dorsal highest anteriorly where it nearly equals that of the body, the posterior rays from about the fifth are not quite 1/3 of the height of the anterior: second dorsal with its last ray prolonged. Pectoral as long as the head behind the front nostril. Ventral reaches above 1/2 way to the anal and equals about 1/6 of the entire length of the fish. First anal fin commences under about the 25th dorsal ray, it is highest anteriorly where it equals 4/5 of that of the body above it, its lower edge is very concave: second anal below but rather shorter than the second dorsal, its last ray prolonged. Caudal deeply forked. *Scales*—dermal productions lanceolate. *Lateral-line*—forms rather a strong curve to above the middle of the pectoral fin where it becomes straight: two keels on either side of the free portion of the tail, the superior being more developed than the inferior one. *Colours*—grayish superiorly, becoming dull beneath, tip of first dorsal and end of pectoral edged with black.

Habitat.—? East coast of Africa, seas of India, perhaps New Zealand, the largest specimen I saw in the Madras Museum was 4 feet 4 inches in length. I have to thank Dr. Bidie for procuring me the interesting specimen from which the figure has been made, it also was taken at Madras and is a little over 4 feet in length.

H. brevirostris, Playfair, is stated to have D. 38/7, A. 12/7, and the last portion of the dorsal and the ventral fins are shown as much lower, the second dorsal and both anals rather higher than in the specimen described above; still it must not be overlooked that his fish was a more adult specimen (being 10 feet 4 inches in length), and in such the posterior portion of the first dorsal has a tendency to decrease in height with age. It is closely allied to *Tetrapterus Lessonii*, Canest. Arch. Zool. 1861, i, p. 259, pl. 7, from the Mediterranean.

Family, XIV—TRICHIURIDÆ, *Günther*.

Trichiurinæ, *Swainson*.

Branchiostegals seven to eight: pseudobranchiæ. Body elongated and compressed. Gill openings wide. Eyes lateral. Cleft of mouth deep. Teeth in jaws or palate, several being strong and conical. Dorsal and anal fins many rayed: there may be finlets behind the dorsal or anal fins: ventrals, when present, thoracic, but sometimes they are rudimentary: caudal absent or present. Scales when present rudimentary. No prominent papilla behind the vent. Air-vessel present. Pyloric appendages few or many.

Uses.—These fishes are held in various estimation in different places. In Beloochistan and where salt is cheap no one will touch them, but along the coasts of India where the salt tax has ruined the fish curers' trade, they are more esteemed, mostly because being thin or ribbon-shaped they can be dried without salting. Russell observed that in his time they were esteemed by the European soldiers. Jerdon states that "they afford very delicate eating when fresh though never brought to the table of Europeans."

Geographical distribution.—Tropical seas and extending into more temperate regions.

Cantor observes that neither *Trichiurus haumela* nor *T. savala* are "electrical, but both give at certain seasons, like many other fishes, a vivid phosphorescent light."

SYNOPSIS OF INDIVIDUAL GENUS.

Genus, 1—Trichiurus,* *Linn.*

Eachelyopus, Klein: *Lepturus* (Art.) Gill, and *Eupleurogrammus*, Gill.

Branchiostegals seven: pseudobranchiæ. Body very elongate, strongly compressed, ribbon-shaped, tapering to a finless point at the tail. Cleft of mouth deep. Teeth in jaws and palatines, those in the premaxillaries being arched and very strong, whilst the lateral ones are lancet-shaped. A single long dorsal fin extending the whole length of the back: ventrals, when present, in the form of a pair of scales: anal spines minute, sometimes concealed beneath the skin. Scales absent. Air-vessel present. Pyloric appendages numerous.

SYNOPSIS OF SPECIES.

1. *Trichiurus muticus*, D. 140-150. Ventral fins in the form of two rudimentary scales. Silvery.
2. *Trichiurus haumela*, D. 127-133. Anal fin in the form of minute spines. Eyes from $1\frac{2}{3}$ to $2\frac{1}{3}$ diameters from end of snout. Silvery, upper third of dorsal fin dark. Seas and estuaries of India to China.
3. *Trichiurus savala*, D. 112-120. Eyes $2\frac{1}{4}$ to $3\frac{1}{2}$ diameters from end of snout. Anal fin in the form of spines. Silvery. Seas and estuaries of India to China.

1. **Trichiurus muticus**, Plate XLVII, fig. 5.

Gray, Zool. Misc. p. 10; Griffith, Cuv. Anim. King. Fishes, p. 349, pl. 6, f. 2; Günther, Catal. ii, p. 348.
? *Trichiurus intermedius*, Gray, l. c. p. 10; Richards. Ich. China, p. 268.
? *Trichiurus medius*, Griffith, l. c. pl. 6, fig. 3.

B. vii, D. 140-150, P. 11.

Length of head $10\frac{1}{2}$ to $11\frac{1}{3}$, height of body 1/16 to 2/33 of the total length. *Eyes*—diameter $6\frac{1}{2}$ in length of head, 2 diameters from end of snout, and nearly 1 apart. The height of the head equals 1/2 its length. The lower jaw slightly produced beyond the upper: the maxilla reaches to below the middle of the eye: interorbital space with a keeled ridge along its centre. *Teeth*—about 20 sharp compressed ones laterally in the upper jaw, whilst anteriorly are two pairs of large, curved, and usually (but not invariably) slightly barbed fangs: there are two similar but much smaller ones above the symphysis of the lower jaw, and which are anterior to the snout when the mouth is closed; laterally there are about 15 or 16 teeth similar to those in the upper jaw but smaller. *Fins*—the dorsal fin commences above the hind edge of the preopercle, its first rays are short, their length being about equal to one diameter of the orbit, the longest rays are only about equal to 1/2 the height of the body: the rudimentary ones have been enumerated in the numbers given above. Pectoral 1/3 as long as the head. Ventrals indicated by two small rounded scale-like productions on the lower surface of the abdomen, about 3/4 the length of the head posterior to the opercle. Anal spine almost or entirely concealed in the skin. *Lateral-line*—almost straight and a little below the middle of the body especially in the last part of its course. *Colours*—burnished silver, fins yellowish.

Habitat.—Seas of India to China, it is very common in Orissa up to about 25 inches in length. The one figured is $20\frac{1}{2}$ inches long and from Orissa.

* *Nar-sah-rus*, Mugh.: *Savaryi*, Tel.

2. Trichiurus haumela.

Clupea haumela, Forsk. p. 72; Gmel. Linn. p. 1408.

Trichiurus lepturus, Lacep. ii, pl. 7, fig. 1; Russell, Fish. Vizag. i, p. 30, *Savala*, pl. 41; Ham. Buch. Fish. Ganges, pp. 31, 364.

Trichiurus haumela, Cuv. and Val. viii, p. 249; Rüpp. N. W. Fische, p. 41; Swainson, Fishes, ii, p. 254; Cantor, Catal. p. 113; Bleeker, Makr. p. 41; Jerdon, M. J. L. and Sc. 1851, p. 139; Günther, Catal. ii, p. 345; Day, Fishes of Malabar, p. 66; Kner. Novara Fische, p. 140; Klunz. Verh. z. b. Ges. Wien, 1871, p. 471.

Trichiurus Malabaricus, Day, Fish. Malabar, p. 65, pl. v.

Eupleurogrammus haumela, Bleeker, Bintang. 1868, p. 4.

Puttiah, Ooriah: *Savalu*, Tel.: *Sowa-ka-wahlah*, Tam.: *Pa-pa-dah*, Andam.

B. vii. D. 127-133, P. 11.

Length of head from 2/13 to 1/8, height of body from 1/12 to 1/15 of the total length. *Eye*—diameter $4\frac{3}{4}$ to $6\frac{1}{2}$ in length of head, $1\frac{1}{3}$ to $2\frac{1}{3}$ diameters from the end of snout, and 3/4 of a diameter apart: its height is at least 1/2 of that of the head where it is situated. Lower jaw considerably the longer, the posterior extremity of the maxilla reaches to below the middle of the orbit. Dorsal profile, between the end of the snout and the eye, rather concave. Height of head equals 2/5 of its length. *Teeth*—upwards of 10 to 12 sharp compressed ones laterally in either side of upper jaw, usually increasing in size posteriorly, whilst anteriorly in the premaxillaries are two pairs of large curved and barbed canines, there are two similar but smaller teeth above the symphysis* of the lower jaw (and in advance of the end of the snout when the mouth is closed), most distinct in the adult, and 8 lateral ones also of less size than those in the upper jaw, and some of which are occasionally barbed. Teeth also in the palatines. *Fins*—the first few dorsal rays are of less height than those near the middle of the fin which about equal that of the body. Pectoral nearly or quite as long as the height of the head. Behind the anus the anal fin is seen in the form of short spines, often entirely concealed or else blunted at their external extremities: in one specimen I count 74, in another 80. *Lateral-line*—gradually descends until above the commencement of the anal fin, where it is in the lower third of the body. *Colours*—grayish along the back, becoming silvery on the sides and beneath: a dark mark along the edge of the preorbital. Fins of a pale yellow, the upper half of the dorsal dark, due to numerous fine black dots.

Habitat.—East coast of Africa, seas and estuaries of India, and the Malay Archipelago to China, attaining at least 3 feet in length. It is extremely voracious, devouring its own species, as well as other kinds of fish and crustacea. It is much more common than *T. savala*.

3. Trichiurus savala, Plate XLVII, fig. 4.

Cuv. and Val. viii, p. 251, pl. 224; Cantor, Ann. and Mag. ix, p. 15, and Catal. p. 115; Bleeker, Makr. p. 41; Jerdon, M. J. L. and Sc. 1851, p. 139; Günther, Catal. ii, p. 347; Day, Fishes of Malabar, p. 67.

Trichiurus armatus, Gray, Zool. Misc. p. 9, and Ill. Ind. Zool. pl. 93, f. 1; Richards. Ich. China, p. 268; Griffith, in Cuv. Anim. Kingdom, Fishes, p. 340, pl. 6, f. 1.

Eupleurogrammus savala, Bleeker, Bintang. 1868, p. 14.

B. vii, D. 112-120, P. 11.

Length of head $7\frac{1}{2}$, height of body 1/16 of the total length. *Eye*—diameter 2/13 to 1/7 of length of head, $2\frac{1}{4}$ to $2\frac{1}{2}$ in the length of snout, and 1 apart; its height is about 1/3 of that of the head where it is situated. The height of the head equals $2\frac{1}{4}$ to $2\frac{1}{2}$ in its length. The lower jaw considerably prolonged beyond the upper: the maxilla reaches to below the middle of the eye. Interorbital space nearly flat: dorsal profile between upper surface of eyes and end of snout slightly concave. The distance from the eye to the upper jaw nearly equals the diameter of the orbit. *Teeth*—about 8 sharp and compressed ones laterally in the upper jaw, whilst anteriorly are two or three pairs of large, curved, and barbed fangs: there are two similar and rather smaller ones above the symphysis of the lower jaw, and which are anterior to the snout when the mouth is closed: laterally there are about 9 similar to those in the upper jaw but smaller. *Fins*—the dorsal fin commences over the hind edge of the preopercle, its first rays are short, being about equal to 1 diameter of the orbit, the longest rays are about equal to the height of the body. Pectoral 4/11 of the length of the head. No rudiment of ventral fins. Anal in the form of about 76 to 82 free spines which may be concealed in the skin but are generally distinct, especially the first, which is twice as long as seen in *T. haumela*. *Lateral-line*—passes downwards to the lower third of the side. *Colours*—silvery, fins yellowish white.

Habitat.—Seas and estuaries of India, the Malay Archipelago, and China, attaining at least 16 inches in length. The specimen figured is 12 inches long, and from Bombay, it has 113 dorsal rays.

* In a specimen from Orissa, nearly 19 inches long, only one such tooth exists, it is however upwards of 1/2 the diameter of the eye in length and barbed posteriorly.

FAMILY, XV—ACANTHURIDÆ, (pt.) *Richards.*

Acanthurinæ, pt. Swains.: *Acanthuroidei*, Bleeker: *Acronuridæ*, Günther.

Branchiostegals from four to seven: pseudobranchiæ. Body oblong or elevated and compressed. Eyes of moderate size and lateral. Cleft of mouth very slight. Teeth in both jaws in a single compressed row, often lobate or serrated, and tapering incisors may be present. Palate edentulous. A single dorsal fin with fewer spines than rays: anal with two or three spines: ventrals thoracic. Scales minute. Lateral line complete and continuous. The side of the free portion of the tail usually armed with one or more bony plates or spines, these are small or absent in the immature, developing with age. Air-vessel present, forked posteriorly. Pyloric appendages few.

SYNOPSIS OF GENERA.

1. *Acanthurus.* An erectile spine on either side of the free portion of the tail: ventral usually with one spine and five rays. Scales small or even rudimentary. Red Sea, East coast of Africa, through the seas of India, and the tropics.

2. *Naseus.* One to three non-erectile spines on either side of the free portion of the tail: ventral with one spine and three rays. Scales minute or rudimentary. From the East coast of Africa through the seas of India to Polynesia.

Genus, 1—ACANTHURUS,* *(Forsk.) Bl.*

Opisotomus, Comm.: *Harpurus*, Forster: *Acronurus*, Cuv. (young): *Keris*,† pt., Cuv. (? young): *Ctenodon* and *Zebrasoma*, Swains.: *Scopas*, Kner: *Rhombotides*, Bleeker.

Branchiostegals five: pseudobranchiæ well developed. Body and head elevated and strongly compressed. Eyes high up. Teeth in a single row with lobate or serrated edges. A single dorsal fin with fewer spines than rays: anal with three spines: ventral usually with one spine and five rays. Scales small or minute, cycloid or ctenoid, sometimes spinate. A moveable spine exists in a groove on the side of the free portion of the tail, just below the lateral-line. Air-vessel large, posteriorly forked. Pyloric appendages few (5-7).

The caudal fin generally becomes more lobed or emarginate in the adults than it is in the young. In some instances (see *A. hepatus*, p. 206) the rays in the ventral fin are decreased in number and rather altered in character.

The young of this genus have no scales, but the skin is vertically striated, sometimes with small rough points. In a specimen (*Acanthurus melanurus*, Cuv. and Val.) from Malabar, 1½ inches in length, the most distinct appearance of scales is to be seen along the bases of the dorsal and anal fins. There are two parallel raised serrated ridges from the snout to opposite the nostril, whilst the anterior edge of the second spine of the dorsal fin is serrated. In a second specimen, although slightly smaller, little sharp points or rudimentary scales are to be seen, or appearing as if each ridge of the skin were ctenoid in places. In a specimen 2¾ inches in length, the serrations adverted to have disappeared and rudimentary scales are visible all over the body.

SYNOPSIS OF SPECIES.

A. Broad teeth fixed in the jaws: 8 or 9 dorsal spines: 5 ventral rays. *(Rhombotides.)*

1. *Acanthurus lineatus.* D. [illegible]. A. [illegible]. Upper two-thirds of body canary yellow, which, as well as the head, have 9 or 10 oblique blue bands. A semilunar blue band in the centre of the caudal. Seas of India to the Malay Archipelago.

2. *Acanthurus leucosternon.* D. [illegible]. A. [illegible]. Blue, head dark brown, chest white as is also a ring round the lower part of the mouth. A black band along base and either side of caudal fin, a second in its last fourth. East coast of Africa, seas of India to the Malay Archipelago.

3. *Acanthurus annulineatus.* D. [illegible]. A. [illegible]. Bluish, with about 12 horizontal yellow bands, dorsal and anal fins likewise banded. Coromandel coast of India.

4. *Acanthurus triostegus.* D. [illegible]. A. [illegible]. Greenish, with a black ocular band, four more down the body and an interrupted one across the free portion of the tail.

5. *Acanthurus Tennentii.* D. [illegible], A. [illegible]. Brown, white hind edge to the caudal fin, and ? a dark ring on the shoulder. Ceylon.

6. *Acanthurus matoides.* D. [illegible], A. [illegible]. Brown, sometimes with blue lines on the body and fins, and a white ring at the base of the caudal fin. Red Sea, seas of India to the Malay Archipelago and beyond.

* *Kehli-meen*, Tam.

† The Genus *Keris*, C.V. appears to consist of the young of *Acanthurus*, or *Naseus*, or both.

7. *Acanthurus mata.* D. $\frac{9}{24-27}$, A. $\frac{3}{23-25}$. Brown, with black fins. Red Sea, seas of India to the Malay Archipelago.

8. *Acanthurus Celebicus.* D. $\frac{9}{26-27}$, A. $\frac{3}{24}$. L. l. 80. Brown, fins dark. Madras, Malay Archipelago.

9. *Acanthurus melanurus.* D. $\frac{9}{25-26}$, A. $\frac{3}{25}$. Scales rudimentary or absent. Black band over occiput, another across free portion of the tail. Seas of India to the Malay Archipelago.

B. Broad teeth fixed in the jaws: 8 or 9 dorsal spines: ventrals not fully developed.

10. *Acanthurus hepatus.* D. $\frac{9}{19-20}$, V. 1/2, A. $\frac{3}{19}$. Slatey gray, covered by a deep brown band in the upper half of its back, leaving an oval blotch of ground colour above the pectoral fin. Fins gray, spines and rays orange, caudal yellow. Seas of India to New Guinea.

C. Setiform moveable teeth dilated at their extremities: 8 or 9 dorsal spines: 5 ventral rays. *(Ctenodon.)*

11. *Acanthurus strigosus.* D. $\frac{8}{27-30}$, A. $\frac{3}{24-27}$. Teeth setiform with dilated extremities. Body brown lineated with bluish lines, red spots on the head. Red Sea, East coast of Africa, seas of India to the Malay Archipelago and beyond.

D. Broad teeth fixed in the jaws: 1 to 4 dorsal spines: 5 ventral rays. *(Harpurus.)*

12. *Acanthurus xanthurus.* D. $\frac{4}{26-28}$, A. $\frac{3}{26-27}$. Scales rudimentary, rough. Blackish, caudal yellow. Red Sea, East coast of Africa and Ceylon.

13. *Acanthurus velifer.* D. $\frac{4}{28-30}$, A. $\frac{3}{22-23}$. Scales rudimentary. Dorsal and anal fins much elevated. Brown, banded with narrow blue lines. Red Sea, East coast of Africa to the Malay Archipelago and beyond.

A. Broad teeth fixed in the jaws: 8 or 9 dorsal spines: 5 ventral rays. *(Rhombotides.)*

1. Acanthurus lineatus.

Chætodon lineatus, Linn. Nat. Hist. i, p. 1246.

Acanthurus lineatus, Bl. Schn. p. 214, t. xlix; Lacép. iv, pp. 547, 549; Cuv. and Val. x, p. 223; Bleeker, Sumatra, ii, p. 263; Günther, Catal. iii, p. 333; Kner, Novara Fische, p. 210.

Ctenodon lineatus, Swainson, Fishes, ii, p. 256.

Acanthurus vittatus, Benn. Fish. Ceylon, p. 2, pl. ii.

Rhombotides lineatus, Bleeker, Arou, 1873, p. 3.

B. v, D. $\frac{9}{27-28}$, P. 15, V. 1/5, A. $\frac{3}{25}$, C. 17.

Length of head $5\frac{1}{4}$ to $5\frac{1}{2}$, of caudal 2/7, height of body 1/3 of the total length. *Eyes*—diameter 2/9 of length of head, 3 to $3\frac{1}{2}$ diameters from end of snout, and $1\frac{1}{2}$ apart. Profile from dorsal fin to snout obtuse. The maxilla reaches 1/3 of the distance to below the orbit. *Teeth*—six or seven lobate incisors on either side of the upper jaw. *Fins*—dorsal spines rather weak and a little shorter than the rays, interspinous membrane scarcely notched. Pectoral as long as or slightly longer than the head. Caudal lobed, the upper the longer. *Scales*—about eight rows between the lateral-line and the base of the last dorsal spine. Lancet-shaped spine with a posterior process. Least depth of the free portion of the tail equal to 1/2 the length of the head. *Colours*—head and upper two-thirds of body canary yellow, traversed by nine or ten more or less oblique blue bands going from the head to the back and caudal fin: lower third of body reddish-gray. Two or three blue bands pass down the summit of the head and the anterior edge of the eye towards the snout, whilst about seven more pass across the cheeks to the bands on the body. Other blue bands pass upwards and backwards from the hind edge of the eye to the bands on the body. Dorsal and anal fins dark with a gray margin. Pectoral having its upper ray blue, and just internal to it a white line ascending 1/2 way up the ray: an arched white band on lower half of pectoral fin on its inferior side. Ventral with its outer ray blue, its inner ones red. Caudal with a semilunar blue band in its centre and a blue posterior edge. Bennett observes of Ceylon examples that amongst six or seven specimens no two were alike in the arrangement of the blue and yellow streaks near the caudal fin.

Habitat.—Seas of India to the Malay Archipelago: common at the Andamans in December and January up to 10 inches in length. Bennett says: "the *Seeryah (Acanthurus lineatus)* is an extremely scarce fish on the southern coast of Ceylon: inhabits rocky situations, and is not in request but for the gratification of the naturalist. It seldom exceeds 16 or 17 inches in length." (p. 2.)

2. Acanthurus leucosternon.

Benn. Proc. Zool. Soc. 1832, p. 183; Bleeker, Batoe, iii, p. 237; Günther, Catal. iii, p. 340.

Acanthurus Delisiana, Cuv. and Val. x, p. 193; Guér. Icon. Poiss. pl. xxxv, fig. 2; Griffith, in Cuv. Anim. Kingdom, Fishes, pl. xxxiii, fig. 2.

B. v, D. $\frac{9}{29-30}$, P. 16, V. 1/5, A. $\frac{3}{24-25}$, C. 17.

Length of head $4\frac{2}{3}$, of caudal $5\frac{1}{2}$, height of body about 2/5 of the total length. *Eyes*—diameter 2/7 of length of head, $2\frac{2}{3}$ diameters from end of snout, and $1\frac{1}{4}$ apart. Profile from the upper edge of the eye to the snout rather concave. *Teeth*—five truncated and lobate ones on either side of the upper jaw, and six in the lower. *Fins*—last dorsal spine as high as the rays, and equal to about 4/13 of the height of the body, the posterior extremity of the soft dorsal and anal fins rather angular. Pectoral as long as the head. Anal as high as the soft dorsal: caudal emarginate. *Scales*—very small, rough and rudimentary on head and chest. Lancet-shaped spine with a posterior process. Least depth of free portion of the tail equals 3/7 of the length of the head. *Colours*—blue, head dark brown or black, chest white, as is also a ring on the lower part of the mouth, ascending to its angle. A broad bluish band passes down the shoulder to the axilla, which last has a triangular brown patch. A narrow crescentic black band across the base of the caudal, and continued along the upper and lower edges of the fin, a second wide one along the last fourth of the fin, and having a white outer border. Other fins stained gray at their edges.

Habitat.—East coast of Africa, Mauritius, Ceylon, to the Malay Archipelago. The above description is taken from the type specimen sent by Dr. Sibbald to the British Museum.

3. Acanthurus aurolineatus, Plate XLVIII, fig. 3.

B. v, D. $\frac{9}{27}$, P. 18, V. 1/5, A. $\frac{3}{25}$, C. 17.

Length of head $4\frac{1}{4}$, of caudal $5\frac{1}{2}$, height of body 2/5 of the total length. *Eyes*—high up, diameter 1/3 of length of head, $1\frac{1}{2}$ diameters from end of snout, and 1 apart. Preopercle entire. Upper profile of head rather convex. *Teeth*—on either side eight lobate ones in the upper, and eight or nine in the lower jaw. *Fins*—last dorsal spine 2/5 of the height of the body and of about the same length as the rays, last portion of the fin and of the anal rather angular, interspinous membrane very slightly emarginate. Pectoral about as long as the head; third anal spine rather above half the length of the head. Caudal emarginate. *Scales*—on head minute, very small on the body, about twenty rows between the lateral-line and base of the last dorsal spine. Lancet-shaped spine with a posterior process. Least depth of the free portion of the tail equal to 1 diameter of the orbit. *Colours*—a general yellowish tinge, with yellow horizontal lines along the body about 1/2 the width of the ground colour, which is bluish. A narrow lightish band over the base of the caudal. Dorsal and anal fins bluish, with several longitudinal yellow bands as seen on the body.

The specimen, figured life-size, is from the collection of Sir W. Elliot, K.C.S.I., and was captured at Waltair some years since.

Habitat.—Coromandel coast of India.

4. Acanthurus triostegus, Plate XLVIII, fig. 2.

Chætodon triostegus, Linn. Sys. i, p. 463.

Acanthurus triostegus, Bl. Schn. p. 215; Cuv. and Val. x, p. 197; Swainson, Fishes, ii, p. 255; Bleeker, Teuth. p. 13; Jenyns, Voy. Beagle, Fishes, p. 75; Jerdon, M. J. L. and Sc. 1851, p. 138; Günther, Catal. iii, p. 327.

Chætodon meotah, Russell, Fish. Vizag. i, p. 66, pl. 84.

Harpurus fasciatus, Forst. Desc. Anim. ed. Licht. p. 216.

Chætodon zebra, Lacép. iii, pl. 25, f. 3.

Acanthurus zebra, Lacép. iv, p. 546, pl. vi, f. 3.

Chætodon couagga, Lacép. iv, p. 727.

Acanthurus hirudo, Benn. Fish. Ceylon, p. 11, pl. xi.

Teuthis Australis, Gray in King's Survey Australia, ii, p. 435.

Acanthurus subarmatus, Benn. Whaling Voy. ii, p. 278.

Rhombotides triostegus, Bleeker, Solor, 1868, p. 2.

Mootah, Tel.: *Kuru-pamoorah*, Cing.

B. v, D. $\frac{9}{22-23}$, P. 15, V. 1/5, A. $\frac{3}{21-22}$, C. 17.

Length of head $3\frac{3}{4}$ to 1/4, of caudal 1/5, height of body $2\frac{1}{4}$ to $2\frac{2}{3}$ in the total length. *Eyes*—diameter 2/7 of length of head, 2 to $2\frac{1}{2}$ diameters from end of snout, and 1 to $1\frac{1}{4}$ apart. Profile from above the orbit to the snout rather concave. *Teeth*—eight lobate incisors on either side of the upper jaw, and nine or ten on either side of the lower. *Fins*—dorsal spines moderately strong, the last 1/5 higher than the longest ray, and equal to $3\frac{2}{3}$ or 1/4 of the height of the body. Pectoral 4/5 as long as the head. Caudal lunated. *Scales*—rudimentary and cycloid on the head, small and ctenoid on the body: about twenty rows between the lateral-line and the last dorsal spine. Lancet-shaped spine with a sharp posterior process. Least depth of free portion of the tail equal to about $1\frac{1}{2}$ diameters of the orbit. *Colours*—greenish, with a brownish tinge along the back. One vertical dark band along the snout, a second through the orbit, four down the body, and one over the base of the caudal fin, the last being in the form of two rounded blotches, one above, the other below the lateral-line. Fins stained darkish.

Habitat.—Seas of India, to the Malay Archipelago and beyond. The specimen figured is from the Andaman islands, where it is common. As Jerdon observes this species is rare at Madras.

5. Acanthurus Tennentii.

Günther, Catal. iii, p. 337.

B. v, D. $\frac{9}{24}$, P 17, V. 1/5, A. $\frac{3}{23}$, C. 17.

Length of head 2/9, of caudal 2/11, height of body 2/5 of the total length. *Eyes*—diameter 2/7 of length of head, $2\frac{1}{2}$ diameters from the end of snout. Nostrils 2/3 the length of the head from the end of the snout. *Teeth*—eight lobate incisors on either side of the upper, and eight on either side of the lower jaw.

Fins—last dorsal spine nearly 1/3 the height of the body, and about equal to the rays: posterior extremity of the soft dorsal and anal rather angular. Pectoral as long as the head. Caudal emarginate. *Scales*—about fourteen rows between the lateral-line and the base of the last dorsal spine. A posterior process to the lancet-shaped spine. *Colours*—brown, caudal with a broad white posterior edge, having a dark base behind it. The skin in the British Museum has a dark ring on the shoulder, considered normal, but which appears very like an ink mark: the pectoral seems to have been tinged with yellow in its posterior half on the lower side.

Habitat.—An immature specimen from Ceylon in the British Museum.

6. Acanthurus matoides.

Chætodon nigrofuscus, Forsk. p. 64.
? *Chætodon nigricans*, Gmel. Linn. p. 1245.
Acanthurus nigricans, Bl. Schn. p. 211 (pt.).
? *Acanthurus rasi*, Cuv. and Val. x, p. 203.
Acanthurus matoides, Cuv. and Val. x, p. 204; Bleeker, Teuth. p. 12; Günther, Catal. iii, p. 330; Day. Fish. Malabar, p. 126; ? Kner, Novara Fische, p. 210; Playfair, P. Z. Soc. 1867, p. 858; Klunz. Verh. z. b. Ges. Wien, 1871, p. 508.
Acanthurus annularis, Cuv. and Val. x, p. 209 (with a whitish basal caudal band).
Acanthurus nigrofuscus, Cuv. and Val. x, p. 214 (not Günther, Catal.).
Acanthurus xanthopterus, Cantor, Catal. p. 206, pl. iv.
Rhombotides matoides, Bleeker, Sanger, 1868, p. 1.

B. v, D. $\frac{9}{24-27}$, P. 17, V. 1/5, A. $\frac{3}{23-25}$, C. 16, Vert. 9/13.

Length of head 4½ to 1/5, of caudal 4½, height of body 2½ in the total length. *Eyes*—diameter 3½ to 3¾ in the length of head, 2¼ diameters from end of snout, and 1 apart. Profile from snout to dorsal fin much elevated, and having a slight depression above the orbits. The distance from the anterior nostril to the front edge of the upper jaw equals about 2/3 of the length of the head: from the eye to the angle of the mouth 2/3 to 3/5 of the length of the head. Opercle striated. *Teeth*—eight or nine lobate or serrated incisors on either side of the upper jaw, and the same in the lower. *Fins*—dorsal spines of moderate strength, the last not quite so high as the first few rays, and equal to nearly 1/3 the height of the body: the interspinous membrane scarcely emarginate: the posterior extremity of the fin and also of the anal angularly rounded: pectoral nearly as long as the head. Ventral pointed, 4/5 as long as the pectoral. Third anal spine equals 2 diameters of the orbit in length: rays not quite so long as those of the dorsal. Caudal emarginate: in the adult as upwards of a foot in length its outer rays become elongated causing the fin to be deeply lunated in its last half. *Scales*—rudimentary and cycloid on head and over shoulders, chest, and in a band along the base of the dorsal fin: ctenoid, and in irregular rows on the body, about 18 to 20 rows between the lateral-line and base of the last dorsal spine. Lancet-shaped spine with a posterior process. Free portion of the tail at its lowest part equal to 1/2 the length of the head. *Colours*—brown, sometimes with narrow light bands across the cheeks and along the body; lips black: dorsal and anal fins with several longitudinal bands: caudal with a white band across its base, sometimes the rest of the fin is light-coloured with a crescentic dark mark at its posterior extremity. Outer half of pectoral yellowish-green.

Habitat.—Red Sea, seas of India to the Malay Archipelago and beyond. It is reputed to attain to 3 feet in length at Madras. The largest obtained by me was 22½ inches long. It is said to be good eating but not brought to the tables of Europeans.

7. Acanthurus mata, Plate XLVIII, fig. 1.

Chætodon nigrofuscus ?, Russell, i, p. 64, and *Mata*, pl. 82 (not *C. nigrofuscus*, Forsk.).
Acanthurus mata, Cuv. and Val. x, p. 202; Bleeker, Java, ii, p. 432.
Acanthurus rasi, Jerdon, M. J. L. and Sc. 1851, p. 138 (not Cuv. and Val.).
Acanthurus Bleekeri, Günther, Catal. iii, p. 331; Klunz. Verh. z. b. Ges. Wien, 1871, p. 509.
Koli, Tam.

B. v, D. $\frac{9}{24-27}$, P. 17, V. 1/5, A. $\frac{3}{23-25}$, C. 16.

Length of head 4⅔, of caudal 4⅗, height of body 2⅔ in the total length. *Eyes*—diameter 3¼ in length of head, 2½ diameters from end of snout, and 1½ apart. Profile from snout to dorsal fin nearly straight. The distance from the anterior nostril to the front edge of the upper jaw equals not quite 1/2 the length of the head, whilst it is about the same distance from the lower edge of the eye to the angle of the mouth. Opercle strongly striated, more strongly so and with a larger number of elevations than in *A. matoides*. *Teeth*—eight or nine incisors in the upper jaw serrated along 3/4 of their external edge, and the same in the lower. *Fins*—dorsal spines increase in length to the last which is nearly or as high as the anterior rays and equals 1/3 in that of the body: the interspinous membrane scarcely emarginate; the posterior portion of the fin and also of the anal angularly rounded. Pectoral as long as the head. Third anal spine equal to about 1⅓ diameters of the orbit and the rays similar to those of the soft dorsal. Caudal emarginate, upper lobe the longer. *Scales*—rudimentary on head and over the nape, becoming ctenoid and in angular rows on the body, there appear to be about 150 to 160 rows descending to the lateral-line: and about 16 or 18 rows between the lateral-line and base of the last dorsal spine. Lancet-shaped spine on the side of the free portion of the tail with a posterior process. *Colours*—blackish-brown: lips and fins black.

Variety (? *A. Dussumieri*, C. and V. x, p. 201) with numerous rather undulating narrow brown bands, the intermediate colour being bluish. Dorsal and anal fins with three or four longitudinal bands: a light band across the base of the caudal.

A. mata, has been separated from *A. matoides* owing to the upper profile of its snout not being so convex, and to the distance of its nostril from the edge of the upper jaw equalling 1/2 (instead of 2/3) the length of the head. The affinities are so great that probably they might with justice be considered varieties.

Habitat.—Red Sea, seas of India to the Malay Archipelago. The specimen figured ($7\frac{1}{4}$ inches in length) was taken at Madras, it is said to attain 18 inches in length.

8. Acanthurus Celebicus.

Bleeker, Celebes, iii, p. 761; Günther, Catal. iii, p. 339; Kner, Novara Fische, p. 211.

? *Acanthurus fuscus*, Steind. Verh. z. b. Ges. Wien, 1861, p. 176, t. v.; Günther, Catal. iii, p. 339 (? adult).

B. v, D. $\frac{9}{24-26}$, P. 16, V. 1/5, A. $\frac{3}{23}$, C. 16.

Length of head $4\frac{1}{4}$, of caudal $3\frac{1}{4}$, height of body nearly 1/3 in the total length. *Eyes*—diameter about $3\frac{1}{4}$ in the length of head. Profile of snout concave. *Teeth*—about 16 lobate incisors in the upper and 20 in the lower jaw. *Fins*—last dorsal spine the longest: dorsal and anal rays of about the same height and equal to about $2\frac{1}{2}$ in that of the body, the posterior extremity of both fins obtusely rounded. Ventral and caudal lobes pointed. *Scales*—small, ctenoid, but much larger than in *A. matoides* or *A. mata*, there being about 80 rows. *Colours*—brownish, darkest about the head, lips black, a white ring round the mouth. Dorsal, anal, and ventral fins blackish brown: outer half of pectoral yellowish. Caudal blackish, posteriorly yellowish.

Habitat.—Malay Archipelago. Kner states that he received a single specimen from Madras.

9. Acanthurus melanurus.

Cuv. and Val. x, p. 240; Bleeker, Amb. and Ceram, p. 271.

Acronurus melanurus, Günther, Catal. iii, p. 346.

B. v, D. $\frac{9}{25-26}$, P. 15, V. 1/5, A. $\frac{3}{24}$, C. 16.

Length of head 2/7, of caudal 1/5, height of body 1/2 the total length or 2/3 of that of the oval portion. *Eyes*—diameter $2\frac{1}{2}$ in the length of head, 1 diameter from end of snout (see p. 202). *Fins*—second dorsal spine longest and strongest, being nearly equal to 1 diameter of the orbit. Caudal cut square or slightly emarginate. *Scales*—rudimentary or absent. *Colours*—brownish-white with a black band over the occiput and another over the free portion of the tail. From the whole of the space below the eye and opercle a silvery band passes downwards to the chest. One specimen has a dark mark on the shoulder.

As the longest specimen I could obtain is only $1\frac{1}{2}$ inches in length it appears reasonable to believe that this may be the fry of some known form as *A. matoides*, of which I have small specimens, giving the following:

1. *Acanthurus melanurus*, $1\frac{1}{2}$ inches long: height of body 1/2 of the total length.
2. *Acanthurus melanurus*, $1\frac{1}{2}$ " : " $2\frac{1}{2}$ " "
3. *Acanthurus matoides*, $2\frac{1}{2}$ " : " $2\frac{1}{4}$ " "
4. *Acanthurus matoides*, $2\frac{3}{4}$ " : " $2\frac{1}{3}$ " "

In Cuv. and Val. this species is said to come from Pondicherry and to be obtained up to 2 inches in length. It is also found in the Malay Archipelago.

Acanthurus melas, Cuv. and Val. x, p. 241, appears to be the same, but having the colours of *A. matoides*.

Habitat.—Seas of India to the Malay Archipelago.

B. Broad teeth fixed in the jaws: 8 or 9 dorsal spines: ventrals not fully developed.

10. Acanthurus hepatus.

Teuthis hepatus, Linn. Syst. Nat. i, p. 507; Gmel. Linn. i, p. 1362.

Acanthurus hepatus, Bl. Schn. p. 211; Cuv. and Val. x, p. 183, pl. 288; Bleeker, Floris, p. 325; Günther, Catal. iii, p. 341.

Acanthurus theuthis, Lacép. iv, pp. 549, 553.

B. v, D. $\frac{9}{19-20}$, P. 15, V. 1/2, A. $\frac{3}{18}$, C. 17.

Length of head 2/9, of caudal 1/6, height of body $2\frac{3}{4}$ in the total length. *Eyes*—diameter 1/5 of length of head, $3\frac{1}{4}$ diameters from end of snout, and 2 apart. Upper profile of head rather convex. Preopercle entire. *Teeth*—six lobate incisors on either side of both the upper and lower jaws. *Fins*—last dorsal spine higher than the first ray, beyond which the height of the rays gradually diminishes, the end of the fin being rather angular; the interspinous membrane scarcely emarginate. Pectoral 4/5 the length of the head. Ventral spine strong, nearly 1/2 as long as the head, its inner ray also spinate at its commencement, but having a bifurcated rayed extremity. Caudal emarginate, its outer rays being prolonged. *Scales*—the dermal productions are stellate and rough, about 12 rows exist between the lateral-line and the base of the last dorsal spine; none on the fins. Lancet-shaped spine on side of tail, without any exposed posterior process. *Colours*—slatey-gray along the back, becoming dashed with brownish-gray along the abdomen. A deep brown band ascends from the posterior-superior angle of the eye, and passing backwards gradually widens until below the fifth or sixth dorsal spine it extends over the upper half of the back, leaving an oval spot of ground colour as long as the head, uncovered in the middle of the first part of its course. Just before reaching the lancet-shaped process it divides into two portions, which rapidly narrow, and pass along either side of the lobes of the tail. Dorsal spines orange-brown, the membrane light slate colour, having the upper edge of the fin stained with black. Pectoral blackish-gray, with a large yellow oval spot on its last fourth. Anal similar to dorsal. Caudal canary-yellow, which colour extends on to the free portion of the tail, as far as the lancet-shaped spine.

Habitat.—Seas of India to New Guinea.

C. Setiform moveable teeth, dilated at their extremities. (*Ctenodon.*)

11. Acanthurus strigosus, Plate XLVII, fig. 2.

Acanthurus strigosus, Bennett, Zool. Journal, Fasc. xiii, p. 41; Cuv. and Val. x, p. 243; Günther, Catal. iii, p. 342; Bleeker, Nat. Tyds. Ned. Ind. iv, p. 264, and vi, p. 102; Kner, Novara Fische, p. 211.

Acanthurus ctenodon, Cuv. and Val. x, p. 241, pl. 289; Günther, Catal. iii, p. 342; Bleeker, Solor, 1858, p. 2; Klunz. Verh. z. b. Ges. Wien, 1871, p. 509.

B. v, D. [illegible], P. 17, V. 1/5, A. [illegible], C. 17, L. l. ca. 120.

Length of head 4½ to 4⅔, of caudal 1/4 to 4½, height of body 2⅔ in the total length. *Eyes*—high up, diameter 1/4 of length of head, nearly 2½ diameters from end of snout, and 1½ apart. Profile of snout very gibbous. Mouth compressed so as to become angular. *Teeth*—setiform, moveable, having their outer third dilated and spoon-shaped, with three deep clefts causing them to appear to be laterally serrated: about twenty-one in the upper and twenty in the lower jaw. *Fins*—last dorsal spine 1/5 shorter than the longest ray, and 1/2 the length of the head; soft portions of the dorsal and anal fins rather angular posteriorly. Pectoral nearly as long as the head. Caudal deeply lunated. *Scales*—rounded, small and cycloid on the head, ctenoid on the body, about nine rows between the lateral-line and the base of the last dorsal spine. Lancet-shaped spine with a sharp posterior process. Free portion of the tail in its least depth equal to 2½ in the length of the head. *Colours*—body horizontally lineated with narrow bluish lines on a yellow ground colour, the latter being somewhat the wider: numerous dull red spots about the head, more especially around the eyes. Dorsal and anal fins also lineated, and a light vertical band on the middle of the caudal.

Although the typical specimens of *A. strigosus* have more teeth in the lower jaw (about 25 on either side) than in *A. ctenodon*, and one or two more rows of scales between the lateral-line and base of the last dorsal spine, whilst the horizontal bands are more distinct, they appear to be otherwise the same, and only varieties of one species.

Habitat.—Red Sea, East coast of Africa, seas of India to the Malay Archipelago, and beyond: the specimen figured was captured at the Andaman islands.

D. Broad teeth fixed in the jaws, 1 to 4 dorsal spines: 5 ventral rays. (*Harpurus.*)

12. Acanthurus xanthurus.

Blyth, Fauna Ceylon, Appendix, p. 50; Günther, Catal. iii, p. 343; Playfair, Fish. Zanzibar, p. 57, pl. viii, f. 4; Klunz. Verh. z. b. Ges. Wien, 1871, p. 504.

B. v, D. [illegible], P. 15, V. 1/5, A. [illegible], C. 17.

Length of head 2/9, of pectoral 1/5, height of body 2/5 of the total length. *Eyes*—diameter 1/4 of head, 2½ diameters from end of snout, and 1½ apart. *Teeth*—in a single row, 10 lobate incisors on either side of the upper jaw. *Fins*—last dorsal spine longest, almost equalling the length of the longest ray, and 2/5 of the height of body: dorsal rays nearly half as high as the body, the posterior end of it and of the anal rather angular; third anal spine the longest and strongest: caudal slightly emarginate. *Scales*—on the head very rough, somewhat similar to what is seen in *Balistes*, those on the body are likewise rough, but in a less degree: some of these roughnesses are continued on to the rays of the dorsal and anal fins, and a few between the spines and rays of the former, but more at the base only of the anal fin. No posterior process to the lancet-shaped spine, but two or three elevations near its base. *Colours*—blackish, caudal canary-yellow, head and shoulders reticulated with gray: end of the pectoral stained with yellow.

Habitat.—Red Sea, East coast of Africa, and Ceylon. Grows to at least 8 inches in length.

13. Acanthurus velifer.

Bloch, t. 427, f. 1; Bl. Schn. p. 215; Lacép. iv, pp. 547, 553; Cuv. and Val. x, p. 251; Rüpp. Atl. Fische, p. 58, t. xv, f. 2; Bleeker, Cocos, iv, p. 451, and Batoe, p. 315; Jerdon, M. J. L. and Sc. 1851, p. 138; Günther, Catal. iii, p. 344; Klunz. Verh. z. b. Ges. Wien, 1871, p. 505.

Zebrasoma velifer, Swainson, Fishes, ii, p. 256.

Acanthurus Rüppellii, Benn. Proc. Z. S. 1835, p. 207; Bleeker, Batoe, p. 316; Günther, Catal. iii, p. 345.

Acanthurus Desjardinii, Bennett, l. c. p. 127; Günther, Catal. iii, p. 344.

Acanthurus Blochii, Bennett, P. Z. S. 1835, p. 207.

B. v, D. [illegible], P. 17, V. 1/5, A. [illegible], C. 17, Vert. 9/13, Cæc. pyl. 7.

Length of head 1/4 to 4½, of pectoral 1/4, of caudal 1/5, height of body from 1/2 to 1/3 of the total length. *Eyes*—diameter 1/3 of length of head, $1\frac{1}{2}$ diameters from end of snout, and 1 apart. Profile over snout concave. *Teeth*—six lobate incisors on each side of the upper jaw. *Fins*—dorsal very elevated, fourth dorsal ray highest, and equal to from 1/2 to 1/3 of the length of the body; anal also elevated, but not so much so as the dorsal, it begins under ninth dorsal ray. *Scales*—rudimentary, ctenoid. *Lateral-line*—present. *Colours*—grayish, with nine vertical bands, having white edges, from the back to the abdomen. The ocular band passes through the eye and to the base of the ventral fin; the second band through the base of the pectoral to the anus. Head sometimes with white spots. Dorsal with four curved blue or white bands, six on the anal and four on the caudal. These bands being more or less continuations of those on the body but more vertically curved. Caudal usually spotted with white or a light colour.

Jerdon observes of this species "*Graudua*, Tam. rare. I have only seen a dried skin procured by W. Elliot, Esq." A specimen in the Calcutta Museum from the Andamans is $8\frac{3}{4}$ inches in length. One in the British Museum 16 long and 14 high.

Col. Playfair (Fish. Zanzibar, p. 57) observes of *A. Desjardinii*, "this may prove to be only the adult state of *Acanthurus velifer*, Bloch." But as his two specimens of *A. Desjardinii*=$6\frac{1}{2}$ and 7 inches respectively, and the type in the British Museum only 5 inches, and these are the whole of those present, it is hardly a tenable conclusion that they are the adult form, when an *A. velifer*, 16 inches long, exists in the collection.

Habitat.—From the Red Sea and East coast of Africa, through the seas of India to New Guinea.

Genus, 2—Naseus, *Commer.*

Monoceros, Bl. Schn.; *Naso*, Lacép.; *Aspisurus*, (Lacép.) Rüpp.; *Axinurus* and *Priodon*, Cuv. and Val.; ? *Keris*, part Cuv. and Val.; *Callicanthus*, Swainson.

Branchiostegals four or five: pseudobranchiæ well developed. Body rather elevated and compressed. Eyes high up, anterior to which there is a bony prominence, frontal horn, or crest-like protuberance. Teeth in the jaws in a single row and sometimes having their edges serrated: palate edentulous. A single dorsal fin having few spines (4-6) *and many rays. Anal with two spines, its rays similar to those of the dorsal. Ventral with one spine and three rays. Scales rudimentary in the form of roughnesses of the skin like shagreen. Free portion of the tail having from* 1 *to* 3 *keeled bony plates on either side in the adult, which are indistinct or even absent in young specimens. Air-vessel large, posteriorly forked. Pyloric appendages few* (5-8).

These fishes are said to have a very convoluted intestinal tract and to be herbivorous. They appear to be found in Ceylon and probably may be taken at the Andamans.

Geographical distribution.—Red Sea, East coast of Africa, seas of India to Polynesia.

SYNOPSIS OF SPECIES.

1. *Naseus tuberosus.* D. [illegible], A. [illegible]. Teeth smooth. Anterior surface of forehead prominent. Gray, dorsal and anal fins banded, pectoral and caudal edged with white. Mauritius and Ceylon to Polynesia.

2. *Naseus brevirostris.* D. [illegible], A. [illegible]. Teeth finely serrated. A horn from opposite lower portion of eye. Gray, with short transverse spots on the hind portion of the body. Caudal with a light edge. Seas of India to the Malay Archipelago and beyond.

3. *Naseus unicornis.* D. [illegible], A. [illegible]. Teeth smooth. Forehead with a long horn from opposite upper third of eye. Dorsal and anal fins with longitudinal bands: caudal yellowish. Red Sea, East coast of Africa, seas of India to Polynesia.

1. Naseus tuberosus.

Naso tuberosus, Lacép. iii, p. 111, t. vii, f. 3.
Acanthurus nasus, Shaw, Zool. v, p. 376, pl. 51.
Naseus tuber, Cuv. and Val. x, p. 290.
Naseus tuberosus, Günther, Catal. iii, p. 353.

B. v, D. [illegible], P. 18, V. 1/3, A. [illegible], C. 16.

Length of head $4\frac{1}{2}$ to 1/5, of caudal $5\frac{1}{2}$ to 1/6, height of body 1/3 to $3\frac{1}{2}$ in the total length. *Eyes*—diameter $3\frac{1}{2}$ to 1/5 of the length of head, $2\frac{1}{2}$ to $3\frac{1}{4}$ diameters from end of snout, and $1\frac{1}{4}$ to $1\frac{1}{2}$ apart. Anterior profile of the snout convex, forming a crest-like prominence in the adult. *Teeth*—rather compressed, pointed, and from 18 to 20 on either side of both jaws. *Fins*—in young specimens the dorsal spines appear to be comparatively longer than in adults; in one of the latter the length of the fourth spine equalled its distance from the base of the first. Pectoral equals 3/4 of the length of the head. Caudal emarginate, but subject to great variation, in some being almost truncated, whilst in others the outer rays are considerably produced. Free portion of the tail with two strong sharp lancet-shaped spines, one behind the other on either side in the adult. *Colours*—gray, becoming dull yellow along the abdomen and covered with small dark spots. Dorsal and anal fins with a narrow dark base, external to which is a broad orange band, margined with black and externally edged with white. Pectoral and caudal edged with white.

Habitat.—From the Mauritius and Ceylon to Polynesia.

2. Naseus brevirostris, Plate XLVIII, fig. 4.

Cuv. and Val. x, p. 277, pl. 291; Bleeker, Celebes, iv, p. 165, and Celebes, viii, p. 306; Günther, Catal. iii, p. 349; Klunz. Verh. z. b. Ges. Wien, 1871, p. 71.

Naseus Hoedtii, Bleeker, Amboina, iv, p. 339.

B. v, D. $\frac{6}{27-29}$, P. 16, V. 1/3, A. $\frac{2}{27-29}$, C. 16.

Length of head $4\frac{1}{2}$, of caudal $5\frac{3}{4}$ to one-sixth, height of body $2\frac{3}{4}$ in the total length. *Eyes*—diameter $3\frac{3}{4}$ in the length of head, $2\frac{1}{2}$ diameters from the end of snout, and $1\frac{1}{4}$ apart. Profile from the snout to above the orbits very abrupt, with a large horizontal horn in front of the eyes, varying in size with age. *Teeth*—small, about 40 in either jaw, and finely serrated. *Fins*—the height of the fifth dorsal spine equals its distance from the base of the first, the spines not quite so high as the rays. Anal rays not so high as those of the soft dorsal. Caudal emarginate. Free portion of the tail with two moderately strong spines on either side. *Colours*—grayish, with numerous short blue transverse spots or lines in the last half of the body. Caudal with a light edge.

Habitat.—Seas of India to the Malay Archipelago and Polynesia.

3. Naseus unicornis.

Monoceros piscis et minor, Willughby, pp. 150, 216, t. O. 4.

Chætodon unicornis, Forsk. p. 63, and Icones, t. xxiii; Gmel. Linn. i, p. 1268.

Monoceros raii et biaculeatus, Bl. Schn. pp. 180, 181, t. xlii.

Naso fronticornis, Lacép. iii, pp. 105, 106, t. vii, f. 2.

Acanthurus unicornis, Shaw, Zool. iv, p. 374, pl. 50.

Aspisurus unicornis, Rüpp. Atl. Fische, p. 60.

Naseus fronticornis (Comm.) Cuv. and Val. x, p. 259; Temm. and Schleg. Fauna Japon. Poiss. p. 129, t. lxix; Richards. Ich. China, p. 244; Bleeker, Batoe, iii, p. 238, and Waigou, 1868, p. 3; Cuv. Règ. Anim. Ill. Poiss. pl. 72, f. 2.

Naseus longicornis, Cuv. in Guér. Icon. Poiss. pl. 35, f. 3; Griffith in Cuv. Anim. King. Fishes, pl. 33, f. 3.

Naseus olivaceus, (Solander) Cuv. and Val. x, p. 288 (young).

Harpurus monoceros, Forst. Desc. Anim. ed. Licht. p. 219.

Acronurus Ægyptius, Gronov. ed. Gray, p. 191.

Acronurus cringer, Gronov. ed. Gray, p. 192.

Naseus unicornis, Günther, Catal. iii, p. 348; Klunz. Verh. z. b. Ges. Wien, 1871, p. 72.

B. iv, D. $\frac{5}{27}$ | $\frac{6}{30}$, P. 17, V. 1/3, A. $\frac{2}{27-30}$, C. 16.

Length of head $4\frac{1}{4}$ to $4\frac{1}{2}$, of caudal $5\frac{1}{2}$, height of body $2\frac{3}{4}$ in the total length. *Eyes*—diameter one-fourth to $5\frac{1}{2}$ in the length of head, $3\frac{1}{2}$ to 4 diameters from the end of snout, and $1\frac{1}{2}$ apart. Forehead with a long horn-like production on a level with the middle or upper edge of the eye, and increasing in length with age: in one 10 inches long it is 1/2 an inch, another at 14 inches it is 1 inch, whilst in a third a little over 20 inches it is $3\frac{1}{4}$. *Teeth*—rather compressed, pointed, with smooth edges, and about 15 on either side of both jaws. *Fins*—fifth dorsal spine equals its length from the base of the first spine and 1/4 higher than the rays. Pectoral 2/3 as long as the head. Anal rays not quite so high as those of the soft dorsal. Caudal slightly emarginate. Free portion of the tail with two strong lancet-shaped spines on either side. *Colours*—grayish superiorly, becoming tinged with yellow on the abdomen: dorsal and anal fins with longitudinal orange stripes and a blue outer edge: tail yellowish.

Habitat.—Red Sea, East coast of Africa, seas of India to Polynesia.

Family, XVI—CARANGIDÆ, *Günther*.

Scomberoidei, pt., et *Squamipinnes*, pt., Cuv.: *Scombridæ*, pt., Richardson.

Branchiostegals usually seven, occasionally less: pseudobranchiæ as a rule present, but absent in *Lichia* and *Trachynotus*. Body oblong, elevated, or sub-cylindrical and compressed. Gill-openings wide. Eyes lateral. Infraorbital bones do not articulate with the preopercle. Dentition varied. The length of the base of the spinous portion of the dorsal fin is of less extent than that of the soft, and is sometimes formed by isolated spines: the spinous may be continuous with or distinct from the soft portion: the posterior portion both of the dorsal and anal sometimes consists of detached finlets: the soft dorsal and the anal of nearly equal extent. Anal spines, when present, may or may not be continuous with the soft portion. Ventrals, when present, thoracic, sometimes rudimentary. Scales usually small, unless absent. Lateral-line may be wholly, partially, or not at all armed with shield-like plates. Air-vessel present. Pyloric appendages usually in large numbers. Vertebræ 10/14 (Naucrates 10/16).

SYNOPSIS OF GENERA.

1. *Caranx*. Lateral-line wholly or only partially formed of plate-like scales, each of which is armed with a lateral spinate keel.
2. *Micropteryx*. Lateral-line smooth: abdomen trenchant.
3. *Seriola*. Lateral-line smooth: abdomen rounded.
4. *Seriolichthys*. Lateral-line smooth: a finlet behind the dorsal and anal fins.
5. *Naucrates*. Lateral-line smooth: dorsal fin reduced to a few spines: no finlets: pre-anal spines in the young. A keel on either side of the tail.
6. *Chorinemus*. First dorsal formed of isolated spines: posterior rays of dorsal and anal fins in the form of finlets: dermal productions usually lanceolate.
7. *Trachynotus*. First dorsal formed of isolated spines: no finlets behind dorsal and anal fins. Scales rounded.
8. *Psettus*. No pre-anal spines: ventrals rudimentary: no finlets: vertical fins scaled.
9. *Platax*. No pre-anal spines: ventrals well developed: no finlets: vertical fins scaled.
10. *Psenes*. No pre-anal spines: two separate dorsal fins: no finlets behind dorsal or anal fins.
11. *Equula*. No pre-anal spines. Mouth very protractile. Teeth small and of equal size. Scales cycloid.
12. *Gazza*. No pre-anal spines. Mouth very protractile. Canine-like teeth in the jaws. Lower edge of preopercle serrated.
13. *Lactarius*. No pre-anal spines. One or two pairs of canines. Lower edge of preopercle entire.

Genus, 1—Caranx, *Lacép.*

Trachurus, *Olistus*, *Blepharis*, *Gallichthys*, *Scyris*, et *Hynnis*, Cuv. and Val.:* *Megalaspis*, *Decapterus*, *Selar*, *Carangichthys*, *Carangoides*, *Leioglossus*, *Uraspis*, *Selaroides*, *Gnathanodon*, and *Hemicaranx*, Bleeker: *Carangus* (C. and V.) Girard: *Trachurops*, *Caranxops*, and *Paratractus*, Gill.

Branchiostegals seven: pseudobranchiæ. Body oblong, sub-cylindrical, and more or less compressed. Eyes lateral. Dentition feeble. Two dorsal fins: the first continuous, having about eight weak spines, which are sometimes rudimentary, at its base anteriorly is a recumbent spine directed forwards: the second dorsal longer than the first and similar to the anal: sometimes the last rays of both these fins wholly or only semi-detached: two preanal spines (which may be rudimentary) they are separated by an interspace from the rays. Scales minute. Lateral-line with an anterior curved portion, whilst the posterior is straight, having large plate-like scales, which are usually keeled and sometimes spinate. Air-vessel bifurcated posteriorly. Pyloric appendages in large numbers.

* The following are the principal distinctions of the genera instituted by Cuv. and Val., which are included in Genus *Caranx* of Lacépède.

1. *Trachurus*. Lateral-line entirely covered by plate-like, keeled scales.
2. *Caranx*. Subdivided into (1) those with several finlets; (2) a single finlet: (3) no finlets, form but little elevated and profile nearly straight: (4) those having the skull elevated and compressed, and the dorsal profile forming the arc of a circle, or the *Carangues*: (5) the last group with the points of the dorsal and anal very prolonged, or *Citulas*.
3. *Olistus* are *Citulas* with several of their dorsal and anal rays being unbranched and having filamentous terminations.
4. *Blepharis*. Body as high as long, and a very elevated profile. A rudimentary first dorsal fin. A portion of the anterior dorsal and anal rays filamentous.
5. *Gallichthys*. Body less elevated. A rudimentary first dorsal fin. Anterior dorsal and anal rays prolonged into filaments. Ventrals very long.
6. *Scyris*. Profile more like the last, with short ventrals.
7. *Hynnis*. No first dorsal fin. No filamentous prolongation of the rays. Ventrals short.

The Genus *Caranx* contains so many species and varieties of forms that it is not surprising it has been numerously subdivided. If we examine these living in the Indian seas, we find the dentition modified in various ways, each of which has been made to constitute a genus.*

The forms of the fins have been employed as generic characters, as to whether the soft dorsal and anal have or have not finlets posteriorly, if several *Megalaspis*, if only one *Decapterus*. Or the first dorsal, present in the young, may disappear with age, as in *Blepharis*, *Scyris*, and *Gallichthys*. Or some of the dorsal and anal rays may be elongated, as *Olistus*, &c.

The preopercle may be serrated or entire, but certainly in one species (*C. oblongus*) that bone is serrated in the young, but not distinctly so in the adult, and consequently Genus *Carangichthys* cannot be valid.

The scales of the lateral-line also have given generic characters, thus if the keeled scales exist along its whole extent, the term *Trachurus* has been used. In some the body is almost scaleless, *C. ciliarus* and *C. gallus*: in others though the body is scaled the chest may be scaled or scaleless. The latter again may be subdivided into, first, those in which this scaleless portion extends as high up the breast as the base of the pectoral fins, and appears to continue so through life as in *C. gymnostethoides*, *C. Malabaricus*, *C. nigrescens*, *C. atropus*, and *C. armatus*; or, secondly, such species wherein the chest is equally scaleless in the immature, but a portion of this space becomes partially scaled in the adult, as *C. carangus* and *C. oblongus*.

The eyes in some have a well developed adipose eyelid on both sides, or only on one: or adipose lids may be minute or entirely absent.

I propose subdividing the Genus *Caranx* into (1) those species which have the palate toothed, and (2) such as have it toothless.

SYNOPSIS OF SPECIES.

A. Teeth on the palate.

a. Several finlets behind dorsal and anal fins.

1. *Caranx Rottleri*, D. 6-8 | $\frac{1}{9-11}$ + viii-x, A. 2 | $\frac{1}{8-9}$ + vii-viii, L. l, 55.† A dark opercular spot. Red Sea, seas of India, Malay Archipelago, and beyond.

b. A single finlet behind dorsal and anal fins.

2. *Caranx kurra*, D. 8 | $\frac{1}{25-26}$ + i, A. 2 | $\frac{1}{21-22}$ + i, L. l. 33. A dark opercular spot. Red Sea, seas of India to the Malay Archipelago.

c. No finlets, outer row of premaxillary teeth distinctly enlarged: a single row in lower jaw, with often two or four canines.

3. *Caranx melampygus*, D. 8 | $\frac{1}{21-23}$, A. 2 | $\frac{1}{17-19}$, L. l. 34-36. Height of body 2/7 of total length. Eye with a broad posterior adipose lid. Second dorsal anteriorly 2/3 the height of the body. Lateral-line arches to below seventh dorsal ray. Chest scaled. A small black opercular spot. Seas of India to the Malay Archipelago.

4. *Caranx jarra*, D. 8 | $\frac{1}{21}$, A. 2 | $\frac{1}{17}$, L. l. 33-36. Height of body $3\frac{2}{3}$ in the total length. Eye with a broad posterior adipose lid. Second dorsal anteriorly 3/5 the height of the body. Lateral-line forms an undulating curve to below seventh dorsal ray. Scaleless below the ventral fin. No opercular spot. Seas of India to the Malay Archipelago.

5. *Caranx carangus*, D. 8 | $\frac{1}{19-21}$, A. 2 | $\frac{1}{16-17}$, L. l. 33-37. Height of body 1/3 of the total length. Eye with a narrow posterior adipose lid. Second dorsal anteriorly about 1/2 as high as the body. Lateral-line curves to below sixth dorsal ray. Scaleless before the ventral fin and sometimes as high laterally as the base of the pectoral. No opercular spot. Seas of India to the Malay Archipelago and beyond.

* The following Genera have been proposed by Bleeker in his Ich. of Amboina, p. 408, and Fish. Madag.

A. *Finlets present.*

Megalaspis. Teeth in lower jaw in many rows. Teeth on vomer, palate, and tongue. Dorsal and anal fins with several finlets posteriorly.

Decapterus. Teeth in upper and lower jaws in a single row. Teeth on vomer, palate, and tongue. Dorsal and anal fins with a single finlet posteriorly.

B. *Finlets absent.*

Selar. A single row of teeth in both jaws. Teeth on vomer, palate, and tongue.

Caranx. Several rows of teeth in premaxillaries, the outer of which is enlarged. A single row in the lower jaw, with two or four canines anteriorly. Teeth on vomer, palate, and tongue.

Carangichthys. Preopercle serrated. Several rows of teeth in both jaws, the outer being the larger, several of those anteriorly in the lower jaw canine-like. Teeth on vomer, palate, and tongue.

Carangoides. Several rows of equal sized teeth in both jaws. Teeth on vomer, palate, and tongue.

Leioglossus. A single row of equal sized teeth in either jaw. Teeth on vomer and palatines, none on tongue.

Uraspis. Two rows of teeth in either jaw. Vomer, palatines, and tongue edentulous.

Selaroides. A single row of teeth on lower jaw and tongue. Premaxillaries, vomer, and palate edentulous.

Gnathanodon. Tongue scabrous. Jaws, vomer, and palate edentulous.

Hemicaranx. A single row of equal sized teeth in both jaws. Teeth on tongue. Vomer and palate edentulous.

† L. l. or lateral-line in this genus only refers to the number of keeled scales along its course.

6. *Caranx hippos*, D. 7-8 | [illegible], A. 2 | [illegible], L. l. 30-36. Height of body 1/3 to 3/10 of total length. Eye with a broad posterior adipose lid. Cleft of mouth commences anteriorly opposite the middle or lower third of eye. Second dorsal anteriorly $2\frac{1}{4}$ in the height of the body. Lateral-line curves to below the sixth dorsal ray. Chest scaled. A small dark spot on opercle at commencement of the lateral-line, upper angle of soft dorsal and tip of upper caudal lobe black. Red Sea, seas of India to the Malay Archipelago and beyond.

7. *Caranx sansun*, D. 8 | [illegible], A. 2 | [illegible], L. l. 30-32. Height of body 1/3 of total length. Eye with a narrow posterior adipose lid. Cleft of mouth commences anteriorly below the level of the eye. Second dorsal anteriorly $2\frac{1}{4}$ in the height of the body. Lateral-line curves to below sixth dorsal ray. Chest scaled. No opercular spot. Red Sea, seas of India.

d. No finlets, teeth in jaws in one or more rows, and of nearly equal size.

8. *Caranx gymnostethoides*, D. 8 | [illegible], A. 2 | [illegible], L. l. 22-25. Height of body 1/4 of total length. Eye with a narrow posterior adipose lid. Villiform teeth in the jaws. Second dorsal anteriorly 2/5 of the height of the body. Lateral-line curves to below 16th dorsal ray. Chest and breast as high as the pectoral scaleless. A dull opercular spot. Seas of India to the Malay Archipelago.

9. *Caranx ferdau*, D. 7-8 | [illegible], A. 2 | [illegible], L. l. 25. Height of body $3\frac{3}{5}$ to $4\frac{1}{2}$ in the total length. Eye with a narrow posterior adipose lid. Villiform teeth in the jaws. Second dorsal anteriorly 2/5 of the height of the body. Lateral-line curves to below the 13th dorsal ray. Chest in front of the ventral fin scaleless. No opercular spot. Red Sea and seas of India.

10. *Caranx crumenophthalmus*, D. 8 | [illegible], A. 2 | [illegible], L. l. 27-32. Height of body $4\frac{1}{2}$ to $4\frac{3}{4}$ in the total length. Eye with very broad anterior and posterior adipose lids. Teeth in a single row in both jaws. The arched portion of the lateral-line passes into the straight part below the tenth dorsal ray. Chest scaled. Usually no opercular spot. Red Sea, seas of India to the Malay Archipelago and beyond.

11. *Caranx boops*, D. 8 | [illegible], A. 2 | [illegible], L. l. 46. Height of body 1/4 of the total length. Eye with a broad posterior adipose lid. Teeth in a narrow band, or single row in both jaws. Lateral-line becomes straight below the sixth dorsal spine. Chest scaled. A small opercular spot. Andamans to the Malay Archipelago.

12. *Caranx Djeddaba*, D. 8 | [illegible], A. 2 | [illegible], L. l. 46-53. Height of body $3\frac{1}{2}$ in the total length. Eye with a broad posterior adipose lid. Teeth in a single row in both jaws. Lateral-line becomes straight below the first dorsal ray. Chest scaled. A well-marked opercular spot. Red Sea, seas of India to the Malay Archipelago and beyond.

13. *Caranx affinis*, D. 7-8 | [illegible], A. 2 | [illegible], L. l. 42-47. Height of body $3\frac{3}{4}$ to $4\frac{1}{4}$ in the total length. Eye with a broad anterior and posterior adipose lid. Teeth in a narrow band anteriorly, a single row posteriorly. Lateral-line becomes straight below the seventh dorsal ray. Chest scaled. A well-marked opercular spot. Red Sea, seas of India to the Malay Archipelago and beyond.

14. *Caranx kalla*, D. 8 | [illegible], A. 2 | [illegible], L. l. 40-44. Height of body from 1/3 to 2/7 of the total length. Eye with a broad posterior adipose lid. Teeth in a single row in both jaws. Lateral-line becomes straight below the fifth dorsal ray. Chest scaled. A large opercular spot. Red Sea, seas of India to China.

15. *Caranx ire*, D. 8 | [illegible], A. 2 | [illegible], L. l. 26-28. Height of body $3\frac{3}{5}$ to 1/4 of the total length. Eye with a narrow posterior adipose lid. Teeth anteriorly in a villiform band in both jaws, in a single row laterally. Lateral-line becomes straight below the eighth dorsal ray. Chest scaled. No opercular spot. A black blotch at summit of soft dorsal fin. Seas of India to the Malay Archipelago.

16. *Caranx compressus*, D. 8 | [illegible], A. 2 | [illegible], L. l. 13. Height of body $3\frac{1}{4}$ to $3\frac{1}{3}$ in total length. Eye without adipose lids. Teeth in both jaws in villiform bands. Lateral-line becomes straight below the twelfth dorsal ray. Chest scaled. A small opercular spot. Red Sea, Andaman islands.

17. *Caranx atropus*, D. 8 | [illegible], A. 2 | [illegible], L. l. 32-35. Height of body 2/5 of total length. Eye without adipose lids. Teeth in two rows in either jaw. Second dorsal anteriorly 1/3 height of body. Lateral-line becomes straight below the fifth dorsal ray. Chest and breast scaleless. An opercular spot. Seas of India to the Malay Archipelago.

18. *Caranx Malabaricus*, D. 7-8 | [illegible], A. 2 | [illegible], L. l. 28. Height of body $2\frac{2}{3}$ in the total length. Eye without adipose lids. Teeth villiform in either jaw. Second dorsal fin anteriorly $2\frac{2}{3}$ in height of body. Lateral-line becomes straight below the thirteenth dorsal ray. Chest and breast scaleless. Red Sea, seas of India to the Malay Archipelago.

19. *Caranx oblongus*, D. 8 | [illegible], A. 2 | [illegible], L. l. 34-40. Height of body $3\frac{1}{2}$ in the total length. Eye without adipose lids. Teeth in villiform bands in upper, a single row in the lower jaw. Second dorsal anteriorly 3/4 height of body. Lateral-line becomes straight below ninth dorsal ray. Chest scaleless. No opercular spot.

20. *Caranx nigrescens*, D. 8 | [illegible], A. 2 [illegible], L. l. 23. Height of body 2/7 of the total length. Eye without adipose lids. Teeth in villiform rows in both jaws. Second dorsal anteriorly $1\frac{1}{4}$ in height of body. Lateral-line becomes straight below thirteenth dorsal ray. Breast and chest scaleless. An opercular spot. Andamans.

21. *Caranx armatus*, D. 6-8 | [illegible], A. 2 | [illegible], L. l. 20. Height of body 2/5 of the total length. Eye with a narrow posterior adipose lid. Teeth villiform in both jaws. Second dorsal anteriorly nearly as high as the body. Lateral-line becomes straight below the middle of the second dorsal. Breast and a portion of the chest scaleless. An opercular spot. Red Sea, seas of India to the Malay Archipelago.

22. *Caranx gallus*, D. 0-6 | $\frac{1}{20}$, A. 0-2 | $\frac{1}{16}$, L. l. 8-10. Height of body from $1\frac{3}{4}$ to 1/3 of the total length. Height of preorbital $1\frac{1}{3}$ to $1\frac{2}{3}$ in diameter of orbit. Eye without adipose lids. Teeth villiform in the young, obtuse in adults. Anterior rays of second dorsal and anal filiform and prolonged. Lateral-line becomes straight below twelfth dorsal ray. Scaleless except along lateral-line. A small opercular spot in adults. Red Sea, seas of India to the Malay Archipelago.

23. *Caranx ciliaris*, D. 6 | $\frac{1}{19}$, A. 2 | $\frac{1}{16}$, L. l. 15. Height of body $1\frac{1}{2}$ to $1\frac{3}{4}$ in the total length. Height of preorbital from 3/4 to 1 diameter of orbit. Eye without adipose lids. Teeth villiform in both jaws. Anterior rays of second dorsal and anal filiform and prolonged. Lateral-line becomes straight below tenth dorsal ray. Scaleless except along the lateral-line. An opercular spot. From the Red Sea, through those of India.

B. No teeth on the palate.

24. *Caranx leptolepis*, D. 8 | $\frac{1}{24-25}$, A. 2 | $\frac{1}{21}$, L. l. 24-28. Height of body $3\frac{3}{4}$ to $4\frac{1}{4}$ in the total length. Eye with a broad posterior and narrow anterior adipose lid. Teeth in a single row in both jaws. Second dorsal anteriorly $2\frac{1}{4}$ in height of body. Lateral-line becomes straight below seventh dorsal ray. Chest scaled. Seas of India to the Malay Archipelago.

25. *Caranx nigripinnis*, D. 7-8 | $\frac{1}{24-27}$, A. 2 | $\frac{1}{20-22}$, L. l. 55-60. Height of body 2/7 of the total length. Eyes with wide anterior and posterior adipose lids. Teeth in a single row in both jaws. Second dorsal anteriorly 1/3 height of body. Lateral-line becomes straight below fifth dorsal ray. Chest scaled. Seas of India.

26. *Caranx speciosus*, D. 7-8 | $\frac{1}{18-20}$, A. 2 | $\frac{1}{15-16}$, L. l. 13-15. Height of body $3\frac{1}{2}$ in the total length. Eyes without adipose lids. Teeth absent. Second dorsal anteriorly $2\frac{1}{3}$ in height of body. Lateral-line becomes straight below eighth dorsal ray. Chest scaled. Red Sea, seas of India to the Malay Archipelago.

A. Teeth on the palate.

a. Several finlets behind dorsal and anal fins.

1. Caranx Rottleri.

Scomber Rottleri, Bloch, x, p. 40, t. 346; Bl. Schn. p. 25; Shaw, Zool. iv, p. 598.

Scomber woragoo, Russell, Fish. Vizag. ii, p. 33, pl. 143.

?*Scomber gnara*, Lacép. ii, p. 604.

Caranx Rotleri, Rüpp. Atl. p. 102, and N. W. Fische, pp. 48 and 52; Cuv. and Val. ix, p. 29; Richards. Ich. China, p. 273.

Caranx Rottleri, Cantor, Catal. p. 124; Jerdon, M. J. L. and Sc. 1851, p. 136; Günther, Catal. ii, p. 424; Day, Fishes of Malabar, p. 80; Kner, Novara Fische, p. 150; Klunz. Verh. z. b. Ges. Wien, 1871, p. 453.

Megalaspis Rottleri, Bleeker, Makr. p. 40.

Sora parah, Tel.: *Komara parah*, Tam.

B. vii, D. 6-8 | $\frac{1}{10-11}$ + viii-x, P. 21, V. 1/5, A. 2 | $\frac{1}{8-9}$ + vii-viii, C. 18, L. l. 55.*

Length of head $4\frac{3}{4}$ to $5\frac{1}{4}$, of caudal $5\frac{1}{2}$, height of body $4\frac{1}{4}$ to $4\frac{3}{4}$ in the total length. *Eye*—with a broad anterior and posterior adipose lid, both covering a portion of the pupil: diameter of eyes from $3\frac{3}{4}$ to $4\frac{1}{2}$ in the length of the head, 1 to $1\frac{1}{4}$ diameters from end of snout, and 1 apart. There is a very gradual ascent from the snout to the first dorsal fin, and the dorsal and abdominal profiles are about equally convex. The greatest width of the head equals 4/7 of its length, and its height its length behind the front nostril. Cleft of mouth very slightly oblique, commencing opposite the lower edge of the eye, lower jaw slightly the longer and the maxilla reaches to below the middle of the eye. The greatest depth of the preorbital equals about 1/2 the diameter of the orbit. *Teeth*—villiform in the upper jaw, with an outer row of rather widely separated and slightly conical ones: in the lower jaw two or three rows above the symphysis and a single lateral one. In a triangular patch on the vomer, in a long elliptical band on the palatines, and a wide one along the tongue. *Fins*—spines of first dorsal of moderate strength, the third to the fifth highest and equal to 2/5 of the height of the body: second dorsal highest anteriorly where it equals from $1\frac{3}{4}$ to about 1/2 the height of the body. Posteriorly it has from eight to ten detached rays. Pectoral falciform and longer than the head, reaching to about the 20th plate on the lateral-line. Ventral reaches rather above 1/2 way to the pre-anal spines. Anal similar in form to the second dorsal but rather lower and having from 7 to 8 free rays posterior to it. Caudal deeply forked. *Scales*—consist of about 78 rows, 55 of which are large plates. They are on the cheeks, upper edge of opercle, and top of head, there is only a narrow band in the central line in front of the ventral fin, otherwise the chest in front of it is scaleless: they also form a low sheath over the bases of the soft dorsal and anal fins. *Lateral-line*—at first makes a strong curve, the height of which equals half its length, it becomes straight below the middle of the first dorsal fin where wide plates commence, the highest equalling from 1/2 to 2/5 of the height of the body, they are most strongly keeled over the free portion of the tail which is strongly depressed. *Colours*—back glossy-green, abdomen silvery tinged with yellow: a large black spot on the upper and posterior portion of the opercle. Fins yellow, dorsal and anal tipped with black: upper half of pectoral darker than the lower.

In a young specimen $1\frac{7}{10}$ inches in length the angle and lower edge of the preopercle are crenulated, and crenulations are still visible in one 4 inches long.

* L. l. or lateral-line in this genus only refers to the number of keeled scales along its course.

Habitat.—From the Red Sea and East coast of Africa, through the seas of India to the Malay Archipelago and beyond. It is said by fishermen to attain 5 feet in length.

b. A single finlet behind dorsal and anal fins.

2. **Caranx kurra**, Plate XLVIII, fig. 5.

Scomber, Russell, Fish. Vizag. ii, p. 30, and *Kurra vodagawah*, pl. 139.
Caranx Russellii, Rüpp. Atl. Fische, p. 99.
Caranx kurra, Cuv. and Val. ix, p. 44; Jerdon, M. J. L. and Sc. 1851, p. 137; Günther, Catal. ii, p. 427; Day, Fishes of Malabar, p. 81; Klunz. Verh. z. b. Ges. Wien, 1871, p. 453.
Caranx pseudopterygius, Bleeker, Makr. p. 50.
? *Caranx kiliche*, Cuv. and Val. ix, p. 43.
Decapterus kurra, Bleeker, Makr. p. 50, and Nat. Tyds. Ned. Ind. 1851, p. 358.

B. vii, D. 8 | $\frac{1}{29-30}$ + i, P. 22, V. 1/5, A. 2 | $\frac{1}{25-27}$ + i, C. 17, L. l. 88.

Length of head 3¾ to 1/4, of pectoral 1/5, of caudal 1/6, height of body 1/5 to 2/11 of the total length. *Eye*—with a broad anterior and posterior adipose lid, each of which reaches nearly or quite to the pupil: diameter of the eyes 1/4 of length of head, 1 diameter from end of snout and also apart. Greatest width of the head equals 1/2, and its height 4/5 of its length. Lower jaw the longer, the cleft of the mouth commences opposite the middle of the orbit, the maxilla reaches to below the front edge of the eye. The greatest height of the preorbital equals 1/2 the diameter of the orbit, it has three or four well marked raised ridges radiating from its centre. *Teeth*—villiform in both jaws, becoming a single row laterally, in a triangular spot on the vomer, having a narrow row posteriorly in the median line, a row on either palatine, and in three rows along the middle of the tongue. *Fins*—spines of first dorsal weak, the third longest and equal to 3/5 of the height of the body: anterior portion of the second dorsal the highest where it equals 2/5 of that of the body, posteriorly it has a detached ray: anal similar to second dorsal. Ventral reaches nearly half way to the base of the anal. Caudal forked. *Scales*—on the upper surface of the head, cheeks, and opercles, also all over the body including the chest. A low sheath along the second dorsal and anal fins. *Lateral-line*—consisting of 88 scales, it continues nearly straight until opposite the end of the first dorsal where it gradually descends, and below the 15th ray it goes direct to the centre of the tail. The keeled scales at first are moderately so, the broadest equals from 1/5 to 2/11 of the height of the body. Free portion of the tail as high at its base as it is long. *Colours*—bluish superiorly, becoming silvery below. A deep black spot on the upper margin of the opercle: upper surface of head minutely dotted with black. Fins yellow, darkest at their edges.

Caranx kiliche, Cuv. and Val. from Pondicherry, is probably this species: its fin rays are D. 8 | $\frac{1}{30}$ + i, A. 2 | $\frac{1}{28}$ + i, L. l. 30. The teeth are not referred to. Klunzinger observes that the type of *C. Russellii* is not in the Senkenberg Museum. Amongst Sir Walter Elliot's figures of Madras fishes is this species, termed *Moonda kun kilchi*, Tam.

Habitat.—From the Red Sea, throughout those of India to the Malay Archipelago. It is a small species, attaining 6 or 7 inches in length: it arrives in Madras about October.

c. No finlets. Outer row of teeth in premaxillaries distinctly enlarged: a single row in the lower jaw, often with 2 or 4 canines.

3. **Caranx melampygus**, Plate L, fig. 3.

Scomber, Russell, Fish. Vizag. ii, p. 34, and *Kuramoo parah*, pl. 145.
Caranx melampygus, Cuv. and Val. ix, p. 116; Bleeker, Gilolo, p. 58; Jerdon, M. J. L. and Sc. 1851, p. 137; Günther, Catal. ii, p. 446.
Carangus melampygus, Bleeker, Madagas. 1871, p. 99.

B. vii, D. 8 | $\frac{1}{21-23}$, P. 22, V. 1/5, A. 2 | $\frac{1}{17-19}$, C. 19, L. l. 34-36.

Length of head from 4¼ to 4½, of caudal 1/4 to 4½, height of body 2/7 of the total length. *Eye*—with a broad posterior adipose lid, extending 2/3 of the distance across the iris, diameter of eyes 3½ to 4½ in length of head, 1½ diameters from end of snout, and 1 apart. Dorsal profile rather more convex than that of the abdomen. The greatest width of the head equals about 1/2, and its height its entire length. Lower jaw slightly the longer. Cleft of mouth commences opposite the lower third of the eye, the maxilla reaches to below the middle of the orbit. The greatest width of the preorbital nearly equals one diameter of the eye. *Teeth*—in a villiform band in the premaxillaries having an outer row of conically enlarged ones, a single row in the lower jaw, also present on vomer, palatines, and tongue. *Fins*—dorsal spines of moderate strength, the third the highest and equal to 1/3 that of the body: soft dorsal having its anterior rays elongated, and equal to 2/3 of the height of the body: anal similar to it but rather lower. Pectoral falciform and equal to 2/7 of the total length. Caudal deeply forked. *Scales*—on upper margin of head, cheeks, chest, and body: a low sheath along the bases of the soft dorsal and anal fins. *Lateral-line*—consists of 90 to 95 rows of scales, at first it slightly ascends, then curves to below the 6th or 8th dorsal ray, the height of the arch is not quite 1/4 of its length: it has keeled scales along most of its straight portion, the highest of which equals 1/8 or 1/9 of that of the body. Free portion of the tail half higher at its base than it is long. *Colours*—greenish gold along the back, becoming silvery along the abdomen: a small black spot on the opercle: dorsal and anal fins dark anteriorly.

In one specimen about 13 inches in length, from the Andamans, there are small scattered black spots over the body.

Habitat.—Seas of India to the Malay Archipelago and beyond. The largest specimen I have seen is 2 feet in length. The one figured (8 inches long) is from the Andamans.

4. Caranx jarra.

Scomber, Russell, Fish. Vizag. ii, p. 35, and *Jarra-dandee parrah*, pl. 147.

Caranx jarra, Cuv. and Val. ix, p. 109; Bleeker, Makr. p. 58; Jerdon, M. J. L. and Sc. 1851, p. 137; Günther, Catal. ii, p. 446.

B. vii, D. 8 | $\frac{1}{22}$, P. 21, V. 1/5, A. 2 | $\frac{1}{18}$, C. 18, L. l. 33-36.

Length of head $4\frac{1}{3}$, of caudal $4\frac{1}{2}$, height of body $3\frac{2}{3}$ in the total length. *Eye*—with a broad posterior adipose lid extending 2/3 of the distance across the iris, diameter of eye $4\frac{2}{3}$ in length of head, $1\frac{1}{2}$ diameters from end of snout, and rather above 1 apart. Dorsal profile a little more convex than that of the abdomen, the ascent from the snout to occiput rather abrupt. Greatest width of the head equals half, and its height almost equals its entire length. Cleft of the mouth commences opposite the lower edge of the eye, the jaws are of about the same length anteriorly, the maxilla reaches to below the middle of the orbit. The greatest height of the preorbital equals 1 diameter of the eye. *Teeth*—villiform in the premaxillaries, with an external conically enlarged row: villiform in the lower jaw, on the vomer, palatines, and tongue. *Fins*—dorsal spines increase to the third which equals $2\frac{3}{4}$ in the height of the body: the first few rays of the second dorsal elevated, the highest being equal to $1\frac{2}{3}$ in that of the body. Pectoral falciform, its length equal to 3/10 of that of the total. Ventral reaches 1/2 way to the anal. Anal similar to soft dorsal, its first few rays 1/2 as high as the body. Caudal forked. *Scales*—cover the cheeks, upper portion of the opercles and behind the eyes, but none exist along the median longitudinal crest on the head, which is well developed. Present over the body, but absent from the chest in front of the base of the ventral fins. They form a distinct sheath to the bases of the soft dorsal and anal fins. *Lateral-line*—consisting of 99 scales, in its first half it forms a low, undulating arch, which terminates below the seventh dorsal ray, the height of the arch equals 2/9 of the length of its base. The keeled scales begin at the commencement of the straight portion of the lateral-line, becoming largest below the end of the second dorsal, where they equal 1/9 of the height of the body. Free portion of the tail 2/3 as high at its base as it is long. *Colours*—greenish above, becoming of a dull white on the sides and below. No opercular spot.

This species is termed *Karandilli parah*, Tam., in Sir W. Elliot's collection of drawings of Indian Fishes.

Habitat.—Seas of India to the Malay Archipelago, attaining at least a foot in length.

5. Caranx carangus, Plate L, fig. 4.

Scomber carangus, Bl. t. 340; Bl. Schn. p. 28.

Scomber ekala parah, Russell, Fish. Vizag. ii, p. 35, pl. 146.

Caranx carangus, Cuv. and Val. ix, p. 91; Günther, Catal. ii, p. 448; Kner, Novara Fische, p. 157; Steind. Ak. d. Wiss. 1869, p. 36.

Caranx chrysos, Cuv. and Val. ix, p. 117.

Caranx ekala, Cuv. and Val. ix, p. 117; Bleeker, Makr. p. 59; Day, Fish. Malabar, p. 86.

Caranx xanthopygus, Cuv. and Val. ix, p. 109.

Trachurus cordyla, Gronov. ed. Gray, p. 124.

B. vii, D. 8 | $\frac{1}{20-21}$, P. 21, V. 1/5, A. 2 | $\frac{1}{17-18}$, C. 19, L. l. 33-37.

Length of head $4\frac{1}{4}$, of caudal $4\frac{1}{2}$, height of body one-third in the total length. *Eye*—with a narrow posterior adipose lid, diameter 2/7 of length of head, 1 diameter from end of snout, and also apart. Dorsal profile rather more convex than that of the abdomen. Greatest width of head nearly equals 1/2 its length, and its height rather more than its length. Lower jaw slightly the longer, the cleft of the mouth commences opposite the lower 1/3 of the front edge of the eye, the maxilla extends to beneath the middle of the eye. Central longitudinal crest on the head well-developed. Greatest height of the preorbital equals 2/3 of the diameter of the eye. The lower edges of the sub- and inter- opercles more or less crenulated. *Teeth*—villiform in the premaxillaries, with an outer enlarged and conical row: a single row in the lower jaw, some of which are larger than the others: in a triangular spot on the vomer, a band on the palatines, and also along the middle of the tongue. *Fins*—dorsal spines of moderate strength, the third the longest, and equal to 1/3 of the height of the body, or 3/4 that of the anterior dorsal rays. Pectoral slightly longer than the head. Ventral does not reach 1/2 way to the anal. Caudal rather deeply forked. *Scales*—a few round the eye on the hind portion of the opercle, on the body, in a patch in front of the ventral fins, but usually none anterior to the base of the pectoral or below its anterior half, the skin however is puckered and wrinkled into little pits, and occasionally the scales extend half-way to between the ventral and anal fins. *Lateral-line*—containing 90 to 95 scales, the arched portion terminates rather abruptly below the third or fifth dorsal ray, the height of the arch equals 3/10 of the length of its base, whilst that of its base equals 3/5 that of the straight portion. Keeled scales commence at the beginning of the straight portion, becoming well developed below the last third of the second dorsal, where they equal 1/8 to 1/9 of the height of the body. Free portion of the tail rather longer than high at its base. *Colours*—silvery along the back, golden on the sides and below. Four or five broad vertical bands on the body in immature specimens. Fins golden, except the first dorsal, which is gray, the tip, and sometimes the entire upper edge of the second dorsal and end of the upper lobe of the caudal black. Usually no opercular spot in Indian specimens, and when present mostly small.

Habitat.—Seas of India, Malay Archipelago to the Atlantic coasts of tropical America: the specimen figured ($5\frac{3}{4}$ inches long) is from Madras where they attain a large size.

6. Caranx hippos.

Scomber hippos, Linn. Syst. Nat. i, p. 494; Bl. Schn. p. 28; Forster, Desc. Anim. ed. Licht. p. 199.
Scomber Kleinii, Bl. t. 347, f. 2; Bl. Schn. p. 30.
Scomber wodia parah, Russell, ii, p. 36, pl. 148.
Caranx sem, Cuv. and Val. ix, p. 105; Jerdon, M. J. L. and Sc. 1851, p. 137.
Caranx Forsteri, Cuv. and Val. ix, p. 107; Cantor, Catal. p. 127; Bleeker, Makr. p. 57, and Nat. Tyds. Ned. Ind. 1852, iii, p. 164; Kner, Novara Fische, p. 158.
Caranx sexfasciatus, Quoy and Gaim. Voy. Freyc. p. 358, pl. 65, f. 4; Cuv. and Val. ix, p. 110 (*young*).
Caranx Peronii, Cuv. and Val. ix, p. 112.
Caranx Lessonii and *Belengeri*, Cuv. and Val. ix, pp. 113, 116.
Caranx hippos, Günther, Catal. ii, p. 449; Day, Fishes of Malabar, p. 86; Klunz. Verh. z. b. Ges. Wien, 1871, p. 465.
Carangus hippos, Bleeker, Waigou, 1868, p. 3.

B. vii, D. 7-8 | $\frac{1}{19-21}$, P. 22, V. 1/5, A. 2 | $\frac{1}{16-17}$, C. 21, L. l. 30-36.

Length of head 1/4, of caudal 2/9, height of body 1/3 to $3\frac{1}{4}$* in the total length. *Eye*—with a posterior adipose lid reaching half way or two-thirds of the distance to the pupil, diameter 3/11 of length of head, 1 diameter from end of snout, and also apart. Dorsal and abdominal profiles about equally convex and forming a gradual slope. Greatest width of head equals 1/2 its length, and its height equals nearly its length. Lower jaw slightly the longer, the cleft of the mouth commences opposite the middle or lower third of the front edge of the eye, the maxilla reaches to below the last third of the orbit. Greatest height of preorbital equals 1/2 the diameter of the eye. *Teeth*—villiform, with an outer enlarged row in the premaxillaries: in a single row in the lower jaw, amongst which occasionally are a few larger ones, a pair of well-marked canines above the symphysis: in a triangular patch on the vomer, in a band on the palatines, also along the tongue. *Fins*—the third dorsal spine the longest and equal from 1/3 to $3\frac{1}{4}$ in the height of the body: the anterior dorsal rays equal to $2\frac{1}{4}$ in the height of the body. Pectoral 1/5 longer than the head. Anal similar to, but lower than, the second dorsal. Caudal deeply forked. *Scales*—on cheeks, body, and chest. *Lateral-line*—consisting of 80 scales, forms an arch, 1/3 as high as long, ending below the sixth dorsal ray, the length of the arch equalling 2/3 of that of the straight portion: keeled plates extend the whole distance along the horizontal portion of the lateral-line, the largest being below the last portion of the second dorsal fin, and equal 1/10 of the height of the body. *Colours*—body golden, having a tinge of gray along the back. A small black spot on the opercle just before the commencement of the lateral-line. Fins yellow, summit of second dorsal and point of the upper caudal lobe deep black, sometimes the whole of the posterior border of the caudal fin is black edged. Eyes, bright orange. Usually a dark spot behind the base of the pectoral fin. The *young* are golden, with four or five broad vertical bands on the body.

Caranx Heberi, Benn. Fish. Ceylon (p. 26, pl. xxvi.) is probably this species: if so the mouth is shown too low down.

Habitat.—Seas of India to the Malay Archipelago, China, and beyond. It attains a large size, as 3 feet or more in length. When captured it grunts like a young pig, and this is repeated whenever it is moved, so long as vitality remains.

7. Caranx sansun, Plate L, fig. 5.

Scomber sansun, Forsk. p. 56.
Scomber gaudi-parah, Russell, ii, p. 33, and pl. 144.
Caranx sansun, Rüpp. Atl. Fische, p. 101, and N. W. Fische, p. 48, t. xiii, f. 3; Günther, Catal. ii, p. 447; Klunz. Verh. z. b. Ges. Wien, 1871, p. 446.
Carangus sansun, Bleeker, Fauna de Madag. 1874, p. 99.

B. vii, D. 8 | $\frac{1}{19-20}$, P. 20, V. 1/5, A. 2 | $\frac{1}{16-17}$, C. 19, L. l. 30-32.

Length of head 1/4, of caudal 1/4 to 2/9, height of body 1/3 of the total length. *Eye*—with a narrow posterior adipose lid, diameter $3\frac{3}{5}$ in the length of head, 1 to $1\frac{1}{4}$ diameters from end of snout, and 1 apart. Dorsal profile more convex than that of the abdomen, the profile of the anterior surface of the head somewhat obtuse. The greatest width of the head equals 4/9 of its length, and its height its entire length. Lower jaw a little the longer, the cleft of the mouth commences below the level of the orbit, the maxilla reaches to below the last third of the eye. Greatest depth of preorbital equals 3/4 in the young to $1\frac{1}{3}$ in the adult diameters of the eye. *Teeth*—villiform, with an outer row of enlarged but irregularly sized ones in the premaxillaries, in a single row of irregularly sized ones in the lower jaw, some being much larger than the others, and a pair of minute canines at the symphysis: in a triangular spot on the vomer, in a band on the palatines and in a narrow patch

* In a specimen $1\frac{8}{10}$ inches long, the height of the body equals 2/5 of the total length.

along the middle of the tongue. *Fins*—third dorsal spine the highest, equalling 1/3 of that of the body and 2/3 as high as the commencement of the second dorsal. Pectoral 1/4 longer than the head. Ventral reaches nearly 1/2 way to the anal. Caudal deeply forked. *Scales*—on body, chest, and cheeks. *Lateral-line*—consisting of ninety-five scales, its arched portion ending below the sixth dorsal ray, the height of the arch being equal to 1/4 of its length, and its length equal to $1\frac{2}{3}$ or $1\frac{1}{4}$ in the straight portion. Keeled scales commence about the third scale of the horizontal portion, becoming well developed beneath the last part of the soft dorsal, where their height equals 1/8 to 1/9 of that of the body. Free portion of the tail longer than high at its base. *Colours*—silvery along the back, becoming golden below, all the fins yellow, first dorsal grayish. No opercular spot.

Habitat.—Red Sea, seas of India. The specimen figured ($6\frac{7}{8}$ inches long) is from Madras. Russell's specimen was 1 foot long, and he says that it is a dry, insipid fish.

d. No finlets. Teeth in jaws in one or more rows of nearly equal size.

8. Caranx gymnostethoides, Plate XLVIII, fig. 6.

? *Caranx gymnostethus*, Cuv. and Val. ix, p. 73.
Carangoides gymnostethoides, Bleeker, Makr. p. 365.
Caranx gymnostethoides, Günther, Catal. ii, p. 431; Kner, Novara Fische, p. 153.

B. vii, D. 8 | $\frac{1}{20-21}$, P. 21, V. 1/5, A. 2 | $\frac{1}{17-17}$, C. 17, L. l. 22-25.

Length of head 1/4, of caudal 2/9, height of body 1/4 of the total length. *Eye*—with a narrow posterior adipose lid, diameter $5\frac{1}{3}$ in length of head, 2 diameters from end of snout, and $1\frac{3}{4}$ apart. Abdominal profile rather more convex than the dorsal, a slight rise from the snout to the base of the first dorsal fin. Greatest width of head equals half its length, and its height equals its length posterior to the nostrils. Lower jaw somewhat the longer. Cleft of the mouth commences opposite the middle of the eyes, the maxilla reaches to nearly below the front edge of the orbit. The preorbital in its deepest part equals 1 diameter of the orbit. *Teeth*—villiform in both jaws, on the vomer, palatines, and along the middle of the tongue. *Fins*—dorsal spines not strong, the third and fourth the longest and equal to 2/7 of the height of the body: the first portion of the soft dorsal the highest, and equal to 2/5 of that of the body. Pectoral rather longer than the head. Anal similar to soft dorsal. Caudal forked. *Scales*—extended over the cheeks and body, but none on the chest from below the pectoral fin. *Lateral-line*—at first makes a long, low curve to below the 16th dorsal ray, the length of the arch equals that of the straight portion, the height of the more developed plates equals 1/14 of that of the body. Free portion of the tail 2/3 as high at its base as it is long. *Colours*—greenish along the back, becoming dull silvery-white below: an indistinct opercular spot present. Soft dorsal and anal stained with black in their highest portions.

Habitat.—Seas of India to the Malay Archipelago. The largest specimen in the Madras Museum is 28 inches in length. The one figured is 17 inches long and from Madras.

9. Caranx ferdau.

Scomber ferdau, Forsk. p. 55.
Caranx bajad, Rüpp. Atl. Fische, p. 98, t. 25, f. 5; Günther, Catal. ii, p. 438.
Caranx fulvoguttatus, Cuv. and Val. ix, p. 73.
Carangoides fulvoguttatus, Bleeker, Makr. p. 89.
Caranx ferdau, Klunz. Verh. z. b. Ges. Wien, 1871, p. 462 (not Rüppell or Günther).

B. vii, D. 7-8 | $\frac{1}{21-22}$, P. 21, V. 1/5, A. 2 | $\frac{1}{17}$, C. 17, L. l. 25.

Length of head $4\frac{1}{4}$, of caudal 1/5, height of body $3\frac{7}{8}$ to $4\frac{1}{3}$ in the total length. *Eye*—with a narrow posterior adipose lid, diameter from $4\frac{1}{2}$ to $4\frac{3}{4}$ of length of head, $1\frac{1}{2}$ to 2 diameters from end of snout. Dorsal and abdominal profiles about equally convex, a slight ascent from the snout to the base of the dorsal fin. Height of head equals its length. Cleft of mouth commences opposite the middle of the front edge of the eyes, jaws of about equal length: the maxilla reaches to below the middle of the orbit. Greatest height of preorbital equals 3/4 of a diameter of the orbit. *Teeth*—villiform in both jaws, on vomer, and palate, tongue scabrous. *Fins*—spines of first dorsal increase in length to the third which equals 2/7 in the height of the body: the anterior portion of the second dorsal equals 2/5 the height of the body. Pectoral falciform and equal to $3\frac{1}{3}$ in the total length. Anterior portion of the anal commences below the seventh dorsal ray, and is as high as the first portion of that fin. Caudal deeply forked. *Scales*—in 140 rows, present on cheeks, upper portion of opercle, behind the eyes, also on the body, but not on the chest in front of the base of the ventral fin. A scaly sheath along bases of soft dorsal and anal fins. *Lateral-line*—in its first half makes a long low curve to below the 13th dorsal ray, the height of the arch being equal to 1/5 or 1/6 of its length. The keeled scales developed below the end of the second dorsal fin. *Colours*—greenish along the back, the young having five transverse oval spots or bars on the side of the body. No opercular spot.

Habitat.—Red Sea, East coast of Africa, seas of India to the Malay Archipelago.

10. Caranx crumenophthalmus, Plate XLIX, fig. 1.

Scomber crumenophthalmus, Bloch, t. 343.
Scomber balantiophthalmus, Bl. Schn. p. 29.

Caranx crumenophthalmus, Lacép. iv, p. 107; Cuv. and Val. ix, p. 62; Günther, Catal. ii, p. 429.
Caranx macrophthalmus, Rüpp. Atl. Fische, p. 97, t. 25, f. 4; Klunz. Verh. z. b. Ges. Wien, 1871, p. 458.
Caranx Mauritianus, Quoy and Gaim. Voy. Freyc. Zool. p. 359; Cuv. and Val. ix, p. 60.
Caranx torvus, Jenyns, Voy. Beagle, Fishes, p. 69, pl. 15; Günther, Catal. ii, p. 431; Kner, Novara Fische, p. 152.
Selar torvus, Bleeker, Makr. p. 51.

B. vii, D. 8 | $\frac{1}{24-26}$, P. 21, V. 1/5, A. 2 | $\frac{1}{21-23}$, C. 21, L. l. 27-32.

Length of head $3\frac{3}{4}$ to 1/4, of caudal 1/5 to $5\frac{1}{2}$, height of body $4\frac{1}{2}$ to $4\frac{3}{4}$ of the total length. *Eye*—with a broad posterior and also anterior adipose lid, diameter 1/3 to $3\frac{1}{4}$ in the length of head, 1 diameter from end of snout, and 3/4 of a diameter apart. Dorsal and abdominal profiles about equally convex. The greatest width of the head equals nearly half its length: its height is rather greater than its length excluding the snout. Lower jaw the longer: the cleft of the mouth commences opposite the upper third of the orbit: the maxilla reaches to below the first third of the eye. Height of the preorbital scarcely equals the diameter of the eye. *Teeth*—a single row in both jaws, in a Λ-shaped band on the vomer, a narrow one on the palatines, also along the centre of the tongue. *Fins*—dorsal spines weak, the third and fourth the longest, equal to 1/2 or 3/5 the height of the body and rather more than the rays at the commencement of the soft dorsal fin, of which the last is thickened and slightly prolonged. Pectoral $4\frac{1}{4}$ in the length of the body, not being so long as the head. Ventral reaches half way to the anal fin. Caudal rather deeply forked. *Scales*—on body, chest, and cheeks. *Lateral-line*—88 scales, forming a very long, low arched portion running into the straight part below the tenth dorsal ray, but the keeled scales do not commence until under the middle of that fin, becoming strongest under its termination, where they equal 1/8 to 1/10 the height of the body, in the arched portion of the lateral-line they are rounded and plate-like. Free portion of the tail nearly as high at its base as it is long. *Colours*—silvery, becoming golden below: usually no opercular spot, but present in some specimens from Madras. Fins golden, with fine dots. Caudal tipped with black.

Habitat.—Red Sea, seas of India to the Malay Archipelago, and also found in West Africa and Atlantic coasts of Tropical America, attaining at least 12 inches in length. The specimen figured is 8 inches long and from the Andamans.

11. **Caranx boops,** Plate XLIX, fig. 2.

Cuv. and Val. ix, p. 46; Günther, Catal. ii, p. 431; Bleeker, Obi, 1868, p. 5.
Selar boops, Bleeker, Makr. p. 51.

B. vii, D. 8 | $\frac{1}{24-25}$, P. 19, V. 1/5, A. 2 | $\frac{1}{20-21}$, C. 17, L. l. 46.

Length of head $3\frac{3}{4}$ to 1/4, of caudal 2/9, height of body 1/4 of the total length. *Eye*—with a broad posterior adipose lid and a narrower anterior one, diameter $2\frac{3}{4}$ to 1/3 of length of head, 3/4 to 1 diameter from end of snout, and rather less apart. Snout pointed: lower jaw rather the longer: commencement of cleft of mouth on a level with the middle of eye: the posterior extremity of the maxilla reaches to below the centre of the orbit: interorbital space nearly flat: preorbital narrow, its height in its deepest part being equal to 2/5 or 1/2 of that of the orbit. Dorsal and abdominal profiles equally convex: the width of the head equalling half its length. Lower edge of pre- sub- and interopercles roughened. *Teeth*—in a narrow band or single row on both jaws: in a Λ-shaped patch on the vomer, in a band on the palate, and also on the tongue. *Fins*—dorsal spines weak, the third and fourth the longest, equal to rather more than half the height of the body at the commencement of the second dorsal fin: anterior portion of second dorsal rather the highest, but a little lower than the longest dorsal spines. Pectoral not quite so long as the head: ventral reaches nearly 2/3 of the way to the anal, which latter fin is similar to but rather lower than the soft dorsal. Caudal deeply forked. *Scales*—over body, chest, cheeks, and upper jaw: a very low sheath on bases of soft dorsal and anal fins. *Lateral-line*—with 69 rows of scales, forming a rather strong curve anteriorly and becoming straight below the sixth dorsal spine, where the plates immediately begin to be developed, they are large and 1/4 of the height of the body in their broadest part. Free portion of the tail not quite so high at its base as it is long. *Colours*—silvery, darkest along the back, and shot with gold along the abdomen: a small but well developed opercular spot: dorsal and caudal fins with dark spots.

Habitat.—Andamans, (where the specimen figured, $7\frac{1}{4}$ inches in length, was captured) to the Malay Archipelago.

12. **Caranx Djeddaba,** Plate XLIX, fig. 3.

Scomber Djeddaba, Forsk. p. 56.
Caranx Djeddaba, Rüpp. Atl. p. 97, pl. xxv, fig. 3; Cuv. and Val. ix, p. 51; Günther, Catal. ii, p. 432; Klunz. Verh. z. b. Ges. Wien, 1871, p. 458.
Caranx rottleri, Cuv. and Val. ix, p. 48; Cantor, Catal. p. 125.
Selar Kuhlii, Bleeker, Makr. p. ~~86~~ 54
Selar rottleri, Bleeker, Beng. en Hind. p. 44.
Caranx xanthurus, Kner, Novara Fische, p. 154 (not C. and V.).

B. vii, D. 8 | $\frac{1}{22-24}$, P. 21, V. 1/5, A. 2 | $\frac{1}{18-20}$, C. 17, L. l. 46-53.

Length of head $4\frac{2}{3}$ to 1/5, of caudal $4\frac{3}{4}$, height of body $3\frac{1}{2}$ in the total length. *Eye*—having a broad posterior adipose covering, extending on to the pupil in the adult; diameter of eyes 1/4 to 2/9 of length of head, 1 to $1\frac{1}{4}$ diameters from end of snout, and $1\frac{1}{2}$ apart. Dorsal and abdominal profiles about equally convex.

Greatest width of head equals 3/5 of its length, whilst its height is nearly equal to its length. Lower jaw a little the longer: cleft of the mouth commences opposite the centre of the orbit: the maxilla reaches to below the first third of the eye. Depth of preorbital equal to 2/3 of the diameter of the eye. Central crest along the head well developed. *Teeth*—a fine row of pointed ones in either jaw, a triangular patch on the vomer, a narrow band along the palatines, also a bony plate on the centre of the tongue, which is finely toothed. *Fins*—dorsal spines of moderate strength, the third a little the longest and equal to 4/11 or 1/3 of the height of the body, and nearly as high as the anterior rays of the second dorsal. Pectoral falciform, equal to 1/4 or 2/7 of the entire length of the fish, and reaching to below the tenth or twelfth dorsal ray: ventral reaches half way to the anal. Anal commences under the third or fourth dorsal ray. Caudal deeply forked. *Scales*—over body, chest, cheeks, and above the hind third of the eye, also forming a well developed sheath to both the dorsal and anal fins. *Lateral-line*—with 86 to 90 scales, strongly curved anteriorly, becoming straight below the first dorsal ray, the height of its arch equals about 1/3 of its length: the length of its arch is 2¼ in that of the straight part: keeled plates commence on the first scale of the straight portion, becoming most developed below the last third of the second dorsal fin, where they equal 1/8 to 1/9 of the height of the body. Free portion of the tail about twice as long as it is deep at its base. *Colours*—silvery blue along the back, becoming golden on the sides and below: a large black blotch on the opercle at its posterior-superior angle. Fins yellow, the first dorsal tinged with gray, as is also the upper edge of the second dorsal, except its most elevated portion which is white: upper lobe of caudal darker than the lower. In a specimen over 13 inches in length, the summit of the soft dorsal is white and the rest of the fin black: the first dorsal is dark: the anal has a black spot at the base of its first six rays.*

Habitat.—Red Sea, East coast of Africa, seas of India to the Malay Archipelago and beyond. It is common in Madras and considered fair eating: it attains at least 13 inches in length.

13. **Caranx affinis**, Plate XLIX, fig. 4.

Caranx affinis, Rüpp. N. W. Fische, p. 49, t. xiv, f. 1; Kner, Novara Fische, p. 151; Klunz. Verb. z. b. Ges. Wien, 1871, p. 459.

Caranx mate, Cuv. and Val. ix, p. 54; Cantor, Catal. p. 125; Day, Fishes of Malabar, p. 82.

Caranx xanthurus, (Kuhl. and v. Hass.), Cuv. and Val. ix, p. 55; Günther, Catal. ii, p. 434; Bleeker, Bintang, 1868, p. 5.

Selar Hasseltii, Bleeker, Makr. p. 360.

Caranx Hasseltii, Günther, Catal. ii, p. 439.

B. vii, D. 7-8 | $\frac{1}{24}$, P. 24, V. 1/5, A. 2 | $\frac{1}{19-20}$, C. 17, L. l. 42-47, Cæc. pyl. 20.

Length of head 4½, of caudal 5¼, height of body 3¾ to 4¼ in the total length. *Eye*—with a broad anterior and posterior adipose lid, both reaching the pupil; diameter 1/4 of length of head, rather more than 1 diameter from end of snout, and 1½ apart. Dorsal and abdominal profiles about equally convex, snout rather pointed. Lower jaw the longer: the maxilla reaches to below the front edge or first third of the orbit. Interorbital space with a raised ridge along its centre. Greatest width of head equals rather more than half its length: its height equals its length behind the posterior nostril. Preorbital in its deepest part, equal to nearly 1 diameter of the orbit. *Teeth*—villiform and in more than one row at symphysis of either jaw, laterally in a single row of moderately large ones: in a Λ-shaped or lozenge-shaped patch on vomer, also on the palatines, and in a very narrow band along the centre of the tongue. *Fins*—fourth dorsal spine rather the longest, and equal to 1/3 the height of the body, and nearly as high as the commencement of the soft dorsal, the last ray of which is rather prolonged. Pectoral falciform and 1 diameter of the eye longer than the head: ventral reaches half way to the anal, the spine of which fin is well developed, and nearly half as long as the first ray: the base of the last ray is rather distant from the one preceding it. Caudal deeply forked. *Scales*—over body, chest, cheeks, but not on the upper jaw, or occipital crest which is moderately developed. *Lateral-line*—with a long irregular curve (which is 3/4 as long as the straight portion) becoming straight below the sixth or seventh dorsal ray: the plates begin about the fifth or eighth scale on the straight portion, becoming well developed near the end of the dorsal fin, below which they equal 1/7 of the height of the body. About 100 rows of scales along the lateral-line, and 125 rows descend from the back to it along its whole course. Free portion of tail rather longer than high. *Colours*—silvery along the back, becoming golden on the abdomen, a series of short vertical bands, as wide as the ground colour, cross the lateral-line along its whole extent. A black shoulder spot extending on to the opercle. Fins yellow, tip of second dorsal anteriorly white, posteriorly with rather a dark summit: anal with a white edge.

This species is figured amongst Sir W. Elliot's Fishes of Madras, as *Warri pirah*, Tam.

Habitat.—Red Sea, seas of India, Andamans, to the Malay Archipelago and beyond. The specimen figured, nearly 8 inches long, is from Madras, where it is common, especially during the cold months. I have found some full of developed ova as early as March.

14. **Caranx kalla**, Plate XLIX, fig. 5.

Cuv. and Val. ix, p. 49; Day, Fish. Malabar, p. 83.

Selar brevis, Bleeker, Makr. p. 54.

Selar kalla, Bleeker, Beng. en Hind. p. 44.

* In a young specimen, 3½ inches long, crenulations are visible on the angle and lower limb of the preopercle.

Caranx calla, Günther, Catal. ii, p. 433.
Caranx brevis, Günther, Catal. ii, p. 435.
Kalla parah, Tam.

B. vii, D. 8 | [illegible] P. 20, V. 1/5, A. 2 | [illegible] C. 17, L. l. 40-44.

Length of head $4\frac{1}{2}$ to 1/5, of caudal $4\frac{2}{3}$, height of body from 1/3 to $3\frac{1}{2}$ of the total length. *Eye*—with a developed posterior adipose lid, diameter 1/3 of length of head, 2/3 of a diameter from end of snout, and 3/4 of a diameter apart. The abdominal profile more convex than that of the back. The greatest width of the head is 4/7 of its length, its height nearly equals its length. Lower jaw the longer: the maxilla reaches to below the first third of the eye. Greatest depth of preorbital equal to half the diameter of the eye. *Teeth*—in the jaws in a single row, in a Λ-shaped spot on the vomer, in a band on the palatines, also along the middle of the tongue. *Fins*—dorsal spines of moderate strength, the third and fourth the longest and equal to 1/3 the height of the body, and 1/4 less than the anterior portion of the second dorsal fin. Pectoral falciform, from 4/5 to as long as the body is high: ventral short, not reaching half way to the anal. Anal commences below the fourth dorsal ray, its last ray as well as that of the dorsal a little elongated. Caudal deeply forked, upper lobe the longer. *Scales*—over the body, chest, and some on the cheeks: a well developed sheath to dorsal and anal fins. *Lateral-line*—having 80 scales, rather strongly curved anteriorly, but not ending abruptly, the height of its arch equals 1/3 of its length, whilst its length equals $1\frac{1}{2}$ in that of the straight portion, which last commences below the fourth or fifth dorsal ray. Its keeled plates begin at the commencement of the straight portion, and below the end of the second dorsal they equal 1/7 of the height of the body. The free portion of the tail longer than high. *Colours*—bluish-green above, shot with silver, sides and abdomen silvery, with numerous reflections: a distinct black spot on the opercle. The tail and the caudal fin brilliant yellow, the upper lobe being tinged with green: the other fins white, excepting the dorsal which has some black upon it.

Caranx para, Cuv. and Val. ix, p. 58, and ? *C. cambon*, C.V. ix, p. 60; *Selar para*, Bleeker, Makr. p. 56, may be this species.

Habitat.—Red Sea, seas of India and China, attaining at least 8 inches in length. The specimen figured ($5\frac{1}{2}$ inches long) is from Madras.

15. **Caranx ire**, Plate XLIX, fig. 6.

Cuv. and Val. ix, p. 57; Günther, Catal. ii, p. 436.

Caranx praeustus, Bennett, Life of Raffles, p. 689; Günther, Catal. ii, p. 436; Peters, Monats. Ak. Berlin, 1868, p. 262.

Carangoides praeustus, Bleeker, Makr. p. 364, and Verh. Bat. Gen. xxiv, Makr. p. 60, and Bintang, 1868, p. 5.

Selar ire, Bleeker, Beng. en Hind. p. 44.
Citula praeusta, Bleeker, Bintang, 1868, p. 5.
Caranx melanostethos, Day, Proc. Zool. Soc. 1865, p. 23, and Fish. Malabar, p. 83, pl. vi.
Ire-parah, Tam.; *Oolin-parah*, Mal.

B. vii, D. 8 | [illegible] P. 20, V. 1/5, A. 2 | [illegible] C. 19, L. l. 26-28.

Length of head $4\frac{1}{2}$ to $4\frac{2}{3}$, of pectoral 1/5, of caudal 2/9, height of body $3\frac{3}{4}$ to 1/4 of the total length. *Eye*—having a narrow posterior adipose lid extending not quite half way to the pupil,* diameter of eye $3\frac{1}{2}$ to 1/4 in length of head, from 1 to $1\frac{1}{3}$ diameter from end of snout, and nearly 4/5 of a diameter apart. Dorsal and anal profiles about equally convex: snout slightly elevated. Greatest width of head equals nearly half its length, whilst its height is about the same as its length. Jaws of about equal length anteriorly, or the lower slightly the longer: the maxilla reaches to below the front edge or first third of the eye. Preorbital in its deepest part equals rather more than 1/2 a diameter of the orbit. *Teeth*—in villiform bands in both jaws, which become a single row laterally in the lower: the outer row in the upper jaw being a little enlarged. In a semilunar spot anteriorly on the vomer, whilst posteriorly there exists a long narrow band along the median line: in a band on the palatines and also along the middle of the tongue. *Fins*—spines of first dorsal weak, the third slightly the longest and equal to about 1/3 of the height of the body. Second dorsal highest anteriorly where its rays equal from 1/2 to $2\frac{1}{3}$ in the height of the body. Pectoral reaches to above the commencement of the anal fin, which last is similar to the soft dorsal. Caudal deeply forked, upper lobe usually the longer. *Scales*—cover the body except just in front of the ventral fins: superiorly they extend forwards on the head to above the eyes, cheeks, and upper portion of the opercle, but there are none on the snout, preorbital, nor occipital crest: the soft dorsal and anal fins have a high scaly sheath. *Lateral-line*—consists of about 102 scales, at first it is moderately curved, becoming straight below the eighth dorsal ray, but the keeled scales do not commence until underneath the fifteenth ray, they are well developed but not very strong, the highest equalling about 1/10 of that of the body. Free portion of the tail rather longer than high. *Colours*—gray along the back, becoming lighter on the abdomen, the whole glossed with purple and gold. Head and chest are occasionally brownish-black. No opercular spot. Fins yellow, with black points, the anterior portion of the second dorsal black with a white tip, the rest of the fin and of the anal more or less dark. Caudal sometimes with black tips and a white edge.

This species is named *Nuar parah* and *Karumunji parah*, Tam., in Sir W. Elliot's collection.

* This varies with age, also in individual specimens, in one at 3 inches in length it reaches the pupil.

Habitat.—Seas of India to the Malay Archipelago. Grows to upwards of a foot in length. In Malabar it is mostly captured during the cold months.

16. Caranx compressus, Plate L, fig. 1.

Caranx ferdau, Rüppell, Atl. Fische, p. 99, t. xxv, f. 6; Cuv. and Val. ix, p. 56; Günther, Catal. ii, p. 439 (not Forsk.).

Caranx compressus, Day, Proc. Zool. Soc. 1870, p. 689.

Caranx brevicarinatus, Klunz. Verh. z. b. Ges. Wien, 1871, p. 461.

B. vii, D. 8 | [illegible], P. 21, V. 1/5, A. 2 | [illegible], C. 21, L. l. 13.

Length of head 1/4 to 4¼, of caudal 1/5, height of body 3¼ to 3½ in the total length. *Eyes*—without adipose lids, situated just above the centre of the height of the head and 1 vertical diameter from the upper profile, diameter of eyes 3½ to 1/4 of length of head, 1⅓ to 1½ diameters from end of snout, and 1 apart. Body rather strongly compressed, dorsal and abdominal profiles equally convex: occipital crest well developed. Greatest width of head equals 1/5, and its height the entire length of the head. Lower jaw the longer: cleft of mouth commences opposite the middle or upper third of the eye, and the maxilla reaches to below the front edge or first third of the orbit. Greatest depth of preorbital equals 2/3 to 3/4 of the diameter of the eye. *Teeth*—villiform in both jaws, becoming in a single narrow band laterally in the lower, also present on the vomer, palate, and tongue. *Fins*—third dorsal spine longest, and equal to 1/3 or 2/7 of the height of the body, and only 2/3 as high as the anterior portion of second dorsal fin. Pectoral falciform and 1/4 longer than the head. Ventral reaches 1/2 way to the anal. Anal similar to but lower than the second dorsal. Caudal forked. *Scales*—present on the cheeks, round the posterior edge of the eye, the body and chest, also forming a low groove along the bases of second dorsal and anal fins. *Lateral-line*—containing about 150 scales, it forms a very gradual curve to below the 12th dorsal ray when it becomes straight, the keels are most developed on the free portion of the tail, where the largest equal 1/28 of the height of the body. Free portion of the tail 1/2 longer than high at its base. *Colours*—silvery, with a minute opercular spot: vertical margin of preopercle dark.

Habitat.—Red Sea and Andamans, where the specimen (16 inches long) which is figured was captured.

17. Caranx atropus.

Brama atropus, Bl. Schn. p. 98, t. 23.

Scomber wait-parah, Russell. Fish. Vizag. ii, p. 38, pl. 152.

Caranx nigripes, Cuv. and Val. ix, p. 122; Richards. Ich. China, p. 275, Cantor, Catal. p. 129; Jerdon. M. J. L. and Sc. 1851, p. 137; Kner, Novara Fische, p. 159.

Olistus atropus, Cuv. and Val. ix, p. 141.

Carangoides atropus, Bleeker, Makr. p. 66.

Caranx atropus, Cantor, Catal. p. 130; Günther, Catal. ii, p. 450; Day, Fish. Malabar, p. 88.

Kuadi parah, Tam.

B. vii, D. 8 | [illegible], P. 22, V. 1/5, A. 2 | [illegible], C. 16, L. l. 32-35, Vert. 10/14.

Length of head 1/4 to 2/7, of pectoral 2/7, of caudal 1/4 to 2/7, height of body 2/5 of the total length. *Eyes*—without adipose lids, diameter 3/10 to 2/7 of length of head, 2/3 of a diameter from end of snout, and also apart. Body oval, strongly compressed, with the crest on the summit of the head well developed. Greatest width of the head equals rather more than half its length, and its height 1/5 more than its length. Cleft of mouth commences anteriorly opposite the centre of the front edge of the eye, and the maxilla reaches to below the middle of the orbit: lower jaw the longer. The greatest depth of the preorbital equals about 1/2 the diameter of the eye. *Teeth*—in two rows in both jaws, the outer in the premaxillaries very slightly the larger: in the lower jaw the teeth laterally form only a single row: in a triangular patch on the vomer, in a narrow band on the palatines, and also along the middle of the tongue. *Fins*—spines of first dorsal weak, the third and fourth the longest, and equal to 1/5 of the height of the body: second dorsal highest anteriorly, its second ray being equal to 1/3 of the height of the body. Pectoral falciform. Ventral with a weak spine and elongated rays which reach as far as the anal fin, and are receivable into a groove, at the bottom of which are inserted the two pre-anal spines. Caudal deeply lobed. *Scales*—a few on the cheeks and below the eye, none on the remainder of the head; body scaled except on the chest and from between the bases of the pectoral and ventral fins to the head. They form a rather high scaly sheath to the second dorsal and anal fins. *Lateral-line*—consists of about 75 rows, it curves to below the fifth ray of the dorsal fin, subsequent to which the keeled scales commence, the widest below the last fourth of the dorsal fin being equal to 1/17 of the height of the body. *Colours*—bluish-green along the back, becoming silvery shot with purple on the sides and beneath: a well marked black opercular spot; ventrals deep black. The *young* are vertically banded, and the opercular spot indistinct or absent.

In a specimen 3½ inches in length the angle and lower edge of the preopercle are crenulated.

Habitat.—Seas of India to the Malay Archipelago, attaining at least a foot in length.

18. Caranx Malabaricus, Plate L, fig. 2.

Scomber Malabaricus, Bl. Schn. p. 31.

Scomber tolum parah, Russell, ii, p. 37, pl. 150.

Caranx cæruleo-pinnatus, Rüpp. Atl. Fische, p. 100, and N. W. Fische. p. 47, t. xiii, fig. 2 (not Cuv. and Val.).

Caranx Malabaricus, Cuv. and Val. ix, p. 121; Richards. Ich. China, p. 275; Cantor, Catal. p. 128; Jerdon, M. J. L. and Sc. 1851, p. 137; Günther, Catal. ii, p. 437; Kner, Novara Fische. p. 155; Klunz. Verh. z. b. Ges. Wien, 1871, p. 463.

Carangoides tilampareh, Bleeker, Makr. p. 64.

Carangoides Malabaricus, Bleeker, en Pisc. p. 69.

Citula Malabarica, Bleeker, Madagas. p. 99.

B. vii, D. 7-8 | $\frac{1}{21-22}$, P. 21, V. 1/5, A. 2 | $\frac{1}{17-19}$, C. 21, L. l. 28.

Length of head $3\frac{4}{5}$ to 1/4, of caudal $4\frac{1}{2}$ to $4\frac{2}{3}$, height of body $2\frac{1}{2}$ in the young to $2\frac{1}{3}$ in the adult of the total length. *Eyes*—without distinct adipose lids, but the skin rather projects over the eye; diameter of eyes 1/3 of length of head, 1 diameter from end of snout, and 3/4 of a diameter apart. Body oval and strongly compressed, dorsal and anal profiles equally convex, a slight concavity, most distinct in the adult, opposite the middle of the eyes: the occipital crest well developed. Greatest width of the head equals nearly 1/2 its length: the height of the head is a little more than its length. Cleft of the mouth commences opposite the lower edge of the orbit: the lower jaw slightly the longer: the maxilla reaches to below the first third of the eye. Greatest depth of the preorbital nearly equals 1 diameter of the orbit. *Teeth*—villiform in both jaws, in a somewhat triangular spot on the vomer, an elongated band along the palatines, and likewise along the centre of the tongue being widest anteriorly. *Fins*—dorsal spines of moderate strength, the second, third, and fourth being of about the same height, and equal to 2/5 of that of the body: second dorsal highest anteriorly, where the rays equal $2\frac{2}{3}$ in that of the body and are similar to those in the anal. Pectoral rather longer than the head. Ventral small, reaching 2/3 of the way to the pre-anal spines. Caudal deeply forked. *Scales*—on the head there are merely a few behind the middle of the eye, none on the chest. Only a low groove along the first part of the soft dorsal fin. *Lateral-line*—having about 90 to 105 scales, it forms a low curve to below the twelfth or thirteenth dorsal ray. Its plates only commence under about the twentieth ray, becoming most developed on the side of the free portion of the tail, when their greatest depth only equals 1/20 to 1/30 of the height of the body, being proportionately smaller in the adults. Free portion of the tail 1/2 longer than high at its base. *Colours*—back bluish, sides and abdomen silvery shot with purple: a dull black mark in axilla. The whole of the posterior half and upper edge of the opercle stained black or brown (said to be sometimes absent). Dorsal usually stained darkest at its outer edge, the other fins pale yellow.

Jerdon observes that this fish is termed *Tolloo parah*, Tam.

I have two young *Caranx's*, $1\frac{3}{4}$ and $2\frac{1}{2}$ inches long, which appear to be the young of this species, the height of the body of the smallest is $1\frac{7}{8}$ in the total length, its ventrals reach the anal fin: it is vertically banded, the first dorsal and ventral black. In the larger specimen the height of the body is $2\frac{1}{4}$ in the total length, the ventrals reach the pre-anal spines, whilst the vertical bands have begun to disappear. The first dorsal and ventral are black.

Habitat.—Red Sea, seas of India to the Malay Archipelago and beyond, attaining at least a foot in length, the specimen figured is from Madras, it is nearly 8 inches long.

19. Caranx oblongus, Plate LI, fig. 1.

Cuv. and Val. ix, p. 128; Cantor. Catal. p. 132; Günther, Catal. ii, p. 452.

Carangoides oblongus, Bleeker, Makr. p. 62.

Ra-thel-dah, Andam.

B. vii, D. 8 | $\frac{1}{27-28}$, P. 21, V. 1/5, A. 2 | $\frac{1}{25-26}$, C. 18, L. l. 34-40.

Length of head 1/4 to 2/9, of caudal $4\frac{1}{2}$, height of body $3\frac{1}{2}$ in the total length. *Eyes*—without distinct adipose lids, diameter $3\frac{1}{4}$ in the young to $4\frac{1}{2}$ in the adult in length of head, nearly 1 diameter from end of snout, and 3/4 to 1 diameter apart. Body oval, with the dorsal profile rather more convex than that of the abdomen, a slight concavity in the profile opposite the upper third of the eye. Greatest width of head 4/7 of its length, its height rather more than its length. Occipital crest moderately developed. Upper edge of eye rather close to the dorsal profile. Lower jaw the longer. Cleft of mouth oblique, commencing opposite the upper third or centre of the front edge of the orbit, the maxilla reaching to below the middle of the eye. Greatest width of preorbital equals 1/2 in the young to 3/4 in the adult of the diameter of the orbit. Preopercle with some rather strong denticulations along both limbs, which become almost imperceptible in the adult. *Teeth*—in a narrow villiform band, or in two rows in the premaxillaries, having the outer slightly enlarged: in a single row in the lower jaw, except at its anterior portion where they are the largest, and have a few villiform ones posteriorly. In a triangular spot on the vomer, and in a band along the palatines, and on the tongue. *Fins*—dorsal spines low, the longest equal to $3\frac{1}{3}$ or 1/4 in the height of the body: second dorsal very much elevated anteriorly, where its rays equal from 3/4 to the height of the body. Pectoral as long or longer than the head. Ventral almost reaches the pre-anal spines. Anterior rays of anal elongated and equal to 3/5 of the height of the body. Caudal deeply forked. *Scales*—along the upper and hind edge of the eyes, on the cheeks and body, except on the chest as high as the pectoral fin, which is scaleless in the young, but in the adult this scaleless portion is confined to the chest anterior to the ventral fin, and about half the distance to the base of the pectoral. A low sheath to second dorsal and anal fins. *Lateral-line*—in about 105 rows, at first in the form of plate-like rounded scales it goes directly backwards and commences to descend below the commencement of the second dorsal, becoming straight beneath its ninth ray; the height of the arch equals 2/9 of its length: the keeled scales extend along the whole of its keeled portion, the widest equalling about 1/13 of the height of the body. Free portion of the tail as high at its commencement as it is long. *Colours*—golden in the young, with vertical bluish bands, which soon fade after death: the adults are more olive, becoming dull white beneath. No opercular spot. Fins yellow, stained at their edges, due to innumerable fine dots: caudal orange, with its last half black, having a light tip to either lobe.

Habitat.—Seas of India to the Malay Archipelago and beyond. Largest specimen from Madras, 5 inches long. Cantor's type is $4\frac{1}{2}$ inches in length, and these two specimens with their serrated preopercles approach very closely to *Carangichthys typus*, Bleeker, which has D. 8 | $\frac{1}{20}$, A. 2 | $\frac{1}{17}$, L. l. 22. The one figured (5 inches long) is from the Andaman islands.

20. **Caranx nigrescens**, Plate L, fig. 6.

Day, Proc. Zool. Soc. 1867, p. 704.

Tarja parah, Tam.

B. vii, D. 8 | $\frac{1}{22}$, P. 19, V. 1/5, A. 2 | $\frac{1}{17}$, C. 19, L. l. 23.

Length of head nearly 1/4, of caudal 2/9, height of body 2/7 of the total length. *Eyes*—without any adipose lids, diameter 1/5 of length of head, nearly 2 diameters from end of snout, and $1\frac{1}{2}$ apart. Dorsal profile slightly more convex than that of the abdomen, interorbital crest well developed. Greatest width of head equals half of its length, and its height equals its length. Lower jaw very slightly the longer, cleft of mouth commences anteriorly below the level of the eye, it is very slightly oblique, the maxilla reaches to below the front edge of the eye. Lower limb of preopercle, also sub- and interopercles crenulated. *Teeth*—in numerous villiform rows in both jaws, a triangular patch on the vomer, in a long narrow band on the palatines, none on the tongue. *Fins*—third dorsal spine the longest, equal to 2/7 of the height of the body and rather above 1/2 as high as the anterior dorsal rays, which fin is elevated in its first part. Pectoral falciform, a little longer than the head and reaching to below the middle of the soft dorsal fin. Anal similar in form, but a little lower than the second dorsal. Caudal deeply forked. *Scales*—on cheeks round the eyes, upper portion of opercle and body, none on the chest as high as the base of the pectoral fin. *Lateral-line*—contains 140 scales, at first it forms a very low long curve to below the thirteenth dorsal ray, from whence it gradually becomes straight, the length of the base of the arch equalling that of the straight portion of the fin. Keeled scales are but slightly developed, being only distinct in the last 8 scales where the largest equals 1/20 of the height of the body. Free portion of the tail at its base nearly equals its length. *Colours*—of a dusky-grayish, having innumerable fine black points, and generally glossed with purple. A well marked black opercular spot. Fins nearly black, especially the dorsal.

This species appears to be allied to *C. chrysophrys*, Cuv. and Val. which has D. 8 | $\frac{1}{20}$, A. 2 | $\frac{1}{16}$, but the figure shows a much higher body ($2\frac{1}{2}$ of the total length) and the eye placed more in the centre of the depth of the head. No opercular spot.

Habitat.—Madras, where the specimen figured (a male, 24 inches long) was captured in March, 1867. The fishermen asserted that it annually arrived from the deep sea about March.

21. **Caranx armatus**, Plate LI, fig. 2.

Sciæna armata, Forsk. p. 53; Gmel. Linn. p. 1306.

Scomber, Russell, ii, p. 38, and *Tchawil parah*, pl. 151 *(young)*.

Citula plumbea, Quoy and Gaim. Voy. Freyc. Zool. Poiss. p. 361.

Citula ciliaria, Rüpp. Atl. Fische, p. 102, t. xxv, f. 3; Kner, Novara Fische, p. 156.

Citula armata, Rüpp. Atl. Fische, p. 103, and N. W. Fische, p. 50; Bleeker, Madagas. p. 99.

Caranx citula et cirrhosus (Ehren.) Cuv. and Val. ix, p. 126, pl. 250.

Caranx armatus, Cuv. and Val. ix, p. 127; Cantor, Catal. p. 131; Günther, Catal. ii, p. 453; Day, Fishes of Malabar, p. 89; Klunz. Verh. z. b. Ges. Wien, 1871, p. 455.

Caranx ciliaris, Cuv. and Val. ix, p. 129 *(young)*; Temm. and Schleg. Fauna Japon. Poiss. p. 112: Richards. Ich. China, p. 276; Jerdon, M. J. L. and Sc. 1851, p. 137.

Olistus Malabaricus, Cuv. and Val. ix, p. 137, pl. 251; Cuv. Règ. Anim. Ill. Poiss. pl. 58, f. 1.

Olistus Rüppellii, Cuv. and Val. ix, p. 144.

Carangoides citula, Bleeker, Makr. p. 65.

Carangoides armatus, Bleeker, en Pisc. p. 67.

Tarja parah, Tam.

B. vii, D. 6-8 | $\frac{1}{20-21}$, P. 21, V. 1/5, A. 2 | $\frac{1}{17-18}$, C. 19, L. l. 20.

Length of head 2/9 to 1/5, of pectoral 2/7, height of body 2/5 to 4/11 of the total length. *Eye*—with a very narrow posterior adipose lid, diameter $3\frac{1}{4}$ to $3\frac{1}{2}$ in the length of head, 3/4 to 1 diameter from end of snout, and also apart. Body oval, the dorsal and anal profiles about equally convex. Greatest width of the head equals 3/5 of its length, its height 1/4 more than its length. Lower jaw the longer, cleft of mouth commences opposite the middle of the eyes: the maxilla reaches posteriorly to below the anterior 1/3 or centre of the eye. Greatest depth of the preorbital equals 2/3 of the diameter of the orbit. *Teeth*—villiform in both jaws, with an outer somewhat enlarged row in the premaxillaries: they are also present in a triangular spot on the vomer, and in an elongated band along the palatines and middle of the tongue. *Fins*—second to fourth dorsal spines subequal in length and about 2/9 of the height of the body: second dorsal much elongated anteriorly, the first few rays occasionally reaching the caudal fin: in some specimens all the rays have prolongations, usually only the first few. Pectoral falciform, extending to at least below the middle of the soft dorsal. Ventral reaches rather above half way to the anal. Caudal deeply forked. *Scales*—a few on the hind portion of the head, round the eyes and on the cheeks, also over the body except the chest and the portion anterior to the bases of the pectoral and ventral fins. They also form a groove for the soft dorsal and anal fins. *Lateral-line*—consists of 104 scales, it makes a long low curve becoming straight beneath the middle of the second dorsal, the keeled plates are developed in the last half of the horizontal portion of the lateral-line, but are not large. Free portion of the tail hardly so high at its base as it is long. *Colours*—upper surface of head and back bluish-green, sides of the head and body golden, with purple reflections. Opercular spot moderately distinct. First dorsal blackish, second and anal yellowish, with darker edges. Pectoral dark behind its base. The *young* vertically banded.

Habitat.—Red Sea, East coast of Africa, seas of India to the Malay Archipelago and beyond, attaining at least 20 inches in length. The specimen figured (8 inches long) is from the Andamans.

22. **Caranx gallus**, Plate LI, fig. 3.

Zeus gallus, Linn. Sys. i, p. 454; Bloch, t. 192, and Gmel. Linn. p. 1222; Bl. Schn. p. 94; Russell, Fish. Vizag. i, p. 45, and *Gurrah parah*, pl. 57.

Zeus vomer, Russell, l. c. p. 46, and *Cheeroola parah*, pl. 58 (not *Zeus vomer*, Linn.).

Gallus virescens, Lacép. iv, pp. 583, 584.

Gallichthys major, Cuv. and Val. ix, p. 168, pl. 254; Cantor, Catal. p. 136; Richards. Ich. China, p. 271.

Gallichthys cheroda, Cuv. and Val. ix, p. 175.

Scyris Indica, Rüpp. Atl. Fische, p. 128, t. 33, f. 1 *(young)*; Cuv. and Val. ix, p. 145, pl. 252 *(adult ?)*; Rüpp. N. W. Fische, p. 51; Swainson, Fishes, ii, p. 251; Richards. Ich. China, p. 270; Cantor, Catal. p. 134.

Blepharis gallichthys, Swainson, Fishes, ii, p. 250.

Scyris Ruppellii, Swainson, *l. c.* p. 251.

Carangoides gallichthys, Bleeker, Makr. p. 68.

Caranx gallus, Günther, Catal. ii, p. 455; Day, Fish. Malabar, p. 91; Klunz. Verh. z. b. Ges. Wien, 1871, p. 454.

Citula gallus, Bleeker, Bintang, 1868, p. 5.

B. vii, D. 0-6 | [illegible], P. 17, V. 1/5, A. 0-2 | [illegible], C. 19, L. l. 8-10, Vert. 10/14.

Length of head from $3\frac{1}{2}$ at 6 inches to $4\frac{2}{3}$ at 23 inches in the total length: of caudal $3\frac{1}{2}$ to $4\frac{1}{2}$, height of body $1\frac{3}{4}$ to 1/3 of the total length. *Eye*—without or with only a small posterior adipose lid, diameter $3\frac{3}{4}$ to 1/4 in length of head, $1\frac{1}{2}$ to $1\frac{3}{4}$ diameters from end of snout. Body much elevated, especially in the young, and strongly compressed: central longitudinal crest on the head much raised, causing the dorsal profile before the eyes to be concave. Lower jaw the longer, cleft of mouth commences below the level of the eye, the maxilla reaches to nearly below the ventral from the front edge of the orbit. Preorbital very high, equalling from $1\frac{1}{4}$ to $1\frac{1}{3}$ diameters of the orbit. *Teeth*—apparently villiform in the *young* in jaws, vomer, palatines, and tongue, but in adults (as at 23 inches long) it is seen that they assume an entirely different (or *Sparoid*) character, having rounded crowns, 5 rows in the premaxillaries, and 4 in the lower jaw, decreasing to 2 or 1 posteriorly: whilst the vomer has only a single row across it. *Fins*—the spinous first dorsal in the young appears in a rudimentary form, becoming absorbed as age advances: the second dorsal commences at the most elevated point of the back, its rays, especially the first 7 or 8, are elongated and have filiform terminations. Pectoral rather longer than the head. Ventral with its two outer rays elongated in the young, not so in the adult. The pre-anal spines are apparent in the immature. First two or three anal rays elongated, but not so much so as those of the dorsal fin. Caudal deeply forked. *Scales*—rudimentary or absent except along the lateral-line: at the free portion of the tail they are keeled, anteriorly they are small and rounded. A low keel on either side of base of the tail in adults. *Lateral-line*—first ascends, then curves to below the 12th dorsal ray when it becomes straight. *Pyloric appendages*—numerous. *Colours*—silvery glossed with purple and gold: the young with five wide vertical bands which disappear with age. A small, dark opercular spot in the adult. Filamentous prolongations of fins dark or black.

Habitat.—Red Sea, through those of India to the Malay Archipelago and beyond, attaining at least 2 feet in length (said to reach 5 feet) and is not uncommon.

23. **Caranx ciliaris.**

Zeus ciliaris, Bloch, t. 191; Gmel. Linn. p. 1223; Bl. Schn. p. 94; Shaw, Zool. iv, p. 283; Lacép. iv, pp. 570, 572.

Scomber filamentosus, Mungo Park, Trans. Linn. Soc. iii, p. 36; Bl. Schn. p. 34.

Blepharis Indicus, Cuv. and Val. ix, p. 154; Tem. and Schleg. Fauna, Japon. Poiss. p. 113, pl. 60, f. 2; Cuv. Règ. Anim. Ill. Poissons, pl. 58, f. 3; Richards. Ich. China, p. 271.

Blepharis fasciatus, Rüpp. Atl. Fische, p. 129, t. 33, f. 2.

Carangoides blepharis, Bleeker, Makr. p. 67.

Caranx ciliaris, Günther, Catal. ii, p. 454; Day, Fish. Malabar, p. 90; Klunz. Verh. z. b. Ges. Wien, 1871, p. 454.

B. vii, D. 6 | [illegible], P. 18, V. 1/5, A. 2 | [illegible], C. 19, L. l. 15.

Length of head $3\frac{1}{3}$ to $3\frac{1}{2}$, of caudal 2/9, height of body $1\frac{1}{2}$ to $1\frac{3}{4}$ in the total length. *Eyes*—without adipose lids, diameter 1/3 of length of head, 3/4 to 1 diameter from end of snout. Body elevated and compressed, a swelling in the dorsal profile opposite the eyes, causing a slight concavity below and also above them. Lower jaw the longer, cleft of mouth commences just below, or level with, the lower edge of the orbit: the maxilla reaches to below the front edge or first third of the eyes. Greatest height of preorbital equalling from 3/4 to 1 diameter of the orbit. *Teeth*—villiform in jaws, vomer, palatines, and tongue. *Fins*—spinous first dorsal rudimentary: the second dorsal commencing at the most elevated point of the back, has its first five or six rays elongated and with filiform terminations. Pectoral as long as the head. Ventral reaches the anal. Anterior rays of anal elongated similarly to the second dorsal. Caudal deeply forked. *Scales*—absent except on the lateral-line. *Lateral-line*—with a strong bend anteriorly, becoming straight below the ninth or tenth dorsal ray. *Colours*—silvery, with five or six vertical bands on the body. Anterior portion of soft dorsal and anal black. An opercular spot.

Habitat.—From the Red Sea, through those of India to the Malay Archipelago and beyond. This species is not nearly so common as *C. gallus.*

B. No teeth on the palate.

24. Caranx leptolepis, Plate LI, fig. 4.

Caranx leptolepis et *Mertensii*, Cuv. and Val. ix, pp. 63, 64.
Caranx leptolepis, Cantor, Catal. p. 127; Günther, Catal. ii, p. 440.
Letaspis leptolepis, Bleeker, Makr. p. 71.
Selaroides leptolepis, Bleeker, l. c. p. 87.
Caranx Bidii, Day, Proc. Zool. Soc. 1873, p. 237.
Ramah parah, Tam.

B. vii, D. 8 | [illegible], P. 20, V. 1/5, A. 2 | $\frac{1}{21}$, C. 17, L. l. 24-28.

Length of head $4\frac{2}{3}$ to $4\frac{1}{2}$, of caudal 1/5 to 2/11, height of body $3\frac{3}{4}$ to $4\frac{1}{4}$ in the total length. *Eye*—with a broad posterior adipose lid which covers the hind third of the pupil, an anterior eyelid extends half the distance across the iris: diameter 2/7 of length of head, 1 to $1\frac{1}{3}$ diameters from the end of snout, and also apart. The greatest width of the head equals half its length, its height nearly equals its length; jaws of about the same length, or lower slightly the longer: the maxilla reaches to below the anterior edge of first third of the orbit. Preorbital in its deepest part equals 2/3 of the diameter of the orbit.* *Teeth*—fine ones in the anterior portion of the lower jaw, none on the upper, the vomer, or palate: a fine band on the tongue. *Fins*—dorsal spines weak, the third and fourth the longest and equal to 1/2 the height of the body: anterior portion of soft dorsal the highest and equal to $2\frac{1}{2}$ in that of the body. Pectoral rather longer than the head and reaching to above the fourth anal ray: ventral nearly reaches to the pre-anal spines. Last dorsal and anal ray somewhat elongated. Caudal forked. *Scales*—over body, chest, cheeks, and superiorly on the head to above the middle of the eye. *Lateral-line*—ninety-five scales, it makes a very gentle curve, becoming straight from below the first third of the second dorsal fin: keeled scales begin so gradually under the last portion of the second dorsal that it is difficult to decide where they commence, the longest are below the commencement of the free portion of the tail, and equal about $\frac{1}{15}$ of the height of the body. Free portion of the tail one-fourth higher at its base than it is long. *Colours*—silvery, a broad golden stripe from above the eye to the upper edge of the tail, lower two-third of dorsal fin yellow, upper third dark. Anal having its outer third white, the rest yellow: a large deep black spot on the shoulder, said to be sometimes absent (*C. Mertensii*).

This species is termed *Nama parah*, Tam., in Sir Walter Elliot's figures of Madras Fishes.

Habitat.—Seas of India to the Malay Archipelago. The specimen figured ($6\frac{1}{4}$ inches in length) is from Madras.

25. Caranx nigripinnis, Plate LI, fig. 5.

? *Scomber wori-parah*,† Russell, ii, p. 40, pl. 155.

B. vii, D. 7-8 | [illegible], P. 23, V. 1/5, A. 2 | [illegible], C. 19, L. l. 55-60.

Length of head $4\frac{1}{2}$ to $4\frac{2}{3}$, of caudal 4 to $4\frac{1}{3}$, height of body $3\frac{1}{4}$ in the total length. *Eye*—with a wide anterior and posterior adipose lid; in one specimen with only a very broad posterior one reaching to across a portion of the pupil: diameter of eyes $3\frac{1}{2}$ to $3\frac{1}{4}$ in the length of head, 1 diameter from end of snout, and $1\frac{1}{3}$ apart. Dorsal and abdominal profiles about equally convex. Greatest width of head equals 4/7 of its length, and its height slightly less than its entire length. Snout and lower jaw rather broad and rounded, the width of the gape being rather more than the depth of the cleft, lower jaw somewhat the longer, the cleft of the mouth commences opposite the middle of the eye, the maxilla reaching to below the front edge of the eye. Greatest depth of preorbital equals 2/3 of the diameter of the orbit. *Teeth*—in both jaws in a single row of equal size, none on the vomer or palate, some on the tongue. *Fins*—dorsal spines of moderate strength, the third the longest, and equal to from 3/8 to 1/3 of the height of the body, and from 1/4 shorter to as long as

* In a specimen $3\frac{1}{2}$ inches long the lower edge of the preopercle is crenulated.

† Bleeker considers this species as *Carangoides* or *Caranx praeustus*, Bennett=*C. ire*, C. V., but the curve of its lateral-line and its black first dorsal fin would make it more suitable to *C. nigripinnis*. Russell says it has no scales and that the skin is singularly striated. Swainson, Fishes, ii, p. 245, names Russell's figure *Alepes melanoptera*.

the first rays, last dorsal ray thickened but not prolonged. Pectoral falciform, and from as long as, to slightly longer than the head. Ventral reaches half-way to the anal. Caudal rather deeply forked. *Scales*—over body, chest, behind the eyes, and on the upper portion of the opercles. No sheath to the soft dorsal and anal fins. *Lateral-line*—consisting of 105 scales, anteriorly moderately bent and becoming straight below the fourth or fifth dorsal rays where the plates commence, they soon become pretty well developed, the depth of the largest equalling from 1/11 to 1/13 of that of the body. Free portion of the tail longer than high. *Colours*—silvery, shot with gold: first dorsal deep black, anal with a white edge. A wide dark band along the second dorsal, having its upper anterior corner white.

Selar or *Caranx malam*, Bleeker, Makr. p. 363, and Bintang, 1868, p. 5, should from its generic name have teeth on the vomer and palate. This species would be a *Hemicaranx*, Bleeker.

Habitat.—Madras and Andamans. The specimen figured is 9 inches long, and from the Andamans.

26. Caranx speciosus.

Scomber speciosus, Forsk. p. 54; Gmel. Linn. 1332; Shaw, Zool. iv, p. 663.

Caranx speciosus, Lacép. iii, p. 72, pl. i, fig. 1; Cuv. and Val. ix, p. 130; Cantor, Catal. p. 133; Jerdon, M. J. L. and Sc. 1851, p. 137; Peters, Wieg. Arch. 1855, p. 245; Günther, Catal. ii, p. 444; Day, Fishes of Malabar, p. 84; Klunz. Verh. z. b. Ges. Wien, 1871, p. 455.

Scomber, Russell, Fish. Vizag. ii, p. 36, and *Polooroo parah*, pl. 149.

Caranx petaurista, Geoff. Desc. Eg. pl. 23, f. 1 (not Rüppell).

Zonichthys subcarinata, Swainson, Fishes, ii, p. 248.

Gnathanodon speciosus, Bleeker, Makr. p. 72.

Caranx poloosoo, Richards. Voy. Erebus and Terror, Ich. pl. 58, f. 4, 5.

B. vii, D. 7-8 | $\frac{1}{18-20}$, P. 22, V. 1/5, A. 2 | $\frac{1}{15-17}$, C. 19, L. l. 13-15.

Length of head $4\frac{1}{4}$, of caudal $4\frac{1}{2}$, height of body $3\frac{1}{2}$ in the total length. *Eyes*—in the centre of the depth of the head, without anterior or posterior adipose lids, but the skin extends slightly over the edge of the eye all round: diameter of eyes 1/4 to 2/9 of length of head, $1\frac{1}{2}$ diameters from end of snout. Body oval and strongly compressed. Interorbital space much elevated, having a crest along its centre. The greatest width of the head equals $2\frac{1}{4}$ in its length: whilst its height equals its length. Jaws of equal length anteriorly. The cleft of the mouth commences from opposite the lower edge of the eye, and the posterior extremity of the maxilla reaches to below the first third or centre of the orbit. Greatest depth of preorbital equals 1 diameter of eye. Pre- sub- and inter-opercles finely serrated in the young, crenulated or entire in the adult. *Teeth*—absent from jaws and palate. *Fins*—spines of first dorsal weak, the length of the third or the highest being equal to 1/4 of that of the body, interspinous membrane rather deeply emarginate: the recumbent spine anterior to the fin is very distinct in the young. Anterior portion of second dorsal the highest, decreasing to the ninth, from whence it remains the same height, the anterior rays equal $2\frac{1}{3}$ in the height of the body, upper edge of fin emarginate. Pectoral falcate longer than the head, and reaching to above the eleventh dorsal ray. The second of the anal free spines the longest. Anal fin commences on the vertical below the fifth dorsal ray and is of similar form to the second dorsal. Caudal deeply forked. *Scales*—small, some on cheeks, upper edge of opercle, and superiorly to above the hind third of the eye, none on the interorbital crest. Body and chest scaled. *Lateral-line*—about 106 rows along its whole course, the first portion of the lateral-line to below the sixth or eighth dorsal ray forms a long curve, from thence it proceeds direct to the centre of the tail, in the first portion of its straight course the plates are small, the last thirteen to fifteen are pretty well developed, and equal about 1/15 of the height of the body. *Colours*—golden, with vertical black bands alternately narrow and wide, going from the dorsal to the ventral surfaces. The first wide band descends obliquely through the eye, whilst on the body are five more wide bands, the first going over the shoulder touching the hind edge of the opercle, and the last over the free portion of the tail, between these wide ones are intermediate narrow ones. Dorsal fin minutely dotted with fine black points: upper edge of soft dorsal gray, end of caudal lobes black: anal golden. Adults are said to become of an uniform colour, a statement I have not been able to verify.

This species is termed *Pathi parah* and *Pilli parah*, Tam., in Sir W. Elliot's collection of drawings of fish.

Habitat.—From the Red Sea throughout the seas of India to the Malay Archipelago and beyond: it attains at least three feet in length, and at which size I have observed the colours to be still distinct.

Genus, 2—Micropteryx, *Agass.*

Seriola, sp. Cuv.: *Chloroscombrus*, Gir.: *Micropus*, Kner (not Gray).

Branchiostegals seven. Body compressed; abdomen prominent and trenchant. Gape of mouth rather small. Teeth feeble, present on vomer and palatines. Two dorsal fins, the first with 7 spines, and a recumbent, anteriorly-directed one in front of the base of the fin: the second and the anal considerably more developed and without finlets posteriorly: two pre-anal spines. Scales small. Lateral-line smooth. Air-vessel bifurcated posteriorly. Pyloric appendages in moderate numbers.

SYNOPSIS OF INDIVIDUAL SPECIES.

1. *Micropteryx chrysurus*, D. 7 | $\frac{1}{26-27}$, A. 2 | $\frac{1}{27-28}$. Colour of body uniform, a dark square blotch on the back of the tail. Ventrals white. Pondicherry, West coast of Africa, Atlantic coasts of temperate and tropical America.

1. Micropteryx chrysurus.

Scomber chrysurus, Linn. Syst. i, p. 494; Bl. Schn. p. 33.
Scomber chloris, Bloch, t. 339; Bl. Schn. p. 27.
Micropteryx cosmopolita, Agass. in Spix, Pisc. Bras. p. 104, t. lix.
Seriola cosmopolita, Cuv. Règ. Anim.; Cuv. and Val. ix, p. 219, pl. 259; Dekay, New York, Fauna, Fishes, p. 129; Holbr. Ich. South Carolina, p. 77, pl. xi, f. 1; Guich. Poiss. in Sagra, Hist. Cuba, p. 117; Jerdon, M. J. L. and Sc. 1851, p. 137.
Scomber latus, Gronov. ed. Gray, p. 127.
Chloroscombrus cosmopolita, Girard, Proc. Acad. Nat. Sc. Phil. 1858, p. 168.
Chloroscombrus Caribbæus, Girard, l. c.
Micropteryx chrysurus, Günther, Catal. ii, p. 460; Kner, Novara Fische, p. 161; Bleeker, Fish. New Guinea, p. 84.

B. vii, D. 7 | [illegible], P. 18, V. 1/5, A. 2 | [illegible], C. 17, Cæc. pyl. 10-15, Vert. 10/14.

Length of head $4\frac{1}{2}$ to $5\frac{1}{4}$, of caudal $4\frac{1}{2}$ to one-fifth, height of body $2\frac{3}{4}$ to one-third in the total length. *Eyes*—diameter $3\frac{1}{4}$ in the length of head, 1 diameter from end of snout, and 3/4 apart. Body high and very compressed: the abdominal more convex than the dorsal profile. Greatest width of the head equals 2/5 of its length; its height equals its length. Cleft of mouth almost vertical, it commences opposite the upper edge of the orbit, the lower jaw the longer and its end forming part of the dorsal profile when the mouth is closed: the maxilla reaches to below the first third of the eye. *Teeth*—fine ones on both jaws, vomer, palate, and tongue. *Fins*—dorsal spines weak, increasing in length to the third which is nearly as high as the anterior portion of the soft dorsal, and 1/5 of the height of the body. Pectoral falciform and $3\frac{1}{2}$ to $3\frac{3}{4}$ in the total length. Ventral short and equal to 1/5 the height of the body. Anal similar to second dorsal. Caudal forked. *Scales*—small, present behind the eyes and over the body, also forming a sheath for the bases of the dorsal and anal fins. *Lateral-line*—forms rather a strong curve in the first third of its course. *Colours*—greenish along the back, becoming silvery on the sides and beneath. A dark blotch over the free portion of the tail. Ventrals white.

Jerdon observed that this species is termed *Tergaree parah*, Tam. at Madras.

Habitat.—This fish frequents the West coast of Africa and the Atlantic coasts of America: it has also been captured at Pondicherry.

Genus, 3—Seriola, *Cuv.*

Branchiostegals seven: pseudobranchiæ. Body oblong and moderately compressed: abdomen rounded. Cleft of mouth sometimes deep. Preopercle entire. Villiform teeth in the jaws, vomer, and palatine bones. First dorsal fin continuous, its spines not strong, the second dorsal and anal with many more rays: as a rule a pair of preanal spines, remote from the rest of the fin. Scales small or rudimentary. Lateral-line unarmed. Air-vessel simple. Pyloric appendages many.

Geographical distribution.—Nearly all temperate and tropical seas.

SYNOPSIS OF INDIVIDUAL SPECIES.

1. *Seriola nigrofasciata*, D. 5-6 | [illegible], A. [illegible]. Five or six broad vertical bands on the body: a dark spot on either lobe of caudal. Red Sea, through the seas of India, to the Malay Archipelago and beyond.

1. Seriola nigrofasciata, Plate LI, fig. 6.

Nomeus nigrofasciatus, Rüpp. Atl. Fische, p. 92, t. xxiv, f. 2.
Seriola binotata? Cuv. and Val. ix, p. 215; Cantor, Catal. p. 137.
Seriola Rüppellii, Cuv. and Val. ix, p. 216; Bleeker, Makr. p. 73.
Seriola nigrofasciata, Rüpp. N. W. Fische, p. 51; Günther, Catal. ii, p. 465; Klunz. Verh. z. b. Ges. Wien, 1871, p. 450.

B. vii, D. 5-6 | [illegible], P. 19, V. 1/5, A. [illegible], C. 19.

Length of head from $3\frac{3}{4}$ in the young to $4\frac{1}{2}$ in the adult, of caudal $5\frac{3}{4}$ to one-sixth, height of body $3\frac{1}{2}$ to one-fourth of the total length. *Eyes*—diameter 1/4 of length of head, 1 diameter from end of snout. Dorsal profile more convex than that of the abdomen; snout rather obtuse; abdomen broad. Lower jaw rather the longer. Cleft of mouth commences opposite the centre or lower third of the front edge of the eye, the maxilla reaches to below the middle or hind third of the eye. *Teeth*—villiform in jaws, vomer, palate, and on the tongue. *Fins*—first dorsal spines weak, low, from 1/3 to 1/2 the height of the second dorsal, the anterior portion of which latter equals from 1/2 to 2/3 of that of the body. Pectoral 2/3 as long as the head. Ventral nearly as long as the head. Anal commences below the middle of the soft dorsal. Caudal forked. *Scales*—minute. *Colours*—bluish gray, with five vertical black bands from the back down the body, and which have a rather anterior direction above the lateral-line: one or two similar but narrower bands on the head. First dorsal fin black, second dorsal dark, becoming black near its summit and with a white tip. Pectoral yellow. Ventral and anal black, the latter with a white tip. Caudal yellowish, the young having a black blotch in the last portion of either caudal lobe.

Jerdon (M. J. L. and Sc. 1851, p. 137) observes on the affinity of the Madras fish with *S. binotata*, C.V. and terms it *Mouskoom parah*, Tamil.

2 G 2

Seriola Dussumieri, C.V. ix, p. 217, D. 5 | $\frac{1}{31}$, A. 2 | $\frac{1}{28}$, may be the young of this species, the specimens from the Bay of Bengal being only 2 inches in length, but having 7 vertical brown bands. There is however in the Madras Museum a stuffed specimen 22 inches in length, having D. 5 | $\frac{1}{30}$, A. 2 | $\frac{1}{19}$. Eyes, diameter 2/7 of length of head, 1 diameter from end of snout, a slight keel on the side of the tail, and which appears different from *S. nigrofasciata*. I have also a skin 12 inches long, in a bad state, from the same place. The ventrals are shorter than in *S. nigrofasciata*.

Habitat.—Red Sea, East coast of Africa, seas of India to the Malay Archipelago and beyond. The one figured (life-size) was captured in Madras in February, 1867, they are not rare.

Genus, 4—Seriolichthys, *Bleeker*.

Decaptus, Poey.

Branchiostegals seven. Body oblong, compressed: abdomen rounded. Cleft of mouth of moderate depth. Preopercle slightly crenulated or entire. Villiform teeth on the jaws, vomer, and palatines. First dorsal fin continuous, the second and the anal with many more rays, and each having one or two finlets posteriorly: a pair of pre-anal spines remote from the rest of the fin may be present or absent. Scales cycloid, small. Lateral-line unarmed.

Geographical distribution.—From the East coast of Africa, through the seas of India, to the Malay Archipelago and beyond.

SYNOPSIS OF INDIVIDUAL SPECIES.

1. *Seriolichthys bipinnulatus*, D. 6 | $\frac{1}{25-27}$ + I, A. 0-2 | $\frac{1}{15-17}$ + i. Two longitudinal bands, one from the eye to the end of the dorsal, the second to the middle of the caudal fin. Seas of India.

1. Seriolichthys bipinnulatus, Plate LI, A. fig. 1.

Seriola bipinnulata, Quoy and Gaim, Voy. Uranie, Zool. i, p. 363, pl. 61, f. 3; Cuv. Règ. Anim. Ill. Poiss. p. 130; Jenyns, Voy. Beagle, Fishes, p. 72.

Elagatis bipinnulatus, Benn. Whaling Voyage, ii, p. 283.

Seriolichthys bipinnulatus, Bleeker, Nat. Tyds. Ned. Ind. vi, p. 196; Günther, Catal. ii, p. 468; Klunz. Verh. z. b. Ges. Wien, 1871, p. 452.

Seriolichthys lineolatus, Day, Proc. Zool. Soc. 1867, p. 559.

Kulal, Tam.

B. vii, D. 5 | $\frac{1}{25-26}$ + i, P. 21, V. 1/5, A. 0-2 | $\frac{1}{15-17}$ + i, C. 18, L. l. 95, L. tr. 16/28.

Length of head 1/5, of caudal 1/4 to 4/17, height of body 1/5 of the total length. *Eyes*—diameter 1/4 of length of head, 1¼ diameters from end of snout, and also apart. Body elongated and compressed, its greatest height being opposite the origin of the soft dorsal fin. Lower jaw slightly the longer, gape of mouth rather narrow, the maxilla reaches to below the front edge of the eye. Gill-openings cleft as far forwards as to below the anterior edge of the orbit. *Teeth*—villiform in jaws, vomer, palatines, and on the tongue. *Fins*—dorsal spines of moderate strength, low, with the interspinous membrane deeply cleft. Anterior portion of second dorsal highest, equalling 2/5 of that of the body, at a short distance behind this fin are two rays placed close together and forming a finlet, they are rather elongated and reach the root of the caudal fin. Pectoral short, equalling 1/9 of the total length. Anal of the same form but anteriorly lower than the soft dorsal, being 2/7 of the height of the body, it has similarly a posterior finlet. Caudal deeply forked, its middle rays being only equal to 2/7 of its outer ones. *Scales*—on cheeks, upper edge of opercles, behind the eyes, and over the body. *Colours*—two longitudinal blue bands pass from the eye, the upper to the dorsal finlet, and the lower to the centre of the base of the caudal fin.

Günther (Catal. l. c.) gives two pre-anal spines. Not finding any in Madras specimens, I concluded they belonged to a distinct species; however, since then I see in the "Fishes of Zanzibar," p. 62, that it is observed, "Bleeker's statement that there are two pre-anal spines separate from the remainder of that fin requires further confirmation." The fish mentioned by Jerdon, M. J. L. and Sc. 1851, p. 136, as *Poon kulal*, Tamil, is this species.

Habitat.—From the East coast of Africa, through the seas of India, to the Malay Archipelago and beyond. It attains several feet in length. The specimen figured (nearly 12 inches long) is from Madras.

Genus, 5—Naucrates, *Cuv.*

Nauclerus, Cuv. and Val. (*young*).

Branchiostegals seven. Body oblong, sub-cylindrical. Cleft of mouth moderate. In the very young there is a spine at the angle of the preopercle, which becomes absorbed as age advances. Villiform teeth in the jaws, vomer, and palatine bones. The first dorsal fin, which is continuous in the young, becomes reduced to a few spines in the adult; the second dorsal and anal with many rays; no spurious fins: in the young two pre-anal spines remote from the soft fin, and which become lost with age. Scales small; lateral-line unarmed; a keel on either side of the tail. Air-vessel present. Pyloric appendages in moderate numbers.

The natural position of this Genus has been subjected to several changes. It is amongst the *Scombridæ* in Cuv. and Val.'s grand work, and Günther in his "Catalogue of Fishes," left *Naucrates* in the same family, but included *Naucleras* amongst the *Carangidæ*. Gill and Kner distinctly proved *Naucleras* to be the young of *Naucrates*, in which the authors of the "Fishes of Zanzibar," p. 63, acquiesced and referred the Genus to *Carangidæ*.*

Habitat.—These "pilot fishes" are spread through all the seas of temperate and tropical regions. Most travellers in sailing vessels have seen them as close attendants upon sharks, leading them, as the sailors consider, to their prey.

SYNOPSIS OF INDIVIDUAL SPECIES.

1. *Naucrates ductor*, D. 3-6 | $\frac{1}{26-28}$, A. 0-2 | $\frac{2}{16-17}$. Five to seven broad bluish vertical bands on the body.

1. Naucrates ductor, Plate LI, A. fig. 2.

Gasterosteus ductor, Linn. Syst. Nat. p. 489; Brun. Pisc. Mass. p. 67; Bennett, Whaling Voyage, ii, p. 274.

Gasterosteus antecessor, Dahl. Skrivt. Nat. Selsk. Kjob. ii, p. 166.

Scomber ductor, Bl. t. 338; Hasselq. Iter, p. 336; Mitchell, Trans. Lit. and Phil. Soc. New York, i, p. 424.

Scomber Koelreuteri, Bl. Schn. p. 570.

Centronotus conductor, Lacép. iii, p. 311; Risso. Ich. Nice, p. 428, and Eur. Merid. iii, p. 193; Couch. Trans. Linn. Soc. xiv, p. 82.

Naucrates ductor, Cuv. and Val. viii, p. 312, pl. 232; Yarrell, Brit. Fish. i, p. 170; Guichen, Exp. Algér. Poiss. p. 60; Günther, Catal. ii, p. 374; Klunz. Verh. z. b. Ges. Wien, 1871, p. 445.

Naucrates Noveboracensis, Cuv. and Val. viii, p. 325.

Naucrates Indicus, Cuv. and Val. viii, p. 326; Cuv. Règ. Anim. Ill. Poiss. pl. 54, f. 1; Less. Voy. Coq. Zool. Poiss. p. 157, pl. xiv; Richards. Ich. China, p. 269; Kner, Novara Fische, p. 145.

Naucrates Koelreuteri, Cuv. and Val. viii, 327.

Naucleras compressus, Cuv. and Val. ix, p. 249, pl. 263; Günther, Catal. ii, p. 469 (? *young*).

Thynnus pompilus, Gronov. ed. Gray, p. 123.

B. vii. D. 3-6 | $\frac{1}{26-28}$, P. 21, V. 1/5, A. 0-2 | $\frac{2}{16-17}$, C. 17, Cæc. pyl. 12-15, Vert. 10/16.

Length of head 1/5 to 2/9, of pectoral 1/8, of caudal 2/11, height of body 1/4 to 2/9 of the total length. *Eyes*—diameter 1/5 of length of head, 1½ diameters from end of snout. The greatest width of the head equals 3/5 of its length, and its height equals its length behind the posterior nostril. The maxilla extends to below the anterior edge of the orbit. *Teeth*—villiform in jaws, in a pyriform band on vomer, and a long patch on the palatines, tongue rough. *Fins*—first dorsal spine short, second dorsal highest anteriorly, anal commences under the middle of the second dorsal. Pectoral as long as the ventral, which reaches 2/5 of way to the base of the anal. Caudal deeply forked. *Scales*—cycloid. *Lateral-line*—a little raised on the side of the tail. *Colours*—bluish, with five or six dark vertical bands: caudal sometimes with the ends of the lobes white, and having a dark band across their last third. Basal half of anal and centre of dorsal dark gray.

Naucleras abbreviatus, C.V. Lowe, Günther: *N. brachycentrus*, *triacanthus*, *annularis*, and *leucurus*, C.V. and Günther, are all probably young of this or closely allied species, having two pre-anal spines, and a more or less serrated preopercle, &c.

Habitat.—Seas of temperate and tropical regions. A specimen 7 inches long of the "pilot fish" is in the Calcutta Museum, taken in the Indian Ocean by J. Hart, Esq., of the "Inflexible."

Genus, 6—Chorinemus, *Cuv. and Val.*

Scomberoides, Lacép.

Branchiostegals seven or eight: pseudobranchiæ. Body oblong and compressed. Eyes lateral. Cleft of mouth moderate or deep. Teeth in jaws, also present on vomer, palatines, and tongue. Two dorsal fins, the first (preceded by an immoveable, recumbent spine, directed forwards) has a groove at its base for its reception, it is formed by a few free spines, but in a less number than the rays of the second dorsal or anal, the posterior rays of both of which last are either detached or semi-detached; a pair of pre-anal spines separated by an interspace from the remainder of the fin. Dermal scales mostly lanceolate. Lateral-line continuous, not keeled. Air-vessel bifurcated posteriorly. Pyloric appendages numerous.

Geographical distribution.—Red Sea, seas of India to the Malay Archipelago: also found in tropical parts of the Atlantic.

Although this Genus is as a rule marine, the young ascend estuaries and tidal rivers, and it is not uncommon to find them in the Hoogly at Calcutta. As food they are dry and rather tasteless, in this respect resembling *Trachynotus*.

* "A second question arises, whether *Naucrates* should be referred to *Scombridæ* or *Carangidæ*. The two anal spines of the young are separate from the soft portion: and although the number of caudal vertebræ is increased by two, yet the number of abdominal vertebræ remains the same: we are therefore inclined to remove this genus from the *Scombridæ* to the *Carangidæ*." (Fish. Zanz. p. 63.) Bleeker in the Family Lichioidei includes *Naucrates*, *Chorinemus*, *Trachynotus*, and *Elacate*.

SYNOPSIS OF SPECIES.

1. *Chorinemus Sancti-Petri*, D. 7 | $\frac{1}{19-21}$, A. 2 | $\frac{1}{18-19}$. Height of body $4\frac{1}{4}$ to $4\frac{2}{3}$ in the total length. Maxilla reaches to below hind edge of orbit. No enlarged teeth: in a triangular patch on the vomer elongated posteriorly. Dorsal spines flattened and do not overlap in the adult. Scales lanceolate and pointed. A single row of dark blotches above the lateral-line and sometimes a second below it: summit of soft dorsal black. Red Sea, seas of India to the Malay Archipelago and beyond.

2. *Chorinemus moadetta*, D. 7 | $\frac{1}{21}$, A. 2 | $\frac{1}{19-20}$. Height of body $5\frac{1}{4}$ in the total length. Maxilla reaches to below last third of orbit. Canine-like teeth in front of either jaw: an elongated oval patch on vomer. Dorsal spines rounded and overlap. Scales like needles lying close together. A single row of dark blotches above the lateral-line: summit of soft dorsal black. Seas of India.

3. *Chorinemus lysan*, D. 7 | $\frac{1}{19-20}$, A. 2 | $\frac{1}{17-19}$. Height of body 1/4 of the total length. Maxilla reaches to beyond the hind edge of the orbit. No enlarged teeth in jaws: in a triangular spot on vomer, having a posterior prolongation. Dorsal spines overlap. Scales lanceolate; six or eight large, round, gray marks on the side: summit of soft dorsal black. Red Sea, seas of India to the Malay Archipelago and beyond.

4. *Chorinemus tala*, D. 7 | $\frac{1}{23}$, A. 2 | $\frac{1}{21}$. Height of body $3\frac{1}{4}$ in the total length. Maxilla reaches to below hind edge of the eye. Strong canines in either jaw: in a quadrangular patch of villiform ones on the vomer. Dorsal spines overlap. Scales lanceolate and pointed. A row of dark spots along the sides. Summit of second dorsal black. Seas of India.

5. *Chorinemus toloo*, D. 7 | $\frac{1}{19-20}$, A. 2 | $\frac{1}{17-18}$. Height of body $3\frac{1}{2}$ to $3\frac{3}{4}$ in the total length. Maxilla reaches to nearly or quite below the hind edge of the eye. No enlarged teeth in the jaws: in a triangular patch on the vomer. Dorsal spines overlap. Scales lanceolate. A row of dark spots along the sides. Vertical fins darkish. Seas of India to the Andamans.

1. Chorinemus Sancti-Petri.

Cuv. and Val. viii, p. 379, pl. 236; Bleeker, Makr. p. 45; Jerdon, M. J. L. and Sc. 1851, p. 136; Peters, Wieg. Arch. 1855, p. 245; Günther, Catal. ii, p. 473 (part).

Thynnus Malaccensis, Gronov. ed. Gray, p. 121.

Scomberoides sancti-petri, Bleeker, Bintang, 1868, p. 4.

B. viii, D. 7 | $\frac{1}{19-21}$, P. 17, V. 1/5, A. 2 | $\frac{1}{18-19}$, C. 15.

Length of head $5\frac{1}{4}$ to $5\frac{2}{3}$, of pectoral $4\frac{1}{2}$, of caudal $4\frac{1}{3}$, height of body $4\frac{1}{4}$ to $4\frac{2}{3}$ in the total length. *Eyes*—diameter one-fourth to $4\frac{1}{2}$ in length of head, 1 to $1\frac{1}{4}$ diameters from end of snout, and also apart. Greatest width of head equals 2/5 of its length, and its height its length posterior to the hind nostril. Profile above orbit slightly concave. The maxilla reaches to beneath the hind edge of the orbit, it is concealed by the preorbital except in the last third of its course. Central longitudinal crest on the skull scarcely elevated. Angle of preopercle slightly produced. *Teeth*—in several villiform rows anteriorly in both jaws, becoming a single one in the last 2/3 of the premaxillaries; in two rows in the lower jaw: in a triangular patch, elongated posteriorly, on the vomer: in a pyriform band, largest anteriorly, on the palatines, and also on the tongue. *Fins*—the spines of the first dorsal are flattened, laterally expanded into a lanceolate form, and have a keel along their centre: in the adult one spine does not extend so far as to the base of the next before it, but they slightly overlap in the young. Second dorsal commences midway between the snout and the front nostril, its first portion is elevated and equals 4/9 of that of the body, and is 1/3 higher than the commencement of the anal. Ventral reaches half way to the anal. Caudal deeply lobed. *Scales*—lanceolate and pointed in their exposed portions, which have a line along their centre and the posterior part depressed, behind the exposed lanceolate portion each scale ends in a narrow pedicle rather more than half its entire length. In the young they are not quite so pointed and when removed appear much like a spoon. *Lateral-line*—makes an obtuse angle opposite the middle of the pectoral fin, from thence it gradually slopes downwards, becoming straight beneath the first dorsal ray. *Colours*—a bluish-gray spot on the opercle, and a row of from 6 to 8 dark blotches above the lateral-line: sometimes, more especially in the adult, a second row beneath it. Summit of soft dorsal black.

Habitat.—Red Sea, East coast of Africa, seas of India to the Malay Archipelago and beyond. It attains at least 20 inches in length.

2. Chorinemus moadetta, Plate LI, B. fig. 1.

Scomber tol parah, Russell, Fish. Vizag. ii, p. 29, pl. 138.

Chorinemus moadetta, Cuv. and Val. viii, p. 382; Rüpp. N. W. Fische, p. 45; Klunz. Verh. z. b. Ges. Wien, 1871, p. 448.

Chorinemus tol, Cuv. and Val. viii, p. 385; Cantor, Catal. p. 119; Jerdon, M. J. L. and Sc. 1851, p. 136; Günther, Catal. ii, p. 473; Day, Fish. Malabar, p. 93; Kner, Novara Fische, p. 162.

Chorinemus Sancti-Petri, Günther, Catal. ii, p. 473 (pt.); Day, Fish. Malabar, p. 95.

B. viii, D. 7 | $\frac{1}{21}$, P. 19, V. 1/5, A. 2 | $\frac{1}{18-19}$, C. 17.

Length of head $5\frac{2}{3}$ to $5\frac{3}{4}$, of caudal $6\frac{1}{2}$, height of body $5\frac{1}{4}$ in the total length. *Eyes*—diameter $4\frac{3}{4}$ to one-fifth in length of head, $1\frac{1}{2}$ diameters from end of snout, and also apart. Dorsal profile rather more convex than that of the abdomen, and rather concave above the orbits, the central and lateral ridges on the summit of the head well developed. The lower jaw somewhat the longer, the cleft of the mouth commences opposite the middle of the eyes, the maxilla (which is uncovered from beneath the first third of the eyes) reaches to beneath the last third of the orbit.* Greatest depth of preorbital equals 1/3 of the diameter of the orbit. *Teeth*—in the premaxillaries in a single row, the two anterior ones of which are large and rather canine-like, posteriorly to these are some villiform ones: teeth in the lower jaw in two rows, the outer of which is curved rather outwards and upwards, whilst there are enlarged ones on either side of the symphysis: an elongated ovate patch on the vomer having an anterior-posterior direction: in a long pyriform band on the palate largest anteriorly, also on the tongue. *Fins*—dorsal spines rounded, not flattened, overlapping and twisting laterally when elevated. Second dorsal commences midway between the anterior edge of the eye and the base of the caudal fin, its first portion is the highest equalling 2½ in that of the body, and 1/3 higher than the first part of the anal. Pectoral as long as the head behind the middle of the eye. Ventral reaches 2/5 of the way to the anal. Caudal deeply forked. *Scales*—are peculiar, resembling needles sharp at both ends, lying close together and interdigitating, it is only near the free portion of the tail that they become at all scale-like. *Lateral-line*—rather indistinct and almost straight, making one slight angular elevation above the last third of the pectoral. *Colours*—silvery along the upper third of the body, becoming white on the sides and below, a series of 6 or 8 blotches along the sides, mostly above the lateral-line. A black blotch at the highest point of the second dorsal and the ends of either lobe of the caudal, the other fins yellow.

This species in its external form resembles *C. Sancti-Petri*, C. V., but its scales are entirely different, corresponding apparently to *C. Mauritianus*, in which they are said to be smooth requiring a magnifying glass to detect, as under the naked eye they merely resemble pores. Likewise it appears to be *C. tol*, in which the mode of scaling as existing in this species is described, but the mouth is said only to be cleft below the front edge of the eye. Russell observes that *Scomber tol parah* is without scales. *Chorinemus tol* of Cantor and Jerdon is identical with the *C. moadetta*. It is also termed *Tool parah* or "leather skin" by the natives.

Habitat.—Red Sea, east coast of Africa, and seas of India, attaining upwards of 15 inches in length. As food its flesh is dry and tasteless.

3. Chorinemus lysan.

Scomber lysan, Forsk. No. 67, pl. 54.
Scomber Forsteri, Bl. Schn. p. 26.
Scomberoides Commersonianus, Lacép. ii, pl. 20, f. 3.
Scomber aken parah, Russell, Fish. Vizag. ii, p. 31, pl. 141.
Scomber Madagascariensis, Shaw, Zool. iv, p. 590, pl. 85; Bennett, Life of Raffles, p. 689.
Lichia lysan, Rüpp. Atl. Fische, p. 91.
Chorinemus Commersonianus, Cuv. and Val. viii, p. 370; Bleeker, Makr. p. 44; Jerdon, M. J. L. and Sc. 1851, p. 136.
Chorinemus lysan, Cuv. and Val. viii, p. 387; Rüppell, N. W. Fische, p. 44; Cantor, Catal. p. 118; Günther, Catal. ii, p. 471; Day, Fish. Malabar, p. 92; Kner, Novara Fische, p. 163; Klunz. Verh. z. b. Ges. Wien, 1871, p. 448.
? *Chorinemus Forkhorii*, Cuv. and Val. viii, p. 388.
Chorinemus aculeatus, Cuv. and Val. viii, p. 384.
Tool parah, Tam.; *Parah*, Hind.

B. viii, D. 7 | $\frac{1}{19-20}$, P. 19, V. 1/5, A. 2 | $\frac{1}{17-18}$, C. 19, Vert. 10/16.

Length of head 5½ to one-sixth, of caudal two-ninths, height of body 3¼ to one-fourth in the total length. *Eyes*—diameter 1/4 of length of head, 1/2 to 2/3 of a diameter from end of snout, and rather above 1 apart. Greatest width of head 2¼ in its length, whilst its height almost equals its length. Body rather strongly compressed, profile over nape slightly concave. Cleft of mouth deep, the maxilla extending nearly half a diameter behind the orbit, the maxilla is narrow and uncovered by the preorbital from beneath the first third of the eye. The length of the premaxillary is 4/7 of that of the head. *Teeth*—anteriorly in two rows, posteriorly in one in the premaxillaries: in two rows in the lower jaw, the outer of which is directed outwards and upwards in the young, some of the anterior teeth in both jaws are rather enlarged: in a triangular spot rather prolonged posteriorly in the vomer: in a pyriform band, largest anteriorly, on the palatines, also on the tongue. *Fins*—the anterior portions of the soft dorsal and anal elevated, equalling 4/5 of the length of the head, the last 8 or 10 rays semi-detached, the last rather elongated. Caudal deeply forked. *Scales*—distinct and lanceolate. *Lateral-line*—has a slight angular elevation soon after its commencement. *Colours*—six to eight large, round, gray spots like finger-marks on the side, the lateral-line sometimes going through the two first, while the others are all above it: summit of soft dorsal black.

Habitat.—Red Sea, seas of India to the Malay Archipelago and beyond; it attains a considerable size.

4. Chorinemus tala.

Scomber tala parah, Russell, Fish. Vizag. ii, p. 30, pl. 140.

* Mouth cleft to below front edge of eye in *C. tol*, according to Russell, Cuv. and Val., Günther, &c.

Chorinemus tala, Cuv. and Val. viii, p. 377; Jerdon, M. J. L. and Sc. 1851, p. 136; Günther, Catal. ii. p. 473; Day, Fish. Malabar, p. 93.

B. viii, D. 7 | $\frac{1}{20}$, P. 19, V. 1/5, A. 2 | $\frac{1}{17}$, C. 17.

Length of head $5\frac{1}{3}$, of caudal $4\frac{3}{4}$, height of body $3\frac{7}{8}$ in the total length. *Eyes*—diameter 1/4 of length of head, 1 diameter from end of snout, and $1\frac{1}{4}$ apart. Greatest width of head equals 3/7, and its height equals 7/8 of its length. Dorsal and abdominal profiles equally convex. Lower jaw prominent: cleft of mouth commences opposite the upper third of the eye: the maxilla (which is uncovered from below the middle of the eye) extends to beneath the hind edge of the eye. Greatest depth of preorbital equals 3/7 of width of orbit. Posterior limb of preopercle nearly vertical, and its angle not produced. *Teeth*—two strong canines directed a little outwards at the symphysis in either premaxillary, and several villiform rows behind them, laterally a single row of rather distantly placed pointed teeth: in the lower jaw at the symphysis are two canines anteriorly pointing a little forward, posteriorly two more directed upwards, laterally two rows of teeth, the inner being considerably the larger: in a quadrangular spot on the vomer, in a pyriform band larger anteriorly on the palatines, and also on the tongue. *Fins*—dorsal spines overlapping and twisting slightly laterally when elevated. Second dorsal commences midway between the nostrils and the base of the caudal, its first portion equals $2\frac{1}{2}$ in the height of the body, and is 1/5 longer than the anterior part of the anal. Pectoral as long as the head without the snout. Ventral reaches 2/5 of the distance to the anal. Caudal deeply forked. *Scales*—rhomboidal, and more or less pointed posteriorly, on being removed the outer half is found to be lanceolate, the posterior more contracted. *Lateral-line*—becomes straight below the middle dorsal spine, in this course it has an angular elevation above the last 2/3 of the pectoral fin. *Colours*—leaden-silvery in the upper third of the back, silvery-white on the sides and below, a series of 7 spots above the middle of the sides, the two first being intersected by the lateral-line. Summit of second dorsal black.

Habitat.—Seas of India, attaining at least $6\frac{1}{2}$ inches in length.

5. Chorinemus toloo, Plate LI, A. fig. 3.

Scomber toloo parah, Russell, Fish. Vizag. ii, p. 29, pl. 137.

Chorinemus toloo, Cuv. and Val. viii, p. 377; Günther, Catal. ii, p. 473; Day, Fish. Malabar, p. 96; Klunz. Verh. z. b. Ges. Wien, 1871, p. 447.

B. viii, D. 7 | $\frac{1}{19-20}$, P. 20, V. 1/5, A. 2 | $\frac{1}{17-18}$, C. 19.

Length of head $5\frac{2}{3}$, of pectoral 1/8 to $8\frac{1}{2}$, of caudal $4\frac{1}{2}$ to one-fifth, height of body $3\frac{1}{2}$ to $3\frac{2}{3}$ in the total length. *Eyes*—diameter 2/9 of length of head, 1 diameter from end of snout, and also apart. Body elliptical, compressed; a gradual rise to the first dorsal. Greatest width of head equals $2\frac{1}{3}$ in its length, and its height almost its length. Cleft of mouth commences opposite the upper third of the eye. The maxilla extends to nearly or quite below the posterior margin of the orbit: upper jaw only uncovered in the last 1/3 of its extent: premaxillaries equal to 4/7 of the length of the head. Preorbital narrow, but covering the first 2/3 of the maxilla: preopercle narrow, having its angle rounded and produced. Central crest of the skull distinct. *Teeth*—comparatively large, in a single row in the upper jaw and in two in the lower, the outer of which last is directed somewhat outwards, whilst there are two canine-like teeth on either side of the symphysis of the lower jaw: in a triangular patch on the vomer: an elongated pyriform band, largest anteriorly on the palatines, and on the tongue. *Fins*—the anterior portion of the soft dorsal elevated, similar to the anal, and 1/2 the height of the body, the posterior 8 or 10 rays of either fin semi-detached, and the last rather elongated. Caudal deeply forked. *Scales*—small but distinct, and lanceolate in their exposed portion. *Lateral-line*—has a very slightly raised angle in the first part of its course, but its general direction is straight. *Colours*—greenish tinge along the back shot with blue, becoming of a dull silvery below the lateral-line. Six to eight moderately sized, oval, and indistinct vertical spots or blotches on the side, usually intersected by the lateral-line. Vertical fins darkish.

Habitat.—Seas of India, the specimen figured (11 inches long) is from the Andamans; it is said to attain eighteen inches in length.

Genus, 7—Trachynotus,* (*Lacép.*) *Cuv. and Val.*

Acanthinion and Caesiomorus, Lacép.

Branchiostegals seven: pseudobranchiæ absent. Body compressed, more or less elevated, with the frontal region prominent. Eyes lateral. Snout obtuse and swollen: cleft of mouth small. Teeth on the jaws, vomer, and palatines, usually lost with age. Two dorsal fins, the first composed of spines having a small connecting membrane (receivable into a groove at their base), and a horizontal one, directed forwards, anterior to the fin: second dorsal and anal with more rays than spines in the first dorsal: the anterior portion of the second dorsal and anal pointed and elongated: two pre-anal spines separated by an interspace from the remainder of the fin: no finlets. Scales small. Lateral-line unarmed. An air-vessel bifurcated posteriorly. Pyloric appendages numerous, or in moderate numbers.

Geographical distribution.—From the Red Sea, through the seas of India to the Malay Archipelago and beyond.

* *Cuttalli*, Tamil.

SYNOPSIS OF SPECIES.

1. *Trachynotus Baillonii*, D. 6-7 | 1/[illegible], A. 2 | 1/[illegible]. Short ventral fins, caudal from $3\frac{1}{2}$ to $3\frac{3}{4}$ in the total length; 3 to 5 small black spots on the lateral-line. Red Sea, seas of India to the Malay Archipelago.

2. *Trachynotus Russellii*, D. 6 | 1/[illegible], A. 2 | 1/[illegible]. Comparatively long ventral fins; caudal $4\frac{1}{4}$ to $4\frac{1}{2}$ in the total length: 3 to 5 large and dull roundish blotches above the lateral-line. Seas of India to the Malay Archipelago.

3. *Trachynotus ovatus*, D. 6-7 | 1/[illegible], A. 2 | 1/[illegible]. Golden, without blotches. Red Sea, seas of India to the Malay Archipelago and beyond. Also found in the Atlantic, between Africa and America.

1. Trachynotus Baillonii, Plate LI, A. fig. 4.

Cæsiomorus Baillonii, Lacép. iii, p. 93, pl. 3, fig. 1.
Cæsiomorus quadripunctatus, Rüpp. Atl. Fische, p. 90, pl. 24, f. 1.
Trachinotus quadripunctatus, Cuv. and Val. viii, p. 434; Cantor, Catal. p. 122.
Trachinotus Baillonii, Cuv. and Val. viii, p. 431; Günther, Catal. ii, p. 484; Day, Fish. Malabar, p. 98; Klunz. Verh. z. b. Ges. Wien, 1871, p. 449.
Vella oodoo and *Parrwra*, Mal.; *Mookaler*, Tamil.

B. vii, D. 6-7 | 1/[illegible], P. 17, V. 1/5, A. 2 | 1/[illegible], C. 19, Cæc. pyl. 12, Vert. 9/12.

Length of head $5\frac{1}{2}$ to $5\frac{3}{4}$, of pectoral one-eighth, of caudal $3\frac{1}{3}$ to $3\frac{1}{2}$, height of body from one-third to $3\frac{1}{2}$ in the total length. *Eyes*—diameter 2/7 to 1/4 of length of head, 1 diameter from end of snout, and $1\frac{1}{4}$ apart. Body elevated and strongly compressed: jaws of equal length: the maxilla nearly reaches to beneath the centre of the orbit. *Teeth*—card-like in both jaws, on vomer, and palatines. *Fins*—the first dorsal spines moderately strong: second dorsal and anal are very much produced in front, and if laid backwards those of the dorsal reach to nearly the end of that fin; those of the anal to its posterior extremity: whilst the last fifteen rays are parallel with the back and abdomen. Pectoral as long as the head, excluding the snout. Ventral small, equalling $1\frac{1}{2}$ diameters of the orbit. Caudal with deeply produced lobes, the upper slightly the longer, the central rays 1/4 the length of the outer ones. *Scales*—small, placed in sinuous lines. *Lateral-line*—nearly straight, and in simple tubes. *Colours*—upper surface of head and back of a silvery yellowish-green, becoming lighter on the sides, and silvery-white on the abdomen, opercles, and cheeks. Lobes of dorsal, anal, and caudal black, some white likewise on those of the tail: a row of three to five deep black blotches along the sides and on the lateral-line.

Habitat.—Red Sea, East coast of Africa, seas of India to the Malay Archipelago: it attains at least 20 inches in length. The specimen figured is 13 inches long and from Aden.

2. Trachynotus Russellii, Plate LI, B. fig. 3.

Scomber latla parah, Russell, Fish. Vizag. ii, p. 32, pl. 142.
Scomber botla, Shaw, Zool. iv, p. 591.*
Trachinotus Russellii, Cuv. and Val. viii, p. 436; Jerdon, M. J. L. and Sc. 1851, p. 136.
Trachinotus oblongus, Cuv. and Val. viii, p. 437; Günther, Catal. ii, p. 484.

B. vii, D. 6 | 1/[illegible], P. 17, V. 1/5, A. 2 | 1/[illegible], C. 17.

Length of head one-fifth to $5\frac{1}{4}$, of caudal one-fourth to $4\frac{1}{2}$, height of body $3\frac{1}{4}$ to $3\frac{2}{3}$ in the total length. *Eyes*—diameter $3\frac{1}{2}$ to $3\frac{3}{4}$ in the length of head, about 1 diameter from end of snout, and $1\frac{1}{2}$ apart. Dorsal and abdominal profiles about equally convex, snout obtuse. Height of head equals its length. Jaws of about equal length, the cleft of the mouth commences opposite the middle or lower third of the front edge of the orbit, and the maxilla reaches to beneath the centre of the eye. Preorbital at its widest part equals the width of the maxilla. Central longitudinal crest on the head well developed. *Teeth*—fine ones on jaws, vomer, and palatines, even in fish 22 inches long. *Fins*—spines of first dorsal of moderate strength: anterior rays of second dorsal prolonged, equalling 2/3 or 3/4 of the length of the base of the fin, and being similar to those of the anal. Pectoral rounded, as long as the head without the snout, or behind the middle of the eyes. Ventrals as long as the postorbital portion of the head in the adult, rather longer in the young, they reach above halfway to the anal in the young, but are not quite so long in the adult. Caudal deeply forked, the central rays equalling 1/3 of those of the longest outer ones in the young, but 1/4 or even less in the adult. *Scales*—in irregular rows, small. *Lateral-line*—nearly straight. *Colours*—greenish, dashed with yellow on the back, becoming more golden on the sides and beneath: usually a dark blotch at the upper margin of opercle and commencement of the lateral-line. From 3 to 5 large, dull, rounded blotches a little distance above the lateral-line, but which often disappear after death: they are much darker and more persistent in the adult than in the young: elongated portions of dorsal and anal fins, also lobes of caudal, orange stained with black.

This species can at once be distinguished from *T. Baillonii* by the spots being above, not on, the lateral-line, and by its much longer ventral fins.

Amongst Sir Walter Elliot's drawings of Indian Fishes is one of this genus, having the dorsals black, and a black band along the anal. The soft dorsal is scarcely higher than the spinous, but the figure is scarcely 2 inches in length.

Habitat.—Seas of India to the Malay Archipelago. It is not uncommon at Madras, my largest specimen being 22 inches long, from Canara: specimen figured 13 inches long.

* Shaw observes "var. ? pl. 137" in Russell's Fish. Vizag. which is *Chorinemus toloo*.

3. **Trachynotus ovatus,*** Plate LI. B. fig. 2.

Gasterosteus ovatus, Lin. Syst. Nat. i, p. 490.
Caesiomorus Blochii, Lacép. iii, p. 95, pl. iii, f. 2.
Centronotus ovalis, Lacép. iii, pp. 309, 316.
Scomber falcatus, Forsk. p. 57.
Scomber mooduhlee-parah, Russell, Fish. Vizag. ii, p. 39, pl. 154.
Trachinotus falcatus, Lacép. iii, p. 79; Rüpp. Atl. Fische, p. 89; Cuv. and Val. viii, p. 430.
Trachinotus mookalee, Cuv. and Val. viii, p. 423; Cantor, Catal. p. 129; Jerdon, M. J. L. and Sc. 1851, p. 136.
Trachinotus Blochii, Cuv. and Val. viii, p. 425.
Trachinotus affinis and *falcifer*, Cuv. and Val. viii, p. 428.
Trachinotus drepanis, Cuv. and Val. viii, p. 429.
Trachynotus ovatus, Gunther, Catal. ii, p. 481; Day, Fish. Mal. p. 97; Steind. Ak. Wien, 1869, p. 709; Kner, Novara Fische, p. 164; Klunz. Verh. z. b. Ges. Wien, 1871, p. 449.
Kootili, Tamil.

B. vii, D. 6-7 | $\frac{1}{19-20}$, P. 17, V. 1/5, A. 2 | $\frac{1}{17-18}$, C. 17, Cæc. pylori 12.

Length of head 2/9, of pectoral 1/8, of caudal 1/4, height of body 1/2 to 3/7 of the total length. *Eyes*—in centre of height of head, diameter 1/3 to 2/9 of length of head, 1/2 of a diameter in the young to 1½ in the adult from end of snout, and 1½ apart. Body elliptical and compressed, snout obtuse; a considerable rise from it to the first dorsal, but superior and inferior profiles of body equally convex. Mouth oblique: maxilla reaching to beneath the centre of the orbit. *Teeth*—in young specimens a band of card-like ones in both jaws, but as the fish increases in size (as eight inches in length) they disappear, as well as those on the vomer and palatine bones. *Fins*—second dorsal having its first ray highest, and equalling 1/2 the height of the body, its last portion or two-thirds parallel with the curve of the back. Ventrals in the young as long as the head behind the middle of the eyes. Caudal with deep lobes, its central rays equal 2/5 of its outer ones. *Scales*—minute. *Lateral-line*—at first very slightly ascends, and then forms a slight curve to opposite the eleventh dorsal ray, from whence it proceeds straight to the centre of the caudal. *Colours*—more or less golden colour: the upper half of the first five dorsal rays tipped with black, and the fin generally with minute black points; sometimes the anal and caudal are similarly marked. Pectoral gray in its first three quarters, its last fourth yellow.

Amongst Sir Walter Elliot's drawings of Indian Fishes is one of the young of this species (2 inches long) showing the soft dorsal black, and a dark band along the anal.

Habitat.—Red Sea, East coast of Africa, through the seas of India to the Malay Archipelago and beyond: it attains at least 20 inches in length. This fish salts well, but when fresh is dry and insipid.

Genus, 8—Psettus† *(Commers.)*, *Cuv. and Val.*

Monodactylus, Lacép.

Branchiostegals six: pseudobranchiæ. Body much compressed and elevated. Eyes lateral. Cleft of mouth small, snout short. Teeth villiform on jaws, vomer, palatine bones, and tongue. A single dorsal fin with seven or eight spines: anal with three, continuous with the rest of the fin: ventrals rudimentary. Scales small, covering the vertical fins. Lateral-line unarmed. Air-vessel present, bifurcated posteriorly. Cæcal appendages numerous.

Geographical distribution.—Red Sea, East coast of Africa, seas of India to the Malay Archipelago and beyond.

SYNOPSIS OF SPECIES.

1. *Psettus falciformis*, D. $\frac{7-8}{28-30}$, A. $\frac{3}{29}$, L. l. 100. Height of body half to 2½ in the total length. Silvery. Red Sea, seas of India and beyond.

2. *Psettus argenteus*, D. $\frac{7-8}{27-30}$, A. $\frac{3}{27-30}$, L. l. 75. Height of body 2/3 of the total length. Silvery. A black ocular band and a second from the dorsal spine to opercle. Red Sea, seas of India and beyond.

1. **Psettus falciformis,** Plate LI, A. fig. 6.

Monodactylus falciformis, Lacép. iii, pp. 131, 132, 133.
Psettus Commersonii, Cuv. and Val. vii, p. 250.
Psettus falciformis, Günther, Catal. ii, p. 488; Day, Fish. Malabar, p. 100.
Parrundee, Mal.

B. vi, D. $\frac{7-8}{28-30}$, P. 16, V. 1/3-5, A. $\frac{3}{29}$, C. 17, L. l. 100.

Length of head one-fourth to 4⅓, of caudal 4⅓ to one-fifth, height of body half to 2¼ in the total length. *Eyes*—diameter 2½ in length of head, 1/2 a diameter from end of snout, and 1 apart. Cleft of mouth oblique,

* The synonymy of the Atlantic species is not inserted amongst the above, see *Chætodon rhomboides*, Bl. t. 209: *Acanthinion rhomboides*, Lacép.: *Trachinotus rhomboides*, *fuscus* and *teraia*, C. and V.: *T. spinosus*, Dekay: *Lichia spinosa*, Baird: *Doliodon spinosus*, Girard.

† Family Psettoidei, Bleeker.

the maxilla reaches to below the front edge or first third of the eye. Angle of preopercle rounded and finely serrated. Greatest depth of preorbital equals 1/3 of the diameter of the eye. *Teeth*—villiform and in numerous rows in both jaws, present on vomer, palate, and tongue. *Fins*—dorsal spines nearly concealed, anterior rays elevated anteriorly. Pectoral 2/3 as long as the head. Ventrals placed close together like two spines, the rays being minute. Anal of the same form as the dorsal, its anterior portion as high as the head is long. Caudal rather deeply emarginate. *Scales*—about 120 rows descend to the lateral-line. *Lateral-line*—forms a long arch becoming straight on free portion of the tail. *Colours*—silvery, soft dorsal and anal tinged with black.

Habitat.—Red Sea, seas of India and beyond: attaining at least 9 inches in length. The specimen figured (from Madras) is 6½ inches in length.

2. **Psettus argenteus**, Plate LI, B. fig. 5.

Chætodon argenteus, Linn. Amœn. Acad. iv, p. 249; Bl. Schn. p. 230.
Scomber rhombeus, Forsk. p. 58; Shaw, Zool. iv, p. 595.
Centrogaster rhombeus, Gmel. Linn. p. 1338.
Acanthopodus argenteus, Lacép. iv, pp. 558, 559.
Centropodus rhombeus, Lacép. iii, pp. 303, 304.
Zeus kauki-moodaou, Russell, Fish. Vizag. i, p. 47, pl. 59.
Psettus rhombeus, Cuv. and Val. vii, p. 245; Cuv. Règ. Anim. Ill. Poiss. pl. xlii, f. 2; Bleeker, Chætod. p. 29; Peters, Wieg. Arch. 1855, p. 247.
Monodactylus rhombeus, Griffith in Cuv. An. King. Fishes, pl. 55, f. 2; Swainson, Fishes, ii, p. 212; Cantor, Catal. p. 172.
Psettus argenteus, Richards. Voy. Erebus and Terror, Fishes, p. 57, pl. 35, f. 1-3; Günther, Catal. ii, p. 487; Day, Fishes of Malabar, p. 99; Kner, Novara Fische, p. 164; Klunz. Verh. z. b. Ges. Wien, 1871. p. 794.
Monodactylus argenteus, Bleeker, Fish. Madagascar, p. 65.
Nga-pus-soond, Mugh.; *Oo-chra-dah*, Andam.

B. vi, D. [illegible], P. 17, V. [illegible], A. [illegible], C. 17, L. l. [illegible].

Length of head one-fourth to 4⅓, of caudal 4⅓, height of body 1⅓ in the total length. *Eyes*—diameter 2⅓ in length of head, 1/3 of a diameter from end of snout, and 1 apart. Cleft of mouth oblique, lower jaw the longer, the maxilla reaches to below the front edge of the eye. Angle of preopercle rather angular and finely serrated. Greatest depth of preorbital equals 2/7 of the diameter of the eye. *Teeth*—villiform and in numerous rows in both jaws: present on vomer, palatines, and tongue. *Fins*—anterior dorsal rays elevated, equalling 1/5 more than those of the anal. Pectoral as long as the head excluding the snout. Ventrals placed close together like two spines, the rays being minute. Anterior anal rays as long as the head. Caudal emarginate. *Lateral-line*—makes a long, low curve, becoming straight nearly below the last fourth of the dorsal fin. *Colours*—silvery with purplish reflections, especially about the anal fin: the back is of a yellowish green, which after death rapidly assumes a leaden hue. One rather wide black band passes directly downwards from the nape to the centre of the eye; a second from opposite the three first dorsal spines goes as far as the opercle. Some of the dorsal is stained with black, as is also the anterior portion of the anal though to a less extent. Pectoral and ventral colourless: caudal yellow, with a narrow black posterior edge.

Habitat.—Red Sea, East coast of Africa, seas of India to the Malay Archipelago and beyond: it attains at least seven inches in length. Most common in Malabar during the monsoon months. The specimen figured (life-size) is from Madras.

Genus, 9—PLATAX, *Cuv.* and *Val.*

Branchiostegals six: pseudobranchiæ. Body compressed and much elevated. Eyes lateral. Cleft of mouth small: snout short. Teeth setiform, trilobed at their summits, some also present on the vomer. A single dorsal fin with from three to seven spines, which are nearly hidden: anal with three continuous with the rest of the fin: ventrals well developed. Scales ctenoid, of moderate or small size, extended on to the vertical fins. Lateral-line unarmed. Air-vessel simple. Pyloric appendages few.

These fishes appear to alter considerably with age, their anterior profile becoming more obtuse and their fins comparatively shorter.

SYNOPSIS OF SPECIES.

1. *Platax teira*, D. [illegible], A. [illegible], L. l. 60-65. Snout obtuse, profile from snout to above eyes vertical. Young with an ocular band as wide as the eye, a second from dorsal spines to between ventral and anal fins: a broad one covers the last half of the back and sides. Seas of India to Malay Archipelago and beyond.

2. *Platax vespertilio*, D. [illegible], A. [illegible], L. l. 55. Snout not quite vertical. Young with a narrow ocular band 1/3 as wide as eye: a second from dorsal spines to just before anal: another at commencement of free portion of tail. Red Sea, East coast of Africa, seas of India to the Malay Archipelago and beyond.

1. **Platax teira**, Plate LI, B. fig. 4.

Chætodon teira, Forsk. p. 60, t. 22; Bl. t. 199, f. 1; Gmel. Linn. p. 1265; Bl. Schn. p. 221; Shaw, Zool. iv, p. 345, pl. 48.

Chætodon kiki sandawa, Russell, Fish. Vizag. i, p. 68, pl. 87.

Platax teira, Cuv. Règ. Anim.; Rüpp. Atl. Fische, p. 68, and N. W. Fische, pp. 33, 37; Cuv. and Val. vii, p. 226; Cantor, Catal. p. 168; Bleeker, Chætod. p. 28; Jerdon, M. J. L. and Sc. 1851, p. 133; Peters, Wieg. Arch. 1855, p. 247; Günther, Catal. ii, p. 492; Day, Fish. Malabar, p. 101; Klunz. Verh. z. b. Ges. Wien, 1870, p. 123.

Platax Leschenaldi, Cuv. and Val. vii, p. 223.

Platax vespertilio, Tem. and Schleg. Fauna Japon. Poiss. p. 83, pl. 43.

B. vi, D. [illegible], P. 17, V. 1/5, A. [illegible], C. 17, L. l. [illegible].

The height of the body, excluding the vertical fins, is rather more than, or equal to, its length* excluding the caudal fin. *Eyes*—diameter about 1/3 of length of head, rather above 1 diameter from end of snout, and 1½ apart. Dorsal profile more convex than that of the abdomen, it is very obtuse from the snout to above the eyes. Angle of preopercle rounded and entire. Greatest depth of preorbital equals 2/3 of the diameter of the eye. *Fins*—anterior portions of dorsal and anal fins very prolonged in the young extending (at 6 inches in length) nearly 1/2 the length of the entire fish beyond the end of the caudal fin, and the ventral to the end of the caudal. These fins become comparatively much shorter as age advances. Caudal with its central rays slightly prolonged, making the posterior end of the fin concave in either half. *Colours*—in the *young* grayish, with an ocular band about as wide as the eye passing downwards to the ventral fin: a second broad one from the spines and first few dorsal rays passes downwards behind the head, half going in front the other half behind the pectoral fin, and it is lost between the ventral and anal: a very broad band passes from the last 2/3 of the dorsal fin to the same part of the anal: a narrow band over root of caudal fin. Fins black, exclusive of the pectoral and ventral which are yellow except at their bases. The bands disappear with age.

In a specimen 9 inches long the dorsal, anal, and ventral fins have decreased in length so as to closely resemble the young *P. vespertilio*, (Pl. 51 A, f. 5), but the snout is more obtuse and the scales more numerous.

Habitat.—Seas of India to the Malay Archipelago and beyond. Attaining at least 20 inches in length. Russell says their flavour is excellent, and Cantor makes the same remark.

2. Platax vespertilio, Plate LI, A. fig. 5.

Chætodon vespertilio, Bloch, t. 199, f. 2; Gmel. Linn. p. 1257; Bl. Schn. p. 228; Shaw, Zool. iv, p. 344; Bennett, Fish. Ceylon, p. 5, pl. v.

Platax vespertilio, Cuv. Règ. Anim.; Rüpp. Atl. Fische, p. 143, and N. W. Fische, p. 33; Cantor, Catal. p. 166; Jerdon, M. J. L. and Sc. 1851, p. 133; Peters, Wieg. Arch. 1855, p. 247; Günther, Catal. ii, p. 489.

Platax Guiwardi, Cuv. and Val. vii, p. 216.

Platax guttulatus, Cuv. and Val. vii, p. 227, pl. 186 (*young*).

Platax Reynaldi, Cuv. and Val. vii, p. 219; Jerdon, M. J. L. and Sc. 1851, p. 133; Günther, Catal. ii, p. 490.

Platax albipunctatus, Rüpp. Atl. Fische, p. 69, t. 18, f. 4 (*young*).

Platax Blochii, Cuv. and Val. vii, p. 222; Bleeker, Chætod. p. 27.

Platax Ehrenbergii, Cuv. and Val. vii, p. 221; Rüpp. N. W. Fische, p. 23; Richards. Ich. China, p. 245; Cuv. Règ. Anim. Ill. Poiss. pl. 42, f. 1.

B. vi, D. [illegible], P. 17, V. 1/5, A. [illegible], C. 17, L. l. [illegible].

The height of the body, excluding the vertical fins, is rather more than its length excluding the caudal fin. *Eyes*—diameter 1/3 of length of head, 1 diameter from end of snout, and also apart. The dorsal profile more convex than that of the abdomen, it is not quite vertical from the occiput to the snout.† Angle of preopercle rounded, and its lower edge feebly serrated. *Fins*—the anterior portion of the dorsal fin is elevated, and its height exceeds the length of its base by about 1/3 the distance between the snout and its front edge. Pectoral nearly as long as the head. Ventral reaches to about the middle of the base of the anal fin, its length being nearly equal to the anterior portion of the anal, which is 4/5 as high as that of the dorsal. Caudal slightly emarginate. *Scales*—about 65 rows descend to the lateral-line, which contains about 55 tubes: the upper point of the lateral-line below the base of the first dorsal ray is at nearly the junction of the upper and middle third of the height of the body. *Colours*—brownish, fins black, and last two-thirds of pectoral yellow. In the *young* there is a narrow ocular band‡ scarcely above 1/3 the width of the orbit, passing through the eye to the base of the ventral fin: a second, also narrow, from just anterior to the base of the dorsal, descends behind the base of the pectoral towards the anal: a third is over the commencement of the free portion of the tail, and occasionally a fourth at the base of the caudal which is yellow.

I think that Dr. Günther is correct in suggesting *Platax orbicularis* as the adult of this species (see *Chætodon orbicularis*, Forsk. p. 59; *C. pentacanthus*, Lacép. iv, p. 454, pl. 9, f. 2; *Platax orbicularis*, Cuv. and

* Bleeker states both dimensions to be equal: Günther, that the height of the body is more than its length: consequently it may be assumed to vary slightly one way or the other.

† This becomes more pronounced as age advances, when the profile from the eye to the snout is less vertical than in young subjects.

‡ These bands gradually become detached from the specimen if preserved in spirit.

Val. vii, p. 232; Rüpp. Atl. p. 67, t. xviii, f. 3; Bleeker, Sumatra, iv, p. 81; Günther, Catal. ii, p. 490; Klunz. Verh. z. b. Ges. Wien. 1870, p. 793).

Habitat.—Red Sea, East coast of Africa, through the seas of India to the Malay Archipelago and beyond. The one figured (life-size) is from the Andamans.

Genus, 10—Psenes, *Cuv. and Val.*

Branchiostegals, six. Body compressed and elevated, with the frontal region swollen. Eyes lateral. Cleft of mouth shallow, with a short snout. A row of fine teeth in the jaws, none on the palate. Two dorsal fins, the first continuous: the second with more rays and similar to the anal, which last has two or three spines joined to the soft portion of the fin: no finlets. Lateral-line unarmed. Air-vessel bifurcated posteriorly.

Geographical distribution.—Seas of India to the Malay Archipelago and beyond.

SYNOPSIS OF SPECIES.

1. *Psenes Javanicus*, D. 9-10 | $\frac{1}{21-23}$, A. $\frac{3}{21-23}$, L. l. 55. Leaden colour, with dark fins except the pectoral which is yellow. Seas of India to the Malay Archipelago.
2. *Psenes Indicus*, D. 10 | $\frac{1}{14-15}$, A. $\frac{3}{15}$, L. l. 41-43. Silvery. Madras, in the sea.

1. Psenes Javanicus, Plate LI, C. fig. 1.

Cuv. and Val. ix, p. 264; Bleeker, Makr. p. 74, and Amboina, 1857, p. 60; Günther, Catal. ii, p. 494.

B. vi, D. 9-10 | $\frac{1}{21-23}$, P. 19, V. 1/5, A. $\frac{3}{21-23}$, C. 17, L. l. 55, L. tr. 15/18.

Length of head 1/4, of pectoral 1/6, of caudal 1/4, height of body 1/3 of the total length. *Eyes*—diameter 1/3 of length of head, 1/2 a diameter from end of snout, and 2/3 of a diameter apart. Dorsal profile elevated, especially above the nostrils. Body compressed. Lower jaw the longer. Cleft of mouth very oblique, commencing opposite the middle or upper third of the front edge of the eye: the maxilla reaches to below the first third of the eye. *Teeth*—in a single row of comparatively large ones in either jaw, palate edentulous. *Fins*—the first dorsal commences above the hind edge of the opercle, the spines are weak, the third being the longest and equal to the anterior dorsal rays or 2/5 the height of the body, the interspinous membrane deeply emarginate. Second dorsal highest anteriorly, the upper margin of its fin rather concave. Pectoral rather pointed. Ventral 1/3 shorter than the pectoral, and almost reaching to the base of the anal fin. Caudal deeply lunated. *Scales*—small and cycloid. *Lateral-line*—nearly straight. *Colours*—generally leaden, dorsal and anal fins black. Pectoral yellow. Caudal with a yellowish tinge.

Psenes auratus, Cuv. and Val. ix, p. 264, has the same number of spines and rays, but the eye is said to be a little larger. M. Dussumier observed that the body is of a golden yellow, tinged with greenish on the snout. The fins greenish, except the pectoral, which is yellow. The specimens were up to 5 inches (French) in length.

Habitat.—Madras, in the sea where it is not uncommon, but the largest specimen I obtained (October, 1867) was 4½ inches in length.

2. Psenes Indicus, Plate LIV, fig. 2.

Cubiceps Indicus, Day, Proc. Zool. Soc. 1870, p. 690.

B. vi, D. 10 | $\frac{1}{14-15}$, P. 23, V. 1/5, A. $\frac{3}{15}$, C. 18, L. l. 41-43.

Length of head 3½ to 3⅔, of caudal 4½ to 5, height of body 2⅔ to 2¾ in the total length. *Eyes*—diameter 2¾ to 3 in length of head, 1/3 to 1/2 of a diameter from end of snout, and about 1 apart. Abdominal profile rather more convex than that of the back, body compressed: snout short. Lower jaw the longer, the maxilla reaches to below the front edge of the eye. Cleft of mouth equals half its gape. Preopercle entire: opercle ending in a rounded point and spineless. *Teeth*—in a fine single row in either jaw. *Fins*—dorsal spines feeble, from the second to the fifth subequal in length, 1/3 higher than the soft dorsal fin. Pectoral as long as the head excluding the snout. Ventral reaches above half way to the anal, the spines of which last are low. Caudal deeply forked. *Scales*—very deciduous: some extended on to soft dorsal, anal, and caudal fins. *Lateral-line*—on a row of plate-like scales, the tubes are branched posteriorly. *Colours*—silvery, with a purplish gloss. Spinous dorsal rather dark in its upper part.

Habitat.—Madras, where several specimens were captured in the sea (up to 4½ inches in length) during the month of October.

Genus, 11—Equula,* *Cuv. and Val.*

Leiognathus, Lacép.†

Branchiostegals from five to six: pseudobranchiæ. Body oblong or elevated and strongly compressed. Eyes lateral. Mouth very protractile. Lower edge of preopercle serrated. Minute teeth of equal size in the jaws, some

* Fishes of this Genus are termed *Carupatty* in Madras, and are eaten salted by natives who are suffering from malarious fevers. At Akyab they are called *Nga-dan-pak*.

† In Cuv. and Val. it is observed that this Generic term was given under the supposition of the jaws being toothless, but as they are invariably toothed it is inadmissible.

times in a single row; palate edentulous. A single dorsal fin, having less spines (8-10) than rays (15-17): anal with three spines continuous with the soft portion, which has less rays (13-14) than the soft dorsal: no pinlets: ventrals thoracic. Scales small, cycloid, and sometimes deciduous. Lateral-line curved, usually complete, but in some species ceasing beneath the middle or end of the dorsal fin. Air-vessel terminating anteriorly in two horns. Pyloric appendages few.

The species included in this Genus are very similar one with another, but are chiefly to be distinguished by the following points. The comparative length of the head and height of the body to that of the total length. Likewise the length of the dorsal and anal spines. (The length given of these spines in the following species is comparative, as they are liable to considerable variation.) Whether the supraorbital edge is smooth or serrated. If the breast and chest are scaled or scaleless.* If the teeth are in one or more rows. Whilst some have, others have not, a black blotch on the spinous dorsal fin.

Geographical distribution.—Red Sea, seas of India to the Malay Archipelago and beyond.

Uses.—These small fish are extensively sun-dried in India. The salt tax renders refined salt too expensive to be employed in fish-curing by the poorer classes, or the value of the article would be beyond the reach of the consumers. It is also illegal (except along a portion of the Western coast) to collect salt earth for preserving fish. Consequently, as a rule, fish have to be consumed fresh, or if preserved, are mostly only sun-dried. These thin and bony forms are soaked in sea water (which is sometimes partially evaporated previously) and dried in the open air. Of course, being only very slightly cured, they rapidly become putrid, or at any rate greatly deteriorate in moist weather, and if consumed during the monsoon months, are liable to set up visceral irritation as diarrhœa and dysentery.

SYNOPSIS OF SPECIES.

1. *Equula edentula.* Length of head 1/4, height of body half to $2\frac{1}{4}$ in the total length. Supraorbital edge serrated. No scales on chest. No black mark on dorsal fin. Red Sea, seas of India to the Malay Archipelago and beyond.

2. *Equula Dussumieri.* Length of head $4\frac{1}{3}$, height of body $2\frac{1}{2}$ in the total length. Supraorbital edge not serrated. No scales on chest. No black mark on dorsal fin. Seas of India to the Malay Archipelago.

3. *Equula splendens.* Length of head one-fourth, height of body $2\frac{1}{4}$ to $2\frac{1}{3}$ in the total length. Supraorbital edge coarsely serrated. Scales on chest. A deep black blotch on spinous dorsal. Red Sea, seas of India to the Malay Archipelago.

4. *Equula daura.* Length of head $4\frac{1}{2}$, height of body $3\frac{2}{3}$ in the total length. Supraorbital edge not serrated. No scales on chest. Upper half of spinous dorsal black. Seas of India to the Malay Archipelago.

5. *Equula bindus.* Ventral fin very short. Upper half of spinous dorsal orange, with a narrow black basal edging. Coromandel coast of India.

6. *Equula Blochii.* Length of head $4\frac{1}{3}$, height of body $2\frac{1}{4}$ to $3\frac{1}{4}$ in the total length. Supraorbital edge serrated. Chest scaled. A brown blotch over the nape. Seas of India.

7. *Equula brevirostris.* Length of head $4\frac{1}{2}$, height of body $2\frac{2}{3}$ in the total length. Supraorbital edge serrated. Chest scaleless. A brown blotch over the nape. Seas of India.

8. *Equula lineolata.* Length of head $4\frac{1}{4}$, height of body $2\frac{3}{4}$ in the total length. Supraorbital edge not serrated. Chest scaled. No black blotch on spinous dorsal.

9. *Equula insidiatrix.* Length of head from $4\frac{2}{3}$ to one-fifth, height of body from $2\frac{1}{3}$ to $2\frac{2}{3}$ in the total length. Supraorbital edge finely serrated. Chest scaled. A black blotch on upper portion of spinous dorsal: back with rows of spots. Seas of India to the Malay Archipelago.

10. *Equula ruconius.* Length of head $4\frac{1}{3}$, height of body one-half of the total length. Supraorbital edge serrated. Scales very deciduous, much larger than in the last species. Vertical blackish streaks on back: a black blotch on spinous dorsal. Seas of India to the Malay Archipelago.

11. *Equula fasciata.* Length of head 1/4, height of body 2/5 of the total length. Supraorbital edge not serrated. Chest scaleless. No black blotch on spinous dorsal. Seas of India to the Malay Archipelago.

12. *Equula oblonga.* Length of head 4 to $4\frac{1}{3}$, height of body $3\frac{1}{2}$ to 4 in the total length. Supraorbital edge not serrated. Chest scaleless. No black blotch on spinous dorsal. Seas of India to the Malay Archipelago.

1. Equula edentula, Plate LII, fig. 1.

Scomber edentulus, Bl. t. 428; Bl. Schn. p. 36.
Scomber equula, Forsk. p. 58; Bl. Schn. p. 36; Shaw, Zool. iv, p. 587.
Centrogaster equula, Gmel. Linn. p. 1337.
Zeus tottah karah, Russell, Fish. Vizag. i, p. 49, f. 52.
Cæsio equulus, Lacép. iii, pp. 85, 90.
Leiognathus argenteus, Lacép. iv, pp. 448, 449.
Equula ensifera, Cuv. and Val. x, p. 66; Bleeker, Makr. p. 80.

* The chest being scaleless may occasionally be due to the specimen being immature. Sometimes the skin is quite smooth after the scales have been rubbed off. It may be that their presence or absence has no specific value.

Equula caballa, Cuv. and Val. x, p. 73; Rüpp. N. W. Fische, p. 51; Cantor, Catal. p. 146; Jerdon, M. J. L. and Sc. 1851, p. 138; Günther, Catal. ii, p. 499; ? Klunz. Verh. z. b. Ges. Wien, 1871, p. 467.

Equula edentula, Günther, Catal. ii, p. 498; Day, Fish. Malabar, p. 103; Kner, Novara Fische, p. 166; Klunz. Verh. z. b. Ges. Wien, 1871, p. 467.

Equula raconius, Day, P. Z. S. 1869, p. 302 (not H. B.).

Leiognathus edentulus, Bleeker, Ann. 1873, p. 3.

Tauba chandee, Ooriah: *Nga-kper-sea*, Burm.

B. v, D. $\frac{8}{15-16}$, P. 20, V. 1/5, A. $\frac{3}{14}$, C. 17, L. l. 60.

Length of head 1/4, of caudal 1/4, height of body 1/2 to two and a fourth of the total length. *Eyes*—diameter 1/3 of length of head, about 1 diameter from end of snout, and also apart. Dorsal profile rather more convex than that of the abdomen: snout obtuse. Interorbital cavity anteriorly rather wide, not quite twice as long as broad. A pair of small spines at the anterior-superior angle of the orbits: the distance between the outer edges of the spines on the orbits in the young equal 2/5 of the length of the head, in the adult 1/3 of the same distance: supraorbital edge minutely serrated. The maxilla reaches to below the front edge of the eye. Lower edge of preopercle very finely serrated. Mandible very concave. *Teeth*—fine. *Fins*—dorsal spines moderately strong, the second is arched, compressed, and nearly equal to 3/4 the length of the head, or 1/6 of the total length: the third and fourth spines anteriorly serrated in their lower portions. Pectoral as long as the head excluding the snout. Ventral nearly, or in the young quite, reaches to the anal. The length of the second anal spine equals that of the head behind the middle of the eyes, or even a little more, the third spine is rather strongly serrated anteriorly in its lower half. *Scales*—small, but distinct, except on the chest or breast, and to a little above the base of the pectoral fin, in which localities they are absent or indistinct:* a large scale at the base of the ventral fin. *Lateral-line*—in about 60 tubes, it first curves upwards, its highest point being below the third dorsal spine, then it arches to below the end of the dorsal fin. Free portion of the tail about as long as high. *Colours*—silvery, grayish along the lateral-line: fine vertical lines from the back down the sides: the soft dorsal stained with gray on its upper edge: base of pectoral stained gray.

Large specimens, as at 8 inches in length, have the height of the body $1\frac{4}{5}$ of the total length, the eye is 2/7 of the length of the head, and $1\frac{1}{4}$ diameters from the end of snout. In one specimen the second dorsal spine is 1/4 longer than the head. It is termed *Soorookoo neat karé*, Tam. Jerdon, *l. c.*

Habitat.—Red Sea, seas of India to the Malay Archipelago and beyond: attaining 10 inches and more in length: it ascends rivers far above tidal reach, but only apparently whilst young.

2. Equula Dussumieri, Plate LII, fig. 2.

Cuv. and Val. x, p. 77, pl. 283; Cuv. Règ. An. Ill. Poiss. pl. 62, f. 1; Swainson, Fishes, ii, p. 250; Jerdon, M. J. L. and Sc. 1851, p. 138; Günther, Catal. ii, p. 500.

B. v, D. $\frac{8}{16}$, P. 21, V. 1/5, A. $\frac{3}{14-15}$, C. 17, L. l. 65.

Length of head $4\frac{1}{4}$, of caudal $4\frac{1}{4}$, height of body $2\frac{1}{2}$ in the total length. *Eyes*—diameter 2/5 of length of head, 3/4 of a diameter from end of snout, and 1 apart. Dorsal and abdominal profiles equally convex. Interorbital cavity anteriorly rather broad, and not twice as long as wide. A pair of small spines at the anterior-superior angle of the orbit. The distance between the two outer spines is $2\frac{3}{4}$ in the length of the head. Orbital margin not serrated. The maxilla reaches to below the first third of the eye. Mandibles inferiorly slightly concave. Lower margin of preopercle rather strongly serrated. *Teeth*—fine, and in several rows in both jaws. *Fins*—the second dorsal spine almost straight and as long as the head excluding the snout, or 1/5 of the total length, the third nearly as long, the front edge of both third and fourth spines serrated in their lower portion. Pectoral as long as the head excluding ohe snout. Ventral does not quite reach the anal. Second anal spine rather weak, it equals the length of the head behind the first third or middle of the eye,† third anal spine a little shorter than the second and serrated anteriorly. Caudal forked. *Scales*—small but distinct, except on the breast and chest, which are scaleless. A moderately strong scale at the base of the ventral. *Lateral-line*—in tubes which anteriorly are distinct, but posteriorly run into one another. *Colours*—silvery, no black spot on dorsal fin: base of pectoral dark, sometimes black. Dark and narrow vertical lines pass from the back over the lateral-line.

Termed *Vori karé*, Tamil. Jerdon, *l. c.*

Habitat.—Seas of India to the Malay Archipelago; attaining at least 8 inches in length.

3. Equula splendens, Plate LII, fig. 3.

Zeus goomorah kurah, Russell, Fish. Vizag. i, p. 48, pl. 61.

Equula splendens, Cuv. Règ. Anim.; Cantor, Catal. p. 140; Jerdon, M. J. L. and Sc. 1851, p. 138; Kner, Novara Fische, p. 168; Peters, Mon. Akad. Berlin, 1868, p. 262; Day, Fish. Malabar, p. 104; Klunz. Verh. z. b. Ges. Wien, 1871, p. 467.

* Russell's figure, pl. 63, termed *Equula coma*, C.V. is a *Gazza*. Russell distinctly remarks "The teeth larger than in the former (*E. caballa*—*E. edentula*) and somewhat curved."

† In a specimen $5\frac{3}{4}$ inches long.

Equula gomorah, Cuv. and Val. x, p. 80; Rüpp. N. W. Fische, p. 51; Bleeker, Makr. p. 82.
Equula caballa, Bleeker, Oost-Java, (not C. V.)
Leiognathus splendens, Bleeker, Arou, 1873, p. 2.

B. v, D. [illegible], P. 17, V. 1/5, A. [illegible], C. 17, L. l. 55-60.

Length of head one-fourth, of caudal 4¾, height of body 2¼ to 2½ in the total length. *Eyes*—diameter 1/3 of length of head, nearly 1 diameter from end of snout, and also apart. Dorsal profile much more convex than that of the abdomen. Snout obtuse. Interorbital cavity nearly twice as long as wide. A pair of fine spines at the anterior-superior angle of the orbit, and which are sometimes bifurcated, the distance between the bases of the outer orbital spines equals one-third of the length of the head. Supra-orbital edge rather coarsely serrated. The maxilla reaches to below the middle of the eye. Lower preopercular edge strongly serrated. Mandibles slightly concave. *Teeth*—in a single row in either jaw. *Fins*—dorsal spines strong, the second equals about 1/3 of the height of the body, the third is strongly serrated along the anterior edge of its lower third, the fourth and fifth are also serrated. Pectoral as long as the head excluding the snout. Ventral spine strong, the fin nearly reaches the base of the anal: second anal spine strong, equalling about 1/3 of the height of the body, the third serrated anteriorly along its lower third. Caudal deeply forked. *Scales*—distinct, in irregular rows, and extended over the breast and chest: a large one at base of ventral fin. *Lateral-line*—consisting of 60 or 70 short tubes, and does not quite reach the base of the caudal fin. *Colours*—silvery, with a deep black blotch in the upper half of the spinous dorsal: a black mark over snout: axilla dark, and the base of the pectoral black posteriorly.

It is termed *Kalli kari*, Tam., Jerdon, *l. c.*

Habitat.—Red Sea, seas of India to the Malay Archipelago; attaining at least 5 inches in length.

4. Equula daura, Plate LII, fig. 4.

Zeus daeer karah, Russell, Fish. Vizag. i, p. 51, pl. 65.
Equula daura, Cuv. Règ. Anim.; Cantor, Catal. p. 150; Jerdon, M. J. L. and Sc. 1851, p. 138; Günther, Catal. ii, p. 502; Day, Fish. Malabar, p. 105.
Equula daeer, Cuv. and Val. x, p. 83; Bleeker, Makr. p. 81.
Equula brevirostris, Bleeker, Batav. and Oost-Java (not Cuv. and Val.).

B. v, D. [illegible], P. 20, V. 1/5, A. [illegible], C. 17.

Length of head 4¼, of caudal 4½, height of body 2⅔ in the total length. *Eyes*—diameter 1/3 of length of head, 1 diameter from end of snout, and nearly 1 apart. Dorsal profile slightly more convex than that of the abdomen. Interorbital cavity a little more than twice as long as wide. A pair of very small spines at the anterior-superior angle of the orbit. Distance between the outer margins of orbital spines equals 2/5 of the length of the head. Orbital edge not serrated. The maxilla reaches to below the front edge of the eye. Mandibles slightly concave: lips thick. Lower preopercular margin finely serrated. *Teeth*—fine. *Fins*—dorsal spines of moderate strength, the second equal to nearly 1/2 the height of the body, the third is slightly serrated anteriorly near its base. Pectoral as long as the head excluding the snout. Ventral does not reach the anal. Anal spines comparatively weak, the second equals 3/10 of the height of the body, the third is serrated anteriorly in its lower third. Caudal forked. *Scales*—small but distinct, none on breast or chest: an elongated one at base of ventral. *Lateral-line*—in about 60 short tubes, placed on rounded plate-like scales; it does not extend on to the caudal fin. Free portion of the tail as long as high. *Colours*—silvery, with a golden stripe along the side. A dark line along the base of the dorsal: a darkish triangular spot between the occiput and dorsal fin: upper half of spinous dorsal black from the second to the fifth spines.

It is termed *Rama kari*, Tam., Jerdon, *l. c.*

Habitat.—Ceylon and Coromandel coast to the Malay Archipelago; attaining at least 5 inches in length. The specimen figured (life-size) is from Madras.

5. Equula bindus.

Zeus bindoo-karah, Russell, Fish. Vizag. i, p. 50, pl. 64.
Equula bindus, Cuv. and Val. x, p. 78; ? Cantor, Catal. p. 148; Jerdon, M. J. L. and Sc. 1851, p. 138.

B. iv, D. [illegible], P. 15, V. 1/5, A. [illegible].

Length of head 4½, of caudal 4¼, height of body 2½ in the total length. Abdominal profile more convex than the dorsal, which is rather concave over the orbits. *Fins*—second dorsal spine equal to about 1/3 of the height of the body. Ventrals short, scarcely reaching half way to the anal (Russell did not detect any spine in them.) Second anal spine weaker and a little shorter than the second dorsal one. *Colours*—silvery-olive over the nape, fins hyaline, the upper third of the spinous dorsal orange edged inferiorly with black.

Amongst Sir W. Elliot's figures of Indian Fishes, is one marked by Jerdon as belonging to this species, and its proportions and colours are very similar to *Equula bindoides*, Bleeker, Makr. p. 375 and p. 83; Günther, Catal. ii, p. 501; Kner, Novara Fische, p. 168.

Sir W. Elliot's fish is termed *Tetaoo kari*, Tam. Unfortunately I have mislaid my specimens, so am unable to give a full description.

Habitat.—Coromandel coast.

6. Equula Blochii, Plate LII, fig. 5.

Zeus notatus, (Bloch, MSS.) Cuv. and Val.
Equula Blochii, Cuv. and Val. x, p. 84; Day, Fish. Malabar, p. 105.

B. v, D. $\frac{8}{16}$, P. 18, V. 1/5, A. $\frac{3}{14}$, C. 17.

Length of head $4\frac{1}{3}$, of caudal $4\frac{3}{4}$ to 5, height of body $2\frac{3}{4}$ to $3\frac{1}{4}$ in the total length. *Eyes*—diameter 1/3 of length of head, 1 diameter from end of snout, from 3/4 to 1 apart. Dorsal profile rather more convex than that of the abdomen, a slight concavity over the occiput, the snout is rather pointed and not truncated. Upper surface of orbit serrated, which serrations appear to become obsolete in some old specimens: a pair of small spines at its anterior-superior angle, the distance between the outer edges of the supraorbital spines equals 2/5 of the length of the head. The posterior margin of the maxilla reaches to below the first third or middle of the eye. Lower edge of preopercle strongly serrated. Cavity on upper surface of head at least twice as long as wide. *Teeth*—in a single row in the jaws. *Fins*—dorsal spines of moderate strength, the second rather the longest, and equal or nearly equal, to 1/2 the height of the body, the third and fourth serrated anteriorly in their lower halves. Pectoral as long as the head excluding the snout. Ventral reaches to the anal. Second anal spine $2\frac{1}{4}$ in the height of the body: the third finely serrated anteriorly. *Scales*—on body (except base of pectoral fin), breast, and chest: a rather large one at base of ventral. *Lateral-line*—in about 60 tubes, situated on rounded scales. *Colours*—silvery, with a dark brown blotch over the nape, and a black mark in the upper half of the spinous dorsal fin from the third to the sixth spines. Vertical zig-zag yellow lines on the back and sides, which fade soon after death: base of pectoral posteriorly dark coloured.

Habitat.—Seas of India, where it is common. I have it from Bombay, Malabar, Madras, Calcutta, and Akyab, and many young from the Sunderbunds. The specimen figured (life-size) is from Bombay.

7. Equula brevirostris.

Cuv. and Val. x, p. 84 (not Bleeker, Batav. and Oost Java).

B. v, D. $\frac{8}{16}$, P. 18, V. 1/5, A. $\frac{3}{14}$, C. 17.

Length of head $4\frac{1}{3}$, of caudal $4\frac{1}{3}$, height of body $2\frac{2}{3}$ in the total length. *Eyes*—diameter nearly $2\frac{3}{4}$ in length of head, 3/4 of a diameter from end of snout, and 1 apart. Body oval, dorsal and abdominal profiles equally convex: snout pointed, not obtuse except just at its anterior extremity. Interorbital cavity nearly twice as long as broad. A pair of well developed spines at the anterior-superior angle of the eye; supraorbital edge finely serrated. The distance from the external sides of the bases of the orbital spines equals 1/2 the length of the head. The maxilla reaches to below the first third of the eye: lower jaw very concave inferiorly. Lower limb of preopercle finely serrated. *Teeth*—in a single fine row in either jaw. *Fins*—dorsal spines moderately strong and compressed, the second equals 4/9 (sometimes 1/3) of the height of the body: the third is strongly serrated in its lower half, whilst the fourth is in its lower fourth. Pectoral as long as the head excluding the snout. Ventral reaches 2/3 of way to the anal. Second anal spine 2/5 of height of body, the third is strongly serrated in its lower half. Caudal forked. Free portion of tail as high at its base as it is long. *Scales*—extended over body, but not on breast or chest. *Lateral-line*—in from 58 to 64 distinct tubes, and not quite reaching to the base of the caudal fin. *Colours*—an oval black blotch on the upper half of the spinous dorsal fin, from the third to the seventh spines (it is sometimes very faint), and a dark brown transverse blotch across the nape of the neck. Pectoral posteriorly black at its base. A narrow yellow band passes from above the eye to the centre of the base of the caudal fin.

There are two Indian *Equula's* (? species) very similar, the one described above, *E. brevirostris*, which is destitute of scales on the breast and chest, but which is otherwise similar to the second or *E. Blochii*. The latter was described from a stuffed specimen still at Berlin, and they may prove to be varieties of the same species.

E. nuchalis, Tem. and Schleg. is very similar, but the dorsal and anal spines appear to be usually shorter, but this again is subject to considerable variation. Dr. Hubrecht at Leyden having kindly examined the type, observes that the breast and chest are apparently scaleless: still microscopic scales may perhaps exist partly hidden in the integument.

Habitat.—Seas of India to China: attaining at least $4\frac{1}{2}$ inches in length.

8. Equula lineolata, Plate LI, C. fig. 3.

Cuv. and Val. x, p. 86; Bleeker, Makr. p. 83; Günther, Catal. ii, p. 502.

B. v, D. $\frac{8}{16}$, P. 19, V. 1/5, A. $\frac{3}{14}$, C. 17.

Length of head $4\frac{1}{3}$, of caudal $4\frac{2}{3}$, height of body $2\frac{2}{3}$ in the total length. *Eyes*—diameter 1/3 of length of head, 3/4 of a diameter from end of snout, and 1 apart. Body of an oblong form, with the dorsal and abdominal profiles equally convex, a slight concavity over the occiput. Interorbital cavity at least twice as long as wide. A pair of minute spines over the anterior third of the orbit, and the distance between their outer margins equals $3\frac{1}{4}$ in the length of the head: supraorbital edge serrated or only a little rough to the feel. Maxilla reaches to below front third of the eye: inferior edge of mandible very slightly concave. Lower edge of preopercle minutely serrated. *Teeth*—fine and in a single row. *Fins*—dorsal spines weak, the second arched, and equal to 2 or $2\frac{1}{2}$ in the height of the body, the third and fourth anteriorly serrated in their lower halves. Pectoral as long as the head excluding the snout. Ventral does not quite reach the anal. Second anal spine arched,

1/3 to 2/5 of the height of the body, its third spine anteriorly serrated. Caudal forked. *Scales*—small but distinct, present on breast and chest. *Lateral-line*—becomes lost at nearly the end of the free portion of the tail: it consists of above 60 tubes placed on a row of plate-like, rounded scales. *Colours*—silvery, with vertical zigzag lines passing down the back: base of pectoral posteriorly black: upper edge of dorsal darkish.

Habitat.—Seas of India to the Malay Archipelago. The specimen figured (life-size) is from Madras.

9. **Equula insidiatrix**, Plate LI, C. fig. 5.

Zeus insidiator, Bloch, t. cxcii, f. 2, 3; Gmel. Linn. p. 1221; Bl. Schn. p. 95; Shaw, Zool. iv, p. 284, pl. 41; Lacép. iv, pp. 572, 574.

Equula insidiatrix, Cuv. and Val. x, p. 98; Cantor, Catal. p. 151; Bleeker, Makr. p. 84; Jerdon, M. J. L. and Sc. 1851, p. 138; Peters, Mon. Akad. Berlin, 1868, p. 262; Günther, Catal. ii, p. 504; Day, Fish. Malabar, p. 102.

Paarl coorchee, Mal.

B. v, D. $\frac{8}{16-17}$, P. 18, V. 1/5, A. $\frac{3}{14}$, C. 17.

Length of head from 4$\frac{4}{5}$ to 5, of caudal 5, height of body from 2$\frac{1}{4}$ to 2$\frac{2}{3}$ in the total length. The young are much more elongated. *Eyes*—diameter 2$\frac{1}{2}$ in length of head, 3/4 of a diameter from end of snout, and 3/4 to 1 apart. Abdominal profile more convex than the dorsal one. Premaxillaries very protractile, the length of their hind limb equalling 1/8 of that of the total length: and when fully protracted the mouth remains directed somewhat upwards, when closed the mandible is almost vertical and not concave. Interorbital cavity triangular. The middle third of the supraorbital edge finely serrated. One or two minute supraorbital spines at the anterior-superior edge of the orbit directed backwards, the external when two are present the stronger. The maxilla reaches to below the front third of the eye. Lower edge of preopercle minutely serrated, occasionally almost smooth. *Teeth*—minute, in 1 or 2 rows. *Fins*—dorsal spines weak, smooth: the first minute, the second, third, and fourth subequal in length and equal 1/3 the height of the body. Pectoral nearly as long as the head. Second anal spine equals the diameter of the orbit. Ventral minute, reaching 1/2 way to anal. Caudal forked. *Scales**—minute over the body, breast, and chest, but not at the base of the pectoral fin. *Lateral-line*—passes nearly level with the back and is generally lost near the tail, but sometimes as far forwards as below the middle or last third of the dorsal fin. *Colours*—back bluish-silver, abdomen whitish-silver, the whole being glossed over with a slightly golden tint. The upper surface of the head, cheeks, and lower jaw, all of burnished silver, often a black streak from the eye to the throat, joining that of the opposite side: a dark mark in the axilla. Three or four horizontal lines of black spots, with bronze reflections, form from eight to ten vertical bands descending along the upper half of the body. Spinous dorsal tipped with black: ventral white: pectoral light yellow: caudal yellowish, and stained at the end with brown.

Habitat.—Seas of India and the Malay Archipelago: it is said to be occasionally captured in fresh water.

10. **Equula ruconius**, Plate LI, C, fig. 4.

Chanda ruconius, Ham. Buch. Fish. Ganges, pp. 106, 371, pl. xii, f. 35.

Equula interrupta, Cuv. and Val. x, p. 102; Bleeker, Ich. Fauna Beng. 1853, p. 96, and Makr. p. 85; Günther, Catal. ii, p. 504; Peters, Monats. Ak. Berlin, 1868, p. 262; Kner, Novara Fische, p. 169.

Equula ruconius, Cuv. and Val. x, p. 79 (not Day, P. Z. S. 1869, p. 302).

B. v, D. $\frac{8}{16}$, P. 18, V. 1/5, A. $\frac{3}{14}$, C. 17.

Length of head 4$\frac{1}{3}$, of caudal 4$\frac{3}{4}$, height of body (1$\frac{1}{2}$ to 1$\frac{3}{4}$ in the young) one half of the total length. *Eyes*—diameter 1/3 of length of head, 1 diameter from end of snout, and also apart. Abdominal profile much more convex than that of the abdomen, a concavity over the occiput. Premaxillaries very protractile, the length of their hind limbs equalling 1/12 of the total length, the mouth as in *E. insidiatrix*. Last half of supraorbital edge minutely serrated; one or two spines close to hind nostril. The maxilla reaches to below the front edge of the orbit. Lower edge of preopercle serrated, most coarsely so anteriorly. *Teeth*—in a single, minute, and deciduous row. *Fins*—second dorsal spine the longest, equal to 2/7 of the height of the body, the third serrated anteriorly in its lower third. Pectoral 3/4 the length of the head. Ventral reaches half way to anal, second anal spine equals the diameter of the orbit. Caudal forked. *Scales*—very deciduous, apparently often absent and usually so above the lateral-line, they are from two to three times the size of those in *E. insidiatrix*, and are often extended on to the chest. *Lateral-line*—in single tubes, usually ceasing below the middle of soft dorsal, but sometimes continued to its last third. *Colours*—back bluish-silvery, abdomen silvery-white. A well marked black streak from the anterior edge of the eye to the throat, joining that of the opposite side. A dark spot on the upper part of the opercle, back of the base of the pectoral black. Vertical lines of black marks having bronze reflections descend down the upper third of the body, and are often subdivided into spots. Spinous dorsal tipped with black.

This is much more frequently captured in estuaries and tidal rivers than *E. insidiatrix*, it is common in the Hooghly at Calcutta. *Chanda (ambassis) ruconius*, McClelland, C. J. N. H. ii, p. 586, has erroneously been referred to this species. His specimens came from the Punjab, where no *Equula* exists. It is doubtless an *Ambassis*, and probably the *A. ranga*, H. B.

* In a specimen from Akyab, only 1$\frac{3}{4}$ inches long and 7/10 high, the lower edge of the preopercle is rather coarsely serrated, and there are no scales on the body.

Habitat.—Seas of India to the Malay Archipelago and beyond; the specimen figured (life-size) is from Madras.

11. Equula fasciata, Plate LI, C. fig. 2.

Zeus karah, Russell, Fish. Vizag. i, p. 51, pl. 66.
Clupea fasciata, Lacép. v, p. 463.
Equula filigera, longispinis and *carah*, Cuv. and Val. x, pp. 92, 94, 95, pl. 284.
Equula fasciata, Cuv. and Val. x, p. 96; Günther, Catal. ii, p. 498; Day, Fish. Malabar, p. 106; Kner. Novara Fische, p. 167; Klunz. Verh. z. b. Ges. Wien, 1871, p. 467.
Equula filigera, Cuv. Mém. Mus. i, p. 402, pl. 23, f. 1; Swainson, Fishes, ii, p. 250; Cantor, Catal. p. 150; Bleeker, Makr. p. 79; Jerdon, M. J. L. and Sc. 1851, p. 138.
Equula setigera, Agass. Poiss. Foss. v, p. 24, t. B.
Leiognathus fasciatus, Bleeker, Bintang, 1868, p. 5.

B. v, D. $\frac{8}{16}$, P. 19, V. 1/5, A. $\frac{3}{14}$, C. 17, Cæc. pyl. (3).

Length of head 4 to four and a fourth, of caudal 4, height of body 2½ in the total length. *Eyes*—diameter 1/3 of length of head, 3/4 to 1 diameter from end of snout, and nearly 1 apart. Dorsal profile rather more convex than the abdominal. A concavity over the occiput. Interorbital cavity nearly twice as long as wide, the posterior limb of premaxillary equals 2/3 of the length of the head. A pair of spines above the anterior-superior angle of the orbit. Orbital edge not serrated. The distance between the outer edges of the orbital spines equals 2⅔ in the length of the head. The maxilla reaches to below the first third of the eye. Lower edge of preopercle nearly straight, and very finely serrated. Mandibula slightly concave inferiorly. *Teeth*—in a single row in the upper jaw; in villiform bands in the lower. *Fins*—dorsal spines of moderate strength, the second elongated, usually about 4/5 as high as the body, the third and fourth serrated anteriorly. Pectoral as long as the head excluding the snout. Ventral reaches 3/4 of the way to the anal. Second anal spine strong, equalling about 2/5 of the height of the body, but sometimes much longer. Caudal forked. Free portion of the tail about as high as long. *Scales*—cover body, absent or exceedingly indistinct on the chest. *Lateral-line*—consists of about 65 tubes, it ceases just before the base of the caudal fin. *Colours*—silvery, with irregular vertical streaks on the body.

Habitat.—Red Sea, seas of India to the Malay Archipelago and beyond.

12. Equula oblonga.

? *Scomber equula*, var. Forsk. p. 58.
Equula oblonga, Cuv. and Val. x, p. 85; Bleeker, Makr. p. 84; Günther, Catal. ii, p. 502; Day, Fish. Malabar, p. 106; Klunz. Verh. z. b. Ges. Wien, 1871, p. 467.
Equula berbis, Cuv. and Val. x, p. 85.

B. v, D. $\frac{8}{16-17}$, P. 16, V. 1/5, A. $\frac{3}{14-15}$, C. 16.

Length of head 4 to 4½, of caudal 5½, height of body 3½ to 4 in the total length. *Eyes*—diameter 1/3 of length of head, 1 diameter from end of snout, and 1 apart. Abdominal profile rather more convex than that of the back. Snout rather pointed. Posterior limb of preopercle equal to 6½ in the total length: an interorbital cavity much longer than wide. Orbital edge not serrated: two spines above the anterior edge of the eye: the distance between the outer edges of orbital spines equals half the length of the head. Lower preopercular edge finely serrated. Lower edge of mandible slightly concave. *Teeth*—in a single row in either jaw. *Fins*—dorsal spines moderately strong, the second equal to 2/3 the height of the body. Pectoral 4/7 of the length of the head. Ventral reaches 2/3 of way to anal, the second spine of which latter fin equals 1/2 the height of the body. Caudal forked. *Scales*—very minute, none on chest. *Colours*—grayish on the back, becoming silvery below: a silvery band along the side, irregular angular bands over the back to as low as the lateral-line. No black on the dorsal fin.

Habitat.—Red Sea, seas of India to Malay Archipelago and beyond.

Genus, 12—Gazza, *Rüpp.*

Equula, sp. Cuv. and Val.

Branchiostegals five: pseudobranchiæ. Body oblong, elevated, and compressed. Mouth very protractile. Lower preopercular margin serrated. Teeth, a pair of canines in the upper, a conical row in the lower jaw. A single dorsal fin, having less spines (8) than rays (16): anal with three spines continuous with the soft portion which has less rays (14) than the soft dorsal: no finlets. Lateral-line unarmed.

These fishes were included by Cuv. and Val. with the *Equula* as one genus, Rüppell observing their strong teeth and the presence of canines, separated them, but Kner has again considered them as one genus.

Geographical distribution.—Red Sea, seas of India to the Malay Archipelago and beyond.

SYNOPSIS OF SPECIES.

1. *Gazza minuta*. Length of head 3¾, height of body 2¼ to 2½ in the total length. Dorsal spines 2½ in height of body. Silvery, axilla black. Seas of India to the Malay Archipelago and beyond.

2. *Gazza equulæformis.* Length of head 3½ to 4, height of body 2⅓ to 3 in the total length. Dorsal spines 2 to 2½ in height of body. Silvery, axilla usually brown or black: a silvery lateral streak in the young. Red Sea, seas of India to the Malay Archipelago.

1. **Gazza minuta**, Plate LIII, fig. 1.

Scomber minutus, Bl. t. 429, f. 2; Bl. Schn. p. 36.
Zeus komah-karah, Russell, Fish. Vizag. i, p. 50, pl. 63.
Equula coma et *minuta*, Cuv. and Val. x, pp. 76, 88; Jerdon, M. J. L. and Sc. 1851, p. 138.
Equula dentex, Cuv. and Val. x, p. 91; Kner, Novara Fische, p. 170.
Gazza minuta, Bleeker, Sumatra, p. 259, and Makr. p. 85; Günther, Catal. ii, p. 506.
Gar-chusa, Belouch.

B. v, D. $\frac{8}{16}$, P. 17, V. 1/5, A. $\frac{3}{14}$, C. 19.

Length of head 3¼, of caudal 4⅔ to 5, height of body 2½ to 2¾ in the total length. *Eyes*—diameter 2¾ to 2½ in length of head, 2/3 of a diameter from end of snout, and 3/4 apart. Dorsal profile from snout to base of fin ascending in an almost straight line. Supraorbital edge serrated, two spines above the anterior third of the eye. The maxilla reaches to below the first third of the eye. Lower edge of preopercle coarsely serrated, especially anteriorly. *Teeth*—a row of pointed ones in the premaxillaries, and two canines opposite the symphysis: villiform in the lower jaw, with an outer row of large conical ones, increasing in size with age. *Fins*—dorsal spines weak, the second and third of about the same height, and equalling 2½ in that of the body. Pectoral as long as the head excluding the snout. Ventral reaches two-thirds of the way to the anal. Second anal spine from 2½ to 3 in the height of the body. *Scales*—on body, but absent from or very inconspicuous on the chest. *Lateral-line*—on a row of plate-like scales and in about 60 tubes, it ceases either below the end of the dorsal or close to the base of the caudal fin. *Colours*—silvery, with irregular bluish or yellowish lines descending from the back to the lateral-line, the axilla black; anterior portion of the dorsal fin dark.

In external appearance *Zeus kossa karah*, Russell=*Equula coma*, C.V. strongly resembles *E. edentula*, Bl. (see p. 238). It is termed *Kotoo kare*, Tam. Jerdon, *l. c.*

Habitat.—Seas of India to the Malay Archipelago and beyond: the specimen figured (6 inches long) is from the Andamans.

2. **Gazza equulæformis.**

Rüpp. N. W. Fische, p. 4, t. i, f. 3; Bleeker, Sumatra, ii, p. 261; Cantor, Catal. p. 153; Günther, Catal. ii, p. 506; Klunz. Verh. z. b. Ges. Wien, 1871, p. 468.

B. v, D. $\frac{8}{16}$, P. 15, V. 1/5, A. $\frac{3}{14}$, C. 17.

Length of head 3½ to 4, of caudal 4½, height of body 2⅓ to 3 in the total length. *Eyes*—diameter 2¾ in length of head, 3/4 of a diameter from end of snout, and 1 diameter apart. Dorsal and abdominal profiles about equally convex. Supraorbital edge serrated, sometimes coarsely so (in one specimen it only feels rough to the touch), two spines above the front third of the eye, the distance between the outer edges of the spines on either side of the orbit equals 2/5 of the length of the head. The length of the hind limb of the premaxillary equals 5½ in the total length. The maxilla reaches to below the anterior 1/3 of the eye. Inferior surface of mandible scarcely concave. Lower margin of preopercle rather strongly serrated. *Teeth*—in a row of pointed ones in the upper jaw, having two canines in the median line: villiform in the lower jaw, with an outer row of curved and pointed ones, which increase in size anteriorly, becoming like canines on either side of the symphysis. *Fins*—dorsal spines weak, second and third of about the same length, and equal to from 2 to 2½ in the height of the body. Pectoral as long as the head behind the middle of the eye. Ventral reaches 2/3 of the way to the anal. Second anal spine stronger than those of the dorsal, and equal to about 1/3 of the height of the body, the third rough anteriorly in its lower third. Caudal forked. *Scales*—over body, none on breast and chest. *Lateral-line*—in single tubes, ceasing opposite the last third of the soft dorsal. *Colours*—grayish along the back, silvery on the sides and beneath, zigzag irregular bluish bands descend from the back to as low as the lateral-line. Spinous dorsal fin with brown spots, especially between the second and third spines: axilla usually brown or black. The young have a silvery band along the sides.

Habitat.—Red Sea, seas of India to the Malay Archipelago: attaining at least 6 inches in length. It is very common along all the coasts of India as far as Sind.

Genus, 13—Lactarius, *Cuv. and Val.*

Branchiostegals seven; pseudobranchiæ. Body oblong, compressed. Eyes lateral. Cleft of mouth deep, with the lower jaw prominent. Preopercular margins entire. Teeth in jaws small, with one or two pairs of strong canines. Two dorsal fins, the first with seven or eight feeble spines, second and the anal with many rays, but no finlets: anal with three spines joined to the remainder of the fin. Scales cycloid, of moderate size, some over the second dorsal and anal fins. Lateral-line continuous, unarmed. Air-vessel bifurcated both anteriorly and posteriorly. Pyloric appendages few.

Lactarius, as observed by Günther (Catal. ii, p. 507), "approaches the family of *Sciænidæ*, and especially the Genus *Otolithus*, by several characters, namely, by the structure of the mouth, and by the air-bladder, by the muciferous cavities of the skull, and by the anal spines, which are continuous with the soft fin."

Geographical distribution.—Seas of India to the Malay Archipelago.

SYNOPSIS OF INDIVIDUAL SPECIES.

1. *Lactarius delicatulus*, D. 7-8 | [illegible], A. [illegible], L. l. 74-80. A black spot at the upper and posterior part of the opercle. A dark band sometimes present along the soft dorsal and anal fins. Seas of India to the Malay Archipelago.

1. Lactarius delicatulus, Plate LIII, fig. 2.

Scomber lactarius, Bl. Schn. p. 31.
Sparus chundawah, Russell, Fish. Vizag. ii, p. 6, pl. 108.
Lactarius delicatulus, Cuv. and Val. ix, p. 238, pl. 261; Cantor, Catal. p. 138; Günther, Catal. ii, p. 507; Day, Malabar Fishes, p. 107.
Purrimeah, Mal.; *Sudumu*, Telugu (Gopaulpore).

B. vii, D. 7-8 | [illegible], P. 17, V. $\frac{1}{5}$, A. [illegible], C. 17, L. l. 74-80, Cæc. pyl. 6.

Length of head 1/6, of caudal 2/9 to 1/4, height of body 2/7 of the total length. *Eyes*—diameter 1/3 of length of head, 1/2 to 2/3 of a diameter from end of snout, 4/5 of a diameter apart. Profile with a gradual rise to the first dorsal. The end of the lower jaw, when the mouth is closed, appears on the upper profile. Mouth oblique and large: the upper jaw extending to below the centre of the orbit. Preorbital narrower than the maxillary: preopercle narrow, with its margin entire and angle rounded. Opercle ending in a soft point. Interorbital space convex. Occipital crest well developed, the lateral ridges moderately so. *Teeth*—a curved canine on each side of the symphysis of the upper jaw, and laterally a single series of fine ones: a central canine (occasionally two) in lower jaw, and laterally a single row of curved teeth. Teeth on vomer, palatines, and tongue. *Fins*—first dorsal spine weak, the third the longest: membrane rather deeply notched. Second dorsal highest anteriorly, where it nearly equals the first dorsal, and is about 1/2 the height of the body. Anal similar to the second dorsal. In many specimens taken in Malabar, the fin rays were invariably A. 3/26, but amongst several taken in Madras they were in all instances A. 3/28. Caudal rather deeply lobed. *Scales*—cycloid, small, and deciduous. *Lateral-line*—in short single tubes. *Colours*—the upper surface of the head and the back as low as the lateral-line of a leaden colour: a black spot exists on the upper and posterior part of opercle. Fins diaphanous, marginal halves of dorsals and caudal minutely dotted with black, sometimes the base is also dark. Iris silvery, upper portion darkish.

Habitat.—Seas of India, Malay Archipelago, and China. Grows to at least 10 inches in length, is eaten by the natives either fresh or salted, but is insipid. It appears in Malabar in shoals during the months of February and March, but a few are present throughout the year.

FAMILY, XVII—STROMATEIDÆ.

Stromateinæ, **Swainson.**

Branchiostegals from five to seven: pseudobranchiæ. Body oblong or slightly elongated and compressed Gill-openings wide. Eyes lateral. The infraorbital bones do not articulate with the preopercle. Small teeth in the jaws, palate edentulous: barbed teeth extend into the œsophagus. One long dorsal fin without any distinct spinous division, or with rudimentary spines anteriorly: ventrals, when present, thoracic. No prominent papilla near the vent. Air-vessel, when present, small. Pyloric appendages few, in moderate numbers, or numerous. Vertebræ exceed 10-14.

Geographical distribution.—Found in most tropical and temperate seas.

SYNOPSIS IN INDIVIDUAL GENUS.

Genus, 1—STROMATEUS, *Artedi.*

Peprilus, Cuv.: *Apolectus*, Cuv. and Val. (young having ventral fins): *Rhombus* (ventrals reduced to a spine), (Lacép.) Cuv. and Val.: *Seserinus* (with minute ventrals), Cuv. and Val.: *Stromateoides*, Bleeker: *Chondroplites* and *Poronotus*, Gill.

Branchiostegals from five to seven: pseudobranchiæ. Body compressed, more or less elevated. Cleft of mouth narrow or of moderate depth. Teeth small, in a single row in the jaws: palate and tongue edentulous: œsophagus armed with numerous barbed teeth. A single long dorsal and anal fin, having rudimentary spines anteriorly: ventral fins not present in the adult stage. Scales small, covering the vertical fins. Lateral-line, as a rule, smooth (keeled in S. niger). Air-vessel absent. Pyloric appendages numerous.

After examining very numerous specimens of fish of this genus in the fish markets of India, I could not resist the belief that reduced as the number of species had been from what were formerly recognized, a still further reduction might still be necessary. I have been unable to convince myself of more than three distinct species, which may be recognised in the fry and immature by the following characters.

SYNOPSIS OF SPECIES.

1. *Stromateus Sinensis*, D. 43-50, A. 39-42. Caudal lobes of about equal length. No free spines before dorsal or anal fins. Seas of India to China.

2. *Stromateus cinereus*, D. 5-9 | [illegible], A. 5-6 | [illegible]. Lower caudal lobe much the longer. Free, truncated, spines before both dorsal and anal fins. Seas of India to China.

3. *Stromateus niger*, D. [illegible], A. [illegible]. Ventral fins present in the young. Last portion of lateral-line keeled. Deep brown colour. Seas of India to China.

1. Stromateus Sinensis, Plate LI, C. fig. 6 (*young*).

Euphrasin, Vetensk. Acad. Nya Handl. Stockh. ix, p. 49, t. ix; Bl. Schn. p. 492; Cantor, Catal. p. 140; Day, Fish. Malabar, p. 76.

Stromateus otoo boia, Russell, Fish. Vizag. i, p. 33, pl. 44.

Stromateus atous, Cuv. and Val. ix, p. 389; Richards. Ich. China, p. 273; Jerdon, M. J. L. and Sc. 1851, p. 137; Günther, Catal. ii, p. 399.

Stromateus albus, Cuv. and Val. ix, p. 388; Cantor, Ann. and Mag. ix, p. 15.

Stromateus candidus, Bleeker, Ich. M. O. Java, p. 9 (not Cuv. and Val.).

Stromateoides atokoia, Bleeker, Makr. p. 369, and Makr. p. 76.

Vella avoolee, Mal.; *Mogang varal*, Tam.; *White pomfret.*

B. vi, D. 43-50, P. 25, A. 39-42, C. 19.

Length of head 4½ to 5, of pectoral 3½ to 4, of caudal 4¼ to 5, height of body 1⅔ to 1½ in the total length. *Eyes*—diameter 3½ to 4½ in length of head, 2/3 to 1 diameter from end of snout, and 1⅔ apart. Dorsal and abdominal profiles about equally convex. The lower jaw the longer, especially in young specimens: the maxilla reaches to beneath the first third of the eye. *Teeth*—in a fine single row in each jaw, becoming lost with age. *Fins*—first four or five dorsal rays very short, and not appearing above the skin, its anterior portion is similar to that of the anal and equals the length of the pectoral fin. First five anal rays short but not appearing above the skin. Caudal with equal lobes, in the young it is slightly emarginate. Even in the young there is no trace of any ventral fins. *Scales*—small and very deciduous, especially in the immature, in the adult they cover the vertical fins. *Colours*—upper surface of head and body as far as the lateral-line of a deep neutral-tint, the rest of the body with a mixture of brownish-gray, having metallic reflections, becoming lighter and silvery towards the abdomen: it is dotted all over with brown, the larger spots having a silvery point in their centre. Fins silvery-gray, marginal half blackish. Cavity of the mouth and tongue pale bluish-gray with brown dots, silvery in the centre. Iris reddish-silver or copper coloured, minutely dotted with brown. The *young* are gray, the head covered with irregularly star-shaped spots, and the fins nearly black, especially at their edges.

Jerdon observes, *l. c.*, "this is by far the finest eating of all the genus." Russell, however, says, "though alike in colour, this fish is very different from the *Stromateus cinereus* of Bloch; which is specifically characterized by the length of the lower lobe of the caudal fin," (p. 34.)

Habitat.—Seas of India, Malay Archipelago, and China. This species of Pomfret is that most esteemed for eating: in Malabar it is by no means rare during the S. W. monsoon (from June till September.) It should be cooked when quite fresh. The young are common round the coasts and ascend estuaries. I found them numerous during March in the Sunderbunds. The one figured (life-size) is from Bombay. Russell's figure of the adult is a very good representation of the fish.

2. Stromateus cinereus, Plate LIII, fig. 3.

Bloch, xii, p. 90, t. ccccxx. (*semi-adult*); Cantor, Catal. p. 143; Günther, Catal. ii, p. 400; Day, Fish. Malabar, p. 78 (*immature*).

Stromateus argenteus, Bloch, xii, p. 92, t. ccccxxi; Russell, Fish. Vizag. i, p. 35; Cuv. and Val. ix, p. 393; Cantor, Catal. p. 142; Günther, Catal. ii, p. 400; Day, Fish. Malabar, p. 77 (*adult*).

Stromateus sudi sandawah, Russell, Fish. Vizag. i, p. 34, pl. 45 (*immature*).

Stromateus tella sandawah, Russell, l. c. i, p. 31; pl. 42 (*adult*).

Stromateus candidus, Cuv. and Val. ix, p. 391; Jerdon, M. J. L. and Sc. 1851, p. 137.

Stromateus securifer, Cuv. and Val. ix, p. 394, pl. 273 (*immature*).

Stromateus griseus, Cuv. and Val. ix, p. 395; Jerdon, l. c. p. 138.

Stromateoides cinereus, Bleeker, Makr. p. 368.

Vella vowal, Tam.; *Silver-pomfret* (*immature*); *Gray-pomfret*, (*adult*).

B. vii, D. 5-9 | [illegible], P. 27, A. 5-6 | [illegible], C. 19.

Length of head 4 to $4\frac{1}{2}$, of pectoral $2\frac{1}{4}$ to $2\frac{1}{2}$, height of body $1\frac{1}{3}$ to $1\frac{1}{2}$ in the total length excluding the caudal fin. *Eyes*—diameter 1/4 to 1/5 of length of head, 1 diameter from end of snout, and $1\frac{1}{2}$ to 2 apart. Snout projecting over the mouth: the maxilla reaches to below the first third of the orbit. *Teeth*—in a single row in either jaw. *Fins*—the dorsal spines appear in a truncated form above the skin, as do also those of the anal: anterior portion of soft dorsal elevated, but not to so great an extent as the anterior part of the anal which in the immature reaches to below the middle of the caudal fin, but as age advances it gradually becomes shortened. Pectoral rather pointed. Caudal deeply forked, the lower lobe much the longer in the immature, sometimes being twice as long as the upper. *Scales*—small and very deciduous. *Colours*—upper surface of head and back as low as the lateral-line of a grayish neutral-tint with purplish reflections, sides of head and body silvery-gray, fading to white on the abdomen, and everywhere covered with minute black dots: a dark spot on upper portion of the opercle. Dorsal and anal gray minutely dotted with black, the outer half being the darker. Caudal and pectoral yellowish-white, also minutely dotted with black, the outer half being the darker. Iris silvery. The *young* are much darker, the vertical fins being nearly black.

The occiput in the adult of this species is striated almost horizontally as shown in Russell's figure, but the commencement of these furrows is apparent in the immature.

The larger specimens (Gray-pomfrets) are considered superior to the immature (silver-pomfrets) for eating.

Habitat.—Seas of India to the Malay Archipelago and beyond, attaining at least a foot in length. The specimen figured is a little over 7 inches long.

3. Stromateus niger, Plate LIII, fig. 4.

? *Stromateus paru*, Linn. Syst. Nat. xii, I, p. 432; Bloch, v, p. 75, (*Stromateus fiatola*), t. 160; Bl. Schn. p. 491; Lacép. ii, p. 319; Shaw, Zool. iv, p. 108.

Stromateus niger, Bloch, t. 422; Bl. Schn. p. 492, t. xciii; Shaw, Zool. iv, p. 111; Cuv. and Val. ix, p. 385; Cantor, Ann. and Mag. ix, p. 15, and Catal. p. 139; Richards. Ich. China, p. 272; Bleeker, Makr. p. 370, and Makr. p. 77; Jerdon, M. J. L. and Sc. 1851, p. 138; Günther, Catal. ii, p. 401; Day, Fish. Malabar, p. 79.

Stromateus nala sandawah, Russell, Fish. Vizag. i, p. 32, pl. 43.

Apolectus stromateus, Cuv. and Val. viii, p. 439, pl. 238 (*immature*); Cantor, Catal. p. 123.

Nala-sanda-wah, Tel.; *Baal*, Ooriah; *Curroopoo-voval*, Tam.; *Kar-aroodee*, Mal.; *Ko-lig-dah*, And.

B. vii, D. [illegible], P. 22, A. [illegible], C. 19.

Length of head 2/9, of caudal 1/4, height of body 3/7 to 3 in total length. *Eyes*—diameter $4\frac{1}{2}$ to 5 in length of head, $1\frac{1}{2}$ diameters from end of snout, and nearly 2 apart. Dorsal and abdominal profiles equally angular. The lower jaw the longer: the maxilla extends to beneath the anterior margin to the orbit. *Teeth*—in a fine single series in both jaws. *Fins*—the dorsal and anal are much elevated anteriorly, very low posteriorly, with concave external margins. Pectoral 1/2 longer than the head, and falciform: ventrals only apparent in the young, in a specimen $3\frac{1}{10}$ inches in length they are jugular, and equal 1/8 of the total length. The spines, before the dorsal and anal fins, which are concealed in the adult fish, are apparent in the young specimens. *Scales*—small, and extended over the vertical fins. *Lateral-line*—gently curves downwards, and in its last fourth passes straight to the centre of the caudal, in the form of a raised keeled line with lateral shields as perceived in the genus *Caranx*. *Colours*—deep brown or grayish-brown with blue reflections: cheeks, opercles, and abdomen pale-neutral or brownish-neutral. Dorsal and anal grayish-brown, stained black towards their margins: pectoral and caudal brownish, edged with black. Iris brownish-blue: in the young it is gray. The dorsal and anal fins black, and the tail yellow, with three brown cross bands.

Habitat.—Seas of India to the Malay Archipelago and China. Grows to two feet in length, is excellent eating. John observes that the people of Tranquebar dislike it, because a species of parasite similar to a wood-louse is often found in its mouth. It appears in Malabar about the same time as the *S. Sinensis*. It comes in shoals, and disappears as suddenly as it arrives. The specimen figured is from Madras and about 15 inches long.

Family, XVIII—CORYPHÆNIDÆ, (pt.) *Swainson.*

Branchiostegals from five to seven: pseudobranchiæ present or absent. Body oblong or elevated and compressed. Gill-openings wide. Eyes lateral. The infraorbital bones do not articulate with preopercle. Teeth in the jaws, present or absent on the palate, none in the œsophagus. One long dorsal fin, without distinct spinous division: ventrals thoracic, (except in *Pteraclis*, when they are jugular). No prominent papilla near the vent. Air-vessel present or absent.* Pyloric appendages few or many. Vertebræ exceed 10/40.

SYNOPSIS OF GENERA.

1. *Coryphæna.* Dorsal fin commencing on occiput: scales present.
2. *Mene.* Dorsal fin commencing on the back: scales absent.

Genus, 1—Coryphæna, *Cuv. and Val.*

Lampugus (immature), Cuv. and Val. Dolphins.

Branchiostegals seven; pseudobranchiæ absent. Body rather elongated and compressed. Preopercle entire. Teeth in the jaws, on vomer, palatines, and tongue. A single long dorsal fin extending from the occiput nearly to the caudal, but without distinct spines, neither are they apparent in the anal: ventral thoracic and well developed. Scales small, cycloid. Air-vessel absent. Pyloric appendages numerous.

Geographical distribution.—Seas of temperate and tropical regions.

Cuvier remarks upon the relative height of the crest on the neck, and suggests the possibility of its being partly due to sex. Günther considers "that the crest and the anterior part of the dorsal fin become gradually higher with age," Catal. ii, p. 405.

SYNOPSIS OF INDIVIDUAL SPECIES.

1. *Coryphæna hippurus*, D. 58-63, A. 25-27. Gray, becoming golden on the sides and beneath, and covered with small blue spots. Seas of tropical and temperate regions.

1. **Coryphæna hippurus**, Plate LIII, fig. 6.

Linn. Syst. p. 446. Bloch, t. 174; Bl. Schn. p. 295; Lacép. iii, pp. 173, 178; Shaw, Zool. iv, p. 212, pl. 32, f. 1; Cuv. and Val. ix, p. 278, pl. 266; Guichen, Explor. Sc. Algér. Poiss. p. 63; Lowe, Trans. Zool. Soc. ii, p. 183, iii, p. 6, and Proc. Z. S. 1839, p. 80; Günther, Catal. ii, p. 406; Steind. Sitz. Ak. Wiss. 1868, p. 370; Klunz. Verh. z. b. Ges. Wien, 1871, p. 446.

Coryphæna chrysurus, Lacép. ii, pl. 18, f. 2; Cuv. and Val. ix, p. 309.
Coryphæna dorado, Cuv. and Val. ix, p. 303; Cuv. Règ. An. Ill. Poiss. pl. 65, f. 1.
Coryphæna dolfyn, virgata, and *argyrurus*, Cuv. and Val. ix, pp. 305, 308, 314.
Lampugus pelagica and *? immaculatus*, Cuv. and Val. ix, pp. 318, 329 *(immature)*.
Coryphæna Japonica, Schleg. Fauna Japon. Poiss. p. 120, pl. 64.
Badaklan, Tam.: *Dolphin.*

B. vii, D. 58-63, P. 21, V. 1/5, A. 25-27, C. 19.

Length of head $5\frac{1}{4}$ to 6, of caudal $4\frac{2}{3}$ to $4\frac{1}{2}$, height of body $5\frac{1}{4}$ to $6\frac{1}{4}$ in the total length. *Eyes*—diameter 1/4 to 1/6 of length of head, 3 diameters from end of snout, and $1\frac{1}{2}$ apart. Body elongated and compressed: occipital crest well developed. Cleft of mouth rather oblique, the lower jaw the longer, the maxilla extends to below the middle or last third of the orbit. Opercles and shoulder bones striated but entire. *Teeth*—in numerous villiform rows in either jaw, with an outer somewhat enlarged one: they are also present on the vomer, palatines, and tongue. *Fins*—dorsal commences over the posterior edge of the orbit, its first seven or eight rays gradually increase in length, whilst the last in the fin is not quite 1/3 that of the highest, the fin reaches to a short distance anterior to the root of the caudal. Pectoral falcated: the anal commences midway between the anterior margin of the orbit and the base of the caudal fin, it is highest in front, but after the third or fourth rays it becomes parallel with the abdomen: caudal with deeply pointed lobes. *Lateral-line*—curved to opposite the end of the pectoral from whence it goes straight to the centre of the caudal. *Colours*—back grayish, shot with gold: abdomen golden, covered with blue spots, which become black after death: dorsal fin light blue at the base, becoming black towards the summit.

February 22nd, 1867, I found in the stomach of one of these fishes a *Clupea Neohowii* and the anterior half of an *Elops machnata.*

Habitat.—Seas of India, Malay Archipelago, &c.; the one figured (34 inches long) is from Madras: it attains 5 feet or more in length. These dolphins are not uncommon in Madras, and are eaten by the natives.

Genus, 2—Mene, *Lacép.*

Branchiostegals seven. Body oval, strongly compressed, with a prominent and sharp-edged abdomen. Mouth very protractile. Villiform teeth in the jaws, palate edentulous. A single long dorsal fin, without any distinct spinous portion, commencing on the back and extending nearly to the caudal: anal spineless, having many rays which are enveloped in skin and have very broad free extremities: ventral thoracic, with one spine and five rays, the first of which is very elongate. Scales absent. Air-vessel large and bifurcated posteriorly. Pyloric appendages numerous.

SYNOPSIS OF INDIVIDUAL SPECIES.

1. *Mene maculata*, D. [illegible], A. 30-33. Two rows of the blue spots along the back. Seas of India, to the Malay Archipelago and beyond.

1. **Mene maculata**, Plate LIII, fig. 5.

Zeus maculatus, Bl. Schn. p. 95, pl. 22.
Mene anna carolina, Lacép. v, pp. 479, 480, pl. xiv, f. 2.
Zeus ambate kuttee, Russell, Fish. Vizag. i, p. 47, pl. 60.
Mene maculata, Cuv. and Val. x, p. 104, pl. 285; Temm. and Schleg. Fauna Japon. Poiss. p. 127. p. 67, f. 3; Richards. Ich. China, p. 276; Cantor, Catal. p. 154; Bleeker, Makr. p. 86; Cuv. Règ. Anim. Ill. Poiss. pl. 62, t. 2; Jerdon, M. J. L. and Sc. 1851, p. 138; Günther, Catal. ii, p. 415.
Ambuton parah, Tam.

B. vii, D. [illegible], P. 15, V. 1/5, A. 30-33, C. 18, Cæc. pyl. 25-30.

Length of head 4, of caudal 4, height of body $1\frac{3}{4}$ to 2 in the total length. *Eyes*—diameter 2/7 to 1/3 of length of head, 4/5 of a diameter apart, and 1 to $1\frac{1}{3}$ from end of snout. Body ovoid, highest anteriorly. Dorsal profile nearly horizontal, the abdominal very abruptly descending to the base of the ventral fin, from whence it gently curves so far as the commencement of the caudal. Mouth oblique, the lower jaw being anterior, cleft twice as long as the gape: anterior portion of the upper jaw formed by the premaxillaries, the maxilla smooth and S-shaped extends to below the anterior edge of the orbit. Opercles entire. Occipital crest high. *Teeth*—in villiform rows in the jaws. *Fins*—dorsal highest anteriorly, its first few rays undivided and more elevated than the remainder. Pectoral as long as the head excluding the snout, rays flat: ventral spine short, its first ray compressed and very long. Anal rudimentary, its rays forming short, wide, and flat processes: caudal deeply lobed. *Lateral-line*—sometimes ceases below the end of the dorsal fin, or on reaching the upper caudal lobe it may divide into two branches, the lower of which descends. *Colours*—deep blue along the back, becoming silvery white on the sides and abdomen: from two to three rows of large spots along the superior half of the body above the level of the pectoral fin.

This fish is termed "*Amatti katti*," Tam. *i. e.* "*razor*," Jerdon, *l. c.*

Habitat.—Seas of India to the Malay Archipelago and beyond: attaining at least $8\frac{1}{2}$ inches in length.

FAMILY, XIX—SCOMBRIDÆ, *Cuv.*

Branchiostegals seven or eight: pseudobranchiæ. Body oblong or slightly elongated and compressed. Gill-openings wide: eyes lateral. The infraorbital bones do not articulate with the preopercle. Teeth present in the jaws, absent or present on the palate. Two dorsal fins, the first being distinct from the soft, which has more rays than the first has spines: finlets present or absent: ventrals thoracic (jugular in *Hypsiptera*): no prominent papilla near the vent. Side of tail sometimes keeled. Scales, if present, small. Air-vessel present or absent. Pyloric appendages moderate, numerous, or dendritical. Vertebræ exceed 10/14.

SYNOPSIS OF GENERA.

1. *Scomber.* Teeth small, present in jaws. Five or six finlets: a low ridge on either side of base of tail. Body equally scaled. Red Sea, through those of India to the Malay Archipelago and beyond, also in most temperate and tropical seas.

2. *Thynnus.* Teeth small, present in jaws, vomer, and palate. Six to nine finlets: a central keel along either side of free portion of tail. Scales in the anterior region of the body forming a corselet. Red Sea, through those of India to the Malay Archipelago; also in most open temperate and tropical seas.

3. *Cybium.* Teeth large in jaws, small on vomer and palate. Seven to ten finlets: a central keel along either side of free portion of tail. Scales when present rudimentary. Red Sea, seas of India to the Malay Archipelago; also in the Atlantic.

4. *Elacate.** No finlets. First dorsal fin as free spines. A low keel along either side of free portion of the tail. Red Sea, seas of India to the Malay Archipelago; also in tropical parts of the Atlantic.

5. *Echeneis.*† No finlets. First dorsal in the form of a sucking disk on the summit of the head. No keel on side of tail. Found in most seas.

Genus, 1—SCOMBER, *Artedi.*

Branchiostegals seven: pseudobranchiæ. Body rather elongated and compressed. Eyes with adipose lids. Cleft of mouth deep. Small deciduous teeth on the jaws; deciduous ones present or absent on the vomer, and palatine bones. Two dorsal fins, the first spinous and separated by an interspace from the second, behind which and also posterior to the anal are five or six finlets: less spines in the first dorsal than there are rays in the second dorsal or in the anal: ventrals thoracic. Two slight keels on either side of the root of the caudal fin. Scales small. Air-vessel, when present, simple. Pyloric appendages numerous.

Although the young of the *Cybium*, *Elacate*, &c. are common all along the coasts of India, I have never obtained the fry of any species of *Scomber*. Sars has observed that the Mackerel deposits its ova in the open sea, where it floats near the surface (see Ann. and Mag. Nat. Hist. 1868, ii, p. 330).

Geographical distribution.—Red Sea, seas of India to the Malay Archipelago and beyond; also in most temperate and tropical seas.

SYNOPSIS OF SPECIES.

1. *Scomber microlepidotus*, D. 10 | $\frac{1}{12}$ + v-vi. A. $\frac{1}{12}$ + v-vi. Length of head $3\frac{3}{4}$ to $4\frac{1}{4}$, height of body 4 to $4\frac{1}{2}$ in the total length. A black spot covered by the pectoral fin in the young, bands along the back and sides in the adult. Red Sea, through those of India to the Malay Archipelago.

2. *Scomber brachysoma*, D. 10 | $\frac{1}{11}$ + v. A. $\frac{1}{11}$ + v. Length of head $3\frac{4}{5}$, height of body $3\frac{3}{4}$ in the total length. Andamans to the Malay Archipelago.

1. Scomber microlepidotus, Plate LIV, fig. 3 *(young)*, 4 *(immature)*, and 5 *(adult)*.

Rüpp. N. W. Fische, p. 38, t. xi, f. 2; Cantor, Catal. p. 105; Günther, Catal. ii, p. 361; Kner, Novara Fische, p. 143; Steind. Ak. Wiss. Wien, 1868, lvii, p. 987; Klunz. Verh. z. b. Ges. Wien, 1871, p. 443.

Scomber kanagurta, Russell, Fish. Vizag. ii, p. 28, pl. 136; Rüpp. Atl. Fische, p. 93, and N. W. Fische, p. 37; Cuv. and Val. viii, p. 49; Cuv. Règ. Anim.; Bleeker, Makr. p. 35; Peters, Weigm. Arch. 1855, p. 245; Jerdon, M. J. L. and Sc. 1851, p. 135; Günther, Catal. ii, p. 360; Day, Fish. Malabar, p. 68; Kner, Novara Fische, p. 142; Klunz. Verh. z. b. Ges. Wien, 1871, p. 441.

Scomber chrysozonus, Rüpp. N. W. Fische, t. xi, f. 1; Günther, Catal. ii, p. 360.

Scomber Reani, Day, Proc. Z. S. 1870, p. 690 *(adult)*.

Kurna-kita or *Kurnang-kullutan*, Tam.: *Kanagurta*, Tel.: *Ila*, Mal.: *Nga-congree*, "Large head," Mugh.: *Look-wa-dah*, Andam.

* A portion of Fam. LICHIOIDEI, Bleeker (see note, page 229).
† Forming a distinct Family, ECHENEOIDEI, Bleeker.

B. vi, D. 8-10 | $\frac{1}{12}$ + v-vi, P. 21, V. 1/5, A. $\frac{1}{11}$ + v-vi, C. 24, L. l. 130 to 150, L. tr. 10/28, Vert. 13/16.

Length of head 3¾ to 4¼, of caudal 4¾ to 5, height of body 4 to 4¾ in the total length. *Eye*—with a broad anterior and posterior adipose lid extending 1/3 across the eye. Diameter of eye 4 to 4¼ in length of head, 1 to 1¼ diameters from end of snout, and also apart. Lower jaw slightly the longer, cleft of mouth deep, the maxilla reaches to below the hind edge of the eye. Length of preorbital 1/2 that of the head, its greatest depth equals half the diameter of the eye. Interorbital space flat. *Teeth*—minute* in both jaws, none on vomer or palate. *Fins*—dorsal spines weak and receivable into a groove, the second to the eighth subcqual and about 1/2 the height of the body, posteriorly they rapidly decrease in length. The distance between the two dorsal fins equals half the length of the base of the latter, the upper edge of which last is concave. Finlets commence just behind the fin and are opposite to and similar to those behind the anal. Pectoral short, nearly equalling half the length of the head. Caudal with deeply pointed lobes. *Scales*—smaller above than below the lateral-line, and largest just beneath the pectoral fin: the first few rows beneath the lateral-line are parallel with it, those below the pectoral are irregularly concave. Minute scales on second dorsal and anal fins. *Lateral-line*—very slightly curved. *Air-vessel*—present. *Pseudobranchiæ*—largely developed. *Colours*—back greenish, sides and abdomen iridescent, a row of sixteen spots along the summit of the back, close to the base of the dorsal fin: summit of head spotted: sides shot with bluish-purple. Dorsal fins yellowish, tipped with black: caudal bright yellow, stained with black at its extremity. Pectoral bright yellow, with a dark mark on the body below it which shows through the fin: ventral and anal finely dotted with black, but which fades soon after death, when all the shot colours also disappear, and it becomes of a dull green with the abdomen of a lighter colour. Posterior edge of caudal sometimes blackish with a white outer margin. In large specimens the colours differ, there are from five to eight dark longitudinal bands along the back and upper half of the body, the superior of which is occasionally broken up into spots. There are usually two golden bands below the lateral-line, and one along its course. In this stage it appears to closely resemble the description of *S. loo*,† C.V. viii, p. 52, which is said to grow to a larger size than *S. kanagurta*, and to be destitute of teeth. Günther observes of *S. Moluccensis*, Bleeker, that "this species is probably identical with *S. loo*, C.V."

Habitat.—Red Sea, through those of India to the Malay Archipelago. Along the coasts of India it is very rarely seen above 10 inches in length, but at the Andamans I obtained what appeared to be a distinct species a foot long, and differently coloured as described above. This fish I have captured at Madras, with fully developed ova in March. In Malabar it is very common throughout the cold season, and is extensively salted and dried. Although good eating, it is seldom brought to the table of Europeans, as it rapidly taints, and if eaten in that state gives rise to visceral irritation. Fig. 3 is from a Sind specimen 6½ inches long: fig. 4 is from a Madras specimen 8 inches long: and fig. 5 from an Andamanese one 12 inches in length.

2. Scomber brachysoma.

? *Scomber brachysoma*, Bleeker, Makr. p. 356; Günther, Catal. ii, p. 361.

B. vii, D. 10 | $\frac{1}{11}$ + v, P. 22, V. 1/5, A. $\frac{1}{11}$ + v, C. 21, L. l. 135, L. tr. 13/.

Length of head 3½, of caudal 5½, height of body 3¾ in the total length. *Eyes*—with a broad anterior and posterior adipose lid, diameter of eye 4⅓ in length of head, 1⅓ diameters from end of snout, and 1¼ apart. Greatest width of head 2¼ in its length. Lower jaw slightly the longer: cleft of mouth deep, the maxilla reaches to below the hind edge of the eye. Length of preorbital 4/7 of that of the head, its greatest depth equalling 2/3 of that of the orbit. Hind edge of suboperclo is vertically behind the level of the hind edge of the opercle. *Teeth*—minute in both jaws, none on vomer or palate. *Fins*—dorsal spines weak and receivable into a groove, the second and third the highest and rather above 1/2 that of the body, the upper edge of second dorsal fin concave, finlets commence just behind the fin and are opposite to and similar to those behind the anal. Pectoral half as long as the head. Caudal with deeply pointed lobes. *Colours*—similar to *S. microlepidotus*, except that there are two shining light spots above and behind either eye, and the spinous dorsal is posteriorly edged with black.

The height of the body in *S. brachysoma*, Bleeker, is said to be a little above three times in the total length. In the single specimen (if identical) from the Andaman islands it is 3½.

Habitat.—The specimen described is 7½ inches long and from the Andamans.

Genus, 2—Thynnus, *Cuv. and Val.*

Orcynus, Cuv.; *Grammatorcynus*, Gill.

Branchiostegals seven: pseudobranchiæ. Body oblong, somewhat compressed. Cleft of mouth deep. Small teeth on the jaws, vomer, and palatine bones. Two dorsal fins, the spines weak, finlets behind the soft dorsal and anal. Scales small; those in the anterior portion of the body form a kind of corselet. Lateral-line incomplete, a longitudinal keel along either side of the free portion of the tail. Air-vessel, when present, simple. Pyloric appendages numerous.

Geographical distribution—the "tunny fishes" are found from the Red Sea, throughout those of India to the Malay Archipelago and beyond. Also in most open tropical and temperate seas. They are very voracious, and may often be observed in schools pursuing the *Exocœti*, "flying fishes," or *Clupeidæ* as "sardines." As food

* Teeth in the upper jaw more or less disappear with age, except at the symphysis, where they are usually persistent.

† Steind. l. c. considers *S. microlepidotus* as the young of *S. loo*.

they are moderately esteemed: in the "Fauna Japonica," their flesh if eaten fresh is said to cause diarrhœa, therefore they are more commonly salted or dried.

SYNOPSIS OF SPECIES.

1. *Thynnus thunnina*, D. 15 | $\frac{2}{12-13}$ + viii, A. $\frac{3}{11}$ + viii. Length of pectoral from $6\frac{1}{4}$ to $6\frac{1}{2}$ in that of the total to the end of the centre of caudal fin. Undulating oblique dark bands along the back. Seas of India to the Malay Archipelago, also in the Mediterranean and tropical parts of the Atlantic.

2. *Thynnus pelamys*, D. 15 | $\frac{1}{12}$ + viii, A. $\frac{2}{12}$ + viii. Length of pectoral 1/6 of that of the total to the end of the centre of the caudal fin. Four or five concave longitudinal bands along the lower half of the sides of the body. Indian and Atlantic Oceans.

3. *Thynnus macropterus*, D. 14 | $\frac{2}{12}$ + ix, A. 12 + ix. Length of pectoral $3\frac{3}{4}$ in that of the total to the end of the centre of the caudal fin. Grayish above, becoming silvery on the sides and beneath. Tips of elongated dorsal and anal fins, also finlets, yellow. Seas of India to China.

1. Thynnus thunnina, Plate LIV, fig. 6.

Scomber quadripunctatus, Geof. Desc. Eg. Poissons, t. xxiv, f. 3.

Thynnus thunnina, Cuv. and Val. viii, p. 104, pl. 212; Temm. and Schleg. Fauna Japon. Poiss. p. 95, pl. 48; Cuv. Règ. Anim. Ill. Poiss. pl. 46, f. 1; Bleeker, Makr. p. 36, and Fische, Madag. p. 100; Guichen, Exp. Alg. Poiss. p. 57; Günther, Catal. ii, p. 364; Nilss. Æfvers. Sven. Vet. Ak. Förh. 1864, p. 409, t. 5.

Thynnus Brasiliensis, Cuv. and Val. viii, p. 110.

Thynnus affinis, Cantor, Catal. p. 106; Jerdon, M. J. L. and Sc. 1851, p. 136; Günther, Catal. ii, p. 363.

Suraly, Tam.

B. vii, D. 15 | $\frac{2}{12-13}$ + viii, P. 26, V. 1/5, A. $\frac{3}{11}$ + viii, C. 17.

Length of head $3\frac{1}{2}$ to $3\frac{3}{4}$, of pectoral $6\frac{1}{4}$ to $6\frac{1}{2}$, of caudal lobes $6\frac{1}{4}$, height of body $4\frac{1}{2}$ in the distance between the snout and the centre of the posterior edge of the caudal fin. *Eyes*—diameter $6\frac{1}{2}$ in length of head, $1\frac{1}{2}$ diameters from end of snout, and also apart. Head rather compressed, snout pointed: the maxilla reaches to below the middle of the orbit. Vertical or posterior border of the preopercle short, its angle rounded, and its lower edge at least twice as long as its vertical one. *Teeth*—in a single row in either jaw, also on vomer and palate. *Fins*—first dorsal spine the broadest, equal in height to the second, or 1/2 as long as the head. In some specimens the first dorsal is continued to within a short distance of the second, in others (as in the one figured) the last few spines are nearly or quite hidden in the integument. Second dorsal highest anteriorly, having a concave upper edge, its three spines are short and concealed by the skin: finlets rather large. Pectoral rather short. Ventral having an oval or elongated lamella between the two fins and under which they can be partially received. Anal similar to the second dorsal, commencing on the vertical behind that fin, its three spines equally concealed. Caudal broad and pointed. *Scales*—forming a corselet anteriorly in three portions separated by two deep emarginations. Superiorly the corselet embraces the two dorsal fins, and is divided from its central portion by an emargination which reaches to below the eighth dorsal spine. The central portion of the corselet is mostly beneath the pectoral fin, and the emargination which divides it from the inferior portion extends to below the base of the pectoral. The lowest portion goes to below and behind the ventral fins. *Colours*—bluish along the back having a number of undulating oblique dark bands, silvery below the lateral-line; sometimes black spots on the chest or breast.

Jerdon observes that this fish is called *Choori min*, Tam.

Geographical distribution.—Seas of India to the Malay Archipelago, where it is common during the cold months; also found in the Mediterranean, tropical parts of the Atlantic, and in Scandinavian seas. The specimen figured is from Bombay, where it is often seen in the markets during the cold season up to two feet in length.

2. Thynnus pelamys.

Scomber pelamys,* Linn. Syst. Nat. i, p. 492; Bl. Schn. p. 23; Shaw, Zool. iv, p. 588.

Scomber pelamides, Lacép. iii, p. 14 (pt.) ii, pl. xx, f. 2.

Thynnus pelamys, Cuv. and Val. viii, p. 113, pl. 214; Temm. and Schleg. Fauna Japon. Poiss. p. 96, pl. 49; Richards. Ich. China, p. 267; Cuv. Règ. Anim. Ill. Poiss. pl. 47, f. 2; Bleeker, Amboina, p. 41; Günther, Catal. ii, p. 365.

The Bonito.

B. vii, D. 15 | $\frac{1}{12}$+viii, P. 27, V. 1/5, A. $\frac{2}{12}$+vii.

Length of head $3\frac{1}{2}$, of pectoral 6, height of body $3\frac{1}{2}$ to $3\frac{3}{4}$ in the distance between the snout and the centre of the posterior margin of the caudal fin. *Eyes*—diameter 1/5 to 1/6 of length of head, $1\frac{1}{2}$ diameters from end of snout. The vertical border of the preopercle is 3/5 the length of its horizontal margin. *Fins*—dorsal spines rather weak, anteriorly 2/3 of height of body and nearly twice as high as the second dorsal. Pectoral

* See also Bennett, Whaling Voyage, ii, p. 281; De la Roche, Ann. Mus. xiii, p. 315. Farlatta, Humboldt, Obs. Zool. ii, p. 120. *T. pelamys*, Yarrell, Fennell, Couch. *Thynnus vagans*, Less. Voy. Coq. Zool. ii, p. 162, pl. 32.

reaches to below the tenth dorsal spine. Anal similar to second dorsal, it commences on the vertical behind its last ray. Caudal with pointed lobes. *Scales*—forming a corselet anteriorly, which extends from the base of the pectoral along the whole length of that of the spinous dorsal. *Colours*—back bluish, becoming silvery on the sides and beneath. Four or five concave, longitudinal, dark bluish bands pass along the lower half of the abdomen posteriorly, ending on the lateral-line below the finlets.

I have not seen this species in India, but in Cuv. and Val. it is observed that it has been received from that locality.

Habitat.—Indian and Atlantic Oceans; attaining a considerable size.

3. Thynnus macropterus.

Temm. and Schleg. Fauna Japon. Poiss. p. 98, pl. 51; Bleeker, Makr. p. 37.

B. vii, D. 14 | $\frac{1}{13}$ + ix, P. 31, V. 1/5, A. 12 + ix, C. 28.

Length of head and height of body each $3\frac{3}{4}$ in the distance between the snout and the centre of the posterior margin of the caudal fin. *Eyes*—diameter 1/5 of length of head, $1\frac{3}{4}$ diameters from end of snout, and also apart. Maxilla reaches to below the first third of the eye: lower jaw a little the longer. Preopercle with its posterior margin somewhat irregular in shape, angle pretty well developed, the length of its vertical 1/3 longer than its horizontal margin. *Teeth*—in a fine single row in either jaw, in an angular patch prolonged posteriorly on the vomer, and in a band on the palatines. *Fins*—the anterior dorsal spines equal about $2\frac{1}{4}$ in the height of the body: second dorsal considerably longer than the spinous and falciform. Pectoral nearly or quite as long as the head. Anal similar to soft dorsal. Caudal with pointed lobes. Corselet with three distinct posterior prolongations, the upper commencing below the seventh dorsal spine, is continued along the base of the two dorsal fins: the second ceases below the eleventh dorsal spine, and a little above the middle of the body: the lowest extends along the abdomen to midway between the end of the ventral and commencement of the anal. A well developed keel on the lateral-line commencing from opposite the tenth finlet. *Colours*—grayish along the back becoming silvery below, tips of soft dorsal and anal, as well as the finlets, yellow.

Amongst the specimens sent me by Sir Walter Elliot is the one described above, it is a skin 27 inches long and probably Jerdon's specimen from Tellicherry. This is "*Thynnus (Orcynus)*? Jerdon, M. J. L. and Sc. 1851, p. 136." Dr. Günther observes of *T. macropterus* that it is closely allied to, and perhaps identical with, *T. albacora*, Lowe, P. Z. Soc. 1839, p. 77, and Trans. Z. S. iii, p. 4.

Habitat.—Seas of India to Japan.

Genus, 3—PELAMYS, *Cuv. and Val.*

Gymnosarda and *Orcynopsis*, Gill.

Branchiostegals seven: pseudobranchiæ. Body rather elongate and slightly compressed. Cleft of mouth deep. Rather strong teeth in jaws, none on vomer, present on palatines. Two dorsal fins, the spines feeble, or of moderate strength, finlets behind soft dorsal and anal fins. Scales small, those in the anterior portion of the body form a kind of corselet. Lateral-line unarmed, a longitudinal keel along either side of the free portion of the tail. Air-vessel absent. Pyloric appendages dendritical.

SYNOPSIS OF INDIVIDUAL SPECIES.

1. *Pelamys Orientalis*, D. 18 | $\frac{1}{14}$ + viii, A. $\frac{1}{14}$ + vi. About eight longitudinal blue lines pass backwards and a little upwards in the upper half of the body. Seas of India to Japan and beyond.

1. Pelamys Chilensis, Plate LVI, fig. 1.

Pelamys Chilensis, Cuv. and Val. viii, p. 163; Gay, Chili, Zool. ii, p. 224; Günther, Catal. ii, p. 368: Steind. Sitz. Ak. Wiss. Wien, lvii, p. 353.

Pelamys Orientalis, Temm. and Schleg. Fauna Japon, p. 99, pl. 52; Günther, Catal. ii, p. 368.

B. vii, D. 18 | $\frac{1}{14}$-viii, P. 24, V. 1/5, A. $\frac{1}{14}$ + vi, C. 20.

Length of head $3\frac{1}{2}$, height of body $4\frac{1}{2}$ in the distance between the snout and the centre of the posterior edge of the caudal fin: caudal lobes 1/6 of the same distance. *Eyes*—diameter $8\frac{1}{2}$ in length of head, $2\frac{1}{2}$ diameters from end of snout and 2 apart. Snout pointed, the greatest width of head equals $2\frac{1}{2}$, and its height $1\frac{1}{2}$ in its length. The maxilla reaches to below the hind edge of the eye. Angle of preopercle rounded, its lower border rather above 1/2 the length of its vertical one. *Teeth*—in a single row in either jaw with some rather large ones above the symphysis of the lower. *Fins*—dorsal spines weak, second to fourth subequal and about $2\frac{1}{2}$ in height of body and very slightly higher than the second dorsal, it is continued nearly close up to the second fin. Pectoral $2\frac{1}{4}$ in length of head; ventral 3/4 of pectoral. Anal commences on the vertical below first finlet and is similar to second dorsal. Caudal with pointed lobes. *Scales*—forming a corselet anteriorly in three portions, separated by two deep emarginations. Superiorly the corselet embraces the whole length of the first dorsal fin: its central portion is narrow and pointed ending close to the end of the pectoral fin: its lower portion is small and just embraces the ventrals which have a small scale between them. *Lateral-line*—makes a low curve to below commencement of second dorsal fin, where its becomes straight.

Colours—the upper half of the body with about eight broad, straight, blue lines passing backwards and a little upwards, silvery below the lateral-line, where however there are similar lines but very faint.

Habitat.—Seas of India to Japan and beyond. The specimen figured (17 inches long) is from Bombay.

Genus, 4—Cybium, *Cuv.*

Apodontis and *Apolectus*, Bennett; *Lepidocybium* and *Acanthocybium*, Gill.

Seer-fishes.

Branchiostegals seven: pseudobranchiæ. Body somewhat elongated. Cleft of mouth deep. Teeth large and strong in the jaws: villiform on vomer, palatines, and tongue. Two dorsal fins, the first with feeble spines, extending to the commencement of the second, more rays in the second dorsal than spines in the first: seven or more finlets behind the second dorsal and anal fins. Scales, when present, rudimentary. A slight keel on either side of the caudal lobes. Air-vessel present.

The seer-fishes of India, when of the proper size, are considered as amongst the most delicate for eating of the marine forms. If small, as under a foot in length, they are dry, resembling *Trachynotus* and *Chorinemus*: from $1\frac{1}{2}$ to $2\frac{1}{2}$ foot in length they are at their primest size, above this they become coarse.

SYNOPSIS OF SPECIES.

1. *Cybium Kuhlii*, D. 16 | [illegible] + viii, A. [illegible] + vii. Head $5\frac{1}{2}$ to 6, height of body 5 in the total length. Lateral-line with a gradual curve. Sides silvery: first dorsal black. Seas of India.

2. *Cybium interruptum*, D. 16 | [illegible] + viii-ix, A. [illegible] + viii-ix. Head $5\frac{1}{4}$, height of body $5\frac{1}{2}$ in the total length. 28 to 30 teeth in upper, and about 24 in lower jaw. Body with three rows of horizontally elongated blotches: first dorsal nearly black. Seas of India.

3. *Cybium guttatum*, D. 16-17 | [illegible] + viii-x, A. [illegible] + vii-ix. Head 5 to $5\frac{1}{2}$, height of body 5 in the total length. 10 to 12 teeth in either jaw. Body with three rows of elongated blotches: first dorsal black to the eighth spine, the rest pure white edged with black. Seas of India.

4. *Cybium Commersonii*, D. 16-17 | [illegible] + ix-x, A. [illegible] + ix-x. Head 4 to 5, height of body $5\frac{1}{2}$ to 7 in the total length. Lateral-line with a strong bend below twelfth dorsal ray. Undulating vertical spots and lines on the sides. First dorsal black to the end of seventh spine, behind pure white with a black upper edge. Red Sea, seas of India to the Malay Archipelago and beyond.

5. *Cybium lineolatum*, D. 16 | [illegible] + ix, A. [illegible] + x. Head 5, height of body $6\frac{1}{2}$ in the total length. Several rows of horizontally elongated dark spots along the sides. Seas of India to ? the Malay Archipelago.

1. Cybium Kuhlii, Plate LVI, fig. 2.

Cybium Kuhlii, Cuv. and Val. viii, p. 178.

B. vii, D. 16 | [illegible] + viii, P. 29, V. 1/5, A. [illegible] + vii, C. 21.

Length of head $5\frac{1}{2}$ to 6, of caudal $3\frac{3}{4}$ to 4, height of body 5 in the total length. *Eyes*—diameter 1/5 of length of head, $1\frac{1}{4}$ diameters from end of snout, and also apart. Greatest width of head equals 1/2, and its height equals 4/5 of its entire length. Maxilla reaches to below the hind edge of the eye. Preopercle emarginate along its vertical border, with the lower limb almost as long as the hind one. *Teeth*—conical and rather compressed, from 15 to 20 in either jaw, those in the lower much the larger: vomerine patch anteriorly rounded, in a band along the palatines. *Fins*—first dorsal spines weak, second dorsal anteriorly equals 3/4 of the height of the body below it, there are six unarticulated rays at its commencement hidden in the skin, the anal which commences on a vertical line below its centre is similar to it but not so high. Pectoral as long as the head behind the middle of the eye. Ventrals equal $1\frac{1}{2}$ diameters of the eye in length. Caudal with deeply pointed lobes. *Lateral-line*—containing about 200 plate-like rounded scales, each having a simple tube, is straight until it arrives opposite the end or middle of the base of the second dorsal, where it curves to below the third finlet and then becomes rather wavy, its central keel well-developed. *Colours*—bluish above becoming silvery on the side and below. After death the sides assume a dark hue and have neither bands or spots. First dorsal black: second dorsal and also anal with dark bases: pectoral with a light outer edge, tips of caudal dark.

Habitat.—Seas of India. The specimen figured (from Bombay) is $14\frac{1}{4}$ inches in length, but it attains a much larger size.

2. Cybium interruptum, Plate LVI, fig. 3.

Scomber wingeram, Russell, Fish. Vizag. ii, p. 26, pl. 134.

Scomber leopardus, Shaw, Zool. iv, p. 591.

Cybium interruptum, Cuv. and Val. viii, p. 172; Jerdon, M. J. L. and Sc. 1851, p. 136; Günther, Catal. ii, p. 371.

Buck-ku, Gwadur.

B. vii, D. 16 | [illegible] + viii-ix, P. 21, V. 1/5, A. [illegible] + viii-ix, C. 21.

Length of head $5\frac{1}{4}$, of caudal 5, height of body $5\frac{1}{4}$ in the total length. *Eyes*—diameter $4\frac{1}{2}$ in length of head, $1\frac{1}{2}$ diameters from end of snout, and also apart. Greatest width of head equals $2\frac{1}{4}$ in its length, and its height equals its length behind the posterior nostril. Maxilla reaches to below the middle of the eye. Vertical limb of preopercle emarginate. *Teeth*—comparatively small, equal sized, conical and somewhat compressed, about 28 or 30 in the upper, and 24 rather larger ones in the lower jaw, they are placed close together as shown in Russell's figure: in a patch rounded anteriorly and slightly emarginate laterally on the vomer, and in a band along the palatines. *Fins*—dorsal spines weak: second dorsal commences midway between the anterior nostril and the base of the caudal fin, anteriorly it is 1/2 the height of the body, its upper edge concave: anal commences below the first third of the second dorsal which fin it resembles. Caudal deeply forked. *Lateral-line*—with a gradual descent. *Colours*—bluish along the back becoming white on the sides and below, three rows of elongated blotches along the sides, almost forming interrupted bands, the two upper sets of blotches cross the lateral-line below the second or third finlet: first dorsal dark, its outer edge nearly black.

The above appears to be Russell's fish, the number of teeth separates it from the *C. guttatum*, (Bl. Schn.) C. V. It is also most probably *C. interruptum*, C. V., from Pondicherry, which is said to have 28 teeth in the upper and 16 in the lower jaw.

Habitat.—Seas of India. The specimen figured (from Madras) is a little over 15 inches, it attains at least 3 feet in length.

3. Cybium guttatum, Plate LV, fig. 1 (*young*) and LVI, fig. 4 (*adult*).

Scomber guttatus, Bl. Schn. p. 23, f. v.

Cybium guttatum, Cuv. and Val. viii, p. 173; Richards. Ich. China, p. 268 (pt.); Cantor, Catal. p. 111; Bleeker, Makr. p. 38; Günther, Catal. ii, p. 371; Day, Fish. Malabar, p. 71; Kner, Novara Fische, p. 143.

Cybium lineolatum, Cantor. Catal. p. 110.

B. vii, D. 16-17 | [illegible] + viii-x, P. 21, V. 1/5, A. [illegible] + vii-ix, C. 26.

Length of head 5 to 5½, of caudal 4¾ to 5, height of body 5 in the total length. *Eyes*—diameter 5¼ to 5½ in the total length, 2 diameters from end of snout, and 1½ apart. Greatest width of head equals 1/2 its length, and its height equals its length behind the anterior nostril. The maxilla reaches to below the hind edge of the eye. Vertical limb of preopercle slightly emarginate. *Teeth*—lancet-shaped, laterally compressed, and somewhat wide apart, about 10 to 12 in either jaw and frequently some smaller ones likewise present for taking the place of any lost; they are much longer in the lower jaw: in a triangular patch on the vomer, and in a band on the palatines. *Fins*—first dorsal spines weak, and ending in soft points; second dorsal highest anteriorly where it equals 4/7 of that of the body below it, and has a concave upper edge: anal commences below the first third of the soft dorsal. *Lateral-line*—having a very gradual descent, it becomes somewhat undulating opposite the commencement of the second dorsal, and very much so below the third and fourth finlets. The keel on the lateral-line well developed. *Colours*—bluish above, silvery beneath: back and sides with three rows of round or rather horizontally oval spots, which become most apparent after death: the membrane between the first and eighth spines black, the rest pure white edged with black: in the young the first dorsal is occasionally almost wholly black.

Habitat.—Seas of India, Malay Archipelago, and China. Grows to 6 feet in length, is good eating, and salts well. Specimens under a foot in length are dry, from two to two-and-a-half feet long they are in the best condition, above that they become coarse. They should be cooked when quite fresh. They are also one of the best fish for "Tamarind fish." Are captured in numbers from October throughout the cold months along all the Indian coasts.

Cantor's specimen of *C. lineolatum*, in the British Museum, has the formula of the fins as above, and 11 or 12 teeth in either jaw. The specimen figured, Pl. LV, f. 1 (from Canara) is 9 inches long, the older one Pl. LVI, fig. 4, is from Madras.

4. Cybium Commersonii, Plate LVI, fig. 5.

Scomber Commersonii, Lacép. ii, p. 600, pl. 20, f. 1; Shaw, Zool. iv, pp. 589 and 590, pl. 83.

Scomber maculosus, Shaw, Nat. Misc. No. 982, and Zool. iv, p. 592.

Scomber konam, Russell, ii, p. 27, pl. 135.

Cybium Commersonii, Cuv. Règ. Anim.; ? Rüpp. Atl. Fische, p. 94, t. 25, f. 1; Cuv. and Val. viii, p. 165; Rüpp. N. W. Fische, p. 41 (pt.); Richards. Ich. China, p. 268; Cantor, Catal. p. 108; Jerdon, M. J. L. and Sc. 1851, p. 136; Günther, Catal. ii, p. 370; Day, Fish. Malabar, p. 69; Klunz. Verh. z. b. Ges. Wien, 1871, p. 444.

Cybium konam, Bleeker, Makr. p. 357; ? Kner, Novara Fische, p. 144.

Chumbum, Mal.; *Konam*, *Mah-wu-laachi*, or *Ah-ku-lah*, Tam.

B. vii, D. 16-17 | [illegible] + ix-x, P. 20-23, V. 1/5, A. [illegible] + ix-x, C. 21.

Length of head 1/4 to 1/5, of caudal 1/5 to 2/11, height of body 2/11 to 1/7 of the total length. *Eyes*—diameter 2/9 to 1/5 of length of head, 1½ to 2 diameters from end of snout, and 1½ apart. Greatest width of head equals 3/7, and its height 3/5 of its length. The maxilla reaches to below the centre or hind edge of the orbit. Posterior border of preopercle rather emarginate, and its angle rounded and slightly produced. *Teeth*—strong, conical, compressed laterally, those in the upper jaw varying in number from about 11 to 25, the posterior ones being rather the smallest. In the lower jaw there are from 10 to 15 of the same shape, but the posterior ones are the largest. A triangular group of villiform teeth on the vomer, and a long narrow band on the palatines.

Fins—the spines of the first dorsal are weak, and end in thin filamentous points projecting beyond the membrane, which is deeply notched. The second dorsal highest in front with its upper margin concave, it is situated opposite the anal which it resembles. Ventral small: pectoral pointed: caudal with pointed lobes each with a raised soft oblique ridge along its base. *Lateral-line*—at first in upper third of body, opposite the twelfth or thirteenth dorsal ray it bends down, making a second strong curve from opposite the first to the third pairs of finlets, beyond which it passes direct to the centre of the caudal where it ends in a soft raised keel between the bases of either lobe. *Colours*—bluish above, silvery below: first dorsal black to the end of the seventh spine, behind which it is pure white, having a narrow black upper edge: basal half of pectoral black. After death numerous vertical undulating lines and spots appear on the sides, in the specimen figured (from Madras) they are very distinct, but during life they are rather indistinct.

Habitat.—Red Sea, East coast of Africa, seas of India to the Malay Archipelago and beyond; it attains at least 4 feet in length.

5. Cybium lineolatum.

Cuv. and Val. viii, p. 170; Belanger, Voy. p. 366, pl. 2, f. 1; Griffith in Cuv. An. Kingdom, Fishes, pl. 48, f. 1; Bleeker, Makr. p. 40; Günther, Catal. ii, p. 370.

B. vii, D. 16 | $\frac{1}{17}$ + ix, P. 21, V. 1/5, A. $\frac{1}{17}$ + x, C. 15.

Length of head 1/5, of caudal 1/5, height of body 2/13 of the total length. *Eyes*—diameter 4½ in length of head, 1½ apart. *Teeth*—about 18 in either jaw, triangular and strongly compressed, the central ones in the lower being the largest: in a triangular pointed patch on the vomer, and in a band on the palatines. *Fins*—spines of first dorsal slender. Pectorals 8½ in the total length: ventrals 1/3 of pectoral. *Lateral-line*—at first in upper fourth of body, descends gradually towards the end of the second dorsal fin until it arrives below the fifth finlet. *Colours*—bluish above, silvery on the sides and beneath: several rows of elongated black blotches on the body, three rows of them, like interrupted lines, being below the lateral-line.

Cuv. and Val.'s specimen was in a bad state, and a difficulty occurred in counting the number of rays, the species appears to somewhat resemble *C. guttatum*, C. V. (it has fewer teeth than in *C. interruptum*, C. V.) but is stated to have less rays. Bleeker, Beng. en Hind. (1853, p. 42) places it as a synonym of *C. interruptum*, C. V.? Cantor's type specimen also appears to be *C. interruptum*.

Habitat.—Seas of India to ? Malay Archipelago.

Genus, 5—Elacate, *Cuv.*

Meladerma, Swainson.

Branchiostegals seven: pseudobranchiæ. Body fusiform: head depressed. Cleft of mouth of moderate depth. Villiform teeth on the jaws, vomer, palatine bones, and tongue. The first dorsal reduced to a few free spines: the second with many rays and somewhat similar to the anal: no finlets. Scales very small. No keel on the side of the tail. Air-vessel absent. Pyloric appendages dendritical.

The immature of this fish, as seen in the seas of India, has its central caudal rays exceedingly prolonged: as age advances, as 8½ inches, the fin becomes more obtuse, but still the central rays are rather the longest: in a specimen 12 inches long that fin is obtuse, in another 11 inches long it is slightly emarginate: in the adult it becomes concave or almost lobed, the lower being usually the longer.

SYNOPSIS OF INDIVIDUAL SPECIES.

1. *Elacate nigra*, D. 8 | 28-36. A. $\frac{2}{23\text{-}26}$. Brown, with two longitudinal black bands. Seas of India to Japan and beyond.

1. Elacate nigra, Plate LV, fig. 2.

Scomber niger, Bloch, t. 337; Bl. Schn. p. 35.

Centronotus Gardenii, Lacép. iv, p. 357.

Scomber peddah mottah, Russell, Fish. Vizag. ii, p. 39, pl. 153.

Elacate Pondiceriana, Cuv. and Val. viii, p. 329; Rüpp. N. W. Fische, p. 43, t. xii, f. 3; Jerdon, M. J. L. and Sc. 1851, p. 139.

Elacate motta, Cuv. and Val. viii, p. 332; Bleeker, Makr. p. 42.

Elacate Malabarica, Cuv. and Val. l. c.; Cuv. Règ. An. Ill. Poiss. pl. 54, f. 2.

Elacate bivittata, Cuv. and Val. viii, p. 338; Temm. and Schleg. Fauna Japon. Poissons, p. 104, pl. 56; Richards. Ich. China, p. 269; Cantor, Catal. p. 116; Jerdon, M. J. L. and Sc. 1851, p. 139.

Meladerma nigerrima, Swainson, Fishes, ii, p. 243.

Elacate Canada, Holb. Ich. South Carol. p. 95, pl. 14, f. 1.

Elacate nigra, Günther, Catal. ii, p. 375; Day, Fish. Malabar, p. 73; Klunz. Verh. z. b. Ges. Wien, 1871, p. 445; Bleeker, Madagascar, p. 98.

Cubbul verari, Tam.

B. vii, D. 8 | 28-36, P. 21, V. 1/5, A. $\frac{2}{25\text{-}26}$, C. 17, Vert. 12/13.

Length of head $4\frac{3}{4}$ to 5, of caudal $5\frac{1}{2}$ to 6, height of body $7\frac{3}{4}$ to 8 in the total length. *Eyes*—diameter $4\frac{1}{2}$ to 5 in the length of head, $1\frac{1}{4}$ to 2 diameters from end of snout, and about 2 apart. Mouth wide, the maxilla reaches to below the anterior edge or first third of the eye. Greatest width of head equals its height, or its length excluding the snout. Upper surface of head flat, and stellately rugose. *Teeth*—villiform. *Fins*—dorsal free spines with a very short interspinous membrane. Second dorsal highest anteriorly where its rays equal the height of the body, its upper edge slightly concave. Anal similar to second dorsal, but rather lower, it arises on the vertical below the seventh or eighth dorsal ray, its two first rays are short and undivided. Pectoral $1\frac{1}{2}$ longer than ventral, and equalling the length of head without the snout. Caudal with its central rays much the longest in the immature, becoming moderately or deeply lunated in the adult. *Colours*—olivaceous brown, having a dark band along the back below the base of the dorsal fin and another along the centre of the side. Fins brownish, with dark or black edges. Outer edges of caudal lobes white.

Habitat.—Seas of India to Japan, also stated to be found in the tropical parts of the Atlantic and along the shores of the United States. The one figured (from Madras) is $13\frac{1}{2}$ inches in length. A specimen 4 feet 10 inches in length exists in the Madras Museum. March, 1867, I took a female, 30 inches long, full of well developed ova. In February, 1867, I examined the contents of the stomach of one, and found the remains of numerous small fishes.

Genus, 6—Echeneis, *Artedi.**

Remoropsis, *Rhombochirus*, *Remilegia*, *Leptecheneis*, *Phtheirichthys*, Gill.

Branchiostegals seven or eight: pseudobranchiæ. Body elongated, fusiform: head depressed and superiorly furnished with an adhesive organ. Eyes lateral or directed downwards and outwards. Cleft of mouth deep. Villiform teeth on the jaws, vomer, palatine bones, and generally on the tongue. The first dorsal fin modified on the summit of the head and occiput, into an adhesive disk; a long second dorsal and anal; no finlets: ventrals thoracic. Scales very small. No keel on the side of the tail. Air-vessel absent. Pyloric appendages in moderate numbers.

Geographical distribution.—These fishes appear to be inhabitants of nearly all seas. In those of India they are most commonly captured adhering to sharks, and are consequently considered to be parasitic on those animals. Van Beneden (Bull. Ac. Belg. 1870, xxx, pp. 181-185) has however shown that sometimes, at least, they prey upon fishes.

The shape of the caudal fin in these fishes changes with age, as observed in *Elacate*.

SYNOPSIS OF SPECIES.

1. *Echeneis neucrates*, D. 22-25 | 33-41, A. 32-38. A dark band along the body. Seas of temperate and tropical reigons.
2. *Echeneis remora*, D. 17-18 | 22-24, A. 24-25. General brown colour. Seas of temperate and tropical regions.
3. *Echeneis brachyptera*, D. 15-16 | 26-32, A. 24-27. Light brown, end of caudal whitish. Seas of India to China, also Madeira, and the coast of North America, and the Brazils.
4. *Echeneis albescens*, D. 12-13 | 17-22, A. 19-22. Seas of India, Japan, and the Cape.

1. Echeneis neucrates, Plate LVII, fig. 1.

Linn. Syst. i, p. 446; Gmel. Linn. p. 1188; Forsk. p. xvi, No. 7; Bloch, ii, p. 131, t. 171; Bl. Schn. p. 239; Shaw, Zool. iv, p. 209, pl. 31; Bennett, Life Raffles, p. 692; Bleeker, Fish. Madag. p. 98.

Echeneis naucrates, Lacép. iii, pp. 146, 162, pl. ix, f. 2; Cuv. Règ. Anim.; Cantor, Catal. p. 199; Tem. and Schleg. Fauna Japon. p. 270, pl. 120, f. 1; Richards. Ich. China, p. 203; Günther, Ann. and Mag. Nat. Hist. May, 1860, p. 395, and Catal. ii, p. 384 (see syn.); Day, Fish. Malabar, p. 75; Kner, Novara Fische, p. 146; Klunz. Verh. z. b. Ges. Wien, 1871, p. 446.

Echeneis neucrates, Russell, Fish. Vizag. i, p. 39, and *Ale wattah*, pl. 40.

Echeneis albicauda, Mitchell, Am. Monthly Mag. ii, p. 244.

Echeneis lunata, Bancroft, Proc. Zool. Soc. i, p. 134, and Zool. Journ. v, p. 411, pl. xviii.

Echeneis Australis, Griffith, in Cuv. An. King. Fishes, p. 504.

Echeneis vittata, Lowe, Proc. Zool. Soc. 1839 p. 89, 1850 p. 252, and Trans. Zool. Soc. iii, p. 17; Rüpp. N. W. Fische, p. 82.

Echeneis fusca, Gronov. ed. Gray, p. 92.

Putthu-wurlay, "Catching mouth," Mal.: *Ubloy*, Tam.

B. vii, D. 22-25 | 33-41, P. 20, V. 1/5, A. 32-38, C. 17.

Length of head $5\frac{1}{4}$ to 6, including disk $3\frac{1}{2}$ to $4\frac{1}{2}$, of disk $4\frac{1}{2}$ to 5, of pectoral $7\frac{3}{4}$ to 8, of caudal 8, width between pectorals $10\frac{1}{2}$ to $11\frac{1}{2}$, height of body $11\frac{1}{2}$ to $12\frac{1}{2}$ in the total length. *Eyes*—transversely oval, directed obliquely outwards and downwards, $2\frac{1}{2}$ to 3 diameters in the postorbital length of head, 2 to 3 diameters from end of snout, $3\frac{1}{2}$ to $4\frac{1}{2}$ apart superiorly, and 3 to 4 inferiorly. The disk or modified first dorsal fin is situated on the summit of the head and occiput, is about 2/5 as wide as long, containing from twenty-one to twenty-five

* The fishes of this Genus form the sub-family ECHENEIDINA, Cantor, or the Family ECHENEOIDEI, Bleeker. Cantor observes that the Malays consider these fish to be a powerful manure for fruit trees.

transverse laminæ, having a tooth-like posterior margin to each, whilst along the central line runs a smooth elevation so that the vacuum may be confined to only one half of the disk. The most anterior of the laminæ are directed slightly forwards, the second quarter are nearly transverse, and the posterior go backwards, the difference between each and the one succeeding it being very gradual. External to this disk is a wide fleshy membrane, which posteriorly extends to over the occiput, but anteriorly does not reach as far as the end of the upper jaw, the whole acting as a sucker. Maxilla extending about as far as the anterior margin of the orbit in the immature, or to only beneath the third lamina in a specimen 2½ feet in length. Mandibula pointed and covered superiorly with numerous rows of villiform teeth, forming a triangular toothed space in advance of the upper jaw, which last is pointed. *Fins*—pectoral situated over the posterior margin of the opercle, and opposite the posterior quarter of the bony disk. First dorsal forming the disk: second dorsal and anal opposite one another, both highest in front, where the rays equal from 2½ to 2¾ the length of the disk, outer edge of both fins rather concave, and the last rays slightly produced. Ventral pointed, and placed almost horizontally. Caudal with its posterior margin straight, but having four short notches at its extremity. *Scales*—minute. *Lateral-line*—rather undulating. *Colours*—generally brownish gray, with the external margins of the caudal and the anterior tips of the dorsal and anal fins edged with white: pectoral of a deep brown: anal tipped with dark brown: centre of caudal nearly black. Sometimes a blackish band along the middle of the side.

Habitat.—Red Sea, seas of India, Malay Archipelago, and tropical and temperate seas generally: attains at least 3 feet in length: this is the commonest form in the Indian seas, the one figured is 8 inches in length.

2. Echeneis remora.

Remora imperati, Willughby, Append. p. 5, t. ix, f. 2.

Echeneis remora, Linn. Syst. i, p. 446; Gmel. Linn. 1187; Bloch, ii, p. 134, pl. 172; Bl. Schn. p. 240; Lacép. iii, pp. 146, 147, t. ix, f. 1; Shaw, Zool. iv. p. 202, pl. 31; Temm. and Schleg. Fauna Japon. Poissons, p. 271; Lowe, Trans. Zool. Soc. iii, p. 16; Jenyns, Voy. Beagle, p. 142; Günther, Ann. and Mag. May, 1860, p. 390, and Catal. ii, p. 378 (see Synon.); Kner, Novara Fische, p. 146; Bleeker, Madagascar, p. 99.

Echeneis Jacobæa and *pallida*, Lowe, P. Z. S. 1839, p. 89.

Echeneis remoroides, Bleeker, Batoe, ii, p. 70.

Echeneis parva, Gronov. ed. Gray, p. 92.

? *Echeneis borboniensis*, Guich. in Maillard, Reunion, Append. p. 19.

B. vii, D. 17-18 | 22-24, P. 20, V. 1/5, A. 24-25, C. 17, Cæc. pyl. 6, Vert. 12/15.

Length of head 4½, with disk 1/3, of disk alone 3¼, of caudal 1/6, height of body 1/9, breadth between pectoral fins 1/6 to 1/7, length of pectorals 7¼, of ventrals 8¼ in the total length. *Eyes*—situated in the centre of the length of the head, 3½ diameters from end of snout, and 5 apart superiorly. Mouth rounded. *Teeth*—the outer lateral row in the lower jaw enlarged. *Fins*—first dorsal or disk in its widest part equals half its length. Second dorsal commences midway between the base of the pectoral and the base of the caudal, its highest rays equal the length of the head excluding the snout. Anal opposite the second dorsal. Caudal forked in a specimen 9 inches long. *Colours*—brown.

Habitat.—Seas of temperate and tropical regions.

3. Echeneis brachyptera, Plate LV, fig. 3.

Lowe, Proc. Zool. Soc. 1839, p. 89; and Trans. Zool. Soc. p. 17; Günther, Ann. and Mag. May, 1860, p. 399, and Catal. ii, p. 378.

Echeneis sexdecim-lamellata, Eydoux et Gervais, Voy. Favor. v, Zool. p. 77, pl. xxxi.

Echeneis pallida, Temm. and Schleg. Fauna Japon. Poiss. p. 271, pl. 120, f. 2, 3.

Echeneis Nieuhofii, Bleeker, Sumatra, ii, p. 279.

B. vii, D. 15-16 | 26-32, P. 20, V. 1/5, A. 24-27, C. 17.

Length of head 4⅔, including disk 3½, of disk alone 4⅔, of caudal 6½, height of body 8¼, width at pectorals 6¾ to 7½, length of pectoral 1/10, of ventral 7½ in the total length. *Eyes*—diameter 2½ in the postorbital portion of the head, 2½ diameters from end of snout, 3½ apart superiorly, and 3 inferiorly. Upper jaw rather angular: the maxilla reaches posteriorly to below the front edge of the eye or beneath the fourth lamina of the disk. *Teeth*—the outer lateral row in the lower jaw is somewhat enlarged. *Fins*—greatest width of disk equals half its length. The second dorsal commences midway between the posterior edge of the eye and the base of the caudal, its highest portion equals the postorbital length of the head. The anal commences on a vertical below the third or fourth dorsal ray to which fin it is similar. Caudal very slightly emarginate. *Scales*—rudimentary. *Colours*—of a light brown with the posterior edge of the caudal whitish.

Habitat.—Seas of India to China, also Madeira, and the coasts of North America and Brazil. The specimen figured (life-size) is from Madras.

4. Echeneis albescens, Plate LVII, fig. 2.

Echeneis albescens, Temm. and Schleg. Fauna Japon. p. 272, pl. 120, f. 3; Günther, Catal. ii, p. 377.

Echeneis clypeata, Günther, Ann. and Mag. Nat. Hist. May, 1860, p. 401; and Catal. ii, p. 376.

? *Echeneis lophioides*, Guich. in Maill. Reunion, App. p. 20.

Remora albescens, Bleeker, Ternate, 1863, p. 2.

B. vii, D. 12-13 | 17-22, P. 19, V. 1/5, A. 19-22, C. 15.

Length of head $4\frac{3}{5}$, including disk $3\frac{1}{2}$, of disk 4, width of body between pectorals $5\frac{1}{3}$, of caudal $8\frac{1}{2}$ in the total length. *Eyes*—$2\frac{1}{2}$ diameters in the postorbital portion of the head, $2\frac{1}{3}$ from end of snout, 6 apart superiorly, and slightly less inferiorly. Body wide anteriorly, width of sucker equals 2/3 of its length. Mouth obtuse: lower jaw the longer, the maxilla reaches to below the hind nostril or the third lamina of the disk. *Teeth*—villiform in jaws, vomer, and palatines: an outer enlarged series in lower jaw and vomer. *Fins*—second dorsal commences in the second third of the distance between the bases of pectoral and caudal fins, and opposite the anal. Ventral equals the distance between the eye and base of pectoral. Caudal very slightly emarginate. *Scales*—rudimentary. *Colours*—uniform brown.

The specimen figured (12 inches in length and stuffed) is from Sir W. Elliot's collection, and very curiously resembles partly Dr. Günther's species and partly *E. albescens*, Temm. and Schleg. Agreeing with the latter, it has 13 laminæ, the length of the disk 1/4 of the total, mouth obtuse, angle of mouth below the third lamina, the length of the ventrals equals the distance between the base of the pectoral and the posterior margin of the eye. But instead of 22 rays in the second dorsal it has 17, and A. 19 instead of 22, still this variation is not more than is observed in some of the other species.

Habitat.—Seas of India, Japan, and the Cape.

FAMILY, XX—URANOSCOPIDÆ, *Richardson.*

Korukè, Tamil.

Branchiostegals from five to seven: pseudobranchiæ. Body low and more or less cylindrical. Gill-openings wide. Eyes on the upper surface of the head. Head mostly cuirassed with bony plates. Infraorbital ring of bones does not articulate with the preopercle. Usually villiform teeth in both jaws, canines present or absent, but no molars. One or two dorsal fins, the spines being fewer in number than the rays. Ventral with one spine and five rays. Pectoral rays branched. No prominent papilla near the vent. Scales when present rudimentary. Lateral line continuous. Air-vessel absent. Pyloric appendages when present few or in moderate numbers.

In Cuv. and Val. the genus *Uranoscopus* was divided into (1) those with two dorsal fins; and (2) those with one.

SYNOPSIS OF GENERA.

1. *Uranoscopus.* Two dorsal fins. Scales small. Seas of India.
2. *Ichthyscopus.* A single dorsal fin. Head armed with bony plates. Scales rudimentary. Seas of India.

Genus, 1—URANOSCOPUS, *Cuv.*

Branchiostegals six: pseudobranchiæ. Body somewhat cylindrical. Head large, broad, and partly covered with bony plates. The opercles and shoulder-bones usually armed. Besides the posterior gill-opening there is generally a rounded orifice above the opercle. Eyes on the upper surface of the head. Cleft of mouth vertical, with a filament below, or before the tongue. Villiform or cardiform teeth on the jaws, vomer, and palatine bones, no canines. Two dorsals, the first with from three to five spines: ventrals jugular. Scales small and rudimentary. Lateral-line continuous. Air-vessel absent. Pyloric appendages in moderate numbers.

SYNOPSIS OF INDIVIDUAL SPECIES.

1. *Uranoscopus guttatus*, D. 4-5 | 12-13, A. 13. Strong shoulder spines. Chestnut or slaty-brown, with light spots in the upper half of its body and head: a black blotch at upper portion of spinous dorsal fin. Seas of India.

1. **Uranoscopus guttatus,*** Plate LV, fig. 4.

Cuv. and Val. iii, p. 305; Cuv. Règ. Anim. Ill. Poissons, pl. 17, f. 2; Bleeker, Beng. en Hind. p. 34; Griffith in Cuv. An. King. Fishes, p. 128, pl. 24, f. 3; Jerdon, M. J. L. and Sc. 1851, p. 142; Günther, Catal. ii, p. 228.

Uranoscopus marmoratus, Jerdon, M. J. L. and Sc. 1851, p. 142; Day, Proc. Zool. Soc. 1867, p. 702, (? Cuv. and Val. iii, p. 304.)

B. vi, D. 4-5 | 12-13, P. 17, V. 1/5, A. 13, C. 13.

Length of head $3\frac{1}{4}$ to $3\frac{1}{2}$, of pectoral 4 to $4\frac{1}{2}$, of caudal 5 to $5\frac{1}{2}$, height of body 4 to $4\frac{1}{2}$ in the total length. *Eyes*—on the upper surface of the head, 1/2 a diameter from end of snout, and $1\frac{1}{2}$ apart. Greatest width of head rather exceeds its height. Cleft of mouth nearly vertical: lips with a narrow fringe: nostrils situated in front of the centre of the eye. Four to seven spines along the lower edge of the preopercle, and one on subopercle. Two large spines on shoulder-bone, the lower the larger and equalling 2 diameters of the orbit. Posterior border of occiput with one central and on either side two more little bony lobes, the posterior of which has one or two spines. Bones of the head roughened like the impressions of a thimble. *Teeth*—two or three rows of cardiform ones in either jaw, becoming laterally a single one in the lower: smaller teeth on vomer and palatines. *Fins*—dorsal spines weak, the first the longest, but only 2/3 as high as the soft dorsal. Caudal rather rounded. *Scales*—present on the body, except above the first part of the lateral-line, and on the breast and chest to the commencement of the anal fin: they are not imbricated but covered by skin, and are in rows bounded by muciferous channels. *Lateral-line*—goes from the shoulder to the base of the second dorsal, along which it is continued, it has a few rounded scales above it behind the base of the second dorsal spine. *Colours*—chestnut or slaty-brown, with two or three rows of bluish white spots along the back and half way down the sides. First dorsal pure white, with its upper two-thirds black, from the first to midway between the third and fourth spines: second dorsal black along its upper two-thirds: caudal with a wide

* *Uranoscopus affinis*, C. V. iii, p. 304; Günther, Catal. ii, p. 227, appears to be closely allied to *U. cognatus*, Cantor. It is said to have D. 5 | 12, A. 13. The spine at the shoulder is 2/3 the length of the pectoral, and the black dorsal blotch extends from the second to the fourth dorsal spines. It is stated to have come from the Indian Ocean, but India is not distinctly indicated.

vertical black band covering its middle third: anal white with a black base: pectoral dark, its lower margin edged with white.

Habitat.—Seas of India, said to attain a foot in length: the largest I captured at Madras is 7½ inches, the one figured (life-size) is from the same locality.

Genus, 2—Ichthyscopus, *Swainson.*

Uranoscopus, sp., Cuv. and Val.: *Anema*, Günther.

Branchiostegals six: pseudobranchiæ. Body somewhat cylindrical. Head large, broad, and partly covered with bony plates. Gill-openings without any superior orifice. Eyes on the upper surface of the head. Cleft of mouth vertical. Some of the bones of the head may be armed. No filament below or before the tongue. Villiform teeth on upper jaw, vomer, and palatines, in a single conical row in the lower jaw. One continuous dorsal fin with less spines than branched rays, the latter portion similar to the anal: ventrals jugular. Scales rudimentary. Air-vessel absent. Pyloric appendages in moderate numbers.

SYNOPSIS OF INDIVIDUAL SPECIES.

1. *Ichthyscopus inermis*, D. $\frac{3}{12}|\frac{1}{12}$, A. 16-19. Canary-yellow, with buffy markings along the back and sides, enclosing pure white round or oval spots. Seas of India to Japan.

1. Ichthyscopus inermis, Plate LV, fig. 5.

Uranoscopus le Beck, Bloch, Syst. p. 47.

Uranoscopus inermis, Cuv. and Val. iii, p. 310, pl. 65; Temm. and Schleg. Fauna Japon. Poissons, p. 27, pl. 10 A; Jerdon, M. J. L. and Sc. 1851, p. 142; Günther, Catal. ii, p. 230; Day, Fish. Malabar, p. 46.

Ichthyscopus inermis, Swainson, Fishes, ii, p. 269.

Nillam kornajan, "A diver into the mud," Tam.

B. vii, D. 8 | $\frac{3}{12}|\frac{1}{12}$, P. 18, V. 1/5, A. 16-19, C. 11, Cæc. pyl. 9 (8).

Length of head 3 to 3½, of caudal 5½, height of body 4 to 4¼ in the total length. *Eyes*—situated considerably before the middle of the length of the head and on its upper surface. Greatest width of head equals 3/4 of its length, and its height 5/6 of the same extent. Cleft of mouth nearly vertical: lips covered with numerous branched papillæ. Anterior nostril round, situated in front of the centre of the eye and surrounded with papillæ resembling those on the lips, similar ones likewise surround the large oval posterior nostril which is situated along the inner side of the orbit. No spines on the head or shoulder: the posterior edge of the occiput straight and entire: posterior edge of opercle fringed. An elongated angular flap edged with papillæ behind the shoulder. *Teeth*—in villiform rows in the upper jaw; in a single row of widely separated conical ones in the lower jaw, and sometimes a few villiform ones posteriorly above the symphysis: villiform on vomer and palatines. *Fins*—dorsal spines weak, and not so high as the rays. Pectoral 4⅔ and ventral 5½ in the total length. Caudal slightly rounded. *Scales*—present on the body, except above the lateral-line, on the breast, chest, and to about the sixth anal ray, they are not imbricated but covered by the skin, and are laid in rows, each being bounded by a muciferous channel. *Lateral-line*—goes from the shoulder to the base of third dorsal spine, and is continued close to the base of that fin in its whole length. *Colours*—canary-yellow, with buffy-brown markings along the sides, enclosing pure white round or oval spots, also some of the same white colour on the pectoral and dorsal fins. Upper surface of the head brownish: caudal brownish-yellow with dark extremities, a dark bar across the pectoral and caudal fins.

On March 23rd, 1868, a fine male specimen was brought to me alive, and placed in water having a bed of mud, into which it rapidly worked itself, first depressing one side and then the other, until only the top of its head and mouth remained above the mud, whilst a constant current was kept through its gills. If lifted out of the water, it squirted fluid from its mouth for some distance; whilst in the mud it looked like a frog. It made a curious noise, half snapping and half croaking, when removed from its native element.

Habitat.—Seas of India to Japan, said to live in the mud and be taken with difficulty. The specimen figured (about 12 inches in length) is from Canara.

Family, XXI—TRACHINIDÆ, (*Swains.*) *Günther.*

Branchiostegals from five to seven: pseudobranchiæ. Body more or less elongated, posteriorly compressed: head often large. Eyes more or less lateral. Cleft of mouth, almost horizontal, lateral, or even nearly vertical. Some of the bones of the head usually armed: the suborbital ring of bones articulates with the preopercle. Teeth in the jaws, present or absent on the vomer and palatines. Dorsal fins sometimes in two distinct portions but more or less connected: the spines may be in excess of the rays, but as a rule there are more of the latter: anal generally similar to the soft dorsal: ventrals thoracic: pectorals with or without appendages. Body scaleless, scaled, or with a single series of plate-like scales. Lateral-line continuous. Air-vessel present or absent. Pyloric appendages few.

SYNOPSIS OF GENERA.

1. *Percis.* A single dorsal fin, the spines (4 or 5) short and continuous at their base with the soft portion. Ventrals a little anterior to the pectorals. Canine teeth: no palatine teeth. Red Sea, throughout those of India to the Malay Archipelago.

2. *Sillago.* Two dorsal fins, the first with 9 to 12 spines, slightly separated from the second. Muciferous system of head well developed. Ventrals thoracic. No palatine teeth. Red Sea, seas of India to the Malay Archipelago and beyond.

Genus, 1—Percis, *Bl. Schn.*

Parapercis, Bleeker.

Branchiostegals six: pseudobranchiæ. Body rather elongated and subcylindrical: head a little depressed. Eyes lateral, directed somewhat upwards. Cleft of mouth slightly oblique: lower jaw the longer. Opercle with one or two spines: pre- and sub- opercles are sometimes slightly serrated. Villiform teeth in the jaws, with an outer enlarged row, some of which are canine-like: teeth also on the vomer, but not in the palatines. The first dorsal fin with four or five spines, more or less continuous with the second dorsal, which has a moderate number of rays, and is similar to the anal: ventrals slightly anterior to the pectorals, the rays of which are branched. Scales ctenoid, rather small. Air-vessel absent. Pyloric appendages, when present, few.

Geographical distribution.—From the Red Sea and East coast of Africa, through the seas of India to the Malay Archipelago and beyond. The common forms on the Coromandel coast of India are small, the larger, *P. hexophthalma*, I have only taken at the Andamans, and it is not figured in Sir W. Elliot's collection of Indian Fishes.

SYNOPSIS OF SPECIES.

1. *Percis punctata*, D. 5 | 21-22, A. [illegible], L. l. 58-60, L. tr. 5/16. Pre- and sub- opercles serrated. Diameter of eyes 1/4 of length of head. Caudal rather rounded. Vertically banded, a few black spots in the bands. Soft dorsal with three rows of black spots: caudal with two grayish bands: ventral slate-coloured. Seas of India.

2. *Percis pulchella*, D. 5 | 21-22, A. [illegible], L. l. 60-62, L. tr. 5/18. Preopercle entire, a few serrations may exist on subopercle. Diameter of eye $3\frac{4}{5}$ in length of head. Caudal cut square, with its upper ray a little prolonged. Body with six vertical bands: head with dark spots superiorly, three blue bands go from the eye over the sub- and inter- opercles. A row of spots along the soft dorsal fin: five rows of yellow spots along the anal. Lower half of caudal darker than the upper, which is barred. East coast of Africa, seas of India to Japan.

3. *Percis hexophthalma*, D. 5 | 19-21, A. 17-18, L. l. 62, L. tr. 7/21. Pre- and sub- opercles entire. Diameter of eye 1/5 of length of head. Caudal cut square, with its upper ray a little prolonged. Upper part of body gray with vertical lines: a row of three white spots each having a black centre along the abdomen: opercles with narrow stripes below the eyes. A black blotch on caudal fin. Red Sea, East coast of Africa, seas of India to the Malay Archipelago and beyond.

1. **Percis punctata,** Plate LVIII, fig. 1.

? *Percis punctata*, Cuv. and Val. iii, p. 264; Günther, Catal. ii, p. 238.

B. vi, D. 5 | 21-22, P. 16-17, V. 1/5, A. [illegible], C. 15, L. l. 58-60, L. tr. 5/16.

Length of head from $4\frac{1}{2}$ to 5, of caudal 7 to $7\frac{1}{2}$, height of body 6 to $6\frac{1}{2}$ in the total length. *Eyes*—diameter 1/4 of length of head, 1 to $1\frac{1}{2}$ diameters from end of snout, and 1/4 of a diameter apart. Greatest width of head equals its length behind the middle of the eye, its height equals 1/2 its length. Snout sharp: cleft of mouth somewhat oblique, lower jaw a little the longer, the maxilla reaches to nearly below the front edge of the eye. Greatest depth of preorbital equals half the diameter of the eye. Preopercle coarsely serrated along its posterior limb: operele with a well marked spine, the edge of the suboperele serrated. A shoulder spine. *Teeth* above the symphysis of the lower jaw an outer enlarged row of about eight curved teeth, the external of which is the largest: a villiform band on the vomer. *Fins*—spines of first dorsal of moderate strength, the fourth the longest equalling $1\frac{1}{4}$ diameters of the eye in length, the third is a quarter shorter, the fifth spine midway between the height of the first and second. Pectoral as long as the head excluding the snout: ventral reaches the vent. Caudal cut square or a little rounded. *Scales*—four entire and two half rows between the lateral-line and the base of the first dorsal fin. *Colours*—whitish with reddish-brown vertical bands and blotches above the lateral-line, which are interrupted along the middle of the body; on these bands are a few black spots. A bright golden line goes from below the orbit to the base of the dorsal fin, and another from the centre of the eye to the snout. Spinous dorsal with or without a row of black spots: soft dorsal with three rows on the rays: caudal with two grayish bands, one at its base the other at its posterior third, and sometimes an ocellus at the upper part of the base of the caudal fin: anal yellowish: ventrals slate-coloured.

There are three objections to uniting *P. punctata* with Dr. Günther's fish, (1) its having five instead of four spines to the first dorsal fin, but the latter being only a single specimen such may be an individual anomaly: likewise (2) the height of its body is 6—$6\frac{1}{2}$ instead of $7\frac{3}{4}$ in the total length; lastly (3) the colours differ. But as Dr. Günther's type is, at least, semi-putrid, the existence of colours could not be expected. The preoperele and operele are both serrated in *P. millepunctata*, whilst the fish described above is common along the Coromandel coast of India, and would doubtless extend to Ceylon.

A figure of this fish exists amongst Sir W. Elliot's drawings termed *Kul ooloovα*.

P. punctata, C. V., has no characters or colours assigned to it that do not exist in this species.

Habitat.—Coromandel coast of India and (? Ceylon): attaining at least 5 inches in length at Madras.

2. **Percis pulchella,** Plate LVIII. fig. 2.

? *Percis maculata*, Bl. Schn. p. 179, pl. 38.

Percis pulchella, Temm. and Schleg. Fauna Japon. Poiss. p. 24, pl. 10, f. 2; Richards. Ich. China, p. 211; Günther, Catal. ii, p. 240.

B. vi, D. 5 | 21-22, P. 18, V. 1/5, A. $\frac{1}{17}$, C. 17, L. l. 60-62, L. tr. 5/18.

Length of head $4\frac{1}{3}$ to $4\frac{1}{2}$, of caudal 7, height of body $6\frac{1}{2}$ in the total length. *Eyes*—diameter $3\frac{3}{4}$ in length of head, 1 diameter from end of snout, and 1/4 of a diameter apart. Greatest width of head equals its length behind the middle of the eye, its height equals half its length. Snout not so pointed as in *P. punctata*. Cleft of mouth somewhat oblique, lower jaw slightly the longer, the maxilla reaches to below first third of eye. Greatest depth of preorbital equals half the diameter of the eye. Preopercle entire: subopercle with two or three serrations just below the opercle, which latter has a well marked spine. *Teeth*—anterior row in front of upper jaw enlarged as are likewise those in the lower consisting of 6 or 8, which are strong and recurved, also there are some enlarged teeth laterally in the mandibles: in a band on vomer. *Fins*—spines of first dorsal rather strong, first short, the fourth the longest and equal to the diameter of the eye, the fifth about equals the second. Pectoral as long as the head without the snout. Ventral does not quite reach the vent. Caudal cut square with its upper ray a little prolonged. *Scales*—four entire and two half rows between the lateral-line and the base of the first dorsal fin. *Colours*—reddish, with six crossbands of a darker colour: a light pinkish band along the side, becoming yellow along the centre of the caudal fin, head spotted with dark purplish black marks superiorly: three well-marked vertical blue bands across the sub- and inter- opercles, and sometimes a fourth crosses the breast in front of and to below the pectoral fin. Dorsal fins yellow, black in their lower halves: the soft with a single row of spots along its upper half: anal yellowish in its lower two-thirds, with five rows of round canary-coloured spots: its outer third reddish: ventrals reddish, stained at their edges. Caudal yellow along its centre, dark reddish in its lower half, some fine vertical bars in its upper half.

Both *P. punctata* and *P. pulchella* are found at Tranquebar, from whence *P. maculata*, Bl. Sch. was obtained. Its preopercle is shown serrated as in *P. punctata*, the markings on the head, body, and caudal fin agree with *P. pulchella*, but the colours on dorsal and anal fins resemble neither. Dr. Günther, Catal. ii. p. 237, refers it with doubt to *P. nebulosa*. *P. pulchella* is the fish referred to by Jerdon (M. J. L. and Sc. 1851, p. 144.) "*Bupiscartes*—one of Swainson's subgenus occurs at Madras." Sir W. Elliot's figure is thus named by Jerdon, it is said to be termed *Varen aolinoli*, Tam.

Habitat.—East coast of Africa, seas of India to Japan. The specimen figured (life-size) is from Madras.

3. **Percis hexophthalma,** Plate LVII, fig. 4.

(Ehrenb.) Cuv. and Val. iii, p. 271, vii, p. 507; Günther, Catal. ii, p. 239, Fish. Zanz. p. 68.

Percis cylindrica, Rüpp. Atl. Fische, p. 19, t. v, f. 2, (not *Sciæna cylindrica*, Bl.=*P. cylindrica*, C. V.)

Percis caudimaculata, Rüpp. N. W. Fische, p. 98; Bleeker, Perc. p. 54.

Parapercis hexophthalmus, Bleeker, Guébé, 1868, p. 2.

Percis polyophthalma, Klunz. Verh. z. b. Ges. Wien, 1870, p. 816.

B. vi, D. 5 | 19-21, P. 17, V. 1/5, A. 17-18, C. 15, L. l. 62, L. tr. 7/21.

Length of head 4, of caudal $6\frac{1}{4}$, height of body $6\frac{1}{2}$ in the total length. *Eyes*—diameter 1/5 of length of head, $1\frac{1}{2}$ diameters from end of snout, and nearly 2/3 of a diameter apart. Greatest width of head equals its length without the snout, and its height equals 4/7 of its length. Snout somewhat pointed. Cleft of mouth rather oblique, the maxilla reaches to below the front edge of the eye. Greatest depth of preorbital equals 1 diameter of the eye. Preopercle entire: a spine on opercle and another at shoulder. *Teeth*—outer row in upper jaw enlarged, as are also 8 or 10 of the anterior ones in the lower jaw, also four or five of the outer ones in the middle of the lateral teeth: teeth on vomer. *Fins*—fourth dorsal spine longest and equal to 1 diameter of the orbit. Pectoral equals 3/4 of the length of the head. Ventral reaches the anal. Caudal cut square, having its upper ray a little prolonged. *Colours*—upper half of body and head grayish-brown with irregular vertical gray lines, also one or two narrow and interrupted or entire lines along the side: three or more white spots each having a black centre along either side of the abdomen. Some narrow dark lines pass obliquely backwards and downwards from the eye over the sides of the head, others go directly backwards. A black spot on the base of the first dorsal, its edges also dark: three rows of black spots along the soft dorsal which also has a dark edge, one along the anal. A large black blotch on the caudal extending half its length, and having a large white blotch behind it, the whole of the caudal vertically barred with spots.

In the "Catal. of Fishes of the British Museum," *P. polyophthalmus* is united with *P. hexophthalmus*, but in the Fishes of Zanzibar they are again separated for the reasons advanced in Cuv. and Val.: that all the specimens with three ocellated spots on each side (*P. hexophthalmus*), have about ten narrow oblique brown lines radiating from the lower part of the eye, over the opercles, whilst the specimens with six or seven ocelli on each side (*P. polyophthalmus*) have the sides of the head dotted.

Habitat.—Red Sea, East coast of Africa, seas of India to the Malay Archipelago and beyond. The specimen figured (from the Andamans) is 8 inches in length.

Genus, 2—Sillago,* *Cuv.*

Sillaginodes and *Sillaginopsis*, Gill.

Branchiostegals six: pseudobranchiæ. Body elongated, somewhat cylindrical. Head conical, with its muciferous system well developed. Gill-openings wide: eyes lateral or directed slightly upwards. Cleft of mouth short: the upper jaw the longer. Preopercle serrated or crenulated: opercle ending in a point. Villiform teeth in the jaws with the outer row rather conical, also present on vomer, none on the palatines. Two dorsal fins, the first with nine to twelve spines, which are less than the rays (19-27) of the soft dorsal, which last is similar to the anal: ventrals thoracic, with one spine and five rays: lower pectoral rays branched. Scales ctenoid. Lateral-line not continued on to the caudal fin. Air-vessel simple. Pyloric appendages few.

These fishes having much the appearance of *Sciæna* and placed in that genus by Bloch, are esteemed light and wholesome food: as they ascend rivers and tidal estuaries they may be captured almost throughout the year.

Geographical distribution.—Red Sea, seas of India to the Malay Archipelago and beyond.

SYNOPSIS OF SPECIES.

1. *Sillago domina*, D. 9 | [illegible], A. [illegible], L. l. 90. Second dorsal spine very elongate. Upper portion of Bay of Bengal to Burma and the Malay Archipelago.

2. *Sillago sihama*, D. 10-11 | [illegible], A. [illegible], L. l. 70-74, L. tr. 5-6/12. Eyes, diameter 4 to 5 in length of head. A silvery longitudinal band: minute black points on dorsal and anal fins. Red Sea, seas of India to the Malay Archipelago and beyond.

3. *Sillago maculata*, D. 11 | [illegible], A. [illegible], L. l. 70, L. tr. 6/10. Eyes, diameter $2\frac{3}{4}$ in length of head. Dark blotches along the sides, first dorsal superiorly black. Andamans and the Malay Archipelago to S.E. Australia.

1. **Sillago domina**, Plate LVIII, fig. 3.

Cuv. and Val. iii, p. 415, pl. 69; Cuv. Règ. Anim. Ill. Poiss. pl. 13, f. 1; Swainson, Fishes, ii, p. 205; Cantor, Catal. p. 21; Günther, Catal. ii, p. 246.

Sillaginopsis domina, Gill. Proc. Nat. Hist. Soc. Phil. 1861, p. 505.

Yerra-soring, Tel.: *Tool-dauti*, Ooriah.

B. vi, D. 9 | [illegible], P. 24, V. 1/5, A. [illegible], C. 19, L. l. 90, L. tr. 5-6/14, Cæc. pyl. 4.

Length of head $3\frac{3}{4}$ to 4, of pectoral 6, of caudal 7 to 8, height of body 7 to 8 in the total length. *Eyes*—situated in the commencement of the anterior half of the head, $3\frac{1}{2}$ to 4 diameters from end of snout, and $1\frac{2}{3}$ to 2 apart. Body, subcylindrical. Head depressed, pyriform: cheeks, swollen. Greatest width of head equals $2\frac{1}{4}$, and its height $2\frac{1}{3}$ in its length: upper jaw the longer: the maxilla extends to half way between the snout and the anterior extremity of the orbit: opercle with a very small spine in the centre of its posterior margin: other opercles entire. *Teeth*—villiform in both jaws with an external conical row, the largest (four) being in the centre of the upper jaw. A transverse semicircular band of villiform ones on the vomer. *Fins*—dorsal commences slightly behind the pectoral, its first spine short, its second of varying length, but in large specimens appears usually to extend to the base of the caudal fin, there are some fine scales on the interspinous membrane between it and the third spine. Second dorsal rather highest in front where it equals 2/3 of the height of the body: pectoral rounded. The first two rays of the anal are undivided and have articulated extremities, form of fin similar to that of the second dorsal: caudal lobed, the upper the longer. *Scales*—strongly ctenoid, in regular horizontal rows, extending over cheeks, and between the eyes, as far forwards as the anterior nostril. Some fine ones over the base of the pectoral and nearly to the extremity of caudal. *Lateral-line*—descends very gently

* Family, Sillaginidæ, Richardson.

to opposite about the seventh ray of anal fin, from whence it proceeds direct to the centre of the caudal. *Colours*—greenish-yellow shot with purple.

Habitat.—Coromandel coast of India, where it is caught in droves in October, Bay of Bengal as low as Pondicherry,* and also in the Ganges, Burma, and Malay Archipelago. It attains at least 10 inches in length, the one figured is from Calcutta.

2. Sillago sihama, Plate LVII, fig. 3.

Atherina sihama, Forsk. p. 70.
Sciæna Malabarica, Bl. Schn. p. 81, t. xix.
Platycephalus sihamus, Bl. Schn. p. 60.
Sparus soring, Russell, ii, p. 9, pl. 113.
Sillago sihama, Rüpp. Atl. Fische, p. 9, t. iii, f. 1, and N. W. Fische, p. 100; Gunther, Catal. ii, p. 243; Day, Fish. Malabar, p. 47; Klunz. Verh, z. b. Ges. Wien, 1870, p. 818; Bleeker, Revis. Sill. 1874, p. 67.
Sillago acuta, Cuv. and Val. iii, p. 400; Jerdon, M. J. L. and Sc. 1851, p. 131; Bleeker, Perc. p. 61; Kner, Novara Fische, p. 128.
Sillago erythræa, Cuv. and Val. iii, p. 409.
Sillago Malabarica, Cantor, Catal. p. 21; Bleeker, Bali, iii, p. 157.
Soring, or *Tella-soring*, or *Arriti-ki*, Tel.: *Culingah*, Tam.: *Cudeerah*, Mal.: *Thol-o-dah*, And.: *Nga-rai*, Mugh.

B. vi, D. 10-11 | $\frac{1}{20-22}$, P. 20, V. 1/5, A. $\frac{2}{22-23}$, C. 19, L. l. 70-74, L. tr. 5-6/12, Cæc. pyl. 3-4,† Vert. 19/15.

Length of head 1/4 to 2/9, of caudal 1/8 to 1/9, height of body 1/6 to 2/15 of the total length. *Eyes*—diameter 4 to 5 in length of head,‡ 1¼ to 2¼ diameters from end of snout, and 1 to 1½ apart. Snout pointed. Greatest width of head equals its height or half of its length. Upper jaw slightly the longer: the maxilla reaches nearly half way to below the front edge of the eye. Vertical limb of preopercle serrated in its lower half. Opercle with a well developed spine. *Teeth*—villiform in both jaws, the outer row sometimes a little enlarged: in a semicircular band on the vomer. *Fins*—dorsal spines of moderate strength, second and third subequal in length and as high as the body below them: second dorsal highest anteriorly where it equals 4/7 of that of the body. Pectoral as long as the head excluding the snout, and rather longer than the ventral. Anal below and similar to soft dorsal but not so high. Caudal emarginate or obtuse. *Scales*—about six rows between the lateral-line and the last dorsal spine. *Air-vessel*—extends posteriorly to opposite the first third of the anal fin. *Colours*—olive-green along the back, becoming light on the abdomen, the whole having a brilliant purple reflection: a silvery longitudinal band: minute black points on the dorsal and anal fins.

Habitat.—Red Sea, seas of India to the Malay Archipelago and beyond, it ascends tidal rivers. It is known as *Whiting* at Madras. Native women who have young babies are advised to eat it, as it is said to be even more nourishing than shark's flesh. It attains a foot in length. M. Leschenault asserted that he had seen them, although seldom, 3 feet long. The one figured is from Madras.

3. Sillago maculata, Plate LVIII, fig. 4.

Quoy and Gaim. Voy. Freyc. Zool. p. 261, pl. 53, f. 2; Cuv. and Val. iii, p. 411; Bleeker, Perc. p. 62, and Revis. Sill. 1874, p. 71; Günther, Catal. ii, p. 245; Kner, Novara Fische, p. 127.
Sillago Bassensis, Cuv. and Val. iii, p. 412; Quoy and Gaim. Voy. Astrol. Poiss. p. 672, pl. i, f. 2.

B. vi, D. 11 | $\frac{1}{21-22}$, P. 17, V. 1/5, A. $\frac{2}{20-21}$, C. 18, L. l. 70, L. tr. 6/10.

Length of head 3¾, of caudal 7½, height of body 5½ in the total length. *Eyes*—diameter 2¾ in length of head, 1½ diameters from end of snout, and 3/4 of a diameter apart. Greatest width of head equals 2¾, and its height 1½ in its length. Snout rather pointed, upper jaw a little the longer: the maxilla reaches nearly half way to below the front edge of the eye. Vertical limb of preopercle finely serrated opercle with a small spine. *Teeth*—villiform in either jaw, the outer row a little enlarged: also in a band on the vomer. *Fins*—dorsal spines weak, third to fifth subequal in length, nearly as high as the body, and rather higher than the soft portion of the fin. Pectoral as long as the head excluding the snout: ventral a little shorter. Anal similar to second dorsal. Caudal lobed. *Colours*—grayish along the back, becoming dull white on the abdomen: some irregular blackish blotches along the sides, also a silvery median longitudinal band. Upper half of first dorsal black, outer edges of second dorsal and anal dark, and a gray band along the upper third of soft dorsal.

Habitat.—Andamans, Malay Archipelago to South-East Australia. The specimen figured (life-size) is from the Andamans. It is said to attain 8 or 9 inches in length.

* In Cuv. and Val. this species is termed "Pêche Malame de Pondicherry." Jerdon observes, "I never saw a specimen of the *Sillago domina* at Madras, and the fishermen to whom I showed the drawing said they did not know it. Pondicherry is only 80 miles from Madras, and I doubt therefore if it was sent from thence: most probably it is more from the mouths of the Ganges." I have taken it at Coconada but that is the lowest point in the Bay of Bengal where I have observed it. Some might however easily stray down to Pondicherry.

† Cuv. and Val. found 2 cæcal appendages, I have sometimes found 4, occasionally 3, 2 being short and 1 long.

‡ Respecting the diameter of the eye in the length of the head, I have found it 4¾ at 4 inches; 4 at 5 inches; 4¼ at 5½ inches; 4¼ at 7¼ inches; 4¾ at 9 inches; 4¾ at 9½ inches; 5¼ at 9 inches; and 5 at 10 inches or the total length of the specimen.

FAMILY, XXII—PSEUDOCHROMIDES, *Mull. and Trosch.*

Branchiostegals from five to seven: pseudobranchiæ. Body more or less elongated. Eyes more or less lateral. Cleft of mouth oblique. Bones on the head unarmed or obtuse points on the opercle: head not cuirassed. The suborbital ring of bones articulates with the preopercle. Teeth in the jaws, present or absent on the vomer or palatines. Dorsal fin consisting of two portions which are connected, usually more rays than spines: anal similar to, or of less extent than the soft dorsal: ventrals thoracic or jugular: pectorals without appendages. Body scaled. Scales feebly cycloid or ctenoid. Lateral-line interrupted or incomplete. Air-vessel present or absent. Pyloric appendages, when present, in small numbers.

Bleeker, with much reason, objects to the union of the Genus *Opisthognathus* with the *Pseudochromides.* He considers the OPISTHOGNATHIDÆ as forming a distinct family, intermediate between the BLENNIIDÆ and PSEUDOCHROMIDES, and distinguished by having a scaleless head, cycloid scales, edentulous palate. Ventral fins well developed and jugular, possessing five soft rays, the two anterior of which are simple, thick, and elongated: dorsal and anal spines very weak and flexible, whilst the number of rays in the anal about equals those of the soft dorsal: caudal with twelve branched rays.

SYNOPSIS OF GENERA.

1. *Opisthognathus.* Cleft of mouth large. Palate edentulous. Scales cycloid. Lateral-line incomplete. Red Sea, those of India to the Malay Archipelago, also Brazils.

2. *Pseudochromis.* Lower jaw the longer. Teeth in jaws, vomer, and palate. Scales ctenoid. Lateral-line interrupted.

Genus, 1—OPISTHOGNATHUS, *Cuv.*

Gnathypops, Gill.

Branchiostegals six: pseudobranchiæ. Body more or less elongated, and posteriorly rather compressed. Upper profile of snout parabolic. Eyes lateral, large. Cleft of mouth deep, the upper jaw being either produced in a styliform process to beyond the angle of the preopercle, or truncated a little behind the level of the hind edge of the eye. Fine teeth in jaws, with an outer enlarged row: palate edentulous. Dorsal and anal spines weak and flexible (10-13), rays (15-17) similar to those of the anal: anal with two flexible spines: ventrals jugular: pectoral rays branched. Scales cycloid, small. Lateral-line not continued so far as the caudal fin. Air-vessel small. Cæcal appendages absent.

Geographical distribution.—Red Sea, those of India to the Malay Archipelago and beyond, also Brazil.

This Genus has been subdivided by Mr. Gill into (1) those species in which the maxilla is produced backwards into a styliform process, (2) such as have the maxilla truncated (*Gnathypops*).

SYNOPSIS OF SPECIES.

1. *Opisthognathus nigromarginatus*, D. $\frac{11}{16}$, A. 16-18. Maxilla produced backwards to beyond angle of preopercle. Buff marbled with darker. Dorsal fin light with a black ovate spot between the fourth and eighth dorsal spines. Red Sea to the Malay Archipelago.

2. *Opisthognathus Rosenbergii*, D. $\frac{11}{17}$, A. $\frac{2}{?}$. Maxilla truncated, reaching to just behind posterior edge of eye. Marbled: dorsal and anal fins black edged, the former with four or five large blotches along its base. Madras to the Malay Archipelago.

1. Opisthognathus nigromarginatus, Plate LVII, fig. 5.

Rüppell. Atl. Fische, p. 114, t. xxviii, f. 4; Swainson, Fishes, ii, p. 278; Günther, Catal. ii, p. 254; Klunz. Verh. z. b. Ges. Wien, 1871, p. 486.

Opisthognathus Sonneratii, Cuv. Règ. Anim.; Cuv. and Val. xi, p. 498; Swainson, Fishes, ii, p. 278; Jerdon, M. J. L. and Sc. 1851, p. 144.

Opisthognathus Cuvieri,* Val. Cuv. Règ. Anim. Ill. Poiss. pl. 78, f. 3 (? C. and V. xi, p. 498).

B. vi, D. $\frac{11}{16}$, P. 20, V. 1/5, A. 16-18, C. 12.

* Some error may have occurred in Cuv. and Val. as the figure, pl. 78, f. 3, does not represent the colours attributed to *O. Cuvieri.* I obtained the *O. Cuvieri* at Madras, but have mislaid it. Amongst Sir W. Elliot's drawings are three of this species, D. 25, A. 17. The maxilla is produced backwards, as in *O. nigromarginatus*, and the membrane has the same black marks. Body buff colour, with an irregular chestnut band along the side, and two or three more of whitish spots: head with white spots. Dorsal fin

Length of head 1/4, of caudal 1/9 to 1/10, height of body 1/6 of the total length. *Eyes*—diameter 1/4 of length of head, 1/2 a diameter from end of snout, and 1/4 of a diameter apart. Greatest width of the head is rather above 1/2 its length. Snout obtuse: cleft of mouth commences anteriorly opposite the middle of the eyes: the maxilla is elongated and reaches at its posterior extremity to the base of the pectoral fin, it has a membraneous connection with the cheek. Opercles entire. *Teeth*—in a rather large row of curved ones in either jaw, with a few villiform ones posteriorly at the symphysis. *Fins*—dorsal spines weak, not quite so high as the rays. Pectoral as long as 4/9 of length of head: ventral slightly longer. Caudal rounded. *Scales*—small. *Lateral-line*—ceases below middle of dorsal fin. *Colours*—yellowish marbled with brown, inside of upper jaw with two deep bluish bands on a white ground, one of which shows along the upper edge of the maxilla. Dorsal fin with a dark blue ovate spot between its fourth and eighth spines, cloudy marks and spots over the fin: base of anal light coloured, externally dark.

Habitat.—Red Sea, seas of India.

2. Opisthognathus Rosenbergii, Plate LVIII, fig. 5.

Bleeker, Nias, p. 220; Günther, Catal. ii, p. 256.
Gnathypops Rosenbergii, Bleeker, Opisthognathoidei (1873), p. 9, fig. 1.
Natsudi, Tam.

B. vi, D. $\frac{11}{14}$, P. 21, V. 1/5, A. $\frac{3}{14}$, C. 12, L. l. 76.

Length of head $4\frac{1}{4}$, of caudal $6\frac{1}{4}$, height of body 5 in the total length. *Eyes*—diameter $3\frac{3}{4}$ in length of head, 1/2 a diameter from end of snout, and 1/6 of a diameter apart. Greatest width of head equals 4/7 of its length, and its height its length excluding the snout. Snout obtuse. Cleft of mouth commences anteriorly opposite the middle of the eye: the maxilla (the length of which equals that of the postorbital portion of the head) reaches to rather beyond the vertical from the hind edge of the eye, it is truncated and does not nearly extend to the angle of the preopercle. Opercles entire. *Teeth*—villiform opposite the symphysis in either jaw, with an outer row of enlarged and somewhat curved ones in either jaw (largest in the upper), which are continued along their rami. *Fins*—dorsal spines weak, and not so high as the rays. Pectoral as long as the head behind the eye. Ventral reaches more than half way to vent. Caudal rounded. *Scales*—about 26 rows below the lateral-line to the commencement of the anal fin, none above it so far as the end of the spinous dorsal. *Lateral-line*—on raised scales, smaller than those on the body, the tubes are short and unbranched. *Colours*—appear to vary somewhat, the one figured (life-size) from Madras, has the body somewhat blotched, the dorsal and anal fins edged with black, and four large black blotches on the lower two-thirds of that fin: ventrals black. In a drawing amongst Sir W. Elliot's collection the dorsal and caudal are blacker, with five white bands on the former, and two white spots on the latter fin. Bleeker's figure shows five black blotches along the lower half of the dorsal fin, and the caudal white with two wide black bands.

Habitat.—Seas of India to the Malay Archipelago. The one figured is the only one I obtained at Madras. It is probably a small species, and apparently rare.

Genus, 2—Pseudochromis, *Rüpp.*

Labristoma, Swains.; *Leptochromis*, Bleeker.

Branchiostegals six: pseudobranchiæ. Body rather elongated and compressed. Eyes lateral. Cleft of mouth slightly oblique, lower jaw the longer. Jaws with a single row of teeth laterally, an outer enlarged row anteriorly in premaxillaries, canines in the lower jaw: teeth on vomer and palate. Preopercle entire. A single dorsal fin having a few (2-7) spines anteriorly: pectoral rays branched: ventrals thoracic. Scales of moderate size. Air-vessel present. Pyloric appendages absent.

Geographical distribution.—Red Sea, seas of India to the Malay Archipelago.

SYNOPSIS OF INDIVIDUAL SPECIES.

1. *Pseudochromis xanthochir*, D. $\frac{3}{26}$, A. $\frac{3}{15}$, L. l. 41, L. tr. $\frac{5}{12}$. First six dorsal rays unbranched. Olive colour: dorsal with yellow spots, anal and base of caudal with brown ones, outer half of caudal yellow.

1. Pseudochromis xanthochir, Plate LVIII, fig. 6.

Bleeker, Celebes, p. 443, and Revis. Pseudochr. p. 17, t. 1, f. 3, 4; Günther, Catal. ii, p. 257.

B. vi, D. $\frac{3}{26}$, P. 17, V. 1/5, A. $\frac{3}{15}$, C. 17, L. l. 41, L. tr. $\frac{5}{12}$.

Length of head $3\frac{3}{4}$, of caudal $5\frac{1}{4}$, height of body $3\frac{2}{3}$ in the total length. *Eyes*—diameter $4\frac{1}{2}$ in length of head, 1 to $1\frac{1}{2}$ diameters from end of snout, and 1 apart. Greatest width of head equals 1/2 its length, and its height equals its length excluding the snout. The maxilla reaches to below the first third of the eye. Preopercle slightly crenulated at its angle: four rows of scales between the eye and angle of the preopercle. *Teeth*—in a

blackish with white spots, and a large blue ocellus, having a circular white edge extending from the fourth to the ninth dorsal spines. Anal black, with a white base. Caudal light in two specimens, dark in the third. They are from $1\frac{1}{2}$ to 5 inches in length. Jerdon, from his remarks, evidently considered that this is merely a variation in the colours of *O. Sonneratii*=*O. nigromarginatus*; Dr. Günther considers it "a very different species."

single row laterally in either jaw, anteriorly an enlarged outer row in the premaxillaries, and two large canines in the mandibles: a little obtuse on vomer: with rounded crowns on palatines. *Fins*—dorsal spines short, third the longest, and about half as high as the first ray, the first 11 to 15 of which are unbranched: the end of the fin rather pointed. Pectoral as long as the head excluding the snout, ventral slightly longer. Caudal rounded. *Scales*—finely ctenoid. *Colours*—of a dull olive, the upper half of the soft dorsal with numerous yellow spots, the outer half of anal with brown ones. Caudal yellow in its last half, its base with brown spots between the rays.

This species appears to be closely allied to if not identical with *Pseudochromis fuscus*, Mull. and Trosch. Hor. Ich. 1849. p. 24, t. iv, f. 2, but the base of the pectoral is said to be black, and the dorsal and anal spots blue-streaks. None appear to exist on the caudal fin. The height of the body and length of head are given at 1/4 each of the total, and the snout is less than the diameter of the eye.

Black finned variety, D. $\frac{3}{[illegible]}$, A. $\frac{3}{15}$, L. l. 41. Dorsal and anal fins black edged, last half of caudal black.

Pseudochromis adustus, Mull. and Trosch. Hor. Ich. iii, p. 23, t. iv, f. 2, differs in that most of its dorsal rays are said to be branched, if such can be considered a sufficient reason for constituting a species. In some specimens a few or even a single ray is here and there divided, but it does not appear to me that any strict rule exists.*

Habitat.—Andaman islands where it is not rare, to perhaps the Philippines: the specimen figured (life-size) is from the former locality.

* I gave the British Museum specimens from the Andamans, they are labelled *P. adustus*.

FAMILY, XXIII—BATRACHIDÆ, *Swainson*.

Pediculati, pt., Cuv.

Branchiostegals six: pseudobranchiæ present. Body low and more or less elongated: head large: the muciferous system well developed. Gills three. The gill-openings narrow, in the form of a slit before the pectoral fin. Opercles armed. Teeth conical, and of moderate size or small. First dorsal with few spines: the second and the anal with many rays: ventral with two rays, jugular: pectorals not pediculated. Scales, when present, small. Air-vessel present.

Swainson formed the Family BATRACHIDÆ (Fishes, ii, p. 282), or "Bleany Bullheads," as he termed them, in 1839.

Geographical distribution.—Coasts of tropical and temperate regions.

These carnivorous fishes apparently delight in mud and dirty water, they frequent the shores ascending tidal rivers and estuaries. Dr. Cantor observes that at Pinang "the natives attribute poisonous qualities to these fishes, and reject them even as manure," Catal. p. 206. They are, however, eaten at Bombay by the poorer classes. Dr. Günther observes in the Zool. Record (1864, p. 155). "Dr. Günther has described a second species of this Genus (*Thalassophryne* belonging to this family) *Th. reticulatus* from the Pacific coast of Panama (Proc. Zool. Soc. 1864, p. 150). On examining this fish, he discovered a most singular apparatus which structurally is as perfect a poison-organ as that of the venomous serpents. Each operculum terminates in a long spine similar to the two dorsal spines: each spine is perforated at the extremity and at the base, and has a canal in its interior. The canal leads to a sac at the base of each spine, in which a considerable quantity of the poisonous substance was found: on the slightest pressure it flowed freely from the opening of the spine. The sacs are not the secretory organs, but merely the reservoirs in which the fluid secreted accumulates. The author believes he has found evidence that the real organ of secretion is the system of muciferous channels, or at least some portion of it." Captain Dow remarks (Proc. Zool. Soc. 1865, p. 667), "The natives seemed quite familiar with the existence of the spines, and of the emission from them of a poison, which, when introduced into a wound, caused fever; but in no case was a wound caused by one of them known to result seriously. The slightest pressure of the finger at the base of the spine caused the poison to jet a foot or more from the opening of the spine."

SYNOPSIS OF INDIVIDUAL GENUS.

1. *Batrachus*, as defined.

GENUS, 1—BATRACHUS, *Bl. Schn.*

Branchiostegals six. Body anteriorly somewhat cylindrical, and posteriorly compressed; head broad, depressed. Gill-openings narrow. Eyes lateral. Gape of mouth wide. Gill covers with several spines. Teeth on jaws, vomer, and palate. No distinct canines. First dorsal with three strong spines. Scales, if present, very minute. Air-vessel divided into two lateral parts. Pyloric appendages absent. Vertebræ [illegible].

Cantor observes that these fishes live some period after removal from the water.

SYNOPSIS OF SPECIES.

1. *Batrachus grunniens*, D. 3 | 20-22, A. 15-18. Four, occasionally only three, opercular spines. A foramen in the axilla. Brown, marbled. Seas of India to the Malay Archipelago.
2. *Batrachus Gangene*, D. 3 | 20-22, A. 16-18. Four opercular spines. No foramen in axilla. Reddish-brown, marbled. Estuaries of the Ganges and large Burmese rivers.

1. **Batrachus** grunniens, Plate LIX, fig. 1.

Cottus grunniens, Var. B. Linn. Mus. Ad. Fr. ii, p. 65, and Syst. p. 1209.
Cottus grunniens, Bloch, t. 179; Lacép. iii, p. 232; Shaw, Zool. iv, p. 256.
Batrachus grunniens, Bl. Schn. p. 43; Cuv. Règ. Anim.; Cuv. and Val. xii, p. 466; Cantor, Catal. p. 20[illegible]; Bleeker, Rioaw. p. 487; Peters, Monats. Ak. Wiss. Berlin, 1868, p. 270; Steind. Ak. Wien, ix, 1870, p. 561.
Batrachus trispinosus, Günther, Catal. iii, p. 169; Day, Fish. Malabar, p. 120; Kner, Novara Fische, p. 189.

Batrachus Dussumieri, Jerdon, M. J. L. and Sc. 1851, p. 144; ? Cuv. and Val. xii, p. 474, pl. 367.

B. vi, D. 3 | 20-22, P. 21, V. 1/2, A. 15-18, C. 15.

Length of head 3½, of caudal 5½, height of body 5 in the total length. *Eyes*—diameter 1/5 of length of head, nearly 1 diameter from end of snout, and 1½ apart. Head depressed, its greatest width equals its length behind the middle of the eyes. Gill covers with four backwardly directed spines, two on the opercle and two on the subopercle, the inferior of these last being often indistinct (*B. trispinosus*), sometimes only two spines are visible on the opercles. Snout broad and depressed, surrounded by a wreath of tentacles, those above the orbit very distinct. The maxilla extends to below the posterior margin of the orbit. A round foramen in the upper part of the axilla. *Teeth*—in several sharp, pointed rows in both jaws, becoming a single row laterally, also present in one or two rows on vomer and in a single row on palatines. *Fins*—first dorsal triangular, spines moderately strong, the second the longest: caudal wedge-shaped. *Air-vessel*—in two rounded lateral portions, connected across the body of the vertebra. *Colours*—yellowish, marbled with darker.

B. Dussumieri, C. V., may be a distinct species, known by having narrow bands of villiform teeth on the palatines.

Habitat.—Seas of India (most numerous along the Malabar coast) to the Malay Archipelago. The specimen figured is 7½ inches in length.

2. **Batrachus Gangene,** Plate LX, fig. 1.

Batrachoides Gangene, Ham. Buch. Fish. Ganges, pp. 34, 365, pl. 14, f. 8.
Batrachus grunniens, Günther,* Catal. iii, p. 168 (not Bl. Schn.); Day, Fishes of Malabar, p. 119.

B. vi, D. 3 | 20-22, P. 21, V. 1/2, A. 16-18, C. 15.

Length of head 3⅓, of caudal 7½ to 8, height of body 4 to 4¼ in the total length. *Eyes*—diameter 1/7 to 1/8 of length of head, 3 diameters from end of snout, and 3½ apart. Head broad, depressed, its greatest width nearly equal to its length. Maxilla reaches to below the hind edge of the orbit. Four backwardly directed spines on the gill-covers, two being on the opercle, and the other two on the subopercle. Snout broad, depressed, surrounded by tentacles which are most distinct along the edge of the mandibles, some are also round the eye, and numerous fine ones over the surface of the head. No foramen in axilla. *Teeth*—two or more rows of teeth in the centre of either jaw, a single row laterally, those in the mandibles the largest and directed a little inwards: two rows of teeth on vomer: a single one on palatines. *Fins*—as in the last species. *Colours*—light reddish-brown, marbled with darker.

Hamilton Buchanan observes that this fish "is found in the salt-water estuaries of the Ganges, is an ugly animal, does not exceed a span in length, and when frightened emits a remarkable croaking noise."

Habitat.—Estuaries of the Ganges and other large Indian and Burmese rivers; attaining at least a foot in length. The specimen figured is from Calcutta.

* See note on dentition of palate, Günther, An. and Mag. 1872, ix, p. 459.

FAMILY, XXIV—PEDICULATI, *Cuv.*

Branchiostegals five or six: pseudobranchiæ absent. Skeleton fibro-osseus. Head and anterior portion of the body large, the former depressed or compressed. Gills two and a half or three and a half: gill-opening reduced to a small foramen, situated in or near the axilla. Eyes superior or lateral. Teeth minute, villiform, or cardiform. The spinous dorsal, when present, composed of a few isolated spines: the carpal bones prolonged, forming a sort of arm for the pectoral fin: ventrals, when present, jugular, with four or five soft rays. Skin smooth, or covered with small spines or tubercles. Air-vessel present or absent. Pyloric appendages few or absent.

Bleeker agrees with Gill in considering the LOPHIOIDEI, CHIRONECTEOIDEI, and MALTHEOIDEI as forming distinct families. *Antennarius* belonging to the CHIRONECTEOIDEI, and *Halieutæa* to the MALTHEOIDEI.

SYNOPSIS OF GENERA.

1. *Antennarius.* Head and body compressed. Teeth on palate. Gills lateral. Three isolated dorsal spines, the anterior of which may be rudimentary or absent. Air-vessel present. Seas of tropical regions.

2. *Halieutæa.* Head and body strongly compressed. No teeth on palate. Gills on upper surface of body. No air-vessel. Seas of India to the Malay Archipelago and beyond.

Genus, 1—ANTENNARIUS, *(Comm.) Cuv.*

Chironectes, pt. Cuv.

Head large, elevated, and compressed. Only one half of the anterior branchial arch provided with lamellæ. Cleft of mouth nearly vertical. Eyes lateral. Gill-openings lateral. Cardiform teeth in the jaws and palate. The spinous dorsal in the form of three isolated spines, the anterior of which, situated upon the snout, is modified into a tentacle; the second dorsal of moderate length; anal short. Body smooth, granulated, or covered with minute spines, and sometimes with cutaneous tentacles. Air-vessel large and simple. Pyloric appendages absent.

These fishes, due to their mode of progression, have a wide geographical range. Their pediculated pectoral fins allow them to walk or hop over moist ground, or slimy rocks in quest of their prey, and even clasp pieces of wood or seaweeds, attached to which they often become carried away from the shore by currents, and are sometimes observed far out at sea. Although bad swimmers, M. Dussumier observes that they inflate themselves and float on the water like a *Diodon*. Sir Emerson Tennent gives a figure of *A. nummifer*, from Ceylon, and observes that it belongs to the Family of "Anglers" which conceal themselves in the mud, displaying only the erectile first ray, situated on the head, and which bears an excrescence on its extremity resembling a worm or piece of meat. By agitating this, smaller fishes are attracted and fall a prey to the artful angler.

These fishes, owing to the diversities of colour in the same species, to the change of the form of spines on the body with age, and to the abnormal increase or decrease in the number of rays are difficult to discriminate one from another. The *A. nummifer*, for instance, has P. 13 in Madras specimens. I have examined some in the British Museum and find the following: in one from Aden 6½ inches long P. 12: in one from N.W. coast of Africa P. 11: one from St. Helena P. 10: in others from the Malay Archipelago and China P. 10: at once showing that such variations should not be admitted in constituting species.

SYNOPSIS OF SPECIES.*

1. *Antennarius hispidus*, D. 3 | 12, P. 10, A. 7. Skin rough. Yellow, with brown spots and streaks radiating from the eye and over the body and fins. Seas of India to the Malay Archipelago and beyond.

2. *Antennarius nummifer*, D. 3 | 12, P. 10-13, A. 7. Skin rough. Grayish-brown, with a black ocellus on the side, another at base of middle of dorsal fin. Fins spotted. East coast of Africa, seas of India to the Malay Archipelago and beyond.

3. *Antennarius marmoratus*, D. 3 | 12, P. 10, A. 7. Skin smooth, but with fleshy excrescences. Colours various. Red Sea, East coast of Africa, seas of India, to the Malay Archipelago and beyond.

1. **Antennarius hispidus**, Plate LX, fig. 2.

Lophius hispidus, Bl. Schn. p. 142.
Lophius histrio, Russell, Fish. Vizag. i, p. 12, and *Kappa mura moia*, pl. xix.
Chironectes hispidus, Cuv. Mém. Mus. iii, p. 428, t. xvii, f. 2.
Chironectes hispidus, Cuv. and Val. xii, p. 407.

* Dr. Günther's list of Ceylon Fishes in Sir Emerson Tennent's Nat. Hist. of Ceylon, p. 361, includes, besides those named below, *A. pinniceps*, *A. Commersonii*, *A. multiocellatus*, and *A. bigibbus*, but *A. nummifer* is not included unless as *A. multiocellatus*.

Antennarius hispidus, Cantor, Catal. p. 203; Bleeker, Moluk. p. 289, and Atl. Ich. v, p. 14, t. cxciv, f. 2. and cxcviii, f. 1; Günther, Catal. ii, p. 189.

B. vi, D. 3 | 12, P. 10, V. 5, A. 7, C. 9.

Mouth subvertical, lower jaw a little compressed, the width of the gape of the mouth exceeding that of the cleft. *Eyes*—high up, from 2 to 2½ diameters from end of snout. *Teeth*—cardiform in both jaws and on the palatines. *Fins*—first dorsal spine about as long as the second, and ending in fleshy knob, second about as long as the third, and each with a skinny flap posteriorly, that from the third nearly or quite joining the second dorsal fin, the last three rays of which latter fin are branched. Pectoral and ventral rays unbranched. Last six anal rays branched, as are also those of the caudal. *Scales*—skin universally roughened, with spinate points extending over the fins, except some of the rays of the pectoral, ventral, and caudal. *Lateral-line*—ceases below middle of second dorsal. *Colours*—yellow, with brown spots and streaks, some radiating from the eye, others descending from the back and many down the sides. Small ones and blotches or spots on the fins.

Habitat.—Seas of India to the Malay Archipelago and beyond.

2. Antennarius nummifer, Plate LIX, fig. 2.

Chironectes nummifer, Cuv. Mém. Mus. iii, p. 430, pl. xvii, fig. 4; Cuv. and Val. xii, p. 425; Rüpp. N. W. Fische, p. 141.

? *Chironectes chlorostigma*, (Ehrenb.) Cuv. and Val. xii, p. 421.

Antennarius nummifer, Günther, Catal. iii, p. 195; Day, Fish. Malabar, p. 121; Bleeker, Atl. Ich. v, p. 18, t. 198, f. 2; Klunz. Verh. z. b. Ges. Wien, 1871, p. 499.

B. vi, D. 3 | 12, P. 10-13, V. 5, A. 7, C. 9.

Mouth almost vertical, with the lower jaw compressed towards its extremity, the width of the gape equalling the extent of the cleft. Length of lower jaw equals the length of the third spine of the dorsal fin. *Eye*—high up, but little more than 1 diameter from end of snout. *Teeth*—cardiform in both jaws and on the palatines. *Fins*—first dorsal spine not quite so long as the second, and ending in a fringed extremity, second rather above 1/2 as long as third, which latter has a flap of skin posteriorly, which does not extend so far as to the base of the second dorsal, the last two rays of which are divided at their outer extremities. Pectoral with 13 unbranched rays. Ventral with five unbranched rays. Anal, commencing under middle of second dorsal, has branched rays, its last just reaches the base of the caudal. Caudal rounded, its rays branched: last dorsal rays just reach the base of the caudal fin. *Scales*—skin universally roughened, with points extending over fins except some of the rays of the pectoral, ventral, and caudal. *Lateral-line*—ceases below the commencement of the second dorsal. *Colours*—grayish-brown, having a purplish tinge: a black ocellus having a yellow edge behind and above the end of the base of the pectoral fin. Fins yellow, the dorsal with a black yellow-edged ocellus below its seventh and eighth rays, its end with black bands and spots, as have also the pectoral, ventral, caudal, and anal fins. Tongue whitish, with green marks: eyes golden.

Bleeker, also Günther in Catal. ii, p. 195, give P. 10 to this species. Playfair, in the "Fishes of Zanzibar," states 12. I find 13 in the Madras species, this variation has already been referred to (p. 271).

Habitat.—Red Sea, East coast of Africa, seas of India to the Malay Archipelago and beyond. Grows to at least 6¾ inches in length. The one figured (life-size) is from Madras.

3. Antennarius marmoratus.

Lophius histrio, var. *marmoratus*, Bl. Schn. p. 142.

Chironectes laevigatus, Cuv. Mém. Mus. iii, p. 423, pl. xvi, f. 1; Cuv. and Val. xii, p. 399.

Lophius geographicus, Quoy and Gaim. Voy. Uranie, i, p. 355, pl. 65, f. 3.

Chironectes marmoratus, Less. Voy. Coq. Zool. ii, p. 145, Poiss. pl. xvi, f. 2; Cuv. and Val. xii, p. 402; Tem. and Schleg. Fauna Japon. Poissons, p. 159, pl. 81, f. 1.

Chironectes pictus, Cuv. and Val. xii, p. 393, pl. 364.

Chironectes tumidus, Cuv. and Val. xii, p. 397.

Chironectes nesogallicus, Cuv. and Val. xii, p. 401.

Antennarius nitidus, Bennett, Zool. Journ. iii, p. 375, t. ix, f. 2.

Chironectes pictus, var. *villosus*, Richards. Voy. Ereb. and Terr. Fishes, p. 15, pl. ix, f. 3, 4.

Lophius histrio, Gronov. ed. Gray, p. 48 (not syn.).

Antennarius marmoratus, Günther, Catal. iii, p. 185; Day, Fish. Malabar, p. 121; Bleeker, Atl. Ich. v, p. 23, t. 198, f. 4, t. 199, fig. 1 (see synonyms); Kner, Novara Fische, p. 192.

B. vi, D. 3 | 12, P. 9-10, V. 5, C. 9, A. 7, Vert. 9/9.

The variations in this species due to age or locality are so considerable that two specimens are very rarely found possessing complete similarity. *Eyes*—about 1 diameter from end of snout. The skin may be smooth, minutely or distinctly granulated, whilst the length of the third dorsal spine varies from one-half to less than one-third of the height of the body. The anterior dorsal spine is short, slender, and terminating in a small knob having a minute tentacle attached to it, sometimes it is very short, or it may be entirely absent, the second and third spines are fringed on their summits. The last two dorsal rays branched, the last if laid backwards extends to or slightly beyond the root of the caudal. Skin usually smooth or sometimes granular, rarely rough. Head and body with cutaneous tentacles, those at the angle of the mouth and on the abdomen being the largest. Stomach a large sac. *Air-vessel*—large and simple. *Colours*—

vary, generally reddish-yellow marbled with brown, and brown spots mostly edged with white, radiating from the eye. Round white spots on sides, and on abdomen. In some the fins are banded. Iris golden, with radiating brown lines.

Habitat.—Red Sea, East coast of Africa, through the seas of India to the Malay Archipelago and beyond.

Genus, 2—Halieutæa, *Cuv. and Val.*

Astrocanthus, Swainson.

Branchiostegals six. Body and head depressed, the latter very large and broad, anteriorly forming the arc of a circle. Eyes antero-lateral. Cleft of mouth horizontal, rather wide, with the upper jaw rather protractile. A transverse bony ridge across snout, beneath which is a retractile tentacle. Gill opening near the axilla on the upper surface of the body. Gills two and a half: the anterior branchial arch destitute of laminæ, small teeth on jaws and tongue, palate edentulous. A short dorsal and also anal fin: fin rays unbranched. Body and head covered with small spines. Air-vessel and pyloric appendages absent.

"The union of the interopercle with the preorbital" is said by Dr. Günther to be "very singular, and unique in this order of fishes. A little before the suture between the inter- and sub- opercle the preopercle is joined to the former; it is the smallest of all the opercular pieces, and its limbs meet at a somewhat acute angle." (Catal. iii, p. 204.)

Bleeker found that the intestinal tract was much longer than the fish, and contained the remains of shells. (*Verh. Acad. Wetensch. Amsterdam, i, Japan*, p. 10.)

SYNOPSIS OF INDIVIDUAL SPECIES.

1. *Halieutæa stellata*, D. 4, A. 4. Superiorly and laterally covered with spines. Pinkish. Seas of India to the Malay Archipelago and beyond.

1. **Halieutæa stellata**, Plate LIV, fig. 1.

Lophius stellatus, Wahl. Skr. Nat. Kjöb. iv, p. 214, t. iii, fig. 3, 4; Bl. Schn. p. 142.

Lophius faujas, Lacép. i, p. 318, t. xi, fig. 2, 3.

Lophius muricatus, Shaw, Zool. v, p. 382, pl. 162.

Halieutæa stellata, Cuv. and Val. xii, p. 456, pl. 366; Temm. and Schlegel, Fauna Japon. Poissons, p. 160, pl. 72; Jerdon, M. J. L. and Sc. 1851, p. 150; Bleeker, Japan, p. 10, and Atl. Ich. vi, p. 4, t. 198, f. 3, and 200, f. 2; Günther, Catal. iii, p. 203.

Astrocanthus stellatus, Swainson, Fishes, ii, p. 331, fig. 108.

B. vi, D. 4, P. 13, V. 1/5, A. 4, C. 9, Vert. 7/10.

Eyes—lateral, with the interorbital space rather concave. A retractile tentacle at snout above the mouth and which has a trefoil extremity. Gill openings above the axilla in about the middle of the total length. *Fins*—dorsal fin situated in the third fifth of the total length, and slightly behind the pectorals. All the fin rays unbranched. *Scales*—body covered with rather distantly placed spines, each of which as a rule, has four or more roots, the lateral spines are the largest, and in the anterior half of the body have three or even four points at their outer edges. *Colours*—pinkish.

Jerdon observes that he only procured two specimens of this fish whilst in Madras. Whilst I was there it was by no means rare, but not attaining the size at which Bleeker has taken it in the Malay Archipelago.

Habitat.—Seas of India to the Malay Archipelago and beyond; it attains at least 8 inches in length. The one figured (life-size) is from Madras.

FAMILY, XXV—COTTIDÆ,* *Günther.*

Platicephalinæ (Sub. Fam.) **Swainson.**

Branchiostegals five to seven: pseudobranchiæ. Body oblong, compressed, or subcylindrical. Eyes lateral or partly directed upwards and outwards. Cleft of mouth lateral. Some of the bones of the head armed. Infraorbital bones articulate with the preopercle. Teeth villiform, no canines. Two separate dorsal fins or in two distinct portions, the spinous less developed than the soft or than the anal: ventrals thoracic, sometimes scarcely developed. Air-vessel generally absent. Pyloric appendages few, or in moderate numbers.

SYNOPSIS OF GENERA.

1. *Platycephalus*, as defined.

Genus, 1—PLATYCEPHALUS,† *Bl. Schn.*

Flat heads, or Crocodile Fishes.

Branchiostegals seven: pseudobranchiæ. Head broad, depressed, and armed with spines. Lower jaw the longer. Eyes lateral or superior. Villiform teeth in the jaws, vomer, and palatines, with larger ones sometimes internixed. Two dorsal fins, the first having a small isolated spine anterior to it: the soft portion similar to the anal: ventrals thoracic: no pectoral appendage. Scales present, ctenoid, small or rather so. Lateral-line complete, in some species armed with spines. Air-vessel absent. Pyloric appendages in moderate numbers.

These fishes are termed "Crocodile fishes" in Malabar, and wounds from their spines are dreaded because of the violent irritation they occasion. Immediately on being captured they are knocked on the head.

Their eyes are peculiar, in that the iris possesses two semicircular flaps, one above, the other below, the upper being usually the larger, they can be brought close one to the other, probably due to the stimulus of light.

The comparative width of the head to its length differs in individuals, also with age, becoming broader in the adult. In *P. insidiator* at 5½ and 6¾ inches the width of the head between the inner edges of the preopercular spines equals its length behind the eyes; at 14¼ inches it equals that of the head excluding the snout.

I have captured specimens full of well developed ova as early as February. These fishes are eaten by the lower classes of natives.

The subdivision of this genus into those having (1) two spines, or those (2) with more than two spines at the angle of the preopercle is open to this objection, some count the small one usually present at the base of the large spine, others consider it as forming the end of the spinate ridge. I have therefore thought it better to follow the division of whether the lateral-line is spined or smooth.

SYNOPSIS OF SPECIES.

A. *Lateral-line armed with spines.*

1. *Platycephalus scaber*, D. 1 | 7-8 | 12, A. 12, L. r. 105. Spines 55. Ridges on head spined. Largest preopercular spine if laid forwards would reach 1/2 way to orbit. Brownish. Seas of India to the Malay Archipelago.

2. *Platycephalus tuberculatus*, D. 1 | 7-8 | 11-12. A. 11-12, L. l. 53-55, having 15 to 20 spines in its first third. Ridges on head spined or serrated. Largest preopercular spine if laid forwards would reach 1/2 way to orbit. Brownish, with vertical bands. Seas of India.

* This family is not identical with the sub-Family *Cottini* of Dr. Sauvage (N. Arch. Mus. 1873, see p. 148 ante) who has divided the Family Triglidæ into the following groups:

I. SCORPÆNIDÆ. Dentition feeble, teeth villiform without canines. Infraorbital bones articulated moveably with the preopercle, never entirely covering the cheeks. Nasal bones small and free. Skin scaleless or scaled, sometimes spiny, never cuirassed. Ventrals thoracic, supported by a long pelvic bone, the two bones being in contact and fused together.
   a. *Scorpænii*:—as *Sebastes, Scorpæna, Pterois, Tæniunotus*, and group of *Apistes*.
   b. *Cottini*:—as *Hemitripterus, Synanceidium, Synanceia, Minous, Pelor*, group of *Cottus, Icelus, Triglops, Polycaulus, Hemilepidotus.*

II. PLATYCEPHALIDÆ. Head flattened and as if crushed. Body anteriorly depressed. Dentition feeble, no canines. Two dorsals: ventrals thoracic and widely separated. Pelvic bones wide asunder.
   a. *Platycephalus.*

III. TRIGLIDÆ. Infraorbital bones articulated in an almost immoveable manner with the preopercle and covering the entire cheek. Nasals soldered into a great plate and almost covering the snout. Ventrals thoracic and in contact.
   a. *Triglini*:—(1) body covered with ordinary scales, as *Trigla, Lepidotrigla, Prionotus, Bembras.*
   (2) body having scales and plates, as *Hoplichthys.*
   b. *Cataphracti*:—(1) an interparietal, as *Dactylopterus. Cephalacanthus.*
   (2) no interparietal, as *Agonus, Aspidophorus, Peristhedion.*

† *Uiu parti*, Tam.

3. *Platycephalus macracanthus*, D. 1 | 8 | 12, A. 12, L. l. 75, having 15 spines. Ridges on head spined or serrated. Largest preopercular spine if laid forwards would reach orbit. Brownish. Seas of India to Amboina.

B. *Lateral-line smooth.*

4. *Platycephalus insidiator*, D. 1 | 7 | 13, A. 13, L. l. 120. Ridges on head slightly spined. Two large spines at angle of preopercle. Brownish, caudal yellow with oblique black bands. Red Sea, seas of India to the Malay Archipelago and beyond.

5. *Platycephalus punctatus*, D. 1 | 8 | 12, A. 11-12, L. l. 110. Ridges on head spinate. Largest preopercular spine about 1/7 of length of head. Brown, banded and with black spots. Seas of India to Malay Archipelago.

6. *Platycephalus serratus*, D. 1 | 8 | 11-12, A. 11. Ridges on head serrated not spinate. Brownish, with vertical bands. Trincomalee.

7. *Platycephalus carbunculus*, D. 1 | 8 | 11-12, A. 11-12, L. l. 75-80. Brownish spotted. Seas of India to the Malay Archipelago.

A. *Lateral-line armed with spines.*

1. Platycephalus scaber, Plate LX, fig. 4.

Cottus scaber, Linn. Mus. Ad. Fred. ii, p. 66, and Syst. Nat. i, p. 451; Bloch, t. clxxx; Gmel. Linn. p. 1209.

Platycephalus scaber, Bl. Schn. p. 58; Cuv. and Val. iv, p. 249; Bleeker, Sclerop. p. 6; Jerdon, M. J. L. and Sc. 1851, p. 142; (Günther, Catal. ii, p. 187, not syn.); Kner, Novara Fische, p. 123; Peters, Monats. Akad. Berlin, 1868, p. 258; Sauvage, Mém. Mus. 1874, p. 59.

Callionymus, Russell, Fish. Vizag. i, p. 37, and *Irroa*, fig. xlvii.

Platycephalus vittatus, Cuv. and Val. ix, p. 462.

Platycephalus neglectus, Trosch. Wiegm. Arch. 1840, p. 187; Günther, Catal. ii, p. 187.

Vet-ool-pa-thy, Tam.

B. vi, D. 1 | 7-8 | 12, P. 21, V. 1/5, A. 12, C. 15, L. r. 105. Spines 55.

Length of head $3\frac{1}{2}$ to $3\frac{3}{4}$, of pectoral $7\frac{1}{2}$ to 8, of caudal 8, height of body 8 in the total length. *Eyes*—diameter $4\frac{1}{2}$ to $5\frac{3}{4}$ in length of head, $1\frac{1}{2}$ to $1\frac{3}{4}$ diameters from end of snout, and 2/3 of a diameter apart. Interorbital space concave. Greatest width of head equals $1\frac{3}{4}$ in its length, and its height equals 1/3 of its length. The maxilla extends to under the anterior 1/3 of the orbit: a sharp spine at the anterior superior edge of the orbit. Supraorbital margin serrated, and from it a spinate ridge goes to the occiput. A similar ridge passes from the hind edge of the eye to the shoulder: a third spiny ridge extends from the preorbital to the angle of the preopercle where there are two spines, the upper if laid forwards reaching 1/2 or 2/3 of the distance to the orbit, it has a third short spine anteriorly at its base. In a specimen 5 inches long the preopercular spine if laid forwards would reach as far as the orbit. No spines at nostrils, but in some specimens on the median ridge, opposite the nostrils are two small ones. Two opercular spines. *Teeth*—small in jaws, in two oval parallel patches, about as long as the diameter of the eye on the vomer: in an elongated band on either palatine. *Fins*—second dorsal spine equals $2\frac{1}{2}$ to 3 in the length of the head, and is not quite so high as the two next, second dorsal of about the same height as the first. Ventral nearly reaches the anal which commences slightly behind the vertical from that of the first dorsal ray. Caudal cut nearly square. *Scales*—from 4 to 5 rows between the lateral-line and base of first dorsal fin, each of those on the cheeks is furnished with a small spinate point, which in old individuals is occasionally subdivided into several as if serrated. *Lateral-line*—with about 55 rather strong spines directed backwards, and extending along its entire length, one being on every alternate scale. *Colours*—brownish, becoming dull white beneath, more or less distinct vertical bands pass from the back to the sides. First dorsal clouded with black, second dorsal spotted. Pectoral and ventral usually dark externally. Caudal greyish in its last half.

Platycephalus scaber, Günther=*P. rodericensis*, C. V. iv, p. 253. It is said of *P. punctatus*, C. V. (iv, p. 245) this species makes a sort of transition to the *scaber*: but it has not like the *scaber* the lateral-line spiny.

Habitat.—Seas of India to the Malay Archipelago and beyond. The specimen figured (7 inches long) is from Madras where it is common.

2. Platycephalus tuberculatus, Plate LX, fig. 5.

Cuv. and Val. iv, p. 258; Günther, Catal. ii, p. 186.

B. vi, D. 1 | 7-8 | 11-12, P. 21, V. 1/5, A. 11-12, C. 15, L. l. 53-55.

Length of head 1/3 to 4/13, of pectoral 1/8, of caudal 1/7, height of body 1/6 in the total length. *Eyes*—directed upwards and somewhat outwards, diameter $3\frac{3}{4}$ to 4 in the length of head, $1\frac{1}{4}$ to $1\frac{1}{2}$ diameters from end of snout, and 1/4 of a diameter apart. Interorbital space concave. Width of head between the preopercular spines equals $1\frac{1}{4}$ in its length. The maxilla extends to below the front quarter of the eye. Supraorbital margin serrated, and having two sharp spines anteriorly, from it posteriorly passes a serrated ridge towards the occiput, whilst a second goes from behind the eye to the upper opercular spine: a third serrated ridge passes from the preorbital to the angle of the preopercle. A few spines in the median line midway between eye and snout: a spinate ridge passes forwards from them on either side above the limbs of the premaxillaries. A serrated bony ridge goes across the opercle to a strong spine at the middle of its hind edge. Angle of preopercle with a strong spine which equals half the distance between its base and the orbit. This spine has one superiorly at its base at the end of the serrated ridge, and another a little longer inferiorly, and situated on the lower margin of the preopercle, which contains from 2 to 4 more decreasing in size anteriorly and all pointing backwards. The number and size of these lower spines varies. Several spines at the shoulder, and a strong one above the axilla. *Teeth*—villiform in jaws, in two oval parallel patches on the vomer, and in an elongated band on the palatines. *Fins*—second dorsal spine 2¼ in length of head, and not quite so high as the third, soft dorsal as high as the spinous. Ventral nearly reaches the anal, which last arises below the second dorsal: caudal slightly rounded. *Scales*—from 4 to 5 rows between the lateral-line and base of first dorsal fin: most of those on the cheeks have a rudimentary spine. *Lateral-line*—with from 15 to 20 spines in the first third of its course. *Colours*—brown, becoming lighter beneath, vertical bands pass from the back to the sides. First dorsal blackish brown: second dorsal spotted. Pectoral with brown spots in its upper two-thirds, and a black margin with a white edge along its lower border: outer half of ventrals gray.

The objection to considering this Cuv. and Val. fish is that it is observed that the lateral-line is nearly as spinate as in *P. scaber*. It is identical with the species thus named in the British Museum. *P. spinosus* according to a communication from Dr. Hubrecht has from 36 to 38 scales along the lateral-line.

Habitat.—Seas of India.

3. Platycephalus macracanthus, Plate LIX, fig. 3.

Bleeker, Versl. and Meded. Ak. Wet. Amsterd. 1867, p. 7, c fig.

B. vii, D. 1 | 8 | 12, P. 23, V. 1/5, A. 12, C. 13, L. l. [illegible], L. tr. 4/15, Spines 15.

Length of head 3⅓, of caudal 7½, height of body 7½ in the total length. *Eyes*—diameter 4¼ in length of head, 1½ diameters from end of snout, and about 1/2 a diameter apart. Interorbital space concave. Width of head between the preopercular spines equal to about 1/2 its length. Lower jaw the longer: the maxilla extends to below the first third of the eye. Supraorbital margin with six strong denticulations, and the ridge from it to occiput with about five more: ridge from eye to shoulder with about five spines: the one from preorbital to preopercular spine with six, (besides being serrated), its lower edge serrated. A small spine internal to the front nostril which is furnished with a cirrus. Spine at angle of preopercle reaching to the base of the pectoral, and having a short one inferiorly succeeded by another still more minute. *Teeth*—villiform in two parallel patches on vomer, and in a narrow band along either palatines. *Fins*—second dorsal spine 2¼ in length of head, and nearly as high as the commencement of the second dorsal. Pectoral 2¼ in length of head, ventral slightly longer. Anal commences below second ray of dorsal: caudal cut square. *Scales*—those on the head not spinate. *Lateral-line*—with about 15 small spines in the first portion of its course. *Colours*—brownish above, becoming dull white beneath, first dorsal and end of caudal darkish, second dorsal with brown spots on the rays.

Habitat.—Madras, Amboina. The specimen figured (life-size) is from Madras.

B. *Lateral-line smooth.*

4. Platycephalus insidiator.

Cottus insidiator, Forsk. p. 25; Gmel. Linn. 1213; Shaw, Zool. iv, p. 260.

Callionymus Indicus, Gmel. Linn. p. 1153; Russell, Fish. Vizag. ii, p. 36, and *Irrwa*, pl. xlvi.

Cottus spatula, Bl. t. 424.

Platycephalus insidiator, Bl. Schn. p. 59; Cuv. and Val. iv, p. 227; Rüpp. N. W. Fische, p. 102; Bleeker, Sclerop. p. 6; Temm. and Schleg. Fauna Japon. Poiss. p. 39, pl. 15, f. 1; Cantor, Catal. p. 37; Richards. Ich. China, p. 216; Jerdon, M. J. L. and Sc. 1851, p. 142; Günther, Catal. ii, p. 177; Day, Fishes of Malabar, p. 43; Kner, Novara Fische, p. 121; Klunz. Verh. z. b. Ges. Wien, 1870, p. 815.

Batrachus Indicus, Bl. Schn. p. 43.

Platycephalus spatula, Bl. Schn. p. 59.

Callionymus Indicus, Lacép. ii, p. 343.

Cottus Madagascariensis, Lacép. iii, p. 248, t. xi, f. 12; Shaw, Zool. iv, p. 261, pl. 37.

Callionymus chaca, Ham. Buch. pp. 133, 373.

Platycephalus endrachtensis, Quoy and Gaim. Voy. Freyc. Zool. p. 353; Cuv. and Val. iv, p. 240.

? *Platycephalus cultellatus*, Richards. Ich. China, p. 217.

Platycephalus chacca, Gray and Hard. Ind. Zool. ii, pl. 93, f. 2.

Irrwa, Tel.: *Ool-pa-thy*, Tam.: *Nga-paying-ki*, Mugh.: *A-ra-wul-dah or Chow-ara-dah*, And.

B. vii, D. 1 | 7 | 13, P. 17, V. 1/5, A. 13, C. 15, L. r. [illegible], L. tr. 12/24, Cæc. Pyl. 14, Vert. 12/15.

Length of head 3⅘, of caudal 7, height of body 7 in the total length. *Eyes*—superior, diameter 6¾ to 7 in length of head, 1⅓ diameters from end of snout, and 2 apart. Head strongly depressed, its upper surface being of a triangular shape, the base being a line drawn from one preopercular spine to its fellow, width of head at this place 3/4 of its length. Lower jaw slightly the longer: the maxilla reaches to below the middle of the orbit. Interorbital space flat or slightly concave, two ridges extending backwards from the orbit, the internal dividing over the occiput, whilst the external or temporal terminates at the shoulder in two blade-like spines. One spine exists at the anterior-superior angle of the orbit, none at nostrils, which are patent but not tubular. Preorbital with three raised grooves starting in a stellated form from a common centre. Preopercle with most of its surface forming a portion of the flattened upper plane of the head, and having two very strong spines at its angle, the inferior of which is the longest and sometimes equals the diameter of the eye. Opercle with two spines. *Fins*—first dorsal spines weak, the first slightly the longest, interspinous membrane very slightly emarginate. A small, stout, single spine before the first dorsal, and sometimes another fine one between it and second dorsal, the rays of which anteriorly are as high as the spines of the first dorsal. Caudal obtuse or even rounded. *Colours*—brownish above, becoming dirty white beneath: fins spotted. Caudal yellow, with a deep black band, having a white border obliquely crossing its upper lobe, a second along its lower lobe.

The specimen of *P. tasmanius* "(?) Half-grown, Madras, Presented by T. C. Jerdon, Esq., M.D." in the B. M. catalogue, is a young *P. insidiator* nearly 6 inches long.

Habitat.—Red Sea, East coast of Africa, seas of India to the Malay Archipelago and beyond; attaining at least a foot and a half in length.

5. Platycephalus punctatus, Plate LX, fig. 3.

Cuv. and Val. iv, p. 243; Bleeker, Sclerop. p. 25; Quoy and Gaim. Voy. Astrol. Poissons, p. 682, pl. x, f. 2; Günther, Catal. ii, p. 180.

Platycephalus Malabaricus, Cuv. and Val. iv, p. 245 (Günther, Catal. ii, p. 181, not synon.); Day, Fish. Malabar, p. 45; Kner, Novara Fische, p. 121.

B. vii, D. 1 | 8 | 12, P. 21, V. 1/5, A. 11-12, C. 13, L. l. [illegible], L. tr. 8/25.

Length of head $3\frac{1}{2}$ to $3\frac{2}{3}$, of caudal 8 to 9, height of body $6\frac{1}{2}$ in the total length. *Eyes*—diameter from 5 to $5\frac{1}{2}$ in the length of head, $1\frac{1}{2}$ to 2 diameters from end of snout, and 1/2 to 2/3 of a diameter apart. Interorbital space slightly concave. Width of head between the preopercular spines equals half its length. The maxilla extends to below first third of eye. Supraorbital margin with four or five teeth, the ridge from it towards occiput with two more small ones: ridge from eye to shoulder spine with three to four teeth: ridge from preorbital to preopercular spine with two or three teeth. A small spine internal to either front nostril. Spine at angle of preopercle strong, its length equalling about 1/7 of that of the head, superiorly it has a small one at its base, and inferiorly a large one directed slightly downwards as well as backwards. Posterior nostril rather tubular, anterior also tubular and with a valve which sometimes terminates in a short filament. A small spine above the axilla. *Teeth*—villiform in jaws, in two parallel bands on vomer, and in a long narrow patch along palatines. *Fins*—second spine of first dorsal not so high as the third to the sixth which are subequal in length, and 1/2 the length of the head: second dorsal anteriorly 3/4 the height of the spinous. Pectoral 1/2 and ventral 3/4 of length of head. Anal commences before second or third ray of dorsal. Caudal cut square. *Scales*—about 10 rows between the lateral-line and base of the spinous dorsal: those on the head and cheeks have no trace of any spine. *Lateral-line*—smooth in its entire extent, tubes with one or two simple branches. *Colours*—brown, becoming lighter beneath: four or five wide and dark bands pass from the back to the middle of the sides, and numerous black spots over head and body. First dorsal stained nearly black, second dorsal and anal yellowish, the first with brown points. Pectoral covered with dark markings so as to appear almost black. Ventral dark in its last two-thirds. Caudal dark.

The distinction between *P. punctatus* and *P. Malabaricus* is said to be that the latter has one more spine on the ridge of the infraorbital bone. The type specimen of the latter at Paris has L. l. [illegible]. The specimen figured has only two spines along each infraorbital bone.

Habitat.—Seas of India to the Malay Archipelago; the specimen figured ($9\frac{1}{2}$ inches long) is from Malabar, it attains at least 15 inches in length.

6. Platycephalus serratus.

Cuv. and Val. iv, p. 259; Günther, Catal. ii, p. 183.

B. vii, 1 | 8 | 11-12, P. 19, V. 1/5, A. 11, C. 13.

Length of head 1/4 of the total length. Interorbital space 1/4 of the transverse diameter of the eye. The crests on the various bones of the head and suborbital ring are serrated but destitute of spines. The supraorbital ridge is elevated: that across the opercle is smooth. The ridge from the eye to the angle of the preopercle is elevated and finely denticulated, above it is another less pronounced and smooth. Upper spine at the angle of the preopercle the largest, it is succeeded by a shorter one, and on the border of the interopercle are two more small ones, it does not appear to have any spine directed anteriorly, or if it has it is but a little one. *Teeth*—fine. *Scales*—with rough borders. *Lateral-line*—smooth. *Colours*—reddish-brown, with six or eight irregular brown bands descending from the back to the white abdomen. Fins gray, with black points. On the top of the dorsal a black blotch. Ventrals bluish above and whitish below.

Habitat.—Trincomalee, to 7 inches in length.

7. Platycephalus carbunculus.

Cuv. and Val. ix, p. 461; Cantor, Catal. p. 39.
Platycephalus Malabaricus, Günther, Catal. ii, p. 181, pt. (not synon.)

B. vii, D. 1 | 8 | 11-12, P. 20, V. 1/5, A. 11-12, C. 13, L. l. [illegible], L. tr. 6/25.

Length of head 3 to $3\frac{1}{2}$, of caudal 5 to 6, height of body $6\frac{1}{2}$ in the total length. *Eyes*—diameter 1/4 of length of head, 1 diameter from end of snout, and 1/4 of a diameter apart. Supraorbital edge with one or two spines anteriorly, and a strongly serrated edge, posteriorly from the orbit the line to the occiput has six, and the one to the shoulder spine five more spines. From the preorbital exists a raised line armed with 10 or 12 spines going to the two preopercular spines, the upper (which has a small one at its base) is longer than the lower. A pair, or even three, of turbinal spines, no nasal tentacle. Two well marked opercular spines, and another in the axilla. *Fins*—ventral reaches the origin of the anal: caudal cut square. *Scales*—ctenoid, present on the head, but destitute of spines or raised points. *Lateral-line*—smooth. *Colours*—brownish, with numerous brown spots: three vertical bands on the body, one broad one through the anterior half of the first dorsal to the abdomen, the second through the middle of the second dorsal, and the third over the free portion of the tail: opercle dark: posterior half of first dorsal black: second dorsal spotted: pectoral with several lines of spots and a dark mark near its base: caudal dark, with one or two ill-defined vertical bands.

Habitat.—Western coast of India to the Malay Archipelago. Cantor observes that it occurs, although not numerously, at all seasons at Pinang, and it is eaten by the natives: his specimens were up to $6\frac{1}{2}$ inches in length.

FAMILY, XXVI—CATAPHRACTI, *Cuv.*

Branchiostegals one to six: pseudobranchiæ present or absent. Infraorbital bones articulate with the preopercle. Head and body more or less angular, cuirassed with plates, or keeled scales entirely cover the body. The opercular pieces may or may not be anchylosed to one another. Teeth present or absent in the jaws, in one species present on the vomer. One or two dorsal fins: pectorals may be simple, with or without free rays, or they may be divided by a notch into two portions, and elongated or not so: ventrals thoracic, with five or less rays. Lateral-line present, or absent. Air-vessel present or absent. Pyloric appendages, when present, in small, moderate numbers, or numerous.

SYNOPSIS OF GENERA.

1. *Dactylopterus.* A long spine at angle of preopercle. Dorsal fin with detached rays anteriorly: pectorals very elongate, with the anterior portion detached and shorter than the rest of the fin.

2. *Pegasus.* No spine at angle of preopercle. Pectorals rather elongate and with unbranched rays.

Genus, 1—DACTYLOPTERUS* (*Lacèp.*).

Branchiostegals six. Head with its surfaces more or less flattened, and laterally and superiorly bony. The angle of the preopercle and the shoulder bone each produced into the form of a long spine. Granular teeth in the jaws only. Two dorsal fins of nearly equal length: pectorals much elongated, with the anterior portion detached from and shorter than the upper. Scales on body keeled and of a moderate size. Lateral-line absent. Air-vessel in two lateral portions, each furnished with a large muscle. Pyloric appendages in moderate numbers or numerous.

SYNOPSIS OF INDIVIDUAL SPECIES.

1. *Dactylopterus Orientalis*, D. 1 | 1 | 5 | 8, A. 6. Pectoral fin very long: dorsal, caudal, and pectoral rays spotted. Seas of India to the Malay Archipelago and beyond.

Dactylopterus Orientalis, Plate LX, fig. 6.

Cuv. and Val. iv, p. 134, pl. 76; Richardson, Ich. China, p. 218; Bleeker, Amb. and Ceram. p. 264; Temm. and Schleg. Fauna Japon. Poissons, p. 37, pl. 15, A.; Jerdon, M. J. L. and Sc. 1851, p. 141; Günther, Catal. ii, p. 222, and Proc. Z. S. 1871, p. 663.

Dactylopterus Japonicus, Bleeker, Japan, p. 396.

Dactylopterus chirophthalmus, Bleeker, Nat. Tyds. Ned. Ind. 1854, iv, p. 494; Günther, Catal. ii, p. 223.

B. vi, D. 1 | 1 | 5-6 | 8, P. 30, V. 6, A. 6, C. 9, Vert. 9/13, Cæc. pyl. 18-19.

Length of head (including preopercular spine) 3 to 3½, of caudal 5½, height of body 5¾ to 6 in the total length. *Eyes*—nearly 1 diameter from end of snout, and also apart. Interorbital space concave transversely. A strong spine at the angle of the preopercle more than half the length of the rest of the head. Bony covering of the head produced backwards a little below the back to as far as below second or third dorsal spine. A shoulder spine. *Fins*—an elongated filament arises over occiput and is 1/2 longer than the head: a second midway between it and the first dorsal spine than which it is half shorter, it is detached from the fin. Fin rays unbranched except the last few of the dorsal, and sometimes of the anal, also those of the caudal which are bifid. Pectoral reaching to the end of the caudal, its first few rays are short, and rather detached from the remainder of the fin, its middle ones are the longest. *Scales*—with a ridge along each, and a large one forms an oblique keel along either side of the base of the caudal fin. *Colours*—pinkish, having a tinge of blue along the abdomen: dorsal and caudal rays spotted: pectoral gray along its centre, and the whole of the fin spotted, in the young it appears to have a large round black spot edged with white.

Jerdon observes of this fish "*Ana tonubi*, Tam. rare at Madras." I did not procure it whilst there, but have received the remains of a dried Madras specimen from Sir W. Elliot.

Habitat.—Seas of India to the Malay Archipelago and beyond. The figure is taken from a specimen in the British Museum.

Genus, 2—PEGASUS, *Linn.*

Fam. *Pegasidæ*, Richards.

Branchiostegals one: pseudobranchiæ absent. Gills four: gill-opening narrow, in front of the pectoral fin. Body broad and depressed, covered with bony plates, which are anchylosed on the trunk and moveable on the tail. Gill-cover formed of one bony plate, and a small interopercle concealed by it. No teeth. One short dorsal and anal fin opposite to one another: pectorals horizontal and long, composed of simple rays, some of which may be spinous: ventral with one or two rays, the outer being elongated. Air-vessel absent.

* Part of Family TRIGLOIDEI, Bleeker.

SYNOPSIS OF INDIVIDUAL SPECIES.

1. *Pegasus draconis*, D. 5, A. 5. Lateral edges of snout serrated. Body with brown markings; snout and last caudal rings black: pectoral with a white band and white edge.

1. Pegasus draconis, Plate LXI, fig. 1.

Pisciculus Amboinensis, Gronov. Mus. Ich. i, p. 65, No. 146.

Pegasus draconis, Linn. Syst. Nat. i, p. 418; Bloch, t. 109, figs. 1 and 2; Lacép. ii, pp. 77, 78, pl. 2, f. 3; Günther, Catal. viii, p. 147.

Pegasus volans, Lacép. ii, p. 83; Bleeker, Nat. Tyds. Ned. Ind. iii, p. 307.

? *Pegasus latirostris*, Richards. Ich. Chin., p. 293.

Cataphractus draco, Gronov. ed. Gray, p. 144.

Pegasus draco, Swainson, Fishes, ii, p. 332; Kaup. Lopho. p. 5, and *P. natans*, pl. i, f. 3; Jerdon, M. J. L. and Sc. 1851, p. 150; Günther, Fish. Zanz. p 138.

B. i, D. 5, P. 11, V. 2, A. 5, C. 8.

Body broad and depressed. *Eyes*—$2\frac{1}{2}$ diameters from end of snout, and 2 apart. Interorbital space transversely concave, two deep grooves on the neck. Under surface of body nearly flat, the expanded body portion with two median and two lateral ridges, whilst there are three cross ridges: at the meeting points of the various ridges are obtuse points. Caudal portion composed of eight rings, most of the anterior five of which have a lateral spinate elevation. Lateral edges of snout denticulated: a serrated ridge runs along the upper edge of orbit, and is continued along the snout to its end. *Fins*—pectorals horizontal, the anterior rays the shortest, all the fin rays simple. Vent situated midway behind the posterior edge of the orbit and the root of the caudal fin. *Colours*—body with brown reticulations, snout and last caudal ring black. Pectoral gray, with its rays spotted, having a white outer edge and sometimes a white band.

Richardson observes that *P. latirostris*, has the form of *draco*, but the back is nearly as broad as it is long.

My single specimen was taken at Port Blair by Dr. Rean. I never captured one alive, although several times at the Andamans I observed them skimming a short distance above the surface of the water.

Habitat.—Seas of India to the Malay Archipelago and beyond. Specimen figured life-size.

FAMILY, XXVII—GOBIIDÆ.

Pseudobranchiæ present, sometimes rudimentary. Gill-openings varying from extremely narrow to wide: the gill membranes attached to the isthmus: four gills. Body generally elongated. Eyes lateral, occasionally prominent, and mostly without free orbital margins, the skin being continued directly over their surface. The infraorbital ring of bones does not articulate with the preopercle. Teeth of varying characters, canines present or absent: inferior pharyngeal bones may be separated, or coalesced with a median suture. A single rayed dorsal fin, sometimes divided into two portions, the spines are flexible, and this part of the fin has less rays than the remainder: anal similar to the soft dorsal: ventrals sometimes united so as to form a disk, or arising close together. Scales and lateral-line present or absent. Air-vessel generally absent. Pyloric appendages, if present, few.

This Family has been subject to numerous subdivisions, due to the great variations observable amongst those species of which it is composed. Bleeker in his elaborate paper divides them as follows:—

I. *Eleotriformes*, with the ventrals free and completely separated.
II. *Gobiiformes*, with the ventrals entirely united together, or only in their basal halves: two dorsals separated or only united at their bases.
III. *Amblyopodiformes*, with the vertical fins united, a single dorsal which occupies the entire length of the back.
IV. *Luciogobiiformes*, with a single short dorsal situated in the last half of the body.

SYNOPSIS OF GENERA.

A. Gobiina.* Ventrals forming a disk, being united along their whole extent, or only in their basal halves: two separate dorsal fins.

1. *Gobius*. Ventrals only adherent to the abdomen at their bases. Scales more or less present. Simple teeth in the jaws in one or more rows: canines present or absent.

2. *Gobiodon*. Body oblong, compressed. Scales absent. Teeth in jaws in several rows; usually two canines near symphysis of lower jaw.

3. *Sicydium*. Ventrals short, adherent to the abdomen. Scales present. Teeth in the jaws moveable, being situated in the gums or lips.

4. *Apocryptes*. Ventrals only adherent to the abdomen at their bases. Scales present. Teeth in the jaws in a single row, those in the lower jaw subhorizontal: a pair of posterior canines above the mandibular symphysis.

5. *Apocryptichthys*. No posterior canines above the mandibular symphysis.

6. *Periophthalmus*. Eyes very prominent. Base of pectorals very muscular. Scales present. Teeth erect in both jaws in one or two rows, some of which are canine-like.

7. *Boleophthalmus*. Eyes very prominent. Base of pectorals very muscular. Scales present. Teeth in jaws in a single row, those in the lower jaw horizontal, having a pair of posterior canines.

B. Eleotrina.† Ventrals not united together.

8. *Bostrichthys*. Eyes not prominent. Vomerine teeth. Scales present.

9. *Eleotris*. Eyes not prominent. Teeth small and usually without canines: none on palate. Scales present. Anal papilla distinct.

* GOBIIFORMES, Bleeker, is thus primarily divided—
1. *Gobiodontini*. Teeth in the jaws in several rows, fixed: the outer row in the premaxillaries the longer.
2. *Gymnogobiini*. Teeth in the jaws fixed.
3. *Latrunculini*. Teeth in lower jaw in a single row.
4. *Triænophorichthyini*. Part of the teeth in the jaws tricuspidate.
5. *Sicydiini*. Moveable teeth in the gums or lips.
6. *Gobiini*. Simple teeth in the jaws, neither clubbed nor incised at their extremities: from one to many rows in the premaxillaries: from two to many rows in the lower jaw.
7. *Periophthalmini*. Teeth in the jaws conical, fixed and in one or two rows: conical and sharp in the pharyngeals.
8. *Apocryptini*. Teeth in a single row in either jaw, those in the lower jaw sub-horizontal, whilst there are also two erect canines above the symphysis of the lower jaw and behind the outer row.

† ELEOTRIFORMES, Bleeker, is thus primarily divided:—
1. *Eleotrini*:—
   a. *Philypni*. Several rows of teeth in jaws: vomerine teeth.
   b. *Eleotrii*. Palate and tongue edentulous.
   c. *Butii*. Several rows of teeth in jaws without canines. Palate and tongue edentulous.
2. *Hypseleotrini*. Teeth in the jaws in several rows, the external slender and moveable.
3. *Pareleotrini*. Teeth in the jaws fixed: none on the palate or tongue.

C. Amblyopina.* **Vertical fins united, a single dorsal occupying the whole length of the back.**

10. *Gobioides.* Anterior teeth very strong: no cavity above the opercle. Scales, when present, rudimentary.

11. *Trypauchen.* Several rows of teeth in each jaw, the outer the longer. No canines. A cavity above the opercle.

A. Gobiina. Ventrals forming a disk, being united along their whole extent or in their basal halves. Two separate dorsal fins.

Genus, 1—Gobius,† *Artedi.*

Branchiostegals five: pseudobranchiæ. Gill-openings of moderate width. Body low and elongated. Opercles

* Amblyopodiformes, Bleeker, is thus primarily divided—
  1. *Amblyopodini*, B. v, body very elongate, no post-temporal fossa.
  2. *Trypauchini*, B. iv, several rows of teeth in either jaw, the outer row the longer and very sharp, internal row of a conical grain shape. A post-temporal fossa.

† Although in my opinion minutely sub-dividing this large Genus will not conduce to aiding the enquirer in determining the species of a specimen, still I consider it necessary to give a synopsis of Bleeker's elaborate paper on the densition of the Gobiini, many of which fishes are included in Genus *Gobius*, Artedi.

Gobiini:—Teeth in jaws simple, their apices being neither clubbed nor incisal: in one or two rows in upper, in two or more in lower, jaw.

I. *Brachygobii.* No canines.
1. *Lophogobius*, Gill. Body compressed. Teeth in both jaws in many villiform rows, the outer the longer. Scales ctenoid.

II. *Platygobii.* Teeth in many rows in both jaws. No true canines.
2. *Gillichthys*, Coop.=*Gillia*, Günther. Teeth villiform in both jaws. Scales small, cycloid.
3. *Gobiopsis*, Steind. Teeth, the outer row the larger. Scales large, ctenoid.
4. *Glossogobius*, Gill=*Cephalogobius*, Bleeker. Outer row of teeth the longer, curved, not crowded together, unequal. Upper jaw not produced posteriorly.
5. *Platygobius*, Bleeker. Teeth, outer row in premaxillaries scarcely enlarged, in the lower jaw not enlarged.

III. *Eugobii.* Teeth in jaws fixed.

a. Teeth in both jaws sharp, in many rows, with the outer one enlarged: no canines.

6. *Gobius*, Artedi=*Pomatoschistus*, Gill. Teeth in the outer row conical and subequal: caudal obtuse. Scales ctenoid. Abdomen scaled. Snout short.
7. *Acanthogobius*, Gill. Teeth in the outer row subequal: caudal obtuse. Scales ctenoid. Snout conical.
8. *Brachygobius*, Bleeker=*Hypogymnogobius*, Bleeker. Teeth in the outer row subequal. Abdomen scaleless.
9. *Eucyclogobius*, Gill. Teeth in the outer row subequal. Scales cycloid, none on the head.
10. *Lepidogobius*, Gill=*Cyclogobius*, Steind. Teeth in the outer row subequal. Scales cycloid. Head scaled.
11. *Callogobius*, Bleeker. Teeth in the outer row, slender, subequal. Caudal lanceolate. Head depressed, convex.
12. *Stenogobius*, Bleeker. Teeth in the outer row, conical, subequal. Caudal obtusely lanceolate, longer than the head.
13. *Actinogobius*, Bleeker. Teeth in the outer row unequal. Caudal acute, shorter than the head.

b. Teeth in each jaw in many rows, the outer the longer: some truncated.

14. *Hemigobius*, Bleeker. Some of the middle teeth of the outer row in the premaxillaries truncated.

c. Teeth in each jaw in many rows, pointed, subequal, the outer row erect and not elongated. No canines.

15. *Awaous*, Val. Scales 50 to 60.
16. *Enisogobius*, Gill=*Chonophorus*, Poey. Scales 28.

d. Teeth in either jaw in many pointed rows, the outer the longer: in the lower jaw laterally a posterior curved canine.

17. *Ctenogobius*, Bleeker. Head scaleless. Scales 14 to 30.
18. *Centrogobius*, Bleeker=*Cyclogonus*, Steind. First dorsal spine pungent.
19. *Acentrogobius*, Bleeker=*Porogobius*, Bleeker. Head scaled. No pungent dorsal spine. Caudal lanceolate.
20. *Amblygobius*, Bleeker=*Odontogobius*, Bleeker. Scales 52 to 56.
21. *Cryptocentrus*, Ehr.=*Paragobius*, Bleeker. Scales 65 to more than 100.

e. Teeth in both jaws pointed, and in two rows.

22. *Zonogobius*, Bleeker. Outer row of teeth in upper and inner in lower jaw the longer.
23. *Lophiogobius*, Günther. Teeth in two rows in each jaw, the outer row the longer, placed wide apart and sub-horizontal. No canines.

f. Teeth pointed, in one or less than two rows in the upper and many in the lower jaw. Canines present or absent.

24. *Stigmatogobius*, Bleeker. Teeth in one row in the upper jaw: outer row in the lower jaw the longer, and posteriorly above the symphysis two canines.
25. *Euctenogobius*, Gill. A single row of teeth in the premaxillaries, few rows in lower jaw: no canines.
26. *Oxyurichthys*, Bleeker=*Gobiichthys*, Klunz. Teeth in premaxillaries in one or less than two rows, the inner of which is rudimentary: many rows in the lower jaw, the outer being the longer: no canines. Caudal lanceolate.

IV. *Chæturichthyi.* No canines: barbels on lower jaw.
27. *Chæturichthys*, Rich. Teeth in two rows in either jaw, the outer row close together, the longest, and consisting of fixed, curved, subulate teeth directed obliquely inwards.
28. *Amblychæturichthys*, Bleeker. Teeth in the premaxillaries in few rows, the outer the longer, fixed, straight, subulate: three or laterally two rows in the lower jaw, the outer the longer, moveable, straight, and directed obliquely inwards.
29. *Parachæturichthys*, Bleeker. Many rows of teeth in both jaws, the outer row close together, consisting of elongated, straight, and fixed ones.

V. *Gobionelli.* Teeth in both jaws in many rows.
30. *Synechogobius*, Gill. Pointed fixed teeth in both jaws, the outer the longer.
31. *Gobionellus*, Gir.=*Smaragdus*, Poey. Teeth small, the outer row setaceous and moveable.

unarmed. Simple teeth in one or more rows in the upper, and two or more in the lower jaw: canines sometimes present. Anterior portion of the dorsal fin, with from five to six flexible spines: the posterior more developed and of the same character as the anal: ventrals united, forming a disk, which is only attached by its base, each has one spine and four or five rays. Caudal rounded or pointed. Scales present or absent, and either cycloid or ctenoid. Lateral-line absent. Air-vessel, when present, generally small. Pyloric appendages usually absent.

The fishes comprised in this Genus have the form of the body variously modified, some being much deeper than others. They are either wholly scaled, the head may be scaleless, and even the body partially or entirely devoid of scales. Barbels or warts on the head or a crest on the occiput may be present or absent.

The dentition also is subject to considerable modification, canines being present or absent, most distinctly in the form of a recurved one on the outer side of the enlarged lateral row in the lower jaw, and more commonly found in the marine than in the fresh-water species. Variations may also occur in specimens of the same species. Amongst a series of *G. striatus* exists one in which the outer row of teeth in both jaws is abnormally enlarged, thus occasioning canines where they are not normally to be found.

In some the two dorsal fins are almost united at their bases, in others there is a longer or shorter interspace between them, whilst the form of the fins and the character of the spines are subject to great variations.

These fishes are found in numbers along the shores and estuaries of India, but due to their rapidly decomposing after death full collections have yet to be made. Amongst Sir Walter Elliot's figures of the Gobies captured at Waltair, are two or three which I am unable to recognise, but it would be manifestly unsafe to found new species upon drawings alone.

Amongst the fresh-water Gobies, the *G. giuris*, H. B. is largely bred in tanks and shows considerable diversity not only in its proportions, but also in its colours, this has occasioned its having been subdivided into several species.

SYNOPSIS OF SPECIES.

A. Lateral, recurved canines, present in the lower jaw: dorsal spines flexible.

1. *Gobius Bynoensis*, D. 6 | $\frac{1}{10}$, A. $\frac{1}{11-12}$, L. l. 65, L. tr.* 16. Two longitudinal bands, and some cross bars from the back. Andamans to Malay Archipelago and beyond.

2. *Gobius sexfasciatus*, D. 6 | 11, A. 10. Scales minute. Six vertical bands. Madras.

3. *Gobius brevirostris*, D. 6 | $\frac{1}{10}$, A. 10, L. l. 44, L. tr. 14. Scales very small to below the commencement of second dorsal fin. Olive, with a dark median band. Sind and China.

4. *Gobius griseus*, D. 6 | $\frac{1}{10}$, A. 10, L. l. 42, L. tr. 14. Olivaceous, with black spots. Madras.

5. *Gobius polynema*, D. 6 | 11, A. 10, L. l. 28-30, L. tr. 8. Purplish-black: a yellow-edged ocellus at upper portion of base of caudal fin. Seas of India to China and beyond.

6. *Gobius macrostoma*, D. 6 | 11, A. 10, L. l. 33. Vertical fins with dark streaks. Bombay.

7. *Gobius viridipunctatus*, D. 6 | $\frac{1}{10}$, A. $\frac{1}{9}$, L. l. 34-38, L. tr. 9. Olive, with some blotches along the sides, and some of the scales with brilliant green centres. Seas of India.

8. *Gobius ocellatus*, D. 6 | $\frac{1}{10}$, A. $\frac{1}{10}$, L. l. 33, L. tr. 8. Olive, with small green spots, blotches along the sides: vertical fins spotted: a yellow ocellus at top of last half of caudal fin. Bombay.

9. *Gobius Masoni*, D. 6 | $\frac{1}{10-11}$, A. $\frac{1}{9}$, L. l. 28, L. tr. 10. Gray with black fins, and blue spots on the body. Bombay.

10. *Gobius cyanomos*, D. 6 | $\frac{1}{10}$, A. 10, L. l. 28-30, L. tr. 8. Olive, many scales with blue spots, a blue mark on shoulder. Seas of India to the Malay Archipelago.

11. *Gobius criniger*, D. 6 | 10, L. l. 26-32, L. tr. 12-13. No scales before the first dorsal fin. Olivaceous with black blotches and spots. East coast of Africa, seas of India to the Malay Archipelago and beyond.

12. *Gobius puntang*, D. 6 | $\frac{1}{10}$, A. 10, L. l. 28-29, L. tr. 8-9. Olive with rusty spots, fin rays yellow, spotted and barred with purplish-red. Andamans to the Malay Archipelago.

13. *Gobius Bleekeri*, D. 6 | $\frac{1}{9}$, A. $\frac{1}{9}$, L. l. 32, L. tr. 11. With cloudy dark markings, upper half of first dorsal dusky, a large bluish spot from first to fourth spine. Madras.

14. *Gobius semidoliatus*, D. 6 | $\frac{1}{9}$, A. $\frac{1}{8}$, L. l. 27, L. tr. 6. A blue spot on opercle, body with angular bands. Madras.

15. *Gobius biocellatus*, D. 6 | $\frac{1}{9}$, A. $\frac{1}{8}$, L. l. 28-30, L. tr. 7-8. Some large blotches along the sides, a black ocellus with a white edging in hind portion of first dorsal fin, dorsal fins white spotted. Seas of India to the Malay Archipelago.

16. *Gobius Madraspatensis*, D. 6 | $\frac{1}{9}$, A. $\frac{1}{9}$, L. l. 28-29, L. tr. 7. Irregular vertical brown bands: vertical fins spotted. Madras.

17. *Gobius Neilli*, D. 6 | $\frac{1}{9}$, A. 9, L. l. 28, L. tr. 7. Ochreous, upper two-thirds of body blotched and with dark marks: upper portion of first dorsal white, some of the fins barred. Madras.

18. *Gobius melanosticta*, D. 6 | $\frac{1}{10}$, A. 9, L. l. 24, L. tr. 7. Light brown, scales of body with dark marks: vertical fins spotted. Madras.

* By L. tr. is signified the number of horizontal rows of scales existing between the commencement of the base of the second dorsal and that of the anal fins.

B. No lateral recurved canines in the lower jaw: dorsal spines flexible.

19. *Gobius cristatus*, D. 6 | 14, A. 14, L. l. 50-60, L. tr. 11-12. Scales cycloid. A light ocellus at base of pectoral fin: body spotted and blotched: caudal spotted in its upper half. Bombay.

20. *Gobius tentacularis*, D. 6 | $\frac{1}{11}$, A. $\frac{1}{10}$, L. l. 60, L. tr. 10. An orbital tentacle. Scales ctenoid. Dull green with reddish spots: vertical fins spotted. Seas of India to the Malay Archipelago.

21. *Gobius acutipinnis*, D. 6 | $\frac{1}{10-11}$, A. $\frac{1}{11}$, L. l. 25-28, L. tr. 6-7. Some blotches along the body, a brown band from the eye over the cheeks: dorsal fins longitudinally barred. Seas of India to the Andamans.

22. *Gobius striatus*, D. 6 | $\frac{1}{10}$, A. 10, L. l. 55-60, L. tr. 14. Yellowish, with some blotches along the sides: fins barred in spots. Fresh waters of India.

23. *Gobius personatus*, D. 6 | $\frac{1}{10}$, A. $\frac{1}{10}$, L. l. 55, L. tr. 14. Light brown, with vermiculated markings. Seas of India to the Malay Archipelago.

24. *Gobius Malabaricus*, D. 6 | $\frac{1}{9}$, A. $\frac{1}{9}$, L. l. 50, L. tr. 9. First dorsal with a black crescentic mark. Malabar.

25. *Gobius planifrons*, D. 6 | $\frac{1}{10}$, A. 10, L. l. 46, L. tr. 15. Head wide. Olive, fins dark gray, a black mark at base of pectoral. Bombay.

26. *Gobius elegans*, D. 6 | $\frac{1}{9}$, A. 10, L. l. 36, L. tr. 9. Blotched and banded. Seas of India to the Malay Archipelago.

27. *Gobius ornatus*, D. 6 | $\frac{1}{10}$, A. $\frac{1}{9}$, L. l. 26-28, L. tr. 7. Many oblong brown spots and yellow dots: fins dotted with black. Red Sea to the Malay Archipelago.

28. *Gobius gutum*, D. 6 | $\frac{1}{10}$, A. 11. Dark spots clustered into cloud-like blotches: vertical fins spotted. Lower portions of Hooghly.

29. *Gobius albopunctatus*, D. 6 | $\frac{1}{9}$, A. $\frac{1}{8}$, L. l. 35-40, L. tr. 11-12. Brownish, irregularly marbled, head and body spotted, some of the spots white. Red Sea, seas of India to Australia.

30. *Gobius giuris*, D. 6 | $\frac{1}{8-9}$, A. $\frac{1}{8-9}$, L. l. 30-34, L. tr. 9. Brown, with blotches along the sides: dorsal and caudal barred in spots. Fresh waters of India to the Malay Archipelago, China, and beyond.

31. *Gobius semidoliatus*, D. 6 | $\frac{1}{8}$, A. 8, L. l. 28, L. tr. 9. Chestnut, with red bands on the head and below the first dorsal fin. Red Sea, Andamans.

32. *Gobius magniloquus*, D. 6 | $\frac{1}{8}$, A. 9, L. l. 38, L. tr. 10. Maxilla reaches to below hind edge of eye. Brown spotted. Madras.

33. *Gobius planiceps*, D. 6 | $\frac{1}{8}$, A. 9, L. l. 38, L. tr. 10. Maxilla reaches to below first third of eye. Dark brown angular bands on the body. Madras.

34. *Gobius sadanundio*, D. 6 | $\frac{1}{9}$, A. $\frac{1}{8}$, L. l. 28-30, L. tr. 8. Greenish, with large black spots. Estuaries of the Ganges to Burma.

35. *Gobius melanosoma*, D. 6 | $\frac{1}{8}$, A. 10, L. l. 22, L. tr. 9. Black. Andamans to the Malay Archipelago.

36. *Gobius nanus*, D. 5 | $\frac{1}{8}$, A. 9, L. l. 30, L. tr. 10. Six black belts round the head and body. Hooghly and Burma.

A. Lateral recurved canines present in the lower jaw: dorsal spines flexible.

1. Gobius Bynoensis, Plate LXI, fig. 3.

Richardson, Ich. Erebus and Terror, p. 4, pl. 1, f. 1, 2; Günther, Catal. iii, p. 70; Peters, Monats. Akad. Berlin, 1868, p. 266.

Gobius stethophthalmus, Bleeker, Nat. Tyd. Ned. Ind. i, p. 249, f. 17, and xv, p. 236.

Odontogobius Bynoensis, Bleeker, Gobioides (1874), p. 35 = *Amblygobius Bynoensis*, Bleeker, *MSS.*

B. v, D. 6 | $\frac{1}{10}$, P. 19, V. 1/5, A. $\frac{1}{10-11}$, L. l. 65, L. tr.* 16.

Length of head $4\frac{1}{2}$ to 5, height of body 5 to $5\frac{1}{2}$ in the total length. *Eyes*—diameter 1/4 to 1/5 of length of head, 1 diameter from end of snout, and 1/2 a diameter apart. Head rather higher than broad: snout obtuse: cleft of mouth a little oblique, commencing opposite the centre of the eyes, the maxilla reaches to below anterior edge or first-third of the orbit. *Teeth*—two or three rows in either jaw, with an outer row of about 10 large ones in the premaxillaries: outer row in the lower jaw enlarged, elongated, and sub-horizontal, the outer one or two of which on either side are large, obliquely placed, canines. *Fins*—dorsal spines weak, having filiform terminations, the two dorsals of about equal height, and the bases of the two separated by a very short interspace. Pectoral nearly as long as the head. Caudal rounded, its central rays the longest. *Scales*—ctenoid, 16 rows between the bases of the second dorsal and anal: anterior to the dorsal fin they are very small, and are continued forwards to opposite the middle of the eyes, whilst there are a few on the upper portion of the opercle: those on the free portion of the tail are the largest. *Colours*—greenish, back with from eight to ten darkish cross bars. Two longitudinal bands, the superior from the snout through the eye, at first black, becoming yellow on the body and ending at the extremity of the soft dorsal: the second from the mouth to the pectoral, forming a dark band across the opercles, becoming a black spot at the base of the pectoral, and continued as a golden band to the centre of the base of the caudal, which last fin has a dark spot at the upper part of its base: anal with a dark margin.

* By L. tr. is signified in the Gobies the number of rows of scales between the origins of the second dorsal and anal fins.

Habitat.—Andamans, Malay Archipelago to Australia: the specimen figured (life-size) is from the Andamans.

2. Gobius sexfasciatus, Plate LIX, fig. 4.

B. v, D. 6 | 11, P. 19, V. 1/5, A. 10, C. 15, Sc. minute.

Length of head $4\frac{1}{3}$, of caudal $4\frac{1}{2}$, height of body 6 in the total length. *Eyes*—diameter $3\frac{1}{2}$ in length of head, not 1/2 a diameter from end of snout, and 1/6 of a diameter apart. Greatest width of head equals 4/7 of its length, and its height equals its length excluding the snout. Anterior profile of head very obtuse. Lower jaw the longer: cleft of mouth oblique, the anterior extremity of the mouth commencing opposite the lower third of the eye: the maxilla reaches to below the hind edge of the eye. Preopercle without any spine. *Teeth*—in several villiform rows, and an outer enlarged one in either jaw, those in the mandibles being the smaller and confined to about 16 at its anterior extremity, the outer of which is recurved. *Fins*—dorsal spines weak and filiform, the third being about as long as the body is high. Anterior dorsal rays not half so long as the spines, its last rays the longest. Pectoral as long as the head excluding the snout. Ventral not adherent to the abdomen, it does not reach the vent. Anal commencing below the second dorsal ray, and is similar to that fin. Caudal wedge-shaped. *Scales*—minute over body, becoming somewhat larger towards the tail. *Colours*—grayish-brown, with six bands descending from the back towards the middle of the sides: opercle covered with a large dull blotch. Fins grayish, stained darker at their edges. Upper half of caudal yellow, and barred with light brown spots. A black mark between the two first dorsal spines, about the centre of their height.

Habitat.—The specimen figured (life-size) was captured at Madras in June, 1867.

3. Gobius brevirostris, Plate LXIII, fig. 5.

Günther, Catal. iii, p. 41.

B. v, D. 6 | $\frac{1}{10-11}$, P. 17, V. 1/5, A. 10, C. 13, L. l. 44, L. tr. 14.

Length of head $4\frac{1}{3}$, of caudal $5\frac{1}{2}$, height of body 6 in the total length. *Eyes*—1/5 of length of head, 1 diameter from end of snout and apart. Upper profile of head parabolic. Width of head equals its height, and its length behind the middle of the orbit. Lower jaw slightly the longer. Mouth oblique, its cleft commencing opposite the lower edge of the eye, the maxilla extends to below the anterior third of the orbit. No tentacles or barbels on the scaleless head. *Teeth*—in several villiform bands with an outer enlarged row: a recurved canine at either extremity of the enlarged row in the lower jaw. *Fins*—dorsal spines flexible, the second or longest equals the length of the postorbital portion of the head. Caudal wedge-shaped. Pectoral as long as the head without the snout. Ventral extends half way to anus: caudal rounded. *Scales*—ctenoid, increasing in size posteriorly: a few rows on the head in old specimens, none in small ones: about 25 rows before base of dorsal fins: 13 rows between the second dorsal and anal fins. *Colours*—olivaceous, with a blotched irregular band running from the mouth to the centre of the base of the caudal fin: a narrow brown band from the eye to above the opercle, terminating above the axilla in a large light blue ocellus. Two small bluish spots on the opercle at its upper margin, another at the upper edge of the base of the caudal. Dorsal fins with a violet coloured basal half. Anal white, having a violet band along its centre, lightish blue superiorly and white externally. Caudal with blackish margins.

Habitat.—Kurrachee, where the specimen figured (life-size) was obtained, to China.

4. Gobius griseus, Plate LXIII, fig. 3.

B. v, D. 6 | $\frac{1}{10}$, P. 17, V. 1/5, A. 10, C. 14, L. l. 42, L. tr. 14.

Length of head $4\frac{2}{3}$, of caudal $5\frac{1}{2}$, height of body $4\frac{1}{2}$ in the total length. *Eyes*—upper margin near the dorsal profile; diameter $4\frac{1}{2}$ in length of head, 1 diameter from end of snout, and 1/4 of a diameter apart. Head as wide as high or as its length without the snout. Lower jaw the longer, cleft of mouth rather oblique, the maxilla reaches to below the first-third of the eye. Numerous rows of warts on the cheeks and opercles, which are but little apparent in the young. No barbels. *Teeth*—in several very fine villiform rows in both jaws, the outer row in the premaxillaries much enlarged, especially near the symphysis: the outer eight or ten in the front of the lower jaw are still larger, and the external on either side is a large recurved canine. *Fins*—spines of first dorsal ending in filamentous prolongations, and being rather higher than the body, its base ends close to the commencement of the second dorsal, the last ray of which reaches the base of the caudal. Pectoral as long as the head: ventral reaches half way to the anal. Caudal wedge-shaped, the central rays being the longest. *Scales*—ctenoid and angular, largest in the posterior portion of the body, very small (20 or 30 rows) anterior to the dorsal fin, they extend as far as to the eyes: 14 rows between the bases of the second dorsal and anal fins. A few very fine ones on the upper part of the opercles: the scales do not show the sudden increase in size from under the commencement of the second dorsal fin as seen in *G. brevirostris*. *Colours*—olivaceous, with bands and many well marked deep brown or black spots. Pectoral fin and contiguous portions of the body finely dotted with small chestnut spots. Base of first dorsal yellowish with three or four horizontal brown bands and usually a dark mark near its posterior extremity: second dorsal yellowish with a dark outer edge. Ventral, anal, and caudal with dark outer edges.

Due to an error, one of the smaller specimens was given to the artist to figure, it does not show the dorsal spines so elongate, whilst the scales extend forward anteriorly to only midway between the base of the dorsal and posterior edge of the eye, and a series of specimens conclusively shows that the scaled space increases anteriorly with age.

Habitat.—Madras, in the backwaters, up to $3\frac{1}{2}$ inches in length. It dies when placed in fresh water.

5. Gobius polynema, Plate LXI, fig. 8.

Chaeturichthys polynema, Bleeker, Japan, p. 44, f. 4.
Gobius polynema, Günther, Catal. iii, p. 46.
Parachaeturichthys polynema, Bleeker, Gobioides, 1874, p. 37.

B. v, D. 6 | 11, P. 21, V. 1/5, A. 10, C. 13, L. l. 28-30, L. tr. 8.

Length of head 1/5, of caudal 1/4, height of body 1/6 to 1/8 of the total length. *Eyes*—diameter 4 to $4\frac{1}{2}$ in the length of head, about 1 diameter from end of snout, and 2/3 of a diameter apart. Head rather flat superiorly, as broad as high and equalling its length excluding the snout. Snout moderately rounded, cleft of mouth oblique, commencing opposite the lower edge of the eye, jaws of equal length anteriorly: the maxilla reaches to below the first third of the orbit. *Barbels*—several small ones below the lower jaw, and nearer its posterior than its anterior extremity. *Teeth*—villiform, the outer row the largest, a small recurved canine tooth on each side of the enlarged row in the lower jaw. *Fins*—the first dorsal about half as high as the body below it, lower than the second which equals the height of the body: pectoral as long as the head: ventrals reach two-thirds of the distance to the base of the anal: caudal pointed. *Scales*—ctenoid, they extend forwards to the snout and on to the sides of the head: about 19 rows before dorsal fin, eight rows between the bases of the second dorsal and anal fins. *Colours*—purplish-black, fins blackish: a black ocellus edged with white or yellow on the upper portion of the base of the caudal fin.

Habitat.—Seas of India to China and Japan: the specimen figured (life-size) is from Madras.

6. Gobius macrostoma.

Gobiopsis macrostomus, Steind. Sitz. Wien, Acad. 1860, xlii, p. 291, t. i, f. 6.
Gobius macrostoma, Günther, Catal. iii, p. 548.

B. v, D. 6/11, A. 10, L. l. 33.

Length of head from $3\frac{1}{3}$ to $3\frac{3}{4}$, height of body $7\frac{1}{2}$ in the total length. *Eyes*—diameter $6\frac{3}{4}$ in length of head, 1 to $1\frac{1}{2}$ diameters apart. Head depressed, broader than high. Cleft of mouth extending to behind the posterior margin of the orbit. *Teeth*—an outer enlarged row: canines present. *Scales*—cycloid anteriorly, ctenoid posteriorly. *Fins*—spines of first dorsal flexible with filamentous terminations, but not so high as the body, soft dorsal higher than the spinous, or than the body, the two dorsal fins at a short distance apart. Pectorals $5\frac{1}{4}$ in the total length. Caudal rounded. *Colours*—vertical fins with dark streaks.

Habitat.—Bombay.

7. Gobius viridipunctatus, Plate LXI, fig. 4, LXIII, fig. 4 (*abnormal*), and LIX, fig. 5 (*male.*)

Gobius swan nottah, Russell, Fish. Vizag. i, p. 41, pl. 52.
Gobius viridipunctatus, Cuv. and Val. xii, p. 62; Jerdon, M. J. L. and Sc. 1851, p. 143; Günther, Catal. iii, p. 24; Day, Fish. Malabar, p. 110.
Gobius cematus, Cuv. and Val. xii, p. 85; Günther, Catal. iii, p. 38.
Bichu gende, Tam. "Scorpion goby."

B. v, D. 6 | $\frac{1}{10}$, P. 20, V. 1/5, A. $\frac{1}{9}$, C. 15, L. l. 34-38, L. tr. 9.

Length of head $4\frac{1}{2}$ to $4\frac{3}{4}$, of caudal $5\frac{1}{2}$, height of body $4\frac{3}{4}$ to $5\frac{1}{2}$ in the total length. *Eyes*—diameter 1/4 of length of head, rather above 1 diameter from end of snout, and 1/3 of a diameter apart. Head as broad as high, and equalling the length of the head behind the middle of the eyes. Cheeks swollen, having many rows of warts, and also pitted in large specimens: a large open pore in interorbital space. Lower jaw the longer, cleft of mouth oblique, commencing anteriorly opposite the lower edge of the eye: the maxilla reaching to below middle of orbit. *Teeth*—in both jaws villiform, with an external enlarged row in the premaxillaries, and two or four canines; in the lower jaw there are from 12 to 16 enlarged teeth, the outer of which is a recurved canine, likewise there are from two to four canine-like teeth in the internal row above the symphysis, and some of the internal row laterally are conical. *Fins*—dorsal spines moderately flexible and with short filamentous endings, its height 2/3 that of the body: the second dorsal and anal vary considerably, as seen in plates 61, fig. 4, and 59, f. 5, which show the two extremes, the last ray may reach only 2/3 of the way to the caudal, or even be lengthened to beyond the commencement of that fin. Pectoral as long as the head without the snout. Caudal rounded. *Scales*—ctenoid, smallest anteriorly, about 32 rows existing between the dorsal fin and hind edge of the orbit, a few on the upper portion of the opercle. *Colours*—olive, with a series of four or five large badly defined blotches along the sides: many scales with a light centre, which in life is of an emerald green colour; dorsals dark at their bases, usually having light edges with a dark basal band. Ventral, anal, and caudal gray, the last with a light upper edge.

Plate 61, fig. 4 (life-size from Bombay) is *G. venenatus*, Cuv. and Val.: plate 59, f. 5, is *G. viridipunctatus*, C. V. from Madras: plate 63, fig. 4, is a curious abnormal form showing a deficiency of two anal rays.

Habitat.—Sind, through the seas of India, it is most common at Bombay and Madras, up to at least 5 inches in length.

8. Gobius ocellatus, Plate LXI, fig. 7.

Day, Proc. Zool. Soc. 1873, p. 107.

B. v, D. 6 | $\frac{1}{10}$, P. 20, V. 1/5, A. $\frac{1}{9}$, C. 12, L. l. 33, L. tr. 8.

Length of head $4\frac{1}{3}$ to $4\frac{1}{2}$, of caudal 5 to 6, height of body 6 to 7 in the total length. *Eyes*—somewhat superior, diameter 5 to 6 in the length of head, $1\frac{1}{2}$ diameters from end of snout, and 1 apart. Head slightly broader than high, its greatest width being equal to the length of its postorbital portion, the summit of which is somewhat flat and snake-shaped. No occipital crest, nor warts on the head: a pair of short barbels under the symphysis of the lower jaw. Cleft of mouth somewhat oblique, commencing opposite the middle of the eye: the lower jaw a little the longer: the posterior extremity of the maxilla extends to beneath the anterior margin of the orbit. *Teeth*—several rows in both jaws, an enlarged outer one in the mandibles, the external of which on either side is a moderately or small recurved canine: outer row in premaxillaries likewise enlarged, and a lateral canine in large specimens. *Fins*—the two dorsals not widely separated, the distance of the first dorsal from the orbit equals the distance from the snout to the base of the pectoral fin, its second spine is elongated in some specimens, being nearly as long as the head, last dorsal ray divided to its base. Pectoral rays silk-like, second dorsal and anal of about equal development and highest posteriorly: caudal wedge-shaped: ventral reaches half way to the vent. *Scales*—ctenoid on the body, cycloid on the head, they are much smaller anterior to the dorsal fin than posterior to it: they cover the cheeks and opercles, and on the top of the head as far as the snout: are in rather irregular rows, eight being between the origin of the second dorsal and anal fins, where they are angular: about 28 rows before the dorsal fin. *Colours*—olive, a dark green spot above the upper margin of the opercle, about six indistinct blotches along the sides: dorsal and caudal fins stained with dark, and having some indistinct spots or bars:* a yellow ocellus, with a black centre, at the top of the caudal fin in its last half: anal whitish, basal half covered with fine black dots: ventrals yellow.

Habitat.—Bombay and Sind, to 6 inches in length. The specimen figured (life-size) is from Bombay.

9. Gobius Masoni, Plate LXI, fig. 6.

Day, Proc. Zool. Soc. 1873, p. 107.

B. vii, D. 6 | $\frac{1}{10-11}$, P. 19, V. 1/5, A. $\frac{1}{9}$, C. 12, L. l. 28, L. tr. 10.

Length of head $4\frac{1}{2}$, of caudal 5 to $5\frac{1}{2}$, height of body 5 in the total length. *Eyes*—somewhat superior, diameter $5\frac{1}{2}$ to 6 in the length of head, $1\frac{1}{2}$ diameters from end of snout, and 1 to $1\frac{1}{4}$ apart. Profile of head bluntly rounded, its greatest width equalling its length excluding the snout, its height a little more: cleft of mouth oblique, commencing opposite lower edge of eye: lower jaw anterior, the posterior extremity of the maxilla extends to below the middle of the orbit. Numerous rows of fine wart-like glands along the opercles, nape, and mandibles. *Teeth*—in villiform rows in both jaws, there is an external enlarged row in the upper jaw, with two large canines: from 12 to 15 also enlarged in front of the lower jaw, on either side of the outer row is a very large recurved canine. *Fins*—first dorsal low, its spines filiform, and the longest about half the height of the body below it: the second dorsal rays increase in length posteriorly: pectoral destitute of silk-like rays: caudal wedge-shaped. *Scales*—ctenoid, before the first dorsal fin there are 25 rows, anterior to which they are rounded and smaller than those in the remainder of the body, where they are angular: none on the cheeks, a few along the upper margin of the opercles, superiorly they do not extend so far forwards as to above the posterior margin of the orbit: 10 rows between the origin of the second dorsal and anal fins. *Air-vessel*—large. *Colours*—olive, with numerous brilliant blue spots on the nape and behind the pectoral fin: some blackish ones along the sides. Dorsal, anal, ventral, and caudal black: pectoral yellow, margined with black.

Habitat.—Bombay, to 4 inches in length.

10. Gobius cyanosmos, Plate LXI, fig. 5.

Bleeker, Blen. en Gob. p. 25; Günther, Catal. iii, p. 39.

Gobius setosus, Jerdon, M. J. L. and Sc. 1851, p. 143 (not Cuv. and Val.).

Acentrogobius cyanosmos, Bleeker, MSS.

B. v, D. 6 | $\frac{1}{10}$, P. 18, V. 1/5, A. 10, C. 11, L. l. 28-30, L. tr. 8.

Length of head $4\frac{1}{2}$, of caudal $5\frac{1}{2}$, height of body $6\frac{1}{4}$ in the total length. *Eyes*—somewhat superior, diameter 1/5 to 1/6 of length of head, $1\frac{1}{4}$ diameters from end of snout, and 1/2 a diameter apart. Greatest width of head 2/3 of length, height equals its length without the snout. Cheeks swollen. No warts on cheeks, no crest on nape, nor tentacles above the orbit. The orifice of a canal behind posterior-inferior angle of eye. Mouth anterior, oblique, commencing opposite the lower edge of the eye, jaws of equal length, the maxilla

* Specimens from Sind are more barred than are those from Bombay.

extends posteriorly to below the anterior third of the orbit. *Barbels*—below the symphysis of the mandible are a short pair. *Teeth*—in villiform rows in both jaws, with an outer enlarged one in both, the anterior 10 in the premaxillaries being large and canine-like, the outer 10 or 12 in the lower jaw are also enlarged, but not to the same size as in the upper jaw, the external one on either side is a recurved canine. *Fins*—dorsal spines, especially the second and third, filiform and prolonged far beyond the membrane: rays increase in length to the last which reaches to the base of the caudal fin, and is as high as the body, it is divided to its base. Pectoral as long as the head excluding the snout. Anal similar to soft dorsal. Caudal wedge-shaped or rather rounded. *Scales*—small, rounded, and cycloid anteriorly: about 20 rows existing anterior to the dorsal fin, none on the head; those on the remainder of the body are angular and feebly ctenoid, eight rows between the second dorsal and anal fins. *Colours*—olive, many of the scales with light bluish spots, a deep blue spot on the shoulder, second dorsal and anal dark, each with a reddish outer edge: ventral and last two-thirds of caudal gray.

A beautifully finished coloured drawing of this species* exists amongst Sir W. Elliot's collection, and was named by Jerdon as above.

Habitat.—Seas of India to the Malay Archipelago, the specimen figured (life-size) is from Madras.

11. Gobius criniger, Plate LXII, fig. 2.

? *Gobius nebulosus*, Forsk. p. 24; Bl. Schn. p. 72; Cuv. and Val. xii, p. 84.

Gobius criniger, Cuv. and Val. xii, p. 82; Cantor, Catal. p. 184; Bleeker, Banka, p. 453; Richards. Erebus and Terror, p. ii, pl. i, figs. 3 and 4; Günther, Catal. iii, p. 29; Day, Fish. Malabar, p. 111.

Gobius brevifilis,† Cuv. and Val. xii, p. 90; Day, Proc. Zool. Soc. 1867, p. 940.

Gobius Kraffii, Steind. Verh. z. b. Ges. Wien, 1867, p. 326.

Gobius caninus, Günth. and Playfair, Fish. Zanz. p. 71, pl. ix, f. 1 (not Cuv. and Val.).

B. v, D. 6 | 10, P. 19, V. 1/5, A. 10, C. 13, L. l. 26-32, L. tr. 12-13.

Length of head 4, of caudal $5\frac{1}{2}$, height of body $4\frac{1}{2}$ in the total length. *Eyes*—diameter $3\frac{1}{2}$ to 4 in the length of head, 1 diameter from end of snout, and 1/2 a diameter apart. Snout obtuse: jaws of about the same length anteriorly. Cleft of mouth oblique, commencing anteriorly opposite the middle of the eyes, the depth of its cleft equalling the width of its gape: the maxilla reaches to below front edge or first third of the eye. Greatest width of head equals its height, or its length excluding the snout. Several rows of fine warts across the cheeks, opercles, upper surface of head, and nape of neck: an open pore between the eyes. *Teeth*—in several villiform rows in both jaws, an outer enlarged row in anterior portion of the lower jaw, the outer of which is a small recurved canine: an anterior enlarged row in premaxillaries. *Fins*—the two dorsals with a narrow interspace between their bases, and of about the same height or 1/6 of the total length, the second and third spines often with filamentous terminations: last dorsal ray divided to its base. Pectoral as long as the head excluding the snout, and of similar length to the ventral. Caudal rounded. *Scales*—ctenoid, none on the head nor in front of base of first dorsal fin. *Colours*—pale ochreous: head, body, dorsal, and caudal fins irregularly spotted and blotched with black: caudal and anal with dark edges.

This is "*Gobius* ——," Jerdon, M. J. L. and Sc. 1851, p. 143.

Habitat.—East coast of Africa, seas of India to the Malay Archipelago and beyond. The specimen figured (life-size) is from Madras, where it is common all the year round in the sea and backwaters.

12. Gobius puntang, Plate LXII, fig. 1.

Bleeker, Nat. Tyds. Ned. Ind. iii, p. 692 (? ii, p. 486): Günther, Catal. iii, p. 19.

Gobius puntangoides, Bleeker, Ceram, iii, p. 242.

Gobius Andamanensis, Day, Proc. Zool. Soc. 1870, p. 691.

B. v, D. 6 | $\frac{1}{10}$, P. 17, V. 1/5, A. 10, C. 11, L. l. 28-29, L. tr. 8-9.

Length of head $4\frac{1}{2}$ to $5\frac{1}{2}$, of caudal $3\frac{1}{2}$, height of body $4\frac{2}{3}$ to $5\frac{1}{2}$ in the total length. *Eyes*—diameter 1/4 of length of head, $1\frac{1}{2}$ diameters from end of snout, and 1/2 a diameter apart. Jaws of the same length anteriorly. Upper profile of head rounded, a considerable rise from the snout to the forehead. Greatest width of head two-thirds and its height three-fourths of its length. Cleft of mouth very slightly oblique, the maxilla reaches to below the middle of the orbit: two open pores between the orbits. *Teeth*—in several villiform rows, the outer row in the premaxillaries rather enlarged, as is also the external row in the lower jaw which ends laterally in a small canine. *Fins*—dorsal spines flexible, with filamentous terminations, the first three

* I am unable to find any record that *Gobius caninus*, C.V. has been taken in India unless it is this species. The type has L. l. 33, L. tr. 8, and 18 rows of scales anterior to the dorsal fin, which are not much smaller than those on the body. Width of head 3/4 its height. Glands on head, but no scales. It appears to have been found in the Malay Archipelago and beyond, but it is by no means improbable that it frequents the seas of India.

G. grandinosus, Val. Voy. Bonite, Poiss. p. 177, pl. 5, f. 4, is very similar, it has D. 6 | 11, A. 10, L. l. 30, L. tr. 9. Head $4\frac{2}{3}$, caudal and body each $5\frac{1}{2}$ in the total length. *Eyes*—diameter 1/4 of head, $1\frac{1}{2}$ diameters from end of snout, and 1/4 apart. Width of head equals its height. Lines of warts on scaleless cheeks. *Teeth*—one or two recurved but not very large canines on either side of lower jaw. *Scales*—25 rows of small ones between dorsal and occiput, a few on upper edge of opercle.

† Bleeker, "Fishes of Madagascar," p. 77, observes "*Gobius auchenolenia*, Bleeker=*Gobius brevifilis*, C.V. ?"

the longest and much more than the second, the hind rays of which equal the height of the body and reach the base of the caudal; anal similar to second dorsal. Pectoral as long as the head and half longer than the ventral. Caudal pointed, its central rays being the longest. *Scales*—ctenoid, extending as far forwards as the orbits, also on the cheeks and opercles. Eleven rows anterior to the dorsal fin: nine between the origins of the second dorsal and anal fins. *Colours*—olive, spotted all over with rusty, fin-rays yellow, barred and dotted with purplish red. Anal with a yellow margin and sometimes with transverse purplish-red streaks.

Habitat.—Andamans to the Malay Archipelago: it appears to prefer brackish water. The specimen figured (life-size) is from the Andamans. Genus *Acentrogobius*, Bleeker, MSS.

13. Gobius Bleekeri, Plate LXII, fig. 5.

Day, Proc. Zool. Soc. 1868, p. 195.

B. v, D. 6 | $\frac{1}{9}$, P. 16, V. 1/5, A. 1/8, C. 13, L. l. 32, L. tr. 11.

Length of head 1/5, of caudal 1/6, height of body 1/5 of the total length. *Eyes*—directed upwards and slightly outwards, closely approximating superiorly, diameter $3\frac{3}{4}$ in length of head, 3/4 of a diameter from end of snout. Height of head equal to its length excluding the snout. Lower jaw the longer, cleft of mouth oblique, commencing opposite the middle of the eyes, the maxilla reaches to beneath the anterior half of the orbit. *Teeth*—in villiform rows having an external enlarged row in either jaw, with the outer on either side in the mandibles being a recurved conical canine. *Fins*—dorsal spines slender, with filamentous prolongations, and higher than the second dorsal. Pectoral 1/4 longer than the head, the ventral does not reach the origin of the anal: anal and second dorsal similar: caudal wedge-shaped. *Scales*—ctenoid, extending as far forwards as the posterior margin of the orbit, none on the cheeks or base of pectoral, sixteen rows anterior to the dorsal fin which are rather smaller than those on the remainder of the body. Eleven rows between the bases of the second dorsal and anal. *Colours*—olivaceous, clouded with darker blotches and irregular spots, very fine black spots on the scales: first dorsal dusky in its upper half, with a large bluish spot extending from the first to the fourth spine, and a light mark along its base from thence to the end of the fin, the spines orange: second dorsal studded with black points most numerous towards its base, its first half minutely edged with white, and some blue spots on its posterior half: anal covered with minute black points: pectoral orange, with a blue ocellus on the upper half of its base, its lowest ray deep blue: ventral blackish. Caudal nearly black, having from three to four rows of bluish-white spots between each ray.

Habitat.—Madras, to $2\frac{1}{2}$ inches long. Genus *Acentrogobius*, Bleeker, MSS.

14. Gobius zonalternans.

B. v, D. 6 | $\frac{1}{9}$, P. 17, V. 1/5, A. $\frac{1}{9}$, C. 13, L. l. 27, L. tr. 6.

Length of head $4\frac{1}{3}$, of caudal $4\frac{1}{2}$, height of body $6\frac{1}{3}$ in the total length. *Eyes*—diameter $3\frac{1}{4}$ in length of head, 1/2 a diameter from end of snout, and 1/6 of a diameter apart. Greatest width of head equals half its length, and its height equals its length excluding the snout. Lower jaw slightly the longer, the maxilla reaches to below the first third of the eye. No warts or barbels on the head. *Teeth*—in several cardiform rows, directed rather inwards, and having an external enlarged row, the outer of which in the lower jaw is a large recurved canine. *Fins*—spines of first dorsal very thin having filamentous terminations, and much higher than the body: last dorsal and anal rays long and reach the caudal fin. Pectoral and ventral reach the anal. Caudal pointed. *Scales*—cycloid, very small ones before the first dorsal fin, and not extending to so far as the hind edge of the eyes. *Colours*—a large blue spot surrounded with black on the opercle: body with brown bands going from the dorsal to the abdominal surface, they are of an angular form, the angle directed backwards: a dark band over the free portion of the tail just before the base of the caudal fin, which has a black basal band, whilst its outer half is gray. First dorsal with a white band along its base, and a dark blotch between the last dorsal spines. Other fins dark gray.

Habitat.—Madras: two specimens up to $1\frac{1}{4}$ inches, from brackish water (Adyair river).

15. Gobius biocellatus, Plate LXIII, fig. 8.

Cuv. and Val. xii, p. 73; Günther, Catal. iii, p. 20; Day, Proc. Zool. Soc. 1868, p. 154.

Gobius Celebicus, Cuv. and Val. xii, p. 74; Bleeker, Bant. p. 318.

Gobius sublitus, Cantor, Catal. p. 181; Günther, Catal. iii, p. 24.

Cephalogobius sublitus, Bleeker, Gobioides, p. 32=*Glossogobius sublitus*, Bleeker MSS.

B. v, D. 6 | $\frac{1}{9}$, P. 19, V. 1/5, A. $\frac{1}{8}$, C. 15, L. l. 28-30, L. tr. 7-8.

Length of head 4 to $4\frac{3}{4}$, of caudal 6, height of body 6 in the total length. *Eyes*—high up, diameter 1/4 to 1/5 of length of head, 1 to $1\frac{1}{4}$ diameters from end of snout, 1/4 of a diameter apart. Height and breadth of head equal, and as long as the head behind the middle of the eyes. Cleft of mouth rather oblique, lower jaw the longer: the maxilla reaches to below the middle of the orbit, nearest point from eye to angle of preopercle 1/2 longer than the snout. A large open pore in the posterior third of the interorbital space. Several rows of fine warts on the cheeks. *Teeth*—several cardiform rows in the centre of the upper jaw directed inwards, becoming two laterally, the outer one enlarged: a narrow cardiform band in the lower jaw, also directed inwards and becoming two rows laterally, irrespective of these is an outer enlarged row and about ten enlarged teeth in front of the lower jaw, the external of which is slightly recurved and canine-like in large specimens. *Fins*—first dorsal spines weak, the fifth slightly the longest, the first as high as the second dorsal, the last ray of which is as long as the head. Pectoral as long as the head excluding the snout: ventral extends beyond the vent. *Scales*—ctenoid, 18 to 20 rows between orbit and base of dorsal fin: none on cheeks: some on opercle, much smaller than those on the rest of the body, where they are angular. *Colours*—these vary, generally grayish-brown, with some large irregular blotches along the sides, and a slight brownish line along the centre of each row of scales: under surface of cheeks and jaws lineated with circuitous brownish lines. Dorsal fin generally yellowish, with a grayish tinge, and having several irregular whitish lines along its lower half, and usually also a black blotch with a white edge between its fifth and sixth spines: second dorsal with several rows of irregular white spots: pectoral, ventral, and anal grayish, the last with some white dots: caudal dark gray, with some lines of dark spots.

Habitat.—Coasts of India as high as Sind, and to the Malay Archipelago. Genus *Glossogobius*, Bleeker MSS.

16. Gobius Madraspatensis, Plate LXII, fig. 3.

Day, Proc. Zool. Soc. 1868, p. 152.

B. v, D. 6 | $\frac{1}{10}$, P. 17, V. 1/4, A. $\frac{1}{9}$, C. 13, L. l. 28-29, L. tr. 7.

Length of head 5 to $5\frac{1}{4}$, caudal $5\frac{1}{2}$ to 6, height of body 4 to $4\frac{1}{2}$ in the total length. *Eyes*—their upper margin near the profile, diameter 1/4 of length of head, 2/3 of a diameter from end of snout, 1/4 of a diameter apart. Width of head equals its postorbital length: height of head equals its length without the snout. Some rows of warts across the cheeks: two open glands in the interorbital space. Cleft of mouth oblique, commencing opposite the upper third of the eye, the lower jaw the longer, the maxilla extending to beneath the anterior margin of the orbit. *Teeth*—villiform in both jaws, with an outer enlarged row in the upper, and about 14 enlarged ones anteriorly in the lower jaw, ending in a large external recurved canine. *Fins*—dorsal spines flexible, the first with a filamentous termination, the fin ending near the commencement of the second dorsal which is rather the highest. Pectoral as long as the head, and of equal length to the ventrals. Anal commences below second or third dorsal ray. Caudal rounded. *Scales*—ctenoid, they extend forwards to nearly as far as the posterior margin of the orbit, and are smaller on the nape than on the remainder of the body: none on the head, about 12 rows anterior to the base of the dorsal fin: seven rows between the origin of the second dorsal and anal. *Colours*—olivaceous, with irregular, ill defined brownish blotches and dots. From five to eight very narrow vertical black lines pass from the back to the abdomen, commencing opposite the base of the ventrals and terminating about the middle of the anal. Fins grayish, first dorsal with two rows of black blotches, and sometimes a black blotch covering one-third of the membrane between the fifth and sixth spines, which may be continued to the end of the fin: second dorsal irregularly blotched and dotted. Pectoral and anal unspotted. Ventrals tipped with black. Caudal minutely dotted in rows.

Habitat.—Madras backwaters, up to about 3 inches in length. Genus *Acentrogobius*, Bleeker MSS.

17. Gobius Neilli, Plate LXII, fig. 4.

Day, Proc. Zool. Soc. 1868, p. 152.

B. v, D. 6 | $\frac{1}{10}$, P. 17, V. 1/5, A. 9, C. 13, L. l. 28, L. tr. 7.

Length of head 2/7, of caudal 1/5, height of body 1/4 of the total length. *Eyes*—directed upwards and slightly outwards, diameter 2/7 of length of head, 1 diameter from end of snout, and less than 1/6 of a diameter apart. Head as broad as high, equalling its length behind the middle of the eye. Cheeks swollen. No warts or barbels but an open pore in front of the interorbital space and another at the posterior inferior angle of the eye: cleft of mouth very oblique, commencing opposite the upper third of the eye: the posterior extremity of the maxilla extends to beneath the anterior third of the orbit. *Teeth*—in two or three rows in either jaw, an outer row of enlarged ones anteriorly in the upper, and a much larger outer series of twelve or fourteen in the lower jaw, the external of which on either side is a large recurved canine. *Fins*—first dorsal spines flexible and prolonged, the termination of the second in the adult being filamentous. Pectoral as long as the head: ventrals reach the anal: caudal somewhat pointed. *Scales*—in regular rows, ctenoid, anteriorly they extend (in about 12 rows, the first eight of which are small), three-fourths of the distance from the first dorsal to the orbits: seven rows between the bases of the second dorsal and anal: none on the head, gill-opening extending inferiorly to rather below the base of the pectoral fin. *Colours*—superiorly ochreous, becoming dirty white on the abdomen, cheeks, head, and upper two-thirds of the body being blotched over with various sized rusty brown dots of irregular shape, forming oblique bands on the head. Pectoral and ventrals unspotted. First dorsal with a black mark between its first and fifth spine to about half the height of the fin, above this it is yellow, the ends of the spine black, last two spines brown spotted. Second dorsal brown externally, with a longitudinal yellow and black band dividing it from the lower three-fourths of the fin which is spotted with light brown: caudal barred with eight or nine chestnut spots.

Habitat.—Madras, up to $3\frac{1}{2}$ inches in length. Genus *Acentrogobius*, Bleeker MSS.

18. Gobius melanosticta, Plate LXIII, fig. 2.

B. v, D. 6 | $\frac{1}{10}$, P. 17, V. 1/5, A. 9, C. 13, L. l. 24, L. tr. 7.

Length of head 5 to $5\frac{1}{2}$, of caudal $4\frac{1}{2}$, height of body $4\frac{1}{2}$ in the total length. *Eyes*—diameter 1/3 of length of head, 1/2 diameter from end of snout, and 1/3 apart. Greatest width of head equals its height, or its length excluding the snout. Upper jaw slightly the longer: cleft of mouth oblique, commencing opposite the lower edge of the eye: the maxilla reaches to below the last third or middle of the eye. No barbels. Scales cover opercles. *Teeth*—in villiform rows with an outer enlarged series, the outer tooth of the enlarged row in the lower jaw a small recurved canine. *Fins*—first dorsal spines with filamentous terminations, the fin rather higher than the second, the last rays of which latter equals the height of the body. Pectoral as long as the head: ventral reaches half way to the vent. Caudal rounded. *Scales*—scarcely ctenoid, about 9 rows between the dorsal fin and the hind edge of the eyes. *Colours*—light brown, most of the scales on the body with a dark spot or vertical mark; a dark blotch on the opercles, and another below the eye. Dorsal and caudal fins with numerous dark spots forming bars. Pectoral with a dark mark at its base.

Habitat.—Backwaters of Madras, up to 2 inches in length.

B. *No lateral recurved canine in the lower jaw: dorsal spines flexible.*

19. Gobius cristatus, Plate LXII, fig. 8.

Ectenogobius cristatus, Day, Proc. Zool. Soc. 1873, p. 109.

B. v, D. 6/14, P. 21, V. 1/5, A. 14, C. 13, L. l. 50-60, L. tr. 11-12.

Length of head 5½, of caudal 3 to 4, height of body 6 in the total length. *Eyes*—rather superior, with a very narrow and concave interorbital space, diameter 1/4 of length of head, 1 diameter from end of snout. Greatest width of head equals its length behind the middle of the eyes, whilst its height is a little more. Cleft of mouth oblique, lower jaw the longer, the maxilla reaches to below the middle of the orbit, the width of the gape of the mouth is 1/4 less than the length of its cleft. Several rows of fine warts across the cheeks. Barbels absent, no tentacle at the orbit. A low black-stained crest extends from the nape to the base of the first dorsal fin. *Teeth*—in a single row in the upper jaw, in above two in the lower, the outer of which is directed somewhat outwards. No canines. Inferior pharyngeal bones in close juxtaposition along the median line, the two have a T-shape, and a single row of teeth. *Fins*—all the spines in the first dorsal flexible and elongated beyond the membrane: last rays of second dorsal the longest in the fin, the two fins are close together at their bases. Anal similar to second dorsal: caudal pointed and elongated. Ventral reaches the vent. *Scales*—cycloid, in irregular rows and very small anterior to the second dorsal fin: about 18 rows anterior to the dorsal fin. *Colours*—olivaceous: one or two black spots on the posterior-superior angle of the eye: a light ocellus having a brown edge at the base of the pectoral fin: body blotched and spotted: some black bars on upper half of dorsal, and a badly defined violet ocellus edged with yellow on its last ray: caudal spotted in its upper half.

The Madras specimens differ somewhat in having a light edge to the anal fin, ventral dark gray, and no ocellus on the dorsal, whilst the caudal fin is longer: it has a dark spot under the eye. Doubtless this species is very similar to *G. tentacularis*, and although it wants the tentacle on the eye, it has a black spot at the same place. Genus *Oxyurichthys*, Bleeker MSS.

Habitat.—Madras and Bombay, where in the month of March they were breeding.

20. Gobius tentacularis, Plate LXIV, fig. 4.

Cuv. and Val. xii, p. 128; Bleeker, Java, ii, p. 434; Günther, Catal. iii, p. 48.
Gobius macrurus, Bleeker, Blenn. en Gob. p. 35.
Oxyurichthys tentacularis, Bleeker, En. Spec. p. 120.

B. v, D. 6 | 1/11, P. 20, V. 1/5, A. 1/11, C. 15, L. l. 60, L. tr. 10.

Length of head 5½ to 6½, of caudal 3¾, height of body 7 to 8 (9½) in the total length. *Eyes*—high up and close together, diameter 3¾ in length of head, 1 diameter from end of snout. Width of head equals its length behind the middle of the eye: its height equals its length excluding the snout. Snout somewhat obtuse and rounded, cleft of mouth oblique, commencing opposite the lower edge of the orbit, lower jaw the longer, the maxilla reaches to below last third of eye. A simple tentacle above the posterior third of the eye, and about 2/3 of the length of the orbit. *Teeth*—in a single row of rather pointed ones in the premaxillaries: in two or three rows in the lower jaw without any canines. *Fins*—dorsal spines flexible, extending far beyond the membrane and equal to the height of the body, second dorsal about equally high, the distance between the bases of the two fins is not so much as one diameter of the eye. Pectoral as long as the head, and 1/4 longer than the ventral. Anal commences below origin of second dorsal: caudal acutely pointed. *Scales*—ctenoid in the posterior part of the body, they extend forward nearly to the eyes, none on the crest going from the base of the first dorsal fin or on the head, there are about 20 rows anterior to the dorsal fin. They are very much smaller anterior to the second dorsal fin, and on the breast and chest before the anal fin. An anal papilla. *Colours*—dull green, with some reddish spots. First dorsal with four to six narrow bands of horizontal spots, and six or eight along the second dorsal. Caudal gray, with some spots on its upper half. Anal gray, with a narrow white band at its base.

Habitat.—Seas of India to the Malay Archipelago. The specimen figured (life-size) is from the Andamans.

21. Gobius acutipinnis, Plate LXI, fig. 2.

Cuv. and Val. xii, p. 80; Günther, Catal. iii, p. 44; Day, Fish. Malabar, p. 112.
Gobius setosus, Cuv. and Val. xii, p. 81.

Many-woo-yoo-du-lah-dah, Andam.

B. v, D. 6 | $\frac{1}{10-11}$, P. 19, V. 1/5, A. $\frac{1}{9}$, C. 19, L. l. 25-28, L. tr. 6-7.

Length of head from 5 to 6, of pectoral 4½ to 5, of caudal 3 to 3½, height of body 5 to 6, of first dorsal 3 to 4, of second dorsal 5 to 5½ in the total length. *Eyes*—diameter 3¼ to 3½ in length of head, 1 diameter from end of snout, and 1/6 of a diameter apart. Snout obtuse and rounded: cleft of mouth oblique, its anterior extremity commencing opposite the lower edge of the eye, the width of gape equalling length of cleft. The maxilla reaches to beneath the anterior edge of the eye. Greatest width of head equals its length behind the middle of the eye, whilst its height equals its length excluding the snout. A narrow row of warts across the cheeks, a large opening of mucous canals opposite the posterior inferior angle of the orbit. *Teeth*—villiform in two or three rows in the upper and several in the lower jaw, the outer of which is very slightly enlarged: no canines.* *Fins*—spines of first dorsal weak, with filamentous terminations: last dorsal ray divided at its base. Caudal lanceolate. *Scales*—angular, ctenoid, none on the head or in front of the base of the first dorsal fin. *Colours*—grayish-brown superiorly, becoming dull white beneath: four or five (sometimes more) dull blotches almost forming bands pass from the back down the sides: a dark mark at the base of the caudal fin. A brown band goes from the corner of the eye down the cheeks to behind the angle of the mouth. Four lines of spots or bands along both dorsal fins: some obscure brownish bands sometimes present on the caudal, especially on its central rays; the fins generally dark gray with a light outer edge. Pectoral, ventral, and anal stained of a slate colour.

Habitat.—Seas of India to the Andaman islands, is very common up to 3½ inches in length. The specimen figured (life-size) is from Madras. Genus *Acentrogobius*, Bleeker MSS.

22. Gobius striatus, Plate LXII, fig. 6.

Rhinogobius striatus, Day, Proc. Zool. Soc. 1868, p. 272 c. fig.
Coondalloon, Tam.: *Mahtoei*, *Nuolli (young)*, Ooriah.

B. v, D. 6 | $\frac{1}{10}$, P. 15, V. 1/5, A. 10, C. 15, L. l. 56-60, L. tr. 14, Vert. 11/16.

Length of head 4 to 4½, of caudal 5 to 5¾, height of body 5½ to 6¾ in the total length. *Eyes*—not prominent, directed upwards and outwards, diameter 1/6 to 1/7 of length of head, 2 to 2½ diameters from end of snout, and 1/2 a diameter apart. Body elongated: sides compressed. Snout elongated, cheeks inflated: head 4/7 as broad as long, height equals 1/2 of length: no tentacles. Jaws of equal length, or the lower slightly the longer. Cleft of mouth nearly horizontal, the maxilla reaches to nearly below front edge of the eye. *Teeth*—in one row in the upper and in two or three rows in the centre of the lower jaw, becoming one or two laterally, as a rule no canines, but present in one specimen; also on the inferior pharyngeal bones which are of an elongated triangular shape, having a median longitudinal suture. *Fins*—first dorsal spines weak, not filamentous, and 3/4 the height of the body: second dorsal rays of about equal height: last dorsal ray divided to its root, it only reaches 1/2 way to the base of the caudal: caudal slightly rounded. *Scales*—ctenoid, those anterior to the dorsal fin smaller than the rest on the body: none on the cheeks and head: 30 rows between occiput and dorsal fin: 14 rows between the origin of the second dorsal and anal fins. *Colours*—generally light fulvous, with a bluish tinge along the sides, becoming dirty-white beneath: some irregular bands pass from the back towards the middle of the body, also some thin black lines proceed upwards on the abdomen opposite to the anal fin: cheeks glossed with silver: pectoral, ventral and anal whitish-yellow: both dorsals diaphanous, with five or six rows of brown dots: caudal with eight or nine vertical rows of spots in its upper half or two-thirds.

Dr. Bleeker, who has been good enough to go through my plates of Gobies, suggests that this species of Genus *Awaous*, is very closely allied to, if not identical with, *Gobius stamineus*, Val. Voy. Bonite, Poissons, p. 179, pl. 5, f. 5, from the Sandwich islands.

A very good coloured figure exists amongst Sir W. Elliot's drawings marked "*Kel Oolooa*, Tam. Fresh water, *Gobius Russellii*, Russell, pl. 53."

Habitat.—Fresh and backwaters of Madras and Canara.

23. Gobius personatus, Plate LXIII, fig. 6.

Gobius melanocephalus, Bleeker, Blen. en Gob. p. 33.
Gobius personatus, Bleeker, l. c. p. 34, and Nat. Tyds. Ned.-Ind. 1851, f. 4.
Gobius grammepomus, Bleeker, l. c. p. 34; Günther, Catal. iii, pp. 64, 554.
Gobius litteratus, (Heck.) Steind. Sitz. Wien Acad. 1861, p. 289, f. 4, 5.
Gobius Stoliczkae, Day, Proc. Zool. Soc. 1870, p. 692.

B. v, D. 6 | $\frac{1}{10}$, P. 16, V. 1/5, A. $\frac{1}{10}$, C. 12, L. l. 55, L. tr. 14.

Length of head 3¾ to 4, of caudal 5 to 5½, height of body 5½ to 6½ in the total length. *Eyes*—diameter 1/6 of length of head, 2 diameters from end of snout, and nearly 1 diameter apart. Greatest width of head equals its length behind the middle of the eyes, its height equals half its length. No warts or tentacles on the head. Cleft of mouth slightly oblique, commencing opposite the lower edge of the eye, upper jaw a little the longer: the maxilla reaches to below the front edge of the eye. *Teeth*—in several fixed rows in the upper jaw,

* In one specimen there is a small canine internally on either side of the symphysis of the lower jaw.

the outer of which is the longer: in many villiform rows in the lower jaw, the outer of which are fine, rather elongated and slightly horizontal. *Fins*—dorsal spines weak, with filamentous terminations as high as the body and equalling the last rays of the dorsal fin, which are the longest and extend to the base of the caudal fin. Pectoral 3/4 of length of head, and 1/4 longer than the ventral. Caudal cut nearly square. *Scales*—ctenoid, those anterior to the dorsal fin in about 22 rows of rounded ones, which are much smaller than those on the body, and extend forwards as far as the eye, some exist on the upper portion of the opercles: those on the body angular. *Colours*—of a light brown, a little darkest along the back and upper surface of the head, a black spot at posterior superior angle of opercle, the head and upper two-thirds of the body with numerous vermiculated black lines and spots, the dorsal fin with three or four rows of spots forming bars, and sometimes a dark mark in its outer half from the fifth spine to the end of the fin. Anal with a white outer edge. Caudal with five or six angular bars or irregularly placed spots.

Habitat.—Seas of India to the Malay Archipelago, apparently preferring brackish waters, as estuaries and backwaters, due to which cause its colours appear subject to considerable variation. The specimen figured (life-size) is from the Andamans. Genus *Amoya*, Bleeker MSS.

24. Gobius Malabaricus.

Day, Proc. Zool. Soc. 1865, p. 27, and Fishes of Malabar, p. 111, pl. vii, f. 2.

B. v, D. 6 | $\frac{1}{8}$, P. 13, V. 1/5, A. $\frac{1}{8}$, C. 13, L. l. 50, L. tr. 9.

Length of head 1/5, of caudal 1/4, height of body 1/5 of the total length. *Eyes*—diameter 1/6 of length of head, 1 diameter from end of snout, 1/2 a diameter apart. Height of head 2/3 of its length, snout obtuse: cleft of mouth oblique, the lower jaw the longer, the maxilla extends backwards to beneath the anterior third of the orbit. *Teeth*—an external enlarged row in either jaw, no canines. *Fins*—dorsal spines weak, not filiform, not quite so long as the second dorsal, the last rays of which reach the base of the caudal, which last is rounded with the middle rays rather the longest. *Scales*—ctenoid, angular, nine rows between the origin of the second dorsal and anal fins, none on the head. *Colours*—light brown, with irregular dusky bands on the back and sides, a dark band descends from the eye, and some brown blotches about the head. A deep black crescentic mark on the first dorsal fin, commencing between the second and third spines and continued to the last, above this is a white curved band bordered with black. Second dorsal, anal, and caudal brownish, barred with several rows of darker spots.

Gobius neglectus, Jerdon, M. J. L. and Sc. 1849, p. 148, may be this species, or *Gobius striatus*, p. 292. Neither *Gobius Malabaricus* or *G. striatus*, so far as I have observed, ever attain to nearly eight inches in length as *G. neglectus* is said to, irrespective of which Jerdon considered *striatus* as *G. Russellii*, C. V. (See p. 295.)

Habitat.—Backwaters in Madras, also in some of the rivers of Malabar, to about 4 inches in length.

25. Gobius planifrons, Plate LXIII, fig. 9.

Day, Proc. Zool. Soc. 1873, p. 108.

B. v, D. 6 | $\frac{1}{10}$, P. 19, V. 1/5, A. 10, C. 13, L. l. 46, L. tr. 15.

Length of head $4\frac{1}{2}$, of caudal $5\frac{1}{2}$, height of body $5\frac{3}{4}$ in the total length. *Eyes*—very high up, diameter 1/6 of length of head, 1 diameter from end of snout, and $1\frac{1}{3}$ apart. Greatest width of head equals its length excluding the snout, and its height equals half its length. Upper surface of head flat. Cleft of mouth horizontal, with the jaws anteriorly of about the same length; width of the gape equals about half the length of the head, the maxilla reaches to two diameters of the orbit behind its posterior edge. Fine tentacles near the nostrils, and rows of warty glands along the scaleless head. *Teeth*—in numerous villiform rows, the outer of which are a little enlarged: no canines. *Fins*—first dorsal low, about half as high as the body beneath it: the second higher. Pectoral as long as the head without the snout: ventral reaches half way to the anal: caudal rounded. Anal papilla rather large. *Scales*—those on the body finely ctenoid, about 18 rows before the dorsal fin: the rows on the body very irregular, anteriorly they reach to half way between the first dorsal and the hind edge of the eye. *Colours*—olive, fins very dark gray, second dorsal spotted: a black blotch at the base of the pectoral.

Habitat.—Bombay, where the specimen figured (life-size) was obtained.

26. Gobius elegans.

(Kuhl and v. Hass.) Cuv. and Val. xii, p. 58; Bleeker, Nat. Tyds. Ned. Ind. 1851, i, f. 10; Cantor, Catal. p. 179; Gunther, Catal. iii, p. 18.

B. v, D. 6 | $\frac{1}{10}$, P. 18, V. 1/5, A. $\frac{1}{9}$, C. 18, L. l. 36, L. tr. 9.

Length of head 1/5, height of body 1/6 of the total length. Snout obtuse. *Teeth*—small and of equal size. *Fins*—first dorsal rather lower than the second, which equals that of the body. Caudal rounded. *Colours*—buff, with a tinge of olive, minutely dotted with brown: the upper half of the sides with three or four indistinct lines, each formed by a series of very short brown streaks, beneath which are a series of indistinct brown spots: a blackish spot at the posterior margin of the orbit: a second at the upper part of the root of the pectoral fin, and a third at the lower part of the root, spreading on to the gill-membrane. Near the lower part of the root of the pectoral is a faint trace of a fourth brown spot. The membranes of the fins are of a very pale bluish-green, minutely clouded with brown: those of the dorsals, particularly the second, with three or four indistinct series of blackish spots, and a few similar on the caudal membrane. The rays of the anterior dorsal have two or three series of brown spots. Iris pale greenish-silvery, minutely dotted with brown. (Cantor.)

Habitat.—Bombay to the Malay Archipelago, it appears to be a small marine or estuary species.

27. Gobius ornatus, Plate LXIII, fig. 1.

Gobius ornatus, Rüpp. Atl. Fische, p. 135, and N. W. Fische, p. 137; Günther, Catal. iii, p. 21; Peters, Monats. Akad. Berlin, 1868, p. 263; Day, Proc. Zool. Soc. 1870, p. 691; Kner, Novara Fische, p. 173; Klunz. Verh. z. b. Ges. Wien, 1871, p. 473.

Gobius centralis, (Ehren.) Cuv. and Val. xii, p. 113.

Gobius interstinctus, Richards. Erebus and Terror, p. 3, pl. 5, fig. 3-6; Bleeker, Amb. and Ceram. p. 275.

Gobius periophthalmoides, Bleek. Nat. Tyd. Ned. Ind. 1851, i, p. 249.

B. v, D. 6 | $\frac{1}{10}$, P. 21, V. 1/5, A. $\frac{1}{9}$, C. 13, L. l. 26-28, L. tr. 7.

Length of head 4 to $4\frac{1}{2}$, of caudal 5, height of body 6 to 7 in the total length. *Eyes*—diameter 1/3 to 2/7 of length of head, 1 diameter from end of snout, 1/4 of a diameter apart. Snout obtuse, convex. Head as broad as high, and equalling two-thirds of its length. Jaws of about equal length. Cleft of mouth very slightly oblique, the maxilla reaching to below first third of orbit. *Teeth*—in villiform rows, no canines. *Fins*—first dorsal somewhat lower than the second or than the body. Pectoral as long as the head: caudal rounded. *Scales*—ctenoid, they extend on to the crown of the head, 13 rows before the base of the dorsal fin: seven rows between the bases of the second dorsal and anal fins. *Colours*—green, with numerous oblong brown spots, generally in three or four rows, also yellow dots in the centre of some of the scales: all the fins, except the ventral, dotted with black.

Some specimens in the Calcutta Museum were marked *Gobius maculatus*, Blyth, but I have been unable to ascertain if such a name was ever published. Genus *Acentrogobius*, Bleeker MSS.

Habitat.—Red Sea to the Malay Archipelago, the specimen figured is from the Andamans.

28. Gobius gutum.

Ham. Buch. Fish. Ganges, pp. 50, 366; Cuv. and Val. xii, p. 139.

D. 6 | $\frac{1}{10}$, P. 13, V. 5/5, A. 11, C. 17.

Head small, narrower than the body. *Eyes*—small. Mouth large, the upper jaw the longer. *Teeth*—sharp. *Fins*—pectoral and caudal rounded. *Scales*—ctenoid. *Colours*—greenish, with many black dots clustered into irregular spots resembling clouds in form: dorsal and caudal fins spotted. A figure of this species $2\frac{1}{10}$ inches in length exists amongst Hamilton Buchanan's MSS. drawings at Calcutta.

Habitat.—Lower portion of the Hooghly, to three or four inches in length.

29. Gobius albo-punctatus, Plate LXIII, fig. 7.

Cuv. and Val. xii, p. 57; Blyth, Proc. Asiat. Soc. Beng. 1860, p. 111; Günther, Catal. iii, p. 25; Kner, Novara Fische, p. 174; Klunz. Verh. z. b. Ges. Wien, 1871, p. 473.

? *Gobius nebulo-punctatus*, Rüpp. N. W. Fische, p. 139; Cuv. and Val. xii, p. 58; Klunz. Verh. z. b. Ges. Wien, 1871, p. 472.

Gobius punctillatus, Rüpp. Atl. Fische, p. 138, and N. W. Fische, p. 138.

? *Gobius fuscus*, Rüpp. Atl. Fische, p. 137.

Gobius Padangensis, Bleeker, Bleun. en Gob. p. 249.

Gobius breviceps, Blyth, Proc. Asiat. Soc. Beng. 1858, p. 271.

B. v, D. 6 | $\frac{1}{9}$, P. 21, V. 1/5, A. $\frac{1}{8}$, C. 13, L. l. 35-40, L. tr. 11-12.

Length of head $4\frac{1}{4}$ to $4\frac{3}{4}$, of caudal $4\frac{2}{3}$, height of body $5\frac{1}{4}$ in the total length. *Eyes*—diameter 2/9 to 1/5 of length of head, $1\frac{1}{4}$ diameters from end of snout, and 3/4 of a diameter apart. Greatest width of head equals its length excluding the snout, whilst its height equals its length behind the eye. Cleft of mouth slightly oblique, the maxilla reaching to below the first third of the eye. *Teeth*—in villiform rows in both jaws, the outer row of which is slightly enlarged. No canines. No glands, warts, or barbels on the head. *Fins*—first dorsal lower than, or of equal height to, the second, the anterior rays of which equal the height of the body. Pectoral as long as the head excluding the snout. Ventral does not quite reach the anus. Caudal rounded. *Scales*—those on the nape rounded, cycloid, and in about 20 rows anterior to the dorsal fin, those on the rest of the body feebly ctenoid, and in 11 or 12 rows between the bases of the second dorsal and anal fins. An anal papilla. *Colours*—brownish, irregularly marbled: sides of head and body studded with white spots: dorsal and caudal grayish, dotted with black, forming three rows on the first and second dorsal fins: the other fins unspotted. In some instances the dorsal, caudal, and pectoral are blackish, with a row of white dots.

Habitat.—Red Sea, Andamans, Mauritius, Feejee islands, and Port Essington. The specimen figured (life-size) is from Port Blair.

30. Gobius giuris, Plate LXVII, fig. 1.

Gobius korah mottah, Russell, Fish. Vizag. i, p. 40, pl. 50.

Gobius koku, Russell, l. c. p. 41, pl. 51.

Gobius bulle kokah, Russell, l. c. p. 42, pl. 53.

Gobius giuris, Ham. Buch. Fish. Ganges, pp. 51, 366, pl. 33, fig. 15; Cuv. and Val. xii, p. 72; Bleeker, Blenn. en Gob. p. 24; Günther, Catal. iii, p. 21; Peters, Monats. Akad. Berlin, 1868, p. 263, and Reise nach Mosambique, p. 20; Day, Fish. Malabar, p. 109; Kner, Novara Fische, p. 173.

Gobius kurpah, Sykes, Tr. Zool. Soc. ii, p. 352, pl. 61, f. 1.

Gobius kokius, Cuv. and Val. xii, p. 68; Jacq. Atl. t. xiv, f. 3; Jerdon, M. J. L. and Sc. 1849, p. 148; Bleeker, Verb. Bat. Gen. xxii, 24, 3; Cantor, Catal. p. 180.

Gobius catebus, Cuv. and Val. xii, p. 76; Jerdon, M. J. L. and Sc. 1851, p. 143.

Gobius kora, Cuv. and Val. xii, p. 77.

Gobius platycephalus, Peters. Monats. Akad. Berlin, 1852, p. 681, and Reise nach Mosambique, t. iii, f. 2.

Gobius spectabilis, Günther, Catal. iii, p. 45.

Wartee-poolah, *Pooan*, and *Kurdán*, Mal.; *Nullatan*, *Oolooway*, Tam.; *Tsikkdrondoa* and *Isnakee* [illegible], Tel.; *Gulah*, Ooriah; *Nga-tha-boh*, Burmese; *Poo-dah*, Andam.; *Ab-bro-my*, Canarese; *Goo-loo-wah*, and *B*[illegible], Punj.; *Gooloo*, Sind. and N. W. Prov.

B. iv, D. 6 | $\frac{1}{9-10}$, P. 20, V. 1/5, A. $\frac{1}{8-9}$, C. 17, L. l. 30-34, L. tr. 8-9, Vert. 11/16.

Length of head 3¼ to 4, of caudal 4 to 5½, height of body 5 to 6¼ in the total length. *Eyes*—diameter 1/6 to 1/8 of length of head, 2 to 2½ diameters from end of snout, and 1/3 to 3/4 of a diameter apart. Interorbital space slightly concave, with an open gland. Greatest width of head* equals from 1/2 to 3/5 of the length of the head, whilst its height equals about 1/2 its length. Lower jaw the longer, the maxilla extends to below the anterior edge of the orbit. *Teeth*—in villiform rows, with an outer enlarged row in the upper jaw, laterally in two rows of which the inner is sometimes the larger: in the lower jaw a large row anteriorly, laterally two rows. *Fins*—these are subject to very great variations as to the length of the spines and rays, as might be anticipated in a fish which is so extensively used for stocking ponds, and as far as I have seen the variety *G. giuris*, or *G. spectabilis*, is that in which they are most lengthened. I have a specimen from Calcutta in which the caudal fin is 1/4 of the total length, and another from Assam in which it is 4½, as shown in Ham. Buch. In some the spines of the first dorsal are a little higher than the body, in others a little lower: the posterior rays of the second dorsal reach to the caudal, in others not above 1/2 way to that fin. Caudal somewhat pointed or rounded. *Scales*—extend superiorly to nearly as far as the hind edge of the eyes, and from 25 to 30 rows before the base of the dorsal fin, where they are smaller than those on the body which are angular and ctenoid. *Colours*—vary both with the localities and also with the colour of the water, they may generally be said to be of a fawn-colour, with cloudy markings on the head, and irregular bands, spots, or blotches, on the back and sides of the body. Vertical fins spotted.

This fish may be divided as follows:—

Gobius giuris, H. B.=*G. catebus*, C. V.=*G. spectabilis*, Günther. As a rule there is no distinct black blotch on the first dorsal spine, but both the dorsal fins have from six to eight or even more rows of spots: the caudal is closely banded in spots, as in *G. puntang*. This form is most common in the freshwaters of Bengal, Assam, and Burma, but it does not exclude either of the two next.

Gobius kora motteh, Russell=*G. kora*, C. V. In this form, the tail fin is entirely, or almost entirely destitute of spots, but instead has dark edges.

Gobius bullee kokah, Russell=*G. kurpah*, Sykes=*G. Russellii*, C. V.=*G. platycephalus*, Peters. There are usually only three or four rows of spots along the dorsal fins, and a deep black blotch on the first dorsal spine anteriorly, which extends on to the interspinous membrane. The caudal has distinct black bands, from four to six or eight, but is not so closely barred as in the Bengal variety.

Gobius koku, Russell=*G. kokius*, C. V. is an entirely marine form, and probably a distinct species. Its snout is narrower at its base where it only equals its length. The last rays of the dorsal fin are short. It has four or five large blotches along the sides, and intermediate above them usually three more. Its fins are spotted in about three or four rows, there is no black blotch on the first dorsal spine: its caudal is spotted in rows.

This fish is much esteemed by the natives of India as being very light and wholesome, but unless elaborately cooked is not relished by Europeans, because of its deficiency in or earthy taste. It is very voracious and takes a bait freely.

Habitat.—East coast of Africa, also in all pieces of fresh water throughout the plains of India, Ceylon, Burma, Sind, to the Malay Archipelago and beyond: attaining a foot and a half in length. The variety (? species) *kokius* never exceeds a span, and appears to be entirely confined to the sea and estuaries all along the coasts of India, and also at the Andamans.

31. Gobius semidoliatus, Plate LIX, fig. 6 ($\frac{4}{1}$).

Cuv. and Val. xii, p. 67; Günther, Catal. iii, p. 31; Klunz. Verh. z. b. Ges. Wien, 1871, p. 475.

B. v, D. 6 | $\frac{1}{9}$, P. 17, V. 1/5, A. 8, C. 13, L. l. 28, L. tr. 9.

Length of head 4½, of caudal 4¾, height of body 4½ in the total length. *Eyes*—diameter 3½ in length of

* This is one of the freshwater species of Indian fishes in which but little reliance can be placed upon the "width of the head," because they frequently die with their mouths distended, as is so often seen in *Gudgeons* in Europe. All Museum specimens of GOBIIDÆ should be examined to see whether they have stiffened with their gills distended, as such alters the shape of the head.

head, 3/4 of a diameter from end of snout, and 1/2 a diameter apart. Dorsal profile more convex than that of the abdomen. Greatest width of head equals its length behind the middle of the eyes, whilst its height is slightly more. Lower jaw the longer, cleft of mouth oblique, commencing opposite the upper third of the eye, the maxilla reaches to below the middle of the orbit. Neither scales, rows of warts, or barbels on the head. *Teeth*—in villiform rows, the outer of which is enlarged, and the last of the outer row in the lower jaw is slightly recurved, but can scarcely be considered a canine.* *Fins*—dorsal spines flexible, having filamentous terminations, the fin is as high as the body, and 1/3 higher than the second. Pectoral as long as the head. Caudal rounded. *Scales*—strongly ctenoid. *Colours*—chestnut, with three rather wide transverse interorbital bands: between the eye and the dorsal fin are three more bands which cross the back, and four or five more descend from below the commencement of the second dorsal fin to 1/3 down the sides. Three bands descend from the eye, another over the opercle and one in front of the pectoral fin. Both dorsal fins with brown spots.

Habitat.—Red Sea to the Andamans. I obtained two small specimens of this species at the Andamans, the one figured is twice life-size.

32. Gobius magniloquus.

B. v, D. 6 | $\frac{1}{9}$, P. 17, V. 1/5, A. 9, C. 13, L. l. 38, L. tr. 10.

Length of head $4\frac{1}{4}$, of caudal $5\frac{1}{3}$, height of body $6\frac{1}{2}$ in the total length. *Eyes*—diameter $3\frac{3}{4}$ in length of head, 1/2 a diameter from end of snout, and 2/3 of a diameter apart. Greatest width of head equals half its length: its height equals its length behind the eyes. Snout slightly depressed. Cleft of mouth rather oblique, commencing opposite the lower edge of the eye, lower jaw the longer, the maxilla reaches to below the hind edge of the eye. *Teeth*—villiform, outer row enlarged, but without canines, two or three posterior canines in the middle line above the symphysis of the lower jaw. *Fins*—dorsal spines with filamentous terminations, and 2/3 as high as the body, an interspace of five scales between the bases of the two dorsal fins: last dorsal rays two-thirds the height of the body, and reach half way to the base of the caudal. Pectoral as long as the head behind the eyes. Caudal wedge-shaped. *Scales*—ctenoid, extending forwards to opposite the hind edge of the eyes, where there exists a large one (as in an *Ophiocephalus*) and 15 rows between it and the base of the first dorsal fin, which are scarcely smaller than those on the body. Opercles scaled. *Colours*—light brown, covered with fine black dots and spots on the scales. A dark band from the eye across the opercles. A dark spot on upper edge of base of pectoral. Dorsal and caudal spotted in rows.

Habitat.—Madras, to $1\frac{1}{4}$ inches in length.

33. Gobius planiceps.

B. v, D. 6 | $\frac{1}{9}$, P. 17, V. 1/5, A. 9, C. 13, L. l. 38, L. tr. 10.

Length of head $4\frac{1}{2}$, of caudal $4\frac{3}{4}$, height of body $4\frac{3}{4}$ in the total length. *Eyes*—diameter $3\frac{1}{2}$ in length of head, 3/4 of a diameter from end of snout, and $1\frac{1}{2}$ apart. Head broad and flattened superiorly, its greatest width equalling its length behind the middle of the eyes, its height rather less. Cleft of mouth oblique, commencing opposite the upper edge of the eye, the maxilla extends to below the middle of the eye. *Teeth*—villiform, with the outer row enlarged, no canines. *Fins*—dorsal spines 2/3 the height of the body, a distance equal to four scales between the bases of the two dorsal fins: last dorsal ray divided to its base, and nearly as high as the body. Caudal rounded. *Scales*—ctenoid, 19 rows before the first dorsal fin, they suddenly become larger below the second dorsal fin, where they are angular. *Colours*—dark brown, every scale on the body with a dark purplish band down its centre. A dark spot above the axilla. A black band across the base of the pectoral. Caudal with eight angular bars of spots.

Habitat.—Madras, up to $1\frac{1}{2}$ inches in length.

34. Gobius sadanundio, Plate LXIII, fig. 10.

Ham. Buch. Fish. Ganges, pp. 56, 366; Bleeker, Verh. Bat. Gen. xxv, Beng. en Hind. p. 102, t. 2, f. 2; Günther, Catal. iii, 29.

Oontee-nounsl, Mugh. (Akyab.)

B. v, D. 6 | $\frac{1}{9}$, P. 19, V. $\frac{1}{5}$, A. $\frac{1}{8}$, C. 15, L. l. 28-30, L. tr. 8.

Length of head $4\frac{1}{2}$, of pectoral 4, of caudal 5 to 6, height of body $4\frac{1}{2}$ to 5, of first dorsal up to 3, of second dorsal and anal each $5\frac{1}{2}$ to 6 in the total length. *Eyes*—diameter from 1/3 to 2/7 of the length of head, 1/4 to 1/2 a diameter from the end of the snout, and $1\frac{1}{2}$ apart. Greatest width of head equals its length excluding the snout, and its height is a little more. Mouth almost horizontal, cleft commencing opposite the lower edge of the eye: jaws of equal length. The maxilla reaches to below the middle or last third of the orbit. *Teeth*—villiform, without canines, outer row in premaxillaries enlarged. *Fins*—the second and third dorsal spines elongated, filamentous: four rows of scales between the two dorsal fins, the bases of which are 1 diameter of the orbit apart; about 10 rows anterior to the base of the first dorsal fin. Caudal rounded. *Scales*—ctenoid, eight rows between the origin of the second dorsal and anal fins: they exist on the opercles and are extended on the head to between the eyes, on the cheeks they are rudimentary. *Colours*—olive, with very large deep

* If this fish attains any size the probability is that a posterior lateral canine will be present in the lower jaw, judging from the dentition in specimens of other species of the same size and what exists when they become large.

black, white-edged blotches scattered over the body: first dorsal black, with a white ring on its last three rays; second dorsal with two rows of black spots along its base, and a third of white dots along its centre. Ventral black in the centre, and having orange edges. Anal dark olive, margined with black. Caudal with numerous fine black dots.

Habitat.—Mouths of the Ganges, and along the Chittagong and Burmese coasts, attaining at least 3 inches in length.

35. Gobius melanosoma, Plate LXIV, fig. 1, ($\frac{2}{1}$).

Bleeker, Ceram. ii, p. 703; Peters, Monats. Ak. Berlin, 1868, p. 265.
Gobius gobiodon, Day, Proc. Zool. Soc. 1869, p. 516.
Paragobiodon melanosoma, Bleeker, Gobioides, 1874, p. 21.

B. v, D. 6 | $\frac{1}{9}$, P. 21, V. 1/5, A. 10, C. 15, L. l. 22-25, L. tr. 8-9.

Length of head 3 to $3\frac{1}{3}$, of caudal 5, height of body $3\frac{1}{2}$ in the total length. *Eyes*—diameter $3\frac{2}{3}$ in length of head, 1/2 to 2/3 of a diameter from end of snout, and $1\frac{1}{4}$ diameters apart. Form of body elevated and compressed. Anterior portion of head and jaws covered with warty tubercles and fine hairy barbels. Cleft of mouth very oblique, commencing opposite the middle of the eyes: the maxilla reaching to below the front margin of the eyes. Height of head equals its length without the snout. *Teeth*—villiform, with one or two posterior canines above the symphysis of the lower jaw. *Fins*—first dorsal somewhat higher than the second, but not quite half of that of the body, the last dorsal ray reaches rather above half-way to the base of the caudal. Pectoral as long as the head excluding the snout; ventral reaches half-way to the anal. Caudal rounded. *Scales*—ctenoid, extending forwards to opposite the middle of the first dorsal fin, eight or nine rows between the bases of second dorsal and anal. *Colours*—brownish, the head may be light-coloured: dorsal, anal, and caudal very dark, ventrals nearly black having a reddish edge, caudal reddish.

Habitat.—Andamans and Nicobars to the Malay Archipelago. It appears to be a small species, the one figured (from the Andamans) is twice the natural size.

36. Gobius nunus.

Ham. Buch. Fish. Ganges, pp. 54, 366; Cuv. and Val. xii, p. 138.

B. v, D. 5 | $\frac{1}{9}$, P. 17, V. 1/5, A. 9, C. 15, L. l. 30, L. tr. 7.

Length of head $4\frac{1}{2}$, of caudal 5, height of body 5 in the total length. *Eyes*—small, in the anterior part of the head, 1 diameter from end of snout. Greatest width of head equals its height and half its length. Cleft of mouth very oblique, lower jaw the longer, the maxilla reaches to below the hind edge of the eye. *Teeth*—external row in lower jaw enlarged, the outer tooth being rather recurved. *Fins*—first dorsal spines with filamentous prolongations: caudal wedge-shaped. *Scales*—ctenoid, extended to over head and cheeks, ten rows before the dorsal fin. *Colours*—reddish-brown with seven black belts, the first through the eye, the second over the opercles, and five more down the body, the last being at the root of the caudal fin, these bands are extended on to the vertical fins.

Habitat.—River Hooghly, also Burma; the one described is hardly an inch in length, and was captured by the late Dr. Stoliczka in a freshwater stream, near Moulmein.

Genus, 2—Gobiodon, *Bleeker*.

Gill-openings of moderate width. Body oblong and compressed: head large. Teeth conical and fixed; a pair of posterior canines generally present near the symphysis of the lower jaw. Two dorsal fins, the first with six spines and united at its base to the second; ventrals united. Scales absent.

SYNOPSIS OF SPECIES.

1. *Gobiodon quinque-strigatus*, D. 6 | $\frac{1}{10-11}$, A. $\frac{1}{9-10}$. Eyes 1 to $1\frac{1}{4}$ diameters from end of snout. Two small posterior canines above symphysis of lower jaw. Head with five vertical orange stripes: two or three similar bands or rows of blotches on the body. Andamans to the Malay Archipelago.

2. *Gobiodon erythrospilus*, D. 6 | $\frac{1}{10-11}$, A. $\frac{1}{9}$. Eyes less than 1 diameter from end of snout. Two small posterior canines above symphysis of lower jaw. Brown, with black fins. Ceylon, Andamans, Nicobars, to the Malay Archipelago.

3. *Gobiodon citrinus*, D. 6 | $\frac{1}{10}$, A. $\frac{1}{9}$. Eyes 3/4 of a diameter from end of snout. An inner enlarged row of teeth in the lower jaw, and a posterior lateral recurved canine. Four blue black-edged vertical streaks on the head and before the base of the pectoral fin: a similar band along the bases of dorsal and anal fins. Red Sea, Andamans, and Nicobars.

1. Gobiodon quinque-strigatus.

Gobius quinque-strigatus, Cuv. and Val. xii, p. 134; not Bleeker, Blenn. en Gob. p. 29, and Solor. p. 82.
Gobiodon quinque-strigatus, Bleeker, Gobioideorum, 1874, p. 17, not Boero, p. 408; Günther, Catal. iii, p. 87.
Gobius and *Gobius erythrophaios*, Bleeker, Gob. p. 29, and Boero, p. 409 (part.)
Gobius Ceramensis, Bleeker, Ceram. p. 704.

D. 6 | $\frac{1}{10-11}$, P. 19, V. 1/5, A. $\frac{1}{9-10}$, C. 15.

Length of head 1/4, of caudal 1/5, height of body 1/3 to 2/7 of the total length. *Eyes*—diameter 1/4 to

1/5 of length of head, 1 to $1\frac{1}{2}$ diameters from end of snout, and 1 apart. Body elevated and strongly compressed. Cleft of mouth commences opposite the lower edge of the orbit: the maxilla reaches to below the first third of the eye. Head as high as long, its anterior profile parabolic. No tubercles on forehead. *Teeth*—two large posterior canines above the symphysis of the lower jaw. *Fins*—first dorsal only half as high as the second, which latter equals the length of the head behind the middle of the eyes. Pectoral as long as the head. Ventrals reach 1/3 of the way to the anal. Caudal rounded. *Colours*—head with five vertical orange stripes: two irregular bands of the same colour pass along the body, breaking up into blotches, and a row of spots exists along the posterior third of the body, sometimes there is a black spot at the tip of the opercle. In my specimens, which have been only five or six years in spirit, the colours have almost entirely faded. Those described were observed in the recently captured fish.

Habitat.—Andamans and Nicobars, to $2\frac{1}{2}$ inches in length: is also found in the Malay Archipelago.

2. Gobiodon erythrospilus.

Gobius quinquestrigatus, Bleeker, Gob. p. 29, and Soler, p. 82 (not C. and V.)
Gobiodon Ceramensis, Günther, Catal. iii, p. 88 (not Bleeker).
Gobiodon erythrospilus, Bleeker, Gobioid. 1874, p. 22.

D. 6 | $\frac{1}{10-11}$, P. 19, V. 1/5, A. $\frac{1}{9}$, C. 15.

Length of head $4\frac{1}{2}$ to $4\frac{3}{4}$, of caudal 5, height of body 3 to $3\frac{1}{2}$ in the total length. *Eyes*—diameter $3\frac{1}{2}$ in length of head, less than 1 diameter from end of snout, and 1/2 to 2/3 of a diameter apart. Head compressed, as high as long. Cleft of mouth slightly oblique, the maxilla reaches to below the middle of the eyes. No tubercles on forehead. *Teeth*—two small posterior canines above the symphysis of the lower jaw. *Fins*—in some specimens the first dorsal spine is somewhat produced, otherwise the two dorsal fins are of about the same height or half of that of the body. Pectoral as long as the head. Ventral reaches 1/3 of the way to the anal. Caudal rounded. *Colours*—body brown, covered with small black spots, fins blackish. Caudal sometimes with a white base, or entirely white.

Habitat.—Ceylon, Andamans, Nicobars, to the Malay Archipelago.

3. Gobiodon citrinus, Plate LXIV, fig. 2.

Gobius citrinus, Rüpp. N. W. Fische, p. 139, t. xxxii, f. 4.
Gobius coryphaenula, Blyth, P. A. S. of B., 1858, p. 272 (? Cuv. and Val. xii, p. 131.)
Gobiodon citrinus, Günther, Catal. iii, p. 87; Klunz. Verh. z. b. Ges. Wien, 1871, p. 49.
Pseudogobiodon citrinus, Bleeker, Gobioides, 1874, p. 21.

D. 6 | $\frac{1}{10}$, P. 20, V. 1/5, A. $\frac{1}{9}$, C. 13.

Length of head 4, of caudal $4\frac{1}{2}$, height of body 3 to $3\frac{1}{4}$ in the total length. *Eyes*—diameter $3\frac{1}{4}$ in length of head, 3/4 of a diameter from end of snout, and also apart. Cleft of mouth slightly oblique, commencing anteriorly opposite the lower edge of the eye. *Teeth*—in a single row in the upper jaw: a posterior enlarged row in the lower jaw, the external of which is a lateral recurved canine. *Fins*—dorsals of about the same height, and equalling the length of the head excluding the snout, the last rays of the second dorsal and anal almost reach the base of the caudal. Pectoral as long as the head. Ventral reaches half way to the anal. Caudal rounded. *Colours*—yellow, a blue black-edged horizontal streak goes along the bases of the dorsal and anal fins, in some specimens higher than in others: there are four similar vertical bands, two descending from the eye, one from the summit of the head to the opercles, and a fourth in front of the pectoral fins. A black spot at the posterior extremity of the opercle.

Habitat.—Red Sea, Andamans, and Nicobars. The specimen figured (life-size) is from the Andamans.

Genus, 2—Sicydium,* *Cuv. and Val.*

Sicyopterus, Gill; *Cotylopus*, Guich.; *Sicydiops* and *Microsicydium*, Bleeker.

Branchiostegals four: pseudobranchiæ, a slit behind the fourth gill: gill-openings of moderate width.

* Bleeker in his revision of the Gobioides, 1874, has:—

Sicydiini. Moveable teeth in the gums and lips.

a. Two rows of teeth in each jaw.

1. *Tridentiger*, Gill. Inner row of teeth elongated, curved, the outer having their apices dilated and tricuspidate.

b. Teeth in the premaxillaries in a crowded row: two rows in the lower jaw, the outer of which is fine and moveable.

2. *Sicydium*, Val. Teeth in premaxillaries pointed and curved: in the lower jaw the inner row is conical and very unequal. Barbels on the lower jaw.
3. *Sicyopterus*, Gill. Inner row of teeth in lower jaw pointed, curved, and wide apart. No barbels on lower jaw.
   α. *Sicyopterus*, Gill. Teeth in premaxillaries pointed, their apices neither compressed, swollen, nor incised.
   β. *Cotylopus*, Guich. Teeth in premaxillaries having their apices compressed, dilated, and bilobed.
   γ. *Sicydiops*, Bleeker. Teeth in premaxillaries with their apices compressed and dilated.
4. *Microsicydium*, Bleeker. Teeth in premaxillaries with their apices compressed and obtuse: inner row of teeth in the lower jaw small and of equal size. No scales on head or anterior portion of body.

c. Teeth in a single row in either jaw. Scaleless.

5. *Lentipes*, Günther=*Sicyogaster*, Gill. Front teeth in premaxillaries tricuspidate, lateral ones simple: all simple in the lower jaw.

Body subcylindrical. Eyes of moderate size. Upper jaw rather prominent, cleft of mouth nearly horizontal. Teeth in the upper jaw small, in one row, mostly implanted in the gums, and as a rule moveable, their apices may be compressed and dilated or bilobed: in the lower jaw they are in one or two rows, if two the outer is fine and moveable. Two dorsal fins, the first with six flexible spines: the caudal not united to the dorsal or the anal: ventrals united, forming a disk, which is more or less adherent to the abdomen. Scales ctenoid, of varying size. Air-vessel absent.

Geographical distribution.—This genus has a wide range in fresh and brackish waters, having been captured in the Mauritius, Bourbon, Burma, to the Malay Archipelago and beyond; also in the West Indies.

SYNOPSIS OF INDIVIDUAL SPECIES.

1. *Sicydium fasciatum*, D. 6 | $\frac{1}{10}$, A. 11, L. l. 67, L. tr. 19. Brown, banded, spotted, and with dark fins. Burma.

1. Sicydium fasciatum, Plate LXIV, fig. 7.

B. iv, D. 6 | $\frac{1}{10}$, P. 17, V. 6, A. 11, C. 13, L. l. 67, L. tr. 19.

Length of head $5\frac{1}{3}$, of caudal $5\frac{1}{2}$, height of body $5\frac{1}{2}$ in the total length. *Eyes*—diameter 2/9 of length of head, nearly $1\frac{1}{2}$ diameters from end of the snout, and $1\frac{1}{4}$ apart. Body subcylindrical: head rather flattened superiorly, and broader than high, its breadth being equal to its length without the snout. Cleft of mouth horizontal, extending to below the centre of the orbit: lips rather thick: snout overhanging the mouth. No barbels. *Teeth*—in the upper jaw small, and implanted in the gums in a single row: the inner row in the lower jaw large, conical, recurved, some distance apart, there being two canines near the symphysis, also a minute row of sharp ones on the lower lip. *Fins*—dorsal spines rather filiform, and projecting beyond the membrane, being 3/4 as high as the body beneath, and 1/3 higher than the second dorsal. Pectorals nearly as long as the head: ventrals short, forming a complete disk, and not reaching half-way to the anal fin, which latter is beneath the soft dorsal but lower than it. Caudal rounded. *Scales*—strongly ctenoid, somewhat irregularly arranged, they extend forwards nearly as far as the eyes: those anterior to the dorsal fin (about 30 rows) and also in front of the anal, smaller than the others, and more or less cycloid. None on opercles or cheeks. *Colours*—reddish-brown, with about six vertical darker bands on the body wider than the ground colour: there are also some dark spots: its under surface is dirty yellowish-brown. Fins nearly black, with a light, nearly white, edge.

This *Sicydium* or *Sicyopterus*, Gill, is the most westerly species I am aware of on the continent of Asia.

Habitat.—Burma, to $2\frac{1}{4}$ inches in length, the specimen figured is life-size.

Genus, 3—APOCRYPTES,* *Cuv. and Val.*

Branchiostegals four: pseudobranchiæ rudimentary: gill-openings of moderate width. Body elongated. Teeth conical in a single fixed row in either jaw, with usually a pair of canines in the lower, and above the symphysis posterior to the fixed row: sometimes canines in the upper jaw. The first portion of the dorsal fin containing five or six flexible spines, and either distinct from or continuous with the soft portion, which is similar to the anal. Ventrals united, forming a disk, and only attached by their bases. Scales, when present, small, becoming larger posteriorly.

Geographical distribution.—Coasts of India, Burma, Andamans, and through the Malay Archipelago. They ascend estuaries and rivers, sometimes even above tidal influence.

SYNOPSIS OF SPECIES.

1. *Apocryptes serperaster*, D. 6 | 27, A. 27, L. l. 65-70, L. tr. 20. Whitish, with gray vertical bands. Seas of India and China.

2. *Apocryptes rictuosus*, D. 6 | 24-27, A. 25-29, L. l. ca. 75. Gray, with ill-defined oblique bands passing down from the back: usually a black, yellow-edged ocellus on last dorsal rays. Seas and estuaries of India.

3. *Apocryptes Bleekeri*, D. 6 | 22-25, A. 22-23, L. l. 50-55, L. tr. 13. Gray, with brown spots or blotches along the sides. Pectorals dark, with a light edge. Seas of India to the Malay Archipelago.

4. *Apocryptes batoides*, D. 6 | 23, A. 23. Teeth pointed. Head 1/2 as wide as long. Grayish. Moulmein.

5. *Apocryptes lanceolatus*, D. 5 | 31-32, A. 29-30. Greenish superiorly, with numerous brown spots and bands, dorsal and caudal spotted and barred. Seas of India to the Malay Archipelago.

6. *Apocryptes dentatus*, D. 5 | 32, A. 31. Said to have larger teeth than *A. lanceolatus*. Coromandel coast.

* Bleeker's APOCRYPTINI consists of Gobies possessing a single row of teeth in either jaw, those in the mandibles being sub-horizontal, with two erect posterior canines above the symphysis.

I. APOCRYPTEI—

1. *Apocryptodon*, Bleeker. Teeth in premaxillaries partly truncated, partly sharp canines: in the lower jaw truncated or bilobed.
2. *Parapocryptes*, Bleeker. Teeth subulate and sharp in both jaws, partly canines in premaxillaries.
3. *Apocryptes*, Val.=*Gobileptes*, Swains. Teeth in both jaws, with their apices incised: no canines in the premaxillaries.
4. *Pseudapocryptes*, Bleeker. Teeth in both jaws with their apices obtuse, swollen, not incised: no canines in the premaxillaries.

7. *Apocryptes lato*, D. 5 | 21-22, A. 23. Teeth notched. Head 2/3 as wide as long. Light greenish, with ill-defined vertical bands. Orissa and lower Bengal, within tidal reach.

1. Apocryptes serperaster, Plate LXVI, fig. 2.

Richardson, Ich. China, p. 206; Günther, Catal. iii, p. 82.

B. iv, D. 6 | 27, P. 21, V. 1/5, A. 27, C. 13, L. l. 65-70, L. tr. 20.

Length of head 6½, of caudal 5, height of body 7 in the total length. *Eyes*—diameter 4½ to 5 in length of head, 1 to 1½ diameters from end of snout, and 1/4 of a diameter apart. Snout obtuse, convex. Lower jaw slightly the longer. Cleft of mouth oblique, the maxilla reaching to below the hind edge of the eye. Greatest width of head equals its height, and its height its length behind the eye. *Teeth*—villiform in the upper jaw, with an outer enlarged row directed downwards of from four to eight on either side of the symphysis of the upper jaw: in a single row in the lower jaw of teeth directed outwards, and a single or a pair of large canines internally above the symphysis. *Fins*—dorsal fins not continuous, the first twice as high as the second, its spines weak and having filamentous terminations, the last dorsal ray reaches to beyond the commencement of the caudal fin. Pectoral as long as the head excluding the snout. Ventrals not having a posterior attachment to the abdomen and reaching as far as the pectorals extend. Anal commences under the vertical from the second ray of the dorsal, which fin it resembles, but is slightly lower. Caudal lanceolate. *Scales*—over body and head, excluding the interorbital space, snout, and jaws, the smallest are between the occiput and fourth dorsal spine, and anteriorly to a line drawn from thence to the base of the anal fin, posterior to this they are in regular rows: they are much larger in the hinder portion of the body, there being only six rows between the last dorsal ray and base of anal fin. *Colours*—of a dull greenish along the upper surface of the head and back, becoming dull white on the sides and abdomen: five or six irregular bands pass from the back to half-way down the sides. A narrow gray band along the lower third of both dorsals, which are also dark externally. Caudal gray, with a light yellowish outer edge. Pectoral gray, with its upper and five lower rays yellowish white. Anal with a narrow gray band along its centre, its outer edge dark, and its last rays nearly black.

Habitat.—Seas and estuaries of India and China. The specimen figured (life-size) is from Madras, where it is not rare up to five or six inches in length.

2. Apocryptes rictuosus.

Cuv. and Val. xii, p. 151; Jerdon, M. J. L. and Sc. 1851, p. 143; Günther, Catal. iii, p. 82; Day, Fish. Malabar, p. 113.

B. iv, D. 6 | 24-27, P. 20, V. 1/5, A. 25-29, C. 13, L. l. ca. 75.

Length of head 7½, of caudal 3, height of body 11 to 13 in the total length. *Eyes*—diameter 1/6 to 1/7 of length of head, about 1 diameter from end of snout, and 1/3 of a diameter apart. Greatest width of head equals half its length and its height equals its length behind the eyes. Snout rather obtuse, lower jaw a little the longer, cleft of mouth deep, extending at least 1 diameter of the eye beyond the hind edge of orbit. *Teeth*—from 20 to 28 pointed ones in either ramus of the lower jaw, the most external of which is recurved: a rather large number also of pointed ones in the upper jaw: a pair of small canines, internally, above the symphysis of the lower jaw. *Fins*—dorsals continuous at their bases, spines of first dorsal with filamentous prolongations, but not much higher than the second dorsal: last dorsal ray extends to as far as the base of the caudal. Pectoral as long as the head excluding the snout, and of equal length with the ventral. Anal commences on the vertical below the second or third dorsal ray. Caudal pointed and very elongate. *Scales*—in irregular rows, very small anterior to the dorsal fin, becoming larger posteriorly. *Colours*—grayish, lighter towards the abdomen, with badly defined oblique bands passing downwards and forwards from the base of the dorsal fin half way to the abdomen. Ventral whitish. Pectoral, anal, first and second dorsal whitish, externally stained with gray, sometimes spotted with brown: usually a black spot surrounded by a yellow ring on the last few dorsal rays. The inside of the mouth with black spots.

Habitat.—Seas and estuaries of India, attaining 7 inches in length.

3. Apocryptes Bleekeri, Plate LXIV, fig. 3.

Apocryptes Madurensis, Day, Proc. Zool. Soc. 1873, p. 109 (not Bleeker, Blenn. en Gob. p. 35; Günther, Catal. iii, p. 84).

B. iv, D. 6 | 22-25, P. 19, V. 1/5, A. 22-23, C. 13, L. l. 55-60, L. tr. 13.

Length of head 4½ to 5, of caudal 5 to 5½, height of body 7 to 8 in the total length. *Eyes*—diameter 1/5 to 1/6 of length of head, 1 to 1½ diameters from end of snout, and 1/2 a diameter apart: interorbital space concave. Greatest width of head equals half its length, and its height equals its length behind the eyes. Snout somewhat compressed, jaws of about equal length, cleft of mouth nearly horizontal: the maxilla reaches to about the length of one or two diameters of the orbit behind the posterior edge of the eye: extent of the gape 1/4 less than that of the cleft. *Teeth*—25 to 30 teeth notched at their extremities in the anterior half of the lower jaw on either side: 15 or 20 pointed ones on either side of the premaxillaries extending further backwards than in the mandibles, whilst they are not placed so closely together. *Fins*—first dorsal higher than the second, and equal from 2/3 to the height of the body, the membrane of the first dorsal extends to the commencement of the second, which latter fin is higher than the anal. Pectoral as long as the head without the snout: ventral reaches nearly half way to the anal. Caudal pointed. *Scales*—cycloid and arranged in regular rows, largest in the posterior portion of the body, they are extended on to the head and cheeks, 13 rows between the origin of the second dorsal and anal fins. *Colours*—grayish or olive brown, with five light brown spots along the sides, usually forming bands over the back: numerous fine dots over the head and body. Pectoral deep olive or nearly black, with a white lower edge. First dorsal mostly with a dark mark in its upper fourth between its third and fifth spines. Second dorsal and caudal with some rows of fine dots. Ventrals white.

From the description it appeared to me that this species might be identical with *A. glyphidodon*, Bleeker, but Dr. Bleeker observes that the figure has a physiognomy very different from *Apocryptodon glyphidodon*, Bleeker. I therefore propose naming it after that learned ichthyologist.

Variety.—Without scales on the head, an ocellus at end of soft dorsal fin, and last third of anal with a gray band along its base.

Habitat.—Seas of India to the Malay Archipelago, attaining at least 4 inches in length. The one figured (life-size) is from Madras.

4. **Apocryptes batoides**, Plate LXVI, fig. 3.

B. iv, D. 6 | 23, P. 21, V. 1/5, A. 23, C. 13.

Length of head 6½, of caudal 3¾, height of body 12 in the total length. *Eyes*—high up, diameter 6½ in length of head, 2 diameters from end of snout, and 3/4 of a diameter apart. Greatest width of head equals its height or 1/2 its length. Cleft of mouth nearly horizontal: upper jaw slightly the longer; width of the gape exceeds that of the cleft: the maxilla reaches to below the front edge of the eye. *Teeth*—eight to ten pointed ones on either side of both jaws, none are notched, whilst all are of a brown colour, two moderately sized posterior canines in the lower jaw. *Fins*—the two dorsals of about the same height, and equal to that of the body. Pectoral half as long as the head: ventral reaches half way to the anal. Caudal lanceolate. *Scales*—cycloid, large and small ones intermixed, becoming largest posteriorly, they are extended on to the head. *Colours*—grayish along the back, becoming whitish below: fins without marks.

This species reminds one of *A. bato*, which however has notched teeth, whereas *A. batoides* has sharp ones, or *Pseudapocryptes*, Bleeker.

Habitat.—Moulmein, where the example, 10 inches long, was obtained.

5. **Apocryptes lanceolatus**, Plate LXIV, fig. 5.

Eleotris lanceolata, Bl. Schn. p. 67, t. 15.
Gobius chaguna, Ham. Buch. Fish. Ganges, pp. 41, 365, pl. 5, f. 10.
Apocryptes changua, Cuv. and Val. xii, p. 145; Bleeker, Blenn. en Gob. pp. 5, 36.
Scartelaos cantoris, Swains. Fishes, ii, p. 280.
Apocryptes lanceolatus, Cantor, Catal. p. 187; Jerdon, M. J. L. and Sc. 1851, p. 143; Günther, Catal. iii, p. 89; Kner, Novara Fische, p. 180.
Pseudapocryptes lanceolatus, Bleeker, Gobioides, 1874, p. 40.
Nallah ramah, Tel.

B. iv, D. 5 | 31-32, P. 21, V. 1/5, A. 29-30, C. 11.

Length of head 7 to 7½, of caudal 4½ to 6½, height of body 7 to 9 in the total length. *Eyes*—diameter 1/6 to 1/7 of length of head, 1¼ diameters from the end of snout, and 1 apart. Greatest width of head equals half or more than half of its length, and its height 3/5 of its length. Jaws of nearly equal length anteriorly, the maxilla reaches to beneath the middle or hind edge of the orbit. *Teeth*—of moderate size in the upper jaw, with blunt free extremities as if cut off, or else slightly swollen; those in the lower jaw horizontal, occasionally the outer one is slightly recurved and a little enlarged: a pair of posterior canines above the symphysis. *Fins*—the membrane of the first dorsal fin scarcely reaches to the base of the second dorsal, the two fins of about the same height and equal to half that of the body. Pectoral two-thirds as long as the head: ventral reaches about 1/3 of the way to the anal. Caudal lanceolate. *Scales*—minute, becoming most distinct in the posterior portion of the body. *Colours*—dull greenish superiorly, with numerous fine brown spots and usually many dark bands descend from the back towards the abdomen: dorsals with several rows of fine spots: caudal barred in a few or many rows as observed in *Gobius giuris*, and this seems the form figured amongst Sir W. Elliot's drawings of Fishes of India named by Jerdon *Apocryptes dentatus*?

Habitat.—Seas of India to the Malay Archipelago; attaining at least 8 inches in length. The specimen figured (life-size) is from Calcutta.

6. **Apocryptes dentatus.**

Cuv. and Val. xii, p. 148; Jerdon, M. J. L. and Sc. 1851, p. 143; Günther, Catal. iii, p. 81.

B. iv, D. 5/32, A. 31, Vert. 12/15.

Length of head 1/8, of caudal 2/9, height of body 1/14 of the total length. *Eyes*—diameter 1/6 of length of head, rather more than 1 diameter from end of snout, and 1/2 a diameter apart. Snout rounded: jaws of equal length anteriorly, the cleft of the mouth horizontal and extending to behind the posterior margin of the orbit. *Teeth*—20 in each jaw, the central ten the largest, a pair of canines near the symphysis. *Fins*—

dorsal low, the first connected by its membrane to the base of the second. Caudal lanceolate. *Scales*—very small. *Colours*—olive or brownish, palest below: caudal reddish dotted with brown.

This fish appears from the description (as yet I have not seen the type) to be identical with *A. lanceolatus*. It is said to be remarkable by the largeness of its teeth and the smallness of its eyes; this last character bringing it nearly to the genus *Amblyopus*. However its eyes are stated as 1/6 of the length of the head, and *A. lanceolatus* is said to have them of exactly the same size. As regards the size of its teeth these vary exceedingly in different specimens.

Habitat.—Coromandel coast of India.

7. Apocryptes bato, Plate LXIV, fig. 6.

Gobius bato, Ham. Buch. Fish. Ganges, pp. 40, 365, pl. 37, f. 10.

Apocryptes bato, Cuv. and Val. xii, p. 143, pl. 369; Bleeker, Beng. en Hind. p. 103, and Gobioides, 1874, p. 39; Günther, Catal. iii, p. 82.

Rutta, Ooriah.

B. iv, D. 5 | 21-22, P. 23, V. 1/5, A. 23, C. 13.

Length of head 6 to $6\frac{1}{2}$, of caudal $4\frac{2}{3}$, height of body 7 in the total length. *Eyes*—rather high up, diameter $5\frac{1}{2}$ to 6 in the length of head, 1 to $1\frac{1}{2}$ diameters from end of snout, and 1 apart. Interorbital space slightly concave. Greatest width of head equals its height or 2/3 of its length: snout rounded. Upper jaw slightly the longer: cleft of mouth nearly horizontal; the gape slightly exceeds the extent of the cleft: the maxilla reaches to below the first third or centre of the eye. *Teeth*—about 24 on either side of both jaws, all of which are notched at their extremities, those in the mandible horizontal: two moderately sized posterior canines in the lower jaw. *Fins*—dorsal and anal fins of about the same height, and equal to 2/3 of that of the body. Pectoral half as long as the head, ventral reaches half way to the anal. Caudal lanceolate, most expanded in examples from Orissa. *Scales*—cycloid, large and small ones intermixed, becoming largest posteriorly, and extended on to the head. *Colours*—greenish-white, with about twelve ill-defined narrow bands, descending from the back towards the abdomen: scales with brown points: fins white, but also with minute dots: a dark band at the base of the pectoral.

Habitat.—Orissa and Lower Bengal within tidal reach, attaining $6\frac{1}{2}$ inches length. The specimen figured (life-size) is from Calcutta.

Genus, 4—Apocryptichthys.

Branchiostegals five. Gill-openings rather small. Body elongated. Teeth in a single fixed row in either jaw, those in the premaxillaries curved, pointed, elongated, and with a long canine on either side of the symphysis: those in the lower jaw sub-horizontal, rather swollen at their free extremities, and no posterior canines. Two separate dorsal fins, the first with six flexible spines, the second elongated and similar to the anal. Ventrals united, forming a disk and only connected to the body by their bases. Caudal lanceolate. Scales cycloid, absent from the head, becoming largest posteriorly.

The fish for which this Genus is proposed is rather peculiar in possessing or being deficient in characters appertaining to the *Apocryptina* and *Amblyopina*.

It can hardly be an *Apocryptes* as it has no posterior canines above the symphysis of the lower jaw, whilst the teeth in its premaxillaries are very elongate: its eyes are not prominent, and are larger than in the *Amblyopina*; its dorsal fins likewise are distinct.

SYNOPSIS OF INDIVIDUAL SPECIES.

1. *Apocryptichthys Cantoris*, D. 6 | 27, A. 26, L. l. ca. 90, L. tr. 17. Grayish-olive with dark fins. Andamans and Madras.

1. Apocryptichthys Cantoris, Plate LXII, fig. 7.

Apocryptes Cantoris, Day, Proc. Zool. Soc. 1870, p. 693.

B. v, D. 6 | 27, P. 19, V. 1/5, A. 26, C. 17, L. l. ca. 90, L. tr. 17.

Length of head 1/4, of caudal 1/5, height of body 1/9 of the total length. *Eyes*—not prominent, diameter 1/6 of length of head, 1 diameter from end of snout, and 2/3 of a diameter apart. Head rather depressed, its lower surface flat: greatest width equals its height or 2/5 of its length. Cleft of mouth slightly oblique, commencing anteriorly opposite the lower edge of the eye, the maxilla reaches to 1 diameter of the orbit behind its posterior edge. An angular pendulous flap of skin from the preorbital falls to over the teeth on the side of the upper jaw. No barbels. *Teeth*—fixed, curved, and elongated, about 13 on either side of both jaws, the two central ones in the premaxillaries being long pointed canines curving downwards extending far beyond the lips; those in the lower jaw sub-horizontal and curved slightly upwards, whilst their extremities are rather enlarged, no posterior canines. *Fins*—first and second dorsals of about the same height: the membrane of the first dorsal continued almost to the base of the second. Base of the pectoral not muscular, the fin as long as the head behind the eyes: ventrals with a well developed basal membrane, not adherent to abdomen. Caudal lanceolate. *Scales*—cycloid, about 90 rows along the body much smallest anteriorly; 17 rows between bases of second dorsal and anal. None on the head. Gill-opening rather small, before the lower half of the base of the pectoral fin. *Colours*—grayish-olive: first dorsal dark, longitudinally banded: caudal dark with some spots in its upper half.

Habitat.—Madras and Andamans. The specimen figured (life-size) is from the latter locality.

Genus, 5—Periophthalmus,* *Bl. Schn.*

Mud-skippers.

Branchiostegals five: pseudobranchiæ rudimentary. Gill-openings rather narrow. Body elongated, subcylindrical anteriorly. Profile from eyes to snout very steep. Eyes placed close together, very prominent, and the eyelids well developed. Teeth in both jaws, erect, conical, fixed, and in one or two rows. Two dorsal fins, the first with a varying number of flexible spines: base of pectoral muscular: ventrals more or less united in their lower two-thirds: caudal with its inferior edge obliquely truncated. Air-vessel absent. Scales small or of moderate size, cycloid or feebly ctenoid, covering the body and the base of the pectoral fins.

These fishes, due to the muscular development at the base of the pectoral fins, are able to use them for progression as mud-skippers or climbers. I made the following remarks on the *P. Schlosseri* in the Irrawaddi river:—It is most curious to see these little fishes along the side of the Burmese rivers, at a distance they at first appear between large tadpoles, stationary, contemplating all passing objects, or else snapping at flies or insects: suddenly startled by something, away they go with a hop, skip, and a jump, either inland among the trees, or on to the water like a flat stone or a piece of slate sent skimming by a schoolboy. They climb on to trees and large pieces of grass, leaves and sticks, holding on by their pectoral fins exactly as if they were arms. Now and then they plant these firmly as an organ of support, the same as one places one's elbows on a table, then they raise their heads and take a deliberate survey of surrounding objects.

They are not very timid, in fact my interpreter captured several by means of quietly creeping up to them and knocking them over with a stick. Occasionally, when moored, they crawled up to the boat's rope, and even on to its sides. Some looked light brown with dark bands, others darker, whilst a few were of a brilliant emerald green, probably due to the position of the body and the reflection of the light. One morning when at anchor I saw close to the side of my boat a snake in the water watching one of these fish, which was intently occupied capturing flies: with a stick I saved it from its reptilian foe, but its colours were so vivid I could not resist giving it a place in one of my collecting bottles. They are extensively used in Burma for live bait, a purpose for which they appear to be well adapted.

SYNOPSIS OF SPECIES.

1. *Periophthalmus Koelreuteri*, D. 10-15 | 12-13, A. 10-14, L. l. 75. First dorsal fin variously formed, being produced or not so. Second dorsal generally banded, and first dorsal mostly with a black intramarginal edge. Seas and estuaries of India to the Malay Archipelago and beyond.

2. *Periophthalmus Schlosseri*, D. 9-15 | $\frac{1}{12}$, A. $\frac{1}{10}$, L. l. 55, L. tr. 11-12. Banded, with emerald green spots: dorsal blackish, having a scarlet band, edged with blue and tipped with white. Coasts and large rivers of India, Burma, Andamans, to the Malay Archipelago and beyond.

1. Periophthalmus Koelreuteri, Plate LXIV, fig. 8.

Gobius Koelreuteri, Pall. Spic. viii, p. 8, t. ii, f. 1.

Periophthalmus Koelreuteri, Bl. Schn. p. 65; Cuv. and Val. xii, p. 181; Rüpp. N. W. Fische, p. 140; Bleeker, Blenn. en Gob. p. 252; Günther, Catal. iii, p. 97; Kner, Novara Fische, p. 182; Steind. Ak. Wien, 1869, p. 945; Klunz. Verh. z. b. Ges. Wien, 1871, p. 485.

Periophthalmus papilio, Bl. Schn. p. 63, t. xiv; Cuv. and Val. xii, p. 190, plate 353; Bleeker, Gobioides, 1874, p. 38.

Periophthalmus argentilineatus, Cuv. and Val. xii, p. 191; Bleeker, Amb. and Ceram. p. 276.

Periophthalmus kalolo, Less. Voy. Coq. Zool. ii, p. 146.

Periophthalmus modestus, Cantor, Ann. and Mag. 1842, ix, p. 29; Richards. Ich. China, pp. 208, 309; Temm. and Schleg. Fauna Japon. p. 147, pl. 76, f. 2; Bleeker, Japan, vi, p. 82.

Periophthalmus dipus, Bleeker, BanT. p. 320.

Periophthalmus fuscatus, Blyth, Journ. Asi. Soc. of Beng. 1859, p. 271, and 1860, p. 111.

Euchoristopus Koelreuteri, Bleeker, Gobioides, 1874, p. 38.

Chaud-naud-dah, Andam.

B. v, D. 10-15 | 12-13, P. 15, V. 1/5, A. 11-14, C. 11, L. l. 75.

Length of head 4 to $4\frac{2}{3}$, of caudal $4\frac{1}{4}$, height of body 7 in the total length. *Eyes*—elevated, and close together, diameter 1/4 of length of head, and 1 diameter from end of snout. Greatest width of head equals its

* The Periophthalmini, Bleeker.

1. *Periophthalmus*, Bl. Sch. Teeth in a single row in both jaws, partly canines: in many rows of mainly fine, sharp ones in the pharyngeals.
2. *Euchoristopus*, Gill. Teeth in a single row in both jaws. No canines: in few rows of mostly conical ones in the pharyngeals.
3. *Periophthalmodon*, Bleeker. Anterior teeth in premaxillaries in two rows, the outer canines: in a single row in the lower jaw, a portion of which are canines.

height, and $1\frac{3}{4}$ in its length. Profile from eyes to end of snout very abrupt, cleft of mouth nearly horizontal, the maxilla reaching to below the middle of the eye. Skin of the snout forms fleshy flaps. *Teeth*—about 24 conical, pointed ones in each jaw. In some specimens they laterally decrease in size by degrees, as in one from the Andamans of the same length as the specimen figured, which latter, however, has the teeth of unequal sizes and distinct curved canines present in both jaws. In a smaller specimen from the latter locality only one canine has appeared, this seems due to an opposite tooth in the lower jaw having become lost. When teeth are regular, canines are absent, and the greater development of a tooth seems due to the loss of an opposite one. *Fins*—the first dorsal fin is much more elevated in some specimens than in others, being shortest in the immature. Ventrals short, connected with one another in their basal two-thirds. *Colours*—head sometimes with blue spots. Body olive brown, with white or blue dots: first dorsal bluish with a dark edge, having a white tip and occasionally white spots at its base: second dorsal generally with a black-white-edged longitudinal band in its upper half or upper third, whilst its lowest portion has white dots. Pectoral and caudal often with brown dots.

Steindachner, *l. c.* observes that *Periophthalmus Gabonicus* and *P. erythronemus* of Duméril and Guichenot are identical with *P. Kœlreuteri*.

Bleeker considers *P. papilio* as the type of Genus *Periophthalmus* (as restricted) possessing canines and many fine rows of sharp teeth in the pharyngeals, and *P. Kœlreuteri* as the type of *Euchoristopus*, having no canines, and a few rows of mostly conical ones in the pharyngeals. Günther observes "the size of the teeth varies considerably in this species, not only according to age, but in specimens of the same size, and from the same locality, and even on both sides of the same individual." (Catal. iii, p. 98.)

Habitat.—Seas and coasts of India, ascending estuaries and tidal rivers, also found at the Andamans, to the Malay Archipelago and beyond. The specimen figured (life-size) is from Sind, and has five enlarged, curved, canines in the lower, and four in the upper jaw much larger than the remainder of the teeth.

Periophthalmus Schlosseri, Plate LXVI, fig. 4.

Gobius Schlosseri, Pall. Spic. viii, p. 3, pl. 1, f. 1-4; Gmel. Linn. i, p. 1201; Lacép. ii, p. 573; Shaw, Zool. iv, p. 246.

Periophthalmus Schlosseri, Bl. Schn. p. 64; Cuv. and Val. xii, p. 192; Swainson, Fishes, ii, p. 280; Bleeker, Blenn. en Gob. p. 39; Cantor, Catal. p. 191; Cuv. Règ. Anim. Ill. Poisson. pl. 81, f. 1; Günther, Catal. iii, p. 100.

Gobius tredecem-radiatus, septem-radiatus, et *novem-radiatus*, Ham. Buch. Fish. Ganges, pp. 46, 47, 48, 366, pl. ii, f. 14.

Periophthalmus tredecem-radiatus, septem-radiatus, et *novem-radiatus*, Cuv. and Val. xii, pp. 189, 196; Swainson, Fishes, ii, p. 280.

Periophthalmus Freycineti, Cuv. and Val. xii, p. 197. Quoy and Gaim. Voy. Freyc. Poiss. p. 257; Swainson, Fishes, ii, p. 280.

? *Periophthalmus Borneensis*, Bleeker, Born. i, p. 11.

Periophthalmodon Schlosseri, Bleeker, Gobioides, 1874, p. 39.

B. v, D. 0-15 | $\frac{1}{12}$, P. 9, V. 1/5, A. $\frac{1}{12}$, C. 12, L. l. 55, L. tr. 11-12.

Length of head 4 to $4\frac{1}{2}$, of caudal 5 to 6, height of body 5 to 6 in the total length. *Eyes*—high up, diameter $4\frac{1}{4}$ to $4\frac{1}{2}$ in length of head, $1\frac{1}{2}$ diameters from end of snout, and 1/4 of a diameter apart. Greatest width of head equals $1\frac{1}{4}$ in its length and rather exceeds its height. Cleft of mouth nearly horizontal, the maxilla reaches to below the middle of the eye. *Teeth*—in both jaws, pointed, erect, the front six in the premaxillaries the longest. *Fins*—the first dorsal fin may be entirely absent, composed of very short spines, or of moderate development, or the anterior spine elongated as in the males. Pectorals with a strong muscular base. Ventrals united in their basal third or entirely separated. Lower edge of caudal obliquely truncated. *Colours*—when alive, brownish banded, with emerald green spots most distinct on the head, but in certain lights all over the body. First dorsal black, which becomes bluish superiorly, and edged with white, it has a scarlet band along its centre with a white dot between each ray. Second dorsal the same, but the base lighter and spotted; and edged with white. In the *male* the first dorsal fin has a black band, becoming cobalt externally and with a scarlet edging.

Habitat.—Coasts and large rivers of Bengal, Burma, Andamans, to the Malay Archipelago and beyond, attaining at least 9 inches in length. The specimen figured (life-size) is from the Irrawaddi.

Genus, 7—Boleophthalmus,* *Cuv. and Val.*

Branchiostegals five: pseudobranchiæ, a slit behind the fourth gill. Gill-openings narrow. Body subcylindrical: head oblong. Eyes very prominent, situated close together, the outer eyelids well developed. Cleft of mouth nearly horizontal, the upper jaw sometimes slightly the longer. Teeth in a single row, the anterior ones in the

* Bleeker divides his Boleophthalmi thus:—

1. *Scartelaos*, Swains. Anterior teeth in the premaxillaries unequal sized, curved, subulate, canines: in the lower jaw sharp, simple, and of medium size.
2. *Boleophthalmus*, Val. Anterior teeth in the premaxillaries, simple, conical, sharp and curved canines: in the lower jaw with their apices dilated, truncated or emarginate.

upper jaw enlarged and stronger than the others; those in the lower jaw, in a single horizontal row, of about equal size and having a pair of posterior canines near the symphysis. Two dorsal fins, the anterior with five flexible spines; the second many rayed and of about equal number to, or rather more than those in the anal; pectoral with its basal portion muscular and generally free; ventrals more or less united; caudal with its inferior edge obliquely truncated. Air-vessel present or absent. Scales when present rudimentary or small, generally largest posteriorly.

It should be remarked that although the eyes are very prominent during life, this peculiarity is not so well seen after death. Had the eyes of *B. Dussumieri, tenuis, Boddaerti* and *glaucus* in my figures been a little more prominent than delineated, accuracy as to what exists during life would not have been infringed upon.

These fishes are essentially dwellers in the mud, and if placed in an aquarium in deep water appear to be rapidly drowned.

SYNOPSIS OF SPECIES.

1. *Boleophthalmus tenuis*, D. 5/28-29, A. 26. Height of body 10 in total length. Teeth pointed. Gray along the back, white beneath, black spots on head, bands and blotches on body, end of dorsal and upper edge of caudal with black margins. Sind.

2. *Boleophthalmus Dussumieri*, D. 5/27-28, A. 26. Teeth in lower jaw with a slight lobe. First dorsal nearly as high as body, not attached to second dorsal. Gray, black spots on first dorsal and white ones on second dorsal. Bombay and Sind.

3. *Boleophthalmus dentatus*, D. 5/27, A. 26-27. Teeth on lower jaw with a slight lobe. First dorsal higher than the body and connected to the second. Gray, black spots on first dorsal and white ones on second dorsal. Bombay and Sind.

4. *Boleophthalmus glaucus*, D. 5/27, A. 25. Thirteen large teeth in front of upper jaw and 13 lateral ones; 25 sub-horizontal, equal sized, and pointed ones in lower jaw. Height of second dorsal half length of head. Greenish, dorsals longitudinally banded: upper two-thirds of caudal dark and spotted. Andamans.

5. *Boleophthalmus viridis*, D. 5/26, A. 26. Fourteen large teeth in front of upper jaw, laterally a few minute ones; 30 sub-horizontal and pointed ones in lower jaw, the outer the largest. First dorsal high. Height of second dorsal $3\frac{1}{2}$ in length of head. Greenish, with black spots on head, back, and dorsal fins. Upper two-thirds of caudal dark with black angular bands.

6. *Boleophthalmus Boddaerti*, D. 5/24-25, A. 24. Height of body 5 or 6 in total length. Vertical dark bands, body covered with opaque blue spots: dorsals with blue spots. Pectoral orange, with a dark edge.

7. *Boleophthalmus sculptus*, D. 5/25, A. 24. Scales on head and anterior portion of body in the form of flat, rounded tubercles. Greenish-olive along the back, lighter below: six vertical body bands. India.

8. *Boleophthalmus pectinirostris*, D. 5/23-24, A. 23-24. Greenish spots on body. Vertical blue spots on first dorsal fin, transverse ones on second, spots on caudal. Burma to the Malay Archipelago and beyond.

1. Boleophthalmus tenuis, Plate LXV, fig. 1.

B. v, D. 5/28-29, P. 13, V. 1/5, A. 26, C. 13.

Length of head $5\frac{1}{2}$ to $6\frac{1}{4}$, of caudal $4\frac{1}{3}$ to $4\frac{3}{4}$, height of body 10 in the total length. *Eyes*—elevated, projecting above the dorsal profile during life time, situated close together, diameter 1/6 of length of head, 1 diameter from end of snout. Greatest width of head equals $2\frac{1}{4}$ in its length, and its height equals its width. Upper jaw the longer, snout rounded in both senses, its skin loose but without any angular flap. The extent of the gape of the mouth exceeds its cleft, the maxilla reaches to below the last third of the eye. Eight or ten short barbels along the lower edge of each ramus of the lower jaw, but no central barbels under symphysis. *Teeth*—from 7 to 9 large, pointed, canines in the centre of the upper jaw on either side directed downwards, whilst laterally on either side of them are about 10 more one-third of their size, and also pointed; those in the lower jaw are compressed, sub-horizontal, pointed and about 17 on either side, two moderately sized posterior canines above the symphysis. *Fins*—first dorsal about 1/3 higher than the second, and about as high as the body, the interspace between the two fins in a large specimen equals the height of the first dorsal fin: second dorsal reaches nearly to the base of the caudal, which is lanceolate and inferiorly truncated. Pectoral as long as the head, excluding the snout: ventral one-fourth shorter and the two fins united in their whole extent. Anal beneath, but not so high as, second dorsal. Gill-opening small, before the lower half of the base of the pectoral. *Scales*—absent, a few crypts in the skin in the last part of the body. *Colours*—grayish superiorly, becoming white along the abdomen: numerous black spots on the upper surface of the head and commencement of the body, which latter has cloudy marks and bands from the second dorsal fin. First dorsal black superiorly and with some dark bands inferiorly: second dorsal with about nine or ten oblique black bands in its lower two-thirds continued on to the body, posteriorly its upper edge white with a black margin as is also upper edge of caudal. Pectoral and ventral gray, anal white: caudal blackish with white spots each having a black centre.

Habitat.—Estuaries of Kurrachee. The one figured is life-size. Largest specimen obtained $6\frac{1}{2}$ inches in length. It is common in Sind, but does not appear to extend so far east as Bombay.

2. Boleophthalmus Dussumieri, Plate LXIV, fig. 9.

Cuv. and Val. xii, p. 207, pl. 354; Gunther, Catal. iii, p. 104.

B. v, D. 5/27-28, P. 19, V. 1/5, A. 26, C. 13, L. l. ca. 125.

Length of head $5\frac{1}{4}$, of caudal $4\frac{1}{2}$ to $4\frac{3}{4}$, height of body $7\frac{3}{4}$ to 8 in the total length. *Eyes*—rather prominent, diameter 1/7 of length of head, 1 diameter from end of snout, and 1/3 of a diameter apart. Greatest width of head equals $2\frac{1}{4}$ in its length, and its height equals 1/2 its length. Snout obtuse, descending almost vertically from the eyes, the anterior end of the cleft of the mouth below the middle of the height of the head, its cleft slightly oblique, and the maxilla reaches to below the hind margin of the orbit. *Barbels*—absent. *Teeth*—three on either side of the middle of the upper jaw, pointed, and directed downwards, about 25 small, conically shaped ones along either branch of the upper jaw: about 25 truncated and notched sub-horizontal ones along either side of the lower jaw, and a pair of posterior canines. *Fins*—first dorsal nearly or as high as the body, its base slightly longer than its height, it does not extend so far as to the base of the second dorsal: the second dorsal commences midway between the anterior margin of the orbit and the base of the caudal fin, its rays are about half as high as those of the first dorsal and equal throughout. Pectoral as long as the head without the snout: ventrals entirely united, more than half as long as the head, and extending half way to the vent: anal commencing under the fourth dorsal ray, its posterior rays slightly the longest and about half as high as those of the second dorsal; caudal pointed, its lower rays truncated. *Scales*—distinct on the body, but somewhat indistinct on the head. *Colours*—gray, first dorsal purplish, covered with round black spots: the second with two or three rows of oblong white spots: caudal black.

Habitat.—Bombay and coast of Sind, to 6 inches in length.

3. **Boleophthalmus dentatus**, Plate LXIV, fig. 10.

Cuv. and Val. xii, p. 208, pl. 355.

B. v, D. 5 | 27, P. 19, V. 1/5, A. 26-27, C. 15.

Length of head 5 to $5\frac{1}{4}$, of caudal 4 to $4\frac{1}{2}$, height of body $7\frac{1}{2}$ to $8\frac{1}{2}$ in the total length. *Eyes*—rather prominent, diameter 1/7 of length of head, $1\frac{1}{2}$ to 2 diameters from the end of snout, and half a diameter or less apart. Head, its breadth equals its height and half its length. Snout somewhat obtuse, the anterior end of the cleft of the mouth is opposite about the middle of the height of the head, its cleft is slightly oblique, and the maxilla reaches to below the hind margin of the orbit. *Barbels*—absent. *Teeth*—three on either side of the middle of the upper jaw, elongate, directed downwards and slightly forwards, about 25 conical ones along either branch of the upper jaw. A pair of enlarged, recurved canines internally and behind symphysis of the lower jaw, and from 35 to 40 nearly horizontal teeth, on either branch of the lower jaw, with their summits tricuspidate, or else with a slight lobe on the outer side. *Fins*—first dorsal one fourth higher than the body below it, its rays extend beyond the membrane, which last reaches posteriorly as far as the base of the second dorsal: the second dorsal fin commences midway between the snout and the base of the caudal, its rays are about half as high as those of the first dorsal, and of equal height throughout. Pectoral as long as the head posterior to the orbit: ventrals entirely united, half as long as the head, and not extending half way to the vent: anal commencing under the fourth ray of the second dorsal, has its posterior rays a little the longest and rather above half the height of those of the second dorsal: caudal pointed, its lower rays shorter than the upper. *Scales*—only distinct in a narrow band on the abdomen, along either side of the anal fin, some along the sides below the second dorsal fin, and a few towards the head, elsewhere they look like rough points. *Air-vessel*—small, but present. *Colours*—olive gray, with dull vertical bands on the body, six or eight of which are continued to the lower half of the second dorsal fin. First dorsal purplish, covered with black spots, having whitish edges, whilst the upper margin of the fin is yellowish: second dorsal with about five rows of oblong white spots, and some black ones having white edges along the first-half of its base. Upper margin of the caudal with a white band and yellow spots between its black rays.

Whether this species and *B. Dussumieri* are in reality distinct species may be open to question, they commence to appear in Bombay, where however they are not so common as *B. Boddaerti*, but in Sind they have completely superseded it.

Habitat.—Bombay and Kurrachee, to $7\frac{1}{2}$ inches in length.

4. **Boleophthalmus glaucus**, Plate LXV, fig. 3.

B. v, D. 5 | 27, P. 19, V. 1/5, A. 25, C. 13.

Length of head 5 to $5\frac{1}{2}$, of caudal $4\frac{1}{2}$, height of body 8 to 9 in the total length. *Eyes*—prominent (more so during life than is shown in the figure), situated close together at the summit of the head, diameter 1/5 of length of head, $1\frac{1}{2}$ diameters from end of snout. Greatest width of head equals its length behind the eyes, its height is a little less. Profile from eyes to snout rather abrupt. The maxilla reaches to below the middle of the eyes. A few short tentacles along the lower edge of each ramus of the mandibles, none below the symphysis. *Teeth*—13 large, pointed, canine-like ones in front of the upper jaw, the outer of which on either side is a little enlarged and recurved, internally there are 13 more teeth as large as those in the mandibles. Twenty-five sub-horizontal and pointed teeth in the lower jaw, all of about the same size: a pair of posterior canines above the symphysis. *Fins*—first dorsal elevated, its height being from 1/5 to 1/6 in the total length, second dorsal about 2/3 the height of the body, or half the length of the head, posteriorly it is not connected by membrane to the base of the caudal. Pectoral equals half the length of the head. Ventrals united along their whole extent. Caudal lanceolate. *Scales*—minute, but visible in the last half of the body. *Colours*—greenish, tinged with violet along the abdomen, cloudy bands on head, a few widely scattered black spots on the cheeks and upper fourth of body. Second dorsal with dark horizontal lines, most distinct posteriorly. Pectoral gray, with a yellowish outer edge. Anal yellowish. Caudal light in its lower third, whilst superiorly it is dotted or covered with white spots surrounded by a black ring.

This fish differs from *B. viridis* in having a wider first dorsal fin, a higher second dorsal, in its dentition and colours, &c.

Habitat.—Andamans, where the specimen figured (life-size) was obtained; it, along with *Periophthalmus Koelreuteri* and other allied forms, frequents in hundreds the large mud flats, but it is most difficult to capture any as they dive down instantaneously into the semifluid mud on the slightest sign of danger. It is said that crows and birds of prey never trouble themselves to pursue them, as catching is an almost hopeless task.

5. Boleophthalmus viridis, Plate LXVI, fig. 5.

Gobius viridis, Ham. Buch. Fish. Ganges, pp. 42, 366, pl. 32, f. 12.
Boleophthalmus viridis, Cuv. and Val. xii, p. 213; Cantor, Catal. p. 195; Günther, Catal. iii, p. 104.
Boleophthalmus histophorus, Cuv. and Val. xii, p. 210.
Boleophthalmus aucupatorius, Richards. Voy. Sulph. Fishes, p. 148, pl. 62, f. 1, 2, and Ich. China, p. 208.
Scartelaos viridis, Bleeker, Gobioides, 1874, p. 40.

B. v, D. 5 | 26, P. 21, V. 1/5, A. 26, C. 15.

Length of head $5\frac{1}{2}$, of caudal $4\frac{1}{2}$, height of body 10 in the total length. *Eyes*—very protuberant, close together, diameter 1/6 of length of head, and $1\frac{1}{4}$ diameters from end of snout. Greatest width of head equals its height, or 1/2 its length. Profile from eye to snout rounded. The maxilla reaches to below the hind edge of the eye. A few short tentacles along the lower edge of each ramus of the lower jaw, and a larger one under the symphysis. *Teeth*—14 large, pointed, canine-like ones in front of the upper jaw, the outer of which is the largest but not recurved, laterally there are some small pointed ones. About 30 sub-horizontal and pointed teeth in the lower jaw, the outermost of which is the longest. A pair of posterior canines above the symphysis. *Fins*—first dorsal from two to three times as high as the body, and with a very narrow base: second dorsal low, its height equalling $3\frac{1}{2}$ in the length of the head, whilst posteriorly it has a membraneous connection between its last ray and the base of the caudal. Pectoral as long as the head excluding the snout. Ventrals connected together for almost their entire length. Caudal lanceolate. *Scales*—microscopic. *Colours*—greenish, becoming white beneath. Some black spots rather widely separated upon the head, body, and dorsal fins: caudal with its upper two-thirds having dark angular bands, its lower third white. In two specimens in the British Museum there are some narrow, vertical, dark bands on the sides.

Habitat.—Estuaries and coasts of Bengal to the Malay Archipelago and beyond. Specimen figured (life-size) is from Akyab.

6. Boleophthalmus Boddaerti, Plate LXV, fig. 2.

Gobius Boddaerti, Pall. Spicil. viii, p. 11, pl. 2, f. 4, 5; Gmel. Linn. i, p. 1201; Shaw, Zool. iv, p. 238.
Eleotris Boddaerti, Bl. Schn. p. 66.
Gobius striatus, Bl. Sch. p. 71, t. 16 (fem.).
Gobius Russell, i, p. 42, and *Nettee kandu mottah*, pl. 54.
Gobius plinianus, Ham. Buch. pp. 45, 366, pl. 35, f. 13.
Boleophthalmus Boddaerti, Cuv. and Val. xii, p. 199; Bleeker, Blenn. en Gob. pp. 5, 40, and Gobioides, 1874, p. 40; Cantor, Catal. p. 192; Jerdon, M. J. L. and Sc. 1851, p. 144; Günther, Catal. iii, p. 102; Kner, Novara Fische, p. 182.
Boleophthalmus plinianus, Cuv. and Val. xii, p. 205.
Apocryptes punctatus, Day, Proc. Zool. Soc. 1867, p. 941.

B. v, D. 5 | 24-25, P. 17, V. 1/5, A. 24, C. 13, L. l. 70, L. tr. 19-21.

Length of head $4\frac{1}{4}$ to 5, of caudal 5 to 6, height of body 5 to 6 in the total length. *Eyes*—high up, projecting, diameter from 6 to 7 in the length of head, 1 to $1\frac{1}{2}$ diameters from end of snout, and 1/4 of a diameter apart. Greatest width of head about equals its height, or its length excluding the snout. Jaws of about equal length, the maxilla reaches to below the hind edge of the eye. *Barbels*—absent. *Teeth*—the six central ones in the premaxillaries are canines pointing downwards, there are about 30 more pointed ones, but of much smaller size laterally. In the lower jaw the teeth are horizontal, about 30 on either ramus, truncated at their summits, whilst some have a slight lobe on either side: above the symphysis are a pair of posterior canines. Inferior pharyngeal bones spoon-shaped, approximating along the inner side, where a fine row of teeth exists merely at the opposed edges. *Scales*—cycloid, scarcely, if at all, imbricate on the head although extended all over it, on each scale on the head and anterior portion of the body is a rough elevation, sometimes pitted in the centre, and as the fish becomes older it appears as if in place of scales its anterior portion were covered instead with small rough elevations. 19 to 21 rows of scales between the front margins of dorsal and anal fins, and eight between their posterior margins. *Air-vessel*—present, but small. *Colours*—greenish blue, with seven or eight vertical black bands; body covered with opaque blue spots: first dorsal likewise blue-spotted, and three rows on the second, with four large series along its base. Pectoral orange, with a black edge: or dark, with an orange margin: anal and caudal blackish: ventrals purplish. In some specimens I find a few large white spots along the bases of either dorsal fin, whilst the whole of the first dorsal is densely dotted with round blue spots, and there are four rows of blue ones along the second dorsal as seen in *B. pectinirostris*. It climbs up rocks and pieces of wood, when it resides in shallow estuaries. If kept damp it lives some time out of water, and is brought in considerable numbers to Bombay markets, in baskets covered with wet cloths.

Habitat.—Coasts and estuaries of India and Burma to the Malay Archipelago. I have not taken it West of Bombay, it being replaced in Sind by *B. tenuis, Dussumieri*, and *dentatus*. Burmese specimens have usually a black edge to the pectoral fin.

7. Boleophthalmus sculptus.

Günther, Catal. iii, p. 104.

B. v, D. 5 | 25, P. 15, V. 1/5, A. 24, C. 15.

Length of head $4\frac{1}{2}$, of caudal $5\frac{1}{4}$, height of body 6 in the total length. *Eyes*—diameter $4\frac{1}{2}$ in length of head, 1 diameter from end of snout, and close together. Greatest width of the head equals its length behind the eyes, whilst its height is a little less. The maxilla reaches to below the last third of the eye. *Teeth*—six large, vertical, pointed teeth in front of premaxillaries, laterally a row of fine pointed ones: those in the lower jaw truncated at their summits, some having a slight lobe on either side; a pair of posterior canines above the symphysis. *Fins*—third dorsal spine with a filamentous prolongation. Pectoral rather short. Caudal truncated. *Scales*—cycloid, those on the head and anterior portion of the body rudimentary, with flat, rounded tubercles, having a depression in their centres. In the last portion of the body they become more distinct, there are about 12 rows between the anterior portion of the bases of the second dorsal and anal fins. *Colours*—"greenish-olive, yellowish on the belly: six rather distinct darker bands descend obliquely from the back towards the belly: the anterior dorsal grayish, the other fins reddish." Günther, *l. c.*

Habitat.—India, from whence one specimen was brought by General Hardwicke.

8. Boleophthalmus pectinirostris.

Gobius pectinirostris, Gmel. Linn. i, p. 200; Bl. Schn. p. 70; Lacép. ii, p. 542; Shaw, Zool. iv, p. 245.
Apocryptes pectinirostris, Cuv. and Val. xii, p. 150.
Boleophthalmus pectinirostris, Rich. Ich. China, p. 208; Cantor, Catal. p. 193; Günther, Catal. iii, p. 103.
Boleophthalmus Boddaertii, Rich. l. c.; Temm. and Schleg. Fauna Japon. Poissons, p. 148, pl. 76, f. 3.
Boleophthalmus inornatus, Blyth, J. A. S. of B. 1860, p. 148.

B. v, D. 5 | 23-24, P. 18, V. 1/5, A. 23-24, C. 14, Vert. 11-14.

Length of head $4\frac{2}{3}$, of caudal 5, height of body 6 in the total length. *Eyes*—approximating, diameter 1/4 to 1/5 of length of head, 2/3 of a diameter from end of snout. The greatest width of the head equals a little above 1/2 its length, and its height equals its length without the snout. The maxilla extends to below the hind edge of the orbit. *Teeth*—three large, pointed, and vertically placed teeth on either side of the centre of the upper jaw, and about 40 small conical ones laterally: teeth in lower jaw horizontal, about 38 or 40 truncated and notched ones along either ramus, also a pair of posterior canines. *Fins*—spines of first dorsal filamentous and extending some distance beyond the membrane, their height being nearly twice that of the body: last dorsal rays 3/4 height of body. Pectoral as long as the head excluding the snout: ventrals reach half way to the anal, and are united in their entire extent. Caudal pointed. *Scales* cycloid, anteriorly rudimentary, those in the posterior portion of the body are more developed, but in irregular rows, there being about 17 between the posterior extremities of the second dorsal and anal fins. *Colours*—the body with small, dark tubercles, and verdigris spots. Vertically placed blue spots on the first dorsal fin, and six or seven transverse ones on the second, where they sometimes form bands: some also on the caudal: the other fins brownish.

There are seven specimens up to 3 inches in length in the Calcutta Museum, received from the Tenasserim Provinces, where they were collected by the late Major Berdmore, and are the type of Blyth's *B. inornatus*. It seems to be a more Westerly form than most of the Indian species of this genus.

Habitat.—Coast of Burma to the Malay Archipelago and beyond.

Genus, 8—Bostrichthys,* (*Lacép.*) *C. Duméril.*

Bostrychus, Lacép.; *Philypnus*, Val.; *Bostrictis* and *Ictiopogon*, Raf.; *Philypnodon*, Bleeker; *Bostrichthys*, C. Dum.; *Lembus*, Günther.

Branchiostegals four to six: pseudobranchiæ. Gill-opening of moderate width. Body moderately elongated, sub-cylindrical anteriorly: head somewhat depressed. Eyes lateral, of moderate size, not prominent. Teeth in the jaws in many rows without canines, present on the vomer, present or absent on palate and tongue. Two dorsal fins, the anterior with 6 or 7 spines, the second and the anal of about the same length (10-13). *Base of pectoral slightly muscular: ventrals placed close together but not united. Scales of moderate or small size, cycloid or ctenoid, head scaled or scaleless.*

* The Philypni, Bleeker, which possess vomerine teeth, consist of:—

1. Philypnodon, Bleeker. Teeth on palatines and tongue. Scales ctenoid. Head scaleless.
2. Bostrichthys, C. Dum. Palatines and tongue edentulous. Scales cycloid. Head scaled.
3. Philypnus, Val. Palatines and tongue edentulous. Scales ctenoid. Head scaled

SYNOPSIS OF SPECIES.

1. *Bostrichthys Sinensis*, D. 6 | $\frac{1}{10-12}$, A. $\frac{1}{9}$, L. l. 140. Anterior nostril long and tubular. Dark brown with a large black white-edged ocellus at the upper part of the base of the caudal fin. Andamans to China.

Bostrichthys Sinensis, Plate LXV, fig. 4.

Bostrychus Sinensis, Lacép. iii, p. 141, pl. 14, f. 2.
Gobius Sinensis, Cuv. and Val. xii, p. 94.
Philypnus ocellicauda, Richards. Voy. Sulphur, Fishes, pp. 58, 149, pl. 56, f. 15, 16.
Philypnus Sinensis, Richards. Ich. China, p. 210.
Philypnus ophicephalus, Bleeker, Verh. Bat. Gen. xxii, Blen. en Gob. p. 29.
Bostrichthys Sinensis, Gill, Proc. Acad. Nat. Sc. Phil. 1860, p. 125; Kner, Novara Fische, p. 1[illegible]; Bleeker, Gobioides, 1874, p. 13.
Eleotris Sinensis, Günther, Catal. iii, p. 127.
Bostrychus Sinensis, Bleeker, Diutang, 1868, p. 5, and *Eleotriformes*, 1874, p. 4.
Lee-mee-jo-dodah, Andam.

B. v, D. 6 | $\frac{1}{10-12}$, P. 15, V. 1/5, A. $\frac{1}{9}$, C. 13, L. l. 140, Vert. 12/15.

Length of head from $4\frac{2}{3}$ to $4\frac{3}{4}$, of caudal $6\frac{1}{2}$ to 7, height of body $7\frac{1}{2}$ to 8 in the total length. *Eyes*—diameter 1/5 of length of head, $1\frac{1}{2}$ diameters from end of snout, and 2 diameters apart. Head obtuse, broad, depressed. Lower jaw the longer, the maxilla reaches to below the hind edge of the eye. Greatest width of head equals its length excluding the snout, its height equals about 1/2 its length. Anterior nostril tubular and long. *Teeth*—in equal sized villiform rows in both jaws, also on a semi-oval spot on the vomer. *Fins*—first dorsal not so high as the second, a rather considerable interspace between the two fins. Pectoral and ventral of about the same length, and equalling the head excluding the snout. Caudal rounded or wedge-shaped. *Scales*—cycloid, rudimentary on the top of the head and the nape: small on the cheeks, larger on the opercles. On the body they are irregular. *Colours*—dark brown marbled, a black white-edged ocellus at the upper part of the root of the caudal fin: three bands formed of spots along the dorsal fin, caudal also vertically banded by spots.

Habitat.—Andamans, to the Malay Archipelago and China. The specimen figured (life-size) is from the Andamans, where it is not uncommon in the brackish waters, feeding on small crustacea.

Genus, 9—Eleotris,* Gronovius.

Branchiostegals from four to six, occasionally terminating anteriorly in a spine: pseudobranchiæ present. Gill-openings of moderate width. Body sub-cylindrical: head oblong. Eyes lateral, not prominent, and of moderate size. Teeth small, none on vomer or palatines. Two dorsal fins, the anterior with few (5-8) spines, and these sometimes filamentous: base of pectoral slightly muscular: ventrals placed close together but not united. Scales present. Air-vessel large. Anal papilla distinct. Pyloric appendages generally absent.

As in the Genus *Gobius* I considered it unadvisable to adopt minute subdivisions, for the purpose of forming Genera, I cannot but think that the same plan had better be continued for Genus *Eleotris*, or Gobies with separated ventral fins and no teeth on the palate. Those which have an outer barbed row are likewise properly removed to separate genera, as *Megaxoda*, Gill.

Geographical distribution.—These fishes are generally found in the seas of the tropics, mostly along the shores, in estuaries, or tidal rivers, but not above tidal influence. The only one I have observed that appears

* Many of the following Genera which comprise *Eleotrii* and *Butii* of Bleeker are comprised in the above:—
No crests or serrated ridges on the head: teeth in *many rows in both jaws*, *Eleotris*, Gronov. = *Gobiomoroides*, Lacép. = *Eleotris*, Poey: anterior canines also in both jaws and the inner row in the lower enlarged, *Odontoeleotris*, Gill: or simply the outer row enlarged, *Guavina*, Bleeker: head scaleless, *Dolobranchus*, Bleeker: or the inner row in the lower jaw may be slightly enlarged (scales 35 to 40, isthmus narrow) *Ophiocara*, Gill: or the outer row in the upper jaw, and anteriorly the outer in the lower, which also has its inner row posteriorly enlarged (a preopercular spine), *Cheilodipterus*, H. B. = *Culius*, Bleeker: or the teeth may be subequal and slender (upper surface of head scaled) *Gobiomorphus*, Gill.
Or the teeth may be in *few rows in both jaws*, the outer being enlarged in the upper, and also anteriorly in the lower as is also its posterior inner row (isthmus of medium size) *Oxyeleotris*, Bleeker.
Or the teeth may be in many rows *in the upper*, and only a *single one in the lower jaw*, as *Poyoneleotris*, Bleeker, and *Gymnoeleotris*, Bleeker.
Osseous crests or serrated ridges on the head: teeth in *many rows in both jaws*, crowded and of equal size, *Butis*, Bleeker: or unequal in size (head scaleless) *Gymnobutis*, Bleeker: or the outer row enlarged in either jaw (head osseous) *Prionobutis*, Bleeker: or slender and not crowded, with the outer row slightly enlarged, *Odontobutis*, Bleeker.
Or there may be *many rows of teeth in both jaws*, the outer being slender and moveable, as *Dormitator*, Gill: *Asterropteryx*, Rüpp.
Or the teeth in the jaws may be fixed in *many rows in both jaws*, the outer enlarged, in the lower a posterior lateral canine. Scales large and ctenoid, *Brachyeleotris*, Bleeker: or cycloid *Hetereleotris*, Bleeker.
Or the scales may be small: teeth in *many rows in both jaws*, the outer the longer, and partly canine-like, *Eleotriodes*, Gill: or with only two canines at the symphysis of the premaxillaries, and posterior canines above the symphysis of the lower jaw, *Oxymetopon*, Bleeker.
Or the teeth may be in *one or more rows in the premaxillaries*, the inner being rudimentary, or in *many in the lower jaw*, the outer the longer and unequal, a posterior lateral canine, *Valenciennesia*, Bleeker: or a *single row* in the upper jaw, an enlarged outer unequal row in the lower, and a large posterior curved canine, *Eleotriodes*, Bleeker.

to live in fresh water as well as brackish or saline is the *E. fusca*, which though most numerous near the coasts, is still found a hundred miles and more from the sea.

SYNOPSIS OF SPECIES.

1. *Eleotris macrolepidota*, D. 7 | $\frac{1}{8}$, A. $\frac{1}{10}$, L. l. 30. Brownish, dorsal, anal, and caudal spotted. India.

2. *Eleotris muralis*, D. 6 | $\frac{1}{9}$, A. $\frac{1}{9}$, L. l. 100. No scales on head. Two or three red longitudinal bands along the body, some on head, several on dorsal fins, and a black mark at the summit of the first dorsal, between its third and fourth spines. Seas of India to the Malay Archipelago.

3. *Eleotris sexguttata*, D. 6 | $\frac{1}{9}$, A. $\frac{1}{9}$, L. l. 75-80. Blue spots, with dark edges on the sides of the head, a black upper edge to first dorsal fin, and six violet stripes along the second, anal with two: caudal spotted. Ceylon to the Malay Archipelago.

4. *Eleotris fuliceps*, D. 6 | $\frac{1}{8}$, A. 11, L. l. 27, L. tr. 12. Brownish-white, irregularly spotted and blotched with a darker colour, fins spotted. Andamans.

5. *Eleotris macrodon*, D. 6 | $\frac{1}{9}$, A. $\frac{1}{8}$, L. l. 120, L. tr. 30. Canines in jaws. Brownish. A dark ocellus at upper part of base of caudal fin: fins spotted. Estuaries of Bengal and Burma.

6. *Eleotris porocephalus*, D. 6 | $\frac{1}{8-9}$, A. $\frac{1}{8}$, L. l. 36-37, L. tr. 12-13. Twenty-five to thirty rows of scales before the dorsal fin. Brown, marbled with darker. Dorsals spotted, anal with a dark band. Andamans, Burma, and to the Malay Archipelago.

7. *Eleotris ophiocephalus*, D. 6 | $\frac{1}{8-9}$, A. $\frac{1}{8}$, L. l. 31-34, L. tr. 10-11. Fifteen rows of scales before the dorsal fin. Brown, blotched and marbled with darker. Fins banded. Africa, Andamans, and to the Malay Archipelago.

8. *Eleotris cavifrons*, D. 6 | $\frac{1}{8}$, A. $\frac{1}{8}$, L. l. 65, L. tr. 17. A preopercular spine. Scales extend to the snout, 55 rows before the dorsal fin. Brown, with a few spots on the body, dorsal and caudal barred in spots. Andamans.

9. *Eleotris fusca*, D. 6 | $\frac{1}{8}$, A. $\frac{1}{8}$, L. l. 60-65, L. tr. 16. A preopercular spine. Scales extend to the snout, 48 rows before the dorsal fin. Leaden-black, and of various colours, fins spotted. Coast of Africa and India to the Malay Archipelago.

10. *Eleotris Canarensis*, D. 6 | $\frac{1}{8}$, A. $\frac{1}{9}$, L. l. 58, L. tr. 17. Forty-two rows of scales before the dorsal fin. Dark brown, mottled: fins spotted. Mangalore.

11. *Eleotris lutea*, D. 6 | $\frac{1}{8}$, A. $\frac{1}{8}$, L. l. 50, L. tr. 12. A preopercular spine. Scales do not extend to so far as the eyes, 23 rows before the dorsal fin. Dirty-gray, with vertical bands: fins spotted. Andamans.

12. *Eleotris scintillans*, D. 6 | $\frac{1}{8}$, A. $\frac{1}{8}$, L. l. 42, L. tr. 15. Thirty-four rows of scales before the dorsal fin. Brownish, marbled with darker, a dark ocellus at upper part of base of caudal fin. Dorsals spotted, anal with a dark band. Akyab and the Andamans.

13. *Eleotris litoralis*, D. 6 | $\frac{1}{8}$, A. $\frac{1}{8}$, L. l. 35, L. tr. 11. Thirty rows of scales before the dorsal fin. Brownish, marbled with darker, dorsal and caudal fins spotted. Andamans.

14. *Eleotris caperata*, D. 6 | $\frac{1}{8}$, A. $\frac{1}{8}$, L. l. 30, L. tr. 9. Serrated ridges on the head. Interorbital space scaleless. Brown, a black blotch edged with scarlet at base of pectoral fin: vertical fins spotted. Coasts of India to the Malay Archipelago and beyond.

15. *Eleotris butis*, D. 6 | $\frac{1}{8}$, A. $\frac{1}{8}$, L. l. 28, L. tr. 9-10. Maxilla extends to below middle of the eye. Serrated ridges on head. Interorbital space scaled. Brownish, with a black blotch edged with scarlet at base of the pectoral fin: fins spotted. Seas and estuaries of India to the Malay Archipelago.

16. *Eleotris Amboinensis*, D. 6 | $\frac{1}{8}$, A. $\frac{1}{8}$, L. l. 28, L. tr. 9. Maxilla scarcely reaches to below front edge of the eye. Serrated ridges on the head. Interorbital space scaled. Brownish, a black blotch edged with yellow at base of the pectoral fin: fins spotted. Seas and estuaries of India to the Malay Archipelago.

1. Eleotris macrolepidota.

Sciæna macrolepidota, Bl. t. 298; Bl. Schn. p. 89.
Eleotris tumifrons, Cuv. and Val. xii, p. 241.
Eleotris macrolepidota, Günther, Catal. iii, p. 111.
Dormitator macrolepidota, Bleeker, Eleotriformes, 1874, p. 6.

B. vi, D. 7 | $\frac{1}{8}$, P. 13, V. 1/5, A. $\frac{1}{10}$, C. 16, L. l. 30.

Length of head, of caudal fin, and height of body, each nearly 1/4 of the total length. *Eyes*—diameter 1/4 of length of head, 1 diameter from end of snout, 3 diameters apart. Height of head 3/4 of its length. Interorbital space swollen: otherwise the upper surface of the head is flat. Cleft of mouth very oblique. The maxilla reaches to beneath the anterior margin of the orbit. *Teeth*—villiform. *Scales*—finely ctenoid on the body, those on the upper surface of the head small. *Colours*—brownish, with brown spots on the second dorsal. Bloch in his figure gives it six vertical bands on the body, and both dorsals, anal, and caudal spotted.

Habitat.—The specimen from which Bloch took his figure is stated to have come from India, and to attain 9 inches in length.

2. Eleotris muralis, Plate LXIX, fig. 1.

(Quoy and Gaim.) Cuv. and Val. xii, p. 253, pl. 357; Bleeker, Amb. and Ceram. p. 276; Günther, Catal. iii, p. 130.

Valenciennea muralis, Bleeker, Boeroe, p. 412, and Electriformes, 1874, p. 6.
Eleotrioides muralis, Bleeker, Gorum. p. 212.

B. v, D. 6 | $\frac{1}{11}$, P. 19, V. 1/5, A. $\frac{1}{12}$, C. 13, L. l. ca. 100.

Length of head $4\frac{1}{2}$, of caudal $4\frac{1}{2}$, height of body $6\frac{3}{4}$ in the total length. *Eyes*—diameter 1/5 of length of head, $1\frac{1}{4}$ diameters from end of snout, and 1 apart. Greatest width of head equals its height or its length behind the middle of the eyes. Cleft of mouth oblique, commencing anteriorly opposite the middle of the eye: the maxilla reaches to below the front edge of the orbit. *Teeth*—a single row of pointed, rather curved, and large teeth in the premaxillaries: villiform in the lower jaw, with anteriorly an outer row of curved teeth ending laterally in one or two canines. *Fins*—dorsal spines with filamentous terminations, the third being half higher than the body: the last dorsal ray as high as the body. Pectoral nearly as long as the head: ventral reaches half way to the anal. Caudal pointed. *Scales*—none on the head, those on the body ctenoid, about 39 rows between the anterior portion of the bases of the second dorsal and anal fins. *Colours*—two or three longitudinal red bands along the upper half of the body, and which may be broken up into spots, sometimes there are also a few vertical red bands crossing the horizontal rows at right angles: three or four red bands on the head, those on the opercle being tortuous. Several rows of red spots on the first dorsal fin forming bands, and a black blotch at its summit between the third and fourth spines. Two or three red lines along the second dorsal, and one along the anal fin: caudal with red spots.

Amongst Sir Walter Elliot's collection of drawings is a coloured one of the fish captured inside a *Murex*, at Madras, and referred to by Jerdon in the M. J. L. and Sc. 1851, p. 143, it may perhaps be the species described above. Dr. Günther identified one of Sir Emerson Tennent's drawings of Ceylon Fishes with *E. muralis*, therefore it would appear to be found off that island. Bleeker places *E. lineato-oculatus*, Kner, as a synonym of this species.

Habitat.—Seas of India to the Malay Archipelago.

3. Eleotris sexguttata.

Cuv. and Val. xii, p. 254; Bleeker, Blen. en Gob. p. 253, and Sumatra, p. 52; (Jerdon, M. J. L. and Sc. 1851, p. 143 not synon.); Günther, Catal. p. 130.
Valenciennea sexguttata, Bleeker, Boeroe, p. 412, Aroe, 1873, p. 2, and Eleotriformes, 1874, p. 6.
Eleotriodes sexguttata, Bleeker, Gorum. p. 212.

B. iv-v, D. 6 | $\frac{1}{12}$, P. 21, V. 1/5, A. $\frac{1}{12}$, L. l. 75-80.

Height of body 7 to 8 in the total length. *Eyes*—not one diameter apart. Jaws of equal length anteriorly. *Teeth*—in a single row of unequal size. *Fins*—dorsal spines, from the second to the fourth inclusive, produced into filaments. *Colours*—greenish, shot with rosy: blue spots, with dark edges on the side of the head: occasionally a violet spot before the dorsal fin, which latter has a black superior margin: second dorsal with six longitudinal violet stripes, anal with two: caudal with pearl-coloured ocelli edged with violet.

Jerdon's fish can hardly be identical with Cuv. and Val. The figure amongst Sir W. Elliot's drawings represents a fish with D. 6/11. Body gray, with six vertical bands, six black spots at the base of the caudal fin, and a large black yellow-edged ocellus at the base of the pectoral. First dorsal white in its lower 1/3, black in its upper two-thirds: second dorsal white along its base, gray in its outer three-fourths. Caudal with a white tip. First dorsal about 1/2 the height of the second, which equals that of the body. It is marked "*Eleotris 6 guttata* ? C.V. ? *Natsooli* Tamil. *Batis*." It appears similar to *E. Amboinensis*.

Habitat.—Ceylon to the Malay Archipelago.

4. Eleotris feliceps.

Blyth, J. A. S. of Beng. 1860, p. 146; Day, Proc. Zool. Soc. 1869, p. 517.

B. v, D. 6 | $\frac{1}{9}$, P. 15, V. 1/5, A. 11, C. 13, L. l. 27, L. tr. 12.

Length of head 1/4, of caudal 1/5, height of body 1/5 of the total length. *Eyes*—close together, 1 diameter from end of snout. Head slightly depressed, snout pointed. Lower jaw the longer. Cleft of mouth short, the maxilla only extends half way to below the orbit: no preopercular spine. *Teeth*—villiform. *Fins*—dorsal spines filiform: central caudal rays the longest. *Scales*—cycloid as far as the base of the anal fin, where they become strongly ctenoid: anteriorly they reach to the posterior margin of the orbit, and also cover the cheeks and opercles: twelve rows between the bases of the second dorsal and anal fins. *Colours*—brownish-white, irregularly spotted and blotched with a darker colour: dark bands pass downwards from the orbit: fins more or less spotted.

Habitat.—Andamans, from whence the Calcutta Museum received one specimen $1\frac{1}{2}$ inches in length.

5. Eleotris macrodon, Plate LXV, fig. 3.

Bleeker, Beng. en Hind. p. 104, t. 2, f. 1; Günther, Catal. iii, p. 129.
Odontoleotris macrodon, Gill, Bleeker, Eleotriformes, 1874, p. 14.

B. v, D. 6 | $\frac{1}{9}$, P. 17, V. 1/5, A. $\frac{1}{8}$, C. 13, L. l. 120, L. tr. 30.

Length of head $4\frac{1}{2}$, of caudal 6, height of body 6 in the total length. *Eyes*—diameter $6\frac{1}{2}$ in length of head, $1\frac{1}{4}$ diameters from end of snout, and 2 apart. Upper surface of head flattened, snout slightly elevated.

Greatest width of head equals its length behind the eyes, and its height equals half its length. Lower jaw the longer. Cleft of mouth oblique, commencing anteriorly opposite the middle of the eyes, the maxilla reaching to below the centre of the orbit. No spine on preopercle. Anterior nostril tubular. A small barbel is said to exist on each side of the upper jaw. *Teeth*—several villiform rows in both jaws, an outer row of enlarged conical ones in front of the premaxillaries, consisting of from eight to ten, two of which are large canines: in the lower jaw from four to six conical canines anteriorly, whilst the inner row of the villiform ones is very slightly the largest. *Fins*—dorsals of about the same height and equal to half of that of the body. Pectoral as long as the head behind the eyes: ventral reaching a little above half way to the anal. Caudal rounded. *Scales*—cycloid, extending in irregular rows over body and head, except at front of snout and lower jaw, about 70 rows in front of dorsal fin. The posterior half of caudal scaled. *Colours*—brownish, second dorsal with several brown spots. A dark ocellus edged with light at the upper part of the base of the caudal fin.

Habitat.—Estuaries and mouths of large rivers in lower Bengal and Burma, attaining at least $4\frac{1}{2}$ inches in length.

6. Electris porocephalus, Plate LXVII, fig. 1.

Eleotris porocephala, Cuv. and Val. xii, p. 237; Cantor, Catal. p. 195; Bleeker, Amboina, p. 344.
Eleotris porocephaloides, Bleeker, Sumatra, p. 511; Günther, Catal. iii, p. 109.
Eleotris Cantoris, Günther, Catal. iii, p. 108.
Ophiocara porocephala, Bleeker, Eleotriformes, 1874, p. 5.

B. v, D. 6 | $\frac{1}{8-9}$, P. 15, V. 1/5, A. $\frac{1}{8}$, C. 15, L. l. 36-37, L. tr. 12-13.

Length of head $3\frac{1}{2}$ to $3\frac{2}{3}$, of caudal 5 to 6, height of body $4\frac{2}{3}$ to $5\frac{1}{4}$ in the total length. *Eyes*—diameter from 1/5 to 1/6 in length of head, $1\frac{1}{2}$ to $1\frac{1}{2}$ diameters from end of snout, and 2 to $2\frac{1}{2}$ diameters apart. Head obtuse, flat, depressed. Greatest width of head equals its length excluding the snout, and its height equals its length behind the eye. Lower jaw the longer, the maxilla reaches to rather behind the centre of the eye. Anterior nostril tubular. *Teeth*—in villiform rows, the outer row in the lower jaw slightly the longest and pointed. *Fins*—the two dorsals of about equal height or two-thirds that of the body, the last dorsal ray scarcely reaches the base of the caudal fin. Pectoral equals the length of the head behind the middle of the eyes, the ventral is rather shorter. Caudal rounded. *Scales*—ctenoid, extended over the head, except on front portion of snout, those on the upper surface of the head smaller than those on the body and from 25 to 30 rows anterior to the base of the dorsal fin, there are about 12 rows between the eye and angle of the preopercle, seven or eight across the opercle, and 13 to 14 between the anterior portions of the bases of the second dorsal and anal fins. *Colours*—deep blackish-brown, marbled with darker: second dorsal with three or four rows of spots: a dark band along the anal. The body may have numerous light spots upon it and also on the second dorsal fin.

Habitat.—Andamans, Burma, to the Malay Archipelago. The specimen figured (life-size) is from the Andamans.

7. Electris ophiocephalus, Plate LXVII, fig. 2.

Eleotris ophiocephalus, (Kuhl. and v. Hass.) Cuv. and Val. xii, p. 239; Bleeker, Bonn. en Gob. p. 22; Cantor, Catal. p. 196; Günther, Catal. iii, p. 107; Day, Proc. Zool. Soc. 1870, p. 694.
Eleotris margaritacea, Cuv. and Val. xii, p. 240.
Eleotris viridis, Bleeker, Madura, p. 22.
Ophiocara ophicephala, Bleeker, Eleotriformes, 1874, p. 15.
A-rig-dah and *Mu-took-dah*, Andam.

B. v, D. 6 | $\frac{1}{9}$, P. 17, V. 1/5, A. $\frac{1}{8}$, C. 15, L. l. 31-34, L. tr. 10-11, Cæc. pyl. 2.

Length of head $3\frac{3}{4}$ to $4\frac{1}{4}$, of caudal $5\frac{1}{2}$ to 6, height of body 4 to 5 in the total length. *Eyes*—diameter 1/5 to 1/6 of length of head, 1 to $1\frac{1}{2}$ diameters from end of snout, and 2 to 3 apart. Head obtuse and depressed, its upper surface flat, its greatest width equalling its length without the snout, and its height being a little less. Lower jaw the longer, cleft oblique, commencing anteriorly opposite the middle of the eyes, the maxilla reaches to below the front edge of the orbit. Anterior nostril tubular. *Teeth*—in numerous villiform rows in both jaws, the outer being rather enlarged and pointed: palate edentulous. *Fins*—first dorsal spines rather fine, and equalling about 1/2 the height of the body, last dorsal rays prolonged, reaching to nearly or quite the base of the caudal fin. Pectoral as long as the head excluding the snout, the ventral equally long and reaching the vent. Caudal rounded. *Scales*—finely ctenoid, 15 rows in front of first dorsal fin and reaching to the snout, also covering the cheeks and opercles: those on the top of the head as large as those on the body. *Pyloric appendages*—two. *Colours*—olive brown, some irregular blotches along the sides, whilst three black bands radiate from the eye: sometimes a light ocellus edged with dark at the upper half of the base of the pectoral fin, or some dark markings: vertical fins with light margins: a darkish band along the second dorsal, anal, and ventral fins: soft dorsal sometimes with two narrow darkish bands.

Dr. Bleeker observes that yellow spots are very well marked on the second dorsal and anal fin in this species of *Ophiocara*. I did not see such at the Andamans where I captured many, but was only there in December and January, and season may affect their colours.

Habitat.—Andamans, the coast of Africa, and Malay Archipelago, to at least $9\frac{1}{2}$ inches in length.

8. Electris cavifrons, Plate LXV, fig. 6.

Blyth, J. A. S. of Beng. 1860, p. 145; Day, Proc. Zool. Soc. 1869, p. 517.

B. v, D. 6 | $\frac{1}{9}$, P. 13, V. 1/5, A. $\frac{1}{8}$, C. 15, L. l. 65, L. tr. 17.

Length of head $3\frac{1}{4}$ to $3\frac{1}{2}$, of caudal 5 to $5\frac{1}{4}$, height of body $5\frac{1}{2}$ to $6\frac{1}{2}$ in the total length. *Eyes*—diameter 1/5 to 1/6 of length of head, 1 to $1\frac{1}{2}$ diameters from end of snout, and 1 to $1\frac{1}{2}$ apart. Head depressed. Its greatest width equals its length excluding the snout, and its height equals half its length. A deep depression exists over the orbits. Lower jaw the longer, cleft of mouth oblique, commencing anteriorly opposite the upper edge of the eye, the maxilla reaches to below the hind edge of the orbit. A well marked spine pointing downwards at the angle of the preopercle. Anterior nostril somewhat tubular. *Teeth*—villiform in both jaws, the outer row in the premaxillaries rather enlarged, whilst the inner row is likewise a little larger than the outer ones and directed somewhat inwards. Four or five large canine-like teeth in the front of the lower jaw, whilst its inner row is also enlarged, terminating laterally in a canine-like tooth. *Fins*—first dorsal not quite so high as the second, the last rays of which equal the height of the body. Pectoral as long as the head behind the middle of the eyes, ventral extends half way to the anal. Caudal obtusely rounded. *Scales*—cycloid and small anteriorly, ctenoid on the body, about 55 rows before the dorsal fin, they extend forwards to the snout and over the opercle and subopercle, but there are none on the cheeks, which however have little rows of warts. *Colours*—light brown, with dark bands radiating from the orbits: a few dark spots on the body: dorsals and caudal barred in spots.

This fish appears to be an *Oxyeleotris*, Bleeker.

Habitat.—Andamans, up to 4 inches in length.

9. Electris fusca, Plate LXV, fig. 7.

Pœcilia fusca, Bl. Schn. p. 453.
Cobitis pacifica, Forst. Desc. Anim. ed. Licht. p. 235.
Cheilodipterus culius, Ham. Buch. pp. 55, 367, pl. 5, f. 16.
Eleotris nigra, Quoy and Gaim, Voy. Freyc. Zool. p. 259, pl. 6, f. 2; Cuv. and Val. xii, p. 233; Bleeker, Beng. p. 105, t. i, f. 3; Jerdon, M. J. L. and Sc. 1848, p. 149.
Eleotris Mauritianus, Benn. Proc. Zool. Soc. i, p. 166.
Culius niger, Bleeker, Boeroe, p. 411.
Eleotris incerta, Blyth, J. A. S. of Beng. 1860. p. 146.
Eleotris fusca, Günther, Catal. iii, p. 125; Day, Fish. Mal. p. 115, and Proc. Z. S. 1869, p. 517; Kner, Novara Fische, p. 186; Playfair, Fish. Zanz. p. 74.
Eleotris Soaresi, Playfair, Fish. Zanz. p. 74, pl. ix, fig. 4.
Culius fuscus, Bleeker, Eleotriformes, 1874, p. 15.
Poollan, Mal.: *Bundi* and *Baloh kera*, Ooriah.

B. vi, D. 6 | $\frac{1}{8}$, P. 18, V. 1/5, A. $\frac{1}{8}$, C. 12, L. l. 60-65, L. tr. 16, Vert. 11/14.

Length of head 4, of caudal $5\frac{3}{4}$ to 6, height of body 5 to 6 in the total length. *Eyes*—diameter 1/6 to 1/7 of length of head, 1 to $1\frac{1}{2}$ diameters from end of snout, and $1\frac{1}{2}$ to 2 diameters apart. Head depressed, its greatest width slightly exceeding its height and equalling its length excluding the snout. Lower jaw rather the longer: the maxilla reaches to below the middle of the orbit. Angle of preopercle armed with a short spine directed downwards and forwards, which usually becomes blunted with age. *Teeth*—in many villiform rows, the outer in the upper jaw being rather wide asunder and twice the size of the inner ones. In the lower jaw there are usually, not invariably, a few enlarged ones anteriorly in an outer row, whilst laterally there are some rather larger sized, pointed teeth. *Fins*—first dorsal spines weak, more than half as high as the body, but 1/4 less than the rays of the second dorsal. Pectoral as long as the head excluding the snout. Anal similar to the second dorsal. Caudal wedge-shaped. *Scales*—cover the body, and head superiorly as far forwards as the snout, the opercles and cheeks: occasionally those below the eyes and on the sub- and inter-opercles are rudimentary or even absent, in such cases lines of fine warts are usually seen. There are about 48 rows anterior to the dorsal fin, and they are rather minute between the eyes: 16 rows between the anterior extremities of second dorsal and anal fins, and 14 between their posterior extremities. Those on the body are ctenoid. *Colours*—leaden-black, lighter on the abdomen, which sometimes has a yellow tinge: horizontal bars on the dorsal fins, sometimes vertical ones on the caudal. Occasionally its upper surface is of a light stone-colour. Its markings and colours are subject to great variation.

Jerdon remarks that it conceals itself under stones and amongst weeds, remaining motionless for hours. Its movements are slow and it is fond of attaching itself vertically, with its head downwards, to the side of the vessel in which it may be confined.

Habitat.—Coasts of India to the Malay Archipelago, also the African coast, &c. to 8 inches in length.

10. Electris Canarensis, Plate LXIX, fig. 2.

B. vi, D. 6 | $\frac{1}{8}$, P. 16, V. 1/5, A. $\frac{1}{7}$, C. 15, L. l. 38, L. tr. 17.

Length of head $3\frac{3}{4}$, of caudal $6\frac{1}{2}$, height of body $6\frac{1}{2}$ in the total length. *Eyes*—diameter $4\frac{1}{2}$ in length of head, 3/4 of a diameter from end of snout, and nearly 1 apart. Greatest width of head equals its length behind the middle of the eye, and its height equals half its length. Upper surface of the head flat. Snout elevated. Lower jaw the longer: cleft of mouth very oblique, commencing opposite the upper edge of the eye: the maxilla reaches to below the middle of the orbit. Interorbital space flat. No serrated ridges on the head, nor any preopercular spine. *Teeth*—in numerous villiform rows, very small, and equal sized. *Fins*—first dorsal spines weak, not produced, equal to two-thirds of the height of the body, and nearly as long as the posterior rays of the second dorsal. Pectoral nearly as long as the head, and longer than the ventral. Caudal pointed. *Scales*—strongly ctenoid behind the head and base of first dorsal fin, those on the upper surface of the head are nearly as large as those on the body, they extend forwards to the snout, and cover the cheeks and opercles. There are 42 rows anterior to the base of the first dorsal fin, six rows between the orbit, 17 rows between the anterior portions of the origins of the second dorsal and anal fins, and 15 between their posterior portions. *Colours*—dark brown, mottled with black: pectoral yellow, with several black bands of spots: first dorsal black, with a white band along its lower third: second dorsal with six or seven bands of spots: anal with bands of spots: caudal reticulated with black spots, and having a black band at its base: ventral spotted.

Habitat.—Mangalore, where the specimen figured (life-size) was obtained.

11. Eleotris lutea.

B. vi, D. 6 | $\frac{1}{9}$, P. 15, V. 1/5, A. $\frac{1}{8}$, C. 15, L. l. 50, L. tr. 12.

Length of head $3\frac{1}{2}$, of caudal $5\frac{1}{2}$, height of body 4 in the total length. *Eyes*—diameter 1/4 of length of head, 3/4 of a diameter from end of snout, and also apart. Greatest width of head equals its length behind the eyes, and its height equals about the same. Upper surface of head and interorbital space flattened, snout slightly elevated. Lower jaw the longer, cleft of mouth oblique, commencing opposite the upper edge of the eye, the maxilla reaches to below the middle of the orbit. Anterior nostril tubular. A spine directed downwards at the angle of the preopercle. *Teeth*—in numerous villiform rows, the outer in the upper jaw being rather enlarged, as are also a few anteriorly in the lower jaw, whilst laterally its inner row is likewise enlarged. *Fins*—first dorsal spines with filamentous terminations extending a short distance beyond the membrane, height equals half that of the body, second dorsal highest anteriorly, where it equals 2/3 of that of the body, and is similar to the anal. Pectoral as long as the head without the snout: ventral of similar length. Caudal wedge-shaped. *Scales*—ctenoid on the body, superiorly they do not extend so far forwards as the eye, whilst there are none on the sides of the head: 23 rows before the dorsal fin: 12 between the origins of second dorsal and anal, and 10 between their posterior extremities. *Colours*—of a dirty-grayish, with vertical bands most distinct in the posterior half of the body: many dark spots on head: dorsals and anal with bands of black spots: caudal nearly black, and slightly reticulated.

This species of *Culius*, Bleeker, differs from *E. fusca* in the fewer number of scales on the body, scaleless head, and lesser width of interorbital space.

Habitat.—Andamans.

12. Eleotris scintillans, Plate LXV, fig. 8.

Blyth, J. A. S. of Bengal, 1860, p. 146; Day, Proc. Zool. Soc. 1869, p. 517, and 1870, p. 693.

B. v, D. 6 | $\frac{1}{8}$, P. 15, V. 1/5, A. $\frac{1}{8}$, C. 13, L. l. 42, L. tr. 15.

Length of head $3\frac{3}{4}$, of caudal $4\frac{1}{3}$, height of body $4\frac{1}{2}$ in the total length. *Eyes*—diameter 1/5 of length of head, $1\frac{1}{4}$ diameters from end of snout, and also apart. Head rather obtuse, flattened superiorly, its greatest width equals its height or its length behind the eyes. Lower jaw the longer. Cleft of mouth oblique, commencing anteriorly opposite the upper third of the eye the maxilla reaches to below the middle of the orbit. Anterior nostril in a short tube. No spine on preopercle. *Teeth*—villiform, the outer row in the lower jaw somewhat the larger. *Fins*—first dorsal fin equals about half the height of the body, and terminates only a short distance anterior to the base of the second dorsal, the posterior rays of which reach to the base of the caudal, and equal 4/5 of the height of the body. Pectoral as long as the head behind the middle of the eyes: ventral reaches more than half way to the anal. Caudal rounded. *Scales*—on body and head excluding the front of the snout and the lower jaw, they are ctenoid except on the head, 34 rows anterior to the base of the first dorsal fin, 15 between the anterior portion of the bases of the second dorsal and anal. *Colours*—brownish, marbled with darker, and the scales shot with light spots when in a certain position. Both dorsals with about three rows of spots, and a dark edge having a light margin. Anal with a dark band in its outer half having a light edge. Caudal dark, with a white edge, sometimes it and the anal are spotted: a dark ocellus at upper part of base of caudal fin.

This fish belongs to Genus *Ophiocara*, Bleeker, MSS. It is very closely allied to *E. porocephalus*, of which it may be the young.

Habitat.—Akyab and the Andamans, the one figured is life-size.

13. Eleotris litoralis.

B. vi, D. 6 | $\frac{1}{8}$, P. 15, V. 1/5, A. $\frac{1}{8}$, C. 13, L. l. 35, L. tr. 11.

Length of head $3\frac{3}{4}$, of caudal 5, height of body 5 in the total length. *Eyes*—diameter $3\frac{3}{4}$ in length of head, 3/4 of a diameter from end of snout, and $1\frac{1}{2}$ apart. Greatest width of head equals its height or its length behind the eye. Upper surface of head nearly flat. Snout slightly elevated. Lower jaw the longer. Cleft of mouth rather oblique, commencing opposite the upper edge of the eye. The maxilla reaches to below the middle of the eye. No serrated ridge on the head or preopercular spine. Anterior nostril tubular. *Teeth*—in numerous closely set villiform rows in both jaws, the inner of which is slightly the larger. *Fins*—spines of first dorsal weak, extending slightly beyond the membrane, two-thirds as high as the body and equal to the posterior rays of the second dorsal. Pectoral as long as the head behind the middle of the eyes, ventral a little shorter, but reaching more than half-way to the base of the anal. Caudal wedge-shaped. *Scales*—ctenoid on the body, those on the upper surface of the head extend forwards to the snout, there are 30 rows before the dorsal fin not much smaller than those on the body, seven rows between the orbits, eleven between the origins of second dorsal and anal fins, and eight between their posterior extremities. Large scales on the cheeks and opercles. *Colours*—brownish, marbled with darker, fins very dark due to fine black dots, and three or four bars of spots on the dorsal spines and rays. Caudal blackish. Anal with a black band along its centre and an external white edge.

Habitat.—One specimen, a little over 3 inches in length, from the Andaman islands.

14. Eleotris caperata.

Eleotris caperatus, Cantor, Catal. p. 197.
Eleotris koilomatodon, Bleeker, Blen. en Gob. p. 21.
Eleotris caperata, Günther, Catal. iii. p. 117; Day, Proc. Zool. Soc. 1870, p. 694.
Prionobutis koilomatodon, Bleeker, Eleotriformes, 1874, p. 5.
Oosuf-foo, Mugh.

B. v, D. 6 | 1/9, P. 21, V. 1/5, A. 1/8, C. 15, L. l. 30, L. tr. 9.

Length of head 4, of caudal 4½, height of body 5¾ in the total length. *Eyes*—diameter 1/4 of length of head, 1 diameter from end of snout, and 1/2 a diameter apart. Greatest width of the head equals its height or its length behind the middle of the eyes. Snout rather elevated, with a slight transverse depression posterior to it: the maxilla reaches to below the first third of the eye. Supraorbital margin rather strongly serrated, likewise a serrated ridge along either side of the posterior limb of the premaxillary. *Teeth*—in villiform rows in both jaws, with the outer enlarged. *Fins*—first dorsal spines weak, and 3/4 the height of the body: the last rays of the second dorsal equal to the height of the body. Caudal rounded. *Scales*—ctenoid, about 12 rows anterior to the dorsal fin, none on the interorbital space. No rudimentary scales as a rule at the base of those on the body. *Colours*—leaden brown, fins blackish, especially the first dorsal: a deep black blotch, edged with scarlet, at the base of the pectoral fin: the second dorsal, caudal, and anal more or less spotted.

Habitat.—Coasts of India, the Andamans, to the Malay Archipelago, China, and beyond.

15. Eleotris butis, Plate LXVII, fig. 3.

Cheilodipterus butis*, Ham. Buch. Fish. Ganges, pp. 57, 367; Gray and Hard. Ill. Ind. Zool. ii, pl. 93, f. 3 (from H. B. MSS.).
Eleotris humeralis, Cuv. and Val. xii, p. 246; Bleeker, Blen. en Gob. pp. 5, 22.
Eleotris butis, Cantor, Catal. p. 186; Günther, Catal. iii, p. 116; Day, Fish. Malabar, p. [illegible].
? *Eleotris melanopterus*, Bleeker, Ceram. p. 707.
Eleotris prismatica, Bleeker, Madura, p. 23.
Butis butis, Bleeker, Eleotriformes, 1874, p. 16.
Kullahray, Mal.

B. v, D. 6 | 1/8, P. 21, V. 1/5, A. 1/8, C. 13, L. l. 28, L. tr. 9-10.

Length of head 3 to 3½, of caudal 6, height of body 5¼ to 5½ in the total length. *Eyes*—diameter 5 to 6 in length of head, 1¼ diameters from end of snout, and also apart. Head broad and anteriorly depressed, the dorsal profile rather concave from the occiput to the snout. The greatest width of head equals a little more than half its length, and its height is slightly less. Lower jaw the longer. Cleft of mouth commences opposite the upper edge of the eye. The maxilla reaches to below the middle of the eye. A finely serrated ridge passes along the posterior and superior edges of the orbit, from which it is divided by two rows of fine scales: serrated ridges also exist on either side of the snout, but all these serrations appear liable to variation, being usually mostly distinct in the young. *Teeth*—in numerous fine villiform rows, none of which are enlarged. *Fins*—first dorsal 2/3 of the height of the body, not so high as the second, the posterior rays of which equal 3/4 of the height of the body. Pectoral as long as the head without the snout: ventral reaches rather above half-way to the anal. Caudal cut rather square. *Scales*—ctenoid on the body, in large specimens there are generally about five or even more rudimentary ones at the base of each large one. They cover the head except the front of the snout and its under surface, there are about 25 rows between the base of the first dorsal fin and the hind edge of the eye. Interorbital space nearly flat and covered with small scales, those on the preorbital and below the eyes are usually smaller than those on the preopercle.

* I overlooked the fact (see p. 264, ante) that *Cheilodipterus panijus*, Ham. Buch. pp. 57, 367, belongs to an entirely different family, and is *Sillago domina*, C. V., or perhaps should be termed *Sillago panijus*, Ham. Buch. The figure had been abstracted from Ham. Buch. original collection in Calcutta, but a duplicate of it, with the name omitted, is present amongst the copies of the missing ones.

Nine or ten rows between the bases of the second dorsal and anal fins. *Colours*—depend very much on locality, generally leaden or brownish, sometimes blotched with darker. A scarlet spot at the base of the pectoral fin, divided in the centre by a round black mark. First dorsal nearly black: the second, the anal, and the caudal yellowish with bands of spots, upper edge of caudal sometimes reddish.

Habitat.—Seas and estuaries of India to the Malay Archipelago, attaining about 4 inches in length. The specimen figured (life-size) is from Calcutta.

16. Electris Amboinensis.

? Bleeker, Amboina, iv, p. 343; Günther, Catal. iii, p. 117; Day, Proc. Zool. Soc. 1869, p. 303.
Electris buccata, Blyth, J. A. S. of Beng. 1860, p. 145.
? *Butis Amboinensis*, Bleeker, Electriformes, 1874, p. 5.
Prionobutis buccata, Bleeker, Electriformes, 1874, p. 5.
Gagi-dalah-kera, Ooriah.

B. v, D. 6 | $\frac{1}{9}$, P. 19, V. 1/5, A. $\frac{1}{8}$, C. 13, L. l. 28, L. tr. 9.

Length of head $3\frac{2}{3}$, of caudal 5 to $5\frac{1}{4}$, height of body 7 in the total length. *Eyes*—diameter 1/5 of length of head, $1\frac{1}{2}$ diameters from end of snout, and $1\frac{1}{4}$ apart. Dorsal profile nearly horizontal, snout depressed. Greatest width of head equals its length without the snout, and its height equals nearly half its length. Lower jaw somewhat the longer: cleft of mouth commences opposite the upper edge of the eye: the maxilla reaches to nearly below the front edge of the eye. Upper and hind edge of orbit minutely serrated, also two serrated ridges along either side of the snout. *Teeth*—in numerous villiform rows in both jaws, the outer row in the premaxillaries consists of widely separated pointed ones, much larger than the villiform bands, and its inner row is rather horizontal: the outer row in the lower jaw is anteriorly similar to that in the premaxillaries; whilst the inner row laterally is enlarged. *Fins*—dorsal spines weak, about 1/2 the height of the body: anterior rays of second dorsal as high as the body and higher than the posterior ones. Pectoral nearly as long as the head: ventral reaches above half way to vent. Caudal rounded. *Scales*—feebly ctenoid on the body, more strongly so on the cheeks: 18 rows between the base of the dorsal fin and hind edge of the eye, anteriorly they extend forwards to the snout, those in the interorbital space not being very small. Nine rows between the second dorsal and anal. A few scales on the body have a rudimentary one at their base. *Colours*—brownish, sometimes vertically banded, first dorsal dark, second yellowish, with rows of brown spots on the rays. A large black spot surrounded by yellow at the base of the pectoral fin: anal and caudal brown dotted, and having reddish margins.

This species differs from *E. asperata* in having no elevation of snout, and the interorbital space being scaled. From *E. butis* in having an outer, widely set, enlarged row of teeth. Bleeker's species *E. Amboinensis* is in a group having "*Dentes utrinque maxilla æquales conferti*," consequently the above may not be his species.

Habitat.—Seas and estuaries of India to the Malay Archipelago.*

Genus, 10—Gobioides, *Lacépède*.

? *Tænioides*, Lacép.; *Amblyopus*, Cuv. and Val.; *Oxyichodes* and *Psilosomus*, Swains.; *Odontamblyopus*, Bleeker.

Branchiostegals five; gills four; pseudobranchiæ absent. Body elongated: head oblong: no cavity above the opercles. Lower jaw prominent, causing the cleft of the mouth to be directed upwards. Eyes lateral, minute or indistinct. Teeth in a band, with a single anterior row of large, curved, conical, and distantly placed ones: a pair of posterior canines above the symphysis of the lower jaw may be present or absent. The first portion of the dorsal fin, consisting of five undivided rays is separated by an interval from the soft portion, in the centre of which is a single sixth undivided ray. Second portion of dorsal and anal with many rays and more or less confluent with the caudal: ventrals united. Scales rudimentary or absent. Air-vessel, when present, small or large.

Bleeker separates *Gobioides*, Lacép., from *Tænioides*, Lacép., partly due to their being deficient in posterior canines which *G. Broussonetti* is said to be without. But Lacépède's type of *Gobioides* is *G. anguillaris*, which has posterior canines, whilst his *Tænioides* is stated to have no caudal fin.

Geographical distribution.—These fishes are found along the coasts, estuaries and within tidal influence throughout India to the Malay Archipelago, China, and Japan. They mostly delight in muddy localities and use their teeth very freely as organs of attack or defence.

These following seven species may be thus subdivided:—

A. *A pair of posterior canines above the symphysis of the lower jaw.*

a. Vertical fins densely enveloped in skin, *G. anguillaris*.
b. Vertical fins not enveloped in skin, *G. Buchanani*, *G. rubicundus*, *G. tenuis*.

* *Atherina danius*, Ham. Buch. Fish. Ganges, pp. 222, 381; *Eleotris danius*, Bleeker, Beng. en Hind.; *Cestreus minutus*, McClell. Cal. Journ. Nat. Hist. ii, p. 151, pl. iv, f. 2, may belong to this genus. D. 4-5 | 8-9, P. 7, V. 6, A. 10-12, C. 13. Appearance that of a *Mugil*, elongated, compressed. Upper surface of head flat: three protuberances on the nape. *Eyes*—large, prominent. *Teeth*—in two rows of forked ones. *Fins*—caudal ends in a crescent. *Scales*—ctenoid, very thin, none on the head. *Colours*—back dotted, silvery-white on the abdomen. *Habitat*—Mahanaddi and Ganges rivers, to one inch in length.

B. *No posterior canines above the centre of the lower jaw.*

a. Vertical fins densely enveloped in skin, *G. gracilis*, *G. cæculus*, *G. cirratus*.

SYNOPSIS OF SPECIES.

1. *Gobioides gracilis*, D. 6 | 47-49, A. 47-49. Height of body 18½ to 20 times in the total length. No posterior canines in the lower jaw. Vertical fins enveloped in skin and continuous with the dorsal. Pectoral short. Bluish or tinged with red. Seas of India to the Malay Archipelago.

2. *Gobioides anguillaris*, D. 6 | 45-47, A. 44-45. Height of body 14 to 18 times in the total length. Fourteen to 16 large teeth in either jaw: a pair of posterior canines in the lower. Vertical fins enveloped in skin and continuous with the caudal. Pectoral short. Pinkish, caudal dark.

3. *Gobioides cæculus*, D. 6 | 40-44, A. 38-45. No posterior canines in the lower jaw. Vertical fins enveloped in skin and separated from the caudal by a notch. Pectoral short. Bluish or reddish. Seas, estuaries and coasts of India.

4. *Gobioides cirratus*, D. 6 | 43, A. 43. Height of body 12½ times in the total length. From 8 to 10 large teeth in the upper and 6 to 8 in the lower jaw: no posterior canines. Vertical fins enveloped in skin and separated from the caudal by a notch. Pectoral short. Bright pink. Hooghly.

5. *Gobioides Buchanani*, D. 6 | 42, A. 36. Height of body 12 to 14 times in the total length. Eight large teeth anteriorly in either jaw: a pair of posterior canines. Vertical fins not enveloped in skin, continuous with the caudal. Pectoral short. Brownish, fins black. Coasts of the Bay of Bengal to Burma.

6. *Gobioides rubicundus*, D. 6 | 35-39, A. 33-36. Height of body 12 times in the total length. A pair of posterior canines in the lower jaw. Vertical fins not enveloped in skin and more or less continuous with the caudal. Pectoral of moderate length. Greenish olive, caudal black.

7. *Gobioides tenuis*, D. 6 | 33, A. 32. Height of body 20½ times in the total length. A pair of posterior canines in the lower jaw. Vertical fins not enveloped in skin and continuous with the caudal. Pectoral of moderate length. Roseate, caudal dark.

1. Gobioides gracilis.

Amblyopus gracilis, Cuv. and Val. xii. p. 166; Bleeker, Blen. en Gob. p. 38; Günther, Catal. iii, p. 134.

B. v, D. 6 | 47-49, P. 17, V. 1/5, A. 47-49, C. 11.

Length of head 10½ to 11, of caudal 10½, height of body 18½ to 20 times in the total length. *Eyes*—minute. Greatest width of head equals one-third of its length and its height rather above half of its length. Cleft of mouth oblique, lower jaw the longer and with several barbels on its anterior surface. *Teeth*—about ten almost vertical and large pointed teeth in the outer row in either jaw, posterior to which are several rows of small pointed teeth, no posterior canines. *Fins*—densely enveloped in skin, dorsal and anal continuous with the caudal. Pectoral short, 33 times in the total length: ventral 10½ in the total length. Caudal pointed. *Scales*—absent. *Colours*—olive, with the fins, especially the caudal, rather darker.

Habitat.—Seas of India to the Malay Archipelago. This is not I believe a common species in India, my single specimen from Madras is 7 inches long. I saw a species at Calcutta which I believe to be the same, it came from the Hooghly, but I have mislaid it. It is not figured amongst Sir W. Elliot's fishes.

2. Gobioides anguillaris, Plate LXVII, fig. 4.

Gobius anguillaris, Linn. Syst. i, p. 450; Gmel. Linn. p. 1201; Bl. Schn. p. 71.

? *Tænioides Hermanni*, Lacép. ii, pp. 532, 533, pl. 14, f. 1; Bleeker, Gobioides, 1875, p. 42.

Gobioides anguilliformis, Lacép. ii, pp. 576, 577.

Cepola Hermanniana, Shaw, Zool. iv, p. 191.

Amblyopus Hermannianus, Cuv. and Val. xii, p. 159, pl. 350; Swainson, Fishes, ii, p. 279; Bleeker, Beng. en Hind. p. 103; Cantor, Catal. p. 190; Jerdon, M. J. L. and Sc. 1851, p. 144; Day, Fish. Malabar, p. 116.

Ahra ramah, Tel.

B. v, D. 6 | 45-47, P. 15, V. 1/5, A. 44-45, C. 13.

Length of head 7½, of caudal 10 to 10½, height of body 14 to 18 in the total length. *Eyes*—minute. Greatest width of head equals 2/3 to 3/5 of its length, and its height equals 3/4 of the same extent. Lower jaw the longer and anterior, with its cleft nearly vertical. A tubercle at the symphysis of the lower jaw with a pair of short barbels, sometimes two more posteriorly. *Teeth*—of comparatively moderate size, about 16 large ones in the anterior row in the premaxillaries, and 14 in the lower jaw, behind these there are villiform ones, and a pair of posterior canines above the symphysis of the lower jaw. *Fins*—dorsal enveloped in skin and not so high as the body, it is not separated from the caudal (as a rule) by any notch, but in some instances is half, in others entirely notched. Pectoral fleshy in its basal half, and not quite half so long as the ventral which is 1/4 shorter than the head. Anal not quite so high as the second dorsal, and usually not separated from the caudal by a notch. Caudal rhomboidal. *Scales*—absent. *Colours*—pinkish, caudal darkest in its centre.

Tænioides Hermanni, Lacép. is said to be destitute of a caudal fin.

Habitat.—Seas of India to the Malay Archipelago and beyond. The specimen figured (from Calcutta) is nearly 15 inches long.

3. Gobioides cæculus, Plate LXVIII, fig. 1.

Cepola cæcula, Bl. Schn. p. 241, t. 54.
Amblyopus cæculus, Cuv. and Val. xii, p. 165; Jerdon, M. J. L. and Sc. 1851, p. 144; Günther, Catal. iii, p. 133; Day, Fish. Malabar, p. 117.
Gogee rasah, Tel.

B. v, D. 6 | 40-44, P. 15, V. 1/5, A. 38-45, C. 13.

Length of head 7 to 7½, of pectoral 16½ to 18, of caudal 10, height of body 13½ to 15 in the total length. *Eyes*—high up, minute, in the anterior third of the head, and 5 diameters from the end of the snout. The greatest width of the head equals its height or 1/2 its length. Body rounded, head as wide as the body. Lower jaw the longer, with some small barbels on it: cleft of mouth oblique. *Teeth*—an outer row of more or less curved teeth in either jaw, varying from 16 to 18 in the upper and 10 to 13 in the lower jaw, several villiform rows internally: no posterior canines in the lower jaw. *Fins*—dorsal and anal only united to the caudal at their bases in some specimens, in half the height of the last rays in others: the fins enveloped in skin. Ventral as long as the head. Caudal short and pointed. *Scales*—absent. *Colours*—vary, those at Madras are mostly of a leaden hue, becoming light on the abdomen (Schneider shows several vertical black bands which I have not observed): vertical fins gray, central caudal rays black: pectorals and ventrals reddish, or they may be of a coppery colour along the back, shot with blue along the sides, fins reddish except the caudal which is deep brown with reddish outer edges. Some are of a general reddish-brown colour.

Amongst Sir Walter Elliot's drawings of Waltair fishes is one of this species marked *Gagiliam* or *Rhua*, Tel. taken from a tank January 10th, 1854.

This fish, like many others related to it, is exceedingly vicious, and when captured snaps at everything near it: should its tail be touched it springs round and anything it seizes, it holds on to in the most determined manner.

Habitat.—Seas, estuaries, tidal rivers and tanks along the coasts of India and the Andamans. The one figured (life-*size*) is from Madras.

4. Gobioides cirratus, Plate LXIX, fig. 4.

Amblyopus cirratus, Blyth, J. A. S. of Beng. 1860, p. 147.
Amblyopus brachygaster, Günther, Catal. iii, 1861, p. 134.

B. v, D. 6 | 43-47, P. 13, V. 1/5, A. 43-46, C. 13.

Length of head 7¼, of caudal 9, height of body 8 to 12½ in the total length. *Eyes*—exceedingly minute, sometimes almost invisible. Blyth says they are "undiscernible in an adult preserved in spirit." Günther says "eyes invisible." Greatest width of head equals 2/3 of its length, and its height equals slightly more. Lower jaw anterior, its end forming a portion of the dorsal profile: cleft of mouth almost vertical. A pair of barbels under the symphysis of the lower jaw, and two more along either ramus. *Teeth*—much larger and more curved than in *G. anguillaris*, from eight to ten in the upper and six or eight in the lower jaw: internal to this outer row are several more of pointed, scarcely villiform, teeth: no posterior canines above the symphysis of the lower jaw. *Fins*—dorsal densely enveloped in skin and not quite so high as the body, it is separated from the caudal by a notch. Pectoral fleshy in its basal three-fourths and not quite half as long as the ventrals, which latter are nearly as long as the head. Anal not quite so high as the dorsal and like it enveloped in dense skin and separated from the caudal by a deep notch. Caudal rhomboidal. *Colours*—bright pinkish, caudal dark except its outer edges which are pink.

A. brachygaster, Günther, appears to be the same. Length of head 6¼ to 6¾, of caudal 8, height of body 7½ to 10* in the total length. Outer row of teeth in upper jaw from 10 to 20, in lower from 6 to 9. The adult specimen referred to is 10 not 14 inches in length.

Habitat.—Hooghly. The specimen figured is rather above 10 inches long, and from Calcutta. Its less numerous enlarged anterior row of teeth, comparatively shorter head and less height of body separate it from *G. anguillaris*, to which however it is very closely allied.

5. Gobioides Buchanani, Plate LXVII, fig. 5.

Amblyopus Buchanani, Day, Proc. Zool. Soc. 1873, p. 110.

B. v, D. 6 | 42, P. 19, V. 1/5, A. 36, C. 17.

Length of head 7 to 7½, of caudal 8, height of body 12 to 14 in the total length. *Eyes*—distinct. Greatest width of head equals its height, or half its length. Lower jaw prominent, its cleft rather oblique. The posterior nostril opens just before the eye, and the anterior one, which is tubular, close to the front edge of the snout. A minute pair of barbels below the symphysis of the lower jaw, and a still smaller pair behind them. *Teeth*—a front row of eight large and curved teeth in either jaw, several villiform rows posterior to them: a pair of posterior canines above the symphysis of the lower jaw. *Fins*—vertical ones continuous, their posterior

* In Blyth's type the height of the body is 1/8 of the total.

portions scarcely enveloped in skin: caudal elongate and pointed. Pectoral not enveloped in skin, half as long as the ventrals and 2/7 of the length of the head. *Air-vessel*—large and oval. *Scales*—a few crypts containing some rudimentary ones exist in the posterior part of the body. *Colours*—brownish-olive superiorly, reddish inferiorly. Pectoral and ventral yellow, with their outer halves black. Vertical fins blackish.

An excellent coloured figure, 10 inches in length, marked *Amblyopus cæculus*, Nat. size, exists of this species amongst Sir W. Elliot's drawings of fish. It was captured at Waltair, September, 1852.

Habitat.—Calcutta, Lower Bengal, and along the coasts of the Bay of Bengal at least as low as Waltair, also Burma, certainly so far as Moulmein. The specimen figured is from Calcutta.

6. **Gobioides rubicundus**, Plate LXVII, fig. 6.

Ham. Buch. Fish. Ganges, pp. 37, 365, pl. 5, f. 9.
Amblyopus Mayenna, Cuv. and Val. xii, p. 163.
Amblyopus rubicunda, Swainson, Fishes, ii, p. 279.
Amblyopus anguillaris, Richards. Ich. China, p. 207.
Amblyopus Hermannianus, Günther, Catal. iii, p. 135.
Amblyopus tenuis, Günther, Catal. iii, p. 135.
Odontamblyopus rubicundus, Bleeker, Gobioides, 1875, p. 42.

B. v, D. 6 | 35-39, P. 30, V. 1/5, A. 33-36, C. 15.

Length of head $7\frac{1}{2}$ to 8, of caudal 5 to 6, height of body 12 in the total length. *Eyes*—high up in the front third of the head, almost concealed. Greatest width of head equals half its length, and its height equals its length behind the eyes. Cleft of mouth oblique, and of moderate depth. *Barbels*—absent.* *Teeth*—an outer row of about eight long, curved, pointed ones in the premaxillaries, and of about twelve similar ones in the lower jaw, posterior to these are one or two villiform rows in both jaws. A pair of posterior canines exist above the symphysis of the lower jaw. *Fins*—dorsal and anal fins not enveloped in skin, but both continuous with the caudal, the anal (as shown in the figure) is often only connected to the caudal by its base. The dorsal fin is about 1/2 the height of the body. Pectoral as long as the head behind the eyes, and the ventral nearly as long. Caudal lanceolate. *Scales*—in the form of crypts on the head, minute ones begin to appear on the body in its last half, and become more distinct near the tail. *Colours*—greenish-olive superiorly, becoming dull white below, vertical fins diaphanous: caudal black.

The proportions differ greatly with age. In one from Sind, $7\frac{1}{2}$ inches long, D. 6 | 33, the head is $9\frac{1}{2}$, caudal $3\frac{1}{3}$ in the total length.

Habitat.—Seas of India and estuaries, very common in the Hooghly at Calcutta, where it attains at least 11 inches in length. The specimen figured (life-size) is from Calcutta.

7. **Gobioides tenuis**, Plate LXIX, fig. 3.

? *Amblyopus roseus*, Cuv. and Val. xii, p. 164.

B. v, D. 6 | 33, P. 50, V. 1/5, A. 32, C. 17.

Length of head $8\frac{1}{2}$, of caudal $4\frac{1}{2}$, height of body $20\frac{1}{2}$ in the total length. *Eyes*—small but distinct in the anterior third of the head. Greatest width of head equals its height and nearly half its length. Body very compressed. Lower jaw the longer, but not so distinctly forming the front of the head as in the other species, the maxilla reaches to about 1 diameter behind the hind edge of the eye. Some small barbels below the symphysis of the lower jaw. *Teeth*—the outer row in the upper jaw consisting of about twelve curved canines not so large as those in the lower jaw, where there exists the same number: two or three rows of fine pointed teeth in either jaw behind the canines; and two posterior canines above the symphysis of the lower jaw. *Fins*—vertical ones not enveloped in skin, the dorsal continuous with the caudal, its height rather exceeds that of the body. Pectoral 2/3 as long as the head, with about 50 branched rays: ventral slightly longer. Caudal lanceolate. *Scales*—a few rudimentary ones present on the last part of the body. *Colours*—of a general roseate tinge, fins colourless except the caudal which is dark with a light outer edge.

The proportions of this fish, except as regards the pectoral fin, agree with *A. roseus*, C.V. which came from Bombay, it however is said to have D. 6 | 48, A. 1 | 41, and the pectoral $8\frac{1}{2}$ times in the total length.

Habitat.—Sind, where the specimen figured ($7\frac{3}{4}$ inches long) was captured.

Genus, 11—Trypauchen, *Cuv. and Val.*

Branchiostegals four: pseudobranchiæ. A deep blind cavity above the opercle, and which is not in communication with that of the branchiæ. Body elongated and compressed: head likewise compressed. Eyes lateral, minute, not elevated. Teeth in a band: no canines. Dorsal fin single, the anterior portion consisting of six spines, the soft with many rays, as has also the anal, whilst both are confluent with the caudal: ventrals with four or five rays, united forming a disk. Scales small, cycloid.

* In some young specimens from Madras I find rudimentary barbels.

SYNOPSIS OF INDIVIDUAL SPECIES.

1. *Trypauchen vagina*, D. 6 | 48-49, A. 40-46. Pinkish. Coasts of India to the Malay Archipelago and China.

1. Trypauchen vagina, Plate LXVIII, fig. 2.

Gobius vagina, Bl. Schn. p. 73, No. 20.
Gobioides ruber, Ham. Buch. pp. 33, 365.
Trypauchen vagina, Cuv. and Val. xii, p. 153, pl. 351; Cantor, Catal. p. 190; Günther, Catal. iii, p. 137; Day, Fishes, Malabar, p. 118; Kner, Novara Fische, p. 187.
Na-vattee, Tam.

B. iv, D. 6 | 40-49, P. 15, V. 1/5, A. 40-46, C. 13, L. r. 80-85, L. tr. 21.

Length of head 1/7 to 1/8, of caudal 1/8, height of body 2/15 to 1/11 of the total length. *Eyes*—small, in the anterior fourth of the length of the head from the snout, and the same distance apart. Body elongated and compressed, occipital crest elevated. The greatest width of the head a little above 1/2 of its length, and its height equals its length behind the eyes. Lower jaw the longer, cleft of mouth oblique, the maxilla reaches to below the front edge of the eye. *Teeth*—an outer row of rather distantly placed, moderately long, conical and rather curved ones in either jaw, posterior to which is a fine row in the upper and two in the lower jaw. *Fins*—first dorsal spine rather wide at its base, the height of the fin is from 2 to 2½ in that of the body: dorsal and anal confluent with the caudal. Pectoral 1/3 of the length of the head, its lower five rays short and unbranched: ventrals a little longer. Caudal pointed or rounded. *Scales*—cycloid, in rather irregular rows, lightest at their edges, sometimes depressed in their centres. *Colours*—white with a rosy tinge, much brighter at some seasons than at others: dorsal and anal with their outer edges gray: caudal, pectoral, and ventral white, or tinged with yellow.

Habitat.—Coasts of India through the Malay Archipelago to China. The specimen figured (from Calcutta) is 8¾ inches in length, and probably full grown. It is a very common fish, and eaten by the lower classes.

END OF VOL. I.

ALPHABETICAL INDEX TO VOLUME I.

2 T

2 U

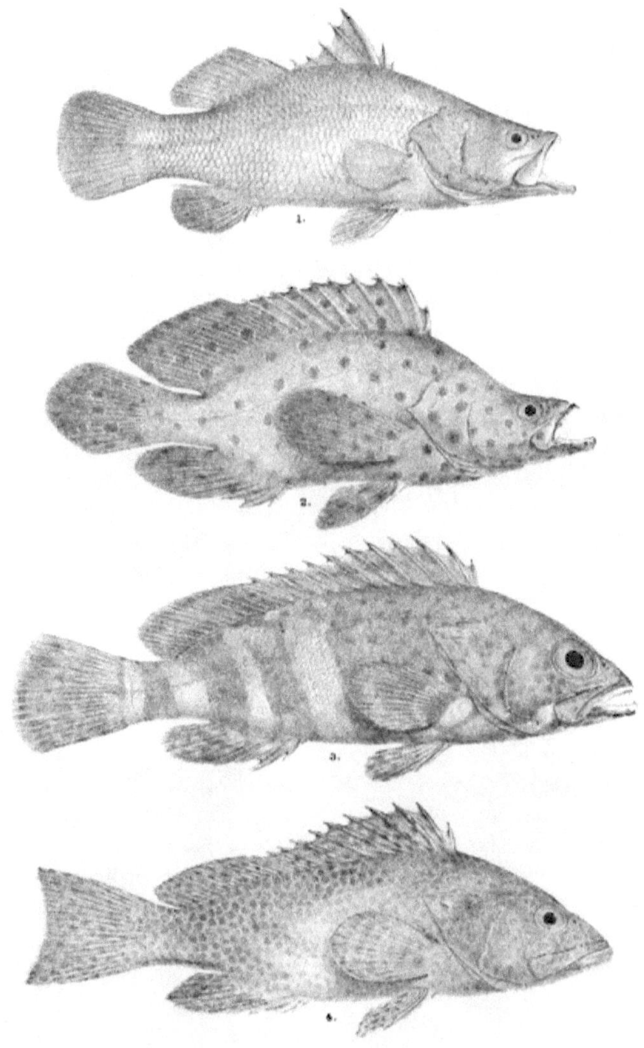

1. LATES CALCARIFER. 2 CROMILEPTES ALTIVELIS. 3 SERRANUS STOLICZKÆ. 4 S AREOLATUS.

J. N. Fonn del. C. L. Griesbach lith.

1 SERRANUS UNDULOSUS. 2 S. MERRA. 3 S. HEXAGONATUS. 4 S. MACULATUS.

1.
2.
3.
4.

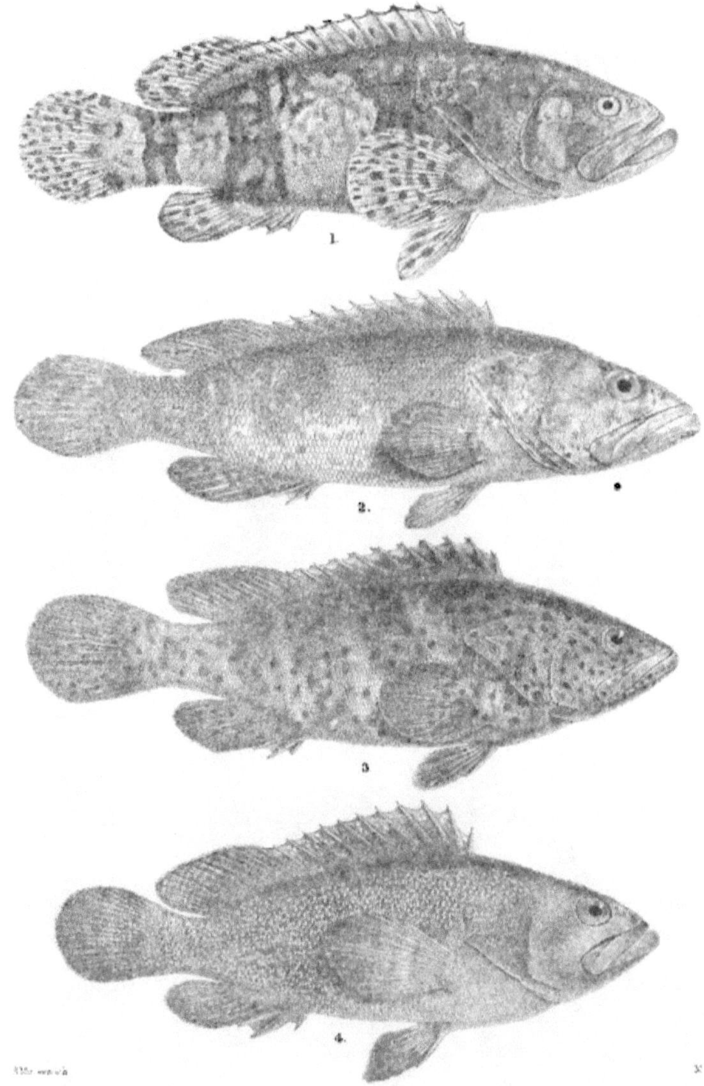
1.
2.
3.
4.

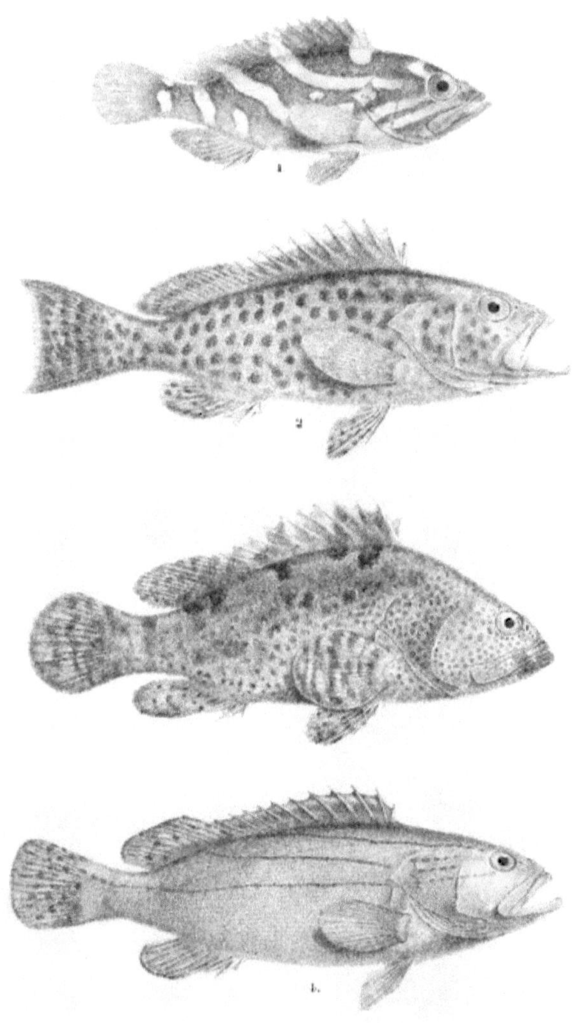

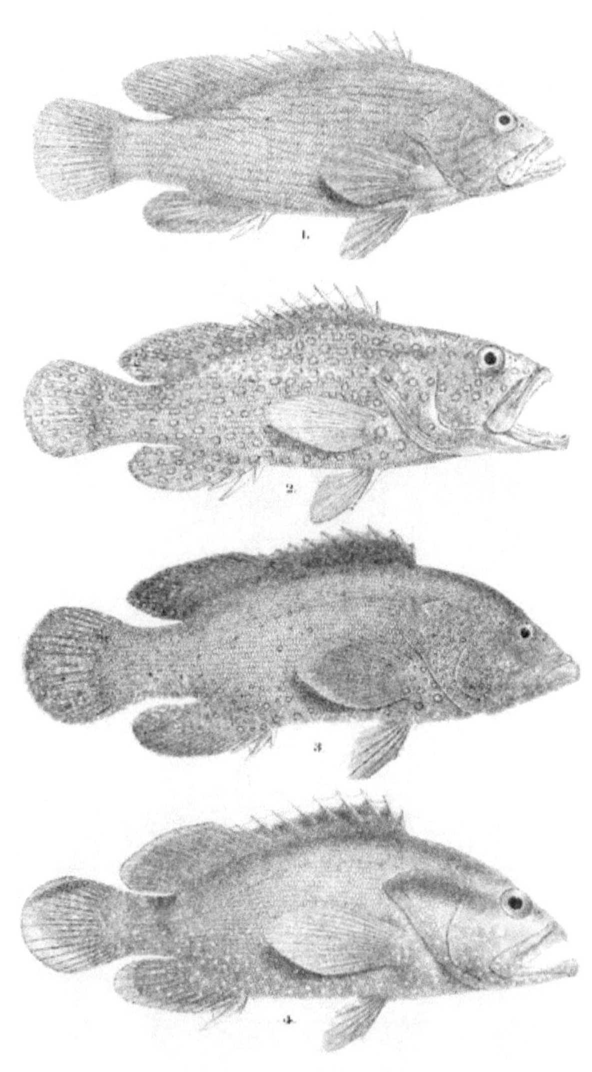

G. H. Ford del. C. L. Griesbach lith.

1. SERRANUS SONNERATI. 2. S. BOELANG. 3. VARIOLA LOUTI. 4. ANTHIAS MULTIDENS.

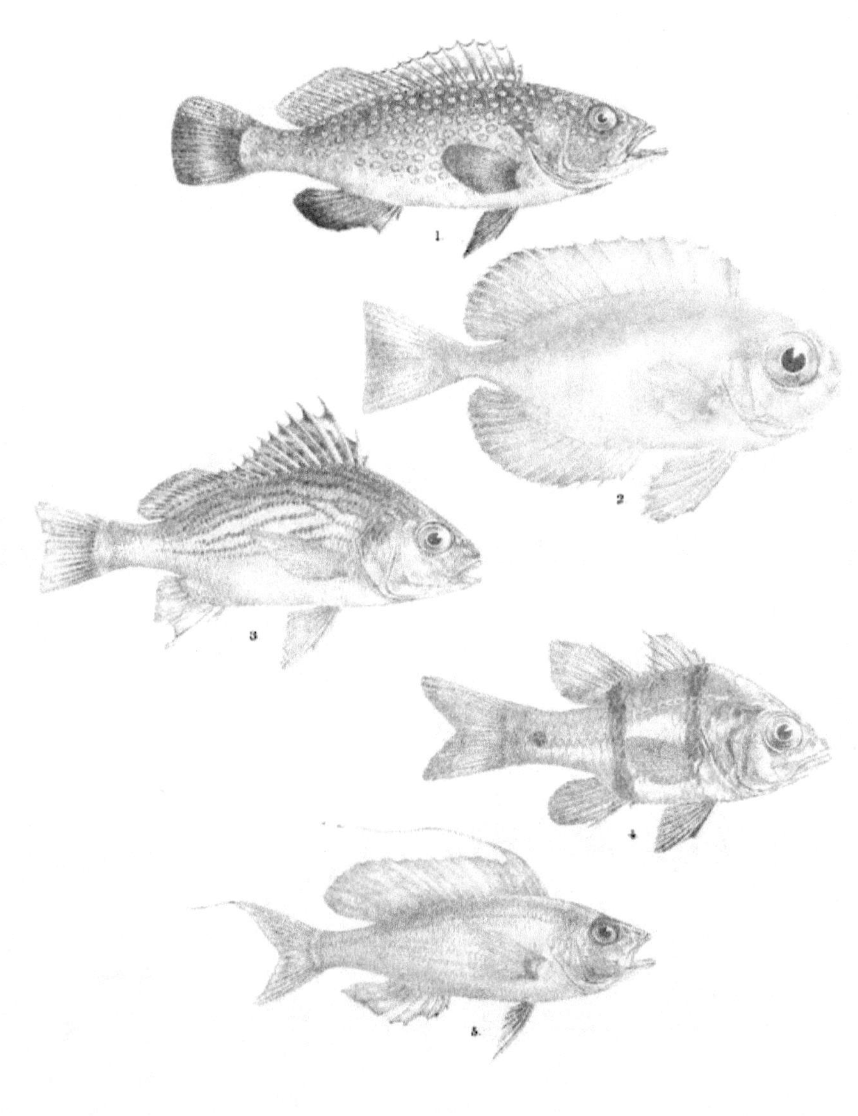

GRAMMISTES ORIENTALIS. 2. DIPLOPRION BIFASCIATUM 3. LUTIANUS SEBÆ.
4. L. MALABARICUS.

1.
2.
3.
4.
5.
6.

G.H. Ford del. J.R. King lith.

Mintern Bros. imp.

Jnl Ford del. R. Mintern lith. Mintern Bros. imp.

1. LUTIANUS LIOGLOSSUS. 2. L. SILLAO. 3. L. QUINQUELINEATUS 4. L. LUNULATUS
5. 4 FULVIFLAMMA (VAR. RUSSELLII) 6. L. FULVIFLAMMA.

G.H. Ford del. J.R. King lith. Mintern Bros imp.

1. LUTIANUS JOHNII. 2. L. GIBBUS (ADULT) 3. L. GIBBUS (YOUNG) 4. L. BOHAR
5. L. MARGINATUS. 6. L. YAPILLI

1.
2.
3
4.
5
6.

G. H. Ford del. J. R. Keulemans lith. Mintern Bros. imp.

1. AMBASSIS BACULIS. 2. A. THOMASSI. 3. A. COMMERSONII. 4. A. NALUA. 5. A. INTERRUPTA. 6. A. GYMNOCEPHALUS. 7. A. DAYI. 8. A. UROTÆNIA.

J.H.Ford del. R.Mintern lith. Mintern Bros. imp.

G.H. Ford del. R. Mintern lith. Mintern Bros imp.

1. PRISTIPOMA OLIVACEUM 2. P. FURCATUM 3. P. HASTA 4. P. HASTA (YOUNG $\frac{2}{1}$)
5. P. MACULATUM 6. P. DUSSUMIERI

1. PRISTIPOMA GUORAKA 2 P. OPERCULARE. 3 HAPALOGENYS PETERSI. 4 DIAGRAMMA CRASSISPINUM.
5. D. LINEATUM. 6 D. ORIENTALE.

1.
2.
3.
4.
5.

G. H. Ford del. R. Mintern lith.

Mintern Bros. imp.

1 SCOLOPSIS BIMACULATUS. 2 S. PHÆOPS. 3 S. BILINEATUS. 4 S. GHANAM
5 S. MONOGRAMMA. 6 S. CANCELLATUS.

1.

2.

3.

4.

5.

6.

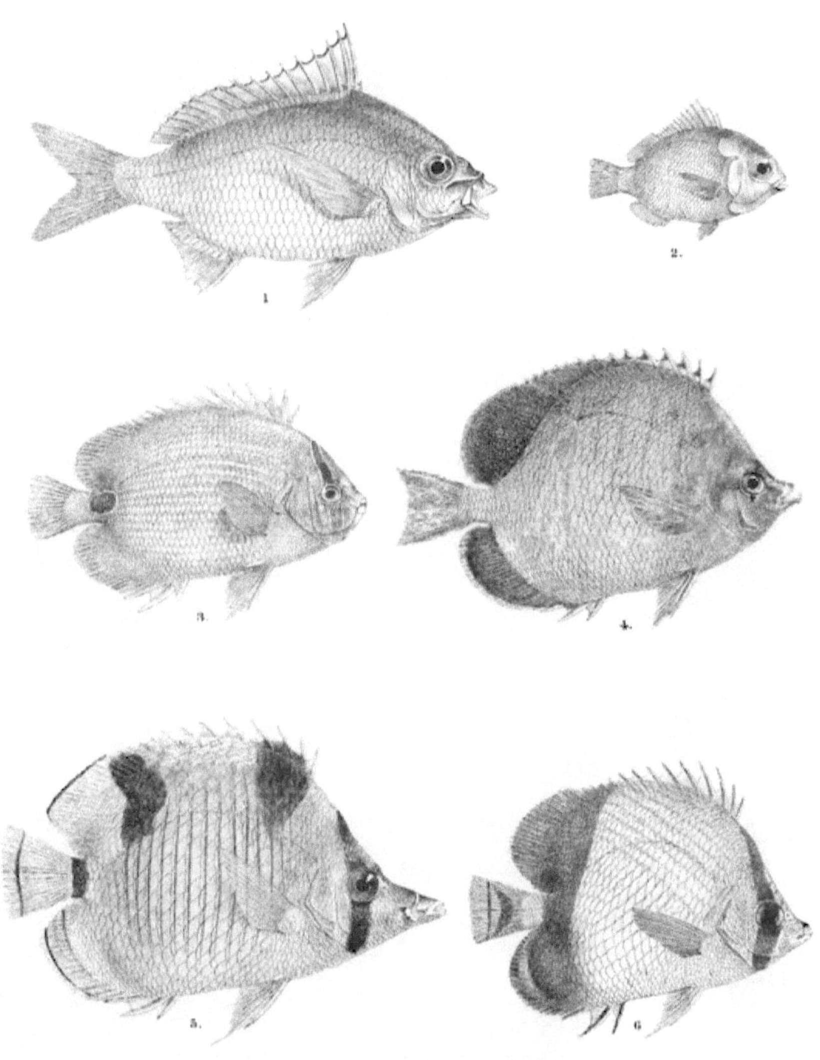
1
2.
3.
4.
5.
6

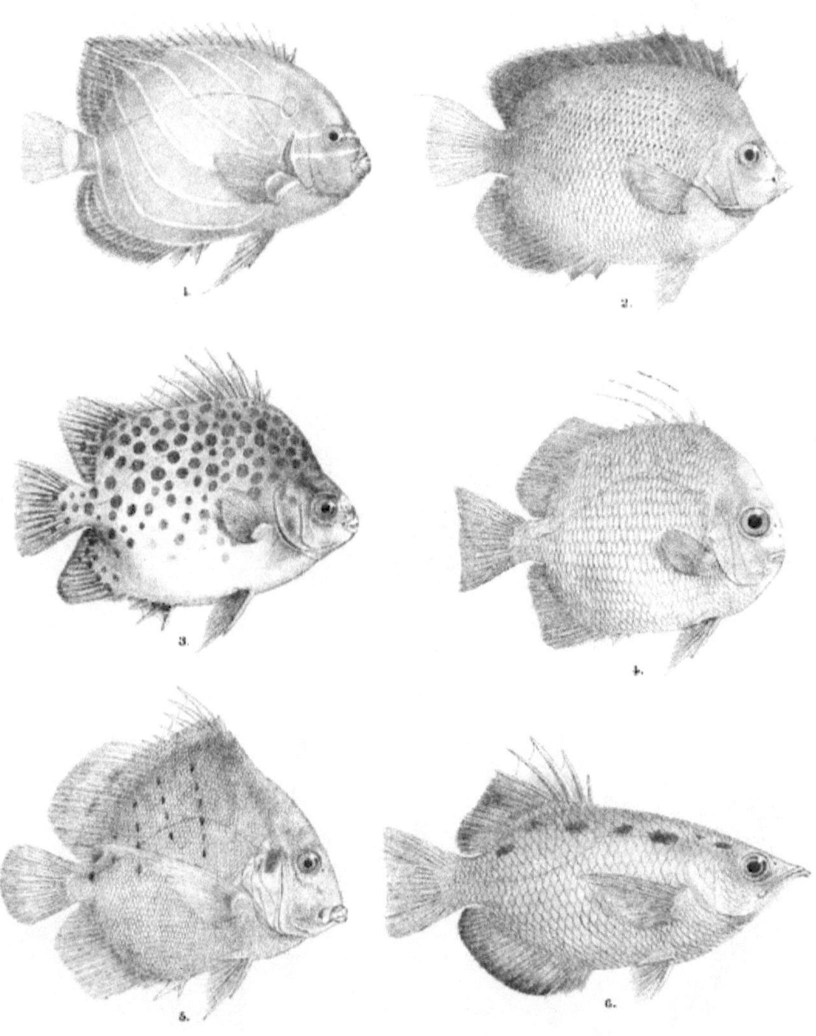
1.
2.
3.
4.
5.
6.

1.
2.
3.
4.
5.
6.

1.
2.
3.
4.
5
6.

1.
2.
3.
4.
5.

1. LETHRINUS ROSTRATUS 2. L. KARWA. 3. L. HARAK. 4. L. NEBULOSUS.
5. PAGRUS SPINIFER.

T.H. Ford del. B. Mintern lith.

Mintern Bros. imp.

1
2
3
4
5

1.
2.
3.
4.
5

1.
2.
3.
4.
5.

G. H. Ford del. F. Mintern lith. Mintern Bros. imp.

1, GYMNAPISTUS DRACÆNA. 2, CENTROPOGON INDICUS. 3, AMBLYAPISTUS MACRACANTHUS.
4, A. LONGISPINIS. 5, A. TÆNIANOTUS. 6, MICROPUS ZEYLONICUS. 7, MINOUS MONODACTYLUS.
8, COCOTROPUS ROSEUS.

1
2.
3.
4.
5
6.

1.
2.
3.
4.
5
6.

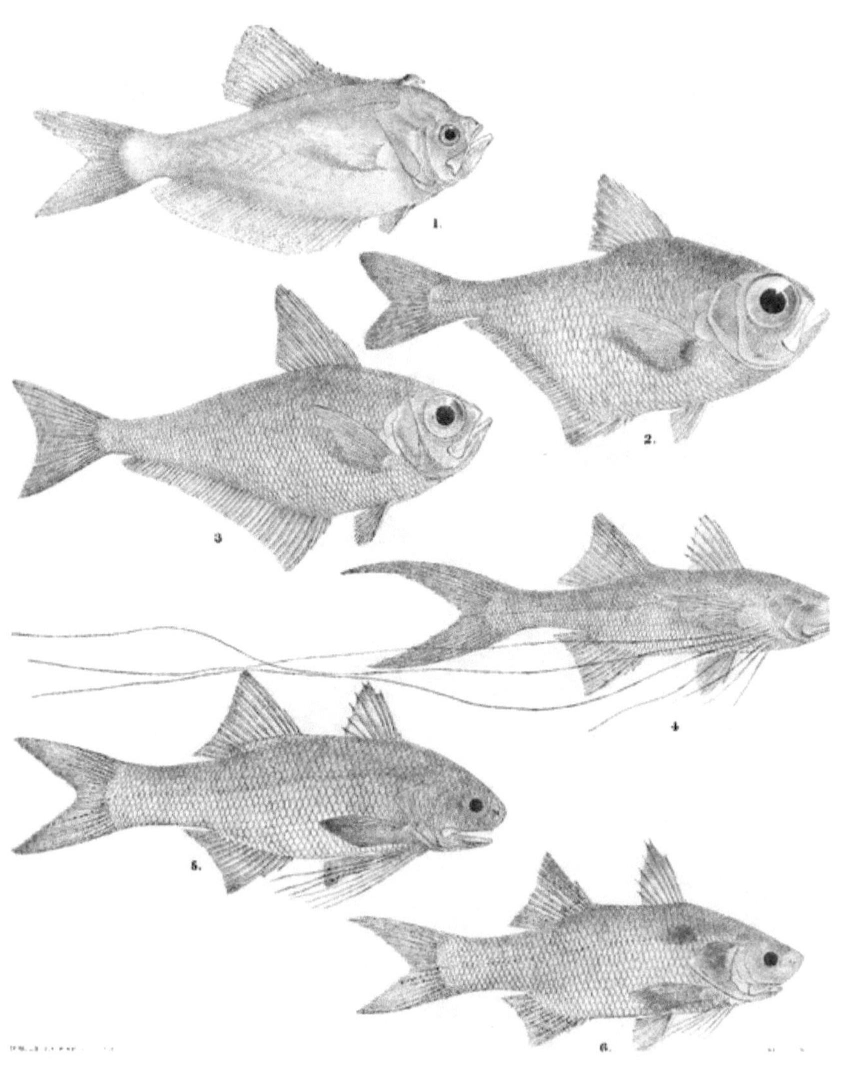

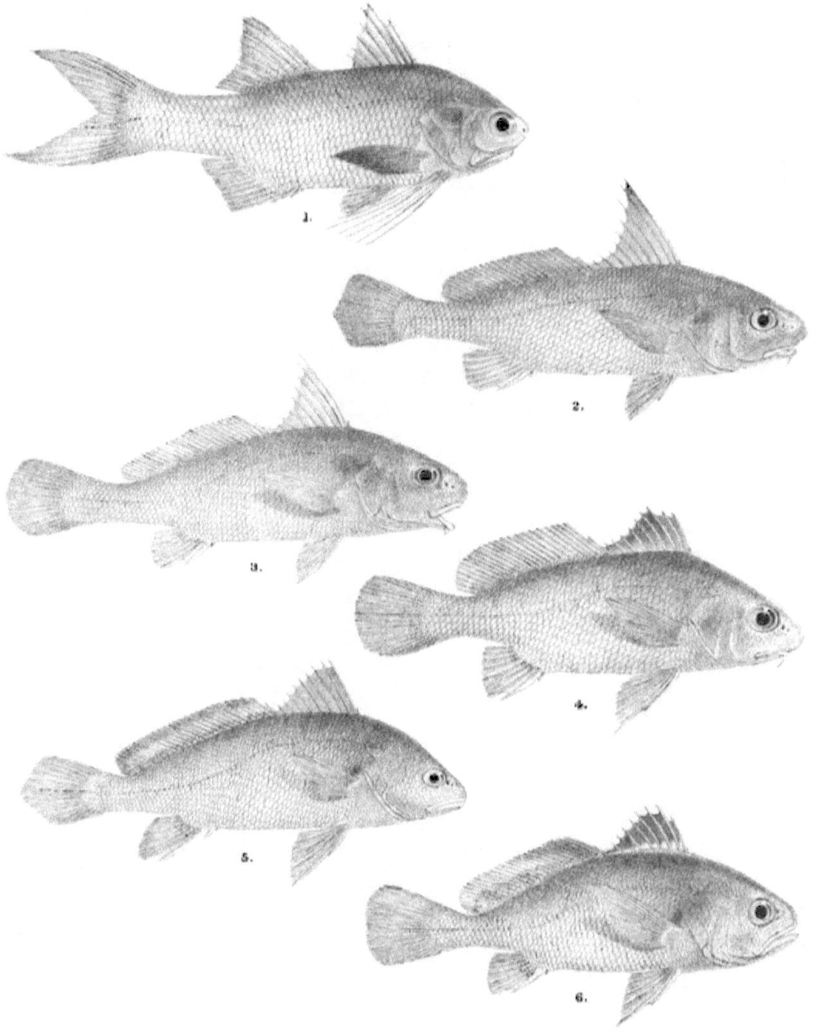

Mintern Bros. imp.

1.
2.
3
4.
5
6.

1
2
3
4.

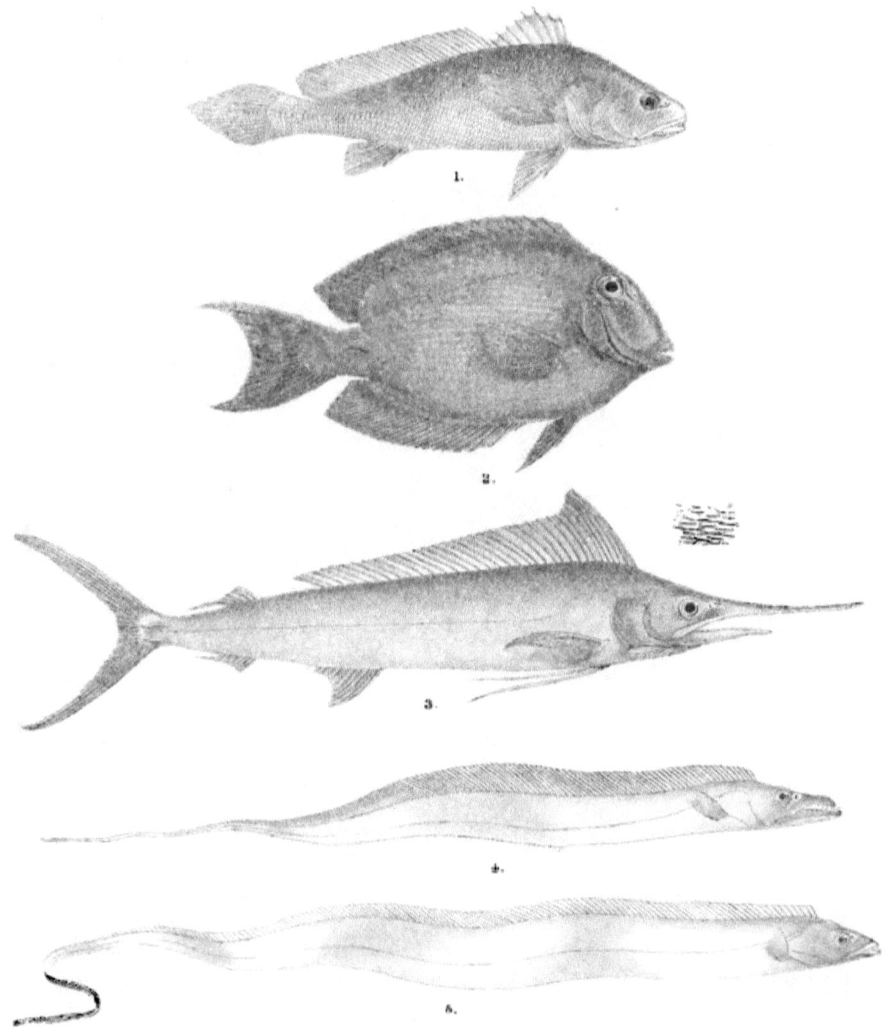
1.
2.
3.
4.
5.

1.
2.
3
4.
5.
6

1 CARANX CRUMENOPHTHALMUS 2. C. BOOPS 3. C. DJEDDABA 4. C. AFFINIS.
5. C. KALLA 6. C. IRE.

1 CARANX COMPRESSUS. 2. C. MALABARICUS 3. C. MELAMPYGUS. 4. C. CARANGUS. 5. C. SAUSUN. 6. C. NIGRESCENS.

G. H. Ford del. Dugan lith. Mintern Bros. imp.

1. CARANX OBLONGUS. 2. C. ARMATUS. 3. C. GALLUS. 4. C. LEPTOLEPIS.
5. C. NIGRIPINNIS. 6. SERIOLA NIGRO-FASCIATA.

1.
2.
3.
4.
5.
6.

G. H. Ford del. Mintern Bros. imp.

1. CHORINEMUS MOADETTA. 2. TRACHYNOTUS OVATUS. 3. T. RUSSELLII. 4. PLATAX TEIRA. 5. PSETTUS ARGENTEUS.

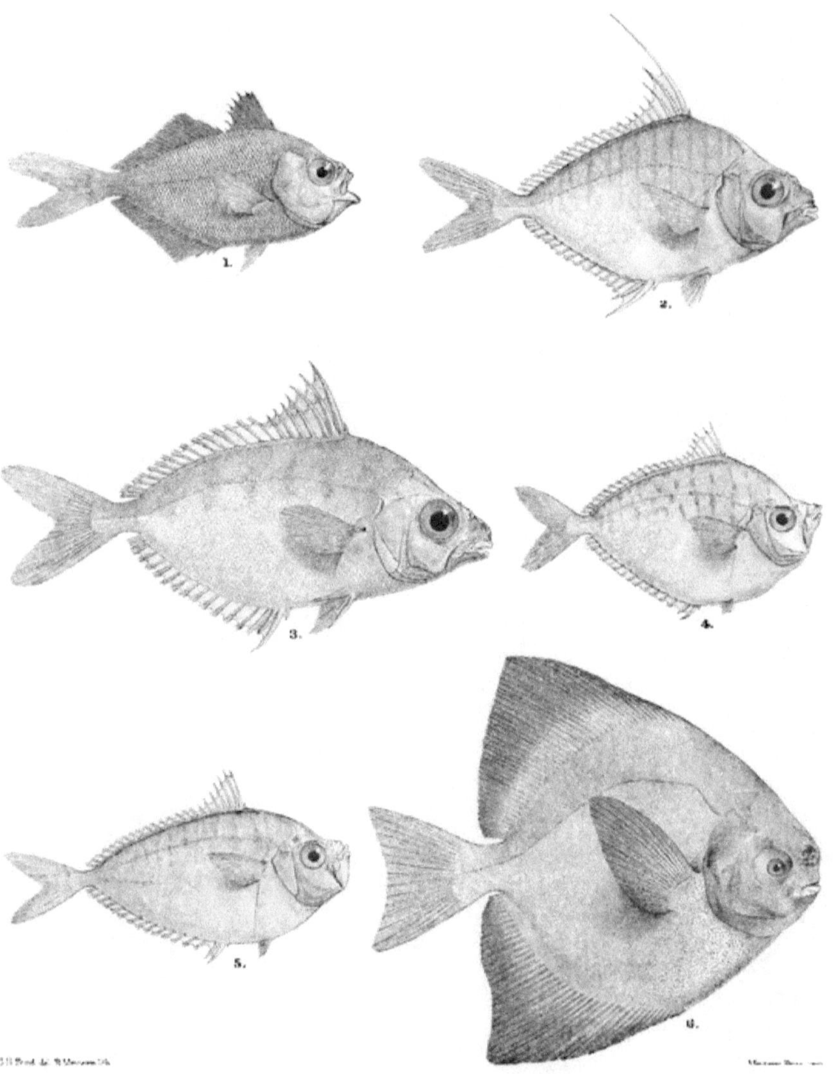

1.
2
3.
4.
5.
6.

G. H. Ford del. R. Mintern lith. Mintern Bros imp.

GAZZA MINUTA. 2. LACTARIUS DELICATULUS. 3. STROMATEUS CINEREUS (IMMATURE.
4 S. NIGER. 5 MENE MACULATA. 6. CORYPHÆNA HIPPURUS.

1.
2.
3.
4.
5.
6.

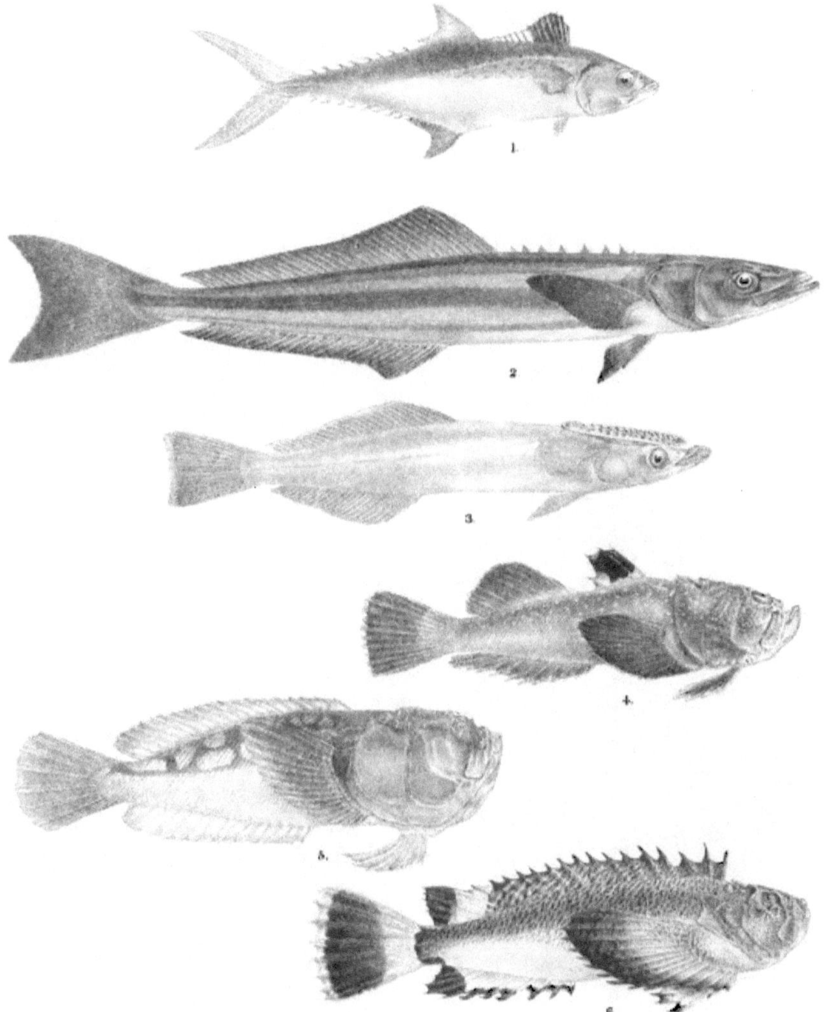
1.
2
3.
4.
5.
6.

G.H. Ford del. R. Mintern lith. Mintern Bros. imp.

1. PELAMYS CHILENSIS. 2. CYBIUM KUHLII. 3. C. INTERRUPTUM. 4. C. GUTTATUM.
5. C. COMMERSONII.

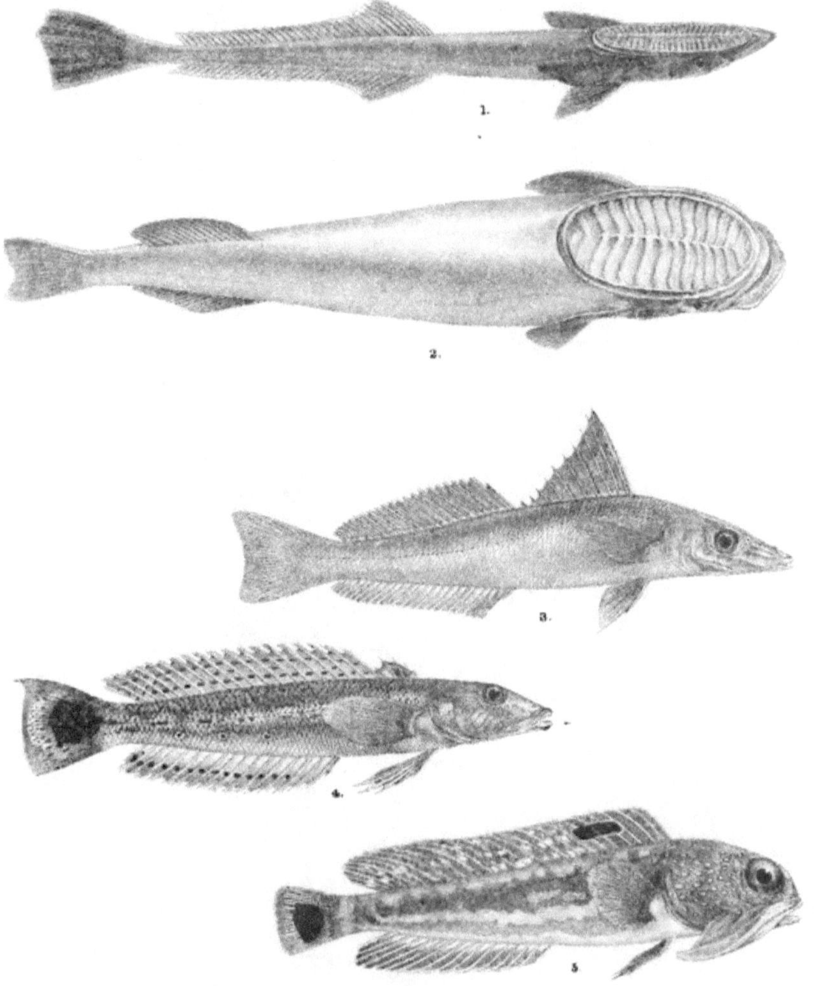

Mintern Bros imp.

1. ECHENEIS NEUCRATES   2. E. ALBESCENS   3. SILLAGO SIHAMA   4. PERCIS HEXOPHTHALMA
5. OPISTHOGNATHUS NIGROMARGINATUS

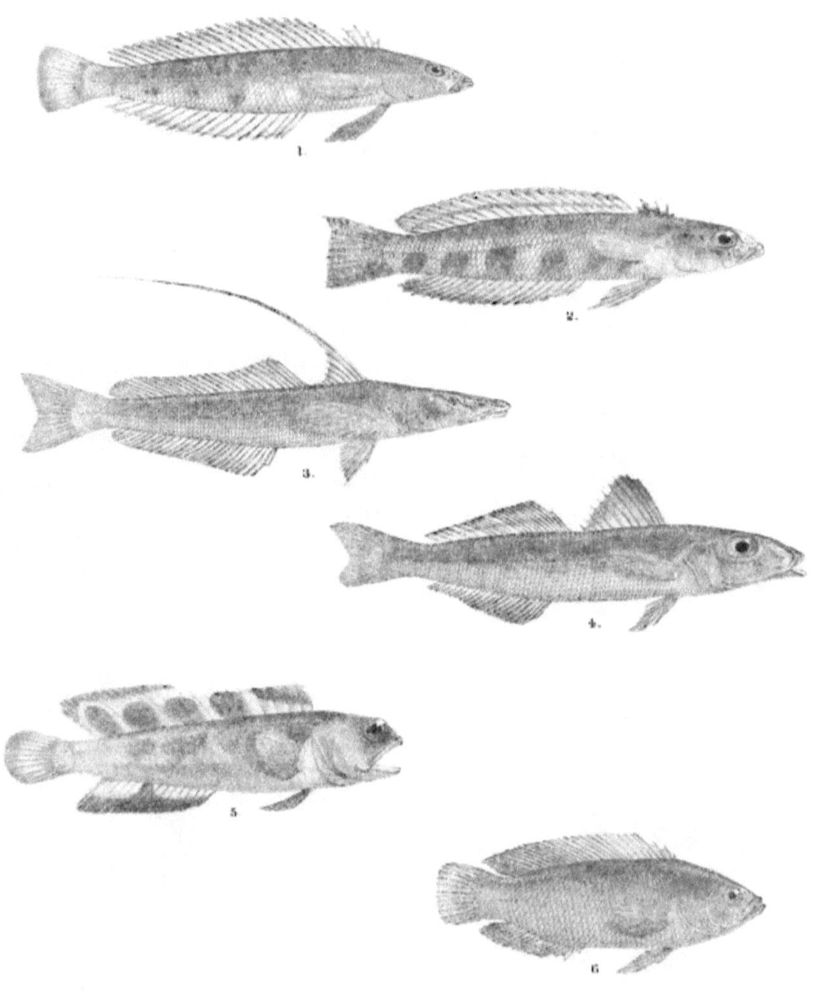
1.
2.
3.
4.
5
6

1.
2.
3
4.
5.
6.
7.
8.

Mintern Bros. imp.

1. GOBIUS PUNGTANG 2. G. CRINIGER 3. G. MADRASPATENSIS 4. G. NEILLI 5. G. BLEEKERI
6. G. STRIATUS 7. APOCRYPTICHTHYS CANTORI 8. GOBIUS CRISTATUS

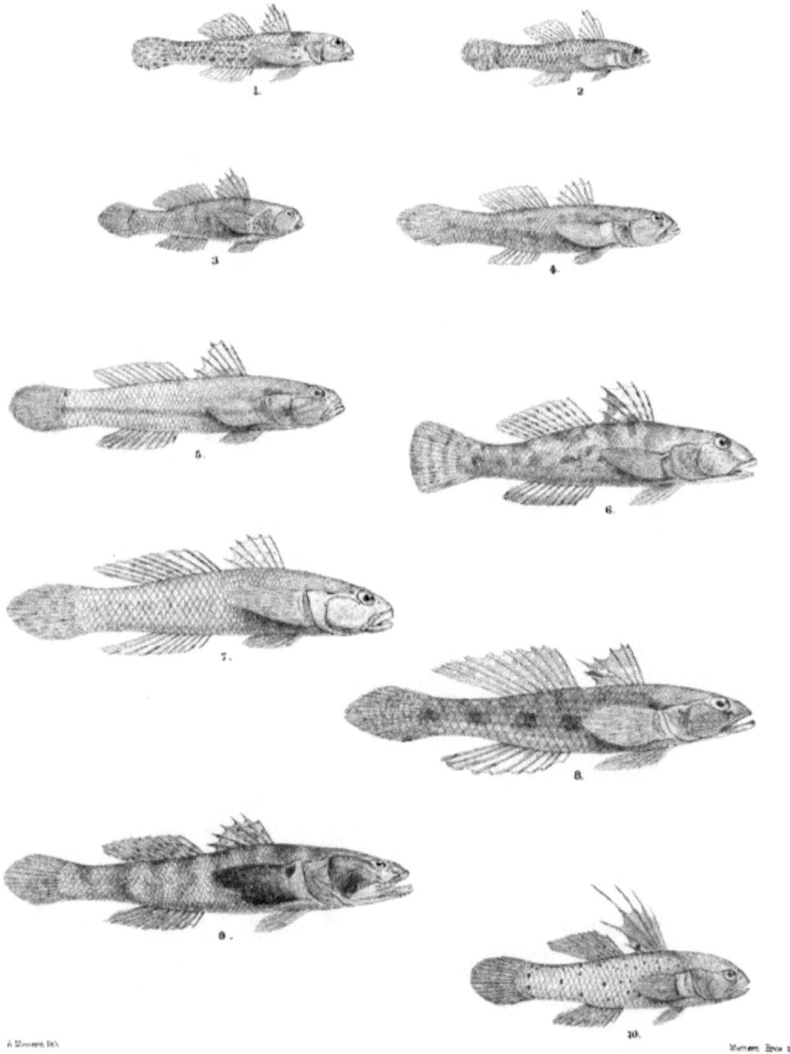
1.
2
3
4.
5.
6.
7.
8.
9.
10.

G. H. Ford del. P. Mintern lith.

Mintern Bros. imp.

1. GOBIUS MELANOSOMA. 2. GOBIODON CITRINUS. 3. APOCRYPTES BLEEKERI. 4. GOBIUS TENTACULARIS. 5. APOCRYPTES LANCEOLATUS. 6. A. BATO. 7. SICYDIUM FASCIATUM. 8. PERIOPHTHALMUS KOELREUTERI. 9. BOLEOPHTHALMUS DUSSUMIERI. 10. B. DENTATUS.

1. 2. 3. 4. 5. 6. 7. 8.

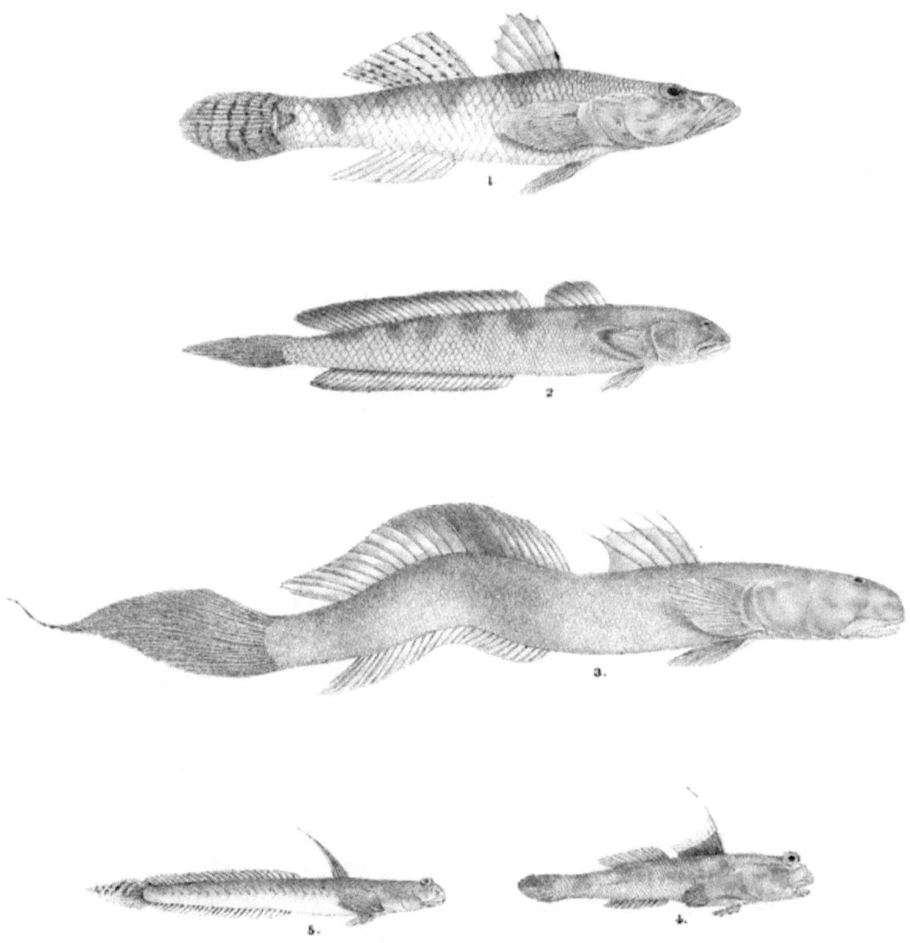

G.H.Ford del. P.Mazzara lith. Mintern imp.

1. GOBIUS GIURIS 2. APOCRYPTES SERPERASTER 3. A. BATOIDES 4. PERIOPHTHALMUS SCHLOSSERI
5. BOLEOPHTHALMUS VIRIDIS

J H Ford del. R Mintern lith.

Mintern Bros imp.

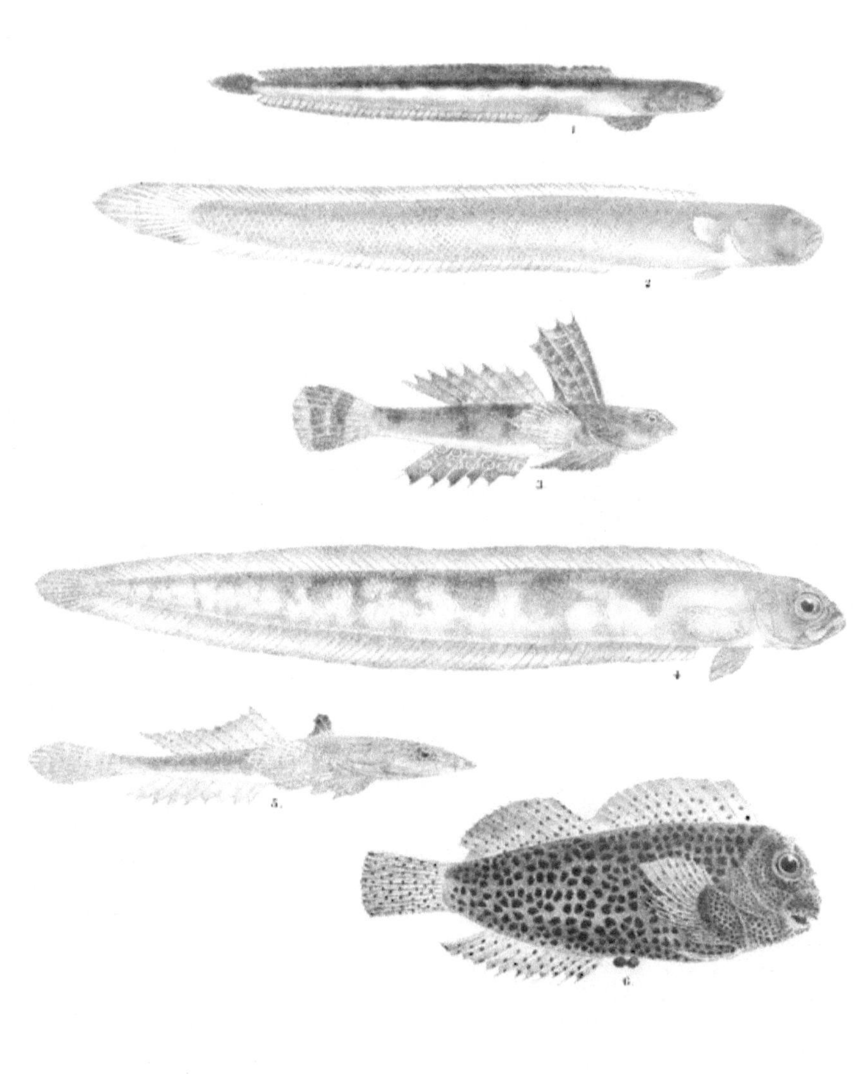
1
2
3
4
5
6

www.ingramcontent.com/pod-product-compliance
Lightning Source LLC
Chambersburg PA
CBHW022057300426
44117CB00007B/491

* 9 7 8 3 3 3 7 2 4 1 1 3 1 *